E-commerce

business. technology. society.

TWELFTH EDITION

Kenneth C. Laudon
New York University

Carol Guercio Traver
Azimuth Interactive, Inc.

PEARSON

Boston   Columbus   Indianapolis   New York   San Francisco
Amsterdam   Cape Town   Dubai   London   Madrid   Milan   Munich   Paris   Montreal   Toronto
Delhi   Mexico City   São Paulo   Sydney   Hong Kong   Seoul   Singapore   Taipei   Tokyo

Vice President, Business Publishing: Donna Battista
Editor-In-Chief: Stephanie Wall
Acquisitions Editor: Nicole Sam
Editorial Assistant: Olivia Vignone
Vice President, Product Marketing: Maggie Moylan
Director of Marketing, Digital Services and Products:
　Jeanette Koskinas
Executive Field Marketing Manager: Adam Goldstein
Field Marketing Manager: Lenny Ann Raper
Product Marketing Assistant: Jessica Quazza
Team Lead, Program Management: Ashley Santora
Program Manager: Denise Weiss
Team Lead, Project Management: Jeff Holcomb
Project Manager: Karalyn Holland
Operations Specialist: Carol Melville
Creative Director: Blair Brown
Sr. Art Director: Janet Slowik
Cover Designer: DePinho Design

Cover Image: Shutterstock VLADGRIN
Chapter and Part Opener Images: Marinini/Fotolia
Vice President, Director of Digital Strategy & Assessment:
　Paul Gentile
Manager of Learning Applications: Paul Deluca
Digital Editor: Brian Surette
Director, Digital Studio: Sacha Laustsen
Digital Studio Manager: Diane Lombardo
Digital Studio Project Manager: Robin Lazrus
Digital Studio Project Manager: Alana Coles
Digital Studio Project Manager: Monique Lawrence
Digital Studio Project Manager: Regina DaSilva
Full Service Project Management: Azimuth Interactive, Inc.
Composition: Azimuth Interactive, Inc.
Printer/Binder: LSC Communications
Cover Printer: Phoenix Color/Hagerstown
Text Font: ITC Veljovic Std. Book, 9.5pt

Library of Congress Cataloging-in-Publication Information is available.

2　16

PEARSON

ISBN 10: 0-13-393895-6
ISBN 13: 978-0-13-393895-1

PREFACE

E-commerce. Business. Technology. Society. 12E provides you with an in-depth introduction to the field of e-commerce. We focus on key concepts, and the latest empirical and financial data, that will help you understand and take advantage of the evolving world of opportunity offered by e-commerce, which is dramatically altering the way business is conducted and driving major shifts in the global economy.

Just as important, we have tried to create a book that is thought-provoking and current. We use the most recent data available, and focus on companies that you are likely to encounter on a daily basis in your everyday life, such as Facebook, Google, Twitter, Amazon, YouTube, Pinterest, eBay, Uber, WhatsApp, Snapchat, and many more that you will recognize, as well as some exciting startups that may be new to you. We also have up-to-date coverage of the key topics in e-commerce today, from privacy and piracy, to government surveillance, cyberwar, social, local, and mobile marketing, Internet sales taxes, intellectual property, and more. You will find here the most up-to-date and comprehensive overview of e-commerce today.

The e-commerce concepts you learn in this book will make you valuable to potential employers. The e-commerce job market is expanding rapidly. Many employers expect new employees to understand the basics of e-commerce, social and mobile marketing, and how to develop an e-commerce presence. Every industry today is touched in at least some way by e-commerce. The information and knowledge you find in this book will be valuable throughout your career, and after reading this book, we expect that you will be able to participate in, and even lead, management discussions of e-commerce for your firm.

WHAT'S NEW IN THE 12TH EDITION

Currency

The 12th edition features all new or updated opening, closing, and "Insight on" cases. The text, as well as all of the data, figures, and tables in the book, have been updated through October 2015 with the latest marketing and business intelligence available from eMarketer, Pew Research Center, Forrester Research, comScore, Gartner Research, and other industry and government sources.

In addition, we have added new, expanded, and/or updated material throughout the text on a number of e-commerce topics that have appeared in the headlines during 2015, including the following:

- On-demand service companies such as Uber, Airbnb, Instacart, and many others (Chapters 1, 2, and 9)
- Elevator pitches; equity crowdfunding; subscription-based sales revenue models (Chapter 2)

- Public, private, and hybrid clouds; Amazon Web Services; proposed changes in Internet governance; Internet access drones; the Internet of Things, wearable computing (Apple Watch), smart houses, and connected cars (Chapter 3)

- A/B and multivariate testing; open source Web and app development tools; mobile-first and responsive design (Chapter 4)

- New security threats (such as XcodeGhost; FREAK; Beebone botnet; Anthem, IRS, OPM, Sony hack, JPMorgan Chase, and other data breaches; IoT and connected car risks; Superfish adware); encryption; HTTPS; new chip cards; mobile wallets; Bitcoin; P2P (Venmo; Facebook Messenger) and mobile payment systems (Chapter 5)

- Ad blocking software; mobile supercookies and cross-device tracing methods; Google's new Mobilegeddon algorithm; changes to Facebook's Graph Search; IAB rich media Rising Star ad units; new IAB standards for video ads; IAB research on impact of interactive digital video; FTC position on native advertising; content marketing; rise in ad fraud; Google research on ad viewability and revised MRC guidelines; personalization and targeting in e-mail marketing; increase in retargeting ads; consumer reactions to personalized marketing messages; new Big Data tools such as Spark; online video and native advertising ad metrics; cross-platform attribution issues (Chapter 6)

- New social marketing and social e-commerce tools from Facebook, Twitter, Pinterest, Instagram; proximity marketing; BLE; and Apple iBeacons (Chapter 7)

- New Facebook privacy policies; Dirtboxes; USA Freedom Act; CalECPA; White House draft Consumer Privacy Bill of Rights; measuring privacy policies ; EU court invalidates U.S. data transfer safe harbor; new EU data protection law; new fair use and DMCA cases; impact of new gTLDs on trademarks; new FCC net neutrality regulations; online fantasy sports betting (Chapter 8)

- The rise of social e-commerce; Millenials' use of mobile and online financial services; consolidation in the online real estate and travel services markets; online recruitment industry trends in 2015; on-demand service companies (Chapter 9)

- Digital-first newspapers and explosive growth of digital news sites; Facebook Instant Articles; online magazine resurgence; Apple News app; e-book revenues; Amazon-Hatchette e-book pricing issues; social TV; binge viewing; Apple Music and other streaming music services; e-Sports (Chapter 10)

- Social network monetization; social e-commerce becomes a reality; Facebook at Work; Google+ retreats; eBay goes it alone; Yahoo continues to struggle (Chapter 11)

- Impact of B2C e-commerce on B2B e-commerce; supply chain visibility; cloud-based B2B; Amazon Business; mobile B2B (Chapter 12)

Themes

E-commerce has significantly evolved over the last decade. The iPhone was introduced in 2007. The iPad tablet was first introduced in 2010 and has already gone through several generations! Cloud services for storing and streaming content, and hosting thousands of apps, were not widely available until 2011. Smartphone and tablet devices have changed e-commerce into a social, local, and mobile experience. The 12th edition spotlights the following themes and content:

Headlines

- Social, Mobile, Local: We include an entire chapter describing social, mobile, and local marketing. Content about social networks, the mobile platform, and local e-commerce appears throughout the book.
    - » Social networks such as Facebook, Twitter, Pinterest, Instagram, and LinkedIn continue their rapid growth, laying the groundwork for a social network marketing platform
    - » The mobile platform composed of smartphones and tablet computers takes off and becomes a major factor in search, marketing, payment, retailing and services, and online content, as well as on-demand service companies. Mobile device use poses new security and privacy issues as well.
    - » Location-based services lead to explosive growth in local advertising and marketing.
- Online privacy continues to deteriorate, driven by a culture of self-revelation and powerful technologies for collecting personal information online without the knowledge or consent of users. A growing number of consumers adopt ad blockers.
- Internet security risks increase; cyberwarfare becomes a new way of conducting warfare among nation-states and a national security issue. A growing perception of online risk supports a growing lack of trust in e-commerce firms and transactions.

Business

- E-commerce revenues surge, despite slow economic growth.
- Internet advertising growth continues to outpace traditional advertising, including television.
- Social marketing grows faster than traditional online marketing like search and display advertising.
- E-books sales plateau but continue as a major channel for books. Consumers increasingly use smartphones and tablets as reader devices.
- Newspapers struggle to define a digital first news service
- Streaming of popular TV shows and movies (Netflix, Amazon, YouTube, and Hulu. com) becomes a reality, as Internet distributors and Hollywood and TV producers strike deals for Web distribution that also protects intellectual property.
- "Free" and "freemium" business models compete to support digital content. Subscription services show unexpected strength.
- New mobile payment platforms emerge to challenge PayPal.
- B2B e-commerce exceeds pre-recession levels as firms become more comfortable with digital supply chains.

Technology

- Smartphones, tablets, and e-book readers, along with associated cloud-based software applications, and coupled with 4G cellular network expansion, fuel rapid growth of the mobile platform.
- Investment in cloud computing increases, providing the computing infrastructure for a massive increase in online digital information content, and e-commerce.
- Cloud-based streaming services for music and video challenge sales of downloads and physical product.
- Software apps fuel growth in app sales, marketing, and advertising; transforming software production and distribution.
- The cost of developing sophisticated Web sites continues to drop due to declining software and hardware prices and open source software tools.
- Internet and cellular network capacity is challenged by the rapid expansion in digital traffic generated by mobile devices; the use of bandwidth caps tier-pricing expands.

Society

- The mobile, "always on" culture in business and family life continues to grow.
- Congress considers legislation to regulate the use of personal information for behavioral tracking and targeting consumers online.
- European countries develop much stronger privacy policies, including Right to be Forgotten laws, and expand the rights of citizens viz-a-viz Internet data giants.
- States heat up the pursuit of taxes on Internet sales by e-commerce firms.
- Intellectual property issues remain a source of conflict with significant movement toward resolution in some areas, such as Google's deals with Hollywood and the publishing industry, and Apple's and Amazon's deals with e-book and magazine publishers.
- Net neutrality regulations forbid Internet providers from discriminating against types of content, or providing differential service to large players
- P2P piracy traffic declines as paid streaming music and video gains ground, although digital piracy of online content remains a significant threat to Hollywood and the music industry.
- Governments around the world increase surveillance of Internet users and Web sites in response to national security threats; Google continues to tussle with China and other countries over censorship and security issues. Europe ends safe harbor protections for U.S. Internet firms.
- Venture capital investing in e-commerce explodes for social, mobile, and local software applications. Crowdfunding becomes a new source of funding for e-commerce start-ups.

WELCOME TO E-COMMERCE 2016

Since it began in 1995, electronic commerce has grown in the United States from a standing start to a $531 billion retail, travel, and media business and a $6.2 trillion business-to-business juggernaut, bringing about enormous change in business firms, markets, and consumer behavior. Economies and business firms around the globe are being similarly affected. During this relatively short time, e-commerce has itself been transformed from its origin as a mechanism for online retail sales into something much broader. Today, e-commerce has become the platform for media and new, unique services and capabilities that aren't found in the physical world. There is no physical world counterpart to Facebook, Twittter, Google search, or a host of other recent online innovations from Pinterest and iTunes to Tumblr. The Internet is about to replace television as the largest entertainment platform. Welcome to the new e-commerce!

E-commerce is projected to continue growing at double-digit rates over the next five years, remaining the fastest growing form of commerce. Just as automobiles, airplanes, and electronics defined the twentieth century, so will e-commerce of all kinds define business and society in the twenty-first century. The rapid movement toward an e-commerce economy and society is being led by both established business firms such as Walmart, Ford, IBM, Macy's, and General Electric, and online firms such as Google, Amazon, Apple, Facebook, Yahoo, Twitter, and YouTube. Students of business and information technology need a thorough grounding in e-commerce in order to be effective and successful managers in the next decade.

While firms such as Facebook, Tumblr, YouTube, Twitter, Pinterest, and Uber have grown explosively in the last two years and grab our attention, the traditional forms of retail e-commerce and services also remain vital and have proven to be more resilient than traditional retail channels in facing the economic recession. The experience of these firms from 1995 to the present is also a focus of this book. The defining characteristic of these firms is that they are profitable, sustainable, efficient, and innovative, with powerful brand names. Many of these now-experienced retail and service firms, such as eBay, Amazon, E*Trade, Priceline, and Expedia, are survivors of the first era of e-commerce. These surviving firms have evolved their business models, integrated their online and offline operations, and changed their revenue models to become profitable. Understanding how these online businesses succeeded will help students to manage their own firms in the current omni-channel business environment.

It would be foolish to ignore the lessons learned in the early period of e-commerce. Like so many technology revolutions in the past—automobiles, electricity, telephones, television, and biotechnology—there was an explosion of entrepreneurial efforts, followed by consolidation. By 2005, the survivors of the early period were moving to establish profitable businesses while maintaining rapid growth in revenues. In 2015, e-commerce is in the midst of a new period of explosive entrepreneurial activity focusing on on-demand services, social networks and the mobile platform created by smartphones and tablet computers. These technologies and social behaviors are bringing about extraordinary changes to our personal lives, markets, industries, individual businesses, and society as a whole. E-commerce is generating thousands of new jobs in all fields from marketing to management, entrepreneurial studies, and information systems. Today, e-commerce has moved into the mainstream life of established businesses that have the market brands and financial muscle required for the long-term deployment of e-commerce technologies and methods. If you are working in an established business, chances are the firm's e-commerce capabilities are important factors for its success. If you want to start a new business, chances are very good that the knowledge you learn in this book will be very helpful.

BUSINESS. TECHNOLOGY. SOCIETY.

We believe that in order for business and technology students to really understand e-commerce, they must understand the relationships among e-commerce business concerns, Internet technology, and the social and legal context of e-commerce. These three themes permeate all aspects of e-commerce, and therefore, in each chapter, we present material that explores the business, technological, and social aspects of that chapter's main topic.

Given the continued growth and diffusion of e-commerce, all students—regardless of their major discipline—must also understand the basic economic and business forces driving e-commerce. E-commerce has created new digital markets where prices are more transparent, markets are global, and trading is highly efficient, though not perfect. E-commerce has a direct impact on a firm's relationship with suppliers, customers, competitors, and partners, as well as how firms market products, advertise, and use brands. Whether you are interested in marketing and sales, design, production, finance, information systems, or logistics, you will need to know how e-commerce technologies can be used to reduce supply chain costs, increase production efficiency, and tighten the relationship with customers. This text is written to help you understand the fundamental business issues in e-commerce.

We spend a considerable amount of effort analyzing the business models and strategies of both online companies and established businesses now employing "bricks-and-clicks" business models. We explore why e-commerce firms fail and the strategic, financial, marketing, and organizational challenges they face. We also discuss how e-commerce firms learned from the mistakes of early firms, and how established firms are using e-commerce to succeed. Above all, we attempt to bring a strong sense of business realism and sensitivity to the often exaggerated descriptions of e-commerce.

The Web and mobile platform have caused a major revolution in marketing and advertising in the United States. We spend two chapters discussing online marketing and advertising. Chapter 6 discusses "traditional" online marketing formats like search engine marketing, display advertising, and e-mail, as well as various Internet marketing technologies underlying those efforts, and metrics for measuring marketing success. Chapter 7 provides an in-depth examination of social, mobile, and local marketing, which relies on mobile devices and social networks.

E-commerce is driven by Internet technology. Internet technology, and information technology in general, is perhaps the star of the show. Without the Internet, e-commerce would be virtually nonexistent. Accordingly, we provide three chapters specifically on the Internet and e-commerce technology, and in every chapter we provide continuing coverage by illustrating how the topic of the chapter is being shaped by new information technologies. For instance, Internet technology drives developments in security and payment systems, marketing strategies and advertising, financial applications, media distribution, business-to-business trade, and retail e-commerce. We discuss the rapid growth of the mobile platform, the emergence of cloud computing, new open source software tools and applications, and new types of Internet-based information systems that support digital business-to-business markets.

E-commerce is not only about business and technology, however. The third part of the equation for understanding e-commerce is society. E-commerce and Internet technologies have important social consequences that business leaders can ignore only at their peril. E-commerce has challenged our concepts of privacy, intellectual property, and even our ideas about national sovereignty and governance. Google, Facebook, Amazon, and assorted advertising networks maintain profiles on millions of shoppers and consumers worldwide. The proliferation of illegally copied music, videos, and books on the Internet, and the growth of social network sites often based on displaying copyrighted materials without permission, are challenging the intellectual property rights of record labels, Hollywood studios, artists, and writers. And many countries—including the United States—are demanding to control the content of Web sites displayed within their borders for political and social reasons. Tax authorities in the United States and Europe are demanding that e-commerce sites pay sales taxes just like ordinary brick and mortar stores on Main Street. As a result of these challenges to existing institutions, e-commerce and the Internet are the subject of increasing investigation, litigation, and legislation. Business leaders need to understand these societal developments, and they cannot afford to assume any longer that the Internet is borderless, beyond social control and regulation, or a place where market efficiency is the only consideration. In addition to an entire chapter devoted to the social and legal implications of e-commerce, each chapter contains material highlighting the social implications of e-commerce.

FEATURES AND COVERAGE

Strong Conceptual Foundation The book emphasizes the three major driving forces behind e-commerce: business development and strategy, technological innovations, and social controversies and impacts. Each of these driving forces is represented in every chapter, and together they provide a strong and coherent conceptual framework for understanding e-commerce. We analyze e-commerce, digital markets, and e-business firms just as we would ordinary businesses and markets using concepts from economics, marketing, finance, sociology, philosophy, and information systems. We strive to maintain a critical perspective on e-commerce and avoid industry hyperbole.

Some of the important concepts from economics and marketing that we use to explore e-commerce are transaction cost, network externalities, information asymmetry, social networks, perfect digital markets, segmentation, price dispersion, targeting, and positioning. Important concepts from the study of information systems and technologies play an important role in the book, including Internet standards and protocols, client/server computing, cloud computing, mobile platform and wireless technologies, and public key encryption, among many others. From the literature on ethics and society, we use important concepts such as intellectual property, privacy, information rights and rights management, governance, public health, and welfare.

From the literature on business, we use concepts such as business process design, return on investment, strategic advantage, industry competitive environment, oligopoly, and monopoly. We also provide a basic understanding of finance and accounting issues, and extend this through an "E-commerce in Action" case that critically examines the financial statements of Amazon. One of the witticisms that emerged from the early years of e-commerce and that still seems apt is the notion that e-commerce changes everything except the rules of business. Businesses still need to make a profit in order to survive in the long term.

Currency Important new developments happen almost every day in e-commerce and the Internet. We try to capture as many of these important new developments as possible in each annual edition. You will not find a more current book for a course offered for the 2016 academic year. Many other texts are already six months to a year out of date before they even reach the printer. This text, in contrast, reflects extensive research through October 2015, just weeks before the book hits the press.

Real-World Business Firm Focus and Cases From Akamai Technologies to Google, Microsoft, Apple, and Amazon, to Facebook, Twitter, and Tumblr, to Netflix, Pandora, and Elemica, this book contains hundreds of real-company examples and over 60 more extensive cases that place coverage in the context of actual e-commerce businesses. You'll find these examples in each chapter, as well as in special features such as chapter-opening, chapter-closing, and "Insight on" cases. The book takes a realistic look at the world of e-commerce, describing what's working and what isn't, rather than presenting a rose-colored or purely "academic" viewpoint.

In-depth Coverage of Marketing and Advertising The text includes two chapters on marketing and advertising, both traditional online marketing and social, mobile, and local marketing. Marketing concepts, including market segmentation, personalization, clickstream analysis, bundling of digital goods, long-tail marketing, and dynamic pricing, are used throughout the text.

In-depth Coverage of B2B E-commerce We devote an entire chapter to an examination of B2B e-commerce. In writing this chapter, we developed a unique and easily understood classification schema to help students understand this complex arena of e-commerce. This chapter covers e-distributors, e-procurement companies, exchanges, and industry consortia, as well as the development of private industrial networks and collaborative commerce.

Current and Future Technology Coverage Internet and related information technologies continue to change rapidly. The most important changes for e-commerce include dramatic price reductions in e-commerce infrastructure (making it much less expensive to develop a sophisticated e-commerce presence), the explosive growth in the mobile platform such as iPhones, iPads, and tablet computers, and expansion in the development of social technologies, which are the foundation of online social networks. What was once a shortage of telecommunications capacity has now turned into a surplus, PC prices have continued to fall, smartphone and tablet sales have soared, Internet high-speed broadband connections are now typical and are continuing to show double-digit growth, and wireless technologies such as Wi-Fi and cellular broadband are transforming how, when, and where people access the Internet. While we thoroughly discuss the current Internet environment, we devote considerable attention to describing emerging technologies and applications such as the Internet of Things, advanced network infrastructure, fiber optics, wireless Web and 4G technologies, Wi-Fi, IP multicasting, and future guaranteed service levels.

Up-to-Date Coverage of the Research Literature This text is well grounded in the e-commerce research literature. We have sought to include, where appropriate, references and analysis of the latest e-commerce research findings, as well as many classic articles, in all of our chapters. We have drawn especially on the disciplines of economics, marketing, and information systems and technologies, as well as law journals and broader social science research journals including sociology and psychology.

We do not use references to Wikipedia in this text, for a variety of reasons. Most colleges do not consider Wikipedia a legitimate or acceptable source for academic research and instruct their students not to cite it. Material found on Wikipedia may be out of date, lack coverage, lack critical perspective, and cannot necessarily be trusted. Our references are to respected academic journals; industry sources such as eMarketer, comScore, Hitwise, Nielsen, and Gartner; newspapers such as the *New York Times* and *Wall Street Journal*; and industry publications such as *Computerworld* and *InformationWeek*, among others. Figures and tables sourced to "authors' estimates" reflect analysis of data from the U.S. Department of Commerce, estimates from various research firms, historical trends, revenues of major online retailers, consumer online buying trends, and economic conditions.

Special Attention to the Social and Legal Aspects of E-commerce We have paid special attention throughout the book to the social and legal context of e-commerce. Chapter 8 is devoted to a thorough exploration of four ethical dimensions of e-commerce: information privacy, intellectual property, governance, and protecting public welfare on the Internet. We have included an analysis of the latest Federal Trade Commission and other regulatory and nonprofit research reports, and their likely impact on the e-commerce environment.

A major theme throughout this chapter, and the remainder of the book, is the impact of social, mobile, and local commerce on how consumers use the Internet.

Writing That's Fun to Read Unlike some textbooks, we've been told by many students that this book is actually fun to read and easy to understand. This is not a book written by committee—you won't find a dozen different people listed as authors, co-authors, and contributors on the title page. We have a consistent voice and perspective that carries through the entire text and we believe the book is the better for it.

OVERVIEW OF THE BOOK

The book is organized into four parts.

Part 1, "Introduction to E-commerce," provides an introduction to the major themes of the book. Chapter 1 defines e-commerce, distinguishes between e-commerce and e-business, and defines the different types of e-commerce. Chapter 2 introduces and defines the concepts of business model and revenue model, describes the major e-commerce business and revenue models for both B2C and B2B firms, and introduces the basic business concepts required throughout the text for understanding e-commerce firms including industry structure, value chains, and firm strategy.

Part 2, "Technology Infrastructure for E-commerce," focuses on the technology infrastructure that forms the foundation for all e-commerce. Chapter 3 traces the historical development of the Internet and thoroughly describes how today's Internet works. A major focus of this chapter is mobile technology, new software applications, and the near-term future Internet that is now under development and will shape the future of e-commerce. Chapter 4 builds on the Internet chapter by focusing on the steps managers need to follow in order to build an e-commerce presence. This e-commerce infrastructure chapter covers the process that should be followed in building an e-commerce presence; the major decisions regarding outsourcing site development and/or hosting; how to choose software, hardware, and other tools that can improve Web site performance, and issues involved in developing a mobile Web site and mobile applications. Chapter 5 focuses on e-commerce security and payments, building on the e-commerce infrastructure discussion of the previous chapter by describing the ways security can be provided over the Internet. This chapter defines digital information security, describes the major threats to security, and then discusses both the technology and policy solutions available to business managers seeking to secure their firm's sites. This chapter concludes with a section on e-commerce payment systems. We identify the various types of online payment systems (credit cards, stored value payment systems such as PayPal, digital wallets such as Google Wallet, and others), and the development of mobile and social payment systems such as Apple Pay, Venmo, and Facebook Messenger.

Part 3, "Business Concepts and Social Issues," focuses directly on the business concepts and social-legal issues that surround the development of e-commerce. Chapter 6 focuses on e-commerce consumer behavior, the Internet audience, and introduces the student to the basics of online marketing and branding, including traditional online marketing technologies and marketing strategies. Topics include the Web site as a marketing platform, search engine marketing and advertising, display ad marketing, e-mail campaigns, affiliate and lead generation marketing programs, multichannel marketing, and various customer retention strategies such as personalization (including interest-based advertising, also known as behavioral targeting) and customer service tools. The chapter also covers other marketing strategies such as pricing and long-tail marketing. Internet marketing technologies (Web transaction logs, tracking files, data mining, and Big Data) and marketing automation and CRM systems are also explored. The chapter concludes with a section on understanding the costs and benefits of various types of online marketing, including a new section on Web analytics software. Chapter 7 is devoted to an in-depth analysis of social, mobile, and local marketing. Topics include Facebook, Twitter, and Pinterest marketing platforms, the evolution of mobile marketing, and the growing use of geo-aware technologies to support proximity marketing. Chapter 8 provides a thorough introduction to the social and legal environment of e-commerce. Here, you will find a description of the ethical and legal dimensions of e-commerce, including a thorough discussion of the latest developments in personal information privacy, intellectual property, Internet governance, jurisdiction, and public health and welfare issues such as pornography, gambling, and health information.

Part 4, "E-commerce in Action," focuses on real-world e-commerce experiences in retail and services, online media, auctions, portals, and social networks, and business-to-business e-commerce. These chapters take a sector approach rather than the conceptual approach used in the earlier chapters. E-commerce is different in each of these sectors. Chapter 9 takes a close look at the experience of firms in the retail marketplace for both goods and services, as well as on-demand service companies such as Uber and Airbnb. Chapter 9 also includes an "E-commerce in Action" case that provides a detailed analysis of the business strategies and financial operating results of Amazon, which can be used as a model to analyze other e-commerce firms. Chapter 10 explores the world of online content and digital media and examines the enormous changes in online publishing and entertainment industries that have occurred over the last two years, including streaming movies, e-books, and online newspapers and magazines. Chapter 11 explores the online world of social networks, auctions, and portals. Chapter 12 concentrates on the world of B2B e-commerce, describing both Net marketplaces and the less-heralded, but very large arena of private industrial networks and the movement toward collaborative commerce.

PEDAGOGY AND CHAPTER OUTLINE

The book's pedagogy emphasizes student cognitive awareness and the ability to analyze, synthesize, and evaluate e-commerce businesses. While there is a strong data and conceptual foundation to the book, we seek to engage student interest with lively writing about e-commerce businesses and the transformation of business models at traditional firms.

Each chapter contains a number of elements designed to make learning easy as well as interesting.

Learning Objectives A list of learning objectives that highlights the key concepts in the chapter guides student study.

Chapter-Opening Cases Each chapter opens with a story about a leading e-commerce company that relates the key objectives of the chapter to a real-life e-commerce business venture.

The Uber-ization of Everything

If you were trying to pick iconic examples of e-commerce in the two decades since it began in 1995, it is likely that companies such as Amazon, eBay, Google, Apple, and Facebook would be high on the list. Today, there's a new company that may become the face of e-commerce as it enters its third decade: Uber. Uber and other firms with similar business models, such as Lyft (a ride service similar to Uber's), Airbnb (rooms for rent), Heal (doctor home visits), Handy and Homejoy (part-time household helpers), Instacart (grocery shopping), Washio (laundry service), and BloomThat (flower delivery), are the pioneers of a new on-demand service e-commerce business model that is sweeping up billions of investment dollars in 2015, and disrupting major industries from transportation, to hotels, real estate, house cleaning, maintenance, and grocery shopping. On-demand service firms have collected over $26 billion in venture capital funding over the last five years, making this the hottest business model in e-commerce for 2015.

© Lenscap/Alamy

Uber provides two major services: UberTaxi (also called UberX), which provides taxi service, and UberBlack, which provides a higher-priced town car service for business executives. UberPool is a ride-sharing service that allows users to share a ride with another person who happens to be going to same place. Google is working with Uber on developing this new service. In several cities, Uber is developing UberEats, a food delivery service; UberRush, a same-day delivery service; and UberCargo, a trucking service.

Uber, headquartered in San Francisco, was founded in 2009 by Travis Kalanick and Garrett Camp, and has grown explosively since then to over 300 cities and 60 countries. Drivers are signing up at an exponential rate, doubling every year; as of the beginning of 2015, there were over 160,000. Over 44% of Uber drivers have college degrees (compared to 15% of taxi drivers), 71% say they have boosted their income and financial security by driving for Uber, and 73% say they prefer a job where they choose their hours rather than a 9-to-5 job, according to an Uber-sponsored survey. In 2015, Uber's revenue is estimated to be $10 billion, with profits (after paying its drivers) of $2 billion. This is five times as much as it made in 2014, when net revenue was about $400 million, which itself is about four times as much as its net revenue in 2013. Uber appears to be growing

3

"Insight on" Cases Each chapter contains three real-world cases illustrating the themes of technology, business, and society. These cases take an in-depth look at relevant topics to help describe and analyze the full breadth of the field of e-commerce. The cases probe such issues as the ability of governments to regulate Internet content, how to design Web sites for accessibility, the challenges faced by luxury marketers in online marketing, and smartphone security.

Margin Glossary
Throughout the text, key terms and their definitions appear in the text margin where they are first introduced.

Real-Company Examples
Drawn from actual e-commerce ventures, well over 100 pertinent examples are used throughout the text to illustrate concepts.

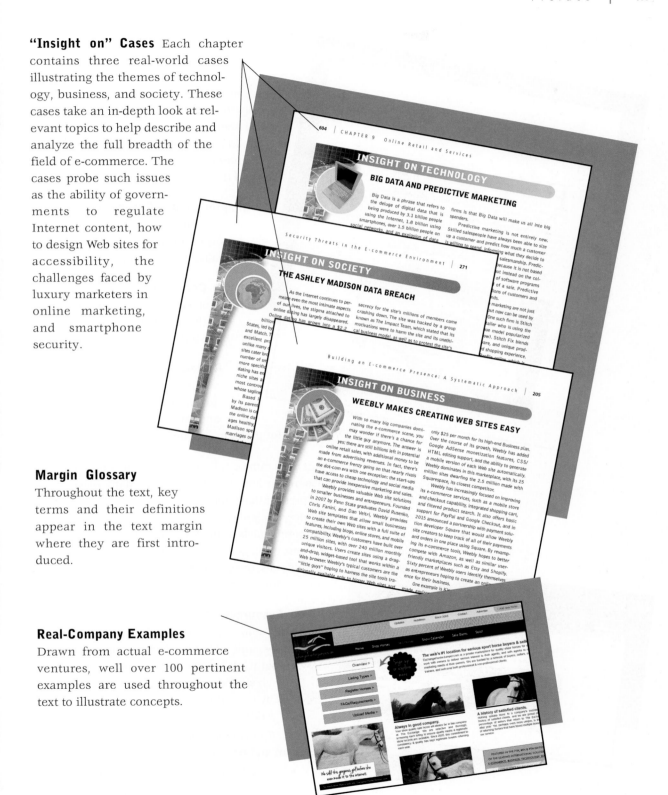

2.5 CASE STUDY

Freemium
Takes Pandora Public

Pandora is the Internet's most successful radio service. As of May 2014, it had over 250 million registered users (200 million of which access the service via a mobile device) and 77 million active listeners. Pandora now accounts for more than 70% of all Internet radio listening hours and a 9% share of total U.S. radio listening (both traditional and Internet).

At Pandora, users select a genre of music based on a favorite musician, and a computer algorithm puts together a personal radio station that plays not only the music of the selected artist but also closely related music by different artists. A team of professional musicians listens to new songs each day and classifies the music according to more than 450 musical criteria. These criteria are used in a computer algorithm to classify new songs into various genres. Within each of these genres are hundreds of subgenres. Altogether, Pandora has a database of over 1 million analyzed songs from over 100,000 artists.

Pandora's founders, Will Glaser and Tim Westergren, launched Pandora in 2005. Their biggest challenge was how to make a business out of a totally new kind of online

© NetPhotos / Alamy

Chapter-Closing Case Studies Each chapter concludes with a robust case study based on a real-world organization. These cases help students synthesize chapter concepts and apply this knowledge to concrete problems and scenarios such as evaluating Pandora's freemium business model, Exchange-HunterJumper's efforts to build a brand, and the evolution of eBay.

Chapter-Ending Pedagogy Each chapter contains extensive end-of-chapter materials designed to reinforce the learning objectives of the chapter.

Key Concepts Keyed to the learning objectives, Key Concepts present the key points of the chapter to aid student study.

Review Questions Thought-provoking questions prompt students to demonstrate their comprehension and apply chapter concepts to management problem solving.

Projects At the end of each chapter are a number of projects that encourage students to apply chapter concepts and to use higher level evaluation skills. Many make use of the Internet and require students to present their findings in an oral or electronic presentation or written report. For instance, students are asked to evaluate publicly available information about a company's financials at the SEC Web site, assess payment system options for companies across international boundaries, or search for the top 10 cookies on their own computer and the sites they are from.

E-commerce 2016
business. technology. society.
Kenneth C. Laudon
Carol Guercio Traver

Welcome to the Companion Website for E-commerce
Business. Technology. Society. 12th edition

This site contains a variety of student resources, including:
• additional projects, exercises, tutorials, and links to useful e-commerce resources
• links to tech tutorials
• information on building a business plan and raising capital
• career information

To access these resources, click on a chapter number on the navigation bar above.

Instructors: For faculty resources, including the instructor's manual and PowerPoint presentations, please visit the instructor resource center for this book.

Web Resources Web resources that can extend students' knowledge of each chapter with projects, exercises, and additional content are available at www.azimuth-interactive.com/ecommerce12e. The Web site contains the following content provided by the authors:

• Additional projects, exercises, and tutorials
• Information on how to build a business plan and revenue models
• Essays on careers in e-commerce

INSTRUCTOR RESOURCES

At the Instructor Resource Center, www.pearsonhighered.com/irc, instructors can easily register to gain access to a variety of instructor resources available with this text in downloadable format. If assistance is needed, our dedicated technical support team is ready to help with the media supplements that accompany this text. Visit http://247.pearsoned.com for answers to frequently asked questions and toll-free user support phone numbers.

The following supplements are available with this text:

- **Instructor's Resource Manual**
- **Test Bank**
- **TestGen® Computerized Test Bank**
- **PowerPoint Presentation**
- **Learning Tracks** These additional essays, created by the authors, provide instructors and students with more in-depth content on selected topics in e-commerce.

  Chapter 1
  1.1 Global E-commerce Europe
  1.2 Global E-commerce Latin America
  1.3 Global E-commerce China

  Chapter 6
  6.1 Basic Marketing Concepts
  6.2 Consumer Behavior: Cultural, Social, and Psychological Background Factors
  6.3 Social Media Marketing—Blogging

  Chapter 7
  Social Media Marketing: Facebook
  Social Media Marketing: Twitter

- **Video Cases** The authors have created a collection of video case studies that integrate short videos, supporting case study material, and case study questions. Video cases can be used in class to promote discussion or as written assignments.

  Chapter 1
  1.1 The Importance of the Internet for E-commerce
  1.2 The Future of E-commerce

  Chapter 2
  2.1 Twitter for Business
  2.2 Angel Investing
  2.3 Deals Galore at Groupon

  Chapter 3
  3.1 How Freshdesk Uses Amazon Web Services
  3.2 Google Data Center Efficiency Best Practices
  3.3 NBA: Competing on Global Delivery

Chapter 4
4.1 WL Gore Expands Using Demandware
4.2 ESPN Goes to eXtreme Scale

Chapter 5
5.1 Cyberespionage: The Chinese Threat
5.2 Stuxnet and Cyberwarfare
5.3 Apple Pay vs. Google Wallet vs. PayPal

Chapter 6
6.1 Nielsen Online Campaign Ratings
6.2 Pandora's Recommendation System

Chapter 7
7.1 The Power of Like
7.2 Pinterest Users Engage with Sephora

Chapter 8
8.1 The Right to Be Forgotten
8.2 Facebook Privacy
8.3 What Net Neutrality Means for You

Chapter 9
9.1 Etsy: A Marketplace and a Community
9.2 Amazon Echo

Chapter 10
10.1 YouTube's 7th Birthday
10.2 Vox Media

Chapter 11
11.1 Facebook Graph Search
11.2 Mint Returns for Goodwill's eBay Auctions of Thrift-Store Finds

Chapter 12
12.1 Flextronics Uses Elementum's Cloud-based Mobile Supply Chain Apps
12.2 Walmart Retail Link

ACKNOWLEDGMENTS

Pearson Education sought the advice of many excellent reviewers, all of whom strongly influenced the organization and substance of this book. The following individuals provided extremely useful evaluations of this and previous editions of the text:

Deniz Aksen, Koç University (Istanbul)

Carrie Andersen, Madison Area Technical College

Christine Barnes, Lakeland Community College

Dr. Shirley A. Becker, Northern Arizona University

Prasad Bingi, Indiana-Purdue University, Fort Wayne

Joanna Broder, Pima Community College

James Buchan, College of the Ozarks

Ashley Bush, Florida State University

Cliff Butler, North Seattle Community College

Adnan Chawdhry, California University of Pennsylvania

Mark Choman, Luzerne City Community College

Andrew Ciganek, Jacksonville State University

Daniel Connolly, University of Denver

Tom Critzer, Miami University

Dursan Delen, Oklahoma State University

Abhijit Deshmukh, University of Massachusetts

Brian L. Dos Santos, University of Louisville

Robert Drevs, University of Notre Dame

Akram El-Tannir, Hariri Canadian University, Lebanon

Kimberly Furumo, University of Hawaii at Hilo

John H. Gerdes, University of California, Riverside

Philip Gordon, University of California at Berkeley

Allan Greenberg, Brooklyn College

Bin Gu, University of Texas at Austin

Norman Hahn, Thomas Nelson Community College

Peter Haried, University of Wisconsin-La Crosse

Sherri Harms, University of Nebraska at Kearney

Sharon Heckel, St. Charles Community College

David Hite, Virginia Intermont College

Gus Jabbour, George Mason University

Kevin Jetton, Texas State University, San Marcos

Ellen Kraft, Georgian Court University

Gilliean Lee, Lander University

Zoonky Lee, University of Nebraska, Lincoln

Andre Lemaylleux, Boston University, Brussels

Haim Levkowitz, University of Massachusetts, Lowell

Yair Levy, Nova Southeastern University

Richard Lucic, Duke University

John Mendonca, Purdue University

Dr. Abdulrahman Mirza, DePaul University

Barbara Ozog, Benedictine University

Kent Palmer, MacMurray College

Karen Palumbo, University of St. Francis

James Pauer, Lorain County Community College

Wayne Pauli, Dakota State University

Sam Perez, Mesa Community College

Jamie Pinchot, Thiel College

Kai Pommerenke, University of California at Santa Cruz

Barry Quinn, University of Ulster, Northern Ireland

Michelle Ramim, Nova Southeastern University

Jay Rhee, San Jose State University

Jorge Romero, Towson University

John Sagi, Anne Arundel Community College

Patricia Sendall, Merrimack College

Dr. Carlos Serrao, ISCTE/DCTI, Portugal

Neerja Sethi, Nanyang Business School, Singapore

Amber Settle, DePaul CTI

Vivek Shah, Texas State University-San Marcos

Wei Shi, Santa Clara University

Seung Jae Shin, Mississippi State University

Sumit Sircar, University of Texas at Arlington

Hongjun Song, University of Memphis

Pamela Specht, University of Nebraska at Omaha

Esther Swilley, Kansas State University

Tony Townsend, Iowa State University

Bill Troy, University of New Hampshire

Susan VandeVen, Southern Polytechnic State University

Hiep Van Dong, Madison Area Technical College

And Michael Van Hilst, Nova Southeastern University

Mary Vitrano, Palm Beach Community College

Andrea Wachter, Point Park University

Catherine Wallace, Massey University, New Zealand

Biao Wang, Boston University

Haibo Wang, Texas A&M International University

Harry Washington, Lincoln University

Rolf Wigand, University of Arkansas at Little Rock

Erin Wilkinson, Johnson & Wales University

Alice Wilson, Cedar Crest College

Dezhi Wu, Southern Utah University

Gene Yelle, SUNY Institute of Technology

David Zolzer, Northwestern State University

We would like to thank eMarketer, Inc. and David Iankelevich for their permission to include data and figures from their research reports in our text. eMarketer is one of the leading independent sources for statistics, trend data, and original analysis covering many topics related to the Internet, e-business, and emerging technologies. eMarketer aggregates e-business data from multiple sources worldwide.

In addition, we would like to thank all those at Pearson who have worked so hard to make sure this book is the very best it can be. We want to thank Nicole Sam, Acquisitions Editor of the Pearson MIS list, and Karalyn Holland, Project Manager, for their support; Jeff Holcomb for overseeing production of this project; and DePinho Design for the outstanding cover design. Very special thanks to Megan Miller, Will Anderson, and Robin Pickering at Azimuth Interactive, Inc., for all their hard work on the production of, and supplements for, this book.

A special thanks also to Susan Hartman, Executive Editor for the first and second editions and to Frank Ruggirello, Publisher at Addison-Wesley when we began this project, and now Vice President and Editorial Director at Benjamin-Cummings.

Finally, last but not least, we would like to thank our family and friends, without whose support this book would not have been possible.

Kenneth C. Laudon
Carol Guercio Traver

Brief Contents

PART 1 Introduction to E-commerce

PART 2 Technology Infrastructure for E-commerce

PART 3 Business Concepts and Social Issues

PART 4 E-commerce in Action

Contents

PART 2 Technology Infrastructure for E-commerce

PART 3   Business Concepts and Social Issues

6   E-COMMERCE MARKETING AND ADVERTISING CONCEPTS   332

---

7   SOCIAL, MOBILE, AND LOCAL MARKETING   420

PART 4 E-commerce in Action

9   ONLINE RETAIL AND SERVICES   572

11   SOCIAL NETWORKS, AUCTIONS, AND PORTALS   708

12   B2B E-COMMERCE: SUPPLY CHAIN MANAGEMENT AND COLLABORATIVE COMMERCE   750

Introduction to E-commerce

The Revolution Is Just Beginning

After reading this chapter, you will be able to:

- Define e-commerce and describe how it differs from e-business.
- Identify and describe the unique features of e-commerce technology and discuss their business significance.
- Describe the major types of e-commerce.
- Understand the evolution of e-commerce from its early years to today.
- Describe the major themes underlying the study of e-commerce.
- Identify the major academic disciplines contributing to e-commerce.

The Uber-ization of Everything

I f you were trying to pick iconic examples of e-commerce in the two decades since it began in 1995, it is likely that companies such as Amazon, eBay, Google, Apple, and Facebook would be high on the list. Today, there's a new company that may become the face of e-commerce as it enters its third decade: Uber. Uber and other firms with similar business models, such as Lyft (a ride service similar to Uber's), Airbnb (rooms for rent), Heal (doctor home visits), Handy and Homejoy (part-time household helpers), Instacart (grocery shopping), Washio (laundry service), and BloomThat

© Lenscap/Alamy

(flower delivery), are the pioneers of a new on-demand service e-commerce business model that is sweeping up billions of investment dollars in 2015, and disrupting major industries from transportation, to hotels, real estate, house cleaning, maintenance, and grocery shopping. On-demand service firms have collected over $26 billion in venture capital funding over the last five years, making this the hottest business model in e-commerce for 2015.

Uber provides two major services: UberTaxi (also called UberX), which provides taxi service, and UberBlack, which provides a higher-priced town car service for business executives. UberPool is a ride-sharing service that allows users to share a ride with another person who happens to be going to same place. Google is working with Uber on developing this new service. In several cities, Uber is developing UberEats, a food delivery service; UberRush, a same-day delivery service; and UberCargo, a trucking service.

Uber, headquartered in San Francisco, was founded in 2009 by Travis Kalanick and Garrett Camp, and has grown explosively since then to over 300 cities and 60 countries. Drivers are signing up at an exponential rate, doubling every year; as of the beginning of 2015, there were over 160,000. Over 44% of Uber drivers have college degrees (compared to 15% of taxi drivers), 71% say they have boosted their income and financial security by driving for Uber, and 73% say they prefer a job where they choose their hours rather than a 9-to-5 job, according to an Uber-sponsored survey. In 2015, Uber's revenue is estimated to be $10 billion, with profits (after paying its drivers) of $2 billion. This is five times as much as it made in 2014, when net revenue was about $400 million, which itself is about four times as much as its net revenue in 2013. Uber appears to be growing at 300% a year! As a result, in 2015, Uber is the most richly valued start-up in history and is currently valued at more than $50 billion.

Uber has a compelling value proposition for both customers and drivers. Customers can sign up for free, request and pay for a ride (at a cost Uber claims is 40% less than a traditional taxi) using a smartphone and credit card, and get picked up within a few minutes. No need to stand on a street corner frantically waving, competing with others, or waiting and waiting for an available cab to drive by, without knowing when that might happen. Instead, customers can use the Uber app to secure a ride, and they know just how long it will take for the ride to arrive, and how much it will cost. With UberPool ride-sharing, the cost of a ride drops by 50%, making it cost-competitive with owning a car in an urban area, according to Uber. For drivers, Uber's value proposition is: set your own hours, work when you like, and put your own car to use generating revenue.

Uber is the current poster child for "digital disruption." It is easy see to why Uber has ignited a firestorm of opposition from existing taxi services both in the United States and around the world. Who can compete in a market where a new upstart firm offers a 50% price reduction? If you've paid $1 million for a license to drive a taxi in New York City, what is it worth now that Uber has arrived? Even governments find Uber to be a disruptive threat. Cities and states do not want to give up regulatory control over passenger safety, driver training, nor the healthy revenue stream generated by charging taxi firms for a taxi license and sales taxes.

Uber's business model differs from traditional retail e-commerce. Uber doesn't sell goods. Instead it has created a smartphone-based platform that enables people who want a service—like a taxi—to find a provider with the resources, such as a personal automobile that spends much of its time parked and a driver with available time, to fill the demand. It's important to understand that although Uber and similar firms were initially called "sharing economy" companies, this is a misnomer. Uber drivers are selling their services as drivers and the temporary use of their car. Uber the company is not in the sharing business either: it charges a hefty fee for every transaction on its platform. Uber is not an example of "peer-to-peer" e-commerce because Uber transactions involve an online intermediary: a third party that takes a cut of all transactions and arranges for the marketplace to exist in the first place.

Uber has disrupted the traditional taxi business model because it offers a superior, fast, convenient taxi-hailing service when compared to traditional taxi companies that rely on the telephone, a central dispatcher using antiquated radio communications to direct cabs, or, as in many urban areas such as New York City, customers standing on street corners frantically waving their hands. With traditional taxi services there is no guarantee you will find a cab, or that a cab will arrive when you really need one. Customers have no way of knowing how long a traditional taxi will take to arrive. Uber reduces that uncertainty: using a smartphone, the customer enters a request for pickup, and nearly instantly (under the best of circumstances) a provider will be found by Uber, and the estimated time of arrival established, along with the price. Riders can accept the price, or find an alternative.

Uber's business model is much more efficient than a traditional taxi firm. Uber does not own taxis and has no maintenance and financing costs. It does not have employees, but instead calls its drivers "independent contractors." Uber is not encumbered with the costs for workers compensation, minimum wage requirements, background checks on drivers, driver training, health insurance, or commercial licensing.

Quality control would seem to be a nightmare with over 160,000 contract drivers. But Uber relies on user reviews of drivers and the ride experience to identify problematic drivers, and driver reviews of customers to identify problematic passengers. It also sets standards for cleanliness. The reviews can be used to discipline drivers: drivers are evaluated by riders on a 5-point scale, and if drivers fall below 4.5 they are warned and may be dropped if they don't improve. Anything less than a 5 is a sign to the company that something was not right about the ride experience. Customers are also rated with a 5-point system. Drivers can refuse to pick up troublesome customers, and the Uber server can delay service to problematic people with low ratings, or ban them entirely. Uber does not publicly report on how many poorly rated drivers or passengers there are in its system. Academic articles have found that in similar on-demand companies, such as Airbnb, there's a built-in bias for both sellers and buyers to give good reviews regardless of the actual experience. If you routinely give low reviews to sellers (drivers), they will think you are too demanding and not service you in the future. If a driver gives low reviews to passengers, they might not rate you highly in return.

Rather than having a dispatcher in every city, Uber has an Internet-based app service running on cloud servers located throughout the world. It does not provide radios to its drivers, who instead must use their own smartphones and cell service, which the drivers pay for. It does not provide insurance or maintenance for its drivers' cars. Uber has shifted the costs of running a taxi service entirely to the drivers. Uber charges prices that vary dynamically with demand: the higher the demand, the greater the price of a ride. Therefore, it is impossible using public information to know if Uber's prices are lower than traditional taxis. Clearly, in high-demand situations they are higher, sometimes ten times higher, than a regulated taxi. There is no regulatory taxi commission setting uniform per mile fares. Consumers do face some traditional uncertainties regarding availability: during a rain storm, a convention, or a sports event, when demand peaks, not enough drivers may be available at any price.

What could be wrong with Uber's apparent over-the-top success? It is digitally disrupting a staid, highly regulated, and decidedly non-digital industry that employs over 200,000 people, most of whom are full-time employees, and who have a median pay of $22,820 per year, or about $11 an hour. In the not so distant future, Uber's part-time drivers will outnumber full-time taxi drivers in the United States, and likely the entire world.

If Uber is the poster child for the new on-demand service economy, it's also the iconic example of the social costs and conflicts associated with this new kind of e-commerce. Uber has been accused by attorney generals in several states of misclassifying its drivers as contractors as opposed to employees, thereby denying the drivers the benefits of employee status, such as minimum wages, social security, workers compensation, and health insurance. In June 2015, the California Labor Commission ruled that Uber's drivers were, in

SOURCES: "Twisting Words to Make 'Sharing' Apps Seem Selfless," by Natasha Singer, *New York Times,* August 9, 2015; "Uber Valued at More Than $50 Billion," by Douglas Macmillan and Telis Demos, *Wall Street Journal,* July 31, 2015; "Uber Dealt Setback on Labor Rules," by Lauren Weber, *Wall Street Journal,* June 18, 2015; "The $50 Billion Question: Can Uber Deliver?," by Douglas Macmillan, *Wall Street Journal,* June 15, 2015; "George Zimmer Starts an 'Uber for Tailors,'" by David Gelles, *New York Times,* May 31, 2015; "Coming Next: The On-Demand Sales Force," by Christopher Mims, *Wall Street Journal,* May 31, 2015; "How Everyone Misjudges the Sharing Economy," by Christopher Mims, *Wall Street Journal,* May 25, 2015; "Icahn Puts Big Wager on Uber Rival Lyft," by Douglas Macmillan, *Wall Street Journal,* May 16, 2015; "An Uber for Doctor Housecalls," by Jennifer Jolly, *New York Times,* May 5, 2015; "Uber Expands Funding Round as Revenue Growth Accelerates," by Douglas Macmillan, *Wall Street Journal,* February 18, 2015; "The On-Demand Economy Is Reshaping Companies and Careers," *The Economist,* January 4, 2015; "The On-Demand Economy: Workers on Tap," *The Economist,* January 3, 2015.

fact, employees under the direct, detailed supervision and control of Uber management, notwithstanding Uber's claims that it merely provides a "platform."

Uber has also been accused of violating public transportation laws and regulations throughout the United States and the world; abusing the personal information it has collected on users of the service; seeking to use personal information to intimidate journalists; failing to protect public safety by refusing to do adequate criminal, medical, and financial background checks on its drivers; taking clandestine actions against its chief competitor Lyft in order to disrupt its business; and being tone-deaf to the complaints of its own drivers against the firm's efforts to reduce driver fees in 2015. Uber drivers went on strike in New York City in October 2014, claiming that Uber had reduced their fares by 25%, and that most drivers were making less than $7–$12 per hour. Expenses for owning and operating the car reduce this wage even further. Uber has been banned in several European cities.

Critics also fear the long-term impact of on-demand service firms, because of their potential for creating a society of part-time, low-paid work, temp work, displacing traditionally full-time, secure jobs—the so-called Uber-ization of work. As one critic put it, Uber is not the Uber for rides so much as it is the Uber for low-paid jobs. Uber responds to this fear by claiming that it is lowering the cost of transportation, making better use of spare human and financial resources, expanding the demand for ride services, and expanding opportunities for car drivers, whose pay is about the same as other taxi drivers. In reality, the point is moot: on-demand service companies will continue to grow explosively until the supply of part-time workers is exhausted. This means, inevitably, the continued growth of a part-time work economy, and growing political pressure to bring benefits to these workers.

Does Uber have a sustainable business model? Is the company really worth over $50 billion based on $2 billion in net revenue a year? If the company continues to triple its net revenue every year, the answer is yes. But Uber does have a few competitors already, such as Lyft in the United States, and local firms in Asia and Europe, and many more emerging monthly. Lyft is currently about one-tenth the size of Uber, but growing rapidly. Lyft and Uber are in a financing war. Lyft is financially backed by Alibaba, Carl Icahn (the billionaire investor), Marc Andreessen (Silicon Valley venture capital), and a number of venture firms. Uber faces a bevy of new, smaller competing firms, including Sidecar, Via, Tripda, and Shuddle, all of whom offer app-based hailing services. China has its own cab hailing services, Kuaidi Dache and Didi Dache. Uber does not have unique technology although it does have a strong brand. Large taxi firms in New York City are launching their own hailing apps, and trumpet their fixed-rate prices without surges: rain, snow, ice or sun, it's all the same price. Half of the U.S. taxi business is concentrated in three cities: New York, Los Angeles, and San Francisco, with New York accounting for about one-third. In New York City, where cabs are plentiful, many critics of Uber's high valuation believe the quickest way from point A to point B is to just hail a cab on the street. Others prefer the certainty of a ride arranged through Uber, or Lyft, regardless of price.

I n 1994, e-commerce as we now know it did not exist. In 2015, just 21 years later, around 172 million American consumers are expected to spend about $531 billion, and businesses around $6.3 trillion, purchasing goods, services, and digital content online or via a mobile device. A similar story has occurred throughout the world. And in this short period of time, e-commerce has been reinvented not just once, but twice.

The early years of e-commerce, during the late 1990s, were a period of business vision, inspiration, and experimentation. It soon became apparent, however, that establishing a successful business model based on those visions would not be easy. There followed a period of retrenchment and reevaluation, which led to the stock market crash of 2000–2001, with the value of e-commerce, telecommunications, and other technology stocks plummeting. After the bubble burst, many people were quick to write off e-commerce. But they were wrong. The surviving firms refined and honed their business models, and the technology became more powerful and less expensive, ultimately leading to business firms that actually produced profits. Between 2002–2008, retail e-commerce grew at more than 25% per year.

Today, we are in the middle of yet another transition. Social networks such as Facebook, Twitter, YouTube, Pinterest, and Tumblr, which enable users to distribute their own content (such as videos, music, photos, personal information, commentary, blogs, and more), have rocketed to prominence. Never before in the history of media have such large audiences been aggregated and made so accessible. Businesses are grappling with how best to approach this audience from a marketing, advertising, and sales perspective. At the same time, the traditional desktop platform and Web browser that most consumers have used to access the Internet in the past is being augmented by mobile devices such as smartphones and tablet computers, and mobile apps. Facilitated by technologies such as cloud computing, mobile devices have become advertising, shopping, reading, and media viewing machines, and in the process, consumer behavior is being transformed yet again. Mobile, social, and local have become driving forces in e-commerce. The mobile platform infrastructure is also giving birth to yet another e-commerce innovation: on-demand services that are local and personal. From hailing a taxi, to shopping, to washing your clothes, these new businesses are creating a marketspace where owners of resources such as cars, spare bedrooms, and spare time can find a market of eager consumers looking to buy a service in a few minutes using their smartphones. The opening case on Uber is a leading example of these new on-demand service firms that are disrupting traditional business models.

1.1 E-COMMERCE: THE REVOLUTION IS JUST BEGINNING

Table 1.1 describes the major trends in e-commerce in 2015–2016. The mobile platform based on smartphones and tablet computers has finally arrived with a bang, making true mobile e-commerce a reality. Social networks are enabling social e-commerce by providing search, advertising, and payment services to vendors and customers. More

TABLE 1.1	MAJOR TRENDS IN E-COMMERCE 2015–2016

BUSINESS

- Retail e-commerce in the United States continues double-digit growth (over 14%), with global growth rates even higher in Europe and emerging markets such as China, India, and Brazil.
- Mobile e-commerce explodes and is estimated to reach around $128 billion in the United States in 2015.
- The mobile app ecosystem continues to grow, with almost 200 million U.S. consumers using mobile apps.
- Social e-commerce, based on social networks and supported by advertising, emerges and grows by 25% from 2013 to 2014, generating over $3.3 billion in revenue for the top 500 social media retailers in the United States.
- Local e-commerce, the third dimension of the mobile, social, local e-commerce wave, also is growing in the United States, fueled by an explosion of interest in on-demand services such as Uber, to over $25 billion in 2015.
- On-demand service firms like Uber and Airbnb attract billions in capital, garner multi-billion dollar valuations, and show explosive growth.
- Mobile and social advertising platforms show strong growth and begin to challenge search engine marketing.
- Small businesses and entrepreneurs continue to flood into the e-commerce marketplace, often riding on the infrastructures created by industry giants such as Apple, Facebook, Amazon, Google, and eBay.
- B2B e-commerce in the United States continues to strengthen and grow to $6.3 trillion.

TECHNOLOGY

- A mobile computing and communications platform based on smartphones, tablet computers, and mobile apps becomes a reality, rivaling the PC platform and creating an alternative platform for online transactions, marketing, advertising, and media viewing. Mobile messaging services like WhatsApp and Snapchat are used by 40% of smartphone users.
- Cloud computing completes the transformation of the mobile platform by storing consumer content and software on Internet servers and making it available to any consumer-connected device from the desktop to a smartphone.
- Computing and networking component prices continue to fall dramatically.
- As firms track the trillions of online interactions that occur each day, a flood of data, typically referred to as Big Data, is being produced.
- In order to make sense out of Big Data, firms turn to sophisticated software called business analytics (or Web analytics) that can identify purchase patterns as well as consumer interests and intentions in milliseconds.

SOCIETY

- User-generated content, published online as social network posts, tweets, blogs, and pins, as well as video and photo-sharing, continues to grow and provides a method of self-publishing that engages millions.
- The amount of data the average American consumes continues to increase, more than doubling from an average of about 34 gigabytes in 2008 to an estimated 74 gigabytes by 2015.
- Social networks encourage self-revelation, while threatening privacy.
- Participation by adults in social networks increases; Facebook becomes ever more popular in all demographic categories.
- Conflicts over copyright management and control continue, but there is substantial agreement among online distributors and copyright owners that they need one another.
- Taxation of online sales becomes more widespread and accepted by large online merchants.
- Surveillance of online communications by both repressive regimes and Western democracies grows.
- Concerns over commercial and governmental privacy invasion increase.
- Online security continues to decline as major sites are hacked and lose control over customer information.
- Spam remains a significant problem despite legislation and promised technology fixes.
- On-demand service e-commerce produces a flood of temporary, poorly paid jobs without benefits.

and more people and businesses are using the Internet and mobile devices to conduct commerce; smaller, local firms are taking advantage of the Internet and mobile platform as e-commerce technologies become less and less expensive. New e-commerce brands have emerged while traditional retail brands such as Walmart and Macy's are further extending their omnichannel strategies and retaining their dominant retail positions by strengthening their e-commerce operations. At the societal level, other trends are apparent. The Internet and mobile platform provide an environment that allows millions of people to create and share content, establish new social bonds, and strengthen existing ones through social network, photo- and video-posting, and blogging sites and apps, while at the same time creating significant privacy issues. The major digital copyright owners have increased their pursuit of online file-sharing services with mixed success, while reaching broad agreements with the big technology players like Apple, Amazon, and Google to protect intellectual property rights. Governments have successfully moved toward taxation of e-commerce sales. Sovereign nations have expanded their surveillance of, and control over, online communications and content as a part of their anti-terrorist activities and their traditional interest in snooping on citizens. Privacy seems to have lost some of its meaning in an age when millions create public online personal profiles.

THE FIRST 30 SECONDS

It is important to realize that the rapid growth and change that has occurred in the first 21 years of e-commerce represents just the beginning—what could be called the first 30 seconds of the e-commerce revolution. Technology continues to evolve at exponential rates. This underlying ferment presents entrepreneurs with new opportunities to both create new businesses and new business models in traditional industries, and also to destroy old businesses. Business change becomes disruptive, rapid, and even destructive, while offering entrepreneurs new opportunities and resources for investment. For instance, on-demand service firms such as Uber and Airbnb threaten the traditional taxi and low-cost hotel industries.

Improvements in underlying information technologies and continuing entrepreneurial innovation in business and marketing promise as much change in the next decade as was seen in the previous decade. The twenty-first century will be the age of a digitally enabled social and commercial life, the outlines of which we can barely perceive at this time. Analysts estimate that by 2019, consumers will be spending over $775 billion and businesses over $8.5 trillion in digital transactions. It appears likely that e-commerce will eventually impact nearly all commerce, and that most commerce will be e-commerce by the year 2050.

Can e-commerce continue to grow indefinitely? It's possible that at some point, e-commerce growth may slow simply as a result of overload: people may just not have the time to watch yet another online video, open another e-mail, or read another blog, tweet, or Facebook update. However, currently, there is no foreseeable limit to the continued rapid development of e-commerce technology, or limits on the inventiveness of entrepreneurs to develop new uses for the technology. Therefore, for now at least, it is likely that the disruptive process will continue.

Business fortunes are made—and lost—in periods of extraordinary change such as this. The next five years hold out exciting opportunities—as well as risks—for new and traditional businesses to exploit digital technology for market advantage. For society as a whole, the next few decades offer the possibility of extraordinary gains in social wealth as the digital revolution works its way through larger and larger segments of the world's economy, offering the possibility of high rates of productivity and income growth in an inflation-free environment.

As a business or technology student, this book will help you perceive and understand the opportunities and risks that lie ahead. By the time you finish, you will be able to identify the technological, business, and social forces that have shaped, and continue to shape, the growth of e-commerce, and ready to participate in, and ultimately guide, discussions of e-commerce in the firms where you work.

WHAT IS E-COMMERCE?

e-commerce

the use of the Internet, the Web, and mobile apps and browsers running on mobile devices to transact business. More formally, digitally enabled commercial transactions between and among organizations and individuals

Our focus in this book is **e-commerce**—the use of the Internet, the World Wide Web (Web), and mobile apps and browsers running on mobile devices to transact business. Although the terms Internet and Web are often used interchangeably, they are actually two very different things. The *Internet* is a worldwide network of computer networks, and the *Web* is one of the Internet's most popular services, providing access to billions of Web pages. An *app* (short-hand for application) is a software application. The term is typically used when referring to mobile applications, although it is also sometimes used to refer to desktop computer applications as well. A *mobile browser* is a version of Web browser software accessed via a mobile device. (We describe the Internet, Web, and mobile platform more fully later in this chapter and in Chapters 3 and 4.) More formally, we focus on digitally enabled commercial transactions between and among organizations and individuals. Each of these components of our working definition of e-commerce is important. *Digitally enabled transactions* include all transactions mediated by digital technology. For the most part, this means transactions that occur over the Internet, the Web, and/or via mobile devices. *Commercial transactions* involve the exchange of value (e.g., money) across organizational or individual boundaries in return for products and services. Exchange of value is important for understanding the limits of e-commerce. Without an exchange of value, no commerce occurs.

The professional literature sometimes refers to e-commerce as digital commerce. For our purposes, we consider e-commerce and digital commerce to be synonymous.

THE DIFFERENCE BETWEEN E-COMMERCE AND E-BUSINESS

There is a debate about the meaning and limitations of both e-commerce and e-business. Some argue that e-commerce encompasses the entire world of electronically based organizational activities that support a firm's market exchanges—including a firm's entire information system's infrastructure (Rayport and Jaworski, 2003). Others argue, on the other hand, that e-business encompasses the entire world of internal and external electronically based activities, including e-commerce (Kalakota and Robinson, 2003).

We think it is important to make a working distinction between e-commerce and e-business because we believe they refer to different phenomena. E-commerce is not

FIGURE 1.1	THE DIFFERENCE BETWEEN E-COMMERCE AND E-BUSINESS

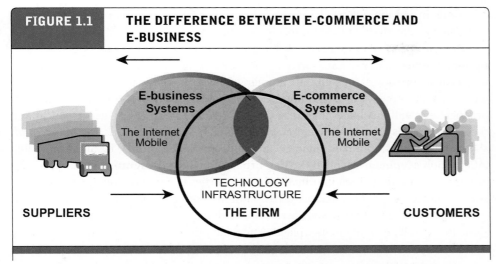

E-commerce primarily involves transactions that cross firm boundaries. E-business primarily involves the application of digital technologies to business processes within the firm.

"anything digital" that a firm does. For purposes of this text, we will use the term **e-business** to refer primarily to the digital enabling of transactions and processes *within* a firm, involving information systems under the control of the firm. For the most part, in our view, e-business does not include commercial transactions involving an exchange of value across organizational boundaries. For example, a company's online inventory control mechanisms are a component of e-business, but such internal processes do not directly generate revenue for the firm from outside businesses or consumers, as e-commerce, by definition, does. It is true, however, that a firm's e-business infrastructure provides support for online e-commerce exchanges; the same infrastructure and skill sets are involved in both e-business and e-commerce. E-commerce and e-business systems blur together at the business firm boundary, at the point where internal business systems link up with suppliers or customers (see **Figure 1.1**). E-business applications turn into e-commerce precisely when an exchange of value occurs (see Mesenbourg, U.S. Department of Commerce, 2001, for a similar view). We will examine this intersection further in Chapter 12.

e-business
the digital enabling of transactions and processes within a firm, involving information systems under the control of the firm

WHY STUDY E-COMMERCE?

Why are there college courses and textbooks on e-commerce when there are no courses or textbooks on "TV Commerce," "Radio Commerce," "Railroad Commerce," or "Highway Commerce," even though these technologies had profound impacts on commerce in the twentieth century and account for far more commerce than e-commerce?

The reason for the interest specifically in e-commerce is that e-commerce technology (discussed in detail in Chapters 3 and 4) is different and more powerful than any of the other technologies we have seen in the past century. E-commerce technologies—and the digital markets that result—have brought about some fundamental, unprecedented shifts in commerce. While these other technologies transformed economic life in the twentieth century, the evolving Internet and other information technologies are shaping the twenty-first century.

Prior to the development of e-commerce, the marketing and sale of goods was a mass-marketing and sales force–driven process. Marketers viewed consumers as passive targets of advertising campaigns and branding "blitzes" intended to influence their long-term product perceptions and immediate purchasing behavior. Companies sold their products via well-insulated channels. Consumers were trapped by geographical and social boundaries, unable to search widely for the best price and quality. Information about prices, costs, and fees could be hidden from the consumer, creating profitable information asymmetries for the selling firm. **Information asymmetry** refers to any disparity in relevant market information among parties in a transaction. It was so expensive to change national or regional prices in traditional retailing (what are called *menu costs*) that one national price was the norm, and dynamic pricing to the marketplace let alone to individuals in the marketplace—changing prices in real time—was unheard of. In this environment, manufacturers prospered by relying on huge production runs of products that could not be customized or personalized. One of the shifts that e-commerce is bringing about is a reduction in information asymmetry among market participants (consumers and merchants). Preventing consumers from learning about costs, price discrimination strategies, and profits from sales becomes more difficult with e-commerce, and the entire marketplace potentially becomes highly price competitive. At the same time, online merchants gain considerable market power over consumers by using consumer personal information in ways inconceivable 10 years ago to maximize their revenues.

information asymmetry
any disparity in relevant market information among parties in a transaction

EIGHT UNIQUE FEATURES OF E-COMMERCE TECHNOLOGY

Figure 1.2 illustrates eight unique features of e-commerce technology that both challenge traditional business thinking and explain why we have so much interest in e-commerce. These unique dimensions of e-commerce technologies suggest many new possibilities for marketing and selling—a powerful set of interactive, personalized, and rich messages are available for delivery to segmented, targeted audiences. E-commerce technologies make it possible for merchants to know much more about consumers and to be able to use this information more effectively than was ever true in the past. Online merchants can use this new information to develop new information asymmetries, enhance their ability to brand products, charge premium prices for high-quality service, and segment the market into an endless number of subgroups, each receiving a different price. To complicate matters further, these same technologies make it possible for merchants to know more about other merchants than was ever true in the past. This presents the possibility that merchants might collude on prices rather than compete and drive overall average prices up. This strategy works especially well when there are just a few suppliers (Varian, 2000a). We examine these different visions of e-commerce further in Section 1.2 and throughout the book.

Each of the dimensions of e-commerce technology illustrated in Figure 1.2 deserves a brief exploration, as well as a comparison to both traditional commerce and other forms of technology-enabled commerce.

FIGURE 1.2	EIGHT UNIQUE FEATURES OF E-COMMERCE TECHNOLOGY

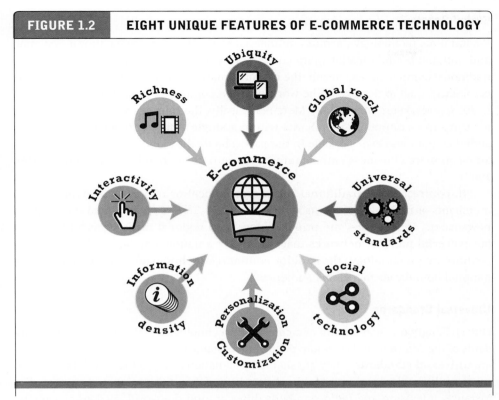

E-commerce technologies provide a number of unique features that have impacted the conduct of business.

Ubiquity

In traditional commerce, a **marketplace** is a physical place you visit in order to transact. For example, television and radio typically motivate the consumer to go someplace to make a purchase. E-commerce, in contrast, is characterized by its **ubiquity**: it is available just about everywhere, at all times. It liberates the market from being restricted to a physical space and makes it possible to shop from your desktop, at home, at work, or even from your car, using mobile e-commerce. The result is called a **marketspace**—a marketplace extended beyond traditional boundaries and removed from a temporal and geographic location. From a consumer point of view, ubiquity reduces *transaction costs*—the costs of participating in a market. To transact, it is no longer necessary that you spend time and money traveling to a market. At a broader level, the ubiquity of e-commerce lowers the cognitive energy required to transact in a marketspace. *Cognitive energy* refers to the mental effort required to complete a task. Humans generally seek to reduce cognitive energy outlays. When given a choice, humans will choose the path requiring the least effort—the most convenient path (Shapiro and Varian, 1999; Tversky and Kahneman, 1981).

marketplace
physical space you visit in order to transact

ubiquity
available just about everywhere, at all times

marketspace
marketplace extended beyond traditional boundaries and removed from a temporal and geographic location

Global Reach

E-commerce technology permits commercial transactions to cross cultural, regional, and national boundaries far more conveniently and cost-effectively than is true in traditional commerce. As a result, the potential market size for e-commerce merchants is roughly equal to the size of the world's online population (an estimated 3.1 billion in 2015) (eMarketer, Inc., 2015a). More realistically, the Internet makes it much easier for start-up e-commerce merchants within a single country to achieve a national audience than was ever possible in the past. The total number of users or customers an e-commerce business can obtain is a measure of its **reach** (Evans and Wurster, 1997).

reach
the total number of users or customers an e-commerce business can obtain

In contrast, most traditional commerce is local or regional—it involves local merchants or national merchants with local outlets. Television and radio stations, and newspapers, for instance, are primarily local and regional institutions with limited but powerful national networks that can attract a national audience. In contrast to e-commerce technology, these older commerce technologies do not easily cross national boundaries to a global audience.

Universal Standards

One strikingly unusual feature of e-commerce technologies is that the technical standards of the Internet, and therefore the technical standards for conducting e-commerce, are **universal standards**—they are shared by all nations around the world. In contrast, most traditional commerce technologies differ from one nation to the next. For instance, television and radio standards differ around the world, as does cell phone technology. The universal technical standards of e-commerce greatly lower *market entry costs*—the cost merchants must pay just to bring their goods to market. At the same time, for consumers, universal standards reduce *search costs*—the effort required to find suitable products. And by creating a single, one-world marketspace, where prices and product descriptions can be inexpensively displayed for all to see, *price discovery* becomes simpler, faster, and more accurate (Banerjee et al., 2005; Bakos, 1997; Kambil, 1997). Users, both businesses and individuals, also experience *network externalities*—benefits that arise because everyone uses the same technology. With e-commerce technologies, it is possible for the first time in history to easily find many of the suppliers, prices, and delivery terms of a specific product anywhere in the world, and to view them in a coherent, comparative environment. Although this is not necessarily realistic today for all or even most products, it is a potential that will be exploited in the future.

universal standards
standards that are shared by all nations around the world

Richness

Information **richness** refers to the complexity and content of a message (Evans and Wurster, 1999). Traditional markets, national sales forces, and small retail stores have great richness: they are able to provide personal, face-to-face service using aural and visual cues when making a sale. The richness of traditional markets makes them a powerful selling or commercial environment. Prior to the development of the Web,

richness
the complexity and content of a message

there was a trade-off between richness and reach: the larger the audience reached, the less rich the message. E-commerce technologies have the potential for offering considerably more information richness than traditional media such as printing presses, radio, and television because they are interactive and can adjust the message to individual users. Chatting with an online sales person, for instance, comes very close to the customer experience in a small retail shop. The richness enabled by e-commerce technologies allows retail and service merchants to market and sell "complex" goods and services that heretofore required a face-to-face presentation by a sales force to a much larger audience.

Interactivity

Unlike any of the commercial technologies of the twentieth century, with the possible exception of the telephone, e-commerce technologies allow for **interactivity**, meaning they enable two-way communication between merchant and consumer and among consumers. Traditional television, for instance, cannot ask viewers questions or enter into conversations with them, or request that customer information be entered into a form. In contrast, all of these activities are possible on an e-commerce site and are now commonplace with smartphones, social networks, and Twitter. Interactivity allows an online merchant to engage a consumer in ways similar to a face-to-face experience.

interactivity
technology that allows for two-way communication between merchant and consumer

Information Density

E-commerce technologies vastly increase **information density**—the total amount and quality of information available to all market participants, consumers, and merchants alike. E-commerce technologies reduce information collection, storage, processing, and communication costs. At the same time, these technologies greatly increase the currency, accuracy, and timeliness of information—making information more useful and important than ever. As a result, information becomes more plentiful, less expensive, and of higher quality.

information density
the total amount and quality of information available to all market participants

A number of business consequences result from the growth in information density. In e-commerce markets, prices and costs become more transparent. *Price transparency* refers to the ease with which consumers can find out the variety of prices in a market; *cost transparency* refers to the ability of consumers to discover the actual costs merchants pay for products (Sinha, 2000). But there are advantages for merchants as well. Online merchants can discover much more about consumers; this allows merchants to segment the market into groups willing to pay different prices and permits them to engage in *price discrimination*—selling the same goods, or nearly the same goods, to different targeted groups at different prices. For instance, an online merchant can discover a consumer's avid interest in expensive exotic vacations, and then pitch expensive exotic vacation plans to that consumer at a premium price, knowing this person is willing to pay extra for such a vacation. At the same time, the online merchant can pitch the same vacation plan at a lower price to more price-sensitive consumers. Merchants also have enhanced abilities to differentiate their products in terms of cost, brand, and quality.

Personalization/Customization

personalization
the targeting of marketing messages to specific individuals by adjusting the message to a person's name, interests, and past purchases

customization
changing the delivered product or service based on a user's preferences or prior behavior

E-commerce technologies permit **personalization**: merchants can target their marketing messages to specific individuals by adjusting the message to a person's name, interests, and past purchases. Today this is achieved in a few milliseconds and followed by an advertisement based on the consumer's profile. The technology also permits **customization**—changing the delivered product or service based on a user's preferences or prior behavior. Given the interactive nature of e-commerce technology, much information about the consumer can be gathered in the marketplace at the moment of purchase. With the increase in information density, a great deal of information about the consumer's past purchases and behavior can be stored and used by online merchants. The result is a level of personalization and customization unthinkable with traditional commerce technologies. For instance, you may be able to shape what you see on television by selecting a channel, but you cannot change the contents of the channel you have chosen. In contrast, the online version of the *Wall Street Journal* allows you to select the type of news stories you want to see first, and gives you the opportunity to be alerted when certain events happen. Personalization and customization allow firms to precisely identify market segments and adjust their messages accordingly.

Social Technology: User-Generated Content and Social Networks

In a way quite different from all previous technologies, e-commerce technologies have evolved to be much more social by allowing users to create and share content with a worldwide community. Using these forms of communication, users are able to create new social networks and strengthen existing ones. All previous mass media in modern history, including the printing press, used a broadcast model (one-to-many) where content is created in a central location by experts (professional writers, editors, directors, actors, and producers) and audiences are concentrated in huge aggregates to consume a standardized product. The telephone would appear to be an exception but it is not a mass communication technology. Instead the telephone is a one-to-one technology. E-commerce technologies have the potential to invert this standard media model by giving users the power to create and distribute content on a large scale, and permit users to program their own content consumption. E-commerce technologies provide a unique, many-to-many model of mass communication.

Table 1.2 provides a summary of each of the unique features of e-commerce technology and their business significance.

TYPES OF E-COMMERCE

There are several different types of e-commerce and many different ways to characterize them. **Table 1.3** on page 18 lists the major types of e-commerce discussed in this book.[1] For the most part, we distinguish different types of e-commerce by the nature of

[1] For the purposes of this text, we subsume business-to-government (B2G) e-commerce within B2B e-commerce, viewing the government as simply a form of business when it acts as a procurer of goods and/or services.

TABLE 1.2	BUSINESS SIGNIFICANCE OF THE EIGHT UNIQUE FEATURES OF E-COMMERCE TECHNOLOGY
E-COMMERCE TECHNOLOGY DIMENSION	**BUSINESS SIGNIFICANCE**
Ubiquity—E-commerce technology is available everywhere: at work, at home, and elsewhere via mobile devices, anytime.	The marketplace is extended beyond traditional boundaries and is removed from a temporal and geographic location. "Marketspace" is created; shopping can take place anywhere. Customer convenience is enhanced, and shopping costs are reduced.
Global reach—The technology reaches across national boundaries, around the earth.	Commerce is enabled across cultural and national boundaries seamlessly and without modification. "Marketspace" includes potentially billions of consumers and millions of businesses worldwide.
Universal standards—There is one set of technology standards.	There is a common, inexpensive, global technology foundation for businesses to use.
Richness—Video, audio, and text messages are possible.	Video, audio, and text marketing messages are integrated into a single marketing message and consuming experience.
Interactivity—The technology works through interaction with the user.	Consumers are engaged in a dialog that dynamically adjusts the experience to the individual, and makes the consumer a co-participant in the process of delivering goods to the market.
Information density—The technology reduces information costs and raises quality.	Information processing, storage, and communication costs drop dramatically, while currency, accuracy, and timeliness improve greatly. Information becomes plentiful, cheap, and accurate.
Personalization/Customization—The technology allows personalized messages to be delivered to individuals as well as groups.	Personalization of marketing messages and customization of products and services are based on individual characteristics.
Social technology—User-generated content and social networks.	New online social and business models enable user content creation and distribution, and support social networks.

the market relationship—who is selling to whom. Mobile, social, and local e-commerce can be looked at as subsets of these types of e-commerce.

Business-to-Consumer (B2C) E-commerce

The most commonly discussed type of e-commerce is **business-to-consumer (B2C) e-commerce**, in which online businesses attempt to reach individual consumers. B2C commerce includes purchases of retail goods, travel services, and online content. Even though B2C is comparatively small (an estimated $531 billion in 2015 in the United States), it has grown exponentially since 1995, and is the type of e-commerce that most

business-to-consumer (B2C) e-commerce
online businesses selling to individual consumers

TABLE 1.3	MAJOR TYPES OF E-COMMERCE
TYPE OF E-COMMERCE	**EXAMPLE**
B2C—business-to-consumer	Amazon is a general merchandiser that sells consumer products to retail consumers.
B2B—business-to-business	Go2Paper is an independent third-party marketplace that serves the paper industry.
C2C—consumer-to-consumer	Auction sites such as eBay, and listing sites such as Craigslist, enable consumers to auction or sell goods directly to other consumers. Airbnb and Uber provide similar platforms for services such as room rental and transportation.
M-commerce—mobile e-commerce	Mobile devices such as tablet computers and smartphones can be used to conduct commercial transactions.
Social e-commerce	Facebook is both the leading social network and social e-commerce site.
Local e-commerce	Groupon offers subscribers daily deals from local businesses in the form of Groupons, discount coupons that take effect once enough subscribers have agreed to purchase.

consumers are likely to encounter (see **Figure 1.3**). Within the B2C category, there are many different types of business models. Chapter 2 has a detailed discussion of seven different B2C business models: portals, online retailers, content providers, transaction brokers, market creators, service providers, and community providers.

Business-to-Business (B2B) E-commerce

business-to-business (B2B) e-commerce

online businesses selling to other businesses

Business-to-business (B2B) e-commerce, in which businesses focus on selling to other businesses, is the largest form of e-commerce, with around $6.3 trillion in transactions in the United States in 2015 (see **Figure 1.4** on page 20). There is an estimated $14.6 trillion in business-to-business exchanges of all kinds, online and offline, suggesting that B2B e-commerce has significant growth potential. The ultimate size of B2B e-commerce is potentially huge. There are two primary business models used within the B2B arena: Net marketplaces, which include e-distributors, e-procurement companies, exchanges and industry consortia, and private industrial networks.

Consumer-to-Consumer (C2C) E-commerce

consumer-to-consumer (C2C) e-commerce

consumers selling to other consumers

Consumer-to-consumer (C2C) e-commerce provides a way for consumers to sell to each other, with the help of an online market maker (also called a platform provider) such as eBay or Etsy, the classifieds site Craigslist, or on-demand service companies such as Airbnb and Uber. Given that in 2014, eBay by itself generated around $83 billion in gross merchandise volume around the world, it is probably safe to estimate that the size of the global C2C market in 2015 is more than $100 billion (eBay, 2015). In C2C e-commerce, the consumer prepares the product for market, places the product for auction or sale, and relies on the market maker to provide catalog, search engine, and transaction-clearing capabilities so that products can be easily displayed, discovered, and paid for.

Mobile E-commerce (M-commerce)

Mobile e-commerce, or m-commerce, refers to the use of mobile devices to enable online transactions. Described more fully in Chapter 3, m-commerce involves the use of cellular and wireless networks to connect laptops, smartphones such as the iPhone and Android phones, and tablet computers such as the iPad to the Internet. Once connected, mobile consumers can conduct transactions, including stock trades, in-store price comparisons, banking, travel reservations, and more. M-commerce purchases are expected to reach around $128 billion in 2015 and to grow rapidly in the United States over the next five years (eMarketer, Inc., 2015b).

mobile e-commerce (m-commerce)
use of mobile devices to enable online transactions

Social E-commerce

Social e-commerce is e-commerce that is enabled by social networks and online social relationships. It is sometimes also referred to as Facebook commerce, but in actuality is a much larger phenomenon that extends beyond just Facebook. The growth

social e-commerce
e-commerce enabled by social networks and online social relationships

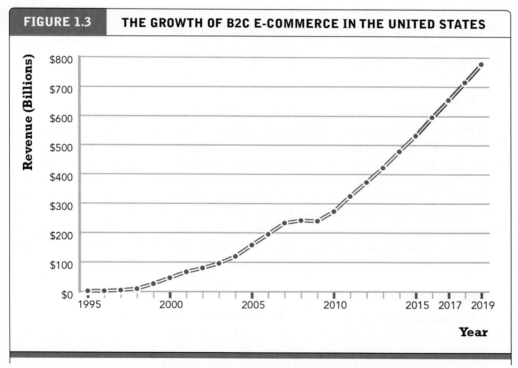

| FIGURE 1.3 | THE GROWTH OF B2C E-COMMERCE IN THE UNITED STATES |

In the early years, B2C e-commerce was doubling or tripling each year. Although B2C e-commerce growth in the United States slowed in 2008–2009 due to the economic recession, it resumed growing at about 13% in 2010 and since then, has continued to grow at double-digit rates.

SOURCES: Based on data from eMarketer, Inc., 2015c, 2015d; authors' estimates.

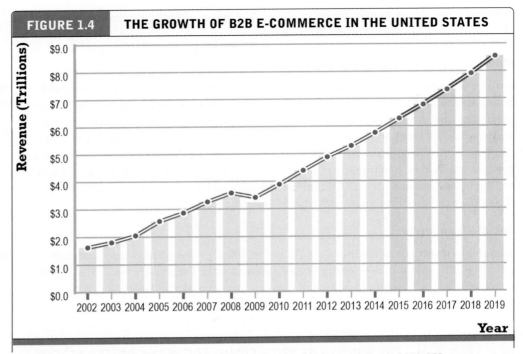

| FIGURE 1.4 | THE GROWTH OF B2B E-COMMERCE IN THE UNITED STATES |

B2B e-commerce in the United States is about 10 times the size of B2C e-commerce. In 2019, B2B e-commerce is projected to be over $8.5 trillion. (Note: Does not include EDI transactions.)
SOURCES: Based on data from U.S. Census Bureau, 2015; authors' estimates.

of social e-commerce is being driven by a number of factors, including the increasing popularity of social sign-on (signing onto Web sites using your Facebook or other social network ID), network notification (the sharing of approval or disapproval of products, services, and content via Facebook's Like button or Twitter tweets), online collaborative shopping tools, and social search (recommendations from online trusted friends). Social e-commerce is still in its infancy, but in 2014, the top 500 retailers in Internet Retailer's Social Media 500 earned about $3.3 billion from social commerce, a 25% increase over 2013, and shoppers clicking from social networks to Social Media 500 retailers' Web sites accounted for about 5.8% of all traffic to those Web sites in 2014, up from about 5.4% in the previous year (Zaroban, 2015).

Local E-commerce

local e-commerce
e-commerce that is focused on engaging the consumer based on his or her current geographic location

Local e-commerce, as its name suggests, is a form of e-commerce that is focused on engaging the consumer based on his or her current geographic location. Local merchants use a variety of online marketing techniques to drive consumers to their stores. Local e-commerce is the third prong of the mobile, social, local e-commerce wave, and fueled by an explosion of interest in local on-demand services such as Uber, is expected to grow in the United States to over $25 billion in 2015.

Figure 1.5 illustrates the relative size of all of the various types of e-commerce.

GROWTH OF THE INTERNET, WEB, AND MOBILE PLATFORM

The technology juggernauts behind e-commerce are the Internet, the Web, and increasingly, the mobile platform. We describe the Internet, Web, and mobile platform in some detail in Chapter 3. The **Internet** is a worldwide network of computer networks built on common standards. Created in the late 1960s to connect a small number of mainframe computers and their users, the Internet has since grown into the world's largest network. It is impossible to say with certainty exactly how many computers and other wireless access devices such as smartphones are connected to the Internet worldwide at any one time, but the number is clearly more than 1 billion. The Internet links businesses, educational institutions, government agencies, and individuals together, and provides users with services such as e-mail, document transfer, shopping, research, instant messaging, music, videos, and news.

One way to measure the growth of the Internet is by looking at the number of Internet hosts with domain names. (An *Internet host* is defined by the Internet Systems Consortium as any IP address that returns a domain name in the in-addr.arpa

Internet
worldwide network of computer networks built on common standards

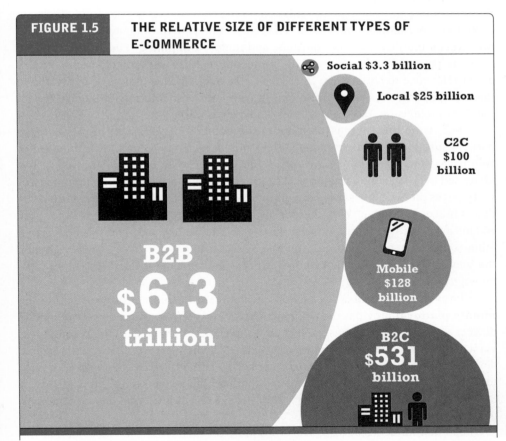

| FIGURE 1.5 | THE RELATIVE SIZE OF DIFFERENT TYPES OF E-COMMERCE |

Social $3.3 billion

Local $25 billion

C2C $100 billion

B2B $6.3 trillion

Mobile $128 billion

B2C $531 billion

B2B e-commerce dwarfs all other forms of e-commerce; mobile, social, and local e-commerce, although growing rapidly, are still relatively small in comparison to "traditional" e-commerce.

domain, which is a special part of the DNS namespace that resolves IP addresses into domain names.) In July 2015, there were more than 1 billion Internet hosts in over 245 countries, up from just 70 million in 2000 (Internet Systems Consortium, 2015).

The Internet has shown extraordinary growth patterns when compared to other electronic technologies of the past. It took radio 38 years to achieve a 30% share of U.S. households. It took television 17 years to achieve a 30% share. It took only 10 years for the Internet/Web to achieve a 53% share of U.S. households once a graphical user interface was invented for the Web in 1993.

World Wide Web (the Web)
provides access to billions of Web pages

The **World Wide Web (the Web)** is one of the most popular services that runs on the Internet infrastructure. The Web was the original "killer app" that made the Internet commercially interesting and extraordinarily popular. The Web was developed in the early 1990s and hence is of much more recent vintage than the Internet. We describe the Web in some detail in Chapter 3. The Web provides access to billions of Web pages indexed by Google and other search engines. These pages are created in a language called *HTML (HyperText Markup Language)*. HTML pages can contain text, graphics, animations, and other objects. You can find an exceptionally wide range of information on Web pages, ranging from the entire collection of public records from the Securities and Exchange Commission, to the card catalog of your local library, to millions of music tracks and videos. The Internet prior to the Web was primarily used for text communications, file transfers, and remote computing. The Web introduced far more powerful and commercially interesting, colorful multimedia capabilities of direct relevance to commerce. In essence, the Web added color, voice, and video to the Internet, creating a communications infrastructure and information storage system that rivals television, radio, magazines, and even libraries.

There is no precise measurement of the number of Web pages in existence, in part because today's search engines index only a portion of the known universe of Web pages, and also because the size of the Web universe is unknown. Google has identified over 60 trillion unique URLs, up from 1 trillion in 2008, although many of these pages do not necessarily contain unique content (Google, 2014). In addition to this "surface" or "visible" Web, there is also the so-called deep Web that is reportedly 500 to 1,000 times greater than the surface Web. The deep Web contains databases and other content that is not routinely indexed by search engines such as Google. Although the total size of the Web is not known, what is indisputable is that Web content has grown exponentially since 1993.

mobile platform
provides the ability to access the Internet from a variety of highly mobile devices such as smartphones, tablets, and other ultra-lightweight laptop computers

The mobile platform is the newest development in Internet infrastructure. The **mobile platform** provides the ability to access the Internet from a variety of mobile devices such as smartphones, tablets, and other ultra-lightweight laptop computers via wireless networks or cell phone service. In 2015, there are over 350 million mobile devices in the United States that can be connected to the Internet (more than 1 device for each person in the United States), and that number is expected to grow to around 370 million by 2019 (eMarketer, Inc., 2015e). **Figure 1.6** illustrates the rapid growth of mobile Internet access.

Read *Insight on Technology: Will Apps Make the Web Irrelevant?* for a look at the challenge that apps and the mobile platform pose to the Web's dominance of the Internet ecosphere.

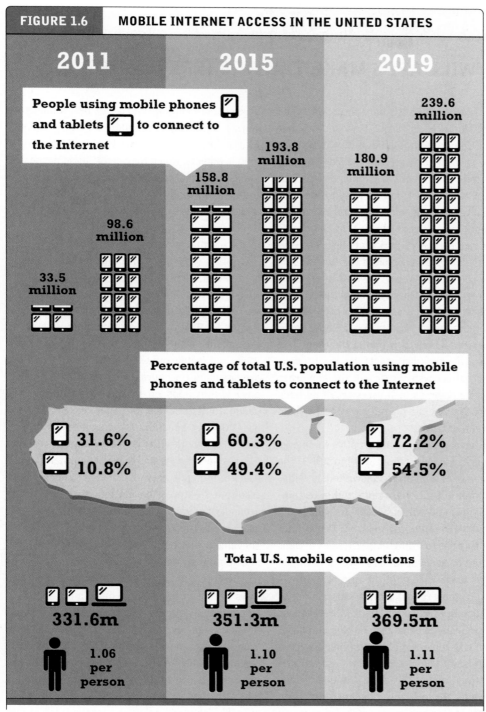

FIGURE 1.6   MOBILE INTERNET ACCESS IN THE UNITED STATES

Continued growth in the number of people using mobile phones and tablets to connect to the Internet will provide a significant stimulus to m-commerce.

SOURCES: Based on data from eMarketer, Inc., 2013a, 2013b, 2013c, 2015e, 2015f, 2015g.

INSIGHT ON TECHNOLOGY

WILL APPS MAKE THE WEB IRRELEVANT?

Nowadays, it's hard to recall a time before the Web. How did we get along without the ability to pull up a Web browser and search for any item, learn about any topic, or play just about any type of game? Though the Web has come a remarkably long way from its humble beginnings, many experts claim that the Web's best days are behind it, and that there's a new player on the field: apps. Opinions vary widely over the future role of the Web in a world where apps have become an ever larger portion of the Internet marketspace. In 10 years, will Web browsers be forgotten relics, as we rely entirely on apps to do both our work and our play on the Internet? Will the Web and apps coexist peacefully as vital cogs in the Internet ecosystem? Or will the app craze eventually die down as tech users gravitate back toward the Web as the primary way to perform Internet-related tasks?

Apps have grown into a disruptive force ever since Apple launched its App Store in 2008. The list of industries apps have disrupted is wide-ranging: communications, media and entertainment, logistics, education, healthcare, and most recently, with Uber, the taxi industry. Despite not even existing prior to 2008, in 2015, sales of apps are expected to account for well over $30 billion in revenues worldwide, and the app economy is continuing to show robust growth, with estimates of $70 billion in revenue by 2017. More of those revenues are likely to come from in-app purchases than from paid app downloads. Not only that, but the growth is not coming from more users trying the same small number of apps. Although usage of apps tends to be highly concentrated, with nearly 80% of smartphone app minutes spent on an individual's top 3 apps, consumers are trying new apps all the time and visit about 25 apps per month, leaving plenty of room for new app

developers to innovate and create best-selling apps. In fact, according to mobile advertising company Flurry, 280 million people worldwide qualify as mobile addicts, which they define as someone who launches a smartphone app more than 60 times a day. According to Flurry, the number of such addicts has increased by about 350% from 2013 to 2015.

In January 2014, for the first time ever, Americans used apps more than desktop computers to access the Internet. The time U.S. adults are spending using mobile apps has exploded, growing by 90% over the past two years, and now accounting for 53.8% of total digital media time spent; time spent on the desktop now accounts for just 38%, and mobile browsers just 8.2%. U.S. adults are spending 68 hours a month (over 2 hours a day) within apps on their smartphones, while young adults between the ages of 18–24 spend over 90 hours a month (3+ hours a day). Consumers have gravitated to apps for several reasons. First, smartphones and tablet computers enable users to use apps anywhere, instead of being tethered to a desktop or having to lug a heavy laptop around. Of course, smartphones and tablets enable users to use the Web too, but apps are often more convenient and boast more streamlined, elegant interfaces than mobile Web browsers.

Not only are apps more appealing in certain ways to consumers, they are much more appealing to content creators and media companies. Apps are much easier to control and monetize than Web sites, not to mention they can't be crawled by Google or other services. On the Web, the average price of ads per thousand impressions is falling, and after twenty years, many content providers are still mostly struggling to turn the Internet into a profitable content delivery platform. Much of software and media companies' focus has shifted to developing mobile apps for this reason.

These trends are why some pundits boldly proclaim that the Web is dead, and that the shift from the Web to apps has only just started. These analysts believe that the Internet will be used to transport data, but individual app interfaces will replace the Web browser as the most common way to access and display content. Even the creator of the Web, Tim Berners-Lee, feels that the Web as we know it is being threatened. That's not a good sign.

But there is no predictive consensus about the role of the Web in our lives in the next decade and beyond. Many analysts believe the demise of the Web has been greatly exaggerated, and that the Web boasts many advantages over today's apps that users will be unwilling to relinquish. Although apps may be more convenient than the Web in many respects, the depth of the Web browsing experience trumps that of apps. The Web is a vibrant, diverse array of sites, and browsers have an openness and flexibility that apps lack. The connections between Web sites enhance their usefulness and value to users, and apps that instead seek to lock users in cannot offer the same experience.

Other analysts who are more optimistic about the Web's chances to remain relevant in an increasingly app-driven online marketplace feel this way because of the emergence of HTML5. HTML5 is a new markup language that will enable more dynamic Web content and allow for browser-accessible Web apps that are as appealing as device-specific apps. In fact, there is another group of analysts who believe that apps and the Web are going to come together, with HTML5 bringing the best of the app experience to the Web, and with apps developing new Web-like capabilities. Already, work is underway to create more "smart" apps that handle a wider array of tasks than today's apps can handle, such as apps with Siri integration.

A shift towards apps and away from the Web could have a ripple effect on e-commerce firms. As the pioneer of apps and the market leader in apps, smartphones, and tablet computers, Apple stands to gain from a shift towards apps, and although it will also face increasing opposition from other companies, including Google, the established success of the App Store will make it next to impossible to dethrone Apple. While Google's Google Play store has dwarfed the App Store in downloads in 2015, Apple nevertheless maintains a strong lead in app revenues. Google's search business is likely to suffer from all of the "walled garden" apps that it cannot access, but it also has a major stake in the world of smartphones, tablets, and apps itself with its Android operating system, which is used by over 80% of smartphones worldwide. Facebook has already seen its members make the transition from using its site on the Web to using its mobile app and has made, and continues to make, significant investments in standalone apps, such as Instagram and WhatsApp. Web-based companies that fail to find an answer to the growth of the mobile platform may eventually fall by the wayside.

SOURCES: "Smartphone OS Market Share, 2015 Q2," Idc.com, accessed September 24, 2015; "The 2015 U.S. Mobile App Report," by comScore, September 2015; "Mobile Addicts Multiply Across the Globe," by Simon Khalaf, Flurrymobile.tumblr.com, July 15, 2015; "App Annie Report: Google Play's Downloads Dwarf the App Store as Apple Retains Revenue Lead," by Jackie Dove, Thenextweb.com, July 15, 2015; "Mobile Apps Poised to Hit $70B in Revenues by 2017," by Per Petterson, Impactradius.com, December 3, 2014; "More People Are Opening More Mobile Apps Every Day," by Ewan Spence, Forbes.com, April 24, 2014; "The Rise of the Mobile Addict," by Simon Khalaf, Flurry.com, April 22, 2014; "How Apps Won the Mobile Web," by Thomas Claburn, Informationweek.com, April 3, 2014; "Apps Solidify Leadership Six Years into the Mobile Revolution," by Simon Khalaf, Flurry.com, April 1, 2014; "Mobile Apps Overtake PC Internet Usage in U.S.," by James O'Toole, Money.cnn.com, February 28, 2014; "Convergence of User Experiences," Savas.me, April 4, 2013; "Flurry Five-Year Report: It's an App World. The Web Just Lives in It," by Simon Khalaf, Flurry.com, April 3, 2013; "Here's Why Google and Facebook Might Completely Disappear in the Next 5 Years," by Eric Jackson, Forbes.com, April 30, 2012; "Is The Web Dead In the Face of Native Apps? Not Likely, But Some Think So," by Gabe Knuth, Brianmadden.com, March 28, 2012; "Imagining the Internet," by Janna Quitney Anderson and Lee Rainie, Pew Internet and American Life Project, March 23, 2012; "The Web Is Dead. Long Live the Internet," by Chris Anderson and Michael Wolff, Wired.com, August 17, 2010; "The Web Is Dead? A Debate," by Chris Anderson, Wired.com, August 17, 2010.

ORIGINS AND GROWTH OF E-COMMERCE

It is difficult to pinpoint just when e-commerce began. There were several precursors to e-commerce. In the late 1970s, a pharmaceutical firm named Baxter Healthcare initiated a primitive form of B2B e-commerce by using a telephone-based modem that permitted hospitals to reorder supplies from Baxter. This system was later expanded during the 1980s into a PC-based remote order entry system and was widely copied throughout the United States long before the Internet became a commercial environment. The 1980s saw the development of Electronic Data Interchange (EDI) standards that permitted firms to exchange commercial documents and conduct digital commercial transactions across private networks.

In the B2C arena, the first truly large-scale digitally enabled transaction system was deployed in France in 1981. The Minitel was a French videotext system that combined a telephone with an 8-inch screen. By the mid-1980s, more than 3 million Minitels were deployed, and more than 13,000 different services were available, including ticket agencies, travel services, retail products, and online banking. The Minitel service continued in existence until December 31, 2006, when it was finally discontinued by its owner, France Telecom.

However, none of these precursor systems had the functionality of the Internet. Generally, when we think of e-commerce today, it is inextricably linked to the Internet. For our purposes, we will say e-commerce begins in 1995, following the appearance of the first banner advertisements placed by AT&T, Volvo, Sprint, and others on Hotwired in late October 1994, and the first sales of banner ad space by Netscape and Infoseek in early 1995. Since then, e-commerce has been the fastest growing form of commerce in the United States.

The data suggests that, over the next five years, B2C e-commerce in the United States will grow by over 10% annually, much faster than traditional retail sales (which are growing at only about 3.5% a year). There is tremendous upside potential. Today, for instance, B2C retail e-commerce is still a very small part (around 7%) of the overall $4.8 trillion retail market in the United States, and under current projections, in 2019, will only be about 10% higher than Walmart's fiscal 2015 revenue ($485 billion). There is obviously much room to grow (see **Figure 1.7**). However, it's not likely that B2C e-commerce revenues will continue to expand forever at double-digit rates. As online sales become a larger percentage of all sales, online sales growth will likely eventually decline to that growth level. This point still appears to be a long way off. Online content sales, everything from music, to video, medical information, games, and entertainment, have an even longer period to grow before they hit any ceiling effects.

1.2 E-COMMERCE: A BRIEF HISTORY

Although e-commerce is not very old, it already has a tumultuous history. The history of e-commerce can be usefully divided into three periods: 1995–2000, the period of invention; 2001–2006, the period of consolidation; and 2007–present, a period of

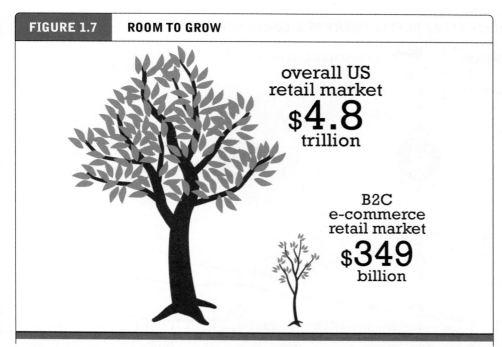

| FIGURE 1.7 | ROOM TO GROW |

overall US
retail market
$4.8
trillion

B2C
e-commerce
retail market
$349
billion

The B2C e-commerce retail market is still just a small part of the overall U.S. retail market, but with much room to grow in the future.

reinvention with social, mobile, and local expansion. The following examines each of these periods briefly, while **Figure 1.8** places them in context along a timeline.

E-COMMERCE 1995–2000: INVENTION

The early years of e-commerce were a period of explosive growth and extraordinary innovation, beginning in 1995 with the first widespread use of the Web to advertise products. During this Invention period, e-commerce meant selling retail goods, usually quite simple goods, on the Internet. There simply was not enough bandwidth for more complex products. Marketing was limited to unsophisticated static display ads and not very powerful search engines. The Web policy of most large firms, if they had one at all, was to have a basic static Web site depicting their brands. The rapid growth in e-commerce was fueled by over $125 billion in venture capital. This period of e-commerce came to a close in 2000 when stock market valuations plunged, with thousands of companies disappearing (the "dot-com crash").

The early years of e-commerce were also one of the most euphoric of times in American commercial history. It was also a time when key e-commerce concepts were developed. For computer scientists and information technologists, the early success of e-commerce was a powerful vindication of a set of information technologies that had developed over a period of 40 years—extending from the development of the early Internet, to the PC, to local area networks. The vision was of a universal

| FIGURE 1.8 | PERIODS IN THE DEVELOPMENT OF E-COMMERCE |

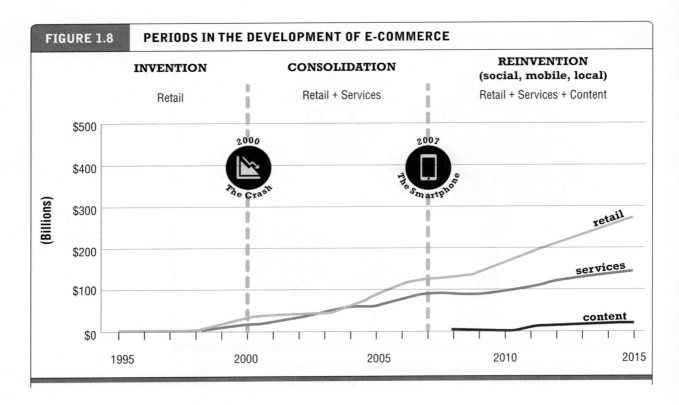

communications and computing environment that everyone on Earth could access with cheap, inexpensive computers—a worldwide universe of knowledge stored on HTML pages created by hundreds of millions of individuals and thousands of libraries, governments, and scientific institutes. Technologists celebrated the fact that the Internet was not controlled by anyone or any nation, but was free to all. They believed the Internet—and the e-commerce that rose on this infrastructure—should remain a self-governed, self-regulated environment.

For economists, the early years of e-commerce raised the realistic prospect of a nearly perfect competitive market: where price, cost, and quality information are equally distributed, a nearly infinite set of suppliers compete against one another, and customers have access to all relevant market information worldwide. The Internet would spawn digital markets where information would be nearly perfect—something that is rarely true in other real-world markets. Merchants in turn would have equal direct access to hundreds of millions of customers. In this near-perfect information marketspace, transaction costs would plummet because search costs—the cost of searching for prices, product descriptions, payment settlement, and order fulfillment—would all fall drastically (Bakos, 1997). For merchants, the cost of searching for customers would also fall, reducing the need for wasteful advertising. At the same time, advertisements could be personalized to the needs of every customer. Prices and even costs would be increasingly transparent to the consumer, who could now know exactly and instantly the worldwide best price, quality, and availability of most products. Information asymmetry would be greatly reduced. Given the instant nature of Internet communications, the availability of powerful sales information systems, and the low cost involved in changing prices on a Web site (low menu costs), producers could dynamically price their products to reflect actual demand, ending the idea of one national price, or one suggested manufacturer's list price. In turn, market middlemen—the distributors and wholesalers who are intermediaries between producers and consumers, each demanding a payment and raising costs while adding little value—would disappear (**disintermediation**). Manufacturers and content originators would develop direct market relationships with their customers. The resulting intense competition, the decline of intermediaries, and the lower transaction costs would eliminate product brands, and along with these, the possibility of *monopoly profits* based on brands, geography, or special access to factors of production. Prices for products and services would fall to the point where prices covered costs of production plus a fair, "market rate" of return on capital, plus additional small payments for entrepreneurial effort (that would not last long). Unfair competitive advantages (which occur when one competitor has an advantage others cannot purchase) would be reduced, as would extraordinary returns on invested capital. This vision was called **friction-free commerce** (Smith et al., 2000).

For real-world entrepreneurs, their financial backers, and marketing professionals, e-commerce represented an extraordinary opportunity to earn far above normal returns on investment. This is just the opposite of what economists hoped for. The e-commerce marketspace represented access to millions of consumers worldwide who used the Internet and a set of marketing communications technologies (e-mail and Web pages) that was universal, inexpensive, and powerful. These new technologies would permit marketers to practice what they always had done—segmenting the market into groups with different needs and price sensitivity, targeting the segments with branding and promotional messages, and positioning the product and pricing for each group—but with even more precision. In this new marketspace, extraordinary profits would go to **first movers**—those firms who were first to market in a particular area and who moved quickly to gather market share. In a "winner take all" market, first movers could establish a large customer base quickly, build brand name recognition early, create an entirely new distribution channel, and then inhibit competitors (new entrants) by building in *switching costs* for their customers through proprietary interface designs and features available only at one site. The idea for entrepreneurs was to create near monopolies online based on size, convenience, selection, and brand. Online businesses using the new technology could create informative, community-like features unavailable to traditional merchants. These "communities of consumption" also would add value and be difficult for traditional merchants to imitate. The thinking was that once customers became accustomed to using a company's unique Web interface and feature set, they could not easily be switched to competitors. In the best case, the entrepreneurial firm would invent proprietary technologies and techniques that almost everyone adopted, creating a network effect. A **network effect** occurs where all participants receive value from the fact that everyone else uses the same tool or product (for example, a common operating system, telephone system, or software application such as a proprietary instant

disintermediation
displacement of market middlemen who traditionally are intermediaries between producers and consumers by a new direct relationship between producers and consumers

friction-free commerce
a vision of commerce in which information is equally distributed, transaction costs are low, prices can be dynamically adjusted to reflect actual demand, intermediaries decline, and unfair competitive advantages are eliminated

first mover
a firm that is first to market in a particular area and that moves quickly to gather market share

network effect
occurs where users receive value from the fact that everyone else uses the same tool or product

messaging standard or an operating system such as Windows), all of which increase in value as more people adopt them.[2]

To initiate this process, entrepreneurs argued that prices would have to be very low to attract customers and fend off potential competitors. E-commerce was, after all, a totally new way of shopping that would have to offer some immediate cost benefits to consumers. However, because doing business on the Web was supposedly so much more efficient when compared to traditional "bricks-and-mortar" businesses (even when compared to the direct mail catalog business) and because the costs of customer acquisition and retention would supposedly be so much lower, profits would inevitably materialize out of these efficiencies. Given these dynamics, market share, the number of visitors to a site ("eyeballs"), and gross revenue became far more important in the earlier stages of an online firm than earnings or profits. Entrepreneurs and their financial backers in the early years of e-commerce expected that extraordinary profitability would come, but only after several years of losses.

Thus, the early years of e-commerce were driven largely by visions of profiting from new technology, with the emphasis on quickly achieving very high market visibility. The source of financing was venture capital funds. The ideology of the period emphasized the ungoverned "Wild West" character of the Web and the feeling that governments and courts could not possibly limit or regulate the Internet; there was a general belief that traditional corporations were too slow and bureaucratic, too stuck in the old ways of doing business, to "get it"—to be competitive in e-commerce. Young entrepreneurs were therefore the driving force behind e-commerce, backed by huge amounts of money invested by venture capitalists. The emphasis was on *disrupting* (destroying) traditional distribution channels and disintermediating existing channels, using new pure online companies who aimed to achieve impregnable first-mover advantages. Overall, this period of e-commerce was characterized by experimentation, capitalization, and hypercompetition (Varian, 2000b).

E-COMMERCE 2001–2006: CONSOLIDATION

In the second period of e-commerce, from 2000 to 2006, a sobering period of reassessment of e-commerce occurred, with many critics doubting its long-term prospects. Emphasis shifted to a more "business-driven" approach rather than being technology driven; large traditional firms learned how to use the Web to strengthen their market positions; brand extension and strengthening became more important than creating new brands; financing shrunk as capital markets shunned start-up firms; and traditional bank financing based on profitability returned.

During this period of consolidation, e-commerce changed to include not just retail products but also more complex services such as travel and financial services. This period was enabled by widespread adoption of broadband networks in American homes and businesses, coupled with the growing power and lower prices of personal

---

[2] The network effect is quantified by Metcalfe's Law, which argues that the value of a network grows by the square of the number of participants.

computers that were the primary means of accessing the Internet, usually from work or home. Marketing on the Internet increasingly meant using search engine advertising targeted to user queries, rich media and video ads, and behavioral targeting of marketing messages based on ad networks and auction markets. The Web policy of both large and small firms expanded to include a broader "Web presence" that included not just Web sites, but also e-mail, display, and search engine campaigns; multiple Web sites for each product; and the building of some limited community feedback facilities. E-commerce in this period was growing again by more than 10% a year.

E-COMMERCE 2007–PRESENT: REINVENTION

Beginning in 2007 with the introduction of the iPhone, to the present day, e-commerce has been transformed yet again by the rapid growth of **Web 2.0** (a set of applications and technologies that enable user-generated content, such as online social networks, blogs, video and photo sharing sites, and wikis), widespread adoption of consumer mobile devices such as smartphones and tablet computers, the expansion of e-commerce to include local goods and services, and the emergence of an on-demand service economy enabled by millions of apps on mobile devices and cloud computing. This period can be seen as both a sociological, as well as a technological and business, phenomenon.

Web 2.0
set of applications and technologies that enable user-generated content

The defining characteristics of this period are often characterized as the "social, mobile, local" online world. Entertainment content has developed as a major source of e-commerce revenues and mobile devices have become entertainment centers, as well as on-the-go shopping devices for retail goods and services. Marketing has been transformed by the increasing use of social networks, word-of-mouth, viral marketing, and much more powerful data repositories and analytic tools for truly personal marketing. Firms have greatly expanded their online presence by moving beyond static Web pages to social networks such as Facebook, Twitter, Pinterest, and Instagram in an attempt to surround the online consumer with coordinated marketing messages. These social networks share many common characteristics. First, they rely on user-generated content. "Regular" people (not just experts or professionals) are creating, sharing, and broadcasting content to huge audiences. They are inherently highly interactive, creating new opportunities for people to socially connect to others. They attract extremely large audiences (about 1.5 billion monthly active users worldwide as of June 2015 in the case of Facebook). These audiences present marketers with extraordinary opportunities for targeted marketing and advertising.

More recently, the re-invention of the Web and e-commerce has resulted in a new set of on-demand, personal service businesses such as Uber, Airbnb, Instacart, Handy, and Homejoy. These businesses have been able to tap into a large reservoir of unused assets (cars, spare rooms, and personal spare time) and to create lucrative markets based on the mobile platform infrastructure. The *Insight on Business* case, *Start-up Boot Camp,* takes a look at Y Combinator, which has mentored a number of these new social, mobile, and local e-commerce ventures.

Table 1.4 on page 34 summarizes e-commerce in each of these three periods.

INSIGHT ON BUSINESS

START-UP BOOT CAMP

By now we've all heard the story of some lines of code written by Mark Zuckerberg in a Harvard dorm room blossoming into a multi-billion dollar business. These days, it's harder than ever to keep track of all the tech start-ups being valued at millions and even billions of dollars, often even without a cent of revenue to show for themselves. A number of them have something in common—they have been nurtured, and in some cases, whipped into shape, with the help of an "incubator."

As entrepreneurs continue to launch a growing number of e-commerce companies, incubators have come to occupy a vital role in Silicon Valley, helping new businesses move from little more than a great idea to an established, vibrant business. Founded in 2005 by programmer and venture capitalist Paul Graham, Y Combinator is Silicon Valley's best known incubator. Twice a year the company provides a three-month boot camp, complete with seed funding and mentorship from an extensive network of highly regarded tech entrepreneurs. Every boot camp ends with a demonstration day, known as Demo Day or D Day, where all of the entrepreneurs, known as "founders," pitch their fledgling businesses to a group of wealthy venture capitalists hoping to unearth the next Facebook or Google. In 2014, Graham stepped down from a leadership role at the company, replaced by Sam Altman, former CEO of Loopt, a location-based mobile services provider and a successful Y Combinator graduate company. Altman is aiming to expand Y Combinator's focus beyond the Internet to energy, biotechnology, medical devices, and other "hard technology" start-ups that solve concrete problems.

When companies are admitted to Y Combinator after a rigorous selection progress (the Winter 2015 program had 5,600 applications and just 2% (114 companies) were accepted), they are given $120,000 in cash in exchange for a 7% stake in the company. Founders have regular meetings with Y Combinator partners, and have free access to technology, technical advice, emotional support, and lessons in salesmanship. As of August 2015, Y Combinator has helped launch 940 start-up companies, which together have a net worth of more than $65 billion. Its graduates have raised more than $7 billion, and eight of them have attained once rare, but now increasingly common, "unicorn" status, with a valuation in excess of $1 billion. More than 40 are worth over $100 million.

Y Combinator has been so successful that it is sometimes referred to as a "unicorn breeder." Graduates that have achieved unicorn status include Airbnb, an on-demand room rental service (with a valuation of $25.5 billion); Dropbox, a cloud-based file storage service ($10 billion); Zenefits, a cloud-based employee benefits manager ($4.5 billion); Stripe, a digital payment infrastructure company ($3.5 billion), Machine Zone, a massively multi-player online gaming company ($3 billion); Instacart, an on-demand grocery delivery service ($2 billion); Twitch, a streaming video game network (acquired by Amazon for $1 billion), and Docker, an open source software company ($1 billion). Other well-known graduates include Reddit, a social news site; Weebly, a Web site building platform; Coinbase, a Bitcoin wallet; Scribd, a digital library subscription service; and Codecademy, an online education service that teaches people how to program.

There is no shortage of entrepreneurs with visions of guiding their companies to becoming the next billion-dollar business. Mike Chen and four friends from Oberlin College originally had an idea about creating an app that helps people keep track of their blood pressure. They were accepted into the Winter 2015 Y Combinator session, and one weekend, while brainstorming, came up with a totally different idea for an SMS-based service that they called Magic, which enables users to text a single number to get anything delivered on-demand. The service acts as an intermediary, and piggy-backs off other on-demand delivery services springing up like hot cakes, such as Instacart, GrubHub, Eat24, and Postmates. In the first 48 hours after going live, after being featured on the Web site Product Hunt, the service received over 17,000 text messages, and within one month, was valued at $40 million, securing $12 million in venture capital from Sequoia.

Y Combinator's Summer 2015 session featured start-ups such as Lugg (an Uber for moving large items, such as furniture); Instant eSports (an ESPN for competitive e-sports in the form of a mobile app created by three University of California at Berkeley undergraduate students); and Luna (a smart mattress cover that connects your bed to the Internet of Things). By August 2015, Lugg had already raised $3.8 million in seed funding from a number of investors, while Luna had taken in $1.3 million, and Instant eSports had entered into partnerships with multiple e-sports organizations.

Not every company that makes it through Y Combinator's boot camps is this successful or successful at all. Companies that fail to attract sufficient investor interest at Demo Day can try again with a different company or go their own way and "grow organically," which is practically a death sentence in today's Silicon Valley. Some skeptics believe that incubators like Y Combinator might not be the best idea for every start-up. For start-ups with solid, but not eye-popping products, services, or growth metrics, Y Combinator's D Day might actually hurt their chances of getting funding. Having to compete against an extremely qualified field of start-up companies diminishes the appeal for less flashy businesses. Once you've failed at acquiring funding at Y Combinator, other prospective investors might become concerned. There is also the concern founders may fixate on raising more money in seed funding rounds than necessary. According to Altman, founders should initially focus on making their company work on as little capital as possible, and that Y Combinator's best companies have been able to make great strides even with just relatively small amounts of seed funding.

As part of its own continuing evolution, Y Combinator announced in October 2015 that it would begin to make later-stage investments in its graduates as well. Together with Stanford University's endowment fund and Willett Advisors, it has created a new $700 million Y Combinator Continuity Fund. Its first investment was leading a $30 million round for Checkr, a Summer 2014 graduate that runs background checks on workers used by on-demand service companies such as Uber. Y Combinator has said that it hopes to participate in later funding rounds for all of its graduates that are being valued in the funding at $300 million or less, in part to help further guide them as they mature.

SOURCES: "Stanford, Michael Bloomberg Now Back Every Y Combinator Startup," by Douglas Macmillan, *Wall Street Journal,* October 15, 2015; "Y Combinator Will Fund Later-Stage Companies," by Mike Isaac, *New York Times,* October 15, 2015; "Startups Are Complaining That They're Only Able to Raise $1 Million Seed Rounds," by Maya Kosoff, Businessinsider.com, October 13, 2015; "YC Stats," by Sam Altman, Ycombinator.com, August 26, 2015; "Lugg, An App for On-Demand, Short-Distance Moves, Raises $3.8 Million," by Sarah Perez, Techcrunch.com, August 26, 2015; "The 50 Startups that Launched at Y Combinator Summer 2015 Demo Day 1," by Josh Constine, Techcrunch.com, August 18, 2015; "YC-Backed Instant eSports is ESPN for Competitive Gaming," by Fitz Tepper, Techcrunch.com, June 29, 2015; "Meet Y Combinator's Bold Whiz Kid Boss," by Jason Ankeny, Entrepreneur.com, April 25, 2015; "The Y Combinator Chronicles: Y Combinator President Sam Altman Is Dreaming Big," by Max Chafkin, Fastcompany.com, April 16, 2015; "Sources: Magic is Raising $12M from Sequoia at a $40M Valuation," by Jordan Crook, Techcrunch.com, March 26, 2015; "Magic Is a Startup That Promises to Bring You Anything – If You're Willing to Pay for It," by Sarah Buhr, Techcrunch.com, February 23, 2015; "The 13 Y Combinator Startups Worth Over $50 Billion," Cbinsights.com, January 5, 2015; "Y Combinator Known for Picking Winners," by Heather Somerville, San Jose Mercury News, May 8, 2014; "Each New Y Combinator Class Worth More Than a Billion Dollars, President Says," by Erin Griffith, Tech.fortune.com, May 5, 2014; "Y Combinator's New Deal for Startups: More Money, Same 7% Equity," by Kia Kokalitcheva, Venturebeat.com, April 22, 2014; "The New Deal," by Sam Altman, Blog.ycombinator.com, April 22, 2014; "Silicon Valley's Start-up Machine," by Nathaniel Rich, New York Times, May 2, 2013; "What's the Secret Behind Y Combinator's Success?," by Drew Hansen, Forbes.com, February 18, 2013.

TABLE 1.4	EVOLUTION OF E-COMMERCE	
1995–2000 INVENTION	2001–2006 CONSOLIDATION	2007–PRESENT REINVENTION
Technology driven	Business driven	Mobile technology enables social, local, and mobile e-commerce
Revenue growth emphasis	Earnings and profits emphasis	Audience and social network connections emphasis
Venture capital financing	Traditional financing	Return of venture capital financing; buy-outs of start-ups by large firms
Ungoverned	Stronger regulation and governance	Extensive government surveillance
Entrepreneurial	Large traditional firms	Entrepreneurial social, mobile, and local firms
Disintermediation	Strengthening intermediaries	Proliferation of small online intermediaries renting business processes of larger firms
Perfect markets	Imperfect markets, brands, and network effects	Continuation of online market imperfections; commodity competition in select markets
Pure online strategies	Mixed "bricks-and-clicks" strategies	Return of pure online strategies in new markets; extension of bricks-and-clicks in traditional retail markets
First-mover advantages	Strategic-follower strength; complementary assets	First-mover advantages return in new markets as traditional Web players catch up
Low-complexity retail products	High-complexity retail products and services	Retail, services, and content

ASSESSING E-COMMERCE: SUCCESSES, SURPRISES, AND FAILURES

Looking back at the evolution of e-commerce, it is apparent that e-commerce has been a stunning technological success as the Internet and the Web ramped up from a few thousand to billions of e-commerce transactions per year, and this year will generate an estimated $531 billion in total B2C revenues and around $6.3 trillion in B2B revenues, with around 172 million online buyers in the United States. With enhancements and strengthening, described in later chapters, it is clear that e-commerce's digital infrastructure is solid enough to sustain significant growth in e-commerce during the next decade. The Internet scales well. The "e" in e-commerce has been an overwhelming success.

From a business perspective, though, the early years of e-commerce were a mixed success, and offered many surprises. Only about 10% of dot-coms formed since 1995 have survived as independent companies in 2015. Only a very tiny percentage of these survivors are profitable. Yet online B2C sales of goods and services are still growing very rapidly. Contrary to economists' hopes, online sales are increasingly concentrated in the top ten retailers who account for over 50% of all online retail sales (Internet Retailer, 2015). So thousands of firms have failed, and those few that have survived dominate the market. The idea of thousands of suppliers competing on price has been replaced by a market dominated by giant firms. Consumers have learned to use the Web as a powerful source of information about products they actually purchase through other channels, such as at a traditional bricks-and-mortar store. For instance, a 2014 study found that almost 90% of those surveyed "webroomed" (researched a product online before purchasing at a physical store) (Interactions Consumer Experience Marketing, Inc., 2014). This is especially true of expensive consumer durables such as appliances, automobiles, and electronics. This offline "Internet-influenced" commerce is very difficult to estimate, but is believed to be somewhere around $1.5 trillion in 2015 (Forrester Research, 2014). Altogether then, B2C retail e-commerce (actual online purchases) and purchases influenced by online shopping but actually buying in a store (Internet-influenced commerce) are expected to amount to almost $1.9 trillion in 2015, or almost 40% of total retail sales in the United States. The "commerce" in e-commerce is basically very sound, at least in the sense of attracting a growing number of customers and generating revenues and profits for large e-commerce players.

Although e-commerce has grown at an extremely rapid pace in customers and revenues, it is clear that many of the visions, predictions, and assertions about e-commerce developed in the early years have not have been fulfilled. For instance, economists' visions of "friction-free" commerce have not been entirely realized. Prices are sometimes lower online, but the low prices are sometimes a function of entrepreneurs selling products below their costs. In some cases, online prices are higher than those of local merchants, as consumers are willing to pay a small premium for the convenience of buying online. Consumers are less price sensitive than expected; surprisingly, the Web sites with the highest revenue often have the highest prices. There remains considerable persistent and even increasing price dispersion: online competition has lowered prices, but price dispersion remains pervasive in many markets despite lower search costs (Levin, 2011; Ghose and Yao, 2010). In a study of 50,000 goods in the United Kingdom and the United States, researchers found Internet prices were sticky even in the face of large changes in demand, online merchants did not alter prices significantly more than offline merchants, and price dispersion across online sellers was somewhat greater than traditional brick and mortar stores (Gorodnichenko, et al., 2014). The concept of one world, one market, one price has not occurred in reality as entrepreneurs discover new ways to differentiate their products and services. While for the most part Internet prices save consumers about 20% on average when compared to in-store prices, sometimes online prices are higher than for similar products purchased offline, especially if shipping costs are considered. For instance, prices on books and CDs vary by as much as 50%, and prices for airline tickets as much as 20% (Alessandria, 2009; Aguiar and Hurst, 2008; Baye, 2004; Baye et al., 2004; Brynjolfsson and Smith, 2000; Bailey, 1998a, b). Merchants have adjusted to the competitive Internet environment by engaging in "hit-and-run pricing" or changing prices every day or hour (using "flash pricing" or "flash sales") so competitors never know what they are charging (neither do customers); by making their prices hard to discover and sowing confusion among consumers by "baiting and switching" customers from low-margin products to high-margin products with supposedly "higher quality." Finally, brands remain very important in e-commerce—consumers trust some firms more than others to deliver a high-quality product on time and they are willing to pay for it (Rosso and Jansen, 2010).

The "perfect competition" model of extreme market efficiency has not come to pass. Merchants and marketers are continually introducing information asymmetries. Search costs have fallen overall, but the overall transaction cost of actually completing a purchase in e-commerce remains high because users have a bewildering number of new questions to consider: Will the merchant actually deliver? What is the time frame of delivery? Does the merchant really stock this item? How do I fill out this form? Many potential e-commerce purchases are terminated in the shopping cart stage because of these consumer uncertainties. Some people still find it easier to call a trusted catalog merchant on the telephone than to order on a Web site. Finally, intermediaries have not disappeared as predicted. Most manufacturers, for instance, have not adopted the manufacturer-direct sales model of online sales, and some that had, such as Sony, have returned to an intermediary model. Dell, one of the pioneers of online manufacturer-direct sales, has moved toward a mixed model heavily reliant on in-store sales where customers can "kick the tires;" Apple's physical stores are among the most successful stores in the world. People still like to shop in a physical store.

If anything, e-commerce has created many opportunities for middlemen to aggregate content, products, and services and thereby introduce themselves as the "new" intermediaries. Third-party travel sites such as Travelocity, Orbitz, and Expedia are an example of this kind of intermediary. E-commerce has not driven existing retail chains and catalog merchants out of business, although it has created opportunities for entrepreneurial online-only firms to succeed.

The visions of many entrepreneurs and venture capitalists for e-commerce have not materialized exactly as predicted either. First-mover advantage appears to have succeeded only for a very small group of companies, albeit some of them extremely well-known, such as Google, Facebook, Amazon, and others. Getting big fast sometimes works, but often not. Historically, first movers have been long-term losers, with the early-to-market innovators usually being displaced by established "fast-follower" firms with the right complement of financial, marketing, legal, and production assets needed to develop mature markets, and this has proved true for e-commerce as well. Many e-commerce first movers, such as eToys, FogDog (sporting goods), Webvan (groceries), and Eve.com (beauty products), failed. Customer acquisition and retention costs during the early years of e-commerce were extraordinarily high, with some firms, such as E*Trade and other financial service firms, paying up to $400 to acquire a new customer. The overall costs of doing business online—including the costs of technology, site design and maintenance, and warehouses for fulfillment—are often no lower than the costs faced by the most efficient bricks-and-mortar stores. A large warehouse costs tens of millions of dollars regardless of a firm's online presence. The knowledge of how to run the warehouse is priceless, and not easily moved. The start-up costs can be staggering. Attempting to achieve or enhance profitability by raising prices has often led to large customer defections. From the e-commerce merchant's perspective, the "e" in e-commerce does not stand for "easy."

On the other hand, there have been some extraordinary, and unanticipated surprises in the evolution of e-commerce. Few predicted the impact of the mobile platform. Few anticipated the rapid growth of social networks or their growing success as advertising platforms based on a more detailed understanding of personal behavior than even Google has achieved. And few, if any, anticipated the emergence of on-demand e-commerce, which enables people to use their mobile devices to order up everything from taxis, to groceries, to laundry service.

1.3 UNDERSTANDING E-COMMERCE: ORGANIZING THEMES

Understanding e-commerce in its totality is a difficult task for students and instructors because there are so many facets to the phenomenon. No single academic discipline is prepared to encompass all of e-commerce. After teaching the e-commerce course for several years and writing this book, we have come to realize just how difficult it is to "understand" e-commerce. We have found it useful to think about e-commerce as involving three broad interrelated themes: technology, business, and society. We do not mean to imply any ordering of importance here because this book and our thinking freely range over these themes as appropriate to the problem we are trying to understand and describe. Nevertheless, as in previous technologically driven commercial revolutions, there is a historic progression. Technologies develop first, and then those developments are exploited commercially. Once commercial exploitation of the technology becomes widespread, a host of social, cultural, and political issues arise, and society is forced to respond to them.

TECHNOLOGY: INFRASTRUCTURE

The development and mastery of digital computing and communications technology is at the heart of the newly emerging global digital economy we call e-commerce. To understand the likely future of e-commerce, you need a basic understanding of the information technologies upon which it is built. E-commerce is above all else a technologically driven phenomenon that relies on a host of information technologies as well as fundamental concepts from computer science developed over a 50-year period. At the core of e-commerce are the Internet and the Web, which we describe in detail in Chapter 3. Underlying these technologies are a host of complementary technologies: cloud computing, desktop computers, smartphones, tablet computers, local area networks, relational and non-relational databases, client/server computing, data mining, and fiber-optic switches, to name just a few. These technologies lie at the heart of sophisticated business computing applications such as enterprise-wide information systems, supply chain management systems, manufacturing resource planning systems, and customer relationship management systems. E-commerce relies on all these basic technologies—not just the Internet. The Internet, while representing a sharp break from prior corporate computing and communications technologies, is nevertheless just the latest development in the evolution of corporate computing and part of the continuing chain of computer-based innovations in business. **Figure 1.9** illustrates the major stages in the development of corporate computing and indicates how the Internet and the Web fit into this development trajectory.

To truly understand e-commerce, you will need to know something about packet-switched communications, protocols such as TCP/IP, client/server and cloud computing, mobile digital platforms, Web servers, HTML5, CSS, and software programming tools such as Flash and JavaScript on the client side, and Java, PHP, Ruby on Rails, and ColdFusion on the server side. All of these topics are described fully in Part 2 of the book (Chapters 3–5).

BUSINESS: BASIC CONCEPTS

While technology provides the infrastructure, it is the business applications—the potential for extraordinary returns on investment—that create the interest and excitement in e-commerce. New technologies present businesses and entrepreneurs with new ways of organizing production and transacting business. New technologies change the strategies and plans of existing firms: old strategies are made obsolete and new ones need to be invented. New technologies are the birthing grounds where thousands of new companies spring up with new products and services. New technologies are the graveyard of many traditional businesses. To truly understand e-commerce, you will need to be familiar with some key business concepts, such as the nature of digital markets, digital goods, business models, firm and industry value chains, value webs, industry structure, digital disruption, and consumer behavior in digital markets, as well as basic concepts of financial analysis. We'll examine these concepts further in Chapters 2, 6, 7, and 9 through 12.

SOCIETY: TAMING THE JUGGERNAUT

With almost 260 million Americans now using the Internet, many for e-commerce purposes, and more than 3.1 billion users worldwide, the impact of the Internet and e-commerce on society is significant and global. Increasingly, e-commerce is subject to the laws of nations and global entities. You will need to understand the pressures that global e-commerce places on contemporary society in order to conduct a successful

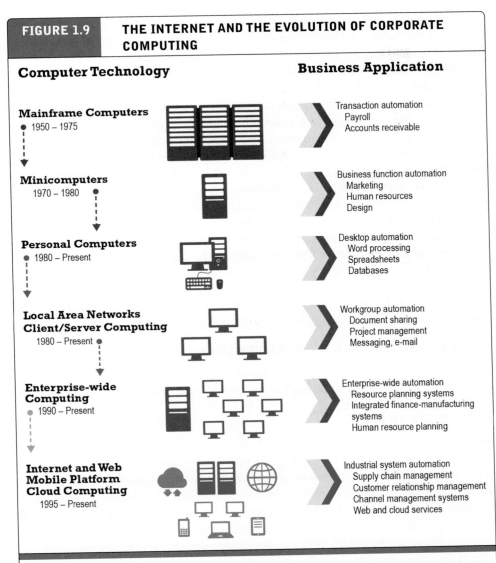

| FIGURE 1.9 | THE INTERNET AND THE EVOLUTION OF CORPORATE COMPUTING |

Computer Technology

Business Application

Mainframe Computers
● 1950 – 1975

Transaction automation
Payroll
Accounts receivable

Minicomputers
1970 – 1980 ●

Business function automation
Marketing
Human resources
Design

Personal Computers
● 1980 – Present

Desktop automation
Word processing
Spreadsheets
Databases

**Local Area Networks
Client/Server Computing**
1980 – Present ●

Workgroup automation
Document sharing
Project management
Messaging, e-mail

**Enterprise-wide
Computing**
● 1990 – Present

Enterprise-wide automation
Resource planning systems
Integrated finance-manufacturing
systems
Human resource planning

**Internet and Web
Mobile Platform
Cloud Computing**
1995 – Present

Industrial system automation
Supply chain management
Customer relationship management
Channel management systems
Web and cloud services

The Internet and Web, and the emergence of a mobile platform held together by the Internet cloud, are the latest in a chain of evolving technologies and related business applications, each of which builds on its predecessors.

e-commerce business or understand the e-commerce phenomenon. The primary societal issues we discuss in this book are individual privacy, intellectual property, and public welfare policy.

Because the Internet and the Web are exceptionally adept at tracking the identity and behavior of individuals online, e-commerce raises difficulties for preserving privacy—the ability of individuals to place limits on the type and amount of information collected about them, and to control the uses of their personal information. Read the *Insight on Society* case, *Facebook and the Age of Privacy,* to get a view of some of the ways e-commerce sites use personal information.

Because the cost of distributing digital copies of copyrighted intellectual property—tangible works of the mind such as music, books, and videos—is nearly zero on the Internet, e-commerce poses special challenges to the various methods societies have used in the past to protect intellectual property rights.

The global nature of e-commerce also poses public policy issues of equity, equal access, content regulation, and taxation. For instance, in the United States, public telephone utilities are required under public utility and public accommodation laws to make basic service available at affordable rates so everyone can have telephone service. Should these laws be extended to the Internet and the Web? If goods are purchased by a New York State resident from a Web site in California, shipped from a center in Illinois, and delivered to New York, what state has the right to collect a sales tax? Should some heavy Internet users who consume extraordinary amounts of bandwidth by streaming endless movies be charged extra for service, or should the Internet be neutral with respect to usage? What rights do nation-states and their citizens have with respect to the Internet, the Web, and e-commerce? We address issues such as these in Chapter 8, and also throughout the text.

ACADEMIC DISCIPLINES CONCERNED WITH E-COMMERCE

The phenomenon of e-commerce is so broad that a multidisciplinary perspective is required. There are two primary approaches to e-commerce: technical and behavioral.

Technical Approaches

Computer scientists are interested in e-commerce as an exemplary application of Internet technology. They are concerned with the development of computer hardware, software, and telecommunications systems, as well as standards, encryption, and database design and operation. Operations management scientists are primarily interested in building mathematical models of business processes and optimizing these processes. They are interested in e-commerce as an opportunity to study how business firms can exploit the Internet to achieve more efficient business operations. The information systems discipline spans the technical and behavioral approaches. Technical groups within the information systems specialty focus on data mining, search engine design, and artificial intelligence.

Behavioral Approaches

From a behavioral perspective, information systems researchers are primarily interested in e-commerce because of its implications for firm and industry value chains, industry structure, and corporate strategy. Economists have focused on online consumer behavior, pricing of digital goods, and on the unique features of digital electronic markets. The marketing profession is interested in marketing, brand development and extension, online consumer behavior, and the ability of e-commerce technologies to

INSIGHT ON SOCIETY

FACEBOOK AND THE AGE OF PRIVACY

In a January 2010 interview, Mark Zuckerberg, the founder of Facebook, proclaimed that the age of privacy had to come to an end. According to Zuckerberg, people were no longer worried about sharing their personal information with friends, friends of friends, or even the entire Web. Supporters of Zuckerberg's viewpoint believe the twenty-first century is a new era of openness and transparency. If true, this is good news for Facebook because its business model is based on selling access to a database of personal information.

However, not everyone is a true believer. Privacy—limitations on what personal information government and private institutions can collect and use—is a founding principle of democracies. A decade's worth of privacy surveys in the United States show that well over 80% of the American public fear the Internet is a threat to their privacy.

With about 1.5 billion monthly users worldwide, and around 165 million in North America, Facebook's privacy policies are going to shape privacy standards on the Internet for years to come. The economic stakes in the privacy debate are quite high, involving billions in advertising and transaction dollars. Facebook's business model is based on building a database of billions of users who are encouraged, or even perhaps deceived, into relinquishing control over personal information, which is then sold to advertisers and other third parties. The less privacy Facebook's users want or have, the more Facebook profits. Eliminating personal information privacy is built into Facebook's DNA.

Facebook's current privacy policies are quite a flip-flop from its original policy in 2004, which promised users near complete control over who could see their personal profile. However,

every year since 2004, Facebook has attempted to extend its control over user information and content, often without notice. For instance, in 2007, Facebook introduced the Beacon program, which was designed to broadcast users' activities on participating Web sites to their friends. After a public outcry, Facebook terminated the Beacon program, and paid $9.5 million to settle a host of class action lawsuits. In 2009, undeterred by the Beacon fiasco, Facebook unilaterally decided that it would publish users' basic personal information on the public Internet, and announced that whatever content users had contributed belonged to Facebook, and that its ownership of that information never terminated. However, as with the Beacon program, Facebook's efforts to take permanent control of user information resulted in users joining online resistance groups and it was ultimately forced to withdraw this policy as well.

In 2011, Facebook began publicizing users' "likes" of various advertisers in Sponsored Stories (i.e., advertisements) that included the users' names and profile pictures without their explicit consent, without paying them, and without giving them a way to opt out. This resulted in yet another class action lawsuit, which Facebook settled for $20 million in June 2012. (Facebook dropped Sponsored Stories in April 2014.) In 2011, Facebook enrolled all Facebook subscribers into its facial recognition program without notice. This too raised the privacy alarm, forcing Facebook to make it easier for users to opt out.

In May 2012, Facebook went public, creating even more pressure to increase revenues and profits to justify its stock market value. Shortly thereafter, Facebook announced that it was launching a mobile advertising product that pushes ads to the mobile news feeds of

(continued)

users based on the apps they use through the Facebook Connect feature, without explicit permission from the user to do so. It also announced Facebook Exchange, a program that allows advertisers to serve ads to Facebook users based on their browsing activity while not on Facebook. Privacy advocates raised the alarm yet again and more lawsuits were filed by users. In 2013, Facebook agreed to partner with several data marketing companies that deliver targeted ads based on offline data. The firms provide customer data to Facebook, which then allows Facebook advertisers to target their ads to those users based on that data.

In December 2013, another class action lawsuit was filed against Facebook by users alleging that it violated their privacy by scanning users' private Facebook messages and mining them for data such as references to URLs that Facebook could then sell to advertisers. In May 2014, an enhancement to Facebook's mobile app that allows the app to recognize the music, television show, or movie playing in the background when a user makes a status update raised a new privacy alarm. In 2015, Facebook implemented a "new" privacy policy that allows it to share user personal data across partner sites and apps, including WhatsApp and Instagram. Also in 2015, Facebook admitted that its Facebook Messenger app collected and shared user geo-location as the default setting. After negative publicity, it changed the default to "do not share."

After all these lawsuits and online public protests, one might think that Facebook's privacy policy would improve. But an academic analysis of Facebook's privacy policies from 2008 to 2015 found that on most measures of privacy protection, Facebook's policies have worsened. Since 2008, Facebook has made it more difficult for users to find out what information is being shared with whom, how it builds profiles, or how to change privacy settings. Its privacy policies have become less readable, even inscrutable, according to the researchers.

Facebook is certainly aware of consumer suspicion of its privacy policies, and it changes its policies almost yearly in response to criticism. But the response is often not helpful for users, and typically extends the company's claims to do whatever it wants with personal information. Its latest privacy policy, implemented in 2015, claims to switch its default privacy settings for new users from Public to Friends, provide a Privacy Checkup tool for users, and give users the ability to see the data it keeps on their likes and interests, and enable users to change, delete, or add to that data. Facebook argues this new policy gives users more control of the ads they are shown. Analysts point out, however, that using these new features requires users to navigate a maze of check boxes and menus that are difficult to understand even for expert Facebook users. Facebook's growth in North America has steadily declined in part because users have come to realize that everything they post or say on Facebook will be given over to advertisers. There is no privacy on Facebook. People who are concerned about their privacy, analysts have concluded, should delete their Facebook accounts.

SOURCES: "Facebook Rescinds Internship to Harvard Student Who Exposed a Privacy Flaw in Messenger," by Robert Gabelhoff, *Washington Post,* August 14, 2015; "Did You Really Agree to That? The Evolution of Facebook's Privacy Policy," by Jennifer Shore and Jill Steinman, *Technology Science,* August 11, 2015; "Facebook's Privacy Incident Response: A Study of Geolocation Sharing on Facebook Messenger," by Aran Khanna, *Technology Science,* August 11, 2015; "Sharing Data, but Not Happily," by Natasha Singer, *New York Times,* June 4, 2015; "How Your Facebook Likes Could Cost You a Job," by Anna North, *New York Times,* January 20, 2015; "Facebook Stops Irresponsibly Defaulting Privacy of New Users' Posts to 'Public,' Changes to 'Friends,'" by Josh Constine, Techcrunch.com, May 22, 2014; "Facebook Users Revolt Over Privacy Feature—Enables Microphone in Apps," by Jan Willem Aldershoff, Myce.com, June 9, 2014; "Didn't Read Those Terms of Service? Here's What You Agreed to Give Up," by Natasha Singer, *New York Times,* April 28, 2014; "Facebook Eliminates Sponsored Stories—Will It Matter to Advertisers?," by Amy Durbin, Mediapost.com, February 25, 2014; "Facebook Sued for Allegedly Intercepting Private Messages," by Jennifer Van Grove, Cnet.com, January 2, 2014; "Facebook to Partner with Data Brokers," by Bob Sullivan, Redtape.nbcnews.com, February 26, 2013; "Facebook Exchange Ads Raise Privacy Concerns," by Mikal E. Belicove, Cnbc.com, June 21, 2012; "Facebook Suit Over Subscriber Tracking Seeks $15 Billion," by Kit Chellel and Jeremy Hodges, Bloomberg.com, May 19, 2012; "How Facebook Pulled a Privacy Bait and Switch," by Dan Tynan, *PC World,* May 2010.

segment and target consumer groups, and differentiate products. Economists share an interest with marketing scholars who have focused on e-commerce consumer response to marketing and advertising campaigns, and the ability of firms to brand, segment markets, target audiences, and position products to achieve above-normal returns on investment.

Management scholars have focused on entrepreneurial behavior and the challenges faced by young firms who are required to develop organizational structures in short time spans. Finance and accounting scholars have focused on e-commerce firm valuation and accounting practices. Sociologists—and to a lesser extent, psychologists—have focused on general population studies of Internet usage, the role of social inequality in skewing Internet benefits, and the use of the Web as a social network and group communications tool. Legal scholars are interested in issues such as preserving intellectual property, privacy, and content regulation.

No one perspective dominates research about e-commerce. The challenge is to learn enough about a variety of academic disciplines so that you can grasp the significance of e-commerce in its entirety.

Pinterest:
A Picture Is Worth a Thousand Words

Like all successful e-commerce companies, Pinterest taps into a simple truth. In Pinterest's case, the simple truth is that people love to collect things, and show off their collections to others. Founded in 2009 by Ben Silbermann, Evan Sharp, and Paul Sciarra and launched in March 2010, Pinterest allows you to create virtual scrapbooks of images, video, and other content that you "pin" to a virtual bulletin board or pin board on the Web site. Categories range from Animals to Videos, with Food & Drink, DIY & Crafts, Home Décor, and Women's Fashion among the most popular. Find something that you particularly like? In addition to "liking" and perhaps commenting on it, you can re-pin it to your own board, or follow a link back to the original source. Find someone whose taste you admire or who shares your passions? You can follow one or more of that pinner's boards to keep track of everything she or he pins. As of April 2015, there were over 50 billion pins on Pinterest on more than 1 billion different boards.

Pinterest originally positioned itself as a social network. Recently, however, it has changed its tune. It now describes itself as a visual bookmarking tool for discovering and

© Blaize Pascall / Alamy

saving creative ideas (and potential purchases), with less emphasis on sharing with friends. Search has become the core part of its mission, with Google, rather than Facebook, Twitter, or Instagram, viewed as its primary competition.

In September 2015, Pinterest announced that it had reached the 100 million monthly active member mark. About 70% of those members are women, but men are its fastest growing demographic, growing by almost 75% in 2014. Pinterest is one of the "stickiest" sites on the Web, with women spending over 1.5 hours (96 minutes) per session, and men about 1.25 hours (75 minutes). According to a recent survey by the Pew Research Center, the percentage of online adults in the United States who use Pinterest has more than doubled since 2012.

Over the past five years, investors such as well-known Silicon Valley venture capital firms Andreessen Horowitz and Bessemer Venture Partners, hedge fund Valiant Capital Partners, and Japanese e-commerce company Rakuten have poured $1.3 billion in venture capital into Pinterest, with its latest round of funding in March 2015 valuing the company at $11 billion, more than double its 2014 valuation. Like Facebook, Twitter, and many other start-up companies, Pinterest focused initially on refining its product and building its user base, but not surprisingly, its investors have begun to push it to begin generating revenue. Pinterest's first step was to offer business accounts that provided additional resources for brands. In 2013, it introduced Rich Pins, which allowed companies to embed information, such as current pricing and availability, as well as a direct link to a product page. In 2014, Pinterest took the official leap into the advertising arena, launching a beta version of ads it called Promoted Pins that appear in search results and category feeds. Around the same time, Pinterest also introduced a search engine, called Guided Search, which suggests related terms to refine a search. Guided Search is based on user metadata, such as board titles, captions, and comments related to pins, to create different categories and subcategories. In January 2015, Pinterest further enhanced Guided Search by allowing users to personalize search results based on gender. According to Pinterest, the number of searches has increased by 80% over the last year.

In 2015, Pinterest has gotten serious about monetization. In January 2015, it rolled out Promoted Pins to all its U.S.-based partners. Pinterest claims that these ads are perceived as less intrusive than ads on other social networks and that the average customer coming from Pinterest spends 50% more than regular customers. In May 2015, it added paid video ads (Cinematic Pins), with brands such as Unilever, Target, Walgreens, L'Oréal, Wendy's and Visa among the first takers. Unlike Facebook's autoplay video ads, Cinematic Pins display a short animation when the user scrolls down through the ad, and only play a full-length version when the user clicks on the ad, providing more user control over the experience. Pinterest also introduced new ad-targeting and pricing options. Advertisers can target users by interests, life stage, or persona such as Millennial, prospective parent, or foodie, and rather than being limited to paying for ads on just a pay-per-view or pay-per-click basis, can now also choose a cost-per-engagement (CPE) or cost-per-action (CPA) model. Using the CPE model, advertisers only pay when a user engages with a pin, such as through re-pinning, and with the CPA model, only when the user clicks through to a Web site and makes a purchase or downloads an app. Pinterest had previously partnered

SOURCES: "Pinterest & Retailers Agree: Buyable Pins Are Driving New Customer Acquisition," by Martin Beck, Marketingland.com, September 25, 2015; "Pinterest Crosses User Milestone of 100 Million," by Mike Isaac, *New York Times,* September 17, 2015; "Pinterest Hits 100 Million Users," by Erin Griffith, *Fortune,* September 17, 2015; "Pinterest Hits 100 Million Monthly Users in Bid for Ad-Search Dollars," by Yoree Koh, *Wall Street Journal,* September 17, 2015; "Mobile Messaging and Social Media 2015," by Maeve Duggan, Pewinternet.org, August 19, 2015; "In Lawsuit Against Pinterest, Artist Continues a Crusade for Copyright on the Internet," by Kate Lucas, Grossmanllp.com, July 23, 2015; "With Buyable Pins, Pinterest Lets You Buy Stuff Right in the App," by JP Mangalindan, Mashable.com, June 2, 2015; "Why $11 Billion Pinterest Thinks It Has the 'Best Kind of Business Model'," by Jillian D'Onfrio, Businessinsider.com, May 19, 2015; "Pinterest Doubles Down on Making Money, Rolls Out

Video Ads," by JP Mangalindan, Mashable.com, May 19, 2015; "Pinterest Puts Its Own Spin on Video Ads with These Cinematic Pins," by Garret Sloane, Adweek.com, May 19, 2015; "Pinterest Bolsters Ads with 'Cinematic Pins'," by Yoree Koh, *Wall Street Journal*, May 19, 2015; "How Pinterest Plans to Spend Its New Millions and Why It Only Hires Nice Employees, According to Its Cofounder," by Jillian D'Onfrio, Businessinsider.com, May 11, 2015; "Why Pinterest Updates Its Mobile App Every 3 Weeks," by Chris Murphy, Informationweek.com, April 1, 2015; "80 Percent of Pinterest's Traffic Comes From Mobile Devices," by Jordan Novet, Venturebeat.com, March 31, 2015; "Pinterest Valued at $11 Billion after Latest Funding," by Yoree Koh, *Wall Street Journal*, March 16, 2015; "Pinterest Beefs Up Security with Full HTTPS Support and Bug Bounty Program," by Jordan Novet, Venturebeat.com, March 13, 2015; "Fighting Spam at Pinterest," Engineering. pinterest.com, February 20, 2015; "Aiming to Ease App Discovery, Apple Pairs with Pinterest," by Mike Isaac, *New York Times*, February 12, 2015; "As Social Media Matures, Pinterest Looks Stronger," by Ed Arnold, Bizjournals.com, February 4, 2015; "Pinterest Goes After the Male Demographic with Debut of New Search Filters," by Sarah Perez, Techcrunch.com, January 23, 2015; "Pinterest Becomes More Search Engine-Like with the Launch of Guided Search on the Web," by Sarah Perez, Techcrunch.com, June 11, 2014; "Pinterest Tests Do-It-Yourself Promoted Pins for Small and Medium-Sized Businesses," by Ryan Lawler, Techcrunch.com, June 5, 2014; "Can Pinterest Be Found in Translation," by Sarah Frier, Businessweek.com, May 22, 2014; "On Pins and Needles over Pinterest," by Erika Morphy, Ecommercetimes.com, May 19, 2014; "Pinterest's Next Big Move: A Clever New Take on Search," by Kyle VanHemert, Wired.com, April 24, 2014; "Paying for Pin-Ups," by Sarah Laskow, *Columbia Journalism Review*, November 7, 2013; "Pinning Down Pinterest: Addressing Copyright and Other IP

with Apple to introduce App Pins, which allows users to discover new iOS apps that can be downloaded directly from Pinterest.

In June 2015, Pinterest launched Buyable Pins, which allow users to directly purchase products by clicking a blue Buy It button within the pin, for its iPhone and iPad apps; versions for Android devices and desktop computers are still in the works. According to Pinterest, 30 billion of its 50 billion pins are buyable, from merchants both large (such as Macy's, Nordstrom, Neiman Marcus) and small. Pinterest says its data shows that Buyable Pins are generating a significant percentage of brand-new customers for merchants.

The fact that Pinterest launched Buyable Pins on its iOS mobile platform rather than the desktop is just one indication of how important the mobile platform is to Pinterest. Pinterest provides apps for iPhone, iPad, Android, and Windows Phone, as well as a mobile version of its Web site using HTML5. Pinterest Mobile runs inside the smartphone's browser rather than as a stand-alone program. Mobile has been a huge success for Pinterest, with 80% of its traffic coming from mobile devices in 2015. Pinterest releases a new version of its iOS and Android mobile apps every few weeks, enabling it to quickly test new features. According to Pinterest co-founder Evan Sharp, the smartphone is the platform Pinterest focuses on when it develops new features and products.

International expansion is another major focus in 2015. Pinterest introduced its first localized site, for the United Kingdom in May 2013, and it is now available in 31 different languages. Pinterest is aiming to make its platform feel more regional, focusing specifically on the United Kingdom, France, Germany, Japan, and Brazil. Currently about 55% of its user base is located in the United States, with 45% coming from other parts of the world. Looking to the future, Pinterest believes that eventually, a majority of its users will be from outside the United States, and that international expansion will provide it with the greatest growth opportunities.

Despite all the good news for Pinterest, there are some issues lurking just behind the scenes that may cloud its future, such as the issue of copyright infringement. The basis of Pinterest's business model involves users potentially violating others' copyrights by posting images without permission and/or attribution. Although Pinterest's Terms of Service puts the onus on its users to avoid doing so, the site knowingly facilitates such actions by, for example, providing a Pin It tool embedded in the user's browser toolbar. Much content on the site reportedly violates its Terms of Service. Pinterest has provided an opt-out code to enable other sites to bar its content from being shared on Pinterest, but some question why they should have to take action when Pinterest is creating the problem. Another thing Pinterest has done to try to ameliorate the problem is to automatically add citations (attribution) to content coming from certain specified sources, such as Flickr, YouTube, Vimeo, Etsy, Kickstarter, and SlideShare, among others. In 2013, it entered into an agreement with Getty Images in which it agreed to provide attribution for Getty content and pay Getty a fee. Pinterest says it complies with the Digital Millennium Copyright Act, which requires sites to remove images that violate copyright, but this too requires the copyright holder to be proactive and take action to demand the images be removed. Christopher Boffoli, a well-known photographer, filed a federal lawsuit against Pinterest in late 2014 alleging that Pinterest users have used his photographs without his permission, and Pinterest has failed to take adequate measures to remove them. How this issue is resolved may have a significant impact on Pinterest's ultimate success.

Pinterest is also not immune to the spam and scams that plague many e-commerce initiatives. Security analysts believe Pinterest will have to adapt its systems to deal with scammers and warn users to be wary of requests to pin content before viewing it and to be suspicious of "free" offers, surveys, and links with questionable titles. Pinterest has acknowledged the problem and has promised to improve its technology. In 2015, for instance, Pinterest migrated its Web site to the HTTPS protocol, which provides more security than the more common HTTP protocol typically used to access Web pages. Pinterest also employs a system known as Stingray that enables it to quickly react to spam and other types of malicious behavior, and has created a program that pays a bounty to white hat hackers who discover security issues.

At the moment, however, the future looks very bright for Pinterest. Although it may encounter some growing pains in the process of implementing its new business model, it has the potential to generate significant revenue based on advertising.

Issues," by Jennifer L. Barry, Lexology.com, October 22, 2013; "Pinterest (Officially) Jumps the Pond," by Zak Stambor, Internetre-tailer.com, May 10, 2013; "Pinterest Gives Copyright Credit to Etsy, Kickstarter, SoundCloud," by Sarah Kessler, Mashable.com, July 19, 2012; "Pinterest Whets Consumer Desire with Images that Turn Window Shoppers into Online Buyers," by Matt Butter, *Forbes,* June 6, 2012; "A Site That Aims to Unleash the Scrapbook Maker in All of Us," by Jenna Wortham, *New York Times,* March 11, 2012; "Pinterest Releases Optional Code to Prevent Unwanted Image Sharing," by Andrew Webster, Theverge.com, February 20, 2012; "A Scrapbook on the Web Catches Fire," by David Pogue, *New York Times,* February 15, 2012.

Case Study Questions

1. Why does Pinterest view Google as its primary competitor?

2. Why does Pinterest focus on the smartphone platform when it develops new features and products?

3. Why is copyright infringement a potential issue for Pinterest?

1.5 REVIEW

KEY CONCEPTS

■ **Define e-commerce and describe how it differs from e-business.**

- E-commerce involves digitally enabled commercial transactions between and among organizations and individuals. Digitally enabled transactions include all those mediated by digital technology, meaning, for the most part, transactions that occur over the Internet, the Web, and/or via mobile devices. Commercial transactions involve the exchange of value (e.g., money) across organizational or individual boundaries in return for products or services.

- E-business refers primarily to the digital enabling of transactions and processes within a firm, involving information systems under the control of the firm. For the most part, e-business does not involve commercial transactions across organizational boundaries where value is exchanged.

■ **Identify and describe the unique features of e-commerce technology and discuss their business significance.**

There are eight features of e-commerce technology that are unique to this medium:

- *Ubiquity*—available just about everywhere, at all times, making it possible to shop from your desktop, at home, at work, or even from your car.
- *Global reach*—permits commercial transactions to cross cultural and national boundaries far more conveniently and cost-effectively than is true in traditional commerce.
- *Universal standards*—shared by all nations around the world, in contrast to most traditional commerce technologies, which differ from one nation to the next.
- *Richness*—enables an online merchant to deliver marketing messages in a way not possible with traditional commerce technologies.
- *Interactivity*—allows for two-way communication between merchant and consumer and enables the merchant to engage a consumer in ways similar to a face-to-face experience, but on a much more massive, global scale.
- *Information density*—is the total amount and quality of information available to all market participants. The Internet reduces information collection, storage, processing, and communication costs while increasing the currency, accuracy, and timeliness of information.
- *Personalization* and *customization*—the increase in information density allows merchants to target their marketing messages to specific individuals and results in a level of personalization and customization unthinkable with previously existing commerce technologies.
- *Social technology*—provides a many-to-many model of mass communications. Millions of users are able to generate content consumed by millions of other users. The result is the formation of social networks on a wide scale and the aggregation of large audiences on social network platforms.

■ **Describe the major types of e-commerce.**

There are six major types of e-commerce:
- *B2C e-commerce* involves businesses selling to consumers and is the type of e-commerce that most consumers are likely to encounter.
- *B2B e-commerce* involves businesses selling to other businesses and is the largest form of e-commerce.
- *C2C e-commerce* is a means for consumers to sell to each other. In C2C e-commerce, the consumer prepares the product for market, places the product for auction or sale, and relies on the market maker to provide catalog, search engine, and transaction clearing capabilities so that products can be easily displayed, discovered, and paid for.
- *Social e-commerce* is e-commerce that is enabled by social networks and online social relationships.
- *M-commerce* involves the use of wireless digital devices to enable online transactions.
- *Local e-commerce* is a form of e-commerce that is focused on engaging the consumer based on his or her current geographic location.

■ **Understand the evolution of e-commerce from its early years to today.**

E-commerce has gone through three stages: innovation, consolidation, and reinvention.
- The early years of e-commerce were a technological success, with the digital infrastructure created during the period solid enough to sustain significant growth in e-commerce during the next decade, and a mixed business success, with significant revenue growth and customer usage, but low profit margins.
- E-commerce entered a period of consolidation beginning in 2001 and extending into 2006.
- E-commerce entered a period of reinvention in 2007 with the emergence of the mobile digital platform, social networks, and Web 2.0 applications that attracted huge audiences in a very short time span.

■ **Describe the major themes underlying the study of e-commerce.**

E-commerce involves three broad interrelated themes:
- *Technology*—To understand e-commerce, you need a basic understanding of the information technologies upon which it is built, including the Internet, the Web, and mobile platform, and a host of complemen-

tary technologies—cloud computing, desktop computers, smartphones, tablet computers, local area networks, client/server computing, packet-switched communications, protocols such as TCP/IP, Web servers, HTML, and relational and non-relational databases, among others.

- *Business*—While technology provides the infrastructure, it is the business applications—the potential for extraordinary returns on investment—that create the interest and excitement in e-commerce. Therefore, you also need to understand some key business concepts such as electronic markets, information goods, business models, firm and industry value chains, industry structure, and consumer behavior in digital markets.

- *Society*—Understanding the pressures that global e-commerce places on contemporary society is critical to being successful in the e-commerce marketplace. The primary societal issues are intellectual property, individual privacy, and public policy.

■ **Identify the major academic disciplines contributing to e-commerce.**

There are two primary approaches to e-commerce: technical and behavioral. Each of these approaches is represented by several academic disciplines. On the technical side, this includes computer science, operations management, and information systems. On the behavioral side, it includes information systems as well as sociology, economics, finance and accounting, management, and marketing.

QUESTIONS

1. What is e-commerce? How does it differ from e-business? Where does it intersect with e-business?
2. What is information asymmetry?
3. What are some of the unique features of e-commerce technology?
4. What is a marketspace?
5. What are three benefits of universal standards?
6. Compare online and traditional transactions in terms of richness.
7. Name three of the business consequences that can result from growth in information density.
8. What is Web 2.0? Give examples of Web 2.0 sites and explain why you included them in your list.
9. Give examples of B2C, B2B, C2C, and social, mobile, and local e-commerce besides those listed in the chapter materials.
10. How are e-commerce technologies similar to or different from other technologies that have changed commerce in the past?
11. Describe the three different stages in the evolution of e-commerce.
12. Define disintermediation and explain the benefits to Internet users of such a phenomenon. How does disintermediation impact friction-free commerce?
13. What are some of the major advantages and disadvantages of being a first mover?
14. What is a network effect, and why is it valuable?
15. Discuss the ways in which the early years of e-commerce can be considered both a success and a failure.
16. What are five of the major differences between the early years of e-commerce and today's e-commerce?
17. Why is a multidisciplinary approach necessary if one hopes to understand e-commerce?
18. What are some of the privacy issues that Facebook has created?
19. What are those who take a behavioral approach to studying e-commerce interested in?

PROJECTS

1. Choose an e-commerce company and assess it in terms of the eight unique features of e-commerce technology described in Table 1.2. Which of the features does the company implement well, and which

features poorly, in your opinion? Prepare a short memo to the president of the company you have chosen detailing your findings and any suggestions for improvement you may have.

2. Search the Web for an example of each of the major types of e-commerce described in Section 1.1 and listed in Table 1.3. Create a presentation or written report describing each company (take a screenshot of each, if possible), and explain why it fits into the category of e-commerce to which you have assigned it.

3. Given the development and history of e-commerce in the years from 1995–2015, what do you predict we will see during the next five years of e-commerce? Describe some of the technological, business, and societal shifts that may occur as the Internet continues to grow and expand. Prepare a brief presentation or written report to explain your vision of what e-commerce will look like in 2019.

4. Prepare a brief report or presentation on how companies are using Instagram or another company of your choosing as a social e-commerce platform.

5. Follow up on events at Uber since October 2015 (when the opening case was prepared). Prepare a short report on your findings.

REFERENCES

Aguiar, Mark and Erik Hurst. "Life-Cycle Prices and Production." *American Economic Review* 97:5, 1533–1559. (January 1, 2008).

Alessandria, George. "Consumer Search, Price Dispersion, and International Relative Price Fluctuations." *International Economic Review* 50:3, 803–829 (September 1, 2009).

Bailey, Joseph P. *Intermediation and Electronic Markets: Aggregation and Pricing in Internet Commerce.* Ph.D., Technology, Management and Policy, Massachusetts Institute of Technology (1998a).

Bakos, Yannis. "Reducing Buyer Search Costs: Implications for Electronic Marketplaces." *Management Science* (December 1997).

Banerjee, Suman and Chakravarty, Amiya. "Price Setting and Price Discovery Strategies with a Mix of Frequent and Infrequent Internet Users." (April 15, 2005). SSRN: http://ssrn.com/abstract=650706.

Baye, Michael R. "Price Dispersion in the Lab and on the Internet: Theory and Evidence." *Rand Journal of Economics* (2004).

Baye, Michael R., John Morgan, and Patrick Scholten. "Temporal Price Dispersion: Evidence from an Online Consumer Electronics Market." *Journal of Interactive Marketing* (January 2004).

Brynjolfsson, Erik, and Michael Smith. "Frictionless Commerce? A Comparison of Internet and Conventional Retailers." *Management Science* (April 2000).

eBay, Inc. "eBay Inc. Reports Fourth Quarter and Full Year Results." (January 21, 2015).

eMarketer, Inc. "Internet Users and Penetration, 2013–2019." (April 2015a).

eMarketer, Inc. (Yory Wurmser). "US Mobile Commerce Forecast and Trends." (May 2015b).

eMarketer, Inc. "US Retail Ecommerce Sales, 2013–2019." (June 2015c).

eMarketer, Inc. "US Digital Travel Metrics, 2013–2019." (May 1, 2015d).

eMarketer, Inc. "US Mobile Connections, 2013–2019." (February 2015e)."

eMarketer, Inc. "US Mobile Phone Internet Users and Penetration, 2013–2019." (February 2015f).

eMarketer, Inc. "US Tablet Users and Penetration, 2013–2019." (February 2015g).

eMarketer, Inc. "US Mobile Connections, 2011–2017." (March 2013a).

eMarketer, Inc. "US Mobile Phone Internet Users and Penetration, 2011–2017." (March 2013b).

eMarketer, Inc. "US Tablet Users and Penetration, 2011–2017." (March 2013c).

Evans, Philip, and Thomas S. Wurster. "Getting Real About Virtual Commerce." *Harvard Business Review* (November-December 1999).

Evans, Philip, and Thomas S. Wurster. "Strategy and the New Economics of Information." *Harvard Business Review* (September-October 1997).

Forrester Research. "U.S. Cross-Channel Retail Forecast, 2012 to 2017." (March 27, 2014).

Ghose, Anindya, and Yuliang Yao. "Using Transaction Prices to Re-Examine Price Dispersion in Electronic Markets." *Information Systems Research*, Vol. 22 No. 2. (June 2011).

Google. "How Search Works: From Algorithms to Answers." (accessed June 17, 2014).

Gorodnichenko, Yuriy, et al. "Price Setting in Online Markets: Does IT Click?" NBER Working Paper No. 20819 (December 2014).

Interactions Consumer Experience Marketing, Inc., "The Rise of Webrooming." (May 2014).

Internet Retailer. "Top 500 Guide 2015 Edition." (2015).

Internet Systems Consortium, Inc. "ISC Internet Domain Survey." (July 2015).

Kalakota, Ravi, and Marcia Robinson. *e-Business 2.0: Roadmap for Success, 2nd edition*. Reading, MA: Addison Wesley (2003).

Kambil, Ajit. "Doing Business in the Wired World." *IEEE Computer* (May 1997).

Levin, Jonathon. "The Economics of Internet Markets." Stanford University, Draft, February 18, 2011.

Mesenbourg, Thomas L. "Measuring Electronic Business: Definitions, Underlying Concepts, and Measurement Plans." U. S. Department of Commerce Bureau of the Census (August 2001).

Rayport, Jeffrey F., and Bernard J. Jaworski. *Introduction to E-commerce, 2nd edition*. New York: McGraw-Hill (2003).

Rosso, Mark and Bernard Jansen. "Smart Marketing or Bait & Switch: Competitors' Brands as Keywords in Online Advertising." Proceedings of the 4th Workshop on Information Credibility. ACM (2010).

Shapiro, Carl, and Hal R. Varian. *Information Rules. A Strategic Guide to the Network Economy*. Cambridge, MA: Harvard Business School Press (1999).

Sinha, Indrajit. "Cost Transparency: The Net's Threat to Prices and Brands." *Harvard Business Review* (March-April 2000).

Smith, Michael, Joseph Bailey, and Erik Brynjolfsson. "Understanding Digital Markets: Review and Assessment." In Erik Brynjolfsson and Brian Kahin (eds.), *Understanding the Digital Economy*. Cambridge, MA: MIT Press (2000).

Tversky, A., and D. Kahneman. "The Framing of Decisions and the Psychology of Choice." *Science* (January 1981).

U.S. Census Bureau. "E-Stats." (May 28, 2015).

Varian, Hal R. "When Commerce Moves On, Competition Can Work in Strange Ways." *New York Times* (August 24, 2000a).

Varian, Hal R. "5 Habits of Highly Effective Revolution." *Forbes ASAP* (February 21, 2000b).

Zaroban, Stefany. "Social Networks Deliver for Retailers, But at a Price." Internetretailer.com (January 13, 2015).

CHAPTER 2

E-commerce Business Models and Concepts

After reading this chapter, you will be able to:

- Identify the key components of e-commerce business models.
- Describe the major B2C business models.
- Describe the major B2B business models.
- Understand key business concepts and strategies applicable to e-commerce.

Tweet Tweet:

Twitter's Business Model

Twitter, the social network based on 140-character text messages, continues in the long tradition of Internet developments that appeared to spring out of nowhere and take the world by storm. Twitter began as a Web-based version of text messaging services provided by cell phone carriers. The basic idea was to marry short text messaging on cell phones with the Web and its ability to create social groups.

Since then, Twitter has expanded beyond simple text messages to article previews, photographs, videos, and even animated images, and today has over 315 million active users worldwide (as of

© Kennedy Photography / Alamy

September 2015). The 5,000 tweets a day that it began with in 2006 has turned into a deluge of around 500 million daily tweets worldwide. Special events, such as the Super Bowl, tend to generate an explosion of tweets, with a total of 28.4 million tweets during the course of the game in 2015. Some celebrities, such as the pop star Katy Perry, have millions of followers (in Perry's case, over 75 million as of 2015).

Like many social network firms, Twitter began operating without any revenue stream. However, it quickly developed some important assets, such as user attention and audience size (unique visitors). Another important asset is its database of tweets, which contain the real-time comments, observations, and opinions of its audience, and a search engine that can mine those tweets for patterns. In addition, Twitter has become a powerful alternative media platform for the distribution of news, videos, and pictures. Twitter has sought to monetize its platform via three primary advertising options, Promoted Tweets, Promoted Trends, and Promoted Accounts, although it is rolling out more and more variations on these products every day.

Promoted Tweets are Twitter's version of Google's text ads. In response to a query to Twitter's search function for tablet computers, for example, a Best Buy tweet about tablets will be displayed. Promoted Tweets look the same as regular tweets and are available on a cost-per-engagement basis (advertisers only pay when users interact with the tweet by clicking, replying, or retweeting it) or on an objective-based campaign basis that focuses on a specific goal such as a click-through to the advertiser's Web site, lead generation, or the installation of an app. Promoted Tweets typically cost between 20 cents and $4. Twitter also offers geo-targeted and keyword targeting functionality, which enables advertisers to send Promoted Tweets to specific users in specific locations or based on keywords in their recent tweets or tweets with which they have interacted. Twitter's research indicates that users are much more likely to engage with such Promoted Tweets, and that Promoted Tweets produce greater engagement with viewers than do traditional Web advertisements.

Promoted Trends is the second major Twitter advertising product. "Trends" is a section of the Twitter home page that identifies what people are talking about. A company can place a Promoted Trends banner at the top of the Trends section, and when users click on the banner, they are taken to the follower page for that company or product. A Promoted Trend must be purchased for an entire market for a day (for example, the United States) for a flat fee. In the United States, the fee is now $200,000, up from $80,000 when Promoted Trends were first introduced in 2010. Promoted Trends are available for purchase in 50 different countries.

Twitter's third primary advertising product is Promoted Accounts, which are suggestions to follow various advertiser accounts based on the list of accounts that the user already follows. Like Promoted Tweets, Promoted Accounts can be geo-targeted at both the country level and the Nielsen DMA (Designated Marketing Area, roughly equivalent to a city and its suburb) level. Promoted Accounts are priced on a cost-per-follower basis, with advertisers only paying for new followers gained. Prices range from $.50 to $2.50. Twitter also offers Enhanced Profile Pages for brands. For a reported $15,000 to $25,000, companies get their own banner to display images, and the ability to pin a tweet to the top of the company's Twitter stream.

In 2013, Twitter began a natural progression into the video ad market. Video clips that include video ads can now be embedded within tweets. Known as the Twitter Amplify program, the program now includes more than 80 media partners such as CBS, ESPN, Condé Nast, MLB.com, Warner Music, and others in 10 countries. Twitter also launched a television ad targeting product in 2013 that allows marketers to show Promoted Tweets to people who have been tweeting about a television show. The product leverages "video fingerprinting" technology created by Bluefin Labs, which Twitter acquired in 2013 for $90 million. In 2014, building on the Amplify program, Twitter announced a beta test of Promoted Video, which allows advertisers to distribute videos on the Twitter platform and in 2015, it began allowing advertisers to use Promoted Video to link directly to app installations, as well as an ad purchasing feature for videos called "optimized action bidding." This allows marketers to customize ad purchases to improve their return on investment.

But it is mobile that is proving to be the primary driver of Twitter's business and the source of most of its revenue. Twitter began testing Promoted Tweets and Promoted Accounts on mobile devices in March 2012, and by June 2012, reported that it was generating the majority of its revenues from ads on mobile devices rather than on its Web site. Twitter has acquired companies like MoPub and TapCommerce to bolster its mobile capabilities, and in 2015 made its largest acquisition yet, spending $533 million to acquire digital ad platform TellApart. Twitter hopes that TellApart's technology will help improve its mobile ad targeting. Currently, Twitter derives over 80% of its advertising revenue from mobile.

SOURCES: "Twitter Adds a New 'Buy' Button," by Emily Price, Blog.sfgate.com, September 16, 2015; "Here's Another Area Where Twitter Appears to Have Stalled: Tweets Per Day," by Alexei Oreskovic, Businessinsider.com, June 15, 2015; "Twitter Is Now Letting Apps Advertise With Video," by Garett Sloane, Adweek.com, July 8, 2015; "Twitter To Pay About $533 Million For TellApart, Largest Acquisition To Date," by Zach Rodgers, Adexchanger.com, April 30, 2015; "Where Did Dick Costolo Go Wrong?" by Erin Griffith, *Fortune*, June 12, 2015; "Twitter's Evolving Pans to Make Money From its Data," by Vindu Goel, *New York Times*, April 11, 2015; "Twitter Launches New Ad Product, Promoted Video, into Beta," by Sarah Perez, Techcrunch.com, August 12, 2014; "Twitter Changes Pricing Model for Advertisers," by Mark Bergan, Adage.com, August 7, 2014; "Twitter Hopes Its New Marketing Partnership Will Translate to Mobile Ad Growth," by Richard Byrne Reilly, Venturebeat.com, July 5, 2014; "Twitter 'Buy Now' Button Appears for First Time," by Kurt Wagner, Mashable.com, June 30, 2014; "Twitter Buys TapCommerce, a Mobile Advertising Start-up," by Mike Isaac, *New York Times*, June 30, 2014; "Twitter Now Supports Animated GIFs Online and On Mobile," by Sarah Perez, Tech-crunch.com, June 18, 2014; "In a Single Tweet, as Many Pieces of Metadata as There Are Characters," by Elizabeth Dwoskin, *Wall Street*

Twitter went public in November 2013 with a valuation of about $14 billion, raising $1.8 billion on top of the $1.2 billion it had previously raised from private investors and venture capital firms. The public offering was viewed as a rousing success, with the stock price jumping almost 75% on its opening day, despite the fact that at the time, Twitter had not generated a profit. However, its share price has declined significantly from its high of over $74 in December 2013 down to approximately $27 as of Fall 2015, threatening to dip below its IPO price of $26. Analysts have reiterated concerns that Twitter's growth rate in the United States is slowing. Only 25% of Americans with an Internet connection use Twitter, compared to the over 60% that use Facebook. The vast majority of its users (over 75%) are located outside the United States, although the United States is the source of 75% of its ad revenues.

Another issue is user engagement. Research indicates that the vast majority of tweets are generated by a small percentage of users: one study found that the top 15% of users account for 85% of all tweets. This is problematic because Twitter only makes money when a user engages with an ad. User retention is another problem. One study found that Twitter had only a 40% retention rate: 60% of users failed to return the following month. Only about 11% of the accounts created in 2012 are still tweeting. And while Twitter boasted that its users generated 500 million tweets per day in 2013, the company still hasn't announced that it has reached the 600 million daily tweet threshold, further suggesting that its growth has stalled. Acknowledging a need for a change in direction, CEO Dick Costolo stepped down in 2015, replaced by co-founder Jack Dorsey.

Twitter recognizes that one of its problems is that it is perceived to be more confusing to use than Facebook. In 2014, it rolled out a new profile page design, and it has been experimenting with a variety of ways to make its service easier to use. Twitter continues to refine its data mining capability, recognizing that its most valuable resource may be customer sentiment about products, services, and marketing efforts. In 2013, Twitter purchased Big Data start-up Lucky Sort and since then has acquired a number of companies such as Topsy Labs and Gnip that will help it improve its ability to provide information about its users' behavior. In 2015, Twitter stopped allowing third-party resellers to buy access to the full stream of daily messages on the site, hoping that direct relationships with companies interested in that data will prove more lucrative.

Twitter has also been working on a social e-commerce strategy that will allow its users to purchase products without having to leave the site to help diversify its revenue stream. It partnered with Amazon in 2014 to allow users to add products directly to their Amazon shopping cart by responding to a tweet with a hashtag and began a beta test of a Buy Now button within tweets. In 2015, it rolled out the Buy Now button to all users on all platforms, and made it available globally to any company that wants to use it, partnering with payments company Stripe. Brands such as Burberry, Home Depot, Saks Fifth Avenue, Warby Parker, and many others have already begun to implement the button into their tweets, and Twitter hopes it will become a significant revenue generator in the future.

Journal, June 6, 2014; "Making Twitter Easier to Use," by Vindu Goel, *New York Times*, May 28, 2014; "Twitter's Growth Shifts to Developing Countries," by Vindu Goel, *New York Times*, May 27, 2014; "Tweet to Buy: How Amazon and Twitter's Social Shopping Cart Works," by Nathan Oliyarez-Giles," *Wall Street Journal*, May 5, 2014; "Twitter's New Profile Pages: A Guide to the New Settings and Styles," by Nathan Olivarez-Giles, *Wall Street Journal*, April 22, 2014; "Twitter Pushes Further Into Mobile Ads with MoPub Integration," by Yoree Koh, *Wall Street Journal*, April 17, 2014; "Twitter Goes After a Facebook Cash Cow," by Vindu Goel, *New York Times*, April 17, 2014; "Twitter Acquires Gnip, Bringing a Valuable Data Service In-House," by Ashwin Seshagiri, *New York Times*, April 15, 2014; "Only 11% of New Twitter Users in 2012 Are Still Tweeting," by Yoree Koh, *Wall Street Journal*, March 21, 2014; "Twitter's Big Battle is Indifference," by Yoree Koh, *Wall Street Journal*, February 10, 2014; "A Sneak Peek at Twitter's E-commerce Plans," by Yoree Koh, *Wall Street Journal*, January 31, 2014; "#Wow! Twitter Soars 73% in IPO," by Julianne Pepitone, Money.cnn.com, November 7, 2013; "Twitter Amplify Partnerships: Great Content, Great Brands, Great Engagement," by Glenn Brown, Blog.twitter.com, May 23, 2013; "TV Ad Targeting Uses 'Video Fingerprinting'," by Christopher Heine, Adweek.com, May 23, 2013; "Twitter's Latest Buy: Big Data Startup Lucky Sort," by Daniel Terdiman, News.cnet.com, May 13, 2013; "Twitter's New Video Plan: Ads, Brought to You by Ads," by Peter Kafka, Allthingsd.com, April 16, 2013; "Report: Twitter Now Charges $200,000 for Promoted Trends," by Seth Fiegerman, Mashable.com, February 11, 2013; "How Twitter Makes Money," by Harry Gold, Clickz.com, April 26, 2011, "Twitter to Launch Geo-targeted Promoted Tweets and Data for Marketers," by Sarah Shearman, Brandrepublic.com, April 7, 2011.

T he story of Twitter illustrates the difficulties of turning a good business idea with a huge audience into a successful business model that produces revenues and even profits.

Thousands of firms have discovered that they can spend other people's invested capital much faster than they can get customers to pay for their products or services. In most instances of failure, the business model of the firm is faulty from the beginning. In contrast, successful e-commerce firms have business models that are able to leverage the unique qualities of the Internet, the Web, and the mobile platform, provide customers real value, develop highly effective and efficient operations, avoid legal and social entanglements that can harm the firm, and produce profitable business results. In addition, successful business models must scale. The business must be able to achieve efficiencies as it grows in volume. But what is a business model, and how can you tell if a firm's business model is going to produce a profit?

In this chapter, we focus on business models and basic business concepts that you must be familiar with in order to understand e-commerce.

2.1 E-COMMERCE BUSINESS MODELS

INTRODUCTION

business model
a set of planned activities designed to result in a profit in a marketplace

A **business model** is a set of planned activities (sometimes referred to as *business processes*) designed to result in a profit in a marketplace. A business model is not always the same as a business strategy, although in some cases they are very close insofar as the business model explicitly takes into account the competitive environment (Magretta, 2002). The business model is at the center of the business plan. A **business plan** is a document that describes a firm's business model. A business plan always takes into account the competitive environment. An **e-commerce business model** aims to use and leverage the unique qualities of the Internet, the Web, and the mobile platform.

business plan
a document that describes a firm's business model

e-commerce business model
a business model that aims to use and leverage the unique qualities of the Internet and the World Wide Web

EIGHT KEY ELEMENTS OF A BUSINESS MODEL

If you hope to develop a successful business model in any arena, not just e-commerce, you must make sure that the model effectively addresses the eight elements listed in **Figure 2.1**. These elements are value proposition, revenue model, market opportunity, competitive environment, competitive advantage, market strategy, organizational development, and management team. Many writers focus on a firm's value proposition and revenue model. While these may be the most important and most easily identifiable aspects of a company's business model, the other elements are equally important when evaluating business models and plans, or when attempting to understand why a particular company has succeeded or failed (Kim and Mauborgne, 2000). In the following sections, we describe each of the key business model elements more fully.

FIGURE 2.1 THE EIGHT KEY ELEMENTS OF A BUSINESS MODEL

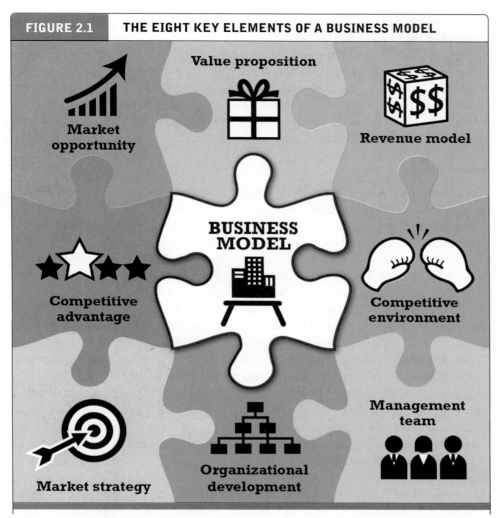

A business model has eight key elements. Each element must be addressed if you hope to be successful.

Value Proposition

A company's value proposition is at the very heart of its business model. A **value proposition** defines how a company's product or service fulfills the needs of customers (Kambil, Ginsberg, and Bloch, 1998). To develop and/or analyze a firm's value proposition, you need to understand why customers will choose to do business with the firm instead of another company and what the firm provides that other firms do not and cannot. From the consumer point of view, successful e-commerce value propositions include personalization and customization of product offerings, reduction of product search costs, reduction of price discovery costs, and facilitation of transactions by managing product delivery.

value proposition
defines how a company's product or service fulfills the needs of customers

For instance, before Amazon existed, most customers personally traveled to book retailers to place an order. In some cases, the desired book might not be available, and the customer would have to wait several days or weeks, and then return to the bookstore to pick it up. Amazon makes it possible for book lovers to shop for virtually any book in print from the comfort of their home or office, 24 hours a day, and to know immediately whether a book is in stock. Amazon's Kindle takes this one step further by making e-books instantly available with no shipping wait. Amazon's primary value propositions are unparalleled selection and convenience.

Revenue Model

revenue model

describes how the firm will earn revenue, produce profits, and produce a superior return on invested capital

A firm's **revenue model** describes how the firm will earn revenue, generate profits, and produce a superior return on invested capital. We use the terms *revenue model* and *financial model* interchangeably. The function of business organizations is both to generate profits and to produce returns on invested capital that exceed alternative investments. Profits alone are not sufficient to make a company "successful" (Porter, 1985). In order to be considered successful, a firm must produce returns greater than alternative investments. Firms that fail this test go out of existence.

Although there are many different e-commerce revenue models that have been developed, most companies rely on one, or some combination, of the following major revenue models: advertising, subscription, transaction fee, sales, and affiliate.

advertising revenue model

a company provides a forum for advertisements and receives fees from advertisers

In the **advertising revenue model**, a company that offers content, services, and/or products also provides a forum for advertisements and receives fees from advertisers. Companies that are able to attract the greatest viewership or that have a highly specialized, differentiated viewership and are able to retain user attention ("stickiness") are able to charge higher advertising rates. Yahoo, for instance, derives a significant amount of revenue from display and video advertising.

subscription revenue model

a company offers its users content or services and charges a subscription fee for access to some or all of its offerings

In the **subscription revenue model**, a company that offers content or services charges a subscription fee for access to some or all of its offerings. For instance, the digital version of *Consumer Reports* provides online and mobile access to premium content, such as detailed ratings, reviews, and recommendations, only to subscribers, who have a choice of paying a $6.95 monthly subscription fee or a $30.00 annual fee. Experience with the subscription revenue model indicates that to successfully overcome the disinclination of users to pay for content, the content offered must be perceived as a high-value-added, premium offering that is not readily available elsewhere nor easily replicated. Companies successfully offering content or services online on a subscription basis include eHarmony (dating services), Ancestry (genealogy research), Microsoft's Xbox Live (video games), Pandora, Spotify, and Rhapsody (music), Scribd, and Amazon's Kindle Unlimited program (e-books), and Netflix and Hulu (television and movies). See **Table 2.1** for examples of various subscription services.

freemium strategy

companies give away a certain level of product or services for free, but then charge a subscription fee for premium levels of the product or service

Recently, a number of companies have been combining a subscription revenue model with a freemium strategy. In a **freemium strategy**, the companies give away a certain level of product or services for free, but then charge a subscription fee for premium levels of the product or service. See the case study, *Freemium Takes Pandora Public*, at the end of the chapter, for a further look at the freemium strategy.

TABLE 2.1	EXAMPLES OF SUBSCRIPTION SERVICES
NAME	**DESCRIPTION**
eHarmony (dating)	• Free: Create profile and view profiles of matches • Basic (see photos, send and receive messages): $165–$170 for 6 months; $225–$230 for 1 year • Total Connect (Basic plus additional services such as identification validation): $180 for 6 months; $288 for 1 year • Premier (Basic/Total Connect plus additional services such as if you do not find match within a year, get another year for free) : $500/year
Ancestry (genealogical research)	• All U.S. records: $19.99/month or $99 for 6 months • All U.S. and international records: $34.99/monthly or $149 for 6 months • All records on Ancestry and also Fold3 and Newspapers.com: $44.99/month or $199 for 6 months
Scribd (e-books)	• Unlimited books for $8.99/month (over 1 million e-books, audio books, and comic books from which to choose)
Spotify (music)	• Many different permutations, depending on device (mobile, tablet, or desktop) and plan chosen (Free, Unlimited or Premier)

In the **transaction fee revenue model**, a company receives a fee for enabling or executing a transaction. For example, eBay provides an auction marketplace and receives a small transaction fee from a seller if the seller is successful in selling the item. E*Trade, a financial services provider, receives transaction fees each time it executes a stock transaction on behalf of a customer.

In the **sales revenue model**, companies derive revenue by selling goods, content, or services to customers. Companies such as Amazon (which sells books, music, and other products), L.L.Bean, and Gap all have sales revenue models. A number of companies are also using a subscription-based sales revenue model. Birchbox, which offers home delivery of beauty products for a $10 monthly or $100 annual subscription price, is one example.

In the **affiliate revenue model**, companies that steer business to an "affiliate" receive a referral fee or percentage of the revenue from any resulting sales. For example, MyPoints makes money by connecting companies with potential customers by offering special deals to its members. When they take advantage of an offer and make a purchase, members earn "points" they can redeem for freebies, and MyPoints receives a fee. Community feedback companies typically receive some of their revenue from steering potential customers to Web sites where they make a purchase.

Table 2.2 on page 62 summarizes these major revenue models. The *Insight on Society* case, *Foursquare: Check Your Privacy at the Door,* examines some of the issues associated with Foursquare's business and revenue model.

transaction fee revenue model
a company receives a fee for enabling or executing a transaction

sales revenue model
a company derives revenue by selling goods, information, or services

affiliate revenue model
a company steers business to an affiliate and receives a referral fee or percentage of the revenue from any resulting sales

INSIGHT ON SOCIETY

FOURSQUARE: CHECK YOUR PRIVACY AT THE DOOR

Foursquare is one of a host of companies that combine a social network business model with location-based technology. Foursquare offers mobile social applications that know where you are located and can provide you with information about popular spots nearby, as well as reviews from other Foursquare users. These apps also allow you to check in to a restaurant or other location, and automatically let friends on Facebook and other social networks learn where you are.

Founded in 2008 by Dennis Crowley and Naveen Selvadurai, Foursquare has over 60 million registered users and more than 50 million monthly active users worldwide, split fairly evenly between the United States and the rest of the world, who have checked in over 7.5 billion times.

Foursquare shares many similarities with other social networks like Facebook and Twitter that began operating without a revenue model in place. Like those companies, Foursquare has been able to command high valuations from venture capital investors, despite unimpressive revenue and profits. How is this possible? The answer lies in the coupling of its social network business model with smartphone-based technology that can identify where you are located within a few yards. There's potentially a great deal of money to be made from knowing where you are. Location-based data has extraordinary commercial value because advertisers can then send you advertisements, coupons, and flash bargains, based on where you are located.

Just as Facebook and Twitter are monetizing their user bases with advertising and social commerce, so too is Foursquare. In one of its first efforts, Foursquare partnered with American Express to offer discounts to cardholders when they check in on their cell phone to certain shops and restaurants. Foursquare has continued to develop new location-based features, including Local

Updates, which allow retailers to deliver location-based updates to customers, Foursquare Ads, which are paid advertisements targeted by location and by prior behavior, Check-In Retargeting, which uses location and behavioral data to retarget ads to users on third-party Web sites, and Post Check-In Units, which serve advertisements to users after checking in with the Foursquare app. In 2015, Foursquare launched Pinpoint, an advertising product that allows marketers unprecedented ability to target users based on its accumulated historical location data. Pinpoint has the ability to filter out inaccurate data and can even reach mobile users without the Foursquare app. Brands interested in Pinpoint include Coors, FedEx, Jaguar Land Rover, Olive Garden, and Samsung.

In 2015, Foursquare's main focus is to continue on a path to profitability by expanding and monetizing its trove of location data. Analysts estimated that Foursquare earned $15 to $20 million in 2013, a significant increase over the $2 million it earned in 2012, and in 2014 and 2015, Foursquare's revenue has continued to double on a year-to-year basis. In 2014, Foursquare struck a multiyear data licensing agreement with Microsoft, which may use the data to customize Bing on a user-by-user basis with specific search results and advertisements based on their location data. In 2015, Foursquare has continued these efforts, partnering with Twitter to provide location-based tagging features on tweets, which enables users to tag tweets with their precise location. Foursquare has also partnered with Google, Yahoo, and Pinterest to provide location-based functions and to share location data, increasing the richness and accuracy of its own data in the process.

In 2014, Foursquare made a major change to its business model, splitting its app into two separate apps with different focuses. Its redesigned Foursquare app became a recommender system using passive location tracking to offer suggestions to users for where to eat or visit. A separate app, Swarm, absorbed Foursquare's check-in feature. CEO Crowley envisions the new Foursquare app as a service that lets you know what places you might enjoy when you travel somewhere new. The redesigned app asks the user to identify things he or she likes, known as "tastes," from over 10,000 possibilities (ranging from barbecue to museums to board games), and then provides recommendations. Rather than earn badges, users are encouraged to add tips to work toward becoming an expert. Many loyal Foursquare users were driven away by the change, particularly Swarm users, who missed many of the old app's lighthearted, collectible elements. In 2015, the company added many of those old features back to Swarm, such as status levels, mayorships, and leaderboards, awards offered to users with the most check-ins at a particular location.

As the popularity of location-based services like Foursquare has grown, so too have concerns about privacy. Privacy advocates point out that many apps have no privacy policy, that most of the popular apps transmit location data to their developers, after which the information is not well controlled, and that these services are creating a situation where government, marketers, creditors, and telecommunications firms will end up knowing nearly everything about citizens, including their whereabouts.

As a case in point, in April 2012, Foursquare was hit by a privacy landmine when an app called Girls Around Me surfaced that used Foursquare's application programming interface to show Facebook photos of women currently checked in around a particular neighborhood. Foursquare quickly shut down the app and shortly thereafter made changes to its API to eliminate the ability of users to see strangers checked into a venue without being checked into the same place themselves. Illustrating the continuing issues Foursquare faces on the privacy front, the version of its mobile app introduced in June 2012 allowed users to see all of their friends' check-ins from the prior two weeks. Many users may not truly understand how much of their location history is available to their friends. One advantage Foursquare does have, though, is that many of its users are actually interested in having their location tracked and their data collected – users are less likely to revolt when they find that Foursquare is collecting and sharing their data.

The redesigned Foursquare and Swarm apps also continue to raise privacy concerns. The Foursquare app tracks a user's location even when the app is closed. Instead, by default, the app automatically provides Foursquare with the phone's GPS coordinates any time the phone is turned on, unless the user specifically opts out of such tracking. In contrast, Facebook's Nearby Friends feature requires users to opt in. Persistent location tracking of this sort further enhances the value of Foursquare's location data. Foursquare claims that the services it provides are a fair trade for the data it collects; privacy experts are concerned that tracking is always on by default, and that users cannot delete archived location data from Foursquare's servers.

SOURCES: "Swarm Gets Back into the Game with Leaderboards," by Jordan Crook, Techcrunch.com, August 20, 2015; "Foursquare by the Numbers: 60M Registered Users, 50M MAUs, and 75M Tips to Date," by Harrison Weber and Jordan Novet, Venturebeat.com, August 18, 2015; "Foursquare Returns to Its Roots in Bid to Win Back Users," by Jason Cipriani, *Fortune*, May 13, 2015; "Foursquare Brings Back Check-in Badges with Swarm Update," by Karissa Bell, Mashable.com, May 4, 2015; "Foursquare Unveils Pinpoint for Location-Based Ad Targeting," by Melanie White, Clickz.com, April 14, 2015; "Foursquare Unveils Pinpoint to Show You Ads Based on Where You've Been," by Harrison Weber, Venturebeat.com, April 14, 2015; "Foursquare Knows Where You've Been, Wants to Offer You a Sick Deal at Olive Garden," by John Paul Titlow, *Fast Company,* April 14, 2015; "Why Twitter and Foursquare Just Struck a Deal," by Erin Griffith, *Fortune*, March 23, 2015; "Twitter Teaming with Foursquare for Location Tagging in Tweets," by Darrell Etherington, Techcrunch.com, March 23, 2015; "Foursquare Now Tracks Your Every Move," by Ryan Tate and Kristin Burnham, *Information Week*, August 7, 2014; "Radical New Foursquare App Thinks You Want Even Less Privacy," by Jason Cipriani, Wired.com, August 6, 2014; "Foursquare Launches Its Redesigned Mobile App Focused on Location-based Recommendations," by Nick Summers, Thenextweb.com, August 6, 2014; "Foursquare Now Tracks Users Even When the App is Closed," by Douglas Macmillan, *Wall Street Journal*, August 6, 2014; "Foursquare Updates Swarm to Soothe Check-in Blues," by Caitlin McGarry, Techhive.com, July 8, 2014; "How Foursquare Uses Location Data to Target Ads on PCs, Phones," by Cotton Delo, Adage.com, February 27, 2014; "With Foursquare Deal, Microsoft Aims for Supremacy in Hyper-Local Search," by Ryan Tate, Wired.com, February 5, 2014; "Foursquare Goes Beyond the Check-in with Passive Tracking," by John McDermott, Digiday.com, December 18, 2013; "A Start-Up Matures, Working With AmEx," by Jenna Wortham, *New York Times*, June 22, 2011; "Telling Friends Where You Are (or Not)," by Jenna Wortham, *New York Times,* March 14, 2010.

TABLE 2.2	**FIVE PRIMARY REVENUE MODELS**	
REVENUE MODEL	EXAMPLES	REVENUE SOURCE
Advertising	Yahoo	Fees from advertisers in exchange for advertisements
Subscription	eHarmony Consumer Reports Online Netflix	Fees from subscribers in exchange for access to content or services
Transaction Fee	eBay E*Trade	Fees (commissions) for enabling or executing a transaction
Sales	Amazon L.L.Bean Birchbox iTunes	Sales of goods, information, or services
Affiliate	MyPoints	Fees for business referrals

Market Opportunity

market opportunity
refers to the company's intended marketspace and the overall potential financial opportunities available to the firm in that marketspace

The term **market opportunity** refers to the company's intended **marketspace** (i.e., an area of actual or potential commercial value) and the overall potential financial opportunities available to the firm in that marketspace. The market opportunity is usually divided into smaller market niches. The realistic market opportunity is defined by the revenue potential in each of the market niches where you hope to compete.

marketspace
the area of actual or potential commercial value in which a company intends to operate

For instance, let's assume you are analyzing a software training company that creates online software-learning systems for sale to businesses. The overall size of the software training market for all market segments is approximately $70 billion. The overall market can be broken down, however, into two major market segments: instructor-led training products, which comprise about 70% of the market ($49 billion in revenue), and computer-based training, which accounts for 30% ($21 billion). There are further market niches within each of those major market segments, such as the Fortune 500 computer-based training market and the small business computer-based training market. Because the firm is a start-up firm, it cannot compete effectively in the large business, computer-based training market (about $15 billion). Large brand-name training firms dominate this niche. The start-up firm's real market opportunity is to sell to the thousands of small business firms that spend about $6 billion on computer-based software training. This is the size of the firm's realistic market opportunity (see **Figure 2.2**).

Competitive Environment

competitive environment
refers to the other companies operating in the same marketspace selling similar products

A firm's **competitive environment** refers to the other companies selling similar products and operating in the same marketspace. It also refers to the presence of substitute products and potential new entrants to the market, as well as the power of customers and suppliers over your business. We discuss the firm's environment

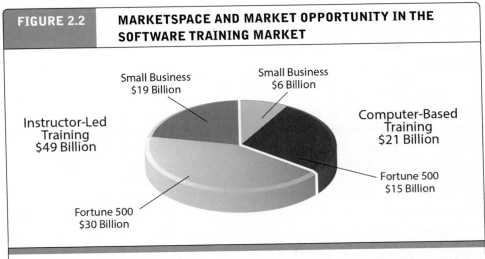

| FIGURE 2.2 | **MARKETSPACE AND MARKET OPPORTUNITY IN THE SOFTWARE TRAINING MARKET** |

Marketspaces are composed of many market segments. Your realistic market opportunity will typically focus on one or a few market segments.

later in the chapter. The competitive environment for a company is influenced by several factors: how many competitors are active, how large their operations are, what the market share of each competitor is, how profitable these firms are, and how they price their products.

Firms typically have both direct and indirect competitors. Direct competitors are companies that sell very similar products and services into the same market segment. For example, Priceline and Travelocity, both of whom sell discount airline tickets online, are direct competitors because both companies sell identical products—cheap tickets. Indirect competitors are companies that may be in different industries but still compete indirectly because their products can substitute for one another. For instance, automobile manufacturers and airline companies operate in different industries, but they still compete indirectly because they offer consumers alternative means of transportation. CNN, a news outlet, is an indirect competitor of ESPN, not because they sell identical products, but because they both compete for consumers' time online.

The existence of a large number of competitors in any one segment may be a sign that the market is saturated and that it may be difficult to become profitable. On the other hand, a lack of competitors could signal either an untapped market niche ripe for the picking, or a market that has already been tried without success because there is no money to be made. Analysis of the competitive environment can help you decide which it is.

Competitive Advantage

Firms achieve a **competitive advantage** when they can produce a superior product and/or bring the product to market at a lower price than most, or all, of their

competitive advantage achieved by a firm when it can produce a superior product and/or bring the product to market at a lower price than most, or all, of its competitors

competitors (Porter, 1985). Firms also compete on scope. Some firms can develop global markets, while other firms can develop only a national or regional market. Firms that can provide superior products at the lowest cost on a global basis are truly advantaged.

Firms achieve competitive advantages because they have somehow been able to obtain differential access to the factors of production that are denied to their competitors—at least in the short term (Barney, 1991). Perhaps the firm has been able to obtain very favorable terms from suppliers, shippers, or sources of labor. Or perhaps the firm has more experienced, knowledgeable, and loyal employees than any competitors. Maybe the firm has a patent on a product that others cannot imitate, or access to investment capital through a network of former business colleagues or a brand name and popular image that other firms cannot duplicate. An **asymmetry** exists whenever one participant in a market has more resources—financial backing, knowledge, information, and/or power—than other participants. Asymmetries lead to some firms having an edge over others, permitting them to come to market with better products, faster than competitors, and sometimes at lower cost.

For instance, when Apple announced iTunes, a service offering legal, downloadable individual song tracks for 99 cents a track that would be playable on any digital device with iTunes software, the company had better-than-average odds of success simply because of Apple's prior success with innovative hardware designs, and the large stable of music firms that Apple had meticulously lined up to support its online music catalog. Few competitors could match the combination of cheap, legal songs and powerful hardware to play them on.

One rather unique competitive advantage derives from being a first mover. A **first-mover advantage** is a competitive market advantage for a firm that results from being the first into a marketplace with a serviceable product or service. If first movers develop a loyal following or a unique interface that is difficult to imitate, they can sustain their first-mover advantage for long periods (Arthur, 1996). Amazon provides a good example. However, in the history of technology-driven business innovation, most first movers often lack the **complementary resources** needed to sustain their advantages, and often follower firms reap the largest rewards (Rigdon, 2000; Teece, 1986). Indeed, many of the success stories we discuss in this book are those of companies that were slow followers—businesses that gained knowledge from failure of pioneering firms and entered into the market late.

Some competitive advantages are called "unfair." An **unfair competitive advantage** occurs when one firm develops an advantage based on a factor that other firms cannot purchase (Barney, 1991). For instance, a brand name cannot be purchased and is in that sense an "unfair" advantage. Brands are built upon loyalty, trust, reliability, and quality. Once obtained, they are difficult to copy or imitate, and they permit firms to charge premium prices for their products.

In **perfect markets**, there are no competitive advantages or asymmetries because all firms have access to all the factors of production (including information and knowledge) equally. However, real markets are imperfect, and asymmetries leading to competitive advantages do exist, at least in the short term. Most competitive

---

asymmetry

exists whenever one participant in a market has more resources than other participants

first-mover advantage

a competitive market advantage for a firm that results from being the first into a marketplace with a serviceable product or service

complementary resources

resources and assets not directly involved in the production of the product but required for success, such as marketing, management, financial assets, and reputation

unfair competitive advantage

occurs when one firm develops an advantage based on a factor that other firms cannot purchase

perfect market

a market in which there are no competitive advantages or asymmetries because all firms have equal access to all the factors of production

advantages are short term, although some can be sustained for very long periods. But not forever. In fact, many respected brands fail every year.

Companies are said to **leverage** their competitive assets when they use their competitive advantages to achieve more advantage in surrounding markets. For instance, Amazon's move into the online grocery business leverages the company's huge customer database and years of e-commerce experience.

Market Strategy

No matter how tremendous a firm's qualities, its marketing strategy and execution are often just as important. The best business concept, or idea, will fail if it is not properly marketed to potential customers.

Everything you do to promote your company's products and services to potential customers is known as marketing. **Market strategy** is the plan you put together that details exactly how you intend to enter a new market and attract new customers.

For instance, Twitter, YouTube, and Pinterest have a social network marketing strategy that encourages users to post their content on the sites for free, build personal profile pages, contact their friends, and build a community. In these cases, the customer becomes part of the marketing staff!

Organizational Development

Although many entrepreneurial ventures are started by one visionary individual, it is rare that one person alone can grow an idea into a multi-million dollar company. In most cases, fast-growth companies—especially e-commerce businesses—need employees and a set of business procedures. In short, all firms—new ones in particular—need an organization to efficiently implement their business plans and strategies. Many e-commerce firms and many traditional firms that attempt an e-commerce strategy have failed because they lacked the organizational structures and supportive cultural values required to support new forms of commerce (Kanter, 2001).

Companies that hope to grow and thrive need to have a plan for **organizational development** that describes how the company will organize the work that needs to be accomplished. Typically, work is divided into functional departments, such as production, shipping, marketing, customer support, and finance. Jobs within these functional areas are defined, and then recruitment begins for specific job titles and responsibilities. Typically, in the beginning, generalists who can perform multiple tasks are hired. As the company grows, recruiting becomes more specialized. For instance, at the outset, a business may have one marketing manager. But after two or three years of steady growth, that one marketing position may be broken down into seven separate jobs done by seven individuals.

For instance, eBay founder Pierre Omidyar started an online auction site, according to some sources, to help his girlfriend trade Pez dispensers with other collectors, but within a few months the volume of business had far exceeded what he alone could handle. So he began hiring people with more business experience to help out. Soon the company had many employees, departments, and managers who were responsible for overseeing the various aspects of the organization.

leverage
when a company uses its competitive advantages to achieve more advantage in surrounding markets

market strategy
the plan you put together that details exactly how you intend to enter a new market and attract new customers

organizational development
plan that describes how the company will organize the work that needs to be accomplished

Management Team

management team

employees of the company responsible for making the business model work

Arguably, the single most important element of a business model is the **management team** responsible for making the model work. A strong management team gives a model instant credibility to outside investors, immediate market-specific knowledge, and experience in implementing business plans. A strong management team may not be able to salvage a weak business model, but the team should be able to change the model and redefine the business as it becomes necessary.

Eventually, most companies get to the point of having several senior executives or managers. How skilled managers are, however, can be a source of competitive advantage or disadvantage. The challenge is to find people who have both the experience and the ability to apply that experience to new situations.

To be able to identify good managers for a business start-up, first consider the kinds of experiences that would be helpful to a manager joining your company. What kind of technical background is desirable? What kind of supervisory experience is necessary? How many years in a particular function should be required? What job functions should be fulfilled first: marketing, production, finance, or operations? Especially in situations where financing will be needed to get a company off the ground, do prospective senior managers have experience and contacts for raising financing from outside investors?

Table 2.3 summarizes the eight key elements of a business model and the key questions that must be answered in order to successfully develop each element.

RAISING CAPITAL

Raising capital is one of the most important functions for a founder of a start-up business and its management team. Not having enough capital to operate effectively is a primary reason why so many start-up businesses fail. Many entrepreneurs initially "bootstrap" to get a business off the ground, using personal funds derived from savings,

TABLE 2.3	KEY ELEMENTS OF A BUSINESS MODEL
COMPONENTS	KEY QUESTIONS
Value proposition	Why should the customer buy from you?
Revenue model	How will you earn money?
Market opportunity	What marketspace do you intend to serve, and what is its size?
Competitive environment	Who else occupies your intended marketspace?
Competitive advantage	What special advantages does your firm bring to the marketspace?
Market strategy	How do you plan to promote your products or services to attract your target audience?
Organizational development	What types of organizational structures within the firm are necessary to carry out the business plan?
Management team	What kinds of experiences and background are important for the company's leaders to have?

TABLE 2.4	KEY ELEMENTS OF AN ELEVATOR PITCH
ELEMENT	DESCRIPTION
Introduction	Your name and position; your company's name, and a tagline in which you compare what your company does to a well-known company. Example: "My name is X, I am the founder of Y, and we are the Uber/Amazon of Z."
Background	The origin of your idea and the problem you are trying to solve.
Industry size/market opportunity	Brief facts about the (hopefully very large) size of the market.
Revenue model/numbers/ growth metrics	Insight into your company's revenue model and results thus far, how fast it is growing, and early adopters, if there are any.
Funding	The amount of funds you are seeking and what it will help you achieve.
Exit strategy	How your investors will achieve a return on their investment.

credit card advances, home equity loans, or from family and friends. Funds of this type are often referred to as **seed capital**. Once such funds are exhausted, if the company is not generating enough revenue to cover operating costs, additional capital will be needed. Traditional sources of capital include incubators, commercial banks, angel investors, venture capital firms, and strategic partners. One of the most important aspects of raising capital is the ability to boil down the elements of the company's business plan into an **elevator pitch**, a short two-to-three minute (about the length of an elevator ride, giving rise to its name) presentation aimed at convincing investors to invest. **Table 2.4** lists the key elements of an elevator pitch.

Incubators (sometimes also referred to as accelerators) such as Y Combinator (profiled in Chapter 1's *Insight on Business* case) typically provide a small amount of funding, but more importantly, also provide an array of services to start-up companies that they select to participate in their programs, such as business, technical, and marketing assistance, as well as introductions to other sources of capital. Well-known incubator programs include TechStars, DreamIt, and Capital Factory.

Obtaining a loan from a commercial bank is often difficult for a start-up company without much revenue, but it may be worthwhile to investigate programs offered by the U.S. Small Business Administration, and its state or local equivalents. The advantage of obtaining capital in the form of a loan (debt) is that, although it must be repaid, it does not require an entrepreneur to give up any ownership of the company.

Angel investors are typically wealthy individuals (or a group of individuals) who invest their own money in an exchange for an equity share in the stock in the business. In general, angel investors make smaller investments (typically $1 million or less) than venture capital firms, are interested in helping a company grow and succeed, and invest on relatively favorable terms compared to later stage investors. The first round of external investment in a company is sometimes referred to as Series A financing.

seed capital

typically, an entrepreneur's personal funds derived from savings, credit card advances, home equity loans, or from family and friends

elevator pitch

short two-to-three minute presentation aimed at convincing investors to invest

incubators

typically provide a small amount of funding and also an array of services to start-up companies

angel investors

typically wealthy individuals or a group of individuals who invest their own money in exchange for an equity share in the stock of a business; often are the first outside investors in a start-up

venture capital investors

typically invest funds they manage for other investors; usually later-stage investors

Venture capital investors typically become more interested in a start-up company once it has begun attracting a large audience and generating some revenue, even if it is not profitable. **Venture capital investors** invest funds they manage for other investors such as investment banks, pension funds, insurance companies, or other businesses, and usually want to obtain a larger stake in the business and exercise more control over the operation of the business. Venture capital investors also typically want a well-defined "exit strategy," such as a plan for an initial public offering or acquisition of the company by a more established business within a relatively short period of time (typically 3 to 7 years), that will enable them to obtain an adequate return on their investment. Venture capital investment often ultimately means that the founder(s) and initial investors will no longer control the company at some point in the future.

crowdfunding

involves using the Internet to enable individuals to collectively contribute money to support a project

Crowdfunding involves using the Internet to enable individuals to collectively contribute money to support a project. The concepts behind crowdfunding have been popularized by Kickstarter and Indiegogo (see the *Insight on Business* case, *Crowdfunding Takes Off*), but they were not able to be used for equity investments in for-profit companies in the United States due to securities regulations. However, the passage of the Jumpstart Our Business Startups (JOBS) Act in 2012 and issuance of regulations by the Securities and Exchange Commission in July 2013 has enabled companies to use the Internet to solicit wealthy ("accredited") investors to invest in small and early-stage start-ups in exchange for stock. Regulation A+, which enables equity crowdfunding investments by non-accredited investors (people with a net worth of less than $1 million and who earned less than $200,000 a year in the previous two years), took effect in June 2015. Regulations implementing even broader-based equity crowdfunding authorized by the JOBS Act, which would allow investments by people with annual income or net worth of less than $100,000, remain a work in progress.

CATEGORIZING E-COMMERCE BUSINESS MODELS: SOME DIFFICULTIES

There are many e-commerce business models, and more are being invented every day. The number of such models is limited only by the human imagination, and our list of different business models is certainly not exhaustive. However, despite the abundance of potential models, it is possible to identify the major generic types (and subtle variations) of business models that have been developed for the e-commerce arena and describe their key features. It is important to realize, however, that there is no one correct way to categorize these business models.

Our approach is to categorize business models according to the different major e-commerce sectors—B2C and B2B—in which they are utilized. You will note, however, that fundamentally similar business models may appear in more than one sector. For example, the business models of online retailers (often called e-tailers) and e-distributors are quite similar. However, they are distinguished by the market focus of the sector in which they are used. In the case of e-tailers in the B2C sector, the business model focuses on sales to the individual consumer, while in the case of the e-distributor, the business model focuses on sales to another business. Many companies use a variety of

INSIGHT ON BUSINESS

CROWDFUNDING TAKES OFF

Think you have the next big idea but lack the resources to make it happen? Crowdfunding sites might be your best shot. Sites such as Kickstarter, Indiegogo, RocketHub, and Crowdtilt have led the growth of crowdfunding from $530 million in 2009 to over $34 billion in 2015. A World Bank study predicts that capital raised via crowdfunding will exceed $93 billion by 2025. The Internet is the ideal medium for crowdfunding because it allows individuals and organizations in need of funds and potential backers to find one another around the globe.

How do sites like Kickstarter and Indiegogo work? The idea is simple—an inventor, artist, or activist looking to raise money for a project uses the site to create a page for that project. People can pledge to support the project, but at Kickstarter, money actually only changes hands once the project fully reaches its funding goal (other sites, such as Indiegogo and RocketHub, allow project creators to keep the money they raise even if they do not achieve their goal). The sites take a small commission, usually about 5%, on completed projects. Backers do not receive any ownership interest in the project, but typically receive some type of reward, often corresponding to the size of their contribution to the project.

Crowdfunding projects are diverse, ranging from inventions to art installations, movies, video games, and political action projects. All you need is an idea that captures the attention of the crowd and for which people are willing to contribute funds. Crowdfunding is quickly becoming a mainstay in nearly all of these fields. For instance, among the most funded Kickstarter invention projects to date are Pebble, a customizable e-paper watch that connects to a smartphone

(over $20 million) and the Micro, a consumer 3-D printer ($3.4 million). Kickstarter has financed more installation art projects than the National Endowment for the Arts, and several of the biggest Kickstarter projects have been movie projects that have struggled to gain traction at Hollywood studios, like the Veronica Mars movie project ($5.7 million) and Zach Braff's film "Wish I Was Here" ($3.1 million), as well as a project to reboot the popular educational TV show Reading Rainbow, which garnered over $5 million in financing in 2015. In 2014, a man from Ohio solicited $10 in donations to make a batch of potato salad as a joke, but after his campaign went viral, he raised over $55,000, much of which he used to support local charities. The applications for crowdfunding are limited only by the imagination.

Successful crowdfunding projects typically share some common elements. One of the most important is a clear and concise presentation of the idea, especially through the use of video. One major crowdfunding site reports that campaigns with great videos get significantly more investment than those without. The crowdfunding campaign is in many ways similar to presenting a business plan, and should touch on the same eight elements of a business model, such as the project's value proposition, its target market, and so on. A whole ecosystem of video producers, editors, and other services has sprung up to support crowdfunding projects. Not every crowdfunding project gets off the ground—Kickstarter reports that only about 40% of its approximately 207,000 projects thus far have reached their funding goals. Sometimes projects that do get off the ground simply flame out, disappointing their backers. Although this is no different than investing in stocks, Kickstarter has sought to ease concerns by improving

(continued)

communication with respect to the risk inherent in the projects posted on its site. For instance, it now requires fundraisers to disclose the risks associated with their project, and for inventions, now requires photos of prototype products instead of simply drawings, simulations, or renderings.

There also is some worry that the lack of privacy involved with donating to crowdfunding sites has a negative effect on the process. In the art world, many artists are concerned that they will make enemies within their industry if they ignore requests for crowdfunding donations, not to mention the possibility of the focus on fundraising corrupting the artistic process. Another common criticism is that those who need Kickstarter the least, such as projects launched by established Hollywood actors and producers, are the ones benefitting the most. Kickstarter counters that a high-profile project draws attention to the site and helps lesser-known artists in their own fundraising efforts.

A new use of crowdfunding is to provide seed capital for startup companies. Under the JOBS Act passed by Congress in 2012, a company will be able to crowdfund up to $1 million over a 12-month period. More than twenty states have also enacted their own rules allowing local businesses to raise money via crowdfunding, and more are following suit. Many expect the use of crowdfunding for this purpose to skyrocket once federal regulations allowing it are fully implemented. However, some critics worry that there will be a steep learning curve and that a period of chaos is likely to ensue, until all participants (entrepreneurs, investors, crowdfunding platforms, and regulators) become familiar with all the potential benefits and risks of equity crowdfunding. For example, in 2012, a project for a virtual reality video gaming headset known as the Oculus Rift raised nearly $2.5 million. In 2014, Facebook paid $2 billion to acquire the start-up company that developed the headset. The thousands of backers who supported the project did not benefit from the Facebook purchase in any way. In the future, sites that are registered as "funding portals" with the Securities and Exchange Commission will allow crowdfunding equity backers who support projects like Oculus Rift to profit when those companies are acquired.

Kickstarter currently has no plans to allow creators to offer equity in Kickstarter projects, but in the meantime, many companies, such as Indiegogo, Crowdfunder, AngelList, and StartEngine are laying the groundwork for an expected explosion of activity. Niche companies are also springing up, with varying degrees of success. For instance, SeedInvest is a company that caters to investors who may have concerns about crowdfunding privacy by offering better privacy controls. CircleUp is focused on consumer products. AlumniFinder is aimed at bringing alumni together to back college entrepreneurs. Many of these fledgling services have failed to gain traction as the more prominent sites continue to grow, but as crowdfunding becomes more widely recognized by the general public, more specialty sites are likely to find success.

SOURCES: "Indiegogo Is Getting Ready for Equity Crowdfunding," by Harry McCracken, *Fast Company,* October 2015; "Kickstarter Basics," Kickstarter.com, accessed September 15, 2015; "Tired of Waiting for U.S. to Act, States Pass Crowdfunding Laws and Rules," by Stacy Cowley, *New York Times,* June 3, 2015; "Keeping Up With Kickstarter," by Stephen Heyman, *New York Times,* January 15, 2015; "Leverage Video to Cut Through the Crowdfunding Clutter," by Ben Chodor, Entrepeneur.com, August 13, 2014; "Why Investors are Pouring Millions into Crowdfunding," by Katherine Noyes, *Fortune,* April 17, 2014; "Invest in Next Facebook...For a Few Bucks," by Patrick M. Sheridan, CNNMoney.com, April 14, 2014; "How You'll Fund – And Wildly Profit From – The Next Oculus Rift," by Ryan Tate, Wired.com, April 4, 2014; "If You Back a Kickstarter Project That Sells for $2 Billion, Do You Deserve to Get Rich?," by Adrianne Jeffries, Theverge.com, March 28, 2014; "Crowdfunding Tips for Turning Inspiration into Reality," by Kate Murphy, *New York Times,* January 22, 2014; "World Bank: Crowdfunding Investment Market to Hit $93 Billion by 2025," by Richard Swart, PBS.org, December 10, 2013; "SEC Finally Moves on Equity Crowdfunding, Phase 1," by Chance Barnett, Forbes.com, July 19, 2013; "SeedInvest Raises $1M to Help Angels Invest Online – Privately," by Lora Kolodny, *Wall Street Journal,* June 28, 2013; "The Trouble with Kickstarter," by Ellen Gamerman, *Wall Street Journal*, June 21, 2013; "AngelList Commits to Crowdfunding," by Lora Kolodny, *Wall Street Journal*, April 24, 2013.

different business models as they attempt to extend into as many areas of e-commerce as possible. We look at B2C business models in Section 2.2 and B2B business models in Section 2.3.

A business's technology platform is sometimes confused with its business model. For instance, "mobile e-commerce" refers to the use of mobile devices and cellular and wide area networks to support a variety of business models. Commentators sometimes confuse matters by referring to mobile e-commerce as a distinct business model, which it is not. All of the basic business models we discuss below can be implemented on both the traditional Internet/Web and mobile platforms. Likewise, although they are sometimes referred to as such, social e-commerce and local e-commerce are not business models in and of themselves, but rather subsectors of B2C and B2B e-commerce in which different business models can operate.

You will also note that some companies use multiple business models. For instance, Amazon has multiple business models: it is an e-retailer, content provider, market creator, e-commerce infrastructure provider, and more. eBay is a market creator in the B2C and C2C e-commerce sectors, using both the traditional Internet/Web and mobile platforms, as well as an e-commerce infrastructure provider. Firms often seek out multiple business models as a way to leverage their brands, infrastructure investments, and assets developed with one business model into new business models.

Finally, no discussion of e-commerce business models would be complete without mention of a group of companies whose business model is focused on providing the infrastructure necessary for e-commerce companies to exist, grow, and prosper. These are the e-commerce enablers. They provide the hardware, operating system software, networks and communications technology, applications software, Web design, consulting services, and other tools required for e-commerce (see **Table 2.5** on page 72). While these firms may not be conducting e-commerce per se (although in many instances, e-commerce in its traditional sense is in fact one of their sales channels), as a group they have perhaps profited the most from the development of e-commerce. We discuss many of these players in the following chapters.

2.2 MAJOR BUSINESS-TO-CONSUMER (B2C) BUSINESS MODELS

Business-to-consumer (B2C) e-commerce, in which online businesses seek to reach individual consumers, is the most well-known and familiar type of e-commerce. **Table 2.6** on page 73 illustrates the major business models utilized in the B2C arena.

E-TAILER

Online retail stores, often called **e-tailers**, come in all sizes, from giant Amazon to tiny local stores that have Web sites. E-tailers are similar to the typical bricks-and-mortar storefront, except that customers only have to connect to the Internet or use their

e-tailer
online retail store

TABLE 2.5	E-COMMERCE ENABLERS
INFRASTRUCTURE	**PLAYERS**
Hardware: Web Servers	HP • Dell • Lenovo
Software: Web Server Software	Microsoft • IBM • Red Hat Linux (Apache) • Oracle
Cloud Providers	Amazon Web Services • Google • IBM • Rackspace
Hosting Services	Rackspace • WebIntellects • 1&1 • HostGator • Hostway
Domain Name Registration	GoDaddy • Network Solutions • Dotster
Content Delivery Networks	Akamai • Limelight
Site Design	Weebly • Wix • Squarespace
E-commerce Platform Providers	Magento • IBM • Oracle • Demandware
Mobile Commerce Hardware Platform	Apple • Samsung • LG
Mobile Commerce Software Platform	Apple • Google • Adobe • Usablenet • Unbound Commerce
Streaming, Rich Media, Online Video	Adobe • Apple • Easy2 Technologies
Security and Encryption	VeriSign • Checkpoint • GeoTrust • Entrust • Thawte • McAfee
Payment Systems	PayPal • Authorize.net • Chase Paymentech • Cybersource
Web Performance Management	Compuware • SmartBear • Keynote
Comparison Engine Feeds/Marketplace Management	ChannelAdvisor • CommerceHub • CPC Strategy
Customer Relationship Management	Oracle • SAP • Salesforce • NetSuite
Order Management	JDA Software • Jagged Peak • Monsoon Commerce
Fulfillment	JDA Software • Jagged Peak • CommerceHub
Social Marketing	Buffer • HootSuite • SocialFlow
Search Engine Marketing	iProspect • ChannelAdvisor • Merkle/RKG
E-mail Marketing	Constant Contact • Experian CheetahMail • Bronto Software • MailChimp
Affiliate Marketing	CJ Affiliate • Rakuten LinkShare
Customer Reviews and Forums	Bazaarvoice • PowerReviews • BizRate
Live Chat/Click-to-Call	LivePerson • BoldChat • Oracle
Web Analytics	Google Analytics • Adobe Analytics • IBM Digital Analytics • Webtrends

smartphone to place an order. Some e-tailers, which are referred to as "bricks-and-clicks," are subsidiaries or divisions of existing physical stores and carry the same products. REI, JCPenney, Barnes & Noble, Walmart, and Staples are examples of companies with complementary online stores. Others, however, operate only in the virtual world, without any ties to physical locations. Amazon, Blue Nile, and Bluefly are examples of this type of e-tailer. Several other variations of e-tailers—such as online versions of direct mail catalogs, online malls, and manufacturer-direct online sales—also exist.

Given that the overall retail market in the United States in 2015 is estimated to be around $4.8 trillion, the market opportunity for e-tailers is very large. Every Internet and smartphone user is a potential customer. Customers who feel time-starved are even better prospects, because they want shopping solutions that will eliminate the

TABLE 2.6	B2C BUSINESS MODELS			
BUSINESS MODEL	**VARIATIONS**	**EXAMPLES**	**DESCRIPTION**	**REVENUE MODELS**
E-tailer	Virtual Merchant	Amazon Blue Nile Bluefly	Online version of retail store, where customers can shop at any hour of the day or night without leaving their home or office	Sales of goods
	Bricks-and-Clicks	Walmart Sears	Online distribution channel for a company that also has physical stores	Sales of goods
	Catalog Merchant	L.L.Bean LillianVernon	Online version of direct mail catalog	Sales of goods
	Manufacturer-Direct	Dell Mattel	Manufacturer uses online channel to sell direct to customer	Sales of goods
Community Provider		Facebook LinkedIn Twitter Pinterest	Sites where individuals with particular interests, hobbies, common experiences, or social networks can come together and "meet" online	Advertising, subscription, affiliate referral fees
Content Provider		Wall Street Journal Apple iTunes CNN ESPN Rhapsody	Information and entertainment providers such as newspapers, sports sites, and other online sources that offer customers up-to-date news and special interest how-to guidance and tips and/or information sales	Advertising, subscription fees, sales of digital goods
Portal	Horizontal/ General	Yahoo AOL MSN Facebook	Offers an integrated package of content, content-search, and social network services: news, e-mail, chat, music downloads, video streaming, calendars, etc. Seeks to be a user's home base	Advertising, subscription fees, transaction fees
	Vertical/ Specialized (Vortal)	Sailnet	Offers services and products to specialized marketplace	Advertising, subscription fees, transaction fees
	Search	Google Bing Ask	Focuses primarily on offering search services	Advertising, affiliate referral
Transaction Broker		E*Trade Expedia Monster Travelocity Orbitz	Processors of online sales transactions, such as stockbrokers and travel agents, that increase customers' productivity by helping them get things done faster and more cheaply	Transaction fees
Market Creator		eBay Etsy Amazon Priceline	Businesses that use Internet technology to create markets that bring buyers and sellers together	Transaction fees
Service Provider		VisaNow Wave RocketLawyer	Companies that make money by selling users a service, rather than a product	Sales of services

need to drive to the mall or store (Bellman, Lohse, and Johnson, 1999). The e-tail revenue model is product-based, with customers paying for the purchase of a particular item.

barriers to entry

the total cost of entering a new marketplace

This sector, however, is extremely competitive. Because **barriers to entry** (the total cost of entering a new marketplace) into the e-tail market are low, tens of thousands of small e-tail shops have sprung up. Becoming profitable and surviving is very difficult, however, for e-tailers with no prior brand name or experience. The e-tailer's challenge is differentiating its business from existing competitors.

Companies that try to reach every online consumer are likely to deplete their resources quickly. Those that develop a niche strategy, clearly identifying their target market and its needs, are best prepared to make a profit. Keeping expenses low, selection broad, and inventory controlled is key to success in e-tailing, with inventory being the most difficult to gauge. Online retail is covered in more depth in Chapter 9.

COMMUNITY PROVIDER

community provider

creates an online environment where people with similar interests can transact (buy and sell goods); share interests, photos, and videos; communicate with like-minded people; and receive interest-related information

Although community providers are not a new phenomenon, the Internet has made such sites for like-minded individuals to meet and converse much easier, without the limitations of geography and time to hinder participation. **Community providers** create an online environment where people with similar interests can transact (buy and sell goods); share interests, photos, videos; communicate with like-minded people; receive interest-related information; and even play out fantasies by adopting online personalities called avatars. The social network sites Facebook, LinkedIn, Twitter, and Pinterest, and hundreds of other smaller, niche sites all offer users community-building tools and services.

The basic value proposition of community providers is to create a fast, convenient, one-stop site where users can focus on their most important concerns and interests, share the experience with friends, and learn more about their own interests. Community providers typically rely on a hybrid revenue model that includes subscription fees, sales revenues, transaction fees, affiliate fees, and advertising fees from other firms that are attracted by a tightly focused audience.

Community providers make money from advertising and through affiliate relationships with retailers. Some of the oldest online communities are The Well, which provides a forum for technology and Internet-related discussions, and The Motley Fool, which provides financial advice, news, and opinions. The Well offers various membership plans ranging from $10 to $15 a month. Motley Fool supports itself through ads and selling products that start out "free" but turn into annual subscriptions.

Consumers' interest in communities is mushrooming. Community is, arguably, the fastest growing online activity. While many community sites have had a difficult time becoming profitable, many have succeeded over time, with advertising as their main source of revenue. Both the very large social network sites such as Facebook, Twitter, and LinkedIn, as well as niche sites with smaller dedicated audiences, are ideal marketing and advertising territories. Traditional online communities such as The Motley Fool and WebMD (which provides medical information to members) find that breadth and depth of knowledge at a site is an important factor. Community members frequently request knowledge, guidance, and advice. Lack of experienced personnel can severely hamper the growth of a community, which needs facilitators and managers to keep discussions on course and relevant. For the newer community social network sites, the most important ingredients of success appear to be ease and flexibility of use, and a strong customer value proposition. For instance, Facebook leapfrogged over its rival MySpace by encouraging the development of third-party revenue-producing applications.

Online communities benefit significantly from offline word-of-mouth, viral marketing. Online communities tend to reflect offline relationships. When your friends say they have a profile on Facebook, and ask you to "friend" them, you are encouraged to build your own online profile.

CONTENT PROVIDER

Content providers distribute information content, such as digital video, music, photos, text, and artwork. It is estimated that U.S. consumers will spend more than $22 billion for online content such as movies, music, videos, television shows, e-books, and newspapers during 2015.

content provider
distributes information content, such as digital news, music, photos, video, and artwork

Content providers can make money via a variety of different revenue models, including advertising, subscription fees, and sales of digital goods. For instance, in the case of Rhapsody, a monthly subscription fee provides users with access to thousands of music tracks. Other content providers, such as the *Wall Street Journal* online newspaper, *Harvard Business Review*, and many others, charge customers for content downloads in addition to, or in place of, a subscription fee.

Of course, not all online content providers charge for their information: just look at the Web sites for CBSSports, CIO, CNN, and the online versions of many newspapers and magazines. Users can access news and information at these sites without paying a cent, although sometimes they may be required to register as a member. These popular sites make money in other ways, such as through advertising and partner promotions on the site. Increasingly, however, "free content" may be limited to headlines and text, whereas premium content—in-depth articles or videos—is sold for a fee.

Generally, the key to becoming a successful content provider is owning the content. Traditional owners of copyrighted content—publishers of books and newspapers, broadcasters of radio and television content, music publishers, and movie studios—have powerful advantages over newcomers who simply offer distribution channels and must pay for content, often at very high prices.

Some content providers, however, do not own content, but syndicate (aggregate) and then distribute content produced by others. *Syndication* is a major variation of the standard content provider model. Aggregators, who collect information from a wide variety of sources and then add value to that information through post-aggregation services, are another variation. For instance, Shopzilla collects information on the prices of thousands of goods online, analyzes the information, and presents users with tables showing the range of prices and links to the sites where the products can be purchased. Shopzilla adds value to content it aggregates, and resells this value to advertisers who advertise on its site.

Any e-commerce start-up that intends to make money by providing content is likely to face difficulties unless it has a unique information source that others cannot access. For the most part, this business category is dominated by traditional content providers. The *Insight on Technology* case, *Online Music: Battle of the Titans and Lilliputians,* discusses how changes in Internet technology are driving the development of new business models in the online content market by Internet titans Apple, Google, and Amazon.

Online content is discussed in further depth in Chapter 10.

PORTAL

portal

offers users powerful search tools as well as an integrated package of content and services all in one place

Portals such as Yahoo, MSN, and AOL offer users powerful search tools as well as an integrated package of content and services, such as news, e-mail, instant messaging, calendars, shopping, music downloads, video streaming, and more, all in one place. Initially, portals sought to be viewed as "gateways" to the Internet. Today, however, the portal business model is to be a destination site. They are marketed as places where consumers will hopefully stay a long time to read news, find entertainment, and meet other people (think of destination resorts). Portals do not sell anything directly—or so it seems—and in that sense they can present themselves as unbiased. The market opportunity is very large: in 2015, around 260 million people in the United States accessed the Internet at work or home. Portals generate revenue primarily by charging advertisers for ad placement, collecting referral fees for steering customers to other sites, and charging for premium services.

Although there are numerous portal/search engine sites, the top five sites (Google, Microsoft (Bing), Yahoo, Ask, and AOL) gather more than 95% of the search engine traffic because of their superior brand recognition (comScore, 2015). Many of the top sites were among the first to appear on the Web and therefore had first-mover advantages. Being first confers advantage because customers come to trust a reliable provider and experience switching costs if they change to late arrivals in the market. By garnering a large chunk of the marketplace, first movers—just like a single telephone network—can offer customers access to commonly shared ideas, standards, and experiences (something called *network externalities* that we describe in later chapters).

The traditional portals have company: Facebook and other social network sites are now the initial start or home page (portal) for millions of Internet users in the United States.

Yahoo, AOL, and others like them are considered to be horizontal portals because they define their marketspace to include all users of the Internet. Vertical portals (sometimes called vortals) attempt to provide similar services as horizontal portals, but are focused around a particular subject matter or market segment. For instance, Sailnet specializes in the consumer sailboat market that contains about 8 million Americans who own or rent sailboats. Although the total number of vortal users may be much lower than the number of portal users, if the market segment is attractive enough, advertisers are willing to pay a premium in order to reach a targeted audience. Also, visitors to specialized niche vortals spend more money than the average Yahoo

INSIGHT ON TECHNOLOGY

ONLINE MUSIC: BATTLE OF THE TITANS AND LILLIPUTIANS

Business models are closely related to the technologies available to produce and distribute products and services. Nowhere is this more apparent than the recorded music business, whose foundations since the early 20th century have been based on the technology on hand, from sheet music, to vinyl records, tape cassettes, CDs, and now, the Internet and mobile platform. The music industry provides an excellent example of how technology, along with customer preferences, can, in a very short period, radically alter the competitive landscape.

Thus far, there have been three basic business models in the online music industry. The first model involved making illegal digital copies of copyrighted music available to consumers for a fee, or for free with advertising. From 1995 to 2000, many firms, such as Napster, sprang up to use this model, but most were eventually shut down, with their owners put in jail or heavily fined. Still, illegal sharing of music files on peer-to-peer (P2P) and BitTorrent networks continued to grow, although at a much slower pace. The technologies underlying this business model were MP3 files, PC hard drives, portable MP3 players that could easily play these files, online databases where they could be stored, and the Internet to share them.

In 2003, Apple introduced a legitimate alternative to illegal downloading: the iTunes store, where consumers could download digital copies of individual songs for 99 cents, or entire albums for $12, and play them on their PCs and the newly introduced iPod portable player. Steve Jobs sold this model to the music industry by arguing that it was the industry's only hope to survive the onslaught of illegal sharing and selling of stolen music. The technologies that enabled this business included higher speed Internet services, the iPod player, and advances in digital storage that greatly reduced the cost of storage. Those technologies made it possible and economical for Apple to store millions of songs and distribute them over the Internet to local hard drives on PCs and iPods that could store thousands of songs. The introduction of the iPhone in 2007 strengthened the digital download model, allowing customers to purchase from mobile devices and to use iTunes apps to access their music anytime, using any device. Amazon launched Amazon Music in 2007 and Google followed with its Google Play Music in 2011. This model was strengthened further in 2011 by the introduction of cloud storage (Apple's iCloud), a digital online storage locker.

By 2014, iTunes had 800 million customers, 43 million songs available, and had sold 35 billion tracks! Apple derived an estimated $1.8 billion in revenue from music in 2014. Today, iTunes dominates the digital download model, with a 70% market share. The rest of the digital download model market belongs to Amazon Music and Google Play Music. In 2015, the digital download model accounts for about $2.5 billion (57% of all digital music sales and 37% of all recorded music sales for the entire industry in the United States). By this time, sales of physical CDs had been cut in half, and music industry revenue by a similar amount. The industry has survived, but is only half of its former size.

However, all is not rosy for the download to own/store-in-the-cloud iTunes business model. It is being challenged by a very different business model: music streaming services like Pandora

(continued)

(2005), Spotify (2008), Rdio (2010), Deezer (2007), and Vevo (2009). These are the Lilliputians of the digital music story: start-ups, with venture money, weak revenue models, no profits, but lots of consumer interest.

With streaming music services, consumers do not purchase music, but instead purchase access to millions of songs when and where they want, on any device. These streaming services typically use an ad-supported freemium model to attract early adopters, and then entice them to become paying subscribers. This model had been tried before by firms such as Rhapsody in 1999 without much success because, at that time, few customers wanted to pay for music and few owned MP3 music players.

Today, streaming services have proved to be very popular although not necessarily profitable (as yet). Ad-supported and subscriber streaming revenues in 2014 totaled $1.8 billion, 42% of all digital music sales, and 27% of all music sales. Sales of digital downloads first began falling in 2012, and in 2015, are decreasing by 7% annually, while streaming services are growing at a 30% rate. The digital music game has changed.

The Internet Titans could not ignore the ballooning customer demand for streaming music. In 2012, Google launched its Google Play Music unlimited streaming service that allows users to upload their MP3 files to Google servers for $9.99 a month (but not download new MP3s). In 2014, Amazon launched its Amazon Prime music service, free for Amazon Prime subscribers.

In 2014, Apple purchased Beats Music for $3 billion, a signal that Apple was getting serious about streaming music. Beats had developed its own music streaming service. In June 2015, Apple launched Apple Music, a streaming-only music service that is free for three months and then $9.99 a month after that. Apple and music industry executives claimed that the new service would restore profitability to the music industry by bringing the support of the Apple brand to a music streaming service that would provide more value for consumers. Where Pandora, Spotify, and many other streaming services still struggle, Apple hopes to prosper.

Many musicians remain skeptical that the streaming services will be good for them. In June 2015, Taylor Swift, one of the most popular recording artists in recent memory, wrote an open letter to Apple objecting to Apple Music's plan to not pay royalties for the first three months of the service. She withdrew her popular album "1989" from the service. Taylor Swift argued that Apple should not expect musicians to subsidize customer acquisition costs for Apple's new service, and that musicians didn't ask Apple for free iPhones, so therefore Apple should not ask musicians for free music. A day later Eddy Cue, Apple's senior vice president of Internet software and services, announced that Apple had decided to reverse course and agreed to pay artists and record labels their full royalty: 70% of the revenues Apple collects. Swift agreed to have her music stream on Apple Music. In the end, there is no music without musicians. And they have their own business models.

SOURCES: "Rise of SoundExchange Shows the Growth of Digital Radio Royalties," by Ben Sisario, *New York Times,* August 4, 2015; "Music Artists Take On the Business, Calling for Change," by Ben Sisario, *New York Times,* July 31, 2015; "Taylor Swift Criticism Spurs Apple to Change Royalties Policy," by Ben Sisario, *New York Times*, June 21, 2015; Apple Takes On a Market Full of Streaming Services," by Ben Sisario, *New York Times,* June 3, 2015; "Apple Wants Beats Music Because Transitioning iTunes to Streaming Could Kill Download Sites," by Josh Constine, Techcrunch.com, May 22, 2015; "Streaming Music Services Hear the Sweet Sound of Success," by eMarketer, Inc., March 25, 2015; "News and Notes on 2014 RIAA Music Industry Shipment and Revenue Statistics," by Joshua Friedlander, Recording Industry Association of America, March 18, 2015.

visitor. Google and Ask can also be considered portals of a sort, but focus primarily on offering search and advertising services. They generate revenues primarily from search engine advertising sales and also from affiliate referral fees.

TRANSACTION BROKER

Companies that process transactions for consumers normally handled in person, by phone, or by mail are **transaction brokers**. The largest industries using this model are financial services, travel services, and job placement services. The online transaction broker's primary value propositions are savings of money and time. In addition, most transaction brokers provide timely information and opinions. Companies such as Monster offer job searchers a national marketplace for their talents and employers a national resource for that talent. Both employers and job seekers are attracted by the convenience and currency of information. Online stock brokers charge commissions that are considerably less than traditional brokers, with many offering substantial deals, such as cash and a certain number of free trades, to lure new customers.

Given rising consumer interest in financial planning and the stock market, the market opportunity for online transaction brokers appears to be large. However, while millions of customers have shifted to online brokers, some are still wary about switching from their traditional broker who provides personal advice and a brand name. Fears of privacy invasion and the loss of control over personal financial information also contribute to market resistance. Consequently, the challenge for online brokers is to overcome consumer fears by emphasizing the security and privacy measures in place, and, like physical banks and brokerage firms, providing a broad range of financial services and not just stock trading. This industry is covered in greater depth in Chapter 9.

Transaction brokers make money each time a transaction occurs. Each stock trade, for example, nets the company a fee, based on either a flat rate or a sliding scale related to the size of the transaction. Attracting new customers and encouraging them to trade frequently are the keys to generating more revenue for these companies. Travel sites generate commissions from travel books and job sites generate listing fees from employers up front, rather than charging a fee when a position is filled.

> **transaction broker**
> processes transactions for consumers that are normally handled in person, by phone, or by mail

MARKET CREATOR

Market creators build a digital environment in which buyers and sellers can meet, display and search for products and services, and establish prices. Prior to the Internet and the Web, market creators relied on physical places to establish a market. Beginning with the medieval marketplace and extending to today's New York Stock Exchange, a market has meant a physical space for transacting business. There were few private digital network marketplaces prior to the Web. The Web changed this by making it possible to separate markets from physical space. Prime examples are Priceline, which allows consumers to set the price they are willing to pay for various travel accommodations and other products (sometimes referred to as a reverse auction), and eBay, the online auction site utilized by both businesses and consumers. Market creators make money by either charging a percentage of every transaction made, or charging merchants for access to the market.

> **market creator**
> builds a digital environment where buyers and sellers can meet, display products, search for products, and establish a price for products

For example, eBay's auction business model is to create a digital environment for buyers and sellers to meet, agree on a price, and transact. This is different from transaction brokers who actually carry out the transaction for their customers, acting as agents in larger markets. At eBay, the buyers and sellers are their own agents. Each sale on eBay nets the company a commission based on the percentage of the item's sales price, in addition to a listing fee. eBay is one of the few e-commerce companies that has been profitable virtually from the beginning. Why? One answer is that eBay has no inventory or production costs. It is simply a middleman.

The market opportunity for market creators is potentially vast, but only if the firm has the financial resources and marketing plan to attract sufficient sellers and buyers to the marketplace. As of June 30, 2015, eBay had more than 157 million active buyers, and this makes for an efficient market (eBay Inc., 2015). There are many sellers and buyers for each type of product, sometimes for the same product, for example, laptop computer models. Many other digital auctions have sprung up in smaller, more special-ized vertical market segments such as jewelry and automobiles.

Uber, Airbnb, and Lyft are another example of the market creator business model (although they could also be categorized as service providers). On-demand service companies (also sometimes called sharing economy companies) are market creators that have developed online platforms that allow people to sell services, such as trans-portation or spare rooms, in a marketplace that operates in the cloud and relies on the Web or smartphone apps to conduct transactions. It is important to note that, although referred to as sharing economy or mesh economy companies, these companies do not in fact share resources. Users of these services are either selling something or buying something, and the companies produce revenue by extracting fees for each transac-tion. However, they do unlock the economic value in spare resources (personal cars and rooms) that might otherwise have been lost. In the process they have created huge online markets. For instance, Uber (founded in 2009) currently operates in hundreds of cities in 60 countries around the world. Airbnb, founded in 2008, operates in more than 190 countries and 34,000 cities, lists over 1.5 million rooms available for rent, and has had over 40 million people use its services to book a room. Airbnb has raised around $2.3 billion in funding thus far and is valued at over $25 billion; Uber has raised $8.2 billion and is valued at more than $50 billion!

SERVICE PROVIDER

service provider
offers services online

While e-tailers sell products online, **service providers** offer services online. There's been an explosion in online services that is often unrecognized. Photo sharing, video sharing, and user-generated content (in blogs and social network sites) are all services provided to customers. Google has led the way in developing online applications such as Google Maps, Google Docs, and Gmail. Other personal services such as online medical bill management, financial and pension planning, and travel recommendation are showing strong growth.

Service providers use a variety of revenue models. Some charge a fee, or monthly subscriptions, while others generate revenue from other sources, such as through advertising and by collecting personal information that is useful in direct marketing. Many service providers employ a freemium revenue model, in which some basic services are free, but others require the payment of additional charges. Much like retailers who trade products for cash, service providers trade knowledge, expertise, and capabilities for revenue.

Obviously, some services cannot be provided online. For example, dentistry, plumbing, and car repair cannot be completed via the Internet. However, online arrangements can be made for these services. Online service providers may offer computer services, such as data storage (Dropbox and Carbonite), provide legal services (RocketLawyer), or accounting or bookkeeping services (Wave, Bench). Grocery shopping sites such as FreshDirect and Peapod are also providing services.[1] To complicate matters a bit, most financial transaction brokers (described previously) provide services such as college tuition and pension planning. Travel brokers also provide vacation-planning services, not just transactions with airlines and hotels. Indeed, mixing services with your products is a powerful business strategy pursued by many hard-goods companies (for example, warranties are services).

The basic value proposition of service providers is that they offer consumers valuable, convenient, time-saving, and low-cost alternatives to traditional service providers or provide services that are truly unique. Where else can you search billions of Web pages, or share photos with as many people instantly? Research has found, for instance, that a major factor in predicting online buying behavior is *time starvation*. Time-starved people tend to be busy professionals who work long hours and simply do not have the time to pick up packages, buy groceries, send photos, or visit with financial planners (Bellman, Lohse, and Johnson, 1999). The market opportunity for service providers is as large as the variety of services that can be provided and potentially is much larger than the market opportunity for physical goods. We live in a service-based economy and society; witness the growth of fast-food restaurants, package delivery services, and wireless cellular phone services. Consumers' increasing demand for convenience products and services bodes well for current and future online service providers.

Marketing of service providers must allay consumer fears about hiring a vendor online, as well as build confidence and familiarity among current and potential customers. Building confidence and trust is critical for service providers just as it is for retail product merchants.

2.3 MAJOR BUSINESS-TO-BUSINESS (B2B) BUSINESS MODELS

In Chapter 1, we noted that business-to-business (B2B) e-commerce, in which businesses sell to other businesses, is more than 10 times the size of B2C e-commerce, even though most of the public attention has focused on B2C. For instance, it is estimated that revenues for all types of B2B e-commerce in the United States will total around $6.3 trillion in 2015, compared to about $531 billion for all types of B2C

---

[1] FreshDirect and other e-commerce businesses can also be classified as online retailers insofar as they warehouse commonly purchased items and make a profit based on the spread between their buy and sell prices.

TABLE 2.7	B2B BUSINESS MODELS		
BUSINESS MODEL	**EXAMPLES**	**DESCRIPTION**	**REVENUE MODEL**
(1) NET MARKETPLACE			
E-distributor	Grainger Amazon Business	Single-firm online version of retail and wholesale store; supply maintenance, repair, operation goods; indirect inputs	Sales of goods
E-procurement	Ariba Supplier Network PerfectCommerce	Single firm creating digital markets where sellers and buyers transact for indirect inputs	Fees for market-making services, supply chain management, and fulfillment services
Exchange	Go2Paper	Independently owned vertical digital marketplace for direct inputs	Fees and commissions on transactions
Industry Consortium	TheSeam SupplyOn	Industry-owned vertical digital market open to select suppliers	Fees and commissions on transactions
(2) PRIVATE INDUSTRIAL NETWORK			
	Walmart Procter & Gamble	Company-owned network that coordinates supply chains with a limited set of partners	Cost absorbed by network owner and recovered through production and distribution efficiencies

e-commerce. Clearly, most of the dollar revenues in e-commerce involve B2B e-commerce. Much of this activity is unseen and unknown to the average consumer. **Table 2.7** lists the major business models utilized in the B2B arena.

E-DISTRIBUTOR

e-distributor
a company that supplies products and services directly to individual businesses

Companies that supply products and services directly to individual businesses are **e-distributors**. W.W. Grainger, for example, is the largest distributor of maintenance, repair, and operations (MRO) supplies. In the past, Grainger relied on catalog sales and physical distribution centers in metropolitan areas. Its catalog of equipment went online in 1995. Today, Grainger's e-commerce platform, which includes Web sites and mobile apps, produces about $2.8 billion in sales (about 30% of its total revenue) for the company.

E-distributors are owned by one company seeking to serve many customers. However, as with exchanges (described on the next page), critical mass is a factor. With e-distributors, the more products and services a company makes available on its site, the more attractive that site is to potential customers. One-stop shopping is always preferable to having to visit numerous sites to locate a particular part or product.

E-PROCUREMENT

e-procurement firm
creates and sells access to digital markets

Just as e-distributors provide products to other companies, **e-procurement firms** create and sell access to digital markets. Firms such as Ariba, for instance, have created software that helps large firms organize their procurement process by creating mini-digital markets for a single firm. Ariba creates custom-integrated online catalogs (where supplier firms can list their offerings) for purchasing firms. On the sell side, Ariba helps vendors sell to large purchasers by providing software to handle catalog creation, shipping, insurance, and finance. Both the buy and sell side software is referred to generically as "value chain management" software.

B2B service providers make money through transaction fees, fees based on the number of workstations using the service, or annual licensing fees. They offer purchasing firms a sophisticated set of sourcing and supply chain management tools that permit firms to reduce supply chain costs. In the software world, firms such as Ariba are sometimes also called Software as a Service (SaaS) or Platform as a Service (PaaS) providers; they are able to offer firms much lower costs of software by achieving scale economies. **Scale economies** are efficiencies that result from increasing the size of a business, for instance, when large, fixed-cost production systems (such as factories or software systems) can be operated at full capacity with no idle time. In the case of software, the marginal cost of a digital copy of a software program is nearly zero, and finding additional buyers for an expensive software program is exceptionally profitable. This is much more efficient than having every firm build its own supply chain management system, and it permits firms such as Ariba to specialize and offer their software to firms at a cost far less than the cost of developing it.

> **B2B service provider**
> sells business services to other firms

> **scale economies**
> efficiencies that arise from increasing the size of a business

EXCHANGES

Exchanges have garnered most of the B2B attention and early funding because of their potential market size even though today they are a small part of the overall B2B picture. An **exchange** is an independent digital marketplace where hundreds of suppliers meet a smaller number of very large commercial purchasers (Kaplan and Sawhney, 2000). Exchanges are owned by independent, usually entrepreneurial start-up firms whose business is making a market, and they generate revenue by charging a commission or fee based on the size of the transactions conducted among trading parties. They usually serve a single vertical industry such as steel, polymers, or aluminum, and focus on the exchange of direct inputs to production and short-term contracts or spot purchasing. For buyers, B2B exchanges make it possible to gather information, check out suppliers, collect prices, and keep up to date on the latest happenings all in one place. Sellers, on the other hand, benefit from expanded access to buyers. The greater the number of sellers and buyers, the lower the sales cost and the higher the chances of making a sale. The ease, speed, and volume of transactions are summarily referred to as *market liquidity*.

> **exchange**
> an independent digital marketplace where suppliers and commercial purchasers can conduct transactions

In theory, exchanges make it significantly less expensive and time-consuming to identify potential suppliers, customers, and partners, and to do business with each other. As a result, they can lower transaction costs—the cost of making a sale or purchase. Exchanges can also lower product costs and inventory-carrying costs—the cost of keeping a product on hand in a warehouse. In reality, as will be discussed in Chapter 12, B2B exchanges have had a difficult time convincing thousands of suppliers to move into singular digital markets where they face powerful price competition, and an equally difficult time convincing businesses to change their purchasing behavior away from trusted long-term trading partners. As a result, the number of exchanges has fallen significantly.

INDUSTRY CONSORTIA

industry consortia
industry-owned vertical marketplaces that serve specific industries

Industry consortia are industry-owned *vertical marketplaces* that serve specific industries, such as the automobile, aerospace, chemical, floral, or logging industries. In contrast, *horizontal marketplaces* sell specific products and services to a wide range of companies. Vertical marketplaces supply a smaller number of companies with products and services of specific interest to their industry, while horizontal marketplaces supply companies in different industries with a particular type of product and service, such as marketing-related, financial, or computing services. For example, SupplyOn, founded in 2000 and owned by industrial giants Bosch (one of the world's largest suppliers of automotive components), Continental (a leading automotive manufacturing company), and Schaeffler (a global manufacturer of various types of bearings), among others, provides a shared supply chain collaboration platform for companies in various manufacturing industries. In 2015, in addition to its shareholders, its customers include Airbus, BMW, BorgWarner, Siemens, Thales, and many other major global manufacturing companies.

Industry consortia have tended to be more successful than independent exchanges in part because they are sponsored by powerful, deep-pocketed industry players, and also because they strengthen traditional purchasing behavior rather than seek to transform it.

PRIVATE INDUSTRIAL NETWORKS

private industrial network
digital network designed to coordinate the flow of communications among firms engaged in business together

Private industrial networks constitute about 75% of all B2B expenditures by large firms and far exceed the expenditures for all forms of Net marketplaces. A **private industrial network** (sometimes referred to as a private trading exchange or PTX) is a digital network designed to coordinate the flow of communications among firms engaged in business together. The network is owned by a single large purchasing firm. Participation is by invitation only to trusted long-term suppliers of direct inputs. These networks typically evolve out of a firm's own enterprise resource planning (ERP) system, and are an effort to include key suppliers in the firm's own business decision making. For instance, Walmart operates one of the largest private industrial networks in the world for its suppliers, who on a daily basis use Walmart's network to monitor the sales of their goods, the status of shipments, and the actual inventory level of their goods.

We discuss the nuances of B2B e-commerce in more detail in Chapter 12.

2.4 HOW E-COMMERCE CHANGES BUSINESS: STRATEGY, STRUCTURE, AND PROCESS

Now that you have a clear grasp of the variety of business models used by e-commerce firms, you also need to understand how e-commerce has changed the business environment in the last decade, including industry structures, business strategies, and industry and firm operations (business processes and value chains). We return to these concepts throughout the book as we explore the e-commerce phenomenon. In general, the Internet is an open standards system available to all players, and this

TABLE 2.8	EIGHT UNIQUE FEATURES OF E-COMMERCE TECHNOLOGY
FEATURE	SELECTED IMPACTS ON BUSINESS ENVIRONMENT
Ubiquity	Alters industry structure by creating new marketing channels and expanding size of overall market. Creates new efficiencies in industry operations and lowers costs of firms' sales operations. Enables new differentiation strategies.
Global reach	Changes industry structure by lowering barriers to entry, but greatly expands market at same time. Lowers cost of industry and firm operations through production and sales efficiencies. Enables competition on a global scale.
Universal standards	Changes industry structure by lowering barriers to entry and intensifying competition within an industry. Lowers costs of industry and firm operations by lowering computing and communications costs. Enables broad scope strategies.
Richness	Alters industry structure by reducing strength of powerful distribution channels. Changes industry and firm operations costs by reducing reliance on sales forces. Enhances post-sales support strategies.
Interactivity	Alters industry structure by reducing threat of substitutes through enhanced customization. Reduces industry and firm costs by reducing reliance on sales forces. Enables differentiation strategies.
Personalization/ Customization	Alters industry structure by reducing threats of substitutes, raising barriers to entry. Reduces value chain costs in industry and firms by lessening reliance on sales forces. Enables personalized marketing strategies.
Information density	Changes industry structure by weakening powerful sales channels, shifting bargaining power to consumers. Reduces industry and firm operations costs by lowering costs of obtaining, processing, and distributing information about suppliers and consumers.
Social technologies	Changes industry structure by shifting programming and editorial decisions to consumers. Creates substitute entertainment products. Energizes a large group of new suppliers.

fact inherently makes it easy for new competitors to enter the marketplace and offer substitute products or channels of delivery. The Internet tends to intensify competition. Because information becomes available to everyone, the Internet inherently shifts power to buyers who can quickly discover the lowest-cost provider. On the other hand, the Internet presents many new opportunities for creating value, for branding products and charging premium prices, and for enlarging an already powerful offline physical business such as Walmart or Sears.

Recall Table 1.2 in Chapter 1 that describes the truly unique features of e-commerce technology. **Table 2.8** suggests some of the implications of each unique feature for the overall business environment—industry structure, business strategies, and operations.

INDUSTRY STRUCTURE

industry structure

refers to the nature of the players in an industry and their relative bargaining power

E-commerce changes industry structure, in some industries more than others. **Industry structure** refers to the nature of the players in an industry and their relative bargaining power. An industry's structure is characterized by five forces: *rivalry among existing competitors*, the *threat of substitute products*, *barriers to entry into the industry*, the *bargaining power of suppliers*, and the *bargaining power of buyers* (Porter, 1985). When you describe an industry's structure, you are describing the general business environment in an industry and the overall profitability of doing business in that environment. E-commerce has the potential to change the relative strength of these competitive forces (see **Figure 2.3**).

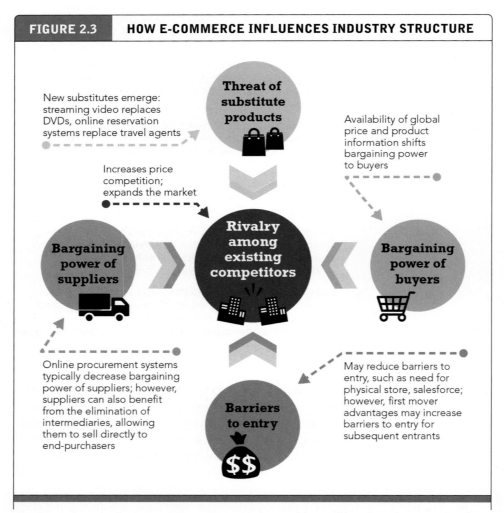

| FIGURE 2.3 | HOW E-COMMERCE INFLUENCES INDUSTRY STRUCTURE |

E-commerce has many impacts on industry structure and competitive conditions. From the perspective of a single firm, these changes can have negative or positive implications depending on the situation. In some cases, an entire industry can be disrupted, while at the same time, a new industry is born. Individual firms can either prosper or be devastated.

When you consider a business model and its potential long-term profitability, you should always perform an industry structural analysis. An **industry structural analysis** is an effort to understand and describe the nature of competition in an industry, the nature of substitute products, the barriers to entry, and the relative strength of consumers and suppliers.

E-commerce can affect the structure and dynamics of industries in very different ways. Consider the recorded music industry, an industry that has experienced significant change because of e-commerce. Historically, the major record companies owned the exclusive rights to the recorded music of various artists. With the entrance into the marketplace of substitute providers such as Napster and Kazaa, millions of consumers began to use the Internet to bypass traditional music labels and their distributors entirely. In the travel industry, entirely new middlemen such as Travelocity entered the market to compete with traditional travel agents. After Travelocity, Expedia, CheapTickets, and other travel services demonstrated the power of e-commerce marketing for airline tickets, the actual owners of the airline seats—the major airlines—banded together to form their own Internet outlet for tickets, Orbitz, for direct sales to consumers (although ultimately selling the company to a private investor group). Clearly, e-commerce creates *new industry dynamics* that can best be described as the give and take of the marketplace, the changing fortunes of competitors.

Yet, in other industries, e-commerce has strengthened existing players. In the chemical and automobile industries, e-commerce is being used effectively by manufacturers to strengthen their traditional distributors. In these industries, e-commerce technology has not fundamentally altered the competitive forces—bargaining power of suppliers, barriers to entry, bargaining power of buyers, threat of substitutes, or rivalry among competitors—within the industry. Hence, each industry is different and you need to examine each one carefully to understand the impacts of e-commerce on competition and strategy.

New forms of distribution created by new market entrants can completely change the competitive forces in an industry. For instance, consumers gladly substituted free access to Wikipedia for a $699 set of World Book encyclopedias, or a $40 DVD, radically changing the competitive forces in the encyclopedia industry. As we describe in Chapter 10, the content industries of newspapers, books, movies, games, and television have been transformed by the emergence of new distribution platforms.

Inter-firm rivalry (competition) is one area of the business environment where e-commerce technologies have had an impact on most industries. In general, e-commerce has increased price competition in nearly all markets. It has been relatively easy for existing firms to adopt e-commerce technology and attempt to use it to achieve competitive advantage vis-à-vis rivals. For instance, e-commerce inherently changes the scope of competition from local and regional to national and global. Because consumers have access to global price information, e-commerce produces pressures on firms to compete by lowering prices (and lowering profits). On the other hand, e-commerce has made it possible for some firms to differentiate their products or services from others. Amazon patented one-click purchasing, for instance, while eBay created a unique, easy-to-use interface and a differentiating brand name. Therefore, although e-commerce has increased emphasis on price competition, it has also enabled businesses to create new strategies for differentiation and branding so that they can retain higher prices.

industry structural analysis
an effort to understand and describe the nature of competition in an industry, the nature of substitute products, the barriers to entry, and the relative strength of consumers and suppliers

It is impossible to determine if e-commerce technologies have had an overall positive or negative impact on firm profitability in general. Each industry is unique, so it is necessary to perform a separate analysis for each one. Clearly, e-commerce has shaken the foundations of some industries, in particular, content industries (such as the music, newspaper, book, and software industries) as well as other information-intense industries such as financial services. In these industries, the power of consumers has grown relative to providers, prices have fallen, and overall profitability has been challenged. In other industries, especially manufacturing, e-commerce has not greatly changed relationships with buyers, but has changed relationships with suppliers. Increasingly, manufacturing firms in entire industries have banded together to aggregate purchases, create industry exchanges or marketplaces, and outsource industrial processes in order to obtain better prices from suppliers. Throughout this book, we document these changes in industry structure and market dynamics introduced by e-commerce.

INDUSTRY VALUE CHAINS

value chain

the set of activities performed in an industry or in a firm that transforms raw inputs into final products and services

While an industry structural analysis helps you understand the impact of e-commerce technology on the overall business environment in an industry, a more detailed industry value chain analysis can help identify more precisely just how e-commerce may change business operations at the industry level. One of the basic tools for understanding the impact of information technology on industry and firm operations is the value chain. The concept is quite simple. A **value chain** is the set of activities performed in an industry or in a firm that transforms raw inputs into final products and services. Each of these activities adds economic value to the final product; hence, the term *value chain* as an interconnected set of value-adding activities. **Figure 2.4** illustrates the six generic players in an industry value chain: suppliers, manufacturers, transporters, distributors, retailers, and customers.

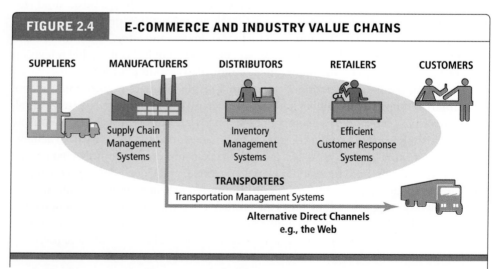

FIGURE 2.4   E-COMMERCE AND INDUSTRY VALUE CHAINS

SUPPLIERS   MANUFACTURERS   DISTRIBUTORS   RETAILERS   CUSTOMERS

Supply Chain Management Systems

Inventory Management Systems

Efficient Customer Response Systems

TRANSPORTERS
Transportation Management Systems

**Alternative Direct Channels
e.g., the Web**

Every industry can be characterized by a set of value-adding activities performed by a variety of actors. E-commerce potentially affects the capabilities of each player as well as the overall operational efficiency of the industry.

By reducing the cost of information, e-commerce offers each of the key players in an industry value chain new opportunities to maximize their positions by lowering costs and/or raising prices. For instance, manufacturers can reduce the costs they pay for goods by developing Internet-based B2B exchanges with their suppliers. Manufacturers can develop direct relationships with their customers, bypassing the costs of distributors and retailers. Distributors can develop highly efficient inventory management systems to reduce their costs, and retailers can develop highly efficient customer relationship management systems to strengthen their service to customers. Customers in turn can search for the best quality, fastest delivery, and lowest prices, thereby lowering their transaction costs and reducing prices they pay for final goods. Finally, the operational efficiency of the entire industry can increase, lowering prices and adding value for consumers, and helping the industry to compete with alternative industries.

FIRM VALUE CHAINS

The concept of value chain can be used to analyze a single firm's operational efficiency as well. The question here is: How does e-commerce technology potentially affect the value chains of firms within an industry? A **firm value chain** is the set of activities a firm engages in to create final products from raw inputs. Each step in the process of production adds value to the final product. In addition, firms develop support activities that coordinate the production process and contribute to overall operational efficiency. **Figure 2.5** illustrates the key steps and support activities in a firm's value chain.

firm value chain
the set of activities a firm engages in to create final products from raw inputs

E-commerce offers firms many opportunities to increase their operational efficiency and differentiate their products. For instance, firms can use the Internet's communications efficiency to outsource some primary and secondary activities to specialized, more efficient providers without such outsourcing being visible to the

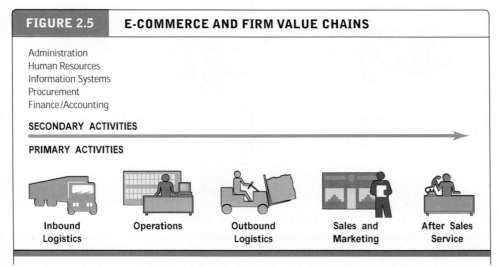

FIGURE 2.5	E-COMMERCE AND FIRM VALUE CHAINS

Administration
Human Resources
Information Systems
Procurement
Finance/Accounting

SECONDARY ACTIVITIES →

PRIMARY ACTIVITIES

| Inbound Logistics | Operations | Outbound Logistics | Sales and Marketing | After Sales Service |

Every firm can be characterized by a set of value-adding primary and secondary activities performed by a variety of actors in the firm. A simple firm value chain performs five primary value-adding steps: inbound logistics, operations, outbound logistics, sales and marketing, and after sales service.

consumer. In addition, firms can use e-commerce to more precisely coordinate the steps in the value chains and reduce their costs. Finally, firms can use e-commerce to provide users with more differentiated and high-value products. For instance, Amazon provides consumers with a much larger inventory of books to choose from, at a lower cost, than traditional book stores. It also provides many services—such as instantly available professional and consumer reviews, and information on buying patterns of other consumers—that traditional bookstores cannot.

FIRM VALUE WEBS

value web

networked business ecosystem that coordinates the value chains of several firms

While firms produce value through their value chains, they also rely on the value chains of their partners—their suppliers, distributors, and delivery firms. E-commerce creates new opportunities for firms to cooperate and create a value web. A **value web** is a networked business ecosystem that uses e-commerce technology to coordinate the value chains of business partners within an industry, or at the first level, to coordinate the value chains of a group of firms. **Figure 2.6** illustrates a value web.

A value web coordinates a firm's suppliers with its own production needs using an Internet-based supply chain management system. We discuss these B2B systems

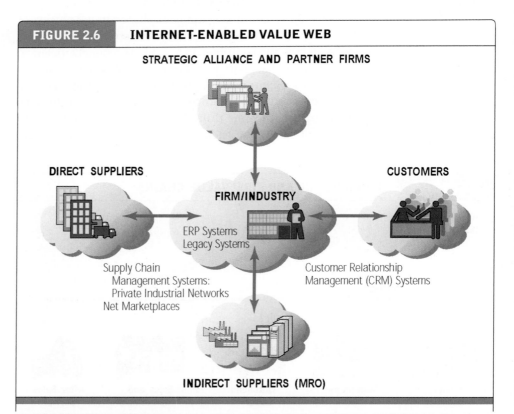

FIGURE 2.6   INTERNET-ENABLED VALUE WEB

STRATEGIC ALLIANCE AND PARTNER FIRMS

DIRECT SUPPLIERS

CUSTOMERS

FIRM/INDUSTRY

ERP Systems
Legacy Systems

Supply Chain
Management Systems:
Private Industrial Networks
Net Marketplaces

Customer Relationship
Management (CRM) Systems

INDIRECT SUPPLIERS (MRO)

Internet technology enables firms to create an enhanced value web in cooperation with their strategic alliance and partner firms, customers, and direct and indirect suppliers.

in Chapter 12. Firms also use the Internet to develop close relationships with their logistics partners. For instance, Amazon relies on UPS tracking systems to provide its customers with online package tracking, and it relies on the U.S. Postal Service systems to insert packages directly into the mail stream. Amazon has partnership relations with hundreds of firms to generate customers and to manage relationships with customers. In fact, when you examine Amazon closely, you realize that the value it delivers to customers is in large part the result of coordination with other firms and not simply the result of activities internal to Amazon. The value of Amazon is, in large part, the value delivered by its value web partners. This is difficult for other firms to imitate in the short run.

BUSINESS STRATEGY

A **business strategy** is a set of plans for achieving superior long-term returns on the capital invested in a business firm. A business strategy is therefore a plan for making profits in a competitive environment over the long term. **Profit** is simply the difference between the price a firm is able to charge for its products and the cost of producing and distributing goods. Profit represents economic value. Economic value is created anytime customers are willing to pay more for a product than it costs to produce. Why would anyone pay more for a product than it costs to produce? There are multiple answers. The product may be unique (there are no other suppliers), it may be the least costly product of its type available, consumers may be able to purchase the product anywhere in the world, or it may satisfy some unique needs that other products do not. Each of these sources of economic value defines a firm's strategy for positioning its products in the marketplace. There are four generic strategies for achieving a profitable business: differentiation, cost, scope, and focus. We describe each of these below. The specific strategies that a firm follows will depend on the product, the industry, and the marketplace where competition is encountered.

Although the Internet is a unique marketplace, the same principles of strategy and business apply. As you will see throughout the book, successful e-commerce strategies involve using the Internet and mobile platform to leverage and strengthen existing business (rather than destroy your business), and to provide products and services your competitors cannot copy (in the short term anyway). That means developing unique products, proprietary content, distinguishing processes (such as Amazon's one-click shopping), and personalized or customized services and products (Porter, 2001). There are five generic business strategies: product/service differentiation, cost competition, scope, focus, and customer/supplier intimacy. Let's examine these ideas more closely.

Differentiation refers to all the ways producers can make their products or services unique and distinguish them from those of competitors. The opposite of differentiation is **commoditization**—a situation where there are no differences among products or services, and the only basis of choosing is price. As economists tell us,

business strategy
a set of plans for achieving superior long-term returns on the capital invested in a business firm

profit
the difference between the price a firm is able to charge for its products and the cost of producing and distributing goods

differentiation
refers to all the ways producers can make their products or services unique and different to distinguish them from those of competitors

commoditization
a situation where there are no differences among products or services, and the only basis of choosing is price

when price alone becomes the basis of competition and there are many suppliers and many customers, eventually the price of the good/service falls to the cost to produce it (marginal revenues from the nth unit equal marginal costs). And then profits are zero! This is an unacceptable situation for any business person. The solution is to differentiate your product or service and to create a monopoly-like situation where you are the only supplier.

There are many ways businesses differentiate their products or services. A business may start with a core generic product or service, but then create expectations among users about the "experience" of consuming the product or using the service— "Nothing equals the experience of driving a BMW." Businesses may also augment products and services by adding features to make them different from those of competitors. And businesses can differentiate their products and services further by enhancing their abilities to solve related consumer problems. For instance, tax programs such as TurboTax can import data from spreadsheet programs, as well as be used to file tax returns online. These capabilities are enhancements to the product that solve a customer's problems. The purpose of marketing is to create these differentiation features and to make the consumer aware of the unique qualities of products and services, creating in the process a "brand" that stands for these features. We discuss marketing and branding in Chapters 6 and 7.

In their totality, the differentiation features of a product or service constitute the customer value proposition we described in earlier sections of this chapter. E-commerce offers some unique ways to differentiate products and services, such as the ability to personalize the shopping experience and to customize the product or service to the particular demands of each consumer. E-commerce businesses can also differentiate products and services by making it possible to purchase the product from home, work, or on the road (ubiquity); by making it possible to purchase anywhere in the world (global reach); by creating unique interactive content, videos, stories about users, and reviews by users (richness and interactivity); and by storing and processing information for consumers of the product or service, such as warranty information on all products purchased through a site or income tax information online (information density).

strategy of cost competition

offering products and services at a lower cost than competitors

Adopting a **strategy of cost competition** means a business has discovered some unique set of business processes or resources that other firms cannot obtain in the marketplace. Business processes are the atomic units of the value chain. For instance, the set of value-creating activities called Inbound Logistics in Figure 2.6 is in reality composed of many different collections of activities performed by people on the loading docks and in the warehouses. These different collections of activities are called *business processes*—the set of steps or procedures required to perform the various elements of the value chain.

When a firm discovers a new, more efficient set of business processes, it can obtain a cost advantage over competitors. Then it can attract customers by charging a lower price, while still making a handsome profit. Eventually, its competitors go out of business as the market decisively tilts toward the lowest-cost provider. Or, when a business discovers a unique resource, or lower-cost supplier, it can also compete effectively on cost. For instance, switching production to low-wage-cost areas of the world is one way to lower costs.

Competing on cost can be a short-lived affair and very tricky. Competitors can also discover the same or different efficiencies in production. And competitors can also move production to low-cost areas of the world. Also, competitors may decide to lose money for a period as they compete on cost.

E-commerce offers some ways to compete on cost, at least in the short term. Firms can leverage ubiquity by lowering the costs of order entry (the customer fills out all the forms, so there is no order entry department); leverage global reach and universal standards by having a single order entry system worldwide; and leverage richness, interactivity, and personalization by creating customer profiles online and treating each individual consumer differently—without the use of an expensive sales force that performed these functions in the past. Finally, firms can leverage information intensity by providing consumers with detailed information on products, without maintaining either expensive catalogs or a sales force.

While e-commerce offers powerful capabilities for intensifying cost competition, which makes cost competition appear to be a viable strategy, the danger is that competitors have access to the same technology. The *factor markets*—where producers buy supplies—are open to all. Assuming they have the skills and organizational will to use the technology, competitors can buy many of the same cost-reducing techniques in the marketplace. Even a skilled labor force can be purchased, ultimately. However, self-knowledge, proprietary tacit knowledge (knowledge that is not published or codified), and a loyal, skilled workforce are in the short term difficult to purchase in factor markets. Therefore, cost competition remains a viable strategy.

Two other generic business strategies are scope and focus. A **scope strategy** is a strategy to compete in all markets around the globe, rather than merely in local, regional, or national markets. The Internet's global reach, universal standards, and ubiquity can certainly be leveraged to assist businesses in becoming global competitors. Yahoo, for instance, along with all of the other top 20 e-commerce companies, has readily attained a global presence. A **focus/market niche strategy** is a strategy to compete within a narrow market segment or product segment. This is a specialization strategy with the goal of becoming the premier provider in a narrow market. For instance, L.L.Bean uses e-commerce to continue its historic focus on outdoor sports apparel; and W.W. Grainger—the Web's most frequently visited B2B site—focuses on the narrow MRO market segment. E-commerce offers some obvious capabilities that enable a focus strategy. Firms can leverage richness and interactivity to create highly focused messages to different market segments; information intensity makes it possible to focus e-mail and other marketing campaigns on small market segments; personalization—and related customization—means the same product can be customized and personalized to fulfill the very focused needs of specific market segments and consumers.

Another generic strategy is **customer intimacy**, which focuses on developing strong ties with customers. Strong linkages with customers increase *switching costs* (the costs of switching from one product or service to a competing product or service)

scope strategy
competing in all markets around the globe, rather than just local, regional, or national markets

focus/market niche strategy
competing within a narrow market or product segment

customer intimacy
focuses on developing strong ties with customers in order to increase switching costs

TABLE 2.9	BUSINESS STRATEGIES	
STRATEGY	DESCRIPTION	EXAMPLE
Differentiation	Making products and services unique and different in order to distinguish them from those of competitors	Warby Parker (Vintage-inspired prescription eyeglasses)
Cost competition	Offering products and services at a lower cost than competitors	Walmart
Scope	Competing in all markets around the globe, rather than merely in local, regional, or national markets	Apple iDevices
Focus/market niche	Competing within a narrow market or product segment	Bonobos (Men's clothing)
Customer intimacy	Developing strong ties with customers	Amazon; Netflix

and thereby enhance a firm's competitive advantage. For example, Amazon's one-click shopping that retains customer details and recommendation services based on previous purchases makes it more likely that customers will return to make subsequent purchases.

Table 2.9 summarizes the five basic business strategies.

Industry structure, industry and firm value chains, value webs, and business strategy are central business concepts used throughout this book to analyze the viability of and prospects for e-commerce sites. In particular, the signature case studies found at the end of each chapter are followed by questions that may ask you to identify the competitive forces in the case, or analyze how the case illustrates changes in industry structure, industry and firm value chains, and business strategy.

E-COMMERCE TECHNOLOGY AND BUSINESS MODEL DISRUPTION

While e-commerce has changed most industries in terms of their structure, processes, and strategies, in some cases e-commerce has radically changed entire industries, driving incumbent firms out of business, greatly altering the economics of an industry, and spawning entirely new firms and value chains (Schumpeter, 1942). When new technologies are at the core of a change in the way business is done, they are referred to as **disruptive technologies**. When the technology involved is digital, the term **digital disruption** is used. Usually it is not the technology per se that is disruptive—in fact, it can be rather ordinary and commonplace. Instead, the disruption occurs when an innovative firm applies the technology to pursue a different business model and strategy than existing firms, perhaps discovering a whole new market that existing firms did not even know existed (Bower and Christensen, 1995; Christensen and Leslie, 2000). For instance, personal computers using off-the-shelf inexpensive processors and technologies disrupted the market for mainframe and mini-computers. All the eight elements of a business model identified previously can be affected by disruptive

disruptive technologies
technologies that underpin a business model disruption

digital disruption
a business model disruption that is driven by changes in information technology

technologies, from the business value proposition to the revenue model, market opportunity, competitive environment, competitive advantage, market strategy, organizational development, and management. In short, it's a whole new world that often confuses and surprises successful companies who tend to dismiss and mock the early disruptive products. For instance, the entrepreneurs who introduced personal computers identified an entire new market of customers that had been ignored by the large computer firms, along with new price points, competitive factors, and market strategy, using new organizational and management teams. Many existing firms could not compete, and dissolved. Similar dynamics can be found in communications (disrupted by e-mail), data storage, music, photography, publishing, and transportation (Lepore, 2014). In 2015, firms like Uber and Airbnb are beginning to have an impact on the taxi and lodging industries, which may be disrupted in several years if these newer firms succeed.

Not all technologies are disruptive. In fact, most successful companies use technology to sustain their current business models, industry structre, processes, and strategies. This use of technology is referred to as **sustaining technology** because it helps companies to cope with competitive pressures and improve their products, and serve their customers with less expensive, more powerful, or unique products. But the same technology can be used by innovative entrepreneurs (**disruptors**) to destroy existing business models. Here's how it works.

Successful companies use whatever technology is available to incrementally improve their products, focusing on the customer by improving quality, price, and service. The incumbent and dominant firms seek to maintain the status quo in an industry, and their firms. In the first disruptive stage, disruptors, often funded by new sources of finance, introduce new products that are less expensive, less capable, and of poorer quality. The first personal computers used relatively unsophisticated technology compared to mainframe computers of the 1970s. These early products nevertheless find a niche in a market that incumbents do not serve or are unaware of. In the second stage, disruptors improve their products at a rapid pace, taking advantage of newer technologies at a faster pace than incumbents, expanding their niche market, and eventually attracting a larger customer base from the incumbents' market. When word processors, and eventually Microsoft Office, were married to the more powerful PC of the 1980s, they attracted a new market of business managers and professionals that was not served by incumbents. The concept was entirely new at the time. The successful incumbents never thought business professionals, let alone people working at home, would like to have a computer at their desk to create documents, build spreadsheets, and make presentation slides. The people and companies that developed personal computers were outsiders to the mainframe computer industry. They were disruptors. They had the vision.

In the third stage, the new products and business model become good enough, and even superior to products offered by incumbents. In the fourth stage, incumbent companies lose market share, and either go out of business or are consolidated into other more successful firms that serve a much more limited customer base. Some incumbents survive by finding new customers for their existing product, adopting some of the newer products and business models in separate divisions of their firms, or moving into other often nearby markets. For instance, mainframe computers are

sustaining technologies
technologies that enable the incremental improvement of products and services

disruptors
the entrepreneurs and their business firms that lead a business model disruption

still made by IBM, but they are one of the few survivors. They survived by sustaining innovation in their traditional market of large-scale computing for Fortune 500 firms, moving into computing services, data centers, enterprise software, and most recently cloud computing, business analytics, data mining, and machine learning. As for the PC industry, it is currently being disrupted by smartphones and tablet computers, created by outsiders who played a small role in the personal computer world, and who have identified huge consumer markets that incumbent PC manufacturers did not realize even existed. They have the vision, for now, but they face new digital disruptors sure to follow.

Why don't the existing companies realize the changes that are coming, and take steps to compete directly with the disruptors? Successful incumbents usually have enormous capital reserves, in-depth technology and intellectual skills, and access to prestigious management consulting firms. Why didn't Kodak see the transition to digital photography? Why didn't Canon see the smartphone camera as a powerful competitor to digital cameras? Why don't firms disrupt their own business models? The answers are complex. Incumbent technologists and professionals may be trained in an *unfit fitness*, having the wrong skills for the current environment. Shareholders expect returns on investment, not destruction of a firm's historic and cherished profitable products. The existing customer base comes to expect continuous improvement in existing products—not a business disruption, but business as usual. These powerful practices, all of which make good business sense, prevent incumbent firms from meeting the challenges of business model disruption. It is unclear at this time if the two most innovative firms in the current e-commerce environment, Apple and Google, will prove any different from previous incumbents.

CASE STUDY

Freemium
Takes Pandora Public

Pandora is the Internet's most successful radio service. As of June 2015, it had over 250 million registered users (225 million of whom access the service via a mobile device) and about 80 million active listeners. Pandora accounts for more than 45% of all Internet radio listening hours, more than double its closest competitor, Spotify, and a 9% share of total U.S. radio listening (both traditional and Internet). In 2014, it streamed over 20 billion hours of music!

At Pandora, users select a genre of music based on a favorite musician, and a computer algorithm puts together a personal radio station that plays not only the music of the selected artist but also closely related music by different artists. As of June 2015, listeners have created over 8 billion different stations. A team of approximately 25 professional musicians listens to new songs each day and classifies the music according to more than 450 musical criteria. These criteria are used in a computer algorithm to classify new songs into various genres. Within each of these genres are hundreds of subgenres. Altogether, Pandora has a database of over 1 million analyzed songs from over 200,000 artists.

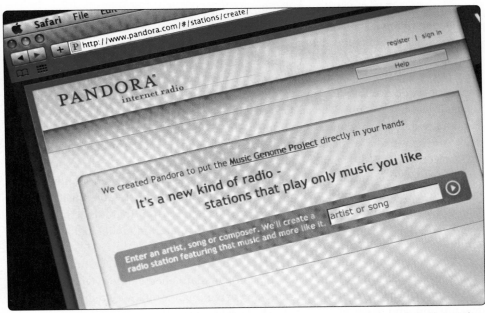

© NetPhotos / Alamy

Pandora's founders, Will Glaser and Tim Westergren, launched Pandora in 2005. Their biggest challenge was making a business out of a totally new kind of online radio station when competing online stations were making music available for free, many without advertising, and online subscription services were streaming music for a monthly fee and finding some advertising support as well. Online music illegally downloaded from P2P networks for free was also a significant factor, as was iTunes, which by 2005 was a roaring success, charging 99 cents a song. The idea of a "personal" radio station playing your kind of music was very new.

Pandora's business strategy is referred to as "freemium." A freemium strategy is based on giving away some products or services for free while relying on a certain percentage of customers to pay for premium versions of the same product or service. As Chris Anderson, author of *Free: The Future of a Radical Price*, has pointed out, because the marginal cost of digital products is typically close to zero, providing free product does not cost much, and potentially enables you to reach many more people. If the market is very large, even getting just 1% of that market to purchase could be very lucrative. Other notable freemium success stories include LinkedIn, a social network for career-oriented and job networking that offers some basic services for free, such as creating a profile and making connections, but which charges for premium services, and Dropbox, a cloud storage and file sharing service that provides 2 gigabytes of cloud storage for free, but charges for additional storage. Freemium has been the standard business model for most apps, with over 65% of the top 100 apps in Apple's App Store using a freemium strategy.

Pandora's first strategy was to give away 10 hours of free access, and then ask subscribers to pay $36 a month for a year after they used up their free 10 hours. The result: 100,000 people listened to their 10 hours for free and then refused to pay for the annual service. People loved Pandora but appeared unwilling to pay for it.

Facing financial collapse, in November 2005 Pandora introduced an ad-supported option. Subscribers could listen to a maximum of 40 hours of music in a calendar month for free. After the 40 hours were used up, subscribers had three choices: (a) pay 99 cents for the rest of the month, (b) sign up for a premium service offering unlimited usage, or (c) do nothing. If they chose (c), the music would stop, but users could sign up again the next month. The ad-supported business model was a risky move because Pandora had no ad server or accounting system, but it attracted so many users that in a few weeks it had a sufficient number of advertisers (including Apple) to pay for its infrastructure. In 2006, Pandora added a "Buy" button to each song being played and struck deals with Amazon, iTunes, and other online retail sites. Pandora now gets an affiliate fee for directing listeners to Amazon where users can buy the music. In 2008, Pandora added an iPhone app to allow users to sign up from their smartphones and listen all day if they wanted. By 2009, this "free" ad-supported model had attracted 20 million users.

After attracting a sufficiently large user base, Pandora turned its attention back to its premium service. In late 2009, the company launched Pandora One, a high-end version of its service that offered no advertising, higher-quality streaming music, a desktop app, and fewer usage limits. The service cost $36 a year. This time around it met with much more success, so much so that Pandora went public in June 2011. By

2015, Pandora had a projected $1.16 billion in revenue with about 80% coming from advertising and the remainder from subscriptions and other sources.

However, Pandora has not yet shown a profit, and its stock price has slowly declined. The company is experiencing slowing growth rates in its number of active users, registering just a 5% increase in users in 2014, compared to an 8% increase the year prior. Music licensing costs are likely to sharply increase in the coming years, clouding their path to profitability further. And the company faces increasingly stiff competition from services such as Spotify, which also is using the freemium strategy. Fully paid services like Apple-backed Apple Music, as well as much-hyped new entrants like Tidal, founded by Jay Z and a slew of other high profile artists, represent threats to Pandora as well. But the picture isn't totally bleak: Pandora has continued to show growth in advertising revenue and in listener hours, as its active users are listening more and more.

While freemium clearly has worked to grow companies like Pandora, LinkedIn, and Dropbox, there is ongoing debate about the effectiveness of the freemium strategy. The crux of the issue is that while freemium can be an efficient way to gather a large group of potential customers, companies have found that it's a challenge to convert eyeballs into those willing to pay. Absent subscriber revenue, firms are forced to rely on advertising revenues.

Apple has led a recent push against freemium music streaming services like Pandora and Spotify. In 2014, Apple, sensing a shift away from paid downloads towards streaming services, acquired Beats, which made trendy headphones and had a streaming music service, for $3 billion. Pandora and Spotify have thrived at the expense of iTunes Music Store, whose revenues have declined steeply for several years, and Apple's first attempt at a streaming service, iTunes Radio, was a bust. In 2015, Apple, after working with Beats, launched its own paid subscription streaming service app, Apple Music.

Music industry executives remain unsure of the profit potential of the freemium model, and many of them have begun to pressure Spotify to remove its free tier of service. Pandora is likely not far behind. The heads of Universal Music Group and Sony Music both expressed skepticism of the long-term prospects of the freemium model in 2015, and in 2014, Taylor Swift removed her entire catalog of music from Spotify in protest of freemium, claiming that it devalued her music. Although Apple's activities have drawn the attention of the U.S. Department of Justice antitrust division, it clearly has no intention of stopping its assault on its freemium competitors, and music labels are optimistic about Apple's ability to make paid streaming work, given Apple's deep pockets and brand cachet. But other industry analysts believe that Pandora and Spotify are headed toward profitability as their subscriber numbers continue to expand. Both Universal and Sony registered strong first-quarter results in 2015, driven by streaming services. It is not clear whether the labels are truly skeptical of freemium, or just Apple.

Whether freemium services continue to breathe life back into the music business remains to be seen, but other companies like MailChimp show how freemium can turn a company's fortunes around. The company lets anyone send e-mail to customers, manage subscriber lists, and track the performance of an e-mail marketing campaign.

SOURCES: "Form 10-Q for the Quarterly Period Ended June 30, 2015," Pandora Media, Inc., July 24, 2015; "No, Apples Music Streaming App Looks Nothing Like Beats," by Liz Stinson, Wired.com, June 11, 2015; "Pandora's Three Biggest Issues Are Both a Blessing and a Curse," by Leon Lazaroff, Thestreet.com, May 20, 2015; "Spotify: Freemium Clampdown Rumours Are 'Completely False,'" by Tim Ingham, Musicbusiness-worldwide.com, May 17, 2015; "Apple, Spotify, and the Battle Over Freemium," by Jingping Zhang, Harvard Business Review, May 13, 2015; "Why Apple Wants to End the Era of Free Music Streaming," by James Cook, Businessinsider. com, May 5, 2015; "Apple Pushing Music Labels to Kill Free Spotify Streaming Ahead of Beats Relaunch," by Micah Singleton, Theverge.com, May 4, 2015; "Pandora Falls on Wider Losses; Future Remains Grim," by Trefis Team, *Forbes*, April 27, 2015; "Pandora Earnings Return to the Same Old Song," by Joan E. Solsman, Cnet.com, April 23, 2015; "Apple and Beats Developing Streaming Music Service to Rival Spotify," by Ben Sisario and Brian X. Chen, *New York Times,* March 25, 2015; "Sony Music Boss Doug Morris: 'In General, Free is Death,'" by Stuart Dredge, Musically.com, March 12, 2015; "Form 10-K for the Fiscal Year Ended December 31, 2014," Pandora Media, Inc., February 11, 2015; "Making 'Freemium' Work," by Vineet Kumar, *Harvard Business Review*, May 2014; "How MailChimp Learned to Treat Data Like Orange Juice and Rethink the Email in the Process," by Derrick Harris, Gigaom.com, May 5, 2013; "Remember Ning? Once-buzzy Social Network Has Relaunched Again as a Publishing Platform," by Eliza Kern, Gigaom.com, March 25, 2013; "When Freemium Fails," by Sarah E. Needleman and Angus Loten, *Wall Street Journal*, August 22, 2012; "Glam Media Completes Ning Acquisition," press release, December 5, 2011; "Pandora IPO Prices at $16; Valuation $2.6 Billion," by Eric Savitz, Blogs. forbes.com, June 14, 2011; "Social-Networking Site Ning: Charging Users Works for Us," by Jennifer Valentino-DeVries, *Wall Street Journal*, April 13, 2011; "Explainer: What Is the Freemium Business Model," by Pascal-Emmanuel Gobry, *San Francisco Chronicle*, April 8, 2011; "Shattering Myths About 'Free-mium' Services: Mobility is Key," by Martin Scott, *WirelessWeek*, April 7, 2011; "Going Freemium: One Year Later," by Ben Chestnut, Blog.mailchimp.com, September 27, 2010; "How to Avoid the Traps

Despite the powerful tools it gives marketers, and its open applications programming interface, after 10 years in business, the company had only 85,000 paid subscribers.

In 2009, MailChimp began giving away its basic tools and charging subscription fees for special features, expecting that users would be more willing to pay for analytics and other services as their e-mail lists grew. In just over a year, MailChimp went from 85,000 to 450,000 users. E-mail volume went from 200 million a month to around 700 million. Most importantly, the number of paying customers increased more than 150%, while profit increased more than 650%!

For MailChimp, freemium has been worth the price. It currently supports more than 8 million subscribers worldwide, sending about 18 billion e-mails a month. However, Ning, a company originally founded to enable companies and individual users to create their own social networks, tried freemium and came to a different conclusion. Venture capitalist Marc Andreessen, founder of Netscape and co-creator of the first Web browser, launched Ning in 2004. With his assistance, the company raised $119 million in funding. Despite being the market's leading social network infrastructure platform, Ning was having a common problem—converting eyeballs into paying customers. While 13% of customers were paying for some premium services, the revenue was not enough. The more free users Ning acquired, the more it cost the company.

In May 2010, Ning announced the impending end of its freemium strategy. The company shed staff, going from 167 to 98, and began using 100% of its resources to capture premium users. Since shifting to a three-tier paid subscription model, Ning has experienced explosive growth, increasing the number of paying customers from 17,000 to more than 100,000 and growing revenue by more than 500%. By September 2011, Ning had more than 100 million registered user social profiles and its social networks reached more than 60 million monthly unique users. After its 2011 acquisition by Glam Media for $200 million and 2013 relaunch, Ning continues to charge users a fee after a free trial period, rather than returning to its old freemium strategy.

So when does it make sense to include freemium in a business plan? It makes sense when the product is easy to use and has a very large potential audience, preferably in the millions. Using a freemium strategy can be a very successful marketing tool, because free features can help attract a user base, and are more attractive to most consumers than 30-day free trials that require a cancellation process. A solid customer value proposition is critical. It's helpful if a large user network increases the perceived value of the product (i.e., a dating service such as Match). Freemium may work when a company has good long-term customer retention rates and the product produces more value over time. An extremely important part of the equation is that the variable costs of providing the product or service to additional customers for free must be low.

Companies also face challenges in terms of determining what products and/or services to offer for free versus what to charge for (this may change over time), the cost of supporting free customers, and how to price premium services. Further, it is difficult to predict attrition rates, which are highly variable at companies using freemium. So, while freemium can be a great way to get early users and to provide a company with a built-in pool for upgrades, it's tough to determine how many users will be willing to pay and willing to stay.

A freemium strategy makes sense for companies such as Pandora, where there is a very low marginal cost, approaching zero, to support free users. It also makes sense for a company where the value to its potential customers depends on a large network, like LinkedIn. Freemium also works when a business can be supported by the percentage of customers who are willing to pay, like Pandora, especially when there are other revenues like advertising fees that can make up for shortfalls in subscriber revenues. The freemium music streaming services don't have to worry about their business model being sound strategy, but they do have to worry about industry goliaths like Apple and the record labels taking a stand against them.

and Make a 'Freemium' Business Model Pay," Anna Johnson, Kikabink.com, June 14th, 2010; "6 Ways for Online Business Directories to Convert More Freemium to Premium," BusinessWeek.com, April 14, 2010; "Case Studies in Freemium: Pandora, Dropbox, Evernote, Automattic and MailChimp," by Liz Gannes, Gigaom.com, March 26, 2010; *Free: The Future of a Radical Price*, by Chris Anderson, Hyperion, 2009.

Case Study Questions

1. Compare Pandora's original business model with its current business model. What's the difference between "free" and "freemium" revenue models?

2. What is the customer value proposition that Pandora offers?

3. Why did MailChimp ultimately succeed with a freemium model but Ning did not?

4. What's the most important consideration when considering a freemium revenue model?

2.6 REVIEW

KEY CONCEPTS

■ **Identify the key components of e-commerce business models.**

A successful business model effectively addresses eight key elements:

- *Value proposition*—how a company's product or service fulfills the needs of customers. Typical e-commerce value propositions include personalization, customization, convenience, and reduction of product search and price delivery costs.
- *Revenue model*—how the company plans to make money from its operations. Major e-commerce revenue models include the advertising model, subscription model, transaction fee model, sales model, and affiliate model.
- *Market opportunity*—the revenue potential within a company's intended marketspace.
- *Competitive environment*—the direct and indirect competitors doing business in the same marketspace, including how many there are and how profitable they are.
- *Competitive advantage*—the factors that differentiate the business from its competition, enabling it to provide a superior product at a lower cost.
- *Market strategy*—the plan a company develops that outlines how it will enter a market and attract customers.
- *Organizational development*—the process of defining all the functions within a business and the skills necessary to perform each job, as well as the process of recruiting and hiring strong employees.
- *Management team*—the group of individuals retained to guide the company's growth and expansion.

■ **Describe the major B2C business models.**

There are a number of different business models being used in the B2C e-commerce arena. The major models include the following:

- *Portal*—offers powerful search tools plus an integrated package of content and services; typically utilizes a combined subscription/advertising revenue/transaction fee model; may be general or specialized (vortal).
- *E-tailer*—online version of traditional retailer; includes virtual merchants (online retail store only), bricks-and-clicks e-tailers (online distribution channel for a company that also has physical stores), catalog merchants (online version of direct mail catalog), and manufacturers selling directly to the consumer.
- *Content provider*—information and entertainment companies that provide digital content; typically utilizes an advertising, subscription, or affiliate referral fee revenue model.
- *Transaction broker*—processes online sales transactions; typically utilizes a transaction fee revenue model.
- *Market creator*—uses Internet technology to create markets that bring buyers and sellers together; typically utilizes a transaction fee revenue model.
- *Service provider*—offers services online.
- *Community provider*—provides an online community of like-minded individuals for networking and information sharing; revenue is generated by advertising, referral fees, and subscriptions.

■ **Describe the major B2B business models.**

The major business models used to date in the B2B arena include:

- *E-distributor*—supplies products directly to individual businesses.
- *E-procurement*—single firms create digital markets for thousands of sellers and buyers.
- *Exchange*—independently owned digital marketplace for direct inputs, usually for a vertical industry group.
- *Industry consortium*—industry-owned vertical digital market.
- *Private industrial network*—industry-owned private industrial network that coordinates supply chains with a limited set of partners.

■ **Understand key business concepts and strategies applicable to e-commerce.**

E-commerce has had a major impact on the business environment in the last decade, and have affected:

- *Industry structure*—the nature of players in an industry and their relative bargaining power by changing the basis of competition among rivals, the barriers to entry, the threat of new substitute products, the strength of suppliers, and the bargaining power of buyers.
- *Industry value chains*—the set of activities performed in an industry by suppliers, manufacturers, transporters, distributors, and retailers that transforms raw inputs into final products and services by reducing the cost of information and other transaction costs.
- *Firm value chains*—the set of activities performed within an individual firm to create final products from raw inputs by increasing operational efficiency.
- *Business strategy*—a set of plans for achieving superior long-term returns on the capital invested in a firm by offering unique ways to differentiate products, obtain cost advantages, compete globally, or compete in a narrow market or product segment.

QUESTIONS

1. What is a business model? How does it differ from a business plan?
2. What are the eight key components of an effective business model?

3. What are Amazon's primary customer value propositions?
4. Describe the five primary revenue models used by e-commerce firms.
5. Why is targeting a market niche generally smarter for a community provider than targeting a large market segment?
6. Would you say that Amazon and eBay are direct or indirect competitors? (You may have to visit the Web sites to answer.)
7. What are some of the specific ways that a company can obtain a competitive advantage?
8. Besides advertising and product sampling, what are some other market strategies a company might pursue?
9. How do venture capitalists differ from angel investors?
10. Why is it difficult to categorize e-commerce business models?
11. Besides the examples given in the chapter, what are some other examples of vertical and horizontal portals in existence today?
12. What are the major differences between virtual storefronts, such as Bluefly, and bricks-and-clicks operations, such as Walmart? What are the advantages and disadvantages of each?
13. Besides news and articles, what other forms of information or content do content providers offer?
14. What is a reverse auction? What company is an example of this type of business?
15. What are the key success factors for exchanges? How are they different from portals?
16. How have the unique features of e-commerce technology changed industry structure in the travel business?
17. Who are the major players in an industry value chain and how are they impacted by e-commerce technology?
18. What are five generic business strategies for achieving a profitable business?
19. What is the difference between a market opportunity and a marketspace?
20. What is crowdfunding and how does it help e-commerce companies raise capital?

PROJECTS

1. Select an e-commerce company. Visit its Web site and describe its business model based on the information you find there. Identify its customer value proposition, its revenue model, the marketspace it operates in, who its main competitors are, any comparative advantages you believe the company possesses, and what its market strategy appears to be. Also try to locate information about the company's management team and organizational structure. (Check for a page labeled "the Company," "About Us," or something similar.)

2. Examine the experience of shopping online versus shopping in a traditional environment. Imagine that you have decided to purchase a digital camera (or any other item of your choosing). First, shop for the camera in a traditional manner. Describe how you would do so (for example, how you would gather the necessary information you would need to choose a particular item, what stores you would visit, how long it would take, prices, etc.). Next, shop for the item on the Web or via a mobile app. Compare and contrast your experiences. What were the advantages and disadvantages of each? Which did you prefer and why?

3. Visit eBay and look at the many types of auctions available. If you were considering establishing a rival specialized online auction business, what are the top three market opportunities you would pursue, based on the goods and auction community in evidence at eBay? Prepare a report or slide presentation to support your analysis and approach.

4. During the early days of e-commerce, first-mover advantage was touted as one way to success. On the other hand, some suggest that being a market follower can yield rewards as well. Which approach has proven to be more successful—first mover or follower? Choose two e-commerce companies that prove your point, and prepare a brief presentation to explain your analysis and position.

5. Select an e-commerce company that has participated in an incubator program such as Y Combinator, TechStars, DreamIt, Capital Factory, or another of your choosing, and write a short report on its business model and the amount and sources of capital it has raised thus far. Include your views on the company's future prospects for success.

6. Create an elevator pitch for the company you select for Project 5.

7. Select a B2C e-commerce retail industry segment such as pet products, sporting goods, or toys, and analyze its value chain and industry value chain. Prepare a short presentation that identifies the major industry participants in that business and illustrates the move from raw materials to finished product.

REFERENCES

Arthur, W. Brian. "Increasing Returns and the New World of Business." *Harvard Business Review* (July–August 1996).

Barney, J. B. "Firm Resources and Sustained Competitive Advantage." *Journal of Management* Vol. 17, No. 1 (1991).

Bellman, Steven, Gerald L. Lohse, and Eric J. Johnson. "Predictors of Online Buying Behavior." *Communications of the ACM* (December 1999).

comScore, "comScore Releases July 2014 U.S. Top 50 Web Property, Search and Online Video Rankings." (August 18, 2014).

eBay, Inc. "eBay Inc. Reports Second Quarter Results." (July 16, 2015).

Kambil, Ajit, Ari Ginsberg, and Michael Bloch. "Reinventing Value Propositions." Working Paper, NYU Center for Research on Information Systems (1998).

Kanter, Elizabeth Ross. "The Ten Deadly Mistakes of Wanna-Dots." *Harvard Business Review* (January 2001).

Kaplan, Steven, and Mohanbir Sawhney. "E-Hubs: The New B2B Marketplaces." *Harvard Business Review* (May–June 2000).

Kim, W. Chan, and Renee Mauborgne. "Knowing a Winning Business Idea When You See One." *Harvard Business Review* (September-October 2000).

Magretta, Joan. "Why Business Models Matter." *Harvard Business Review* (May 2002).

Porter, Michael E. "Strategy and the Internet." *Harvard Business Review* (March 2001).

Porter, Michael E. *Competitive Advantage: Creating and Sustaining Superior Performance.* New York: Free Press (1985).

Rigdon, Joan I. "The Second-Mover Advantage." *Red Herring* (September 1, 2000).

Teece, David J. "Profiting from Technological Innovation: Implications for Integration, Collaboration, Licensing and Public Policy." *Research Policy* 15 (1986).

Technology Infrastructure for E-commerce

CHAPTER 3

E-commerce Infrastructure: The Internet, Web, and Mobile Platform

After reading this chapter, you will be able to:

- Discuss the origins of, and the key technology concepts behind, the Internet.
- Explain the current structure of the Internet.
- Understand the limitations of today's Internet and the potential capabilities of the Internet of the future.
- Understand how the Web works.
- Describe how Internet and Web features and services support e-commerce.
- Understand the impact of m-commerce applications.

The Apple Watch:

Bringing the Internet of Things to Your Wrist

Apple has a rich history of disrupting the technology landscape, dating back to the Mac computer and its revolutionary graphical user interface in the mid-1980s. More recently, we all know about the impact the iPod, iPhone, and iPad have had on our daily lives and on society in general. In 2015, Apple unveiled its most recent attempt at disruptive, groundbreaking technology in the post-Steve Jobs era: the Apple Watch. Apple hopes that the Apple Watch will join these other devices as an indispensable component of our lives.

© Ian Masterton /Alamy

The Apple Watch is one of the latest examples of wearable computing, a fast-emerging field with potential applications in healthcare, medicine, fitness, the military, gaming, and many other areas. Defined broadly as any electronic technology incorporated into clothing and wearable accessories, examples of wearable technology include wristbands and watches, smart clothing and footwear, and smart glasses. Until recently, wearable technology has been too bulky or unwieldy to be useful, but the proliferation of smaller, more compact, more powerful devices and the resulting improvements in computing power have made wearable computing possible. Wearable technology could be invaluable for any job requiring the use of both hands, including field technicians, manufacturing, military personnel, truck drivers, and law enforcement.

Although Google's attempt at smart glasses, Google Glass, fell flat, analysts view wearable computing as an industry primed for explosive growth in the near future. According to market research firm IDC, about 45 million wearable computing devices will be shipped in 2015; that number is projected to grow to 126 million by 2019. Wearable computing is expected to grow into a $34 billion business by 2020. However, the market for wearable computing is so new and evolving so quickly that even these projections could quickly become obsolete.

Sensing these trends earlier than most, Apple has been building and fine-tuning the Apple Watch for several years. Ironically, one of the guiding principles behind the development of the Watch is the idea that we have become increasingly dependent on our smartphones, a trend that Apple itself has fueled. Anywhere you go, you can find people staring down at their phones in a trance instead of interacting with the world around them.

One of Apple's goals for the Watch is to act as a filter to much of the information overload of a smartphone, only notifying users when truly critical information requires attention.

As a result, the Apple Watch prioritizes speed above depth of engagement. In its development, features that required longer than 10 seconds to use were scrapped in favor of shorter, more concise interactions. When it launched, many of the features of the Apple Watch, such as apps, required a nearby iPhone to complete, somewhat defeating the purpose of the Watch as a stand-alone piece of technology. But just as with the iPod and iPhone, Apple designed the Watch as a piece of technology with room to grow and develop. In its first sweeping update for the device, Apple allowed Watch apps to run natively on the device, doing away with the need for an iPhone nearby and dramatically improving the speed of the Watch.

Apple also placed its typical emphasis on elegance and simplicity of design when developing the Watch, both in its outward appearance and its underlying technology. The Watch is equipped with a scrolling wheel called the Digital Crown. This wheel allows users to select apps and other features more quickly than using the touch screen, which is significantly smaller than many iPhone users will be used to. It also functions as a button that returns users to the home screen when pressed. Directly underneath the Digital Crown is the Apple Pay button, which allows Watch wearers to quickly pay for transactions. The prominence of the Apple Pay button on the Watch suggests that Apple wants the Watch to become a popular way to make mobile payments.

The Watch screen is a flexible retina display that uses a feature called Force Touch. Force Touch allows the Watch to detect the strength of each touch of the screen, performing different functions based on the force of the touch. On the back of the watch are four sensors, consisting of sapphire lenses and photodiode sensors that can monitor the user's vital signs and movements. Movement is used to control many functions of the Watch; for example, when receiving an incoming text message by lifting your arm to view the notification, lowering your arm again will hide the notification, saving it for later. The Watch comes in three price ranges, Sport, Watch, and Edition. Most Watch wearers will opt for the Sport, the basic $349 model, while the fashion-conscious (and deep-pocketed) may opt for the Edition, a $17,000 gold plated version of the Watch. There are a wide variety of options for watch faces, straps and strap sizes, and other add-ons.

Perhaps the most unique feature of the Apple Watch with regard to the user experience is the Taptic Engine, a form of haptic technology that applies gentle pressure to the skin to deliver information and alerts to the user. Our bodies are just another user interface for the Watch. Wearers are alerted to different types of incoming information depending on the number, cadence, and force of the taps. Right now, the Taptic Engine gives users a tap to indicate when an Apple Pay transaction has successfully completed, for example. Different taps designate incoming phone calls, upcoming meetings, text messages, and news alerts. When using GPS, different taps can designate different steps on the route. App developers are very excited about the potential uses for this technology. The Apple Watch might someday tap you to let you know that you're leaving the house without a winter coat on a cold day, or that your blood sugar is low and you need to eat.

For the time being, many critics of the device rightly point out that nearly all of what the Watch can do, the iPhone can also do, and often do better. On the other hand, because of its compatibility with apps and the Taptic Engine, the capabilities of the Watch in 2020 may be unrecognizable compared to its capabilities in 2015. In addition to enabling apps to run natively, the first major update to the Watch also allowed developers to use more of the sensors and capabilities of the watch. This will allow the Watch to differentiate itself quickly from the iPhone and iPad, although the future versions of the iPhone will also be equipped with haptic technology. Siri is also much more accurate on the Watch than on any other Apple platform before it, and a new feature called Quickboard automatically suggests sensible responses to incoming messages.

Major retailers and other app developers have lined up in droves to create Apple Watch apps, despite the fact that the mobile shopping experience can be quite limited on the Watch, and that advertising is limited to ten seconds or less along with all of its other features. The device launched with 3,500 apps already available, including many from major retailers such as eBay, Amazon, and Target. Some online retailers are experimenting with the ability to bookmark an item on the Watch for future viewing on a phone or desktop. Bricks-and-mortar retailers like JCPenney and Kohl's have also developed apps, and many of these retailers hope to add features that improve the in-store shopping experience for Watch wearers. Users might be able to use a retailer's Watch app to avoid long lines in stores, find items more efficiently with interactive store maps, and pay for their purchases with Apple Pay.

Although the functionality of the Watch may currently be slightly underwhelming, users appear to be extremely satisfied so far, with 97% of Watch wearers reporting satisfaction with their device. That was better than the first iterations of the iPad and the iPhone. Apple debuted the Watch in the second quarter of 2015, and immediately shipped 3.6 million units. This quickly cemented the device as a success in the wearable computing market, coming in second only behind Fitbit's 4.4 million units. Fitbit is a popular fitness tool, also worn around the wrist, but it's considered a "basic" wearable because it cannot run 3rd party apps. The Apple Watch may grow to have most or all of Fitbit's functionality along with a host of other capabilities. On the other hand, Fitbits sell for as low as $100 for older models, and work with all types of smartphones, including Androids. The Apple Watch will have to contend with Fitbit and other niche devices that may sacrifice some functionality for a much lower cost. Other competitors in the wearables marketspace include low-cost wearable maker Xiaomi, Samsung, and Garmin. Thirty percent of smartphone owners in the United States own or plan to buy a wearable device in the near future, creating a big opportunity for Apple to establish dominance in an emerging market.

Ultimately, the Apple Watch is likely to have the functionality that its users want it to have. Will it be a fitness and health tool? The new frontier in mobile payments? An indispensable in-store shopping buddy? A must-have complement to the iPhone? Or something completely unforeseen? Apple would prefer it be all of these, and become the next great Apple product; but the Watch has a ways to go, both in sales and functionality, until it reaches that level of success.

SOURCES: "Your Guide to Apple's Watch Update," by Dan Graziano, Cnet.com, September 24, 2015; "Apple Improves the Watch, Slightly," by Farhad Manjoo, *New York Times,* September 21, 2015; "Smartwatch Growth Predicted, Thanks Largely to Apple Watch," by Matt Hamblen, Computerworld. com, September 18, 2015; "The Apple Watch Is Already Crushing the Competition, According to a New Study," by Lisa Eadicicco, Businessinsider.com, August 27, 2015; "In Apple Watch Debut, Signs of a Familiar Path to Success," by Farhad Manjoo, *New York Times,* July 22, 2015; "Wearable Computing Market by Application, by Technology, & Geography - Global Forecast to 2020," Prnewswire.com, July 16, 2015; "How Ecommerce Marketers Are Adapting to the Apple Watch," by Eric Samson, Entrepreneur.com, June 03, 2015; "Are Wearables the Next In-Store Shopping Buddies?" eMarketer, Inc., May 29, 2015; "Are We Really Going to Shop From the Apple Watch? What Retail Apps are Trying to Achieve," by Rachel Arthur, *Forbes,* May 7, 2015; "iPhone Killer: The Secret History of the Apple Watch," David Pierce, Wired.com, April 2015; "Apple Watch Is Already Attracting E-Commerce Players," by Rebecca Borison, Thestreet.com, April 24, 2015; "Worldwide Wearables Market Forecast to Reach 45.7 Million Units Shipped in 2015 and 126.1 Million Units in 2019, According to IDC," IDC.com, March 30, 2015; "Wearables: The Next Mobile Payment Device?" eMarketer, Inc., March 3, 2015; "Taptic, Haptics, and the Body Fantastic: The Real Apple Watch Revolution," by Brian S. Hall, Macworld.com, October 3, 2014; "Inside the Apple Watch: The Tech Behind Apple's New Wearable," by Adario Strange, Mashable.com, September 9, 2014.

T his chapter examines the Internet, Web, and mobile platform of today and tomorrow, how it evolved, how it works, and how its present and future infrastructure enables new business opportunities.

The opening case illustrates the importance of understanding how the Internet and related technologies work, and to be aware of what's new. The Internet and its underlying technology are not static phenomena, but instead continue to change over time. Computers have merged with cell phone services; broadband access in the home and broadband wireless access to the Internet via smartphones, tablet computers, and laptops are expanding rapidly; self-publishing on the Web via social networks and blogging now engages millions of Internet users; and software technologies such as cloud computing, and smartphone apps are revolutionizing the way businesses are using the Internet. Looking forward a few years, the business strategies of the future will require a firm understanding of these technologies and new ones, such as different types of wearable technology like the Apple Watch profiled in the opening case, the Internet of Things, and the "smart/connected" movement (smart homes, smart TVs, and connected cars) to deliver products and services to consumers. **Table 3.1** summarizes some of the most important developments in e-commerce infrastructure for 2015–2016.

3.1 THE INTERNET: TECHNOLOGY BACKGROUND

What is the Internet? Where did it come from, and how did it support the growth of the Web? What are the Internet's most important operating principles? How much do you really need to know about the technology of the Internet?

Let's take the last question first. The answer is: It depends on your career interests. If you are on a marketing career path, or general managerial business path, then you need to know the basics about Internet technology, which you'll learn in this and the following chapter. If you are on a technical career path and hope to become a Web designer, or pursue a technical career in Web infrastructure for businesses, you'll need to start with these basics and then build from there. You'll also need to know about the business side of e-commerce, which you will learn about throughout this book.

As noted in Chapter 1, the **Internet** is an interconnected network of thousands of networks and millions of computers (sometimes called *host computers* or just *hosts*) linking businesses, educational institutions, government agencies, and individuals. The Internet provides approximately 3.1 billion people around the world (including about 260 million people in the United States) with services such as e-mail, apps, newsgroups, shopping, research, instant messaging, music, videos, and news (eMarketer, Inc., 2015a, 2015b). No single organization controls the Internet or how it functions, nor is it owned by anybody, yet it has provided the infrastructure for a transformation in commerce, scientific research, and culture. The word *Internet* is derived from the word *internetwork*, or the connecting together of two or more computer networks. The **Web** is one of the Internet's most popular services, providing access to billions, perhaps trillions, of Web pages, which are documents created in a

Internet
an interconnected network of thousands of networks and millions of computers linking businesses, educational institutions, government agencies, and individuals

Web
one of the Internet's most popular services, providing access to billions, and perhaps trillions, of Web pages

TABLE 3.1	TRENDS IN E-COMMERCE INFRASTRUCTURE 2015–2016

BUSINESS

- Mobile devices become the primary access point to social network services and a rapidly expanding social marketing and advertising platform, and create a foundation for location-based Web services and business models.
- Explosion of Internet content services and mobile access devices strains the business models of Internet backbone providers (the large telecommunication carriers).
- The growth in cloud computing and bandwidth capacity enables new business models for distributing music, movies, and television.
- Search becomes more social and local, enabling social and local commerce business models.
- Internet backbone carriers initiate differential pricing models so that users pay for bandwidth usage.
- "Big Data" produced by the Internet creates new business opportunities for firms with the analytic capability to understand it.

TECHNOLOGY

- Mobile devices such as smartphones and tablet computers have become the dominant mode of access to the Internet. The new client is mobile.
- The explosion of mobile apps threatens the dominance of the Web as the main source of online software applications and leads some to claim the Web is dead.
- HTML5 grows in popularity among publishers and developers and makes possible Web applications that are just as visually rich and lively as native mobile apps.
- Cloud computing reshapes computing and storage, and becomes an important force in the delivery of software applications and online content.
- The Internet runs out of IPv4 addresses; the transition to IPv6 continues.
- The decreased cost of storage and advances in database software lead to explosion in online data collection known as Big Data and creates new business opportunities for firms with the analytic capability to understand it.
- The Internet of Things, with millions of sensor-equipped devices connecting to the Internet, starts to become a reality, and is powering the development of smart connected "things" such as televisions, houses, cars, and wearable technology.

SOCIETY

- Governance of the Internet becomes more involved with conflicts between nations; the United States plans to give up control over IANA, which administers the Internet's IP addressing system.
- Government control over, and surveillance of, the Internet is expanded in most advanced nations, and in many nations the Internet is nearly completely controlled by government agencies.
- The growing infrastructure for tracking online and mobile consumer behavior conflicts with individual claims to privacy and control over personal information.

programming language called HTML that can contain text, graphics, audio, video, and other objects, as well as "hyperlinks" that permit users to jump easily from one page to another. Web pages are navigated using browser software.

THE EVOLUTION OF THE INTERNET: 1961—THE PRESENT

Today's Internet has evolved over the last 55 or so years. In this sense, the Internet is not "new;" it did not happen yesterday. Although journalists talk glibly about "Internet" time—suggesting a fast-paced, nearly instant, worldwide global change mechanism—in fact, it has taken about 55 years of hard work to arrive at today's Internet.

The history of the Internet can be segmented into three phases (see **Figure 3.1**). In the first phase, the *Innovation Phase,* from 1961 to 1974, the fundamental building blocks of the Internet were conceptualized and then realized in actual hardware and software. The basic building blocks are packet-switching hardware, a communications protocol called TCP/IP, and client/server computing (all described more fully later in this section). The original purpose of the Internet, when it was conceived in the 1960s, was to link large mainframe computers on different college campuses. This kind of one-to-one communication between campuses was previously only possible through the telephone system or private networks owned by the large computer manufacturers.

In the second phase, the *Institutionalization Phase*, from 1975 to 1995, large institutions such as the U.S. Department of Defense (DoD) and the National Science Foundation (NSF) provided funding and legitimization for the fledging invention called the Internet. Once the concepts behind the Internet had been proven in several government-supported demonstration projects, the DoD contributed $1 million to further develop them into a robust military communications system that could withstand nuclear war. This effort created what was then called ARPANET (Advanced Research Projects Agency Network). In 1986, the NSF assumed responsibility for the development of a civilian Internet (then called NSFNET) and began a 10-year-long $200 million expansion program.

In the third phase, the *Commercialization Phase*, from 1995 to the present, government agencies encouraged private corporations to take over and expand both the Internet backbone and local service to ordinary citizens—families and individuals across America and the world who were not students on campuses. By 2000, the Internet's use had expanded well beyond military installations and research universities. See **Table 3.2** on pages 114–116 for a closer look at the development of the Internet from 1961 on.

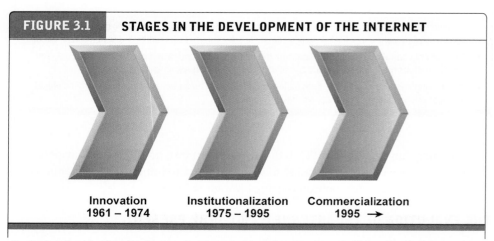

| FIGURE 3.1 | STAGES IN THE DEVELOPMENT OF THE INTERNET |

Innovation
1961 – 1974

Institutionalization
1975 – 1995

Commercialization
1995 →

The Internet has developed in three stages over approximately a 55-year period from 1961 to the present. In the Innovation stage, basic ideas and technologies were developed; in the Institutionalization stage, these ideas were brought to life; in the Commercialization stage, once the ideas and technologies had been proven, private companies brought the Internet to millions of people worldwide.

THE INTERNET: KEY TECHNOLOGY CONCEPTS

In 1995, the Federal Networking Council (FNC) passed a resolution formally defining the term *Internet* as a network that uses the IP addressing scheme, supports the Transmission Control Protocol (TCP), and makes services available to users much like a telephone system makes voice and data services available to the public (see **Figure 3.2**).

Behind this formal definition are three extremely important concepts that are the basis for understanding the Internet: packet switching, the TCP/IP communications protocol, and client/server computing. Although the Internet has evolved and changed dramatically in the last 30 years, these three concepts are at the core of the way the Internet functions today and are the foundation for the Internet of the future.

Packet Switching

Packet switching is a method of slicing digital messages into discrete units called **packets**, sending the packets along different communication paths as they become available, and then reassembling the packets once they arrive at their destination (see **Figure 3.3** on page 117). Prior to the development of packet switching, early computer networks used leased, dedicated telephone circuits to communicate with terminals and other computers. In circuit-switched networks such as the telephone system, a complete point-to-point circuit is put together, and then communication can proceed. However, these "dedicated" circuit-switching techniques were expensive and wasted available communications capacity—the circuit would be maintained regardless of whether any data was being sent. For nearly 70% of the time, a dedicated voice circuit is not being fully used because of pauses between words and delays in assembling the

packet switching
a method of slicing digital messages into packets, sending the packets along different communication paths as they become available, and then reassembling the packets once they arrive at their destination

packets
the discrete units into which digital messages are sliced for transmission over the Internet

---

FIGURE 3.2   **RESOLUTION OF THE FEDERAL NETWORKING COUNCIL**

"The Federal Networking Council (FNC) agrees that the following language reflects our definition of the term 'Internet.'

'Internet' refers to the global information system that—

(i) is logically linked together by a globally unique address space based on the Internet Protocol (IP) or its subsequent extensions/follow-ons;

(ii) is able to support communications using the Transmission Control Protocol/Internet Protocol (TCP/IP) suite or its subsequent extensions/follow-ons, and/or other IP-compatible protocols; and

(iii) provides, uses or makes accessible, either publicly or privately, high level services layered on the communications and related infrastructure described herein."

Last modified on October 30, 1995.

SOURCE: Federal Networking Council, 1995

TABLE 3.2	DEVELOPMENT OF THE INTERNET TIMELINE	
YEAR	EVENT	SIGNIFICANCE
INNOVATION PHASE 1961–1974		
1961	Leonard Kleinrock (MIT) publishes a paper on "packet switching" networks.	The concept of packet switching is born.
1962	J.C.R. Licklider (MIT) writes memo calling for an "Intergalatic Computer Network."	The vision of a global computer network is born.
1969	BBN Technologies awarded ARPA contract to build ARPANET.	The concept of a packet-switched network moves closer toward physical reality.
1969	The first packet-switched message is sent on ARPANET from UCLA to Stanford.	The communications hardware underlying the Internet is implemented for the first time. The initial ARPANET consisted of four routers (then called Interface Message Processors (IMPs)) at UCLA, Stanford, UCSB, and the University of Utah.
1972	E-mail is invented by Ray Tomlinson of BBN. Larry Roberts writes the first e-mail utility program permitting listing, forwarding, and responding to e-mails.	The first "killer app" of the Internet is born.
1973	Bob Metcalfe (XeroxParc Labs) invents Ethernet and local area networks.	**Client/server computing is invented.** Ethernet permitted the development of local area networks and client/server computing in which thousands of fully functional desktop computers could be connected into a short-distance (<1,000 meters) network to share files, run applications, and send messages.
1974	"Open architecture" networking and TCP/IP concepts are presented in a paper by Vint Cerf (Stanford) and Bob Kahn (BBN).	**TCP/IP invented.** The conceptual foundation for a single common communications protocol that could potentially connect any of thousands of disparate local area networks and computers, and a common addressing scheme for all computers connected to the network, are born.
		Prior to this, computers could communicate only if they shared a common proprietary network architecture. With TCP/IP, computers and networks could work together regardless of their local operating systems or network protocols.
INSTITUTIONALIZATION PHASE 1975–1995		
1977	Lawrence Landweber envisions CSNET (Computer Science Network)	CSNET is a pioneering network for U.S. universities and industrial computer research groups that could not directly connect to ARPANET, and was a major milestone on the path to the development of the global Internet.
1980	TCP/IP is officially adopted as the DoD standard communications protocol.	The single largest computing organization in the world adopts TCP/IP and packet-switched network technology.
1980	Personal computers are invented.	Altair, Apple, and IBM personal desktop computers are invented. These computers become the foundation for today's Internet, affording millions of people access to the Internet and the Web.

TABLE 3.2	DEVELOPMENT OF THE INTERNET TIMELINE (CONTINUED)	
YEAR	EVENT	SIGNIFICANCE
1984	Apple Computer releases the HyperCard program as part of its graphical user interface operating system called Macintosh.	The concept of "hyperlinked" documents and records that permit the user to jump from one page or record to another is commercially introduced.
1984	Domain Name System (DNS) introduced.	DNS provides a user-friendly system for translating IP addresses into words that people can easily understand.
1989	Tim Berners-Lee of CERN in Switzerland proposes a worldwide network of hyperlinked documents based on a common markup language called HTML—HyperText Markup Language.	**The concept of an Internet-supported service called the World Wide Web based on HTML pages is born**. The Web would be constructed from"pages" created in a common markup language, with "hyperlinks" that permitted easy access among the pages.
1990	NSF plans and assumes responsibility for a civilian Internet backbone and creates NSFNET.[1] ARPANET is decommissioned.	The concept of a "civilian" Internet open to all is realized through nonmilitary funding by NSF.
1993	The first graphical Web browser called Mosaic is invented by Marc Andreessen and others at the National Center for Supercomputing Applications at the University of Illinois.	Mosaic makes it very easy for ordinary users to connect to HTML documents anywhere on the Web. The browser-enabled Web takes off.
1994	Andreessen and Jim Clark form Netscape Corporation.	The first commercial Web browser—Netscape—becomes available.
1994	The first banner advertisements appear on Hotwired.com in October 1994.	**The beginning of e-commerce**.

COMMERCIALIZATION PHASE 1995–PRESENT

1995	NSF privatizes the backbone, and commercial carriers take over backbone operation.	**The fully commercial civilian Internet is born**. Major long-haul networks such as AT&T, Sprint, GTE, UUNet, and MCI take over operation of the backbone. Network Solutions (a private firm) is given a monopoly to assign Internet addresses.
1995	Jeff Bezos founds Amazon; Pierre Omidyar forms AuctionWeb (eBay).	E-commerce begins in earnest with pure online retail stores and auctions.
1998	The U.S. federal government encourages the founding of the Internet Corporation for Assigned Names and Numbers (ICANN).	Governance over domain names and addresses passes to a private nonprofit international organization.
1999	The first full-service Internet-only bank, First Internet Bank of Indiana, opens for business.	Business on the Web extends into traditional services.
2003	The Internet2 Abilene high-speed network is upgraded to 10 Gbps.	A major milestone toward the development of ultra-high-speed transcontinental networks several times faster than the existing backbone is achieved.

[1] "Backbone" refers to the U.S. domestic trunk lines that carry the heavy traffic across the nation, from one metropolitan area to another. Universities are given responsibility for developing their own campus networks that must be connected to the national backbone.

(continued)

TABLE 3.2	DEVELOPMENT OF THE INTERNET TIMELINE (CONTINUED)	
YEAR	**EVENT**	**SIGNIFICANCE**
2005	NSF proposes the Global Environment for Network Innovations (GENI) initiative to develop new core functionality for the Internet.	Recognition that future Internet security and functionality needs may require the thorough rethinking of existing Internet technology.
2006	The U.S. Senate Committee on Commerce, Science, and Transportation holds hearings on "Network Neutrality."	The debate grows over differential pricing based on utilization that pits backbone utility owners against online content and service providers and device makers.
2007	The Apple iPhone is introduced.	The introduction of the iPhone represents the beginning of the development of a viable mobile platform that will ultimately transform the way people interact with the Internet.
2008	The Internet Society (ISOC) identifies Trust and Identity as a primary design element for every layer of the Internet, and launches an initiative to address these issues.	The leading Internet policy group recognizes the current Internet is threatened by breaches of security and trust that are built into the existing network.
2008	Internet "cloud computing" becomes a billion-dollar industry.	Internet capacity is sufficient to support on-demand computing resources (processing and storage), as well as software applications, for large corporations and individuals.
2009	Internet-enabled smartphones become a major new Web access platform.	Smartphones extend the reach and range of the Internet to more closely realize the promise of the Internet anywhere, anytime, anyplace.
2009	Broadband stimulus package and Broadband Data Improvement Act enacted.	President Obama signs stimulus package containing $7.2 billion for the expansion of broadband access in the United States.
2011	ICANN expands domain name system.	ICANN agrees to permit the expansion of generic top-level domain names from about 300 to potentially thousands using any word in any language.
2012	World IPv6 Launch day.	Major ISPs, home networking equipment manufacturers, and Web companies begin to permanently enable IPv6 for their products and services as of June 6, 2012.
2013	The Internet of Things (IoT) starts to become a reality.	Internet technology spreads beyond the computer and mobile device to anything that can be equipped with sensors, leading to predictions that up to 100–200 billion uniquely identifiable objects will be connected to the Internet by 2020.
2014	Apple introduces Apple Pay and Apple Watch.	Apple Pay is likely to become the first widely adopted mobile payment system; Apple Watch may usher in a new era of wearable Internet-connected technology and is a further harbinger of the Internet of Things.
2015	Federal Communications Commission adopts regulations mandating net neutrality.	ISPs are required to treat all data on the Internet equally and are not allowed to discriminate or charge differentially based on user, content, site, platform, application, type of equipment, or mode of communication.

SOURCES: Based on Leiner et al., 2000; Zakon, 2005; Gross, 2005; Geni.net, 2007; ISOC.org, 2010; Arstechnica.com, 2010; ICANN, 2011a; Internet Society, 2012; IEEE Computer Society, 2013.

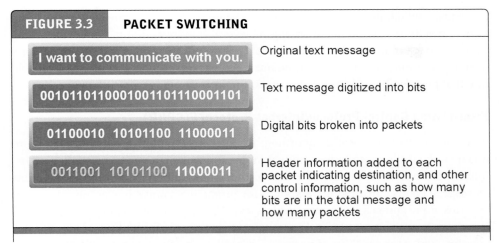

FIGURE 3.3	**PACKET SWITCHING**

I want to communicate with you.	Original text message
00101101100010011011110001101	Text message digitized into bits
01100010 10101100 11000011	Digital bits broken into packets
0011001 10101100 11000011	Header information added to each packet indicating destination, and other control information, such as how many bits are in the total message and how many packets

In packet switching, digital messages are divided into fixed-length packets of bits (generally about 1,500 bytes). Header information indicates both the origin and the ultimate destination address of the packet, the size of the message, and the number of packets the receiving node should expect. Because the receipt of each packet is acknowledged by the receiving computer, for a considerable amount of time, the network is not passing information, only acknowledgments, producing a delay called latency.

circuit segments, both of which increase the length of time required to find and connect circuits. A better technology was needed.

The first book on packet switching was written by Leonard Kleinrock in 1964 (Kleinrock, 1964), and the technique was further developed by others in the defense research labs of both the United States and England. With packet switching, the communications capacity of a network can be increased by a factor of 100 or more. (The communications capacity of a digital network is measured in terms of bits per second.[2]) Imagine if the gas mileage of your car went from 15 miles per gallon to 1,500 miles per gallon—all without changing too much of the car!

In packet-switched networks, messages are first broken down into packets. Appended to each packet are digital codes that indicate a source address (the origination point) and a destination address, as well as sequencing information and error-control information for the packet. Rather than being sent directly to the destination address, in a packet network, the packets travel from computer to computer until they reach their destination. These computers are called routers. A **router** is a special-purpose computer that interconnects the different computer networks that make up the Internet and routes packets along to their ultimate destination as they travel. To ensure that packets take the best available path toward their destination, routers use a computer program called a **routing algorithm**.

router
special-purpose computer that interconnects the computer networks that make up the Internet and routes packets to their ultimate destination as they travel the Internet

routing algorithm
computer program that ensures that packets take the best available path toward their destination

[2] A bit is a binary digit, 0 or 1. A string of eight bits constitutes a byte. A home telephone dial-up modem connects to the Internet usually at 56 Kbps (56,000 bits per second). Mbps refers to millions of bits per second, whereas Gbps refers to billions of bits per second.

protocol

a set of rules and standards for data transfer

Transmission Control Protocol/Internet Protocol (TCP/IP)

the core communications protocol for the Internet

TCP

protocol that establishes the connections among sending and receiving Web computers and handles the assembly of packets at the point of transmission, and their reassembly at the receiving end

IP

protocol that provides the Internet's addressing scheme and is responsible for the actual delivery of the packets

Network Interface Layer

responsible for placing packets on and receiving them from the network medium

Internet Layer

responsible for addressing, packaging, and routing messages on the Internet

Transport Layer

responsible for providing communication with the application by acknowledging and sequencing the packets to and from the application

Application Layer

provides a wide variety of applications with the ability to access the services of the lower layers

Packet switching does not require a dedicated circuit, but can make use of any spare capacity that is available on any of several hundred circuits. Packet switching makes nearly full use of almost all available communication lines and capacity. Moreover, if some lines are disabled or too busy, the packets can be sent on any available line that eventually leads to the destination point.

Transmission Control Protocol/Internet Protocol (TCP/IP)

While packet switching was an enormous advance in communications capacity, there was no universally agreed-upon method for breaking up digital messages into packets, routing them to the proper address, and then reassembling them into a coherent message. This was like having a system for producing stamps but no postal system (a series of post offices and a set of addresses). The answer was to develop a **protocol** (a set of rules and standards for data transfer) to govern the formatting, ordering, compressing, and error-checking of messages, as well as specify the speed of transmission and means by which devices on the network will indicate they have stopped sending and/or receiving messages.

Transmission Control Protocol/Internet Protocol (TCP/IP) has become the core communications protocol for the Internet (Cerf and Kahn, 1974). **TCP** establishes the connections among sending and receiving Web computers, and makes sure that packets sent by one computer are received in the same sequence by the other, without any packets missing. **IP** provides the Internet's addressing scheme and is responsible for the actual delivery of the packets.

TCP/IP is divided into four separate layers, with each layer handling a different aspect of the communication problem (see **Figure 3.4**). The **Network Interface Layer** is responsible for placing packets on and receiving them from the network medium, which could be a LAN (Ethernet) or Token Ring network, or other network technology. TCP/IP is independent from any local network technology and can adapt to changes at the local level. The **Internet Layer** is responsible for addressing, packaging, and routing messages on the Internet. The **Transport Layer** is responsible for providing communication with the application by acknowledging and sequencing the packets to and from the application. The **Application Layer** provides a wide variety of applications with the ability to access the services of the lower layers. Some of the best-known applications are HyperText Transfer Protocol (HTTP), File Transfer Protocol (FTP), and Simple Mail Transfer Protocol (SMTP), all of which we will discuss later in this chapter.

IP Addresses

The IP addressing scheme answers the question "How can billions of computers attached to the Internet communicate with one another?" The answer is that every computer connected to the Internet must be assigned an address—otherwise it cannot send or receive TCP packets. For instance, when you sign onto the Internet using a dial-up, DSL, or cable modem, your computer is assigned a temporary address by your Internet Service Provider. Most corporate and university computers attached to a local area network have a permanent IP address.

| FIGURE 3.4 | THE TCP/IP ARCHITECTURE AND PROTOCOL SUITE |

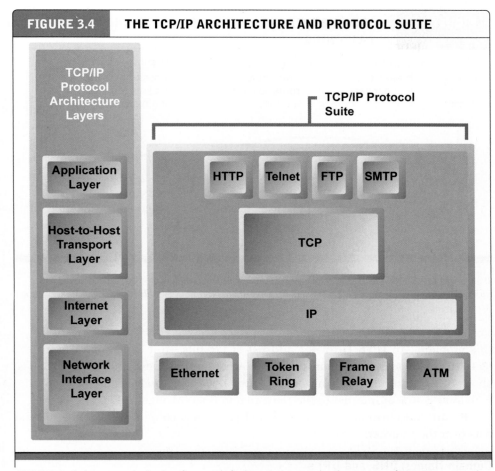

TCP/IP is an industry-standard suite of protocols for large internetworks. The purpose of TCP/IP is to provide high-speed communication network links.

There are two versions of IP currently in use: IPv4 and IPv6. An **IPv4 Internet address** is a 32-bit number that appears as a series of four separate numbers marked off by periods, such as 64.49.254.91. Each of the four numbers can range from 0–255. This "dotted quad" addressing scheme supports up to about 4 billion addresses (2 to the 32nd power). In a typical Class C network, the first three sets of numbers identify the network (in the preceding example, 64.49.254 is the local area network identification) and the last number (91) identifies a specific computer.

Because many large corporate and government domains have been given millions of IP addresses each (to accommodate their current and future work forces), and with all the new networks and new Internet-enabled devices requiring unique IP addresses being attached to the Internet, in 2015, the number of IPv4 addresses available to be assigned has shrunk significantly. In North America, only about 3.4 million remain available from the American Registry for Internet Numbers; registries in Asia and Europe have already essentially run out (McMillan, 2015). IPv6 was created to address

IPv4 Internet address
Internet address expressed as a 32-bit number that appears as a series of four separate numbers marked off by periods, such as 64.49.254.91

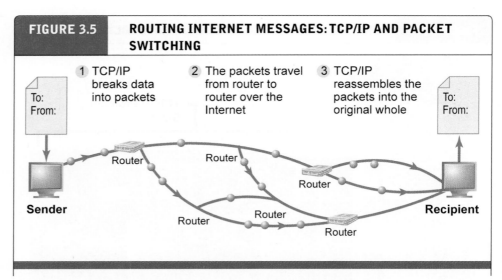

| FIGURE 3.5 | ROUTING INTERNET MESSAGES: TCP/IP AND PACKET SWITCHING |

The Internet uses packet-switched networks and the TCP/IP communications protocol to send, route, and assemble messages. Messages are broken into packets, and packets from the same message can travel along different routes.

IPv6 Internet address
Internet address expressed as a 128-bit number

this problem. An **IPv6 Internet address** is 128 bits, so it can support up to 2^{128} (3.4×10^{38}) addresses, many more than IPv4. According to Akamai, in the United States, about 20% of Internet traffic now occurs over IPv6. Belgium leads the way globally, with almost 40% of Internet traffic converted to IPv6 (Akamai, 2015).

Figure 3.5 illustrates how TCP/IP and packet switching work together to send data over the Internet.

Domain Names, DNS, and URLs

domain name
IP address expressed in natural language

Domain Name System (DNS)
system for expressing numeric IP addresses in natural language

Uniform Resource Locator (URL)
the address used by a Web browser to identify the location of content on the Web

Most people cannot remember 32-bit numbers. An IP address can be represented by a natural language convention called a **domain name**. The **Domain Name System (DNS)** allows expressions such as Cnet.com to stand for a numeric IP address (cnet.com's numeric IP is 216.239.113.101).[3] A **Uniform Resource Locator (URL)**, which is the address used by a Web browser to identify the location of content on the Web, also uses a domain name as part of the URL. A typical URL contains the protocol to be used when accessing the address, followed by its location. For instance, the URL http://www.azimuth-interactive.com/flash_test refers to the IP address 208.148.84.1 with the domain name "azimuth-interactive.com" and the protocol being used to access the address, HTTP. A resource called "flash_test" is located on the server directory path /flash_test. A URL can have from two to four parts; for example, name1.name2.name3.org. We discuss domain names and URLs further in Section 3.4. **Figure 3.6** illustrates the Domain Name System and **Table 3.3** summarizes the important components of the Internet addressing scheme.

---

[3] You can check the IP address of any domain name on the Internet. In Windows 7 or Vista, use Start/cmd to open the DOS prompt. Type ping < Domain Name >. You will receive the IP address in return.

FIGURE 3.6	THE HIERARCHICAL DOMAIN NAME SYSTEM

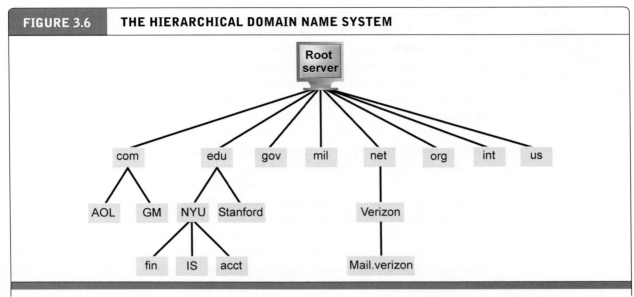

The Domain Name System is a hierarchical namespace with a root server at the top. Top-level domains appear next and identify the organization type (such as .com, .gov, .org, etc.) or geographic location (such as .uk [Great Britain] or .ca [Canada]). Second-level servers for each top-level domain assign and register second-level domain names for organizations and individuals such as IBM.com, Microsoft.com, and Stanford.edu. Finally, third-level domains identify a particular computer or group of computers within an organization, e.g., www.finance.nyu.edu.

Client/Server Computing

While packet switching exploded the available communications capacity and TCP/IP provided the communications rules and regulations, it took a revolution in computing to bring about today's Internet and the Web. That revolution is called client/server computing and without it, the Web—in all its richness—would not exist. **Client/server computing** is a model of computing in which **client** computers are connected in a

client/server computing
a model of computing in which client computers are connected in a network together with one or more servers

client
a powerful desktop computer that is part of a network

TABLE 3.3	PIECES OF THE INTERNET PUZZLE: NAMES AND ADDRESSES
IP addresses	Every device connected to the Internet must have a unique address number called an Internet Protocol (IP) address.
Domain names	The Domain Name System allows expressions such as Pearsoned.com (Pearson Education's Web site) to stand for numeric IP locations.
DNS servers	DNS servers are databases that keep track of IP addresses and domain names on the Internet.
Root servers	Root servers are central directories that list all domain names currently in use for specific domains; for example, the .com root server. DNS servers consult root servers to look up unfamiliar domain names when routing traffic.

server

networked computer dedicated to common functions that the client computers on the network need

network with one or more **servers**, which are computers that are dedicated to performing common functions that the client computers on the network need, such as file storage, software applications, printing, and Internet access. The client computers are themselves sufficiently powerful to accomplish complex tasks. Servers are networked computers dedicated to common functions that the client computers on the network need, such as file storage, software applications, utility programs that provide Web connections, and printers (see **Figure 3.7**). The Internet is a giant example of client/server computing in which millions of Web servers located around the world can be easily accessed by millions of client computers, also located throughout the world.

To appreciate what client/server computing makes possible, you must understand what preceded it. In the mainframe computing environment of the 1960s and 1970s, computing power was very expensive and limited. For instance, the largest commercial mainframes of the late 1960s had 128k of RAM and 10-megabyte disk drives, and occupied hundreds of square feet. There was insufficient computing capacity to support graphics or color in text documents, let alone sound files, video, or hyperlinked documents. In this period, computing was entirely centralized: all work was done by a single mainframe computer, and users were connected to the mainframe using terminals.

With the development of personal computers and local area networks during the late 1970s and early 1980s, client/server computing became possible. Client/server computing has many advantages over centralized mainframe computing. For instance, it is easy to expand capacity by adding servers and clients. Also, client/server networks are less vulnerable than centralized computing architectures. If one server goes down, backup or mirror servers can pick up the slack; if a client computer is inoperable, the rest of the network continues operating. Moreover, processing load is balanced over many powerful smaller computers rather than being concentrated in a single huge computer that performs processing for everyone. Both software and hardware in client/server environments can be built more simply and economically.

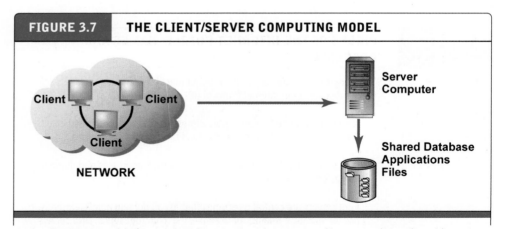

FIGURE 3.7 | **THE CLIENT/SERVER COMPUTING MODEL**

In the client/server model of computing, client computers are connected in a network together with one or more servers.

In 2015, there were about 1.8 billion personal computers in use around the world (Imbert, 2015). Personal computing capabilities have also moved to smartphones and tablet computers (all much "thinner" clients with a bit less computing horsepower, and limited memory, but which rely on Internet servers to accomplish their tasks). In the process, more computer processing will be performed by central servers.

THE NEW CLIENT: THE MOBILE PLATFORM

There's a new client in town. The primary means of accessing the Internet both in the United States and worldwide is now through highly portable smartphones and tablet computers, and not traditional desktop or laptop PCs. This means that the primary platform for e-commerce products and services is also changing to a mobile platform.

The change in hardware has reached a tipping point. The form factor of PCs has changed from desktops to laptops and tablet computers such as the iPad (and more than 100 other competitors). Tablets are lighter, do not require a complex operating system, and rely on the Internet cloud to provide processing and storage. And, while there are an estimated 1.8 billion PCs in the world, the number of cell phones long ago exceeded the population of PCs. In 2015, there are an estimated 4.43 billion worldwide mobile phone users, with 258 million in the United States, around 1 billion in China, and 638 million in India. The population of mobile phone users is almost three times that of PC owners. Around 42%, or 1.84 billion, of the world's mobile phone users are smartphone users. In the United States, about 194 million people access the Internet using mobile devices, mostly smartphones and tablets (eMarketer, Inc., 2015c, 2015d, 2015e). Briefly, the Internet world is turning into a lighter, mobile platform. The tablet is not replacing PCs so much as supplementing PCs for use in mobile situations.

Smartphones are a disruptive technology that radically alters the personal computing and e-commerce landscape. Smartphones have created a major shift in computer processors and software that has disrupted the dual monopolies long established by Intel and Microsoft, whose chips, operating systems, and software applications began dominating the PC market in 1982. Few smartphones use Intel chips, which power 90% of the world's PCs; only a small percentage of smartphones use Microsoft's operating system (Windows Mobile). Instead, smartphone manufacturers either purchase operating systems such as Symbian, the world leader, or build their own, such as Apple's iPhone iOS, typically based on Linux and Java platforms. Smartphones do not use power-hungry hard drives but instead use flash memory chips with storage up to 64 gigabytes that also require much less power.

The mobile platform has profound implications for e-commerce because it influences how, where, and when consumers shop and buy.

THE INTERNET "CLOUD COMPUTING" MODEL: HARDWARE AND SOFTWARE AS A SERVICE

Cloud computing is a model of computing in which computer processing, storage, software, and other services are provided as a shared pool of virtualized resources over the Internet. These "clouds" of computing resources can be accessed on an as-needed

cloud computing
model of computing in which computer processing, storage, software, and other services are provided as a shared pool of virtualized resources over the Internet

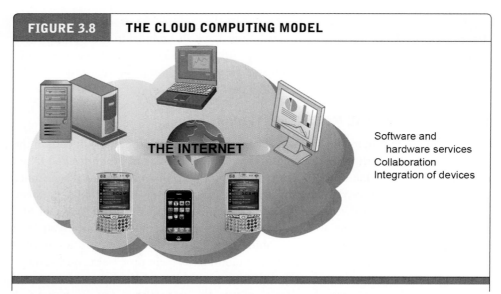

FIGURE 3.8	THE CLOUD COMPUTING MODEL

Software and
  hardware services
Collaboration
Integration of devices

In the cloud computing model, hardware and software services are provided on the Internet by vendors operating very large server farms and data centers.

basis from any connected device and location. **Figure 3.8** illustrates the cloud computing concept.

The U.S. National Institute of Standards and Technology (NIST) defines cloud computing as having the following essential characteristics:

- **On-demand self-service:** Consumers can obtain computing capabilities such as server time or network storage as needed automatically on their own.
- **Ubiquitous network access:** Cloud resources can be accessed using standard network and Internet devices, including mobile platforms.
- **Location-independent resource pooling:** Computing resources are pooled to serve multiple users, with different virtual resources dynamically assigned according to user demand. The user generally does not know where the computing resources are located.
- **Rapid elasticity:** Computing resources can be rapidly provisioned, increased, or decreased to meet changing user demand.
- **Measured service:** Charges for cloud resources are based on the amount of resources actually used.

Cloud computing consists of three basic types of services:

- **Infrastructure as a service (IaaS):** Customers use processing, storage, networking, and other computing resources from third-party providers called cloud service providers (CSPs) to run their information systems. For example, Amazon used the spare capacity of its information technology infrastructure to develop Amazon Web Services, which offers a cloud environment for a myriad of different IT infrastructure services. See **Table 3.4** for a description of the range of services that AWS offers, such as its Simple Storage Service (S3) for storing customers' data and its

TABLE 3.4	AMAZON WEB SERVICES
NAME	**DESCRIPTION**
COMPUTING SERVICES	
Elastic Compute Cloud (EC2)	Scalable cloud computing services
Elastic Load Balancing (ELB)	Distributes incoming application traffic among multiple EC2 instances
STORAGE SERVICES	
Simple Storage Service (S3)	Data storage infrastructure
Glacier	Low-cost archival and backup storage
DATABASE SERVICES	
DynamoDB	NoSQL database service
Redshift	Petabyte-scale data warehouse service
Relational Database Service (RDB)	Relational database service for MySQL, Oracle, SQL Server, and PostgreSQL databases
ElastiCache	In-memory cache in the cloud
SimpleDB	Non-relational data store
NETWORKING AND CONTENT DELIVERY SERVICES	
Route 53	DNS service in the cloud, enabling business to direct Internet traffic to Web applications
Virtual Private Cloud (VPC)	Creates a VPN between the Amazon cloud and a company's existing IT infrastructure
CloudFront	Content delivery services
Direct Connect	Provides alternative to using the Internet to access AWS cloud services
ANALYTICS	
Elastic MapReduce (EMR)	Web service that enables users to perform data-intensive tasks
Kinesis	Big Data service for real-time data streaming ingestion and processing
APPLICATION SERVICES	
AppStream	Provides streaming services for applications and games from the cloud
CloudSearch	Search service that can be integrated by developers into applications
MESSAGING SERVICES	
Simple Email Service (SES)	Cloud e-mail sending service
Simple Notification Service (SNS)	Push messaging service
Simple Queue Service (SQS)	Queue for storing messages as they travel between computers

(continued)

TABLE 3.4	AMAZON WEB SERVICES (CONT.)
DEPLOYMENT AND MANAGEMENT SERVICES	
Identity and Access Management (IAM)	Enables securely controlled access to AWS services
CloudWatch	Monitoring service
Elastic Beanstalk	Service for deploying and scaling Web applications and services developed with Java, .Net, PHP, Python, Ruby, and Node.js
CloudFormation	Service that allows developers an easy way to create a collection of related AWS resources
MOBILE	
Cognito	Allows developers to securely manage and synchronize app data for users across mobile devices
Mobile Analytics	Can collect and process billions of events from millions of users a day
PAYMENT SERVICES	
Flexible Payment Service (FPS)	Payment services for developers
DevPay	Online billing and account management service for developers who create an Amazon cloud application
MISCELLANEOUS	
Amazon Mechanical Turk	Marketplace for work that requires human intelligence
Alexa Web Information Service	Provides Web traffic data and information for developers

Elastic Compute Cloud (EC2) service for running applications. Users pay only for the amount of computing and storage capacity they actually use.

- **Software as a service (SaaS):** Customers use software hosted by the vendor on the vendor's cloud infrastructure and delivered as a service over a network. Leading SaaS examples are Google Apps, which provides common business applications online, and Salesforce.com, which provides customer relationship management and related software services over the Internet. Both charge users an annual subscription fee, although Google Apps also has a pared-down free version. Users access these applications from a Web browser, and the data and software are maintained on the providers' remote servers.

- **Platform as a service (PaaS):** Customers use infrastructure and programming tools supported by the CSP to develop their own applications. For example, IBM offers Bluemix for software development and testing on its cloud infrastructure. Another example is Salesforce.com's Force.com, which allows developers to build applications that are hosted on its servers as a service.

A cloud can be private, public, or hybrid. A **public cloud** is owned and maintained by CSPs, such as Amazon Web Services, IBM, HP, and Dell, and made available to

public cloud

third-party service providers that own and manage large, scalable data centers that offer computing, data storage, and high speed Internet to multiple customers who pay for only the resources they use multiple customers, who pay only for the resources they use. A public cloud offers relatively secure enterprise-class reliability at significant cost savings. Because organizations using public clouds do not own the infrastructure, they do not have to make large investments in their own hardware and software. Instead, they purchase their computing services from remote providers and pay only for the amount of computing power they actually use (utility computing) or are billed on a monthly or annual subscription basis. The term *on-demand computing* is also used to describe such services. As such, public clouds are ideal environments for small and medium-sized businesses who cannot afford to fully develop their own infrastructure; for applications requiring high performance, scalability, and availability; for new application development and testing; and for companies that have occasional large computing projects. Gartner estimates that spending on public cloud services worldwide will grow over 15% in 2015, to $176 billion (Gartner, Inc., 2015a). Companies such as Google, Apple, Dropbox, and others also offer public clouds as a consumer service for online storage of data, music, and photos. Google Drive, Dropbox, and Apple iCloud are leading examples of this type of consumer cloud service.

A **private cloud** provides similar options as a public cloud but is operated solely for the benefit of a single tenant. It might be managed by the organization or a third party and hosted either internally or externally. Like public clouds, private clouds can allocate storage, computing power, or other resources seamlessly to provide computing resources on an as-needed basis. Companies that have stringent regulatory compliance or specialized licensing requirements that necessitate high security, such as financial services or healthcare companies, or that want flexible information technology resources and a cloud service model while retaining control over their own IT infrastructure, are gravitating toward these private clouds.

private cloud
provides similar options as public cloud but only to a single tenant

Large firms are most likely to adopt a **hybrid cloud** computing model, in which they use their own infrastructure for their most essential core activities and adopt public cloud computing for less-critical systems or for additional processing capacity during peak business periods. **Table 3.5** compares the three cloud computing models. Cloud computing will gradually shift firms from having a fixed infrastructure capacity

hybrid cloud
offers customers both a public cloud and a private cloud

TABLE 3.5	CLOUD COMPUTING MODELS COMPARED		
TYPE OF CLOUD	**DESCRIPTION**	**MANAGED BY**	**USES**
Public cloud	Third-party service offering computing, storage, and software services to multiple customers	Third-party service providers (CSPs)	Companies without major privacy concerns Companies seeking pay-as-you-go IT services Companies lacking IT resources and expertise
Private cloud	Cloud infrastructure operated solely for a single organization and hosted either internally or externally.	In-house IT or private third-party host	Companies with stringent privacy and security requirements Companies that must have control over data sovereignty
Hybrid cloud	Combination of private and public cloud services that remain separate entities	In-house IT, private host, third-party providers	Companies requiring some in-house control of IT that are also willing to assign part of their IT infrastructures to a public cloud partition on their IT infrastructures

toward a more flexible infrastructure, some of it owned by the firm, and some of it rented from giant data centers owned by CSPs.

Cloud computing has some drawbacks. Unless users make provisions for storing their data locally, the responsibility for data storage and control is in the hands of the provider. Some companies worry about the security risks related to entrusting their critical data and systems to an outside vendor that also works with other companies. Companies expect their systems to be available 24/7 and do not want to suffer any loss of business capability if cloud infrastructures malfunction. Nevertheless, the trend is for companies to shift more of their computer processing and storage to some form of cloud infrastructure.

Cloud computing has many significant implications for e-commerce. For e-commerce firms, cloud computing radically reduces the cost of building and operating Web sites because the necessary hardware infrastructure and software can be licensed as a service from CSPs at a fraction of the cost of purchasing these services as products. This means firms can adopt "pay-as-you-go" and "pay-as-you-grow" strategies when building out their Web sites. For instance, according to Amazon, hundreds of thousands of customers use Amazon Web Services. For individuals, cloud computing means you no longer need a powerful laptop or desktop computer to engage in e-commerce or other activities. Instead, you can use much less-expensive tablet computers or smartphones that cost a few hundred dollars. For corporations, cloud computing means that a significant part of hardware and software costs (infrastructure costs) can be reduced because firms can obtain these services online for a fraction of the cost of owning, and they do not have to hire an IT staff to support the infrastructure.

OTHER INTERNET PROTOCOLS AND UTILITY PROGRAMS

There are many other Internet protocols and utility programs that provide services to users in the form of Internet applications that run on Internet clients and servers. These Internet services are based on universally accepted protocols—or standards—that are available to everyone who uses the Internet. They are not owned by any organization, but they are services that have been developed over many years and made available to all Internet users.

HyperText Transfer Protocol (HTTP)
the Internet protocol used for transferring Web pages

HyperText Transfer Protocol (HTTP) is the Internet protocol used to transfer Web pages (described in the following section). HTTP was developed by the World Wide Web Consortium (W3C) and the Internet Engineering Task Force (IETF). HTTP runs in the Application Layer of the TCP/IP model shown in Figure 3.4 on page 119. An HTTP session begins when a client's browser requests a resource, such as a Web page, from a remote Internet server. When the server responds by sending the page requested, the HTTP session for that object ends. Because Web pages may have many objects on them—graphics, sound or video files, frames, and so forth—each object must be requested by a separate HTTP message. For more information about HTTP, you can consult RFC 2616, which details the standards for HTTP/1.1, the version of HTTP most commonly used today (Internet Society, 1999). (An RFC is a document published by the Internet Society [ISOC] or one of the other organizations involved in Internet governance that sets forth the standards for various Internet-related technologies. You will learn more about the organizations involved in setting standards for the Internet later in the chapter.)

E-mail is one of the oldest, most important, and frequently used Internet services. Like HTTP, the various Internet protocols used to handle e-mail all run in the Application Layer of TCP/IP. **Simple Mail Transfer Protocol (SMTP)** is the Internet protocol used to send e-mail to a server. SMTP is a relatively simple, text-based protocol that was developed in the early 1980s. SMTP handles only the sending of e-mail. To retrieve e-mail from a server, the client computer uses either **Post Office Protocol 3 (POP3)** or **Internet Message Access Protocol (IMAP)**. You can set POP3 to retrieve e-mail messages from the server and then delete the messages on the server, or retain them on the server. IMAP is a more current e-mail protocol supported by all browsers and most servers and ISPs. IMAP allows users to search, organize, and filter their mail prior to downloading it from the server.

File Transfer Protocol (FTP) is one of the original Internet services. FTP runs in TCP/IP's Application Layer and permits users to transfer files from a server to their client computer, and vice versa. The files can be documents, programs, or large database files. FTP is the fastest and most convenient way to transfer files larger than 1 megabyte, which some e-mail servers will not accept. More information about FTP is available in RFC 959 (Internet Society, 1985).

Telnet is a network protocol that also runs in TCP/IP's Application Layer and is used to allow remote login on another computer. The term Telnet also refers to the Telnet program, which provides the client part of the protocol and enables the client to emulate a mainframe computer terminal. (The industry-standard terminals defined in the days of mainframe computing are VT-52, VT-100, and IBM 3250.) You can then attach yourself to a computer on the Internet that supports Telnet and run programs or download files from that computer. Telnet was the first "remote work" program that permitted users to work on a computer from a remote location.

Secure Sockets Layer (SSL)/Transport Layer Security (TLS) are protocols that operate between the Transport and Application Layers of TCP/IP and secure communications between the client and the server. SSL/TLS helps secure e-commerce communications and payments through a variety of techniques, such as message encryption and digital signatures, that we will discuss further in Chapter 5.

Packet InterNet Groper (Ping) is a utility program that allows you to check the connection between a client computer and a TCP/IP network (see **Figure 3.9**). Ping

Simple Mail Transfer Protocol (SMTP)
the Internet protocol used to send mail to a server

Post Office Protocol 3 (POP3)
a protocol used by the client to retrieve mail from an Internet server

Internet Message Access Protocol (IMAP)
a more current e-mail protocol that allows users to search, organize, and filter their mail prior to downloading it from the server

File Transfer Protocol (FTP)
one of the original Internet services. Part of the TCP/IP protocol that permits users to transfer files from the server to their client computer, and vice versa

Telnet
a terminal emulation program that runs in TCP/IP

Secure Sockets Layer (SSL)/Transport Layer Security (TLS)
protocols that secure communications between the client and the server

Ping
a program that allows you to check the connection between your client and the server

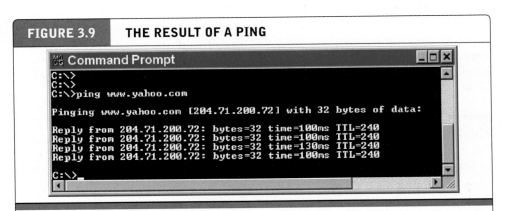

FIGURE 3.9 **THE RESULT OF A PING**

A ping is used to verify an address and test the speed of the round trip from a client computer to a host and back.

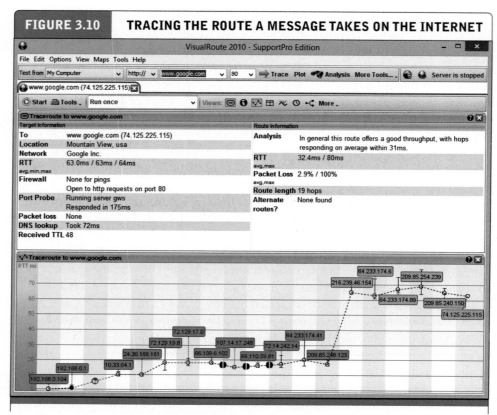

VisualRoute and other tracing programs provide some insight into how the Internet uses packet switching. This particular message traveled to a Google server in Mountain View, California.

SOURCE: Visualware, Inc., 2014.

Tracert
one of several route-tracing utilities that allow you to follow the path of a message you send from your client to a remote computer on the Internet

will also tell you the time it takes for the server to respond, giving you some idea about the speed of the server and the Internet at that moment. You can run Ping from the DOS prompt on a personal computer with a Windows operating system by typing: ping < domain name >. We will discuss Ping further in Chapter 5, because one way to slow down or even crash a domain server is to send it millions of ping requests.

Tracert is one of several route-tracing utilities that allow you to follow the path of a message you send from your client to a remote computer on the Internet. **Figure 3.10** shows the result of a message sent to a remote host using a visual route-tracing program called VisualRoute (available from Visualware).

3.2 THE INTERNET TODAY

In 2015, there are an estimated 3.1 billion Internet users worldwide, up from 100 million users at year-end 1997. While this is a huge number, it represents only about 40% of the world's population (eMarketer, Inc., 2015a). Although Internet user growth has slowed in the United States and Western Europe to about 1%–2% annually, worldwide, the growth rate is about 6.7%, with the highest growth areas being the Asia-Pacific region and the Middle East and Africa (both still growing at over 8%). By 2019, it is expected that there will be almost 3.9 billion Internet users worldwide. One would think the Internet would be overloaded with such incredible growth; however, this has not been true for several reasons. First, client/server computing is highly extensible. By simply adding servers and clients, the population of Internet users can grow indefinitely. Second, the Internet architecture is built in layers so that each layer can change without disturbing developments in other layers. For instance, the technology used to move messages through the Internet can go through radical changes to make service faster without being disruptive to your desktop applications running on the Internet.

Figure 3.11 illustrates the "hourglass" and layered architecture of the Internet. The Internet can be viewed conceptually as having four layers: Network Technology

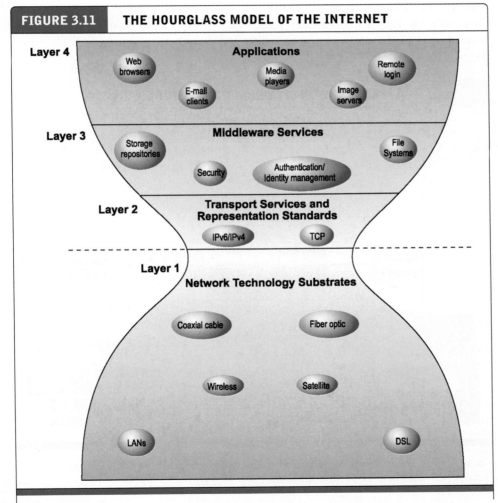

FIGURE 3.11   **THE HOURGLASS MODEL OF THE INTERNET**

The Internet can be characterized as an hourglass modular structure with a lower layer containing the bit-carrying infrastructure (including cables and switches) and an upper layer containing user applications such as e-mail and the Web. In the narrow waist are transportation protocols such as TCP/IP.

Network Technology Substrate layer

layer of Internet technology that is composed of telecommunications networks and protocols

Transport Services and Representation Standards layer

layer of Internet architecture that houses the TCP/IP protocol

Applications layer

layer of Internet architecture that contains client applications

Middleware Services layer

the "glue" that ties the applications to the communications networks and includes such services as security, authentication, addresses, and storage repositories

Substrates, Transport Services and Representation Standards, Middleware Services, and Applications.[4] The **Network Technology Substrate layer** is composed of telecommunications networks and protocols. The **Transport Services and Representation Standards layer** houses the TCP/IP protocol. The **Applications layer** contains client applications such as the World Wide Web, e-mail, and audio or video playback. The **Middleware Services layer** is the glue that ties the applications to the communications networks and includes such services as security, authentication, addresses, and storage repositories. Users work with applications (such as e-mail) and rarely become aware of middleware that operates in the background. Because all layers use TCP/IP and other common standards linking all four layers, it is possible for there to be significant changes in the Network layer without forcing changes in the Applications layer.

THE INTERNET BACKBONE

Figure 3.12 illustrates some of the main physical elements of today's physical Internet. Originally, the Internet had a single backbone, but today's Internet is woven together from numerous privately owned networks comprised of high-bandwidth fiber-optic

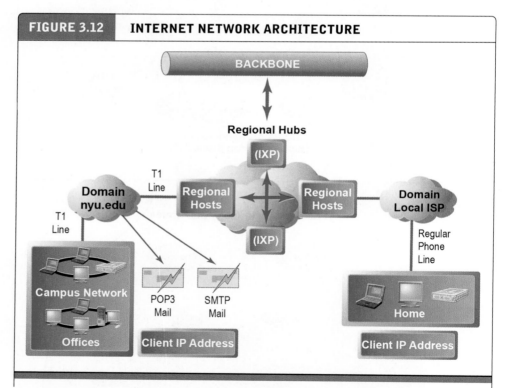

FIGURE 3.12   INTERNET NETWORK ARCHITECTURE

Today's Internet has a multi-tiered open network architecture featuring multiple backbones, regional hubs, campus area networks, and local client computers.

---

[4] Recall that the TCP/IP communications protocol also has layers, not to be confused with the Internet architecture layers.

TABLE 3.6	MAJOR TIER 1 INTERNET SERVICE PROVIDERS	
AT&T	Sprint	
CenturyLink	Verio (NTT Communications)	
Cogent Communications	Verizon	
Level 3 Communications		

cable that are physically connected with each other and that transfer information from one private network to another. These long-haul fiber-optic networks are owned by the major cable providers and firms which are sometimes referred to as **Tier 1 Internet Service Providers (Tier 1 ISPs)** (see **Table 3.6**). For the sake of clarity we will refer to these networks of backbones as a single "backbone." The **backbone** has been likened to a giant pipeline that transports data around the world in milliseconds. In the United States, the backbone is composed entirely of fiber-optic cable with bandwidths ranging from 155 Mbps to 2.5 Gbps. **Bandwidth** measures how much data can be transferred over a communications medium within a fixed period of time and is usually expressed in bits per second (Bps), kilobits (thousands of bits) per second (Kbps), megabits (millions of bits) per second (Mbps), or gigabits (billions of bits) per second (Gbps).

Connections to other continents are made via a combination of undersea fiber-optic cable and satellite links. The backbones in foreign countries typically are operated by a mixture of private and public owners. The backbone has built-in redundancy so that if one part breaks down, data can be rerouted to another part of the backbone. **Redundancy** refers to multiple duplicate devices and paths in a network. A recent study of the Internet's physical structure in the United States has created one of the first maps of the Internet's long-haul fiber network as it currently exists. The map reveals that, not surprisingly, there are dense networks of fiber in the Northeast and coastal areas of the United States, while there is a pronounced absence of infrastructure in the Upper Plains and Four Corners regions. The U.S. Department of Homeland Security has made the map, as well as the data that underlies it, available to government, private, and public researchers, believing that doing so could make the Internet more resilient by improving knowledge (Simonite, 2015; Durairajan et al., 2015).

INTERNET EXCHANGE POINTS

In the United States, there are a number of hubs where the backbone intersects with regional and local networks, and where the backbone owners connect with one another (see **Figure 3.13**). These hubs were originally called Network Access Points (NAPs) or Metropolitan Area Exchanges (MAEs), but now are more commonly referred to as **Internet Exchange Points (IXPs)**. IXPs use high-speed switching computers to connect the backbone to regional and local networks, and exchange messages with one another. The regional and local networks are owned by private telecommunications firms; they generally are fiber-optic networks operating at more than 100 Mbps. The regional networks lease access to ISPs, private companies, and government institutions.

Tier 1 Internet Service Providers (Tier 1 ISPs) own and control the major long-haul fiber-optic cable networks comprising the Internet's backbone

backbone high-bandwidth fiber-optic cable that transports data across the Internet

bandwidth measures how much data can be transferred over a communications medium within a fixed period of time; is usually expressed in bits per second (bps), kilobits per second (Kbps), megabits per second (Mbps), or gigabits per second (Gbps)

redundancy multiple duplicate devices and paths in a network

Internet Exchange Point (IXP) hub where the backbone intersects with local and regional networks and where backbone owners connect with one another

FIGURE 3.13	SOME MAJOR U.S. INTERNET EXCHANGE POINTS (IXPs)		
Region	**Name**	**Location**	**Operator**
EAST	Boston Internet Exchange (BOSIX)	Boston	Markley
	New York International Internet Exchange (NYIIX)	New York	Telehouse
	Peering and Internet Exchange (PAIX)	New York, Virginia, Atlanta	Equinix
	NAP of the Americas	Miami	Verizon Terremark
CENTRAL	Any2 Exchange	Chicago	CoreSite
	Peering and Internet Exchange (PAIX)	Dallas	Equinix
	Midwest Internet Cooperative Exchange (MICE)	Minneapolis	Members
WEST	Peering and Internet Exchange (PAIX)	Seattle, Palo Alto	Equinix
	Los Angeles International Internet Exchange (LAIIX)	Los Angeles	Telehouse
	Any2 Exchange	San Jose, Los Angeles	CoreSite
	Seattle Internet Exchange (SIX)	Seattle	Members

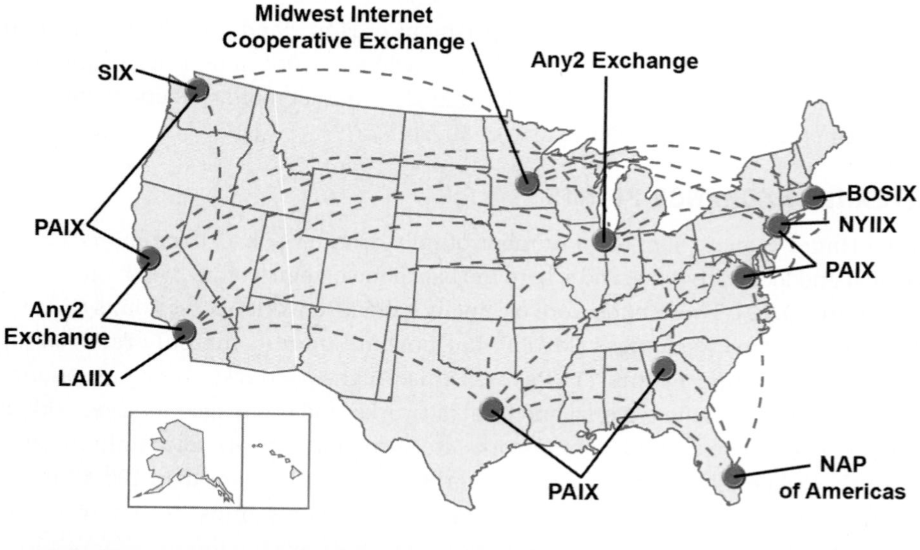

CAMPUS AREA NETWORKS

Campus area networks (CANs) are generally local area networks operating within a single organization—such as New York University or Microsoft Corporation. In fact, most large organizations have hundreds of such local area networks. These organizations are sufficiently large that they lease access to the Web directly from regional and national carriers. These local area networks generally are running Ethernet (a local area network protocol) and have network operating systems such as Windows Server or Linux that permit desktop clients to connect to the Internet through a local Internet server attached to their campus networks. Connection speeds in campus area networks are in the range of 10–100 Mbps to the desktop.

campus area network (CAN)
generally, a local area network operating within a single organization that leases access to the Web directly from regional and national carriers

INTERNET SERVICE PROVIDERS

The firms that provide the lowest level of service in the multi-tiered Internet architecture by leasing Internet access to home owners, small businesses, and some large institutions are called **Internet Service Providers (ISPs)**. ISPs are retail providers. They deal with "the last mile of service" to the curb—homes and business offices. ISPs typically connect to IXPs with high-speed telephone or cable lines (45 Mbps and higher).

There are a number of major ISPs, such as AT&T, Comcast, Cablevision (Optimum), Cox, Time Warner Cable, Verizon, Sprint, and CenturyLink, as well as thousands of local ISPs in the United States, ranging from local telephone companies offering dial-up and DSL telephone access to cable companies offering cable Internet service, to small "mom-and-pop" Internet shops that service a small town, city, or even county with mostly dial-up phone access. If you have home or small business Internet access, an ISP likely provides the service to you. Satellite firms also offer Internet access, especially in remote areas where broadband service is not available.

Table 3.7 summarizes the variety of services, speeds, and costs of ISP Internet connections. There are two types of ISP service: narrowband and broadband. **Narrowband** service is the traditional telephone modem connection now operating at 56.6 Kbps (although the actual throughput hovers around 30 Kbps due to line noise that

Internet Service Provider (ISP)
firm that provides the lowest level of service in the multi-tiered Internet architecture by leasing Internet access to home owners, small businesses, and some large institutions

narrowband
the traditional telephone modem connection, now operating at 56.6 Kbps

TABLE 3.7	ISP SERVICE LEVELS AND BANDWIDTH CHOICES	
SERVICE	COST/MONTH	SPEED TO DESKTOP (DOWNLOAD)
Telephone modem	$10–$25	30–56 Kbps
DSL	$20–$30	1–15 Mbps
FiOS	$50–$300	25 Mbps–500 Mbps
Cable Internet	$35–$199	1 Mbps–500 Mbps
Satellite	$39–$129	5–15 Mbps
T1	$200–$300	1.54 Mbps
T3	$2,500–$10,000	45 Mbps

broadband
refers to any communication technology that permits clients to play streaming audio and video files at acceptable speeds

Digital Subscriber Line (DSL)
delivers high-speed access through ordinary telephone lines found in homes or businesses

FiOS (fiber-optic service)
a form of DSL that provides speeds of up to 500 Mbps

cable Internet
piggybacks digital access to the Internet on top of the analog video cable providing television signals to a home

T1
an international telephone standard for digital communication that offers guaranteed delivery at 1.54 Mbps

T3
an international telephone standard for digital communication that offers guaranteed delivery at 45 Mbps

satellite Internet
high-speed broadband Internet access provided via satellite

causes extensive resending of packets). This used to be the most common form of connection worldwide but it has been largely replaced by broadband connections in the United States, Europe, and Asia. Broadband service is based on DSL (including high speed fiber-optic service), cable, telephone (T1 and T3 lines), and satellite technologies. **Broadband**, in the context of Internet service, refers to any communication technology that permits clients to play streaming audio and video files at acceptable speeds. In January 2015, the U.S. Federal Communications Commission updated its broadband benchmark speeds to 25 Mbps for downloads and 3 Mbps for uploads. According to Akamai, the global average connection speed in 2015 was 5.1 Mbps, and the global average peak connection speed was 32.5 Mbps. The United States ranks 20th with an 11.7 Mbps average connection speed (South Korea leads, at 23.1 Mbps) and 24th with a 50.4 Mbps average peak connection speed (Singapore leads, at 108.3 Mbps). The FCC found that 17% of all Americans lack access to 25 Mbps/3 Mbps service, and that rural America is particularly underserved, with more than half lacking such access (Federal Communication Commission, 2015). In the United States, broadband users surpassed dial-up users in 2004, and in 2015, there are an estimated 91 million broadband households (almost 75% of all households) (eMarketer, Inc., 2015f).

The actual throughput of data will depend on a variety of factors including noise in the line and the number of subscribers requesting service. Service-level speeds quoted are typically only for downloads of Internet content; upload speeds tend to be slower, although a number of broadband ISPs have plans that offer the same upload as download speed. T1 and T3 lines are publicly regulated utility lines that offer a guaranteed level of service, but the actual throughput of the other forms of Internet service is not guaranteed.

Digital Subscriber Line (DSL) service is a telephone technology that provides high-speed access to the Internet through ordinary telephone lines found in a home or business. Service levels typically range from about .5 to 15 Mbps. DSL service requires that customers live within two miles (about 4,000 meters) of a neighborhood telephone switching center. In order to compete with cable companies, telephone companies now also offer an advanced form of DSL called **FiOS (fiber-optic service)** that provides up to 500 Mbps to homes and businesses.

Cable Internet refers to a cable television technology that piggybacks digital access to the Internet using the same analog or digital video cable providing television signals to a home. Cable Internet is a major broadband alternative to DSL service, generally providing faster speeds and a "triple play" subscription: telephone, television, and Internet for a single monthly payment. Cable Internet services typically range from 1 Mbps up to 500 Mbps. Comcast, Time Warner Road Runner, Cox, Charter, and Cablevision (Optimum Online) are some of the major cable Internet providers.

T1 and T3 are international telephone standards for digital communication. **T1** lines offer guaranteed delivery at 1.54 Mbps, while **T3** lines offer 45 Mbps. T1 lines cost about $200–$300 per month, and T3 lines around $2500–$6000 per month. These are leased, dedicated, guaranteed lines suitable for corporations, government agencies, and businesses such as ISPs requiring high-speed guaranteed service levels.

Satellite Internet is offered by satellite companies that provide high-speed broadband Internet access primarily to homes and offices located in rural areas where DSL

TABLE 3.8	TIME TO DOWNLOAD A 10-MEGABYTE FILE BY TYPE OF INTERNET SERVICE	
TYPE OF INTERNET SERVICE	**TIME TO DOWNLOAD**	
NARROWBAND SERVICES		
Telephone modem	25 minutes	
BROADBAND SERVICES		
DSL @ 1 Mbps	1.33 minutes	
Cable Internet @ 10 Mbps	8 seconds	
T1	52 seconds	
T3	2 seconds	

or cable Internet access is not available. Access speeds and monthly costs are comparable to DSL and cable, but typically require a higher initial payment for installation of a small (18-inch) satellite dish. Upload speeds tend to be slower, typically 1–5 Mbps. Satellite providers typically have policies that limit the total megabytes of data that a single account can download within a set period, usually monthly. The major satellite providers are Dish, HughesNet, Exede, and StarBand.

Nearly all business firms and government agencies have broadband connections to the Internet. Demand for broadband service has grown so rapidly because it greatly speeds up the process of downloading Web pages and large video and audio files (see **Table 3.8**). As the quality of Internet service offerings continues to expand, the demand for broadband access will continue to swell.

INTRANETS

The very same Internet technologies that make it possible to operate a worldwide public network can also be used by private and government organizations as internal networks. An **intranet** is a TCP/IP network located within a single organization for purposes of communications and information processing. Internet technologies are generally far less expensive than proprietary networks, and there is a global source of new applications that can run on intranets. In fact, all the applications available on the public Internet can be used in private intranets. The largest provider of local area network software is Microsoft, followed by open source Linux, both of which use TCP/IP networking protocols.

intranet
a TCP/IP network located within a single organization for purposes of communications and information processing

WHO GOVERNS THE INTERNET?

Aficionados and journalists often claim that the Internet is governed by no one, and indeed cannot be governed, and that it is inherently above and beyond the law. What these people forget is that the Internet runs over private and public telecommunications facilities that are themselves governed by laws, and subject to the same pressures as all telecommunications carriers. In fact, the Internet is tied into a complex web of governing bodies, national governments, and international professional societies. There is no one single governing organization that controls activity on the Internet. Instead, there are a number of organizations that influence the system and monitor its operations. Among the governing bodies of the Internet are:

- The *Internet Corporation for Assigned Names and Numbers (ICANN)*, which coordinates the Internet's systems of unique identifiers: IP addresses, protocol parameter registries, and the top-level domain systems. ICANN was created in 1998 as a nonprofit organization and currently manages the Internet Assigned Numbers Authority (IANA), which is in charge of assigning IP addresses, under a contract from the U.S. National Telecommunications and Information Administration (NTIA), an agency of the U.S. Department of Commerce.

- The *Internet Engineering Task Force (IETF)*, which is an open international community of network operators, vendors, and researchers concerned with the evolution of the Internet architecture and operation of the Internet. The IETF has a number of working groups, organized into several different areas, that develop and promote Internet standards, which influence the way people use and manage the Internet.

- The *Internet Research Task Force (IRTF)*, which focuses on the evolution of the Internet. The IRTF has a number of long-term research groups working on various topics such as Internet protocols, applications, applications, and technology.

- The *Internet Engineering Steering Group (IESG)*, which is responsible for technical management of IETF activities and the Internet standards process.

- The *Internet Architecture Board (IAB)*, which helps define the overall architecture of the Internet and oversees the IETF and IRTF.

- The *Internet Society (ISOC)*, which is a consortium of corporations, government agencies, and nonprofit organizations that monitors Internet policies and practices.

- The *Internet Governance Forum (IGF)*, which is a multi-stakeholder open forum for debate on issues related to Internet governance.

- The *World Wide Web Consortium (W3C)*, which is a largely academic group that sets HTML and other programming standards for the Web.

- The *Internet Network Operators Groups (NOGs)*, which are informal groups that are made up of ISPs, IXPs, and others that discuss and attempt to influence matters related to Internet operations and regulation.

While none of these organizations has actual control over the Internet and how it functions, they can and do influence government agencies, major network owners, ISPs, corporations, and software developers with the goal of keeping the Internet operating as efficiently as possible. ICANN comes closest to being a manager of the Internet and reflects the powerful role that the U.S. Department of Commerce has played historically in Internet governance. The United States has been responsible for the IANA function since the beginning of the Internet. After the creation of ICANN, however, the expectation was the function would eventually be transferred out of the U.S. government's control. In 2006, however, the U.S. Department of Commerce announced that the U.S. government would retain oversight over the root servers, contrary to initial expectations. There were several reasons for this move, including the use of the Internet for basic communications services by terrorist groups and the uncertainty that might be caused should an international body take over. In 2008, the Department of Commerce reaffirmed this stance, stating that it did not have any plans to transition management of the authoritative root zone file to ICANN (U.S. Department of Commerce, 2008). At the same time, growing Internet powers China and Russia were lobbying for more functions of the Internet to be brought under the control of the United Nations, raising fears that governance of the Internet could become even more politicized (Pfanner, 2012). In 2014, the United States, under continued pressure from other countries, finally announced its willingness to transition control of IANA, provided that certain stipulations are met, including that the organization managing the IANA functions not be specifically controlled by any other government or inter-governmental organization (such as the United Nations). The transition is intended to take place by September 2016, although it could be extended to as late as September 2019.

In addition to these professional bodies, the Internet must also conform to the laws of the sovereign nation-states in which it operates, as well as the technical infrastructures that exist within each nation-state. Although in the early years of the Internet there was very little legislative or executive interference, this situation is changing as the Internet plays a growing role in the distribution of information and knowledge, including content that some find objectionable.

Read *Insight on Society: Government Regulation and Surveillance of the Internet* for a further look at the issue of censorship of Internet content and substance.

3.3 THE FUTURE INTERNET INFRASTRUCTURE

The Internet is changing as new technologies appear and new applications are developed. The next era of the Internet is being built today by private corporations, universities, and government agencies. To appreciate the potential benefits of the Internet of the future, you must first understand the limitations of the Internet's current infrastructure.

LIMITATIONS OF THE CURRENT INTERNET

Much of the Internet's current infrastructure is several decades old (equivalent to a century in Internet time). It suffers from a number of limitations, including:

- *Bandwidth limitations*. There is insufficient capacity throughout the backbone, the metropolitan switching centers, and most importantly, the "last mile" to the house and small businesses. The result is slow peak-hour service (congestion) and a limited ability to handle high volumes of video and voice traffic.

INSIGHT ON SOCIETY

GOVERNMENT REGULATION AND SURVEILLANCE OF THE INTERNET

Hardly a week goes by without reports that a massive protest has occurred in the streets of a big city somewhere in the world. Invariably, the Internet, social media, and mobile phones are either blamed or praised for enabling these popular expressions of discontent with political regimes, corrupt officials, unemployment, or wealth inequality. Events such as the Jasmine Revolution in Tunisia and the Arab Spring in Egypt in 2010, and more recently, protests in Madrid, Caracas, Moscow, Pakistan, Syria, and even heretofore quiet U.S. Midwestern towns like Ferguson, Missouri, encourage us all to think of the Internet and the Web as an extraordinary technology unleashing torrents of human creativity, innovation, expression, and sometimes, popular rebellion, and even democracy.

How ironic then that the same Internet has spawned an explosion in government control and surveillance of individuals on the Internet. Totalitarian dictators of the mid-twentieth century would have given their eyeteeth for a technology such as this, that can track what millions of people do, say, think, and search for in billions of e-mails, searches, blogs, and Facebook posts every day.

In the early years of the Internet and the Web, many people assumed that because the Internet is so widely dispersed, it must be difficult to control or monitor. But the reality is quite different. We now know that just about all governments assert some kind of control and surveillance over Internet content and messages, and in many nations this control over the Internet and the people who use it is very extensive.

While the Internet is a decentralized network, Internet traffic in all countries runs through large fiber-optic trunk lines that are controlled by national authorities or private firms. In China,

there are three such lines, and China requires the companies that own these lines to configure their routers for both internal and external service requests. When a request originates in China for a Web page in Chicago, Chinese routers examine the request to see if the site is on a blacklist, and then examine words in the requested Web page to see if it contains blacklisted terms. The system is often referred to as "The Great Firewall of China" and is implemented with the assistance of Cisco Systems (the U.S. firm that is the largest manufacturer of routers in the world) and California-based Blue Coat, which provides deep packet inspection software. Other U.S. Internet firms are also involved in China's censorship and surveillance efforts, including Yahoo, Microsoft, and Juniper Networks, among many others.

In 2015, China strengthened and extended its regulation of the Internet in the name of social stability as political unrest in the country has worsened. Recently passed legislation allows Web users to be jailed for up to three years if they post defamatory rumors that are read by more than 5,000 people. China also issued new rules to restrict the dissemination of political news and opinions on instant messaging applications such as WeChat, a text messaging app similar to Twitter and WhatsApp. Users are required to post political opinions and news only to state-authorized media outlets and are required to use their own names when establishing accounts. In 2015, Chinese Internet companies deleted over 60,000 accounts with names that failed to adhere to the new regulations. In 2015, China also issued guidelines to regulate Internet-based financial institutions, such as peer-to-peer lending platforms.

Displeased by China's censorship efforts, Google began to encrypt searches originating in

China in order to prevent surveillance by state agencies in 2014. In response, Chinese authorities severely disrupted Google search access, as well as popular services like Google Maps and Gmail. The disruption occurred on the 25th anniversary of the government's crackdown on the pro-democracy demonstrations in Tiananmen Square. Facebook, Twitter, Flickr, and YouTube have been blocked in China for years. Access to Google was eventually restored, but in 2015 China continued to battle Google, this time over Google's decision to no longer recognize security certificates for Chinese sites issued by major Chinese Internet authorities, instead displaying them as "distrusted sites." Google and China are also battling to bring greater Internet connectivity to Cuba, which ranks near the bottom in Internet penetration worldwide. Google's proposed plan for Cuba would focus on mobile connectivity and favor openness, and China's would allow the Cuban government to conduct significant surveillance on their citizens' Internet activities.

While China is often criticized for its extensive Internet controls, other countries are not far behind. Iran's Internet surveillance of its citizens is considered by security experts to be one of the world's most sophisticated mechanisms for controlling and censoring the Internet, allowing it to examine the content of individual online communications on a massive scale, far more sophisticated than even China's Internet surveillance activities. The Iranian system goes far beyond preventing access to specific sites such as BBC World News, Google, and Facebook. One technique is deep packet inspection of every e-mail, text, or tweet. Deep packet inspection allows governments to read messages, alter their contents for disinformation purposes, and identify senders and recipients. It is accomplished by installing computers in the line between users and ISPs, opening up every digitized packet, inspecting for keywords and images, reconstructing the message, and sending it on. This is done for all Internet traffic including Skype, Facebook, e-mail, tweets, and messages sent to proxy servers. In 2015, Iran acknowledged an overarching effort to surveil social networks, resulting in the elimination of 130 Facebook pages and 12 arrests for crimes such as insulting the Ayatollah Khomeini.

In Russia, a new law took effect in February 2014 that allows the government to close Web sites without a court decision. Sites can be closed if the General Prosecutor's office declares the material on a site to be "extremist." In August 2014, Russia expanded Internet regulations to the blogosphere, requiring bloggers with more than 3,000 daily readers to register their real names and contact information with Russia's communications regulator. In 2015, Russia passed laws requiring domestic Internet companies to store their data on Russian soil, allowing the government to control it and limit access.

In January 2014, the Turkish government shut down the file-sharing site SoundCloud after recordings of Prime Minister Recep Tayyip Erdogan arranging to obtain two villas for his family in return for a zoning change granted to a construction tycoon surfaced. When the recordings moved to YouTube, Turkey shut down YouTube. Turkey already has extensive regulations prohibiting online pornography, gambling, and criticism of the founder of modern Turkey, Mustafa Kemal Attaturk. In April 2014, the Turkish Constitutional Court ordered the government to restore access to YouTube, Twitter, SoundCloud, and other sites because the shutdowns were a violation of freedom of expression, but the culture of censorship remains. In 2015, the Turkish parliament voted to expand Turkish law enforcement's ability to conduct online surveillance without court orders.

Both Europe and the United States have, at various times, also taken steps to control access to Internet sites, censor Web content, and engage in extensive surveillance of communications, although not to the extent of Iran, China, and many other nations nor to attack specific political groups or inhibit the freedom of expression. For instance,

(continued)

Great Britain has a list of blocked sites, as do Germany and France. The Australian Communications and Media Authority has developed a list of several hundred Web sites that have been refused registration in Australia, mostly violent video game and online pornography sites. The United States and European countries generally ban the sale, distribution, and/or possession of online child pornography. Both France and Germany bar online Nazi memorabilia. Even in South Korea, one of the world's most wired countries, there are restrictions on pornographic sites, games sites, and limits on Google Maps.

In response to terrorism threats and other crimes, European governments and the U.S. government also perform deep packet inspection on e-mail and text communications of terrorist suspects. This surveillance is not limited to cross-border international data flows and includes large-scale domestic surveillance and analysis of routine e-mail, tweets, and other messages. In 2013, National Security Agency (NSA) contractor Edward Snowden made headlines by leaking classified NSA documents shedding light on the NSA's PRISM program, which grants the agency unauthorized access to the servers of major Internet companies such as Facebook, Google, Apple, Microsoft, and many others. Additionally, the documents revealed the existence of the NSA's XKeyscore program, which allows analysts to search databases of e-mails, chats, and browsing histories of individual citizens without any authorization. Warrants, court clearance, or other forms of legal documentation are not required for analysts to use the technology. Snowden's documents also showed spy agencies were tapping data from smartphone apps like Candy Crush, and most others, and that the NSA was tapping the flow of personal user information between Google and Yahoo. The NSA claimed that the program was only used to monitor foreign intelligence targets and that the information it collects has assisted in apprehending terrorists. The FBI also has an Internet surveillance unit, the National Domestic Communications Assistance Center. The NDCAC's mission is to assist in the development of new surveillance technologies that will allow authorities to increase the interception of Internet, wireless, and VoIP communications.

However, efforts are underway in the United States to curb domestic and international counterterrorist agencies like the NSA from conducting dragnet surveillance of the entire American population, strengthen court oversight of surveillance, limit surveillance to specific individuals, and ease disclosure rules for Internet firms who receive requests from government agencies. In 2015, Congress passed the USA Freedom Act, which limits the bulk collection of Americans' phone records. However, equally concerted efforts are underway to expand these types of spying powers. In 2015, for instance, the Obama administration expanded the NSA's ability to perform warrantless wiretaps on suspected malicious hackers, allowing them to monitor international Internet traffic from these suspects as well as domestic traffic.

▬ **SOURCES:** "Russian Data Law Fuels Web Surveillance Fears," by Shaun Walker, *The Guardian,* September 1, 2015; "Google and China in Battle Over Cuba's Internet Future," by Michelle Caruso-Cabrera, Cnbc.com, August 12, 2015; "China Looks To Regulate Internet Finance," by Gillian Wong, *Wall Street Journal,* July 20, 2015; "China Passes New National Security Law Extending Control Over Internet," *The Guardian,* July 1, 2015; "Hunting for Hackers, N.S.A. Secretly Expands Internet Spying at U.S. Border," by Charlie Savage et al., *New York Times,* June 4, 2015; "The State of Surveillance In Iran," by Arta Shams, Ifex.org, May 22, 2015; "Why Google and China Are in a War Over the Internet," by Arjun Kharpal, Cnbc.com, April 2, 2015; "House Moves to Curb Government Surveillance of Phone, Internet Records," by Cristina Maza, Csmonitor.com, May 1, 2015; "Turkey's Parliament Issues Contested Security, Surveillance Laws," Bloombergnews.com, March 27, 2015; "China Censorship Sweep Deletes More Than 60,000 Internet Accounts," Reuters.com, February 27, 2015; "China Tightens Message App Rules for Public Information," by Bloomberg.com, September 1, 2014; "Russia Forces Its Popular Bloggers to Register—Or Else," by Ilya Khrennikov, Bloomberg.com, August 19, 2014; "Access to Google Services Within China Returns," by Paul Carsten, Reuters.com, July 10, 2014; "Turkey Lifts Twitter Ban After Court Ruling," by Daren Butler, Reuters.com, April 3, 2014; "NSA Top Lawyer Says Tech Giants Knew About Data Collection," Cnet.com, March 19, 2014; "Documents Say NSA Pretends to Be Facebook in Surveillance," by Reed Albergotti, *Wall Street Journal,* March 12, 2014; "Amid Flow of Leaks, Turkey Moves to Crimp Internet," by Tim Arango and Ceylan Yeginsu, *New York Times,* February 6, 2014; "Spy Agencies Tap Data Streaming From Phone Apps," by James Glanz, Jeff Larson, and Andrew Lehren, *New York Times,* January 27, 2014; "Big Web Crash in China: Experts Suspect Great Firewall," by Nicole Perlroth, *New York Times,* January 22, 2014; "NSA Surveillance Covers 75 Percent of U.S. Internet Traffic: WSJ," by Reuters, News.Yahoo.com, August 20, 2013; "New Snowden Leak: NSA Program Taps All You Do Online," by Amanda Wills, Mashable.com, August 1, 2013; "Snowden: NSA Collects 'Everything,' Including Content of Emails," by Eyder Peralta, NPR.org, June 17, 2013; "FBI Quietly Forms Secret Net-Surveillance Unit," by Declan McCullagh, News.cnet.com, May 22, 2012; "Bullets Stall Youthful Push for Arab Spring," by Michael Slackman, *New York Times,* March 17, 2011.

- *Quality of service limitations.* Today's information packets take a circuitous route to get to their final destinations. This creates the phenomenon of **latency**—delays in messages caused by the uneven flow of information packets through the network. In the case of e-mail, latency is not noticeable. However, with streaming video and synchronous communication, such as a telephone call, latency is noticeable to the user and perceived as "jerkiness" in movies or delays in voice communication. Today's Internet uses "best-effort" quality of service (QOS), which makes no guarantees about when or whether data will be delivered, and provides each packet with the same level of service, no matter who the user is or what type of data is contained in the packet. A higher level of service quality is required if the Internet is to keep expanding into new services, such as video on demand and telephony.

- *Network architecture limitations.* Today, a thousand requests for a single music track from a central server will result in a thousand efforts by the server to download the music to each requesting client. This slows down network performance, as the same music track is sent out a thousand times to clients that might be located in the same metropolitan area. This is very different from television, where the program is broadcast once to millions of homes.

- *Wired Internet.* The Internet is still largely based on cables—fiber-optic and coaxial copper cables. Copper cables use a centuries-old technology, and fiber-optic cable is expensive to place underground. The wired nature of the Internet restricts mobility of users although it is changing rapidly as Wi-Fi hotspots proliferate, and cellular phone technology advances. However, cellular systems are often overloaded due to the growth in the number of smartphones.

Now imagine an Internet at least 1,000 times as powerful as today's Internet, one that is not subjected to the limitations of bandwidth, protocols, architecture, physical connections, and language detailed previously. Welcome to the world of the future Internet, and the next generation of e-commerce services and products!

latency
delays in messages caused by the uneven flow of information packets through the network

THE INTERNET2® PROJECT

Internet2® is an advanced networking consortium of more than 450 member institutions including universities, corporations, government research agencies, and not-for-profit networking organizations, all working in partnership to facilitate the development, deployment, and use of revolutionary Internet technologies. The broader Internet2 community includes more than 93,000 institutions across the United States and international networking partners in more than 100 countries. Internet2's work is a continuation of the kind of cooperation among government, private, and educational organizations that created the original Internet.

The advanced networks created and in use by Internet2 members provide an environment in which new technologies can be tested and enhanced. For instance, Internet2 provides a next-generation, nationwide 100 gigabit-per-second network that not only makes available a reliable production services platform for current high-performance needs but also creates a powerful experimental platform for the development of new network capabilities. See **Table 3.9** to get some sense of just how fast a 100-Gbps network is in terms of data transmission times. The fourth generation of this network, built through a federal stimulus grant from the National Telecommunications

Internet2®
advanced networking consortium of more than 350 member institutions working in partnership to facilitate the development, deployment, and use of revolutionary Internet technologies

TABLE 3.9	HOW FAST IS A 100-GBPS NETWORK?
DATA	TIME TO TRANSMIT
8.5 million electronic records	1 minute
300,000 X-rays	1 minute
1.8 million e-books simultaneously downloaded	2 minute

and Information Administration's Broadband Technology Opportunities Program, has now been deployed. The hybrid optical and packet network provides 8.8 terabits of capacity with the ability to seamlessly scale as requirements grow, includes over 15,000 miles of owned fiber optic cable, and reaches into underserved areas of the country, supporting connectivity for approximately 200,000 U.S. community anchor institutions (schools, local libraries, and museums), and enabling them to provide citizens across the country with telemedicine, distance learning, and other advanced applications not possible with consumer-grade Internet services. The infrastructure supports a wide range of IP and optical services already available today and also will stimulate a new generation of innovative services. The goal is to create an intelligent global ecosystem that will enable researchers, scientists, and others to "turn on" high-capacity network connections whenever and wherever they are needed. **Table 3.10** describes some of the projects that Internet2's 100-Gbps network is enabling. Other initiatives involve science and engineering (advanced network applications in support of distributed lab environments, remote access to rare scientific instruments, and distributed large-scale computation and data access), health sciences and health networks (telemedicine, medical and biological research, and health education and awareness), and arts and humanities (collaborative live performances, master classes, remote auditions, and interactive performing arts education and media events).

THE FIRST MILE AND THE LAST MILE

The Internet2 project is just the tip of the iceberg when it comes to future enhancements to the Internet. In 2007, the NSF began work on the Global Environment for Network Innovations (GENI) initiative. GENI is a unique virtual laboratory for exploring future internets at scale. GENI aims to promote innovations in network science, security technologies, services, and applications. GENI is a partnership of leading academic centers and private corporations such as Cisco, IBM, and HP, among many others. To date, awards have been made to 83 academic/industry teams for various projects to build, integrate, and operate early prototypes of the GENI virtual laboratory (Geni.net, 2014). Over the next two years, GENI will transition from being overseen by NSF's GENI Project Office to a community governance model (Geni.net, 2015).

The most significant privately initiated (but often government-influenced) changes are coming in two areas: fiber-optic trunk line bandwidth and wireless Internet services. Fiber optics is concerned with the first mile or backbone Internet services that carry bulk traffic long distances. Wireless Internet is concerned with the last mile—from the larger Internet to the user's smartphone, tablet computer, or laptop.

TABLE 3.10	PROJECTS BEING ENABLED BY INTERNET2'S 100-GBPS NETWORK
PROJECT	**DESCRIPTION**
XSEDE (Extreme Science and Engineering Discovery Environment)	In 2013, XSEDE upgraded from a 10-Gbps network to Internet2's 100-Gbps network. XSEDE supports over 8,000 members of the global scientific community and 17 supercomputers, and is being used for: • Galaxy, a data-intensive cancer research program, with more than 10,000 users who run 4,000–5,000 DNA sequence analyses daily. • Advanced chemistry research, which has discovered new materials such as two-dimensional metals. • Simulations of the impact of orbital debris on spacecraft and fragment impacts on body armor. • Research into healthcare contract economics.
CloudLab	Cloud computing test beds based at the University of Utah, Clemson, and the University of Wisconsin-Madison, connected by Internet2's 100-Gbps network. Focusing on the development of novel cloud architectures and new cloud computing applications. Will enable researchers to build their own clouds and experiment with applications such as real-time disaster response and medical record security. Awarded $10 milllion NSF grant in 2014.
University of Florida	Support for Compact Muon Solenoid (CMS) experiments at CERN's Hadron collider (contributed to discovery of the Higgs Particle, which earned 2013 Nobel Prize).

Fiber Optics and the Bandwidth Explosion in the First Mile

Fiber-optic cable consists of up to hundreds of strands of glass that use light to transmit data. It often replaces existing coaxial and twisted pair cabling because it can transmit much more data at faster speeds, with less interference and better data security. Fiber-optic cable is also thinner and lighter, taking up less space during installation. The hope is to use fiber optics to expand network bandwidth capacity in order to prepare for the expected increases in Web traffic once next-generation Internet services are widely adopted.

fiber-optic cable
consists of up to hundreds of strands of glass or plastic that use light to transmit data

Telecommunication firms have made substantial investments in fiber optic cross-country and regional cable systems in the last decade. For instance, Verizon has spent over $23 billion since 2004, building and expanding its FiOS fiber-optic Internet service that can provide speeds of up to 500 Mbps, and currently has about 6.6 million FiOS customers. In 2012, Google joined the fray with Google Fiber, a 1-Gbps fiber-optic network, that is currently available in 3 cities. This installed base of fiber-optic cable represents a vast digital highway that is currently being exploited by YouTube (Google), Facebook, and other high-bandwidth applications. But despite the interest in fiber, only about 7.7% of U.S. homes had fiber connections as of 2014, a much lower percentage than a number of other countries around the world (Murphy, 2014). **Table 3.11** illustrates several optical bandwidth standards and compares them to traditional T lines.

The Last Mile: Mobile Internet Access

Fiber-optic networks carry the long-haul bulk traffic of the Internet—and in the future will play an important role in bringing high-speed broadband to the household and

TABLE 3.11	HIGH-SPEED OPTICAL BANDWIDTH STANDARDS
STANDARD	**SPEED**
T1	1.544 Mbps
T3	43.232 Mbps
OC-3	155 Mbps
OC-12	622 Mbps
OC-48	2.5 Gbps
OC-192	9.6 Gbps
OC-768	38.5 Gbps

Note: "OC" stands for Optical Carrier and is used to specify the speed of fiber-optic networks conforming to the SONET standard. SONET (Synchronous Optical Networks) includes a set of signal rate multiples for transmitting digital signals on optical fiber. The base rate (OC-1) is 51.84 Mbps.

small business. The goal of the Internet2 and GENI projects is to bring gigabit and ultimately terabit bandwidth to the household over the next 20 years. But along with fiber optics, arguably the most significant development for the Internet and Web in the last five years has been the emergence of mobile Internet access.

Wireless Internet is concerned with the last mile of Internet access to the user's home, office, car, smartphone, or tablet computer, anywhere they are located. Up until 2000, the last-mile access to the Internet—with the exception of a small satellite Internet connect population—was bound up in land lines of some sort: copper coaxial TV cables or telephone lines or, in some cases, fiber-optic lines to the office. Today, in comparison, high-speed cell phone networks and Wi-Fi network hotspots provide a major alternative.

Today, sales of desktop computers have been eclipsed by sales of smartphones, and tablet and ultramobile laptop computers with built-in wireless networking functionality. Clearly, a large part of the Internet is now mobile, access-anywhere broadband service for the delivery of video, music, and Web search. According to eMarketer, there are almost 194 million mobile Internet users in the United States in 2015 (over 60% of the population), and more than 2.25 billion worldwide (eMarketer, Inc., 2015e; 2015g).

Telephone-based versus Computer Network-based Wireless Internet Access

There are two different basic types of wireless Internet connectivity: telephone-based and computer network-based systems.

Telephone-based wireless Internet access connects the user to a global telephone system (land, satellite, and microwave) that has a long history of dealing with millions of users simultaneously and already has in place a large-scale transaction billing system and related infrastructure. Cellular telephones and the telephone industry are currently the largest providers of wireless access to the Internet today. In 2014, there were almost 1.9 billion mobile phones sold worldwide (of which 1.2 billion were smartphones), with a similar amount expected to be sold in 2015 (Gartner, Inc.,

TABLE 3.12	WIRELESS INTERNET ACCESS TELEPHONE TECHNOLOGIES		
TECHNOLOGY	SPEED	DESCRIPTION	PLAYERS
3G (THIRD GENERATION)			
CDMA2000 EV-DO HSPA (W-CDMA)	144 Kbps–2 Mbps	High-speed, mobile, always on for e-mail, browsing, instant messaging. Implementing technologies include versions of CDMA2000 EV-DO (used by CDMA providers) and HSPDA (used by GSM providers). Nearly as fast as Wi-Fi.	Verizon, Sprint, AT&T, T-Mobile, Vodafone
3.5G (3G+)			
CDMA2000 EV-DO, Rev.B	Up to 14.4 Mbps	Enhanced version of CDMA 2000 EV-DO.	Verizon, Sprint
HSPA+	Up to 11 Mbps	Enhanced version of HSPA.	AT&T, T-Mobile
4G (FOURTH GENERATION)			
Long-Term Evolution (LTE)	Up to 100 Mbps	True broadband on cell phone; lower latency than previous generations.	AT&T, Verizon, Sprint, T-Mobile (in 2013)
5G (FIFTH GENERATION)			
Standards under development; expected by 2020	Up to 10 Gbps	Goals include 1-10 Gbps connectivity; sub-1 millisecond latency enabling services such as autonomous driving, augmented reality, virtual reality, and immersive/tactile Internet.	Ericsson, SK Telecom, Huawei, Samsung, NTT DoCoMo, Verizon, national governments

2015b). **Table 3.12** summarizes the various telephone technologies used and under development for wireless Internet access.

Smartphones combine the functionality of a cell phone with that of a laptop computer with Wi-Fi capability. This makes it possible to combine in one device music, video, Web access, and telephone service. Tablet computers can also access cellular networks.

Wireless local area network (WLAN)-based Internet access derives from a completely different background from telephone-based wireless Internet access. Popularly known as **Wi-Fi**, WLANs are based on computer local area networks where the task is to connect client computers (generally stationary) to server computers within local areas of, say, a few hundred meters. WLANs function by sending radio signals that are broadcast over the airwaves using certain radio frequency ranges (2.4 GHz to 5.875

Wi-Fi
Wireless standard for Ethernet networks with greater speed and range than Bluetooth

TABLE 3.13	WIRELESS INTERNET ACCESS NETWORK TECHNOLOGIES		
TECHNOLOGY	RANGE/ SPEED	DESCRIPTION	PLAYERS
Wi-Fi (IEEE 802.11 a/b/g/n)	300 feet/ 11–70 Mbps	Evolving high-speed, fixed broadband wireless local area network for commercial and residential use	Linksys, Cisco, and other Wi-Fi router manufacturers; entrepreneurial network developers
802.11ac	500 Mbps-1 Gbps		
802.11ad	less than 10 meters/up to 7 Gbps		
WiMax (IEEE 802.16)	30 miles/ 50–70 Mbps	High-speed, medium-range, broadband wireless metropolitan area network	Clearwire, Sprint, Fujitsu, Intel, Alcatel, Proxim
Bluetooth (wireless personal area network)	1–30 meters/ 1–3 Mbps	Modest-speed, low-power, short-range connection of digital devices	Sony Ericsson, Nokia, Apple, HP, and other device makers

GHz, depending on the type of standard involved). The major technologies here are the various versions of the Wi-Fi standard, WiMax, and Bluetooth (see **Table 3.13**).

In a Wi-Fi network, a *wireless access point* (also known as a "hot spot") connects to the Internet directly via a broadband connection (cable, DSL telephone, or T1 line) and then transmits a radio signal to a transmitter/receiver installed in a tablet or laptop computer or smartphone. **Figure 3.14** illustrates how a Wi-Fi network works.

Wi-Fi provided under the 802.11 a/b/g/n specifications offers high-bandwidth capacity from 11 Mbps up to a maximum of 7 Gbps—far greater than any 3G or 4G service currently in existence—but has a limited range of 300 meters, with the exception of WiMax discussed below. Wi-Fi is also exceptionally inexpensive. The cost of creating a corporate Wi-Fi network in a single 14-story building with an access point for each floor is less than $100 an access point. It would cost well over $500,000 to wire the same building with Ethernet cable. IEEE 802.11ac is a version of the 802.11 specification adopted in December 2013 that provides for throughputs of between 500 Mbps to over 1 Gbps. The newest standard, IEEE 802.11ad provides for throughput up to 7 Gbps. The first 802.11ad devices are likely to begin shipping by the end of 2015. Next-generation Wi-Fi standards currently being worked on by the IEEE 802.11 Working Group include 802.11ay, which deals with 60 Ghz wireless operations, and will provide for data rates of up to 20 Gbps, and 802.11ax, aimed at high-efficiency WLANs used for stadiums and other areas where many people want to access a Wi-Fi network at the same time. A next-generation 802.11ah standard aimed at the Internet of Things is also being developed (Weiss, 2015; Hsu, 2015).

FIGURE 3.14	WI-FI NETWORKS

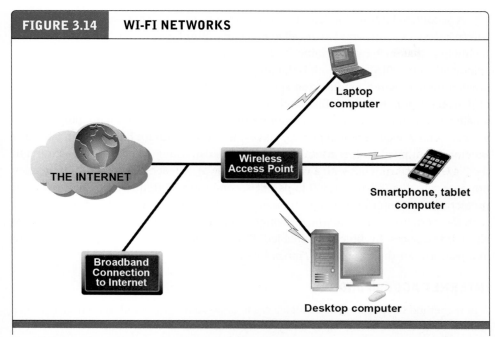

In a Wi-Fi network, wireless access points connect to the Internet using a land-based broadband connection. Clients, which could be laptops, desktops, or tablet computers, connect to the access point using radio signals.

While initially a grass roots, "hippies and hackers" public access technology, billions of dollars have subsequently been poured into private ventures seeking to create for-profit Wi-Fi networks. One of the most prominent networks has been created by Boingo Wireless with more than 1 million hot spots around the globe. Optimum WiFi (available to Optimum Online customers for free) also offers over 1 million hotspots around the world. AT&T Wi-Fi Services (formerly Wayport) created another large network that provides Wi-Fi service at hotels, airports, McDonald's, and IHOP restaurants, and Hertz airport rental offices, with more than 30,000 hot spots in the United States. T-Mobile and Sprint have also established nationwide Wi-Fi services at 2,000 Starbucks coffee shops and thousands of other public locations. Apple, in turn, has made Wi-Fi automatically available to iPhone and iPad devices as an alternative to the more expensive and much slower 3G and 4G cellular systems.

Will WLAN compete directly against far more expensive telephone 4G services? The answer is "eventually, but not right now." Wi-Fi was originally a local area network technology of limited range, for stationary client computers, but with high capacity suitable for most Web surfing and some corporate uses with modest bandwidth demands. Cellular phone systems are wide area networks of nearly unlimited range, for mobile client computers and handhelds, and with modest but rapidly increasing capacity suitable for e-mail, photos, and Web browsing (on very small screens). However, the rock-bottom price of Wi-Fi coupled with ambitious plans for a 30-mile-range WiMax (802.16) service suggests that Wi-Fi could drain significant business from far more capital-intensive cellular systems.

Bluetooth

technology standard for short-range wireless communication under 30 feet

A second WLAN technology for connecting to the Internet, and for connecting Internet devices to one another, is called Bluetooth. **Bluetooth** is a personal connectivity technology that enables links between mobile devices and connectivity to the Internet (Bluetooth.com, 2015). Bluetooth is the universal cable cutter, promising to get rid of the tangled mess of wires, cradles, and special attachments that plague the current world of personal computing. With Bluetooth, users can wear a wireless earbud, share files in a hallway or conference room, synchronize their smartphone with their laptop without a cable, send a document to a printer, and even pay a restaurant bill from the table to a Bluetooth-equipped cash register. Bluetooth is also an unregulated media operating in the 2.4 GHz spectrum but with a very limited range of 30 feet or less. It uses a frequency hopping signal with up to 1,600 hops per second over 79 frequencies, giving it good protection from interference and interception. Bluetooth-equipped devices constantly scan their environments looking for connections to compatible devices. Today, almost all mobile devices are Bluetooth-enabled. Bluetooth may also play a role in the future as a platform for the Internet of Things (see page 152).

INTERNET ACCESS DRONES

A new method of providing Internet access to areas that are not well served by wired or cellular networks is being explored by companies such as Google and Facebook. Both companies have recently purchased companies that make drones (unmanned aircraft/satellites) that may be used to provide Internet access to remote parts of the world.

In April 2014, Google purchased Titan Aerospace, which makes solar-powered drones that can fly for several years at 65,000 feet. In October 2015, Google filed paperwork with the Federal Aviation Administration covering two drones from Project Titan. Google is also experimenting with high-altitude balloons with its Project Loon. Google envisions a network of balloons circling high above the earth in the stratosphere, establishing a ring of uninterrupted connectivity. A pilot test of the concept was conducted over New Zealand in 2013, and in 2014, Google sent a prototype of a networked hot-air balloon around the world in 22 days, even taking photos for its Street View program, and in July 2015, the government of Sri Lanka announced that Sri Lanka would be the first country to use Project Loon to provide universal Internet access across Sri Lanka.

In a similar effort, Facebook has put together the Facebook Connectivity Lab, where engineers will focus on solar-powered drones, satellites, and infrared lasers capable of providing Internet access. To propel that effort, Facebook has purchased the British company Ascenta, whose founders helped create the world's longest flying solar-powered drone. In July 2015, Facebook announced that a prototype of its first Internet access solar-powered drone, Aquila, was complete and ready for testing. Created from carbon fiber, the drone has the wingspan of a Boeing 737 but weighs less than a small car, and is designed to fly at 60,000 to 90,000 feet for up to three months at a time. It reportedly uses a laser communications system that can beam data from the sky.

THE FUTURE INTERNET

The increased bandwidth and expanded wireless network connectivity of the Internet of the future will result in benefits beyond faster access and richer communications.

First-mile enhancements created by fiber-optic networks will enhance reliability and quality of Internet transmissions and create new business models and opportunities. Some of the major benefits of these technological advancements include latency solutions, guaranteed service levels, lower error rates, and declining costs. Widespread wireless access to the Internet will also essentially double or even triple the size of the online shopping marketspace because consumers will be able to shop and make purchases just about anywhere. This is equivalent to doubling the physical floor space of all shopping malls in America. We describe some of these benefits in more detail in the following sections.

Latency Solutions

One of the challenges of packet switching, where data is divided into chunks and then sent separately to meet again at the destination, is that the Internet does not differentiate between high-priority packets, such as video clips, and those of lower priority, such as self-contained e-mail messages. Because the packets cannot yet be simultaneously reassembled, the result can be distorted audio and video streams.

Differentiated quality of service (**diffserv**) is a technology that assigns levels of priority to packets based on the type of data being transmitted. Video conference packets, for example, which need to reach their destination almost instantaneously, receive much higher priority than e-mail messages. In the end, the quality of video and audio will skyrocket without undue stress on the network. Differential service is very controversial because it means some users may get more bandwidth than others, and potentially they may have to pay a higher price for more bandwidth.

differentiated quality of service (diffserv)
a new technology that assigns levels of priority to packets based on the type of data being transmitted

Guaranteed Service Levels and Lower Error Rates

In today's Internet, there is no service-level guarantee and no way to purchase the right to move data through the Internet at a fixed pace. Today's Internet promises only "best effort." The Internet is democratic—it speeds or slows everyone's traffic alike. In the future, it might be possible to purchase the right to move data through the network at a guaranteed speed in return for higher fees.

Declining Costs

As the Internet pipeline is upgraded, the availability of broadband service will expand beyond major metropolitan areas, significantly reducing the cost of access. More users mean lower cost, as products and technology catch on in the mass market. Higher volume usage enables providers to lower the cost of both access devices, or clients, and the service required to use such products. Both broadband and wireless service fees are expected to decline as geographic service areas increase, in part due to competition for that business.

The Internet of Things

No discussion of the future Internet would be complete without mentioning the **Internet of Things (IoT)**, also sometimes referred to as the Industrial Internet. Internet technology is spreading beyond the desktop, laptop, and tablet computer, and

Internet of Things (IoT)
Use of the Internet to connect a wide variety of devices, machines, and sensors

beyond the smartphone, to consumer electronics, electrical appliances, cars, medical devices, utility systems, machines of all types, even clothing—just about anything that can be equipped with sensors that can collect data and connect to the Internet, enabling the data to be analyzed with data analytics software.

IoT builds on a foundation of existing technologies, such as RFID, and is being enabled by the availability of low-cost sensors, the drop in price of data storage, the development of "Big Data" analytics software that can work with trillions of pieces of data, as well as implementation of IPv6, which will allow Internet addresses to be assigned to all of these new devices. Although IoT devices don't necessarily have to be wireless, most use wireless communications technology previously discussed, such as cellular networks, Wi-Fi, Bluetooth, or other wireless protocols such as ZigBee or Z-Wave, to connect either directly or via a mobile app to the Internet (often a cloud service).

IoT technology is powering the development of "smart" connected "things"— televisions, houses, and cars, as well as wearable technology—clothing and devices like the Apple Watch, profiled in the opening case. Smart televisions that integrate the Internet directly into the set and can run apps have become very popular, with 45% of TVs sold in the United States in the second quarter of 2015 being smart, and 50% of U.S. homes with Internet access now owning a connected TV device (NPD, 2015). Smart houses have attracted even more interest, fueled by Google's purchase of Nest Labs for $3.2 billion in 2014. Nest Labs makes smart thermostats, home security cameras, and smoke and carbon monoxide alarms. In October 2015, Nest Labs announced that it was making Nest Weave, a protocol it had developed that enables appliances, thermostats, door locks, and other devices to communicate with each other and other Nest products, available to third-party developers and manufacturers. Apple announced a smart home platform that it calls HomeKit in June 2014. HomeKit is a framework and network protocol for controlling devices in the home that is programmed directly into Apple's iOS software for iPhones and iPads, and is integrated with Siri, Apple's voice-activiated artificial intelligence assistant. By October 2015, a number of devices were designed specifically for use with HomeKit, such as a smart thermostat, a smart deadbolt lock, a home sensor that provides temperature, humidity, and air quality readings, and an iDevices switch that enables you to turn electronic devices on and off using Siri. Many cable companies such as Time Warner Cable, Comcast, and AT&T already offer connected home systems that include appliances and lights. All in all, the global market for smart house products was valued at about $20 billion in 2014, and is expected to grow to over $58 billion by 2020.

In September 2014, as discussed in the chapter-opening case, Apple introduced the Apple Watch. The Apple Watch features a fitness/activity tracker similar to offerings from Fitbit, Nike+, FuelBand, and Jawbone Up, is able to access a wide variety of apps, and also works with Apple Pay, Apple's mobile payment service. A number of other manufacturers, such as Samsung, LG, Motorola, and Swatch, also introduced smartwatches in 2014. Wearable computing is expected to grow into a $34 billion business by 2020.

Connected cars that have built-in Internet access have also arrived. Here too, Google and Apple are major players. In January 2014, Google announced the Open

Automotive Alliance, a group of leading automakers and technology companies focused on bringing the Android platform to cars. In March 2014, Apple announced CarPlay, a software platform that synchronizes iPhones to the car's infotainment system. Android Auto and CarPlay-enabled vehicles began to be introduced in 2015, and will become more widely available in 2016, when GM plans to make both available as an option on all models. Connected cars are likely to be integrated with smart home initiatives in the future. Already, iControl, which provides the software underlying automated home systems from Comcast, TimeWarner, ADT, and others, has entered into a partnership with Zubie, a provider of connected car services.

Despite all of the IoT activity, however, interoperability remains a major concern. As with many technologies in the early stages of development, many organizations are fighting to create the standards that participants in the market will follow. The AllSeen Alliance, formed by Qualcomm in December 2013 with 50 other companies, including Microsoft and Cisco, is one group that hopes to create an open source standard. Membership in the Alliance has soared by over 650% since its initial founding. Another group, the Open Interconnect Consortium, formed by Intel, Broadcom, Dell, and others apparently not happy with the AllSeen effort, formed in July 2014, and has also seen its membership soar to over 100 members. A different group, the Industrial Internet Consortium, has been formed by AT&T, Cisco, GE, IBM, and Intel to focus on engineering standards for industrial assets. The Wolfram Connected Devices Project is aimed at developing a database of IoT devices, and currently includes more than 2,000. And as with many other types of Internet-related technology, Google with its Android operating system and Apple with AirPlay wireless streaming protocol may be trying to create their own standards.

Other concerns include security and privacy. Security experts believe that IoT devices could potentially be a security disaster, with the potential for malware being spread through a connected network, and difficulty in issuing patches to devices, leaving them vulnerable (Internet Society, 2015). Data from stand-alone smart devices can reveal much personal detail about a consumer's life, and if those devices are all ultimately interconnected, there will be little that is truly private.

Although challenges remain before the Internet of Things is fully realized, it is coming closer and closer to fruition, with some experts projecting as many as 100 billion connected IoT devices and global economic impact of more than $11 trillion by 2025 (Internet Society, 2015).

3.4 THE WEB

Without the Web, there would be no e-commerce. The invention of the Web brought an extraordinary expansion of digital services to millions of amateur computer users, including color text and pages, formatted text, pictures, animations, video, and sound. In short, the Web makes nearly all the rich elements of human expression needed to establish a commercial marketplace available to nontechnical computer users worldwide.

While the Internet was born in the 1960s, the Web was not invented until 1989–1991 by Dr. Tim Berners-Lee of the European Particle Physics Laboratory, better known as CERN (Berners-Lee et al., 1994). Several earlier authors—such as Vannevar Bush (in 1945) and Ted Nelson (in the 1960s)—had suggested the possibility of organizing knowledge as a set of interconnected pages that users could freely browse (Bush, 1945; Ziff Davis Publishing, 1998). Berners-Lee and his associates at CERN built on these ideas and developed the initial versions of HTML, HTTP, a Web server, and a browser, the four essential components of the Web.

First, Berners-Lee wrote a computer program that allowed formatted pages within his own computer to be linked using keywords (hyperlinks). Clicking on a keyword in a document would immediately move him to another document. Berners-Lee created the pages using a modified version of a powerful text markup language called Standard Generalized Markup Language (SGML).

Berners-Lee called this language HyperText Markup Language, or HTML. He then came up with the idea of storing his HTML pages on the Internet. Remote client computers could access these pages by using HTTP (introduced earlier in Section 3.1 and described more fully in the next section). But these early Web pages still appeared as black and white text pages with hyperlinks expressed inside brackets. The early Web was based on text only; the original Web browser only provided a line interface.

Information being shared on the Web remained text-based until 1993, when Marc Andreessen and others at the National Center for Supercomputing Applications (NCSA) at the University of Illinois created a Web browser with a graphical user interface (GUI) called **Mosaic** that made it possible to view documents on the Web graphically—using colored backgrounds, images, and even primitive animations. Mosaic was a software program that could run on any graphically based interface such as Macintosh, Windows, or Unix. The Mosaic browser software read the HTML text on a Web page and displayed it as a graphical interface document within a GUI operating system such as Windows or Macintosh. Liberated from simple black and white text pages, HTML pages could now be viewed by anyone in the world who could operate a mouse and use a Macintosh or PC.

Aside from making the content of Web pages colorful and available to the world's population, the graphical Web browser created the possibility of **universal computing**, the sharing of files, information, graphics, sound, video, and other objects across all computer platforms in the world, regardless of operating system. A browser could be made for each of the major operating systems, and the Web pages created for one system, say, Windows, would also be displayed exactly the same, or nearly the same, on computers running the Macintosh or Unix operating systems. As long as each operating system had a Mosaic browser, the same Web pages could be used on all the different types of computers and operating systems. This meant that no matter what kind of computer you used, anywhere in the world, you would see the same Web pages. The browser and the Web have introduced us to a whole new world of computing and information management that was unthinkable prior to 1993.

In 1994, Andreessen and Jim Clark founded Netscape, which created the first commercial browser, **Netscape Navigator**. Although Mosaic had been distributed free of charge, Netscape initially charged for its software. In August 1995, Microsoft

Mosaic
Web browser with a graphical user interface (GUI) that made it possible to view documents on the Web graphically

universal computing
the sharing of files, information, graphics, sound, video, and other objects across all computer platforms in the world, regardless of operating system

Netscape Navigator
the first commercial Web browser

Corporation released its own free version of a browser, called **Internet Explorer**. In the ensuing years, Netscape fell from a 100% market share to less than .5% in 2009. The fate of Netscape illustrates an important e-commerce business lesson. Innovators usually are not long-term winners, whereas smart followers often have the assets needed for long-term survival. Much of the Netscape browser code survives today in the Firefox browser produced by Mozilla, a nonprofit heavily funded by Google.

HYPERTEXT

Web pages can be accessed through the Internet because the Web browser software on your PC can request Web pages stored on an Internet host server using the HTTP protocol. **Hypertext** is a way of formatting pages with embedded links that connect documents to one another and that also link pages to other objects such as sound, video, or animation files. When you click on a graphic and a video clip plays, you have clicked on a hyperlink. For example, when you type a Web address in your browser such as http://www.sec.gov, your browser sends an HTTP request to the sec.gov server requesting the home page of sec.gov.

HTTP is the first set of letters at the start of every Web address, followed by the domain name. The domain name specifies the organization's server computer that is housing the document. Most companies have a domain name that is the same as or closely related to their official corporate name. The directory path and document name are two more pieces of information within the Web address that help the browser track down the requested page. Together, the address is called a Uniform Resource Locator, or URL. When typed into a browser, a URL tells it exactly where to look for the information. For example, in the following URL:

http://www.megacorp.com/content/features/082602.html

http = the protocol used to display Web pages

www.megacorp.com = domain name

content/features = the directory path that identifies where on the domain Web server the page is stored

082602.html = the document name and its format (an HTML page)

The most common domain extensions (known as general top-level domains, or gTLDs) currently available and officially sanctioned by ICANN are shown in **Table 3.14**. Countries also have domain names, such as .uk, .au, and .fr (United Kingdom, Australia, and France, respectively). These are sometimes referred to as country-code top-level domains, or ccTLDs. In 2008, ICANN approved a significant expansion of gTLDs, with potential new domains representing cities (such as .berlin), regions (.africa), ethnicity (.eus), industry/activities (such as .health), and even brands (such as .deloitte). In 2009, ICANN began the process of implementing these guidelines. In 2011, ICANN removed nearly all restrictions on domain names, thereby greatly expanding the number of different domain names available. As of October 2015, about 765 gTLDs have been applied for, acquired, and launched, and another 575

Internet Explorer
Microsoft's Web browser

hypertext
a way of formatting pages with embedded links that connect documents to one another, and that also link pages to other objects such as sound, video, or animation files

TABLE 3.14	EXAMPLES OF TOP-LEVEL DOMAINS		
GENERAL TOP-LEVEL DOMAIN (GTLD)	**YEAR(S) INTRODUCED**	**PURPOSE**	**SPONSOR/ OPERATOR**
.com	1980s	Unrestricted (but intended for commercial registrants)	VeriSign
.edu	1980s	U.S. educational institutions	Educause
.gov	1980s	U.S. government	U.S. General Services Administration
.mil	1980s	U.S. military	U.S. Department of Defense Network Information Center
.net	1980s	Unrestricted (but originally intended for network providers, etc.)	VeriSign
.org	1980s	Unrestricted (but intended for organizations that do not fit elsewhere)	Public Interest Registry (was operated by VeriSign until December 31, 2002)
.int	1998	Organizations established by international treaties between governments	Internet Assigned Numbers Authority (IANA)
.aero	2001	Air-transport industry	Societé Internationale de Telecommunications Aeronautiques SC (SITA)
.biz	2001	Businesses	NeuLevel
.coop	2001	Cooperatives	DotCooperation LLC
.info	2001	Unrestricted use	Afilias LLC
.museum	2001	Museums	Museum Domain Name Association (MuseDoma)
.name	2001	For registration by individuals	Global Name Registry Ltd.
.pro	2002	Accountants, lawyers, physicians, and other professionals	RegistryPro Ltd
.jobs	2005	Job search	Employ Media LLC
.travel	2005	Travel search	Tralliance Corporation
.mobi	2005	Web sites specifically designed for mobile phones	mTLD Top Level Domain, Ltd.
.cat	2005	Individuals, organizations, and companies that promote the Catalan language and culture	Fundació puntCAT
.asia	2006	Regional domain for companies, organizations, and individuals based in Asia	DotAsia Organization
.tel	2006	Telephone numbers and other contact information	ICM Registry
.xxx	2010	New top-level domain for pornographic content	None yet approved

SOURCE: Based on data from ICANN, 2011b.

| FIGURE 3.15 | EXAMPLE HTML CODE (A) AND WEB PAGE (B) |

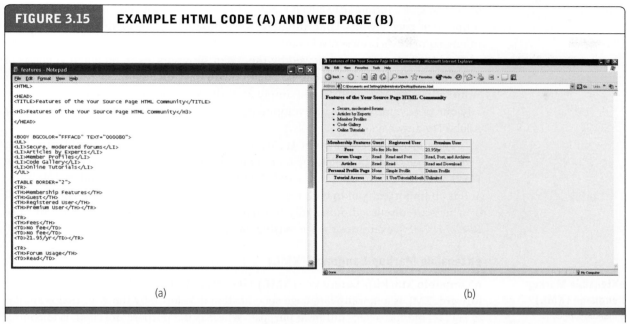

(a)   (b)

HTML is a text markup language used to create Web pages. It has a fixed set of "tags" that are used to tell the browser software how to present the content on screen. The HTML shown in Figure 3.15 (a) creates the Web page seen in Figure 3.15 (b).

---

are currently in the pipeline. The new gTLDs are in multiple languages and scripts/ characters (including Arabic, Chinese, Japanese, and Russian) and include geographic place names such as .nyc, .london, and .paris; business identifiers such as .restaurant, .realtor, .technology, and .lawyer; brand names such as .bmw and .suzuki; and a whole host of other descriptive names.

MARKUP LANGUAGES

Although the most common Web page formatting language is HTML, the concept behind document formatting actually had its roots in the 1960s with the development of Generalized Markup Language (GML).

HyperText Markup Language (HTML)

HyperText Markup Language (HTML) is a GML that is relatively easy to use. HTML provides Web page designers with a fixed set of markup "tags" that are used to format a Web page (see **Figure 3.15**). When these tags are inserted into a Web page, they are read by the browser and interpreted into a page display. You can see the source HTML code for any Web page by simply clicking on the "Page Source" command found in all browsers. In Figure 3.15, the HTML code in the first screen produces the display in the second screen.

HTML defines the structure and style of a document, including the headings, graphic positioning, tables, and text formatting. Since its introduction, the major

HyperText Markup Language (HTML)
GML that is relatively easy to use in Web page design. HTML provides Web page designers with a fixed set of markup "tags" that are used to format a Web page

browsers have continuously added features to HTML to enable programmers to further refine their page layouts. Unfortunately, some browser enhancements may work only in one company's browser. Whenever you build an e-commerce site, you should take care that the pages can be viewed by the major browsers, even outdated versions of browsers. HTML Web pages can be created with any text editor, such as Notepad or WordPad, using Microsoft Word (simply save the Word document as a Web page), or any one of several Web page development tools such as Microsoft Expression Web or Adobe Dreamweaver CC.[5]

The most recent version of HTML is HTML5. HTML5 introduces features like video playback and drag-and-drop that in the past were provided by plug-ins like Adobe Flash. HTML5 is also used in the development of mobile Web sites and mobile apps, and is an important tool in both responsive Web design and adaptive Web delivery, all of which are discussed more fully in Chapter 4. The *Insight on Technology* case, *The Rise of HTML5,* examines the increasing use of HTML5.

eXtensible Markup Language (XML)

eXtensible Markup Language (XML)
a markup language specification developed by the World Wide Web Consortium (W3C) that is designed to describe data and information

eXtensible Markup Language (XML) takes Web document formatting a giant leap forward. XML is a markup language specification developed by the W3C that is similar to HTML, but has a very different purpose. Whereas the purpose of HTML is to control the "look and feel" and display of data on the Web page, XML is designed to describe data and information. For example, consider the sample XML document in **Figure 3.16**. The first line in the sample document is the XML declaration, which is always included; it defines the XML version of the document. In this case, the document conforms to the 1.0 specification of XML. The next line defines the first element of the document (the root element): < note >. The next four lines define four child elements of the root (to, from, heading, and body). The last line defines the end of the root element. Notice that XML says nothing about how to display the data, or how the text should look on the screen. HTML is used for information display in combination with XML, which is used for data description.

FIGURE 3.16	A SIMPLE XML DOCUMENT

```
<?xml version="1.0"?>
<note>
<to>George</to>
<from>Carol</from>
<heading>Just a Reminder</heading>
<body>Don't forget to order the groceries from FreshDirect!</body>
</note>
```

The tags in this simple XML document, such as <note>, <to>, and <from>, are used to describe data and information, rather than the look and feel of the document.

[5] A detailed discussion of how to use HTML is beyond the scope of this text.

INSIGHT ON TECHNOLOGY

THE RISE OF HTML5

In 2010, Apple founder Steve Jobs lambasted Adobe Flash for its poor security, poor performance on mobile devices, and for being an energy hog. Jobs instead trumpeted HTML5 as the preferred method for displaying video online. Flash forward to 2015. A year after its official ratification by the W3C, the Web's standards-setting organization, HTML5 has become a de facto standard, proving once again Jobs' uncanny ability to see and perhaps shape the future.

HTML5 has become a catch-all term that encompasses not only the video element but also the use of the newest versions of Cascading Style Sheets (CSS3) and JavaScript, and another new tool, HTML5 Canvas. Also intended to replace plug-ins, it is used with a set of JavaScript functions to render simple animations, which reduces page load time. Multi-platform Web developers began using HTML5 because these new elements provided device independence, but soon discovered that they could do even more. The built-in functionality of mobile devices, including GPS and swiping, can be accessed, enabling m-commerce sites to build Web-based mobile apps that can replicate the native app experience. Web-based mobile apps (HTML5 apps) work just like Web pages. When a user navigates to the page containing the mobile app, the page content, including graphics, images, and video, are loaded into the browser from the Web server, rather than residing in the mobile device hardware like a native app. This concept has been embraced by mobile developers who naturally dream of being able to reach all platforms with a single product.

For businesses, the cost savings of HTML5 are obvious. A single HTML5 app requires far less effort to build than multiple native apps for the iOS, Android, Windows Phone, and other platforms.

HTML5 apps can more easily be linked to and shared on social networks, encouraging viral distribution. Some HTML5 apps can even be designed so that they can be run on mobile devices when they are offline. Differences in how apps run across different platforms and workarounds are eliminated. It used to be the case that HTML5 apps couldn't approach the smooth and speedy user experience of a native app, but thanks to many advancements in the underlying technologies behind HTML5 and improvements in the expertise of HTML5 developers, that is no longer the case. And plug-ins like Flash require installation, whereas HTML5 does not.

In 2014, the Interactive Advertising Bureau (IAB), together with a number of the largest publishers and advertising firms, urged advertisers to implement HTML5 as the standard for mobile ads in order to guarantee that ads will run and look good on different platforms, and in 2015 released guidelines that fully embrace HTML5, citing interoperability and the improved effectiveness of HTML5 ads. The rise of HTML5 has mirrored the growth of the mobile platform as it supplants Flash, which was developed for the desktop, as the preferred media delivery platform on the Web. In 2015, the number of Flash vulnerabilities reported nearly doubled to 133 from just over 70 in the previous year. Many of the Web's most prominent advertisers responded accordingly. In 2015, Facebook announced it would introduce HTML5 capability to its News Feed, and Google signaled a shift towards HTML5 by blocking Flash advertisements from autoplaying in Chrome, in part due to their notorious security issues. Mozilla followed suit with Firefox, meaning that over 80% of the Web browser market is now blocking Flash. Amazon also switched to HTML5-only promos in

(continued)

2015. The moves from these advertising and tech juggernauts have solidified the downfall of Flash and the rise of HTML5 as the future of advertising.

Retailers have taken notice. In 2015, almost 50% of Internet Retailer's top 500 mobile retailers use HTML5 for their smartphone or tablet mobile sites. One example of a company using HTML5 with success is Rakuten Shopping, an online retailer that offers a wide variety of goods online, and is currently ranked as one of Internet Retailer's top 30 mobile retailers in 2015. Using HTML5 has enabled Rakuten to shift away from using cookies to store customer attributes and has lightened the load on its servers, which are receiving fewer calls from mobile devices because once content is downloaded, it is then stored locally in the device's browser. HTML5's video tag has also enabled Rakuten to embed video within HTML pages on a mobile device.

Another example is the *Financial Times,* whose HTML5 app has proven to be an important driver for FT's business. FT first switched from a native app to HTML5 in 2011, in part to make maintaining the app across multiple platforms and devices easier. In 2013, FT rolled out a redesign of the app, featuring even more videos and personalization features. FT's managing director, Robert Grimshaw, believes that those who have chosen to develop native apps in parallel will struggle with the overhead of maintaining and developing them.

In fact, according to Indeed, which searches millions of jobs from thousands of different job sites, in 2015, "HTML5" continues to be one of the fastest growing keyword found in online job postings, ahead of iOS and Android. As a result, HTML5 projects typically take longer to develop than planned, according to a Forrester survey.

According to Tim Berners-Lee, founder and chief of the W3C and an ardent opponent of native apps because they remove functionality from the Web, HTML5 security and access control issues are currently being addressed. For instance, HTML5 has not consistently supported digital rights management (DRM). In the past, media companies developed their own copy protection standards based on geographical region and/or whether payment had been proffered. These were enforced through their own media players. Because HTML5 does not require plug-ins to play video (or audio), and further, because HTML5 is an official W3C standard charged with remaining vendor neutral, this presents a challenge to the HTML5 working group. HTML5 also allows Web sites to track how much battery power their site visitors have remaining. This feature was implemented so that sites could warn users to recharge their battery, but the reporting is so detailed that sites can determine what sites you've come from last solely based on your battery information. However, the security issues with HTML5 pale in comparison to those associated with Flash, and it's still early in the development cycle for HTML5.

Although HTML5 is being widely adopted on e-commerce and m-commerce sites, native apps aren't going anywhere. Instead, many developers are incorporating HTML5 code into native apps, creating a kind of hybrid or mixed mode app. Gartner expects that more than 50% of mobile applications will be hybrid by 2016.

SOURCES: "Transforming the Web with HTML5," by Christina Mulligan, Sdtimes.com, October 5, 2015; "With Digital Ads Shifting to HTML5, the Industry Now Has a New Set of Guidelines," by Christopher Heine, Adweek.com, September 28, 2015; "HTML5 Looks Good in Light of Google, Facebook and IAB Moves," by Carl Weinschenk, September 22, 2015; "Ad Firms Are The Reason Adobe's Flash Still Exists - Despite Its Many, Many Security Flaws," by Alice Truong, Qz.com, August 6, 2015; "How Your Smartphone's Battery Life Can Be Used to Invade Your Privacy," by Alex Hern, *The Guardian,* August 4, 2015; "Mozilla Firefox Temporarily Blocks Flash by Default," by Ian Paul, Macworld.com, June 14, 2015; "Mobile HTML5 Remains Relevant, But Faces Challenges," by George Lawton, Techtarget.com, August 28, 2014; "RIP Flash: Why HTML5 Will Finally Take Over Video and the Web This Year," by Erika Trautman, Thenextweb. com, April 19, 2014; "Top Mobile Retailers Reap Rewards Using the Magical HTML5," by Bill Siwicki, Internetretailer.com, December 13, 2013; "Financial Times: 'There Is No Drawback to Working in HTML5'," by Stuart Dredge, TheGuardian.com, April 29, 2013; "The HTML5 Promise: Responsive Web Design for Any Screen," by Tom Foremski, Siliconvalleywatcher.com, April 16, 2013; "Adobe's Flash Surrender Proves Steve Jobs and Apple Were Right All Along with HTML5," by Nigam Arora, *Forbes*, November, 9, 2011.

| FIGURE 3.17 | **SAMPLE XML CODE FOR A COMPANY DIRECTORY** |

```xml
<?xml version="1.0"?>
<Companies>
    <Company>
            <Name>Azimuth Interactive Inc.</Name>
        <Specialties>
                    <Specialty>HTML development</Specialty>
                     <Specialty>technical documentation</Specialty>
                <Specialty>ROBO Help</Specialty>
                <Country>United States</Country>
        </Specialties>
        <Location>
                <Country>United States</Country>
             <State />
              <City>Chicago</City>
        </Location>
                <Telephone>301-555-1212</Telephone>
    </Company>
    <Company>
        . . .
    </Company>
    . . .
</Companies>
```

This XML document uses tags to define a database of company names.

Figure 3.17 shows how XML can be used to define a database of company names in a company directory. Tags such as < Company >, < Name >, and < Specialty > can be defined for a single firm, or an entire industry. On an elementary level, XML is extraordinarily easy to learn and is very similar to HTML except that you can make up your own tags. At a deeper level, XML has a rich syntax and an enormous set of software tools, which make XML ideal for storing and communicating many types of data on the Web.

XML is "extensible," which means the tags used to describe and display data are defined by the user, whereas in HTML the tags are limited and predefined. XML can also transform information into new formats, such as by importing information from a database and displaying it as a table. With XML, information can be analyzed and displayed selectively, making it a more powerful alternative to HTML. This means that business firms, or entire industries, can describe all of their invoices, accounts payable, payroll records, and financial information using a Web-compatible markup language. Once described, these business documents can be stored on intranet Web servers and shared throughout the corporation.

WEB SERVERS AND CLIENTS

We have already described client/server computing and the revolution in computing architecture brought about by client/server computing. You already know that a server is a computer attached to a network that stores files, controls peripheral devices, interfaces with the outside world—including the Internet—and does some processing for other computers on the network.

But what is a Web server? **Web server software** refers to the software that enables a computer to deliver Web pages written in HTML to client computers on a network that request this service by sending an HTTP request. Apache, which works with Linux and Unix operating systems, is the most commonly used type of Web server software. Microsoft's Internet Information Services (IIS) also has significant market share (Netcraft, 2015).

Aside from responding to requests for Web pages, all Web servers provide some additional basic capabilities such as the following:

Web server software
software that enables a computer to deliver Web pages written in HTML to client computers on a network that request this service by sending an HTTP request

- *Security services*—These consist mainly of authentication services that verify that the person trying to access the site is authorized to do so. For Web sites that process payment transactions, the Web server also supports SSL and TLS, the protocols for transmitting and receiving information securely over the Internet. When private information such as names, phone numbers, addresses, and credit card data needs to be provided to a Web site, the Web server uses SSL to ensure that the data passing back and forth from the browser to the server is not compromised.

- *FTP*—This protocol allows users to transfer files to and from the server. Some sites limit file uploads to the Web server, while others restrict downloads, depending on the user's identity.

- *Search engine*—Just as search engine sites enable users to search the entire Web for particular documents, search engine modules within the basic Web server software package enable indexing of the site's Web pages and content and permit easy keyword searching of the site's content. When conducting a search, a search engine makes use of an index, which is a list of all the documents on the server. The search term is compared to the index to identify likely matches.

- *Data capture*—Web servers are also helpful at monitoring site traffic, capturing information on who has visited a site, how long the user stayed there, the date and time of each visit, and which specific pages on the server were accessed. This information is compiled and saved in a log file, which can then be analyzed. By analyzing a log file, a site manager can find out the total number of visitors, the average length of each visit, and the most popular destinations, or Web pages.

The term *Web server* is also used to refer to the physical computer that runs Web server software. Leading manufacturers of Web server computers include Lenovo, Dell, and Hewlett-Packard. Although any desktop computer can run Web server software, it is best to use a computer that has been optimized for this purpose. To be a Web server, a computer must have the Web server software installed and be connected to the Internet. Every public Web server computer has an IP address. For example, if you type http://www.pearsonhighered.com/laudon in your browser, the browser software sends a request for HTTP service to the Web server whose domain name is pearsonhighered.com. The server then locates the page named "laudon" on its hard drive, sends the page back to your browser, and displays it on your screen. Of course, firms also can use Web servers for strictly internal local area networking in intranets.

database server
server designed to access specific information within a database

ad server
server designed to deliver targeted banner ads

mail server
server that provides e-mail messages

Aside from the generic Web server software packages, there are actually many types of specialized servers on the Web, from **database servers** that access specific information within a database, to **ad servers** that deliver targeted banner ads, to **mail servers** that provide e-mail messages, and **video servers** that provide video clips. At a small e-commerce site, all of these software packages might be running on a single computer, with a single processor. At a large corporate site, there may be hundreds or thousands of discrete server computers, many with multiple processors, running specialized Web server functions. We discuss the architecture of e-commerce sites in greater detail in Chapter 4.

A **Web client**, on the other hand, is any computing device attached to the Internet that is capable of making HTTP requests and displaying HTML pages. The most common client is a Windows or Macintosh desktop computer, with various flavors of Unix/Linux computers a distant third. However, the fastest growing category of Web clients is not computers at all, but mobile devices. In general, a Web client can be any device—including a printer, refrigerator, stove, home lighting system, or automobile instrument panel—capable of sending and receiving information from a Web server.

WEB BROWSERS

A **Web browser** is a software program whose primary purpose is to display Web pages. Browsers also have added features, such as e-mail and newsgroups (an online discussion group or forum). As of September 2015, the leading Web browser remains Microsoft Internet Explorer, with about 52% of the market. The second most popular browser, with about a 30% market share, is Google's Chrome, a small, yet technologically advanced open source browser. Mozilla Firefox has dropped to third place, with only about 11.5% of the U.S. Web browser market. First released in 2004, Firefox is a free, open source Web browser for the Windows, Linux, and Macintosh operating systems, based on Mozilla open source code (which originally provided the code for Netscape). It is small and fast and offers many features such as pop-up blocking and tabbed browsing. Apple's Safari browser is fourth, with about 5% of the market (Marketshare.hitslink.com, 2015). In July 2015, Microsoft introduced Edge, an entirely new browser bundled with its new operating system, Windows 10. Edge is designed to replace Internet Explorer. However, despite the popularity of Windows 10 (it has already been installed on 110 million devices as of October 2015), Edge has thus far been largely ignored by Windows 10 adopters. Instead, Chrome is the dominant browser on Windows 10 (Keizer, 2015).

3.5 THE INTERNET AND THE WEB: FEATURES AND SERVICES

The Internet and the Web have spawned a number of powerful software applications upon which the foundations of e-commerce are built. You can think of all these as Web services, and it is interesting as you read along to compare these services to other traditional media such as television or print media. If you do, you will quickly realize the richness of the Internet environment.

E-MAIL

Since its earliest days, **electronic mail**, or **e-mail**, has been the most-used application of the Internet. Worldwide, there are an estimated 4.4 billion e-mail accounts, sending

video server
server that serves video clips

Web client
any computing device attached to the Internet that is capable of making HTTP requests and displaying HTML pages, most commonly a Windows PC or Macintosh

Web browser
software program whose primary purpose is to display Web pages

electronic mail (e-mail)
the most-used application of the Internet. Uses a series of protocols to enable messages containing text, images, sound, and video clips to be transferred from one Internet user to another

an estimated 205 billion e-mails a day. There are an estimated 1.4 billion mobile e-mail users worldwide, and their number is expected to almost double, to 2.5 billion, by 2019 (Radicati Group, 2015). Estimates vary on the amount of spam, ranging from 40% to 90%. E-mail marketing and spam are examined in more depth in Chapter 6.

E-mail uses a series of protocols to enable messages containing text, images, sound, and video clips to be transferred from one Internet user to another. Because of its flexibility and speed, it is now the most popular form of business communication—more popular than the phone, fax, or snail mail (the U.S. Postal Service). In addition to text typed within the message, e-mail also allows **attachments**, which are files inserted within the e-mail message. The files can be documents, images, sounds, or video clips.

attachment
a file inserted within an e-mail message

INSTANT MESSAGING

Instant messaging (IM) allows you to send messages in real time, one line at a time, unlike e-mail. E-mail messages have a time lag of several seconds to minutes between when messages are sent and received. IM displays lines of text entered on a computer almost instantaneously. Recipients can then respond immediately to the sender the same way, making the communication more like a live conversation than is possible through e-mail. To use IM, users create a buddy list they want to communicate with, and then enter short text messages that their buddies will receive instantly (if they are online at the time). And although text remains the primary communication mechanism in IM, more advanced systems also provide voice and video chat functionality. Instant messaging over the Internet competes with cell phone Short Message Service (SMS) texting, which is far more expensive than IM.

instant messaging (IM)
displays words typed on a computer almost instantaneously. Recipients can then respond immediately to the sender the same way, making the communication more like a live conversation than is possible through e-mail

The major IM systems are Skype, Yahoo Messenger, Google Talk, and AIM (AOL Instant Messenger). Facebook also offers instant messaging services via Facebook Chat. IM systems were initially developed as proprietary systems, with competing firms offering versions that did not work with one another. Today, there still is no built-in interoperability among the major IM systems. Mobile messaging apps, such as Facebook Messenger, WhatsApp (purchased by Facebook for $22 billion in 2014), Snapchat (which allows users to send pictures, videos, and texts that will disappear after a short period of time), Viber, and others are also becoming very popular, providing competition for both traditional desktop IM systems and SMS text messaging.

SEARCH ENGINES

Search engines identify Web pages that appear to match keywords, also called queries, entered by a user and then provide a list of the best matches (search results). Almost 85% of U.S. Internet users regularly use search engines from either desktop or mobile devices, and they generate around 18 billion queries a month (eMarketer, Inc., 2015h; comScore, 2015a). There are hundreds of different search engines, but the vast majority of the search results are supplied by the top five providers (see **Figure 3.18**).

search engine
identifies Web pages that appear to match keywords, also called queries, entered by the user and then provides a list of the best matches

Web search engines started out in the early 1990s shortly after Netscape released the first commercial Web browser. Early search engines were relatively simple software programs that roamed the nascent Web, visiting pages and gathering information about the content of each Web page. These early programs were called variously crawlers, spiders, and wanderers; the first full-text crawler that indexed the contents of an entire Web page was called WebCrawler, released in 1994. AltaVista (1995), one of the first widely used search engines, was the first to allow "natural language" queries such as "history of Web search engines" rather than "history + Web + search engine."

The first search engines employed simple keyword indexes of all the Web pages visited. They would count the number of times a word appeared on the Web page, and store this information in an index. These search engines could be easily fooled by Web designers who simply repeated words on their home pages. The real innovations in search engine development occurred through a program funded by the Department of Defense called the Digital Library Initiative, designed to help the Pentagon find research papers in large databases. Stanford, Berkeley, and three other universities became hotbeds of Web search innovations in the mid-1990s. At Stanford in 1994, two computer science students, David Filo and Jerry Yang, created a hand-selected list of their favorite Web pages and called it "Yet Another Hierarchical Officious Oracle," or Yahoo!. Yahoo initially was not a real search engine, but rather an edited selection of Web sites organized by categories the editors found useful. Yahoo later developed "true" search engine capabilities.

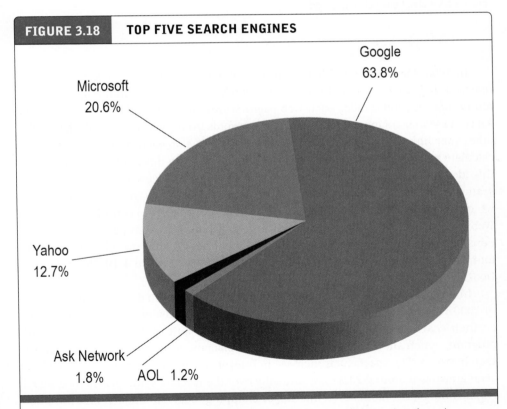

FIGURE 3.18   **TOP FIVE SEARCH ENGINES**

Google 63.8%

Microsoft 20.6%

Yahoo 12.7%

Ask Network 1.8%

AOL 1.2%

Google is, by far, the leading search engine based on its percentage share of the number of searches.
SOURCE: Based on data from comScore, 2015.

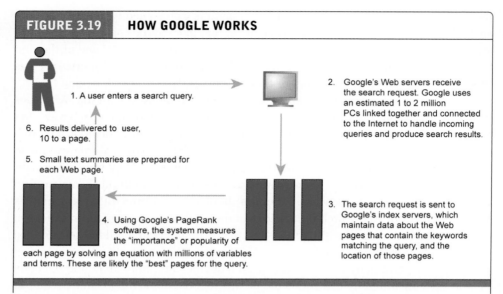

FIGURE 3.19   HOW GOOGLE WORKS

1. A user enters a search query.

2. Google's Web servers receive the search request. Google uses an estimated 1 to 2 million PCs linked together and connected to the Internet to handle incoming queries and produce search results.

6. Results delivered to user, 10 to a page.

5. Small text summaries are prepared for each Web page.

4. Using Google's PageRank software, the system measures the "importance" or popularity of each page by solving an equation with millions of variables and terms. These are likely the "best" pages for the query.

3. The search request is sent to Google's index servers, which maintain data about the Web pages that contain the keywords matching the query, and the location of those pages.

The Google search engine is continuously crawling the Web, indexing the content of each page, calculating its popularity, and caching the pages so that it can respond quickly to your request to see a page. The entire process takes about one-half of a second.

In 1998, Larry Page and Sergey Brin, two Stanford computer science students, released their first version of the Google search engine. This search engine was different: not only did it index each Web page's words, but Page had discovered that the AltaVista search engine not only collected keywords from sites but also calculated what other sites linked to each page. By looking at the URLs on each Web page, they could calculate an index of popularity. AltaVista did nothing with this information. Page took this idea and made it a central factor in ranking a Web page's appropriateness to a search query. He patented the idea of a Web page ranking system (PageRank System), which essentially measures the popularity of the Web page. Brin contributed a unique Web crawler program that indexed not just keywords on a Web page, but combinations of words (such as authors and their article titles). These two ideas became the foundation for the Google search engine (Brandt, 2004). **Figure 3.19** illustrates how Google works.

Initially, few understood how to make money from search engines. That changed in 2000 when Goto.com (later Overture) allowed advertisers to bid for placement on their search engine results, and Google followed suit in 2003 with its AdWords program, which allowed advertisers to bid for placement of short text ads on Google search results. The spectacular increase in Internet advertising revenues (which have been growing at around 20%–25% annually over the last few years) has helped search engines transform themselves into major shopping tools and created an entire new industry called "search engine marketing."

When users enter a search term at Google, Bing, Yahoo, or any of the other Web sites serviced by these search engines, they receive two types of listings: sponsored links, for which advertisers have paid to be listed (usually at the top of the search results page), and unsponsored "organic" search results. Advertisers can also purchase small text ads on the right side of the search results page. In addition, search engines have extended their services to include news, maps, satellite images, computer images, e-mail, group calendars, group meeting tools, and indexes of scholarly papers.

Although the major search engines are used for locating general information of interest to users, search engines have also become a crucial tool within e-commerce sites. Customers can more easily search for the product information they want with the help of an internal search program; the difference is that within Web sites, the search engine is limited to finding matches from that one site. For instance, more online shoppers use Amazon's internal search engine to look for products than conducting a product search using Google, a fact noted by Google's executive chairman Eric Schmidt, who believes that Amazon search poses a significant threat to Google (Mangalindan, 2014).

ONLINE FORUMS

An **online forum** (also referred to as a message board, bulletin board, discussion board, discussion group, or simply a board or forum) is a Web application that enables Internet users to communicate with each other, although not in real time. A forum provides a container for various discussions (or "threads") started (or "posted") by members of the forum, and depending on the permissions granted to forum members by the forum's administrator, enables a person to start a thread and reply to other people's threads. Most forum software allows more than one forum to be created. The forum administrator typically can edit, delete, move, or otherwise modify any thread on the forum. Unlike an electronic mailing list (such as a listserv), which automatically sends new messages to a subscriber, an online forum typically requires that the member visit the forum to check for new posts. Some forums offer an "e-mail notification" feature that notifies users that a new post of interest to them has been made.

online forum
a Web application that allows Internet users to communicate with each other, although not in real time

STREAMING MEDIA

Streaming media enables live Web video, music, video, and other large-bandwidth files to be sent to users in a variety of ways that enable the user to play back the files. In some situations, such as live Web video, the files are broken into chunks and served by specialized video servers to users in chunks. Client software puts the chunks together and plays the video. In other situations, such as YouTube, a single large file is downloaded from a standard Web server to users who can begin playing the video before the entire file is downloaded. Streamed files must be viewed "live;" they cannot be stored on client hard drives without special software. Streamed files are "played" by a software program such as Windows Media Player, Apple QuickTime, Adobe Flash, and RealMedia Player. There are a number of tools used to create streaming files,

streaming media
enables music, video, and other large files to be sent to users in chunks so that when received and played, the file comes through uninterrupted

including HTML5 and Adobe Flash, as well as technologies specifically adapted for the mobile platform such as the Meerkat and Periscope apps.

Sites such as YouTube, Metacafe, and Facebook have popularized user-generated video streaming. Web advertisers increasingly use video to attract viewers. Streaming audio and video segments used in Web ads and news stories are perhaps the most frequently used streaming services. As the capacity of the Internet grows, streaming media will play an even larger role in e-commerce.

COOKIES

cookie

a tool used by Web sites to store information about a user. When a visitor enters a Web site, the site sends a small text file (the cookie) to the user's computer so that information from the site can be loaded more quickly on future visits. The cookie can contain any information desired by the site designers

A **cookie** is a tool used by a Web site to store information about a user. When a visitor enters a Web site, the site sends a small text file (the cookie) to the user's computer so that information from the site can be loaded more quickly on future visits. The cookie can contain any information desired by the Web site designers, including customer number, pages visited, products examined, and other detailed information about the behavior of the consumer at the site. Cookies are useful to consumers because the Web site will recognize returning patrons and not ask them to register again. Cookies are also used by advertisers to ensure visitors do not receive the same advertisements repeatedly. Cookies can also help personalize a Web site by allowing the site to recognize returning customers and make special offers to them based on their past behavior at the site. Cookies allow Web marketers to customize products and segment markets—the ability to change the product or the price based on prior consumer information (described more fully in Chapter 6). As we will discuss throughout the book, cookies also can pose a threat to consumer privacy, and at times they are bothersome. Many people clear their cookies at the end of every day. Some disable them entirely using tools built into most browsers.

WEB 2.0 FEATURES AND SERVICES

Today's broadband Internet infrastructure has greatly expanded the services available to users. These capabilities have formed the basis for new business models. Digital content and digital communications are the two areas where innovation is most rapid. Web 2.0 applications and services are "social" in nature because they support communication among individuals within groups or social networks.

Online Social Networks

Online social networks are services that support communication within networks of friends, colleagues, and entire professions. Online social networks have developed very large worldwide audiences and form the basis for new advertising platforms and for social e-commerce (see Chapters 6, 7, and 11). The largest social networks are Facebook (1.5 billion members worldwide), Instagram (400 million members worldwide), LinkedIn (more than 380 million members worldwide), Twitter (more than 315 million active users worldwide), and Pinterest (around 100 million active users). These networks rely on user-generated content (messages, photos, and videos) and emphasize sharing of content. All of these features require significant broadband Internet connectivity and equally large cloud computing facilities to store content.

Blogs

A **blog** (originally called a **weblog**) is a personal Web page that typically contains a series of chronological entries (newest to oldest) by its author, and links to related Web pages. The blog may include a blogroll (a collection of links to other blogs) and track-backs (a list of entries in other blogs that refer to a post on the first blog). Most blogs allow readers to post comments on the blog entries as well. The act of creating a blog is often referred to as "blogging." Blogs are either hosted by a third-party site such as Blogger, LiveJournal, TypePad, Xanga, WordPress, and Tumblr, or prospective bloggers can download software such as Movable Type to create a blog that is hosted by the user's ISP. Blog pages are usually variations on templates provided by the blogging service or software and hence require no knowledge of HTML. Therefore, millions of people without HTML skills of any kind can post their own Web pages, and share content with friends and relatives. The totality of blog-related Web sites is often referred to as the "blogosphere."

Blogs have become hugely popular. Tumblr, WordPress, and LiveJournal together hosted over 330 million blogs as of October 2015, so it is likely that the total number is significantly higher. According to eMarketer, there are an estimated 28 million active U.S. bloggers, and 79 million U.S. blog readers (eMarketer, Inc., 2015i; 2015j). No one knows how many of these blogs are kept up to date or are just yesterday's news. And no one knows how many of these blogs have a readership greater than one (the blog author). In fact, there are so many blogs you need a search engine just to find them, or you can just go to a list of the most popular 100 blogs and dig in.

Really Simple Syndication (RSS)

The rise of blogs is correlated with a distribution mechanism for news and information from Web sites that regularly update their content. **Really Simple Syndication (RSS)** is an XML format that allows users to have digital content, including text, articles, blogs, and podcast audio files, automatically sent to their computers over the Internet. An RSS aggregator software application that you install on your computer gathers material from the Web sites and blogs that you tell it to scan and brings new informa-tion from those sites to you. Sometimes this is referred to as "syndicated" content because it is distributed by news organizations and other syndicators (or distributors). Users download an RSS aggregator and then "subscribe" to the RSS "feeds." When you go to your RSS aggregator's page, it will display the most recent updates for each channel to which you have subscribed. RSS has rocketed from a "techie" pastime to a broad-based movement. Although Google has closed down Google Reader, a popular RSS product, a number of other RSS reader options remain, including Feedly, Reeder, and NewsBlur.

blog
personal Web page that is created by an individual or corporation to communicate with readers

Really Simple Syndication (RSS)
program that allows users to have digital content, including text, articles, blogs, and podcast audio files, automatically sent to their computers over the Internet

Podcasting

podcast

an audio presentation—
such as a radio show,
audio from a movie, or
simply a personal audio
presentation—stored as an
audio file and posted to
the Web

A **podcast** is an audio presentation—such as a radio show, audio from a movie, or simply a personal audio presentation—stored as an audio file and posted to the Web. Listeners download the files from the Web and play them on their players or computers. While commonly associated with Apple's iPod portable music player, you can listen to MP3 podcast files with any MP3 player. Podcasting has transitioned from an amateur independent producer media in the "pirate radio" tradition to a professional news and talk content distribution channel. For instance, National Public Radio's This American Life's Serial podcast has been downloaded over 90 million times, and in October 2015, WNYC, a major public radio station, announced it would create a new division devoted solely to the production of podcasts.

Wikis

wiki

Web application that allows
a user to easily add and edit
content on a Web page

A **wiki** is a Web application that allows a user to easily add and edit content on a Web page. (The term wiki derives from the "wiki wiki" (quick or fast) shuttle buses at Honolulu Airport.) Wiki software enables documents to be written collectively and collaboratively. Most wiki systems are open source, server-side systems that store content in a relational database. The software typically provides a template that defines layout and elements common to all pages, displays user-editable source code (usually plain text), and then renders the content into an HTML-based page for display in a Web browser. Some wiki software allows only basic text formatting, whereas others allow the use of tables, images, or even interactive elements, such as polls and games. Because wikis by their very nature are very open in allowing anyone to make changes to a page, most wikis provide a means to verify the validity of changes via a "Recent Changes" page, which enables members of the wiki community to monitor and review the work of other users, correct mistakes, and hopefully deter "vandalism."

The most well-known wiki is Wikipedia, an online encyclopedia that contains more than 4.9 million English-language articles on a variety of topics, appears in 288 languages, and has around 500 million unique visitors each month worldwide. The Wikimedia Foundation, which operates Wikipedia, also operates a variety of related projects, including Wikibooks, a collection of collaboratively written free textbooks and manuals; Wikinews, a free content news source; and Wiktionary, a collaborative project to produce a free multilingual dictionary in every language, with definitions, etymologies, pronunciations, quotations, and synonyms.

Music and Video Services

With the low-bandwidth connections of the early Internet, audio and video files were difficult to download and share, but with the huge growth in broadband connections, these files are not only commonplace but today constitute the majority of Web traffic. Spurred on by the worldwide sales of more than 1 billion iOS devices (iPhones, iPads, and iPod Touches) as of January 2015, as well as millions of other smartphones, the Internet has become a virtual digital river of music and video files.

The Apple iTunes store is probably the most well-known repository of digital music tracks online, with a catalog of more than 43 million songs in its catalog as of May 2015. Google Play offers over 30 million, and there are hundreds of other sites offering music downloads as well. In addition, streaming music services (see the *Insight on Technology* case study, *Music: Battle of the Titans and Lilliputians,* in Chapter 2) and Internet radio add to the bandwidth devoted to the delivery of online music.

Online video viewing has also exploded in popularity. In June 2015, for instance, around 193 million U.S. Internet users watched online video content via a desktop computer, while 100 million watched on smartphones and tablet computers (comScore, 2015b). Cisco estimates that consumer Internet video traffic constituted a whopping 64% of all consumer Internet traffic in 2014, not including the video exchanged through P2P file sharing (Cisco, 2015). By far, the most common type of Internet video is provided by YouTube, with more than 1 billion unique visitors worldwide each month who watch more than 6 billion hours of video, most of it short clips taken from television shows, or user-generated content. The largest sources of legal, paid television content are the iTunes Store, where you can purchase specific episodes or entire seasons of TV shows, Netflix, and Hulu.

Internet advertising makes extensive use of streaming video ads. Companies that want to demonstrate use of their products have found video clips to be extremely effective. And audio reports and discussions also have become commonplace, either as marketing materials or customer reports.

Future digital video networks will be able to deliver better-than-broadcast-quality video over the Internet to computers and other devices in homes and on the road. High-quality interactive video and audio makes sales presentations and demonstrations more effective and lifelike and enables companies to develop new forms of customer support. The Internet has become a major distribution channel for movies, television shows, and sporting events (see Chapter 10).

Internet Telephony

If the telephone system were to be built from scratch today, it would be an Internet-based, packet-switched network using TCP/IP because it would be less expensive and more efficient than the alternative existing system, which involves a mix of circuit-switched legs with a digital backbone. In fact, AT&T has begun testing all-digital IP phone networks in several U.S. cities. Likewise, if cable television systems were built from scratch today, they most likely would use Internet technologies for the same reasons.

IP telephony is a general term for the technologies that use **Voice over Internet Protocol (VoIP)** and the Internet's packet-switched network to transmit voice, fax, and other forms of audio communication over the Internet. VoIP can be used over a traditional handset as well as over a mobile device. VoIP avoids the long distance charges imposed by traditional phone companies.

There were about 224 million residential VoIP subscribers worldwide in 2014, and in the United States, more than half of residential customers are now using VoIP, and

IP telephony
a general term for the technologies that use VoIP and the Internet's packet-switched network to transmit voice and other forms of audio communication over the Internet

Voice over Internet Protocol (VoIP)
protocol that allows for transmission of voice and other forms of audio communication over the Internet

this number is expanding rapidly as cable systems provide telephone service as part of their "triple play": voice, Internet, and TV as a single package. This number is dwarfed, however, by the number of mobile VoIP subscribers, which has grown explosively over the last several years, fueled by the rampant growth of mobile messaging apps that now also provide free VoIP services, such as Facebook Messenger, WhatsApp, Viber, WeChat, Line, KakaoTalk, and others (Infonetics Research, 2015; BuddeComm, 2015).

VoIP is a disruptive technology. In the past, voice and fax were the exclusive provenance of the regulated telephone networks. With the convergence of the Internet and telephony, however, this dominance is already starting to change, with local and long distance telephone providers and cable companies becoming ISPs, and ISPs getting into the phone market. Key players in the VoIP market include independent service providers such as VoIP pioneers Vonage and Skype (now owned by Microsoft), as well as traditional players such as telephone and cable companies that have moved aggressively into the market. Skype currently dominates the international market and carries 50 billion minutes (one-third of the world's long distance traffic) each month (Skype for Business Team, 2015).

Video Conferencing, Video Chatting, and Telepresence

Internet video conferencing is accessible to anyone with a broadband Internet connection and a Web camera (webcam). The most widely used Web conferencing suite of tools is WebEx (now owned by Cisco). VoIP companies such as Skype and ooVoo also provide more limited Web conferencing capabilities, commonly referred to as video chatting. Apple's FaceTime is another video chatting technology available for iOS mobile devices with a forward-facing camera and Macintosh computers equipped with Apple's version of a webcam, called a FaceTime camera.

Telepresence takes video conferencing up several notches. Rather than single persons "meeting" by using webcams, telepresence creates an environment in a room using multiple cameras and screens, which surround the users. The experience is uncanny and strange at first because as you look at the people in the screens, they are looking directly at you. Broadcast quality and higher screen resolutions help create the effect. Users have the sensation of "being in the presence of their colleagues" in a way that is not true for traditional webcam meetings. Providers of telepresence software and hardware include Cisco, HP, and Dimension Data (formerly Teliris).

Intelligent Personal Assistants

The idea of having a conversation with a computer, having it understand you and be able to carry out tasks according to your direction, has long been a part of science fiction, from the 1968 Hollywood movie *2001: A Space Odyssey*, to an old Apple promotional video depicting a professor using his personal digital assistant to organize his life, gather data, and place orders at restaurants. That was all fantasy. But Apple's Siri, billed as an intelligent personal assistant and knowledge navigator and released in 2011, has many of the capabilities of the computer assistants found in fiction. Siri has a natural language, conversational interface, situational awareness, and is capable of carrying out many tasks based on verbal commands by delegating requests to a variety of different Web services. For instance, you can ask Siri to find a restaurant nearby that serves Italian food. Siri may show you an ad for a local restaurant in the process. Once you have identified a restaurant you would like to eat at, you can ask Siri to make a reservation using OpenTable. You can also ask Siri to place an appointment on your calendar, search for airline flights, and figure out what's the fastest route between your current location and a destination using public transit. The answers are not always completely accurate, but critics have been impressed with its uncanny abilities. Siri is currently available on the Apple Watch, the iPhone 4S and later versions, iPads with Retina display, the iPad Mini, and iPod Touches (fifth generation and later versions).

In 2012, Google released its version of an intelligent assistant for Android-based smartphones, which it calls Google Now. Google Now is part of the Google Search mobile application. While Google Now has many of the capabilities of Apple's Siri, it attempts to go further by predicting what users may need based on situational awareness, including physical location, time of day, previous location history, calendar, and expressed interests based on previous activity, as described in its patent application (United States Patent Office, 2012). For instance, if you often search for a particular musician or style of music, Google Now might provide recommendations for similar music. If it knows that you go to a health club every other day, Google Now will remind you not to schedule events during these periods. If it knows that you typically read articles about health issues, the system might monitor Google News for similar articles and make recommendations. Other intelligent personal assistants include Samsung's S Voice, LG's Voice Mate, and Microsoft's Cortana.

3.6 MOBILE APPS: THE NEXT BIG THING IS HERE

The use of mobile Internet access devices such as smartphones, iPads and other tablet computers, and laptops in e-commerce has truly exploded. From nearly zero mobile commerce prior to 2007, today, mobile B2C e-commerce revenue (retail and travel) in the United States is expected to be around $128 billion, representing about 25% of all B2C e-commerce sales in 2015. According to market research firm eMarketer, over 80% of all online shoppers are mobile shoppers as well, and this number is expected to increase to over 95% by 2019. In addition, eMarketer also believes that over 120 million people in the United States are expected to make a purchase through a mobile device in 2015, and this number will increase over 160 million by 2019 (eMarketer, Inc., 2015k). While mobile commerce is more widespread among younger consumers, even those over 55 are beginning to use this channel more frequently. Tablets are the preferred mobile shopping device. Almost 90% of tablet owners have reported using their tablets to shop, particularly on nights and weekends, and often from the comfort of couch or bed. Over 70% have made a purchase using their tablet (eMarketer, Inc., 2015k). As a result, companies are rapidly increasing their investment in mobile commerce technologies. For instance, the number of retailers with responsive design Web sites in Internet Retailer's 2015 Mobile 500 increased by 164% in 2015, from 39 to 103. Likewise, the number of commerce-enabled smartphone apps also increased, up more than 12% to 439 from 262 retailers. As with many other aspects of e-commerce, Amazon is a leader, with an estimated $16.8 billion in mobile sales worldwide in 2014. Around $34 billion in mobile sales worldwide were transacted using eBay (Internet Retailer, 2015).

Mobile capabilities include making sure Web sites are compatible with mobile browsers, are optimized for use on various devices (discussed further in Chapter 4), and provide downloadable mobile apps. Although both are important, right now, mobile apps appear to be attracting most of the attention. According to Internet Retailer, mobile shopping done from within a mobile app leads to a 30% higher conversion rate compared to mobile shopping done on a mobile Web site. *Insight on Business: Apps For Everything: The App Ecosystem* gives you some further background on mobile apps.

PLATFORMS FOR MOBILE APPLICATION DEVELOPMENT

Unlike mobile Web sites, which can be accessed by any Web-enabled mobile device, native apps, which are designed specifically to operate using the mobile device's hardware and operating system, are platform-specific. Applications for the iPhone, iPad, and other iOS devices are written in the Objective-C programming language using the iOS SDK (software developer kit). Applications for Android operating system–based phones typically are written using Java, although portions of the code may be in the C or C++ programming language. BlackBerry apps also are written in Java. Applications for Windows mobile devices are written in C or C++. In addition to creating native apps using a programming language such as Objective C or Java, there are also hundreds of low-cost or open source app development toolkits that make creating cross-platform mobile apps relatively easy and inexpensive without having to use a device-specific programming language. See Section 4.6 in Chapter 4 for more information.

APP MARKETPLACES

Once written, applications are distributed through various marketplaces. Android apps for Android-based phones are distributed through Google Play, which is controlled by Google. iPhone applications are distributed through Apple's App Store. BlackBerry applications can be found in RIM's App World, while Microsoft operates the Windows Phone Marketplace for Windows mobile devices. Apps can also be purchased from third-party vendors such as Amazon's Appstore. It is important to distinguish "native" mobile apps, which run directly on a mobile device and rely on the device's internal operating system, from Web apps referred to in Section 3.5, which install into your browser, although these can operate in a mobile environment as well.

INSIGHT ON BUSINESS

APPS FOR EVERYTHING: THE APP ECOSYSTEM

When Steve Jobs introduced the iPhone in January 2007, no one—including himself—envisioned that the device would launch a revolution in consumer and business software, or become a major e-commerce platform, let alone a game platform, advertising platform, and general media platform for television shows, movies, videos, and e-books. In short, it's become the personal computer all over again, just in a much smaller form factor.

The iPhone's original primary functions, beyond being a cell phone, were to be a camera, text messaging device, and Web browser. What Apple initially lacked for the iPhone were software applications that would take full advantage of its computing capabilities. The solution was software developed by outside developers—tens of thousands of outside developers—who were attracted to the mission by potential profits and fame from the sale or free distribution of their software applications on a platform approved by the leading innovator in handheld computing and cellular devices. More than two-thirds of apps are free. Every month, Apple receives thousands of new apps from over 9 million registered developers who may be teenagers in a garage, major video game developers, or major publishers, as well as Fortune 500 consumer products firms using apps for marketing and promotion.

In July 2008, Apple introduced the App Store, which provides a platform for the distribution and sale of apps by Apple as well as by independent developers. Following in the footsteps of the iTunes music store, Apple hoped that the software apps—most free—would drive sales of the iPhone device. It was not expecting the App Store itself to become a major source of revenue. Fast forward to 2015: there are now an estimated 1.5 million approved apps available for download

from the App Store. Other smartphone developers also followed suit: by 2015, there were over 1.6 million apps available for Android devices as well. As of June 2015, more than 100 billion apps had been downloaded from the App Store, and approximately 8 million apps are downloaded from the App Store every day. Apple has reported that customers spent about $15 billion in the App Store in 2014, generating an estimated profit for Apple of nearly $5 billion. Even so, Apple's primary goal in offering apps is not to make money from them, but instead to drive sales of devices—the iPhones, iPads, and iPods that need software to become useful. It's the reverse of printer companies who make cheap printers in order to sell expensive ink. At the same time, apps tie the customer to a hardware platform: the cost of switching to a different platform rises with each new app installed.

The app phenomenon has spawned a new digital ecosystem: tens of thousands of developers, a wildly popular hardware platform, and millions of consumers looking for a computer in their pocket that can replace their now clunky desktop-laptop Microsoft Windows computers, do a pretty good job as a digital media center while on the road, and, by the way, serve as a cell phone. And the mobile platform has even started to usurp TV as the most popular entertainment medium. A 2015 report from Flurry found that the average U.S. consumer now spends nearly 200 minutes per day within apps, well ahead of the 168 minutes spent watching TV. As recently as 2014, TV was still comfortably ahead of apps. More consumers are opting to consume media on their phones than ever before, which is more good news for app developers.

The range of applications among the 1.5 million or so apps on the Apple platform is staggering and defies brief description. Currently, there are 24 different categories. You can use the Genius feature to recommend new apps based on ones you

(continued)

already have. The most popular app categories are games, education, business, lifestyle, and entertainment.

The implications of the app ecosystem for e-commerce are significant. The smartphone in your pocket becomes not only a general-purpose computer, but also an always-present shopping tool for consumers, as well as an entirely new marketing and advertising platform for vendors. Early e-commerce applications using desktops and laptops were celebrated as allowing people to shop in their pajamas. Smartphones extend this range from pajamas to office desktops to trains, planes, and cars, all fully clothed. You can shop anywhere, shop everywhere, and shop all the time, in between talking, texting, watching video, and listening to music.

Almost all of the top 100 brands have a presence in at least one of the major app stores, and more than 90% have an app in the Apple App Store. Here are a few examples of how some different firms are using apps to advance and support their brands:

- Coca-Cola Freestyle: Allows users to create custom drinks by combining choices and use the Location Finder to find a Freestyle machine to actually create the drink
- Benjamin Moore's Color Capture: Enables users to match colors and paints
- Colgate-Palmolive's Max White Photo Recharger: Enables users to whiten their teeth in photos
- Tiffany's Engagement Ring Finder: Lets users view diamonds by size, shape, setting, metal, and design
- Charmin's SitOrSquat Restroom Finder: Provides users with locations of nearest public bathrooms, including cleanliness reviews, availability of changing tables, and handicapped access.

There are, of course, dangers in any ecosystem dominated by a single company. The Apple iOS platform is a closed sandbox, inviting the potential for censorship. Whether that censorship is justified depends upon who you ask. For instance, Apple has removed applications because of sexually themed content. Clearly Apple is concerned the App Store might become an adult digital theme park that would turn off parents and families who are the target audience for iPhone and iPad sales. In 2015, Apple removed all games and apps featuring images of the Confederate flag, including a game intended to teach users about Civil War history. After some backlash, they reinstated many of these games, but required the game developers to remove the flag from screenshots and app icons. Apple has also had to fight to keep malware off of the App Store. For instance, a Russian app entitled "Find and Call" purported to simplify users' contacts lists, but instead stole those contacts and uploaded the address book to a remote server, spamming those addresses. In 2013, researchers at Georgia Tech created an app that was able to elude all of Apple iOS's most current security tools, including sandboxing, code signing, and various anti-exploit technologies. Thus far, most Apple app malware has been targeted toward jailbroken iPhones. However, in 2015, security researchers exposed flaws in the App Store that allow malicious apps to steal passwords and private user data. Clearly, the app ecosystem is not immune to many of the same issues that apply to the Internet and e-commerce at large.

SOURCES: "U.S. Consumers Now Spend More Time in Apps Than Watching TV," by Sarah Perez, Techcrunch.com, September 10, 2015; "Tim Cook Takes Apple Down the Dark Road of Censorship," by Jim Lynch, CIO.com, June 25, 2015; "Zero-day Exploit Lets App Store Malware Steal OS X and iOS Passwords," by Glenn Fleishman, Macworld.com, June 17, 2015; "App Downloads Jump Again as January Sets a New Record," by Heather Newman, Venturebeat.com, February 26, 2015; "Google Play Now Has More Apps Than Apple's App Store, Report Says," by Karissa Bell, Mashable.com, January 15, 2015; "Apple Says App Store Sales Rose 50% in 2014," by Daisuke Wakabayashi, *Wall Street Journal,* January 8, 2015; "Apple's iOS App Store Reaches Record 7.8M Daily Downloads," by Katie Marsal, Appleinsider.com, November 24, 2014; "Global Brands in the Mobile Landscape," by Anne Hezemans, *Distimo,* October 2013; "Researchers Outwit Apple, Plant Malware in App Store," by Gregg Keizer, *Computerworld,* August 20, 2013; "First Instance of iOS App Store Malware Detected, Removed," by Christina Bonnington, Wired.com, July 5, 2012; "The Apps Strategies of the Top 100 Brands," by Haydn Shaughnessy, Forbes.com, October 27, 2011; "Mobile Apps and Consumer Product Brands," by Tobi Elkin, eMarketer, March 2010; "Apple Bans Some Apps for Sex-Tinged Content," by Jenna Wortham, *New York Times,* February 22, 2010; "Inside the App Economy," by Douglas MacMillan, *BusinessWeek,* October 22, 2009.

CASE STUDY

Akamai Technologies:
Attempting to Keep Supply Ahead of Demand

I n 2015, the amount of Internet traffic generated by YouTube alone is greater than the amount of traffic on the entire Internet in 2000. Because of video streaming and the explosion in mobile devices demanding high-bandwidth applications, Internet traffic has increased over 500% since 2010 and is predicted to nearly triple over the next 5 years (see **Figure 3.20**). Internet video is now a majority of Internet traffic and will reach 80% by 2019, according to Cisco. Experts call services like YouTube, Netflix, and high definition streaming video "net bombs" because they threaten the effective operation of the Internet. Mobile platform traffic

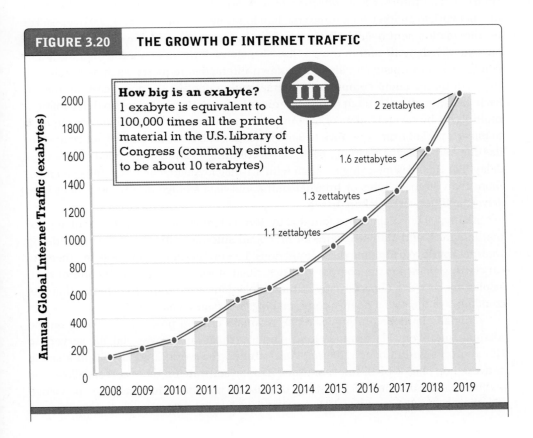

FIGURE 3.20 | **THE GROWTH OF INTERNET TRAFFIC**

How big is an exabyte?
1 exabyte is equivalent to 100,000 times all the printed material in the U.S. Library of Congress (commonly estimated to be about 10 terabytes)

is growing at nearly 70% and will soon push cellular networks and the Internet to their capacities. Cisco estimates that annual global Internet traffic will be around 2 zettabytes in 2019: that's 2,000 exabytes, or, in other words, 20 with 19 zeroes behind it!

Analysts differ on how fast Internet capacity is growing. Large telecommunication companies argue that demand will soon overwhelm capacity, while other experts argue that Internet bandwidth can double every year for a very long time and easily keep up with demand. Perhaps they're both right: Internet capacity can expand to keep up with demand if sufficient capital is invested in backbone and local networks. That's a big "if." As a result, and in order to raise revenue, many large ISPs have bandwidth caps that require heavy users of video to pay more for their Internet service. More charges based on usage are in the pipeline.

In today's broadband environment, the threshold of patience is very low. Increased video and audio customer expectations are bad news for anyone seeking to use the Web for delivery of high-quality multimedia content and high definition video. Akamai is one of the Web's major helpers, and an overwhelming majority of the Web's top companies use Akamai's services to speed the delivery of content. Akamai serves more than 25 terabits of Web traffic per second.

Slow-loading Web pages and Web content sometimes result from poor design, but more often than not, the problem stems from the underlying infrastructure of the Internet. The Internet is a collection of networks that has to pass information from one network to another. Sometimes the handoff is not smooth. Every 1,500-byte packet of information sent over the Internet must be verified by the receiving server and an acknowledgment sent to the sender. This slows down not only the distribution of content such as music, but also slows down interactive requests, such as purchases, that require the client computer to interact with an online shopping cart. Moreover, each packet may go through many different servers on its way to its final destination, multiplying by several orders of magnitude the number of acknowledgments required to move a packet from New York to San Francisco. The Internet today spends much of its time and capacity verifying packets, contributing to a problem called "latency" or delay. For this reason, a single e-mail with a 1-megabyte attached PDF file can create more than 50 megabytes of Internet traffic and data storage on servers, client hard drives, and network backup drives.

Akamai Technologies was founded by Tom Leighton, an MIT professor of applied mathematics, and Daniel Lewin, an MIT grad student, with the idea of expediting Internet traffic to overcome these limitations. Lewin's master's thesis was the theoretical starting point for the company. It described storing copies of Web content such as pictures or video clips at many different locations around the Internet so that one could always retrieve a nearby copy, making Web pages load faster.

Officially launched in August 1998, Akamai's current products are based on the Akamai Intelligent Platform, a cloud platform made up of over 200,000 servers in 110 countries within over 1,400 networks around the world, and all within a single network hop of 85% of all Internet users. Akamai software on these servers allows the platform to identify and block security threats and provide comprehensive knowledge of network conditions, as well as instant device-level detection and optimization.

Akamai's site performance products allow customers to move their Web content closer to end users so a user in New York City, for instance, will be served L.L.Bean pages from the New York Metro area Akamai servers, while users of the L.L.Bean site in San Francisco will be served pages from Akamai servers in San Francisco. Akamai has a wide range of large corporate and government clients: 1 out of every 3 global Fortune 500 companies, the top 30 media and entertainment companies, 97 of the top 100 online U.S. retailers, all branches of the U.S. military, all the top Internet portals, all the major U.S. sports leagues, and so on. In 2015, Akamai delivers between 15% and 30% of all Web traffic, and over 2 trillion daily Internet interactions. Other competitors in the content delivery network (CDN) industry include Limelight Networks, Level 3 Communications, and Mirror Image Internet.

Accomplishing this daunting task requires that Akamai monitor the entire Internet, locating potential sluggish areas and devising faster routes for information to travel. Frequently used portions of a client's Web site, or large video or audio files that would be difficult to send to users quickly, are stored on Akamai's servers. When a user requests a song or a video file, his or her request is redirected to an Akamai server nearby and the content served from this local server. Akamai's servers are placed in Tier 1 backbone supplier networks, large ISPs, universities, and other networks. Akamai's software determines which server is optimum for the user and then transmits the "Akamaized" content locally. Web sites that are "Akamaized" can be delivered anywhere from 4 to 10 times as fast as non-Akamaized content. Akamai has developed a number of other business services based on its Internet savvy, including targeted advertising based on user location and zip code, content security, business intelligence, disaster recovery, on-demand bandwidth and computing capacity during spikes in Internet traffic, storage, global traffic management, and streaming services. Akamai also offers a product called Advertising Decision Solutions, which provides companies with intelligence generated by the Internet's most accurate and comprehensive knowledge base of Internet network activity. Akamai's massive server deployment and relationships with networks throughout the world enable optimal collection of geography and bandwidth-sensing information. As a result, Akamai provides a highly accurate knowledge base with worldwide coverage. Customers integrate a simple program into their Web server or application server. This program communicates with the Akamai database to retrieve the very latest information. The Akamai network of servers is constantly mapping the Internet, and at the same time, each company's software is in continual communication with the Akamai network. The result: data is always current. Advertisers can deliver ads based on country, region, city, market area, area code, county, zip code, connection type, and speed. You can see several interesting visualizations of the Internet that log basic real-time Web activity by visiting the Akamai Web site.

The shift toward cloud computing and the mobile platform as well as the growing popularity of streaming video have provided Akamai with new growth opportunities. As more businesses and business models are moving to the Web, Akamai has seen its client base continue to grow beyond the most powerful Internet retailers and online content providers. In 2014, Akamai made a push to encourage Hollywood studios to

SOURCES: "Facts & Figures," Akamai.com, accessed October 15, 2015; "Akamai in 60 Seconds," Akamai.com, accessed October 15, 2015; "The State of the Internet, 2nd Quarter 2015 Report," by Akamai Technologies, Inc., August 18, 2015; "Akamai Opens Dubai Office to Support Its Growing Middle East Business," Akamai.com, June 14, 2015; "Akamai, Trustwave to Promote, Sell Each Other's Security Services," by Sean Michael Kerner, Eweek.com, June 1, 2015; "Cisco Visual Networking Index, 2014–2019" by Cisco Systems, Inc., May 27, 2015; "Akamai and China Unicom Establish Strategic Cloud Services Partnership," Akamai.com, May 26, 2015; "Akamai Appeals to Hollywood Studios at NAB 2014," by Troy Dreier, Streamingmedia.com, April 7, 2014; "Akamai Completes Acquisition of Prolexic," Akamai.com, February 18, 2014; "You Think the Internet is Big Now? Akamai Needs to Grow 100-Fold," by Mathew Ingram, GigaOM.com, June 20, 2012; "Akamai Eyes Acceleration Boost for Mobile Content," by Stephen Lawson, *Computerworld*, March 20, 2012; "To Cash In on Wave of Web Attacks, Akamai Launches Standalone Security Business," by Andy Greenberg, Forbes.com, February 21, 2012.

use the cloud for feature films. Akamai announced that it was partnering with Aspera, a high-speed file transfer company, to develop the capability to upload and download large video files fast enough for business use, including feature films. Akamai had already developed partnerships with companies that allow movie studios to convert movie files from one format to another as well as to apply DRM protections all in one step. Establishing partnerships with movie studios represents big business for Akamai, with an increasing amount of media consumption taking place on mobile devices through the cloud. To that end, Akamai acquired video streaming optimization start-up Octoshape in 2015, improving its ability to deliver high quality streaming video.

Akamai is also acutely aware of the increase in cybercrime as more traffic migrates to the Internet. Growth in Internet traffic is good news for Akamai, but the company must also now deal with politically motivated cyberattacks, organized crime online, and state-sponsored cyberwarfare. In 2014, Akamai improved its Kona Site Defender tool, which offers a variety of security measures for Akamai clients. The tool protects against Distributed Denial of Service (DDoS) attacks and includes a firewall for Web applications. Akamai also upgraded Site Defender's Web Application Firewall feature and developed modifications to the tool that make it easier for its users to use. Akamai has continued to acquire security companies in 2014, purchasing Prolexic Technologies, a cloud-based security provider specializing in protecting data centers from DDoS attacks. With so many businesses now dependent on the uninterrupted flow of content over the Internet, Akamai is in a very strong position to sell security services to its customers. In 2015, Akamai partnered with top information security firm Trustwave to cross-sell each other's services and products, expanding their offerings and reaching even further. They made a similar agreement with China Unicom, a provider of cloud services in the fast-growing Chinese market. Akamai has also moved into areas of the world with less developed broadband infrastructure, such as the Middle East. In 2015, Akamai opened an office in Dubai, hoping to bolster its presence in an area where the adoption rate for broadband is skyrocketing. However, as impressive as Akamai's operation has become, it may not be nearly enough to cope with the next 5 to 10 years of Internet growth.

Case Study Questions

1. Why does Akamai need to geographically disperse its servers to deliver its customers' Web content?

2. If you wanted to deliver software content over the Internet, would you sign up for Akamai's service? Why or why not?

3. What advantages does an advertiser derive from using Akamai's service? What kinds of products might benefit from this kind of service?

4. Do you think Internet users should be charged based on the amount of bandwidth they consume, or on a tiered plan where users would pay in rough proportion to their usage?

3.8 REVIEW

KEY CONCEPTS

■ **Discuss the origins of, and the key technology concepts behind, the Internet.**

- The Internet has evolved from a collection of mainframe computers located on a few U.S. college campuses to an interconnected network of thousands of networks and millions of computers worldwide.
- The history of the Internet can be divided into three phases: the Innovation Phase (1961–1974), the Institutionalization Phase (1975–1995), and the Commercialization Phase (1995 to the present).
- Packet switching, TCP/IP, and client/server technology are key technology concepts behind the Internet.
- The mobile platform has become the primary means for accessing the Internet.
- Cloud computing refers to a model of computing in which firms and individuals obtain computing power and software applications over the Internet, rather than purchasing the hardware and software and installing it on their own computers.
- Internet protocols and utility programs such as HTTP, SMTP and POP, SSL and TLS, FTP, Telnet, Ping, and Tracert provide a number of Internet services.

■ **Explain the current structure of the Internet.**

- The main structural elements of the Internet are the backbone (composed primarily high-bandwidth fiber optic cable), IXPs (hubs that use high-speed switching computers to connect to the backbone), CANs (campus areas networks), and ISPs (which deal with the "last mile" of service to homes and offices).
- *Governing bodies*, such as IAB, ICANN, IESG, IETF, ISOC, and W3C, have influence over the Internet and monitor its operations, although they do not control it.

■ **Understand the limitations of today's Internet and the potential capabilities of the Internet of the future.**

- To envision what the Internet of tomorrow will look like, we must first look at the limitations of today's Internet, which include bandwidth limitations, quality of service limitations, network architecture limitations, language limitations, and limitations arising from the wired nature of the Internet.
- Internet2 is a consortium working together to develop and test new technologies for potential use on the Internet. Other groups are working to expand Internet bandwidth via improvements to fiber optics. Wireless LAN and 4G technologies are providing users of smartphones and tablet computers with increased access to the Internet and its various services. The increased bandwidth and expanded connections will result in a number of benefits, including latency solutions; guaranteed service levels; lower error rates; and declining costs. The Internet of Things will be a big part of the Internet of the future, with more and more sensor-equipped machines and devices connected to the Internet.

■ **Understand how the Web works.**

- The Web was developed during 1989–1991 by Dr. Tim Berners-Lee, who created a computer program that allowed formatted pages stored on the Internet to be linked using keywords (hyperlinks). In 1993, Marc Andreessen created the first graphical Web browser, which made it possible to view documents on the Web graphically and created the possibility of universal computing.
- The key concepts you need to be familiar with in order to understand how the Web works are hypertext, HTTP, URLs, HTML, XML, Web server software, Web clients, and Web browsers.

■ **Describe how Internet and Web features and services support e-commerce.**

- Together, the Internet and the Web make e-commerce possible by allowing computer users to access product and service information and to complete purchases online.
- Some of the specific features that support e-commerce include e-mail, instant messaging, search engines, online forums (message boards), streaming media, and cookies.
- Web 2.0 features and services include social networks, blogs, RSS, podcasts, wikis, music and video services, Internet telephony, and online software and services.

■ **Understand the impact of m-commerce applications.**

- M-commerce applications are part of the larger $128 billion m-commerce market.
- Smartphone and tablet users spent the majority of their time using mobile apps rather than the mobile Web.
- There are a variety of different platforms for mobile application development including Objective-C (for iOS devices), Java (BlackBerrys and Android smartphones), and C and C++ (Windows mobile devices and some BlackBerry coding).
- Mobile apps for the iPhone are distributed through Apple's App Store, for BlackBerrys through RIM's App World, for Android devices through Google Play, and for Windows mobile devices through Microsoft's Windows Phone Marketplace. There are also third-party vendors such as Amazon's Appstore.

QUESTIONS

1. What are the three basic building blocks of the Internet?
2. What is latency, and how does it interfere with Internet functioning?
3. Explain how packet switching works.
4. How is the TCP/IP protocol related to information transfer on the Internet?
5. What technological innovation made client/server computing possible?
6. What is cloud computing, and how has it impacted the Internet?
7. Why are smartphones a disruptive technology?
8. What types of companies form the Internet backbone today?
9. What function do the IXPs serve?
10. What is the goal of the Internet2 project?
11. Compare and contrast intranets and the Internet as a whole.
12. What are some of the major limitations of today's Internet?
13. What are some of the challenges of policing the Internet? Who has the final say when it comes to content?
14. Compare and contrast the capabilities of Wi-Fi and 3G/4G wireless networks.
15. What are the basic capabilities of a Web server?
16. What are the major technological advancements that are anticipated to accompany the Internet of the future? Discuss the importance of each.
17. Why was the development of the browser so significant for the growth of the Web?
18. What advances and features does HTML5 offer?
19. Name and describe five services currently available through the Web.
20. Why are mobile apps the next big thing?

PROJECTS

1. Review the opening case on Apple Watch. What developments have occurred since this case was written in October 2015?

2. Locate where cookies are stored on your computer. (They are probably in a folder entitled "Cookies" within your browser program.) List the top 10 cookies you find and write a brief report describing the kinds of sites that placed the cookies. What purpose do you think the cookies serve? Also, what do you believe are the major advantages and disadvantages of cookies? In your opinion, do the advantages outweigh the disadvantages, or vice versa?

3. Call or visit the Web sites of a cable provider, DSL provider, and satellite provider to obtain information on their Internet services. Prepare a brief report summarizing the features, benefits, and costs of each. Which is the fastest? What, if any, are the downsides of selecting any of the three for Internet service (such as additional equipment purchases)?

4. Select two countries (excluding the United States) and prepare a short report describing their basic Internet infrastructure. Are they public or commercial? How and where do they connect to backbones within the United States?

5. Investigate the Internet of Things. Select one example and describe what it is and how it works.

REFERENCES

Akamai Inc. "Akamai's State of the Internet Q2 2015 Report." (August 2015).

AllSeen Alliance. "IoT Membership Soars at AllSeen Alliance." (October 14, 2015).

Arstechnica.com. "Capitol Hill, The Internet, and Broadband: An Ars Technica Quarterly Report." (September 2010).

Berners-Lee, Tim, Robert Cailliau, Ari Luotonen, Henrik Frystyk Nielsen, and Arthur Secret. "The World Wide Web." *Communications of the ACM* (August 1994).

Bluetooth.com. "What Is Bluetooth Technology." (2015).

Brandt, Richard. "Net Assets: How Stanford's Computer Science Department Changed the Way We Get Information." *Stanford Magazine* (November/December 2004).

BuddeCom. "BuddeCom Intelligence Report - VoIP and Mobile VoIP Statistics and Insights." (2015).

Bush, Vannevar. "As We May Think." *Atlantic Monthly* (July 1945).

Cerf, V., and R. Kahn, "A Protocol for Packet Network Intercommunication." *IEEE Transactions on Communications*, Vol. COM-22, No. 5, pp 637-648 (May 1974).

Cisco. "Cisco Visual Networking Index: Forecast and Methodology, 2014–2019." (May 27, 2015).

comScore. "comScore Releases August 2015 U.S. Desktop Search Engine Rankings." (September 16, 2015).

Durairajan, Ramakrishnan, Paul Barford, Joel Sommers, and Walter Willinger. "InterTubes: A Study of the US Long-haul Fiber-optic Infrastructure." SIGCOMM '15 (August 17–21, 2015).

eMarketer, Inc. "Internet Users and Penetration Worldwide, 2013–2019." (April 2015a).

eMarketer, Inc. "US Internet Users and Population, 2013–2019." (May 2015b).

eMarketer, Inc. "Mobile Phone Users Worldwide and Penetration, 2013–2019." (May 2015c).

eMarketer, Inc. "Smartphone Users and Penetration Worldwide, 2013–2019." (May 2015d).

eMarketer, Inc. "US Mobile Phone Internet Users and Penetration, 2013–2019." (May 2015e).

eMarketer, Inc. "US Search Users and Penetration, 2013–2019." (February 2015f).

eMarketer, Inc. "US Fixed Broadband Households, 2013–2019." (February 2015g).

eMarketer, Inc. "Mobile Phone Internet Users and Penetration Worldwide, 2013–2019." (May 2015h).

eMarketer, Inc., "US Bloggers and Penetration, 2013–2019." (February 2015i).

eMarketer, Inc. "US Blog Readers and Penetration, 2013–2019." (February 2015j).

eMarketer, Inc. (Yory Wurmser) "US Mcommerce 2015: eMarketer's Forecast and Trends." (May 2015k).

Federal Communications Commission. "FCC Finds U.S. Broadband Deployment Not Keeping Pace." (January 29, 2015).

Federal Networking Council. "FNC Resolution: Definition of 'Internet.'" (October 24, 1995).

Gartner, Inc. Forecast Analysis: Public Cloud Services, Worldwide 1Q15 Update." (June 17, 2015a).

Gartner, Inc. "Gartner Says Smartphone Sales Surpassed One Billion in 2014." (March 3, 2015b).

Geni.net. "Have Your Say: GENI Sustainment and Governance & Future Network Research Infrastructure." (accessed October 12, 2015).

Gross, Grant. "NSF Seeks Ambitious Next-Generation Internet Project." *Computerworld* (August 29, 2005).

Hsu, Jeremy. "What's Next After 25 Years of Wi-Fi?" Spectrum.ieee.org (September 10, 2015).

IDC. "The Internet of Things is Poised to Change Everything, Says IDC." (October 3, 2013).

IEEE Computer Society. "Top Trends for 2013." (2013).

Imbert, Fred. "Hold the R.I.P. PCs Are Not Dead: Michael Dell." Cnbc.com (January 22, 2015).

Infonetics Research. "VoIP and UC Services and Subscribers." (May 2015).

Internet2. "Internet2 Planned 100 Gigabit Infrastructure Topology; Internet2 Network." Internet2.edu (September 2011).

Internet Corporation for Assigned Names and Numbers (ICANN). "ICANN Approves Historic Change to Internet's Domain System." (June 20, 2011a).

Internet Corporation for Assigned Names and Numbers (ICANN). "Top-Level Domains (gTLDs)." (2011b).

Internet Retailer. "2015 Lite Edition Mobile 500 Executive Summary." (2015).

Internet Society. "The Internet of Things: An Overview." (October 2015).

Internet Society. "World IPv6 Launch on June 6, 2012, To Bring Permanent IPv6 Deployment." (January 2012).

Internet Society. "ISOC's Standards Activities." (September 2010).

Internet Society. "RFC 2616: Hypertext Transfer Protocol-HTTP/1.1." (June 1999).

Internet Society. "RFC 0959: File Transfer Protocol." (October, 1985).

Keizer, Greg. "Windows 10 Users Back Away From the Edge Browser." Computerworld.com (October 7, 2015).

Kleinrock, Leonard. *1964 Communication Nets: Stochastic Message Flow and Delay.* New York: McGraw-Hill (1964).

Leiner, Barry M., Vinton G. Cerf, David D. Clark, Robert E. Kahn, Leonard Kleinrock, Daniel C. Lynch, Jon Postel, Larry G. Roberts, and Stephen Wolff. "All About the Internet: A Brief History of the Internet." *Internet Society* (ISOC) (August 2000).

Mangalindan, JP. "In Online Search War, It's Google vs. Amazon." *Fortune* (October 15, 2014).

Marketshare.hitslink.com. "Desktop Top Browser Share Trend." (accessed October 14, 2015).

McMillan, Robert. "Coming This Summer: U.S. Will Run Out of Internet Addresses." Wsj.com (May 13, 2015).

Murphy, Kate. "For the Tech-Savvy With a Need for Speed, a Limited Choice of Towns With Fiber." *New York Times* (April 2, 2014).

National Research Foundation. "NSP Leadership in Discovery and Initiative Sparks White House US Ignite Initiative." (June 13, 2012).

Netcraft. "September 2015 Web Server Survey." (October 2015).

NPD Group. "Half of U.S. Internet Homes Now Own a Connected TV Device, According to The NPD Group." (August 26, 2015).

Pfanner, Eric. "Ethics Fight Over Domain Names Intensifies." *New York Times* (March 18, 2012).

Radicati Group. "Email Statistics Report, 2015–2019." (March 2015).

SANS Institute (John Pescatore). "Security the 'Internet of Things' Survey." (January 2014).

Simonite, Tom. "First Detailed Public Map of U.S. Internet Backbone Could Make It Stronger." Technologyreview.com (September 15, 2015).

Skype for Business Team. "Skype for Business Is Here—and This Is Only the Beginning." Blogs.office.com (March 18, 2015).

U.S. Department of Commerce. "Letter to ICANN Chairman." http://www.ntia.doc.gov/comments/2008/ICANN_080730.html (July 30, 2008).

Visualware, Inc., "VisualRoute Traceroute Server." (2014).

Weiss, Todd R. "802.11ac WiFi Products Gaining Market Share as Older Devices Decline." Eweek.com (April 22, 2015).

Zakon, Robert H. "Hobbes' Internet Timeline v8.1." Zakon.org (2005).

Ziff-Davis Publishing. "Ted Nelson: Hypertext Pioneer." Techtv.com (1998).

CHAPTER 4

Building an E-commerce Presence: Web Sites, Mobile Sites, and Apps

LEARNING OBJECTIVES

After reading this chapter, you will be able to:

- Understand the questions you must ask and answer, and the steps you should take, in developing an e-commerce presence.
- Explain the process that should be followed in building an e-commerce presence.
- Identify and understand the major considerations involved in choosing Web server and e-commerce merchant server software.
- Understand the issues involved in choosing the most appropriate hardware for an e-commerce site.
- Identify additional tools that can improve Web site performance.
- Understand the important considerations involved in developing a mobile Web site and building mobile applications.

The Wall Street Journal:

Redesigning for the Future

For 125 years, the *Wall Street Journal (WSJ)* has been a venerated newspaper with a focus on business and an educated, discerning readership. It consistently ranks as one of the top publications worldwide in terms of number of subscribers (currently close to 2.3 million). Despite its pedigree as one of the most recognizable and respected newspapers in the world, *WSJ* has also made an effort to stay on the cutting edge in an industry that has seen significant disruption in the past decade. It was a pioneer in developing a pay wall for its digital content in 1997, which met with skepticism and even ridicule at first, but is now increasingly common among online newspapers. *WSJ* was also one of the first news organizations with its own app for the iPad, released in 2010.

From 2010 to 2015, however, *WSJ* began to lag behind other newspapers and Web sites as devices have become smaller, more streamlined, and more specialized. Although it was a first mover into the mobile space, other papers like the *Financial Times* and *USA Today* have made sweeping changes to their Web sites and mobile offerings that better suited mobile browsing. *WSJ's* last Web site redesign was in 2008. To make matters worse, in 2015, Google updated its search algorithms to prioritize sites that are optimized for mobile devices, which caused *WSJ's* search results to suffer. The company isn't alone in this regard, with nearly half of the Web sites belonging to Fortune 500 companies failing to achieve "mobile-friendliness" according to Google, including a surprising 29% of retail sites, where mobile search is critical to maintaining revenue growth. However, with many publishing companies already struggling to adjust to the new online world, *WSJ* decided it had no more time to waste.

In 2015, *WSJ* undertook a complete redesign of its Web site and mobile apps across multiple platforms. It released new iPad and Android apps with a variety of new features to improve user experience, and followed those up with the release of an app for the new Apple Watch. It also added its first mobile-only product, an app that features a curated digest of 10 stories that is refreshed during the day, patterned after the What's New news brief column that appears on the front page of the print version. The paper also launched the WSJ.D niche site, which focuses on technology news, analysis, commentary, and product reviews. The overhaul was more than just cosmetic. Organizationally, it also integrated the team that works on new technology products and design elements into the news room, so that the editors themselves can have direct input into shaping the technological future of WSJ. This move has helped WSJ keep pace with other top newspapers, including the *Washington Post*, which has almost 50 engineers working in its newsroom.

One of the most critical objectives of the overhaul was to ensure that the user experience was consistent across all of the different devices that readers use today and in the future. Being able to save an article on the iPad and open the app on your iPhone or log in to the Web site and see the same article with your progress saved was a top priority for *WSJ*. The number of options for navigating articles was reduced for simplicity and ease of use, with the number of exposed navigation options dropping by nearly half on many pages. In the past, options were different on different devices and appeared in different places on the screen, confusing readers attempting to move from one device to another. Using an iOS feature called Handoff, *WSJ* allows users to save stories across all of their devices and to carry over the "graying out" of article headlines that have been read across those devices as well. It also allows users to access its Watchlist stock portfolio service across all devices.

In addition to making the user experience more consistent, *WSJ* hoped to improve it. The app versions of *WSJ* are more responsive and more visually appealing. Graphical elements are more prominent and even interactive. The app loads faster, which had been an area where it trailed its competitors in the past. *WSJ* wanted the reading experience to feel natural on any device, which required it to optimize its apps for the screen size of the latest generation of Apple and Android phones. As devices continue to evolve in size, so too will the *WSJ* app experience.

Most of the feedback on the design changes has been positive in the early going. Elements that many readers had requested were added, including a "market data center" featured prominently on the new Web site home page with essential information on the status of the stock markets that day. The iOS app also includes a Journal widget that places top stories of the day alongside other daily notifications, such as appointments and weather alerts. Users can swipe directly from their widget menu to move straight to the story within the *WSJ* app. From a user perspective, the new site and apps provide a large number of content choices, while also offering a variety of advertising opportunities from *WSJ*'s perspective.

As traffic continues to shift to the mobile platform, providing these advertising opportunities will become increasingly important to WSJ's continued success. In 2008, 10% of *WSJ*'s traffic came via mobile devices. That figure sits at 44% in 2015 and continues to grow quickly. *WSJ* has about 725,000 digital-only subscribers, trailing the *New York Times* (900,000) and coming in ahead of the *Financial Times* (over 500,000), but most of its 1.5 million print edition subscribers also have all-access subscriptions. Although measuring subscription numbers has become more complicated as the number of digital devices and reading platforms has grown, the trend away from print and towards digital has long been clear throughout the industry. But despite the proliferation of the mobile platform, two-thirds of *WSJ*'s subscribers visit the Web site home page each month. Realizing this, *WSJ* included the Web site as a key component of its redesign.

Another effect of the wider array of options for *WSJ* subscribers is that different trends and reading patterns emerge on each platform. To capture this new data, *WSJ* is upgrading its analytics capabilities, with the goal of using them in the newsroom and in its larger business strategy. One example of this approach already delivering results is the breakdown of device usage by *WSJ* readers. Tablet usage of the *WSJ* app is growing at approximately 10% per year, but smartphone usage is growing by 30% to 40%, suggesting that the smartphone app experience should be *WSJ*'s primary area of focus going forward. Additionally, *WSJ* has found that app users are more active and engaged than Web browser users, spending more time in the app and reading more articles than other types of users. App users are also likelier to maintain their subscriptions than any other type of user.

To that end, many of the features that *WSJ* engineers are working on are tailored specifically for the app experience. One goal is to provide live video coverage via mobile devices. Another is to improve push alerts to make them more relevant to users. By analyzing reader data to understand what types of stories are most appealing to individual users or different demographics of users, *WSJ* can provide custom push alerts that are likeliest to motivate readers to swipe and move to the app. Another feature in development is a "read-it-later" button that allows users to tag stories on any platform and view them later within their app. *WSJ* will also continue to optimize its Apple Watch app, which allows users to tilt the watch while looking at a headline to make that story available on the iPhone app.

Going forward, *WSJ* hopes to begin work on other features that will help in the future as early as possible. By integrating their engineering and product teams into the news room, they're much better positioned to achieve this level of development. And with their sweeping redesign across all platforms, *WSJ* has once again solidified its status as an industry leader, even in this brave new world of news media.

SOURCES: "Wall Street Journal Debuts Its 'What's News' App," by Joe Pompeo, Capitalnewyork.com, August 26, 2015; "Push It: How the Wall Street Journal Plans to Make Its Push Alerts More Personal," by Joseph Lichterman, Neimanlab.org, August 13, 2015; "The Wall Street Journal Is Targeting Its Loyal Subscribers with Its New News Digest Mobile App," by Shan Wang, Neimanlab.org, August 5, 2015; "New Google Algorithm Changes Prompts Wall Street Journal Website Redesign," by Steve Odart, Ixxus.com, April 28, 2015; "The Atlantic Unveils Its New, Redesigned Website to Mixed Reader Reviews," by D.B. Hebbard, Talkingnewmedia.com, April 23, 2015; "After the Launch of its Long-Awaited Web Redesign, The Wall Street Journal Hopes to Spur Innovation," by Joseph Lichterman, Niemanlab.org, April 21, 2015; "Newsonomics: The Wall Street Journal Is Playing a Game of Digital Catchup," Niemanlab.org, by Ken Doctor, April 21, 2015; "Wall Street Journal to Launch First Site Redesign in 7 Years," by Abigail Edge, Journalism.co.uk, April 16, 2015; "How the New Wall Street Journal iPad App Is Taking Advantage of New Features in iOS 8," by Joseph Lichterman, Niemanlab.org, September 17, 2014.

I
n Chapter 3, you learned about e-commerce's technological foundation: the Internet, Web, and the mobile platform. In this chapter, you will examine the important factors that a manager needs to consider when building an e-commerce presence. The focus will be on the managerial and business decisions you must make before you begin, and that you will continually need to make. Although building a sophisticated e-commerce presence isn't easy, today's tools are much less expensive and far more powerful than they were during the early days of e-commerce. You do not have to be Amazon or eBay to create a successful Web e-commerce presence. In this chapter, we focus on both small and medium-sized businesses as well as much larger corporate entities that serve thousands of customers a day, or even an hour. As you will see, although the scale may be very different, the principles and considerations are basically the same.

4.1 IMAGINE YOUR E-COMMERCE PRESENCE

Before you begin to build a Web site or app of your own, there are some important questions you will need to think about and answer. The answers to these questions will drive the development and implementation of your e-commerce presence.

WHAT'S THE IDEA? (THE VISIONING PROCESS)

Before you can plan and actually build an e-commerce presence, you need to have a vision of what you hope to accomplish and how you hope to accomplish it. The vision includes not just a statement of mission, but also identification of the target audience, characterization of the market space, a strategic analysis, a marketing matrix, and a development timeline. It starts with a dream of what's possible, and concludes with a timeline and preliminary budget for development.

If you examine any successful Web site, you can usually tell from the home page what the vision that inspires the site is. If the company is a public company, you can often find a succinct statement of its vision or mission in the reports it files with the Securities and Exchange Commission. For Amazon, it's to become the largest marketplace on earth. For Facebook, it's to make the world more open and connected. For Google, it's to organize the world's information and make it universally accessible and useful. The e-commerce presence you want to build may not have such all-encompassing ambitions, but a succinct statement of mission, purpose, and direction is the key factor in driving the development of your project. For instance, the mission of TheKnot is to be the Internet's comprehensive, one-stop wedding planning solution.

WHERE'S THE MONEY: BUSINESS AND REVENUE MODEL

Once you have defined a mission statement, a vision, you need to start thinking about where the money will be coming from. You will need to develop a preliminary idea of your business and revenue models. You don't need detailed revenue and cost projections at this point. Instead, you need a general idea of how your business will generate revenues. The basic choices have been described in Chapter 2. Basic business models are portal, e-tailer, content provider, transaction broker, market creator, service provider, and community provider (social network).

The basic revenue model alternatives are advertising, subscriptions, transaction fees, sales, and affiliate revenue. There's no reason to adopt a single business or revenue model, and in fact, many firms have multiple models. For instance, the New York Times digital business model is to both sell subscriptions and sell ad space. In addition, they sell unique photographs and gifts. At TheKnot, a vertical portal for the wedding industry, you will find ads, affiliate relationships, and sponsorships from major creators of wedding products and services, including a directory to local wedding planners, all of which produce revenue for TheKnot. PetSmart, the most popular pet Web site in the United States, has a more focused sales revenue model, and presents itself almost entirely as an e-tailer of pet supplies.

WHO AND WHERE IS THE TARGET AUDIENCE

Without a clear understanding of your target audience, you will not have a successful e-commerce presence. There are two questions here: who is your target audience and where can you best reach them? Your target audience can be described in a number of ways: demographics, behavior patterns (lifestyle), current consumption patterns (online vs. offline purchasing), digital usage patterns, content creation preferences (blogs, social networks, sites like Pinterest), and buyer personas (profiles of your typical customer). Understanding the demographics of your target audience is usually the first step. Demographic information includes age, income, gender, and location. In some cases, this may be obvious and in others, much less so. For instance, Harley-Davidson sells motorcycles to a very broad demographic range of varying ages, incomes, and locations, from 34-year-olds to 65-year-olds. Although most of the purchasers are middle-aged men, with middle incomes, many of the men ride with women, and the Harley-Davidson Web site has a collection of women's clothing and several Web pages devoted to women riders. While the majority of men who purchase Harley-Davidsons have modest incomes, a significant group of purchasers are professionals with above-average incomes. Hence, the age and income demographic target is quite broad. What ties Harley-Davidson riders together is not their shared demographics, but their love of the motorcycles and the brand, and the lifestyle associated with touring the highways of America on a powerful motorcycle that sounds like a potato popper. In contrast, a company like TheKnot is aimed at women in the 18–34-year-old range who are in varying stages of getting married, with lifestyles that include shopping online, using smartphones and tablets, downloading apps, and using Facebook. This audience is technologically hip. These women read and contribute to blogs, comment on forums, and use Pinterest to find ideas for fashion. A "typical" visitor to TheKnot would be a 28-year-old woman who has an engagement ring, is just starting the wedding planning process, has an income of $45,000, lives in the Northeast, and is interested in a beach wedding. There are, of course, other "typical" profiles. For each profile for your Web site you will need to develop a detailed description.

WHAT IS THE BALLPARK? CHARACTERIZE THE MARKETPLACE

The chances of your success will depend greatly on the characteristics of the market you are about to enter, and not just on your entrepreneurial brilliance. Enter into a declining market filled with strong competitors, and you will multiply your chances of failure. Enter into a market that is emerging, growing, and has few competitors, and you stand a better chance. Enter a market where there are no players, and you will either be rewarded handsomely with a profitable monopoly on a successful product no one else thought of (Apple) or you will be quickly forgotten because there isn't a market for your product at this point in time (the Franklin e-book reader circa 1999).

Features of the marketplace to focus on include the demographics of the market and how an e-commerce presence fits into the market. In addition, you will want to know about the structure of the market: competitors and substitute products.

What are the features of the marketplace you are about to enter? Is the market growing, or receding in size? If it's growing, among which age and income groups? Is the marketplace shifting from offline to online delivery? If so, is the market moving toward traditional Web sites, mobile, and/or tablets? Is there a special role for a mobile presence in this market? What percentage of your target audience uses a Web site, smartphone, or tablet? What about social networks? What's the buzz on products like yours? Are your potential customers talking about the products and services you want to offer on Facebook, Twitter, or blogs? How many blogs focus on products like yours? How many Twitter posts mention similar offerings? How many Facebook Likes (signs of customer engagement) are attached to products you want to offer?

The structure of the market is described in terms of your direct competitors, suppliers, and substitute products. You will want to make a list of the top five or ten competitors and try to describe their market share, and distinguishing characteristics. Some of your competitors may offer traditional versions of your products, while others will offer new renditions or versions of products that have new features. You need to find out everything you can about your competitors. What's the market buzz on your competitors? How many unique monthly visitors (UMVs) do they have? How many Facebook Likes, Twitter followers, and/or Pinterest followers? How are your competitors using social sites and mobile devices as a part of their online presence. Is there something special you could do with social networks that your competitors do not? Do a search on customer reviews of their products. You can find online services (some of them free) that will measure the number of online conversations about your competitors, and the total share of Internet voice each of your competitors receives. Do your competitors have a special relationship with their suppliers that you may not have access to? Exclusive marketing arrangements would be one example of a special supplier relationship. Finally, are there substitutes for your products and services? For instance, your site may offer advice to the community of pet owners, but local pet stores or local groups may be a more trusted source of advice on pets.

WHERE'S THE CONTENT COMING FROM?

Web sites are like books: they're composed of a lot of pages that have content ranging from text, to graphics, photos, and videos. This content is what search engines catalog as they crawl through all the new and changed Web pages on the Internet. The content is why your customers visit your site and either purchase things or look at ads that generate revenue for you. Therefore, the content is the single most important foundation for your revenue and ultimate success.

There are generally two kinds of content: static and dynamic. Static content is text and images that do not frequently change, such as product descriptions, photos, or text that you create to share with your visitors. Dynamic content is content that changes regularly, say, daily or hourly. Dynamic content can be created by you, or increasingly, by bloggers and fans of your Web site and products. User-generated content has a number of advantages: it's free, it engages your customer fan base, and search engines are more likely to catalog your site if the content is changing. Other sources of content, especially photos, are external Web sites that aggregate content such as Pinterest, discussed in the closing case study in Chapter 1.

KNOW YOURSELF: CONDUCT A SWOT ANALYSIS

A **SWOT analysis** is a simple but powerful method for strategizing about your business and understanding where you should focus your efforts. In a SWOT analysis you describe your strengths, weaknesses, threats, and opportunities. In the example SWOT analysis in **Figure 4.1**, you will see a profile of a typical start-up venture that includes a unique approach to an existing market, a promise of addressing unmet needs in this market, and the use of newer technologies (social and mobile platforms) that older competitors may have overlooked. There are many opportunities to address a large market with unmet needs, as well as the potential to use the initial Web site as a home base and spin-off related or nearby sites, leveraging the investment in design and technology. But there are also weaknesses and threats. Lack of financial and human resources are typically the biggest weakness of start-up sites. Threats include competitors that could develop the same capabilities as you, and low market entry costs, which might encourage many more start-ups to enter the marketplace.

Once you have conducted a SWOT analysis, you can consider ways to overcome your weaknesses and build on your strengths. For instance, you could consider hiring

SWOT analysis

describes a firm's strengths, weaknesses, opportunities, and threats

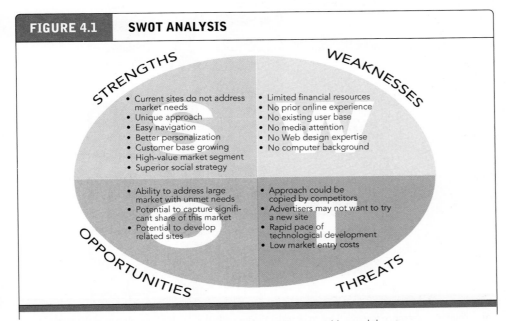

| FIGURE 4.1 | SWOT ANALYSIS |

STRENGTHS
- Current sites do not address market needs
- Unique approach
- Easy navigation
- Better personalization
- Customer base growing
- High-value market segment
- Superior social strategy

WEAKNESSES
- Limited financial resources
- No prior online experience
- No existing user base
- No media attention
- No Web design expertise
- No computer background

OPPORTUNITIES
- Ability to address large market with unmet needs
- Potential to capture significant share of this market
- Potential to develop related sites

THREATS
- Approach could be copied by competitors
- Advertisers may not want to try a new site
- Rapid pace of technological development
- Low market entry costs

A SWOT analysis describes your firm's strengths, weaknesses, opportunities, and threats.

or partnering to obtain technical and managerial expertise, and looking for financing opportunities (including friends and relatives).

DEVELOP AN E-COMMERCE PRESENCE MAP

E-commerce has moved from being a PC-centric activity on the Web to a mobile and tablet-based activity as well. While 75% of e-commerce today is still conducted using desktop computers, increasingly smartphones and tablets will be used for purchasing. Currently, smartphones and tablets are used by a majority of Internet users in the United States to shop for goods and services, explore purchase options, look up prices, and access social sites. Your potential customers use these various devices at different times during the day, and involve themselves in different conversations depending on what they are doing—touching base with friends, tweeting, or reading a blog. Each of these are "touch points" where you can meet the customer, and you have to think about how you develop a presence in these different virtual places. **Figure 4.2** provides a roadmap to the platforms and related activities you will need to think about when developing your e-commerce presence.

Figure 4.2 illustrates four different kinds of e-commerce presence: Web site/App, e-mail, social media, and offline media. For each of these types there are different platforms that you will need to address. For instance, in the case of Web sites and/or apps, there are three different platforms: traditional desktop, tablets, and smartphones, each with different capabilities. And for each type of e-commerce presence there are related activities you will need to consider. For instance, in the case of Web sites

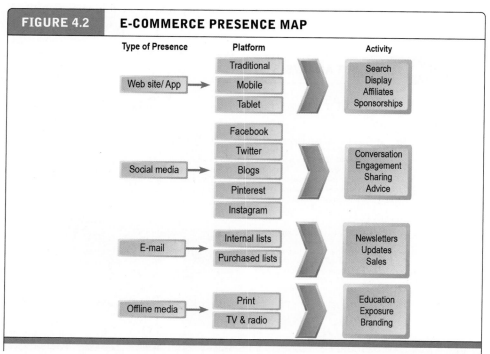

FIGURE 4.2   **E-COMMERCE PRESENCE MAP**

An e-commerce presence requires firms to consider the four different kinds of presence, and the platforms and activities associated with each type of presence.

and apps, you will want to engage in search engine marketing, display ads, affiliate programs, and sponsorships. Offline media, the fourth type of e-commerce presence, is included here because many firms use multiplatform or integrated marketing where print, television, or radio ads refer customers to Web sites and apps. The marketing activities in Figure 4.2 are described in much greater detail in Chapters 6 and 7.

DEVELOP A TIMELINE: MILESTONES

Where would you like to be a year from now? It's a good idea for you to have a rough idea of the time frame for developing your e-commerce presence when you begin. You should break your project down into a small number of phases that could be completed within a specified time. Six phases are usually enough detail at this point. **Table 4.1** illustrates a one-year timeline for the development of a start-up Web site.

Note that this example timeline defers the development of a mobile plan until after a Web site and social media plan have been developed and implemented. There is a growing trend, however, to flip this timeline around, and begin with a mobile plan instead (sometimes referred to as mobile first design). Mobile first design has both advantages and disadvantages that will be examined more fully in Section 4.6.

HOW MUCH WILL THIS COST?

It's too early in the process to develop a detailed budget for your e-commerce presence, but it is a good time to develop a preliminary idea of the costs involved. How much you spend on a Web site, for instance, depends on what you want it to do. Simple Web sites can be built and hosted with a first-year cost of $5,000 or less if all the work is done in-house by yourself and others willing to work without pay. A more reasonable budget for a small Web start-up might be $25,000 to $50,000. Here the firm owner would develop all the content at no cost, and a Web designer and programmer would be hired to implement the initial Web site. As discussed later, the Web site would be

TABLE 4.1	E-COMMERCE PRESENCE TIMELINE	
PHASE	**ACTIVITY**	**MILESTONE**
Phase 1: Planning	Envision e-commerce presence; determine personnel	Mission statement
Phase 2: Web site development	Acquire content; develop a site design; arrange for hosting the site	Web site plan
Phase 3: Web Implementation	Develop keywords and metatags; focus on search engine optimization; identify potential sponsors	A functional Web site
Phase 4: Social media plan	Identify appropriate social platforms and content for your products and services	A social media plan
Phase 5: Social media implementation	Develop Facebook, Twitter, and Pinterest presence	Functioning social media presence
Phase 6: Mobile plan	Develop a mobile plan; consider options for porting your Web site to smartphones	A mobile media plan

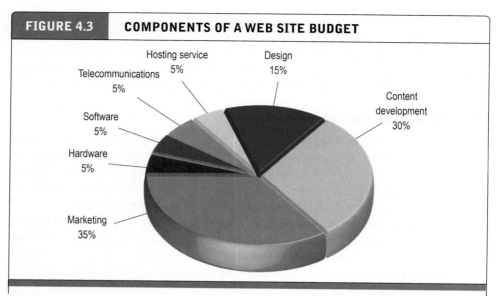

FIGURE 4.3   **COMPONENTS OF A WEB SITE BUDGET**

While hardware and software costs have fallen dramatically, Web sites face significant design, content development, and marketing costs.

hosted on a cloud-based server. The Web sites of large firms that offer high levels of interactivity and linkage to corporate systems can cost several hundred thousand to millions of dollars a year to create and operate.

While how much you spend to build a Web site depends on how much you can afford, and, of course, the size of the opportunity, **Figure 4.3** provides some idea of the relative size of various Web site costs. In general, the cost of hardware, software, and telecommunications for building and operating a Web site has fallen dramatically (by over 50%) in the last decade, making it possible for very small entrepreneurs to build fairly sophisticated sites. At the same time, while technology has lowered the costs of system development, the costs of marketing, content development, and design have risen to make up more than half of typical Web site budgets. The longer-term costs would also have to include site and system maintenance, which are not included here. The costs of developing a mobile site and apps are discussed in Section 4.6.

4.2   BUILDING AN E-COMMERCE PRESENCE: A SYSTEMATIC APPROACH

Once you have developed a vision of the e-commerce presence you want to build, it's time to start thinking about how to build and implement that presence. Building a successful e-commerce presence requires a keen understanding of business, technology, and social issues, as well as a systematic approach. E-commerce is just too important to be left totally to technologists and programmers.

The two most important management challenges are (1) developing a clear understanding of your business objectives and (2) knowing how to choose the right technology to achieve those objectives. The first challenge requires you to build a plan for developing your firm's presence. The second challenge requires you to understand some of the basic elements of e-commerce infrastructure. Let the business drive the technology.

Even if you decide to outsource the development effort and operation to a service provider, you will still need to have a development plan and some understanding of the basic e-commerce infrastructure issues such as cost, capability, and constraints. Without a plan and a knowledge base, you will not be able to make sound management decisions about e-commerce within your firm.

Let's assume you are a manager for a medium-sized industrial parts firm in the United States. You have been given a budget of $100,000 to develop an e-commerce presence for the firm. The purpose will be to sell and service the firm's customers, who are mostly small machine and metal fabricating shops, and to engage your customers through a blog and user forum. Where do you start? In the following sections, we will examine developing an e-commerce Web site, and then, at the end of the chapter, discuss some of the more specific considerations involved in developing a mobile site and building mobile applications.

First, you must be aware of the main areas where you will need to make decisions (see **Figure 4.4**). On the organizational and human resources fronts, you will have to bring together a team of individuals who possess the skill sets needed to build and manage a successful e-commerce presence. This team will make the key decisions about business objectives and strategy, technology, design, and social and information policies. The entire development effort must be closely managed if you hope to avoid the disasters that have occurred at some firms.

You will also need to make decisions about hardware, software, and telecommunications infrastructure. The demands of your customers should drive your choices of technology. Your customers will want technology that enables them to find what they want easily, view the product, purchase the product, and then receive the product from

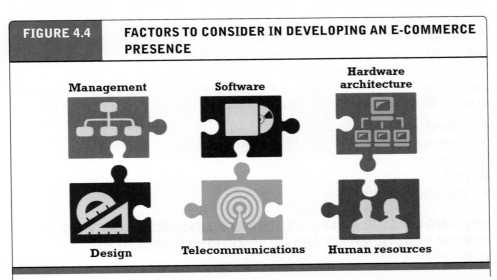

| FIGURE 4.4 | **FACTORS TO CONSIDER IN DEVELOPING AN E-COMMERCE PRESENCE** |

Building an e-commerce presence requires that you systematically consider the many factors that go into the process.

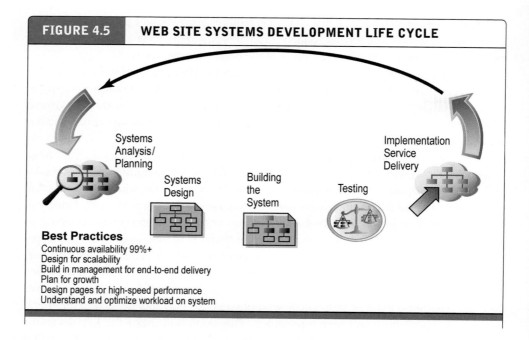

FIGURE 4.5   **WEB SITE SYSTEMS DEVELOPMENT LIFE CYCLE**

Systems Analysis/Planning

Systems Design

Building the System

Testing

Implementation Service Delivery

Best Practices
Continuous availability 99%+
Design for scalability
Build in management for end-to-end delivery
Plan for growth
Design pages for high-speed performance
Understand and optimize workload on system

systems development life cycle (SDLC)

a methodology for understanding the business objectives of any system and designing an appropriate solution

your warehouses quickly. You will also have to carefully consider design. Once you have identified the key decision areas, you will need to think about a plan for the project.

PLANNING: THE SYSTEMS DEVELOPMENT LIFE CYCLE

Your second step in building an e-commerce Web site will be creating a plan document. In order to tackle a complex problem such as building an e-commerce site, you will have to proceed systematically through a series of steps. One methodology is the systems development life cycle. The **systems development life cycle (SDLC)** is a methodology for understanding the business objectives of any system and designing an appropriate solution. Adopting a life cycle methodology does not guarantee success, but it is far better than having no plan at all. The SDLC method also helps in creating documents that communicate objectives, important milestones, and the uses of resources to management. **Figure 4.5** illustrates the five major steps involved in the systems development life cycle for an e-commerce site:

- Systems analysis/planning
- Systems design
- Building the system
- Testing
- Implementation

SYSTEMS ANALYSIS/PLANNING: IDENTIFY BUSINESS OBJECTIVES, SYSTEM FUNCTIONALITY, AND INFORMATION REQUIREMENTS

In the systems analysis/planning step of the SDLC, you try to answer the question, "What do we want this e-commerce site to do for our business?" The key point is to let the business decisions drive the technology, not the reverse. This will ensure that your technology platform is aligned with your business. We will assume here that you have identified a business strategy and chosen a business model to achieve your strategic objectives (see Chapter 2). But how do you translate your strategies, business models, and ideas into a working e-commerce Web site?

One way to start is to identify the specific business objectives for your site, and then develop a list of system functionalities and information requirements. **Business objectives** are simply capabilities you want your site to have.

System functionalities are types of information systems capabilities you will need to achieve your business objectives. The **information requirements** for a system are the information elements that the system must produce in order to achieve the business objectives. You will need to provide these lists to system developers and programmers so they know what you as the manager expect them to do.

Table 4.2 describes some basic business objectives, system functionalities, and information requirements for a typical e-commerce site. As shown in the table, there are ten basic business objectives that an e-commerce site must deliver. These objectives must be translated into a description of system functionalities and ultimately into a set of precise information requirements. The specific information requirements for a system typically are defined in much greater detail than Table 4.2 indicates. To a

business objectives
capabilities you want your site to have

system functionalities
types of information systems capabilities you will need to achieve your business objectives

information requirements
the information elements that the system must produce in order to achieve the business objectives

TABLE 4.2	SYSTEM ANALYSIS: BUSINESS OBJECTIVES, SYSTEM FUNCTIONALITIES, AND INFORMATION REQUIREMENTS FOR A TYPICAL E-COMMERCE SITE	
BUSINESS OBJECTIVE	**SYSTEM FUNCTIONALITY**	**INFORMATION REQUIREMENTS**
Display goods	Digital catalog	Dynamic text and graphics catalog
Provide product information (content)	Product database	Product description, stocking numbers, inventory levels
Personalize/customize product	Customer on-site tracking	Site log for every customer visit; data mining capability to identify common customer paths and appropriate responses
Engage customers in conversations	On-site blog	Software with blogging and community response functionality
Execute a transaction	Shopping cart/payment system	Secure credit card clearing; multiple payment options
Accumulate customer information	Customer database	Name, address, phone, and e-mail for all customers; online customer registration
Provide after-sale customer support	Sales database	Customer ID, product, date, payment, shipment date
Coordinate marketing/advertising	Ad server, e-mail server, e-mail, campaign manager, ad banner manager	Site behavior log of prospects and customers linked to e-mail and banner ad campaigns
Understand marketing effectiveness	Site tracking and reporting system	Number of unique visitors, pages visited, products purchased, identified by marketing campaign
Provide production and supplier links	Inventory management system	Product and inventory levels, supplier ID and contact, order quantity data by product

large extent, the business objectives of an e-commerce site are not that different from those of an ordinary retail store. The real difference lies in the system functionalities and information requirements. In an e-commerce site, the business objectives must be provided entirely in digital form without buildings or salespeople, 24 hours a day, 7 days a week.

SYSTEM DESIGN: HARDWARE AND SOFTWARE PLATFORMS

system design specification
description of the main components in a system and their relationship to one another

logical design
describes the flow of information at your e-commerce site, the processing functions that must be performed, the databases that will be used, the security and emergency backup procedures that will be instituted, and the controls that will be used in the system

physical design
translates the logical design into physical components

outsourcing
hiring an outside vendor to provide the services you cannot perform with in-house personnel

Once you have identified the business objectives and system functionalities, and have developed a list of precise information requirements, you can begin to consider just how all this functionality will be delivered. You must come up with a **system design specification**—a description of the main components in the system and their relationship to one another. The system design itself can be broken down into two components: a logical design and a physical design. A **logical design** includes a data flow diagram that describes the flow of information at your e-commerce site, the processing functions that must be performed, and the databases that will be used. The logical design also includes a description of the security and emergency backup procedures that will be instituted, and the controls that will be used in the system.

A **physical design** translates the logical design into physical components. For instance, the physical design details the specific model of server to be purchased, the software to be used, the size of the telecommunications link that will be required, the way the system will be backed up and protected from outsiders, and so on.

Figure 4.6(a) presents a data flow diagram for a simple high-level logical design for a very basic Web site that delivers catalog pages in HTML in response to HTTP requests from the client's browser, while **Figure 4.6(b)** shows the corresponding physical design. Each of the main processes can be broken down into lower-level designs that are much more precise in identifying exactly how the information flows and what equipment is involved.

BUILDING THE SYSTEM: IN-HOUSE VERSUS OUTSOURCING

Now that you have a clear idea of both the logical and physical designs for your site, you can begin considering how to actually build the site. You have many choices, and much depends on the amount of money you are willing to spend. Choices range from outsourcing everything (including the actual systems analysis and design) to building everything yourself (in-house). **Outsourcing** means that you will hire an outside vendor to provide the services involved in building the site rather than using in-house personnel. You also have a second decision to make: will you host (operate) the site on your firm's own servers or will you outsource the hosting to a Web host provider? These decisions are independent of each other, but they are usually considered at the same time. There are some vendors who will design, build, and host your site, while others will either build or host (but not both). **Figure 4.7** on page 202 illustrates the alternatives.

Build Your Own versus Outsourcing

Let's take the building decision first. If you elect to build your own site, there are a range of options. Unless you are fairly skilled, you should use a pre-built template to create the Web site. For example, Yahoo Store provides templates that merely require

---

FIGURE 4.6	A LOGICAL AND A PHYSICAL DESIGN FOR A SIMPLE WEB SITE

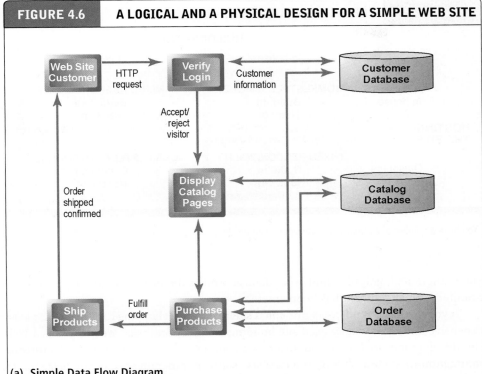

(a) Simple Data Flow Diagram.
This data flow diagram describes the flow of information requests and responses for a simple Web site.

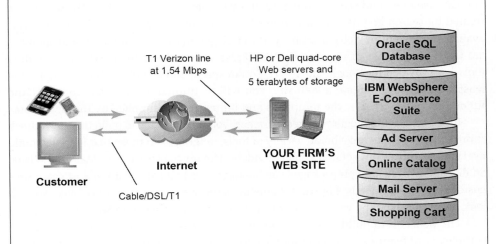

(b) Simple Physical Design.
A physical design describes the hardware and software needed to realize the logical design.

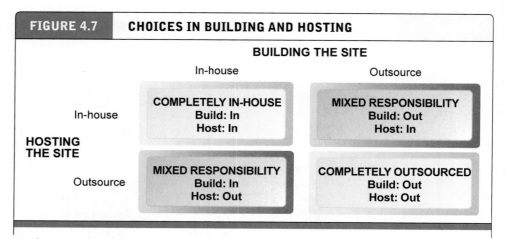

You have a number of alternatives to consider when building and hosting an e-commerce site.

you to input text, graphics, and other data, as well as the infrastructure to run a sales-oriented Web site once it has been created.

WordPress
open source content management and Web site design tool

content management system (CMS)
organizes, stores, and processes Web site content

If your Web site is not a sales-oriented site requiring a shopping cart, one of the least expensive and most widely used site building tools is WordPress. **WordPress** is a Web site development tool with a sophisticated content management system. A **content management system (CMS)** is a database software program specifically designed to manage structured and unstructured data and objects in a Web site environment. A CMS provides Web managers and designers with a centralized control structure to manage Web site content. WordPress also has thousands of user-built plug-ins and widgets that you can use to extend the functionality of a Web site. Web sites built in WordPress are treated by search engines like any other Web site: their content is indexed and made available to the entire Web community. Revenue-generating ads, affiliates, and sponsors are the main sources of revenue for WordPress sites. Other similar Web site building tools are provided by Google Sites, Wix, Squarespace, and Weebly. While these are the least costly ways to create a Web site, you will be limited to the "look and feel" and functionality provided by the templates and infrastructure supplied by these vendors.

If you have some programming experience, you might decide to build the site yourself "from scratch." There are a broad variety of tools, ranging from those that help you build everything truly "from scratch," such as Adobe Dreamweaver CC and Microsoft Visual Studio, to top-of-the-line prepackaged site-building tools that can create sophisticated sites customized to your needs. **Figure 4.8** illustrates the spectrum of tools available. We will look more closely at the variety of e-commerce software available in Section 4.3.

The decision to build a Web site on your own has a number of risks. Given the complexity of features such as shopping carts, credit card authentication and processing, inventory management, and order processing, the costs involved are high, as are the risks of doing a poor job. You will be reinventing what other specialized firms have already built, and your staff may face a long, difficult learning curve, delaying your entry to market. Your efforts could fail. On the positive side, you may be better able to build a site that does exactly what you want, and, more importantly, develop

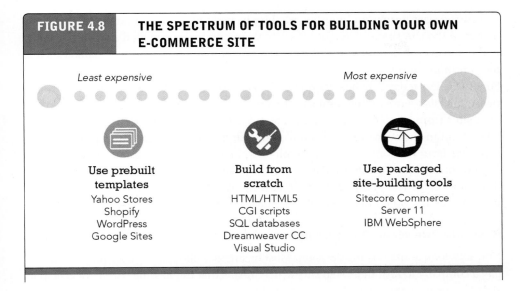

FIGURE 4.8 — **THE SPECTRUM OF TOOLS FOR BUILDING YOUR OWN E-COMMERCE SITE**

Least expensive

Most expensive

Use prebuilt templates
Yahoo Stores
Shopify
WordPress
Google Sites

Build from scratch
HTML/HTML5
CGI scripts
SQL databases
Dreamweaver CC
Visual Studio

Use packaged site-building tools
Sitecore Commerce
Server 11
IBM WebSphere

the in-house knowledge to allow you to change the site rapidly if necessary due to a changing business environment.

If you choose more expensive site-building packages, you will be purchasing state-of-the art software that is well tested. You could get to market sooner. However, to make a sound decision, you will have to evaluate many different packages, and this can take a long time. You may have to modify the package to fit your business needs and perhaps hire additional outside vendors to do the modifications. Costs rise rapidly as modifications mount. A $4,000 package can easily become a $40,000 to $60,000 development project (see **Figure 4.9**).

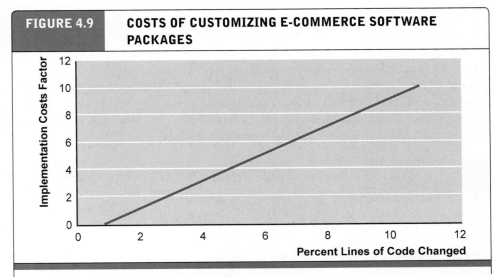

FIGURE 4.9 — **COSTS OF CUSTOMIZING E-COMMERCE SOFTWARE PACKAGES**

While sophisticated site development software packages appear to reduce costs and increase speed to market, as the modifications required to fit the package to your business needs rise, costs rise rapidly.

In the past, bricks-and-mortar retailers in need of an e-commerce site typically designed the site themselves (because they already had the skilled staff in place and had extensive investments in information technology capital such as databases and telecommunications). However, as Web applications have become more sophisticated, larger retailers today rely heavily on vendors to provide sophisticated Web site capabilities, while also maintaining a substantial internal staff. Small start-ups may build their own sites from scratch using in-house technical personnel in an effort to keep costs low. Medium-size start-ups will often purchase a Web site design and programming expertise from vendors. Very small mom-and-pop firms seeking simple storefronts will use templates like WordPress. For e-commerce sites, the cost of building has dropped dramatically in the last five years, resulting in lower capital requirements for all players (see *Insight on Business: Weebly Makes Building Web Sites Easy.*)

Host Your Own versus Outsourcing

Now let's look at the hosting decision. Most businesses choose to outsource hosting and pay a company to host their Web site, which means that the hosting company is responsible for ensuring the site is "live," or accessible, 24 hours a day. By agreeing to a monthly fee, the business need not concern itself with many of the technical aspects of setting up a Web server and maintaining it, telecommunications links, nor with staffing needs.

co-location

when a firm purchases or leases a Web server (and has total control over its operation) but locates the server in a vendor's physical facility. The vendor maintains the facility, communications lines, and the machinery

You can also choose to *co-locate*. With a **co-location** agreement, your firm purchases or leases a Web server (and has total control over its operation) but locates the server in a vendor's physical facility. The vendor maintains the facility, communications lines, and the machinery. Co-location has expanded with the spread of virtualization where one server has multiple processors (4 to 16) and can operate multiple Web sites at once with multiple operating systems. In this case, you do not buy the server but rent its capabilities on a monthly basis, usually at one-quarter of the cost of owning the server itself. See **Table 4.3** for a list of some of the major hosting/co-location/cloud providers. There is an extraordinary range of prices for co-location, ranging from $4.95 a month, to several hundred thousands of dollars per month depending on the size of the Web site, bandwidth, storage, and support requirements.

While co-location involves renting physical space for your hardware, you can think of using a cloud service provider as renting virtual space in your provider's infrastructure. Cloud services are rapidly replacing co-location because they are less expensive, and arguably more reliable. Unlike with co-location, your firm does not own the hardware. Cloud service providers offer a standardized infrastructure, virtualization technology, and usually employ a pay-as-you-go billing system.

TABLE 4.3	KEY PLAYERS: HOSTING/CO-LOCATION/CLOUD SERVICES
Amazon Web Services (AWS) EC2	Hostway
Bluehost	SoftLayer (IBM)
CenturyLink	Rackspace
Digital Realty Trust	Verio
GoDaddy	Verizon Cloud

INSIGHT ON BUSINESS

WEEBLY MAKES CREATING WEB SITES EASY

With so many big companies dominating the e-commerce scene, you may wonder if there's a chance for the little guy anymore. The answer is yes: there are still billions left in potential online retail sales, with additional money to be made from advertising revenues. In fact, there's an e-commerce frenzy going on that nearly rivals the dot-com era with one exception: the start-ups have access to cheap technology and social media that can provide inexpensive marketing and sales.

Weebly provides valuable Web site solutions to smaller businesses and entrepeneurs. Founded in 2007 by Penn State graduates David Rusenko, Chris Fanini, and Dan Veltri, Weebly provides Web site templates that allow small businesses to create their own Web sites with a full suite of features, including blogs, online stores, and mobile compatibility. Weebly's customers have built over 25 million sites, with over 240 million monthly unique visitors. Users create sites using a drag-and-drop, widget-based tool that works within a Web browser. Weebly's typical customers are the "little guys" hoping to harness the site tools traditionally available only to bigger Web sites and retailers.

Weebly is just one option in an increasingly crowded marketplace for website creation services. Today's offerings are a far cry from early services like GeoCities and Angelfire, which look crude by today's standards. Weebly and its competitors, including Squarespace, Wix, and WordPress, offer a much more polished product than their predecessors. The company has a free option with basic features as well as premium plans starting at $4 per month and increasing to only $25 per month for its high-end Business plan. Over the course of its growth, Weebly has added Google AdSense monetization features, CSS/HTML editing support, and the ability to generate a mobile version of each Web site automatically. Weebly dominates in this marketplace, with its 25 million sites dwarfing the 2.5 million made with Squarespace, its closest competitor.

Weebly has increasingly focused on improving its e-commerce services, such as a mobile store and checkout capability, integrated shopping cart, and filtered product search. It also offers basic support for PayPal and Google Checkout, and in 2015 announced a partnership with payment solution developer Square that would allow Weebly site creators to keep track of all of their payments and orders in one place using Square. By revamping its e-commerce tools, Weebly hopes to better compete with Amazon, as well as similar user-friendly marketplaces such as Etsy and Shopify. Sixty percent of Weebly users identify themselves as entrepreneurs hoping to create an online presence for their business.

One example is Kim Beers. Her gifts of handmade, environmentally friendly pet toys were so well received by friends that she decided to start selling them under the name Woof Purr Studio. Beers first tried selling on Etsy and eBay, which enabled her to build an initial following. Dissatisfied with the fees and lack of control offered by those platforms, she decided to create her own Web site with Weebly, starting with Weebly's Basic version and then upgrading to its Business version. Beers reports a much better user experience, with the ability to display larger images and videos, offer coupon codes, and ship items internationally

(continued)

more easily. Even better, her sales have improved, which she attributes to her ability to be able to explain in a video on the site why her toys are better although they cost more than toys made in China from potentially chemical-laced materials.

Although Weebly doesn't disclose its revenue, the company is profitable and has been since 2009. This is an attractive quality for a start-up company, many of which have historically sought growth first and profitability later. In 2014, Weebly received $35 million in venture capital funding that valued the company at $455 million. Weebly is one of the more valuable companies to graduate the technology incubator Y Combinator (featured in the *Insight on Business* case in Chapter 1), which its founders attended in 2007.

Because so many businesses still don't have an online presence, Weebly's prospects for growth are bright. Less than 40% of restaurants have online menus, for example. Although its competitors, such as Squarespace and Wix, are also growing fast, there appears to be enough room in this market for several companies. In 2013, Wix launched an initial public offering, but the response was lukewarm, with investors expressing concern over its lack of profitability. So far, that's an advantage for Weebly, but as Weebly begins an aggressive push for growth, the company's profitability may suffer.

Weebly has continued adapting its platform to mobile devices. It launched a full version of its site creation tool for iPad in late 2014, and for Android in 2015. These tools allow users to create the same high quality Web sites without ever logging on to Weebly's desktop site. Both tools required complete rebuilds of Weebly's site creation system from the ground up, and both use native code to maximize speed. Weebly even developed an app for the Apple Watch that allows users to monitor site traffic and visitor statistics, manage blog comments, check store orders, and other basic functions. Weebly's push to the mobile platform will only help its prospects for future growth, and existing customers will have more options for building and maintaining their sites.

In 2015, Weebly also announced a program that will provide enhanced support for merchants located in the United Kingdom, France, and Germany. It will also now offer localized domain names for Web sites that it hosts, utilizing country-code top level domains (ccTLDs).

Weebly is just one example of a larger trend toward leaner business models that rely on outside help for many of their business functions. Although hardware has become less expensive over time, many startup firms have found that cloud computing and social marketing greatly reduce the costs of starting a company. Market intelligence, public relations, and even design services can be found online for a fraction of the cost of traditional service firms. It's never been cheaper to start an e-commerce company.

SOURCES: "Weebly Targets Europe with Localized Services for Its Drop-and-Drag Websites," by Paul Sawers, Venturebeat.com, October 27, 2015; "About Weebly," Weebly.com, accessed September 21, 2015; "The Whiskey Ball," Weeblystories.com, accessed May 2015; "Weebly for Apple Watch," Weebly. com, April 28, 2015; "Weebly Brings Industry-First App to Android Tablets," *Business Wire*, March 11, 2015; "Weebly and Square Bring Simple, High-Quality Business Solutions to Stores Looking to Get Online," *Business Wire*, February 25, 2015; "Looking Back on a Very Special Year," Weebly.com, November 30, 2014; "Weebly Debuts An iPad App for Building and Managing Websites," by Ryan Lawler, Techcrunch.com, October 9, 2014; "New Weebly App Lets You Build a Website Using the iPad," by Michael Muchmore, Pcmag.com, October 9, 2014; "Weebly Valued at $455 Million Amid Website-Building Boom," by Douglas Macmillan, *Wall Street Journal*, April 22, 2014; "Woof Purr Has Everything You Need for That Special Pet in Your Life," by Tim Goodwin, Theconcordinsider. com, December 31, 2013; "Weebly Website Creator Attracts Online Sellers with Store Features," by Greg Holden, Ecommercebytes.com, December 8, 2013; "A Tiny Web Merchant, But a Global Reach," by Paul Demery, Internetretailer.com, November 19, 2013; "With 30K Active Online Stores, Weebly Launches DIY eCommerce Platform to Take On Amazon and Shopify," by Rip Empson, Techcrunch.com, November 6, 2013; "Weeby Arms Entrepreneurs with Superior eCommerce to Boost Shopper Experience and Sell More Both Online and on Mobile," Reuters.com, November 6, 2013; "As Wix Heads Toward IPO, Weebly Looks to Expand with Big New SF Headquarters, Plans to Add 500+ Employees," by Rip Empson, TechCrunch, August 24, 2013.

Hosting, co-location, and cloud services have become a commodity and a utility: costs are driven by very large providers (such as IBM) who can achieve large economies of scale by establishing huge "server farms" located strategically around the country and the globe. This means the cost of pure hosting has fallen as fast as the fall in server prices, dropping about 50% every year! Telecommunications costs have also fallen. As a result, most hosting services seek to differentiate themselves from the commodity hosting business by offering extensive site design, marketing, optimization, and other services. Small, local ISPs also can be used as hosts, but service reliability is an issue. Will the small ISPs be able to provide uninterrupted service, 24 hours a day, 7 days a week, 365 days a year? Will they have service staff available when you need it?

There are several disadvantages to outsourcing hosting. If you choose a vendor, make sure the vendor has the capability to grow with you. You need to know what kinds of security provisions are in place for backup copies of your site, internal monitoring of activity, and security track record. Is there a public record of a security breach at the vendor? Most Fortune 500 firms have their own private cloud data centers so they can control the Web environment. On the other hand, there are risks to hosting your own site if you are a small business. Your costs will be higher than if you had used a large outsourcing firm because you don't have the market power to obtain low-cost hardware and telecommunications. You will have to purchase hardware and software, have a physical facility, lease communications lines, hire a staff, and build security and backup capabilities yourself.

TESTING THE SYSTEM

Once the system has been built and programmed, you will have to engage in a testing process. Depending on the size of the system, this could be fairly difficult and lengthy. Testing is required whether the system is outsourced or built in-house. A complex e-commerce site can have thousands of pathways through the site, each of which must be documented and then tested. It is important to note that testing is generally under-budgeted. As much as 50% of the budget can be consumed by testing and rebuilding (usually depending on the quality of the initial design). **Unit testing** involves testing the site's program modules one at a time. **System testing** involves testing the site as a whole, in the same way a typical user would when using the site. Because there is no truly "typical" user, system testing requires that every conceivable path be tested. Final **acceptance testing** requires that the firm's key personnel and managers in marketing, production, sales, and general management actually use the system as installed on a test Internet or intranet server. This acceptance test verifies that the business objectives of the system as originally conceived are in fact working.

Another form of testing is called **A/B testing** (or **split testing**). This form of testing involves showing two versions (A and B) of a Web page or Web site to different users to see which one performs better. There are several different types of A/B testing that can be used for a Web site design project. A *template test* compares the same general page content using two different layouts and or design treatments. A *new concept test* compares a control page with one that is very different. A *funnel test* compares the flow through a series of pages (such as a product page, to a registration page, to shopping cart page, versus skipping the registration page) to see which one

unit testing
involves testing the site's program modules one at a time

system testing
involves testing the site as a whole, in a way the typical user will use the site

acceptance testing
verifies that the business objectives of the system as originally conceived are in fact working

A/B testing (split testing)
involves showing two versions of a Web page or Web site to different users to see which one performs better

multivariate testing
involves identifying specific elements, creating versions for each element, and then creating a unique combination of each element and version to test

results in a higher percentage of conversions. **Multivariate testing** is a much more sophisticated form of testing than A/B testing. Multivariate testing involves identifying specific elements, or variables, on a Web page, such as a headline, image, button and text, creating versions for each element, and then creating a unique combination of each element and version to test. So for example, if there are three elements and two versions of each, there will be eight possible combinations ($2*2*2 = 8$) to test. When used correctly, multivariate testing enables designers to identify the most optimal layout, color, content and format.

IMPLEMENTATION AND MAINTENANCE

Most people unfamiliar with systems erroneously think that once an information system is installed, the process is over. In fact, while the beginning of the process is over, the operational life of a system is just beginning. Systems break down for a variety of reasons—most of them unpredictable. Therefore, they need continual checking, testing, and repair. Systems maintenance is vital, but sometimes not budgeted for. In general, the annual system maintenance cost will roughly parallel the development cost. A $40,000 e-commerce site will likely require a $40,000 annual expenditure to maintain. Very large e-commerce sites experience some economies of scale, so that, for example, a $1 million site will likely require a maintenance budget of $500,000 to $700,000.

Why does it cost so much to maintain an e-commerce site? Unlike payroll systems, for example, e-commerce sites are always in a process of change, improvement, and correction. Studies of traditional systems maintenance have found 20% of the time is devoted to debugging code and responding to emergency situations (for example, a new server was installed by your ISP, and all your hypertext links were lost and CGI scripts disabled—the site is down!). Another 20% of the time is concerned with changes in reports, data files, and links to backend databases. The remaining 60% of maintenance time is devoted to general administration (making product and price changes in the catalog) and making changes and enhancements to the system. E-commerce sites are never finished: they are always in the process of being built and rebuilt. They are dynamic—much more so than payroll systems.

The long-term success of an e-commerce site will depend on a dedicated team of employees (the Web team) whose sole job is to monitor and adapt the site to changing market conditions. The Web team must be multi-skilled; it will typically include programmers, designers, and business managers drawn from marketing, production, and sales support. One of the first tasks of the Web team is to listen to customers' feedback on the site and respond to that feedback as necessary. A second task is to develop a systematic monitoring and testing plan to be followed weekly to ensure all the links are operating, prices are correct, and pages are updated. A large business may have thousands of Web pages, many of them linked, that require systematic monitoring.

benchmarking
a process in which the site is compared with those of competitors in terms of response speed, quality of layout, and design

Other important tasks of the Web team include **benchmarking** (a process in which the site is compared with those of competitors in terms of response speed, quality of layout, and design) and keeping the site current on pricing and promotions. The Web is a competitive environment where you can very rapidly frustrate and lose customers with a dysfunctional site.

FIGURE 4.10	FACTORS IN WEB SITE OPTIMIZATION

Page Delivery

Content delivery networks
Edge caching
Bandwidth

Page Generation

Server response time
Device-based accelerators
Efficient resource allocation
Resource utilization thresholds
Monitoring site performance

Page Content

Optimize HTML
Optimize images
Site architecture
Efficient page style

Web site optimization requires that you consider three factors: page content, page generation, and page delivery.

FACTORS IN OPTIMIZING WEB SITE PERFORMANCE

The purpose of a Web site is to deliver content to customers and to complete transactions. The faster and more reliably these two objectives are met, the more effective the Web site is from a commerce perspective. If you are a manager or marketing executive, you will want the Web site operating in a way that fulfills customers' expectations. You'll have to make sure the Web site is optimized to achieve this business objective. The optimization of Web site performance is more complicated than it seems and involves at least three factors: page content, page generation, and page delivery (see **Figure 4.10**). In this chapter, we describe the software and hardware choices you will need to make in building an e-commerce site; these are also important factors in Web site optimization.

Using efficient styles and techniques for *page design* and *content* can reduce response times by two to five seconds. Simple steps include reducing unnecessary HTML comments and white space, using more efficient graphics, and avoiding unnecessary links to other pages in the site. *Page generation* speed can be enhanced by segregating computer servers to perform dedicated functions (such as static page generation, application logic, media servers, and database servers), and using various devices from vendors to speed up these servers. Using a single server or multiple servers to perform multiple tasks reduces throughput by more than 50%. *Page delivery* can be speeded up by using specialized content delivery networks such as Akamai, or by increasing local bandwidth. We will discuss some of these factors throughout the chapter, but a full discussion of optimizing Web site performance is beyond the scope of this text.

4.3 CHOOSING SOFTWARE

Along with telecommunications, software and hardware constitute the infrastructure of an e-commerce presence. As a business manager in charge of creating an e-commerce presence, you will need to know some basic information about both.

SIMPLE VERSUS MULTI-TIERED WEB SITE ARCHITECTURE

system architecture
the arrangement of software, machinery, and tasks in an information system needed to achieve a specific functionality

Prior to the development of e-commerce, Web sites simply delivered Web pages to users who were making requests through their browsers for HTML pages with content of various sorts. Web site software was appropriately quite simple—it consisted of a server computer running basic Web server software. We might call this arrangement a single-tier system architecture. **System architecture** refers to the arrangement of software, machinery, and tasks in an information system needed to achieve a specific functionality (much like a home's architecture refers to the arrangement of building materials to achieve a particular functionality). Many Web sites started this way—there are no monetary transactions. Tens of thousands of sites still perform this way. Orders can always be called in by telephone and not taken online.

However, the development of e-commerce required a great deal more interactive functionality, such as the ability to respond to user input (name and address forms), take customer orders for goods and services, clear credit card transactions on the fly, consult price and product databases, and even adjust advertising on the screen based on user characteristics. This kind of extended functionality required the development of Web application servers and a multi-tiered system architecture to handle the processing loads. *Web application servers*, described more fully later in this section, are specialized software programs that perform a wide variety of transaction processing required by e-commerce.

two-tier architecture
e-commerce system architecture in which a Web server responds to requests for Web pages and a database server provides backend data storage

In addition to having specialized application servers, e-commerce sites must be able to pull information from and add information to pre-existing corporate databases. These older databases that predate the e-commerce era are called *backend* or *legacy* databases. Corporations have made massive investments in these systems to store their information on customers, products, employees, and vendors. These backend systems constitute an additional layer in a multi-tiered site.

multi-tier architecture
e-commerce system architecture in which the Web server is linked to a middle-tier layer that typically includes a series of application servers that perform specific tasks as well as a backend layer of existing corporate systems

Figure 4.11 illustrates a simple two-tier and a more complex multi-tier e-commerce site architecture. In **two-tier architecture**, a Web server responds to requests for Web pages and a database server provides backend data storage. In a **multi-tier architecture**, in contrast, the Web server is linked to a middle-tier layer that typically includes a series of application servers that perform specific tasks, as well as to a backend layer of existing corporate systems containing product, customer, and pricing information. A multi-tiered site typically employs several physical computers, each running some of the software applications and sharing the workload across many physical computers.

The remainder of this section describes basic Web server software functionality and the various types of Web application servers.

FIGURE 4.11	TWO-TIER AND MULTI-TIER E-COMMERCE SITE ARCHITECTURES

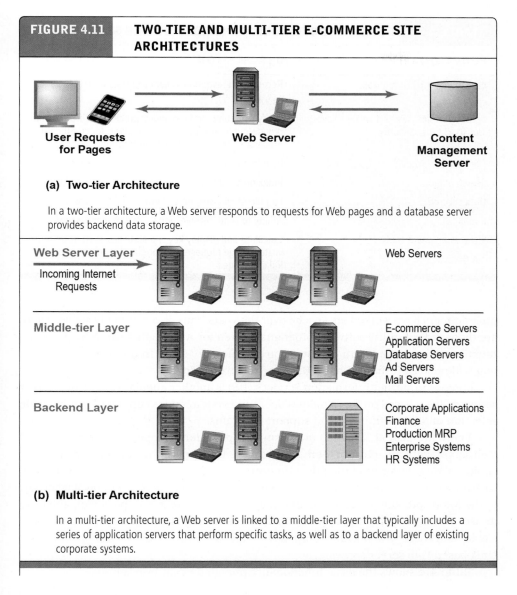

User Requests for Pages   **Web Server**   **Content Management Server**

(a) Two-tier Architecture

In a two-tier architecture, a Web server responds to requests for Web pages and a database server provides backend data storage.

Web Server Layer   Web Servers

Incoming Internet Requests

Middle-tier Layer   E-commerce Servers
Application Servers
Database Servers
Ad Servers
Mail Servers

Backend Layer   Corporate Applications
Finance
Production MRP
Enterprise Systems
HR Systems

(b) Multi-tier Architecture

In a multi-tier architecture, a Web server is linked to a middle-tier layer that typically includes a series of application servers that perform specific tasks, as well as to a backend layer of existing corporate systems.

WEB SERVER SOFTWARE

All e-commerce sites require basic Web server software to answer requests from customers for HTML and XML pages.

When you choose Web server software, you will also be choosing an operating system for your site's computers. Apache, which works with Linux and Unix operating systems, is the leading Web server software (Netcraft, 2015). Unix is the original programming language of the Internet and Web, and Linux is a derivative of Unix designed for the personal computer. Apache was developed by a worldwide community of Internet innovators. Apache is free and can be downloaded from many sites on the Web; it also comes installed on most IBM Web servers. Literally thousands of

TABLE 4.4	BASIC FUNCTIONALITY PROVIDED BY WEB SERVERS
FUNCTIONALITY	DESCRIPTION
Processing of HTTP requests	Receive and respond to client requests for HTML pages
Security services (Secure Sockets Layer)/ Transport Layer Security	Verify username and password; process certificates and private/public key information required for credit card processing and other secure information
File Transfer Protocol	Permits transfer of very large files from server to server
Search engine	Indexing of site content; keyword search capability
Data capture	Log file of all visits, time, duration, and referral source
E-mail	Ability to send, receive, and store e-mail messages
Site management tools	Calculate and display key site statistics, such as unique visitors, page requests, and origin of requests; check links on pages

programmers have worked on Apache over the years; thus, it is extremely stable. There are thousands of utility software programs written for Apache that can provide all the functionality required for a contemporary e-commerce site. In order to use Apache, you will need staff that is knowledgeable in Unix or Linux.

Microsoft Internet Information Services (IIS) is another popular type of Web server software. IIS is based on the Windows operating system and is compatible with a wide selection of Microsoft utility and support programs.

There are also at least 100 other smaller providers or open source versions of Web server software, most of them based on the Unix operating system. Note that the choice of Web server has little effect on users of your system. The pages they see will look the same regardless of the development environment. There are many advantages to the Microsoft suite of development tools—they are integrated, powerful, and easy to use. The Unix operating system, on the other hand, is exceptionally reliable and stable, and there is a worldwide open software community that develops and tests Unix-based Web server software.

Table 4.4 shows the basic functionality provided by all Web servers.

Site Management Tools

site management tools

verify that links on pages are still valid and also identify orphan files

In Chapter 3, we described most of the basic functionality of the Web servers listed in Table 4.4. Another functionality not described previously is site management tools. **Site management tools** are essential if you want to keep your site working, and if you want to understand how well it is working. Site management tools verify that links on pages are still valid and also identify orphan files, or files on the site that are not linked to any pages. By surveying the links on a Web site, a site management tool can quickly report on potential problems and errors that users may encounter. Your customers will not be impressed if they encounter a "404 Error: Page Does Not Exist" message on your Web site. Links to URLs that have moved or been deleted are called dead links; these can cause error messages for users trying to access that link. Regularly checking that all links on a site are operational helps prevent irritation and frustration in users who may decide to take their business elsewhere to a better functioning site.

Even more importantly, site management tools can help you understand consumer behavior on your Web site. Site management software and services, such as those provided by Webtrends, can be purchased in order to more effectively monitor customer purchases and marketing campaign effectiveness, as well as keep track of standard hit counts and page visit information. **Figure 4.12** shows a screenshot that illustrates Webtrends Analytics 10.

Dynamic Page Generation Tools

One of the most important innovations in Web site operation has been the development of dynamic page generation tools. Prior to the development of e-commerce, Web sites primarily delivered unchanging static content in the form of HTML pages.

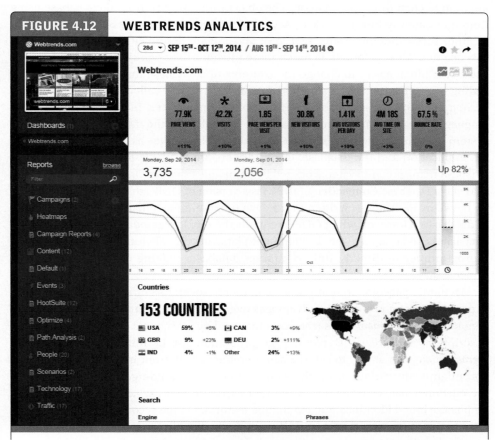

FIGURE 4.12   WEBTRENDS ANALYTICS

Using a sophisticated Web analytics solution such as Webtrends Analytics, managers can quickly understand the return on investment of their online marketing efforts and determine how to improve conversion by drilling down into abandonment paths, product preferences, and successful campaign elements for different types of customers.
SOURCE: Webtrends, Inc., 2014.

While this capability might be sufficient to display pictures of products, consider all the elements of a typical e-commerce site today by reviewing Table 4.2 (on page 199), or visit what you believe is an excellent e-commerce site. The content of successful e-commerce sites is always changing, often day by day. There are new products and promotions, changing prices, news events, and stories of successful users. E-commerce sites must intensively interact with users who not only request pages but also request product, price, availability, and inventory information. One of the most dynamic sites is eBay—the auction site. There, the content is changing minute by minute. E-commerce sites are just like real markets—they are dynamic. News sites, where stories change constantly, also are dynamic.

The dynamic and complex nature of e-commerce sites requires a number of specialized software applications in addition to static HTML pages. Perhaps one of the most important is dynamic page generation software. With **dynamic page generation**, the contents of a Web page are stored as objects in a database, rather than being hard-coded in HTML. When the user requests a Web page, the contents for that page are then fetched from the database. The objects are retrieved from the database using Common Gateway Interface (CGI), Active Server Pages (ASP), Java Server Pages (JSP), or other server-side programs. CGI, ASP, and JSP are described in the last section of this chapter. This technique is much more efficient than working directly in HTML code. It is much easier to change the contents of a database than it is to change the coding of an HTML page. A standard data access method called *Open Database Connectivity (ODBC)* makes it possible for applications written in the C programming language to access data from any database regardless of the database and operating system software being used via an ODBC driver that serves as a translator between the application and the database. ODBC drivers are available for most of the major database management systems offered by companies such as Oracle, SAP, Sybase, and IBM. Java Database Connectivity (JDBC) is a version of ODBC that provides connectivity between applications written in the Java programming language and a wide range of databases. However, while ODBC remains the de facto standard for cross-platform data access, today many web development platforms provide functionality that allows a programmer to directly link to a target database, making ODBC/JDBC drivers unnecessary.

Dynamic page generation gives e-commerce several significant capabilities that generate cost and profitability advantages over traditional commerce. Dynamic page generation lowers *menu costs* (the costs incurred by merchants for changing product descriptions and prices). Dynamic page generation also permits easy online *market segmentation*—the ability to sell the same product to different markets. For instance, you might want variations on the same banner ad depending on how many times the customer has seen the ad. In the first exposure to a car ad, you might want to emphasize brand identification and unique features. On the second viewing you might want to emphasize superlatives like "most family friendly" to encourage comparison to other brands. The same capability makes possible nearly cost-free *price discrimination*—the ability to sell the same product to different customers at different prices. For instance, you might want to sell the same product to corporations and government

dynamic page generation

the contents of a Web page are stored as objects in a database, rather than being hard-coded in HTML. When the user requests a Web page, the contents for that page are then fetched from the database

agencies but use different marketing themes. Based on a cookie you place on client computers, or in response to a question on your site that asks visitors if they are from a government agency or a corporation, you would be able to use different marketing and promotional materials for corporate clients and government clients. You might want to reward loyal customers with lower prices, say on DVDs or musical tracks, and charge full price to first-time buyers. Dynamic page generation allows you to approach different customers with different messages and prices.

Dynamic page generation also enables the use of a content management system (CMS). As previously described, a CMS is used to create and manage Web content. A CMS separates the design and presentation of content (such as HTML documents, images, video, audio) from the content creation process. The content is maintained in a database and dynamically linked to the Web site. A CMS usually includes templates that can be automatically applied to new and existing content, WYSIWYG editing tools that make it easy to edit and describe (tag) content, and collaboration, workflow, and document management tools. Typically, an experienced programmer is needed to install the system, but thereafter, content can be created and managed by non-technical staff. There are a wide range of commercial CMSs available, from top-end enterprise systems offered by HP Autonomy, EMC Documentum, OpenText, IBM, Adobe, and Oracle, to mid-market systems by Sitecore, PaperThin, and EPiServer, as well as hosted software as a service (SaaS) versions by Clickability (Upland) and CrownPeak Technology among others. There are also several open source content management systems available, such as WordPress, Joomla, Drupal, OpenCms, and others.

APPLICATION SERVERS

Web application servers are software programs that provide the specific business functionality required of a Web site. The basic idea of application servers is to isolate the business applications from the details of displaying Web pages to users on the front end and the details of connecting to databases on the back end. Application servers are a kind of middleware software that provides the glue connecting traditional corporate systems to the customer as well as all the functionality needed to conduct e-commerce. In the early years, a number of software firms developed specific separate programs for each function, but increasingly, these specific programs are being replaced by integrated software tools that combine all the needed functionality for an e-commerce site into a single development environment, a packaged software approach.

Table 4.5 illustrates the wide variety of application servers available in the marketplace. The table focuses on "sell-side" servers that are designed to enable selling products on the Web. So-called "buy-side" and "link" servers focus on the needs of businesses to connect with partners in their supply chains or find suppliers for specific parts and assemblies. There are several thousand software vendors that provide application server software. For Linux and Unix environments, many of these capabilities are available free on the Internet from various sites. Most businesses—faced with this bewildering array of choices—choose to use integrated software tools called merchant server software.

Web application server
software program that provides specific business functionality required of a Web site

TABLE 4.5	APPLICATION SERVERS AND THEIR FUNCTION
APPLICATION SERVER	FUNCTIONALITY
Catalog display	Provides a database for product descriptions and prices
Transaction processing (shopping cart)	Accepts orders and clears payments
List server	Creates and serves mailing lists and manages e-mail marketing campaigns
Proxy server	Monitors and controls access to main Web server; implements firewall protection
Mail server	Manages Internet e-mail
Audio/video server	Stores and delivers streaming media content
Chat server	Creates an environment for online real-time text and audio interactions with customers
News server	Provides connectivity and displays Internet news feeds
Fax server	Provides fax reception and sending using a Web server
Groupware server	Creates workgroup environments for online collaboration
Database server	Stores customer, product, and price information
Ad server	Maintains Web-enabled database of advertising banners that permits customized and personalized display of advertisements based on consumer behavior and characteristics
Auction server	Provides a transaction environment for conducting online auctions
B2B server	Implements buy, sell, and link marketplaces for commercial transactions

E-COMMERCE MERCHANT SERVER SOFTWARE FUNCTIONALITY

e-commerce merchant server software
software that provides the basic functionality needed for online sales, including an online catalog, order taking via an online shopping cart, and online credit card processing

E-commerce merchant server software provides the basic functionality needed for online sales, including an online catalog, order taking via an online shopping cart, and online credit card processing.

Online Catalog

online catalog
list of products available on a Web site

A company that wants to sell products on the Web must have a list, or **online catalog**, of its products, available on its Web site. Merchant server software typically includes a database capability that will allow for construction of a customized online catalog. The complexity and sophistication of the catalog will vary depending on the size of the company and its product lines. Small companies, or companies with small product lines, may post a simple list with text descriptions and perhaps color photos. A larger site might decide to add sound, animations, or videos (useful for product demonstrations) to the catalog, or interactivity, such as customer service representatives available via instant messaging to answer questions. Today, larger firms make extensive use of streaming video.

Shopping Cart

Online **shopping carts** are much like their real-world equivalent; both allow shoppers to set aside desired purchases in preparation for checkout. The difference is that the online variety is part of a merchant server software program residing on the Web server, and allows consumers to select merchandise, review what they have selected, edit their selections as necessary, and then actually make the purchase by clicking a button. The merchant server software automatically stores shopping cart data.

shopping cart
allows shoppers to set aside desired purchases in preparation for checkout, review what they have selected, edit their selections as necessary, and then actually make the purchase by clicking a button

Credit Card Processing

A site's shopping cart typically works in conjunction with credit card processing software, which verifies the shopper's credit card and then puts through the debit to the card and the credit to the company's account at checkout. Integrated e-commerce software suites typically supply the software for this function. Otherwise, you will have to make arrangements with a variety of credit card processing banks and intermediaries.

MERCHANT SERVER SOFTWARE PACKAGES (E-COMMERCE SOFTWARE PLATFORMS)

Rather than build your site from a collection of disparate software applications, it is easier, faster, and generally more cost-effective to purchase a **merchant server software package** (also called an **e-commerce software platform**). Merchant server software offers an integrated environment that promises to provide most or all of the functionality and capabilities you will need to develop a sophisticated, customer-centric site. An important element of merchant sofware packages is a built-in shopping cart that can display merchandise, manage orders, and clear credit card transactions. E-commerce software platforms come in three general ranges of price and functionality.

merchant server software package (e-commerce software platform)
offers an integrated environment that provides most or all of the functionality and capabilities needed to develop a sophisticated, customer-centric site

While existing firms often have the financial capital to invest in commercial merchant server software, many small firms and start-up firms do not. There are really two options here, the key factor being how much programming experience and time you have. One option is to utilize the e-commerce merchant services provided by sites such as Yahoo Stores. For instance, for $26 a month and a 1.5% transaction fee for each transaction processed through the store, Yahoo Stores Basic makes it easy to create an e-commerce Web site with customizable templates. An e-commerce template is a predesigned Web site that allows users to customize the look and feel of the site to fit their business needs and provides a standard set of functionalities. Most templates today contain ready-to-go site designs with built-in e-commerce functionality like shopping carts, payment clearance, and site management tools. Yahoo Stores also includes a mobile storefront, search engine optimization tools, social media support,

TABLE 4.6	OPEN SOURCE SOFTWARE OPTIONS
FUNCTIONALITY	OPEN SOURCE SOFTWARE
Web server	Apache (the leading Web server for small and medium businesses)
Shopping cart, online catalog	Many providers: osCommerce, Zen Cart, AgoraCart, X-cart, AspDotNetStorefront
Credit card processing	Credit card acceptance is typically provided in shopping cart software but you may need a merchant account from a bank as well.
Database	MySQL (the leading open source SQL database for businesses)
Programming/scripting language	PHP is a scripting language embedded in HTML documents but executed by the server, providing server-side execution with the simplicity of HTML editing. Perl is an alternative language. JavaScript programs are client-side programs that provide user interface components. Ruby on Rails (RoR, Rails) and Django are other popular open source Web application frameworks.
Analytics	Analytics keep track of your site's customer activities and the success of your Web advertising campaign. You can also use Google Analytics if you advertise on Google, which provides good tracking tools; most hosting services will provide these services as well. Other open source analytic tools include Piwik, CrawlTrack, and Open Web Analytics.

and a variety of other marketing tools. Many others, such as Bigcommerce, Homestead, Vendio, and Shopify offer similar services.

If you have considerable, or at least some, programming background, you can consider open source merchant server software. **Open source software** is software developed by a community of programmers and designers, and is free to use and modify. **Table 4.6** provides a description of some open source options. The advantage of using open source Web building tools is that you get exactly what you want, a truly customized unique Web site. The disadvantage is that it will take several months for a single programmer to develop the site and get all the tools to work together seamlessly. How many months do you want to wait before you get to market with your ideas?

open source software
software that is developed by a community of programmers and designers, and is free to use and modify

Midrange e-commerce software platforms include IBM WebSphere Commerce Express Edition and Sitecore Commerce Server (formerly Microsoft Commerce Server). High-end enterprise solutions for large global firms are provided by IBM Websphere Professional and Enterprise Editions, IBM Commerce on Cloud, Oracle ATG Web Commerce, Demandware, Magento, NetSuite, and others. Many of these e-commerce software platforms are now available on a Software as a Service (SaaS) basis, a model in which the software is hosted in the cloud and run by the client via a Web browser. This model enables a firm to launch an e-commerce site very quickly. For instance, Williams-Sonoma, a housewares retail chain in the United States, used Web-hosted e-commerce software from NetSuite to launch an e-commerce site in Australia in only 3 months time (Dusto, 2014). There are several hundred software firms that provide e-commerce software, which raises the costs of making sensible decisions on this matter.

Choosing an E-commerce Software Platform

With all of these vendors, how do you choose the right one? Evaluating these tools and making a choice is one of the most important and uncertain decisions you will make in building an e-commerce site. The real costs are hidden—they involve training your staff to use the tools and integrating the tools into your business processes and organizational culture. The following are some of the key factors to consider:

- Functionality, including availability on an SaaS basis
- Support for different business models, including m-commerce
- Business process modeling tools
- Visual site management tools and reporting
- Performance and scalability
- Connectivity to existing business systems
- Compliance with standards
- Global and multicultural capability
- Local sales tax and shipping rules

For instance, although e-commerce software platforms promise to do everything, your business may require special functionality—such as streaming audio and video. You will need a list of business functionality requirements. Your business may involve several different business models—such as a retail side and a business-to-business side; you may run auctions for stock excess as well as fixed-price selling. Be sure the package can support all of your business models. You may wish to change your business processes, such as order taking and order fulfillment. Does the platform contain tools for modeling business process and work flows? Understanding how your site works will require visual reporting tools that make its operation transparent to many different people in your business. A poorly designed software package will drop off significantly in performance as visitors and transactions expand into the thousands per hour, or minute. Check for performance and scalability by stress-testing a pilot edition or obtaining data from the vendor about performance under load. You will have to connect the e-commerce platform to your traditional business systems. How will this connection to existing systems be made, and is your staff skilled in making the connection? Because of the changing technical environment—in particular, changes in m-commerce platforms—it is important to document exactly what standards the platform supports now, and what the migration path will be toward the future. Finally, your e-commerce site may have to work both globally and locally. You may need a foreign language edition using foreign currency denominations. And you will have to collect sales taxes across many local, regional, and national tax systems. Does the e-commerce platform support this level of globalization and localization?

4.4 CHOOSING HARDWARE

Whether you host your own site or outsource the hosting and operation of your site, you will need to understand certain aspects of the computing hardware platform. The **hardware platform** refers to all the underlying computing equipment that the system uses to achieve its e-commerce functionality. Your objective is to have enough platform capacity to meet peak demand (avoiding an overload condition), but not so much platform that you are wasting money. Failing to meet peak demand can mean your site is slow, or actually crashes. How much computing and telecommunications capacity is enough to meet peak demand? How many hits per day can your site sustain?

To answer these questions, you will need to understand the various factors that affect the speed, capacity, and scalability of an e-commerce site.

RIGHT-SIZING YOUR HARDWARE PLATFORM: THE DEMAND SIDE

The most important factor affecting the speed of your site is the demand that customers put on the site. **Table 4.7** lists the most important factors to consider when estimating the demand on a site.

Demand on a Web site is fairly complex and depends primarily on the type of site you are operating. The number of simultaneous users in peak periods, the nature of customer requests, the type of content, the required security, the number of items in inventory, the number of page requests, and the speed of legacy applications that may be needed to supply data to the Web pages are all important factors in overall demand on a Web site system.

Certainly, one important factor to consider is the number of simultaneous users who will likely visit your site. In general, the load created by an individual customer on a server is typically quite limited and short-lived. A Web session initiated by the typical user is **stateless**, meaning that the server does not have to maintain an ongoing, dedicated interaction with the client. A Web session typically begins with a page request, then a server replies, and the session is ended. The sessions may last from tenths of a second to a minute per user. Nevertheless, system performance does degrade as more and more simultaneous users request service. Fortunately, degradation (measured as "transactions per second" and "latency" or delay in response) is fairly graceful over a wide range, up until a peak load is reached and service quality becomes unacceptable (see **Figure 4.13** on page 222).

Serving up static Web pages is **I/O intensive**, which means it requires input/output (I/O) operations rather than heavy-duty processing power. As a result, Web site performance is constrained primarily by the server's I/O limitations and the telecommunications connection, rather than the speed of the processor.

hardware platform
refers to all the underlying computing equipment that the system uses to achieve its e-commerce functionality

stateless
refers to the fact that the server does not have to maintain an ongoing, dedicated interaction with the client

I/O intensive
requires input/output operations rather than heavy-duty processing power

TABLE 4.7	FACTORS IN RIGHT-SIZING AN E-COMMERCE PLATFORM				
SITE TYPE	PUBLISH/ SUBSCRIBE	SHOPPING	CUSTOMER SELF-SERVICE	TRADING	WEB SERVICES/ B2B
Examples	WSJ.com	Amazon	Travelocity	E*Trade	Ariba e-procurement exchanges
Content	Dynamic Multiple authors High volume Not user-specific	Catalog Dynamic items User profiles with data mining	Data in legacy applications Multiple data sources	Time sensitive High volatility Multiple suppliers and consumers Complex transactions	Data in legacy applications Multiple data sources Complex transactions
Security	Low	Privacy Nonrepudiation Integrity Authentication Regulations	Privacy Nonrepudiation Integrity Authentication Regulations	Privacy Nonrepudiation Integrity Authentication Regulations	Privacy Nonrepudiation Integrity Authentication Regulations
Percent secure pages	Low	Medium	Medium	High	Medium
Cross session information	No	High	High	High	High
Searches	Dynamic Low volume	Dynamic High volume	Nondynamic Low volume	Nondynamic Low volume	Nondynamic Moderate volume
Unique items (SKUs)	High	Medium to high	Medium	High	Medium to high
Transaction volume	Moderate	Moderate to high	Moderate	High to extremely high	Moderate
Legacy integration complexity	Low	Medium	High	High	High
Page views (hits)	High to very high	Moderate to high	Moderate to low	Moderate to high	Moderate

Other factors to consider when estimating the demand on a Web site are the user profile and the nature of the content. If users request searches, registration forms, and order taking via shopping carts, then demands on processors will increase markedly.

RIGHT-SIZING YOUR HARDWARE PLATFORM: THE SUPPLY SIDE

Once you estimate the likely demand on your site, you will need to consider how to scale up your site to meet demand. We have already discussed one solution that requires very little thought: outsource the hosting of your Web site to a cloud-based service. You can also engage the services of a content delivery network (CDN) such as Akamai. See Chapter 3 for a discussion of cloud-based computing services and a

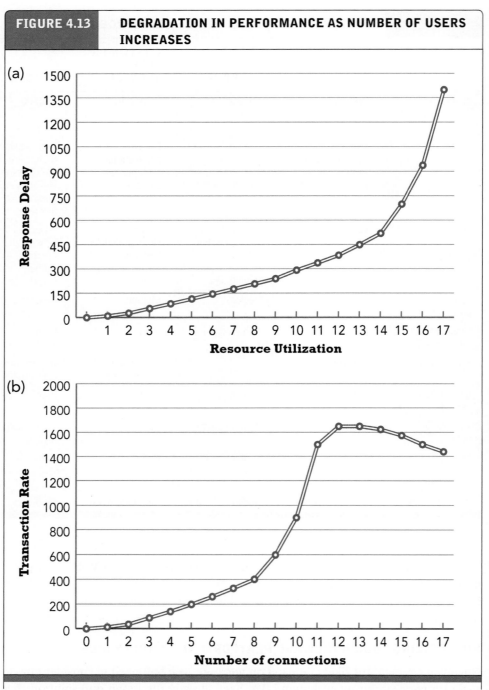

FIGURE 4.13 DEGRADATION IN PERFORMANCE AS NUMBER OF USERS INCREASES

Degradation in Web server performance occurs as the number of users (connections) increases, and as the system's resources (processors, disk drives) become more utilized. In (a), user-experienced delay rises gracefully until an inflection point is reached, and then delay rises exponentially to an unacceptable level. In (b), the transaction rate rises gracefully until the number of users rapidly escalates the transaction rate, and at a certain inflection point, the transaction rate starts declining as the system slows down or crashes.

TABLE 4.8	VERTICAL AND HORIZONTAL SCALING TECHNIQUES
TECHNIQUE	APPLICATION
Use a faster computer	Deploy edge servers, presentation servers, data servers, etc.
Create a cluster of computers	Use computers in parallel to balance loads.
Use appliance servers	Use special-purpose computers optimized for their task.
Segment workload	Segment incoming work to specialized computers.
Batch requests	Combine related requests for data into groups, process as group.
Manage connections	Reduce connections between processes and computers to a minimum.
Aggregate user data	Aggregate user data from legacy applications in single data pools.
Cache	Store frequently used data in cache rather than on the disk.

case study on Akamai. However, if you decide to host your own Web site, scalability is an important consideration. **Scalability** refers to the ability of a site to increase in size as demand warrants. There are three steps you can take to meet the demands for service at your site: scale hardware vertically, scale hardware horizontally, and/or improve the processing architecture of the site (see **Table 4.8**). **Vertical scaling** refers to increasing the processing power of individual components. **Horizontal scaling** refers to employing multiple computers to share the workload and increase the "footprint" of the installation (IBM, 2002).

You can scale your site vertically by upgrading the servers from a single processor to multiple processors. You can keep adding processors to a computer depending on the operating system and upgrade to faster chip speeds as well.

There are two drawbacks to vertical scaling. First, it can become expensive to purchase additional processors with every growth cycle, and second, your entire site becomes dependent on a small number of very powerful computers. If you have two such computers and one goes down, half of your site, or perhaps your entire site, may become unavailable.

Horizontal scaling involves adding multiple single-processor servers to your site and balancing the load among the servers. You can then partition the load so some servers handle only requests for HTML or ASP pages, while others are dedicated to handling database applications. You will need special load-balancing software (provided by a variety of vendors such as Cisco, Microsoft, and IBM) to direct incoming requests to various servers.

There are many advantages to horizontal scaling. It is inexpensive and often can be accomplished using older PCs that otherwise would be disposed of. Horizontal scaling also introduces redundancy—if one computer fails, chances are that another computer can pick up the load dynamically. However, when your site grows from a single computer to perhaps 10 to 20 computers, the size of the physical facility required (the "footprint") increases and there is added management complexity.

scalability
the ability of a site to increase in size as demand warrants

vertical scaling
increasing the processing power of individual components

horizontal scaling
employing multiple computers to share the workload

TABLE 4.9	IMPROVING THE PROCESSING ARCHITECTURE OF YOUR SITE
ARCHITECTURE IMPROVEMENT	**DESCRIPTION**
Separate static content from dynamic content	Use specialized servers for each type of workload.
Cache static content	Increase RAM to the gigabyte range and store static content in RAM.
Cache database lookup tables	Use cache tables used to look up database records.
Consolidate business logic on dedicated servers	Put shopping cart, credit card processing, and other CPU-intensive activity on dedicated servers.
Optimize ASP code	Examine your code to ensure it is operating efficiently.
Optimize the database schema	Examine your database search times and take steps to reduce access times.

A third alternative—improving the processing architecture—is a combination of vertical and horizontal scaling, combined with artful design decisions. **Table 4.9** lists some of the more common steps you can take to greatly improve performance of your site. Most of these steps involve splitting the workload into I/O-intensive activities (such as serving Web pages) and CPU-intensive activities (such as taking orders). Once you have this work separated, you can fine-tune the servers for each type of load. One of the least expensive fine-tuning steps is to simply add RAM to a few servers and store all your HTML pages in RAM. This reduces load on your hard drives and increases speed dramatically. RAM is thousands of times faster than hard disks, and RAM is inexpensive. The next most important step is to move your CPU-intensive activities, such as order taking, onto a high-end, multiple-processor server that is dedicated to handling orders and accessing the necessary databases. Taking these steps can permit you to reduce the number of servers required to service 10,000 concurrent users from 100 down to 20, according to one estimate.

4.5 OTHER E-COMMERCE SITE TOOLS

Now that you understand the key factors affecting the speed, capacity, and scalability of your Web site, we can consider some other important requirements. You will need a coherent Web site design that makes business sense—not necessarily a site to wow visitors or excite them, but to sell them something. You will also need to know how to build active content and interactivity into your site—not just display static HTML pages. You must be able to track customers who come, leave, and return to your site in order to be able to greet return visitors ("Hi Sarah, welcome back!"). You will also want to track customers throughout your site so you can personalize and customize their experience. You will definitely want the ability for customers to generate content and feedback on your site to increase their engagement with your brand. Finally, you

TABLE 4.10	E-COMMERCE WEB SITE FEATURES THAT ANNOY CUSTOMERS
• Requiring user to view ad or Flash introduction before going to Web site content	• Inability to use browser's Back button
• Pop-up and pop-under ads and windows	• No contact information available (Web form only)
• Too many clicks to get to the content	• Unnecessary splash/flash screens, animation, etc.
• Links that don't work	• Music or other audio that plays automatically
• Confusing navigation; no search function	• Unprofessional design elements
• Requirement to register and log in before viewing content or ordering	• Text not easily legible due to size, color, format
• Slow loading pages	• Typographical errors
• Content that is out of date	• No or unclear returns policy

will need to establish a set of information policies for your site—privacy, accessibility, and access to information policies.

In order to achieve these business capabilities, you will need to be aware of some design guidelines and additional software tools that can cost-effectively achieve the required business functionality.

WEB SITE DESIGN: BASIC BUSINESS CONSIDERATIONS

This is not a text about how to design Web sites. (In Chapter 6, we discuss Web site design issues from a marketing perspective.) Nevertheless, from a business manager's perspective, there are certain design objectives you must communicate to your Web site designers to let them know how you will evaluate their work. At a minimum, your customers will need to find what they need at your site, make a purchase, and leave. A Web site that annoys customers runs the risk of losing the customer forever. See **Table 4.10** for a list of the most common consumer complaints about Web sites.

Some critics believe poor design is more common than good design. It appears easier to describe what irritates people about Web sites than to describe how to design a good Web site. The worst e-commerce sites make it difficult to find information about their products and make it complicated to purchase goods; they have missing pages and broken links, a confusing navigation structure, and annoying graphics or sounds that you cannot turn off. **Table 4.11** restates these negative experiences as positive goals for Web site design.

TOOLS FOR SEARCH ENGINE OPTIMIZATION

A Web site is only as valuable from a business perspective as the number of people who visit. The first stop for most customers looking for a product or service is to start with a search engine, and follow the listings on the page, usually starting with the top three to five listings, then glancing to the sponsored ads to the right. The higher you are on the search engine pages, the more traffic you will receive. Page 1 is much better than Page 2. So how do you get to Page 1 in the natural (unpaid) search listings?

TABLE 4.11	THE EIGHT MOST IMPORTANT FACTORS IN SUCCESSFUL E-COMMERCE SITE DESIGN
FACTOR	DESCRIPTION
Functionality	Pages that work, load quickly, and point the customer toward your product offerings
Informational	Links that customers can easily find to discover more about you and your products
Ease of use	Simple foolproof navigation
Redundant navigation	Alternative navigation to the same content
Ease of purchase	One or two clicks to purchase
Multi-browser functionality	Site works with the most popular browsers
Simple graphics	Avoids distracting, obnoxious graphics and sounds that the user cannot control
Legible text	Avoids backgrounds that distort text or make it illegible

While every search engine is different, and none of them publish their algorithms for ranking pages, there are some basic ideas that work well:

- **Metatags, titles, page contents:** Search engines "crawl" your site and identify keywords as well as title pages and then index them for use in search arguments. Pepper your pages with keywords that accurately describe what you say you do in your metatag site "description" and "keywords" sections of your source code. Experiment: use different keywords to see which work. "Vintage cars" may attract more visitors than "antique cars" or "restored cars."

- **Identify market niches:** Instead of marketing "jewelry," be more specific, such as "Victorian jewelry," or "1950s jewelry" to attract small, specific groups who are intensely interested in period jewelry and closer to purchasing.

- **Offer expertise:** White papers, industry analyses, FAQ pages, guides, and histories are excellent ways to build confidence on the part of users and to encourage them to see your Web site as the place to go for help and guidance.

- **Get linked up:** Encourage other sites to link to your site; build a blog that attracts people and who will share your URL with others and post links in the process. List your site with Yahoo Directory for $300 a year. Build a Facebook page for your company, and think about using Twitter to develop a following or fan base for your products.

- **Buy ads:** Complement your natural search optimization efforts with paid search engine keywords and ads. Choose your keywords and purchase direct exposure on Web pages. You can set your budget and put a ceiling on it to prevent large losses. See what works, and observe the number of visits to your site produced by each keyword string.

- **Local e-commerce:** Developing a national market can take a long time. If your Web site is particularly attractive to local people, or involves products sold locally, use keywords that connote your location so people can find you nearby. Town, city, and region names in your keywords can be helpful, such as "Vermont cheese" or "San Francisco blues music."

TOOLS FOR INTERACTIVITY AND ACTIVE CONTENT

The more interactive a Web site is, the more effective it will be in generating sales and encouraging return visitors. Although functionality and ease of use are the supreme objectives in site design, you will also want to interact with users and present them with a lively, "active" experience. You will want to personalize the experience for customers by addressing their individual needs, and customize the content of your offerings based on their behavior or expressed desires. In order to achieve these business objectives, you will need to consider carefully the tools necessary to build these capabilities. Simple interactions such as a customer submitting a name, along with more complex interactions involving credit cards, user preferences, and user responses to prompts, all require special programs. The following sections provide a brief description of some commonly used software tools for achieving high levels of site interactivity.

Common Gateway Interface (CGI)

Common Gateway Interface (CGI) is a set of standards for communication between a browser and a program running on a server that allows for interaction between the user and the server. CGI permits an executable program to access all the information within incoming requests from clients. The program can then generate all the output required to make up the return page (the HTML, script code, text, etc.), and send it back to the client via the Web server. For instance, if a user clicks the My Shopping Cart button, the server receives this request and executes a CGI program. The CGI program retrieves the contents of the shopping cart from the database and returns it to the server. The server sends an HTML page that displays the contents of the shopping cart on the user's screen. Notice that all the computing takes place on the server side (this is why CGI programs and others like it are referred to as "server-side" programs).

CGI programs can be written in nearly any programming language as long as they conform to CGI standards. Currently, Perl is one of the most popular languages for CGI scripting. Generally, CGI programs are used with Unix servers. CGI's primary disadvantage is that it is not highly scalable because a new process must be created for each request, thereby limiting the number of concurrent requests that can be handled. CGI scripts are best used for small to medium-sized applications that do not involve a high volume of user traffic. There are also Web server extensions available, such as FastCGI, that improve CGI's scalability and SCGI, which is a simpler version of FastCGI (Doyle and Lopes, 2005).

CGI scripts also face security issues. In 2014, a major security hole in the command-line shell used by many Linux and Unix operating systems was discovered. Nicknamed Shellshock, the hole allowed hackers to target vulnerable CGI scripts on Apache Web servers. These types of security issues have resulted in some Web hosting services, such as Rackspace, requiring their customers to use alternatives to CGI.

Common Gateway Interface (CGI)
a set of standards for communication between a browser and a program running on a server that allows for interaction between the user and the server

Active Server Pages (ASP) and ASP.NET

Active Server Pages (ASP)
a proprietary software development tool that enables programmers using Microsoft's IIS package to build dynamic pages

Active Server Pages (ASP) is Microsoft's original version of server-side programming for Windows. Invented by Microsoft in late 1996, ASP grew rapidly to become the major technique for server-side Web programming in the Windows environment. ASP enables developers to easily create and open records from a database and execute programs within an HTML page, as well as handle all the various forms of interactivity found on e-commerce sites. Like CGI, ASP permits an interaction to take place between the browser and the server. ASP uses the same standards as CGI for communication with the browser. ASP programs are restricted to use on Windows servers running Microsoft's IIS Web server software. **ASP.NET**, first released in January 2002, and part of Microsoft's .NET framework, is the successor to ASP. As of September 2015, ASP.NET 4.6 is the most current version of ASP.NET. ASP.NET 5, a major rewrite aimed at providing an improved, modern, cross-platform Web framework for cloud and regular application servers, is also under development.

ASP.NET
successor to ASP

Java, Java Server Pages (JSP), and JavaScript

Java
a programming language that allows programmers to create interactivity and active content on the client computer, thereby saving considerable load on the server

Java is a programming language that allows programmers to create interactivity and active content on the client computer, thereby saving considerable load on the server. Java was initially developed by Sun Microsystems as a platform-independent programming language for consumer electronics. The idea was to create a language whose programs (so-called Write Once Run Anywhere [WORA] programs) could operate on any computer regardless of operating system. This would be possible if every operating system at the time (Macintosh, Windows, Unix, DOS, and mainframe MVS systems) had a Java Virtual Machine (VM) installed that would interpret the Java programs for that environment.

By 1995, however, when Sun Microsystems released Java 1.0, the first public version of the language, it had become clear that Java was more applicable to the Web than to consumer electronics. Java programs (known as Java applets) could be downloaded to the client over the Web and executed entirely on the client's computer. Applet tags could be included in an HTML page. To enable this, each browser would have to include a Java VM. Today, the leading browsers include a VM to run Java programs and according to Oracle, which inherited oversight over Java when it acquired Sun Microsystems, Java is used on 97% of enterprise desktop computers. When the browser accesses a page with an applet, a request is sent to the server to download and execute the program and allocate page space to display the results of the program. Java can be used to display interesting graphics, create interactive environments (such as a mortgage calculator), and directly access the Web server. JDK (Java Development Kit) 8 and the Java SE 8 Runtime Environment (for running Java applications) were released in 2014, and Java 9, which reportedly will focus on modularization of the platform, is expected to be released in 2016. Today, Java remains one of the most popular programming languages, with many critical technologies, such as the Google Android mobile platform (although not Apple's iOS), leveraging aspects of the language. However, Java does face some challenges. In recent years, it has been plagued by security flaws, which Oracle has been attempting to address with the frequent release of new versions and security patches (Krill, 2015).

Java Server Pages (JSP), like CGI and ASP, is a Web page coding standard that allows developers to use a combination of HTML, JSP scripts, and Java to dynamically generate Web pages in response to user requests. JSP uses Java "servlets," small Java programs that are specified in the Web page and run on the Web server to modify the Web page before it is sent to the user who requested it. JSP is supported by most of the popular application servers on the market today.

JavaScript is a programming language invented by Netscape that is used to control the objects on an HTML page and handle interactions with the browser. It is most commonly used on the client side to handle verification and validation of user input, as well as to implement business logic. For instance, JavaScript can be used on customer registration forms to confirm that a valid phone number, zip code, or even e-mail address has been given. Before a user finishes completing a form, the e-mail address given can be tested for validity. JavaScript appears to be much more acceptable to corporations and other environments in large part because it is more stable and also it is restricted to the operation of requested HTML pages. JavaScript is also used as part of Node.js, a cross-platform environment for server-side applications (including mobile), which has been used by companies such as PayPal, Walmart, and LinkedIn. In September 2015, Node.js v4.0 was released, combining Node.js and io.js, a variant of the JavaScript platform built on V8, the JavaScript virtual machine used in Google Chrome, into a single codebase for the first time. *Ajax (asynchronous JavaScript and XML)* uses a variety of different tools, including JavaScript, to allow Web pages to be updated asynchronously (i.e., updating only parts of the page rather than having to reload the entire page to change just part of the content).

ActiveX and VBScript

Microsoft invented the **ActiveX** programming language to compete with Java and **VBScript** to compete with JavaScript. When a browser receives an HTML page with an ActiveX control (comparable to a Java applet), the browser simply executes the program. Unlike Java, however, ActiveX has full access to all the client's resources—printers, networks, and hard drives. VBScript performs in the same way as JavaScript. ActiveX and VBScript work only if you are using Internet Explorer. Otherwise, that part of the screen is blank. However, the days of ActiveX and VBScript are numbered. Microsoft has dropped support for both in Microsoft Edge, the browser that has replaced Internet Explorer in the Windows 10 operating system. Microsoft believes that the need for ActiveX and VBScript has been significantly reduced given the capabilities of HTML5, and that eliminating them will enhance browser security.

ColdFusion

ColdFusion is an integrated server-side environment for developing interactive Web and mobile applications. Originally developed by Macromedia and now offered by Adobe, ColdFusion combines an intuitive tag-based scripting language and a tag-based server scripting language (CFML) that lowers the cost of creating interactive features. ColdFusion offers a powerful set of visual design, programming, debugging, and deployment tools. ColdFusion 11, the most recent version of ColdFusion, was released in 2015 and provides enhanced ability to create mobile apps, as well as a number of

Java Server Pages (JSP)
like CGI and ASP, a Web page coding standard that allows developers to dynamically generate Web pages in response to user requests

JavaScript
a programming language invented by Netscape that is used to control the objects on an HTML page and handle interactions with the browser

ActiveX
a programming language created by Microsoft to compete with Java

VBScript
a programming language invented by Microsoft to compete with JavaScript

ColdFusion
an integrated server-side environment for developing interactive Web applications

new security features and programming language enhancements, as well as increased support for interoperability.

PHP, Ruby on Rails (RoR), and Django

PHP
open source, general purpose scripting language

PHP is an open source, general purpose scripting language that is most frequently used in server-side Web applications to generate dynamic Web page content, although it can also be used for client-side graphical user interface applications. PHP is also a part of many Web application development frameworks, such as CakePHP, CodeIgniter, and others, and is also part of the LAMP (Linux, Apache, MySQL, PHP) open source Web development model for building dynamic Web sites and web applications (Perl and Python are sometimes substituted for PHP in some LAMP projects). According to W3Techs, PHP is, by far and away, the most commonly used server-side scripting language (used by over 80% of the Web sites whose server-side programming language it was able to identify), with ASP.NET a distant second, used by around 16.5%, followed by Java, with 3%. ColdFusion, Perl, Ruby on Rails, Python, and JavaScript were all less than 1% (W3techs.com, 2015). Netcraft's Web Server Survey has found PHP on over 240 million sites (Netcraft, 2014). PHP is also popular with hackers; according to Netcraft, nearly all phishing kits are written in PHP (Mutton, 2015).

Ruby on Rails (RoR/ Rails)
open source Web application framework based on Ruby programming language

Ruby on Rails (RoR or Rails) is an open source Web application framework based on the Ruby programming language. RoR is based on a philosophy known as convention over configuration, or coding by convention (CoC), which means that the framework provides a structured layout that minimizes the number of decisions that the programmer needs to make, thereby simplifying and speeding development. JavaScript and Ajax are highly integrated into RoR, which makes it easy to handle Ajax requests for page updates. Some well-known Web sites based on RoR include Shopify, Groupon, Indiegogo, and Airbnb (Codefactory, 2014).

Django
open source Web application framework based on Python programming language

Django is also an open source Web application framework. It is based on the Python programming language. Django is optimized for the creation of complex, database-driven Web sites. It allows for fast development, focuses on automating as much as possible, emphasizes the reusability of various components, and follows the DRY (Don't Repeat Yourself) programming principle. Some well-known Web sites based on Django include Instagram, Pinterest, and the satirical news site, The Onion (Codecondo, 2013).

Other Design Elements

widget
a small, prebuilt chunk of code that executes automatically in your HTML Web page; capable of performing a wide variety of tasks

One easy way to pump up the energy on your Web site is to include some appropriate widgets (sometimes called gadgets, plug-ins, or snippets). **Widgets** are small chunks of code that execute automatically in your HTML Web page. They are prebuilt and many are free. Social networks and blogs use widgets to present users with content drawn from around the Web (news headlines from specific news sources, announcements, press releases, and other routine content), calendars, clocks, weather, live TV, games, and other functionality. You can copy the code to an HTML Web page. You can find widgets at Apple's Dashboard Widgets, Wolfram|Alpha Widgets, and SIMILE Widgets. There are also widgets for specific platforms such as WordPress, Amazon Widgets, and Pinterest's Widget Builder.

Mashups are a little more complicated and involve pulling functionality and data from one program and including it in another. The most common mashup involves using Google Maps data and software and combining it with other data. For instance, if you have a local real estate Web site, you can download Google Maps and satellite image applications to your site so visitors can get a sense of the neighborhood. There are thousands of Google Map mashups, from maps of Myanmar political protests, to maps of the Fortune 500 companies, all with associated news stories and other content. Other mashups involve sports, photos, video, shopping, and news.

PERSONALIZATION TOOLS

You will definitely want to know how to treat each customer on an individual basis and emulate a traditional face-to-face marketplace. *Personalization* (the ability to treat people based on their personal qualities and prior history with your site) and *customization* (the ability to change the product to better fit the needs of the customer) are two key elements of e-commerce that potentially can make it nearly as powerful as a traditional marketplace, and perhaps even more powerful than direct mail or shopping at an anonymous suburban shopping mall. Speaking directly to the customer on a one-to-one basis, and even adjusting the product to the customer is quite difficult in the usual type of mass marketing, one-size-fits-all commercial transaction that characterizes much of contemporary commerce.

There are a number of methods for achieving personalization and customization. For instance, you could personalize Web content if you knew the personal background of the visitor. You could also analyze the pattern of clicks and sites visited for every customer who enters your site. We discuss these methods in later chapters on marketing. The primary method for achieving personalization and customization is through the placement of cookie files on the user's client computer. As we discussed in Chapter 3, a cookie is a small text file placed on the user's client computer that can contain any kind of information about the customer, such as customer ID, campaign ID, or purchases at the site. And then, when the user returns to the site, or indeed goes further into your site, the customer's prior history can be accessed from a database. Information gathered on prior visits can then be used to personalize the visit and customize the product.

For instance, when a user returns to a site, you can read the cookie to find a customer ID, look the ID up in a database of names, and greet the customer ("Hello Mary! Glad to have you return!"). You could also have stored a record of prior purchases, and then recommend a related product ("How about the wrench tool box now that you have purchased the wrenches?"). And you could think about customizing the product ("You've shown an interest in the elementary training programs for Word. We have a special 'How to Study' program for beginners in Office software. Would you like to see a sample copy online?").

We further describe the use of cookies in Chapter 6.

THE INFORMATION POLICY SET

In developing an e-commerce site, you will also need to focus on the set of information policies that will govern the site. You will need to develop a **privacy policy**—a set of

privacy policy
a set of public statements declaring to your customers how you treat their personal information that you gather on the site

accessibility rules
a set of design objectives that ensure disabled users can effectively access your site

public statements declaring to your customers how you treat their personal information that you gather on the site. You also will need to establish **accessibility rules**—a set of design objectives that ensure disabled users can effectively access your site. There are more than 50 million Americans who are disabled and require special access routes to buildings as well as computer systems (see *Insight on Society: Designing for Accessibility*). E-commerce information policies are described in greater depth in Chapter 8.

4.6 DEVELOPING A MOBILE WEB SITE AND BUILDING MOBILE APPLICATIONS

Today, building a Web site is just one part of developing an e-commerce presence. Given that 194 million U.S. Internet users (over 75% of all Internet users) access the Web at least part of the time from mobile devices, businesses today need to develop mobile Web sites, and mobile Web apps, native apps, or hybrid apps, in order to interact with customers, suppliers, and employees. Deciding which of these extended Web presence tools to use is a first step.

mobile Web site
version of a regular desktop Web site that is scaled down in content and navigation

There are different kinds of m-commerce platform offerings to consider, each with unique advantages and costs. A **mobile Web site** is a version of a regular Web site that is scaled down in content and navigation so that users can find what they want and move quickly to a decision or purchase. You can see the difference between a regular Web site and a mobile site by visiting the Amazon Web site from your desktop computer and then a smartphone or tablet computer. Amazon's mobile site is a cleaner, more interactive site suitable for finger navigation, and efficient consumer decision making. Like traditional Web sites, mobile Web sites run on a firm's servers, and are built using standard Web tools such as server-side HTML, Linux, PHP, and SQL. Like all Web sites, the user must be connected to the Web and performance will depend on bandwidth. Generally, mobile Web sites operate more slowly than traditional Web sites viewed on a desktop computer connected to a broadband office network. Most large firms today have mobile Web sites.

mobile Web app
application built to run on the mobile Web browser built into a smartphone or tablet computer

A **mobile Web app** is an application built to run on the mobile Web browser built into a smartphone or tablet computer. In the case of Apple, the native browser is Safari. Generally it is built to mimic the qualities of a native app using HTML5 and Java. Mobile Web apps are specifically designed for the mobile platform in terms of screen size, finger navigation, and graphical simplicity. Mobile Web apps can support complex interactions used in games and rich media, perform real-time, on-the-fly calculations, and can be geo-sensitive using the smartphone's built-in global positioning system (GPS) function. Mobile Web apps typically operate faster than mobile Web sites but not as fast as native apps.

native app
application designed specifically to operate using the mobile device's hardware and operating system

A **native app** is an application designed specifically to operate using the mobile device's hardware and operating system. These stand-alone programs can connect to the Internet to download and upload data, and can operate on this data even when not connected to the Internet. Download a book to an app reader, disconnect from the

INSIGHT ON SOCIETY

DESIGNING FOR ACCESSIBILITY

There are approximately 48 million Americans with significant hearing loss and 20 million with significant vision loss. Millions of others must deal with other issues, such as little or no color perception, limited manual dexterity, reach, or strength, or the need to use prosthetic devices, that impact their ability to use computers, the Internet, and mobile devices. As a result, the Internet and mobile devices have often been relatively inaccessible for many disabled.

Efforts to remedy this problem have taken several fronts, including legislative and regulatory action, lawsuits, industry guidelines, and technical solutions. For instance, in 1998, Congress amended the Rehabilitation Act of 1973 to require that electronic and information technology services provided by federally funded organizations must be accessible to people with disabilities. Early court decisions ruled that the legislation (known as Section 508) applied only to physical spaces, not virtual spaces. In addition, Section 508 is limited to federal procurement and does not provide any enforcement mechanism. However, both the interpretation of the law and public sentiment have resulted in many well-known Web sites attempting to conform to the spirit of Section 508, sometimes voluntarily and sometimes under threat from advocacy groups.

Activists have also focused on the Americans with Disabilities Act (the ADA). In 2006, the National Federation of the Blind (NFB) brought a class-action suit against Target for failing to make its Web site accessible for the blind. In September 2006, a federal district court ruled that the ADA did indeed apply to Web sites. In 2008, Target and the NFB settled the suit, with Target agreeing to bring its Web site into compliance with certain online assistive technology guidelines

and pay damages of $6 million. In 2012, another federal district court ruled that Web sites can be considered "public accommodation," and as such fall under the jurisdiction of the ADA (*National Association of the Deaf, et al., v. Netflix Inc.*). For example, Netflix's "Watch Instantly" feature did not provide equal access, which it must do as a "place of exhibition or entertainment." In October 2012, Netflix settled the case, agreeing to caption all of its streaming videos by 2014. However, other rulings have suggested that the ADA does not apply to online-only companies without an actual physical location.

In 2015, the U.S. Department of Justice (DOJ) signaled a shift in its policy regarding accessibility, stating that public accommodations like universities must make their Web sites accessible, and in the case of a university, not only to potential students, but to all site visitors. Still, as of 2015, the DOJ has yet to issue official regulations for Web accessibility. Nevertheless, rulings issued against H&R Block, online grocery company Peapod, and online education company edX have required these companies to make their Web sites disability compliant, making the DOJ's position on Web site accessibility for online-only companies quite clear. Once the DOJ regulations are released, millions of other Web sites will be forced to follow suit.

The 21st Century Communications and Video Accessibility Act (CVAA), enacted in 2010, has also had a significant impact on accessibility. The CVAA requires that advanced communication services (ACS) must be accessible to users with disabilities. Covered ACS include such products and services as Web-based e-mail, instant messaging, and video services such as Skype. Telecommunications companies, cellphone manufacturers, VoIP service providers and equipment manufacturers,

(continued)

and software companies are all impacted by the statute. A separate part of the statute focuses on the delivery of video programming, requiring that such programming delivered over the Internet or on television include close captioning. The FCC has issued regulations with respect to the CVAA over a three-year period, and as of the beginning of 2014, it is considered to be fully implemented, although the FCC continues to release additional regulations. For instance, in July 2014 it addressed the issue of closed captioning of IP-delivered video clips (previous regulations had applied only to full-length videos).

To ensure accessibility, the FCC has pointed to some acceptable solutions, such as conforming to the World Wide Web Consortium (W3C) Web Content Accessibility Guidelines (WCAG) 2.0. WCAG 2.0 provides organizations with strategies for accommodating people with many different kinds of disabilities. Such strategies include providing text alternatives for any non-text content so that it can be changed to other forms, including large print, braille, speech, or symbols; making content easier to see and hear; and maximizing compatibility with assistive technologies, such as screen reader software. For instance, embedding text descriptions behind images allows screen readers to announce those descriptions. Screen readers such as VoiceOver for Apple and TalkBack for Android work effectively, but only if Web sites are created to ensure compatibility with these tools. Another acceptable solution identified by the FCC involves working with the Accessibility APIs developed for the operating systems of various devices, such as Microsoft Active Accessibility or the Apple's Accessibility APIs for iOS and OS X. Relying on third-party solutions is also acceptable if they are readily available at a low cost. To help identify such solutions for the industry, the FCC presents annual awards for advances in accessibility. In 2014, for instance, it announced awards to a number of innovative products, including Braille Plus 18, the world's first Android device designed specifically for the blind or visually impaired; EasyChirp, a free Web app that makes it easier for users with disabilities to communicate via Twitter; and Capti Narrator, which simplifies Web browsing and makes iOS devices more accessible. In 2015, the W3C announced guidelines for enabling mobile accessibility on government-affiliated sites.

The FCC does not require that every feature and function of every device or service be accessible for every disability, but rather that there be solutions for different types of disabilities across a product line. In addition, providers can claim that certain accessibility solutions are not achievable—i.e., they cannot be accomplished without unreasonable effort or expense. To date, there have not yet been any enforcement actions under the CVAA (the law includes extensive FCC enforcement provisions, unlike Section 508, and for fines of up to $100,000 per day, up to $1 million in total), so it is still unclear exactly how the FCC will interpret its regulations.

SOURCES: "DOJ Shifts Position on Web Access: Stating in Court Filings That Public Accommodations Have a 'Pre-existing' Obligation to Make Websites Accessible," Lexology.com, July 8, 2015; "W3C Prepping Technical Report on Mobile Accessibility," by Molly Bernhart Walker, Fiercemobilegovernment.com, June 24, 2015; "Web-related Bias Rules Up in the Air," by Judy Greenwald, Businessinsurance.com, June 21, 2015; "Looming ADA Rules Could Affect Millions of Websites," by Ron Hurtibise, *Sun Sentinel,* June 26, 2015; "EdX Online Accessibility Settlement Reached," by Tamar Lewin, *New York Times,* April 2, 2015; "DOJ Forces Online Grocer Peapod to Make Website Accessible to Disabled," by Lydia Wheeler, Thehill.com, November 17, 2014; "DOJ Continues Aggressive Enforcement Relating to Website and App Accessibility Under ADA," by Crystal N. Skelton and Gonzalo E. Mon, Adlawaccess.com, December 4, 2014; "Web Accessibility: Is Your Content Ready for Everyone?" by Mindy Charski, Econtentmag.com, March 23, 2015; "Social Media and Tech Sites Must Be Accessible to Everyone," by Alex Howard, Techrepublic.com, July 22, 2014; "FCC Moves to Ensure Online Video Clips Are Accessible to Americans Who Are Deaf or Hard of Hearing," Federal Communications Commission, July 11, 2014; "FCC Announces Awards for Innovations in Accessibility Communications," by Marcus Hedenberg, Broadbandbreakfast.com, June 9, 2014; "FCC Accessible Communications Regulations," by Sam Joehl, Davis Wright Tremaine LLP, February 18, 2014; "Disabled Sue Over Web Shopping," by Joe Palazzolo, *Wall Street Journal,* March 21, 2013; "Netflix and Deaf-Rights Group Settle Suit Over Video Captions," by Dara Kerr, Cnn.com, October 11, 2012; "Can a Web Site Be a Public Accommodation Under the ADA?," Timothy Springer, Webaccessibility.com, June 5, 2012; "W3C Web Accessibility Initiative [Final Draft]," WC3.org, June 2010.

Internet, and read your book. Because the various types of smartphones have different hardware and operating systems, apps are not "one size fits all" and therefore need to be developed for different mobile platforms. An Apple app that runs on an iPhone cannot operate on Android phones. As you learned in Chapter 3, native apps are built using different programming languages depending on the device for which they are intended, which is then compiled into binary code, and which executes extremely fast on mobile devices, much faster than HTML or Java-based mobile Web apps. For this reason, native apps are ideal for games, complex interactions, on-the-fly calculations, graphic manipulations, and rich media advertising.

Increasingly, developers are combining elements of native apps and mobile Web apps into hybrid apps. A **hybrid app** has many of the features of both a native app and a mobile Web app. Like a native app, it runs inside a native container on the mobile device and has access to the device's APIs, enabling it to take advantage of many of the device's features, such as a gyroscope, that are normally not accessible by a mobile Web app. It can also be packaged as an app for distribution from an App store. Like a mobile Web app, it is based on HTML5, CSS3, and JavaScript, but uses the device's browser engine to render the HTML5 and process the JavaScript locally.

hybrid app

has many of the features of both a native app and a mobile Web app

PLANNING AND BUILDING A MOBILE PRESENCE

What is the "right" mobile presence for your firm? The answer depends on identifying the business objectives, and from these, deriving the information requirements of your mobile presence. The same kind of systems analysis and design (SAD) reasoning described earlier in the chapter is needed for planning and building a mobile presence, although there are important differences.

The first step is to identify the business objectives you are trying to achieve. **Table 4.12** illustrates the thought process for the analysis stage of building a mobile presence. Why are you developing a mobile presence? Is it to drive sales by creating

TABLE 4.12	SYSTEMS ANALYSIS FOR BUILDING A MOBILE PRESENCE	
BUSINESS OBJECTIVE	**SYSTEM FUNCTIONALITY**	**INFORMATION REQUIREMENTS**
Driving sales	Digital catalog; product database	Product descriptions, photos, SKUs, inventory
Branding	Showing how customers use your products	Videos and rich media; product and customer demonstrations
Building customer community	Interactive experiences, games with multiple players	Games, contests, forums, social sign-up to Facebook
Advertising and promotion	Coupons and flash sales for slow-selling items	Product descriptions, coupon management, and inventory management
Gathering customer feedback	Ability to retrieve and store user inputs including text, photos, and video	Customer sign-in and identification; customer database

an easily browsed catalog where users can shop and purchase? Strengthen your brand by creating an engaging, interactive experience? Enable customers to interact with your customer community? How are your competitors using their mobile presence? Once you have a clear sense of business objectives, you will be able to describe the kind of system functionality that is needed and specify the information requirements for your mobile presence.

After you have identified the business objectives, system functionality, and information requirements, you can think about how to design and build the system. Now is the time to consider which to develop: a mobile Web site, a mobile Web app, or a native app. For instance, if your objective is branding or building community, a native app might be the best choice because it enables you to deliver a rich, interactive, and immersive experience that can strengthen the emotional connection with the brand. Because native apps are stored locally on the device, they can be accessed even when the user is offline, enabling the user to more deeply engage. In addition, native apps can take advantage of the mobile device's unique characteristics, such as using the gyroscope to deliver a 360-degree view. If your objective, on the other hand, is to create broad awareness, provide specific information on particular products, or drive sales, then a mobile Web site or mobile Web app makes more sense, because it is relatively easy and inexpensive to simply publish information to the mobile Web and consumers are still most comfortable completing transactions on the Web (although this is changing as more and more retailers add e-commerce functionality directly into apps). Increasingly, however, the choice will not be an either/or decision. Mobile apps and mobile Web sites each offer distinct benefits, and in most cases, the best strategy will be to plan to deliver compelling content across all devices.

MOBILE PRESENCE: DESIGN CONSIDERATIONS

Designing a mobile presence is somewhat different from traditional desktop Web site design because of different hardware, software, and consumer expectations. **Table 4.13** describes some of the major differences.

Designers need to take mobile platform constraints into account when designing for the mobile platform. File sizes should be kept smaller and the number of files sent to the user reduced. Focus on a few, powerful graphics, and minimize the number of images sent to the user. Simplify choice boxes and lists so the user can easily scroll and touch-select the options.

Mobile presence has become so important that it is fueling a growing trend to flip the traditional e-commerce development process and begin instead with development of a mobile presence rather than a desktop Web site (known as **mobile first design**). Mobile first design has several advantages. Instead of creating a full-featured design for a desktop Web site that then needs to be scaled back, mobile first design focuses on creating the best possible experience given mobile platform constraints and then adding back elements for the desktop platform, progressively enhancing the functionality of the site. Proponents of mobile first design argue that it forces designers to focus on what is most important, and this helps create a lean

mobile first design

beginning the e-commerce development process with a mobile presence rather than a desktop Web site

TABLE 4.13	UNIQUE FEATURES THAT MUST BE TAKEN INTO ACCOUNT WHEN DESIGNING A MOBILE PRESENCE
FEATURE	IMPLICATIONS FOR MOBILE PLATFORM
Hardware	Mobile hardware is smaller, and there are more resource constraints in data storage and processing power.
Connectivity	The mobile platform is constrained by slower connection speeds than desktop Web sites.
Displays	Mobile displays are much smaller and require simplification. Some screens are not good in sunlight.
Interface	Touch-screen technology introduces new interaction routines different from the traditional mouse and keyboard. The mobile platform is not a good data entry tool but can be a good navigational tool.

and efficient mobile design that functions much better than a design that begins with a traditional platform that must be stripped down to work on mobile. Mobile first design is not without its challenges, however. It can be more difficult for designers who are more comfortable with the more traditional process (Byers, 2013).

Other important trends in the development of mobile Web sites include responsive Web design and adaptive Web design.

Responsive Web design (RWD) tools and design techniques make it possible to design a Web site that automatically adjusts its layout and display according to the screen resolution of the device on which it is being viewed, whether a desktop, tablet, or smartphone. RWD tools include HTML5 and CSS3 and its three key design principles involve using flexible grid-based layouts, flexible images and media, and media queries. RDW uses the same HTML code and design for each device, but uses CSS (which determines the layout of the Web page) to adjust the layout and display to the screen's form factor. RWD sites typically work well for sites with relatively simple functionality (i.e., sites that primarily deliver content) and that users engage with in a similar manner no matter the device being used. However, using RWD can be costly, often requiring a complete redesign of the Web site's interface. Another problem with RDW, particularly if not coupled with mobile first design, is that the responsive Web site still has the size and complexity of a traditional desktop site, sometimes making it slow to load and perform on a mobile device. Another technique, known as adaptive Web design, has been developed to deal with this issue.

With **adaptive Web design (AWD)** (sometimes also referred to as *adaptive delivery or responsive Web design with server-side components (RESS)*), the server hosting the Web site detects the attributes of the device making the request and, using predefined templates based on device screen size along with CSS and JavaScript, loads a version of the site that is optimized for the device. AWD has a number of advantages, including

responsive Web design (RWD)

tools and design principles that automatically adjust the layout of a Web site depending on the screen resolution of the device on which it is being viewed

adaptive Web design (AWD)

server-side technique that detects the attributes of the device making the request and, using predefined templates based on device screen size along with CSS and JavaScript, loads a version of the site that is optimized for the device

faster load times, the ability to enhance or remove functionality on the fly, and typically a better user experience, particularly for businesses where user intent differs depending on the platform being used. For example, creating its mobile Web site with AWD enabled Lufthansa to focus on actions its mobile users are most likely to take, such as checking in, getting flight status information, and looking up travel itineraries, and to provide a differentiated experience from its traditional desktop site (Pratap, 2013). A variation on AWD uses a cloud-based platform to provide similar functionality (Moovweb, 2013).

CROSS-PLATFORM MOBILE APP DEVELOPMENT TOOLS

In addition to creating native apps from scratch using a programming language such as Objective C or Java (as described in Chapter 3), there are hundreds of low-cost or open source app development toolkits that make creating cross-platform mobile apps relatively easy and inexpensive without having to use a device-specific programming language.

Tools include Appery.io, a cloud-based platform that enables you to a drag-and-drop visual builder tool to create HTML5 apps using jQuery Mobile. Appery.io supports Android, iOS, and Windows Phone applications. Codiqa is a similar tool that is even easier to use. It also provides a drag-and-drop interface and builds an app with 100% HTML5 components, without the need to do any coding. For those who are even less technical, Conduit is a free mobile app builder that allows you to include a variety of functionality, including e-commerce, notifications, and a social feed.

On the more technical side, PhoneGap is a mobile development framework that uses software called Apache Cordova to enable building hybrid mobile applications using HTML, CSS, and JavaScript. MoSync is another advanced tool for developing cross-platform apps for iOS, Android, Linux Mobile, Windows Mobile, and Symbian operating systems. Appcelerator is a similar, less technical tool for creating and managing hybrid mobile apps.

MOBILE PRESENCE: PERFORMANCE AND COST CONSIDERATIONS

If you don't have an existing Web site, the most efficient process may be to use a mobile first design philosophy and design a mobile site first. Alternatively, you may choose to build a traditional Web site using RWD or AWD techniques. If you already have a Web site that you don't want to totally redevelop, the least expensive path is to resize it to create a smartphone-friendly mobile site. Doing so typically will not require a complete redesign effort. You will need to reduce the graphics and text, simplify the navigation, and focus on improving the customer experience so you do not confuse people. Because your customers might still need to use a relatively slow cell connection at times, you will need to lighten up the amount of data you send. Also, given the difficulty of customer data entry on a mobile device, you cannot expect customers to happily enter long strings of numbers or text characters. For marketing clarity, make sure the brand images used on the mobile Web site match those on the traditional Web site. The cost of developing a mobile Web site can range widely, from upwards of $1 million for a custom-designed site for a large global enterprise to well under $1,000 for a small business who chooses a company such as Wix or MoFuse that offers a template or mobile Web site creator, as described in the *Insight on Technology* case, *Building a Mobile Presence*.

Building a mobile Web app that uses the mobile device's browser requires more effort and cost than developing a mobile Web site and suffers from the same limitations as any browser-based application. However, it does offer some advantages such as better graphics, more interactivity, and faster local calculations as, for instance, in mobile geo-location applications like Foursquare that require local calculations of position and then communication with the site's Web server.

The most expensive path to a mobile presence is to build a native app. Native apps can require more extensive programming expertise. In addition, virtually none of the elements used in your existing Web site can be reused, and you will need to redesign the entire logic of the interface and carefully think out the customer experience. For instance, there is a fairly stable HTML traditional Web site interface with buttons, graphics, videos, and ads that has developed over the last decade. This is not true for apps. There is no set of standards or expectations even on the part of users—every app looks different from every other app. This means the user confronts large variations in app design, so your interface must be quite simple and obvious. Many of the bells and whistles found on the large desktop Web site screen cannot be used in mobile apps. You'll need even greater simplification and focus. These weaknesses are also native apps' greatest strength: you have the opportunity to create a really stunning, unique customer experience where users can interact with your brand. If you want an intense branding experience with your customers, where interaction between your brand and customers is effortless and efficient, then native apps are the best choice.

INSIGHT ON TECHNOLOGY

BUILDING A MOBILE PRESENCE

Today, almost every company with a Web presence is thinking about or developing mobile applications and a mobile Web site. Customers expect, and even demand, to be able to use a mobile device of their choice to obtain information or perform a transaction anywhere and at any time. So, if a company wants to stay connected to its customers, it needs a mobile presence.

Developing mobile apps or a mobile Web site has some special challenges. The user experience on a mobile device is fundamentally different from that on a desktop computer. There are special features on mobile devices such as location-based services that give a company the potential to interact with customers in new ways. Businesses need to be able to take advantage of those features while delivering an experience that is appropriate to a small screen. You can't just port a Web site or desktop application to a smartphone or tablet. There are multiple mobile platforms to work with—iPhone, Android, Black-Berry, and Windows—and a company may need a different version of an application to run on each of these. Increasingly, mobile-optimized Web sites are "responsive," which means they adapt their displays based on the screen resolution of the mobile device used to view the site. Some mobile sites have tweaks to their layout that factor in the smartphone browsing experience, such as placing company contact information at the top of the screen on every page instead of at the bottom of only certain pages.

It's important to understand how, why, and where customers use mobile devices and how these mobile experiences change business interactions and behavior. For example, do customers who use an app conduct a greater number of transactions (like purchasing) on apps when compared to a mobile browser? When compared to a tablet computer, do customers spend more or less time researching products and shopping from a smartphone?

Local businesses may stand to significantly gain from the shift to mobile. Approximately half of all mobile searches are done in search of a nearby business. The total number of local business searches performed on mobile phones has been growing explosively, along with nearly every other statistic related to mobile devices or mobile apps. Almost 60% of the U.S. population has a smartphone and almost as many (about 50%) own a tablet.

The number of small businesses with Web sites optimized for mobile navigation is trailing behind those numbers. Although almost two-thirds of U.S. small and medium-sized businesses have a professional Web site, only a third of this group (constituting 25% of all those surveyed) had a mobile-optimized site in September 2015. These numbers are expected to rise over time as the businesses that optimize their sites first reap the benefits, such as increased traffic and better standing in Google searches and other search engines. A report by Adobe showed that companies investing in mobile-optimized sites are three times more likely to achieve mobile conversion rates of 5% or higher than companies relying exclusively on traditional desktop Web sites. During the original dot-com boom, companies that were quick to adjust to the new online business environment gained an edge on their competitors. The same thing is happening with the mobile platform today.

Before entering the mobile sphere, companies should develop a clear strategy and goals they hope to accomplish. A mobile strategy involves more than selecting mobile devices, operating systems, and applications. It also involves changes to the way a business interacts with its customers. Mobile technology can streamline processes, make them more portable, and enhance them with capabilities such as touch interfaces, location and mapping features, alerts, texting, cameras, and video functionality. The technology can also create less efficient processes or fail to deliver benefits if the mobile application is not properly designed.

Many small businesses have struggled to adapt to the changes of designing for mobile. Often, businesses design their Web sites with artistic considerations in mind, but mobile users are less interested in presentation and more interested in functionality. Sites with Flash elements are incompatible with the iPhone, which makes the mobile browsing experience incomplete or frustrating for the user. Many times with mobile, less is more when it comes to design. Common features of today's mobile Web sites are a navigation bar at the top of each page that persists throughout browsing, collapsible sets of data that cut down on screen space unless users specifically request to see the complete set of information, such as a restaurant menu or full mailing address, and simple, easy-to-read icons and buttons such as a Facebook Like button.

Many businesses are still getting used to the costs of maintaining a Web site and aren't willing to redo that work and spend more time and resources to incorporate responsive design. In one survey of small businesses, businesses not using any mobile solutions said that the two biggest reasons for staying away from mobile were lack of customer demand and lack of ability to deploy and use them. But the total number of businesses that say they have no intention of entering the mobile arena is going down precipitously. In an eMarketer

survey, 59% of respondents considered improving their mobile Web and m-commerce capability to be one of their highest priorities, while 35% of respondents considered implementing responsive design to be one of their highest priorities.

There are a number of Web site design companies that offer templates that can automatically convert Web sites into mobile-only versions of the same site. For example, you can create a desktop Web site using a template provided by Wix, and it will automatically create a mobile version of the site. A Mobile Editor enables you to change the design of the mobile site without affecting the desktop version of the site, giving businesses more creative freedom. MoFuse is another company that offers an easy-to-use mobile Web site creator. For those who are challenged by even that prospect, MoFuse will create the site for you. Developing mobile apps is probably a bit more daunting for the average small business, but there are a number of platforms that can help you build a mobile app on a budget without any programming knowledge. For example, BiznessApps enables you to use a drag-and-drop template to quickly and easily build iPhone, iPad, Android, and HMTL5 apps that include functionality such as dynamic content, one-touch calling, push notifications, built-in sharing capabilities, a shopping cart, loyalty program, in-app purchases, and much more. It also offers templates optimized for various industries, such as restaurants, bars and clubs, realtors, lawyers, gyms and fitness centers, and spas and salons. A content management system allows the apps to be easily customized and updated. More than 100,000 small businesses around the world have used BiznessApps.

SOURCES: "SMBs Get More Mobile," by eMarketer, Inc., September 22, 2015; "Better Site Optimization Lifts Mobile Conversion Rates," by eMarketer, Inc., May 15, 2015; "Overview," Biznessapps.com, August 22, 2014; "Mobile Madness: Small Business Mobile Adoption on the Rise," by Jason Fidler, Business-2community.com, July 30, 2014; "Making Sure Your Website is Ready for Smartphones," by Eilene Zimmerman, *New York Times*, January 8, 2014; "10 Excellent Platforms for Building Mobile Apps," by Grace Smith, Mashable.com, December 3, 2013; "New Mobile Solution from Wix – Better, Faster and 100% Free Mobile Websites," Wix.com, October 2, 2013; "4 Examples of Stellar Small Business Mobile Websites," by Sebastian Agosta, Experiencedmg.com, April 11, 2013; "45% of Businesses Still Don't Have a Mobile Site or App," by David Moth, Econsultancy.com, May 2, 2013; "Mobility Transforms the Customer Relationship," by Samuel Greengard, *Baseline*, February 2012; "Going Mobile: A Portable Approach to Process Improvement," *Business Agility Insights,* June 2012.

Orbitz Charts

Its Mobile Trajectory

When it comes to mobile apps and gauging their impact on consumers and business, there's no better industry to look at than the online travel industry and its airline and hotel reservation systems. And there's no better company in this industry in developing mobile apps than Orbitz Worldwide Inc., the leading online travel site. Orbitz connects consumers to hundreds of airlines, over 80,000 hotels, 15 rental car agencies, as well as cruises and vacation packages. Orbitz typically has approximately 9 million unique visitors to its Web site each month.

As early as 1999, fledgling Internet travel companies such as Priceline, Expedia, and Travelocity were already transforming the travel industry. Recognizing the threat, and the opportunity, five major airlines—United, Delta, Continental, Northwest, and American—banded together to form a new venture that would become Orbitz. By the

© NetPhotos/Alamy

time the site launched in 2001, six other airlines had invested and anti-trust objections from consumer groups and competitors had been rejected by the U.S. Department of Transportation. Even at that early date, the Orbitz management team was forward-thinking, providing the capability for consumers to access flight updates and cancellations via pagers and mobile phones. By the time the Department of Justice had completely cleared Orbitz for takeoff and it had completed its IPO in November 2003, Orbitz had recruited more than 100 independent hotels in addition to its initial TravelWeb syndicate, which included the big players such as Marriott, Hilton, and Hyatt.

In 2006, Orbitz became the first Internet travel company to offer a WML-only (Wireless Markup Language) mobile Web site in the United States. (Expedia had a mobile site for its UK customers.) Users could check flight statuses for 27 airlines, some of which did not yet have a mobile site, and search for hotels in the 19 largest destination markets in the United States and in Cancun, Mexico. They also had access to a personal page dedicated to itineraries for Orbitz-booked trips and links to autodial Orbitz customer service. Additional services added in 2007 included enabling mobile users to view average wait times to get through security and available Wi-Fi services for a particular airport. A data feedback system was instituted to compute check-in delays and taxi line wait-times based on customer-inputted experiences. In 2008, Orbitz added an iPhone/iPod–specific app with the same capabilities for itinerary, flight status, WiFi availability, and wait-time checking as well as the ability to view weather and traffic conditions, reports from other travelers, and information about where to park and ground transportation. Customers could also now use technology specifically designed for touch-based Safari browsers to book a hotel room during inclement weather.

By 2010, market research had pushed Orbitz to increase its investment in mobile technology. It launched a redesigned mobile Web site and a smartphone app for Google Inc.'s Android operating system along with an updated iPhone app. Users of any Web-enabled device could now access a tool set comparable to the one available on its regular Web site to purchase flights, book car rentals, and secure hotel accommodations, including same-day reservations, as well as Orbitz's Price Assurance service, which guarantees consumers an automatic refund if another Orbitz customer books the same service for less. The native apps and redesigned mobile site were developed in-house with input from an unnamed outside vendor.

In 2011, Orbitz was the first to launch an m-commerce site designed for business users. The site was accessible from any Web-enabled device, which avoided the pitfalls of developing native apps for the wide variety of different devices its customers used. Users could enter and modify their trips via the app and give preference to a preferred vendor, which helped to adhere to company-specific travel policies. They also launched a hotel-booking app for iPad users. The app used the GPS function to display a detailed map of the user's location, with pins denoting nearby hotels and providing hotel details like address, phone number, and cost per night. Barney Harford, CEO of Orbitz Worldwide, touted the ability to book a hotel room in just three taps.

The rollout of the m-commerce site and iPad app prepared Orbitz to create second-generation applications that could meet evolving consumer expectations and adjust to the rapidly expanding and changing mobile environment. Three main improvements were made to the second-generation m-commerce site. First, it was optimized

SOURCES: "Expedia Completes $1.6B Orbitz Acquisition After U.S. Regulators Decide Not to Challenge Deal," by Todd Bishop, Geekwire.com, September 17, 2015; "Orbitz App Now Customized for Apple Watch," Orbitz.com, April 21, 2015; "Orbitz.com Launches Smart Lock for Passwords With Google," Orbitz.com, May 28, 2015; "Orbitz.com Mobile App Bookers Get Exclusive Discounts of Up to 15 Percent off Rental Cars," Orbitz.com, April 27, 2015; "Orbitz Lets Users Resume Searches Across Devices," by Mark Walsh, Mediapost.com, August 19, 2014; "Orbitz for Business See Strong Growth in Best-in-Class Mobile Booking Tool," Orbitz.com, July 29, 2014; "The Orbitz App is on Fire," Orbitz.com, July 25, 2014; "Orbitz Flights, Hotels, Cars App Wins Appy Award for Best Travel App," Marketwatch.com, May 22, 2014; "Orbitz Reports Strong Q1 Growth Backed By Enhanced Mobile and Rewards," Pymnts.com, May 14, 2014; "Orbitz.com Rated #1 Online Travel Provider in ACSI Customer Satisfaction Survey," *Wall Street Journal*, April 23, 2014; "Orbitz for Business Rolls Out Major Update to Best-in-Class Mobile Booking Tool," GlobeNewswire.com, March 26, 2014; "Expedia, Orbitz, Harness Big Data for Next-Generation Mobile Booking," by Chantal Tode, Mobilecommercedaily.com, January 30, 2014; "Orbitz Releases the First Native App for iPad that Allows Consumers to Book Flights, Hotels, and Rental Cars," Orbitz.com, February 25, 2013; "How to Embark upon an M-commerce Redesign," by Kevin Woodward, *Internet Retailer*, August 10, 2012; "Orbitz Revamps iPhone App with Focus on Streamlined Booking, Deals," by Lauren Johnson, *Mobile Commerce Daily*, June 22, 2012; "Orbitz Releases New Travel App," by Emily Brennan, *New York Times*, June 21, 2012; "Orbitz Launches New iPhone App, Bets on Mobile Growth," by Erica Ogg, Gigaom.com, June 21, 2012; "Orbitz Launches Revamped Mobile Site, Daily Deals to Capitalize on Last-Minute Travel,"

to accommodate the small screen size of any Web-enabled mobile device. Second, it was updated to accommodate swiping gestures, and third, it was revamped to expedite touch screen transactions. HTML5 enabled Orbitz to incorporate features traditionally associated with apps, such as swiping and faster browsing. Features were also added, including the ability to book vacation packages, view savings made by booking flight and hotel rooms at once, improved search and filtering capabilities, and linking an online profile to credit cards to hasten the checkout process.

Looking to capitalize on the market research findings that highlighted the burgeoning role of Web-enabled mobile devices in securing same-day accommodations, Orbitz also instituted mobile-exclusive same-day deals. These specials, called Mobile Steals, are available both on the m-commerce site and through the Hotels by Orbitz app, which was also released for the Android and iPhone. Last-minute perishable goods are available in more than 50 markets worldwide, benefitting both lodging proprietors and consumers. Proprietors are able to fill rooms that might otherwise remain vacant, and consumers enjoy savings of up to 50% off the standard rate. In 2015, Orbitz expanded Mobile Steals to include car rentals as well, offering thousands of exclusive deals for app users.

With mobile transaction customers doubling in one year's time, Orbitz decided that an overhaul of its native iPhone app was also in order. When relaunched in June 2012, the iOS app included an improved filtering tool that enabled users to search and compare offerings by cost, distance from destination, and star ratings. Securing flight, lodging, and car rental reservations was simplified, eliminating browser screens and data entry repetition, and allowing users to perform all three operations in a continuous in-app stream unassociated with a mobile Web site. This was the heart of the redesign: to eliminate the mobile Web site and consolidate the entire search and reservation process within the native app so that users would no longer experience disruptive and time-consuming redirects either to Orbitz's mobile site or to an airline, hotel, or car rental agency site to complete the booking. The goal was to trump its competitors on speed and ease of use.

In order to verify that its goals for the app had been achieved, Orbitz commissioned a speed comparison study with Atmosphere Research Group and C + R Research. The travel apps, m-commerce sites, and e-commerce sites of its major competitors, including Kayak, Expedia, Priceline, and Travelocity, were pitted against the Orbitz iPhone app. The study found that Orbitz iPhone app users were able to book a round-trip flight to Hilton Head, South Carolina, a hotel reservation, and a car rental in slightly more than seven minutes, twice as fast as people using its iPhone app competitors. Only 60% of study participants using a competitor's product (aggregated) were able to complete the task as quickly. The Orbitz iPhone app transaction speed also surpassed comparable iPad and Android apps as well as desktop e-commerce site experiences. Study participants overwhelmingly awarded positive marks to the Orbitz iPhone app in comparison to its competitors, at 92% and 30%, respectively.

To speed the identification and fulfillment of future needs, customers' search history, personal information, frequent flyer program data, and travel preferences are saved within the app, enabling one-tap access to recent searches and automatic search suggestions. Itineraries can be accessed even while offline, and flight status and gate change data can be accessed with a single tap. Trips can also be easily added to the Apple Calendar app, formerly called iCal, used by many iPhone and iPod touch users.

Since then, Orbitz has continued to expand its array of apps across different operating systems and platforms. In 2013, it launched a full version of its *Flights, Hotels, Cars* app as a native app optimized for iPad, the first of its kind among travel service providers. Orbitz also fully overhauled the same app for Android, marking the third generation of its Android native app. In October 2013, Orbitz launched Orbitz Rewards, a rewards program that has led to a marked increase in mobile purchases. The program already has over 2 million members, many of which are entirely new customers to Orbitz. In January 2014, Orbitz introduced Orbitz Labs, as part of an effort to use the increasing amount of data its users generate to provide better services and drive more bookings. Orbitz is using Orbitz Labs to test out new features and keep track of which ones are most popular with users, with the intent of incorporating those popular features into the Orbitz mobile app. In March 2014, Orbitz released a new version of its Orbitz for Business mobile site, with a new design that increases ease of use and provides improved speed and touch responsiveness. In addition, it is rolling out a responsive design approach across devices, and has started syncing user searches across devices so that users can pick up where they left off, no matter what device they are using. Orbitz has earned rave reviews for its efforts, winning the APPY Award for best travel app and receiving the top rating in customer satisfaction among all online travel Web sites. The efforts are paying off. Orbitz reports that more than 30% of its hotel bookings now come via a mobile channel, compared to only 3% in 2010, and up from 24% in 2013.

Orbitz continues its mobile development across all platforms, even newer ones such as the Apple Watch. In 2015, Orbitz released a version of its app customized for the Apple Watch, with the ability to see flight status, gate numbers, check-in and check-out information, and rewards points information. Orbitz also became the first travel company to use the Smart Lock password manager system from Google, which automatically signs customers into Orbitz.com whenever they return to the site or the app even on different devices. The system will allow users to quickly shift from device to device to make their travel plans.

In September 2015, Orbitz was acquired by Expedia in a $1.6 billion deal, solidifying Expedia's place as the top digital travel provider in the industry. The move came after Priceline purchased OpenTable in 2014 and Travelocity in 2015, setting up a battle between the two largest online travel services.

by Lauren Johnson, *Mobile Commerce Daily*, December 13, 2011; "Orbitz Travels the M-commerce Site Redesign Route," by Bill Siwicki, *Internet Retailer*, December 13, 2011; "Orbitz for Business Debuts Mobile Booking Site Targeting Corporate Travelers," by Dan Butcher, *Mobile Commerce Daily*, April 15, 2011; "Two Travel Providers Make Mobile Moves," by Katie Deatsch, *Internet Retailer*, November 16, 2010; "Orbitz Goes Mobile," by Russell Buckley, MobHappy.com, September 6, 2007; "Orbitz Mobile," by Dennis Bournique, WAPReview.com, August 15, 2006.

Case Study Questions

1. When compared to traditional desktop customers, why are mobile phone users much more likely to book a room or airline reservation for the same day?

2. In the mobile design project of 2011, why did Orbitz management decide to construct a mobile Web site for corporate users rather than a native app?

3. Why has Orbitz decided to go with native apps for each mobile platform (iOS, Android, and Kindle Fire) instead of a single mobile Web site as it did with the Orbitz for Business mobile site?

4. What issues does syncing recent user searches across devices pose?

4.8 REVIEW

KEY CONCEPTS

■ **Understand the questions you must ask and answer, and the steps you should take, in developing an e-commerce presence.**

- Questions you must ask and answer when developing an e-commerce presence include:
  - What is your vision and how do you hope to accomplish it?
  - What is your business and revenue model?
  - Who and where is the target audience?
  - What are the characteristics of the marketplace?
  - Where is the content coming from?
  - Conduct a SWOT analysis.
  - Develop an e-commerce presence map.
  - Develop a timeline.
  - Develop a detailed budget.

■ **Explain the process that should be followed in building an e-commerce presence.**

- Factors you must consider when building an e-commerce site include hardware, software, telecommunications capacity, Web site and mobile platform design, human resources, and organizational capabilities.
- The systems development life cycle (a methodology for understanding the business objectives of a system and designing an appropriate solution) for building an e-commerce Web site involves five major steps:
  - Identify the specific business objectives for the site, and then develop a list of system functionalities and information requirements.
  - Develop a system design specification (both logical design and physical design).
  - Build the site, either by in-house personnel or by outsourcing all or part of the responsibility to outside contractors.
  - Test the system (unit testing, system testing, acceptance testing, A/B (split) testing, and multivariate testing).
  - Implement and maintain the site.
- The basic business and system functionalities an e-commerce site should contain include a digital catalog, a product database, customer tracking, shopping cart/payment system, an on-site blog, a customer database, an ad server, a site tracking and reporting system, and an inventory management system.
- Advantages of building a site in-house include the ability to change and adapt the site quickly as the market demands and the ability to build a site that does exactly what the company needs.
- Disadvantages of building a site in-house include higher costs, greater risks of failure, a more time-consuming process, and a longer staff learning curve that delays time to market.
- Using design templates cuts development time, but preset templates can also limit functionality.
- A similar decision is also necessary regarding outsourcing the hosting of the site versus keeping it in-house. Relying on an outside vendor places the burden of reliability on someone else in return for a monthly hosting fee. The downside is that if the site requires fast upgrades due to heavy traffic, the chosen hosting company may or may not be capable of keeping up. Reliability versus scalability is the issue in this instance.

- ■ Identify and understand the major considerations involved in choosing Web server and e-commerce merchant server software.

  - Early Web sites used single-tier system architecture and consisted of a single-server computer that delivered static Web pages to users making requests through their browsers. The extended functionality of today's Web sites requires the development of a multi-tiered systems architecture, which utilizes a variety of specialized Web servers, as well as links to pre-existing backend or legacy corporate databases.
  - All e-commerce sites require basic Web server software to answer requests from customers for HTML and XML pages. When choosing Web server software, companies are also choosing what operating system the site will run on. Apache, which runs on the Unix system, is the market leader.
  - Web servers provide a host of services, including processing user HTML requests, security services, file transfer, a search engine, data capture, e-mail, and site management tools.
  - Dynamic server software allows sites to deliver dynamic content, rather than static, unchanging information. Web application server programs enable a wide range of e-commerce functionality, including creating a customer database, creating an e-mail promotional program, and accepting and processing orders, as well as many other services.
  - E-commerce merchant server software is another important software package that provides catalog displays, information storage and customer tracking, order taking (shopping cart), and credit card purchase processing. E-commerce software platforms can save time and money, but customization can significantly drive up costs. Factors to consider when choosing an e-commerce software platform include its functionality, support for different business models, visual site management tools and reporting systems, performance and scalability, connectivity to existing business systems, compliance with standards, and global and multicultural capability.

- ■ Understand the issues involved in choosing the most appropriate hardware for an e-commerce site.

  - Speed, capacity, and scalability are three of the most important considerations when selecting an operating system, and therefore the hardware that it runs on.
  - To evaluate how fast the site needs to be, companies need to assess the number of simultaneous users the site expects to see, the nature of their requests, the type of information requested, and the bandwidth available to the site. The answers to these questions will provide guidance regarding the processors necessary to meet customer demand. In some cases, additional processing power can increase capacity, thereby improving system speed.
  - Scalability is also an important issue. Increasing processing supply by scaling up to meet demand can be done through vertical or horizontal scaling or by improving processing architecture.

- ■ Identify additional tools that can improve Web site performance.

  - In addition to providing a speedy Web site, companies must also strive to have a well-designed site that encourages visitors to buy. Building in interactivity improves site effectiveness, as do personalization techniques.
  - Commonly used software tools for achieving high levels of Web site interactivity and customer personalization include Common Gateway Interface (CGI) scripts, Active Server Pages (ASP) and ASP.NET, Java applets, JavaScript, ActiveX and VBScript, Ajax, PHP, Ruby on Rails (RoR or Rails), and Django.

- ■ Understand the important considerations involved in developing a mobile Web site and building mobile applications.

  - When developing a mobile presence, it is important to understand the difference between a mobile Web site, mobile Web apps, native apps, and hybrid apps.
  - The first step is to identify business objectives, because they help determine which type of mobile presence is best.

- Design should take into account mobile platform constraints. Recent trends include mobile first design, responsive Web design, and adaptive Web delivery.
- Developing a mobile Web site is likely to be the least expensive option; mobile Web apps require more effort and cost; native apps are likely to be the most expensive to develop.

QUESTIONS

1. What are the main factors to consider when developing an e-commerce presence?
2. Define the systems development life cycle and discuss the various steps involved in creating an e-commerce site.
3. Discuss the differences between a simple logical and a simple physical Web site design.
4. Why is system testing important? Name the types of testing and their relation to each other.
5. Compare the costs for system development and system maintenance. Which is more expensive, and why?
6. Why is a Web site so costly to maintain? Discuss the main factors that impact cost.
7. What are the main differences between single-tier and multi-tier site architecture?
8. Name the basic functionalities a Web server should provide.
9. What are the main factors to consider when choosing the best hardware platform for your Web site?
10. Why is Web server bandwidth an important issue for e-commerce sites?
11. Compare and contrast the various scaling methods. Explain why scalability is a key business issue for Web sites.
12. What are the eight most important factors impacting Web site design, and how do they affect a site's operation?
13. What are Java and JavaScript? What role do they play in Web site design?
14. Name and describe three methods used to treat customers individually. Why are they significant to e-commerce?
15. What are some of the policies e-commerce businesses must develop before launching a site, and why must they be developed?
16. What are the advantages and disadvantages of mobile first design?
17. What is the difference between a mobile Web app and a native app?
18. In what ways does a hybrid mobile app combine the functionality of a mobile Web app and a native app?
19. What is PHP and how is it used in Web development?
20. How does responsive Web design differ from adaptive Web delivery?

PROJECTS

1. Go to the Web site of Wix, Weebly, or another provider of your choosing that allows you to create a simple e-tailer Web site for a free trial period. Create a Web site. The site should feature at least four pages, including a home page, product page, shopping cart, and contact page. Extra credit will be given for additional complexity and creativity. Come to class prepared to present your e-tailer concept and Web site.
2. Visit several e-commerce sites, not including those mentioned in this chapter, and evaluate the effectiveness of the sites according to the eight basic criteria/functionalities listed in Table 4.11. Choose one site you feel does an excellent job on all the aspects of an effective site and create an electronic presentation, including screen shots, to support your choice.
3. Imagine that you are in charge of developing a fast-growing start-up's e-commerce presence. Consider your options for building the company's e-commerce presence in-house with existing staff, or outsourcing the entire operation. Decide which strategy you believe is in your company's best interest

and create a brief presentation outlining your position. Why choose that approach? And what are the estimated associated costs, compared with the alternative? (You'll need to make some educated guesses here—don't worry about being exact.)

4. Choose two e-commerce software packages and prepare an evaluation chart that rates the packages on the key factors discussed in the section "Choosing an E-commerce Software Platform." Which package would you choose if you were developing a Web site of the type described in this chapter, and why?

5. Choose one of the open source Web content management systems such as WordPress, Joomla, or Drupal or another of your own choosing and prepare an evaluation chart similar to that required by Project 4. Which system would you choose and why?

REFERENCES

Byers, Josh. "Three Reasons a 'Mobile First' Philosophy Is Critical to Achieving Your Business Goals." Copyblogger.com (May 11, 2013).

Codecondo. "10 Popular Sites Powered by Django Web Framework." (December 21, 2013).

Coderfactory. "Top 15 Sites Built with Ruby on Rails." (February 26, 2014).

Doyle, Barry, and Cristina Videira Lopes. "Survey of Technologies for Web Application Development." *ACM*, Vol. 2., No. 3. (June 2005).

Dusto, Amy. "The Top E-commerce Platform Vendors for Midmarket Retailers." Internetretailer.com (January 10, 2014).

IBM (High Volume Web Sites Team). "Best Practices for High-Volume Web Sites." *IBM Redbooks* (December 2002).

Krill, Paul. "Java at 20: The Programming Juggernaut Rolls On." Infoworld.com (May 18, 2015).

Moovweb. "Responsive Delivery." (accessed August 27, 2014).

Mutton, Paul. "Hostinger Hosts Over 90% of All Steam Phishers." News.netcraft.com (April 28, 2015).

Netcraft. "PHP Just Grows and Grows." (accessed September 21, 2015).

Pratap, Ravi. "Responsive Design vs. Adaptive Delivery: Which One's Right for You?" Venturebeat.com (November 19, 2013).

W3Techs. "Server-side Languages." (accessed September 21, 2015).

Webtrends, Inc. "Webtrends Analytics 10." (2014).

CHAPTER 5

E-commerce Security and Payment Systems

After reading this chapter, you will be able to:

- Understand the scope of e-commerce crime and security problems, the key dimensions of e-commerce security, and the tension between security and other values.
- Identify the key security threats in the e-commerce environment.
- Describe how technology helps secure Internet communications channels and protect networks, servers, and clients.
- Appreciate the importance of policies, procedures, and laws in creating security.
- Identify the major e-commerce payment systems in use today.
- Describe the features and functionality of electronic billing presentment and payment systems.

Cyberwar:

MAD 2.0

From the earliest of days, humans have warred against each other, with the tools of warfare evolving over time from sticks and stones, to arrows and spears, to artillery and bombs. Physical warfare and weaponry are familiar and readily recognizable. But today, there is also another type of warfare that is becoming increasingly common, a type that is conducted by hidden armies of hackers wielding weaponry that consists of algorithms and computer code. Cyberspace has become a new battlefield, one that often involves nations against other nations, and nations against corporations. The targets include defense installations, nuclear facilities, public infrastructure, banks, manufacturing firms, and communications networks. There are two primary objectives of this kind of warfare: obtaining intellectual property (a kind of economic warfare) and attacking the ability of other nations to function.

© Rafal Olechowski / Fotolia

One of the problems of warfare is that your enemy may possess the same weapons as you do. In the context of thermonuclear warfare, politicians have negotiated treaties based on the so-called doctrine of mutually assured destruction (MAD): the recognition that even a first attacker would ultimately perish in the counterattack. Today, cyberwarfare has some striking similarities: an attack by one powerful nation against its enemy's cyberinfrastructure might unleash a counterattack so powerful that critical infrastructure in both nations would be heavily damaged and shut down. Not a shot would be fired, not a bomb dropped, but casualties could be in the millions. The United States, China, Russia, many European nations, and many smaller nations are preparing today for such a cyberwar, hoping it won't happen but developing new weapons and practicing techniques for both cyberdefense and cyberoffense.

Preparations for cyberwar have advanced rapidly in recent years. No longer just a worrisome future issue, cyberwar is now seen as likely, if not inevitable. Unlike a nuclear war that would cost tens of billions to wage, cyberwar is so inexpensive that even small nations can afford it. Many nations are preparing by conducting cyberwar games that in the past were called military exercises. For example, in April 2015, NATO, an alliance of countries from North America and Europe, brought together 400 military and corporate leaders from 16 nations for the 6th annual Locked Shields cyberwar games, the largest such games in the world. Using the Estonian Cyber Range, a sort of firing range for cyberwarriors, the national Blue Teams had to defend their countries against an all-out Red

Team cyberattack, with the emphasis on defensive strategies and keeping the infrastructure of their countries working. The U.S. Department of Defense conducted its 4th Cyber Guard cyberwar games exercise in June 2015. Over 100 organizations and 1,000 people, from both armed forces and private corporations, participated in the games.

A cyberarms race has already started. The big countries in cyberwar are the United States, Great Britain, China, Russia, Iran, Israel, Pakistan, and India, but many smaller countries like Denmark, the Netherlands, Estonia, and tiny Belarus are building their arsenals. A 2015 report documented 29 countries with formal military and intelligence units dedicated to offensive cyberwar, 49 that have purchased off-the-shelf hacking software, and 63 currently engaged in electronic surveillance of their own and other populations. Countries are developing cyberarsenals that include collections of malware for penetrating industrial, military, and critical civilian infrastructure controllers, e-mail lists and text for phishing attacks on important targets, and algorithms for denial of service (DoS) attacks. The computer code has been tested and ready to go for offensive purposes to surprise and cripple enemy systems.

Cyberattacks on information systems, which, while not real cyberwar in the sense of incapacitating infrastructure, nevertheless illustrate the ease with which corporate and government systems can be penetrated, have been on the rise over the past few years. Some of these attacks were likely undertaken by nation states that were practicing their offensive techniques. For instance, at the end of 2014, Sony Pictures' computer system was hacked, revealing information on 47,000 individuals, much of it e-mail correspondence among executives. About 70% of the firm's computers were incapacitated, and confidential e-mails were published by the hackers in an effort to embarrass executives of the firm. North Korea is a major suspect, although North Korean officials deny this. In early 2015, Anthem Health was hacked, exposing virtually all the personal information, from social security numbers to medical information, of 80 million customers. The Chinese government is the leading suspect. Other noteworthy hacks include JPMorgan Chase (76 million records), Home Depot (56 million records), and eBay (145 million records). Most of these were garden-variety hack-for-money attacks by rogue groups in Russia and Eastern Europe, many supported by or certainly tolerated by Russia. In the biggest attack on U.S. government systems thus far, in July 2015, the White House announced that the Office of Personnel Management, the government's human resources agency and database, had been hacked and complete records on over 21 million people were copied, including the names of people in the defense sector. The likely source of the hack was again the Chinese government.

Attacks against physical infrastructure have been less frequent. Infrastructure attacks require detailed knowledge of the infrastructure, which usually requires insider knowledge of industrial controllers (computers that control valves and machines). The most well-known and best documented infrastructure attack was Stuxnet, malware allegedly created by Israeli and American intelligence services in 2010 in an effort to cripple thousands of Iranian nuclear centrifuges. Stuxnet was a malware virus program planted in industrial controller modules of Iranian nuclear fuel centrifuges, causing them to destroy themselves. Stuxnet was precedent-setting: it was the first large-scale cyberattack on infrastructure. More recently, Russian hackers, allegedly employed by the Russian government, have picked up the spirit of Stuxnet and developed malware that gives hackers the ability to take control of industrial control system modules. The hackers have targeted

SOURCES: "Cyberwar Ignites a New Arms Race," by Damian Paletta, Danny Yardon, and Jennifer Valentino-Devries, *Wall Street Journal,* October 11, 2015; "Cataloging the World's Cyberforces," by Jennifer Valentino-Devries and Danny Yardon, *Wall Street Journal,* October 11, 2015; "Obama and Xi Jinping of China Agree to Steps on Cybertheft," by Julie Davis and David Sanger, *New York Times,* September 25, 2015; "U.S. and China Seek Arms Deal for Cyberspace," by David Sanger, *New York Times,* September 19, 2015; "Cyberthreat Posed by China and Iran Confounds White House," by David Sanger, *New York Times,* September 15, 2015; "U.S. vs. Hackers: Still Lopsided Despite Years of Warnings and a Recent Rush," by Michael Shear and Nicole Perlroth, *New York Times,* July 18, 2015; "Hacking of Government Computers Exposed

oil and gas firms. Using a "watering hole attack," the hackers launched a massive e-mail campaign to employees of these firms in an attempt to trick them into visiting a Web site where malware can be downloaded to their computers. The hackers even went so far as to infect local pizza parlor online ordering systems where engineers from the firms typically ordered pizza. While the emphasis of the attackers has been industrial espionage, the same software could be used in a cyberwar attack against oil and gas production and transmission facilities just like the Stuxnet software that crippled Iranian nuclear centrifuges. Over 1,000 organizations, in 84 countries, have discovered the Russian malware. Other infrastructure attacks include weapons known as Flame, which is thought to have caused Iran to disconnect its oil terminals from the Internet, and Snake, a malware tool kit believed to be from Russia that infected many Ukrainian civilian and industrial computer systems and networks. Snake gives attackers full access to remote systems, acts as a two-way conduit that can siphon information from systems, and provides a path for installing additional malware.

Security analysts believe the United States has developed the most powerful cyberwarfare defense and offense capabilities in the world. U.S. efforts are concentrated in the United States Cyber Command located in Fort Meade, Maryland. USCYBERCOM's stated mission is to coordinate and direct the operations and defense of Department of Defense information networks and to prepare for military cyberspace operations in order to enable actions in all domains, ensure US/Allied freedom of action in cyberspace, and deny the same to adversaries. To maintain its cyberwar lead, the United States plans to expand the number of cyberwarriors to 6,000 by 2016 and spend $26 billion developing cyberwarfare capabilities.

A number of diplomatic efforts have been undertaken by American planners to reach some sort of understanding with its cyberenemies that would set limits on cyberwar and prevent civilian casualties. These efforts are similar to nuclear arms treaties. In April 2015, the Pentagon announced a new cyberstrategy outlining the conditions under which the United States would engage in a cyberweapons attack on an adversary. Routine attacks against companies will be defended by companies themselves, but attacks on U.S. government systems, infrastructure systems, defense systems, and intelligence systems that involve significant loss of life, destruction of property, or lasting economic damage, will be grounds for launching a major counterattack that will threaten similar losses to the enemy. This new policy is aimed at Russia, China, Iran, and North Korea, each of whom have been implicated in state-sponsored attacks on U.S. government and corporate systems for several years. Announcing this new policy raises the potential cost of hacking critical American systems, and is the beginning of a deterrence strategy based on the concept of mutual assured destruction.

In September 2015, the Obama administration, frustrated by repeated hacks against government and private sector systems, attempted to arrive at an understanding with Chinese leaders. The presidents of both countries announced their pledge to refrain from computer-enabled theft of intellectual property for commercial gain, but there was no agreement to limit the use of cybertools for traditional espionage. A pledge is hardly a commitment and is certainly not a treaty. Missing from the discussion was an agreement not to attack critical infrastructure, and pledges not to be the first to attack. Today, rather than referring to mutually assured destruction, MAD may mean mutually assured doubt about who is originating attacks, what are their intensions, and how far will they go.

21.5 Million People," by Julie Hirschfield, *New York Times,* July 9, 2015; "U.S. Agencies Conduct Cyberwar Games," by Damian Paletta, *Wall Street Journal,* July 5, 2015; "Defense Infrastructure: Improvements in DOD Reporting and Cybersecurity Implementation Needed to Enhance Utility Resilience Planning." Government Accountability Office, July 2015; "Here's What a Cyber Warfare Arsenal Might Look Like," by Larry Greenemeier, *Scientific American,* May 6, 2015; "Pentagon Announces New Strategy for Cyberwarfare," by David Sanger, *New York Times,* April 23, 2015; "Deterrence Will Keep Lid on Cyberwar, Former Spy Chief Says," by Tim Hornyak, Computerworld. com, April 14, 2015; "State Sponsored Chinese Hackers Suspected in Anthem Breach," by Grant Gross, Computerworld.com, February 25, 2015; "Document Reveals Growth of Cyberwarfare Between the U.S. and Iran," by David Sanger, *New York Times,* February 22, 2015; "NATO Set to Ratify Pledge on Joint Defense in Case of Major Cyberattack," by David Sanger, *New York Times,* August 31, 2014; "Chinese Hackers Extending Reach to Smaller U.S. Agencies, Officials Say," by Michael Schmidt, *New York Times,* July 15, 2014; "Chinese Hackers Pursue Key Data on U.S. Workers," by Michael Schmidt, David Sanger, and Nicole Perlroth, *New York Times,* July 9, 2014; "Russian Hackers Targeting Oil and Gas Companies," by Nicole Perlroth, *New York Times,* June 30, 2014; "2nd China Army Unit Implicated in Online Spying," by Nicole Perlroth, *New York Times,* June 9, 2014; "5 in China Army Face U.S. Charges of Cyberattacks," by Michael Schmidt and David Sanger, *New York Times,* May 19, 2014; "U.S. Tries Candor to Assure China on Cyberattacks," by David Sanger, *New York Times,* April 6, 2014; "Suspicion Falls on Russia as 'Snake' Cyberattacks Target Ukraine's Government," by David Sanger and Steven Erlanger, *New York Times,* March 8, 2014; *Command and Control: Nuclear Weapons, the Damascus Accident, and the Illusion of Safety,* by Eric Schlosser, 2013.

A s *Cyberwar: MAD 2.0* illustrates, the Internet and Web are increasingly vulnerable to large-scale attacks and potentially large-scale failure. Increasingly, these attacks are led by organized gangs of criminals operating globally—an unintended consequence of globalization. Even more worrisome is the growing number of large-scale attacks that are funded, organized, and led by various nations against the Internet resources of other nations. Currently there are few if any steps that individuals or businesses can take to prevent these kinds of attacks. However, there are several steps you can take to protect your business Web sites, your mobile devices, and your personal information from routine security attacks. Reading this chapter, you should also start thinking about how your business could survive in the event of a large-scale "outage" of the Internet.

In this chapter, we will examine e-commerce security and payment issues. First, we will identify the major security risks and their costs, and describe the variety of solutions currently available. Then, we will look at the major payment methods and consider how to achieve a secure payment environment. **Table 5.1** highlights some of the major trends in online security in 2015–2016.

TABLE 5.1	WHAT'S NEW IN E-COMMERCE SECURITY 2015–2016

- Large-scale data breaches continue to expose data about individuals to hackers and other cybercriminals.
- Mobile malware presents a tangible threat as smartphones and other mobile devices become more common targets of cybercriminals, especially as their use for mobile payments rises.
- Malware creation continues to skyrocket and ransomware attacks rise.
- Nations continue to engage in cyberwarfare and cyberespionage.
- Hackers and cybercriminals continue to focus their efforts on social network sites to exploit potential victims through social engineering and hacking attacks.
- Politically motivated, targeted attacks by hacktivist groups continue, in some cases merging with financially motivated cybercriminals to target financial systems with advanced persistent threats.
- Software vulnerabilities, such as the Heartbleed bug and other zero day vulnerabilities, continue to create security threats.
- Incidents involving celebrities raise awareness of cloud security issues.

5.1 THE E-COMMERCE SECURITY ENVIRONMENT

For most law-abiding citizens, the Internet holds the promise of a huge and convenient global marketplace, providing access to people, goods, services, and businesses worldwide, all at a bargain price. For criminals, the Internet has created entirely new—and lucrative—ways to steal from the more than 1.35 billion Internet consumers worldwide in 2015. From products and services, to cash, to information, it's all there for the taking on the Internet.

It's also less risky to steal online. Rather than rob a bank in person, the Internet makes it possible to rob people remotely and almost anonymously. Rather than steal a CD at a local record store, you can download the same music for free and almost without risk from the Internet. The potential for anonymity on the Internet cloaks many criminals in legitimate-looking identities, allowing them to place fraudulent orders with online merchants, steal information by intercepting e-mail, or simply shut down e-commerce sites by using software viruses and swarm attacks. The Internet was never designed to be a global marketplace with billions of users and lacks many basic security features found in older networks such as the telephone system or broadcast television networks. By comparison, the Internet is an open, vulnerable-design network. The actions of cybercriminals are costly for both businesses and consumers, who are then subjected to higher prices and additional security measures. The costs of malicious cyberactivity include not just the cost of the actual crime, but also the additional costs that are required to secure networks and recover from cyberattacks, the potential reputational damage to the affected company, as well as reduced trust in online activities, the loss of potentially sensitive business information, including intellectual property and confidential business information, and the cost of opportunities lost due to service disruptions. Ponemon Institute estimates that the average total cost of a data breach to U.S. corporations in 2014 was $6.5 million (Ponemon Institute, 2015a).

THE SCOPE OF THE PROBLEM

Cybercrime is becoming a more significant problem for both organizations and consumers. Bot networks, DDoS attacks, Trojans, phishing, ransomware, data theft, identity fraud, credit card fraud, and spyware are just some of the threats that are making daily headlines. Social networks also have had security breaches. But despite the increasing attention being paid to cybercrime, it is difficult to accurately estimate the actual amount of such crime, in part because many companies are hesitant to report it due to the fear of losing the trust of their customers, and because even if crime is reported, it may be difficult to quantify the actual dollar amount of the loss. A 2014 study by the Center for Strategic and International Studies examined the difficulties in accurately estimating the economic impact of cybercrime and cyberespionage, with its research indicating a range of between $375 billion to $575 billion worldwide. Further research is planned to try to help determine an even more accurate estimate (Center for Strategic and International Studies, 2014).

One source of information is a survey conducted by Ponemon Institute of 58 representative U.S. companies in various industries. The 2015 survey found that the average annualized cost of cybercrime for the organizations in the study was $15 million, representing a 20% increase from the previous year, and an 82% increase since the first survey in 2009. The average cost per attack was more than $1.9 million, a 22% increase from the previous year. The number of successful cyberattacks also increased, by over 15%. The most costly cybercrimes were those caused by denial of service, malicious insiders, and malicious code. The most prevalent types of attacks were viruses, worms, and Trojans, experienced by 100% of the companies surveyed, followed by malware (97%), Web-based attacks (76%), botnets (66%), phishing and social engineering attacks (59%), and malicious code (52%) (Ponemon Institute, 2015b).

Reports issued by security product providers, such as Symantec, are another source of data. Symantec issues a semi-annual *Internet Security Threat Report*, based on 57.6 million sensors monitoring Internet activity in more than 157 countries. Advances in technology have greatly reduced the entry costs and skills required to enter the cybercrime business. Low-cost and readily available Web attack kits enable hackers to create malware without having to write software from scratch. In addition, there has been a surge in polymorphic malware, which enables attackers to generate a unique version of the malware for each victim, making it much more difficult for pattern-matching software used by security firms to detect. According to Symantec, the number of data breaches increased 23% in 2014, the number of spear-phishing attacks increased by 8%, malware increased by 26%, and ransomware attacks grew by 113% (Symantec, 2015l). However, Symantec does not attempt to quantify actual crimes and/or losses related to these threats.

Online credit card fraud is one of the most high-profile forms of e-commerce crime. Although the average amount of credit card fraud loss experienced by any one individual is typically relatively small, the overall amount is substantial. The overall rate of online credit card fraud is estimated to be about 0.9% of all online card transactions, including both mobile and Web transactions (Cybersource, 2015). The nature of credit card fraud has changed greatly from the theft of a single credit card number and efforts to purchase goods at a few sites, to the simultaneous theft of millions of credit card numbers and their distributions to thousands of criminals operating as gangs of thieves. The emergence of identity fraud, described in detail later in this chapter, as a major online/offline type of fraud may well increase markedly the incidence and amount of credit card fraud, because identity fraud often includes the use of stolen credit card information and the creation of phony credit card accounts.

The Underground Economy Marketplace: The Value of Stolen Information

Criminals who steal information on the Internet do not always use this information themselves, but instead derive value by selling the information to others on the so-called underground or shadow economy market. Data is currency to cybercriminals and has a "street value" that can be monetized. For example, in 2013, Vladislav Horohorin (alias "BadB") was sentenced to over 7 years in federal prison for using online criminal forums to sell stolen credit and debit card information (referred to as "dumps"). At the time of his arrest, Horohorin possessed over 2.5 million stolen credit and debit card numbers. There are several thousand known underground economy marketplaces around the world that sell stolen information, as well as malware, such as exploit kits, access to botnets, and more. **Table 5.2** lists some recently observed prices for various types of stolen data, which typically vary depending on the quantity being purchased, supply available, and "freshness." For example, when credit card information from the Target data breach first appeared on the market, individual card numbers went for up to $120 each. After a few weeks, however, the price dropped

TABLE 5.2	THE CYBER BLACK MARKET FOR STOLEN DATA
DATA	**PRICE***
Individual U.S. card number with expiration date and CVV2 (the three-digit number printed on back of card) (referred to as a CVV)	$0.50–$12
Individual U.S. card number with full information, including full name, billing address, expiration date, CVV2, date of birth, mother's maiden name, etc. (referred to as a Fullz or Fullzinfo)	$30–$100
Dump data for U.S. card (the term "dump" refers to raw data such as name, account number, expiration data, and CVV encoded on the magnetic strip on the back of the card)	$20–$100
Online payment service accounts	$20–$300
Bank account login credentials	$80–$700
Online account login credentials (Facebook, Twitter, eBay)	$10–$15
Medical information/health credentials	$10–$20
1,000 e-mail addresses	$1–$10
Scan of a passport	$1–$2

SOURCES: Based on data from Intel Security, 2015; Symantec, 2015; Maruca, 2015; Infosec Institute, 2015; RAND Corporation, 2014.

*Prices vary based on supply and quality (freshness of data, account balances, validity, etc.).

dramatically (Leger, 2014). Experts believe the cost of stolen information has generally fallen as the tools of harvesting have increased the supply. On the demand side, the same efficiencies and opportunities provided by new technology have increased the number of people who want to use stolen information. It's a robust marketplace.

Finding these marketplaces and the servers that host them can be difficult for the average user (and for law enforcement agencies), and prospective participants are typically vetted by other criminals before access is granted. This vetting process takes place through Twitter, Tor, and VPN services, and sometimes e-mail exchanges of information, money (often Bitcoins, a form of digital cash that we discuss further in Section 5.5 and in the *Insight on Business* case study on pages 315–316), and reputation. There is a general hierarchy of cybercriminals in the marketplace, with low-level, nontechnical criminals who frequent "carder forums," where stolen credit and debit card data is sold, aiming to make money, a political statement, or both at the bottom; resellers in the middle acting as intermediaries; and the technical masterminds who create malicious code at the top.

So, what can we can conclude about the overall size of cybercrime? Cybercrime against e-commerce sites is dynamic and changing all the time, with new risks appearing often. The amount of losses to businesses is significant and growing. The managers of e-commerce sites must prepare for an ever-changing variety of criminal assaults, and keep current in the latest security techniques.

WHAT IS GOOD E-COMMERCE SECURITY?

What is a secure commercial transaction? Anytime you go into a marketplace you take risks, including the loss of privacy (information about what you purchased). Your prime risk as a consumer is that you do not get what you paid for. As a merchant in the market, your risk is that you don't get paid for what you sell. Thieves take merchandise and then either walk off without paying anything, or pay you with a fraudulent instrument, stolen credit card, or forged currency.

E-commerce merchants and consumers face many of the same risks as participants in traditional commerce, albeit in a new digital environment. Theft is theft, regardless of whether it is digital theft or traditional theft. Burglary, breaking and entering, embezzlement, trespass, malicious destruction, vandalism—all crimes in a traditional commercial environment—are also present in e-commerce. However, reducing risks in e-commerce is a complex process that involves new technologies, organizational policies and procedures, and new laws and industry standards that empower law enforcement officials to investigate and prosecute offenders. **Figure 5.1** illustrates the multi-layered nature of e-commerce security.

To achieve the highest degree of security possible, new technologies are available and should be used. But these technologies by themselves do not solve the problem. Organizational policies and procedures are required to ensure the technologies are not subverted. Finally, industry standards and government laws are required to enforce payment mechanisms, as well as to investigate and prosecute violators of laws designed to protect the transfer of property in commercial transactions.

FIGURE 5.1	THE E-COMMERCE SECURITY ENVIRONMENT

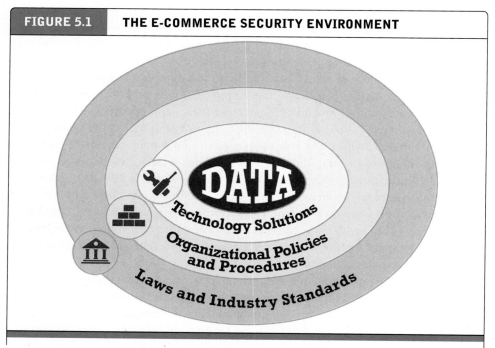

E-commerce security is multi-layered, and must take into account new technology, policies and procedures, and laws and industry standards.

The history of security in commercial transactions teaches that any security system can be broken if enough resources are put against it. Security is not absolute. In addition, perfect security of every item is not needed forever, especially in the information age. There is a time value to information—just as there is to money. Sometimes it is sufficient to protect a message for a few hours or days. Also, because security is costly, we always have to weigh the cost against the potential loss. Finally, we have also learned that security is a chain that breaks most often at the weakest link. Our locks are often much stronger than our management of the keys.

We can conclude then that good e-commerce security requires a set of laws, procedures, policies, and technologies that, to the extent feasible, protect individuals and organizations from unexpected behavior in the e-commerce marketplace.

DIMENSIONS OF E-COMMERCE SECURITY

There are six key dimensions to e-commerce security: integrity, nonrepudiation, authenticity, confidentiality, privacy, and availability.

Integrity refers to the ability to ensure that information being displayed on a Web site, or transmitted or received over the Internet, has not been altered in any way by an unauthorized party. For example, if an unauthorized person intercepts and changes the contents of an online communication, such as by redirecting a bank wire transfer into a different account, the integrity of the message has been compromised because the communication no longer represents what the original sender intended.

Nonrepudiation refers to the ability to ensure that e-commerce participants do not deny (i.e., repudiate) their online actions. For instance, the availability of free e-mail accounts with alias names makes it easy for a person to post comments or send a message and perhaps later deny doing so. Even when a customer uses a real name and e-mail address, it is easy for that customer to order merchandise online and then later deny doing so. In most cases, because merchants typically do not obtain a physical copy of a signature, the credit card issuer will side with the customer because the merchant has no legally valid proof that the customer ordered the merchandise.

Authenticity refers to the ability to identify the identity of a person or entity with whom you are dealing on the Internet. How does the customer know that the Web site operator is who it claims to be? How can the merchant be assured that the customer is really who she says she is? Someone who claims to be someone he is not is "spoofing" or misrepresenting himself.

Confidentiality refers to the ability to ensure that messages and data are available only to those who are authorized to view them. Confidentiality is sometimes confused with **privacy**, which refers to the ability to control the use of information a customer provides about himself or herself to an e-commerce merchant.

E-commerce merchants have two concerns related to privacy. They must establish internal policies that govern their own use of customer information, and they must protect that information from illegitimate or unauthorized use. For example, if hackers break into an e-commerce site and gain access to credit card or other information, this violates not only the confidentiality of the data, but also the privacy of the individuals who supplied the information.

integrity
the ability to ensure that information being displayed on a Web site or transmitted or received over the Internet has not been altered in any way by an unauthorized party

nonrepudiation
the ability to ensure that e-commerce participants do not deny (i.e., repudiate) their online actions

authenticity
the ability to identify the identity of a person or entity with whom you are dealing on the Internet

confidentiality
the ability to ensure that messages and data are available only to those who are authorized to view them

privacy
the ability to control the use of information about oneself

TABLE 5.3	CUSTOMER AND MERCHANT PERSPECTIVES ON THE DIFFERENT DIMENSIONS OF E-COMMERCE SECURITY	
DIMENSION	CUSTOMER'S PERSPECTIVE	MERCHANT'S PERSPECTIVE
Integrity	Has information I transmitted or received been altered?	Has data on the site been altered without authorization? Is data being received from customers valid?
Nonrepudiation	Can a party to an action with me later deny taking the action?	Can a customer deny ordering products?
Authenticity	Who am I dealing with? How can I be assured that the person or entity is who they claim to be?	What is the real identity of the customer?
Confidentiality	Can someone other than the intended recipient read my messages?	Are messages or confidential data accessible to anyone other than those authorized to view them?
Privacy	Can I control the use of information about myself transmitted to an e-commerce merchant?	What use, if any, can be made of personal data collected as part of an e-commerce transaction? Is the personal information of customers being used in an unauthorized manner?
Availability	Can I get access to the site?	Is the site operational?

availability

the ability to ensure that an e-commerce site continues to function as intended

Availability refers to the ability to ensure that an e-commerce site continues to function as intended.

Table 5.3 summarizes these dimensions from both the merchants' and customers' perspectives. E-commerce security is designed to protect these six dimensions. When any one of them is compromised, overall security suffers.

THE TENSION BETWEEN SECURITY AND OTHER VALUES

Can there be too much security? The answer is yes. Contrary to what some may believe, security is not an unmitigated good. Computer security adds overhead and expense to business operations, and also gives criminals new opportunities to hide their intentions and their crimes.

Ease of Use

There are inevitable tensions between security and ease of use. When traditional merchants are so fearful of robbers that they do business in shops locked behind security gates, ordinary customers are discouraged from walking in. The same can be true with respect to e-commerce. In general, the more security measures added to an e-commerce site, the more difficult it is to use and the slower the site becomes. As you will discover reading this chapter, digital security is purchased at the price of slowing down processors and adding significantly to data storage demands on storage devices. Security is a technological and business overhead that can detract from doing business. Too much security can harm profitability, while not enough security can potentially put you out of business.

Public Safety and the Criminal Uses of the Internet

There is also an inevitable tension between the desires of individuals to act anonymously (to hide their identity) and the needs of public officials to maintain public safety that can be threatened by criminals or terrorists. This is not a new problem, or even new to the electronic era. The U.S. government began tapping telegraph wires during the Civil War in the mid-1860s in order to trap conspirators and terrorists, and the first police wiretaps of local telephone systems were in place by the 1890s—20 years after the invention of the phone (Schwartz, 2001). No nation-state has ever permitted a technological haven to exist where criminals can plan crimes or threaten the nation-state without fear of official surveillance or investigation. In this sense, the Internet is no different from any other communication system. Drug cartels make extensive use of voice, fax, the Internet, and encrypted e-mail; a number of large international organized crime groups steal information from commercial Web sites and resell it to other criminals who use it for financial fraud. Over the years, the U.S. government has successfully pursued various "carding forums" (Web sites that facilitate the sale of stolen credit card and debit card numbers), such as Shadowcrew, Carderplanet, and Cardersmarket resulting in the arrest and prosecution of a number of their members and the closing of the sites. However, other criminal organizations have emerged to take their place.

The Internet and mobile platform also provide terrorists with convenient communications channels. Encrypted files sent via e-mail were used by Ramzi Yousef—a member of the terrorist group responsible for bombing the World Trade Center in 1993—to hide plans for bombing 11 U.S. airliners. The Internet was also used to plan and coordinate the subsequent attacks on the World Trade Center on September 11, 2001. The case of Umar Farouk Abdulmutallab further illustrates how terrorists make effective use of the Internet to radicalize, recruit, train, and coordinate youthful terrorists. Abdulmutallab allegedly attempted to blow up an American airliner in Detroit on Christmas Day 2009. He was identified, contacted, recruited, and trained, all within six weeks, according to a Pentagon counterterrorism official. In an effort to combat such terrorism, the U.S. government has significantly ramped up its surveillance of communications delivered via the Internet over the past several years. The extent of that surveillance created a major controversy with National Security Agency contractor Edward Snowden's release of classified NSA documents that revealed that the NSA had obtained access to the servers of major Internet companies such as Facebook, Google, Apple, Microsoft, and others, as well as that NSA analysts have been searching e-mail, online chats, and browsing histories of U.S. citizens without any court approval. The proper balance between public safety and privacy in the effort against terrorism has proven to be a very thorny problem for the U.S. government.

5.2 SECURITY THREATS IN THE E-COMMERCE ENVIRONMENT

From a technology perspective, there are three key points of vulnerability when dealing with e-commerce: the client, the server, and the communications pipeline. **Figure 5.2** illustrates a typical e-commerce transaction with a consumer using a credit card to purchase a product. **Figure 5.3** illustrates some of the things that can go wrong at each major vulnerability point in the transaction—over Internet communications channels, at the server level, and at the client level.

In this section, we describe a number of the most common and most damaging forms of security threats to e-commerce consumers and site operators: malicious code, potentially unwanted programs, phishing, hacking and cybervandalism, credit card fraud/theft, spoofing, pharming, spam (junk) Web sites (link farms), identity fraud,

---

FIGURE 5.2   A TYPICAL E-COMMERCE TRANSACTION

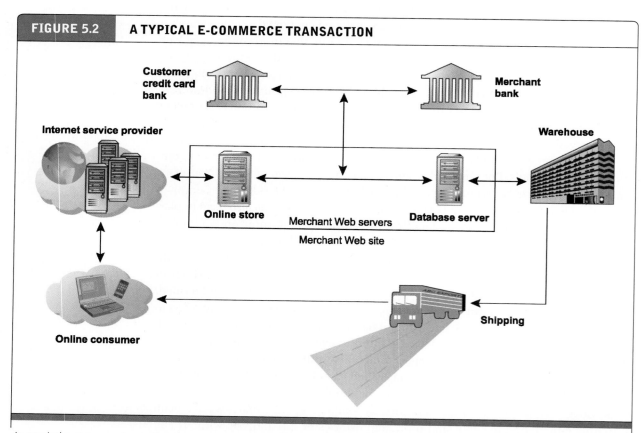

In a typical e-commerce transaction, the customer uses a credit card and the existing credit payment system.

FIGURE 5.3	VULNERABLE POINTS IN AN E-COMMERCE TRANSACTION

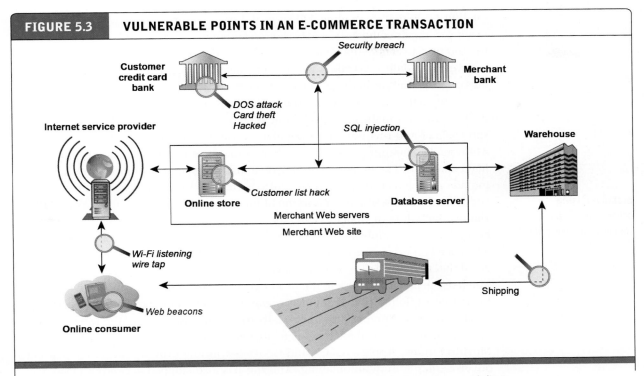

There are three major vulnerable points in e-commerce transactions: Internet communications, servers, and clients.

Denial of Service (DoS) and DDoS attacks, sniffing, insider attacks, poorly designed server and client software, social network security issues, mobile platform security issues, and finally, cloud security issues.

MALICIOUS CODE

Malicious code (sometimes referred to as "malware") includes a variety of threats such as viruses, worms, Trojan horses, ransomware, and bots. Some malicious code, sometimes referred to as an *exploit,* is designed to take advantage of software vulnerabilities in a computer's operating system, Web browser, applications, or other software components. **Exploit kits** are collections of exploits bundled together and rented or sold as a commercial product, often with slick user interfaces and in-depth analytics functionality. Use of an exploit kit typically does not require much technical skill, enabling novices to become cybercriminals. Exploit kits typically target software that is widely deployed, such as Microsoft Windows, Internet Explorer, Adobe Flash and Reader, and Oracle Java. In 2014, according to Cisco, Angler, an exploit kit that uses Flash, Java, Microsoft Internet Explorer, and Microsoft Silverlight vulnerabilities, was one of the exploit kits most observed "in the wild" (Cisco, 2015). According to Symantec, more than 317 million new variants of malware were created in 2014, an average of close to 1 million strains a day, with the overall number of malware variants now

malicious code (malware)
includes a variety of threats such as viruses, worms, Trojan horses, and bots

exploit kit
collection of exploits bundled together and rented or sold as a commercial product

totaling 1.7 billion (Symantec, 2015). In the past, malicious code was often intended to simply impair computers, and was often authored by a lone hacker, but increasingly the intent is to steal e-mail addresses, logon credentials, personal data, and financial information. Malicious code is also used to develop integrated malware networks that organize the theft of information and money.

In the early days of the Internet, malicious code was often delivered by e-mail, in the form of a malicious attachment such as a Microsoft Word document or Excel spreadsheet and this remains a popular distribution method, with 1 in about every 244 e-mails containing mailware, either in the form of a malicious attachment or a malicious URL. The links lead directly to a malicious code download or Web sites that include malicious code (Symantec, 2015). One of the latest innovations in malicious code distribution is to embed it in the online advertising chain (known as **maladvertising**), including in Google, AOL, and other ad networks. As the ad network chain becomes more complicated, it becomes more and more difficult for Web sites to vet ads placed on their sites to ensure they are malware-free. A 2014 research study indicated that as many as 1% of all ads served may be maladvertising (Zarras et al., 2014). Much of the maladvertising in the recent years has been in the form of drive-by downloads that exploited the frequent zero-day vulnerabilities that have plagued Adobe Flash, which is often used for online advertisements. As a result, the Internet Advertising Bureau has urged advertisers to abandon Adobe Flash in favor of HTML5, and Mozilla Firefox, Apple's Safari, and Google's Chrome browser all now block Flash advertisements from autoplaying. Amazon has also stopped accepting Flash ads. A **drive-by download** is malware that comes with a downloaded file that a user intentionally or unintentionally requests. Drive-by is now one of the most common methods of infecting computers. For instance, Web sites as disparate as eWeek (a technology site), to MLB (Major League Baseball), and Yahoo have experienced instances where ads placed on their sites either had malicious code embedded or directed clickers to malicious sites (RAND Corporation, 2014). According to Symantec, drive-by download exploit kits, including updates and 24/7 support, can be rented for between $100 to $700 per week. Malicious code embedded in PDF files also is common. Equally important, there has been a major shift in the writers of malware from amateur hackers and adventurers to organized criminal efforts to defraud companies and individuals. In other words, it's now more about the money than ever before.

A **virus** is a computer program that has the ability to replicate or make copies of itself, and spread to other files. In addition to the ability to replicate, most computer viruses deliver a "payload." The payload may be relatively benign, such as the display of a message or image, or it may be highly destructive—destroying files, reformatting the computer's hard drive, or causing programs to run improperly.

Viruses are often combined with a worm. Instead of just spreading from file to file, a **worm** is designed to spread from computer to computer. A worm does not necessarily need to be activated by a user or program in order for it to replicate itself. The Slammer worm is one of the most notorious. Slammer targeted a known vulnerability in Microsoft's SQL Server database software and infected more than 90% of vulnerable computers worldwide within 10 minutes of its release on the Internet; crashed Bank of America cash machines, especially in the southwestern part of the

---

maladvertising
online advertising that contains malicious code

drive-by download
malware that comes with a downloaded file that a user requests

virus
a computer program that has the ability to replicate or make copies of itself, and spread to other files

worm
malware that is designed to spread from computer to computer

United States; affected cash registers at supermarkets such as the Publix chain in Atlanta, where staff could not dispense cash to frustrated buyers; and took down most Internet connections in South Korea, causing a dip in the stock market there. The Conficker worm, which first appeared in November 2008, is the most significant worm since Slammer, and reportedly infected 9 to 15 million computers worldwide (Symantec, 2010).

Ransomware (scareware) is a type of malware (often a worm) that locks your computer or files to stop you from accessing them. Ransomware will often display a notice that says an authority such as the FBI, Department of Justice, or IRS has detected illegal activity on your computer and demands that you pay a fine in order to unlock the computer and avoid prosecution. In 2013, a new type of ransomware named CryptoLocker emerged. CryptoLocker encrypts victims' files with a virtually unbreakable asymmetric encryption and demands a ransom to decrypt them, often in Bitcoins. If the victim does not comply within the time allowed, the files will not ever be able to be decrypted. Other variants include CryptoDefense and Cryptowall. Ransomware attacks increased by over 113% in 2014, and those involving crypto-ransomware such as CryptoLocker increased astronomically, by 45 times. Crypto-ransomware infections often take place via a malicious e-mail attachment that purports to be an invoice (Symantec, 2015).

A **Trojan horse** appears to be benign, but then does something other than expected. The Trojan horse is not itself a virus because it does not replicate, but is often a way for viruses or other malicious code such as bots or *rootkits* (a program whose aim is to subvert control of the computer's operating system) to be introduced into a computer system. The term *Trojan horse* refers to the huge wooden horse in Homer's *Iliad* that the Greeks gave their opponents, the Trojans—a gift that actually contained hundreds of Greek soldiers. Once the people of Troy let the massive horse within their gates, the soldiers revealed themselves and captured the city. In today's world, a Trojan horse may masquerade as a game, but actually hide a program to steal your passwords and e-mail them to another person. Miscellaneous Trojans and Trojan downloaders and droppers (Trojans that install malicious files to a computer they have infected by either downloading them from a remote computer or from a copy contained in their own code) are a common type of malware. For example, according to Microsoft, the encounter rate for downloaders and droppers spiked in the third quarter of 2014 because of detections of a Trojan downloader known as Tugspay. Tugspay was the most commonly encountered malware family in the second half of 2014, and spread by posing as an installer for legitimate software, such as Java update (Microsoft, 2015). According to Panda Security, Trojans accounted for almost 70% of all malware created in 2014, and 65% of all malware infections. In May 2011, Sony experienced the largest data breach in history up to that time when a Trojan horse took over the administrative computers of Sony's PlayStation game center and downloaded personal and credit card information involving 77 million registered users (Wakabayashi, 2011). Trojan horses are often used for financial malware distributed via botnets. One example is Zeus, which steals information by keystroke logging and has infected over 10 million computers since it first became known in 2007. Other examples include SpyEye, a Trojan that can steal banking information via both a keylogging application and the

ransomware (scareware)
malware that prevents you from accessing your computer or files and demands that you pay a fine

Trojan horse
appears to be benign, but then does something other than expected. Often a way for viruses or other malicious code to be introduced into a computer system

ability to take screenshots on a victim's computer, and which has infected 1.4 million computers as of October 2015; Torpig, a botnet that is spread by a Trojan horse called Meboot; and Vawtrak, a Trojan that spreads via social media, e-mail, and FTP, and is able to hide evidence of fraud by changing bank balances shown to the victim on the fly (Cyphort, 2015).

backdoor

feature of viruses, worms, and Trojans that allows an attacker to remotely access a compromised computer

A **backdoor** is a feature of viruses, worms, and Trojans that allows an attacker to remotely access a compromised computer. Downadup is an example of a worm with a backdoor, while Virut, a virus that infects various file types, also includes a backdoor that can be used to download and install additional threats.

bot

type of malicious code that can be covertly installed on a computer when connected to the Internet. Once installed, the bot responds to external commands sent by the attacker

botnet

collection of captured bot computers

Bots (short for robots) are a type of malicious code that can be covertly installed on your computer when attached to the Internet. Once installed, the bot responds to external commands sent by the attacker; your computer becomes a "zombie" and is able to be controlled by an external third party (the "bot-herder"). **Botnets** are collections of captured computers used for malicious activities such as sending spam, participating in a DDoS attack, stealing information from computers, and storing network traffic for later analysis. The number of botnets operating worldwide is not known but is estimated to be well into the thousands, controlling millions of computers. Bots and bot networks are an important threat to the Internet and e-commerce because they can be used to launch very large-scale attacks using many different techniques. In 2011, federal marshals accompanied members of Microsoft's digital crimes unit in raids designed to disable the Rustock botnet, at that time the leading source of spam in the world with nearly 500,000 slave PCs under the control of its command and control servers located at six Internet hosting services in the United States. Officials confiscated the Rustock control servers at the hosting sites, which claimed they had no idea what the Rustock servers were doing. The actual spam e-mails were sent by the slave PCs under the command of the Rustock servers (Wingfield, 2011). In 2013, Microsoft and the FBI engaged in another aggressive botnet operation, targeting 1,400 of Zeus-derived Citadel botnets, which had been used in 2012 to raid bank accounts at major banks around the world, netting over $500 million (Chirgwin, 2013). In 2014, the Gameover Zeus botnet, used for banking fraud and distribution of CryptoLocker ransomware, was shut down. As a result of efforts such as these, Symantec estimates that the number of bots declined by 18% in 2014, from over 2.3 million in 2013 to 1.9 million in 2014 (Symantec, 2015). In April 2015, an international cybersquad took down the Beebone botnet, made up of 12,000 computers that had been infecting about 30,000 computers a month around the world via drive-by downloads with Changeup, a polymorphic worm use to distribute Trojans, worms, backdoors, and other types of malware (Constantin, 2015).

Malicious code is a threat at both the client and the server levels, although servers generally engage in much more thorough anti-virus activities than do consumers. At the server level, malicious code can bring down an entire Web site, preventing millions of people from using the site. Such incidents are infrequent. Much more frequent malicious code attacks occur at the client level, and the damage can quickly spread to millions of other computers connected to the Internet. **Table 5.4** lists some well-known examples of malicious code.

TABLE 5.4	NOTABLE EXAMPLES OF MALICIOUS CODE	
NAME	TYPE	DESCRIPTION
Cryptolocker	Ransomware/ Trojan	Hijacks users' photos, videos, and text documents, encrypts them with virtually unbreakable asymmetric encryption, and demands ransom payment for them.
Citadel	Trojan/botnet	Variant of Zeus Trojan, focuses on the theft of authentication credentials and financial fraud. Botnets spreading Citadel were targets of Microsoft/FBI action in 2012.
Zeus	Trojan/botnet	Sometimes referred to as king of financial malware. May install via drive-by download and evades detection by taking control of Web browser and stealing data that is exchanged with bank servers.
Reventon	Ransomware worm/Trojan	Based on Citadel/Zeus Trojans. Locks computer and displays warning from local police alleging illegal activity on computer; demands payment of fine to unlock.
Ramnit	Virus/worm	One of the most prevalent malicious code families still active in 2013. Infects various file types, including executable files, and copies itself to removable drives, executing via AutoPlay when the drive is accessed on other computers
Sality.AE	Virus/worm	Most common virus in 2012; still active in 2013. Disables security applications and services, connects to a botnet, then downloads and installs additional threats. Uses polymorphism to evade detection.
Conficker	Worm	First appeared November 2008. Targets Microsoft operating systems. Uses advanced malware techniques. Largest worm infection since Slammer in 2003. Still considered a major threat.
Netsky.P	Worm/Trojan	First appeared in early 2003. It spreads by gathering target e-mail addresses from the computers, then infects and sends e-mail to all recipients from the infected computer. It is commonly used by bot networks to launch spam and DoS attacks.
Storm (Peacomm, NuWar)	Worm/Trojan	First appeared in January 2007. It spreads in a manner similar to the Netsky.P worm. May also download and run other Trojan programs and worms.
Nymex	Worm	First discovered in January 2006. Spreads by mass mailing; activates on the 3rd of every month, and attempts to destroy files of certain types.
Zotob	Worm	First appeared in August 2005. Well-known worm that infected a number of U.S. media companies.
Mydoom	Worm	First appeared in January 2004. One of the fastest spreading mass-mailer worms.
Slammer	Worm	Launched in January 2003. Caused widespread problems.
CodeRed	Worm	Appeared in 2001. It achieved an infection rate of over 20,000 systems within 10 minutes of release and ultimately spread to hundreds of thousands of systems.
Melissa	Macro virus/ worm	First spotted in March 1999. At the time, the fastest spreading infectious program ever discovered. It attacked Microsoft Word's Normal.dot global template, ensuring infection of all newly created documents. It also mailed an infected Word file to the first 50 entries in each user's Microsoft Outlook Address Book.
Chernobyl	File-infecting virus	First appeared in 1998. It wipes out the first megabyte of data on a hard disk (making the rest useless) every April 26, the anniversary of the nuclear disaster at Chernobyl.

POTENTIALLY UNWANTED PROGRAMS (PUPS)

potentially unwanted program (PUP)
program that installs itself on a computer, typically without the user's informed consent

In addition to malicious code, the e-commerce security environment is further challenged by **potentially unwanted programs (PUPs)** such as adware, browser parasites, spyware, and other applications that install themselves on a computer, such as rogue security software, typically without the user's informed consent. Such programs are increasingly found on social network and user-generated content sites where users are fooled into downloading them. Once installed, these applications are usually exceedingly difficult to remove from the computer. One example of a PUP is System Doctor 2014, which infects PCs running Windows operating systems. System Doctor 2014 poses as a legitimate anti-spyware program when in fact it is malware that, when installed, disables the user's security software, alters the user's Web browser, and diverts users to scam Web sites where more malware is downloaded.

adware
a PUP that serves pop-up ads to your computer

browser parasite
a program that can monitor and change the settings of a user's browser

Adware is typically used to call for pop-up ads to display when the user visits certain sites. While annoying, adware is not typically used for criminal activities. A **browser parasite** is a program that can monitor and change the settings of a user's browser, for instance, changing the browser's home page, or sending information about the sites visited to a remote computer. Browser parasites are often a component of adware. In early 2015, Lenovo faced a barrage of criticism when it became known that, since September 2014, it had been shipping its Windows laptops with Superfish adware preinstalled. Superfish injected its own shopping results into the computer's browser when the user searched on Google, Amazon, or other Web sites. In the process, Superfish created a security risk by enabling others on a Wi-Fi network to silently hijack the browser and collect anything typed into it. Lenovo ultimately issued a removal tool to enable customers to delete the adware.

spyware
a program used to obtain information such as a user's keystrokes, e-mail, instant messages, and so on

Spyware, on the other hand, can be used to obtain information such as a user's keystrokes, copies of e-mail and instant messages, and even take screenshots (and thereby capture passwords or other confidential data).

PHISHING

social engineering
exploitation of human fallibility and gullibility to distribute malware

Social engineering relies on human curiosity, greed, and gullibility in order to trick people into taking an action that will result in the downloading of malware. Kevin Mitnick, until his capture and imprisonment in 1999, was one of America's most wanted computer criminals. Mitnick used simple deceptive techniques to obtain passwords, social security, and police records all without the use of any sophisticated technology (Mitnick, 2011).

phishing
any deceptive, online attempt by a third party to obtain confidential information for financial gain

Phishing is any deceptive, online attempt by a third party to obtain confidential information for financial gain. Phishing attacks typically do not involve malicious code but instead rely on straightforward misrepresentation and fraud, so-called "social engineering" techniques. One of the most popular phishing attacks is the e-mail scam letter. The scam begins with an e-mail: a rich former oil minister of Nigeria is seeking a bank account to stash millions of dollars for a short period of time, and requests your bank account number where the money can be deposited. In return, you will receive a million dollars. This type of e-mail scam is popularly known as a "Nigerian letter" scam (see **Figure 5.4**).

FIGURE 5.4	AN EXAMPLE OF A NIGERIAN LETTER E-MAIL SCAM

This is an example of a typical Nigerian letter e-mail scam.
© keith morris / Alamy

Thousands of other phishing attacks use other scams, some pretending to be eBay, PayPal, or Citibank writing to you for account verification (known as *spear phishing,* or targeting a known customer of a specific bank or other type of business). Click on a link in the e-mail and you will be taken to a Web site controlled by the scammer, and prompted to enter confidential information about your accounts, such as your account number and PIN codes. On any given day, millions of these phishing attack e-mails are sent, and, unfortunately, some people are fooled and disclose their personal account information.

Phishers rely on traditional "con man" tactics, but use e-mail to trick recipients into voluntarily giving up financial access codes, bank account numbers, credit card numbers, and other personal information. Often, phishers create (or "spoof") a Web site that purports to be a legitimate financial institution and cons users into entering financial information, or the site downloads malware such as a keylogger to the victim's computer. Phishers use the information they gather to commit fraudulent acts such as charging items to your credit cards or withdrawing funds from your bank account, or in other ways "steal your identity" (identity fraud). Symantec reported that in 2014, about 1 in every 965 e-mails contained a phishing attack. The number of spear-phishing attacks increased by 8%, with the average duration of campaigns reaching 9 days. In 2014, according to Symantec, over 40% of spear-phishing e-mails were directed at large organizations with more than 2,500 employees, and over 80% of large organizations reported they were targeted in spear-phishing campaigns. According to Verizon, more than two-thirds of cyberespionage incidents in 2014 involved spear-phishing (Verizon, 2015; Symantec, 2015).

To combat phishing, in January 2012, leading e-mail service providers, including Google, Microsoft, Yahoo, and AOL, as well as financial services companies such as PayPal, Bank of America, and others, joined together to form DMARC.org, an organization aimed at dramatically reducing e-mail address spoofing, in which attackers use real e-mail addresses to send phishing e-mails to victims who may be deceived because the e-mail appears to orginate from a source the receiver trusts. DMARC offers a method of authenticating the origin of the e-mail and allows receivers to quarantine, report, or reject messages that fail to pass its test. Yahoo and AOL have reported significant success against email fraud as a result of using DMARC, and in October 2015, Google announced that, effective as of June 2016, it was joining them in implementing a stricter version of DMARC, in which e-mail that fails DMARC authentication checks will be rejected (Vijayan, 2015).

HACKING, CYBERVANDALISM, AND HACKTIVISM

hacker
an individual who intends to gain unauthorized access to a computer system

cracker
within the hacking community, a term typically used to denote a hacker with criminal intent

cybervandalism
intentionally disrupting, defacing, or even destroying a site

hacktivism
cybervandalism and data theft for political purposes

A **hacker** is an individual who intends to gain unauthorized access to a computer system. Within the hacking community, the term **cracker** is typically used to denote a hacker with criminal intent, although in the public press, the terms hacker and cracker tend to be used interchangeably. Hackers and crackers gain unauthorized access by finding weaknesses in the security procedures of Web sites and computer systems, often taking advantage of various features of the Internet that make it an open system that is easy to use. In the past, hackers and crackers typically were computer aficionados excited by the challenge of breaking into corporate and government Web sites. Sometimes they were satisfied merely by breaking into the files of an e-commerce site. Today, hackers have malicious intentions to disrupt, deface, or destroy sites (**cybervandalism**) or to steal personal or corporate information they can use for financial gain (data breach).

Hacktivism adds a political twist. Hacktivists typically attack governments, organizations, and even individuals for political purposes, employing the tactics of cybervandalism, distributed denial of service attacks, data thefts, doxing (gathering and exposing personal information of public figures, originating from the term "documents" or "docx"), and more. LulzSec and Anonymous are two prominent hacktivist groups. In 2015, another hacktivist group called the Impact Team allegedly hacked the Ashley Madison Web site to call attention to its weak security, and after its owner Avid Life Media refused to shut it down as they demanded, the group released millions of sensitive customer records. See the *Insight on Society* case study, *The Ashley Madison Data Breach*, for a more in-depth look at implications of this high-profile hack.

white hats
"good" hackers who help organizations locate and fix security flaws

Groups of hackers called *tiger teams* are sometimes used by corporate security departments to test their own security measures. By hiring hackers to break into the system from the outside, the company can identify weaknesses in the computer system's armor. These "good hackers" became known as **white hats** because of their role in helping organizations locate and fix security flaws. White hats do their work under contract, with agreement from clients that they will not be prosecuted for their efforts to break in.

INSIGHT ON SOCIETY

THE ASHLEY MADISON DATA BREACH

As the Internet continues to permeate even the most intimate aspects of our lives, the stigma attached to online dating has largely disappeared. Online dating has grown into a $2.2 billion industry annually in the United States, led by companies like eHarmony, OKCupid, and Match. The online dating industry is one with excellent profit margins and growth potential, unlike many other Internet-based industries. These sites cater broadly to different demographics, and a number of smaller niche sites cater to people with more specific interests or lifestyles. While online dating has entered the mainstream, some of these niche sites are more controversial. Perhaps the most controversial site of all is Ashley Madison.

Based in Canada and launched in 2001 by its parent company, Avid Life Media, Ashley Madison is certainly not emblematic of the rest of the online dating industry at large, which encourages healthy, monogamous relationships. Ashley Madison specifically markets itself to people in marriages or committed relationships, which has earned the site a tawdry reputation. Users purchase credits rather than a monthly subscription, and then redeem the credits to participate in conversations with other members, which can be through messages or real-time chat. Ashley Madison also uses fictitious female profiles to balance out the ratio of men and women on the site, which skews dramatically towards men. Women are also not charged money to create a profile on the site, nor are they charged to send or receive messages, while men are charged for both.

The perception of secrecy is critical for prospective users of Ashley Madison, many of whom undoubtedly want to cheat and get away with it without anyone knowing. But in 2015, the veil of secrecy for the site's millions of members came crashing down. The site was hacked by a group known as The Impact Team, which stated that its motivations were to harm the site and its unethical business model, as well as to protest the site's use of a $19 data deletion fee for users seeking to close their accounts. The Impact Team stated that after creating a plan to make an undetectable breach, they discovered they were easily able to access the entire cache of company data. They released the data in two batches of 10 and 12 gigabytes, and the data is now easily searchable on the Web. Names, street addresses, and dates of birth were all stolen and made public, as well as interests and other personal information. They also stole company documents, including the e-mails of CEO Noel Biderman, many of which caused further damage to the company's shattered reputation. For example, Biderman's e-mails revealed that the CTO of Ashley Madison, Raja Bhatia, had hacked a competitor's database, revealing key security flaws (perhaps he should have been paying more attention to his own company's security systems). Partial credit card information of Ashley Madison users was also leaked, but not enough for identity thieves to use.

Demographic information gleaned from the data dump shows that of the site's 36 million users, 31 million were males, and only 10 million of those were actively involved in site features like chatting with other members. The other 5 million profiles were female, but not even 2,500 of those were involved in chats with other users, suggesting that fake female profiles were the overwhelming majority of female profiles on the site. A full third of the accounts on the site were created with dummy e-mail addresses. North Americans had the highest number of accounts as a percentage of population, with the United States coming in

(continued)

at 5.1%. E-mail addresses associated with government accounts were well-represented, as were big banks, large tech companies, and other high-powered industries. This stands in stark demographic contrast to a service like Tinder, which consists of much younger members; Ashley Madison users tended to be more established financially and willing to pay for what they perceived to be a discreet and upscale service.

How could a site which advertises the ability to discreetly have an affair allow its data to be breached and stolen so easily? Security experts reviewing Ashley Madison's setup claimed that the site lacked even simplistic security measures. For example, all of the data belonging to users who paid the $19 data deletion fee persisted on Ashley Madison servers and was obtained in the hack. Additionally, none of the data was encrypted. Encryption would have incurred hefty additional expense for the company, but it might have saved it considerable embarrassment during a breach like this one.

Most data breaches allow criminals to engage in identity theft and other types of online fraud. But in this case, the Ashley Madison hack has even more significant ramifications on the personal lives of users on the site. There are already multiple reported incidents of suicides committed by former users, and a handful of notable public figures have been publicly embarrassed by the release of their profile data. The hack has the potential to ruin the marriages and personal lives of thousands of people. Of course, one could argue that by creating a profile on a Web site explicitly designed to help people cheat on their spouses and significant others, Ashley Madison's users don't have justification to be upset. But these people were still the victims of a crime and an invasion of privacy that

goes beyond typical data breaches. Spammers have used the now-public data to extort users, demanding Bitcoin in exchange for silence and threatening to share Ashley Madison data with users' families and social media contacts. Ashley Madison can expect a barrage of lawsuits alleging negligence and personal damages. If the company fails to show that it did enough to protect its customers' data, it's likely to be defeated soundly in court.

As a result of the hack, Biderman quickly stepped down from his post as CEO. The company then offered a reward of over $350,000 for information about The Impact Team and its members, though there are no credible leads as of this writing. Going forward, the revelations about fake profiles, impending lawsuits, and overall negative coverage of the breach will likely derail plans for growth. Ashley Madison has already struggled to market its business and raise funds in the past, despite its very solid financial profile. Ashley Madison earned $115.5 million in revenue in 2014 along with $55 million in profits, significant increases over figures from the previous year. The company was growing so fast that Biderman had started investigating launching an IPO in England to fuel its expansion. Although Ashley Madison had been highly profitable, investors and advertisers have unsurprisingly balked at the association with adultery. After the breach, future investments are likely to be much more difficult to come by, and thanks to a hack made possible by its nonexistent security procedures, the site may quickly find profits difficult to come by as well. Ashley Madison's business model was dependent on its users trusting in the site's discretion and ability to keep their accounts a secret; for that reason, they may be particularly susceptible to fallout from a data breach of this magnitude.

SOURCES: "Why the Ashley Madison Hack Is Different & Dangerous," by Saket Modi, Etsmallbiz.com, September 23, 2015; "What to Know About the Ashley Madison Hack," by Robert Hackett, Fortune, August 26, 2015; "Ashley Madison Leak Reveals Its Ex-CTO Hacked Competing Site," by Kim Zetter, Wired, August 24, 2015; "Ashley Madison Hack Exposes (Wait for It) a Lousy Business," by Julia Greenberg, Wired, August 21, 2015; "Ashley Madison Hack: 6 Charts That Show Who Uses the Infidelity Website," by Zachary Davies Boren, Independent.co.uk, August 21, 2015; "Ashley Madison Hackers Speak Out: 'Nobody Was Watching', by Joseph Cox, Motherboard.vice.com, August 21, 2015; "Ashley Madison Hack: Your Questions Answered," by Alex Hern, theguardian.com, August 20, 2015; "The Ashley Madison Hack, Explained," by Timothy B. Lee, Vox.com, August 19, 2015; "Who Is Ashley Madison," by Paul R. LaMonica, CNN Money, July 20, 2015; "Even in the Tinder Era, Adultery Site Ashley Madison Keeps Making Money Hand Over Fist," by Adam Tanner, Forbes, January 21, 2015.

In contrast, **black hats** are hackers who engage in the same kinds of activities but without pay or any buy-in from the targeted organization, and with the intention of causing harm. They break into Web sites and reveal the confidential or proprietary information they find. These hackers believe strongly that information should be free, so sharing previously secret information is part of their mission.

Somewhere in the middle are the **grey hats**, hackers who believe they are pursuing some greater good by breaking in and revealing system flaws. Grey hats discover weaknesses in a system's security, and then publish the weakness without disrupting the site or attempting to profit from their finds. Their only reward is the prestige of discovering the weakness. Grey hat actions are suspect, however, especially when the hackers reveal security flaws that make it easier for other criminals to gain access to a system.

black hats

hackers who act with the intention of causing harm

grey hats

hackers who believe they are pursuing some greater good by breaking in and revealing system flaws

DATA BREACHES

A **data breach** occurs whenever organizations lose control over corporate information to outsiders. According to Symantec, the total number of data breaches in 2014 grew by over 20% compared to 2013 (Symantec, 2015). The number of data breaches tracked by the Identity Theft Resource Center in the United States reached an all-time high of 783 (Dell Inc., 2015). Although fewer "mega" breaches occurred in 2014, data breaches exposed an estimated 348 million U.S. identities. Hackers are the leading cause of data breaches and were responsible for almost 50% of the data breaches that occurred in 2014 and 75% of the identities disposed. Accidental disclosures were the second most common cause, accounting for 22% of breaches, while the theft or loss of a computer or hard drive ranked third, causing 21% of breaches. Among the high profile breaches that occurred in 2014 were those affecting eBay, which announced a breach involving user names, passwords, phone numbers, and addresses in May 2014 affecting 145 million of its users, JPMorgan Chase, which exposed 76 million records, and Home Depot, which announced in September 2014 that data from 56 million cards had been taken in a months-long security breach. In November 2014, in another very high-profile data breach, hackers infiltrated Sony's servers and exposed a wide range of data, including the contents of e-mails and internal documents related to Sony employees and actors. In 2015, the trend has continued, with numerous high-profile data breaches, including several against government agencies such as the Office of Personnel Management and the Internal Revenue Service, as well as others against health-care insurers such as Anthem, retailers such as CVS and Walgreens, and the credit rating agency Experian.

data breach

occurs when an organization loses control over its information to outsiders

CREDIT CARD FRAUD/THEFT

Theft of credit card data is one of the most feared occurrences on the Internet. Fear that credit card information will be stolen prevents users from making online purchases in many cases. Interestingly, this fear appears to be largely unfounded. Incidences of stolen credit card information are actually much lower than users think, around 0.9% of all online card transactions (CyberSource, 2015). Online merchants use a variety of techniques to combat credit card fraud, including using automated fraud detection tools, manually reviewing orders, and rejection of suspect orders.

In addition, federal law limits the liability of individuals to $50 for a stolen credit card. For amounts more than $50, the credit card company generally pays the amount, although in some cases, the merchant may be held liable if it failed to verify the account or consult published lists of invalid cards. Banks recoup the cost of credit card fraud by charging higher interest rates on unpaid balances, and by merchants who raise prices to cover the losses. In 2015, the U.S. credit card system is in the midst of a shift to EMV credit cards, also known as smart cards or chip cards. Already widely used in Europe, EMV credit cards have a computer chip instead of a magnetic strip that can be easily copied by hackers and sold as dump data (see Table 5.2). While EMV technology cannot prevent data breaches from occurring, the hope is that it will make it harder for criminals to profit from stolen cards.

In the past, the most common cause of credit card fraud was a lost or stolen card that was used by someone else, followed by employee theft of customer numbers and stolen identities (criminals applying for credit cards using false identities). Today, the most frequent cause of stolen cards and card information is the systematic hacking and looting of a corporate server where the information on millions of credit card purchases is stored. For instance, in 2010, Albert Gonzalez was sentenced to 20 years in prison for organizing one of the largest thefts of credit card numbers in American history. Along with several Russian co-conspirators, Gonzalez broke into the central computer systems of TJX, BJ's, Barnes & Noble, and other companies, stealing over 160 million card numbers and costing these firms over $200 million in losses (Fox and Botelho, 2013).

International orders have a much higher risk of being fraudulent, with fraud losses twice that of domestic orders. If an international customer places an order and then later disputes it, online merchants often have no way to verify that the package was actually delivered and that the credit card holder is the person who placed the order. As a result, most online merchants will not process international orders.

A central security issue of e-commerce is the difficulty of establishing the customer's identity. Currently there is no technology that can identify a person with absolute certainty. Until a customer's identity can be guaranteed, online companies are at a higher risk of loss than traditional offline companies. The federal government has attempted to address this issue through the Electronic Signatures in Global and National Commerce Act (the "E-Sign" law), which gives digital signatures the same authority as hand-written signatures in commerce. This law also intended to make digital signatures more commonplace and easier to use. Although the use of e-signatures is still uncommon in the B2C retail e-commerce arena, many businesses are starting to implement e-signature solutions, particularly for B2B contracting, financial services, insurance, health care, and government and professional services. DocuSign, Adobe eSign, RightSignature, and Silanis e-SignLive are currently among the most widely adopted e-signature solutions. They use a variety of techniques, such as remote user identification through third-party databases or personal information verification such as a photo of a driver's license; multi-factor user authentication methods (user ID and password, e-mail address verification, secret question and answer); and public/private key encryption to create a digital signature and embedded audit trail that can be used to verify the e-signature's integrity (Silanis Technology, 2014). Mobile e-signature solutions are also beginning to be adopted by early movers (DocuSign, 2015).

IDENTITY FRAUD

Identity fraud involves the unauthorized use of another person's personal data, such as social security, driver's license, and/or credit card numbers, as well as user names and passwords, for illegal financial benefit. Criminals can use such data to obtain loans, purchase merchandise, or obtain other services, such as mobile phone or other utility services. Cybercriminals employ many of the techniques described previously, such as spyware, phishing, data breaches, and credit card theft, for the purpose of identity fraud. Data breaches, in particular, often lead to identity fraud: in 2013, one in three data breach notification recipients later became a victim.

Identity fraud is a significant problem in the United States. In 2014, according to Javelin Strategy & Research, 12.7 million U.S. consumers suffered identity fraud. The total dollar losses as a result of identity fraud were approximately $16 billion (Javelin Research & Strategy, 2015).

> **identity fraud**
> involves the unauthorized use of another person's personal data for illegal financial benefit

SPOOFING, PHARMING, AND SPAM (JUNK) WEB SITES

Spoofing involves attempting to hide a true identity by using someone else's e-mail or IP address. For instance, a spoofed e-mail will have a forged sender e-mail address designed to mislead the receiver about who sent the e-mail. IP spoofing involves the creation of TCP/IP packets that use someone else's source IP address, indicating that the packets are coming from a trusted host. Most current routers and firewalls can offer protection against IP spoofing. Spoofing a Web site sometimes involves **pharming**, automatically redirecting a Web link to an address different from the intended one, with the site masquerading as the intended destination. Links that are designed to lead to one site can be reset to send users to a totally unrelated site—one that benefits the hacker.

Although spoofing and pharming do not directly damage files or network servers, they threaten the integrity of a site. For example, if hackers redirect customers to a fake Web site that looks almost exactly like the true site, they can then collect and process orders, effectively stealing business from the true site. Or, if the intent is to disrupt rather than steal, hackers can alter orders—inflating them or changing products ordered—and then send them on to the true site for processing and delivery. Customers become dissatisfied with the improper order shipment, and the company may have huge inventory fluctuations that impact its operations.

In addition to threatening integrity, spoofing also threatens authenticity by making it difficult to discern the true sender of a message. Clever hackers can make it almost impossible to distinguish between a true and a fake identity or Web address.

> **spoofing**
> involves attempting to hide a true identity by using someone else's e-mail or IP address

> **pharming**
> automatically redirecting a Web link to an address different from the intended one, with the site masquerading as the intended destination

Spam (junk) Web sites (also sometimes referred to as *link farms*) are a little different. These are sites that promise to offer some product or service, but in fact are just a collection of advertisements for other sites, some of which contain malicious code. For instance, you may search for "[name of town] weather," and then click on a link that promises your local weather, but then discover that all the site does is display ads for weather-related products or other Web sites. Junk or spam Web sites typically appear on search results, and do not involve e-mail. These sites cloak their identities by using domain names similar to legitimate firm names, and redirect traffic to known spammer-redirection domains such as topsearch10.com.

> **spam (junk) Web sites**
> also referred to as link farms; promise to offer products or services, but in fact are just collections of advertisements

SNIFFING AND MAN-IN-THE-MIDDLE ATTACKS

sniffer
a type of eavesdropping program that monitors information traveling over a network

A **sniffer** is a type of eavesdropping program that monitors information traveling over a network. When used legitimately, sniffers can help identify potential network trouble-spots, but when used for criminal purposes, they can be damaging and very difficult to detect. Sniffers enable hackers to steal proprietary information from anywhere on a network, including passwords, e-mail messages, company files, and confidential reports. For instance, in 2013, five hackers were charged in another worldwide hacking scheme that targeted the corporate networks of retail chains such as 7-Eleven and the French retailer Carrefour SA, using sniffer programs to steal more than 160 million credit card numbers (Voreacos, 2013).

E-mail wiretaps are a variation on the sniffing threat. An e-mail wiretap is a method for recording or journaling e-mail traffic generally at the mail server level from any individual. E-mail wiretaps are used by employers to track employee messages, and by government agencies to surveil individuals or groups. E-mail wiretaps can be installed on servers and client computers. The USA PATRIOT Act permits the FBI to compel ISPs to install a black box on their mail servers that can impound the e-mail of a single person or group of persons for later analysis. In the case of American citizens communicating with other citizens, an FBI agent or government lawyer need only certify to a judge on the secret 11-member U.S. Foreign Intelligence Surveillance Court (FISC) that the information sought is relevant to an ongoing criminal investigation to get permission to install the program. Judges have no discretion. They must approve wiretaps based on government agents' unsubstantiated assertions. In the case of suspected terrorist activity, law enforcement does not have to inform a court prior to installing a wire or e-mail tap. A 2007 amendment to the 1978 Foreign Intelligence Surveillance Act, known as FISA, provided new powers to the National Security Agency to monitor international e-mail and telephone communications where one person is in the United States, and where the purpose of such interception is to collect foreign intelligence (Foreign Intelligence Surveillance Act of 1978; Protect America Act of 2007). The FISA Amendments Reauthorization Act of 2012 extends the provisions of FISA for five more years, until 2017. NSA's XKeyscore program, revealed by Edward Snowden, is a form of "wiretap" that allows NSA analysts to search through vast databases containing not only e-mail, but online chats, and browsing histories of millions of individuals (Wills, 2013).

The Communications Assistance for Law Enforcement Act (CALEA) requires all communications carriers (including ISPs) to provide near-instant access to law enforcement agencies to their message traffic. Many Internet services (such as Facebook and LinkedIn) that have built-in ISP services technically are not covered by CALEA. One can only assume these non-ISP e-mail operators cooperate with law enforcement. Unlike the past where wiretaps required many hours to physically tap into phone lines, in today's digital phone systems, taps are arranged in a few minutes by the large carriers at their expense.

man-in-the middle (MitM) attack
attack in which the attacker is able to intercept communications between two parties who believe they are directly communicating with one another, when in fact the attacker is controlling the communications

A **man-in-the-middle (MitM) attack** also involves eavesdropping but is more active than a sniffing attack, which typically involves passive monitoring. In a MitM attack, the attacker is able to intercept communications between two parties who believe they are directly communicating with one another, when in fact the attacker is controlling the communications.

DENIAL OF SERVICE (DOS) AND DISTRIBUTED DENIAL OF SERVICE (DDOS) ATTACKS

In a **Denial of Service (DoS) attack**, hackers flood a Web site with useless pings or page requests that inundate and overwhelm the site's Web servers. Increasingly, DoS attacks involve the use of bot networks and so-called "distributed attacks" built from thousands of compromised client computers. DoS attacks typically cause a Web site to shut down, making it impossible for users to access the site. For busy e-commerce sites, these attacks are costly; while the site is shut down, customers cannot make purchases. And the longer a site is shut down, the more damage is done to a site's reputation. Although such attacks do not destroy information or access restricted areas of the server, they can destroy a firm's online business. Often, DoS attacks are accompanied by attempts at blackmailing site owners to pay tens or hundreds of thousands of dollars to the hackers in return for stopping the DoS attack.

A **Distributed Denial of Service (DDoS) attack** uses hundreds or even thousands of computers to attack the target network from numerous launch points. DoS and DDoS attacks are threats to a system's operation because they can shut it down indefinitely. Major Web sites have experienced such attacks, making the companies aware of their vulnerability and the need to continually introduce new measures to prevent future attacks. According to Akamai, the number of DDoS attacks in 2nd quarter of 2015 increased by over 130% compared to same period in 2014. One new technique increasingly being used targets insecure routers and other home devices such as webcams that use UPnP (Universal Plug and Play) to amplify the attacks (Akamai, 2015). In another measure of the prevalence of DDoS attacks, in an Arbor Networks survey of 287 ISP and network operators around the world, respondents noted that DDoS attacks against customers constituted the number one operational threat, with nearly 50% of respondents experiencing DDoS attacks during the survey period. Arbor Networks also reported that the size of reported DDoS attacks in terms of bandwidth consumed continued to increase in 2014, with attackers using reflection/amplification techniques to create attacks reaching 400 Gpbs (Arbor Networks, 2015). Another trend is DDoS smokescreening, in which attackers use DDoS as a distraction while they also insert malware or viruses or steal data. A 2015 survey of 760 security and IT professionals in companies in North America and Europe, the Middle East, and Africa conducted by Neustar found that 36% reported that a virus or malware was installed as a result of the DDoS attack, while nearly 40% also experienced a theft of data or funds (Neustar, 2015). And not surprisingly, now that mobile data connections have become faster and more stable, hackers are beginning to harness mobile devices for mobile-based DDoS attacks. A recent attack originating from China used malicious ads loaded inside mobile apps and mobile browesrs as the attack mechanism (Majkowski, 2015).

China also appears to have been behind another major DDoS attack in March 2015 against the software development platform GitHub, aimed specifically at two Chinese anti-censorship projects hosted on the platform. Researchers say the attack was an example of a new tool they have nicknamed the Great Cannon. Although originally thought to be part of China's Great Firewall censorship system, further investigation revealed that the Great Cannon is a separate distinct offensive system that is co-

Denial of Service (DoS) attack
flooding a Web site with useless traffic to inundate and overwhelm the network

Distributed Denial of Service (DDoS) attack
using numerous computers to attack the target network from numerous launch points

located with the Great Firewall. The Great Cannon enables hackers to hijack traffic to individual IP addresses and uses a man-in-the-middle attack to replace unencrypted content between a Web server and the user with malicious Javascript that would load the two GitHub project pages every two seconds (Kirk, 2015b; Essers, 2015).

INSIDER ATTACKS

We tend to think of security threats to a business as originating outside the organization. In fact, the largest financial threats to business institutions come not from robberies but from embezzlement by insiders. Bank employees steal far more money than bank robbers. The same is true for e-commerce sites. Some of the largest disruptions to service, destruction to sites, and diversion of customer credit data and personal information have come from insiders—once trusted employees. Employees have access to privileged information, and, in the presence of sloppy internal security procedures, they are often able to roam throughout an organization's systems without leaving a trace. Research from Carnegie Mellon University documents the significant damage insiders have done to both private and public organizations (Software Engineering Institute, 2012). Survey results also indicate that insiders are more likely to be the source of cyberattacks than outsiders, and to cause more damage to an organization than external attacks (PWC, 2015). In some instances, the insider might not have criminal intent, but inadvertently exposes data that can then be exploited by others. For instance, a Ponemon Institute study found that negligent insiders are a top cause of data breaches (Ponemon Institute, 2015c). Another study based on an analysis of the behavior of 10 million users during the second quarter of 2015 estimated that 1% of employees are responsible for 75% of cloud-related enterprise security risk, by reusing or sending out plain-text passwords, indiscriminately sharing fiiles, using risky applications, or accidentally downloading malware or clicking phishing links (Korolov, 2015).

POORLY DESIGNED SOFTWARE

Many security threats prey on poorly designed software, sometimes in the operating system and sometimes in the application software, including browsers. The increase in complexity and size of software programs, coupled with demands for timely delivery to markets, has contributed to an increase in software flaws or vulnerabilities that hackers can exploit. For instance, **SQL injection attacks** take advantage of vulnerabilities in poorly coded Web application software that fails to properly validate or filter data entered by a user on a Web page to introduce malicious program code into a company's systems and networks. An attacker can use this input validation error to send a rogue SQL query to the underlying database to access the database, plant malicious code, or access other systems on the network. Large Web applications have hundreds of places for inputting user data, each of which creates an opportunity for an SQL injection attack. A large number of Web-facing applications are believed to have SQL injection vulnerabilities, and tools are available for hackers to check Web applications for these vulnerabilities.

Each year, security firms identify thousands of software vulnerabilities in Internet browsers, PC, Macintosh, and Linux software, as well as mobile device operating systems and applications. According to Microsoft, vulnerability disclosures across the

SQL injection attack
takes advantage of poorly coded Web application software that fails to properly validate or filter data entered by a user on a Web page

software industry in the second half of 2014 increased by 56% compared to the same period in 2013. Over 4,500 vulnerabilities were identified, the highest number in any six-month period in the history of the Common Vulnerabilities and Exposures system that was originally launched in 1999 (Microsoft, 2015). Browser vulnerabilities in particular are a popular target, as well as browser plug-ins such as for Adobe Reader. A **zero-day vulnerability** is one that has been previously unreported and for which no patch yet exists. In 2014, 25 zero-day vulnerabilities were reported, up from 14 in 2013 (Kirk, 2015). The trend continues in 2015. For instance, four zero-day vulnerabilities involving Microsoft's Internet Explorer were disclosed in a single day in July 2015. The very design of the personal computer includes many open communication ports that can be used, and indeed are designed to be used, by external computers to send and receive messages. Ports that are frequently attacked include TCP port 445 (Microsoft-DS), port 80 (WWW/HTTP), and 443 (SSL/HTTPS). Given their complexity and design objectives, all operating systems and application software, including Linux and Macintosh, have vulnerabilities.

zero-day vulnerability
software vulnerability that has been previously unreported and for which no patch yet exists

In April 2014, a flaw in the OpenSSL encryption system, used by millions of Web sites, known as the **Heartbleed bug**, was discovered (see Section 5.3 for a further discussion of SSL). The vulnerability allowed hackers to decrypt an SSL session and discover user names, passwords, and other user data, by using OpenSSL in combination with a communications protocol called the RFC6520 heartbeat that helps a remote user remain in touch after connecting with a Web site server. In the process a small chunk of the server's memory content can leak out (hence the name heartbleed), potentially large enough to hold a password or encryption key that would allow a hacker to exploit the server further. The Heartbleed bug also affected over 1,300 Android apps (Trend Micro, 2014). In September 2014, another vulnerability known as ShellShock or BashBug that affected most versions of Linux and Unix, as well as Mac OS X, was revealed. ShellShock enabled attackers to use CGI (see Chapter 4) to add malicious commands (Symantec, 2015). In March 2015, researchers announced that they had discovered a new SSL/TLS vulnerability that they named FREAK (Factoring Attack on RSA-Export Keys) that allows man-in-the-middle attacks that enable the interception and decryption of encrypted communications between clients and servers, which would then allow the attackers to steal passwords and other personal information. More than one-third of encrypted Web sites were reportedly open to attack via this security vulnerability, including those for the White House, the FBI, and the National Security Agency (Vaughan-Nichols, 2015).

Heartbleed bug
flaw in OpenSSL encryption system that allowed hackers to decrypt an SSL session and discover user names, passwords, and other user data

SOCIAL NETWORK SECURITY ISSUES

Social networks like Facebook, Twitter, LinkedIn, Pinterest, and Tumblr provide a rich and rewarding environment for hackers. Viruses, site takeovers, identity fraud, malware-loaded apps, click hijacking, phishing, and spam are all found on social networks. According to Symantec, the most common type of scam on social media sites in 2014 were manual sharing scams, where victims unwittingly shared videos, stories, and pictures that included links to malicious sites. Fake offerings that invite victims to join a fake event or group with incentives such as free gift cards and that require a user to share his or her information with the attacker were another common technique. Other techniques include fake Like buttons that, when clicked, install malware and post updates to the user's Newsfeed, further spreading the attack, and fake apps (Symantec, 2015). By sneaking in among our friends, hackers can masquerade as friends and dupe users into scams.

Social network firms have thus far been relatively poor policemen because they have failed to aggressively weed out accounts that send visitors to malware sites (unlike Google, which maintains a list of known malware sites and patrols its search results looking for links to malware sites). Social networks are open: anyone can set up a personal page, even criminals. Most attacks are social engineering attacks that tempt visitors to click on links that sound reasonable. Social apps downloaded from either the social network or a foreign site are not certified by the social network to be clean of malware. It's "clicker beware."

MOBILE PLATFORM SECURITY ISSUES

The explosion in mobile devices has broadened opportunities for hackers. Mobile users are filling their devices with personal and financial information, and using them to conduct an increasing number of transactions, from retail purchases to mobile banking, making them excellent targets for hackers. In general, mobile devices face all the same risks as any Internet device as well as some new risks associated with wireless network security. For instance, public Wi-Fi networks that are not secured are very susceptible to hacking. While most PC users are aware their computers and Web sites may be hacked and contain malware, most cell phone users believe their cell phone is as secure as a traditional landline phone. As with social network members, mobile users are prone to think they are in a shared, trustworthy environment.

Mobile cell phone malware (sometimes referred to as malicious mobile apps (MMAs) or rogue mobile apps) was developed as early as 2004 with Cabir, a Bluetooth worm affecting Symbian operating systems (Nokia phones) and causing the phone to continuously seek out other Bluetooth-enabled devices, quickly draining the battery. The iKee.B worm, first discovered in 2009, only two years after the iPhone was introduced, infected jailbroken iPhones, turning the phones into botnet-controlled devices. An iPhone in Europe could be hacked by an iPhone in the United States, and all its private data sent to a server in Poland. IKee.B established the feasibility of cell phone botnets.

By the end of 2014, Symantec had identified more than 1 million apps that it classified as malware, and it expects the growth in mobile malware to continue in 2015 and become more aggressive in targeting mobile payment and mobile banking applications. The majority of mobile malware still targets the Android platform. For instance, Symantec has already discovered Android malware that can intercept text messages with bank authentication codes and forward them to attackers, as well as fake versions of legitimate mobile banking applications. However, the Apple iPhone platform is beginning to be increasingly targeted as well, and in 2015, Chinese hackers infected Xcode, Apple's integrated suite of development tools for creating iOS appps, and as a result, unsuspecting Chinese iOS developers unknowingly created thousands of apps with the malicious code (Keizer, 2015). And it is not just rogue applications that are dangerous, but also popular legitimate applications that simply have little protection from hackers. For instance, in 2014, security researchers revealed that the Starbucks mobile app, the most used mobile payment app in the United States, was storing user names, e-mail addresses, and passwords in clear text, in such a way that anyone with access to the phone could see the passwords and user names by connecting the phone to a computer. According to researchers, Starbucks erred in emphasizing convenience and ease of use in the design of the app over security concerns (Schuman, 2014).

Vishing attacks target gullible cell phone users with verbal messages to call a certain number and, for example, donate money to starving children in Haiti. *Smishing* attacks exploit SMS/text messages. Compromised text messages can contain e-mail and Web site addresses that can lead the innocent user to a malware site. Criminal SMS spoofing services have emerged, which conceal the cybercriminal's true phone number, replacing it with a false alpha-numeric name. SMS spoofing can also be used by cybercriminals to lure mobile users to a malicious Web site by sending a text that appears to be from a legitimate organization in the From field, and suggesting the receiver click on a malicious URL hyperlink to update an account or obtain a gift card. A small number of downloaded apps from app stores have also contained malware. *Madware*—innocent-looking apps that contain adware that launches pop-up ads and text messages on your mobile device—is also becoming an increasing problem. An examination of 2.3 million apps in 2014 that Symantec classified as grayware (programs that do not contain viruses and are not overtly malicious, but which can be annoying or harmful) found that 1.3 million of those ads were madware (Symantec, 2015).

Read the *Insight on Technology* case, *Think Your Smartphone Is Secure?* for a further discussion of some of the issues surrounding smartphone security.

CLOUD SECURITY ISSUES

The move of so many Internet services into the cloud also raises security risks. From an infrastructure standpoint, DDoS attacks threaten the availability of cloud services on which more and more companies are relying. According to Alert Logic, which analyzed 1 billion security events in the IT environments of more than 3,000 enterprise customers, attacks against cloud-based services and applications increased by 45% in 2014. Alert Logic also found a a 36% increase in suspicious activity in cloud environment, such as attempts to scan the infrastructure (Alert Logic, 2015). Safeguarding data being maintained in a public cloud environment is also a major concern. For example, researchers identified several ways data could be accessed without authorization on Dropbox, which offers a popular cloud file-sharing service. In 2014, compromising photos of as many as 100 celebrities such as Jennifer Lawrence were posted online, reportedly stolen from Apple's iCloud. Although initially it was thought that the breach was made possible by a vulnerability in Apple's Find My iPhone API, it instead apparently resulted from lower-tech phishing attacks that yielded passwords that could be used to connect to iCloud. A similar hack into writer Mat Honan's Apple iCloud account using social engineering tactics in 2012 allowed the hackers to wipe everything from his Mac computer, iPhone, and iPad, which were linked to the cloud service, as well as take over his Twitter and Gmail accounts (Honan, 2012). These

INSIGHT ON TECHNOLOGY

THINK YOUR SMARTPHONE IS SECURE?

So far, there have been few publicly identified, large-scale, smartphone security breaches, but just because it hasn't happened yet doesn't mean it won't. With about 190 million smartphone users in the United States, business firms increasingly switching their employees to the mobile platform, and consumers using their phones for financial transactions and even paying bills, the size and richness of the smartphone target for hackers is growing.

Many users believe their smartphones are unlikely to be hacked because Apple and Google are protecting them from malware, and that Verizon and AT&T can keep the cell phone network secure just as they do the land-line phone system. Telephone systems are "closed" and therefore not subject to the kinds of attacks that occur on the open Internet.

But hackers can do to a smartphone just about anything they can do to any Internet device: request malicious files without user intervention, delete files, transmit files, install programs running in the background that can monitor user actions, and potentially convert the smartphone into a robot that can be used in a botnet to send e-mail and text messages to anyone.

Apps are an emerging avenue for potential security breaches. Apple and Google now offer over 3 million apps collectively. Apple claims that it examines each and every app to ensure that it plays by Apple's App Store rules, but risks remain. Most of the known cases that have occurred thus far have involved jailbroken phones. The first iPhone app confirmed to have embedded malware made it past Apple into the App Store in July 2012. However, security company Kaspersky expects the iPhone to face an onslaught of malware going forward. Apple's app rules make some user information available to all apps by default, including the user's GPS position and name. However, a rogue app could easily do much more. Nicolas Seriot, a Swiss researcher, built a test app called SpyPhone that was capable of tracking users and all their activities, then transmitting this data to remote servers, all without user knowledge. The app harvested geolocation data, passwords, address book entries, and e-mail account information. Apple removed the app once it was identified. In 2014, malware known as WireLurker attacked iPhone and iPad users in China via the Mac OS X operating system, representing the first attack on iPhones that were not jailbroken. Apple quickly moved to remove affected apps, but the attack was a warning sign that the iOS system is not likely to be a malware-free environment going forward. That these apps were initially accepted by the App Store staff of reviewers suggests Apple cannot effectively review new apps prior to their use. In addition, companies are increasingly using enterprising provisioning, which allows them to distribute apps to employees without Apple's review so long as the apps are signed with an Apple-issued enterprise certificate. Attackers have been able to hijack this app distribution mechanism to sideload apps on non-jailbroken devices, as demonstrated by both the WireLurker attack noted above and another threat known as XAgent, which can collect data from compromised devices including SMS messages, contacts, photos, and GPS locations, and which can also remotely activate voice recording on compromised devices. And thanks to Apple's walled garden approach to the iOS platform, third parties are not able to develop services to protect Apple devices as easily as they may be able to with Android.

But Android's security future appears just as murky. The amount of malware on the Android platform has skyrocketed over the past few years, with the number of spyware apps quadrupling from its level just a few years ago. According to the Pulse Secure Mobile Threat Center, 97% of all mobile malware in 2014 targeted Android devices, and according to Verizon, more than 5 billion downloaded Android apps are vulnerable to remote attacks, particularly via a vulnerability known as JavaScript-Binding-Over-HTTP (JBOH), which enables an attacker to execute code remotely on Android devices that have affected apps. In part this is due to the fact that security on that platform is much less under the control of Google because it employs an "open" app model compared to Apple's "walled garden" approach, which makes security flaws easier to detect. In addition, in the past, Google did not review Android apps, instead relying on user input and technical hurdles to limit malware. However, in 2013, in response to the growing malware problem, Google launched a universal app-scanning system that instantly checks each app for malicious code at the device level.

Android apps can use any personal information found on a phone but they must also inform the user what each app is capable of doing, and what personal data it requires. Google removes any apps that break its rules against malicious activity. Google can also perform a remote wipe of offending apps from all Droid phones without user intervention. In one incident, Google pulled down dozens of mobile banking apps made by a developer called 09Droid. The apps claimed to give users access to their accounts at many banks throughout the world. In fact, the apps were unable to connect users to any bank, and were removed before they could do much harm. Google does take preventive steps to reduce malware apps such as requiring developers to register and be approved by Google before they can distribute apps through Google Play.

Beyond the threat of rogue apps, smartphones of all stripes are susceptible to browser-based malware that takes advantage of vulnerabilities in all browsers. In addition, most smartphones, including the iPhone, permit the manufacturers to remotely download configuration files to update operating systems and security protections. Unfortunately, flaws in the public key encryption procedures that permit remote server access to iPhones have been discovered, raising further questions about the security of such operations. Attackers have also developed methods of hijacking phones using weaknesses in SIM cards. There are at least 500 million vulnerable SIM cards in use today, and the defects allow hackers to obtain the encryption key that guards users' personal information, granting them nearly complete access over the phone in the process.

In 2015, documents obtained by Edward Snowden indicated that the United States and Great Britain had hacked into Gemalto, a manufacturer of SIM cards, and obtained encryption keys that allowed them to surveil mobile phone users across the globe. The investigation is still ongoing, but suddenly, our smartphones and tablets don't seem quite as safe anymore.

SOURCES: "How Many Smartphone Users Are Officially Addicted?" by eMarketer.Inc, July 31, 2015; "Android Accounts for 97 Percent of All Mobile Malware," by Carly Page, Theinquirer.net, June 25, 2015; "Digital-Security Firm Gemalto Probes Alleged U.S., U.K. Hack," by Amir Mizroch and Lisa Fleisher, *Wall Street Journal*, February 20, 2015; "US and UK Accused of Hacking SIM Card Firm to Steal Codes," Bbc.com, February 20, 2015; "XAgent iPhone Malware Attack Steals Data Without Jailbreaking," by Jeff Gamet, Macobserver.com, February 5, 2015; "2015 Data Breach Investigations Report," by Verizon, 2015; "Enterprise Mobile Security: Managing App Sideloading Threats on iOs," Lookout.com, 2015; "Apple Blocks Apps Infected with WireLurker Malware Targeting iPhones and iPads," by Carly Page, Theinquirer.net, November 6, 2014; "NSA Secretly Broke Smartphone Security," by Cory Doctorow, Boingboing.com, September 8, 2013; "Obama Administration Had Restrictions on NSA Reversed in 2011," by Ellen Nakashima, September 7, 2013; "How Google Just Quietly Made Your Android Phone More Secure," by JR Raphael, *Computerworld*, July 26, 2013; "Crypto Flaw Makes Millions of Smartphones Susceptible to Hijacking," by Dan Goodin, ArsTechnica.com, July 22, 2013; "iPhone Malware: Spam App 'Find and Call' Invades App Store," by Zach Epstein, BGR.com, July 5, 2012.

incidents highlight the risks involved as devices, identities, and data become more and more interconnected in the cloud. A 2014 Ponemon Insititute study found that the majority of IT and IT security practitioners surveyed felt that the likelihood of a data breach increases due to the cloud, in part due to the fact that many organizations do not thoroughly examine cloud security before deploying cloud services (Ponemon Institute, 2014).

INTERNET OF THINGS SECURITY ISSUES

As you learned in Chapter 3, the Internet of Things (IoT) involves the use of the Internet to connect a wide variety of sensors, devices, and machines, and is powering the development of a multitude of smart connected things, such as home electronics (smart TVs, thermostats, home security systems, and more), connected cars, medical devices and industrial equipment that supports manufacturing, energy, transportation, and other industrial sectors. IoT raises a host of security issues that are in some ways similar to existing security issues, but even more challenging, given the need to deal with a wider range of devices, operating in a less controlled, global environment, and with an expanded range of attack. In a world of connected things, the devices, the data produced and used by the devices, and the systems and applications supported by those devices, can all potentially be attacked (IBM, 2015). **Table 5.5** takes a closer look at some of the unique security challenges posed by IoT identified by the Internet

TABLE 5.5	INTERNET OF THINGS SECURITY CHALLENGES
CHALLENGE	POSSIBLE IMPLICATIONS
Many IoT devices, such as sensors, are intended to be deployed on a much greater scale than traditional Internet-connected devices, creating a vast quantity of interconnected links that can be exploited.	Existing tools, methods, and strategies need to be developed to deal with this unprecedented scale.
Many instances of IoT consist of collections of identical devices that all have the same characteristics.	Magnifies the potential impact of a security vulnerability.
Many IoT devices are anticipated to have a much longer service life than typical equipment.	Devices may "outlive" manufacturer, leaving them without long-term support that creates persistent vulnerabilities.
Many IoT devices are intentionally designed without the ability to be upgraded, or the upgrade process is difficult.	Raises the possibility that vulnerable devices cannot or will not be fixed, leaving them perpetually vulnerable.
Many IoT devices do not provide the user with visibility into the workings of the device or the data being produced, nor alert the user when a security problem arises.	Users may believe an IoT device is functioning as intended when in fact, it may be performing in a malicious manner.
Some IoT devices, such as sensors, are unobtrusively embedded in the environment such that a user may not even be aware of the device.	Security breach might persist for a long time before being noticed.

Society (ISOC), a consortium of corporations, government agencies, and nonprofit organizations that monitors Internet policies and practices (Internet Society, 2015).

Already, alarming reports of hacked IoT devices are starting to pop up in the popular press. For example, in July 2015, researchers demonstrated the ability to hack into a Jeep Cherokee through its entertainment system, sending commands to the dashboard, steering, brakes, and transmission system from a remote laptop that turned the steering wheel, disabled the brakes, and shut down the engine (Greenberg, 2015). Fiat Chrysler Automobiles immediately issued a recall notice to fix the software vulnerability involved, but it is almost certain that such incidents will continue to occur, as auto manufacturers add more and more wireless "connected car" features to automobiles. Other reports have surfaced of wireless baby monitors being hacked, as well as medical devices such as hospital lab blood gas analyzers, radiology picture archive and communication systems, drug infusion pumps, and hospital x-ray systems (Storm, 2015a, 2015b).

5.3 TECHNOLOGY SOLUTIONS

At first glance, it might seem like there is not much that can be done about the onslaught of security breaches on the Internet. Reviewing the security threats in the previous section, it is clear that the threats to e-commerce are very real, potentially devastating for individuals, businesses, and entire nations, and likely to be increasing in intensity along with the growth in e-commerce. But in fact a great deal of progress has been made by private security firms, corporate and home users, network administrators, technology firms, and government agencies. There are two lines of defense: technology solutions and policy solutions. In this section, we consider some technology solutions, and in the following section, we look at some policy solutions that work.

The first line of defense against the wide variety of security threats to an e-commerce site is a set of tools that can make it difficult for outsiders to invade or destroy a site. **Figure 5.5** illustrates the major tools available to achieve site security.

PROTECTING INTERNET COMMUNICATIONS

Because e-commerce transactions must flow over the public Internet, and therefore involve thousands of routers and servers through which the transaction packets flow, security experts believe the greatest security threats occur at the level of Internet communications. This is very different from a private network where a dedicated communication line is established between two parties. A number of tools are available to protect the security of Internet communications, the most basic of which is message encryption.

ENCRYPTION

Encryption is the process of transforming plain text or data into **cipher text** that cannot be read by anyone other than the sender and the receiver. The purpose of

encryption
the process of transforming plain text or data into cipher text that cannot be read by anyone other than the sender and the receiver. The purpose of encryption is (a) to secure stored information and (b) to secure information transmission

cipher text
text that has been encrypted and thus cannot be read by anyone other than the sender and the receiver

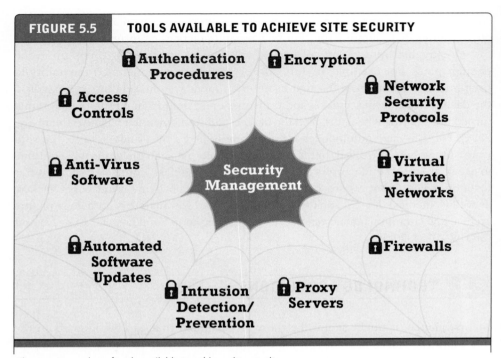

FIGURE 5.5   **TOOLS AVAILABLE TO ACHIEVE SITE SECURITY**

There are a number of tools available to achieve site security.

encryption is (a) to secure stored information and (b) to secure information transmission. Encryption can provide four of the six key dimensions of e-commerce security referred to in Table 5.3 on page 258:

- *Message integrity*—provides assurance that the message has not been altered.
- *Nonrepudiation*—prevents the user from denying he or she sent the message.
- *Authentication*—provides verification of the identity of the person (or computer) sending the message.
- *Confidentiality*—gives assurance that the message was not read by others.

key (cipher)
any method for transforming plain text to cipher text

substitution cipher
every occurrence of a given letter is replaced systematically by another letter

transposition cipher
the ordering of the letters in each word is changed in some systematic way

This transformation of plain text to cipher text is accomplished by using a key or cipher. A **key** (or **cipher**) is any method for transforming plain text to cipher text.

Encryption has been practiced since the earliest forms of writing and commercial transactions. Ancient Egyptian and Phoenician commercial records were encrypted using substitution and transposition ciphers. In a **substitution cipher**, every occurrence of a given letter is replaced systematically by another letter. For instance, if we used the cipher "letter plus two"—meaning replace every letter in a word with a new letter two places forward—then the word "Hello" in plain text would be transformed into the following cipher text: "JGNNQ." In a **transposition cipher**, the ordering of the letters in each word is changed in some systematic way. Leonardo Da Vinci recorded his shop notes in reverse order, making them readable only with a mirror. The word "Hello" can be written backwards as "OLLEH." A more complicated cipher would (a) break all words into two words and (b) spell the first word with every other letter beginning with the first letter, and then spell the second word with all the remaining letters. In this cipher, "HELLO" would be written as "HLO EL."

Symmetric Key Cryptography

In order to decipher (decrypt) these messages, the receiver would have to know the secret cipher that was used to encrypt the plain text. This is called **symmetric key cryptography** or **secret key cryptography**. In symmetric key cryptography, both the sender and the receiver use the same key to encrypt and decrypt the message. How do the sender and the receiver have the same key? They have to send it over some communication media or exchange the key in person. Symmetric key cryptography was used extensively throughout World War II and is still a part of Internet cryptography.

The possibilities for simple substitution and transposition ciphers are endless, but they all suffer from common flaws. First, in the digital age, computers are so powerful and fast that these ancient means of encryption can be broken quickly. Second, symmetric key cryptography requires that both parties share the same key. In order to share the same key, they must send the key over a presumably *insecure* medium where it could be stolen and used to decipher messages. If the secret key is lost or stolen, the entire encryption system fails. Third, in commercial use, where we are not all part of the same team, you would need a secret key for each of the parties with whom you transacted, that is, one key for the bank, another for the department store, and another for the government. In a large population of users, this could result in as many as $n^{(n-1)}$ keys. In a population of millions of Internet users, thousands of millions of keys would be needed to accommodate all e-commerce customers (estimated at about 172 million in the United States). Potentially, 172^2 million different keys would be needed. Clearly this situation would be too unwieldy to work in practice.

Modern encryption systems are digital. The ciphers or keys used to transform plain text into cipher text are digital strings. Computers store text or other data as binary strings composed of 0s and 1s. For instance, the binary representation of the capital letter "A" in ASCII computer code is accomplished with eight binary digits (bits): 01000001. One way in which digital strings can be transformed into cipher text is by multiplying each letter by another binary number, say, an eight-bit key number 0101 0101. If we multiplied every digital character in our text messages by this eight-bit key and sent the encrypted message to a friend along with the secret eight-bit key, the friend could decode the message easily.

The strength of modern security protection is measured in terms of the length of the binary key used to encrypt the data. In the preceding example, the eight-bit key is easily deciphered because there are only 2^8 or 256 possibilities. If the intruder knows you are using an eight-bit key, then he or she could decode the message in a few seconds using a modern desktop PC just by using the brute force method of checking each of the 256 possible keys. For this reason, modern digital encryption systems use keys with 56, 128, 256, or 512 binary digits. With encryption keys of 512 digits, there are 2^{512} possibilities to check out. It is estimated that all the computers in the world would need to work for 10 years before stumbling upon the answer.

symmetric key cryptography (secret key cryptography) both the sender and the receiver use the same key to encrypt and decrypt the message

Data Encryption Standard (DES)

developed by the National Security Agency (NSA) and IBM. Uses a 56-bit encryption key

Advanced Encryption Standard (AES)

the most widely used symmetric key algorithm, offering 128-, 192-, and 256-bit keys

public key cryptography

two mathematically related digital keys are used: a public key and a private key. The private key is kept secret by the owner, and the public key is widely disseminated. Both keys can be used to encrypt and decrypt a message. However, once the keys are used to encrypt a message, that same key cannot be used to unencrypt the message

The **Data Encryption Standard (DES)** was developed by the National Security Agency (NSA) and IBM in the 1950s. DES uses a 56-bit encryption key. To cope with much faster computers, it has been improved by the *Triple DES Encryption Algorithm (TDEA)*—essentially encrypting the message three times, each with a separate key. Today, the most widely used symmetric key algorithm is **Advanced Encryption Standard (AES)**, which offers key sizes of 128, 192, and 256 bits. AES had been considered to be relatively secure, but in 2011, researchers from Microsoft and a Belgian university announced that they had discovered a way to break the algorithm, and with this work, the "safety margin" of AES continues to erode. There are also many other symmetric key systems that are currently less widely used, with keys up to 2,048 bits.[1]

Public Key Cryptography

In 1976, a new way of encrypting messages called **public key cryptography** was invented by Whitfield Diffie and Martin Hellman. Public key cryptography (also referred to as *asymmetric cryptography*) solves the problem of exchanging keys. In this method, two mathematically related digital keys are used: a public key and a private key. The private key is kept secret by the owner, and the public key is widely disseminated. Both keys can be used to encrypt and decrypt a message. However, once the keys are used to encrypt a message, the same key cannot be used to unencrypt the message. The mathematical algorithms used to produce the keys are one-way functions. A *one-way irreversible mathematical function* is one in which, once the algorithm is applied, the input cannot be subsequently derived from the output. Most food recipes are like this. For instance, it is easy to make scrambled eggs, but impossible to retrieve whole eggs from the scrambled eggs. Public key cryptography is based on the idea of irreversible mathematical functions. The keys are sufficiently long (128, 256, and 512 bits) that it would take enormous computing power to derive one key from the other using the largest and fastest computers available. **Figure 5.6** illustrates a simple use of public key cryptography and takes you through the important steps in using public and private keys.

Public Key Cryptography Using Digital Signatures and Hash Digests

In public key cryptography, some elements of security are missing. Although we can be quite sure the message was not understood or read by a third party (message confidentiality), there is no guarantee the sender really is the sender; that is, there is no authentication of the sender. This means the sender could deny ever sending the message (repudiation). And there is no assurance the message was not altered somehow in transit. For example, the message "Buy Cisco @ $16" could have been accidentally or intentionally altered to read "Sell Cisco @ $16." This suggests a potential lack of integrity in the system.

[1] For instance: DESX, GDES, and RDES with 168-bit keys; the RC Series: RC2, RC4, and RC5 with keys up to 2,048 bits; and the IDEA algorithm, the basis of PGP, e-mail public key encryption software described later in this chapter, which uses 128-bit keys.

FIGURE 5.6	PUBLIC KEY CRYPTOGRAPHY—A SIMPLE CASE

STEP	DESCRIPTION
1. The sender creates a digital message.	The message could be a document, spreadsheet, or any digital object.
2. The sender obtains the recipient's public key from a public directory and applies it to the message.	Public keys are distributed widely and can be obtained from recipients directly.
3. Application of the recipient's key produces an encrypted cipher text message.	Once encrypted using the public key, the message cannot be reverse-engineered or unencrypted using the same public key. The process is irreversible.
4. The encrypted message is sent over the Internet.	The encrypted message is broken into packets and sent through several different pathways, making interception of the entire message difficult (but not impossible).
5. The recipient uses his/her private key to decrypt the message.	The only person who can decrypt the message is the person who has possession of the recipient's private key. Hopefully, this is the legitimate recipient.

1 Original message
    Buy XYZ @ $100
Sender

2 Recipient's public key

3 Message encrypted in cipher text
    10101101110001

4

Internet

5 Recipient's private key

Recipient
    Buy XYZ @ $100

In the simplest use of public key cryptography, the sender encrypts a message using the recipient's public key, and then sends it over the Internet. The only person who can decrypt this message is the recipient, using his or her private key. However, this simple case does not ensure integrity or an authentic message.

A more sophisticated use of public key cryptography can achieve authentication, nonrepudiation, and integrity. **Figure 5.7** illustrates this more powerful approach.

To check the integrity of a message and ensure it has not been altered in transit, a hash function is used first to create a digest of the message. A **hash function** is an algorithm that produces a fixed-length number called a *hash* or *message digest*. A hash function can be simple, and count the number of digital 1s in a message, or it can be more complex, and produce a 128-bit number that reflects the number of 0s and 1s, the number of 00s and 11s, and so on. Standard hash functions are available (MD4 and

hash function
an algorithm that produces a fixed-length number called a hash or message digest

FIGURE 5.7	PUBLIC KEY CRYPTOGRAPHY WITH DIGITAL SIGNATURES

STEP	DESCRIPTION
1. The sender creates an original message.	The message can be any digital file.
2. The sender applies a hash function, producing a 128-bit hash result.	Hash functions create a unique digest of the message based on the message contents.
3. The sender encrypts the message and hash result using the recipient's public key.	This irreversible process creates a cipher text that can be read only by the recipient using his or her private key.
4. The sender encrypts the result, again using his or her private key.	The sender's private key is a digital signature. There is only one person who can create this digital mark.
5. The result of this double encryption is sent over the Internet.	The message traverses the Internet as a series of independent packets.
6. The receiver uses the sender's public key to authenticate the message.	Only one person can send this message, namely, the sender.
7. The receiver uses his or her private key to decrypt the hash function and the original message. The receiver checks to ensure the original message and the hash function results conform to one another.	The hash function is used here to check the original message. This ensures the message was not changed in transit.

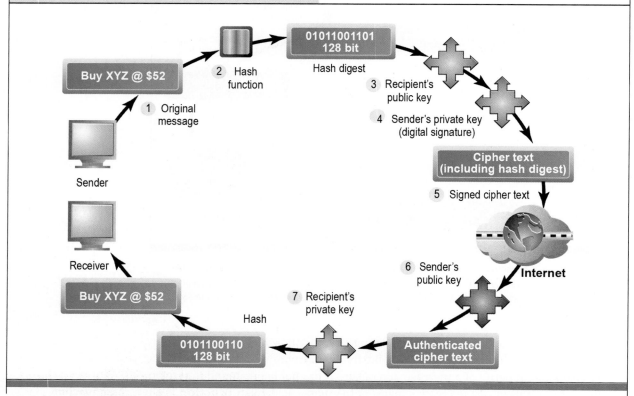

A more realistic use of public key cryptography uses hash functions and digital signatures to both ensure the confidentiality of the message and authenticate the sender. The only person who could have sent the above message is the owner or the sender using his/her private key. This authenticates the message. The hash function ensures the message was not altered in transit. As before, the only person who can decipher the message is the recipient, using his/her private key.

MD5 produce 128- and 160-bit hashes) (Stein, 1998). These more complex hash functions produce hashes or hash results that are unique to every message. The results of applying the hash function are sent by the sender to the recipient. Upon receipt, the recipient applies the hash function to the received message and checks to verify the same result is produced. If so, the message has not been altered. The sender then encrypts both the hash result and the original message using the recipient's public key (as in Figure 5.6 on page 289), producing a single block of cipher text.

One more step is required. To ensure the authenticity of the message and to ensure nonrepudiation, the sender encrypts the entire block of cipher text one more time using the sender's private key. This produces a **digital signature** (also called an *e-signature*) or "signed" cipher text that can be sent over the Internet.

A digital signature is a close parallel to a handwritten signature. Like a handwritten signature, a digital signature is unique—only one person presumably possesses the private key. When used with a hash function, the digital signature is even more unique than a handwritten signature. In addition to being exclusive to a particular individual, when used to sign a hashed document, the digital signature is also unique to the document, and changes for every document.

The recipient of this signed cipher text first uses the sender's public key to authenticate the message. Once authenticated, the recipient uses his or her private key to obtain the hash result and original message. As a final step, the recipient applies the same hash function to the original text, and compares the result with the result sent by the sender. If the results are the same, the recipient now knows the message has not been changed during transmission. The message has integrity.

Early digital signature programs required the user to have a digital certificate, and were far too difficult for an individual to use. Newer programs are Internet-based and do not require users to install software, or understand digital certificate technology. DocuSign, Adobe eSign, and Sertifi are among a number of companies offering online digital signature solutions. Many insurance, finance, and surety companies now permit customers to electronically sign documents.

Digital Envelopes

Public key cryptography is computationally slow. If one used 128- or 256-bit keys to encode large documents—such as this chapter or the entire book—significant declines in transmission speeds and increases in processing time would occur. Symmetric key cryptography is computationally faster, but as we pointed out previously, it has a weakness—namely, the symmetric key must be sent to the recipient over insecure transmission lines. One solution is to use the more efficient symmetric encryption and decryption for large documents, but public key cryptography to encrypt and send the symmetric key. This technique is called using a **digital envelope**. See **Figure 5.8** for an illustration of how a digital envelope works.

In Figure 5.8, a diplomatic document is encrypted using a symmetric key. The symmetric key—which the recipient will require to decrypt the document—is itself encrypted, using the recipient's public key. So we have a "key within a key" (a *digital envelope*). The encrypted report and the digital envelope are sent across the Web.

digital signature (e-signature)
"signed" cipher text that can be sent over the Internet

digital envelope
a technique that uses symmetric encryption for large documents, but public key cryptography to encrypt and send the symmetric key

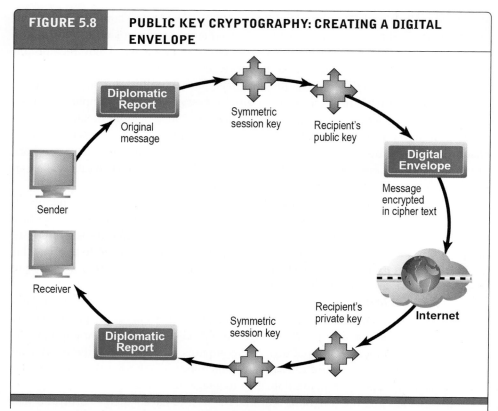

FIGURE 5.8 | **PUBLIC KEY CRYPTOGRAPHY: CREATING A DIGITAL ENVELOPE**

A digital envelope can be created to transmit a symmetric key that will permit the recipient to decrypt the message and be assured the message was not intercepted in transit.

The recipient first uses his/her private key to decrypt the symmetric key, and then the recipient uses the symmetric key to decrypt the report. This method saves time because both encryption and decryption are faster with symmetric keys.

Digital Certificates and Public Key Infrastructure (PKI)

There are still some deficiencies in the message security regime described previously. How do we know that people and institutions are who they claim to be? Anyone can make up a private and public key combination and claim to be someone they are not. Before you place an order with an online merchant such as Amazon, you want to be sure it really is Amazon you have on the screen and not a spoofer masquerading as Amazon. In the physical world, if someone asks who you are and you show a social security number, they may well ask to see a picture ID or a second form of certifiable or acceptable identification. If they really doubt who you are, they may ask for references to other authorities and actually interview these other authorities. Similarly, in the digital world, we need a way to know who people and institutions really are.

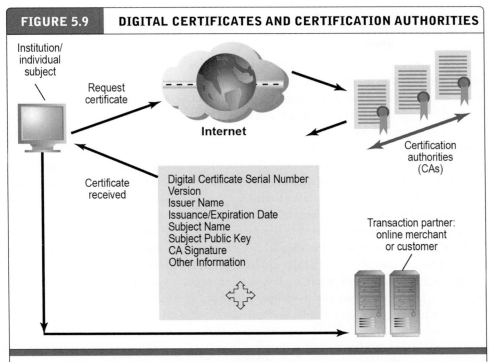

| FIGURE 5.9 | DIGITAL CERTIFICATES AND CERTIFICATION AUTHORITIES |

The PKI includes certification authorities that issue, verify, and guarantee digital certificates that are used in e-commerce to assure the identity of transaction partners.

Digital certificates, and the supporting public key infrastructure, are an attempt to solve this problem of digital identity. A **digital certificate** is a digital document issued by a trusted third-party institution known as a **certification authority (CA)** that contains the name of the subject or company, the subject's public key, a digital certificate serial number, an expiration date, an issuance date, the digital signature of the certification authority (the name of the CA encrypted using the CA's private key), and other identifying information (see **Figure 5.9**).

In the United States, private corporations such as VeriSign, browser manufacturers, security firms, and government agencies such as the U.S. Postal Service and the Federal Reserve issue CAs. Worldwide, thousands of organizations issue CAs. A hierarchy of CAs has emerged with less-well-known CAs being certified by larger and better-known CAs, creating a community of mutually verifying institutions. **Public key infrastructure (PKI)** refers to the CAs and digital certificate procedures that are accepted by all parties. When you sign into a "secure" site, the URL will begin with "https" and a closed lock icon will appear on your browser. This means the site has a digital certificate issued by a trusted CA. It is not, presumably, a spoof site.

To create a digital certificate, the user generates a public/private key pair and sends a request for certification to a CA along with the user's public key. The CA verifies the information (how this is accomplished differs from CA to CA). The CA issues

digital certificate
a digital document issued by a certification authority that contains a variety of identifying information

certification authority (CA)
a trusted third party that issues digital certificates

public key infrastructure (PKI)
CAs and digital certificate procedures that are accepted by all parties

a certificate containing the user's public key and other related information. Finally, the CA creates a message digest from the certificate itself (just like a hash digest) and signs it with the CA's private key. This signed digest is called the *signed certificate*. We end up with a totally unique cipher text document—there can be only one signed certificate like this in the world.

There are several ways the certificates are used in commerce. Before initiating a transaction, the customer can request the signed digital certificate of the merchant and decrypt it using the merchant's public key to obtain both the message digest and the certificate as issued. If the message digest matches the certificate, then the merchant and the public key are authenticated. The merchant may in return request certification of the user, in which case the user would send the merchant his or her individual certificate. There are many types of certificates: personal, institutional, Web server, software publisher, and CAs themselves.

PKI and CAs can also be used to secure software code and content for applications that are directly downloaded to mobile devices from the Internet. Using a technique referred to as code signing, mobile application developers use their private key to encrypt a digital signature. When end users decrypt the signature with the corresponding public key, it confirms the developer's identity and the integrity of the code.

Pretty Good Privacy (PGP)

a widely used e-mail public key encryption software program

You can easily obtain a public and private key for personal, noncommercial use at the International PGP Home Page Web site, Pgpi.org. **Pretty Good Privacy (PGP)** was invented in 1991 by Phil Zimmerman, and has become one of the most widely used e-mail public key encryption software tools in the world. Using PGP software installed on your computer, you can compress and encrypt your messages as well as authenticate both yourself and the recipient. There are also a number of Firefox, Chrome, Internet Explorer, and Safari add-ons, extensions, or plug-ins that enable you to encrypt your e-mail.

Limitations of PKI

PKI is a powerful technological solution to security issues, but it has many limitations, especially concerning CAs. PKI applies mainly to protecting messages in transit on the Internet and is not effective against insiders—employees—who have legitimate access to corporate systems including customer information. Most e-commerce sites do not store customer information in encrypted form. Other limitations are apparent. For one, how is your private key to be protected? Most private keys will be stored on insecure desktop or laptop computers.

There is no guarantee the person using your computer—and your private key—is really you. For instance, you may lose your laptop or smartphone, and therefore lose the private key. Likewise, there is no assurance that someone else in the world cannot use your personal ID papers, such as a social security card, to obtain a PKI authenticated online ID in your name. If there's no real world identification system, there can be no Internet identification system. Under many digital signature laws, you are responsible for whatever your private key does even if you were not the person using the key. This is very different from mail-order or telephone order credit card rules, where you have a right to dispute the credit card charge. Second, there is no guarantee the verifying computer of the merchant is secure. Third, CAs are self-selected organizations seeking to gain access to the business of authorization. They may not be authorities on the corporations or individuals they certify. For instance, how can a CA know about all the corporations within an industry to determine who is or is not legitimate? A related question concerns the method used by the CA to identify the certificate holder. Was this an e-mail transaction verified only by claims of the applicants who filled out an online form? For instance, VeriSign acknowledged in one case that it had mistakenly issued two digital certificates to someone fraudulently claiming to represent Microsoft. Digital certificates have been hijacked by hackers, tricking consumers into giving up personal information. For example, in 2014, India's National Informatics Centre, an intermediate CA that was trusted by the Indian Controller of Certifying Authorities, whose certificates are included in the Microsoft Root Store and thus trusted by the vast majority of programs running on Windows, including Internet Explorer and Chrome, was hacked and a number of unauthorized digital certificates were issued for domains operated by Google and Yahoo (Datta, 2014). Last, what are the policies for revoking or renewing certificates? The expected life of a digital certificate or private key is a function of the frequency of use and the vulnerability of systems that use the certificate. Yet most CAs have no policy or just an annual policy for reissuing certificates. If Microsoft, Apple, or Cisco ever rescinded a number of CAs, millions of users would not be able to access sites. The CA system is difficult and costly to police.

SECURING CHANNELS OF COMMUNICATION

The concepts of public key cryptography are used routinely for securing channels of communication.

Secure Sockets Layer (SSL) and Transport Layer Security (TLS)

The most common form of securing channels is through the *Secure Sockets Layer (SSL)* and *Transport Layer Security (TLS)* protocols. When you receive a message from a server on the Web with which you will be communicating through a secure channel, this means you will be using SSL/TLS to establish a secure negotiated session. (Notice that the URL changes from HTTP to HTTPS.) A **secure negotiated session** is a client-server session in which the URL of the requested document, along with the contents, contents of forms, and the cookies exchanged, are encrypted (see **Figure 5.10**). For instance, your credit card number that you entered into a form would be encrypted. Through a series of handshakes and communications, the browser and the server establish one another's identity by exchanging digital certificates, decide on the strongest shared form of encryption, and then proceed to communicate using an agreed-upon session key. A **session key** is a unique symmetric encryption key chosen just for this single secure session. Once used, it is gone forever. Figure 5.10 shows how this works.

In practice, most private individuals do not have a digital certificate. In this case, the merchant server will not request a certificate, but the client browser will request the merchant certificate once a secure session is called for by the server.

secure negotiated session
a client-server session in which the URL of the requested document, along with the contents, contents of forms, and the cookies exchanged, are encrypted

session key
a unique symmetric encryption key chosen for a single secure session

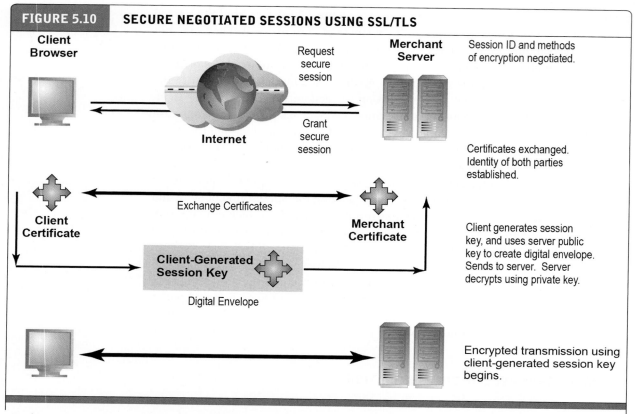

FIGURE 5.10 | **SECURE NEGOTIATED SESSIONS USING SSL/TLS**

Certificates play a key role in using SSL/TLS to establish a secure communications channel.

SSL/TLS provides data encryption, server authentication, optional client authentication, and message integrity for TCP/IP connections. SSL/TLS addresses the issue of authenticity by allowing users to verify another user's identity or the identity of a server. It also protects the integrity of the messages exchanged. However, once the merchant receives the encrypted credit and order information, that information is typically stored in unencrypted format on the merchant's servers. While SSL/TLS provides secure transactions between merchant and consumer, it only guarantees server-side authentication. Client authentication is optional.

In addition, SSL/TLS cannot provide irrefutability—consumers can order goods or download information products, and then claim the transaction never occurred. Recently, social network sites such as Facebook and Twitter have begun to use SSL/TLS for a variety of reasons, including the ability to thwart account hijacking using Firesheep over wireless networks. Firesheep, an add-on for Firefox, can be used by hackers to grab unencrypted cookies used to "remember" a user and allow the hacker to immediately log on to a Web site as that user. SSL/TLS can thwart such an attack because it encrypts the cookie. In June 2015, the White House's Office of Management and Budget issued a memorandum requiring that all publicly accessible federal Web sites and Web services use HTTPS by December 31, 2016.

Virtual Private Networks (VPNs)

A **virtual private network (VPN)** allows remote users to securely access a corporation's local area network via the Internet, using a variety of VPN protocols. VPNs use both authentication and encryption to secure information from unauthorized persons (providing confidentiality and integrity). Authentication prevents spoofing and misrepresentation of identities. A remote user can connect to a remote private local network using a local ISP. The VPN protocols will establish the link from the client to the corporate network as if the user had dialed into the corporate network directly. The process of connecting one protocol through another (IP) is called *tunneling,* because the VPN creates a private connection by adding an invisible wrapper around a message to hide its content. As the message travels through the Internet between the ISP and the corporate network, it is shielded from prying eyes by an encrypted wrapper.

A VPN is "virtual" in the sense that it appears to users as a dedicated secure line when in fact it is a temporary secure line. The primary use of VPNs is to establish secure communications among business partners—larger suppliers or customers, and employees working remotely. A dedicated connection to a business partner can be very expensive. Using the Internet and VPN as the connection method significantly reduces the cost of secure communications.

virtual private network (VPN)
allows remote users to securely access internal networks via the Internet, using the Point-to-Point Tunneling Protocol (PPTP)

Wireless (Wi-Fi) Networks

Accessing the Internet via a wireless (Wi-Fi) network has its own particular security issues. Early Wi-Fi networks used a security standard called Wired Equivalent Privacy (WEP) to encrypt information. WEP was very weak, and easy for hackers to crack. A new standard, Wi-Fi Protected Access (WPA), was developed that provided a higher standard of protection, but this too soon became vulnerable to intrusion. Today, the current standard is **WPA2**, which uses the AES algorithm for encryption and CCMP, a more advanced authentication code protocol.

WPA2
wireless security standard that uses the AES algorithm for encryption and CCMP, a more advanced authentication code protocol

PROTECTING NETWORKS

Once you have protected communications as well as possible, the next set of tools to consider are those that can protect your networks, as well as the servers and clients on those networks.

Firewalls

Firewalls and proxy servers are intended to build a wall around your network and the attached servers and clients, just like physical-world firewalls protect you from fires for a limited period of time. Firewalls and proxy servers share some similar functions, but they are quite different.

A **firewall** refers to either hardware or software that filters communication packets and prevents some packets from entering or exiting the network based on a security policy. The firewall controls traffic to and from servers and clients, forbidding communications from untrustworthy sources, and allowing other communications from trusted sources to proceed. Every message that is to be sent or received from the

firewall
refers to either hardware or software that filters communication packets and prevents some packets from entering the network based on a security policy

network is processed by the firewall, which determines if the message meets security guidelines established by the business. If it does, it is permitted to be distributed, and if it doesn't, the message is blocked. Firewalls can filter traffic based on packet attributes such as source IP address, destination port or IP address, type of service (such as WWW or HTTP), the domain name of the source, and many other dimensions. Most hardware firewalls that protect local area networks connected to the Internet have default settings that require little if any administrator intervention and employ simple but effective rules that deny incoming packets from a connection that does not originate from an internal request—the firewall only allows connections from servers that you requested service from. A common default setting on hardware firewalls (DSL and cable modem routers) simply ignores efforts to communicate with TCP port 445, the most commonly attacked port. The increasing use of firewalls by home and business Internet users has greatly reduced the effectiveness of attacks, and forced hackers to focus more on e-mail attachments to distribute worms and viruses.

There are two major methods firewalls use to validate traffic: packet filters and application gateways. *Packet filters* examine data packets to determine whether they are destined for a prohibited port or originate from a prohibited IP address (as specified by the security administrator). The filter specifically looks at the source and destination information, as well as the port and packet type, when determining whether the information may be transmitted. One downside of the packet filtering method is that it is susceptible to spoofing, because authentication is not one of its roles.

Application gateways are a type of firewall that filters communications based on the application being requested, rather than the source or destination of the message. Such firewalls also process requests at the application level, farther away from the client computer than packet filters. By providing a central filtering point, application gateways provide greater security than packet filters but can compromise system performance.

Next-generation firewalls use an application-centric approach to firewall control. They are able to identify applications regardless of the port, protocol, or security evasion tools used; identify users regardless of device or IP address; decrypt outbound SSL; and protect in real-time against threats embedded in applications.

Proxy Servers

proxy server (proxy)
software server that handles all communications originating from or being sent to the Internet, acting as a spokesperson or bodyguard for the organization

Proxy servers (proxies) are software servers (often a dedicated computer) that handle all communications originating from or being sent to the Internet by local clients, acting as a spokesperson or bodyguard for the organization. Proxies act primarily to limit access of internal clients to external Internet servers, although some proxy servers act as firewalls as well. Proxy servers are sometimes called *dual-home systems* because they have two network interfaces. To internal computers, a proxy server is known as the *gateway*, while to external computers it is known as a *mail server* or *numeric address*.

When a user on an internal network requests a Web page, the request is routed first to the proxy server. The proxy server validates the user and the nature of the request, and then sends the request onto the Internet. A Web page sent by an external Internet server first passes to the proxy server. If acceptable, the Web page passes

---

FIGURE 5.11 **FIREWALLS AND PROXY SERVERS**

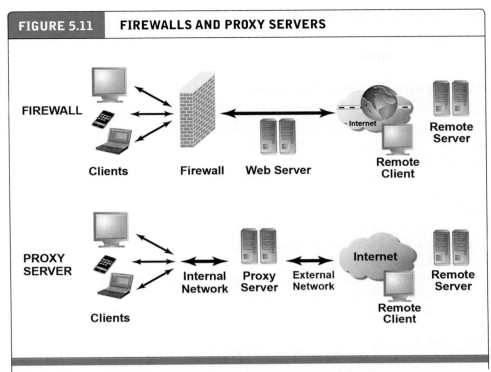

The primary function of a firewall is to deny access by remote client computers to local computers. The primary purpose of a proxy server is to provide controlled access from local computers to remote computers.

onto the internal network Web server and then to the client desktop. By prohibiting users from communicating directly with the Internet, companies can restrict access to certain types of sites, such as pornographic, auction, or stock-trading sites. Proxy servers also improve Web performance by storing frequently requested Web pages locally, reducing upload times, and hiding the internal network's address, thus making it more difficult for hackers to monitor. **Figure 5.11** illustrates how firewalls and proxy servers protect a local area network from Internet intruders and prevent internal clients from reaching prohibited Web servers.

Intrusion Detection and Prevention Systems

In addition to a firewall and proxy server, an intrusion detection and/or prevention system can be installed. An **intrusion detection system (IDS)** examines network traffic, watching to see if it matches certain patterns or preconfigured rules indicative of an attack. If it detects suspicious activity, the IDS will set off an alarm alerting administrators and log the event in a database. An IDS is useful for detecting malicious activity that a firewall might miss. An **intrusion prevention system (IPS)** has all the functionality of an IDS, with the additional ability to take steps to prevent and block suspicious activities. For instance, an IPS can terminate a session and reset a connection, block traffic from a suspicious IP address, or reconfigure firewall or router security controls.

intrusion detection system (IDS)
examines network traffic, watching to see if it matches certain patterns or preconfigured rules indicative of an attack

intrusion prevention system (IPS)
has all the functionality of an IDS, with the additional ability to take steps to prevent and block suspicious activities

PROTECTING SERVERS AND CLIENTS

Operating system features and anti-virus software can help further protect servers and clients from certain types of attacks.

Operating System Security Enhancements

The most obvious way to protect servers and clients is to take advantage of automatic computer security upgrades. The Microsoft, Apple, and Linux/Unix operating systems are continuously updated to patch vulnerabilities discovered by hackers. These patches are autonomic; that is, when using these operating systems on the Internet, you are prompted and informed that operating system enhancements are available. Users can easily download these security patches for free. The most common known worms and viruses can be prevented by simply keeping your server and client operating systems and applications up to date. In April 2014, Microsoft ended security support and updates for its Windows XP operating system. Despite this, many organizations continue to use XP-based systems, and as a result, many security experts anticipate a wave of strikes against such systems. Application vulnerabilities are fixed in the same manner. For instance, most popular Internet browsers are updated automatically with little user intervention.

Anti-Virus Software

The easiest and least-expensive way to prevent threats to system integrity is to install anti-virus software. Programs by McAfee, Symantec (Norton AntiVirus), and many others provide inexpensive tools to identify and eradicate the most common types of malicious code as they enter a computer, as well as destroy those already lurking on a hard drive. Anti-virus programs can be set up so that e-mail attachments are inspected before you click on them, and the attachments are eliminated if they contain a known virus or worm. It is not enough, however, to simply install the software once. Because new viruses are developed and released every day, daily routine updates are needed in order to prevent new threats from being loaded. Some premium-level anti-virus software is updated hourly.

Anti-virus suite packages and stand-alone programs are available to eliminate intruders such as bot programs, adware, and other security risks. Such programs work much like anti-virus software in that they look for recognized hacker tools or signature actions of known intruders.

5.4 | MANAGEMENT POLICIES, BUSINESS PROCEDURES, AND PUBLIC LAWS

Worldwide, in 2015, companies are expected to spend over $75 billion on security hardware, software, and services (Gartner, 2015). However, most CEOs and CIOs believe that technology is not the sole answer to managing the risk of e-commerce. The technology provides a foundation, but in the absence of intelligent management policies, even the best technology can be easily defeated. Public laws and active enforcement

| FIGURE 5.12 | DEVELOPING AN E-COMMERCE SECURITY PLAN |

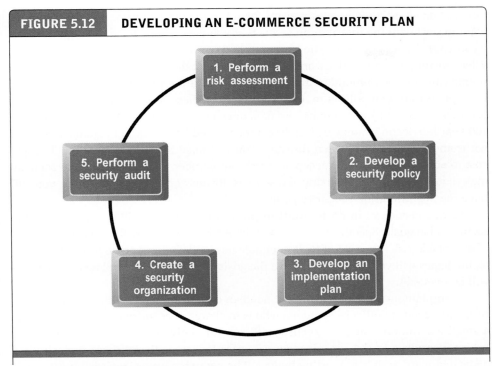

There are five steps involved in building an e-commerce security plan.

of cybercrime statutes also are required to both raise the costs of illegal behavior on the Internet and guard against corporate abuse of information. Let's consider briefly the development of management policy.

A SECURITY PLAN: MANAGEMENT POLICIES

In order to minimize security threats, e-commerce firms must develop a coherent corporate policy that takes into account the nature of the risks, the information assets that need protecting, and the procedures and technologies required to address the risk, as well as implementation and auditing mechanisms. **Figure 5.12** illustrates the key steps in developing a solid security plan.

A security plan begins with **risk assessment**—an assessment of the risks and points of vulnerability. The first step is to inventory the information and knowledge assets of the e-commerce site and company. What information is at risk? Is it customer information, proprietary designs, business activities, secret processes, or other internal information, such as price schedules, executive compensation, or payroll? For each type of information asset, try to estimate the dollar value to the firm if this information were compromised, and then multiply that amount by the probability of the loss occurring. Once you have done so, rank order the results. You now have a list of information assets prioritized by their value to the firm.

Based on your quantified list of risks, you can start to develop a **security policy**— a set of statements prioritizing the information risks, identifying acceptable risk

risk assessment
an assessment of the risks and points of vulnerability

security policy
a set of statements prioritizing the information risks, identifying acceptable risk targets, and identifying the mechanisms for achieving these targets

targets, and identifying the mechanisms for achieving these targets. You will obviously want to start with the information assets that you determined to be the highest priority in your risk assessment. Who generates and controls this information in the firm? What existing security policies are in place to protect the information? What enhancements can you recommend to improve security of these most valuable assets? What level of risk are you willing to accept for each of these assets? Are you willing, for instance, to lose customer credit card data once every 10 years? Or will you pursue a 100-year hurricane strategy by building a security edifice for credit card data that can withstand the once-in-100-year disaster? You will need to estimate how much it will cost to achieve this level of acceptable risk. Remember, total and complete security may require extraordinary financial resources. By answering these questions, you will have the beginnings of a security policy.

implementation plan
the action steps you will take to achieve the security plan goals

Next, consider an **implementation plan**—the steps you will take to achieve the security plan goals. Specifically, you must determine how you will translate the levels of acceptable risk into a set of tools, technologies, policies, and procedures. What new technologies will you deploy to achieve the goals, and what new employee procedures will be needed?

To implement your plan, you will need an organizational unit in charge of security, and a security officer—someone who is in charge of security on a daily basis. For a small e-commerce site, the security officer will likely be the person in charge of Internet services or the site manager, whereas for larger firms, there typically is a dedicated team with a supporting budget. The **security organization** educates and trains users, keeps management aware of security threats and breakdowns, and maintains the tools chosen to implement security.

security organization
educates and trains users, keeps management aware of security threats and breakdowns, and maintains the tools chosen to implement security

access controls
determine who can gain legitimate access to a network

The security organization typically administers access controls, authentication procedures, and authorization policies. **Access controls** determine which outsiders and insiders can gain legitimate access to your networks. Outsider access controls include firewalls and proxy servers, while insider access controls typically consist of login procedures (usernames, passwords, and access codes).

authentication procedures
include the use of digital signatures, certificates of authority, and public key infrastructure

Authentication procedures include the use of digital signatures, certificates of authority, and PKI. Now that e-signatures have been given the same legal weight as an original pen-and-ink version, companies are in the process of devising ways to test and confirm a signer's identity. Companies frequently have signers type their full name and click on a button indicating their understanding that they have just signed a contract or document.

biometrics
the study of measurable biological or physical characteristics

Biometric devices can also be used to verify physical attributes associated with an individual, such as a fingerprint or retina (eye) scan or speech recognition system. (**Biometrics** is the study of measurable biological, or physical, characteristics.) A company could require, for example, that an individual undergo a fingerprint scan before being allowed access to a Web site, or before being allowed to pay for merchandise with a credit card. Biometric devices make it even more difficult for hackers to break into sites or facilities, significantly reducing the opportunity for spoofing. Security tokens are used by millions of corporation and government workers to log on to corporate clients and servers. Newer Apple iPhones (5S and later) feature a fingerprint sensor called the Touch ID built into the iPhone's home button to unlock the phone and authorize purchases from the iTunes, iBooks, and App Stores without requiring users to enter a PIN or other security code. According to Apple, the system does not store an actual fingerprint, but rather biometric data, which will be encrypted and stored only on a chip within the iPhone, and will not be made available to third parties.

Security tokens are physical devices or software that generate an identifier that can be used in addition to or in place of a password. One example is RSA's SecurID token, which continously generates six-digit passwords.

Authorization policies determine differing levels of access to information assets for differing levels of users. **Authorization management systems** establish where and when a user is permitted to access certain parts of a Web site. Their primary function is to restrict access to private information within a company's Internet infrastructure. Although there are several authorization management products currently available, most operate in the same way: the system encrypts a user session to function like a passkey that follows the user from page to page, allowing access only to those areas that the user is permitted to enter, based on information set at the system database. By establishing entry rules up front for each user, the authorization management system knows who is permitted to go where at all times.

The last step in developing an e-commerce security plan is performing a security audit. A **security audit** involves the routine review of access logs (identifying how outsiders are using the site as well as how insiders are accessing the site's assets). A monthly report should be produced that establishes the routine and nonroutine accesses to the systems and identifies unusual patterns of activities. As previously noted, tiger teams are often used by large corporate sites to evaluate the strength of existing security procedures. Many small firms have sprung up in the last five years to provide these services to large corporate sites.

THE ROLE OF LAWS AND PUBLIC POLICY

The public policy environment today is very different from the early days of e-commerce. The net result is that the Internet is no longer an ungoverned, unsupervised, self-controlled technology juggernaut. Just as with financial markets in the last 70 years, there is a growing awareness that e-commerce markets work only when a powerful institutional set of laws and enforcement mechanisms are in place. These laws help ensure orderly, rational, and fair markets. This growing public policy environment is becoming just as global as e-commerce itself. Despite some spectacular internationally based attacks on U.S. e-commerce sites, the sources and persons involved in major harmful attacks have almost always been uncovered and, where possible, prosecuted.

Voluntary and private efforts have played a very large role in identifying criminal hackers and assisting law enforcement. Since 1995, as e-commerce has grown in significance, national and local law enforcement activities have expanded greatly. New laws have been passed that grant local and national authorities new tools and mechanisms for identifying, tracing, and prosecuting cybercriminals. For instance, a majority of states now require companies that maintain personal data on their residents to publicly disclose when a security breach affecting those residents has occurred. **Table 5.6** lists the most significant federal e-commerce security legislation and regulation. In addition, the Federal Trade Commission has asserted that it has authority

security token
physical device or software that generates an identifier that can be used in addition to or in place of a password

authorization policies
determine differing levels of access to information assets for differing levels of users

authorization management system
establishes where and when a user is permitted to access certain parts of a Web site

security audit
involves the routine review of access logs (identifying how outsiders are using the site as well as how insiders are accessing the site's assets)

TABLE 5.6	E-COMMERCE SECURITY LEGISLATION AND REGULATION
LEGISLATION/REGULATION	**SIGNIFICANCE**
Computer Fraud and Abuse Act (1986)	Primary federal statute used to combat computer crime.
Electronic Communications Privacy Act (1986)	Imposes fines and imprisonment for individuals who access, intercept, or disclose the private e-mail communications of others.
National Information Infrastructure Protection Act (1996)	Makes DoS attacks illegal; creates NIPC in the FBI.
Health Insurance Portability and Accountability Act (1996)	Requires certain health care facilities to report data breaches.
Financial Modernization Act (Gramm-Leach-Bliley Act) (1999)	Requires certain financial institutions to report data breaches.
Cyberspace Electronic Security Act (2000)	Reduces export restrictions.
Computer Security Enhancement Act (2000)	Protects federal government systems from hacking.
Electronic Signatures in Global and National Commerce Act (the "E-Sign Law") (2000)	Authorizes the use of electronic signatures in legal documents.
USA PATRIOT Act (2001)	Authorizes use of computer-based surveillance of suspected terrorists.
Homeland Security Act (2002)	Authorizes establishment of the Department of Homeland Security, which is responsible for developing a comprehensive national plan for security of the key resources and critical infrastructures of the United States; DHS becomes the central coordinator for all cyberspace security efforts.
CAN-SPAM Act (2003)	Although primarily a mechanism for civil and regulatory lawsuits against spammers, the CAN-SPAM Act also creates several new criminal offenses intended to address situations in which the perpetrator has taken steps to hide his or her identity or the source of the spam from recipients, ISPs, or law enforcement agencies. Also contains criminal sanctions for sending sexually explicit e-mail without designating it as such.
U.S. SAFE WEB Act (2006)	Enhances FTC's ability to obtain monetary redress for consumers in cases involving spyware, spam, Internet fraud, and deception; also improves FTC's ability to gather information and coordinate investigations with foreign counterparts.
Improving Critical Infrastructure Cybersecurity Executive Order (2013)	After Congress failed to pass cybersecurity legislation in 2012, this executive order issued by the Obama administration directs federal agenices to share cybersecurity threat intelligence with private sector companies that may be targets, and the development and implementation of a cybersecurity framework for private industry, incorporating best practices and voluntary standards.

over corporations' data security practices. The FTC sued the Wyndham hotel chain after hacking attacks in 2008 and 2009 resulted in a data breach that led to fraudulent credit charges of more than $10 million. According to the FTC, its investigation showed that Wyndham had failed to follow basic data security practices, while at the same time assuring customers that their data was safe. In August 2015, the U.S. Court of Appeals for the Third Circuit ruled that the FTC was within the scope of its authority, opening the door for it to take a greater role, especially in light of the failure of Congress to adopt legislation governing data security. By increasing the punishment for cybercrimes, the U.S. government is attempting to create a deterrent to further hacker actions. And by making such actions federal crimes, the government is able to extradite international hackers and prosecute them within the United States.

After September 11, 2001, Congress passed the USA PATRIOT Act, which broadly expanded law enforcement's investigative and surveillance powers. The act has provisions for monitoring e-mail and Internet use. The Homeland Security Act of 2002 also attempts to fight cyberterrorism and increases the government's ability to compel information disclosure by computer and ISP sources. Recent proposed legislation that focuses on requiring firms to report data breaches to the FTC, protection of the national electric grid, and cybersecurity has all failed to pass. However, in October 2015, the U.S. Senate passed the Cybersecurity Information Sharing Act (CISA). The bill, which is intended to create a system that lets companies share evidence about attacks without the risk of being sued, has been opposed by many large technology companies and privacy advocates on the grounds that it does not do enough to protect individual privacy and could lead to increased government surveillance. Before becoming law, the bill must be reconciled with the version passed by the House of Representatives in April 2015, and then signed by the President (Peterson, 2015).

Private and Private-Public Cooperation Efforts

The good news is that e-commerce sites are not alone in their battle to achieve security on the Internet. Several organizations—some public and some private—are devoted to tracking down criminal organizations and individuals engaged in attacks against Internet and e-commerce sites. On the federal level, the Office of Cybersecurity and Communications (CS&C) within the U.S. Department of Homeland Security (DHS), is responsible for overseeing the security, resilience, and reliability of the United States' cyber and communications infrastructure. The National Cybersecurity and Communications Integration Center (NCCIC) acts as a 24/7 cyber monitoring, incident response, and management center. In addition, the DHS also operates the **United States Computer Emergency Readiness Team (US-CERT)**, which coordinates cyber incident warnings and responses across both the government and private sectors. One of the better-known private organizations is the **CERT Coordination Center** (formerly known as the Computer Emergency Response Team) at Carnegie Mellon University. CERT monitors and tracks online criminal activity reported to it by private corporations and government agencies that seek out its help. CERT is composed of full-time and part-time computer experts who can trace the origins of attacks against sites despite the complexity of the Internet. Its staff members also assist organizations in identifying security problems, developing solutions, and communicating with the

US-CERT
division of the U.S. Department of Homeland Security that coordinates cyber incident warnings and responses across government and private sectors

CERT Coordination Center
monitors and tracks online criminal activity reported to it by private corporations and government agencies that seek out its help

TABLE 5.7	GOVERNMENT EFFORTS TO REGULATE AND CONTROL ENCRYPTION
REGULATORY EFFORT	**IMPACT**
Restricted export of strong security systems	Supported primarily by the United States. Widespread distribution of encryption schemes weakens this policy. The policy is changing to permit exports except to pariah countries.
Key escrow/key recovery schemes	France, the United Kingdom, and the United States supported this effort in the late 1990s but now have largely abandoned it. There are few trusted third parties.
Lawful access and forced disclosure	Growing support in U.S. legislation and in OECD countries.
Official hacking	All countries are rapidly expanding budgets and training for law enforcement "technical centers" aimed at monitoring and cracking computer-based encryption activities of suspected criminals.

public about widespread hacker threats. The CERT Coordination Center also provides product assessments, reports, and training in order to improve the public's knowledge and understanding of security threats and solutions.

Government Policies and Controls on Encryption Software

In the United States, both Congress and the executive branch have sought to regulate the uses of encryption and to restrict availability and export of encryption systems as a means of preventing crime and terrorism. At the international level, four organizations have influenced the international traffic in encryption software: the Organization for Economic Cooperation and Development (OECD), G-7 (the heads of state of the top seven industrialized countries in the world, not including Russia, which was suspended from participation in 2014), the European Council, and the Wassenaar Arrangement (which includes 41 countries that produce sensitive industrial equipment or weapons). Various governments have proposed schemes for controlling encryption software or at least preventing criminals from obtaining strong encryption tools (see **Table 5.7**). The U.S. and U.K. governments are also devoting a large amount of resources to cryptography-related programs that will enable them to break encrypted communications collected on the Internet. Documents leaked by former NSA contractor Edward Snowden indicate that both the NSA and its U.K. counterpart, the GCHQ, may be able to break encryption schemes used by SSL/TLS, VPNs, and on 4G smartphones (Vaughan-Nichols, 2013).

5.5 E-COMMERCE PAYMENT SYSTEMS

For the most part, existing payment mechanisms such as cash, credit cards, debit cards, checking accounts, and stored value accounts have been able to be adapted to the online environment, albeit with some significant limitations that have led to efforts

TABLE 5.8	MAJOR TRENDS IN E-COMMERCE PAYMENTS 2015–2016

- Payment by credit and/or debit card remains the dominant form of online payment.
- Mobile retail payment volume skyrockets.
- PayPal remains the most popular alternative payment method online.
- Apple introduces Apple Pay, a mobile payment service that uses near field communication (NFC) chips, with strong support from banks and credit card companies. Samsung and Google follow, with Samsung Pay and Android Pay, respectively.
- Square gains further traction with a smartphone app, credit card reader, and credit card processing service that permits anyone to accept credit card payments.
- Google refocuses Google Wallet, which had met with tepid response, solely on sending and receiving money.
- Mobile P2P payment systems such as Venmo take off.

to develop alternatives. In addition, new types of purchasing relationships, such as between individuals online, and new technologies, such as the development of the mobile platform, have also created both a need and an opportunity for the development of new payment systems. In this section, we provide an overview of the major e-commerce payment systems in use today. **Table 5.8** lists some of the major trends in e-commerce payments in 2015–2016.

U.S. online payments represent a market of almost $530 billion in 2015, and are expected to grow an additional $230 billion to around $760 billion by 2019. Institutions and business firms that can handle this volume of transactions (mostly the large banking and credit firms) generally extract 2%–3% of the transactions in the form of fees, or about $11 to $16 billion a year in revenue. Given the size of the market, competition for online payments is spirited.

In the United States, the primary form of online payment is still the existing credit and debit card system. Alternative payment methods such as PayPal, Amazon Payments, and Bill Me Later are expected to continue to make inroads into traditional payment methods. Mobile payments are also expected to grow significantly (Javelin Strategy & Research, 2014). **Figure 5.13** illustrates the percentage of consumers that use various alternative payment methods in 2015.

In other parts of the world, e-commerce payments can be very different depending on traditions and infrastructure. Credit cards are not nearly as dominant a form of online payment as they are in the United States. If you plan on operating an e-commerce site in Europe, Asia, or Latin America, you will need to develop different payment systems for each region. For instance, in Denmark, Norway, and Finland payment is primarily with debit or credit cards, while in Sweden, payment after being tendered an invoice and by bank transfer are very popular in addition to credit/debit cards. In the Netherlands, the online payments service iDEAL is the most popular retail e-commerce payment method. In Italy, consumers rely heavily on both credit cards and PayPal. In Japan, although credit card is the primary payment method, many consumers still pick up and pay for goods at local convenience stores (konbini) (eMarketer, Inc., 2015).

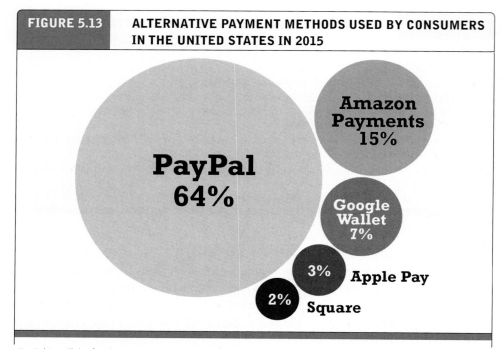

FIGURE 5.13 **ALTERNATIVE PAYMENT METHODS USED BY CONSUMERS IN THE UNITED STATES IN 2015**

PayPal is still, by far, the most popular alternative payment method.
SOURCES: Based on data from eMarketer, 2015a.

ONLINE CREDIT CARD TRANSACTIONS

Because credit and debit cards are the dominant form of online payment, it is important to understand how they work and to recognize the strengths and weaknesses of this payment system. Online credit card transactions are processed in much the same way that in-store purchases are, with the major differences being that online merchants never see the actual card being used, no card impression is taken, and no signature is available. Online credit card transactions most closely resemble Mail Order-Telephone Order (MOTO) transactions. These types of purchases are also called Cardholder Not Present (CNP) transactions and are the major reason that charges can be disputed later by consumers. Because the merchant never sees the credit card, nor receives a hand-signed agreement to pay from the customer, when disputes arise, the merchant faces the risk that the transaction may be disallowed and reversed, even though he has already shipped the goods or the user has downloaded a digital product.

Figure 5.14 illustrates the online credit card purchasing cycle. There are five parties involved in an online credit card purchase: consumer, merchant, clearinghouse, merchant bank (sometimes called the "acquiring bank"), and the consumer's card-issuing bank. In order to accept payments by credit card, online merchants must have a merchant account established with a bank or financial institution. A **merchant account** is simply a bank account that allows companies to process credit card payments and receive funds from those transactions.

merchant account
a bank account that allows companies to process credit card payments and receive funds from those transactions

| FIGURE 5.14 | **HOW AN ONLINE CREDIT CARD TRANSACTION WORKS** |

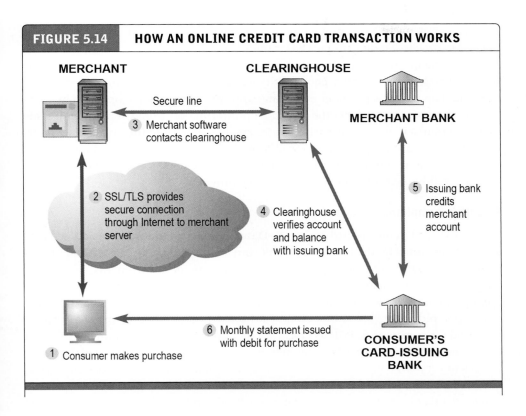

As shown in Figure 5.14, an online credit card transaction begins with a purchase (1). When a consumer wants to make a purchase, he or she adds the item to the merchant's shopping cart. When the consumer wants to pay for the items in the shopping cart, a secure tunnel through the Internet is created using SSL/TLS. Using encryption, SSL/TLS secures the session during which credit card information will be sent to the merchant and protects the information from interlopers on the Internet (2). SSL does not authenticate either the merchant or the consumer. The transacting parties have to trust one another.

Once the consumer credit card information is received by the merchant, the merchant software contacts a clearinghouse (3). As previously noted, a clearinghouse is a financial intermediary that authenticates credit cards and verifies account balances. The clearinghouse contacts the issuing bank to verify the account information (4). Once verified, the issuing bank credits the account of the merchant at the merchant's bank (usually this occurs at night in a batch process) (5). The debit to the consumer account is transmitted to the consumer in a monthly statement (6).

Credit Card E-commerce Enablers

Companies that have a merchant account still need to buy or build a means of handling the online transaction; securing the merchant account is only step one in a two-part process. Today, Internet payment service providers (sometimes referred to as payment gateways) can provide both a merchant account and the software tools needed to process credit card purchases online.

For instance, Authorize.net is an Internet payment service provider. The company helps a merchant secure an account with one of its merchant account provider partners and then provides payment processing software for installation on the merchant's server. The software collects the transaction information from the merchant's site and then routes it via the Authorize.net "payment gateway" to the appropriate bank, ensuring that customers are authorized to make their purchases. The funds for the transaction are then transferred to the merchant's merchant account. CyberSource is another well-known Internet payment service provider.

PCI-DSS Compliance

PCI-DSS (Payment Card Industry-Data Security Standards)
data security standards instituted by the five major credit card companies

The **PCI-DSS (Payment Card Industry-Data Security Standard)** is a data security standard instituted by the five major credit card companies (Visa, MasterCard, American Express, Discover, and JCB). PCI-DSS is not a law or governmental regulation, but an industry-mandated standard. Every online merchant must comply with the appropriate level of PCI-DSS in order to accept credit card payments. Those that fail to comply and are involved in a credit card breach may ultimately be subjected to fines and other expenses. PCI-DSS has various levels, related to the number of credit and/or debit cards processed by the merchant each year. Level 1, the strictest level, applies to very large merchants that process more than 6 million transactions a year, while Level 2 applies to those who process between 1 million and 6 million. Level 3 applies to organizations that process between 20,000 and 1 million transactions, while Level 4 applies to smaller merchants that process less than 20,000 transactions. PCI-DSS has six major control objectives. It requires the merchant to (a) build and maintain a secure network, (b) protect cardholder data, (c) maintain a vulnerability management program, (d) implement strong access control measures, (e) regularly test and monitor networks, and (f) maintain an information security policy. Each of these six broad control objectives has further specific requirements that must be met. The most current version of PCI-DSS is Version 3.1, which went into effect as of April 2015 (PCI Security Standards Council, 2015).

Limitations of Online Credit Card Payment Systems

There are a number of limitations to the existing credit card payment system. The most important limitations involve security, merchant risk, administrative and transaction costs, and social equity.

The existing system offers poor security. Neither the merchant nor the consumer can be fully authenticated. The merchant could be a criminal organization designed to collect credit card numbers, and the consumer could be a thief using stolen or fraudulent cards. The risk facing merchants is high: consumers can repudiate charges even though the goods have been shipped or the product downloaded. The banking industry attempted to develop a secure electronic transaction (SET) protocol, but this effort failed because it was too complex for consumers and merchants alike.

The administrative costs of setting up an online credit card system and becoming authorized to accept credit cards are high. Transaction costs for merchants also are significant—roughly 3.5% of the purchase plus a transaction fee of 20–35 cents per transaction, plus other setup fees.

Credit cards are not very democratic, even though they seem ubiquitous. Millions of young adults do not have credit cards, along with almost 100 million other adult Americans who cannot afford cards or who are considered poor risks because of low incomes.

ALTERNATIVE ONLINE PAYMENT SYSTEMS

The limitations of the online credit card system have opened the way for the development of a number of alternative online payment systems. Chief among them is PayPal. PayPal (purchased by eBay in 2002 and then spun-off as an independent company again in 2015) enables individuals and businesses with e-mail accounts to make and receive payments up to a specified limit. Paypal is an example of an **online stored value payment system**, which permits consumers to make instant, online payments to merchants and other individuals based on value stored in an online account. PayPal has 173 million active customer accounts as of September 2015 and in 2014 processed 4 billion payments, of which 1 billion were on mobile devices. It operates in 203 countries around the world. It allows customers to be paid in more than 100 currencies, to withdraw funds to their bank accounts in 57 currencies, and to hold balances in their PayPal account in 26 currencies. In 2014, PayPal processed $228 billion in payments ($60 billion of which were generated on eBay, and $168 billion elsewhere). PayPal builds on the existing financial infrastructure of the countries in which it operates. You establish a PayPal account by specifying a credit, debit, or checking account you wish to have charged or paid when conducting online transactions. When you make a payment using PayPal, you e-mail the payment to the merchant's PayPal account. PayPal transfers the amount from your credit or checking account to the merchant's bank account. The beauty of PayPal is that no personal credit information has to be shared among the users, and the service can be used by individuals to pay one another even in small amounts. However, one issue with PayPal is its relatively high cost. For example, to send or request money, the cost ranges from 2.9% to 5.99% of the amount (depending on the type of transaction) plus a small fixed fee (typically $0.30) per transaction. PayPal is discussed in further depth in the case study at the end of the chapter.

Although PayPal is by far the most well-known and commonly used online credit/debit card alternative, there are a number of other alternatives as well. Amazon Payments is aimed at consumers who have concerns about entrusting their credit card information to unfamiliar online retailers. Consumers can purchase goods and services at non-Amazon Web sites using the payment methods stored in their Amazon accounts, without having to reenter their payment information at the merchant's site. Amazon provides the payment processing. Visa Checkout (formerly V.me) and MasterCard's MasterPass substitute a user name and password for an actual payment card number during online checkout. Both MasterPass and Visa Checkout are supported by

online stored value payment system
permits consumers to make instant, online payments to merchants and other individuals based on value stored in an online account

a number of large payment processors and online retailers. However, they have not yet achieved the usage of Paypal.

Bill Me Later (owned by PayPal as well) also appeals to consumers who do not wish to enter their credit card information online. Bill Me Later describes itself as an open-ended credit account. Users select the Bill Me Later option at checkout and are asked to provide their birth date and the last four digits of their social security number. They are then billed for the purchase by Bill Me Later within 10 to 14 days. Bill Me Later is currently offered by more than 1,000 online merchants.

WUPay (formerly eBillme, and now operated by Western Union) offers a similar service. WUPay customers who select the WUPay option at firms such as Sears, Kmart, Buy.com, and other retailers do not have to provide any credit card information. Instead they are e-mailed a bill, which they can pay via their bank's online bill payment service, or in person at any Western Union location. Dwolla is a similar cash-based payment network for both individuals and merchants. It bypasses the credit card network and instead connects directly into a bank account. In 2015, Dwolla eliminated its transaction and processing fees, changing its focus from consumer-to-consumer payments to larger businesses. Dwolla has its own network that bypasses the Automated Clearing House (ACH), the traditional system for processing financial transactions in the United States, and in 2015, signed up major U.S. bank BBVA Compass. Earlier in the year, the U.S. Treasury had selected Dwolla (along with PayPal) to process payments to federal agencies, and in October 2015, the Chicago Mercantile Exchange chose Dwolla to replace ACH. Dwolla now processes more than $1 billion a year (Patane, 2015; Leising, 2015).

Like Dwolla, Stripe is another company that is attempting to provide an alternative to the traditional online credit card system. Stripe focuses on the merchant side of the process. It provides simple software code that enables companies to bypass much of the administrative costs involved in setting up an online credit card system, and instead lets companies begin accepting credit card payments almost immediately without the need to obtain a merchant account or use a gateway provider. Unlike PayPal, the customer doesn't need a Stripe account to pay, and all payments are made directly to the company rather than being routed through a third party.

MOBILE PAYMENT SYSTEMS: YOUR SMARTPHONE WALLET

The use of mobile devices as payment mechanisms is already well established in Europe and Asia and is now exploding in the United States, where the infrastructure to support mobile payment is finally being put in place. Total mobile online retail payments are expected to grow from $76 billion in 2014 to $217 billion by 2019. Physical goods are the most common purchase in mobile online shopping, with over 50% of mobile buyers reporting that they had purchased such goods (Javelin Strategy & Research, 2015c; Hernandez, 2015). Near field communication (NFC) is one of the enabling technologies for mobile payment systems. **Near field communication (NFC)** is a set of short-range wireless technologies used to share information among devices within about 2 inches of each other (50 mm). NFC devices are either powered

near field communication (NFC)
a set of short-range wireless technologies used to share information among devices

or passive. A connection requires one powered unit (the initiator), and one target unpowered unit that can respond to requests from the powered unit. NFC targets can be very simple forms such as tags, stickers, key fobs, or readers. NFC peer-to-peer communication is possible where both devices are powered. An NFC-equipped smartphone, for instance, can be swiped by a merchant's reader to record a payment wirelessly and without contact. About 444 million NFC-enabled phones were sold worldwide in 2014, and that number is expected to more than double to over 1 billion by 2016 (IHS Technologies, 2015). Prior to September 2014, Apple's failure to include an NFC chip in the iPhone had slowed the adoption of NFC-based mobile wallet technology in the United States. However, in September 2014, Apple introduced the iPhone 6, which is equipped with NFC chips designed to work with Apple's mobile payments platform, Apple Pay. Building on Apple Passbook and Touch ID biometric fingerprint scanning and encryption that Apple previously introduced in September 2012, Apple Pay is able to be used for mobile payments at the point of sale at a physical store as well as online. It is supported by the major credit card networks and card issuing banks responsible for over 80% of all credit card transactions, as well as many national retailers. Other competitors in NFC-enabled mobile payments include Android Pay and Samsung Pay. PayPal and Square are also attacking the mobile payment market from a different direction, with apps and credit card readers that attach to smartphones. The promise of riches beyond description to a firm that is able to dominate the mobile payments marketplace has set off what one commentator has called a goat rodeo surrounding the development of new technologies and methods of mobile payment. The end-of-chapter case study, *Mobile Payment Marketplace: Goat Rodeo,* provides a further look at the future of online and mobile payment in the United States, including the efforts of Apple, Google, Samsung, Square, PayPal, and others.

SOCIAL/MOBILE PEER-TO-PEER PAYMENT SYSTEMS

In addition to using a mobile device as a vehicle for e-commerce and as a payment method at physical point-of-sale, another type of mobile payment transaction is becoming increasingly popular: social/mobile peer-to-peer payments. Services such as Venmo, Square Cash, Snapcash, the newly refocused Google Wallet, and the new Facebook Messenger Payment service all enable users to send another person money through a mobile application or Web site, funded by a checking account, debit card, credit card, or a digital wallet balance. Currently, these services are the most popular among Millennials, which is the key demographic driving their growth. According to 451 Research, there are about 22 million mobile P2P payment users in 2015 in the United States, a number they expect to grow to over 44 million by 2018. Venmo, owned by PayPal, is particularly popular, with its success in part due to its integration with Facebook and its only social network newsfeed, which lets users see when and why friends are paying other friends. In 2014, almost $2.5 billion in transactions were made over Venmo. Total mobile P2P volume is projected to grow to $17 billion by 2019, according to Forrester Research (eMarketer, Inc., 2015b).

DIGITAL CASH AND VIRTUAL CURRENCIES

digital cash

an alternative payment system in which unique, authenticated tokens represent cash value

Although the terms digital cash and virtual currencies are often used synonymously, they actually refer to two separate types of alternative payment systems. **Digital cash** typically is based on an algorithm that generates unique authenticated tokens representing cash value that can be used "in the real world." Bitcoin is the best known example of digital cash. Bitcoins are encrypted numbers (sometimes referred to as cryptocurrency) that are generated by a complex algorithm using a peer-to-peer network in a process referred to as "mining" that requires extensive computing power. Like real currency, Bitcoins have a fluctuating value tied to open-market trading. Like cash, Bitcoins are anonymous—they are exchanged via a 34-character alphanumeric address that the user has, and do not require any other identifying information. Bitcoins have recently attracted a lot of attention as a potential money laundering tool for cybercriminals, and have also been plagued by security issues, with some high-profile heists. Nonetheless, there are companies now using Bitcoins as a legitimate alternative payment system. Read the *Insight on Business* case, *Bitcoin*, for a further look at Bitcoin and some of the issues surrounding it.

virtual currency

typically circulates within an internal virtual world community or is issued by a specific corporate entity, and used to purchase virtual goods

Virtual currencies, on the other hand, typically circulate primarily within an internal virtual world community, such as Linden Dollars, created by Linden Lab for use in its virtual world, Second Life. Virtual currencies are typically used for purchasing virtual goods.

5.6 ELECTRONIC BILLING PRESENTMENT AND PAYMENT

In 2007, for the first time, the number of bill payments made online exceeded the number of physical checks written (Fiserv, 2007). In the $17.8 trillion U.S. economy with a $12.2 trillion consumer sector for goods and services, there are billions of bills to pay. According to the U.S. Postal Service, U.S. households received about 14 billion bills in 2013 via the mail. No one knows for sure, but some experts believe the life-cycle cost of a paper bill for a business, from point of issuance to point of payment, ranges from $3 to $7. This calculation does not include the value of time to consumers, who must open bills, read them, write checks, address envelopes, stamp, and then mail remittances. The billing market represents an extraordinary opportunity for using the Internet as an electronic billing and payment system that potentially could greatly reduce both the cost of paying bills and the time consumers spend paying them. Estimates vary, but online payments are believed to cost between only 20 to 30 cents to process.

electronic billing presentment and payment (EBPP) system

form of online payment system for monthly bills

Electronic billing presentment and payment (EBPP) systems are systems that enable the online delivery and payment of monthly bills. EBPP services allow consumers to view bills electronically and pay them through electronic funds transfers from bank or credit card accounts. More and more companies are choosing to issue statements and bills electronically, rather than mailing out paper versions. But even those businesses that do mail paper bills are increasingly offering online bill payment

INSIGHT ON BUSINESS

BITCOIN

In recent years, a number of countries around the world have experienced banking crises, eroding trust in the system. Enter Bitcoin, a form of electronic currency that does not exist in physical form and can be transferred from one person to another via peer-to-peer networks, without the need for a bank or other financial institution as intermediary. This ability to operate outside the banking system has made Bitcoin a favorite of narcotics traffickers and buyers and sellers of illicit goods and services; but more recently, it has made Bitcoin a darling among many in the technological elite who believe that Bitcoin and the technology behind it could be the next big thing in the payments industry.

Bitcoin has many unique attributes that differentiate it from traditional currencies. Bitcoins are not physically minted, but have been generated by computer software at a predetermined rate beginning in 2009. A finite amount of coins are "built into the software," such that in the year 2140, all of the coins will be mined and present in the market. The program that is used to generate Bitcoins runs on a peer-to-peer network and requires powerful computer systems to operate. "Mining" a Bitcoin is the result of these powerful computers solving cryptographic problems in tandem with other similar computers—the computer that hits upon the solution is awarded the coin, and a record of all of the involved computers' attempts at mining the coin is logged. Bitcoins derive some of their initial value because of the time and computational effort required to mine them.

There are, however, many reasons to be skeptical of Bitcoin. Law enforcement agencies and governments are justifiably concerned about the emergence of a new currency whose purpose is to avoid regulation. A newly mined Bitcoin can be used with nearly complete anonymity. One report found that a full 5% percent of Bitcoins that were in circulation were collected by the online black market Silk Road, which sold illegal drugs before its closure. Still, by using Bitcoin addresses in tandem with the services used by the individuals in charge of those addresses, law enforcement can catch thieves and apprehend individuals making illegal purchases. For instance, in January 2014, Charlie Shrem, the founding member of a foundation to promote Bitcoin, was arrested for selling $1 million in Bitcoin to Silk Road and for purchasing illegal drugs on the site. The Silk Road's founder, Ross Ulbricht, was convicted in February 2015 of several charges, including money laundering and conspiracy to traffic narcotics.

Nevertheless, the traditional banking system does a better job at curtailing money laundering and illicit money transfers than Bitcoin. As a result, many governments have taken a firm stand against digital cash. In 2014, for instance, China's government announced that it had ordered banks to close their Bitcoin trading accounts. Denmark has also banned digital cash deposits, and other countries like Russia and Israel have warned their citizens that similar regulations may be forthcoming.

Each of these developments has put downward pressure on Bitcoin's value and slowed its growth, although nearly 80% of Bitcoin volume in 2015 is backed by the Chinese yuan, suggesting that China's attempts to limit Bitcoin's usage have been unsuccessful. A 2015 analysis of Bitcoin usage suggested that Bitcoins are still used primarily for gambling, illicit goods, and hoarding by speculators. Security concerns have also crippled the largest Bitcoin exchanges to date, including Mt. Gox and Flexcoin. Hackers

(continued)

stole $425 million and $600,000 in Bitcoins from the two exchanges, respectively. These regulatory pressures and security concerns have driven Bitcoin's dizzying volatility. In 2012, Bitcoin's value was $6; in 2013, it rose to $1,200; and in 2015, it plummeted back down to $225, and is struggling to regain traction.

Despite all of these drawbacks, Bitcoin continues to move forward, and more banks and regulators are recognizing that it may be here to stay. In 2015, Goldman Sachs invested heavily in Circle Internet Financial, a Bitcoin peer-to-peer payment platform, noting that Bitcoin could gain international acceptance over time. In June 2015, the New York State Department of Financial Services released regulations governing the issuance of BitLicenses, which provide a framework for virtual currency businesses to operate within the state of New York. In September 2015, New York issued the first BitLicense to Circle Internet, giving it the right to operate in the state, while subjecting it to strict capital, consumer protection, and anti-money laundering requirements. Many large U.S. banks, the New York Stock Exchange, Japanese telecom giant DoCoMo, and other companies have invested in Coinbase, an intermediary for Bitcoin transactions. In 2015, the first ever legitimate, licensed Bitcoin bank, itBit, went live. Also in 2015, the regulatory agency FINRA allowed the Bitcoin Investment Trust (BIT) to be traded publicly on an electronic platform, making it the first publicly traded Bitcoin investment fund. In 2014, the IRS began taxing Bitcoin earnings, further legitimizing it in the eyes of regulators.

Companies like Circle Internet Financial hope to harness Bitcoin's decentralized network of computers to enable frictionless and inexpensive movement of currencies across international borders. Bitcoins and Bitcoin transactions are all logged on a public ledger known as the blockchain, which is updated and maintained by all of the members of the network. Contrast this with a bank, which is a central hub where all currency and financial information reside. With the blockchain, there isn't a single point of failure or vulnerability the way there may be with a bank, and no single entity must update and maintain the ledger. Businesses like Coinbase also want to "sanitize" the currency, and distance it from its negative association with narcotics and illicit goods. For Bitcoin to truly gain acceptance, regular people will need to begin using it for everyday transactions. In countries where the banking system is less developed than in the United States, this has already begun to happen. In Argentina, the Philippines, Kenya, and other similar countries, excessive banking regulations have made Bitcoin a more appealing alternative for ordinary people making normal commercial transactions.

A number of high-profile online businesses accept Bitcoin, such as Dell and Microsoft, as well as reportedly over 80,000 other merchants around the world. But the total number of businesses adding Bitcoin as a payment method is on the decline. And while the number of individuals with Bitcoin wallets grew from 7.4 million in 2014 to 8.4 million in 2015, Bitcoin trading volume is down from its peak in 2014.

━━ **SOURCES:** "Circle Gets First 'BitLicense,' Releases Circle Pay, New Service," by Paul Vigna, *Wall Street Journal,* September 22, 2015; "Goldman and IDG Put $50 Million to Work in a Bitcoin Company," by Nathaniel Popper, *New York Times,* April 30, 2015; "Bitcoin Behemoth Coinbase launches in the UK," by Alex Hern, *The Guardian,* April 29, 2015; "Can Bitcoin Conquer Argentina?" by Nathaniel Popper, *New York Times,* April 29, 2015; "The World's First Proper Bitcoin Exchange Will Go Live in a Month," by Kieren McCarthy, *The Register,* April 29, 2015; "What Bitcoin Businesses Most Fear Right Now," by Daniel Roberts, *Fortune,* April 28, 2015; "Bitcoin's Q1: Record VC Investment, Falling Prices, and Slow Consumer Adoption," by lex Wilhelm, Techcrunch.com, April 26, 2015; "Final New York Bitcoin Regulation Released: Bitlicense," by P.H. Madore, Cryptocoinnews.com, April 6, 2015; "Bitcoin's Golden Moment: BIT Gets FINRA Approval," by Brian Kelly, Cnbc.com, March 4, 2015; "Is Bitcoin Stalling?" by Mike Orcutt, *Technology Review,* February 18, 2015; "Bitcoin's Price Falls 12%, to Lowest Value Since May," by Sydney Ember, *New York Times,* August 18, 2014; "Tokyo Court: Bitcoin Exchange Mt. Gox Will Liquidate," by Donna Leinwand, *USA Today,* April 16, 2014; "China Cracks Down on Bitcoin," by Chao Deng and Lingling Wei, *Wall Street Journal,* April 1, 2014; "The Mt. Gox Bitcoin Scandal Is the Best Thing to Happen to Bitcoin In Years," by Heidi Moore, Theguardian.com, February 26, 2014; "Israel's Central Bank Warns on Potential Fraud With Bitcoin," by Calev Ben-David, Bloomberg.com, February 19, 2014; "Russian Authorities Say Bitcoin Illegal," by Gabriela Baczynska, Reuters.com, February 9, 2014; "Bitcoin Pitchman Busted for 'Selling $1M in Currency to Silk Road,'" by Kaja Whitehouse and Rich Calder, *New York Post,* January 27, 2014; "Following the Bitcoin Trail," Economist.com, August 28, 2013.

as an option to customers, allowing them to immediately transfer funds from a bank or credit card account to pay a bill somewhere else.

MARKET SIZE AND GROWTH

In 2002, 61% of bill payments were made by check, and only 12% by online bill payments. In 2014, in contrast, online bill payments accounted for more than half of all bill payments, while paper checks now account for less than 25%. Among online households, almost three-quarters pay at least one bill online each month, and almost half receive at least one bill electronically each month. Mobile bill payments are surging, with 27 million U.S. households in 2014 paying at least one bill on a mobile device, up 70% from the previous year. Most consumers cited the convenience and time saved by using mobile bill payment (Fiserv, 2013, 2014a, 2014b).

One major reason for the surge in EBPP usage is that companies are starting to realize how much money they can save through online billing. Not only is there the savings in postage and processing, but payments can be received more quickly (3 to 12 days faster, compared to paper bills sent via regular mail), thereby improving cash flow. Online bill payment options can also reduce the number of phone calls to a company's customer service line. In order to realize these savings, many companies are becoming more aggressive in encouraging their customers to move to EBPP by instituting a charge for the privilege of continuing to receive a paper bill.

Financials don't tell the whole story, however. Companies are discovering that a bill is both a sales opportunity and a customer retention opportunity, and that the electronic medium provides many more options when it comes to marketing and promotion. Rebates, savings offers, cross-selling, and upselling are all possible in the digital realm.

EBPP BUSINESS MODELS

There are two main competing business models in the EBPP marketspace: biller-direct and consolidator. The biller-direct system was originally created by utility companies that send millions of bills each month. Their purpose is to make it easier for their customers to pay their utility bills routinely online. Today, telephone and credit card companies also frequently offer this service, as well as a number of individual stores. Companies implementing a biller-direct system can either develop their own system in-house (usually only an option for the very largest companies), install a system acquired from a third-party EBPP software vendor, use a third-party EBPP service bureau (the service bureau hosts a biller-branded Web site that enables consumers to view and pay bills and handles all customer enrollment, bill presentment, and payment processing), or use an application service provider (similar to a service bureau, but runs on the biller's Web site rather than being hosted on the service provider's Web site).

In the consolidator model, a third party, such as a financial institution or a focused portal such as Intuit's Paytrust, Fiserv's MyCheckFree, Mint Bills, and others, aggregates all bills for consumers and ideally permits one-stop bill payment (pay anyone). Currently, financial institutions have been more successful than portals in attracting online bill payers. The consolidator model faces several challenges. For billers, using the consolidator model means an increased time lag between billing and payment, and also inserts an intermediary between the company and its customer. For consumers,

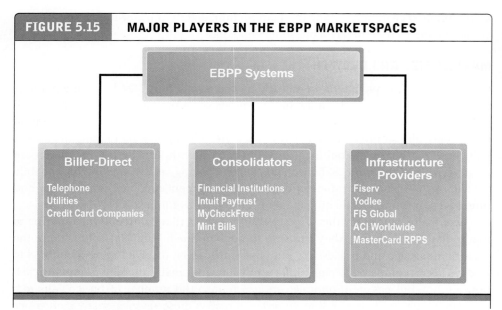

FIGURE 5.15   **MAJOR PLAYERS IN THE EBPP MARKETSPACES**

EBPP Systems

Biller-Direct

Telephone
Utilities
Credit Card Companies

Consolidators

Financial Institutions
Intuit Paytrust
MyCheckFree
Mint Bills

Infrastructure Providers

Fiserv
Yodlee
FIS Global
ACI Worldwide
MasterCard RPPS

The main business models in the EBPP marketspace are biller-direct and consolidator. Infrastructure providers support both of these competing models and sometimes operate their own online payment portals.

security continues to be a major issue. Most consumers are unwilling to pay any kind of fee to pay bills online, and many are concerned about sharing personal financial information with nonfinancial institutions. Today, more and more banks are offering online bill payment free to some or all of their customers as an enticement.

Supporting these two primary business models are infrastructure providers such as Fiserv, Yodlee, FIS Global, ACI Worldwide, MasterCard RPPS (Remote Payment and Presentment Service), and others that provide the software to create the EBPP system or handle billing and payment collection for the biller. **Figure 5.15** categorizes the major players in the EBPP marketspace.

CASE STUDY

The Mobile Payment Marketplace:

Goat Rodeo

Nearly every day, it seems, a new mobile payment system is announced. The mobile payment marketplace is experiencing an explosion of innovative ideas, plans, and announcements, which one commentator has likened to a goat rodeo, a chaotic situation in which powerful players with different agendas compete with one another for public acceptance, and above all, huge potential revenues. It's a battle among the titans of online payment and retailing: PayPal, credit card companies like Visa and Master-Card, Google, Apple, start-up tech companies like Square that offer mobile credit card swiping backed by millions in venture capital, and even large retailers like Walmart, Best Buy, and Target, all of which are developing their own mobile payment systems that they control. Although consumers still prefer to pay with credit cards and cash

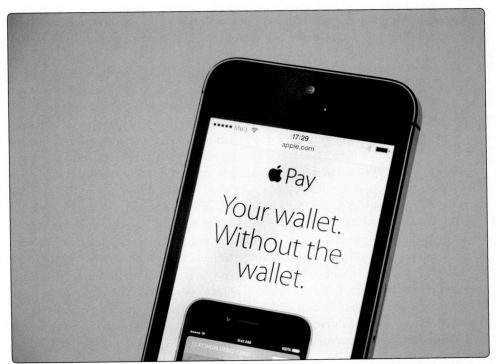

© Anatolii Babii/Alamy

on the go, digital mobile payment systems may finally be poised to deliver on their long-awaited promise.

Apple entered the fray in 2014 with its announcement of Apple Pay for iPhone 6 smartphones, joining Google and others that already had developed a mobile payment system using Near Field Communication (NFC), a short-range radio communications protocol that operates within a range of a few inches, and allows consumers to bump, swipe, or just come close to a merchant's NFC reader to pay for goods and services. What's different about Apple's announcement of an NFC-based payment system is that it's Apple—the firm that revolutionized five different industries and introduced the first smartphones, forever changing how people shop and communicate with one another. Apple's iTunes store already has the credit card information of 800 million users, arguably the largest such collection on earth. In 2015, Apple introduced its Apple Watch, which also includes Apple Pay.

Apple Pay is more than an app or a smartphone feature—it's an ecosystem unto itself. Apple has developed relationships with many of the key players in the payment ecosystem, including credit giants Visa, MasterCard, American Express, and Discover, as well as 11 large bank credit card issuers including JPMorgan Chase, Bank America, Citigroup, and Wells Fargo, which together account for 83% of U.S. credit card payment volume. Apple has also signed up national merchants such as Walgreens, Duane Reade, McDonald's, Disney, Macys, Bloomingdales, Staples, and Whole Foods. Groupon and Uber have integrated Apple Pay into their systems. Unlike the introductions of other mobile payment systems, which tended to reflect the self-interest of those making the introduction, Apple's approach is much more inclusive of the major stakeholders in the marketplace. Target, Walmart, and Best Buy are missing the Apple party because they are developing their own mobile payment systems.

Security is a central issue for all payment systems, and given the evident lack of security for Internet-connected devices and databases, payment security is a major concern for consumers and banks and merchants. The Apple announcement came on the heels of news in August 2014 that several celebrities had their personal iCloud accounts hacked, resulting in the distribution of provocative pictures on social media and the Web. Target, Home Depot, and several major banks reported their customer databases and point of sale terminals had been hacked in 2014 as well, resulting in hackers gaining access to millions of credit card numbers and pin codes. For this reason, the emphasis at Apple Pay's introduction was security.

The Apple Pay system uses several levels of security to avoid the loss of customer information. Apple Pay relies on the customer having a credit card on file with Apple's iTunes, and that card is the financial vehicle for payment. When a customer wants to make a payment, he or she presses the iPhone Touch ID button, which reads the customer's fingerprint and ensures the phone does indeed belong to the person. On the Apple Watch, there's a special button just for Apple Pay transactions. Next, the consumer swipes the device near a merchant's NFC point-of-sale terminal, which begins the transaction process. The iPhone 6 comes with a hardware-defined secure area on a chip that contains a unique device number and the ability to generate a one-time 16-digit code. Together they form a digital token. The token information is encrypted and sent to Apple servers to verify the authenticity of the device and the person. Credit card issuers verify the account owner and available credit. In about one second, the transaction is approved or denied. Credit card information is not shared with the merchant and not transmitted from the iPhone. The 800 million credit cards stored on Apple's servers are also encrypted. If hackers intercept the NFC communication at the point of sale, or intercept the stream of data moving over the cellular network, it would be useless, and incapable of supporting additional transactions because the message is encrypted, and involves a one-time-only code.

Privacy is also an issue. Traditional credit card payment systems gather extensive information on user charges, recording what is purchased, where, and when. Selling credit card purchase information to credit agencies and data brokers is an important income stream for banks that issue credit cards. Apple Pay will not be playing that game. Timothy Cook, Apple's CEO, pointed out in an interview in September 2014 that Apple Pay gathers no consumer information, and that Apple is a technology company and not an advertising company. Apple Pay will not gather any consumer information that could be used to target or track consumers, or expose them to additional targeted advertising.

How will Apple make money from Apple Pay? Credit card companies charge merchants a fee of 2% to 3% of the amount for each transaction. Apple Pay will not charge the merchant or the consumer an additional fee. Instead Apple will charge the credit card issuer bank a .15% fee in return for guaranteeing the authenticity of the transaction. In essence, Apple is providing an insurance policy for the issuers of credit cards. If the transaction is fraudulent, Apple will pay the issuer. Apple Pay could significantly reduce credit card fraud in the United States, benefiting the issuing banks directly.

Apple's .15% fee is a very small charge, but Apple is confident in its system and willing to invest in its own technology. Assuming Apple Pay rings up $1 billion in transactions, how much will the banks and Apple receive as revenue? The banks on average will collect 3%, which works out to $30 million. Apple will receive just .15% or $1.5 million for every $1 billion in transactions, which probably will not clear the costs of operating Apple Pay. The real value to Apple is not the revenue from Apple Pay, but its contribution to the sales of Apple products like the iPhone and iPad, as well as the entire Apple ecosystem of services provided by iTunes. Apple becomes not just your source for music, videos, movies, television, books, and over 1.5 million apps, but also your wallet.

There are some obvious drawbacks to Apple Pay. It works only on Apple devices (and only on the latest iPhone 6 and Apple Watch); merchants need to buy NFC-enabled point-of-sale terminals, and consumers will need to change their behaviors for Apple Pay to achieve widespread acceptance. Finally, merchants lose some of their control over the point-of-payment/purchase moment when they could be upselling customers, offering coupons, ads, and loyalty points.

The overall online payment market in the United States is estimated to be worth about $530 billion in 2015 and is growing at more than 12% a year. While still comparatively small compared to the total e-commerce picture, m-commerce, driven by smartphones, tablets, Wi-Fi, and cellular networks, is growing at more than 30% a year. In 2015, m-commerce is expected to generate $128 billion in revenue. While most of these m-commerce transactions are occurring through the use of credit cards (just as with desktop e-commerce), there is a rapidly growing segment of proximity mobile payments (payments that use a mobile phone as the payment method, via tapping, waving, or similar functionality) which is expected to amount to about $8.7 billion in 2015 and grow astronomically to over $210 billion by 2019. U.S. consumers spent an estimated $5.1 trillion on credit and debit card transactions in 2014. Even if a small percentage of these transactions move from plastic to mobile payments, the potential revenue is very large. This is enough to drive even old goats into a frenzy.

Apple has a number of competitors in mobile payments. Contenders in the NFC-enabled proximity mobile payment market currently include Android Pay, Samsung Pay, and CurrentC, a system being developed by Merchant Customer Exchange (MCX).

Android Pay is a Google app that provides an NFC-based payment system much like Apple Pay. Android Pay replaces Google Wallet, which has been repurposed as a peer-to-peer payment service that allows users to pay friends using only their e-mail address, similar to PayPal. Android Pay is enabled by a prepaid MasterCard. Users must keep a balance with the issuing bank to fund purchases, as with any debit card, and have an Android Pay account. To use Android Pay, customers hold their phone near the merchant's NFC terminal at checkout. Users are asked for their PIN and then choose to pay with either a MasterCard debit card or a balance kept with Android Pay. If the user chooses to pay with MasterCard, the app passes the credit information to the merchant's terminal, which then clears the transaction with MasterCard. Bancorp Bank is the issuing bank. Android Pay is free to credit card companies and merchants. However, Google may offer consumers, rewards, and other loyalty programs through Android Pay that could generate substantial revenue.

Samsung Pay was introduced by Samsung in the United States in September 2015, after an earlier roll-out in Samsung's home country, South Korea. Unlike Apple Pay or Android Pay, Samsung Pay reportedly works in almost all stores, without merchants needing to opt-in to any program or update their point-of-sale terminals, by using Magnetic Secure Transmission, a technology Samsung acquired when it purchased mobile payment company LoopPay earlier in 2015. Samsung Pay works only with certain phones offered by Samsung using AT&T, Sprint, T-Mobile, or US Cellular. An American Express card, or a Visa or MasterCard issued by Bank of America, Citibank, or US Bank, also is required.

Perhaps the strongest competition for both Apple Pay, Android Pay, and Samsung Pay will eventually come from the Merchant Customer Exchange (MCX), a joint venture of 15 of the largest retailers, including Walmart, Target, Sears, 7-Eleven, Sunoco, and 10 other national pharmacies, supermarkets, and restaurant chains. Announced in March 2012, the backers of this effort have annual sales of more than $1 trillion dollars. That's enough to make everyone involved in mobile payments stand up and listen, even Google and Apple. The MCX system, called CurrentC, was pilot tested in 2014, and will be released in a national roll-out in 2016 after plans for a 2015 rollout were delayed. It is the only merchant-owned mobile payment system.

CurrentC is an app-based mobile payment system for both iOS and Android devices that permits customers to pay at the point of sale from credit or debit cards, gift cards, or bank accounts using their smartphone. During the checkout process, merchants can offer coupons, rewards, and loyalty points on the user's payment screen. CurrentC works by allowing users to load value (pre-paid cards or credit cards) into the app. It then generates a QR code unique to each customer that is displayed on the phone screen. After swiping the QR code, an encrypted token is generated and sent to MCX cloud servers, which store the credit card information and make the approval decision. An acceptance token is returned to the merchant. Older point of sale systems can be modified to read this QR code, reducing the need for merchants to upgrade.

Why are these nationwide merchants willing to invest billions in a mobile payment system when financial service firms and technology players also are investing billions in competing systems? The answer is control over the customer during the transaction, and the information on customer purchase history that the apps will be recording. The merchants do not want this valuable marketing asset to flow to financial service firms, or Google, Apple, and Samsung. To some extent, the coming mobile payment battle is one between tech companies like Apple, Google, and Samsung, and the traditional brick and mortar merchants. The banks and credit card companies will benefit no matter who wins.

While NFC-enabled mobile payments may be the future, other types of mobile payments are already here. Currently, the most popular mobile payment systems are offered by PayPal and Square, which do not use NFC. PayPal was late to the mobile payment market, beaten to the punch by Square. Square started in 2009 with Square Reader, a square plastic device that plugged into an iPhone or iPad. Using the Square app, it allows merchants to easily accept credit card payments from customers on the go. Square also developed Square Register (now called Point of Sale), which is a software app that turns a tablet into a point-of-sale terminal and cash register. Square has been very popular with small businesses like coffee shops, newsstands, small retailers, and farmers' market merchants, as well as piano teachers, baby sitters, and taxi drivers, allowing them to accept credit card payments. Square is expected to go public in October 2015, and is reportedly on track to take in $1 billion in revenue in 2015, although it is expected that it will not show a net profit. But a closer analysis reveals that most of its losses resulted from a failed partnership with Starbucks as its exclusive payment processor, and that it makes money on all of its other transactions. The future may be brighter than the present for Square.

PayPal is currently the most successful and profitable mobile payment system. PayPal currently enables mobile payments in three ways. First, PayPal sells to merchants a device that allows them to swipe credit cards using a smartphone or tablet, just like the Square device. Second, the most common mobile PayPal mobile payment occurs when customers use their mobile device browser to make a pur-

SOURCES: "Mobile Payments Will Triple in the US in 2016," by eMarketer, Inc., October 26, 2015; "'Pretty Useless': Consumer Frustrations Grow Over New Credit Card Chip," by Alexandra Zaslow, Todaymoney.com, October 16, 2015; "Square's IPO Filing: It's Complicated," Recode.net, by Jason Del Rey, October 14, 2015; "PayPal Here Launches a Mobile Card Reader That Accepts Android Pay and Apple Pay," by Ruth Reader, Venturebeat.com, September 28, 2015; "Samsung Pay: What You Need to Know (FAQ)," by Lexy Savvides, Cnet. com, September 28, 2015; "Revamped Google Wallet Arrives on iOS," by Stephanie Mlot, Pcmagazine.com, September 22, 2015; "Apple Pay Competitor CurrentC May Not Launch Until Next Year," by Jason Del Rey, Recode.net, August 12, 2015; "PayPal Returns to Market with $52 Billion Valuation," by Devika Krishna Kumar and Mari Saito, Reuters.com, July 20, 2015; "There Are No Transaction Fees for Android Pay, Which Is Good for Us, Bad for Google," by Robert Nazarian, Digitaltrends.com, June 8, 2015; "The State of Mobile Payments in 2015," by James A Martin, CIO.com, April 22, 2015; "Apple Sees Mobile-Payment Service Gaining in Challenge to

PayPal," by Olga Kharif, Bloomberg.com, January 27, 2015; "What Apple Pay Means for Retailers," by Abby Callard, Internetretailer.com, September 12, 2014; "Apple Pay: No Charge for Merchants, But Transaction-Security Fees for Issuers," by Jim Daly, Digitaltransaction.net, September 11, 2014; "Apple Pushes Digital Wallet with Apple Pay," by Associated Press, *Wall Street Journal*, September 10, 2014; "Will Stores Warm Up to Apple Pay," by Daisuke Wakabayashi and Greg Bensinger, *Wall Street Journal*, September 10, 2014; "With Apple Pay and Smartwatch, a Privacy Challenge," by Brian X. Chen and Steve Lohr, *New York Times*, September 10, 2014; "As Questions Linger, Discover Says 'Me Too' to Apple Pay," by Kevin Woodward, Digitaltransactions.net, September 10, 2014; "Apple Unveils an 'Entirely New Payment Process' with Apple Pay," by Jim Daly, Digitaltransactions.net, September 9, 2014; "Endpoint: Not All Mobile-Payment Systems Are Mobile Wallets," Digitaltransactions.net, July 1, 2014; "Apple Pay Leaps Ahead of Mobile Payments Providers," by Spencer Soper, Bloomberg.com, September 10, 2014; "Easier Ways to Make Payments with Smartphones," by Molly Wood, *New York Times*, July 30, 2014; "For Square, Making Money Remains a Challenge," by William Alden, *New York Times*, April 21, 2014.

chase or payment at a Web site. This is not very helpful for merchants like Starbucks, Macys, or local restaurants, who would like customers to be able to purchase goods in their stores and outlets on the fly without keying in information to a smartphone. A third method is PayPal's updated app for iOS and Android devices. On entering a merchant's store that accepts PayPal app payments, the app establishes a link using Bluetooth with the merchant's app that is also running on an iOS or Android device. This step authenticates the user's PayPal account. On checkout, the customer tells the merchant he or she will pay with PayPal. The merchant device charges the customer's PayPal account. After the payment is authorized, a message is sent to the customer's phone. No credit card information is being transmitted or shared with the merchant or the issuing bank. Users do not have to enter a pin code or swipe their phone at a special merchant device, so merchants are not required to purchase an expensive NFC point-of-sale device. However, in 2015, PayPal announced the release of a device that will both read new credit cards equipped with computer chips, as well as accept payments from Android Pay and Apple Pay.

PayPal is currently the largest alternative (non-credit card) online payment service, processing $228 billion in transactions in 2014. PayPal processed $46 billion in mobile payments in 2014, up from $27 billion in 2013. Most of this mobile payment volume involved customers using their mobile phones or tablet browsers to make payments, just as they use PayPal on their PCs at work or home. PayPal has not announced the performance of the PayPal app, but acceptance appears to be very limited in 2015, in part because neither merchants nor customers are familiar with the product.

The future for smartphone mobile payments is assured given the size of the players involved, the potential rewards for successful players, and the demands of consumers for a payment system that does not involve swiping plastic cards and dealing with slips of paper. But it is unlikely that all the payment systems described above will survive, and also quite likely that consumers will remain confused by all their payment options for some time yet to come.

Case Study Questions

1. What is the value proposition that Apple Pay offers consumers? How about merchants?

2. What are some of the limitations of Apple Pay that might prevent its widespread adoption?

3. What advantages do the Square and PayPal mobile card-swiping solutions have in the mobile payment market? What are their weaknesses?

4. What strategies would you recommend that Apple pursue to assure widespread consumer adoption of Apple Pay?

5.8 REVIEW

KEY CONCEPTS

■ **Understand the scope of e-commerce crime and security problems, the key dimensions of e-commerce security, and the tension between security and other values.**

- While the overall size of cybercrime is unclear, cybercrime against e-commerce sites is growing rapidly, the amount of losses is growing, and the management of e-commerce sites must prepare for a variety of criminal assaults.
- There are six key dimensions to e-commerce security: integrity, nonrepudiation, authenticity, confidentiality, privacy, and availability.
- Although computer security is considered necessary to protect e-commerce activities, it is not without a downside. Two major areas where there are tensions between security and Web site operations are:
    - *Ease of use*—The more security measures that are added to an e-commerce site, the more difficult it is to use and the slower the site becomes, hampering ease of use. Security is purchased at the price of slowing down processors and adding significantly to data storage demands. Too much security can harm profitability, while not enough can potentially put a company out of business.
    - *Public safety*—There is a tension between the claims of individuals to act anonymously and the needs of public officials to maintain public safety that can be threatened by criminals or terrorists.

■ **Identify the key security threats in the e-commerce environment**

- The most common and most damaging forms of security threats to e-commerce sites include:
    - *Malicious code*—viruses, worms, Trojan horses, ransomware, and bot networks are a threat to a system's integrity and continued operation, often changing how a system functions or altering documents created on the system.
    - *Potentially unwanted programs (adware, spyware, etc.)*—a kind of security threat that arises when programs are surreptitiously installed on your computer or computer network without your consent.
    - *Phishing*—any deceptive, online attempt by a third party to obtain confidential information for financial gain.
    - *Hacking and cybervandalism*—intentionally disrupting, defacing, or even destroying a site.
    - *Credit card fraud/theft*—one of the most-feared occurrences and one of the main reasons more consumers do not participate in e-commerce. The most common cause of credit card fraud is a lost or stolen card that is used by someone else, followed by employee theft of customer numbers and stolen identities (criminals applying for credit cards using false identities).
    - *Identity fraud*—involves the unauthorized use of another person's personal data, such as social security, driver's license, and/or credit card numbers, as well as user names and passwords, for illegal financial benefit.
    - *Spoofing*—occurs when hackers attempt to hide their true identities or misrepresent themselves by using fake e-mail addresses or masquerading as someone else.
    - *Pharming*—involves redirecting a Web link to an address different from the intended one, with the site masquerading as the intended destination.
    - *Denial of Service (DoS) and Distributed Denial of Service (DDoS) attacks*—hackers flood a Web site with useless traffic to inundate and overwhelm the network, frequently causing it to shut down and damaging a site's reputation and customer relationships.

- *Sniffing*—a type of eavesdropping program that monitors information traveling over a network, enabling hackers to steal proprietary information from anywhere on a network, including e-mail messages, company files, and confidential reports. The threat of sniffing is that confidential or personal information will be made public.
- *Insider jobs*—although the bulk of Internet security efforts are focused on keeping outsiders out, the biggest threat is from employees who have access to sensitive information and procedures.
- *Poorly designed server and client software*—the increase in complexity and size of software programs has contributed to an increase in software flaws or vulnerabilities that hackers can exploit.
- *Social network security issues*—malicious code, PUPs, phishing, data breaches, identity fraud, and other e-commerce security threats have all infiltrated social networks.
- *Mobile platform security issues*—the mobile platform presents an alluring target for hackers and cybercriminals, and faces all the same risks as other Internet devices, as well as new risks associated with wireless network security.
- *Cloud security issues*—as devices, identities, and data become more and more intertwined in the cloud, safeguarding data in the cloud becomes a major concern.

- ■ **Describe how technology helps secure Internet communications channels and protect networks, servers, and clients.**
- Encryption is the process of transforming plain text or data into cipher text that cannot be read by anyone other than the sender and the receiver. Encryption can provide four of the six key dimensions of e-commerce security: message integrity, nonrepudiation, authentication, and confidentiality.
- There are a variety of different forms of encryption technology currently in use. They include:
  - *Symmetric key cryptography*—Both the sender and the receiver use the same key to encrypt and decrypt a message.
  - *Public key cryptography*—Two mathematically related digital keys are used: a public key and a private key. The private key is kept secret by the owner, and the public key is widely disseminated. Both keys can be used to encrypt and decrypt a message. Once the keys are used to encrypt a message, the same keys cannot be used to unencrypt the message.
  - *Public key cryptography using digital signatures and hash digests*—This method uses a mathematical algorithm called a hash function to produce a fixed-length number called a hash digest. The results of applying the hash function are sent by the sender to the recipient. Upon receipt, the recipient applies the hash function to the received message and checks to verify that the same result is produced. The sender then encrypts both the hash result and the original message using the recipient's public key, producing a single block of cipher text. To ensure both the authenticity of the message and nonrepudiation, the sender encrypts the entire block of cipher text one more time using the sender's private key. This produces a digital signature or "signed" cipher text that can be sent over the Internet to ensure the confidentiality of the message and authenticate the sender.
  - *Digital envelope*—This method uses symmetric cryptography to encrypt and decrypt the document, but public key cryptography to encrypt and send the symmetric key.
  - *Digital certificates and public key infrastructure*—This method relies on certification authorities who issue, verify, and guarantee digital certificates (a digital document that contains the name of the subject or company, the subject's public key, a digital certificate serial number, an expiration date, an issuance date, the digital signature of the certification authority, and other identifying information).
- In addition to encryption, there are several other tools that are used to secure Internet channels of communication, including: Secure Sockets Layer (SSL)/Transport Layer Security (TLS), virtual private networks (VPNs), and wireless security standards such as WPA2.

- After communications channels are secured, tools to protect networks, the servers, and clients should be implemented. These include: firewalls, proxies, intrusion detection and prevention systems (IDS/IDP), operating system controls, and anti-virus software.

- **Appreciate the importance of policies, procedures, and laws in creating security.**

- In order to minimize security threats, e-commerce firms must develop a coherent corporate policy that takes into account the nature of the risks, the information assets that need protecting, and the procedures and technologies required to address the risk, as well as implementation and auditing mechanisms.
- Public laws and active enforcement of cybercrime statutes also are required to both raise the costs of illegal behavior on the Internet and guard against corporate abuse of information.
- The key steps in developing a security plan are:
  - *Perform a risk assessment*—an assessment of the risks and points of vulnerability.
  - *Develop a security policy*—a set of statements prioritizing the information risks, identifying acceptable risk targets, and identifying the mechanisms for achieving these targets.
  - *Create an implementation plan*—a plan that determines how you will translate the levels of acceptable risk into a set of tools, technologies, policies, and procedures.
  - *Create a security team*—the individuals who will be responsible for ongoing maintenance, audits, and improvements.
  - *Perform periodic security audits*—routine reviews of access logs and any unusual patterns of activity.

- **Identify the major e-commerce payment systems in use today.**

- The major types of e-commerce payment systems in use today include:
  - *Online credit card transactions,* which are the primary form of online payment system. There are five parties involved in an online credit card purchase: consumer, merchant, clearinghouse, merchant bank (sometimes called the "acquiring bank"), and the consumer's card-issuing bank. However, the online credit card system has a number of limitations involving security, merchant risk, cost, and social equity.
  - *PayPal,* which is an example of an online stored value payment system that permits consumers to make instant, online payments to merchants and other individuals based on value stored in an online account.
  - *Alternative payment services* such as Amazon Payments, Visa Checkout, and Bill Me Later, which enable consumers to shop online at a wide variety of merchants without having to provide credit card information each time they make a purchase.
  - *Mobile payment systems*, using either credit card readers attached to a smartphone (Square, PayPal Here) or near field communication (NFC) chips, which enable proximity mobile payment, used by Apple Pay, Android Pay, and Samsung Pay.
  - *Digital cash* such as Bitcoin, which is based on an algorithm that generates unique authenticated tokens representing cash value, and virtual currencies, that typically circulate within an internal virtual world or are issued by a corporation, and usually used for the purchase of virtual goods.

- **Describe the features and functionality of electronic billing presentment and payment systems.**

- Electronic billing presentment and payment (EBPP) systems are a form of online payment systems for monthly bills. EBPP services allow consumers to view bills electronically and pay them through electronic funds transfers from bank or credit card accounts. Major players in the EBPP marketspace include: biller-direct systems, consolidators, and infrastructure providers.

QUESTIONS

1. Why is it less risky to steal online? Explain some of the ways criminals deceive consumers and merchants.
2. Explain why an e-commerce site might not want to report being the target of cybercriminals.
3. Give an example of security breaches as they relate to each of the six dimensions of e-commerce security. For instance, what would be a privacy incident?
4. How would you protect your firm against a Denial of Service attack?
5. Name the major points of vulnerability in a typical online transaction.
6. How does spoofing threaten a Web site's operations?
7. Why is adware or spyware considered to be a security threat?
8. What are some of the steps a company can take to curtail cybercriminal activity from within a business?
9. Explain some of the modern-day flaws associated with encryption. Why is encryption not as secure today as it was earlier in the century?
10. Briefly explain how public key cryptography works.
11. Compare and contrast firewalls and proxy servers and their security functions.
12. Is a computer with anti-virus software protected from viruses? Why or why not?
13. Identify and discuss the five steps in developing an e-commerce security plan.
14. How do biometric devices help improve security? What particular type of security breach do they reduce?
15. Briefly discuss the disadvantages of credit cards as the standard for online payments. How does requiring a credit card for payment discriminate against some consumers?
16. Describe the major steps involved in an online credit card transaction.
17. Why is Bitcoin so controversial?
18. What is NFC and how does it work?
19. Discuss why EBPP systems are becoming increasingly popular.
20. How are the two main types of EBPP systems both alike and different from each other?

PROJECTS

1. Imagine you are the owner of an e-commerce Web site. What are some of the signs that your site has been hacked? Discuss the major types of attacks you could expect to experience and the resulting damage to your site. Prepare a brief summary presentation.

2. Given the shift toward m-commerce, do a search on m-commerce (or mobile commerce) crime. Identify and discuss the security threats this type of technology creates. Prepare a presentation outlining your vision of the new opportunities for cybercrime that m-commerce may provide.

3. Find three certification authorities and compare the features of each company's digital certificates. Provide a brief description of each company as well, including number of clients. Prepare a brief presentation of your findings.

4. Research the challenges associated with payments across international borders and prepare a brief presentation of your findings. Do most e-commerce companies conduct business internationally? How do they protect themselves from repudiation? How do exchange rates impact online purchases? What about shipping charges? Summarize by describing the differences between a U.S. customer and an international customer who each make a purchase from a U.S. e-commerce merchant.

REFERENCES

Akamai Technologies, Inc. "Akamai's [State of the Internet] Q2 2015 Report." (2015).

Alert Logic. "2015 Cloud Security Report." (2015).

APWG. "APWG Phishing Activity Trends Report, 4th Quarter 2013." (April 7, 2014).

Arbor Networks. "Worldwide Infrastructure Security Report Volume X." (2015).

Center for Strategic and International Studies "Net Losses: Estimating the Global Cost of Cybercrime." (June 2014).

Chirgwin, Richard. "Microsoft and FBI Storm Ramparts of Citadel Botnets." *The Register* (June 6, 2013).

Cisco. "2015 Cisco Annual Security Report." (2015).

Constantin, Lucian. "Police Operation Disrupts Beebone Botnet Used for Malware Distribution." Pcworld.com (April 9, 2015).

Cybersource, Inc. "Online Fraud Management Benchmarks: North American Edition." (2015).

Cyphort. "Cyphort Labs Knocks Down the Top 8 Financial Malware." (October 15, 2015).

Daly, Jim. "Report Documents the March of Online Alternatives to the Payments Mainstream." Digitaltransactions.net (March 9, 2014).

Datta, Saikat. "Security Breach in NIC Allowed Hackers to Issue Fake Digital Certifcates—Hindustan Times." Medianama.com (August 14, 2014).

Dell Inc. "Determining the True Costs of a Data Breach." (2015).

DocuSign. "Going Mobile with Electronic Signatures." (2015).

eMarketer, Inc. (Rahul Chadha). "Global Ecommerce Platforms 2015: A Country-by-Country Look at the Top Retail Ecommerce Sites." (October 2015a).

eMarketer, Inc. "Mobile Peer-to-Peer Payments Catching On Among Millennials." (January 16, 2015).

Essers, Loek. "The 'Great Cannon' of China Enforces Censorship." Computerworld.com (April 10, 2015).

Fiserv. "Seventh Annual Billing Household Survey." (December 15, 2014).

Fiserv. "Sixth Annual Billing Household Survey: The Gen Y Effect and Explosive Growth of the Mobile Channel Fuel Need for Billers to Support More Payment Channels Than Ever Before." (December 2013).

Fiserv. "2007 Consumer Bill Payments Trends Survey: Volume of Electronic Payments." (2007).

Fox, Emily Jane and Greg Botelho. "5 Charged in Credit Card Hacking Scheme Feds Call Largest Ever Prosecuted in the U.S." Cnn.com (July 25, 2013).

Gartner. "Gartner Says Worldwide Information Security Spending Will Grow Almost 4.7 Percent to Reach $75.4 Billion in 2015." (September 23, 2015).

Greenberg, Andy. "Hackers Remotely Kill a Jeep on the Highway—With Me In It." Wired.com (July 21, 2015).

Hernandez, Will. "Mobile Online Retail Payments in Focus." Mobilepaymentstoday.com (July 10, 2015).

Honan, Mat. "How Apple and Amazon Security Flaws Led to My Epic Hacking." Wired.com (August 6, 2012).

IBM. "IBM Point of View: Internet of Things Security." (April 2015).

IHS Technology. "World Shipments of NFC-enabled Cellular Handsets." (June 2015).

Infosec Institute. "A Buyers Guide to Stolen Data on the Deep Web." Darkmatters.norsecorp.com (April 7, 2015).

Internet Society. "The Internet of Things: An Overview." (2015).

Javelin Strategy & Research. "2015 Identity Survey Report." (March 2, 2015a).

Javelin Strategy & Research. "Online Retail Payments Forecast 2015." (October 2015b).

Javelin Strategy & Research. "Mobile Online Retail Payments Forecast 2015." (July 2015c).

Keizer, Greg. "XcodeGhost Used Unprecedented Infection Strategy Against Apple." Computerworld.com (September 26, 2015).

Kirk, Jeremy. "Zero Day, Web Browser Vulnerabilities Spike in 2014." Networkworld.com (March 25, 2015a).

Kirk, Jeremy. "GitHub Recovering from Massive DDoS Attacks." Computerworld (March 29, 2015b).

Korolov, Maria. "Most Corporate Risk Due to Just 1% of Employees." Csoonline.com (August 26, 2015).

Leger, Donna Leinwand. "Credit Card Info Sold on Hacker Sites." *USA Today* (September 4, 2014).

Leising, Matthew. "CME Teams Up with Dwolla to Bring Real-Time Payments to Exchange." Bloomberg.com (October 28, 2015).

Majkowski, Marek. "Mobile Ad Networks as DDoS Vectors: A Case Study." Blog.cloudfare.com (September 25, 2015).

Maruca, William. "Hacked Health Records Prized for their Black Market Value." Hipaahealthlaw.foxrothschild.com (March 16, 2015).

Microsoft. "Microsoft Security Intelligence Report Volume 18: July–December 2014." (May 2015).

Mitnick, Kevin. *Ghost in the Wires.* Little, Brown & Co. (2011).

Neustar. "October 2015 Neustar DDoS Attacks and Protection Report: North America & EMEA." (October 2015).

Panda Security. "PandaLabs Annual Report 2014 Summary." (2015).

Patane, Matthew. "Dwolla Drops Transaction Fees to Gain Ground." *Des Moines Register* (June 4, 2015).

PCI Security Standards Council. "Payment Card Industry (PCI) Data Security Standard: Requirements and Security Assessment Procedure Version 3.1." (April 2015).

Peterson, Andrea. "Senate Passes Cybersecurity Information Sharing Bill Despite Privacy Fears." *Washington Post* (October 27, 2015).

Ponemon Institute. "2015 Cost of Data Breach Study: United States." (May 2015a).

Ponemon Institute. "2015 Cost of Cyber Crime Study: United States." (October 2015b).

Ponemon Institute. "The Unintentional Insider Risk in the United States and German Organizations." (July 2015c).

Ponemon Institute. "Data Breach: The Cloud Multiplier Effect." (June 2014).

PWC. "US Cybersecurity: Progress Stalled. Key Findings from the 2015 US State of Cybercrime Survey." (June 2015).

RAND Corporation. "Markets for Cybercrime Tools and Stolen Data: Hackers' Bazaar." (2014).

Schuman, Evan. "Starbucks Caught Storing Mobile Passwords in Clear Text." *Computerworld* (January 15, 2014).

Schwartz, John. "Fighting Crime Online: Who Is in Harm's Way?" *New York Times* (February 8, 2001).

Silanis Technology. "Security for E-Signatures and E-Transactions: What to Look for in a Vendor." (2014).

Software Engineering Institute. "Common Sense Guide to Mitigating Insider Threats, 4th Edition." Sei.cmu.edu (December 2012).

Stein, Lincoln D. *Web Security: A Step-by-Step Reference Guide*. Reading, MA: Addison-Wesley (1998).

Storm, Darlene. "MEDJACK: Hackers Hijacking Medical Devices Create Backdoors in Hospital Networks." Computerworld.com (June 8, 2015a).

Storm, Darlene. "2 More Wireless Baby Monitors Hacked: Hackers Remotely Spied on Babies and Parents." Computerworld.com (April 22, 2015b).

Symantec, Inc. "Internet Security Threat Report 2015 Volume 20." (April 2015).

Symantec, Inc. "Internet Security Threat Report Volume XV: April 2010." (April 2010).

Vaughan-Nichols, Steven J. "FREAK: Another Day, Another Serious SSL Security Hole." Zdnet.com (March 3, 2015).

Vaughan-Nichols, Steven J. "Has the NSA Broken SSL? TLS? AES?" Zdnet.com (September 6, 2013).

Verizon. "2015 Data Breach Investigations Report." (2015).

Vijayan, Jaikumar. "Google Joins Yahoo, AOL, in Adopting Stricter Email Authentication." Eweek.com (October 20, 2015).

Voreacos, David. "5 Hackers Charged in Largest Data Breach Scheme in U.S." Bloomberg.com (July 26, 2013).

Wakabayashi, Daisuke. "A Contrite Sony Vows Tighter Security." *Wall Street Journal* (May 1, 2011).

Wills, Amanda. "New Snowden Leak: NSA Program Taps All You Do Online." Mashable.com (August 1, 2013).

Wingfield, Nick. "Spam Network Shut Down." *Wall Street Journal* (March 18, 2011).

Zarras, Apostolis, Alexander Krapravelos, Gianluca Stringhini, Thorsten Holz, Christopher Krugel, and Giovanni Vigna. "The Dark Alleys of Madison Avenue: Understanding Malicious Advertisements." ICM '14 Vancouver, BC, Canada (November 5-7, 2014).

Business Concepts and Social Issues

CHAPTER 6

E-commerce Marketing and Advertising Concepts

LEARNING OBJECTIVES

After reading this chapter, you will be able to:

- Understand the key features of the Internet audience, the basic concepts of consumer behavior and purchasing, and how consumers behave online.
- Identify and describe the basic digital commerce marketing and advertising strategies and tools.
- Identify and describe the main technologies that support online marketing.
- Understand the costs and benefits of online marketing communications.

Video Ads:

Shoot, Click, Buy

The age of online video ads is upon us, just in case you haven't noticed. Improvements in video production tools, higher bandwidth, and better streaming quality have fueled an online video surge. Video production is no longer the exclusive province of just a few major players in New York and Hollywood, but instead has expanded to a much larger group of potential creators, including users themselves. In addition, the ways online video can be viewed have also expanded, from desktop PCs and laptops to smartphones, tablet computers, netbooks, and Web-enabled television sets.

© NetPhotos/Alamy

The online audience for videos is huge. In June 2015, over 193 million U.S. Internet users watched online video content via a desktop computer during the month. Over 100 million Americans also watch video on their smartphones and tablet computers. Google Sites (YouTube) is the top online video content site, with over 172 million unique viewers, followed by Facebook, Yahoo, and VEVO.

Because this is where the eyeballs are, video has become an obvious advertising medium. And just in time: Internet users have learned how to avoid traditional banner ads by instinctively moving their eyes to a different part of the screen. Click-throughs on banner ads are miniscule (less than 1 click per 1000 impressions) but videos are another story. Click-through rates for video ads on desktops are more than 5 times higher than for display ads, and the click-through rate is even higher for video ads on tablets and smartphones. In addition, nearly 100% of online spenders are video viewers, and they provide a highly desirable demographic with strong buying power. Research by comScore has found that retail site viewers who view videos are 64% more likely to purchase. As a result, advertisers are jumping on the bandwagon. The leading three online video advertising platforms are BrightRoll (owned by Yahoo), Google Sites, and LiveRail (owned by Facebook). BrightRoll delivers over 17 billion video ad impressions monthly across the Web, mobile devices, and connected TVs, and ranks first in video ad reach, delivering video ads to over 40% of the total U.S. population. Google Sites reaches about 33% of the population, while LiveRail delivers around 10 billion video ads monthly and reaches 32%.

Many large firms have moved into the online video advertising marketplace with sophisticated campaigns and big budgets. As of July 2015, the top 100 global brands

SOURCES: "YouTube Reportedly Prepping for Independent Viewability Measurement," by Ginny Marvin, Marketingland.com, September 8, 2015; "comScore Releases June 2015 U.S. Desktop Online Video Rankings," comScore, July 24, 2015; "YouTube Brings 360-Degree View to TrueView Ads, by Nathalie Tadena, *Wall Street Journal*, July 22, 2015; "Top YouTube Brands Increase Ad Spend by 60 Percent," by Sheila Shayron, Brandchannel.com, July 20, 2015; "Top 100 Global Brands on YouTube—2015 Update," by Alexandra English, Pixability.com, July 20, 2015; "Top 100 Brands Report: Insight into Brand Content on YouTube," Adwordsagency. blogspot.fr, July 19, 2015; "US Mobile Video Advertising," by Jeremy Kressman, eMarketer, Inc., June 2015; "Brands to Publishers: Let Us Check Your Viewability Rates or We'll Stop Buying Ads," by Tim Peterson, Adage.com, May 26, 2015; "Retailers, Google, Shopping Ads Are Coming to YouTube," by Ginny Marvin, Marketingland.com, May 21, 2015; "Google Wants YouTube Viewers to Shop While They Watch," by Alistair Barr, *Wall Street Journal*, May 21, 2015; "Driving Sales for Retailers with YouTube's TrueView for Shopping," Thinkwithgoogle.com, May 2015; "Display Advertising Clickthrough Rates," by Dave Chaffey, Smartinsights.com, April 21, 2015; "Five Years of TrueView: How User Choice is Ushering in the Next Golden Age of Video Advertising," Adwordagency.blogspot.com, April 8, 2015; "YouTube Wants You to Stop and Play with Its Ads," by Lara O'Reilly, Businessinsider.com, April 8, 2015; "YouTube Makes Skippable TrueView Ads More Interactive—And More Lucrative," Adage.com, April 8, 2015; "Five Years of TrueView: How Ads Became the Ones to Watch," Thinkwithgoogle.com, April 2015; "Herein Lies the Tale of a Tongue Toothbrush, YouTube, and 'Reverse Marketing'," by Barry Levine, Venturebeat.com, February 3, 2015; "Orabrush Becomes YouTube Marketing Machine for Katherine Heigl's JustOne," by Laurie Sullivan, Mediapost.com, September 16, 2014; "Orabrush Moves Beyond

collectively have over 2,400 YouTube channels with over 610,000 videos that have attracted 40 billion views. Interest in online ads posted on YouTube has exploded, with the number of views increasing by 85% between June 2014 and June 2015. In fact, four of the top 10 trending videos on YouTube for all of 2014 were branded online advertising content. Collectively, the channels have over 72 million subscribers, who are actively engaging with the content, generating 16 million comments, 90 million Likes (as well as about 9 million Dislikes). The average amount spent by the top 100 brands on YouTube also increased, by around 60% from 2014 to 2015.

Smaller firms are also posting video ads on YouTube. Overall, the number of advertisers running video ads on YouTube increased by more than 40% from 2014 to 2015. Orabrush is an example of a small firm that successfully used video ads on YouTube to build its business from the ground up. Dr. Robert Wagstaff, a dentist who invented a breath-freshening tongue cleaner, was unsuccessful marketing it through traditional channels. Jeffrey Harmon, an MBA student at nearby Brigham Young University, whom Wagstaff had hired on a part-time basis, convinced him to give video ads a try. He initially posted a YouTube video called "How to tell if you have bad breath" on Orabrush's landing page, and found that it tripled Orabrush's conversion rate. From there, they decided to create Orabrush's own YouTube video channel. Today the channel has more than 150 videos, around 190,000 subscribers, and more than 48 million video views (more than major brands such as Colgate and Johnson & Johnson), and more importantly, has resulted in sales of over 3 million units. Orapup, a sister brand for dogs, has also used the same kind of video marketing model with great success, connecting with the pet community and generating more than 24 million views, more than major pet brands Purina, Pedigree, and Iams, combined. YouTube continues to account for 80% of Orabrush's marketing effort, although it now also has a Facebook page. In 2015, Orabrush spun off a new ad technology company named Molio, which is aimed at using proprietary systems to leverage its YouTube marketing model and acting as a consultant to other companies. Initial clients include Wilson Golf's line of Duo golf balls and Stride bicycles.

One of the reasons why advertisers are flocking to place online ads on YouTube is the TrueView ad format, which is available on both the desktop and mobile devices. Launched in 2010, TrueView ads allow viewers to skip the ad after five seconds and go directly to the video they want to watch. The advertiser is not charged unless the viewer watches the full ad or, for longer ads, for at least 30 seconds. TrueView ads, in effect, gives advertisers five free seconds of branding, and also have a lower cost-per-click rate than Google's search ads. As with many other types of online advertising, TrueView ads can be targeted based on audience demographics and other behavioral data. TrueView also allows advertisers to use what Google calls dynamic remarketing (another name for retargeting), which allows advertisers to show ads based on what users previously viewed on the advertiser's Web site. TrueView ads encourage advertisers to deliver ads that people actually want to watch and engage with, and are attractive to advertisers because when viewers actively decide to watch, they are believed to have a greater level of interest. TrueView ads were a rousing success in 2014, representing more than 85% of all of the in-stream ads on YouTube, and used by all of the top 100 global brands.

In 2015, Google took a number of steps to enhance the effectiveness of TrueView ads for advertisers. In April 2015, it added the ability to include an interactive card that overlays extra information, such as a list of related videos or playlists from the advertiser, or links to the advertiser's Web site, on top of the video (typically in a scrollable vertical section that takes up about 35% of the video player screen). The card is not visible (and advertisers are not charged) unless a viewer clicks a button in the top-right corner of the video. TrueView cards work on mobile devices as well as desktops, and eventually will also be available on Internet-connected TVs.

In May 2015, Google announced TrueView for Shopping, which is built on the TrueView cards platform. Advertisers can now include images, product offers with prices, and the ability to click through to a brand's products, allowing viewers to easily purchase items directly from the advertiser's web site. Two advertisers that participated in an early trial were online furniture retailer Wayfair and beauty products retailer Sephora. Wayfair created product-specific videos with tips for decorating, and included product prices, while Sephora created a series of how-to videos, tutorials, and curated product recommendations. Using an attribution system that it developed that allowed it to directly tie revenue back to specific customers exposed to a TrueView ad, Wayfair reported that the ads generated three times as much revenue compared to its traditional video ads. Sephora reported that its ads delivered a 54% lift in ad recall and an 80% lift in brand consideration, with an average view time of two minutes.

In July 2015, Google introduced 360-degree view for TrueView ads, which allows viewers to watch the video from different angles, such as from different parts of the interior of a car. On a desktop, users use a mouse; on a mobile device, just changing the orientation of the device delivers a different view. Budweiser is one advertiser that has already developed TrueView ads using this format, using them for its Bud Light brand to allow viewers to follow along a parade route and be in the middle of a dance floor of a 1920s-themed party.

However, despite the success of the video ads in general, and the TrueView format in particular, video ads still have some hurdles to face. One of advertisers' major concerns is the issue of viewability—whether video ads are actually seen. Currently, industry standards with respect to when a video ad is considered to be viewable are extremely low: just 50% of the ad's pixels must be visible on screen for at least two consecutive seconds. Google research found that of video ads that did not meet this standard, about 75% were in a background tab or not on the screen at all, while the remainder were scrolled off-screen or actively abandoned in fewer than two seconds. In May 2015, Google announced that its research found the average viewability of video ads across the Web was 54%. In contrast, Google said that YouTube had an overall 91% video ad viewability rate. However, Google initially refused to allow independent third-party viewability companies to verify this data, and as a result, some major brands, such as Kellogg, stopped purchasing YouTube ads. In September 2015, Google decided to change its policy and announced that it would begin to allow third-party verification of ad viewability by the end of 2015.

Bad Breath with Sony Executive Hire," by Tessa Curry, Siliconslopes. com, March 4, 2014; "Orabrush Surpasses 50 Million Views on Its YouTube Channel," Orabrush.com, November 15, 2012; "As Seen on YouTube! Orabrush Reinvents the Infomercial," by Joseph Flaherty, Wired.com, May 21, 2012.

Perhaps no area of business has been more affected by Internet and mobile platform technologies than marketing and marketing communications. As a communications tool, the Internet affords marketers new ways of contacting millions of potential customers at costs far lower than traditional media. The Internet also provides new ways—often instantaneous and spontaneous—to gather information from customers, adjust product offerings, and increase customer value. The Internet has spawned entirely new ways to identify and communicate with customers, including search engine marketing, social marketing, behavioral targeting, and targeted e-mail, among others. And the Internet was just the first transformation. Today, the mobile platform based on smartphones and tablet computers is transforming online marketing and communications yet again. **Table 6.1** summarizes some of the significant new developments in online marketing and advertising for 2015–2016.

The subject of online marketing, branding, and market communications is very broad and deep. We have created two chapters to cover the material. In this chapter, we begin by examining consumer behavior on the Web, the major types of online marketing and branding, and the technologies that support advances in online marketing. We then focus on understanding the costs and benefits of online marketing communications. In Chapter 7, we focus on the social, mobile, and local marketing phenomenon in greater depth.

6.1   CONSUMERS ONLINE: THE INTERNET AUDIENCE AND CONSUMER BEHAVIOR

Before firms can begin to sell their products online, they must first understand what kinds of people they will find online and how those people behave in the online marketplace. In this section, we focus primarily on individual consumers in the business-to-consumer (B2C) arena. However, many of the factors discussed apply to the B2B arena as well, insofar as purchasing decisions by firms are made by individuals. For readers who have no background in marketing, we have created an online Learning Track, Learning Track 6.1, that discusses basic marketing and branding concepts.

INTERNET TRAFFIC PATTERNS: THE ONLINE CONSUMER PROFILE

We will start with an analysis of some basic background demographics of Web consumers in the United States. The first principle of marketing and sales is "know thy customer." Who is online, who shops online and why, and what do they buy? In 2015, around 260 million people of all ages had access to the Internet. About 91 million households in the United States (almost 75% of all households) have broadband access to the Internet. By comparison, 98% of all U.S. households currently have televisions and 94% have telephones. Worldwide, around 3.1 billion people are online.

Although the number of new online users increased at a rate of 30% a year or higher in the early 2000s, over the last several years, this growth rate has slowed to about 2% a year in the United States. E-commerce businesses can no longer count on

TABLE 6.1	WHAT'S NEW IN ONLINE MARKETING AND ADVERTISING 2015–2016

BUSINESS

- Online marketing and advertising spending continues to increase (by over 15% in 2015), compared to only about 1% for traditional media marketing and advertising.
- Video advertising continues to be one of the fastest growing formats.
- Search engine marketing and advertising continues in importance, but its rate of growth is slowing somewhat compared to other formats.
- Mobile, social, and local marketing spending all continue to rapidly expand.
- Viewability issues and ad fraud raise increasing concerns for marketers.
- Native advertising and other forms of content marketing rise.

TECHNOLOGY

- Ad blocking software usage increases, creating concern for both online publishers and advertisers.
- Big Data: online tracking produces oceans of data, challenging business analytics programs.
- Cloud computing makes rich marketing content and multi-channel, cross-platform marketing a reality.
- Programmatic advertising (automated, technology-driven method of buying and selling display and video ads) takes off.

SOCIETY

- Targeted advertising based on behavioral tracking leads to growing privacy awareness and fears.

a double-digit growth rate in the online population to fuel their revenues. The days of extremely rapid growth in the U.S. Internet population are over.

Intensity and Scope of Usage

The slowing rate of growth in the U.S. Internet population is compensated for, in part, by an increasing intensity and scope of use. Overall, 71% of all American adults report logging on on a typical day (Pew Research Center, 2014). Internet use by teens is even more pervasive, with over 90% saying they go online daily, and about 25% reporting that they use the Internet almost constantly (Pew Research Center, 2015a). Several studies also show that a greater amount of time is being spent online by Internet users—almost 2 and a half hours a day. In 2015, mobile smartphones and tablets are major access points to the Internet and online commerce. About 194 million people, about 75% of all U.S. Internet users, access the Internet using a mobile phone. Owners of mobile devices spend almost 3 hours a day using them for nontelephone activities such as playing games, viewing videos, and visiting social networks (eMarketer, Inc., 2015a). Engaging in such activities is widespread—in 2015, around 165 million mobile users played games, about 107 million watched videos, 151 million visited a social network, and millions of others listened to music or shopped (eMarketer, Inc., 2015b). The more time users spend online, becoming more comfortable and familiar with

Internet features and services, the more services they are likely to explore, according to the Pew Research Center.

Demographics and Access

The demographic profile of the Internet—and e-commerce—has changed greatly since 1995. Up until 2000, single, white, young, college-educated males with high incomes dominated the Internet. This inequality in access and usage led to concerns about a possible "digital divide." However, in recent years, there has been a marked increase in Internet usage by females, minorities, seniors, and families with modest incomes, resulting in a notable decrease—but not elimination—in the earlier inequality of access and usage.

A roughly equal percentage of men (85%) and women (84%) use the Internet today. Young adults (18–29) form the age group with the highest percentage of Internet use, at 96%. Adults in the 30–49 group (93%) are also strongly represented. Another fast-growing group online is the 65 and over segment, 58% of whom now use the Internet. Teens (12–17) also have a very high percentage of their age group online (97%). The percentage of very young children (0–11 years) online has also spurted, to 50% of that age group. eMarketer predicts that future Internet user growth in the United States will come predominantly from those aged 55 and older and from children in the 0–11 age bracket (eMarketer, Inc., 2015b). Variation across ethnic groups is not as wide as across age groups. Ten years ago, there were significant differences among ethnic groups, but this has receded. In 2015, user participation by whites is 85%, Hispanics, 81%, and African-Americans, 78%.

About 97% of households with income levels above $75,000 have Internet access, compared to only 74% of households earning less than $30,000. Over time, income differences have declined but they remain significant with a 23% gap between the highest category of household income and the lowest. Amount of education also makes a significant difference when it comes to online access. Of those individuals with less than a high school education, only 66% were online in 2015, compared to 95% of individuals with a college degree or more. Even some college education boosted Internet usage, with that segment reaching 90% (Pew Research Center, 2015b).

Overall, the so-called "digital divide" has indeed moderated, but it still persists along income, education, age, and ethnic dimensions. Gender, income, education, age, and ethnicity also impact online behavior. According to the Pew Research Center, adults over the age of 65, those who have not completed high school, those who make less than $30,000 a year, and Hispanics are all less likely to purchase products online. Women are slightly more likely to purchase online than men, but not significantly so. With respect to online banking, the demographics are similar—those 65 and older are less likely than any age group to bank online, while those with at least some college are more likely than those with a high school diploma or less. Online banking is also more popular with men than women. No significant differences were found in terms of ethnicity (Pew Research Center, 2012). Other commentators have observed that children of poorer and less educated families spend considerably more time using their access devices for entertainment (movies, games, Facebook, and texting) than children from wealthier households. For all children and teenagers, the majority of time spent on the Internet is often labeled as "wasted time" because the majority of online use is for entertainment, and not education or learning (Richtel, 2012).

Type of Internet Connection: Broadband and Mobile Impacts

While a great deal of progress has been made in reducing glaring gaps in access to the Internet, there are still inequalities in access to broadband service. In 2015, around 91 million households had broadband service in their homes—75% of all households (eMarketer, Inc., 2015c). Research by the Pew Research Center indicates that broadband adoption levels are lower for older adults, those with low levels of education, and those with low household incomes. Rural residents, African Americans, and Latinos are also less likely to have a home broadband connection (Pew Research Center, 2013). For marketers, the broadband audience offers unique opportunities for the use of multimedia marketing campaigns, and for the positioning of products especially suited for this more educated and affluent audience. It is also important to note that just because a household does not have broadband access, it does not mean that household members do not use the Internet. About 50% of the non-broadband adopters do use the Internet, either from another location or via a smartphone. Certain groups are particularly reliant on smartphones for online access: younger adults in the 18–29 age group, those with low household incomes and levels of education, and non-whites (Pew Research Center, 2013a, 2013b, 2015c). The explosive growth of smartphones and tablet computers connected to broadband cellular and Wi-Fi networks is the foundation for a truly mobile e-commerce and marketing platform, which did not exist a few years ago.

Community Effects: Social Contagion in Social Networks

For a physical retail store, the most important factor in shaping sales is location, location, location. If you are located where thousands of people pass by every day, you will tend to do well. But for Internet retailers, physical location has almost no consequence as long as customers can be served by shipping services such as UPS or the post office or their services can be downloaded to anywhere. What does make a difference for consumer purchases on the Internet is whether or not the consumer is located in "neighborhoods" where others purchase on the Internet. These neighborhoods can be either face-to-face and truly personal, or digital. These so-called neighborhood effects, and the role of social emulation in consumption decisions, are well known for goods such as personal computers. In general, there is a relationship between being a member of a social network and purchasing decisions. Yet the relationship between "connectedness" (either offline or online) and purchase decisions is not straightforward or simple. People who score in the top 10%–15% of connectedness "do their own thing" to differentiate themselves and often do not share purchase decisions with friends. In fact, highly connected users often stop purchasing what their friends purchase. One can think of them as iconoclasts. The middle 50% of connected people very often share purchase patterns of their friends. One can think of these people as "keeping up with the Joneses" (Iyengar et al., 2009). A recent study of 6,000 social network users found that social networks have a powerful influence on shopping and purchasing behavior. An estimated 40% of social media users have purchased an item after sharing or favoriting it on Facebook, Pinterest, or Twitter. Facebook is the network most likely to drive customers to purchase, followed by Pinterest and Twitter. Unexpectedly, social networks increase research online, followed by purchase offline (sometimes referred to as ROPO), driving purchase traffic into physical stores where the product can be seen, tried, and then purchased. This is the opposite of the showrooming effect where consumers shop in stores, and then purchase online. The ROPO effect was found to be as large as the research offline and purchase online effect (Vision Critical, 2013; Schleifer, 2013; Sevitt and Samuel, 2013).

Membership in social networks has a large influence on discovering new independent music, but less influence on already well-known products (Garg, 2009). Membership in an online brand community like Ford's Facebook page and community has a direct effect on sales (Adjei et al., 2009). Amazon's recommender systems ("Consumers who bought this item also bought ...") create co-purchase networks where people do not know one another personally, but nevertheless triple the influence of complementary products (Oestreicher-Singer and Sundararajan, 2008). The value of social networks to marketers rests on the proposition that brand strength and purchase decisions are closely related to network membership, rank, prominence, and centrality (Guo et al., 2011).

CONSUMER BEHAVIOR MODELS

consumer behavior
a social science discipline that attempts to model and understand the behavior of humans in a marketplace

Once firms have an understanding of who is online, they need to focus on how consumers behave online. The study of **consumer behavior** is a social science discipline that attempts to model and understand the behavior of humans in a marketplace. Several social science disciplines play roles in this study, including sociology, psychology, and economics. Models of consumer behavior attempt to predict or "explain" what consumers purchase and where, when, how much, and why they buy. The expectation is that if the consumer decision-making process can be understood, firms will have a much better idea how to market and sell their products. **Figure 6.1** illustrates a general consumer behavior model that takes into account a wide range of factors that influence a consumer's marketplace decisions. Learning Track 6.2 contains further information about the cultural, social, and psychological background factors that influence consumer behavior.

PROFILES OF ONLINE CONSUMERS

Online consumer behavior parallels that of offline consumer behavior with some obvious differences. It is important to first understand why people choose the Internet channel to conduct transactions. **Table 6.2** lists the main reasons consumers choose the online channel.

While price is an important consideration, consumers also shop online because of convenience, which in turn is produced largely by saving them time. Overall transaction cost reduction appears to be a major motivator for choosing the online channel.

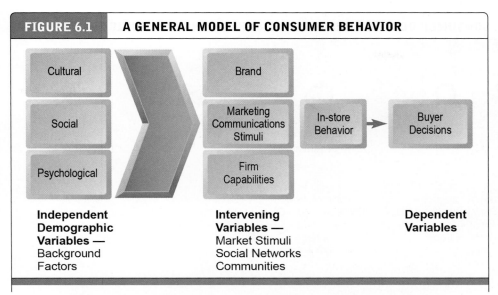

FIGURE 6.1   **A GENERAL MODEL OF CONSUMER BEHAVIOR**

Consumer behavior models try to predict the decisions that consumers make in the marketplace.
SOURCE: Adapted from Kotler and Armstrong, 2009.

THE ONLINE PURCHASING DECISION

Once online, why do consumers actually purchase a product or service at a specific site? Among the most important reasons are price and the availability of free shipping. That the seller is someone whom the purchaser trusts is also a very important factor.

TABLE 6.2   **WHY CONSUMERS CHOOSE THE ONLINE CHANNEL**

REASON	PERCENTAGE OF RESPONDENTS
Lower prices	59%
Shop from home	53%
Shop 24/7	44%
Wider variety of products available	29%
Easier to compare and research products and offers	27%
Products only available online	22%
Online customer reviews	18%
Better product information available	7%
Promotion via e-mail or text	7%
Social media influence	1%

SOURCE: Based on data from eMarketer, Inc., 2014.

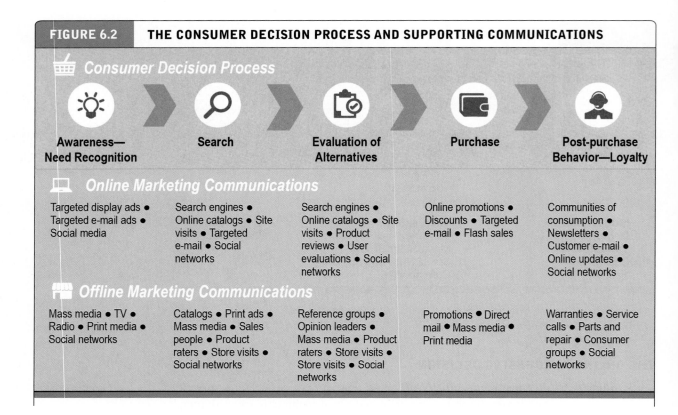

FIGURE 6.2   THE CONSUMER DECISION PROCESS AND SUPPORTING COMMUNICATIONS

The ability to make a purchase without paying tax and the availability of an online coupon are also significant factors.

You also need to consider the process that buyers follow when making a purchase decision, and how the Internet environment affects consumers' decisions. There are five stages in the consumer decision process: awareness of need, search for more information, evaluation of alternatives, the actual purchase decision, and post-purchase contact with the firm. **Figure 6.2** shows the consumer decision process and the types of offline and online marketing communications that support this process and seek to influence the consumer before, during, and after the purchase decision.

The stages of the consumer decision process are basically the same whether the consumer is offline or online. On the other hand, the general model of consumer behavior requires modification to take into account new factors, and the unique features of e-commerce that allow new opportunities to interact with the customer online also need to be accounted for. In **Figure 6.3**, we have modified the general model of consumer behavior to focus on user characteristics, product characteristics, and Web site and mobile platform features, along with traditional factors such as brand strength and specific market communications (advertising) and the influence of both online and offline social networks.

In the online model, Web site and mobile platform features, along with consumer skills, product characteristics, attitudes towards online purchasing, and perceptions

FIGURE 6.3	A MODEL OF ONLINE CONSUMER BEHAVIOR

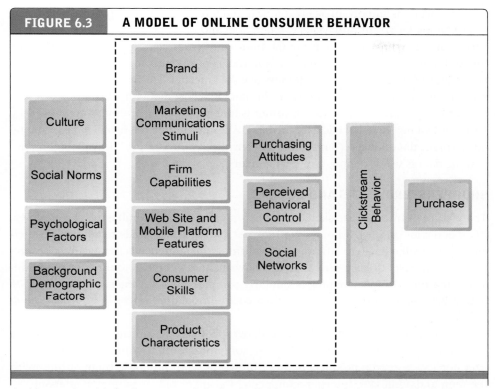

In this general model of online consumer behavior, the decision to purchase is shaped by background demographic factors, several intervening factors, and, finally, influenced greatly by clickstream behavior very near to the precise moment of purchase.

about control over the online environment come to the fore. Web site and mobile platform features include latency (delay in downloads), navigability, and confidence in online security. There are parallels in the analog world. For instance, it is well known that consumer behavior can be influenced by store design, and that understanding the precise movements of consumers through a physical store can enhance sales if goods and promotions are arranged along the most likely consumer tracks. Consumer skills refers to the knowledge that consumers have about how to conduct online transactions (which increases with experience). Product characteristics refers to the fact that some products can be easily described, packaged, and shipped online, whereas others cannot. Combined with traditional factors, such as brand, advertising, and firm capabilities, these factors lead to specific attitudes about purchasing from an e-commerce firm (trust in the firm and favorable customer experience) and a sense that the consumer can control his or her environment online.

Clickstream behavior refers to the transaction log that consumers establish as they move about the Web, from search engine to a variety of sites, then to a single site, then to a single page, and then, finally, to a decision to purchase. These precious moments are similar to "point-of-purchase" moments in traditional retail. A study of over 10,000 visits to an online wine store found that detailed and general clickstream

clickstream behavior
the transaction log that consumers establish as they move about the Web

behavior were as important as customer demographics and prior purchase behavior in predicting a current purchase (Van den Poel and Buckinx, 2005). Clickstream marketing takes maximum advantage of the Internet environment. It presupposes no prior "deep" knowledge of the customer (and in that sense is "privacy-regarding"), and can be developed dynamically as customers use the Internet. For instance, the success of search engine marketing (the display of paid advertisements by search engines) is based in large part on what the consumer is looking for at the moment and how they go about looking (detailed clickstream data). After examining the detailed data, general clickstream data is used (days since last visit, past purchases). If available, demographic data is used (region, city, and gender).

SHOPPERS: BROWSERS AND BUYERS

The picture of Internet use sketched in the previous section emphasizes the complexity of behavior online. Although the Internet audience still tends to be concentrated among the well educated, affluent, and youthful, the audience is increasingly becoming more diverse. Clickstream analysis shows us that people go online for many different reasons. Online shopping is similarly complex. Beneath the surface of the $531 billion B2C e-commerce market in 2015 are substantial differences in how users shop online.

For instance, as shown in **Figure 6.4**, over 75% of U.S. Internet users, age 14 and older, are "buyers" who actually purchase something entirely online via any device. Another 15% research products online ("browsers"), but purchase them offline. With the teen and adult U.S. Internet audience (14 years or older) estimated at about 227 million in 2015, online shoppers (the combination of buyers and browsers, totalling almost 90%) add up to a market size of almost 205 million consumers. Most marketers find this number exciting.

The significance of online browsing for offline purchasing should not be underestimated. Although it is difficult to precisely measure the amount of offline sales

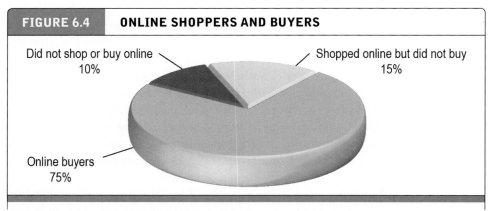

| FIGURE 6.4 | ONLINE SHOPPERS AND BUYERS |

Did not shop or buy online
10%

Shopped online but did not buy
15%

Online buyers
75%

About 90% of U.S Internet users, age 14 and older, shop online on desktop computers and mobile devices, either by researching products or by purchasing products online. The percentage of those actually purchasing has increased to over 75%. Only about 10% do not buy or shop online.
SOURCE: Based on data from eMarketer, Inc., 2015d.

that occur because of online product research, Forrester Research estimates that Web-influenced retail sales will generate over $1.55 trillion in 2015, growing to around $1.8 trillion by 2018 (Forrester Research, 2014a).

E-commerce is a major conduit and generator of offline commerce. The reverse is also true: online traffic is driven by offline brands and shopping. While online research influences offline purchases, it is also the case that offline marketing media heavily influence online behavior including sales. Traditional print media (magazines and newspapers) and television are by far the most powerful media for reaching and engaging consumers with information about new products and directing them to the Web. Online communities and blogging are also very influential but not yet as powerful as traditional media. This may be surprising to many given the attention to social networks as marketing vehicles, but it reflects the diversity of influences on consumer behavior and the real-world marketing budgets of firms that are still heavily dominated by traditional media. Even more surprising in the era of Facebook, face-to-face interactions are a more powerful influence than participation in online social communities.

These considerations strongly suggest that e-commerce and traditional commerce are coupled and should be viewed by merchants (and researchers) as part of a continuum of consuming behavior and not as radical alternatives to one another. Commerce is commerce; the customers are often the same people. Customers use a wide variety of media, sometimes multiple media at once. The significance of these findings for marketers is very clear. Online merchants should build the information content of their sites to attract browsers looking for information, build content to rank high in search engines, put less attention on selling per se, and promote services and products (especially new products) in offline media settings in order to support their online stores.

WHAT CONSUMERS SHOP FOR AND BUY ONLINE

You can look at online sales as divided roughly into two groups: small-ticket and big-ticket items. Big-ticket items include computer equipment and consumer electronics, where orders can easily be more than $1,000. Small-ticket items include apparel, books, health and beauty supplies, office supplies, music, software, videos, and toys, where the average purchase is typically less than $100. In the early days of e-commerce, sales of small-ticket items vastly outnumbered those of large-ticket items. But the recent growth of big-ticket items such as computer hardware, consumer electronics, furniture, and jewelry has changed the overall sales mix. Consumers are now much more confident spending online for big-ticket items. Although furniture and large appliances were initially perceived as too bulky to sell online, these categories have rapidly expanded in the last few years. Free shipping offered by Amazon and other large retailers has also contributed to consumers buying many more expensive and large items online such as air conditioners. Refer to Figure 1.10 to see how much consumers spent online for various categories of goods in 2014.

INTENTIONAL ACTS: HOW SHOPPERS FIND VENDORS ONLINE

Given the prevalence of "click here" display ads, one might think customers are "driven" to online vendors by spur-of-the-moment decisions. In fact, only a tiny percentage of shoppers click on display ads to find vendors. E-commerce shoppers are highly intentional. Typically, they are focused browsers looking for specific products, companies, and services. Once they are online, a majority of consumers use a search engine as their preferred method of research for purchasing a product. Many will go directly to a online marketplace, such as Amazon or eBay, and some will go directly to a specific retail Web site. Merchants can convert these "goal-oriented," intentional shoppers into buyers if the merchants can target their communications to the shoppers and design their sites in such a way as to provide easy-to-access and useful product information, full selection, and customer service, and do this at the very moment the customer is searching for the product. This is no small task.

WHY SOME PEOPLE DON'T SHOP ONLINE

About 10% of Internet users do not shop or buy online. Why not? One of the most important factors cited by those who don't shop or buy online is the "trust factor," the fear that online merchants will cheat you, lose your credit card information, or use personal information you give them to invade your personal privacy, bombarding you with unwanted e-mail and pop-up ads. Secondary factors can be summarized as "hassle factors," like shipping costs, returns, and inability to touch and feel the product.

TRUST, UTILITY, AND OPPORTUNISM IN ONLINE MARKETS

A long tradition of research shows that the two most important factors shaping the decision to purchase online are utility and trust (Brookings Institute, 2011; Kim et al., 2009; Ba and Pavlou, 2002). Consumers want good deals, bargains, convenience, and speed of delivery. In short, consumers are looking for utility. On the other hand, in any seller-buyer relationship, there is an asymmetry of information. The seller usually knows a lot more than the consumer about the quality of goods and terms of sale. This can lead to opportunistic behavior by sellers (Akerlof, 1970; Williamson, 1985; Mishra, 1998). Consumers need to trust a merchant before they make a purchase. Sellers can develop trust among online consumers by building strong reputations of honesty, fairness, and delivery of quality products—the basic elements of a brand. Feedback forums such as Epinions.com (now part of Shopping.com), Amazon's book reviews from reviewers, and eBay's feedback forum are examples of trust-building online mechanisms (NielsenWire, 2012; Opinion Research Corporation, 2009). Online sellers who develop trust among consumers are able to charge a premium price for their online products and services (Kim and Benbasat, 2006, 2007; Pavlou, 2002). A review of the literature suggests that the most important factors leading to a trusting online relationship are perception of Web site credibility, ease of use, and perceived risk (Corritore et al., 2006). An important brake on the growth of e-commerce is lack of trust. Newspaper and television ads are far more trusted than online ads (Nielsen, 2011). Personal friends and family are far more powerful determinants of online purchases than membership in social networks (eMarketer, Inc., 2010). These attitudes have grown more positive over time, but concerns about the use of personal information by online marketers continue to raise trust issues among consumers.

6.2 DIGITAL COMMERCE MARKETING AND ADVERTISING STRATEGIES AND TOOLS

Online marketing has many similarities to, and differences from, ordinary marketing. (For more information on basic marketing concepts, see Learning Tracks 6.1 and 6.2.) The objective of online marketing—as in all marketing—is to build customer relationships so that the firm can achieve above-average returns (both by offering superior products or services and by communicating the brand's features to the consumer). These relationships are a foundation for the firm's brand. But online marketing is also very different from ordinary marketing because the nature of the medium and its capabilities are so different from anything that has come before.

There are four features of online marketing that distinguish it from traditional marketing channels. Compared to traditional print and television marketing, online marketing can be more personalized, participatory, peer-to-peer, and communal. Not all types of online marketing have these four features. For instance, there's not much difference between a marketing video splashed on your computer screen without your consent and watching a television commercial. However, the same marketing video can be targeted to your personal interests, community memberships, and allow you to share it with others using a Like or + tag. Marketers are learning that the most effective forms of online marketing have all four of these features.

STRATEGIC ISSUES AND QUESTIONS

In the past, the first step in building an online brand was to build a Web site, and then try to attract an audience. The most common "traditional" marketing techniques for establishing a brand and attracting customers were search engine marketing, display ads, e-mail campaigns, and affiliate programs. This is still the case: building a Web site is still a first step, and the "traditional" online marketing techniques are still the main powerhouses of brand creation and online sales revenue in 2015. But today, marketers need to take a much broader view of the online marketing challenge, and to consider other media channels for attracting an audience such as social media and mobile devices, in concert with traditional Web sites.

The five main elements of a comprehensive multi-channel marketing plan are: Web site, traditional online marketing, social marketing, mobile marketing, and offline marketing. **Table 6.3** illustrates these five main platforms, central elements within each type, some examples, and the primary function of marketing in each situation. Each of the main types of online marketing is discussed in this section and throughout the chapter in greater detail.

Immediately, by examining Table 6.3, you can understand the management complexity of building brands online. There are five major types of marketing, and a variety of different platforms that perform different functions. If you're a manager of a start-up, or the Web site manager of an existing commercial Web site, you face a number of strategic questions. Where should you focus first? Build a Web site, develop a blog, or jump into developing a Facebook presence? If you have a successful Web site that already uses search engine marketing and display ads, where should you go

TABLE 6.3	THE DIGITAL MARKETING ROADMAP		
TYPE OF MARKETING	**PLATFORMS**	**EXAMPLES**	**FUNCTION**
Web Site	Traditional Web site	Ford.com	Anchor site
Traditional Online Marketing	Search engine marketing	Google; Bing; Yahoo	Query-based intention marketing
	Display advertising	Yahoo; Google; MSN	Interest- and context-based marketing; targeted marketing
	E-mail	Major retailers	Permission marketing
	Affiliates	Amazon	Brand extension
Social Marketing	Social networks	Facebook	Conversations; sharing
	Micro blogging sites	Twitter	News, quick updates
	Blogs/forums	Tumblr	Communities of interest; sharing
	Visual marketing	Pinterest/Instagram	Branding; sharing
	Video marketing	YouTube	Engage; inform
	Game marketing	Chipotle Scarecrow Game	Identification
Mobile Marketing	Mobile site	m.ford.com	Quick access; news; updates
	Apps	2015 Ford Mustang Customizer	Visual engagement
		My Ford	Visual engagement
Offline Marketing	Television	2015 Ford F-150: This Changes Everything	Brand anchoring; inform
	Newspapers	Apple Shot on iPhone 6 campaign	Brand anchoring; inform
	Magazines	Apple Watch/Vogue Magazine	Brand anchoring; inform

next: develop a social network presence or use offline media? Does your firm have the resources to maintain a social media marketing campaign?

A second strategic management issue involves the integration of all these different marketing platforms into a single coherent branding message. Often, there are different groups with different skill sets involved in Web site design, search engine and display marketing, social media marketing, and offline marketing. Getting all these different specialties to work together and coordinate their campaigns can be very difficult. The danger is that a firm ends up with different teams managing each of the four platforms rather than a single team managing the digital online presence, or for that matter, marketing for the entire firm including retail outlets.

A third strategic management question involves resource allocation. There are actually two problems here. Each of the different major types of marketing, and each of the different platforms, has different metrics to measure its effectiveness. In some cases, for new social marketing platforms, there is no commonly accepted metric, and few that have withstood critical scrutiny or have a deep experience base providing empirical data. For instance, in Facebook marketing, an important metric is how many Likes your Facebook page produces. The connection between Likes and sales is still being explored. In search engine marketing, effectiveness is measured by how many clicks your ads are receiving; in display advertising, by how many impressions of your ads are served. Second, each of these platforms has different costs for Likes, impressions, and clicks. In order to choose where your marketing resources should be deployed, you will have to link each of these activities to sales revenue. You will need to determine how much clicks, Likes, and impressions are worth. We address these questions in greater detail in Chapter 7.

THE WEB SITE AS A MARKETING PLATFORM: ESTABLISHING THE CUSTOMER RELATIONSHIP

A firm's Web site is a major tool for establishing the initial relationship with the customer. The Web site performs four important functions: establishing the brand identity and consumer expectations, informing and educating the consumer, shaping the customer experience, and anchoring the brand in an ocean of marketing messages coming from different sources. The Web site is the one place the consumer can turn to find the complete story. This is not true of apps, e-mail, or search engine ads.

The first function of a Web site is to establish the brand's identity and to act as an anchor for the firm's other Web marketing activities, thereby driving sales revenue. This involves identifying for the consumer the differentiating features of the product or service in terms of quality, price, product support, and reliability. Identifying the differentiating features of the product on the Web site's home page is intended to create expectations in the user of what it will be like to consume the product. For instance, Snapple's Web site creates the expectation that the product is a delicious, refreshing drink made from high quality, natural ingredients. Ford's Web site focuses on automobile technology and high miles per gallon. The expectation created by Ford's Web site is that if you buy a Ford, you'll be experiencing the latest automotive technology and the highest mileage. At the location-based social network Web site for Foursquare, the focus is on meeting friends, discovering local places, and saving money with coupons and rewards.

Web sites also function to anchor the brand online, acting as a central point where all the branding messages that emanate from the firm's multiple digital presences, such as Facebook, Twitter, mobile apps, or e-mail, come together at a single online location. Aside from branding, Web sites also perform the typical functions of any commercial establishment by informing customers of the company's products and services. Web sites, with their online catalogs and associated shopping carts, are important elements of the online customer experience. **Customer experience** refers to the totality of experiences that a customer has with a firm, including the search, informing, purchase, consumption, and after-sales support for the product. The concept "customer experience" is broader than the traditional concept of "customer satisfaction" in that a much broader range of impacts is considered, including the customer's cognitive,

customer experience
the totality of experiences that a customer has with a firm, including the search, informing, purchase, consumption, and after-sales support for its products, services, and various retail channels

affective, emotional, social, and physical relationship to the firm and its products. The totality of customer experiences will generally involve multiple retail channels. This means that, in the customer's mind, the Web site, mobile site and apps, Facebook page, Twitter feed, physical store, and television advertisements are all connected as part of his or her experience with the company.

TRADITIONAL ONLINE MARKETING AND ADVERTISING TOOLS

Below we describe the basic marketing and advertising tools for attracting e-commerce consumers: search engine marketing, display ad marketing (including banner ads, rich media ads, video ads, and sponsorships), e-mail and permission marketing, affiliate marketing, viral marketing, and lead generation marketing.

online advertising

a paid message on a Web site, online service, or other interactive medium

Companies will spend an estimated $187.5 billion on advertising in 2015, and an estimated $59 billion of that amount on **online advertising**, which includes display (banners, video, and rich media), search, mobile messaging, sponsorships, classifieds, lead generation, and e-mail, on desktop, laptop, and tablet computers, as well as mobile phones (see **Figure 6.5**) (eMarketer, Inc., 2015e).

In the last five years, advertisers have aggressively increased online spending and cut outlays on traditional channels. By 2018, the amount spent on online advertising is expected to exceed the amount spent on television advertising.

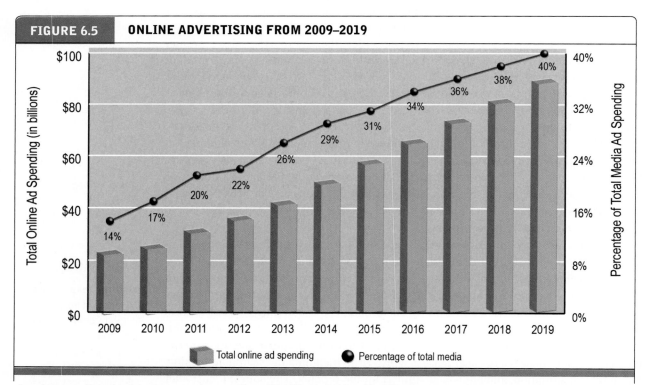

FIGURE 6.5 | **ONLINE ADVERTISING FROM 2009–2019**

Spending on online advertising is expected to grow from $59 billion in 2015 to $91 billion by 2019, and comprise an increasing percentage of total media ad spending.

SOURCE: Based on data from eMarketer, Inc., 2015e.

TABLE 6.4	ONLINE ADVERTISING SPENDING FOR SELECTED FORMATS (IN BILLIONS)		
FORMAT	2015	2019	AVERAGE GROWTH RATE
Search	$25.7	$36.8	9.9%
Banner ads	$12.1	$17.7	10.1%
Video	$7.8	$14.4	20.1%
Rich media	$5.2	$12.1	26.9%
Classifieds	$3.2	$3.9	5.3%
Sponsorships	$2.0	$3.2	12.5%
Lead generation	$2.2	$2.6	5.1%
E-mail	$0.27	$0.34	6.5%

SOURCE: Based on data from eMarketer, Inc., 2015e.

Table 6.4 provides some comparative data on the amount of spending for certain advertising formats. In 2015, the highest amount of spending is for paid search, followed by banner ads, but the fastest growing online ad formats are rich media and video ads.

Spending on online advertising among different industries is somewhat skewed. Retail accounts for the highest percentage (21%), followed by financial services (13%), automotive (12%), telecommunications (9%), leisure travel (9%), consumer electronics and computers (7%), consumer packaged goods (6%), pharmaceuticals and healthcare (5%), media (5%), and entertainment (4%) (Interactive Advertising Bureau/PricewaterhouseCoopers, 2015). Online advertising has both advantages and disadvantages when compared to advertising in traditional media, such as television, radio, and print (magazines and newspapers). One big advantage for online advertising is that the Internet is where the audience has moved, especially the very desirable 18–34 age group. A second big advantage for online advertising is the ability to target ads to individuals and small groups and to track performance of advertisements in almost real time. **Ad targeting**, the sending of market messages to specific subgroups in the population in an effort to increase the likelihood of a purchase, is as old as advertising itself, but prior to the Internet, it could only be done with much less precision, certainly not down to the level of individuals. Ad targeting is also the foundation of price discrimination: the ability to charge different types of consumers different prices for the same product or service. With online advertising, it's theoretically possible to charge every customer a different price.

Theoretically, online advertising can personalize every ad message to precisely fit the needs, interests, and values of each consumer. In practice, as we all know from spam and constant exposure to ads that are of little interest, the reality is very

ad targeting
the sending of market messages to specific subgroups in the population

different. Online advertisements also provide greater opportunities for interactivity—two-way communication between advertisers and potential customers. The primary disadvantages of online advertising are concerns about its cost versus its benefits, how to adequately measure its results, and the supply of good venues to display ads. For instance, the owners of Web sites who sell advertising space ("publishers") do not have agreed-upon standards or routine audits to verify their claimed numbers as do traditional media outlets. We examine the costs and benefits of online advertising as well as research on its effectiveness in Section 6.4.

Search Engine Marketing and Advertising

In 2015, companies will spend an estimated $25.7 billion on search engine marketing and advertising, about 43.5% of all spending for digital marketing. Around 220 million U.S Internet users (almost 85% of all U.S. Internet users) use a search engine at least once a month (eMarketer, Inc., 2015b). Briefly, this is where the eyeballs are (at least for a few moments) and this is where advertising can be very effective by responding with ads that match the interests and intentions of the user. The click-through rate for search engine advertising is generally 1%–4% (with an average of around 2%) and has been fairly steady over the years. The top three search engine providers (Google, Microsoft/Bing, and Yahoo) supply more than 95% of all online searches. **Search engine marketing (SEM)** refers to the use of search engines to build and sustain brands. **Search engine advertising** refers to the use of search engines to support direct sales to online consumers.

> **search engine marketing (SEM)**
> involves the use of search engines to build and sustain brands

> **search engine advertising**
> involves the use of search engines to support direct sales to online

    Search engines are often thought of as mostly direct sales channels focused on making sales in response to advertisements. While this is a major use of search engines, they are also used more subtly to strengthen brand awareness, drive traffic to other Web sites or blogs to support customer engagement, to gain deeper insight into customers' perceptions of the brand, to support other related advertising (for instance, sending consumers to local dealer sites), and to support the brand indirectly. Search engines can also provide marketers insight into customer search patterns, opinions customers hold about their products, top trending search keywords, and what their competitors are using as keywords and the customer response. For example, Pepsico, home of mega brands like Pepsi and Doritos, makes no sales on the Web, but has several branding Web sites aimed at consumers, investors, and shareholders. The focus is on building, sustaining, and updating the Pepsi collection of branded consumer goods. A search on Pepsi will generate numerous search results that link to Pepsi marketing materials.

> **organic search**
> inclusion and ranking of sites depends on a more or less unbiased application of a set of rules imposed by the search engine

Types of Search Engine Advertising Search engine sites originally performed unbiased searches of the Web's huge collection of Web pages and derived most of their revenue from banner advertisements. This form of search engine results is often called **organic search** because the inclusion and ranking of Web sites depends on a more or less "unbiased" application of a set of rules (an algorithm) imposed by the search engine. Since 1998, search engine sites slowly transformed themselves into digital yellow pages, where firms pay for inclusion in the search engine index, pay for keywords to show up in search results, or pay for keywords to show up in other vendors' ads.

Most search engines offer **paid inclusion** programs, which, for a fee, guarantee a Web site's inclusion in its list of search results, more frequent visits by its Web crawler, and suggestions for improving the results of organic searching. Search engines claim that these payments—costing some merchants hundreds of thousands a year—do not influence the organic ranking of a Web site in search results, just inclusion in the results. However, it is the case that page inclusion ads get more hits, and the rank of the page appreciates, causing the organic search algorithm to rank it higher in the organic results.

Google claims that it does not permit firms to pay for their rank in the organic results, although it does allocate two to three sponsored links at the very top of their pages, albeit labeling them as "Sponsored Links." Merchants who refuse to pay for inclusion or for keywords typically fall far down on the list of results, and off the first page of results, which is akin to commercial death.

Pay-per-click (PPC) search ads are the primary type of search engine advertising. In **keyword advertising**, merchants purchase keywords through a bidding process at search sites, and whenever a consumer searches for that word, their advertisement shows up somewhere on the page, usually as a small text-based advertisement on the right, but also as a listing on the very top of the page. The more merchants pay, the higher the rank and greater the visibility of their ads on the page. Generally, the search engines do not exercise editorial judgment about quality or content of the ads although they do monitor the use of language. In addition, some search engines rank the ads in terms of their popularity rather than merely the money paid by the advertiser so that the rank of the ad depends on both the amount paid and the number of clicks per unit time. Google's keyword advertising program is called AdWords.

Network keyword advertising (**context advertising**), introduced by Google as its AdSense product in 2002, differs from the ordinary keyword advertising described previously. Publishers (Web sites that want to show ads) join these networks and allow the search engine to place "relevant" ads on their sites. The ads are paid for by advertisers who want their messages to appear across the Web. Google-like text messages are the most common. The revenue from the resulting clicks is split between the search engine and the site publisher, although the publisher gets much more than half in some cases.

Search engine advertising is nearly an ideal targeted marketing technique: at precisely the moment that a consumer is looking for a product, an advertisement for that product is presented. Consumers benefit from search engine advertising because ads for merchants appear only when consumers are looking for a specific product. Thus, search engine advertising saves consumers cognitive energy and reduces search costs (including the cost of transportation needed to do physical searches for products).

Because search engine marketing can be very effective, companies optimize their Web sites for search engine recognition. The better optimized the page is, the higher a ranking it will achieve in search engine result listings, and the more likely it will appear on the top of the page in search engine results. **Search engine optimization (SEO)** is the process of improving the ranking of Web pages with search engines by altering the content and design of the Web pages and site. By carefully selecting key words used on the Web pages, updating content frequently, and designing the site so

paid inclusion
for a fee, guarantees a Web site's inclusion in its list of sites, more frequent visits by its Web crawler, and suggestions for improving the results of organic searching

pay-per-click (PPC) search ad
primary type of search engine advertising

keyword advertising
merchants purchase keywords through a bidding process at search sites, and whenever a consumer searches for that word, their advertisement shows up somewhere on the page

network keyword advertising (context advertising)
publishers accept ads placed by Google on their Web sites, and receive a fee for any click-throughs from those ads

search engine optimization (SEO)
techniques to improve the ranking of Web pages generated by search engine algorithms

it can be easily read by search engine programs, marketers can improve the impact and return on investment in their Web marketing programs.

Google and other search engine firms make frequent changes to their search algorithms in order to improve the search results and user experience. Google, for instance, reportedly makes over 600 search engine changes in a year. Most are small unannounced tweaks. Recent major changes have included Panda, Penguin, Hummingbird, Knowledge Graph, and an unnamed algorithm that has been nicknamed Mobilegeddon. **Panda** was introduced in 2011 in an effort to weed out low quality sites from search results. Those sites with thin content, duplicate content, content copied from elsewhere on the Web, and content that did not attract high-quality hits from other sources were systematically pushed down in the search results. Google introduced **Penguin** in 2012 in an effort to punish Web sites and their SEO marketing firms who were manipulating links to their site in order to improve their rankings. The Google search engine rewards sites that have links from many other sites. What some marketers discovered is that Google could not tell the quality of these back links, and they began to manufacture links by putting their clients onto list sites, creating multiple blogs to link to their clients' sites, and paying others to link to their clients' sites. Penguin evaluates the quality of links to a site, and pushes down in the rankings those sites that have poor-quality back links.

Many search engines are attempting to capture more of what the user intended, or might like to know about a search subject. This is often referred to as semantic search. Google introduced **Hummingbird** in September 2013. Rather than evaluate each word separately in a search, Google's semantically informed Hummingbird will try to evaluate an entire sentence. Semantic search more closely follows conversational search, or search as you would ordinarily speak it to another human being.

Google introduced **Knowledge Graph** in 2012 as an effort to anticipate what you might want to know more about as you search on a topic or answer questions you might not thought of asking. Since 2013, results of Knowledge Graph appear on the right of the screen and contain more information about the topic or person you are searching on. Not all search terms have a Knowledge Graph result. Google displays information based on what other users have searched for in the past, as well as its database on over 1 billion objects (people, places, and things), and more than 18 billion facts.

In April 2015, Google released a new algorithm update (nicknamed Mobilegeddon) that made the "mobile-friendliness" of Web sites a much stronger ranking factor for mobile searches. Web sites that are not optimized for mobile now have a much lower ranking in mobile search results. And starting in November 2015, Google has announced that it will lower the search rank of mobile Web sites that display an ad that obscures the screen and asks users whether they would like to install the site's mobile app, on the grounds that such ads are less mobile-friendly. Companies that use such ads, such as Yelp, LinkedIn, Pinterest, and others, have charged that Google's new policy is in part an effort to protect its Web search revenue from mobile apps that lure users away from the Web.

Social Search **Social search** is an attempt to use your social contacts (and your entire social graph) to provide search results. In contrast to search engines that use a

Panda
change in the Google algorithm to eliminate low-quality sites from search results

Penguin
change in the Google algorithm to eliminate sites with low-quality back links

Hummingbird
semantic search component of Google's search algorithm

Knowledge Graph
function in Google's search engine that displays a selection of facts related to your search term that you may be interested in knowing more about

social search
effort to provide fewer, more relevant, and trustworthy results based on the social graph

mathematical algorithm to find pages that satisfy your query, social search reviews your friends' (and their friends') recommendations, past Web visits, and use of Like buttons. One problem with traditional search engines is that they are so thorough: enter a search for "smartphone" on Google and in .28 seconds you will receive 569 million results, some of which provide helpful information and others that are suspect. Social search is an effort to provide fewer, more relevant, and trustworthy results based on the social graph. Facebook's first effort to create a social search engine was Facebook Graph Search, which it launched in 2013. Graph Search produced information from within a user's network of friends supplemented with additional results provided by Bing. In December 2014, Facebook introduced a series of changes to Graph Search, dropping its relationship with Bing, rebranding the product as Facebook Search, and providing keyword search functionality that enables users to find people, photos, posts, videos, and links on Facebook by searching for words within a post. Results are ranked using a personalization algorithm based in part on the user's relationship to the poster.

Search Engine Issues While search engines have provided significant benefits to merchants and customers, they also present risks and costs. For instance, search engines have the power to crush a small business by placing its ads on the back pages of search results. Merchants are at the mercy of search engines for access to the online marketplace, and this access is dominated by a single firm, Google. How Google decides to rank one company over another in search results is not known. No one really knows how to improve in its rankings (although there are hundreds of firms who claim otherwise). Google editors intervene in unknown ways to punish certain Web sites and reward others. Using paid sponsored listings, as opposed to relying on organic search results, eliminates some, but not all, of this uncertainty.

Other practices that degrade the results and usefulness of search engines include:

- **Link farms** are groups of Web sites that link to one another, thereby boosting their ranking in search engines that use a PageRank algorithm to judge the "usefulness" of a site. For instance, in the 2010 holiday season, JCPenney was found to be the highest ranked merchant for a large number of clothing products. On examination, it was discovered that this resulted from Penney's hiring a search engine optimization company to create thousands of Web sites that linked to JCPenney's Web site. As a result, JCPenney's Web site became the most popular (most linked-to) Web site for products like dresses, shirts, and pants. No matter what popular clothing item people searched for, JCPenney came out on top. Experts believe this was the largest search engine fraud in history. Google's Panda series of updates to its search algorithms were aimed in part at eliminating link farms (Castell, 2014).

- **Content farms** are companies that generate large volumes of textual content for multiple Web sites designed to attract viewers and search engines. Content farms profit by attracting large numbers of readers to their sites and exposing them to ads. The content typically is not original but is artfully copied or summarized from legitimate content sites.

- **Click fraud** occurs when a competitor clicks on search engine results and ads, forcing the advertiser to pay for the click even though the click is not legitimate. Competitors

link farms
groups of Web sites that link to one another, thereby boosting their ranking in search engines

content farms
companies that generate large volumes of textual content for multiple Web sites designed to attract viewers and search engines

click fraud
occurs when a competitor clicks on search engine results and ads, forcing the advertiser to pay for the click even though the click is not legitimate

can hire offshore firms to perform fraudulent clicks or hire botnets to automate the process. Click fraud can quickly run up a large bill for merchants, and not result in any growth in sales. A study by the National Association of Advertisers estimated that advertisers would lose $6.3 billion in 2015 due to click fraud (Kirk, 2015).

Display Ad Marketing

In 2015, companies will spend around $27.1 billion on all forms of display ad marketing, about 46% of all spending for digital marketing. Around 6 trillion display ads will be served on desktop and mobile devices in 2015. The top five display ad companies are Facebook, Google, Twitter, Yahoo, and AOL, and together they account for 51% of U.S. display ad revenue. The Interactive Advertising Bureau (IAB), an industry organization, has established voluntary industry guidelines for display ads. Publishers are not required to use these guidelines, but many do. One objective of IAB is to give the consumer a consistent experience across all Web sites. The various types of ads are designed to help advertisers break through the "noise" and clutter created by the high number of display ad impressions that a typical user is exposed to within a given day. **Figure 6.6** shows examples of the seven core standard ad units, as specified by the IAB. According to Google, the top performing ad formats are the large rectangle, the medium rectangle, the leaderboard, and the half-page (Google Inc., 2015). Display ads consist of four different kinds of ads: banner ads, rich media ads (animated ads), sponsorships, and video ads.

banner ad
displays a promotional message in a rectangular box at the top or bottom of a computer screen

Banner Ads Banner ads are the oldest and most familiar form of display marketing. They are also the least effective and the lowest cost form of online marketing. A banner ad displays a promotional message in a rectangular box on the screen of a desktop computer or mobile device. A **banner ad** is similar to a traditional ad in a printed publication but has some added advantages. When clicked, it brings potential customers directly to the advertiser's Web site, and the site where the ad appears can observe the user's behavior on the site. The ability to identify and track the user is a key feature of online advertising. Banner ads often feature video and other animations. It's important to note that, although the terms banner ad and display ad are often used interchangeably, banner ads are just one form of display ad. Despite their limited effectiveness, advertisers will still spend about $12.1 billion on banner ads in 2015, about 44% of all spending on display ads, and 21% of total online ad spending.

rich media ad
ad employing animation, sound, and interactivity, using Flash, HTML5, Java, and JavaScript

Rich Media Ads Ads that employ animation, sound, and interactivity, using Flash, HTML5, Java, and JavaScript are referred to as **rich media ads**. Rich media ads are expected to account for about $5.2 billion in online advertising expenditures (about 9% of total online advertising but one of the fastest growing formats) in 2015. They are far more effective than simple banner ads. For instance, one research report that analyzed 24,000 different rich media ads with more than 12 billion impressions served in North America over a six-month period found that exposure to rich media ads boosted advertiser site visits by nearly 300% compared to standard banner ads. Viewers of rich media ads that included video were six times more likely to visit the advertiser's Web site, by either directly clicking on the ad, typing the advertiser's URL, or searching

FIGURE 6.6	TYPES OF DISPLAY ADS

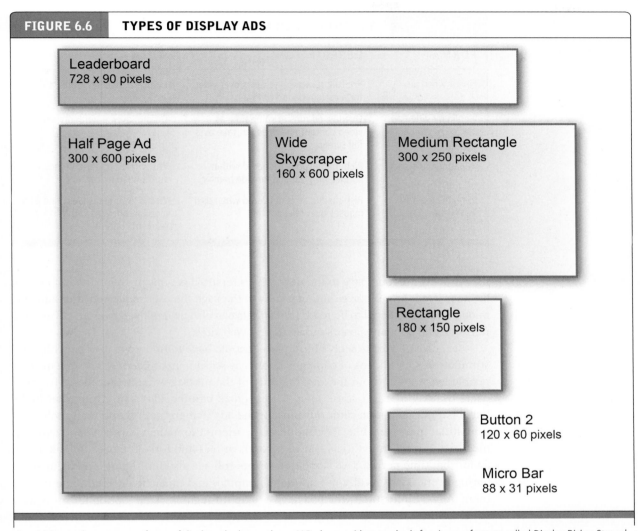

In addition to the seven core forms of display ads shown above, IAB also provides standards for six new formats called Display Rising Star ad units.

SOURCE: Based on data from Interactive Advertising Bureau, 2011.

(MediaMind, 2012a). Recent research by the IAB indicates that its Rising Star ad units that can incorporate rich media elements deliver a 30% stronger brand lift than the traditional IAB core display ads with just one full exposure, increasing to over 40% when a consumer interacts with the ad. Rising Star ads also topped traditional display ads in terms of ad recall and were considered less annoying (IAB, 2015).

The IAB provides guidance for a number of different types of rich media ads, such as those that contain in-banner video, those that are expandable/retractable, pop-ups, floating versions, and interstitials. An **interstitial ad** (interstitial means "in between") is a way of placing a full-page message between the current and destination pages of a user. Interstitials are usually inserted within a single Web site, and displayed as the

interstitial ad
a way of placing a full-page message between the current and destination pages of a user

TABLE 6.5	TYPES OF VIDEO ADS	
FORMAT	DESCRIPTION	WHEN USED
Linear video ad	Pre-roll; takeover; ad takes over video for a certain period of time	Before, between, or after video
Nonlinear video ad	Overlay; ad runs at same time as video content and does not take over full screen	During, over, or within video
In-banner video ad	Rich media; ad is triggered within banner, may expand outside banner	Within Web page, generally surrounded by content
In-text video ad	Rich media; ad is delivered when user mouses over relevant text	Within Web page, identified as a highlighted word within relevant content

user moves from one page to the next. The interstitial is typically contained in its own browser window and moves automatically to the page the user requested after allowing enough time for the ad to be read. Interstitials can also be deployed over an advertising network and appear as users move among Web sites.

Because the Web is such a busy place, people have to find ways to cope with over-stimulation. One means of coping is known as *sensory input filtering*. This means that people learn to filter out the vast majority of the messages coming at them. Internet users quickly learn at some level to recognize banner ads or anything that looks like a banner ad and to filter out most of the ads that are not exceptionally relevant. Interstitial messages, like TV commercials, attempt to make viewers a captive of the message. Typical interstitials last 10 seconds or less and force the user to look at the ad for that time period. IAB standards for pre-roll ads also limit their length. To avoid boring users, ads typically use animated graphics and music to entertain and inform them. A good interstitial will also have a "skip through" or "stop" option for users who have no interest in the message.

The IAB also provides mobile rich media ad interface definitions (MRAID) in an effort to provide a set of standards designed to work with HTML5 and JavaScript that developers can use to create rich media ads to work with apps running on different mobile devices. The hope is make it easier to display ads across a wide variety of devices without having to rewrite code (Interactive Advertising Bureau, 2012).

video ad
TV-like advertisement that appears as an in-page video commercial or before, during, or after content

Video Ads Online **video ads** are TV-like advertisements that appear as in-page video commercials or before, during, or after a variety of content. **Table 6.5** describes some of the IAB standards for video ads. The most widely used format is the "pre-roll" (followed by the mid-roll and the post-roll) where users are forced to watch a video ad either before, in the middle of, or at the end of the video they originally clicked on. In 2014, the IAB released additional standards for five new in-stream and linear interactive video ad formats that enable advertisers to provide additional opportunities for consumer engagement.

Although from a total spending standpoint, online video ads are still very small when compared to the amount spent on search engine advertising, video ads are another fast growing form of online advertisement, accounting for about $7.8 billion in online advertising spending, which is expected to almost double to $14.4 billion by 2019. The rapid growth in video ads is due in part to the fact that video ads are far more effective than other display ad formats. For instance, according to research analyzing a variety of ad formats, in-stream video ads had click-through rates 12 times that of rich media and 27 times that of standard banner ads (MediaMind, 2012). Research by the IAB indicates that interactive digital video has even greater impact than typical, non-interactive video formats, with interaction rates three to four times higher, and brand awareness heightened by more than 50% (Interactive Advertising Bureau, 2014).

There are many specialized video advertising networks that run video advertising campaigns for national advertisers and place these videos on their respective networks of Web sites. Firms can also establish their own video and television sites to promote their products. Retail sites are among the largest users of advertising videos. For instance, Zappos, the largest online shoe retailer, has a video for every one of its over 100,000 products.

Sponsorships A **sponsorship** is a paid effort to tie an advertiser's name to particular information, an event, or a venue in a way that reinforces its brand in a positive yet not overtly commercial manner. In 2015, companies will spend about $2 billion for sponsorship marketing. Sponsorships typically are more about branding than immediate sales. A common form of sponsorship is targeted content (or advertorials), in which editorial content is combined with an ad message to make the message more valuable and attractive to its intended audience. For instance, WebMD, the leading medical information Web site in the United States, displays sponsored pages on the WebMD Web site from companies such as Phillips to describe its home defibrillators, and Lilly to describe its pharmaceutical solutions for attention deficit disorders among children. Social media sponsorships, in which marketers pay for mentions in social media, such as blogs, tweets, or in online video, have also become a popular tactic. Sponsorships have also moved onto the mobile platform. For instance, Subaru sponsors an app called MapMyDogwalk, a GPS-enabled dog walking tool.

sponsorship
a paid effort to tie an advertiser's name to information, an event, or a venue in a way that reinforces its brand in a positive yet not overtly commercial manner

Native Advertising Advertising that looks similar to editorial content is known as **native advertising.** Native advertising is not new. Traditional native advertising includes television infomercials, newspaper advertorials, and entire sections of newspapers and magazines that are given over to advertisers, where the advertising looks similar to the rest of the publication. In the online world, native ads are most often found on social media, especially mobile social media, as part of a Facebook Newsfeed, Twitter Timeline, or Pinterest Promoted Pin. Mobile social networks do not have room for ads on the right side of the screen (the sidebar or right rail), and therefore native ads in the form of posts that look like other posts are the favored option.

Typically, native ads mimic the editorial content around them. They appear outside the normal or expected area for ads and are labeled to indicate they are not editorial content, although in most cases the word "ad" is not used. On the Web or

native advertising
advertising that looks similar to editorial content

mobile screens, native ads are usually distinguished by a "sponsored" tag underneath the headline, often in a different color. Online native advertising is growing rapidly, especially on social networks. In 2015, native ad spending is expected to reach $4.3 billion (eMarketer, Inc., 2015f). Federal Trade Commission researchers found that 73% of online publishers offer native advertising, including the *New York Times*, which began the practice in 2014.

Researchers have found that 35% of online consumers cannot distinguish between editorial content and sponsored ads that look like editorial content, even if the ads are labelled as sponsored or promoted. Most consumers do not know what sponsored or promoted means. In a survey of 10,000 consumers, researchers found that consumers skip over labels like sponsored, and many do not understand the difference between paid and unpaid content (Franklin, 2013). Yet market researchers have found that native ads are far more influential with consumers. Consumers look at native ads 53% more frequently than display ads; native ads raise purchase intent by 18%; and consumers are twice as likely to share a native ad with a family member as a regular ad. Marketers and advertisers are opposed to labeling native advertising with the word "ad" and instead prefer other tags.

Native advertising is controversial. Critics contend that the purpose of native ads is to deceive or fool the consumer into thinking the ad has the same validity as the editorial content in media. The Federal Trade Commission held a conference in December 2013 to explore the native advertising phenomenon because of the potential to deceive consumers. Although the FTC has not as yet issued any specific guidelines with respect to native advertising, it has indicated that if publishers are involved in creating native advertising content, they can potentially be held liable for that content if it is misleading to consumers. Traditionally, the FTC has not held publishers responsible for misleading ads placed by advertisers (Lewis, 2015). Supporters argue that native ads add value by helping consumers, advertisers, and the media in which they are used (Federal Trade Commission, 2013).

Content Marketing Native advertising is usually focused on partnering with a specific publisher. **Content marketing** creates a content campaign for a brand and then tries to secure placement on a variety of Web site. Examples of content include articles, infographics, case studies, interactive graphics, white papers and even traditional press releases. The aim of content marketing is to increase visitors to a company's Web site, organic search rankings, and brand engagement via social media (Libert, 2015).

Advertising Networks In the early years of e-commerce, firms placed ads on the few popular Web sites in existence, but by early 2000, there were hundreds of thousands of sites where ads could be displayed, and it became very inefficient for a single firm to purchase ads on each individual Web site. Most firms, even very large firms, did not have the capability by themselves to place banner ads and marketing messages on thousands of Web sites and monitor the results. Specialized marketing firms called **advertising networks** appeared to help firms take advantage of the powerful marketing potential of the Internet, and to make the entire process of buying and selling

advertising networks
connect online marketers with publishers by displaying ads to consumers based on detailed customer information

FIGURE 6.7	HOW AN ADVERTISING NETWORK SUCH AS DOUBLECLICK WORKS

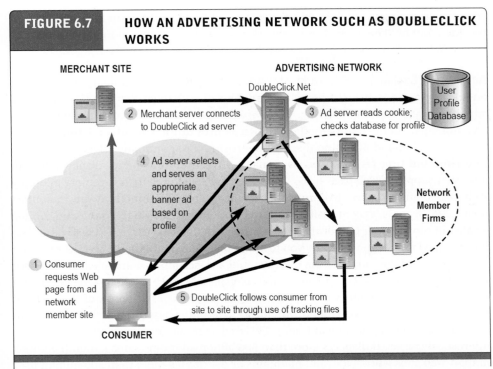

MERCHANT SITE   ADVERTISING NETWORK

DoubleClick.Net

2   Merchant server connects to DoubleClick ad server

3   Ad server reads cookie; checks database for profile

User Profile Database

4   Ad server selects and serves an appropriate banner ad based on profile

Network Member Firms

1   Consumer requests Web page from ad network member site

5   DoubleClick follows consumer from site to site through use of tracking files

CONSUMER

Millions of publishers have audiences to sell, and pages to fill with ads. Thousands of advertisers are looking for audiences. Ad networks are intermediaries that connect publishers with marketers.

online ads more efficient and transparent. These ad networks have proliferated and have greatly increased the scale and liquidity of online marketing.

Advertising networks represent the most sophisticated application of Internet database capabilities to date, and illustrate just how different Internet marketing is from traditional marketing. Advertising networks sell advertising and marketing opportunities (slots) to companies who wish to buy exposure to an online audience (advertisers). Advertising networks obtain their inventory of ad opportunities from a network of participating sites that want to display ads on their sites in return for receiving a payment from advertisers everytime a visitor clicks on an ad. These sites are usually referred to as Web publishers. Marketers buy audiences and publishers sell audiences by attracting an audience and capturing audience information. Ad networks are the intermediaries who make this market work efficiently.

Figure 6.7 illustrates how these systems work. Advertising networks begin with a consumer requesting a page from a member of the advertising network (1). A connection is established with the third-party ad server (2). The ad server identifies the user by reading the cookie file on the user's hard drive and checks its user profile database for the user's profile (3). The ad server selects an appropriate banner ad based on the user's previous purchases, interests, demographics, or other data in the profile (4). Whenever the user later goes online and visits any of the network member sites, the ad server recognizes the user and serves up the same or different ads regardless of the site content. The advertising network follows users from site to site through the use of Web tracking files (5).

Advertising Exchanges, Programmatic Advertising, Real-Time Bidding Today, most online display advertising is being delivered by ad exchanges that use programmatic advertising and real-time bidding. An **ad exchange** is a digital marketplace that uses an automated auction-based method known as **programmatic advertising** to match supply and demand of online display advertising. Programmatic advertising uses a **real-time bidding (RTB) process** to match advertiser demand for display ads with publisher supply of Web page space. Publishers are able to sell their inventory of empty Web pages, often excess inventory that could not be sold directly. Want to contact males age 18 to 34, recent visitors to a car site, unmarried, high risk-taking profile, located in New York or California, urban home, and financial service industry employment? An ad exchange will allow you to bid in real time on this audience against other advertisers, and then manage the placement of ads, accounting, and measurement for your firm. Ad exchanges offer tremendous global scale and efficiency. One of the best known is Google's DoubleClick Ad Exchange, which is based on more than 100 ad networks (the supply side), and provides a computer-based market for buyers to purchase audiences (the demand side). This exchange sells audiences sliced into 1,600 interest categories. It displays more than 300 billion ad impressions a month across 2 million Web sites worldwide, and maintains or distributes more than 500 million user profiles of Internet users (Kantrowitz, 2013, 2015). These profiles are based on Web tracking files, offline purchase information, and social network data. Marketing firms, the buyers from publishers of Web sites, can target their audience and control the frequency and timing of ads during the day. The case study at the end of the chapter, *Programmatic Advertising: Real Time Marketing*, provides you with a further look at ad exchanges and real-time bidding.

Display Advertising Issues As with search engine advertising, online display advertising is not without its issues, which include both ad fraud (similar to click fraud) and concerns about viewability (whether display ads are actually being seen).

   Ad Fraud. According to Interactive Advertising Bureau estimates, about 36% of all Web traffic is fake, and by extension, about the same percentage of clicks on ads are fake as well (Vranica, 2014). A study by the Association of National Advertisers and security company White Ops estimated that $6.3 billion will be lost as a result of ad fraud in 2015 (Kantrowitz, 2015). There are four primary sources of ad fraud. Botnets can be hired by publishers to click on their Web pages to create phony traffic. Second, a browser extension can insert ads into a premium publisher's Web site, and then list the ads as available on a programmatic ad exchange. Third, ad targeting firms can create bots that imitate the behavior of real shoppers, and then charge advertisers for successfully targeting consumers. Fourth, if you are a publisher looking to attract ads to your site, the simplest technique is simply to hire people in low-wage countries to click on your ads using a proxy server (Kantrowitz, 2014).

ad exchanges
auction-based digital marketplace where ad networks sell ad space to marketers

programmatic advertising
automated, auction-based method for matching demand and supply for online display ads

real-time bidding (RTB) process
used to match advertiser demand for display ads with publisher supply of Web page space

Large advertisers have begun to hire online fraud detection firms (a growth industry) to determine the extent of fraud in their campaigns. Verizon Wireless, L'Oreal, and Kellogg are among the firms that found millions of dollars of ad fraud in recent campaigns, and have demanded advertising networks to either reimburse them or generate real Web traffic in the amount of the fraud.

Viewability.   Recent research by Google revealed that 56% of the impressions served across its display advertising platforms, including DoubleClick, are not viewable. Previous research by comScore showed similar results: 54% of display ads, and 57% of video ads, were not in fact seen by people, even though advertisers were charged for generating ad impressions and serving ads (comScore, 2013). There are a number of reasons for this situation. First, there is no mechanism for measuring how many people actually see an online ad that has been served. The same is true of most offline print and TV advertising, although several methods and certifications have been developed over decades to accurately measure audience exposure. There are no such mechanisms for online advertising. Second, a large percentage of ads served appear lower down on the screen where users are less likely to go, or video ads on auto-play are playing in areas the user cannot see. Advertisers are still charged for ads that are served but not viewed. Unscrupulous publishers can place multiple ads on top of each other and charge multiple times for the same page space (Segal, 2014). Third, botnets can be programmed to click on ads on fraudulent Web sites, generating impressions and ad serves, but no one actually sees the ads. The Media Rating Council, an advertising industry group, released a very low standard for "viewability" in 2014: an ad is considered viewable if half of the ad can be viewed for at least one second. For video ads, half of the video needs to be viewable for two seconds (Hof, 2014). A revised version of the guidelines issued in August 2015 addressed some additional specific issues, but did not alter the baseline standard. The advertisers who pay for online ads are beginning to demand guarantees of viewability. Several companies, including comScore, are offering tagging technology that can partially measure viewability (Vranica, 2014). Unviewed ads are just as profitable as viewed ads for Web publishers and advertising agencies. For advertisers, they represent the half of marketing expenditures that is wasted.

Ad Blocking.   Over the past several years, use of ad-blocking software, which can eliminate display ads, pre-roll video ads, retargeted ads, and some types of native ads on desktops and laptops, has been growing. Ad blockers operate in a manner very similar to a firewall, recognizing and eliminating content based on IP address. Ad blockers have become very easy to install, with programs such as Adblock Plus offered as extensions for Firefox, Chrome, and other Web browsers. Currently, about 10% to 15% of Internet users in the United States are estimated to be employing ad blockers, with their most prevalent use among the younger, more technically advanced audience. Gaming, newsgroup/forums, and social network sites are the most frequently affected by ad-blocking. Although advertisers are not yet panicked about ad blocking, it is a trend that they are watching with increasing concern. Some Web sites, such as Wired, The Guardian, and OKCupid have made a direct appeal to their users to turn off their ad-blockers or to make a donation instead.

E-mail Marketing

direct e-mail marketing
e-mail marketing messages sent directly to interested users

When e-mail marketing began, unsolicited e-mail was not common. **Direct e-mail marketing** (e-mail marketing messages sent directly to interested users) was one of the first and most effective forms of online marketing communications. Direct e-mail marketing messages are sent to an opt-in audience of Internet users who, at one time or another, have expressed an interest in receiving messages from the advertiser. By sending e-mail to an opt-in audience, advertisers are targeting interested consumers. By far, in-house e-mail lists are more effective than purchased e-mail lists. Because of the comparatively high response rates and low cost, direct e-mail marketing remains a common form of online marketing communications. Other benefits of e-mail marketing include its mass reach, the ability to track and measure response, the ability to personalize content and tailor offers, the ability to drive traffic to Web sites for more interaction, the ability to test and optimize content and offers, and the ability to target by region, demographic, time of day, or other criteria. In 2015, U.S. companies will spend about $270 million on e-mail marketing, a relatively small amount when compared to search and display ad marketing. But these numbers can be deceiving. E-mail marketing still packs a punch with solid customer response. Click-through rates for legitimate e-mail depend on the promotion (the offer), the product, and the amount of targeting, but average around 3%–4%. Despite the deluge of spam mail, e-mail remains a highly cost-effective way of communicating with existing customers, and to a lesser extent, finding new customers. Mobile devices have become the predominant method for accessing e-mail. A survey by Movable Ink showed that 67% of all email sent on its platform in the first quarter of 2015 were opened on a smartphone or tablet computer, while only 33% were opened on a desktop or laptop (Silverpop, 2015; eMarketer, Inc., 2015g).

E-mail marketing and advertising is inexpensive and somewhat invariant to the number of mails sent. The cost of sending 1,000 e-mails is about the same as the cost to send 1 million. The primary cost of e-mail marketing is for the purchase of the list of names to which the e-mail will be sent. This generally costs anywhere from 5 to 20 cents a name, depending on how targeted the list is. Sending the e-mail is virtually cost-free. In contrast, the cost to acquire the name, print, and mail a 5 x 7-inch direct mail post card is around 75 to 80 cents a name.

While e-mail marketing often is sales-oriented, it can also be used as an integral feature of a multi-channel marketing campaign designed to strengthen brand recognition. Personalization and targeting are major themes in e-mail marketing in 2015. For instance, Jeep created an e-mail campaign to a targeted audience who had searched on SUVs, and visited Chrysler and Jeep Facebook pages. The e-mail campaign announced a contest based on a game users could play online that involved tracking an arctic beast with a Jeep. Recipients could sign up on Facebook, Twitter, or the Jeep blog.

Although e-mail can still be an effective marketing and advertising tool, it faces three main challenges: spam, software tools used to control spam that eliminate much e-mail from user inboxes, and poorly targeted purchased e-mail lists. **Spam** is unsolicited commercial e-mail (sometimes referred to as "junk" e-mail) and *spammers* are people who send unsolicited e-mail to a mass audience that has not expressed any interest in the product. Spammers tend to market pornography, fraudulent deals and

spam
unsolicited commercial e-mail

services, scams, and other products not widely approved in most civilized societies. Legitimate direct opt-in e-mail marketing is not growing as fast as behaviorally targeted display ads and search engine advertising because of the explosion in spam. Consumer response to even legitimate e-mail campaigns has become more sophisticated. In general, e-mail works well for maintaining customer relationships but poorly for acquiring new customers.

While click fraud may be the Achilles' heel of search engine advertising, spam is the nemesis of effective e-mail marketing and advertising. The percentage of all e-mail that is spam averaged around 52.5% in the first 7 months of 2015, down about 10% from the comparable period in 2014 (Symantec, 2015). Most spam originates from bot networks, which consist of thousands of captured PCs that can initiate and relay spam messages (see Chapter 5). Spam volume has declined somewhat since authorities took down the Rustock botnet in 2011. Spam is seasonally cyclical, and varies monthly due to the impact of new technologies (both supportive and discouraging of spammers), new prosecutions, and seasonal demand for products and services.

Legislative attempts in the United States to control spam have been mostly unsuccessful. Thirty-seven states have laws regulating or prohibiting spam (National Conference of State Legislatures, 2015). State legislation typically requires that unsolicited mail (spam) contain a label in the subject line ("ADV") indicating the message is an advertisement, requires a clear opt-out choice for consumers, and prohibits e-mail that contains false routing and domain name information (nearly all spammers hide their own domain, ISP, and IP address).

Congress passed the first national anti-spam law ("Controlling the Assault of Non-Solicited Pornography and Marketing" or CAN-SPAM Act) in 2003, and it went into effect in January 2004. The act does not prohibit unsolicited e-mail (spam) but instead requires unsolicited commercial e-mail messages to be labeled (though not by a standard method) and to include opt-out instructions and the sender's physical address. It prohibits the use of deceptive subject lines and false headers in such messages. The FTC is authorized (but not required) to establish a "Do Not E-mail" registry. State laws that require labels on unsolicited commercial e-mail or prohibit such messages entirely are pre-empted, although provisions merely addressing falsity and deception may remain in place. The act imposes fines of $10 for each unsolicited pornographic e-mail and authorizes state attorneys general to bring lawsuits against spammers. The act obviously makes lawful legitimate bulk mailing of unsolicited e-mail messages (what most people call spam), yet seeks to prohibit certain deceptive practices and provide a small measure of consumer control by requiring opt-out notices. In this sense, critics point out, CAN-SPAM ironically legalizes spam as long as spammers follow the rules. For this reason, large spammers have been among the bill's biggest supporters, and consumer groups have been the act's most vociferous critics.

In contrast, Canada's anti-spam law is one of the toughest in the world. Unlike the CAN-SPAM Act, Canada's law is based on an opt-in model and prohibits the sending of commercial e-mail, texts, and social media messaging unless the recipient has given his or her consent. Violations of the law can lead to penalties of up to $1 million for individuals and $10 million for organizations. The first phase of the law went into effect in July 2014. The law applies anytime a computer within Canada is used to send or access an electronic message, so companies located within the United States that send e-mail to Canada must comply with the law (French, 2014).

There have been a number of state and federal prosecutions of spammers, and private civil suits by large ISPs such as Microsoft. Volunteer efforts by industry are another potential control point. Notably, the Direct Marketing Association (DMA), an industry trade group that represents companies that use the postal mail system as well as e-mail for solicitations, is now strongly supporting legislative controls over spam, in addition to its voluntary guidelines. The DMA would like to preserve the legitimate use of e-mail as a marketing technique. The DMA has formed a 15-person anti-spam group and spends $500,000 a year trying to identify spammers. The DMA is also a supporter of the National Cyber-Forensics & Training Alliance (NCFTA), a nonprofit organization with close ties to the FBI. NCFTA operates a variety of initiatives aimed at combating cybercrime, including digital phishing via spam.

Affiliate Marketing

affiliate marketing
commissions paid by advertisers to affiliate Web sites for referring potential customers to their Web site

Affiliate marketing is a form of marketing where a firm pays a commission, typically anywhere between 4% to 20%, to other Web sites (including blogs) for sending customers to their Web site. Affiliate marketing generally involves pay-for-performance: the affiliate or affiliate network gets paid only if users click on a link or purchase a product. According to Forrester Research, U.S. affiliate marketing spending is expected to reach $4.5 billion annually by 2016 (Robinson, 2014). Industry experts estimate that around 10% of all retail online sales are generated through affiliate programs (as compared to search engine ads, which account for more than 30% of online sales), and affiliate programs run by the Internet Retailer Top 500 have a median of 2,000 participating affiliates.

Visitors to an affiliate Web site typically click on ads and are taken to the advertiser's Web site. In return, the advertiser pays the affiliate a fee, either on a per-click basis or as a percentage of whatever the customer spends on the advertiser's site. Paying commissions for referrals or recommendations long predated the Web.

For instance, Amazon has a strong affiliate program consisting of more than 1 million participant sites, called Associates, which receive up to 10% in advertising fees on sales their referrals generate. Affiliates attract people to their blogs or Web sites where they can click on ads for products at Amazon. Members of eBay's Affiliates Program can earn between 50% and 75% of eBay's revenue on winning bids and Buy It Now transactions as well as between $20 and $35 for each active registered user sent to eBay. Amazon, eBay, and other large e-commerce companies with affiliate programs typically administer such programs themselves. Smaller e-commerce firms who wish to use affiliate marketing often decide to join an affiliate network (sometimes called an affiliate broker), such as CJ Affiliate and Rakuten Linkshare, which acts as an intermediary. Bloggers often sign up for Google's AdSense program to attract advertisers to their sites. They are paid for each click on an ad and sometimes for subsequent purchases made by visitors.

Viral Marketing

viral marketing
the process of getting customers to pass along a company's marketing message to friends, family, and colleagues

Just as affiliate marketing involves using a trusted Web site to encourage users to visit other sites, **viral marketing** is a form of social marketing that involves getting customers to pass along a company's marketing message to friends, family, and colleagues. It's the online version of word-of-mouth advertising, which spreads even faster and further than in the real world. In the offline world, next to television, word of mouth is the second most important means by which consumers find out about new products. And the most important factor in the decision to purchase is the face-to-face recommendations of parents, friends, and colleagues. Millions of online adults in the United States are "influencers" who share their opinions about products in a variety of online settings. In addition to increasing the size of a company's customer base, customer referrals also have other advantages: they are less expensive to acquire because existing customers do all the acquisition work, and they tend to use online support services less, preferring to turn back to the person who referred them for advice. Also, because they cost so little to acquire and keep, referred customers begin to generate profits for a company much earlier than customers acquired through other marketing methods. There are a number of online venues where viral marketing appears. E-mail used to be the primary online venue for viral marketing ("please forward this e-mail to your friends"), but venues such as Facebook, Pinterest, Instagram, Twitter, YouTube, and blogs now play a major role. For example, the most viral video ad of 2014 was a video featuring the singer Shakira that promoted the FIFA World Cup, with over 7.3 million shares and 560 million views as of August 2015 (Koerber, 2014).

Lead Generation Marketing

Lead generation marketing uses multiple e-commerce presences to generate leads for businesses who later can be contacted and converted into customers through sales calls, e-mail, or other means. In one sense, all Internet marketing campaigns attempt to develop leads. But lead generation marketing is a specialized subset of the Internet marketing industry that provides consulting services and software tools to collect and manage leads for firms, and to convert these leads to customers. Companies will spend an estimated $2.2 billion on lead generation marketing in 2015. Sometimes called "inbound marketing," lead generation marketing firms help other firms build Web sites, launch e-mail campaigns, use social network sites and blogs to optimize the generation of leads, and then manage those leads by initiating further contacts, tracking interactions, and interfacing with customer relationship management systems to keep track of customer-firm interactions. One of the foremost lead generation marketing firms is Hubspot, which has developed a software suite for generating and managing leads.

lead generation marketing
uses multiple e-commerce presences to generate leads for businesses who later can be contacted and converted into customers

SOCIAL, MOBILE, AND LOCAL MARKETING AND ADVERTISING

In this section we provide a very brief overview of the social, mobile, and local marketing and advertising landscape. Then, in Chapter 7, we provide a much more in-depth examination of social, mobile, and local marketing and advertising tools.

Social Marketing and Advertising

Social marketing/advertising involves the use of online social networks and communities to build brands and drive sales revenues. There are several kinds of social networks, from Facebook, Twitter, Pinterest, and Instagram, to social apps, social games, blogs, and forums (Web sites that attract people who share a community of interests or skills). In 2015, companies are expected to spend about $9.6 billion on social network marketing and advertising. Next to mobile marketing, it is the fastest growing type of online marketing. Nevertheless, in 2015, it represents only about 16% of all online marketing and is still dwarfed by the amount spent on search engine advertising and display advertising (eMarketer, Inc., 2015h).

Marketers cannot ignore the huge audiences that social networks such as Facebook, Twitter, Pinterest, and Instagram are gathering, which rival television and radio in size. In 2015, there were about 1.5 billion Facebook members, 320 million active Twitter users, around 400 million Instagram users, and around 100 million Pinterest members worldwide. In the United States, in July 2015, Facebook had about 214 million unique visitors. Around 56% of the U.S. population visits social network sites. It's little wonder that marketers and advertisers are joyous at the prospect of connecting with this large audience. Almost 90% of U.S. companies are using social media for marketing purposes in 2015, and research has found that social network users are more likely to talk about and recommend a company or product they follow on Facebook or Twitter.

Social networks offer advertisers all the main advertising formats, including banner ads (the most common), short pre-roll and post-roll ads associated with videos, and sponsorship of content. Having a corporate Facebook page is in itself a marketing tool for brands just like a Web page. Many firms, such as Coca-Cola, have shut down product-specific Web pages and instead use Facebook pages.

Blogs and online games can also be used for social marketing. Blogs have been around for a decade and are a part of the mainstream online culture (see Chapter 3 for a description of blogs). Around 28 million people write blogs, and around 79 million read blogs. Blogs play a vital role in online marketing. Although more firms use Twitter and Facebook, these sites have not replaced blogs, and in fact often point to blogs for long-form content. Because blog readers and creators tend to be more educated, have higher incomes, and be opinion leaders, blogs are ideal platforms for ads for many products and services that cater to this kind of audience. Because blogs are based on the personal opinions of the writers, they are also an ideal platform to start a viral marketing campaign. Advertising networks that specialize in blogs provide some efficiency in placing ads, as do blog networks, which are collections of a small number of popular blogs, coordinated by a central management team, and which can deliver a larger audience to advertisers. For more information on social marketing using blogs, see Learning Track 6.3.

The online gaming marketplace continues to expand rapidly as users increasingly play games on smartphones and tablets, as well as PCs and consoles. The story of game advertising in 2015 is social, mobile, and local: social games are ascendant, mobile devices are the high-growth platform, and location-based advertising is starting to show real traction. The objective of game advertising is both branding and driving customers to purchase moments at restaurants and retail stores. In 2015, around 165 million people play games on their mobile phones, about 49 million play on consoles, while about 116 million play on tablets. Of the online gamers, about 86 million play social games, such as Jackbox Games' You Don't Know Jack. Advertisers are expected to spend about $310 million on in-game social game advertising in 2015 (eMarketer, Inc., 2015i).

Mobile Marketing and Advertising

Marketing on the mobile platform is growing rapidly and becoming a very significant part (49%) of the overall $59 billion online marketing spending. In 2015, spending on all forms of mobile marketing is estimated to be about $29 billion, and it is expected to more than double, to over $65 billion, by 2019 (eMarketer, Inc., 2015e). A number of factors are driving advertisers to the mobile platform, including much more powerful devices, faster networks, wireless local networks, rich media and video ads, and growing demand for local advertising by small business and consumers. Most important, mobile is where the eyeballs are now and increasingly will be in the future: about 194 million people access the Internet at least some of the time from mobile devices.

Mobile marketing includes the use of display banner ads, rich media, video, games, e-mail, text messaging, in-store messaging, Quick Response (QR) codes, and couponing. Mobile is now a required part of the standard marketing budget. In 2015, display ads are expected to be the most popular mobile advertising format, accounting for about 51% of all mobile ad spending. Display ads can be served as a part of a mobile Web site or inside apps and games. Facebook is the leader in mobile display ad revenues, followed by Google and Twitter. Search advertising is also a popular format, and is expected to account for about 44% of mobile ad spending in 2015. Search ads can be further optimized for the mobile platform by showing ads based on the physical location of the user. Mobile messaging generally involves SMS text messaging to consumers offering coupons or flash marketing messages. Messaging is especially effective for local advertising because consumers can be sent messages and coupons as they pass by or visit locations. Video advertising currently accounts for a small percentage of mobile ad spending, but is one of the fastest growing formats. Ad networks such as Google's AdMob, Apple's iAd, Twitter's MoPub, and Millennial Media are also important players in the mobile advertising market.

Apps on mobile devices constitute a marketing platform that did not exist a few years ago. Apps are a nonbrowser pathway for users to experience the Web and perform a number of tasks from reading the newspaper to shopping, searching, and buying. Apps provide users much faster access to content than do multi-purpose browsers. Apps are also starting to influence the design and function of traditional Web sites as consumers are attracted to the look and feel of apps, and their speed of operation. There are over 3 million apps available on Apple's App Store and Google Play and another million apps provided by Internet carriers and third-party storefronts like the Amazon Appstore, GetJar, and Appia. An estimated 2 billion people will use apps in 2015 worldwide (SocialMediaToday.com, 2013).

Local Marketing: The Social-Mobile-Local Nexus

Along with social marketing and mobile marketing, local marketing is the third major trend in e-commerce marketing in 2015–2016. The growth of mobile devices has accelerated the growth of local search and purchasing. New marketing tools like local advertisements on social networks and daily deal sites are also contributing to local marketing growth.

Spending on online local ads in the United States is estimated at around $36 billion in 2015. The mobile portion of local advertising spending is expected to reach $6.6 billion in 2015 (BIA/Kelsey, 2015a). In contrast, spending on traditional local advertising is expected to be flat during the same time period. The most common local marketing tools are geotargeting using Google Maps (local stores appearing on a Google map), display ads in hyperlocal publications like those created by Patch Properties, daily deals, and coupons.

The most commonly used venues include Facebook, Google, Amazon Local, LinkedIn, Yahoo, Bing, and Twitter, as well as more specific location-based offerings such as Google My Business, Yahoo Local, Citysearch, YP, SuperPages, and Yelp. The "daily deal" coupon sites, Groupon and LivingSocial, and location-based mobile firms such as Foursquare are also a significant part of this trend.

We examine social, mobile, and local marketing in much greater depth in Chapter 7.

MULTI-CHANNEL MARKETING: INTEGRATING ONLINE AND OFFLINE MARKETING

Without an audience, marketing is not possible. With the rapid growth of the Internet, media consumption patterns have changed greatly as consumers are more and more likely to engage with online media, from videos and news sites, to blogs, Twitter feeds, Facebook friends, and Pinterest posts. Increasingly, marketers are using multiple online channels to "touch" customers, from e-mail to Facebook, search ads, display ads on mobile devices, and affiliate programs. Forrester Research reports, for instance, that most customers purchased online following some Web marketing influence, and nearly half of online purchases followed multiple exposures to Web marketing efforts (Forrester Research, 2014a).

In 2013, for the first time ever, the average American spent more time with digital media per day than the amount viewing TV. In 2015, the average adult will spend about 5 and a half hours a day online and using a mobile device for something other than telephone calls, compared to about 4 and a quarter hours watching television (see **Figure 6.8**) (eMarketer, Inc., 2015a). An increasing percentage of American media consumers multitask by using several media at once in order to increase the total media exposure. In this environment, marketers increasingly are developing multi-channel marketing programs that can take advantage of the strengths of various media, and reinforce branding messages across media. Online marketing is not the only way, or by itself the best way, to engage consumers. Internet campaigns can be significantly strengthened by also using e-mail, TV, print, and radio. The marketing communications campaigns most successful at driving traffic to a Web site have incorporated both online and offline tactics, rather than relying solely on one or the other. Several research studies have shown that the most effective online advertisements are those that use consistent imagery with campaigns running in other media at the same time.

FIGURE 6.8	AVERAGE TIME SPENT PER DAY WITH MAJOR MEDIA

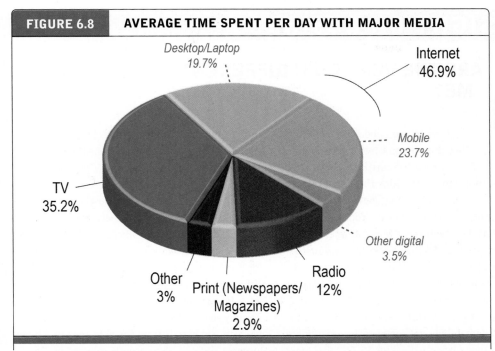

Desktop/Laptop
19.7%

Internet
46.9%

Mobile
23.7%

TV
35.2%

Other digital
3.5%

Other
3%

Print (Newspapers/
Magazines)
2.9%

Radio
12%

Online marketing should be coupled with offline marketing to achieve optimal effectiveness.

SOURCE: Based on data from eMarketer, Inc., 2015a.

Insight on Business: Are the Very Rich Different from You and Me? examines how luxury goods providers use online marketing in conjunction with their offline marketing efforts.

OTHER ONLINE MARKETING STRATEGIES

In addition to the "traditional" online marketing and advertising tools we have previously discussed, such as search engine, display, and e-mail marketing, and the newer social, mobile, and local marketing and advertising tools, there are also a number of other, more focused online marketing strategies. Here we examine tools aimed at customer retention, pricing, and a strategy known as the "long tail."

Customer Retention Strategies

The Internet offers several extraordinary marketing techniques for building a strong relationship with customers and for differentiating products and services.

Personalization, One-to-One Marketing, and Interest-based Advertising (Behavioral Targeting) No Internet-based marketing technique has received more popular and academic comment than "one-to-one" or "personalized marketing." **One-to-one marketing (personalization)** segments the market on the basis of individuals (not

one-to-one marketing (personalization)
segmenting the market based on a precise and timely understanding of an individual's needs, targeting specific marketing messages to these individuals, and then positioning the product vis-à-vis competitors to be truly unique

INSIGHT ON BUSINESS

ARE THE VERY RICH DIFFERENT FROM YOU AND ME?

"Let me tell you about the very rich. They are different from you and me." So observed F. Scott Fitzgerald in the short story, "The Rich Boy." Palm Beach has its Worth Avenue, New York has its Fifth Avenue, Los Angeles has its Rodeo Drive, and Chicago has the Magnificent Mile. So where do the rich go to get that $5,000 cocktail dress or that $3,000 Italian suit online? It turns out they may not be so different from the rest of us: they look for online deals and situations where quality can be had at a bargain. At Net-a-Porter, an online luxury brand store and content site, for instance, you can find a Gucci two-tone silk wrap dress for $1,750 that looks smashing with a pair of Gucci patent-leather knee boots for $1,595. There's free shipping too!

Even experts find it hard to define what it means to be affluent. There are about 24 million households (20% of all U.S. households) with household income of $100,000 or above. These are often referred to as HENRYs (High Earnings, Not Yet Rich). But the really affluent (sometimes called the hyperaffluent) are those 2.4 million (the top 2% of U.S. households) that earn more than $250,000 a year. And then there are the 9 million households (0.7% of households) that earn more than $1 million a year. These are the ultra-rich.

Retail consumption in general is highly skewed: the wealthiest top 10% of households account for about 50% of all retail spending and over 35% of all e-commerce retail spending. Wealthy Americans are opening their wallets to spend on expensive clothing, accessories, jewelry, and beauty products. In fact, in 2014, the United States replaced China as the leader in luxury spending around the world. The trend is continuing in 2015, with 42% of the hyperaffluent intending to purchase more luxury items than in 2014, along with about 33% of the HENRYs, with over 80% indicating they plan to purchase luxury products online. A 2015 McKinsey report notes what consumers hear or see online influences almost 50% of luxury product buying decisions.

One of the largest fashion destinations is Net-a-Porter. Luxury goods designers would not even consider selling to the site when it initially launched in 2000. Affluent women in that period only bought clothes they had seen, touched and tried on. That all has changed in the last decade, and in 2014, Net-a-Porter had revenue of over $800 million. It currently sells over 400 of the world's most fashionable high-end brands from Gucci to Tory Burch and Burberry and was also recently selected by Chanel as the exclusive online vendor for Chanel's first fine jewelry collection. Net-a-Porter's Web site has 9 million visitors a month and it has 4 million followers on social media. The average customer is 39 years old, travels 11 times a year, has an average income of $282,000, and spends $21,000 a year on clothing. On balance, these customers are at the low end of the truly affluent or at the top end of the HENRYs. In 2015, Net-a-Porter launched an app called the Net Set in an effort to create a mobile social commerce network for luxury consumers. The app will provide a live feed of trending luxury items, and provide each designer with its own mobile brand portal.

Even the rich are not immune to the lure of a good deal. The problem is that luxury retailers are typically loath to offer sales because they believe sales detract from their reputations. To get around this problem, luxury retailers often offer "secret" discounts via flash e-mail campaigns and private online sales in which selected online customers are e-mailed alerts. Neiman Marcus calls them Midday Dash sales: two-hour online-only sales with 50% off on luxury goods that can be purchased only by clicking a link in the e-mail.

Luxury retailers have another dilemma: they need to attract not just the ultra-affluent, but also the aspirational HENRYs who are far more numerous and anxious to display their wealth. They need to be both exclusive and accessible. One solution is the so-called Mercedes Benz strategy: build luxurious but affordable cars for the HENRYs while maintaining a focus on high-end truly luxury models for the ultra-affluent. Mercedes Benz combines a dual level product strategy with effective use of social and mobile media. Mercedes' Facebook page is a main hub of interaction between the brand and its customers, with over 18 million fans entertained with sweepstakes, videos, images, news, and links to its blog for additional insight into why Mercedes is unique and worth all that money. Mercedes also uses Twitter, YouTube, Instagram, Pinterest, and a dozen mobile apps to engage a broader range of customers by providing personalized video tours of its cars.

The explosion of social media and the increasing investments in the online channel by luxury companies has reinforced and enlarged the community of those who explore, comment upon, and eventually purchase luxury goods. Luxury companies are more than doubling their fans on Facebook annually in recognition of the link between online and offline purchases. Burberry Group, the United Kingdom's largest luxury goods maker, reports that it obtains the most reach and most response from digital initiatives compared with other media. To promote the Burberry Body fragrance, the London-based company offered exclusive samples to its Facebook fans. It received more than 225,000 requests in little more than a week.

Developing an online marketing approach that increases a company's access to consumers while retaining an image of exclusivity was the challenge faced by Tiffany & Co. The company is in the enviable position of being perhaps the most famous jewelry company in the United States. Tiffany's offline marketing communications seek to engender feelings of beauty, quality, and timeless style—all hallmarks of the Tiffany brand. How does Tiffany maintain its approach on the Web, a medium that often emphasizes speed and flashy graphics over grace and elegance, and low-cost bargains over high-priced exclusive fashion? The Web, for the most part, is all about low prices and great deals—concepts that are anathema to the high-fashion merchants like Tiffany. The answer is apparent in a visit to the Tiffany Web site. The site features limited inventory, with a focus on high-resolution images of its exclusive and original designs in jewelry and apparel. There are no sales, coupons, discounts, or other offers although visitors can choose jewelry in lower price ranges (less than $250 for instance). The Web site and Facebook brand page reflect custom service and design, calm, and simplicity. The prices are equally exclusive: an exquisite Atlas Hinged Bangle in 18k rose gold and round brilliant diamonds for $9,000, and sunglasses for $500.

Today, Tiffany has shifted more of its direct marketing effort from the offline catalog to the online catalog and an increasing social media presence, including Facebook (over 7 million Likes), Instagram, Pinterest, Twitter, Tumblr, and YouTube. It has Web sites in 13 different countries, including Canada, the United Kingdom, Japan, and Australia. Tiffany sites carry over 2,100 products in six categories of goods: engagement, jewelry, watches, designers and collections, gifts, and accessories. In 2014, Tiffany's online sales were $256 million, 6% of its $4.25 billion worldwide sales, placing it in third place in the online jewelry industry.

SOURCES: "Affluents Give Digital the Luxury Treatment," eMarketer, Inc., July 9, 2015; "Net-A-Porter Unveils New Weapon in Luxury E-commerce Battle," by Phil Wahba, Fortune.com, May 12, 2015; "The Opportunity in Online Luxury Fashion," by Jennifer Schmidt et al., McKinsey & Company, February 2015; "Athena Magtail: Net-A-Porter's Porter," by Lucie Green, Lsnglobal.com, April 1, 2014; "Luxury Goods Worldwide Market Study Spring 2014," by Bain & Company, May 19, 2014; "Luxury Report 2014: Ultimate Six-Year Guide to the Luxury Consumer Market," by Unity Marketing Inc., January 2014; "The Luxury Consumer," by Patricia Orsini, eMarketer, Inc., November 2013; "Louis Vuitton Walks the Fine Luxury Line," by Renee Schultes, *Wall Street Journal*, April 14, 2013; "Luxury Marketing: Recreating the One-on-One Experience With Mobile," eMarketer, Inc. (Patricia Orsini), September 2012; "Affluents: Demographic Profile and Marketing Approach," eMarketer, Inc. (Mark Dolliver), January 2012; "Affluent Shoppers and Luxury Brand Retailers Online," eMarketer, Inc. (Jeffrey Grau), September 2011.

groups), based on a precise and timely understanding of their needs, targeting specific marketing messages to these individuals, and then positioning the product vis-à-vis competitors to be truly unique. One-to-one marketing is the ultimate form of market segmentation, targeting, and positioning—where the segments are individuals.

The movement toward market segmentation has been ongoing since the development of systematic market research and mass media in the 1930s. However, e-commerce and the Internet are different in that they enable personalized one-to-one marketing to occur on a mass scale. A recent survey found that over 90% of marketers either use or intend to use personalization for online customer interactions in 2015. Real-time personalization (data-driven personalization that is completed in under one second) is becoming an important tool, used by almost 60% of marketers surveyed (Evergage, 2015).

The Amazon and Barnes & Noble Web sites are good examples of personalization at work. Both sites greet registered visitors (based on cookie files), recommend recent books based on user preferences (stored in a user profile in their database) as well as what other consumers purchased, and expedite checkout procedures based on prior purchases.

behavioral targeting
involves using online and offline behavior of consumers to adjust the advertising messages delivered to them online

Behavioral targeting involves using the online and offline behavior of consumers to adjust the advertising messages delivered to them online, often in real time (milliseconds from the consumer's first URL entry). The intent is to increase the efficiency of marketing and advertising, and to increase the revenue streams of firms who are in a position to behaviorally target visitors. Because behavioral targeting as a label has somewhat unfavorable connotations, the online advertising industry, led by Google, has introduced a new name for behavioral targeting. They call it **interest-based advertising (IBA)**.

interest-based advertising (IBA) (behavioral targeting)
another name for behavioral targeting

One of the original promises of the Web has been that it can deliver a marketing message tailored to each consumer based on this data, and then measure the results in terms of click-throughs and purchases. If you are visiting a jewelry site, you would be shown jewelry ads. If you entered a search query like "diamonds," you would be shown text ads for diamonds and other jewelry. This was taken one step further by advertising networks composed of several thousand sites. An advertising network could follow you across thousands of Web sites and come up with an idea of what you are interested in as you browse, and then display ads related to those interests. For instance, if you visit a few men's clothing sites in the course of a few hours, you will be shown ads for men's clothing on most other sites you visit subsequently, regardless of their subject content. If you search for a certain pair of shoes at Zappos, and Like them to your friends on Facebook, you will be shown ads for the exact same shoes at other sites (including Facebook). Behavioral targeting combines nearly all of your online behavioral data into a collection of interest areas, and then shows you ads based on those interests, as well as the interests of your friends. What's new about today's behavioral targeting is the breadth of data collected: your e-mail content, social network page content, friends, purchases online, books read or purchased, newspaper sites visited, and many other behaviors. And finally, ad exchanges take the marketing of all this information one step further. Most popular Web sites have more than 100 tracking programs on their home pages that are owned by third-party data collector firms who then sell this information in real time to the highest bidding advertiser in real-time online auctions. Ad exchanges make it possible for advertisers to retarget ads at individuals as they roam across the Internet. **Retargeting** involves showing the same or similar ads to individuals across multiple Web sites. Retargeting has become a popular tactic, used by 88% of marketers surveyed in a recent poll, in large part due to its perceived effectiveness. Another recent survey found that over 90% of marketers believe retargeting ads performs equal or better than search advertising or e-mail. However, as more and more consumers use multiple devices, including mobile devices, for online access, the ability to retarget ads across devices is becoming a topic of great interest to marketers (Marin Software, 2014; AdRoll, 2015; eMarketer, Inc., 2015j).

retargeting
showing the same ad to individuals across multiple Web sites

There are four methods that online advertisers use to behaviorally target ads: search engine queries, the collection of data on individual browsing history online (monitoring the clickstream), the collection of data from social network sites, and increasingly, the integration of this online data with offline data like income, education, address, purchase patterns, credit records, driving records, and hundreds of other personal descriptors tied to specific, identifiable persons. This level of integration of both "anonymous" as well as identifiable information is routinely engaged in by Google, Microsoft, Yahoo, Facebook, and legions of small and medium-sized marketing firms that use their data, or collect data from thousands of Web sites using Web beacons and cookies. On average, online information bureaus maintain 2,000 data elements on each adult person in their database. The currency and accuracy of this data are never examined, and the retention periods are not known. Currently, there are no federal laws or regulations governing this data.

Earlier in the chapter we described search engine advertising in some detail. Search engine advertising has turned out to be the most effective online advertising format by several orders of magnitude, and provides more than 95% of the revenue of Google, the world's largest online advertising agency. Why is search engine advertising so effective? Most agree that when users enter a query into a search engine, it reveals a very specific intention to shop, compare, and possibly purchase. When ads are shown at these very moments of customer behavior, they are 4 to 10 times as effective as other formats. The author John Battelle coined the phrase and the notion that the Web is a database of intentions composed of the results from every search ever made and every path that searchers have followed, since the beginning of the Web. In total, this database contains the intentions of all mankind. This treasure trove of intentions, desires, likes, wants, and needs is owned by Google, Microsoft, and to a lesser extent, Yahoo (Battelle, 2003). Battelle later extended the concept of a database of intentions beyond search to include the social graph (Facebook), status updates (Twitter and Facebook), and the "check-in" (Foursquare and Yelp) (Battelle, 2010). The database of intentions can be exploited to track and target individuals and groups. Not only is this capability unprecedented, but it's growing exponentially into the foreseeable future. The potential for abuse is also growing exponentially.

The decline in the growth rate of search engine advertising caused the major search engine firms to seek out alternative forms of future growth, which include display, rich media, and video advertising on millions of Web publisher sites. Web publishers have responded by producing billions of pages of content. In this environment, the effectiveness of display ads has been falling in terms of response rates and prices for ads. Behavioral targeting is an effective way to solve this problem and increase response rates. Behavioral targeting of both search and display advertising is currently driving the expansion in online advertising.

Behavioral targeting seeks to optimize consumer response by using information that Web visitors reveal about themselves online, and if possible, to combine this with offline identity and consumption information gathered by companies such as Acxiom. Behavioral targeting is based on real-time information about visitors' use of Web sites, including pages visited, content viewed, search queries, ads clicked, videos watched, content shared, and products they purchased. Once this information is collected and analyzed on the fly, behavioral targeting programs attempt to develop profiles of individual users, and then show advertisements most likely to be of interest to the user. More than 80% of North American advertisers use some form of targeting in their online display ads (Forrester Research, 2014b).

For a variety of technical and other reasons, this vision has, thus far, not been widely achieved. The percentage of ads that are actually targeted is unknown. Many advertisers use less expensive context ads displayed to a general audience without any targeting, or very minimal demographic targeting. The quality of the data, largely owned by the online advertising networks, is quite good but hardly perfect. The ability to understand and respond—the business intelligence and real-time analytics—is still weak, preventing companies from being able to respond quickly in meaningful ways when the consumer is online. The firms who sell targeted ads to their clients claim the targeted ads are two or three times more effective than general ads. There is not very good data to support these claims from independent sources. Generally these claims confound the impact of brands on targeted audiences, and the impact of the ads placed to this targeted audience. Advertisers target groups that are most likely to buy their product even in the absence of targeting ads at them. The additional impact of a targeted ad is much smaller than ad platforms claim. A research report based on real data from 18 ad campaigns on Yahoo, involving 18.4 million users, found that brand interest is the largest single factor in determining targeted ad effectiveness, and not the targeted ad itself (Farahat and Bailey, 2012). And marketing companies are not yet prepared to accept the idea that there needs to be several hundred or a thousand variations on the same display ad depending on the customer's profile. Such a move would raise costs. Last, consumer resistance to targeting continues. A recent survey found that nearly 70% of Americans are opposed to having companies track their online behavior even if they receive a free service or product. Over 60% of consumers do not believe that viewing more relevant ads is a fair trade-off for being tracked. Almost 90% say people should have the right to control what information is collected online and a significant majority would like to turn tracking off (Consumer-action.org, 2013). Some consumers find marketing messages that are too personalized to be "creepy." For example, suppose you visited the Hanes Web site to look at underclothing. How would you feel about receiving an unsolicited e-mail from Hanes thanking you for your visit and asking you to come back? How would you feel about getting a similar text message or telephone call, or being served a constant array of underclothing ads as you traverse the Web? What if a company mined your Pinterest pins, Facebook posts, or Twitter feed? Although some consumers might not be disturbed by this, many others find it to be "off-putting" at the very least. The public and congressional reaction to behavioral targeting is described more fully in Chapter 8.

Customization and Customer Co-Production Customization is an extension of personalization. **Customization** means changing the product—not just the marketing message—according to user preferences. **Customer co-production** means the users actually think up the innovation and help create the new product.

Many leading companies now offer "build-to-order" customized products on the Internet on a large scale, creating product differentiation and, hopefully, customer loyalty. Customers appear to be willing to pay a little more for a unique product. The key to making the process affordable is to build a standardized architecture that lets consumers combine a variety of options. For example, Nike offers customized sneakers through its Nike iD program on its Web site. Consumers can choose the type of shoe, colors, material, and even a logo of up to eight characters. Nike transmits the orders via computers to specially equipped plants in China and Korea. At the My M&M's Web site, customers can get their own message printed on custom-made M&Ms.

Information goods—goods whose value is based on information content—are also ideal for this level of differentiation. For instance, the *New York Times*—and many other content distributors—allows customers to select the news they want to see on a daily basis. Many Web sites, particularly portal sites such as Yahoo, MSN, and AOL, allow customers to create their own customized version of the Web site. Such pages frequently require security measures such as usernames and passwords to ensure privacy and confidentiality.

Customer Service A Web site's approach to customer service can significantly help or hurt its marketing efforts. Online customer service is more than simply following through on order fulfillment; it has to do with users' ability to communicate with a company and obtain desired information in a timely manner. Customer service can help reduce consumer frustration, cut the number of abandoned shopping carts, and increase sales.

Most consumers want to, and will, serve themselves as long as the information they need to do so is relatively easy to find. Online buyers largely do not expect or desire "high-touch" service unless they have questions or problems, in which case they want relatively speedy answers that are responsive to their individual issue. Researchers have found that online consumers strongly attach to brands when they have a problem with an order. Customer loyalty increases substantially when online buyers learn that customer service representatives are available online or at an 800-number and were willing and able to resolve the situation quickly. Conversely, online buyers who do not receive satisfaction at these critical moments often terminate their relationship with the business and switch to merchants that may charge more but deliver superior customer service (Ba et al., 2010; Wolfinbarger and Gilly, 2001).

There are a number of tools that companies can use to encourage interaction with prospects and customers and provide customer service—FAQs, customer service

customization
changing the product, not just the marketing message, according to user preferences

customer co-production
in the Web environment, takes customization one step further by allowing the customer to interactively create the product

chat systems, intelligent agents, and automated response systems—in addition to the customer relationship management systems described in the preceding section.

frequently asked questions (FAQs)

a text-based listing of common questions and answers

Frequently asked questions (FAQs), a text-based listing of common questions and answers, provide an inexpensive way to anticipate and address customer concerns. Adding an FAQ page on a Web site linked to a search engine helps users track down needed information more quickly, enabling them to help themselves resolve questions and concerns. By directing customers to the FAQs page first, Web sites can give customers answers to common questions. If a question and answer do not appear, it is important for sites to make contact with a live person simple and easy. Offering an e-mail link to customer service at the bottom of the FAQs page is one solution.

real-time customer service chat systems

a company's customer service representatives interactively exchange text-based messages with one or more customers on a real-time basis

Real-time customer service chat systems (in which a company's customer service representatives interactively exchange text-based messages with one or more customers on a real-time basis) are an increasingly popular way for companies to assist online shoppers during a purchase. Chats with online customer service representatives can provide direction, answer questions, and troubleshoot technical glitches that can kill a sale. Leading vendors of customer service chat systems include LivePerson and ClickDesk. Vendors claim that chat is significantly less expensive than telephone-based customer service. However, critics point out this conclusion may be based on optimistic assumptions that chat representatives can assist three or four customers at once, and that chat sessions are shorter than phone sessions. Also, chat sessions are text sessions, and not as rich as talking with a human being over the phone. On the plus side, chat has been reported to raise per-order sales figures, providing sales assistance by allowing companies to "touch" customers during the decision-making process. Evidence suggests that chat can lower shopping cart abandonment rates, increase the number of items purchased per transaction, and increase the dollar value of transactions. "Click to call" or "live call" is another version of a real-time online customer service system, in which the customer clicks a link or accepts an invitation to have a customer service representative call them on the telephone.

Intelligent agent technology is another way customers are providing assistance to online shoppers. Intelligent agents are part of an effort to reduce costly contact with customer service representatives. **Automated response systems** send e-mail order confirmations and acknowledgments of e-mailed inquiries, in some cases letting the customer know that it may take a day or two to actually research an answer to their question. Automated shipping confirmations and order status reports are also common.

automated response system

sends e-mail order confirmations and acknowledgments of e-mailed inquiries

Pricing Strategies

As we noted in Chapter 1, during the early years of e-commerce, many academics and business consultants predicted that the Web would lead to a new world of information symmetry and "frictionless" commerce. In this world, newly empowered customers, using intelligent shopping agents and the nearly infinite product and price information available on the Internet, would shop around the world (and around the clock) with minimal effort, driving prices down to their marginal cost and driving intermediaries out of the market as customers began to deal directly with producers (Wigand and Benjamin, 1995; Rayport and Sviokla, 1995; Evans and Wurster, 1999; Sinha, 2000). The result was supposed to be an instance of the **Law of One Price**: with complete price transparency in a perfect information marketplace, one world price for every product would emerge. Frictionless commerce would, of course, mean the end of marketing based on brands.

But it didn't work out this way. Firms still compete for customers through price as well as product features, scope of operations, and focus. **Pricing** (putting a value on goods and services) is an integral part of marketing strategy. Together, price and quality determine customer value. Pricing of e-commerce goods has proved very difficult for both entrepreneurs and investors to understand.

In traditional firms, the prices of traditional goods—such as books, drugs, and automobiles—are usually based on their fixed and variable costs as well as the market's **demand curve** (the quantity of goods that can be sold at various prices). *Fixed costs* are the costs of building the production facility. *Variable costs* are costs involved in running the production facility—mostly labor. In a competitive market, with undifferentiated goods, prices tend toward their *marginal costs* (the incremental cost of producing the next unit) once manufacturers have paid the fixed costs to enter the business.

Firms usually "discover" their demand curves by testing various price and volume bundles, while closely watching their cost structure. Normally, prices are set to maximize profits. A profit-maximizing company sets its prices so that the *marginal revenue* (the revenue a company receives from the next unit sold) from a product just equals its marginal costs. If a firm's marginal revenue is higher than its marginal costs, it would want to lower prices a bit and sell more product (why leave money on the table when you can sell a few more units?). If its marginal revenue for selling a product is lower than its marginal costs, then the company would want to reduce volume a bit and charge a higher price (why lose money on each additional sale?).

In the early years of e-commerce, something unusual happened. Sellers were pricing their products far below their marginal costs. Some sites were losing money on every sale. How could this be? New economics? New technology? The Internet age? No. Internet merchants could sell below their marginal costs (even giving away products for free) simply because a large number of entrepreneurs and their venture capitalist backers thought this was a worthwhile activity, at least in the short term. The idea was to attract eyeballs with free goods and services, and then later, once the consumer was part of a large, committed audience, charge advertisers enough money to make a profit, and (maybe) charge customers subscription fees for value-added services (the so-called *"piggyback"* strategy in which a small number of users can be convinced to pay for premium services that are piggybacked upon a larger audience that receives standard or reduced value services). To a large extent, social network sites and user-generated content sites have resurrected this revenue model with a focus on the growth in audience size and not short-term profits. To understand the behavior of entrepreneurial firms, it is helpful to examine a traditional demand curve (see **Figure 6.9**).

Law of One Price
with complete price transparency in a perfect information marketplace, there will be one world price for every product

pricing
putting a value on goods and services

demand curve
the quantity of goods that can be sold at various prices

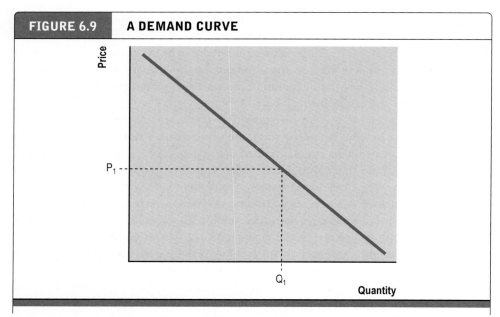

FIGURE 6.9 **A DEMAND CURVE**

A demand curve shows the quantity of product (Q) that could be sold at various prices (P).

A small number of customers are willing to pay a great deal for the product—far above P_1. A larger number of customers would happily pay P_1, and an even larger number of customers would pay less than P_1. If the price were zero, the demand might approach infinity! Ideally, in order to maximize sales and profits, a firm would like to pick up all the money in the market by selling the product at the price each customer is willing to pay. This is called **price discrimination**—selling products to different people and groups based on their willingness to pay. If some people really want the product, sell it to them at a high price. But sell it to indifferent people at a much lower price; otherwise, they will not buy. This only works if the firm can (a) identify the price each individual would be willing to pay, and (b) segregate the customers from one another so they cannot find out what the others are paying. Therefore, most firms adopt a fixed price for their goods (P_1), or a small number of prices for different versions of their products.

What if the marginal cost of producing a good is zero? What should the price be for these goods? It would be impossible then to set prices based on equalizing marginal revenue and marginal cost—because marginal cost is zero. The Internet is primarily filled with information goods—from music to research reports, to stock quotes, stories, weather reports, articles, pictures, and opinions—whose marginal cost of production is zero when distributed over the Internet. Thus, another reason certain goods, such as some information goods, may be free on the Internet is that they are "selling" for what it costs to produce them—next to nothing. Content that is stolen has zero production costs. Content that is contributed by users also has zero production costs for the Web sites themselves.

price discrimination
selling products to different people and groups based on their willingness to pay

Free and Freemium Everyone likes a bargain, and the best bargain is something for free. Businesses give away free PCs, free data storage, free music, free Web sites, free photo storage, and free Internet connections. Free is not new: banks used to give away "free" toasters to depositors in the 1950s. Google offers free office apps, free e-mail, and free collaboration sites. There can be a sensible economic logic to giving things away. Free content can help build market awareness and can lead to sales of other follow-on products. Finally, free products and services knock out potential and actual competitors (the free browser Internet Explorer from Microsoft spoiled the market for Netscape's browser) (Shapiro and Varian, 1999).

Today, "free" is increasingly being implemented online as "freemium" to borrow a phrase from Chris Anderson's book *Free: The Future of a Radical Price.* The freemium pricing model is a cross-subsidy online marketing strategy where users are offered a basic service for free, but must pay for premium or add-on services. The people who pay for the premium services hopefully will pay for all the free riders on the service. Skype uses a freemium model: millions of users can call other Skype users on the Internet for free, but there's a charge for calling a land line or cell phone. Flickr, Google Sites, Yahoo, and a host of others offer premium services at a price in order to support free services. Pandora offers free Internet radio, but it includes advertisements. Premium service without ads costs about $55 a year. (See the Chapter 2 case study, *Freemium Takes Pandora Public,* for more information on Pandora and the freemium pricing strategy.)

"Free" and "freemium" as pricing strategies do have limits. In the past, many e-commerce businesses found it difficult to convert the eyeballs into paying customers. Free sites attract hundreds of millions of price-sensitive "free loaders" who have no intention of ever paying for anything, and who switch from one free service to another at the very mention of charges. The piggyback strategy has not been a universal success. "Free" eliminates a rich price discrimination strategy. Clearly some of the free loaders would indeed pay a small amount each month, and this revenue is lost to the firms who offer significant services for free. Some argue that everything digital will one day be free in part because Internet users expect it to be so. But the history of "free" includes broadcast television, which used to be "free" (it was advertising-supported), but the public eventually had no problem moving to cable television and DVDs as paid services. The exceptions to "free" are really valuable streams of information that are exclusive, expensive to produce, not widely distributed, unique, and have immediate consumption or investment value. Even in the age of the Internet, these digital streams will sell for a price greater than zero. There probably is no free lunch after all, at least not one that's worth eating.

Versioning One solution to the problem of free information goods is **versioning**—creating multiple versions of the goods and selling essentially the same product to different market segments at different prices. In this situation, the price depends on the value to the consumer. Consumers will segment themselves into groups that are willing to pay different amounts for various versions (Shapiro and Varian, 1998).

versioning
creating multiple versions of information goods and selling essentially the same product to different market segments at different prices

Versioning fits well with a modified "free" strategy. A reduced-value version can be offered for free, while premium versions can be offered at higher prices. What are characteristics of a "reduced-value version?" Low-priced—or in the case of information goods, even "free"—versions might be less convenient to use, less comprehensive, slower, less powerful, and offer less support than the high-priced versions. Just as there are different General Motors car brands appealing to different market segments (Cadillac, Buick, Chevrolet, and GMC), and within these divisions, hundreds of models from the most basic to the more powerful and functional, so can information goods be "versioned" in order to segment and target the market and position the products. In the realm of information goods, online magazines, music companies, and book publishers offer sample content for free, but charge for more powerful content. The *New York Times*, for instance, allows you to read 10 articles a month online for free, but if you want to read more, you must have a digital subscription. Some Web sites offer "free services" with annoying advertising, but turn off the ads for a monthly fee.

Bundling "Ziggy" Ziegfeld, a vaudeville entrepreneur at the turn of the twentieth century in New York, noticed that nearly one-third of his theater seats were empty on some Friday nights, and during the week, matinee shows were often half empty. He came up with an idea for bundling tickets into "twofers": pay for one full-price ticket and get the next ticket free. Twofers are still a Broadway theater tradition in New York. They are based on the idea that (a) the marginal cost of seating another patron is zero, and (b) a great many people who would not otherwise buy a single ticket would buy a "bundle" of tickets for the same or even a slightly higher price.

bundling

offers consumers two or more goods for a reduced price

Bundling of information goods online extends the concept of a twofer. **Bundling** offers consumers two or more goods for a price that is less than the goods would cost when purchased individually. The key idea behind the concept of bundling is that although consumers typically have very diverse ideas about the value of a single product, they tend to agree much more on the value of a bundle of products offered at a fixed price. In fact, the per-product price people are willing to pay for the bundle is often higher than when the products are sold separately. Bundling reduces the variance (dispersion) in market demand for goods.

Dynamic Pricing and Flash Marketing The pricing strategies we have discussed so far are all fixed-price strategies. Versions and bundles are sold for fixed prices based on the firm's best effort at maximizing its profits. But what if there is product still left on the shelf along with the knowledge that someone, somewhere, would be willing to pay something for it? It might be better to obtain at least some revenue from the product, rather than let it sit on the shelf, or even perish. Imagine also that there are some people in every market who would pay a hefty premium for a product if they could have it right away. In other situations, such as for an antique, the value of the product has to be discovered in the marketplace (usually because there is a belief that the marketplace would value the product at a much higher price than its owner paid as a cost). In other cases, the value of a good is equal to what the market is willing to pay (and has nothing to do with its cost). Or let's say you want to build frequent visits to your site and offer some really great bargains for a few minutes each day, or the whole day with a set time limit. Here is where dynamic pricing mechanisms come to the fore, and where the strengths of the Internet can be seen. With **dynamic pricing**, the price of the product varies, depending on the demand characteristics of the customer and the supply situation of the seller.

dynamic pricing
the price of the product varies, depending on the demand characteristics of the customer and the supply situation of the seller

There are a number of different kinds of dynamic pricing mechanisms. For instance, *auctions* have been used for centuries to establish the instant market price for goods. Auctions are flexible and efficient market mechanisms for pricing unique or unusual goods, as well as commonplace goods such as computers, flower bundles, and cameras.

Yield management is quite different from auctions. In auctions, thousands of consumers establish a price by bidding against one another. In *yield management*, managers set prices in different markets, appealing to different segments, in order to sell excess capacity. Airlines exemplify yield management techniques. Every few minutes during the day, they adjust prices of empty airline seats to ensure at least some of the 50,000 empty airline seats are sold at some reasonable price—even below marginal cost of production. Amazon and other large online retailers frequently use yield management techniques that involve changing prices hourly to stimulate demand and maximize revenues. Amazon can also track shopping behavior of individuals seeking a specific product, such as a laser printer. As the consumer searches for the best price, Amazon can observe the offering prices on other Web sites, and then adjust its prices dynamically so that when the user visits Amazon again, a lower price will be displayed than all other sites visited.

Yield management works under a limited set of conditions. Generally, the product is perishable (an empty airline seat perishes when the plane takes off without a full load); there are seasonal variations in demand; market segments are clearly defined; markets are competitive; and market conditions change rapidly (Cross, 1997). In general, only very large firms with extensive monitoring and database systems in place have been able to afford yield management techniques.

Surge pricing is a kind of dynamic pricing used by companies such as Uber. Uber uses a dynamic pricing algorithm to optimize its revenue, or as the company claims, to balance supply and demand. Prices have surged from two to ten times or higher during storms and popular holiday periods. Uber was sharply criticized for using this scheme in New York City during Hurricane Sandy in 2012. Critics claim the practice amounts to price gouging, which during an emergency is illegal in some states like New York. Uber counters that the higher prices bring more livery cars onto the streets, increasing supply just when needed. But surge pricing, like most dynamic pricing schemes, is not the same as an open auction, where price movements are transparent to all. Uber does not make its data on supply and demand available to the public. Therefore it is impossible to know if Uber prices go up during holidays and storms because demand exceeds supply or because Uber wants to increase profits. In July 2014, Uber reached an agreement with the New York State Attorney General to limit pricing surges during emergencies (Isaac, 2014).

A third dynamic pricing technique is *flash marketing*, which has proved extraordinarily effective for travel services, luxury clothing goods, and other goods. Using e-mail or dedicated Web site features to notify loyal customers (repeat purchasers), merchants offer goods and services for a limited time (usually hours) at very low prices. JetBlue has offered $14 flights between New York and Los Angeles. Deluxe hotel rooms are flash marketed at $1 a night. Companies like Rue La La, HauteLook, and Gilt Groupe are based on flash marketing techniques. Blink and you can easily miss these great prices. Gilt purchases overstocked items from major fashion brands and then offers them to their subscribers at discounted prices via daily e-mail and SMS flash messages. Typically, the sale of an item lasts for two hours or until the inventory is depleted. On many occasions, Gilt rises to the top of most frequently visited Web sites when it conducts a sale. Critics point out that these sites take advantage of compulsive shoppers and lead to overshopping for unneeded goods. In another example of mass retail dynamic pricing, in 2011, Amazon used its new cloud music service to offer a flash one-day sale of Lady Gaga's latest album for 99 cents. Response was so great that Amazon's cloud servers could not meet the demand, and the offer has not been repeated.

The Internet has truly revolutionized the possibilities to engage in dynamic, and even misleading, pricing strategies. With millions of consumers using a site every hour, and access to powerful databases, merchants can raise prices one minute and drop them another minute when a competitor threatens. Bait-and-switch tactics become more common: a really low price on one product is used to attract people to a site when in fact the product is not available.

Long Tail Marketing

Consider that Amazon sells a larger number of obscure books than it does of "hit" books (defined as the top 20% of books sold). Nevertheless, the hit books generate 80% of Amazon's revenues. Consumers distribute themselves in many markets according to a power curve where 80% of the demand is for the hit products, and demand for nonhits quickly recedes to a small number of units sold. In a traditional market, niche products are so obscure no one ever hears about them. One impact of the Internet and e-commerce on sales of obscure products with little demand is that obscure products become more visible to consumers through search engines, recommendation engines, and social networks. Hence, online retailers can earn substantial revenue selling products for which demand and price are low. In fact, with near zero inventory costs, and a good search engine, the sales of obscure products can become a much larger percentage of total revenue. Amazon, for instance, has millions of book titles for sale at $2.99 or less, many written by obscure authors. Because of its search and recommendation engines, Amazon is able to generate profits from the sale of this large number of obscure titles. This is called the **long tail effect**. See *Insight on Technology: The Long Tail: Big Hits and Big Misses.*

long tail effect
a colloquial name given to various statistical distributions characterized by a small number of events of high amplitude and a very large number of events with low amplitude

---

6.3 INTERNET MARKETING TECHNOLOGIES

Internet marketing has many similarities to and differences from ordinary marketing. The objective of Internet marketing—as in all marketing—is to build customer relationships so that the firm can achieve above-average returns (both by offering superior products or services and by communicating the product's features to the

INSIGHT ON TECHNOLOGY

THE LONG TAIL: BIG HITS AND BIG MISSES

The Long Tail is a name given to various statistical distributions characterized by a small group of events of high amplitude and a large group of events with low amplitude. Coined by *Wired Magazine* writer Chris Anderson in 2004, the Web's Long Tail has since gone on to fascinate academics and challenge online marketers. The concept is straightforward. Think Hollywood movies: there are a few big hits and also thousands of films that no one ever hears about. It's the legion of misses that make up the Long Tail. Anderson claimed to have discovered a new rule: no matter how much content you put online, someone, somewhere will show up to buy it. Rather than 20:80, Anderson suggested that Internet search, recommendation engines, and online social networks all enable niche products to be discovered and purchased. For example, eBay contains millions of items drawn from every Aunt Tilly's closet in the world and still seems to find a buyer somewhere for just about anything, generating revenue that would not be realized without an online marketplace.

On the Internet, where search costs are tiny, and storage and distribution costs are near zero, online retailers like Amazon and Alibaba are able to offer millions of products for sale compared to a typical bricks-and-mortar retailer like Walmart or Sears. Without physical stores to maintain, online merchants can save on overhead and labor costs and load up on inventory. Wherever you look on the Web, you can find a great many items that only a few people are interested in buying. But with over 3 billion people online, even a one-in-a-million product could find over 3,000 buyers. Researchers note that most shoppers have a taste for both popular as well as niche products.

One problem with the Long Tail is that people sometimes have difficulty finding niche products because they are—by definition—largely unknown.

The revenue value of low-demand products is locked up in collective ignorance. Here's where recommender systems come into play: although these systems can skew toward the most popular selections, they can sometimes guide consumers to obscure but wonderful works based on the recommendations of others. Netflix has spent millions in recent years on improving its recommender system, and Pandora's recommender system focuses on generating quality music without regard to popularity.

Search engine optimization is another area where marketers are trying to unlock the power of the Long Tail. Long-Tail keywords are phrases that a small but significant number of people might use to find products. For instance, instead of investing in keywords such as "shoes" or "men's shoes," a marketer focused on the Long Tail might choose a keyword like "purple all-weather running shoes." Google has rolled out various updates to its search algorithm that improve Long Tail searches. According to Google, Long Tail searches comprise as much as 50% of all Web queries, with approximately 20% of searches being extremely unique or never seen before. Google uses textual analysis to deliver better, more focused results for these searches. An increasing number of Internet users are using natural language searches (searches that are phrased in the way we would speak naturally, like "where is the nearest pizza place?") to find products and services. These searches are also a part of the Long Tail, and while big businesses tend to control the more frequently searched keywords, smaller businesses can focus on natural language and other Long Tail searches to dramatically improve their conversion rates.

Social networks also make the Long Tail phenomenon even stronger. A recent study found that popularity information of the sort produced in a social network spurs sales of niche products more than mainstream products because of the higher perceived quality of the niche product.

(continued)

Long Tail search is also pivotal for online sales of rare books. A 2014 study showed that used books sell for higher prices online than in physical stores. The study's authors surmised that book buyers are willing to pay a higher price because without the Web, they wouldn't have found the book they sought.

Anderson claimed that the Internet would revolutionize digital content by making even niche products highly profitable, and that the revenues produced by small niche products would ultimately outweigh the revenues of hit movies, songs, and books. But some newer research casts some doubt on the revenue potential in the Long Tail. Solid best sellers have expanded and produce the vast part of online media revenues. Netflix's most recent earnings report boasted record highs, which it credited to its growing group of original series and recently added blockbuster hits like the television series Friends, not the thousands of titles in its Long Tail. In fact, its DVD business, where most of its Long Tail titles are available, has only 5.5 million subscribers, compared to 62 million subscribers of its streaming service, which consists primarily of more popular movies and shows. Similarly, another study found that while the number of ISBNs of e-books in the Canadian market expanded rapidly in 2014, the number of ISBNs selling at least one copy remained unchanged. The situation is similar in the music industry. As music services compete to offer increasingly large catalogs of songs, the well-known artists do better, while each individual member of the growing Long Tail finds it harder to stand out amidst lesser-known peers. On mobile devices especially, "front end display" for music services and e-books is smaller than on desktop screens, and only the superstars get this valuable marketing real estate.

On the other hand, up-and-coming artists have fewer barriers to entry and more avenues than ever to promote themselves without the aid of major labels. Artists like violinist Lindsey Stirling started out in the Long Tail; she has put up her own videos on YouTube, and has since become a major commercial success. Indie music labels' percentage of the top 200 albums by sales grew from just 13% in 2001 to 35% in 2010. And would-be authors have more options to publish their works and market themselves, despite the low odds of penning a smash hit.

Both the Long Tail and the winner-take-all approaches have implications for marketers and product designers. In the Long Tail approach, online merchants, especially those selling digital goods such as content, should build up huge libraries of content because they can make significant revenues from niche products that have small audiences. In the winner-take-all approach, the niche products produce little revenue, and firms should concentrate on hugely popular titles and services. Surprisingly, contrary to what Anderson originally theorized, the evidence for online digital content increasingly supports a winner-take-all perspective.

SOURCES: "Netflix Wags Its Short Tail," by Justin Fox, Bloombergview.com, April 17, 2015; "Hidden in the Long Tail," *The Economist*, January 10, 2015; "Revisiting the Long Tail Theory as Applied to Ebooks," by Marcello Vena, Publishingperspectives.com, January 8, 2015; "The Long Tail And Why Your SEO Keyword Strategy Is Wrong," by Joshua Steimle, *Forbes*, December 23, 2014; "New Data on the Long Tail Impact Suggests Rethinking History and Ideas About the Future of Publishing," by Mike Shatzkin, Idealog.com, June 25, 2014; "Tales of Long Tail's Death Greatly Exaggerated," by Tracy Maddux, Billboard.com, June 17, 2014; "Why Alibaba's Long Tail Makes Amazon's Look Like a Bobcat's," by Matt Schifrin, *Forbes*, May 8, 2014; "The Death of the Long Tail," Musicindustryblog.com, March 4, 2014; "Winners Take All, But Can't We Still Dream," by Robert H. Frank, *New York Times*, February 22, 2014; "Blockbusters: Why the Long Tail Is Dead and Go-Big Strategies Pay Off," by Ginny Marvin, Marketingland.com, October 23, 2013; "How Google Is Changing Long-Tail Search with Efforts Like Hummingbird," by Rand Fishkin, Moz.com, October 18, 2013; "Microsoft, Apps and the Long Tail," by Ben Bajarin, Time.com, July 8, 2013; "Goodbye Pareto Principle, Hello Long Tail: The Effect of Search Costs on the Concentration of Product Sales," by Eric Brynjolfsson et al., *Management Science*, July 2012; "Recommendation Networks and the Long Tail of Electronic Commerce," by Gail Oestreicher-Singer, New York University, 2012; "Research Commentary—Long Tails vs. Superstars: The Effect of Information Technology on Product Variety and Sales Concentration Patterns," by Erik Brynjolfsson et al., *Information Systems Research*, December 2010; "How Does Popularity Affect Choices? A Field Experiment," by Catherine Tucker and Juanjuan Zhang, *Management Science*, May 2011; "From Niches to Riches: Anatomy of the Long Tail," by Eric Brynjolfsson et al., *MIT Sloan Management Review*, Summer 2006; "The Long Tail," by Chris Anderson, *Wired Magazine*, October 2004.

consumer). But Internet marketing is also very different from ordinary marketing because the nature of the medium and its capabilities are so different from anything that has come before. In order to understand just how different Internet marketing can be and in what ways, you first need to become familiar with some basic Internet marketing technologies.

THE REVOLUTION IN INTERNET MARKETING TECHNOLOGIES

In Chapter 1, we listed eight unique features of e-commerce technology. **Table 6.6** describes how marketing has changed as a result of these new technical capabilities.

TABLE 6.6	IMPACT OF UNIQUE FEATURES OF E-COMMERCE TECHNOLOGY ON MARKETING
E-COMMERCE TECHNOLOGY DIMENSION	SIGNIFICANCE FOR MARKETING
Ubiquity	Marketing communications have been extended to the home, work, and mobile platforms; geographic limits on marketing have been reduced. The marketplace has been replaced by "marketspace" and is removed from a temporal and geographic location. Customer convenience has been enhanced, and shopping costs have been reduced.
Global reach	Worldwide customer service and marketing communications have been enabled. Potentially hundreds of millions of consumers can be reached with marketing messages.
Universal standards	The cost of delivering marketing messages and receiving feedback from users is reduced because of shared, global standards of the Internet.
Richness	Video, audio, and text marketing messages can be integrated into a single marketing message and consuming experience.
Interactivity	Consumers can be engaged in a dialog, dynamically adjusting the experience to the consumer, and making the consumer a co-producer of the goods and services being sold.
Information density	Fine-grained, highly detailed information on consumers' real-time behavior can be gathered and analyzed for the first time. "Data mining" Internet technology permits the analysis of terabytes of consumer data every day for marketing purposes.
Personalization/ Customization	This feature potentially enables product and service differentiation down to the level of the individual, thus strengthening the ability of marketers to create brands.
Social technology	User-generated content and social network sites, along with blogs, have created new, large, online audiences where the content is provided by users. These audiences have greatly expanded the opportunity for marketers to reach new potential customers in a nontraditional media format. Entirely new kinds of marketing techniques are evolving. These same technologies expose marketers to the risk of falling afoul of popular opinion by providing more market power to users who now can "talk back."

On balance, the Internet has had four very powerful impacts on marketing. First, the Internet, as a communications medium, has broadened the scope of marketing communications—in the sense of the number of people who can be easily reached as well as the locations where they can be reached, from desktops to mobile smartphones (in short, everywhere). Second, the Internet has increased the richness of marketing communications by combining text, video, and audio content into rich messages. Arguably, the Web is richer as a medium than even television or video because of the complexity of messages available, the enormous content accessible on a wide range of subjects, and the ability of users to interactively control the experience. Third, the Internet has greatly expanded the information intensity of the marketplace by providing marketers (and customers) with unparalleled fine-grained, detailed, real-time information about consumers as they transact in the marketplace. Fourth, the always-on, always-attached, environment created by mobile devices results in consumers being much more available to receive marketing messages. One result is an extraordinary expansion in marketing opportunities for firms.

WEB TRANSACTION LOGS

transaction log
records user activity at a Web site

How can e-commerce sites know more than a department store or the local grocery store does about consumer behavior? A primary source of consumer information on the Web is the transaction log maintained by all Web servers. A **transaction log** records user activity at a Web site. The transaction log is built into Web server software. Transaction log data becomes even more useful when combined with two other visitor-generated data trails: registration forms and the shopping cart database. Users are enticed through various means (such as free gifts or special services) to fill out registration forms. **Registration forms** gather personal data on name, address, phone, zip code, e-mail address (usually required), and other optional self-confessed information on interests and tastes. When users make a purchase, they also enter additional information into the shopping cart database. The **shopping cart database** captures all the item selection, purchase, and payment data. Other potential additional sources of data are information users submit on product forms, contribute to chat groups, or send via e-mail messages using the "Contact Us" option on most sites.

registration forms
gather personal data on name, address, phone, zip code, e-mail address, and other optional self-confessed information on interests and tastes

shopping cart database
captures all the item selection, purchase, and payment data

For a Web site that has a million visitors per month, and where, on average, a visitor makes 15 page requests per visit, there will be 15 million entries in the log each month. These transaction logs, coupled with data from the registration forms and shopping cart database, represent a treasure trove of marketing information for both individual sites and the online industry as a whole. Nearly all Internet marketing capabilities are based on these data-gathering tools. For instance, here are just a few of the interesting marketing questions that can be answered by examining a site's Web transaction logs, registration forms, and shopping cart database:

- What are the major patterns of interest and purchase for groups and individuals?
- After the home page, where do most users go first, and then second and third?
- What are the interests of specific individuals (those we can identify)?
- How can we make it easier for people to use our site so they can find what they want?

- How can we change the design of the site to encourage visitors to purchase our high-margin products?
- Where are visitors coming from (and how can we optimize our presence on these referral sites)?
- How can we personalize our messages, offerings, and products to individual users?

Businesses can choke on the massive quantity of information found in a typical site's log file. We describe some technologies that help firms more effectively utilize this information below.

SUPPLEMENTING THE LOGS: COOKIES AND OTHER TRACKING FILES

While transaction logs create the foundation of online data collection at a single Web site, marketers use tracking files to follow users across the entire Web as they visit other sites. There are three primary kinds of tracking files: cookies, Flash cookies, and Web beacons. As described in Chapter 3, a cookie is a small text file that Web sites place on the hard disk of visitors' client computers every time they visit, and during the visit, as specific pages are visited. Cookies allow a Web site to store data on a user's computer and then later retrieve it. The cookie typically includes a name, a unique ID number for each visitor that is stored on the user's computer, the domain (which specifies the Web server/domain that can access the cookie), a path (if a cookie comes from a particular part of a Web site instead of the main page, a path will be given), a security setting that provides whether the cookie can only be transmitted by a secure server, and an expiration date (not required). First-party cookies come from the same domain name as the page the user is visiting, while third-party cookies come from another domain, such as ad serving or adware companies, affiliate marketers, or spyware servers. On some Web sites, there are literally hundreds of tracking files on the main pages.

A cookie provides Web marketers with a very quick means of identifying the customer and understanding his or her prior behavior at the site. Web sites use cookies to determine how many people are visiting the site, whether they are new or repeat visitors, and how often they have visited, although this data may be somewhat inaccurate because people share computers, they often use more than one computer, and cookies may have been inadvertently or intentionally erased. Cookies make shopping carts and "quick checkout" options possible by allowing a site to keep track of a user as he or she adds to the shopping cart. Each item added to the shopping cart is stored in the site's database along with the visitor's unique ID value.

Ordinary cookies are easy to spot using your browser, but Flash cookies, beacons, and tracking codes are not easily visible. All common browsers allow users to see the cookies placed in their cookies file. Users can delete cookies, or adjust their settings so that third-party cookies are blocked, while first-party cookies are allowed.

With growing privacy concerns, over time the percentage of people deleting cookies has risen. The more cookies are deleted, the less accurate are Web page and ad server metrics, and the less likely marketers will be able to understand who is visiting their sites or where they came from. As a result, advertisers have sought other methods. One way is using Adobe Flash software, which creates its own cookie files, known as Flash cookies. Flash cookies can be set to never expire, and can store about 5 MB of information compared to the 1,024 bytes stored by regular cookies.

Although cookies are site-specific (a Web site can only receive the data it has stored on a client computer and cannot look at any other cookie), when combined with Web beacons (also called "bugs"), they can be used to create cross-site profiles. Web beacons are tiny (1-pixel) graphic files embedded in e-mail messages and on Web sites. Web beacons are used to automatically transmit information about the user and the page being viewed to a monitoring server in order to collect personal browsing behavior and other personal information. For instance, when a recipient opens an e-mail in HTML format or opens a Web page, a message is sent to a server calling for graphic information. This tells the marketer that the e-mail was opened, indicating that the recipient was at least interested in the subject header. Web beacons are not visible to users. They are often clear or colored white so they are not visible to the recipient. You may be able to determine if a Web page is using Web beacons by using the View Source option of your browser and examining the IMG (image) tags on the page. As noted above, Web beacons are typically one pixel in size and contain the URL of a server that differs from the one that served the page itself.

Using cookies on mobile devices has been less effective. Regular cookies on the mobile Web are reset every time a user closes his or her mobile browser and in-app cookies can't be shared between apps, making both of limited utility. However, with the increasing numbers of people using mobile devices to access the Internet, it is not surprising that telecommunications companies have begun to use tracking files. In late 2014, it was revealed that Verizon Wireless and AT&T were inserting a tracking header called a Unique Identifier Header (UIDH) into HTTP requests issued to Web sites from mobile devices, enabling them to track the online activities of their subscribers. Commentators call these tracking headers zombie cookies, perma-cookies, or supercookies because they cannot be deleted the way that regular browser cookies can. Following an outcry by privacy advocates and an FCC investigation, AT&T reportedly stopped using supercookies, but Verizon continues, although allowing users to opt out of their use. However, a 2015 study found that 15% of mobile users around the world (including the United States) continue to be tracked by supercookies, and their use appears to be increasing.

In an effort to more effectively track consumers across devices, other cross-device tracking methods have begun to be developed. **Deterministic cross-device tracking** relies on personally identifiable information such as e-mail address used to log into an app and Web site on different devices. Facebook, Google, Apple, Twitter, and other companies that have very large user bases and have both desktop and mobile properties that require logins are the most likely to be able to effectively exploit deterministic matching. **Probabilistic cross-device tracking** uses algorithms developed by vendors such as Drawbridge, BlueCava, and Tapad to analyze thousands of anonymous data points, such as device type, operating system, and IP address, to create a possible match. This type of matching is, not surprisingly, less accurate than deterministic matching (Schiff, 2015; Whitener, 2015).

In November 2015, the Federal Trade Commission will host a workshop to examine the privacy issues involved with cross-device tracking, while the Network Advertising Initiative has indicated that it will issue guidance and standards on the

deterministic cross-device tracking
relies on personally identifiable information such as e-mail address used to log into an app and Web site on different devices

probabilistic cross-device tracking
uses algorithms to analyze thousands of anonymous data points to create a possible match

use of such technologies. *Insight on Society: Every Move You Take, Every Click You Make, We'll Be Tracking You* further examines the use of tracking files.

DATABASES, DATA WAREHOUSES, DATA MINING, AND BIG DATA

Databases, data warehouses, data mining, and the variety of marketing decision-making techniques loosely called *profiling* are at the heart of the revolution in Internet marketing. **Profiling** uses a variety of tools to create a digital image for each consumer. This image can be quite inexact, even primitive, but it can also be as detailed as a character in a novel. The quality of a consumer profile depends on the amount of data used to create it, and the analytical power of the firm's software and hardware. Together, these techniques attempt to identify precisely who the online customer is and what they want, and then, to fulfill the customer's criteria exactly. These techniques are more powerful, far more precise, and more fine-grained than the gross levels of demographic and market segmentation techniques used in mass marketing media or by telemarketing.

In order to understand the data in transaction logs, registration forms, shopping carts, cookies, Web bugs, and other unstructured data sources like e-mails, tweets, and Facebook Likes, Internet marketers need massively powerful and capacious databases, database management systems, and analytic tools.

Databases

The first step in interpreting huge transaction streams is to store the information systematically. A **database** is a software application that stores records and attributes. A telephone book is a physical database that stores records of individuals and their attributes such as names, addresses, and phone numbers. A **database management system** (**DBMS**) is a software application used by organizations to create, maintain, and access databases. The most common DBMS are DB2 from IBM and a variety of SQL databases from Oracle, Sybase, and other providers. **Structured query language (SQL)** is an industry-standard database query and manipulation language used in relational databases. **Relational databases** such as DB2 and SQL represent data as two-dimensional tables with records organized in rows, and attributes in columns, much like a spreadsheet. The tables—and all the data in them—can be flexibly related to one another as long as the tables share a common data element.

Relational databases are extraordinarily flexible and allow marketers and other managers to view and analyze data from different perspectives very quickly.

Data Warehouses and Data Mining

A **data warehouse** is a database that collects a firm's transactional and customer data in a single location for offline analysis by marketers and site managers. The data originate in many core operational areas of the firm, such as Web site transaction logs, shopping carts, point-of-sale terminals (product scanners) in stores, warehouse inventory levels, field sales reports, external scanner data supplied by third parties, and financial payment data. The purpose of a data warehouse is to gather all the firm's transaction and customer data into one logical repository where it can be analyzed and modeled by managers without disrupting or taxing the firm's primary transactional systems and databases. Data warehouses grow quickly into storage repositories

profiling
profiling uses a variety of tools to create a digital image for each consumer

database
a software application that stores records and attributes

database management system (DBMS)
a software application used by organizations to create, maintain, and access databases

structured query language (SQL)
industry-standard database query language used in relational databases

relational databases
represent data as two-dimensional tables with records organized in rows and attributes in columns; data within different tables can be flexibly related as long as the tables share a common data element

data warehouse
a database that collects a firm's transactional and customer data in a single location for offline analysis

INSIGHT ON SOCIETY

EVERY MOVE YOU TAKE, EVERY CLICK YOU MAKE, WE'LL BE TRACKING YOU

Advertising-supported Web sites depend on knowing as much personal information as possible about you. One of the main ways ad firms discover your personal information is by placing so-called "tracking files" on your computer's browser. There are several kinds of third-party tracking files on Web pages. Cookies are the best known. These simple text files are placed in your browser and assign a unique number to your computer, which is then used by advertisers to track you across the Web as you move from one site to another (without telling you). Web beacons (sometimes also referred to as Web bugs) are a little more pernicious. Beacons are small software files that track your clicks, choices, and purchases, and even location data from mobile devices, and then send that information, often in real time, to advertisers tracking you. Beacons can also assign your computer a unique number and track you across the Web. Tracking may also occur as you watch Adobe Flash-enabled videos, visit Web sites equipped with HTML5 local storage, and use apps on smartphones. Most Facebook apps, for instance, send personal information, including names, to dozens of advertising and Internet tracking companies. A number of telecommunications companies use supercookies, which are updated whenever a user accesses a Web site with a mobile device. Mobile service carriers then provide those sites with additional information about the user for a cost.

So how common is Web and mobile tracking? In a recent study, researchers found a very widespread surveillance system. Only one site, Wikipedia, had no tracking files. Two-thirds of the tracking files came from companies whose primary business is identifying and tracking Internet users to create consumer profiles that can be sold to advertising firms looking for specific types of customers. The other third came from database firms that gather and bundle the information and then sell it to marketers. Many of the tracking tools gather personal information such as age, gender, race, income, marital status, health concerns, TV shows and movies viewed, magazines and newspapers read, and books purchased. While tracking firms claim the information they gather is anonymous, this is true in name only. Scholars have shown that with just a few pieces of information, such as age, gender, zip code, and marital status, specific individuals can be easily identified. A Web Privacy Census conducted by the University of California Berkeley Center for Law and Technology found that the total number of cookies on the top 100 Web sites had increased by 80%, from 3,600 when first measured in 2009 to over 6,400. The vast majority of these cookies (about 85%) were third-party tracking cookies, from over 450 different third-party hosts. Google's DoubleClick was the top tracker, and the most frequently appearing cookie keys were those associated with Google Analytics. Similar results were observed when looking at the top 1,000 and top 25,000 Web sites.

The Privacy Foundation has issued guidelines for Web beacon usage. The guidelines suggest that Web beacons should be visible as an icon on the screen, the icon should be labeled to indicate its function, and it should identify the name of the company that placed the Web beacon on the page. In addition, if a user clicks on the Web beacon, it should display a disclosure statement indicating what data is being collected, how the data is used after it is collected, what companies receive the data, what other data the Web beacon is combined with, and whether or not a cookie is associated with the Web beacon. Users should be able to opt out of any data collection done by the Web beacon, and the Web beacon should not be used to collect information from Web pages of a sensitive nature, such as medical, financial, job-related, or sexual matters. None of these ideas are found in current law. In 2014, California drafted guidelines for Web sites to disclose all of their privacy practices, but these guidelines are voluntary and attempts to create stricter standards on both the federal and state level have been unsuccessful. Many sites have adopted the Network Advertising Initiative (NAI)'s self-regulatory guidelines, but these too are only voluntary, and these guidelines have done little to assuage fears from Web users that their privacy is at risk.

One roadblock involves the meaning of Do Not Track (DNT). Government and privacy groups have pushed for a DNT feature that would require users to affirmatively allow tracking. The advertising industry, not surprisingly, favors a form of DNT that requires users to affirmatively implement DNT. Nearly all browsers now offer users the option of using a DNT feature, although users have to remember to turn it on. Sites often ignore DNT requests because it is more profitable for them to do so, with advertisers willing to pay up to seven times more for a highly targeted ad. In 2014, major companies such as Yahoo and AOL abandoned the DNT standard, citing the lack of

traction that DNT has encountered across the rest of the Web. Although some bigger Web sites like Twitter and Pinterest do follow DNT guidelines, these prominent defections are setbacks for the standard. Some users have turned instead to ad-blocking browser plug-ins such as AdBlock and Disconnect to avoid ads entirely. This has put additional pressure on Web sites as the pool of Web users that advertisers can reach slowly shrinks.

Major Web sites and the online advertising industry insist their industry can self-regulate and preserve individual privacy, but evidence suggests intervention from a neutral party will be necessary. In 2015, the Electronic Frontier Foundation (EFF), a prominent privacy advocacy group, released a new proposal that allows content publishers and other sites in compliance with DNT to prominently display the EFF's "seal of approval," along with options that allow users to disable ad-blocking software on these sites, enabling them to see ads without being tracked. Social blogging platform Medium and online analytics firm Mixpanel have also pledged not to track users who have enabled DNT, but convincing Google, Facebook, and other industry giants whose revenues depend heavily on Web tracking is more difficult, and thus far, no advertising firms have agreed to the new proposal. As usual, the EFF's new plan is completely voluntary, with minimal legislative backing behind it. Until governments weigh in, Web users will have to be wary of where they go and what they share online.

SOURCES: "Supercookies Are Back, and They're As Unappealing As Ever," by Michael Kassner, Techrepublic.com, August 28, 2015; "New Do Not Track Policy Introduced," by Michael Guta, Smallbiztrends.com, August 10, 2015; "Clear Rules of the Road With the Do Not Track Policy," by Peter Eckersley, Rainey Reitman, and Alan Toner," Eff.org, August 8, 2015; "'Do Not Track Compromise' Is Pitched," by Elizabeth Dwoskin, *Wall Street Journal*, August 5, 2015; "Do Not Track — The Privacy Standard That's Melting Away," by Mark Stockley, Nakedsecurity.sophos.com, August 26, 2014; "California Urges Websites to Disclose Online Tracking," by Vindu Goel, *New York Times*, May 21, 2014; "Yahoo Is the Latest Company Ignoring Web Users' Requests for Privacy," by Jon Brodkin, Arstechnica.com, May 1, 2014; "What Firefox's New Privacy Settings Mean for You," by Sarah A. Downey, Abine.com, March 29, 2013; "The Web Privacy Census," by Chris Jay Hoofnagle and Nathan Good, Berkeley Center for Law & Technology, October 2012; "Online Data Collection Explodes Year Over Year in US," eMarketer, Inc., July 19, 2012; "Online Tracking Ramps Up," by Julia Angwin, *Wall Street Journal*, June 17, 2012; "Microsoft's 'Do Not Track' Move Angers Advertising Industry," by Julia Angwin, *Wall Street Journal*, May 31, 2012; "Opt-Out Provision Would Halt Some, but Not All, Web Tracking," by Tanzina Vega, *New York Times*, February 28, 2012; "How Companies Learn Your Secrets," by Charles Duhigg, *New York Times Magazine*, February 16, 2012; "Study Finds Behaviorally-Targeted Ads More Than Twice as Valuable, Twice as Effective as Non-targeted Online Ads," Network Advertising Initiative, March 24, 2010.

containing terabytes (trillions of bytes) of data on consumer behavior at a firm's stores and Web sites. With a data warehouse, firms can answer such questions as: What products are the most profitable by region and city? What regional marketing campaigns are working? How effective is store promotion of the firm's Web site? Data warehouses can provide business managers with a more complete awareness of customers through data that can be accessed quickly.

data mining

a set of analytical techniques that look for patterns in the data of a database or data warehouse, or seek to model the behavior of customers

Data mining is a set of analytical techniques that look for patterns in the data of a database or data warehouse, or seek to model the behavior of customers. Web site data can be "mined" to develop profiles of visitors and customers. A **customer profile** is simply a set of rules that describe the typical behavior of a customer or a group of customers at a Web site. Customer profiles help to identify the patterns in group and individual behavior that occur online as millions of visitors use a firm's Web site. For example, almost every financial transaction you engage in is processed by a data mining application to detect fraud. Phone companies closely monitor your cell phone use as well to detect stolen phones and unusual calling patterns. Financial institutions and cell phone firms use data mining to develop fraud profiles. When a user's behavior conforms to a fraud profile, the transaction is not allowed or is terminated (Mobasher, 2007).

customer profile

a description of the typical behavior of a customer or a group of customers at a Web site

query-driven data mining

data mining based on specific queries

There are many different types of data mining. The simplest type is **query-driven data mining**, which is based on specific queries. For instance, based on hunches of marketers who suspect a relationship in the database or who need to answer a specific question, such as "What is the relationship between time of day and purchases of various products at the Web site?", marketers can easily query the data warehouse and produce a database table that rank-orders the top 10 products sold at a Web site by each hour of the day. Marketers can then change the content of the Web site to stimulate more sales by highlighting different products over time or placing particular products on the home page at certain times of day or night.

model-driven data mining

involves the use of a model that analyzes the key variables of interest to decision makers

Another form of data mining is model-driven. **Model-driven data mining** involves the use of a model that analyzes the key variables of interest to decision makers. For example, marketers may want to reduce the inventory carried on the Web site by removing unprofitable items that do not sell well. A financial model can be built showing the profitability of each product on the site so that an informed decision can be made.

A more fine-grained behavioral approach that seeks to deal with individuals as opposed to market segments derives rules from individual consumer behavior (along with some demographic information) (Adomavicius and Tuzhilin, 2001a; Chan, 1999; Fawcett and Provost, 1996, 1997). Here, the pages actually visited by specific users are stored as a set of conjunctive rules. For example, if an individual visits a site and typically ("as a rule") moves from the home page to the financial news section to the Asian report section, and then often purchases articles from the "Recent Developments in Banking" section, this person—based on purely past behavioral patterns—might be shown an advertisement for a book on Asian money markets. These rules can be constructed to follow an individual across many different Web sites.

There are many drawbacks to all these techniques, not least of which is that there may be millions of rules, many of them nonsensical, and many others of short-term duration. Hence, the rules need extensive validation and culling (Adomavicius and Tuzhilin, 2001b). Also, there can be millions of affinity groups and other patterns in the data that are temporal or meaningless. The difficulty is isolating the valid, powerful (profitable) patterns in the data and then acting on the observed pattern fast enough to make a sale that otherwise would not have been made. As we see later, there are practical difficulties and trade-offs involved in achieving these levels of granularity, precision, and speed.

Hadoop and the Challenge of Big Data

Up until about five years ago, most data collected by organizations consisted of structured transaction data that could easily fit into rows and columns of relational database management systems. Since then, there has been an explosion of data from Web traffic, e-mail messages, and social media content (tweets, status messages), even music playlists, as well as machine-generated data from sensors. This data may be unstructured or semi-structured and thus not suitable for relational database products that organize data in the form of columns and rows. The popular term "Big Data" refers to this avalanche of digital data flowing into firms around the world largely from Web sites and Internet click stream data. The volumes of data are so large that traditional DBMS cannot capture, store, and analyze the data in a reasonable time. Some examples of Big Data challenges are analyzing 12 terabytes of tweets created each day to improve your understanding of consumer sentiment towards your products; 100 million e-mails in order to place appropriate ads alongside the e-mail messages; or 500 million call detail records to find patterns of fraud and churn. Big Data and the tools needed to deal with it really started with Google and other search engines. Google's problem: it has to deal with 3.5 billion searches a day, and within milliseconds, display search results and place ads. For fun, do a search on "Big Data" and you'll see Google respond with more than 47 million results in .39 seconds. That's much faster than you can read this sentence!

Big Data usually refers to data in the petabyte and exabyte range—in other words, billions to trillions of records, often from different sources. Big Data is produced in much larger quantities and much more rapidly than traditional data collection mechanisms. Even though tweets are limited to 140 characters each, Twitter generates more than 8 terabytes of data daily. According to the IDC technology research firm, data is more than doubling every two years, so the amount of data available to organizations is skyrocketing. The next frontier will be data derived from the Internet of Things (IoT). Making sense out of it quickly in order to gain a market advantage is critical.

Marketers are interested in Big Data because it can be mined for patterns of consumer behavior and contain more interesting anomalies than smaller data sets, with the potential to provide new insights into customer behavior, weather patterns, financial market activity, or other phenomena. For instance, Evrythng, an IoT platform company, is partnering with Trueffect, a digital ad firm, to develop ways that marketers can use data generated by connected appliances and other devices in order to directly communicate with and target advertising with consumers. However, to derive business value from this data, organizations need new technologies and analytic tools capable of managing and analyzing nontraditional data along with their traditional enterprise data. A recent survey found that while marketers say Big Data is their biggest opportunity, only 14% are confident in their use of Big Data (Tadena, 2015).

To handle unstructured and semi-structured data in vast quantities, as well as structured data, organizations are using Hadoop. **Hadoop** is an open source software frame-

Big Data
Big Data refers to very large data sets in the petabyte and exabyte range

Hadoop
a software framework for working with various big data sets

work managed by the Apache Software Foundation that enables distributed parallel processing of huge amounts of data across inexpensive computers. It breaks a Big Data problem down into subproblems, distributes them among up to thousands of inexpensive computer processing nodes, and then combines the result into a smaller data set that is easier to analyze. You've probably used Hadoop to find the best airfare on the Internet, get directions to a restaurant, search on Google, or connect with a friend on Facebook.

Hadoop can process large quantities of any kind of data, including structured transactional data, loosely structured data such as Facebook and Twitter feeds, complex data such as Web server log files, and unstructured audio and video data. Hadoop runs on a cluster of inexpensive servers, and processors can be added or removed as needed. Companies use Hadoop to analyze very large volumes of data as well as for a staging area for unstructured and semi-structured data before it is loaded into a data warehouse. Facebook stores much of its data on its massive Hadoop cluster, which holds an estimated 300 petabytes, about 30,000 times more information than the Library of Congress. Yahoo uses Hadoop to track user behavior so it can modify its home page to fit user interests. Life sciences research firm NextBio uses Hadoop and HBase to process data for pharmaceutical companies conducting genomic research. Top database vendors such as IBM, Hewlett-Packard, Oracle, and Microsoft have their own Hadoop software distributions. Other vendors offer tools for moving data into and out of Hadoop or for analyzing data within Hadoop. In addition, there are many new tools being developed for Big Data analysis in addition to Hadoop. One example is Spark, an open source product being supported by IBM that can deliver results faster than Hadoop.

MARKETING AUTOMATION AND CUSTOMER RELATIONSHIP MANAGEMENT (CRM) SYSTEMS

marketing automation systems

software tools that marketers use to track all the steps in the lead generation part of the marketing process

Marketing automation systems are software tools that marketers use to track all the steps in the lead generation part of the marketing process. The marketing process begins with making the potential customer aware of the firm and product, and recognizing the need for the product. This is the beginning of a lead—someone who might buy. From there, consumers need to find you as they search for products; they will compare your products with your competitors' offerings and at some point, choose to purchase. Software can help in each of these stages of the marketing process. A number of firms sell software packages that can visualize most of the online marketing activities of a firm and then track the progression from exposure to display ads, finding your firm on a search engine, directing follow-up e-mail and communications, and finally a purchase. Once leads become customers, customer relationship management systems take over the maintenance of the relationship.

customer relationship management (CRM) system

a repository of customer information that records all of the contacts that a customer has with a firm and generates a customer profile available to everyone in the firm with a need to "know the customer"

Customer relationship management systems are another important Internet marketing technology. A **customer relationship management (CRM) system** is a repository of customer information that records all of the contacts that a customer has with a firm (including Web sites) and generates a customer profile available to everyone in the firm with a need to "know the customer." CRM systems also supply the analytical software required to analyze and use customer information. Customers come to firms not just over the Web but also through telephone call centers, customer service representatives, sales representatives, automated voice response systems, ATMs and kiosks, in-store point-of-sale terminals, and mobile devices (m-commerce).

Collectively, these are referred to as "**customer touchpoints**." In the past, firms generally did not maintain a single repository of customer information, but instead were organized along product lines, with each product line maintaining a customer list (and often not sharing it with others in the same firm).

In general, firms did not know who their customers were, how profitable they were, or how they responded to marketing campaigns. For instance, a bank customer might see a television advertisement for a low-cost auto loan that included an 800-number to call. However, if the customer came to the bank's Web site instead, rather than calling the 800-number, marketers would have no idea how effective the television campaign was because this Web customer contact data was not related to the 800-number call center data. **Figure 6.10** illustrates how a CRM system integrates customer contact data into a single system.

CRMs are part of the evolution of firms toward a customer-centric and marketing-segment–based business, and away from a product-line–centered business. CRMs

customer touchpoints
the ways in which customers interact with the firm

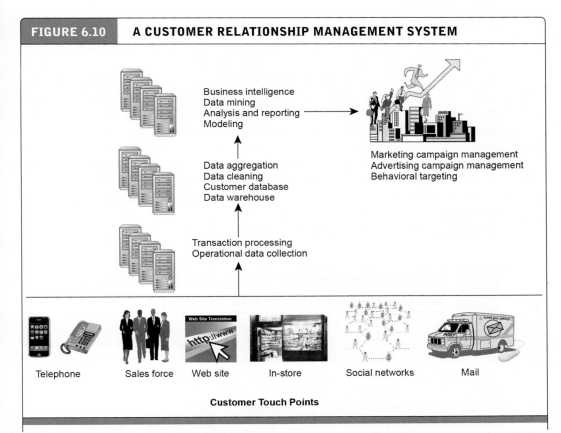

FIGURE 6.10 — A CUSTOMER RELATIONSHIP MANAGEMENT SYSTEM

This is an example of a CRM system. The system captures customer information from all customer touchpoints as well as other data sources, merges the data, and aggregates it into a single customer data repository or data warehouse where it can be used to provide better service, as well as to construct customer profiles for marketing purposes. Online analytical processing (OLAP) allows managers to dynamically analyze customer activities to spot trends or problems involving customers. Other analytical software programs analyze aggregate customer behavior to identify profitable and unprofitable customers as well as customer activities.

are essentially a database technology with extraordinary capabilities for addressing the needs of each customer and differentiating the product or service on the basis of treating each customer as a unique person. Customer profiles can contain the following information:

- A map of the customer's relationship with the institution
- Product and usage summary data
- Demographic and psychographic data
- Profitability measures
- Contact history summarizing the customer's contacts with the institution across most delivery channels
- Marketing and sales information containing programs received by the customer and the customer's responses
- E-mail campaign responses
- Web site visits
- Mobile app downloads

With these profiles, CRMs can be used to sell additional products and services, develop new products, increase product utilization, reduce marketing costs, identify and retain profitable customers, optimize service delivery costs, retain high lifetime value customers, enable personal communications, improve customer loyalty, and increase product profitability. The goal is what is known as a "360-degree" view that enables a company to know what its customers buy, how they browse, what kinds of communications and offers will engage them, and more. Leading CRM vendors include Oracle, SAP, Microsoft, Salesforce.com, and SugarCRM, many of which offer cloud-based versions of their CRM products. One issue facing cloud CRM providers and global companies that use those products is impending European Union data regulations that will require them to reassess how they use CRM data in order to avoid violating those regulations. All the major vendors offer cloud-based SaaS CRM applications.

6.4   UNDERSTANDING THE COSTS AND BENEFITS OF ONLINE MARKETING COMMUNICATIONS

As we noted earlier, online marketing communications still comprise only a small part of the total marketing communications universe. While there are several reasons why this is the case, two of the main ones are concerns about how well online advertising really works and about how to adequately measure the costs and benefits of online advertising. We will address both of these topics in this section. But first, we will define some important terms used when examining the effectiveness of online marketing.

ONLINE MARKETING METRICS: LEXICON

In order to understand the process of attracting prospects via marketing communications and converting them into customers, you will need to be familiar with online marketing terminology. **Table 6.7** lists some terms commonly used to describe the impacts and results of "traditional" online marketing such as display ads and e-mail campaigns. Metrics for social, mobile and local marketing are covered in Chapter 7.

The first nine metrics focus primarily on the success of a Web site in achieving audience or market share by "driving" shoppers to the site. These measures often substitute for solid information on sales revenue as e-commerce entrepreneurs seek to have investors and the public focus on the success of the Web site in "attracting eyeballs" (viewers).

Impressions are the number of times an ad is served. **Click-through rate (CTR)** measures the percentage of people exposed to an online advertisement who actually click on the advertisement. Because not all ads lead to an immediate click, the industry has invented a term for a long-term hit called **view-through rate (VTR)**, which measures the 30-day response rate to an ad. **Hits** are the number of HTTP requests received by a firm's server. Hits can be misleading as a measure of Web site activity because a "hit" does not equal a page. A single page may account for several hits if the page contains multiple images or graphics. A single Web site visitor can generate hundreds of hits. For this reason, hits are not an accurate representation of Web traffic or visits, even though they are generally easy to measure; the sheer volume of hits can be huge—and sound impressive—but not be a true measure of activity. **Page views** are the number of pages requested by visitors. However, with increased usage of Web frames that divide pages into separate sections, a single page that has three frames will generate three page views. Hence, page views per se are also not a very useful metric.

Viewability rate is the percentage of ads (either display or video) that are actually seen by people online. See page 357 for a further discussion of the issue of viewability.

The number of unique visitors is perhaps the most widely used measure of a Web site's popularity. The measurement of **unique visitors** counts the number of distinct, unique visitors to a Web site, regardless of how many pages they view. **Loyalty** measures the percentage of visitors who return in a year. This can be a good indicator of a site's Web following, and perhaps the trust shoppers place in a site. **Reach** is typically a percentage of the total number of consumers in a market who visit a Web site; for example, 10% of all book purchasers in a year will visit Amazon at least once to shop for a book. This provides an idea of the power of a Web site to attract market share. **Recency**—like loyalty—measures the power of a Web site to produce repeat visits and is generally measured as the average number of days elapsed between shopper or customer visits. For example, a recency value of 25 days means the average customer will return once every 25 days.

Stickiness (sometimes called *duration*) is the average length of time visitors remain at a Web site. Stickiness is important to marketers because the longer the amount of time a visitor spends at a Web site, the greater the probability of a purchase. However, equally important is what people do when they visit a Web site and not just how much time they spend there.

The metrics described so far do not say much about commercial activity nor help you understand the conversion from visitor to customer. Several other measures are more helpful in this regard. **Acquisition rate** measures the percentage of visitors who register or visit product pages (indicating interest in the product). **Conversion rate** measures the percentage of visitors who actually purchase something. Conversion

impressions
number of times an ad is served

click-through rate (CTR)
the percentage of people exposed to an online advertisement who actually click on the banner

view-through rate (VTR)
measures the 30-day response rate to an ad

hits
number of http requests received by a firm's server

page views
number of pages requested by visitors

viewability rate
percentage of ads that are actually seen by people online

unique visitors
the number of distinct, unique visitors to a site

loyalty
percentage of purchasers who return in a year

reach
percentage of the total number of consumers in a market who will visit a site

recency
average number of days elapsed between visits

stickiness (duration)
average length of time visitors remain at a site

acquisition rate
percentage of visitors who register or visit product pages

conversion rate
percentage of visitors who purchase something

TABLE 6.7	MARKETING METRICS LEXICON
DISPLAY AD METRICS	**DESCRIPTION**
Impressions	Number of times an ad is served
Click-through rate (CTR)	Percentage of times an ad is clicked
View-through rate (VTR)	Percentage of times an ad is not clicked immediately but the Web site is visited within 30 days
Hits	Number of HTTP requests
Page views	Number of pages viewed
Viewability rate	Percentage of ads that are actually seen online
Unique visitors	Number of unique visitors in a period
Loyalty	Measured variously as the number of page views, frequency of single-user visits to the Web site, or percentage of customers who return to the site in a year to make additional purchases
Reach	Percentage of Web site visitors who are potential buyers; or the percentage of total market buyers who buy at a site
Recency	Time elapsed since the last action taken by a buyer, such as a Web site visit or purchase
Stickiness (duration)	Average length of stay at a Web site
Acquisition rate	Percentage of visitors who indicate an interest in the Web site's products by registering or visiting product pages
Conversion rate	Percentage of visitors who become customers
Browse-to-buy ratio	Ratio of items purchased to product views
View-to-cart ratio	Ratio of "Add to cart" clicks to product views
Cart conversion rate	Ratio of actual orders to "Add to cart" clicks
Checkout conversion rate	Ratio of actual orders to checkouts started
Abandonment rate	Percentage of shoppers who begin a shopping cart purchase but then leave the Web site without completing a purchase (similar to above)
Retention rate	Percentage of existing customers who continue to buy on a regular basis (similar to loyalty)
Attrition rate	Percentage of customers who do not return during the next year after an initial purchase
VIDEO ADVERTISING METRICS	
View time	How long does the ad actually stay in view while it plays
Completion rate	How many viewers watched the complete video
Skip rate	How many viewers skipped the video
E-MAIL METRICS	
Open rate	Percentage of e-mail recipients who open the e-mail and are exposed to the message
Delivery rate	Percentage of e-mail recipients who received the e-mail
Click-through rate (e-mail)	Percentage of recipients who clicked through to offers
Bounce-back rate	Percentage of e-mails that could not be delivered
Unsubscribe rate	Percentage of recipients who click unsubscribe
Conversion rate (e-mail)	Percentage of recipients who actually buy

rates can vary widely, depending on the success of the site. The average conversion rate in the United States for e-commerce sites on traditional desktop computers was about 3.4% in 2014, compared to about 2.75% for tablet computers and 1.1% for smartphones. Clearly, Web sites viewed on desktops still remain the most effective vehicle for converting visitors into purchasers (Monetate, 2015). The **browse-to-buy ratio** measures the ratio of items purchased to product views. The **view-to-cart ratio** calculates the ratio of "Add to cart" clicks to product views. **Cart conversion rate** measures the ratio of actual orders to "Add to cart" clicks. **Checkout conversion rate** calculates the ratio of actual orders to checkouts started. **Abandonment rate** measures the percentage of shoppers who begin a shopping cart form but then fail to complete the form and leave the Web site. Abandonment rates can signal a number of potential problems—poor form design, lack of consumer trust, or consumer purchase uncertainty caused by other factors. Recent studies on shopping cart abandonment found abandonment rates ranging from 68% to 75% (Baymard, 2015). Among the reasons for abandonment were security concerns, customer just checking prices, couldn't find customer support, couldn't find preferred payment option, and the item being unavailable at checkout. Given that more than 80% of online shoppers generally have a purchase in mind when they visit a Web site, a high abandonment rate signals many lost sales. **Retention rate** indicates the percentage of existing customers who continue to buy on a regular basis. **Attrition rate** measures the percentage of customers who purchase once but never return within a year (the opposite of loyalty and retention rates).

Specific types of advertising have their own special metrics. For instance, for video ads, **view time** (how long the ad actually stays in view while it plays) and **completion rate** (how many viewers watch the entire video ad) are important factors. Research has shown that brand recall is significantly higher when the entire ad is watched, making the completion rate metric more meaningful to advertisers than the click-through rate (Adler, 2015).

E-mail campaigns also have their own set of metrics. **Open rate** measures the percentage of customers who open the e-mail and are exposed to the message. Generally, open rates are quite high, in the area of 50% or greater. However, some browsers open mail as soon as the mouse cursor moves over the subject line, and therefore this measure can be difficult to interpret. **Delivery rate** measures the percentage of e-mail recipients who received the e-mail. **Click-through rate (e-mail)** measures the percentage of e-mail recipients who clicked through to the offer. Finally, **bounce-back rate** measures the percentage of e-mails that could not be delivered.

There is a lengthy path from simple online ad impressions, Web site visits, and page views to the purchase of a product and the company making a profit (see **Figure 6.11**). You first need to make customers aware of their needs for your product and somehow drive them to your Web site. Once there, you need to convince them you have the best value—quality and price—when compared to alternative providers. You then must persuade them to trust your firm to handle the transaction (by providing a secure environment and fast fulfillment). Based on your success, a percentage of customers will remain loyal and purchase again or recommend your Web site to others.

browse-to-buy ratio
ratio of items purchased to product views

view-to-cart ratio
ratio of "Add to cart" clicks to product views

cart conversion rate
ratio of actual orders to "Add to cart" clicks

checkout conversion rate
ratio of actual orders to checkouts started

abandonment rate
% of shoppers who begin a shopping cart, but then fail to complete it

retention rate
% of existing customers who continue to buy

attrition rate
% of customers who purchase once, but do not return within a year

view time
how long the video ad actually stays in view while it plays

completion rate
how many viewers watch the complete video ad

open rate
% of customers who open e-mail

delivery rate
% of e-mail recipients who received e-mail

click-through rate (e-mail)
% of e-mail recipients who clicked through to the offer

bounce-back rate
percentage of e-mails that could not be delivered

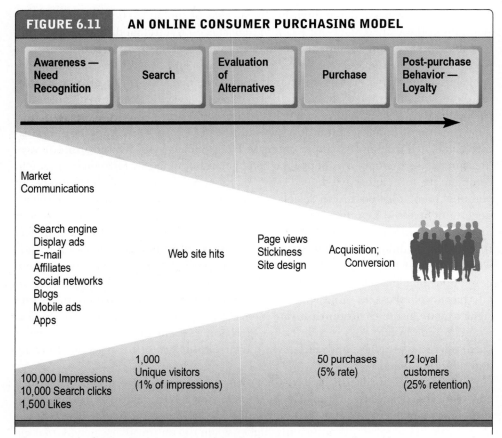

FIGURE 6.11 AN ONLINE CONSUMER PURCHASING MODEL

The conversion of visitors into customers, and then loyal customers, is a complex and long-term process that may take several months.

HOW WELL DOES ONLINE ADVERTISING WORK?

What is the most effective kind of online advertising? How does online advertising compare to offline advertising? The answers depend on the goals of the campaign, the nature of the product, and the quality of the Web site you direct customers toward. The answers also depend on what you measure. Click-through rates are interesting, but ultimately it's the return on the investment (ROI) in the ad campaign that counts. More than 70% of marketing executives said they would spend even more on digital ads if ability to measure ROI improved (Tadena, 2015). Complicating matters is the difficulty of **cross-platform attribution**, which involves understanding how to assign appropriate credit to different marketing initiatives on a variety of platforms that may have influenced a consumer along the way to an ultimate purchase. There is increasing recognition that first-click and last-click models that focus, as their names indicate, on either the first or last marketing channel or advertising format that a consumer engages with prior to a purchase, are no longer sufficient.

cross-platform attribution

understanding how to assign appropriate credit to different marketing initiatives that may have influenced a consumer on the way to a purchase

TABLE 6.8	ONLINE MARKETING COMMUNICATIONS: TYPICAL CLICK-THROUGH RATES
MARKETING METHODS	**TYPICAL CLICK-THROUGH RATES**
Banner ads	.03%–.25%
Google enhanced search ads (Product Listing Ads)	2.8%–3.6%
Search engine keyword purchase	.70–5.0%
Video	.30%–1.65%
Rich media	.13%–.35%
Sponsorships	1.50%–3.00%
Affiliate relationships	.20%–.40%
E-mail marketing in-house list	3.0–5.0%
E-mail marketing purchased list	.01%–1.50%
Social site display ads	.15%–.25%
Mobile display ads	.09%–1.25%

SOURCES: Based on data from The Search Agency, 2014; eMarketer, Inc., 2015k; PointRoll, 2015; Vindico, 2015; industry sources; authors' estimates.

Table 6.8 lists the click-through rates for various types of online marketing communications tools. There is a great deal of variability within any of these types, so the figures should be viewed as general estimates. Click-through rates on all these formats are a function of personalization and other targeting techniques. For instance, several studies have found that e-mail response rates can be increased 20% or more by adding social sharing links. And while the average Google click-through rate is less than 1%, some merchants can hit 10% or more by making their ads more specific and attracting only the most interested people. Permission e-mail click-through rates have been fairly consistent over the last five years, in the 3%–5% range. Putting the recipient's name in the subject line can double the click-through rate. (For unsolicited e-mail and outright spam, response rates are much lower, even though about 20% of U.S. e-mail users report clicking occasionally on an unsolicited e-mail.) The click-through rate for video ads may seem low, but it is twice as high as the rate for banner ads. For instance, research by PointRoll found that adding video to a rich media campaign increased interaction rates by over 17% on average (PointRoll, 2015). "Interaction" means the user clicks on the video, plays it, stops it, or takes some other action.

How effective is online advertising compared to offline advertising? In general, the online channels (e-mail, search engine, display ads, video, and social, mobile, and local marketing) compare very favorably with traditional channels. This explains in large part why online advertising has grown so rapidly in the last five years. Search engine advertising has grown to be one of the most cost-effective forms of marketing communications and accounts for, in large part, the growth of Google. Direct opt-in e-mail is also very cost-effective. This is, in part, because e-mail lists are so inexpensive and because opt-in e-mail is a form of targeting people who are already interested in receiving more information.

A study of the comparative impacts of offline and online marketing concluded that the most powerful marketing campaigns used multiple forms of marketing, including online, catalog, television, radio, newspapers, and retail store. Traditional media like television and print media remain the primary means for consumers to find out about new products even though advertisers have reduced their budgets for print media ads. Consumers who shop multiple channels are spending more than consumers who shop only with a single channel, in part because they have more discretionary income but also because of the combined number of "touchpoints" that marketers are making with the consumers. The fastest growing channel in consumer marketing is the multi-channel shopper.

cost per thousand (CPM)
advertiser pays for impressions in 1,000-unit lots

cost per click (CPC)
advertiser pays prenegotiated fee for each click an ad receives

cost per action (CPA)
advertiser pays only for those users who perform a specific action

THE COSTS OF ONLINE ADVERTISING

Effectiveness cannot be considered without an analysis of costs. Initially, most online ads were sold on a barter or **cost per thousand (CPM)** impressions basis, with advertisers purchasing impressions in 1,000-unit lots. Today, other pricing models have developed, including **cost per click (CPC)**, where the advertiser pays a prenegotiated fee for each click an ad receives; **cost per action (CPA)**, where the advertiser pays a prenegotiated amount only when a user performs a specific action, such as a registration or a purchase; and hybrid arrangements, combining two or more of these models (see **Table 6.9**).

TABLE 6.9	DIFFERENT PRICING MODELS FOR ONLINE ADVERTISEMENTS
PRICING MODEL	DESCRIPTION
Barter	Exchange of ad space for something of equal value
Cost per thousand (CPM)	Advertiser pays for impressions in 1,000-unit lots
Cost per click (CPC)	Advertiser pays prenegotiated fee for each click ad received
Cost per lead (CPL)	Advertiser pays only for qualified leads or contacts
Cost per action (CPA)	Advertiser pays only for those users who perform a specific action, such as registering, purchasing, etc.
Hybrid	Two or more of the above models used together
Sponsorship	Term-based; advertiser pays fixed fee for a slot on a Web site

While in the early days of e-commerce, a few online sites spent as much as $400 on marketing and advertising to acquire one customer, the average cost was never that high. While the costs for offline customer acquisition are higher than online, the offline items are typically far more expensive. If you advertise in the *Wall Street Journal,* you are tapping into a wealthy demographic that may be interested in buying islands, jets, and expensive homes in France. A full-page black and white ad in the *Wall Street Journal* National Edition costs about $270,000, whereas other papers are in the $10,000 to $100,000 range.

One of the advantages of online marketing is that online sales can generally be directly correlated with online marketing efforts. If online merchants can obtain offline purchase data from a data broker, the merchants can measure precisely just how much revenue is generated by specific banners or e-mail messages sent to prospective customers. One way to measure the effectiveness of online marketing is by looking at the ratio of additional revenue received divided by the cost of the campaign (Revenue/Cost). Any positive whole number means the campaign was worthwhile.

A more complex situation arises when both online and offline sales revenues are affected by an online marketing effort. A large percentage of the online audience uses the Web to "shop" but not buy. These shoppers buy at physical stores. Merchants such as Sears and Walmart use e-mail to inform their registered customers of special offers available for purchase either online or at stores. Unfortunately, purchases at physical stores cannot be tied precisely with the online e-mail campaign. In these cases, merchants have to rely on less precise measures such as customer surveys at store locations to determine the effectiveness of online campaigns.

In either case, measuring the effectiveness of online marketing communications—and specifying precisely the objective (branding versus sales)—is critical to profitability. To measure marketing effectiveness, you need to understand the costs of various marketing media and the process of converting online prospects into online customers.

In general, online marketing communications are more costly on a CPM basis than traditional mass media marketing, but are more efficient in producing sales. **Table 6.10** shows costs for typical online and offline marketing communications. For instance, in 2015, the average cost for 30 seconds of commercial time during a prime-time network television broadcast is about $112,000, not including the cost to produce the advertisement. According to Nielsen, such an ad has an average CPM of $24.76. In contrast, a banner ad costs virtually nothing to produce and can be purchased for a cost of from $5–$10 per thousand impressions. Direct postal mail can cost 80 cents to $1 per household drop for a post card, while e-mail can be sent for virtually nothing and costs only $5–$15 per thousand targeted names. Hence, e-mail is far less expensive than postal mail on a CPM basis. **Effective cost-per-thousand (eCPM)** is a metric that measures return on investment from an ad by dividing the total earnings from the ad by the total number of impressions in thousands.

effective cost-per-thousand (eCPM)
measures return on investment from an ad by dividing the total earnings from the ad by the total number of impressions in thousands

TABLE 6.10	TRADITIONAL AND ONLINE ADVERTISING COSTS COMPARED
TRADITIONAL ADVERTISING	
Local television	$1,500–$15,000 for a 30-second commercial; $45,000 for a highly rated show
Network television	$80,000–$600,000 for a 30-second spot during prime time; the average is $112,000
Cable television	$5,000–$8,000 for a 30-second ad during prime time
Radio	$100–$1,000 for a 60-second spot, depending on the time of day and program ratings
Newspaper	$120 per 1,000 circulation for a full-page ad
Magazine	$50 per 1,000 circulation for an ad in a regional edition of a national magazine, versus $120 per 1,000 for a local magazine
Direct mail	$15–$20 per 1,000 delivered for coupon mailings; $25–$40 per 1,000 for simple newspaper inserts
Billboard	$1,500–$30,000 for a large billboard for a 4-week period, with a minimum of 5–20 billboards
ONLINE ADVERTISING	
Banner ads	$5–$10 per 1,000 impressions, depending on how targeted the ad is (the more targeted, the higher the price)
Video and rich media	$20–$25 per 1,000 ads, depending on the Web site's demographics
E-mail	$5–$15 per 1,000 targeted e-mail addresses
Sponsorships	$30–$75 per 1,000 viewers, depending on the exclusivity of the sponsorship (the more exclusive, the higher the price)
Social network ads	$0.50–$3.00 per 1,000 impressions, with news feed ads at the high end of the range
Mobile display ads	$1.50–$3.25 per 1,000 impressions, including media costs, charges for first- or third-party data and service fees

MARKETING ANALYTICS: SOFTWARE FOR MEASURING ONLINE MARKETING RESULTS

A number of software programs are available to automatically calculate activities at a Web site or on a mobile device. Tracking the viewing and behavior of consumers across myriad devices and media channels is a much more difficult task. Other software programs and services assist marketing managers in identifying exactly which marketing initiatives are paying off and which are not.

The purpose of marketing is to convert shoppers into customers who purchase what you sell. The process of converting shoppers into customers is often called a

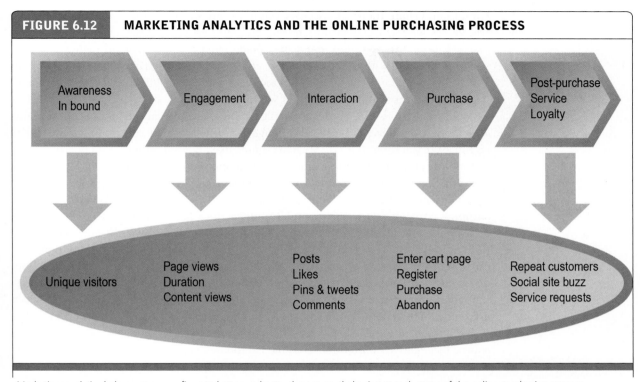

FIGURE 6.12 — MARKETING ANALYTICS AND THE ONLINE PURCHASING PROCESS

Marketing analytics help e-commerce firms to better understand consumer behavior at each stage of the online purchasing process.

"purchasing funnel." We have characterized this as a process rather than a funnel that is composed of several stages: awareness, engagement, interaction, purchase, and post-purchase service and loyalty. **Marketing analytics software** collects, stores, analyzes, and graphically presents data on each of the stages in the conversion of shoppers to customers (see **Figure 6.12**).

Marketing analytics packages can tell business managers how people become *aware* of their site, and where they come from (e.g., search, self-entered URL, e-mail, social campaigns, or off-line traditional print and TV ads), along with demographic, behavioral, and geographic information. Are shoppers coming from mobile devices, Facebook or Pinterest? This information can help managers decide the best ways to drive traffic, the so-called "in-bound" links to a site. Once on the Web site, analytics packages can record how *engaged* visitors are with the site's content, measured in terms of pages viewed and duration on site. This information can allow managers to change the design or their sites, or change the content viewers are seeing. For instance, video testimonials from product users may be much more engaging than expert reviews or user text comments. In a social marketing world, where consumers' opinions and behavior can be harvested and broadcast to their friends, an important intermediate step in the consumer conversion process is to encourage visitors to *interact* with your

marketing analytics software

collects, stores, analyzes, and graphically presents data on each of the stages in the conversion of shoppers to customers process on e-commerce sites

content and share their experiences, opinions, preferences, and behaviors with their friends, as well as other visitors to the site. Marketing analytics packages can track visitor interaction and help managers decide what content leads to higher levels of visitor interaction with friends and other visitors. The *purchase activity* on the shopping cart page is a major focus of analytics tools not just because this is where the revenue is generated, but also because this is where the customer frequently exits the entire site and the firm loses a potential sale. Current shopping cart abandonment is about 75% in the United States, with little change over the last few years, and higher in other countries (eMarketer, Inc., 2015l). This seems like an extraordinary rate but, like most of the indicators discussed in this chapter, abandonment is a complex phenomenon and often not what it seems. Consumers use carts like a shopping list, and don't complete the transaction immediately; they use it for price comparison and to know shipping costs, or taxes; they complete transactions later on a different device, such as a mobile phone. Another measure of near-purchase activity is the add-to-cart rate. Marketing analytics software can help managers tease out the meaning of behavior on a Web site's shopping cart page. Finally, marketing analytics can help managers discover customer *loyalty and post-purchase* behavior. In an increasingly social marketing environment, marketing managers need to know how their products and services are being talked about on other sites, Facebook pages, or Twitter tweets, often called "buzz" or sentiment analysis. Are the comments positive or negative? What is the source of negative comments? Possible candidates are poor quality, high costs, poor warranty service, and shipping issues.

The end objective of marketing analytics packages is to help business managers optimize the return on investment on their marketing efforts, and to do this by building a detailed understanding of how their consumers behave. Marketing analytics also allows managers to measure the impact of specific marketing campaigns involving, say, discounts, loyalty points, and special offers, as well as regional, or demographic-based campaigns. Aside from its role in enhancing management decision making, and optimizing the effectiveness of building an e-commerce presence, marketing analytics packages also enable a near real-time marketing capability where managers are able to change the content of a Web site, respond to customer complaints and comments, and align campaigns with trending topics or news developments, all in a near real-time manner (real-time may be a matter of minutes or at most 24 hours) (MarketingLand, 2015).

While there are a great many marketing analytics firms and software packages on the market, the leaders are Google Analytics, Adobe Analytics, IBM Digital Analytics, and Webtrends. Marketing analytics software is often part of a comprehensive package sold to corporations from hardware, to Web design tools, cloud services, and management expertise.

P r o g r a m m a t i c   A d v e r t i s i n g :
Real-Time Marketing

The holy grail of advertising and marketing is to deliver the right message to the right person at the right time. If this were possible, no one would receive ads they did not want to see, and then no advertising dollars would be wasted, reducing the costs to end users and increasing the efficiency of each ad dollar. In the physical world, only a very rough approximation of this ideal is possible. Advertisers can buy television and radio spots, newspaper ads, and billboards based on broad demographics and interests of likely potential customers. The Internet promised to change this. On the Internet, ads supposedly could be targeted to individual consumers based on their personal characteristics, interests, and recent clickstream behavior. One early vision of e-commerce was a trade-off between privacy and efficiency: let us know more about you, and we will show you only the advertising and products you are interested in seeing, and even offer free content. E-commerce was supposed to end the mass advertising that exploded in the television era.

But contrary to popular impressions and the fears of privacy advocates, most of the display ads shown to site visitors are marvelously irrelevant to visitors' interests, both short-term and long-term. For this reason, the click-through rate for banner advertising is a stunningly low 0.03%, and the price of display ads has fallen to a few cents because of their poor performance. Check this out: visit Yahoo (the largest display advertiser on earth) on a desktop or laptop computer, look at the prominent ads shown on the right,

and ask yourself if you are really interested in the ad content at this moment in time. How about ever? Chances are slim you are interested at this moment, even if the ad is somewhat appropriate to your demographics. Often, it is an ad for something you are totally not interested in and never have been. Researchers have found that only 20% of Internet users find that display ads on Web sites are relevant to their interests. Programmatic advertising promises to improve the targeting of ads, decreasing costs for advertisers, and making the Web less annoying to consumers by showing them ads that really are of interest to them.

Programmatic advertising is an automated method that publishers use to sell their inventory (empty slots on their Web pages) to advertisers who want to buy ad space for their customers (brand and product owners looking to market their products and services). There are two kinds of programmatic advertising: auction-based real time bidding (RTB), and programmatic direct, where advertisers deal directly with publishers in a semi-automated environment.

Programmatic advertising platforms use Big Data repositories that contain personal information on hundreds of millions of online shoppers and consumers; analytic software to classify and search the database for shoppers with the desired characteristics; and machine learning techniques to test out combinations of consumer characteristics that optimize the chance of a purchase resulting from exposure to an ad. All of this technology is designed to lower the cost, increase the speed, and increase the efficiency of advertising in an environment where there are hundreds of millions of Web pages to fill with ads, and millions of online consumers looking to buy at any given moment. Programmatic advertising allows advertisers to potentially show the right ad, at the right time, to just the right person, in a matter of milliseconds. To the extent this is true, display advertising becomes more effective, and perhaps could become as effective as search-based advertising, where it is much more obvious what the searcher is looking for, or interested in, at the moment of search. In 2015, RTB digital display advertising will total an estimated $11 billion, about 42% of all online display advertising. Analysts believe programmatic advertising will grow to about $20 billion by 2016 and that by then, almost two-thirds of all U.S. ads will be placed programmatically.

Currently, 45% of online display advertising is still done in a non-automated, traditional environment that involves e-mail, fax, phone, and text messaging. This is the world of the traditional insertion order: if you want to advertise in a newspaper or magazine, call the ad department and fill out an insertion order. In this environment, firms who want to sell products and services online hire advertising agencies to develop a marketing plan. The ad agencies learn from the firms what kinds of people they would like to contact online. The ad agencies pay data brokers or advertising networks like DoubleClick to help them identify where the online ads should be placed given the nature of the product and the specific characteristics the producer firms are looking for. For instance, let's say a firm wants to market a new mountain bike to men and women, ages 24–35, who live in zip codes where mountain biking is a popular activity. Ad networks traditionally would direct the agency to direct purchases of ad space from Web sites that attract the mountain biking audience.

This traditional environment is expensive, imprecise, and slow, in part because of the number of people involved in the decision about where to place ads. Also, the technology used is slow, and the process of learning which of several ads is optimal could take weeks or months. The ads could be targeted to a more precise group of potential customers. While context advertising on sites dedicated to a niche product is very effective, there are many other Web sites visited by bikers that might be equally effective, and cost much less.

The process is very different in a programmatic environment. Ad agencies have access to any of several programmatic ad platforms offered by Google, Yahoo, AOL, Facebook, and many smaller firms. Working with their clients, the ad agency more precisely defines the target audience to include men and women, ages 24–35, who live in zip codes where mountain biking is a popular activity, have mentioned biking topics on social network sites, have e-mail where mountain biking is discussed, make more than $70,000 a year, and currently do not own a mountain bike. The ad agency enters a bid expressed in dollars per thousand impressions for 200,000 impressions to people who meet the characteristics being sought. The platform returns a quote for access to this population of 200,000 people who meet the characteristics required. The quote is based on what other advertisers are willing to pay for that demographic and characteristics. The quote is accepted or denied. If accepted, the ads are shown to people as they move about the Web, in real-time. As people come on to various Web sites they visit, the automated program assesses whether they meet the desired characteristics, and displays the mountain bike ad with milliseconds to that person. The programmatic platforms also track the responses to the ads in real time, and can change to different ads and test for effectiveness based on the platform's experience. Once the system learns from experience, it will focus on showing the most effective ads on the most productive Web sites. Programmatic direct (or premium) advertising uses the same platform, but publishers sell blocks of inventory to ad agencies rather than single impressions. This stabilizes their income, and puts them in closer contact with advertisers who can also exercise greater oversight over the publishers.

The auto industry is a large user of programmatic advertising. Car brands are highly focused on specific demographic groups, income levels, and aspirations. A programmatic campaign begins with the advertiser picking a demographic target, establishing a total budget for the campaign, and then choosing an RTB platform and competing for the delivery of an ad to that audience against other advertisers who may be other auto companies, retailers, or telecommunications providers. The ads are awarded and served automatically in millisecond-quick transactions handled by machines.

Despite its clear advantages, there are also several risks involved for all parties. Advertisers lose control over where their ads will appear on the Web. This is a threat to a brand if its products are shown on inappropriate sites. Advertisers lose some accountability for their expenditures because they cannot verify that their ads are actually being shown, and they must take the ad platform's word that indeed the ads are being shown to real people. This is a transparency issue. Ghost sites and ad fraud complicate the picture as well. There are thousands of ghost sites on the Web that do nothing but attract clicks using various ruses. Ad networks record this traffic

SOURCES: "Clorox Is Betting Big on Programmatic Advertising," by Jack Marshall, *Wall Street Journal*, September 4, 2015; "New Breed of Digital Publishers Just Say No to Ad Tech," by Mike Shields, *Wall Street Journal*, July 28, 2015; "US Auto Industry Sets Brisk Pace with Mobile Programmatic," by eMarketer, Inc., July 2, 2014; "Creating Ads on the Fly: Fostering Creativity in the Programmatic Era," by Debra Aho Williamson, eMarketer, Inc., April 2015; "Procter & Gamble CMO Pritchard: Programmatic Delivers Business Lift," by Sarah Sluis, Adexchanger. com, March 6, 2015; "Get With the Programmatic: A Primer on Programmatic Advertising," by Or Shani, Marketingland.com, August 22, 2014; "Programmatic Advertising Spreads Quickly Despite Nagging Problems, Says AOL Survey," by Robert Hof, Adage.com, August 13, 2014; "How Big Media Is Adapting to Automated Ad Buying," *Wall Street Journal*, June 27, 2014; "Proctor & Gamble Aims to Buy 70% of Digital Ads Programmatically," Adage.com, June 4, 2014; "Programmatic Buying Roundup," by Lauren Fisher, eMarketer, Inc., June 2014; "Programmatic Guaranteed," by Lauren Fisher, eMarketer Inc., May 2014; "Driving Programmatic Buying: Automotive Industry Will Invest Big in 2014," by Mike Hudson et al., eMarketer, Inc., January 2014; "Programmatic Everywhere? Data, Technology and the Future of Audience Engagement," IAB, November 4, 2013; "RTB Is the Most Overhyped Technology Ever: It's Useful for Extending the Reach of Mediocre Content, but Not for Subtle, Thoughtful Buys," by Joe Mohen, Adage.com, May 30, 2013.

and have little capability to determine if it is legitimate, and may show ads on these sites, which will generate fraudulent clicks that are paid for by the ad network and the advertising firm.

Given the risks, many of the largest advertisers initially did not use programmatic advertising, but that is rapidly changing. It was first used by publishers to sell inventory that was left over after the major ad campaigns had purchased the premium slots on Web pages. Programmatic platforms were inexpensive places to sell excess inventory. However, that is beginning to change as advertisers gain confidence and the platforms themselves improve their abilities to avoid inappropriate Web sites, purge ghost sites, and learn how to detect click fraud. In addition, a number of firms have stepped into the market with tools that address these concerns.

For instance, in 2014, Procter & Gamble announced that, going forward, it planned to buy 70%–75% of its U.S. digital media using programmatic methods. P&G is the largest advertiser in the country, spending $4.6 billion on advertising in the United States in 2014. In the past, P&G purchased premium online inventory at the top 100 comScore sites through several different ad agencies and tracked performance using its internal staff. According to P&G's Chief Marketing Officer Marc Pritchard, programmatic advertising has allowed P&G to more precisely target its advertising at a good price, providing a good return on investment. Other companies are following suit. Cleaning supply company Clorox is devoting about 50% of its entire digital budget to programmatic advertising in 2015.

However, some upstart Web publishers aimed at the millennial demographic are trying to buck the trend. Vox Media, Refinery29, and Mic have all rejected programmatic advertising and will only sell advertising space directly to advertisers. These publishers object on the ground that programmatic advertising can degrade Web site functionality by slowing down how fast Web pages load in browsers while also cluttering the site with ads. Whether other Web publishers will follow this lead remains to be seen.

Case Study Questions

1. Pay a visit to your favorite portal and count the total ads on the opening page. Count how many of these ads are (a) immediately of interest and relevant to you, (b) sort of interesting or relevant but not now, and (c) not interesting or relevant. Do this 10 times and calculate the percentage of the three kinds of situations. Describe what you find and explain the results using this case.

2. Advertisers use different kinds of "profiles" in the decision to display ads to customers. Identify the different kinds of profiles described in this case, and explain why they are relevant to online display advertising.

3. How can display ads achieve search-engine–like results?

4. Do you think instant display ads based on your immediately prior clickstream will be as effective as search engine marketing techniques? Why or why not?

6.6 REVIEW

KEY CONCEPTS

■ **Understand the key features of the Internet audience, the basic concepts of consumer behavior and purchasing, and how consumers behave online.**

• Key features of the Internet audience include the number of users online, the intensity and scope of use, demographics and aspects, the type of Internet connection, and community effects.

• Models of consumer behavior attempt to predict or explain what consumers purchase, and where, when, how much, and why they buy. Factors that impact buying behavior include cultural, social, and psychological factors.

• There are five stages in the consumer decision process: awareness of need, search for more information, evaluation of alternatives, the actual purchase decision, and post-purchase contact with the firm.

• The online consumer decision process is basically the same, with the addition of two new factors: Web site and mobile platform capabilities and consumer clickstream behavior.

■ **Identify and describe the basic digital commerce marketing and advertising strategies and tools.**

• A *Web site* is the major tool for establishing the initial relationship with the customer.

• *Search engine marketing and advertising* allows firms to pay search engines for inclusion in the search engine index (formerly free and based on "objective" criteria), receiving a guarantee that their firm will appear in the results of relevant searches.

• *Display ads* are promotional messages that users can respond to by clicking on the banner and following the link to a product description or offering. Display ads include banner ads, rich media, video ads, and sponsorships.

• *E-mail marketing* sends e-mail directly to interested users, and has proven to be one of the most effective forms of marketing communications.

• *Lead generation marketing* uses multiple e-commerce presences to generate leads for businesses who later can be contacted and converted into customers.

• *Affiliate marketing* involves a firm putting its logo or banner ad on another firm's Web site from which users of that site can click through to the affiliate's site.

• *Viral marketing* is a form of social marketing that involves getting customers to pass along a company's marketing message to friends, family, and colleagues.

• *Social marketing and advertising* involves using the social graph to communicate brand images and directly promote sales of products and services.

• *Mobile and local marketing and advertising* involves using display ads, search engine advertising, video ads, and mobile messaging on mobile devices such as smartphones and tablet computers, often using the geographic location of the user.

• *Multi-channel marketing* (combining offline and online marketing efforts) is typically the most effective. Although many e-commerce ventures want to rely heavily on online communications, marketing communications campaigns most successful at driving traffic have incorporated both online and offline tactics.

• *Customer retention techniques* for strengthening customer relationships include personalization, one-to-one marketing, and interest-based advertising, customization and customer co-production, and customer service (such as CRMs, FAQs, live chat, intelligent agents, and automated response systems).

• *Online pricing strategies* include offering products and services for free, versioning, bundling, and dynamic pricing.

■ **Identify and describe the main technologies that support online marketing.**

- *Web transaction logs*—records that document user activity at a Web site. Coupled with data from the registration forms and shopping cart database, these represent a treasure trove of marketing information for both individual sites and the online industry as a whole.
- *Tracking files*—Various files, like cookies, Web beacons, Flash cookies, and apps, that follow users and track their behavior as they visit sites across the entire Web.
- *Databases, data warehouses, data mining, and profiling*—technologies that allow marketers to identify exactly who the online customer is and what they want, and then to present the customer with exactly what they want, when they want it, for the right price.
- *CRM systems*—a repository of customer information that records all of the contacts a customer has with a firm and generates a customer profile available to everyone in the firm who has a need to "know the customer."

■ **Understand the costs and benefits of online marketing communications.**

- Key terms that one must know in order to understand evaluations of online marketing communications' effectiveness and its costs and benefits include:
    - *Impressions*—the number of times an ad is served.
    - *Click-through rate*—the number of times an ad is clicked.
    - *View-through rate*—the 30-day response rate to an ad.
    - *Hits*—the number of http requests received by a firm's server.
    - *Page views*—the number of pages viewed by visitors.
    - *Stickiness (duration)*—the average length of time visitors remain at a site.
    - *Unique visitors*—the number of distinct, unique visitors to a site.
    - *Loyalty*—the percentage of purchasers who return in a year.
    - *Reach*—the percentage of total consumers in a market who will visit a site.
    - *Recency*—the average number of days elapsed between visits.
    - *Acquisition rate*—the percentage of visitors who indicate an interest in the site's product by registering or visiting product pages.
    - *Conversion rate*—the percentage of visitors who purchase something.
    - *Browse-to-buy ratio*—the ratio of items purchased to product views.
    - *View-to-cart ratio*—the ratio of "Add to cart" clicks to product views.
    - *Cart conversion rate*—the ratio of actual orders to "Add to cart" clicks.
    - *Checkout conversion rate*—the ratio of actual orders to checkouts started.
    - *Abandonment rate*—the percentage of shoppers who begin a shopping cart form, but then fail to complete the form.
    - *Retention rate*—the percentage of existing customers who continue to buy on a regular basis.
    - *Attrition rate*—the percentage of customers who purchase once, but do not return within a year.
    - *Open rate*—the percentage of customers who open the mail and are exposed to the message.
    - *Delivery rate*—the percentage of e-mail recipients who received the e-mail.
    - *Click-through rate (e-mail)*—the percentage of e-mail recipients who clicked through to the offer.
    - *Bounce-back rate*—the percentage of e-mails that could not be delivered.
- Studies have shown that low click-through rates are not indicative of a lack of commercial impact of online advertising, and that advertising communication does occur even when users do not directly respond by clicking. Online advertising in its various forms has been shown to boost brand awareness and brand recall, create positive brand perceptions, and increase intent to purchase.
- Effectiveness cannot be considered without analysis of cost. Typical pricing models for online marketing communications include barter, cost per thousand (CPM), cost per click (CPC), cost per action (CPA), hybrid models, and sponsorships.

- Online marketing communications are typically less costly than traditional mass media marketing. Also, online sales can generally be directly correlated with online marketing efforts, unlike traditional marketing communications tactics.

QUESTIONS

1. Is growth of the Internet, in terms of users, expected to continue indefinitely? What, if anything, will cause it to slow?
2. Other than search engines, what are some of the most popular uses of the Internet?
3. Would you say that the Internet fosters or impedes social activity? Explain your position.
4. Research has shown that many consumers use the Internet to investigate purchases before actually buying, which is often done in a physical storefront. What implication does this have for online merchants? What can they do to entice more online buying, rather than pure research?
5. What are some of the changes that Google has made to its search engine algorithms to improve search results and user experience?
6. Why have advertising networks become controversial? What, if anything, can be done to overcome any resistance to this technique?
7. What is a marketing automation system and how is it used?
8. List the differences among databases, data warehouses, and data mining.
9. Name some of the drawbacks to the four data mining techniques used in Internet marketing.
10. What pricing strategy turned out to be deadly for many e-commerce ventures during the early days of e-commerce? Why?
11. Is price discrimination different from versioning? If so, how?
12. What are some of the reasons that freebies, such as free Internet service and giveaways, don't work to generate sales at a Web site?
13. Explain how versioning works. How is this different from dynamic pricing?
14. Why do companies that bundle products and services have an advantage over those that don't or can't offer this option?
15. What are some reasons why online advertising still constitutes only about 28% of the total advertising market?
16. What are some of the advantages of direct e-mail marketing?
17. Why is offline advertising still important?
18. What is the difference between hits and page views? Why are these not the best measurements of Web traffic? Which is the preferred metric for traffic counts?
19. Define CTR, CPM, CPC, CPA, and VTR.
20. What are Web analytics and how are they used?

PROJECTS

1. Go to www.strategicbusinessinsights.com/vals/presurvey.shtml. Take the survey to determine which lifestyle category you fit into. Then write a two-page paper describing how your lifestyle and values impact your use of e-commerce. How is your online consumer behavior affected by your lifestyle?

2. Visit Net-a-porter.com and create an Internet marketing plan for it that includes each of the following:
   - One-to-one marketing
   - Affiliate marketing
   - Viral marketing

- Blog marketing
- Social network marketing

Describe how each plays a role in growing the business, and create a slide presentation of your marketing plan.

3. Use the Online Consumer Purchasing Model (Figure 6.11) to assess the effectiveness of an e-mail campaign at a small Web site devoted to the sales of apparel to the ages 18–26 young adult market in the United States. Assume a marketing campaign of 100,000 e-mails (at 25 cents per e-mail address). The expected click-through rate is 5%, the customer conversion rate is 10%, and the loyal customer retention rate is 25%. The average sale is $60, and the profit margin is 50% (the cost of the goods is $30). Does the campaign produce a profit? What would you advise doing to increase the number of purchases and loyal customers? What Web design factors? What communications messages?

4. Surf the Web for at least 15 minutes. Visit at least two different e-commerce sites. Make a list describing in detail all the different marketing communication tools you see being used. Which do you believe is the most effective and why?

5. Do a search for a product of your choice on at least three search engines. Examine the results page carefully. Can you discern which results, if any, are a result of a paid placement? If so, how did you determine this? What other marketing communications related to your search appear on the page?

6. Examine the use of rich media and video in advertising. Find and describe at least two examples of advertising using streaming video, sound, or other rich media technologies. (Hint: Check the sites of Internet advertising agencies for case studies or examples of their work.) What are the advantages and/ or disadvantages of this kind of advertising? Prepare a 3- to 5-page report on your findings.

7. Visit Facebook and examine the ads shown in the right margin. What is being advertised and how do you believe it is relevant to your interests or online behavior? You could also search on a retail product on Google several times, and related products, then visit Yahoo or another popular site to see if your past behavior is helping advertisers track you.

REFERENCES

Adjei, Mavis, and Stephanie Noble. "The Influence of C2C Communications in Online Brand Communities On Purchase Behavior." *Journal of the Academy of Marketing Science*, Vol. 38, No. 5 (2009).

Adomavicius, Gediminas, and Alexander Tuzhilin. "Using Data Mining Methods to Build Customer Profiles." *IEEE Computer* (February 2001a).

Adomavicius, Gediminas, and Alexander Tuzhilin. "Expert-Driven Validation of Rule-Based User Models in Personalization Applications." *Data Mining and Knowledge Discovery* (January 2001b).

AdRoll. "The Performance Marketer's Guide to Retargeting: Part 1." (2015).

Akerlof, G. "The Market for 'Lemons' Quality Under Uncertainty and the Market Mechanism." *Quarterly Journal of Economics* (August 1970).

Ba, Sulin, Jan Stallaert, and Zhang. "Balancing IT with the Human Touch: Optimal Investment in IT-Based Customer Service." *Information Systems Research* (September 2010).

Ba, Sulin, and Paul Pavlou. "Evidence on the Effect of Trust Building Technology in Electronic Markets: Price Premiums and Buyer Behavior." *MIS Quarterly* (September 2002).

Bakos, J. Y., and Erik Brynjolfsson. "Bundling and Competition on the Internet: Aggregation Strategies for Information Goods." *Marketing Science* (January 2000).

Battelle, John. "The Database of Intentions Is Far Larger Than I Thought." Battellemedia.com (March 5, 2010).

Battelle, John. "Search Blog." Battellemedia.com (November 13, 2003).

Baymard Research. "31 Cart Abandonment Rate Statistics." Baymard.com (May 8, 2015).

BIA/Kelsey. "U.S. Local Media Forecast 2015 Update." (April 22, 2015).

Brookings Institute. "Online Identity and Consumer Trust: Assessing Online Risk." (January 2011).

Castell, John. "Google Panda Explained for Website Owners." Linkedin.com (June 12, 2014).

Chan, P. K. "A Non-Invasive Learning Approach to Building Web User Profiles." In *Proceedings of ACM SIGKDD International Conference* (1999).

comScore (Andrea Vollman). "Viewability Benchmarks Show Many Ads Are Not In-View but Rates Vary by Publisher." (June 28, 2013).

Consumer-action.org. "Consumer Action 'Do Not Track' Survey Results." (May 5, 2013).

Corritore, C. L., B. Kracher, and S. Wiedenbeck, "On-line Trust: Concepts, Evolving Themes, a Model." *International Journal of Human-Computer Studies* (2006).

Cross, Robert. "Launching the Revenue Rocket: How Revenue Management Can Work For Your Business." *Cornell Hotel and Restaurant Administration Quarterly* (April 1997).

eMarketer, Inc. "US Time Spent with Media: eMarketer's Updated Estimates for Spring 2015." (May 2015a).

eMarketer, Inc. (Alison McCarthy). "US Digital Users: Q1 2015 Forecast." (February 2015b).

eMarketer, Inc. "US Fixed Broadband Households, United States, 2013–2019." (February 2015c).

eMarketer, Inc. "US Digital Shoppers and Buyers, 2013–2019." (June 2015d).

eMarketer, Inc. (Alison McCarthy). "US Ad Spending: Q1 2015 Complete Forecast." (March 2015e).

eMarketer, Inc. (Paul Verna). "Native Video Advertising: Effective, But Still a Work in Progress." (January 20, 2015f).

eMarketer, Inc. (Lauren Fisher). "Email Benchmarks 2015: Are Performance Metrics Revealing Signs of Consumer Fatigue?" (August 12, 2015g).

eMarketer, Inc. "US Social Network Ad Revenues, 2013–2017." (March 9, 2015h)

eMarketer, Inc. "US Social Network Ad Revenues, by Venue, 2013–2017." (March 9, 2015i).

eMarketer, Inc. (Jeremy Kressman). "Cross-Device Search Marketing: As Search Goes Multidevice, Ad Targeting and Measurement Struggle to Keep Pace." (April 9, 2015j).

eMarketer, Inc. "Email CTRs: Nothing New, but Still a Problem." (May 18, 2015k)

eMarketer, Inc. "US Retail Ecommerce Metrics, by Device, Q2 2014 & Q2 2015." (July 30, 2015l).

eMarketer, Inc. "Reasons US Internet Users Buy Products Digitally Rather Than In-Store." (February 23, 2014a).

eMarketer, Inc. (Paul Verna). "Word of Mouth Marketing." (October 2010).

Evans, P., and T. S. Wurster. "Getting Real About Virtual Commerce." *Harvard Business Review* (November-December 1999).

Evergage. "Survey Report: Trends & Priorities in Real-Time Personalization." (June 2015).

Farahat, Ayman, and Michael Bailey. "How Effective is Targeted Advertising." International World Wide Web Conference Committee (April 26–20, 2012).

Fawcett, Tom, and Foster Provost. "Adaptive Fraud Detection." *Data Mining and Knowledge Discovery* (1997).

Fawcett, Tom, and Foster Provost. "Combining Data Mining and Machine Learning for Effective User Profiling." In *Proceedings of the Second International Conference on Knowledge Discovery and Data Mining* (1996).

Federal Trade Commission. "Blurred Lines: Advertising or Content?—An FTC Workshop on Native Advertising." (December 4, 2013).

Forrester Research. "US Cross-Channel Retail Sales Forecast, 2014 to 2018." (July 24, 2014a).

Forrester Research. "Refresh Your Approach to 1:1 Marketing: How Real-Time Automation Elevates Personalization." (August 18, 2014b)

Franklin, David J. "Consumer Recognition and Understanding of Native Advertisements." Federal Trade Commission (December 4, 2013).

French, Violet. "Canada's Tough New Anti-Spam Legislation: Beware Its Extra-Territorial Reach." Americanbar.org (January 2014).

Garg, Rajiv. "Peer Influence and Information Difusion in Online Networks: An Empricial Analysis." Carnegie Mellon University, School of Information Systems and Management, Working Paper, 2009.

Google Inc. "Guide to Ad Sizes." (accessed September 8, 2015).

Guo, Stephen, M. Wang, and J. Leskovec. "The Role of Social Networks in Online Shopping Choice: Information Passing, Price of Trust, and Consumer Choice." Stanford University (June 2011).

Hof, Robert. "The One Second Rule: New Viewability Metrics Exposes How Low Online Advertising Standards Still Are." *Forbes* (March 3, 2014).

Interactive Advertising Bureau. "Rising Stars Ads and Brand Equity." (February 9, 2015).

Interactive Advertising Bureau. "Digital Video Rising Starts Added to IAB Standard Ad Portfolio, Augmenting Sight, Sound & Motion with Interactivity at Scale." (February 10, 2014).

Interactive Advertising Bureau. "Mobile Rich Media Ad Definitions (MRAID)." (September 2012).

Interactive Advertising Bureau. "IAB Standards and Guidelines." Iab.net (September 2011).

Interactive Advertising Bureau (IAB)/PriceWaterhouse-Coopers. "IAB Internet Advertising Revenue Report: 2014 Full Year Results." (April 2015).

Isaac, Mike. "Uber Reaches Deal With New York on Surge Pricing in Emergencies." *New York Times* (July 8, 2014).

Iyengar, Raghuram, S. Han, and S. Gupta. "Do Friends Influence Purchases in a Social Network." Harvard Business School. Working Paper, 2009.

Kantrowitz, Alex. "Inside Google's Secret War Against Ad Fraud." Adage.com (May 18, 2015).

Kantrowitz, Alex. "Digital Ad Fraud is Rampant. Here's Why So Little Has Been Done about It." Adage.com (March 24, 2014).

Kantrowitz, Alex. "Just Look At How Google Dominates Ad Tech." Adage.com (October 18, 2013).

Kim, D., and I. Benbasat. "The Effects of Trust-Assuring Arguments on Consumer Trust in Internet Stores." *Information Systems Research* (2006).

Kim, D., and I. Benbasat. "Designs for Effective Implementation of Trust Assurances in Internet Stores." *Communications of the ACM* (July 2007).

Kim, Dan, Donald Ferrin, and Raghav Rao. "Trust and Satisfaction, Two Stepping Stones for Successful E-Commerce Relationships: A Longitudinal Exploration." *Journal of Information Systems Research* (June 2009).

Kirk, Jeremy. "Online Ad Industry Tries to Stamp Out Click Fraud." Pcworld.com (July 21, 2015).

Koerber, Brian. "The Top 20 Most-Shared Ads of 2014." Mashable.com (November 20, 2014).

Kotler, Philip, and Gary Armstrong. *Principles of Marketing, 13th Edition*. Upper Saddle River, NJ: Prentice Hall (2009).

Lewis, Truman. "FTC Warns Publishers to Be Careful with "Native Advertising." Consumeraffairs.com (June 5, 2015).

Libert, Kelsey. "Comparing the ROI of Content Marketing and Native Advertising." *Harvard Business Review* (July 6, 2015).

Marin Software. "The Performance Marketer's Retargeting Guide: Key Benchmarks, Challenges and Best Practices for Cross-Channel Success." (September 2014).

MediaMind Inc. "Consumers 27 Times More Likely to Click-Through Online Video Ads than Standard Banners." (September 12, 2012).

Mishra, D. P., J. B. Heide, and S. G. Cort. "Information Asymmetry and Levels of Agency Relationships." *Journal of Marketing Research*. (1998).

Mobasher, Bamshad. "Data Mining for Web Personalization." Center for Web Intelligence, School of Computer Science, Telecommunication, and Information Systems, DePaul University, Chicago, Illinois. (2007).

Monetate. "2015 Monetate Ecommerce Quarterly: Merchandise This." (2015)

National Conference of State Legislatures. "State Laws Relating to Unsolicited Commercial of Bulk E-mail (SPAM)." (January 9, 2015).

Nielsen Company. "Global Online Consumer Survey." (May 2011).

Oestreicher-Singer, Gail and Arun Sundararajan. "The Visible Hand of Social Networks." *Electronic Commerce Research* (2008).

Opinion Research Corporation. "Online Consumer Product Reviews Have Big Influence." Opinion Research Corporation (April 16, 2009).

Ostermiller, Jeremy. "After Addressing Initial Viewability, These Are the Metrics That Matter." Mediapost.com (June 26, 2015).

Pavlou, Paul. "Institution-Based Trust in Interorganizational Exchange Relationships: The Role of Online B2B Marketplaces on Trust Formation." *Journal of Strategic Information Systems* (2002).

Pew Research Center. (Amanda Lenhart). "Mobile Access Shifts Social Media Use and Other Online Activities." (April 9, 2015a).

Pew Research Center. (Andrew Perrin and Maeve Duggan). "Americans' Internet Access: 2000–2015." (June 26, 2015b).

Pew Research Center. (Aaron Smith). "U.S. Smartphone Use in 2015." (April 1, 2015c).

Pew Research Center. "Part 1: How the Internet Has Woven Itself into American Life." (February 27, 2014).

Pew Research Center. (Lee Rainie). "The State of the Digital Divides." (November 5, 2013).

Pew Research Center. (Kathryn Zickuhr and Aaron Smith). "Digital Differences." (April 13, 2012).

PointRoll. "2014 Benchmark Report." (March 5, 2015).

Rayport, J. F., and J. J. Sviokla. "Exploiting the Virtual Value Chain." *Harvard Business Review* (November–December 1995).

Richtel, Matt. "Wasting Time Is Divide in Digital Era." *New York Times* (May 29, 2012).

Robinson, Jim. "What You Need to Know About the Changing Affiliate Landscape." Marketingprofs.com (August 8, 2014).

Schiff, Allison. "A Marketer's Guide to Cross-Device Identity." Adexhanger.com (April 9, 2015).

Schleifer, Dan. "Which Social Network Makes Your Customers Buy?" *Harvard Business Review* (April 2, 2013).

Segal, David. "Web Display Ads Often Not Visible." *New York Times* (May 3, 2014).

Sevitt, David, and Alexandra Samuel. "Vision Statement: How Pinterest Puts People in Stores." *Harvard Business Review* (July–August, 2013).

Shapiro, Carl, and Hal Varian. *Information Rules: A Strategic Guide to the Network Economy.* Cambridge, MA: Harvard Business School Press (1999).

Shapiro, Carl, and Hal Varian. "Versioning: The Smart Way to Sell Information." *Harvard Business Review* (November–December 1998).

Silverpop. "2015 Email Marketing Metrics Benchmark Study." (2015).

Sinha, Indrajit. "Cost Transparency: The Net's Real Threat to Prices and Brands." *Harvard Business Review* (March-April 2000).

Socialmediatoday.com. "Mobile Apps: How Many People Use Apps?" (September 3, 2013).

Symantec. "Symantec Intelligence Report." (July 2015).

The Search Agency. "State of Paid Search Report—Q3 2014." (2014).

Tadena, Nathalie. "Marketers Say They Would Spend Even More on Digital Ads If Measurement Improved." *Wall Street Journal* (July 6, 2015).

Tobii/Mediative. "The Effectiveness of Display Advertising on a Desktop PC vs. a Tablet Device." (August 2012).

Van den Poel, Dirk, and Wouter Buckinx. "Predicting Online Purchasing Behavior." *European Journal of Operations Research*, Vol. 166, Issue 2 (2005).

Vindico. "2014 Annual Report." (April 13, 2015).

VisionCritical Corporation. "From Social to Sale: 8 Questions to Ask Your Customers." (June 2013).

Vranica, Suzanne. "A 'Crisis' in Online Ads: One-Third of Traffic is Bogus." *Wall Street Journal* (March 23, 2014).

Whitener, Michael. "Cookies Are So Yesterday; Cross-Device Tracking Is In—Some Tips." Iapp.org (January 27, 2015).

Wigand, R. T., and R. I. Benjamin. "Electronic Commerce: Effects on Electronic Markets." *Journal of Computer Mediated Communication* (December 1995).

Williamson, O. E. *The Economic Institutions of Capitalism.* New York: Free Press (1985).

Wolfinbarger, Mary, and Mary Gilly. "Shopping Online for Freedom, Control and Fun." *California Management Review* (Winter 2001).

CHAPTER 7

Social, Mobile, and Local Marketing

After reading this chapter, you will be able to:

- Understand the difference between traditional online marketing and the new social-mobile-local marketing platforms and the relationships between social, mobile, and local marketing.
- Understand the social marketing process from fan acquisition to sales and the marketing capabilities of social marketing platforms such as Facebook, Twitter, and Pinterest.
- Identify the key elements of a mobile marketing campaign.
- Understand the capabilities of location-based local marketing.

Facebook:

Putting Social Marketing to Work

When Facebook issued its stock for sale in an initial public offering on May 18, 2012, it followed a very long build-up of excitement based on the belief that the company would turn into a marketing behemoth to rival or exceed Google, Yahoo, and Amazon. Facebook was, according to some analysts, the next Google in terms of an advertising platform and possibly even an e-commerce platform that could compete with Amazon. Facebook raised $16 billion in the IPO, placing it in the "Big League" of e-commerce stock offerings. Offered at $38 a share, Facebook's share price fell dramatically in subsequent months to a low of $17.50 in September 2012 on investor fears that Facebook would be unable to increase its advertising revenues fast enough to justify its price. Flash forward to August 2015:

© digitallife/Alamy

Facebook's shares are well on their way to tripling their original offering price. In the past year, Facebook has continually implemented new ways to put targeted ads in front of its increasingly mobile users. It appears to be succeeding, at least for now.

Although Facebook initially flubbed its shift to mobile devices, the social network giant has made steady progress toward an effective mobile strategy. Throughout 2012, Facebook redesigned its Facebook app specifically for smartphones, introducing ads into users' News Feeds, and creating a new kind of ad called "app-install ads," which are ads paid for by Facebook app developers that encourage users to download their apps (usually for free). App-install ads and in-app ads became Facebook's secret weapon that investors had not even heard about. Facebook was aided by a shift away from mobile browsers to apps: in 2015, more than half of mobile users worldwide regularly use brand, product, or store apps, and over 85% of smartphone mobile time is spent inside apps.

Advertisers display ads within these apps, and Facebook shares the ad fees with the app developers. App-install ads, and ads within apps, are the largest single source of Facebook mobile ads. There are an estimated 10 million apps available on Facebook, and users install nearly 30 million apps every day. These apps range from games like Candy Crush Saga, FarmVille, and Words With Friends, to music apps like Spotify and Pandora, to charity-oriented apps like Social Vibe and Charity Trivia. In-app ads have an advantage over standard News Feed ads: they are not perceived to be as disruptive or annoying as News Feed ads, and users are more willing to experience the inconvenience of being exposed to ads in return for a free game.

In 2015, over 500 million Facebook members access the social network solely from their mobile devices, representing about a third of its 1.5 billion monthly active users. Mobile now comprises over 75% of its total advertising revenues, up from 50% in recent years, and from nearly zero just a few years ago. Another factor in Facebook's turnaround in social mobile marketing is its success with small local businesses. Facebook has more than 2 million businesses advertising on its platform in 2015, the majority of which are small businesses, and over 30 million small businesses have Facebook pages.

Facebook has made a number of changes to its advertising toolkit in order to simplify the process of placing and targeting ads on its site for small business owners without professional marketing staffs. Its interface now allows advertisers to specify their objectives, such as increasing likes, or increasing traffic to their Web site, or converting more visitors to sales. They can also choose where to place the ads—either in the Facebook News Feed or the right side column. Advertisers can target demographics, as well as general characteristics that Facebook users indicate in their profile, such as age, gender, education, and employment. Facebook has also added a tracking pixel, which allows advertisers to track customers who visit their Web site as a result of clicking a Facebook ad.

One such business using Facebook's new advertising tools is Little Passports, a firm created by two moms who wanted to design an inspiring and fun way for kids to learn about the United States and other countries. Little Passports is aimed at parents of young children ages 5–12, with newer options available for even younger children. Its business model is a subscription service that sends children monthly packages that take kids on virtual trips where they learn geography, history, and social life. Subscriptions are $11.95 a month.

In 2014, Little Passports began a Facebook advertising campaign. The company ran ads featuring a photo of its Explorer Kit. Surrounding text urged people to subscribe to the service. Co-founder Amy Norman was able to choose who would see the ads based on gender, interests, location, relationship status, education, whether the person was expecting a child, and the type of mobile device used to access the ads (iOS vs Android). She also used a feature called Custom Audience to reach out to mothers who had a college background and read selected parenting magazines. Another tool that proved useful was Facebook's LookAlike Audiences. LookAlike Audiences uses customer e-mail addresses provided by advertisers, looks at the demographic and behavioral trends in that group, and then generates a list of additional prospects based on its database of North American Facebook users (about 260 million people). Facebook pushes the ad to these "look-alikes." If this sounds spooky, it is. But Facebook assures us that all the personal names are replaced with codes.

In just a few months, Little Passport's ads attracted over 1,500 user comments, all positive. In June 2014, the company spent about $30,000 on Facebook ads and its revenue for the month was about $130,000. After running the ad for six months, in December Little Passports spent $150,000 on Facebook advertising and its revenue rose to $700,000. Facebook advertising costs increased five-fold, and revenue advanced by

SOURCES: Facebook, Inc. Report on Form 10-Q for the six months ended June 30, 2015, filed with the Securities and Exchange Commission, July 31, 2015; "Consumers Spend 85% of Their Time on Smartphones in Apps, but Only 5 Apps See Heavy Use," by Sarah Perez, Techcrunch.com, June 22, 2015; "One Million and Counting! Little Passports to Deliver Its Millionth Package This Spring," Marketwired.com, April 16, 2015; "Facebook Counts 2 Million Active Advertisers, Mostly Small Businesses," by Jennifer Saba, Reuters.com, February 24, 2015; "A Year Later, $19 Billion for WhatsApp Doesn't Sound so Crazy," by Josh Constine, Techcrunch.com, February 19, 2015; "How Social Media Can Make Your Small Business Go Gangbusters," by Bruce Freeman, Theweek.com,

5.4 times, a little faster than the cost. Nolan believes the Facebook campaign was worth the expenditure because it tripled Little Passport's customer base in six months. Ms. Norman also felt that Facebook's tracking pixel was a game changer because she could see exactly how well the ads were performing. In 2015, Little Passports sold its millionth subscription package.

Until recently, investors in Facebook wondered if it would be able to continue to grow its advertising revenue. Marketers wondered if Facebook ads really worked. Does it mean anything if millions of Facebook users Like your marketing campaign? Do Likes turn into sales? Is Facebook better for marketing (brand recognition and awareness) than it is for driving sales through advertisements? And, if Facebook's marketing platform does work, how well does it work when compared to other online marketing techniques such as search, e-mail, display ads, and affiliate programs?

Facebook's marketing success on both the desktop and mobile devices is currently based on the insertion of ads in users' News Feeds and display ads in the right column of the home page. Currently an estimated 1 in 20 News Feed items are ads. When the ads reach 1 in 10 News Feed items, how will users react? How about 1 in 5? Zuckerberg, along with investors and marketers, is concerned that putting more ads in the News Feed is not the answer to sustaining future growth. Facebook will have to come up with some other ad opportunities, especially on the mobile platform. The most likely candidate: video advertising using short video clips, and of course, challenging Google's YouTube as a display platform for full-length videos and TV shows. In 2014, Facebook introduced an Autoplay feature, which allows videos to play automatically in the News Feed. Facebook has also reached out to some of Google's video content producers and encouraged them to consider distributing their videos on Facebook. This is yet another sign that Facebook is striving to become much more than just a social network site, and is trying to grow into becoming a video platform, an app platform, and an entire ecosystem. Facebook's purchases of Instagram for $1 billion in 2012 and WhatsApp for $22 billion in 2014 are also a sign that Facebook fully appreciates the urgency to find new sources of revenue, but their commitment to growing these new platforms before monetizing them shows patience and confidence in their long term strategy.

Facebook's financial results in 2014 and 2015 have quieted Wall Street's doubts that it could become a mobile advertising juggernaut. Facebook's 2014 revenue was nearly $12.5 billion, up significantly from $7.8 billion in 2013. In the second quarter of 2015, Facebook earned over $4 billion in revenue, its best quarter ever, and most importantly, registered consistent "stickiness" rates, which had concerned many investors.

Marketers may still have doubts about Facebook's effectiveness, but Facebook has taken a number of steps to prove itself to marketers with better tracking tools. In October 2014 Facebook launched a new advertising platform called Atlas. Atlas is a consumer tracking took suited to the mobile ad platform, where traditional cookies do not work. Atlas will help marketers identify Facebook users who have seen, or interacted with Facebook ads that appear on Facebook, other Web sites, or in Facebook apps. Atlas should go a long way in helping advertisers understand how well Facebook works.

February 16, 2015; "Facebook Reports Fourth Quarter and Full Year 2014 Results," Facebook.com, January 28, 2015; "More Than Half a Billion People Access Facebook Via Mobile," by Anthony Ha, Techcrunch.com, January 28, 2015; "Facebook Extends Reach with New Advertising Platform," Jack Marshall, *Wall Street Journal*, September 22, 2014; "Facebook Tries to Muscle in on YouTube," by Mike Shields and Reed Albergotti, *Wall Street Journal*, September 11, 2014; "Facebook Is Shifting From Being a Social Network to a Mere App Platform," by Ben Austin, *The Guardian*, September 2014; "How Facebook Sold You Krill Oil," by Vindu Goel, *New York Times*, August 2, 2014; Facebook, Inc. Report on Form 10-Q for the six months ended June 30, 2014, filed with the Securities and Exchange Commission, July 24, 2014; "Facebook Answers Critics with a Mobile Ad Surge," by Reed Albergotti, *Wall Street Journal*, July 23, 2014; "When Advertising on Facebook Can be a Waste of Money," by Eilene Zimmerman, *New York Times*, June 23, 2014; "Facebook Says There Are Now 30 Million Small Business with Active Pages, Including 19M on Mobile," by Anthony Ha, Techcrunch.com, June 3, 2014; "A Social Media Marketer Assesses Facebook's Advertising Platform," by Eilene Zimmerman, *New York Times*, January 15, 2014; "Facebook Revamps Ads to Compete With Google," by Eilene Zimmerman, *New York Times*, January 15, 2014; "Facebook's Stock Soars Amid Rosy Growth Expectations," by Vindu Goel, *New York Times*, July 25, 2013; "Why Facebook's Mobile Ads Are Working Better Than Google's," Timothy Senovec, HuffingtonPost.com, July 25, 2013; "Facebook Is Erasing Doubts on Mobile," by Vindu Goel, *New York Times*, July 24, 2013; "The Facebook Ads Benchmark Report," by Salesforce.com, 2013; "Facebook's Growth Slows," by Shayndi Raice, *Wall Street Journal*, July 27, 2012; "Facebook Combats Criticism Over Ads," by Shayndi Raice, *Wall Street Journal*, June 12, 2012.

7.1 INTRODUCTION TO SOCIAL, MOBILE, AND LOCAL MARKETING

Social, mobile, and local marketing have transformed the online marketing landscape. Before 2007, Facebook was a fledgling company limited to college students. Apple had not yet announced the iPhone. Online marketing consisted largely of creating a corporate Web site, buying display ads on Yahoo, purchasing AdWords on Google, and sending e-mail. The workhorse of online marketing was the display ad that flashed brand messages to millions of users who were not expected to respond immediately, ask questions, or make observations. The primary measure of success was how many "eyeballs" (unique visitors) a Web site produced, and how many "impressions" a marketing campaign generated. An impression was one ad shown to one person. Both of these measures were carryovers from the world of television, which measures marketing in terms of audience size and ad views.

FROM EYEBALLS TO CONVERSATIONS

After 2007, everything began to change, with the rapid growth of Facebook and other social network sites, the explosive growth of smartphones beginning with Apple iPhone in 2007, and the growing interest in local marketing. What's different about the new world of social-mobile-local marketing and advertising are the related concepts of "conversations" and "engagement." Marketing today is based on businesses marketing themselves as partners in multiple online conversations with their customers, potential customers, and even critics. Your brand is being talked about on the Web and social media (that's the conversation part). Today, marketing your firm and brands requires you to locate, identify, and participate in these conversations. Social marketing means all things social: listening, discussing, interacting, empathizing, and engaging. Rather than bombarding your audience with fancier, louder ads, instead have a conversation with them and engage them in your brand. The emphasis in online marketing has shifted from a focus on eyeballs to a focus on participating in customer-oriented conversations. In this sense, social marketing and advertising is not simply a "new ad channel," but a collection of technology-based tools for communicating with shoppers.

In the past, businesses could tightly control their brand messaging and lead consumers down a funnel of cues that ended in a purchase. That is not true of social marketing. Consumer purchase decisions are increasingly driven by the conversations, choices, tastes, and opinions of the consumer's social network. Social marketing is all about businesses participating in and shaping this social process.

FROM THE DESKTOP TO THE SMARTPHONE AND TABLET

Today, social, mobile, and local marketing are the fastest growing forms of online marketing (**Figure 7.1**). It's taken eight years for this new landscape to fully emerge since 2007, and firms are still learning how to use the new social and mobile marketing technologies.

By 2012, mobile marketing had already overtaken social marketing using traditional Web browsers on the Web. In 2015, spending on mobile marketing will be

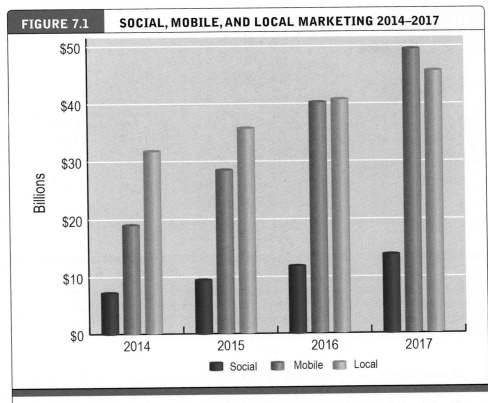

FIGURE 7.1   SOCIAL, MOBILE, AND LOCAL MARKETING 2014–2017

The amount spent on mobile marketing far exceeds the amount spent on social marketing and is rapidly overtaking the amount spent on local online marketing as well.

SOURCE: Based on data from eMarketer, Inc., 2015a, eMarketer, Inc., 2015z; BIA/Kelsey, 2015a.

more than double the amount spent on social marketing. By 2017, it is estimated that mobile marketing spending will account for around $48 billion annually, while social marketing will be about $14 billion. While social marketing is expected to grow by around 30% a year for the next several years, mobile will be growing at almost 60% in 2015, slowing down to 14% in 2017 as the United States market becomes saturated with mobile ads (eMarketer, Inc., 2015a). This figure underestimates the total social marketing spending because of the high percentage of visits to social networks that originate from a mobile device. For instance, Twitter reports that over 75% of their monthly active users access Twitter from a mobile device; about 30% of Facebook's active user base are mobile-only members (eMarketer, Inc., 2015b; Twitter, 2015). A substantial part of the mobile marketing spending should be counted as "social" marketing. Nevertheless, the figure indicates the extraordinary impact that mobile devices are having on marketing expenditures. Local online marketing was almost 70% larger than mobile in 2014, but by 2017, it is estimated that mobile will surpass local online marketing. As with social and mobile, there is significant overlap between local and mobile and social marketing, with much of local marketing also either social or mobile, or both.

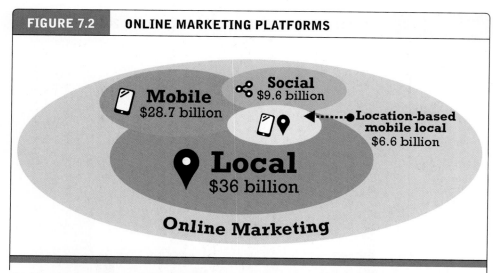

Traditional desktop marketing, including most of local marketing to local audiences, remains the largest part of all online marketing. Mobile marketing is aimed often at local audiences and is the fastest growing form of online marketing, followed closely by social marketing on social networks. Mobile local is in its infancy but it is also growing far faster than traditional desktop marketing.

SOURCE: Based on data from eMarketer, Inc., 2015a; eMarketer, Inc., 2015z; BIA/Kelsey, 2015a.

Figure 7.2 puts the social-mobile-local forms of advertising into the context of the total online advertising market. Here you can see that traditional online marketing (browser-based search and display ads, and e-mail marketing) still constitutes the majority of all online marketing, but it is growing much more slowly than social-mobile-local marketing. By 2017, it is expected that social-mobile-local marketing will be more than 50% of all online marketing. The marketing dollars are following customers and shoppers from the desktop computer to mobile devices, with smartphones having a substantial lead over tablets.

THE SOCIAL, MOBILE, LOCAL NEXUS

Social, mobile, and local digital marketing are self-reinforcing and connected. For instance, as mobile devices become more powerful, they are more useful for accessing Facebook and other social sites. As mobile devices become more widely adopted, they can be used by customers to find local merchants, and for merchants to alert customers in their neighborhood to special offers. Over time, these will become more overlapped as the three platforms become more tightly coupled.

About 78% of Facebook's ad revenue is generated by its mobile audience. Mobile constitutes an even larger share of Twitter's ad revenues—over 90%! Local marketing and mobile are highly related: local advertisers most often target mobile devices. And a considerable amount of mobile ad spending comes from local advertisers. The strong ties among social, mobile, and local marketing have significant implications for managing your own marketing campaign in this new environment. The message is that when you design a social marketing campaign, you must also consider that your customers will be accessing the campaign using mobile devices, and often they will also be looking for local content. Social-mobile-local must be seen in an integrated management framework.

In the sections that follow we will examine social, mobile, and local marketing more closely. The focus will be on describing the primary marketing tools of each platform and how to envision and manage a marketing campaign on each platform.

7.2 SOCIAL MARKETING

Social marketing differs markedly from traditional online marketing. The objectives of traditional online marketing are to put your business's message in front of as many visitors as possible and hopefully encourage them to come to your Web site to buy products and services, or to find out more information. The more "impressions" (ad views) you get, and the more unique visitors to your site, the better. Traditional online marketing never expected to listen to customers, much less have a conversation with them, any more than TV advertisers expected to hear from viewers.

In social marketing, the objective is to encourage your potential customers to become fans of your company's products and services, and engage with your business by entering into a conversation with it. Your further objective is to encourage your business's fans to share their enthusiasm with their friends, and in so doing create a community of fans online. Ultimately, the point is to strengthen the brand and drive sales, and to do this by increasing your "share of online conversation." There is some reason to believe that social marketing is more cost effective than traditional marketing although this is still being explored.

SOCIAL MARKETING PLAYERS

There are hundreds of social network sites in the United States and worldwide, but the most popular sites (Facebook, Instagram, Twitter, LinkedIn, Pinterest, and Tumblr) account for over 90% of all visits. (See Chapter 11, Section 11.1 for a full discussion of social networks.)

While the number of monthly unique visitors is a good measure of market reach, it is not helpful in understanding engagement—the amount and intensity of user involvement in a site. One measure of engagement is the amount of time users spend on a site. **Figure 7.3** illustrates engagement at the top social network sites.

On measures of engagement, Facebook once again dominates, accounting for 85% of the total month visitor minutes, a whopping 230 billion minutes per month in the United States. The average Facebook user spent more than 18 hours a month on Facebook. Tumblr takes second place, followed by Pinterest and Twitter.

For a manager of a social marketing campaign, these findings suggest that in terms of reach and engagement, the place to start a social campaign is Facebook. Yet visitors to the other leading social sites collectively account for an additional 15% of the social market space, and therefore, a social marketing campaign also has to include them at some point. It helps that social network users use multiple social sites. Facebook users

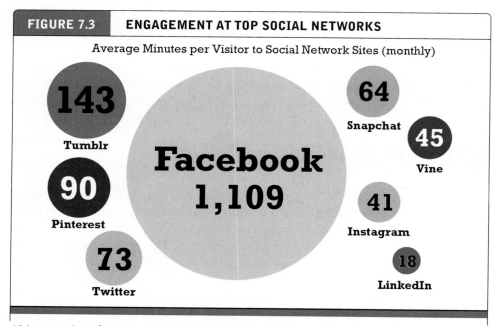

FIGURE 7.3 ENGAGEMENT AT TOP SOCIAL NETWORKS

Average Minutes per Visitor to Social Network Sites (monthly)

143 Tumblr

Facebook 1,109

64 Snapchat

45 Vine

90 Pinterest

41 Instagram

73 Twitter

18 LinkedIn

Visitors spend significantly more time on Facebook than any other social network.

SOURCE: Based on data from comScore, 2015a; comScore, 2015b; Statista.com, 2015; MacMillan and Rusli, 2014; Frommer, 2015.

dark social

those forms of social sharing that occur off the major social networks, through alternative communication tools such as e-mail, instant messages, texts, and mobile messaging apps

are likely to be users at Twitter, Pinterest, LinkedIn, and Instagram. In addition, marketers need to be aware of what has come to be known as dark social. **Dark social** refers to those forms of social sharing that occur off the major social networks, through alternative communication tools such as interpersonal conversations, group meetings, and friendships, not to mention e-mail, instant messages, texts, and mobile messaging apps. While online social network users spend over 30 hours a month on average on all networks combined, there are 720 total hours in a month. Therefore, about 4% of all social life in a month involves online social networks, while 96% does not.

THE SOCIAL MARKETING PROCESS

At first glance the large number of different social sites is confusing, each with a unique user experience to offer, from Twitter's micro blogging text messaging service, to Tumblr's blogging capability, and to graphical social sites like Pinterest and Instagram. Yet they can all be approached with a common framework. **Figure 7.4** illustrates a social marketing framework that can be applied to all social, mobile, and local marketing efforts.

There are five steps in the social marketing process: Fan acquisition, engagement, amplification, community, and brand strength (sales). Each of these steps in the process can be measured. The metrics of social marketing are quite different from those of traditional Web marketing or television marketing. This is what makes social marketing so different—the objectives and the measures. This will become more apparent as we describe marketing on specific social sites.

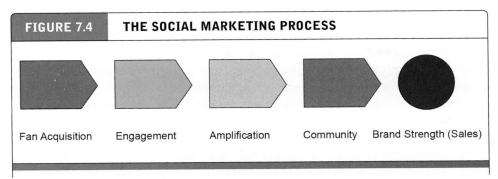

| FIGURE 7.4 | **THE SOCIAL MARKETING PROCESS** |

Fan Acquisition   Engagement   Amplification   Community   Brand Strength (Sales)

The social marketing process has five steps.

Social marketing campaigns begin with **fan acquisition**, which involves using any of a variety of means, from display ads to News Feed and page pop-ups, to attract people to your Facebook page, Twitter feed, or other platform like a Web page. It's getting your brand "out there" in the stream of social messages. Display ads on social sites have a social dimension (sometimes called "display ads with social features" or simply "social ads"). Social ads encourage visitors to interact and do something social, such as participate in a contest, obtain a coupon, or obtain free services for attracting friends.

> **fan acquisition**
> attracting people to your marketing messages

The next step is to generate **engagement,** which involves using a variety of tools to encourage users to interact with your content and brand located on your Facebook or Web pages. You can think of this as "starting the conversation" around your brand. You want your fans to talk about your content and products. You can generate engagement through attractive photos, interesting text content, and blogger reports, with plenty of opportunities for users to express opinions. You can also provide links to Pinterest photos of your products or fan comments on blog sites like Tumblr.

> **engagement**
> encouraging visitors to interact with your content and brand

Once you have engaged visitors, you can begin to use social site features to amplify your messages by encouraging users to tell their friends by clicking a Like or +1 button, or by sending a message to their followers on Twitter. **Amplification** involves using the inherent strength of social networks. On Facebook, the average user has 120 "friends." This includes all people they have ever friended, including people whom they don't really know (and who don't really know them). Facebook users typically have only three to four close friends with whom they can discuss confidential matters, and a larger set of around 20 friends with whom they have two-way communications (mutual friends). Let's use 20 as a reasonable number of mutual friends for marketing purposes. For marketers, this means that if they can attract one fan and encourage that fan to share his or her approval with his or her friends, the message can be amplified twenty times: 20 friends of the one fan can be influenced. Best of all: the friends of fans are free. Marketers pay to attract only the initial fan and they are not charged by social sites (currently) for the amplification that can result.

> **amplification**
> encouraging visitors to share their Likes and comments with their friends

Once you have gathered enough engaged fans, you will have created the foundation for a **community**—a more or less stable group of fans who are engaged and

> **community**
> a stable group of fans engaged and communicating with one another over a substantial period of time about your brand

communicating with one another over a substantial period of time (say several months or more). Marketers have a number of tactics to nurture these communities, including inside information on new products, price breaks for loyalty, and free gifts for bringing in new members. The ultimate goal is to enlarge your firm's "share of the online conversation." The process ends with strengthening the brand and, hopefully, additional sales of products and services. Brand strength can be measured in a variety of ways both online and offline, a subject that is beyond the boundaries of this text (Ailawadi et al., 2003; Aaker, 1996; Simon and Sullivan, 1993; Keller, 1993).

Ultimately, the point of marketing is to drive sales revenue. Measuring the impact of a social marketing campaign on brand strength and sales is still being explored by marketers, social site managers, and researchers, but generally the results are positive: social marketing campaigns drive sales. In 2015, most of the top social network sites, including Facebook, Twitter, Pinterest, and Instagram, have added, or are in the processing of adding, social commerce features, such as Buy buttons and other shopping functionality that makes it even easier for the targets of those social marketing campaigns to act on them and make a purchase.

FACEBOOK MARKETING

Nearly everyone reading this book has a Facebook page. There are power users who spend hours a day on the site, some with thousands of "friends," and there are casual users who have a small set of perhaps 20 friends and relatives. While most have a basic understanding of Facebook, it's worthwhile to review the major features of Facebook before discussing its marketing potential.

Basic Facebook Features

Facebook describes itself as having three pillars: News Feed, Timeline (Profile), and Search. Facebook also has many other features that are equally important to its potential as a marketing platform. **Table 7.1** describes these features.

Reviewing Table 7.1, it is clear that Facebook is built to encourage people to reveal as much personal information about themselves as feasible, including activities, behavior, photos, music, movies, purchases, and preferences. One result is that Facebook is the world's largest repository of deeply personal behavioral information on the Internet. Facebook knows a great deal more about its users than Google does about its users. Second, Facebook's features are built to maximize the connections among people in the form of notifications, tagging, messaging, posting, and sharing. In many instances, the movement of personal information is so widespread that it is beyond the understanding of users and outside observers. The effect of these two factors is to greatly magnify the social density of the Facebook audience. **Social density** refers to the number of interactions among members of a group and reflects the "connectedness" of a group, even if these connections are forced on users. For instance, some natural groups of people are not very "social" and few messages flow among members. Other natural groups are loquacious and chatty with many messages flowing among

social density
refers to the number of interactions among members of a group and reflects the "connectedness" of a group, even if these connections are forced on users

TABLE 7.1	BASIC FACEBOOK FEATURES
FEATURE	DESCRIPTION
Profile	As part of account creation, you create a profile that includes certain personal information. The profile may also include photos and other media. Establishes baseline information that will be shared with friends.
Friend search	Helps you find friends who are already using Facebook, as well as friends who are not, typically by searching your e-mail contact list. Creates your baseline social network based on prior contacts.
Timeline	A history of your actions on Facebook, including photos, history of posts, and comments to your News Feed, as well as life events that you post and want others to see as a part of your profile. Additions you make to your Timeline may appear on your friends' News Feed. Creates additional links with friends.
Tagging	Ability to tag photos, status updates, check-ins, or comments with the names of friends. Tagging links to that person's Timeline and News Feed. Your friends are notified they have been tagged, and you are linked to their Timeline. Friends of your friends may also be notified. Whenever Facebook detects the person in a new image, it notifies all those who have tagged the photo that this friend appears in a new photo that you can link to. The tagging tool is designed to create additional connections among users.
News Feed	The center of the action on Facebook Home pages, News Feed is a continuously updated list of stories from friends and Pages that you have liked on Facebook. Ads running in the News Feed are the major ad revenue producer for Facebook. News Feed stories include status updates, photos, videos, links, app activity, and Likes. Provides a continual stream of messages from friends and advertisers.
Trending	Facebook's version of trending topics; appears at top of right-hand column next to News Feed
Status update	A way to post your comments, observations, and location to all your friends.
Like button	The ubiquitous Like button communicates your support of comments, photos, activities, brands, articles, and products to your friends, and also to the Facebook social graph and third-party marketers. The Like button lives on virtually all Facebook content including status updates, photos, comments, brands, timelines, apps, and even ads. The Like button also appears on external sites, mobile and social apps, and ads. These sites are utilizing Facebook's Like social plug-in, and when you Like something outside of Facebook, it appears on your Timeline, where friends can comment on the activity. The Like button is one way Facebook knows what other sites you visit.
Apps	Facebook apps are built by third-party developers, and add functionality to Facebook. Apps run the gamut from games (Candy Crush Saga; FarmVille) to photos (Instagram, now part of Facebook), music (Spotify), and publications (Washington Post Social Reader). Your personal information and that of your friends is shared with apps that you install. Most Facebook apps are free, and most rely on revenues from advertising that they expose you to.
Open Graph	A feature used by app developers to integrate their apps into the Facebook pages of users who sign up for the app, and in that sense, it opens the Facebook social graph to the developer, who can then use all the features of Facebook in the app. For instance, this feature allows your performance on game apps to be sent to your Friend's News Feeds. Supports the development of social apps and increases links among users.
Search	In July 2013, Facebook introduced Graph Search, a "social" search engine that searched your social network for answers to queries. It was a "semantic" search engine insofar as it provided a single answer rather than a list of links based on an algorithm's estimate of user intentions. It was also a "hybrid" search engine that relied on Bing to supplement results. In 2015, Facebook significantly expanded its Search functionality. It now includes everyone's public posts, Likes, photos, and interests, and makes them available to all users of Facebook, friends or not.

members. The scope, intensity, and depth of Facebook's repository of personal information and rich social network present extraordinary marketing opportunities.

Facebook Marketing Tools

Facebook offers a number of marketing and advertising opportunities and tools for branding and developing community on its site.

Like button

gives users a chance to share their feelings about content and other objects they are viewing

Like Button The Like and Share buttons on Facebook, and similar buttons such as +1 on other social sites, are perhaps the single most important element in the rise of social marketing. "Like" is the engine of social marketing. The Like button was introduced by Facebook on its own Web site in 2009 and rolled out as a plug-in to other Web sites in 2010. Unlike traditional Web advertising, the **Like button** gives users a chance to share their feelings about content and other objects they are viewing and Web sites they are visiting. It's a way for users to express their opinions to their friends about their Web experience. With Like buttons on millions of Web sites, Facebook can track user behavior on other sites and then sell this information to marketers.

Like gives Big Data real meaning. Analysts estimate that each hour, Facebook records 30 million likes and processes 180 million posts and 9 million messages. Facebook's Like and Share buttons are embedded in more than 13 million Web sites worldwide (Bullas, 2015; Facebook, 2015; Lecher, 2015).

Brand Pages Facebook's early efforts at brand marketing focused on the development of brand pages as a means for firms to establish a direct relationship with their current and potential customers. Nearly all Fortune 1000 companies, and hundreds of thousands of smaller firms, have Facebook brand pages, similar to brand Web sites, on Facebook as an adjunct to their main Web site. The purpose of a brand page is to develop fans of the brand by providing users opportunities to interact with the brand through comments, contests, and offerings. Using social calls to action, such as "Like us on Facebook" and "Share," brand pages can escape their isolation and make it more easily into users' social networks, where friends can hear the message. In October 2015, Facebook announced that it would offer a new Shopping/Services tab for Facebook brand pages that will feature products and services, taking it further into the realm of social e-commerce.

Social brand pages have many more social opportunities for fans to like and comment than are typical of traditional Web pages. However, corporate Web sites have, over time, adopted many social features and the two are now often indistinguishable. Brand pages on Facebook typically attract more visitors than a brand's Web site.

Brands can get exposure on Facebook either organically or via paid advertisements. Organic reach is free, and happens when fans see the brand's updates and posts in their News Feed, or when others who are not fans see that content because a fan liked, commented, or shared the post (viral reach). In order to ensure that they get the exposure that they want for their marketing messages, most companies choose one of the paid advertising formats discussed below.

Facebook enables you to choose from a variety of different marketing objectives, including promoting your Page posts/ads (Page Post Engagement); obtaining Likes for your Facebook page to grow your company's audience and brand (Page Likes); getting people to click through to your Web site (Clicks to Web sites); getting people to take certain actions on your Web site (Web site Conversions); getting people to install an app (App Installs); getting people to use an app (App Engagement); creating offers for people to redeem (Offer Claims); and getting people to watch a video (Video Views).

Once you have chosen a marketing objective, the next decision is to whom you want to target the advertisement. Facebook ads can be targeted based on location, age, interest, gender, education level, relationship status, and political views, as well as to custom audiences defined by the marketer. Facebook can also create what it calls a "lookalike audience" based on demographics shared with the custom audience identified by the marketer.

Once the marketing objectives and audience have been determined, the next decision is where to place the advertisement. Facebook has four basic locations from which to choose: the News Feed, the right-hand column or sidebar section of Facebook pages, and the mobile News Feed. Ads can also be placed within apps.

News Feed Page Post Ads The News Feed is the most prominent place for advertisements. The News Feed is the center of the action for Facebook users and where Facebook users spend most of their time because that is where posts from their friends appear. Page Post Ads appear in a user's News Feed along with all of the other posts and status updates that normally appear from friends. Page Post Ads have a tiny tag that indicates that they are sponsored (i.e., are advertisements) but otherwise look very similar to posts from friends. Sometimes the ads have a social context ("John Smith and Jane Doe like Pottery Barn") and can be liked, shared, and commented on, just like any other post. Page Post Ads can contain text, photos, video, and links. They can be used for many of the marketing objectives mentioned above, such as increasing brand engagement, obtaining Likes for the brand's Facebook page, and encouraging app installs and engagement. In 2015, Facebook is also pilot testing a Buy button that will appear in News Feed Page Post Ads that will allow people to purchase items without leaving Facebook. Companies pay to promote or boost Page Post Ads in order to extend their reach. This has become increasingly important as Facebook has reduced the organic reach that brands previously enjoyed for free in an effort to increase advertising revenues (Vahl, 2014; Ernoult, 2014).

Right-Hand Column Sidebar Ads These display ads are located in the right-hand column or sidebar of Facebook pages. They are often used to direct users to off-Facebook content such as Web site landing pages and content offers. Facebook has recently reduced the number of ads that appear in the right-hand column sidebar from seven to two, increased their size, and made them consistent with the format of News Feed Page Post Ads in an effort to enhance their performance.

Mobile Ads Facebook introduced Facebook for Mobile in 2006. It now has nearly 1 billion daily monthly active users as of June 2015. Users can also access Facebook using a mobile browser although it is slower. In 2015, over 75% of Facebook ad revenue will come from its mobile ad platform, and it is its fastest growing revenue stream

TABLE 7.2	BASIC FACEBOOK MARKETING TOOLS
MARKETING TOOL	**DESCRIPTION**
Like Button	Amplification. A feature that allows users to express support for content on social sites to their friends, and friends of friends. The one tool that marketers cannot control. Currently free.
Brand Pages	Engagement and community building. Similar to a business Web page, but much more social by encouraging user interaction and response; ongoing discussions among the community of fans. Brand pages are currently free. Shop/Services tabs for brand pages allow companies to feature products and services for sale.
News Feed Page Post Ads	Fan acquisition. Paid brand messages can be inserted into the News Feed. Requires payment. Buy button that can be embedded in News Feed Page Post Ads currently being tested.
Right-Hand Sidebar Ads	Fan acquisition. Display ads in the right-hand column (sidebar) similar to display ads elsewhere on the Web. Requires payment.
Mobile Ads	Fan acquisition and engagement. Mobile News Feed Page Post Ads are delivered to smartphones and tablets. Requires payment.
Facebook Exchange (FBX)	Facebook's real-time ad exchange, which sells ads and retargets ads through online bidding. Advertisers place cookies on user browsers when they visit a site, and when they return to Facebook, they are shown ads on the right side from the site they visited. Requires payment.

(eMarketer, Inc., 2015c). Mobile app install ads are those paid for by mobile app developers to persuade users to install their app.

Because the smartphone screen is much smaller than regular computer screens, there is no room for sidebar ads on the right-hand column, so all mobile ads need to be displayed in the users' News Feed. Mobile ads can include many of the ad formats described above. Critics complain that the number of ads in the mobile News Feed becomes distracting and annoying. Mobile ads often take up the entire screen. There also is less targeting of mobile ads, which increases the likelihood users will see irrelevant ads. So far, despite the annoyance, Facebook mobile users continue to sign up and view.

Facebook Exchange (FBX)

a real-time bidding system that allows advertisers to target their ads based on personal information provided by Facebook

Facebook Exchange (FBX). **Facebook Exchange (FBX)** is a real-time bidding system that allows advertisers to target their ads based on personal information provided by Facebook. FBX competes with Google's display ad system DoubleClick and other real-time exchanges. Visitors to third-party Web sites are marked with a cookie, and can then be shown ads related to their Web browsing when they return to Facebook.

Table 7.2 summarizes the major tools used by marketers to build their brands on Facebook.

TABLE 7.3	SELECTED FACEBOOK MARKETING CAMPAIGNS
COMPANY	MARKETING CAMPAIGN
Target Stores	Promotes discounts across Facebook, Twitter, and mobile platforms providing access to the Cartwheel.Target.com Web site.
Domino's Pizza	Uses ads to offer discounts to drive sales.
Expedia	Uses its fan base to enlist friends' help to win a free vacation package using a variety of ad types.
Jackson Hewitt	Tax preparation service anchored in Walmart stores used Facebook to increase engagement with its brand by placing ads promoting a dancing game. Winners were given a $25 gift certificate to use at Walmart.

Starting a Facebook Marketing Campaign

Prior to starting a Facebook marketing campaign, there are some basic strategy questions you need to address. While every product presumably could benefit from a social marketing campaign, how is this true of your products? Who is your audience? How can you reach them? How have real-world social networks been used in the past to support sales in your industry? Can you be a "thought leader?" Once you have identified your audience, what content will get them excited and interested? Where are you going to get the content? What will it cost and what impact do you expect it to have on your brand and sales? At this point you do not need a detailed budget, but you should be able to develop estimates of the cost of such a campaign, as well as anticipated revenues.

If you're new to Facebook marketing, start simple and build on your fan base based on experience. A typical marketing campaign for Facebook might include the following elements:

- Establish a Facebook page for your brand. Content is king: have interesting, original content that visitors can be enthusiastic about. Acquire fans.
- Use comment and feedback tools to develop fan comments. You want visitors to engage with your content. You can also encourage bloggers to develop content for your page.
- Develop a community of users. Try to encourage fans to talk with one another, and develop new (free) content for your page.
- Encourage brand involvement through videos and rich media showing products being used by real customers.
- Use contests and competitions to deepen fan involvement.
- Develop display ads for use on Facebook.
- Develop display ads for use in response to social search queries.
- Liberally display the Like button so fans share the experience with their friends.

For more information on social marketing using Facebook, see Learning Track 7.1. **Table 7.3** provides some examples of Facebook marketing campaigns.

Measuring Facebook Marketing Results

There are many ways to measure the success of a Facebook marketing campaign, some very sophisticated. This is a very new field that changes daily. Making matters more complicated is that industry sources sometimes use different names to refer to the same thing! Where this occurs we try to give both the most reasonable name and alternative names you might find in trade literature.

Table 7.4 describes some of the basic metrics to use when evaluating a social marketing campaign. It uses the five steps of the social marketing process found in Figure 7.4—fan acquisition, engagement, amplification, community, and ultimately brand strengthening and sales—as an organizing schema.

While the ultimate goal of Facebook marketing is to drive sales (which typically will take place on your Web site), it is very important to understand what the elements of social marketing that produce these sales are, and how they can be improved.

TABLE 7.4	MEASURING FACEBOOK MARKETING
SOCIAL MARKETING PROCESS	MEASUREMENT
Fan acquisition (impressions)	The number of people exposed to your Facebook brand page posts and paid ads (impressions).
	The percentage of those exposed who become fans based on Likes or comments.
	The ratio of impressions to fans.
Engagement (conversation rate)	The number of posts, comments, and responses.
	The number of views of brand page content.
	The number of Likes generated per visitor.
	The number of users who responded to games, contests, and coupons (participation).
	The number of minutes on average that visitors stay on your page (duration).
	The rate of Likes per post or other content (applause rate).
Amplification (reach)	The percentage of Likes, shares, or posts to other sites (the rate at which fans share your content).
Community	The monthly interaction rate with your content (i.e., the monthly total of posts, comments, and actions on your Facebook brand page).
	The average monthly on-site minutes for all fans.
	The ratio of positive to negative comments.
Brand Strength/Sales	The percentage (or revenue) of your online sales that is generated by Facebook links compared to other platforms, such as e-mail, search engines, and display ads.
	The percentage of Facebook-sourced customer purchases compared to other sources of customers (conversion ratio).
	The conversion ratio for friends of fans.

At the most elementary level, the number of fans (or followers) generated is the beginning of all social marketing. Visitors become fans when they like your content. In the early days of social marketing, firms put a great deal of emphasis on the size of the fan base, and collecting Likes. This is less important today, as social marketing managers have become more sophisticated. Fan engagement in your content and brand is the first step toward developing a truly social experience, and arguably is more important than simply the number of impressions or the number of fans. Fans that you never hear from are not valuable. Engagement relates to how your fans are interacting with your content, how intensely, and how often. Understanding the kinds of content (videos, text, photos, or posts from fans) that create the highest levels of engagement is also very important (Unmetric, 2015).

The ability to amplify your marketing message by tapping into the social network of your fans is also at the core of social marketing. This can be measured very simply as the rate at which fans recommend your content to their friends, and how many of their friends further recommend your content to their friends.

Measuring the strength of a Facebook community is not that much different from measuring the strength of an offline community. In both cases you attempt to measure the collective activities of all in the community. Among your fans, how many actively participate? What is the total number of actions taken by fans in a month? How many minutes of involvement are generated each month? What is the percentage of favorable comments?

Finally, measuring sales that result from social campaigns is also straightforward. First, measure the percentage of sales you receive from the Facebook channel. You can easily measure the number of visits to your Web site that originate on Facebook, and the sales these visits generate. In addition, you can compare purchase rates (conversion rate) for fans and compare these to conversion rates for non-fans from Facebook. More important, you can compare the Facebook conversion rate to other visitors who come from different marketing channels, such as e-mail, display ads, and blogs.

Facebook marketing has entered its second generation even though it's only four years old. The emphasis today in social marketing has gone beyond collecting Likes and more toward building engagement with high-quality content that fans want to share with their friends; nurturing stable communities of intensely involved fans and friends of fans; and ultimately turning these communities of fans into communities of purchasers.

The experience of marketers is tantalizing but still unclear. E-mail, search, and affiliate marketing still drive more sales than Facebook or any social marketing today (eMarketer, 2015; Smith, 2014). Conversion rates for social marketing are less than 1%, while search produces 2.2% and e-mail nearly 4%. Display ads on general Web sites are about as effective for producing sales as those on social network sites. Facebook ads are much less likely to be clicked on than display ads on the Web, and sell for less than half the price of Web display ads. Facebook users join social networks to be social, not to buy or even shop. Despite these limitations, in the space of a few years, Facebook has been able to create a multi-billion dollar business selling ads. Rather than replace other ad venues, Facebook may be creating a whole new venue that it dominates and that has unique value, but nevertheless does not diminish the role of e-mail or search in the marketing mix.

There are a variety of Facebook analytics tools that provide valuable information about your Facebook marketing efforts. Facebook Page Insights, provided by Facebook, tracks total Page Likes, People Talking About This (PTAT) (which tracks the number of unique people who have clicked on, Liked, commented on, or shared a post), Page Tags and Mentions, Page Checkins, and other interactions on a page. It also tracks something it calls Engagement Rate. People are considered to have engaged with a post if they Like it, comment on it, share it, or click it (Simply Measured, 2015; AdRoll, 2015).

Social media management system HootSuite enables teams to execute marketing campaigns across multiple networks from one dashboard, and also provides custom reports. Major analytics providers, such as Google Analytics, Webtrends, and IBM Digital Analytics, also provide Facebook reporting modules. Read the *Insight on Technology* case study *Optimizing Social Marketing with Simply Measured* for a further look at how one organization is using analytics tools to help them better understand social marketing.

TWITTER MARKETING

Twitter is a micro-blogging social network site that allows users to send and receive 140-character messages, as well as news articles, photos, and videos. Twitter has an estimated 315 million active users worldwide as of September 2015, and its 2014 revenue was $1.4 billion, more than double its 2013 revenue. But Twitter lost $577 million in 2014, and has never been profitable since its founding in 2006. Investors have pummeled its stock down 30% in 2015. Over 90% of Twitter's users access the service on mobile devices. Almost all of Twitter's revenue comes from pop-ads that appear in users' timelines (tweet stream), but Twitter also has many other marketing tools in its quiver. The real magic of Twitter, like Facebook, is that Twitter does not pay for the 500 million tweets sent each day. They are supplied for free by active users. Twitter sells ads based on the content of these user messages. Some analysts believe Twitter could easily become the next Google. See the opening case in Chapter 2 for more information on Twitter.

Twitter was designed from the start as a real-time text messaging service. Twitter offers advertisers and marketers a chance to interact and engage with their customers in real time and in a fairly intimate, one-on-one manner. Advertisers can buy ads that look like organic tweets (the kind you receive from friends), and these ads can tie into and enhance marketing events like new product announcements or pricing changes. Twitter is announcing new marketing tools every quarter in an effort to boost its revenues. On the other hand, there may be a limit to how many ads Twitter users will tolerate.

Basic Twitter Features

While most people probably know what a tweet is, Twitter offers marketers many other ways of communicating using Twitter. In fact, Twitter has introduced a whole new vocabulary that is specific to Twitter's platform. **Table 7.5** on page 441 describes the most common Twitter features.

Twitter Marketing Tools

There are many kinds of Twitter marketing products, and the firm is creating new ones every few months. The current major Twitter marketing tools include the following.

INSIGHT ON TECHNOLOGY

OPTIMIZING SOCIAL MARKETING WITH SIMPLY MEASURED

Companies of all shapes and sizes are beginning to tap into the power of social media for marketing and advertising to improve their bottom line and enrich their relationships with their customers. As social media continues to become entrenched in the business and cultural landscape, an ecosystem of companies has sprung up around it to meet growing demand. One major area of growth is in social media analytics – tools that allow companies to track and report social media account performance and generate recommendations on how to optimize social media marketing efforts. Simply Measured is a market leader in this burgeoning field, rating highest in overall customer satisfaction as well as market share.

Founded in 2010, Simply Measured is based in Seattle, Washington, and has quickly grown from humble beginnings (the founders built the original product over a single weekend) to a market-leading company capable of raising almost $30 million in venture capital. It currently has 150 employees and more than 1,000 customers. Its rapid growth is due in part to the similarly rapid growth in social media platforms during that time, as Facebook, Twitter, Instagram, and others have all more than doubled over that span. Marketers and advertisers eager to tap into this emerging channel may not have the tools to understand what techniques are working and which need refinement. That's where Simply Measured comes in.

Simply Measured offers analytics tools for all major platforms, including Twitter, Facebook, Instagram, Tumblr, LinkedIn, YouTube, and Vine. It also offers variations of those products for individual market segments, such as retail, finance and insurance, consumer packaged goods, sports, restaurants, publishing, travel, tech, and telecommunications. Simply Measured's solutions allow companies to plan their social strategy, execute it, and then find out what's working best. Optimizing social marketing techniques in this way leads to better audience engagement and better bottom-line results. Simply Measured generates reports both in Microsoft Excel and on the Web in clear, easily understood formats that can be shared across organizations.

Examples of typical basic reports include Facebook Competitive Analysis, which measures a Facebook page against other competitors in usage and engagement; Traffic Source Analysis, which determines what sources direct the most traffic to your site; and Twitter Follower Analysis, which analyzes an account's followers for demographic information and activity trends. Whatever a company's social marketing needs, odds are good that Simply Measured has solutions to help.

For example, the Seattle Seahawks, winners of the 2014 Super Bowl, are renowned for their passionate fan base, known as "The 12th Man," and for their deafening crowd noise at home games, which held the record for loudest ever recorded at an outdoor stadium until it was surpassed by Kansas City Chiefs fans in 2014. The organization hoped to create a similar atmosphere on social media as well, and turned to Simply Measured to help it achieve this goal. During the team's playoff run in 2014, Simply Measured helped the Seahawks increase social engagement across all major platforms by a whopping 173%.

(continued)

For a team with a large, motivated fan base, managing and understanding that level of social activity is impossible without the assistance of analytics. Using Simply Measured's Cross-Channel Social Performance report, the Seahawks learned which social networks best suited their social media goals and created greater fan engagement. To their surprise, Instagram was extremely effective in this regard, so they focused more energy there. The Twitter Account Report indicated which content was most popular on Twitter and even pointed to particular times of day that were most likely to generate a strong response. And the Twitter Competitive Analysis Report allowed the Seahawks to measure themselves against others, including their opponents in the Super Bowl, the Denver Broncos, as well as the rest of their peers in the NFL, in key metrics like share of overall "voice" and fan engagement.

Simply Measured also offers a variety of reports and e-books detailing the state of social marketing in different market segments. The company identifies and analyzes trends in social marketing campaigns, such as the Montana Department of Tourism's Montana Moment Instagram campaign, which quickly went viral as users shared images of Montana's picturesque countryside with the hashtag #montanamoment. Simply Measured also took notice of the campaign promoting the *Breaking Bad* spinoff television show *Better Call Saul,* which used an aggressive marketing campaign in the weeks leading up to the show to acquire 14,000 followers, to better engage with the show's fans during its run, and to better understand the types of content its followers were most interested in.

Simply Measured is on a growth tear in 2015. Like many start-ups, it is using the money it has raised from venture capital to buy up other firms that can strengthen its main product line, and enable it to branch out into related activities. In September 2015, Simply Measured acquired Inside Social, a small company with 10 employees that helps marketing firms track the return on investment from social marketing campaigns, something which has been difficult to determine, especially with mobile social marketing. Inside Social initially began life as a project at Techstars' Seattle incubator. With this acquisition, Simply Measured can tell its clients not only where to concentrate their efforts in terms of response, but also where they can make the best return on their investment of ad dollars.

In October 2015, Simply Measured acquired Arkansas-based DataRank, a social intelligence platform that helps firms organize and sift through mountains of online comments, helping firms analyze what is being said about them. One of DataRank's offerings is DataRank Sonar, a social media dashboard that visually, in real-time, illustrates how client brands are faring in online social conversations.

Using social media correctly can be difficult (see the Chapter 11 *Insight on Society* case, *The Dark Side of Social Networks,* for examples). With Simply Measured and other social media analytics providers, avoiding these pitfalls and getting the most out of social media become much easier.

SOURCES: "Simply Measured Names ExactTarget Vet as CEO and CRO in Bid to Supercharge Growth," by John Cook, Geekwire.com, October 30, 2015; "Simply Measured Found Right Niche at the Right Time," *Seattle Times,* October 24, 2015; "Simply Measured Acquires DataRank, A Social Intelligence Provider," by Maddy Suresh, Thetechbulletin.com, October 14, 2015; "Simply Measured Acquires Inside Social, as Two Seattle Social Media Data Startups Join Forces," by Jacob Demmitt, Geekwire.com, September 1, 2015; "The Top-Rated Social Analytics Tools by Marketers," by Ayaz Nanji, Marketingprofs.com, July 7, 2015; "How #MontanaMoment Is Capturing Instagram's Heart (and Engagement)," by Lucy Hitz, Simplymeasured.com, July 2, 2015; "What 'Better Call Saul' Can Teach Us About Marketing on Twitter," by Lucy Hitz, Simplymeasured.com, April 8, 2015; "Simply Measured Takes On $20M More to Grow Its Social Media Analytics Service," by Alex Wilhelm, Techcrunch.com, March 18, 2014; "Winning Your Social Community: A Seattle Seahawks Case Study," by Lindzee McCain, Simplymeasured.com, September 4, 2014.

TABLE 7.5	TWITTER FEATURES
FEATURE	DESCRIPTION
Tweet	140-character text message. Messages can be private (to a single person or one to one), public (to everyone, one to many), or to a group of followers.
Followers	You can follow someone's tweets and receive them as soon as they are made. Others can follow your tweets.
Message (DM)	A direct private message (DM) is like an e-mail that only you and the recipient can read.
Hashtag #<word>	Like a Twitter search engine, #<word> organizes the conversations on Twitter around a specific topic. Click on a hashtag and you are taken to the search results for that term.
Mention	A public Tweet that includes another user's name "@username." You can click on mentions and link back to that person's profile. As a public tweet, your followers will be alerted as well.
Moments tab	Curated highlights of what is happening on Twitter at that moment.
Reply	A public response to a tweet using the Reply button. Replies show up on your timeline and that of the person you are responding to.
Timeline	Your timeline is your home page on Twitter listing the tweets you have received in chronological order, the most recent first. Click on a tweet in the timeline and it expands to reveal videos, and photos. Place your mouse over a tweet to reply, retweet, or make it a favorite (which is passed to your followers).
Retweet	Allows you to send along a tweet to all of your followers.
Links	Twitter has a link-shortening feature that allows you to paste in a URL of any link and it will be automatically shortened.

Promoted Tweets. Advertisers pay to have their tweets appear in users' search results. Promoted Tweets are Twitter's version of Google's AdWords. The tweets appear as "promoted" in the search results. Pricing is on a "cost-per-click" basis of between $.50 to $2.00 per click, and based on an auction run by Twitter on the Twitter ad platform. An "ad carousel" allows up to 12 ads to be shown in a single space, enabling users to swipe through the Promoted Tweets. Promoted Tweets can be geo-targeted and also offer keyword targeting that enables advertisers to send the tweets to specific users based on keywords in their recent tweets or tweets with which they have interacted. Buy buttons embedded within Promoted Tweets enable users to purchase without leaving Twitter.

Promoted Trends. Advertisers pay to move their hashtags (# symbol used to mark keywords in a tweet) to the top of Twitter's Trends List. Otherwise, hashtags are found by the Twitter search engine, and only those that are organically popular make it to the Trends List. Promoted Trends cost about $200,000 a day in the United States in 2014, and are also available for purchase in 50 different countries.

Promoted Accounts. Advertisers pay to have their branded account suggested to users who are likely to be interested in the account in the "Who to Follow" list, Twitter's account recommendation engine, on the Twitter home page. Promoted Accounts can be targeted by interest, geography, and gender, and are priced on a cost-per-follower basis, with advertisers paying only for new followers gained. Prices range from $.50 to $2.50.

Enhanced Profile Pages. Companies get their own banner and the ability to pin a tweet to the top of the company's timeline. The price reportedly ranges from $15,000 to $25,000.

Amplify. The Twitter Amplify program provides marketers with a real-time digital dashboard so they can see the resulting tweet activity about the show or the brand. Based on this information, marketers can send Promoted Tweets to users who tweeted about a show. They can alter the copy as well based on other information about the tweeters. For example, Jim Beam used Amplify in 2013 to promote its new Jim Beam Red Stag brand of premium bourbon. The intent was to increase brand awareness, purchase intent, and user engagement. The strength of Twitter, according to Jim Beam marketers, is that it allows the brand to be a part of a real-time conversation, as opposed to Facebook, which is better at reaching a mass audience but not at engaging consumers in real time. The power of social media, including Facebook, is finding consumer advocates who will speak on behalf of the brand.

Promoted Video. In August 2014, building on the Amplify program, Twitter announced a beta test of Promoted Video, which allows advertisers to distribute video on the Twitter platform. In 2015, Twitter began allowing advertisers to use Promoted Video to link directly to app installations and also added an ad purchasing feature for videos called "optimized action bidding" that enables marketers to customize ad purchases to improve return on investment.

Television Ad Retargeting. Millions of users tweet with their friends while watching television, and Twitter can follow the conversation to identify who is watching a particular show. Marketers displaying TV ads can retarget those ads or other messages to tweeters in real time to reinforce their marketing message. Advertisers with video content, like the National Basketball Association, insert in-tweet video clips, which are video replays. Advertisers can precede the video with an ad, or place an ad just below the video on screen. Companies can follow up with a Promoted Tweet.

Lead Generation Cards. Marketers can embed a "card" into business tweeters' standard Twitter messages. When users click on the message, a promotional offer appears and users are asked to sign up. Cards are different from display ads because they are used only by businesses who want to develop new leads, and they always include an offer, such as 50% off your next cup of coffee. This is a one-click process. The users' e-mail and Twitter account names are automatically obtained by Twitter and sent to marketers, who can then follow up with a tweet or an e-mail.

Table 7.6 summarizes these Twitter marketing tools.

Mobile Ads Because over 90% of Twitter users access Twitter on a mobile device, most of the above referenced marketing tools can be considered mobile ads tools. Mobile is also proving to be the primary driver of Twitter's business and the source of most

TABLE 7.6	TWITTER MARKETING TOOLS
TWITTER MARKETING TOOLS	DESCRIPTION
Promoted Tweets	Advertisers pay to have their tweets appear in users' search results and timelines. The tweets appear as "promoted," and the pricing is on a per-click basis, based on an auction run on the Twitter ad platform. Promoted Tweets can be both keyword- and geo-targeted. An "ad carousel" allows up to 12 ads to be shown in a single space, enabling users to swipe through the Promoted Tweets. Buy buttons embedded within Promoted Tweets enable users to purchase without leaving Twitter.
Promoted Trends	Advertisers pay to move their hashtags (# symbol used to mark keywords in a tweet) to the top of Twitter's Trends List. Otherwise, hashtags are found by the Twitter search engine, and only those that are organically popular make it to the Trends List.
Promoted Accounts	Advertisers pay to have their branded account suggested to users likely to be interested in the account in the "Who to Follow" list, Twitter's account recommendation engine, available on the Twitter home page. Promoted Accounts can be specifically targeted and are priced on a cost-per-follower basis.
Enhanced Profile Pages	Companies can get their own banner to display images and the ability to pin a tweet to the top of the company's timeline.
Amplify	A real-time digital dashboard connecting television commercials and tweet activity.
Promoted Video	Advertisers can use distribute videos on the Twitter platform and use Promoted Videos to link directly to app installlations.
TV Ad Retargeting	Tweeting viewers of TV shows with the same ads targeted at them on a show they are watching.
Lead Generation Card	Promotional offers that appear in users' Twitter timeline of messages with a coupon or other offer. Used for lead generation.
Mobile Ads	All of the above formats delivered on mobile devices, as well as mobile app install and app engagement ads.

of its revenue. In addition to all of the above formats, in April 2014, Twitter added mobile app install and app engagement ads, which have been lucrative formats for Facebook as well.

Starting a Twitter Marketing Campaign

If you're new to Twitter marketing, start simple and build on your follower base using experience as a guide for what works. A typical marketing campaign for Twitter may include the following elements:

- Establish a Twitter account. Start following others you are interested in or conversations that you might want to participate with # < topic >. Don't expect any followers at first. Your visibility rises as you follow others, who will begin to tweet back or retweet interesting content. Then start retweeting content you think the group would be interested in, and start encouraging ongoing conversations.

- Try a simple Promoted Tweet. Twitter has a very good online ad facility that will allow you to define an ad, establish the groups you would like to target, and understand the costs. You might start with a regional or metropolitan Promoted Tweet. Test various formats. You don't have to pay for Promoted Tweets unless someone clicks on the tweet, so it is up to you to make those clicks count. Direct users to your Web site and offer a coupon or discount.

- Promoted Trends can be very expensive—around $200,000. If your budget will allow, and your topic is of general interest to a large audience, you can try this tool. Geo-targeting is possible.

- TV ad retargeting is obviously a big business tool for media companies that have television content and television ads. Retargeting these to the Twitter community strengthens the overall brand image, and can direct people to the firm's Web site.

- Lead Generation Cards are something that small and medium-sized businesses can use. If you sell anything locally, from pizza to stationery, make up an offer and build a Lead Generation Card specifying the geo-location where your business is located.

As with Facebook, the objective is to establish your brand identity online and seek out engagement with users, not immediate sales. Encourage others to retweet your content and offers to their friends.

Table 7.7 describes some selected Twitter marketing campaigns.

TABLE 7.7	SELECTED TWITTER MARKETING CAMPAIGNS
COMPANY	MARKETING CAMPAIGN
Adidas	Used Twitter to allow followers to select elements that should be included in New York Fashion Week runway show.
Airbus	Used Twitter to provide details of the first A350 Airbus flight to a global audience, and targeted Promoted Tweets to those most likely to respond.
ESPN/Ford	Used embedded replays of football games in posts sent to Twitter users who have shown an interest in sports. Ads for Ford shown before the video roll.
Starbucks	Used both Promoted Tweets and Lead Generation Cards. Users only need to hit the Submit button and their personal information flows to Starbucks to sign them up for special offers or coupons.
LG Electronics	Used hashtags and Promoted Tweets to promote a treasure hunt and drive awareness of a new smartphone.
Porsche	Used hashtags and Promoted Tweets to enhance awareness of its new 911 sports car launch and support television, newspaper, and magazine campaigns.
Airbnb	The community marketplace for unique accommodations used Promoted Tweets to stimulate interest in a new sublet program with a $200 discount offer.
HubSpot	The online marketing firm used Promoted Accounts and Promoted Tweets to target B2B decision-makers in online marketing.
Lord & Taylor	The luxury goods retail chain used Twitter to promote a giveaway of Rihanna tickets at one of its store locations, and in the process, drive traffic to its stores.

TABLE 7.8	MEASURING TWITTER MARKETING RESULTS
SOCIAL MARKETING PROCESS	**MEASUREMENT**
Fan acquisition (impressions)	The number of people exposed to your Promoted Tweets, Promoted Trends, etc. (impressions). The number of followers and monthly growth.
Engagement (conversation rate)	The number of comments, responses to, and retweets of, your tweets. The number of views of brand page content. The number of users that responded to games, contests, and coupons (participation). The number of minutes on average that followers stay on your page (duration).
Amplification (reach)	The rate at which fans retweet or otherwise share your tweets.
Community	The monthly interaction rate (i.e., the monthly total of comments and responses to, and retweets of, your content). The average monthly onsite minutes for all followers. The ratio of positive to negative tweets.
Brand Strength/Sales	The number of leads generated (people who sign up for news or content). Visitor/lead rate: the number of visitors that become leads to compare campaigns. The percentage (or revenue) of your online sales generated by Twitter links compared to other platforms, such as e-mail, search engines, and display ads. The percentage of Twitter-sourced customer purchases compared to other sources of customers (conversion ratio).

Measuring Twitter Marketing Results

Measuring the results of Twitter marketing is similar to measuring the results of Facebook and other social marketing platforms, with some minor changes to account for the unique qualities of Twitter. **Table 7.8** describes some basic ways to measure the results of a Twitter marketing campaign.

Tools provided by Twitter include a dashboard that provides real-time information on impressions, retweets, clicks, replies, and follows for Promoted Tweets and Promoted Accounts. Twitter's Timeline activity dashboard provides data on how every tweet performs in terms of mentions, follows, and reach. Twitter's Followers dashboard enables marketers to track the growth of the follower base, as well as information about their interests, geography, and engagement.

Third-party tools include TweetDeck, which enables you to track mentions, people, and keywords; Twitalyzer, which provides one-click access to Twitter metrics that analyze followers, mentions, retweets, influencers, and their locations; and Back-Tweets, which allows you to search through a tweet archive for URLs sent via Twitter.

PINTEREST MARKETING

Pinterest is the social network site that provides users with an online board to which they can "pin" interesting pictures (see also the Chapter 1 closing case study, *Pinterest: A Picture Is Worth a Thousand Words*). The success of Pinterest is based in part on a shift in consumer behavior enabled by new technologies: people talk about brands using pictures rather than words. Large numbers of Web users are pinning and insta-gramming about their lives using pictures.

You can think of Pinterest as a highly interactive and social online magazine or "zine." One difference, of course, is that users (including business firms) contribute all the photos. The site currently has 36 categories of boards from gifts, animals, art, cars, and motorcycles to crafts, food, and men's and women's fashion. Users can pin to these boards, create their own boards, and follow other pinners and boards as well. Users have created millions of boards. Firms can create their own brand boards and product pins. See the opening case in Chapter 1 for more information on Pinterest.

Users who pin photos can alert Facebook and Twitter friends and followers who can access their pictures and boards on Pinterest. Pinned photos and photo boards are available to all Pinterest users at this time, although many marketers are pushing Pinterest to develop private boards that can allow marketers to require registration (customer information) as a condition of access to content. But the point of Pinterest, according to its cofounder Ben Silberman, is to share beautiful, interesting photos and graphics as widely as possible across the Web. Everyone can repin images they like to their own boards as well. Pinterest is therefore one of the largest image sharing sites on the Internet.

Pinterest is also one of the fastest growing sites in Web history. In 2010, Pinterest had 10,000 users in the United States, then 12 million by the end of 2011, and 100 million by 2015. Today, about 18% of online adults in the United States use Pinterest. Pinterest's visitors are overwhelmingly female: over 80% are women, but users cover a broad demographic range from grandparents to teenagers, with the largest segment (27%) between 25 and 34. The hope for marketers, and Pinterest, is that its "refer-ral capacity" (the ability to direct users to retail Web sites where they can purchase something) will rapidly increase as its audience grows and intensity of use grows.

One way to look at the millions of pictures on Pinterest is as disguised display ads—click, and off you go to a brand Web site for a purchase. Pinterest pins are much better than display ads because they are unobtrusive, and because they don't look like display ads. Instead, they look like sumptuous catalog or magazine photos. In the future, analysts believe, Pinterest could charge an affiliate fee for any subsequent purchases. Pinterest could also charge businesses for creating brand sites or boards, which currently are free.

Basic Pinterest Features

Marketing on Pinterest requires that you understand the basic features and capa-bilities of Pinterest. While all users of Pinterest understand how to pin photos to an online scrapbook, many other capabilities are less well understood or used. **Table 7.9** provides a list of Pinterest features.

TABLE 7.9	PINTEREST FEATURES
FEATURE	DESCRIPTION
Pins	Used to post a photo to a Pinterest board.
Board	An online scrapbook where photos are organized by the user.
Repins	The ability to pin the photos of other users to your own boards, and to share with your friends.
Hashtags and keywords	Use <#hashtags> in the description of your pins, e.g., #style, #cars, #sports cars. Use keywords people are likely to use when searching for specific content.
Share	Sharing your pinned photos with friends. Options: Twitter, Facebook, e-mail, embed.
Image Hover	A widget you can add to your browser. When your mouse hovers over an online image, the Pin It button pops up and you can pin the photo automatically to your Pinterest boards.
Embed	Code that allows you to embed your pinned photos into your blog automatically.
Me+ Contributors	Allows others to contribute to your boards (only if they are already a follower of yours).
Follow	Users can choose to follow other pinners and boards and receive e-mail updates.
Number of Pins and Followers	A count of the number of pins and the number of followers visible at the top of the brand page.
Link to URL; Link to pinner	Click on the URL of the company who pinned a photo; click on a link to the person who pinned a photo.
Price display	Hover over a product and a display pops up with the price and model information.
Integration with Facebook and Twitter	Login from Facebook, Twitter, and other social sites. Your personal profile (but not your photo) information from Facebook comes over to Pinterest; your pins go onto your Facebook Timeline. Twitter and Pinterest profile pages are also integrated.
Pin It browser button (bookmarklet)	Browsers' red Pin It button. Users drag the button onto their browser screen, allowing them to instantly pin photos they see on the Web.
Apps	Smartphone and tablet apps that allow users to pin photos, browse pins and boards, get ideas while shopping, and display pins.
Pinterest widget	Pin It button on your brand page that makes it easy for people to pin images from your site.

Pinterest Marketing Tools

Pinterest marketing tools are still in an early stage of development. The company is adding new tools every month as Pinterest begins the journey towards monetizing its large user audience. In 2014, Pinterest, following in Facebook's and Twitter's footsteps, took the official leap into paid advertising. It launched Promoted Pins with a select group of national brands and also announced a trial of a Do It Yourself version of Promoted Pins for small and medium-sized businesses, to be paid for on a cost per click basis, similar to the Google AdWords platform. Promoted Pins will appear in

TABLE 7.10	PINTEREST MARKETING TOOLS
MARKETING TOOL	DESCRIPTION
Promoted Pins	A way to promote pins to a targeted audience, and pay for click through to your Web site.
Buyable Pins/Shop Our Picks	Buyable Pins allow users to purchase product featured in pin without leaving Pinterest. Shop our Picks feature highlights hand-picked items for users to consider purchasing.
Add Pin It or Follow button to your Web site (Pinterest widget)	Makes it easy for visitors to pin photos from your Web site, and be notified when you post new photos to your site.
Pin as display ad	The Pinned photo acts as a display ad by directing users back to a firm's Web site.
Create theme-based boards to reflect your brand messaging	Pinterest recommends that business boards not be strictly sales-oriented, but lifestyle-oriented instead.
Brand page	A new Pinterest feature that allows companies to create a corporate brand page. In the past, Pinterest did not distinguish between a personal page and a corporate brand page.
URL Link to stores	Makes it easier for consumers to click through links on brand pages and product pins so they can reliably purchase what they see. The goal is to integrate photos of inventory with Pinterest to make items more easily tracked. What this means is retailers can see a definite link between a sale and a photo they pinned. Currently, after thousands of repins, clicking on the URL sometimes leads to a broken link.
Retail brand Pins (Product Pin; Enhanced Pin)	A new kind of pin for food, retail, and movies. Click on a Retail Pin and you will see the price and where to buy it. Food Pins reveal recipes.
Integration with other social sites	Ask your Facebook fans and Twitter followers to pin photos of your products and tag you. Repin these photos to your brand page on Pinterest. Give a shout-out to your loyal users and fans to show potential customers how much current users like using your product.
Network with users, followers, and others	As with Facebook and Twitter, comment, mention, and communicate with others using Pinterest. Participate in the community and you will become better known, and learn more about potential customers and what they believe and to what they aspire.

search results and category feeds. In 2015, Pinterest added Buyable Pins and a Shop Our Picks feature, allowing users to buy products directly on the Pinterest site, and pay with Apple Pay. The Shop our Picks feature highlights hand-picked items for users to consider purchasing.

Table 7.10 identifies and describes some of the primary Pinterest marketing tools.

For instance, Lands' End has several brand pages on Pinterest, one of which is Lands' End Canvas. Search for Lands' End Canvas and it takes you to the page that Lands' End Canvas created and where Lands' End has pinned some of its catalog photos. On this brand page, only Lands' End Canvas products are pinned, and the company is identified. You can see the number of people who have pinned these photos elsewhere, and the total number of others who follow this line of clothing and have posted their own photos. When you click on a photo, you get a larger version of the photo (sometimes called a photo landing page), and the chance to link to the Web site (canvas.landsend.com) where you can purchase the product and find similar ones. You will also see on this photo landing page a picture of the person who pinned the photo, other boards where it was pinned, and recommendations for related photos and products in a section titled "People who pinned this also pinned ...."

Table 7.11 provides a brief description of Pinterest marketing campaigns of selected retailers.

Starting a Pinterest Marketing Campaign

Before leaping into a Pinterest campaign, ask yourself some questions about your products and services, and then identify some strategic objectives for your Pinterest presence. First, sketch out a vision of what you hope to accomplish with a Pinterest presence. Are you an established brand trying to strengthen your brand? Are you the new kid on the block that no one knows and you want to start a marketing campaign? Are your products visual and can your brand be expressed in a set of pictures? Most products have a visual component, some more compelling than others. Today, most Pinterest marketing campaigns involve clothing, jewelry, home furnishings, food, and art/crafts. If your product is hip implants, for instance, it might be hard to portray your products to likely consumers (but not impossible if you are creative). Is the consumer accustomed to seeing the products in your industry expressed through photos? Food is increasingly a visual experience with the growth of food magazines and Web sites.

Next, consider the target demographic for your products and services, and compare it to the Pinterest demographic. Currently, Pinterest visitors are over 80% women, and while this might change over time, your offerings will have to be attractive to women. Do your products or services appeal to this demographic?

Think about strategy in your marketspace. What are your competitors doing? Are they on Pinterest? Do they have an effective presence? What types of people follow

TABLE 7.11	SELECTED PINTEREST MARKETING CAMPAIGNS
COMPANY	CAMPAIGN
Bank of America	Used to launch its Better Money Habits program aimed at Millennials using boards for different life moments.
Caribou	To promote its newest coffee, Real Inspiration Blend, Caribou asked its followers for help in designing the taste of the new coffee using a hashtag and pictures, a special interest Pinboard, and a video showing how the coffee was made.
Whole Foods	Natural and organic food stores with 57 boards, over 5,300 pins, and over 270,000 followers.
West Elm	Home furnishing company emphasizing simple and elegant designs. 70 boards, over 13,000 Pins, and over 333,000 followers.
Bergdorf Goodman	New York's Fifth Avenue luxury goods department store. 34 boards, over 5,500 pins, and 88,000 followers.
Lands' End	A clothing retailer that started as a mail order business and is now a successful multi-channel retailer of outerwear, footwear, home furnishings, and apparel. 38 boards, 2,900 pins, and almost 13,000 followers.
Etsy	Online-only Web site that sells handmade craft objects, vintage items, and arts and crafts supplies. Provides a platform for small firms to sell their goods on their own storefronts. 120 boards, about 14,000 pins, over 700,000 followers. Arts and Crafts Pinterest boards show both its products and how to use them in everyday life. The emphasis is on attaining a life style, and humanizing the Etsy products to form a deeper bond with their customers.

your competitors and what are the users pinning? How many followers, re-pinners, brand pages, and product pins are there? Because photos are central to a Pinterest presence, where will the photos for your brand pages come from? Are you, or a member of your team, a skilled photographer? You can pin photos from all over the Web, and from other Pinterest boards, but then you're just sharing content, not creating unique and unusual content.

Pinterest is an adjunct to a fully developed marketing plan, both online and offline. You will want to integrate your social and online marketing efforts with a Facebook and Twitter presence. You can share photos from your Web site, and send Web photos to your brand pages. The same photos can be used on your Facebook page and on Twitter. Your customers will be using all these platforms and you will have to follow them to keep up.

Once you have envisioned your Pinterest campaign and developed a marketing plan, you can start implementing your plan. In order to implement your Pinterest plan, you should have a traditional Web site where your products are displayed (a catalog) and can be purchased. Second, you should also have a Facebook brand page to develop followers and a method for informing your followers of new Pins. Once these are in place, you can begin your Pinterest campaign:

- Create a Pinterest brand page and start pinning photos of your products. Grow, and change your pins and board regularly. Be sure your photos are the same quality level or higher than those of your competitors. If necessary, hire a skilled photographer. Brand pages generally do not allow followers to pin photos but only to follow and comment. The idea here is to control the content of your brand page, and develop other boards where followers can pin pictures.

- Improve the quality of your photos. Computer screens limit the resolution that can be displayed to users, but the lighting, composition, and color in your pinned photos are under your control.

- Use URL links and keywords. Make sure your pins have a URL link to your store, or to vendor stores, so followers can easily buy as well as "see." Be sure to use keywords and hashtags to classify each of your photos so they show up in Pinterest searches. Remember, Pinterest cannot "see" a photo or understand its content. It only "knows" the content based on your tags.

- Create a Pinterest product pin. If you are in the food, retail, or movie distribution business, product pins are worth a try if you have a popular product at an attractive price, or if you want to use a specific product as a loss-leader to motivate people to come to your Web site (where you can expose them to your entire catalog of products).

- Use Pin It buttons. Add a Pin It button to your Web site and Facebook page to encourage fans and followers to pin your photos to their own boards, and to recommend them to friends.

- Create multiple theme-based life style boards. Develop several theme-based boards that emphasize life styles or fashions. Pinterest is not just, or even primarily, a selling site. It is also an entertainment and branding site. You want followers to adore your photos. On theme-based boards you will want others besides yourself to be able to pin.

- Use your Facebook and Twitter networks. Start using your Facebook and Twitter networks by adding a Pin It button to Facebook (also called a Pinterest tab), and start sharing your pinned photos with your followers.

- Integrate with Facebook and Twitter. Create Facebook and Twitter logins so that users can go to your pins and boards without leaving the Facebook and Twitter sites.

- Be social. Join the conversation. It's all about being social. Follow other pinners and boards and ask to receive e-mail and Facebook updates.

Measuring Pinterest Marketing Results

Because Pinterest is just beginning to introduce and test its marketing tools, learning how to measure the results of a Pinterest marketing campaign is also in the early stages. Nevertheless, like any social marketing platform, the key dimensions to measure are fan (follower) acquisition, engagement, amplification, community, and sales. **Table 7.12** describes some basic ways to measure the results of a Pinterest marketing campaign.

Pinterest provides a built-in Web Analytics service that offers insights into how people are interacting with pins that originate from their Web sites. There are several

TABLE 7.12	MEASURING PINTEREST MARKETING RESULTS
SOCIAL MARKETING PROCESS	**MEASUREMENT**
Fan acquisition (impressions)	The number of people exposed to your pins.
	The number of followers and the rate of growth.
	The number of people that have pinned your product photos.
	The percentage of those exposed to your pins who also pin them to their own or other boards.
Engagement (conversation rate)	The number of posts, comments, and responses to your brand or pins on Pinterest.
	The number of users who are responding to games, contests, and coupons (participation).
	The number of minutes on average fans stay on your brand or product pages (duration).
	The rate of pins per post or other content (applause rate).
Amplification	The rate at which fans share your pinned photos by sharing or repinning to their own or others' boards.
Community	The monthly interaction rate with your content (i.e., the monthly total of pins, comments, and actions on your Pinterest brand page).
	The average monthly onsite minutes for all fans.
	The ratio of positive to negative comments.
Brand Strength/Sales	The percentage of your online sales that are generated by Pinterest links (referrals) compared to other platforms, such as e-mail, search engines, and display ads.
	The percentage of Pinterest-sourced customer purchases, compared to other sources of customers (conversion ratio).
	The conversion ratio for users receiving repinned photos (friends of followers).

firms that will help produce the metrics referred to in Table 7.12. For instance, Curalate is an online service to measure the impact of Pinterest and other visual social media. It listens and measures visual conversations by seeing what pictures users pin and repin, and also analyzes the colors in the picture. Curalate currently has over 450 brands using its platform.

MARKETING ON OTHER SOCIAL NETWORKS

There are a great many social networks where products and services can be marketed, the largest of which include Instagram and LinkedIn. Instagram is a visual social network: users and advertisers post photos and videos to their friends, potential customers, and the public at large. Instagram (owned by Facebook) has 400 million users worldwide, 77 million of whom are in the United States. Instagram is one of the fastest growing social networks, growing at 20% annually in 2015, compared to only 3% for Facebook. However, its growth is predicted to slow down considerably in the next four years. Instagram is very popular with Millennials (18- to 34-year-olds). In 2015, analysts estimate Instagram will generate around $500 million in mobile ad revenues, increasing to $2.39 billion by 2017 (eMarketer, Inc., 2015d).

As with other social networks, users create a profile. There is a Feed that provides a listing of photos and videos (up to 15 seconds long) posted by friends or advertisers. Using a feature called Direct, users can send photos and videos to specific people. Using Explore, users can search for public profiles and photos. Instagram also has a powerful photo editing suite called Layout.

Similar to Facebook, advertisers have brand profiles and run marketing campaigns by sending posts to users' Feeds. Instagram ad campaigns consist of display ads and video ads of exceptional quality, similar to a printed magazine. Ads can link to advertiser's Web sites and now can include a Buy button. For brands that want to drive mass awareness around premieres, product launches, and key moments, Instagram developed what it calls its Marquee ad product, which reaches millions of people. Marquee ads generally last a single day, promise to deliver a guaranteed number of impressions, and can be posted several times during the day to catch different audiences (eMarketer, Inc., 2015e).

LinkedIn, while generating far less average engagement, nevertheless attracts a highly educated, professional, and managerial audience that is intensively engaged in careers and employment. LinkedIn is a social network focused on professional networking, where users post their resumes, and potential employers hunt for new hires. See the opening case in Chapter 11 for more information on LinkedIn. LinkedIn makes money by charging corporations for corporate brand pages, job ads, and access to its database of users. Users also pay for premium subscriptions called Talent (for employers) and JobSeeker (for individuals). In 2014, LinkedIn generated $2.2 billion in revenue, a 46% leap from 2013 (LinkedIn, 2015).

As with other social networks, users build a profile, but in this case, sharing their professional background, degrees, employment, and skill set. There is a Feed that provides a listing of posts from colleagues and friends, and display ad posts from firms. Display ads are on the right. Users can post updates, send News Signals to learn about contacts that are currently actively using the site, place tags on connections, use the Get Introduced feature to arrange an introduction to a friend of friend, post recommendations, and join groups relevant to their interests.

The primary contribution of LinkedIn is to develop personal brands for professional managers, and to create a marketplace where employers can contact suitable candidates. This is not a site to sell products and services, at least not openly. Advertisers tend to place branding ads in the left margins of the home pages, and are not soliciting sales.

THE DOWNSIDE OF SOCIAL MARKETING

Social marketing is not without its disadvantages. One problem is that brands lose a substantial amount of control over where their ads appear in terms of other content and what people say about their brands on social sites. Ads placed on Facebook according to an algorithm can be placed near content that does not represent the values of the brand. This is not peculiar to social marketing, as advertising using Google's advertising platform faces the same problem. This is very different, however, from TV ads where brands maintain near complete control. Social sites are unique in that disgruntled consumers, or just malicious people, can post material that is inaccurate and/or embarrassing (Vega and Kaufman, 2013).

The *Insight on Society* case, *Marketing to Children of the Web in the Age of Social Networks,* illustrates some additional issues with respect to social marketing.

7.3 MOBILE MARKETING

Although still in an early stage, mobile marketing involves the use of mobile devices such as smartphones and tablet computers to display banner ads, rich media, video, games, e-mail, text messaging, in-store messaging, QuickResponse (QR) codes, and couponing. Mobile is now a required part of the standard marketing budget. Mobile devices represent a radical departure from previous marketing technologies simply because the devices integrate so many human and consumer activities from telephoning or texting friends, to listening to music, watching videos, tracking location, and shopping. The more mobile devices can do, the more people rely on them in daily life. More than 258 million Americans are now using mobile phones, while 190 million of these use smartphones. 159 million Americans also use tablet computers (eMarketer, Inc., 2015f, 2015g). One report found that people look at their mobile devices at least 40 times a day. Most mobile phone users keep their phone within arm's length 24 hours a day. For many, it's the first thing they check in the morning, the last thing they check at night, and the first tool to use when there's a question of where to go, what to do, and where to meet up.

OVERVIEW: M-COMMERCE TODAY

It's a short number of steps from owning a smartphone or tablet, to searching for products and services, browsing, and then purchasing. The rate of growth of m-commerce has skyrocketed over the last several years, growing at 30% annually, but is expected to

INSIGHT ON SOCIETY

MARKETING TO CHILDREN OF THE WEB IN THE AGE OF SOCIAL NETWORKS

In the United States, children influence over $1 trillion in overall family spending. Not surprisingly, marketers are extremely interested in advertising aimed at children.

Today, 93% of all 5- to 15-year-olds use the Internet. Social and mobile marketing provides advertisers with an entirely new arsenal to influence children. Using custom banner ads, product characters, videos, games, virtual worlds, and surveys, marketers are both influencing behaviors and gathering valuable data. A children's digital culture has been created with built-in avenues to the psyche of young minds—in some cases, minds that are so young they are unlikely to know when they are being marketed to and when they are being given misleading or even harmful information.

Marketers have moved aggressively to use social networks and viral marketing to get kids hooked on brands early in life. For instance, Red Bull does little TV advertising and instead uses online contests, games, and apps.

While such moves may be savvy marketing, are they ethical? Some people say no. Research has shown that young children cannot understand the potential effects of revealing their personal information; neither can they distinguish between substantive material on Web sites and the advertisements surrounding it. Experts argue that since children don't understand persuasive intent until they are eight or nine years old, it is unethical to advertise to them before they can distinguish between advertising and the real world. Others believe that fair advertising is an important and necessary part of the maturation process for future adults in today's society.

In 1998, Congress passed the Children's Online Privacy Protection Act (COPPA) after the FTC discovered that 80% of Web sites were collecting personal information from children, but only 1% required their parents' permission. Under COPPA, companies must post a privacy policy on their Web sites, detailing exactly how they collect information from consumers, how they'll use it, and the degrees to which they'll protect consumer privacy. Companies are not permitted to use personal information collected from children under 13 years of age without the prior, verifiable consent of parents.

Since the law took effect, the FTC has obtained a number of settlements and fined a number of companies for violations of COPPA. For instance, Disney's Playdom was fined $3 million, the largest penalty to date, for collecting and disclosing children's information without parental approval.

In 2011, the FTC announced its first-ever COPPA enforcement action involving mobile apps. W3 Innovations was fined $50,000 for collecting personal information such as e-mail addresses from children in connection with numerous apps. Shortly thereafter, in response to the increase in the use of mobile devices by children, the FTC announced revisions to its COPPA regulations in an attempt to keep pace with emerging technology, which finally took effect in July 2013. The revisions expanded the definition of personal information to include a child's location, along with any personal data collected through the use of cookies for the purpose of targeted advertising, and require that Web sites that collect a child's information ensure that they can protect it, hold on to it for only as long as reasonably necessary, and thereafter delete the information. If firms want to use the personal information of children for internal uses only, the FTC requires an e-mail from the parent plus one other form of verification (such as a credit card or phone number). Firms seeking to sell personal information about children are also required to use an additional means of verification, such as a print-and-send consent form, credit card transaction, a toll-free number or video conference staffed by trained personnel, or verification of a parent's identity by checking a form of government-issued identification. Privacy groups applauded the effort, but whether the new regulations have affected the way companies do business is not yet clear, and enforcement is likely to continue to be an issue. For example, in 2014, the FTC fined Snapchat for COPPA violations. Snapchat had falsely claimed that its messages were deleted forever after they were sent and also collected users' contact information without their consent, despite the fact that many of its users were younger than 12 years old. In addition to the fine, Snapchat was required to implement a comprehensive privacy program and will be monitored for 20 years.

Major technology companies have also recently been fined and required to adjust their policies with regard to children signing up for their services. Google settled with the FTC in 2014 and agreed to refund $19 million worth of in-app purchases that were made unwittingly by children. Apple had also agreed to refund $32.5 million in similar purchases earlier in the year, and Amazon is likely to follow suit shortly despite its claim that parents are to blame for these purchases. Yelp was hit with a $450,000 fine despite not having much vested interest in collecting children's information, and even game developers like TinyCo have fallen into the FTC crosshairs, incurring a $300,000 fine for violating children's privacy. The question is whether these FTC fines will be enough to discourage companies from gathering valuable data on future consumers from such a young age. Yelp and TinyCo released statements suggesting their products were now fully COPPA-compliant, but the giants might not budge so easily. In 2015, Google released YouTube Kids, a child-friendly version of YouTube, but consumer advocates found that it still included inappropriate advertising and explicit content.

In 2015, the Senate launched a bipartisan effort to enact amendments to COPPA, which would include children aged 13 to 15 as well as the requirement of an "eraser button" that allows parents or children to permanently erase personal information online for any site collecting information. However, thus far, the bill has not been passed. The FTC has also toughened its policies toward information gathering, forcing software and app makers to reconsider the inclusion of features that allow for data transfer between devices. App developers will also be required to verify parental consent using a credit or debit card number whether or not the app offers items for purchase.

SOURCES: "Significant Amendments to COPPA Proposed in Do Not Track Kids Act," by Ronald London and John Seiver, Jdsupra.com, June 22, 2015; "Following FTC Complaints, Senator Nelson Asks Google for Answers on YouTube Kids App Content," by Sarah Perez, Techcrunch.com, June 17, 2015; "Mapping the Regulations Protecting Children's Privacy Online," by Josh Yaker, Techcrunch.com, June 4, 2015; "FTC Fines Tech Giants for Violating Kids' Privacy," by Bill Snyder, Cio.com, September 18, 2014; "Games Developer TinyCo Fined for Illegally Collecting Children's Data," by Dominic Rushe, *The Guardian*, September 18, 2014; "Amazon Blames Parents for Kids' App Store Purchases," by Jonathan Randles, Law360.com, September 9, 2014; "Google to Refund $19 Million of Children's In-App Purchases," Mashable.com, September 4, 2014; "Round Two for Snapchat: Agreement with the Maryland Attorney General Settling Claims of Consumer Deception and COPPA Violations," by Julia M. Siripurapu, Lexology.com, June 19, 2014; "FTC Changes Privacy Guidelines for Developers of Kids' Apps," by Hayley Tsukayama, Washington Post, July 16, 2014; "FTC to Better Define New COPPA 'Actual Knowledge' Standards," by John Eggerton, Broadcastingcable.com, July 8, 2013; "Child Privacy Online: FTC Updates COPPA Rules," by Mathew Schwartz, Informationweek.com, July 5, 2013; "Revised Children's Online Privacy Protection Rule Goes Into Effect Today," FTC.gov, July 1, 2013; "The Ripple Effects of Stricter Privacy Rules for Kids," by Bryon Acohido, *USA Today*, July 1, 2013; "FTC Announces First-Ever COPPA Enforcement Action Against Mobile Apps," by David Silverman, Privsecblog.com, August 17, 2011; "FTC Fine on App Developer Prompts Calls for Updated Privacy Policies," by Josh Smith, *National Journal*, August 15, 2011; "FTC: Disney's Playdom Violated Child Protection Act," by Don Reisinger, News.cnet.com, May 13, 2011.

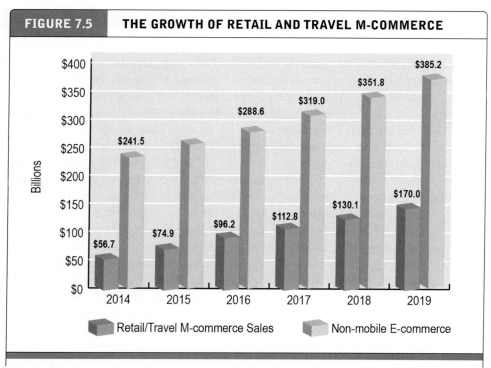

FIGURE 7.5 — THE GROWTH OF RETAIL AND TRAVEL M-COMMERCE

M-commerce in the retail and travel industries is expected to grow to almost $250 billion by 2019.
SOURCE: Based on data from eMarketer, Inc., 2015h, 2015i, 2015j, 2015k.

slow down to 15% annual growth by 2019. Analysts estimate that by 2019, m-commerce will account for about one-third of all e-commerce in the retail and travel industries. **Figure 7.5** illustrates the expected growth of mobile and non-mobile commerce in the retail and travel industries to 2019.

Initially, m-commerce was focused primarily on digital goods, such as music, videos, games, and e-books. Today, however, traditional retail products and travel services are the source of much of the growth in m-commerce. **Figure 7.6** lists the top companies in terms of mobile retail sales in 2014. Not surprisingly, the giant is Amazon, with an expected $16.8 billion in sales through its mobile Web site and Amazon app. Note that the chart does not include eBay, which facilitated $34 billion in m-commerce transactions, nor Apple or Google Play, where most purchases are for digital content.

Increasingly, consumers are using their mobile devices to search for people, places, and things—like restaurants and deals on products they saw in a retail store. The rapid switch of consumers from desktop platforms to mobile devices is driving a surge in mobile marketing expenditures. Because search is so important for directing consumers to purchase situations, the mobile search advertising market is very important for search engines like Google and Bing. Desktop search revenues are slowing for both. Google's mobile ad business is growing rapidly, but the prices it can charge for mobile ads are far less than for desktop computer ads. The challenge facing Google

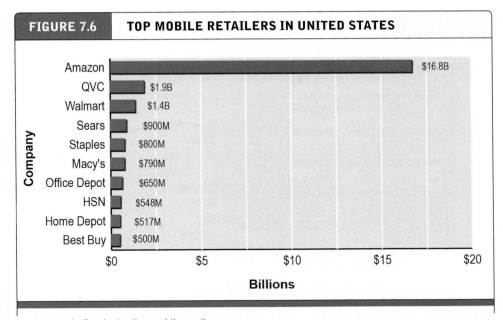

FIGURE 7.6	TOP MOBILE RETAILERS IN UNITED STATES

Amazon is, by far, the leading mobile retailer.

SOURCE: Based on data from Internet Retailer, 2014.

and other mobile marketing firms is how to get more consumers to click on mobile ads, and how to charge marketers more for each click. And the answer lies with the consumer who decides what and when to click.

How People Actually Use Mobile Devices

If you plan a mobile marketing campaign, it's important to understand how people actually use their mobile devices (which may be different from what you do or think others do). For instance, most of us think people use their mobile devices on the go, but in fact, according to one of the very few studies of actual mobile behavior, almost 70% of all mobile minutes actually occur in the home. We know people spend 5.5 hours with digital media on average daily, and nearly three of these hours is spent using mobile devices—smartphones and tablets (eMarketer, Inc., 2015x) What are they doing in these three hours, and on what device?

Recent data show that entertainment, not shopping or buying, is the primary focus (at least in terms of time) for mobile device users. Of the three hours (180 minutes) a day that people are spending using their mobile devices, 27 minutes (15%) is spent on social networks. Smartphones are more popular for this social activity (18 minutes) versus tablets (9 minutes). Watching video accounts for 26 minutes (14%), of which 14 minutes is spent on tablets versus 12 minutes on smartphones. A whopping 44 minutes (24%) is spent listening to music, primarily streaming music services. We have to assume this is mostly on smartphones. Hence, nearly 40% of mobile device use is for entertainment (music and video), with social networks consuming another 15% (eMarketer, Inc., 2015x). Where else does the time go? A recent survey by Pew

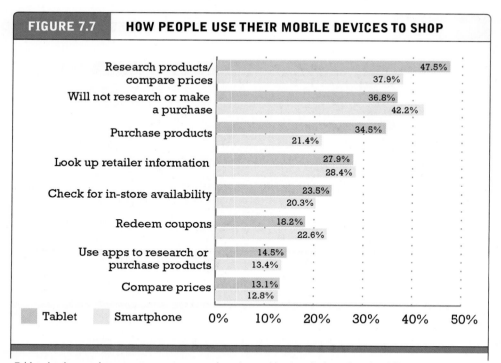

FIGURE 7.7 | **HOW PEOPLE USE THEIR MOBILE DEVICES TO SHOP**

Tablets lead smartphones as an m-commerce shopping and buying platform, but this difference may disappear over time as better tools are developed for smartphones.

Source: Based on data from eMarketer, Inc., 2015y.

Research Center described the broad range of activities that mobile users accomplish on their mobile devices when they are not entertaining themselves or socializing. People use the mobile devices for pretty much the same activities as they do their desktop computers, from getting information, to banking, and looking for places to live. Unfortunately, this survey did not include data on shopping and purchasing behavior, and did not include information on time spent with the activity.

However, a recent National Federation of Retailers survey provides insight into how consumers intend to use their mobile devices and which ones—tablet or smartphone—in the 2015 holiday shopping season (**Figure 7.7**). Researching products and comparing prices tops the list, with tablets (47%) leading smartphones (37%) as a vehicle for purchase. However, a very large percentage (35%–40%) do not plan to use either a tablet or a smartphone for shopping or buying at all. Only around one-third of tablet users and less than 25% of smartphone users plan to purchase anything with their tablets or smartphones.

From this research, we can conclude that, at least in 2015, mobile devices are still primarily used for entertainment, socializing, and communicating, and far less time is spent using them for shopping or buying. None of these patterns are permanent, however, and as mobile payment systems and smartphone screen resolution improves, they may become better shopping and buying platforms. The mobile platform has changed over the past few years, and now there are almost as many tablet users as

FIGURE 7.8	**RETAIL M-COMMERCE REVENUES BY DEVICE**

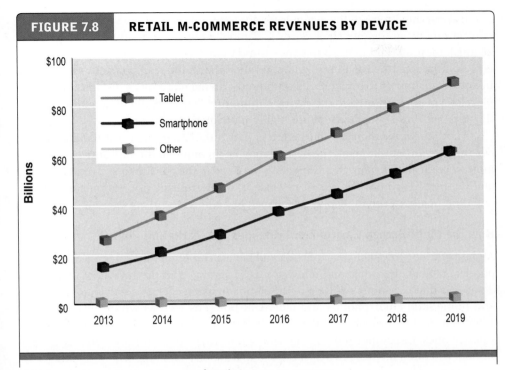

Tablet computers are the largest source of retail m-commerce revenues.
SOURCE: Based on data from eMarketer, Inc., 2015j.

smartphone users in the United States: 158 million Americans use tablets, almost 50% of the U.S. population. Tablets, with their larger screens, are the fastest growing and largest source of m-commerce revenues (**Figure 7.8**).

In-App Experiences and In-App Ads

You may think that using a browser to access the Web on your smartphone is a typical mobile activity. In reality, however, mobile users spend over 71% of their smartphone time using apps and 44% of their total digital time is spent using apps. On average, users use only about 26 apps a month. Over 80% of all app time is spent on a user's top three apps (comScore, 2015c). There may be millions of apps on the iOS and Android cloud servers, but just a handful are actually generating sufficient user traffic to be of interest to general advertisers. More than 50% of users' time is spent on social networks (29%), radio (15%), and games (11%). Facebook (and its related properties like Messenger) is the top app both in audience size and share of time spent. Other top 25 apps in terms of unique visitors include those from Google (YouTube, Google Play, Google Search, Google Maps, Gmail, and Google+), Instagram, Apple Music, Pandora Radio, Yahoo (Stocks, Weather, and Mail), Twitter, Netflix, Snapchat, and Pinterest. Only two retail-oriented apps are in the top 25: Amazon Mobile and eBay (comScore, 2015c).

The implications for marketers are quite clear: if consumers are primarily using apps rather than browsing the Web on their mobile devices, marketers need to place ads in apps where most of the action is for attracting consumers, and that means social, entertainment, and game sites. Second, if mobile consumers only use, on average, 26 apps, then marketers need to concentrate their marketing in these popular apps, let's say, the top 100. Niche marketers, on the other hand, can concentrate their ads in apps that support that niche. A distributor of diving equipment, for instance, could place ads in apps devoted to the diving community. There may not be many users of the app, but those who do use it are highly motivated on the topic.

Another implication for marketers is that rather than focus on mobile display ads that are difficult to read, the best ad may be an app that directly serves customer interest or an ad in an app that is precisely targeted to the consumer's current activities and interests. For instance, ads in newsfeeds, or pre-roll ads prior to music or video, will do much better than display ads placed elsewhere.

How the Multi-Screen Environment Changes the Marketing Funnel

Along with the growth of smartphones and tablets comes a multi-screen world: smartphones, tablets, desktops, and television. The reality, and the future, of computing devices is that consumers will be multi-platform: using desktops and laptops at work and home, and smartphones and tablets at home as well as when moving about. Television will be available all the time, both at home and on the go via tablets and smartphones. Consumer purchasing behavior changes in a multi-screen world. Consumers will often be using two or more screens at once, tweeting when watching a TV show, or moving seamlessly from a TV ad, to a mobile search for more information, to a later tablet purchase screen. Several research studies have found that 90% of multi-device users switch among screens to complete tasks, for instance, viewing an ad on TV, searching on a smartphone for the product, and then purchasing it with a tablet. Consumers move seamlessly among devices, either sequentially or simultaneously. Also, the more screens people use, the more shopping and purchasing they do. One conclusion is that the more screens consumers have, the more consumer touchpoints or marketing opportunities exist (Google, Inc., 2012).

The implications of the multi-device platform, or screen diversity environment, are that marketing needs to be designed for whatever device the consumer is using, and consistent branding across platforms will be important. Screen diversity means that one ad size, for instance, will not fit all situations, and that branding images will need to be adjusted automatically based on the device the consumer is using. From a design perspective, graphics and creative elements will appear differently depending on the screen. This is called responsive design or responsive creative design. Responsive design is a Web design process that allows your marketing content to resize, reformat, and reorganize itself so that it looks good on any screen. You can see responsive design in action if you look at any portal on a desktop, and then compare the screen to that same portal viewed on a smartphone or tablet. You are likely to find there are three versions of the screen, one for each platform (IAB, 2012). The requirement to find customers on multiple screens can add considerably to the cost of marketing online. Companies may find that they need to develop a presence and market not only on Web sites, but on mobile Web sites, and/or smartphone apps as

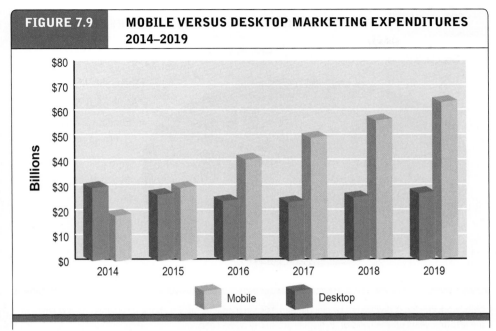

FIGURE 7.9 **MOBILE VERSUS DESKTOP MARKETING EXPENDITURES 2014–2019**

Spending on mobile marketing is growing much more rapidly than spending on advertising aimed at desktop computers. Mobile marketing will be more than twice the size of desktop marketing.
SOURCE: Based on data from eMarketer, Inc. 2015m.

well. Perhaps they may not be able to afford all three, and may want to choose only one. In that case, which is the best? Much depends on what the point of the marketing is. To drive sales, a Web site might be more effective, but to drive brand awareness, and engagement, social and entertainment apps might be better (eMarketer, 2015l).

But even beyond screen adaptability, a multi-screen world means merchants need to be on all platforms, and to be integrated across platforms, in order to send a coherent message and to create a convenient consumer platform. The marketing environment today is much more complex than placing banner ads on pages or on search engine results pages on the Web.

BASIC MOBILE MARKETING FEATURES

As millions of consumers adopt mobile devices, mobile marketing expenditures have rapidly grown and in the next five years will equal marketing on desktop PCs. **Figure 7.9** illustrates how rapidly mobile marketing expenditures have grown, while marketing on desktops is slowing and will eventually decline somewhat.

In 2015, mobile marketing will be about 39% of all online marketing, which is extraordinary given that smartphones appeared only eight years ago, in 2007, and tablets not until 2010. Analysts believe that if current mobile marketing growth rates continue, by 2019, mobile marketing will be over 70% of all online advertising and over twice as large as desktop advertising.

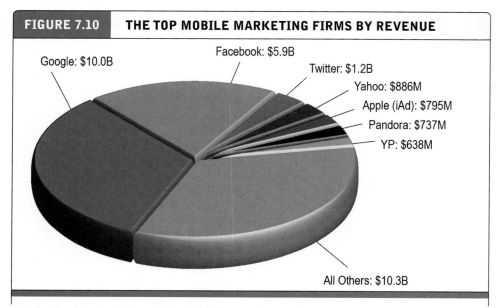

FIGURE 7.10 | **THE TOP MOBILE MARKETING FIRMS BY REVENUE**

Google: $10.0B
Facebook: $5.9B
Twitter: $1.2B
Yahoo: $886M
Apple (iAd): $795M
Pandora: $737M
YP: $638M
All Others: $10.3B

Mobile advertising is dominated by Google and its search engine, but Facebook has gained market share in the last four years on the basis of its display ads in the News Feed.
SOURCE: Based on data from eMarketer, Inc. 2015n.

Mobile advertising is dominated by Google, with an expected $10 billion in mobile ad revenues, constituting about 33% of the entire market, down from 40% the previous year as Facebook and others continue to expand into the mobile market (**Figure 7.10**). On the mobile platform, Google is still the king of search, garnering almost two-thirds of all mobile search ad spending, and expected to total almost $8.5 billion in 2015. Google is also the largest distributor of video ads on the mobile platform because of YouTube, and is expected to earn about $2.2 billion in video ad revenues in 2015. Facebook is second in mobile ads with $5.9 billion, about 20% of mobile ad revenues, of which over 95% ($5.6 billion) is generated by mobile display ads. Facebook is the leading display ad site on mobile devices, accounting for more than 40% of all spending on mobile display ads.

Other players in the mobile marketing marketplace are Twitter (with a 4% share), Yahoo (3%), and Apple (iAd), with 3% (see **Figure 7.10**).

The Technology: Basic Mobile Device Features

Everybody knows the capabilities of smartphones and tablets. But what is it about mobile platforms that make them any different from desktops? Are there any features that make them especially suitable for marketing? **Table 7.13** describes these basic features.

Smartphones today play a much more central role in the personal life of consumers than desktops and laptops in large part because smartphones are always physically with us, or close by. In this sense, they are more personal, and almost "wearable." The "always on, always with us" nature of smartphones has several implications for

TABLE 7.13	FEATURES OF MOBILE DEVICES
FEATURE	DESCRIPTION
Personal communicator and organizer	Telephone plus calendars and clocks to coordinate life on a personal scale.
Screen size and resolution	Resolution of both tablets and phones is high enough to support vibrant graphics and video.
GPS location	Self-locating GPS capability.
Web browser	Standard browsers will operate all Web sites and applications.
Apps	Over a million specialized applications running in native code and extending the functionality of mobile devices.
Ultraportable and personal	Fits into a pocket, or a briefcase for tablets, able to be used anywhere and on the go.
Multimedia capable: video, audio, text	Fully capable of displaying all common media from video to text and sound.

marketers. Because they are perceived as "personal appendages," consumers are less tolerant of commercial intrusion. Have you ever had a telephone conversation interrupted by an advertisement? You probably have not, and if so, you most likely would be annoyed at the interference with a personal conversation. These attitudes extend to any use of the phone or tablet, from reading e-mail, visiting Facebook, or watching a video. Consumers are simply less tolerant of advertising on the small screens of smartphones. Second, the around-the-clock physical proximity of smartphones to our persons greatly expands the time available for marketing materials and increases the supply of screens for marketing materials. This excess supply decreases the price of mobile marketing messages. In turn, there is a tension between marketers and consumers: marketers want to increase the number of mobile ads, while consumers want to see fewer ads, not more, on their mobile devices. Ads inside apps are treated differently by consumers: in return for a free game, consumers are more accepting of ads.

But perhaps the most unique feature of smartphones is that they know users' precise location by virtue of their built-in GPS. This allows marketing messages to be targeted to consumers on the basis of their location, and supports the introduction of location-based marketing and local marketing (described in Section 7.4). While Web sites may know a desktop's general location, it is a very imprecise fix, and the position of the desktop does not change as the user moves about.

MOBILE MARKETING TOOLS: AD FORMATS

Unlike social marketing, mobile marketing does not require much of a new marketing vocabulary. All the marketing formats available on the desktop are also available on mobile devices. With few exceptions, mobile marketing is very much like desktop marketing—except it is smaller. The major marketing opportunities in mobile marketing are search ads, display ads, videos and rich media, messaging (SMS/MMS/PPS), and

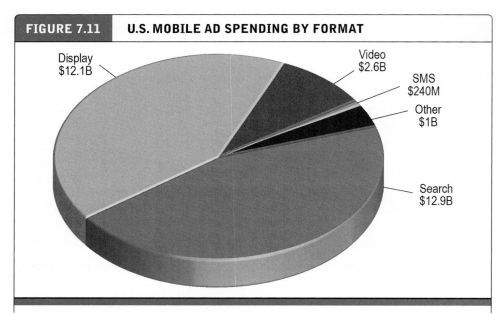

FIGURE 7.11 — **U.S. MOBILE AD SPENDING BY FORMAT**

Display $12.1B
Video $2.6B
SMS $240M
Other $1B
Search $12.9B

Search engine advertising is the most popular mobile marketing format.
SOURCE: Based on data from eMarketer, Inc. 2015o.

some familiar other formats like e-mail, classified, and lead generation. **Figure 7.11** illustrates the relative size of mobile marketing expenditures by format. The marketing formats on mobile devices are search ads, display, video, text/video messaging, and other (including e-mail, classifieds, and lead generation).

In 2015, search engine advertising is estimated to be the most popular mobile marketing format, accounting for over 45% of all mobile ad spending, not surprising given that search is the second most common smartphone application (after voice and text communication). Search engine ads can be further optimized for the mobile platform by showing ads based on the physical location of the user. Display ads (banner ads, rich media, and sponsorships) are the second leading ad format, accounting for about 42% of mobile ad spending. Display ads can be served as a part of a mobile Web site or inside apps and games. Ad networks such as Google's AdMob, Facebook, Apple's iAd, Twitter's MoPub, and MillennialMedia are some of the largest providers of mobile display advertising. Video ads are only about 9% of mobile marketing, but are a fast growing segment because of their very high click rates. Most desktop video ads can be resized for use on mobile phones and tablets. Mobile messaging generally involves SMS text messaging to consumers, with coupons or flash marketing messages. Messaging is especially effective for local advertising because consumers can be sent messages and coupons as they pass by or visit locations (see Section 7.4).

Social networks such as Facebook, Twitter, and Pinterest have generally brought their desktop advertising techniques over to the mobile platform, with some alterations of the interface for use on small-screen smartphones. In the process, social networks have brought real innovation to the mobile marketing experience, including News Feed

TABLE 7.14	SELECTED MOBILE MARKETING CAMPAIGNS
COMPANY	CAMPAIGN
Walmart	Company-wide mobile strategy using mobile applications, mobile Web, augmented reality, mobile advertising, mobile bar codes, social media, location-based services, and push notifications.
eBay	Multiple apps for deals, clothing, and flagship brand app eBay Mobile.
OfficeMax	Uses iPhone and Android platforms for loyalty marketing and daily deals.
Rue La La	Flash sales site for luxury clothing using SMS and Facebook mobile ads saw mobile sales increase to 40% of all online sales.
Ikea	Uses the Apple iAd platform to display banner ads promoting the Ikea catalog.
Starbucks	Early adopter of mobile marketing, now using a number of apps (company app, augmented reality app, and the Square Wallet mobile payment app) along with SMS and QR code campaigns to reach out to customers.

posts on Facebook and Promoted Tweets in Twitter. **Table 7.14** provides selected examples of mobile marketing campaigns and techniques used by several well-known firms.

Mobile marketing is uniquely suited for branding purposes, raising awareness through the use of video and rich interactive media such as games. Read the *Insight on Business* case, *Mobile Marketing: Ford Goes 3-D*, for a further look.

STARTING A MOBILE MARKETING CAMPAIGN

As with all marketing campaigns, start by identifying your objectives and understanding just how a mobile marketing campaign might help your firm. Are you a new unknown start-up seeking to develop a brand image, or an already existing brand looking to strengthen your presence and sell products? Is there something about your products that makes them especially attractive to a mobile audience? For instance, if you sell to local customers walking by your shop, then you might want to use the GPS capabilities of smartphones to target consumers who are nearby.

Next, consider the target demographic for your campaign and products. The most active purchasers on mobile devices are men, and they are more likely to buy consumer electronics equipment and digital content. Women are more likely to cash in coupons and respond to flash sales and deals. Younger consumers are more likely to research products and price on mobile devices, and more likely to share experiences using social media. Mobile shoppers and buyers are more affluent than the online population in general. These demographics are averages, and mobile marketing campaigns do not need to restrict themselves to these averages. Find out where your mobile customers are congregating. Are your mobile customers likely to be using apps, and if so, what are they? Are your customers likely to be on Facebook or use Twitter? Or are your customers most likely to find you on a Google mobile search page?

Finally, consider the marketspace where you hope to succeed. What are your competitors doing on the mobile platform? Is their presence effective? Where do they place their marketing efforts: display ads on Web portals, or display ads in Google search

INSIGHT ON BUSINESS

MOBILE MARKETING: FORD GOES 3-D

Why is mobile marketing any different from ordinary online marketing? In one sense, it isn't. The same kinds of ad formats you find on Web sites are also used on smartphones—in order of importance, search, display, video, and text messages. In another sense, mobile marketing can be very different from other types of online marketing because of the unique features of the smartphone, which include a built-in GPS, a gyroscope, and an accelerometer. This means marketers can know the location of the user, and they can present rich media and video ads where the user can control the action in a way not possible with an ordinary desktop computer. Smartphones use a touch interface, which increases user involvement. Mobile ads can therefore be more engaging and interactive than traditional desktop computer ads. Location information can be used to market local businesses at the very point of consumer purchase, namely, on the street or in the store while browsing. Other unique smartphone features are that people almost always carry them and keep them turned on while moving about. This means that smartphone users can be exposed to marketing messages throughout the day (and sometimes the night).

Mobile devices are used by consumers throughout the purchase cycle: Nearly half of the population uses a mobile device to research products online before purchasing. The use of mobile devices to actually purchase products or services online (as opposed to just shopping and browsing online) is growing. For certain goods that the consumer is familiar with, for sites that have an easy-to-use one-click shopping capability, and for purchases of content like books and

movies, mobile purchasing is particularly convenient. Also, for local marketing, mobile is an ideal platform for merchants to attract consumers in the neighborhood. Restaurants, museums, and entertainment venues are ideal candidates to use mobile marketing aimed at local consumers. What attracts users to mobile purchasing is the ability to access product information now, find deals, and buy all with the swipe of a finger. But mobile is also good for introducing new products and building brand recognition, with sales taking place elsewhere and offline.

One increasingly popular method of mobile advertising among companies with big advertising budgets is 3-D advertising, which consists of advertisements with video and other interactive features that take advantage of the capabilities of modern mobile devices. A good example of this type of advertising in action is Ford's "We Own Work" campaign for its F-150 pickup truck, America's top selling truck for 36 years. Ford used a 3-D mobile advertisement for the 2014 edition of the truck as the centerpiece and "lead creative unit" in the campaign, with the stated goals that the ad be innovative, creative, and compatible with all major platforms and devices. They hoped to simulate a showroom experience within the ad, building brand awareness and user engagement in the process.

Ford's advertising team partnered with Amobee, a three-dimensional mobile advertising platform, to create the virtual showroom experience. The ad displays as a motion-sensitive banner ad that expands across the screen into a full 3-D virtual showroom, complete with fully customizable options for the displayed F-150, embedded videos, and a 360-degree view of the vehicle. Users can change the truck to one of fourteen colors with a quick tap of the screen, and can view the F-150 in different environments at any angle by moving their device. The environments are intended to show the F-150 in action performing a wide array of functions, including construction, hauling, farming, and transporting hazardous materials. Users can also tap the screen to load the bed of the virtual F-150, showcasing its payload capacity. By tilting the mobile device in any direction, users can generate reflections of each environment in the mirrors and windows of the truck via the accelerometer of the device.

Unlike traditional rich media ads, 3-D mobile ads respond to users' actions in real time, changing colors, lighting, shading, and other features. But the 3-D ad format offered by Amobee is actually a more light-weight and user-friendly package than traditional HTML5 rich media ads. Amobee advertisements use WebGL to render interactive 3-D graphics, which allow each ad to run on traditional Web browsers as well as an extensive array of mobile devices.

Amobee also touts that its advertising platform can identify and target individual demographics at scale. Amobee can keep track of engagement with its advertisements in real time, keeping consumers anonymous but measuring how much time different demographics of users spend with individual elements of each ad and how effectively ads engage each type of user. Amobee has an in-house data management platform with over a million profiles with customer information such as gender, age, location, and interests. Needless to say, this capability is extremely useful when measuring the effectiveness of an advertising campaign, and when a brand like Ford is seeking to target specific types of consumers.

Ford rolled out the ad in conjunction with the launch of the F-150. Using Amobee analytics, Ford determined that the F-150 3-D ad registered 20 million impressions and 595,000 expansions. The 2.9% rate of expansions was 4.6 times the industry average, and the 13% overall engagement rate was twice as high as the industry average. Metrics also indicated that the 3-D mobile campaign generated an increase in brand favorability by 19.9%, an increase in purchase consideration by 40.4%, and an increase in brand awareness of the F-150 and Ford by 11.4%. The ad generated a 71.1% association by consumers of the "We Own Work" slogan with Ford.

Amobee requires a minimum investment of $250,000 for a month-long 3-D advertising campaign, so currently this style of ad is available mostly to bigger brands. Retail brands with physical products are great fits for 3-D ads, but companies offering services such as financial institutions may never be interested in 3-D ads. And while these ads currently offer impressive engagement rates, when their novelty wears of and they become more commonplace, those numbers may come back to earth a bit. Still, the trend toward 3-D advertising is undeniable. Facebook users could see similar posts from brands as a result of its $2 billion purchase of VR app developer Oculus Rift, and Ford was so encouraged by its F-150 campaign that they ran a similar one for the 2015 Mustang. With 3-D advertising, consumers can explore products in greater detail than ever before, at their own pace and with an emphasis on interactivity and fun. It could be closer than ever to a marketer's holy grail: advertising that doesn't feel like advertising.

SOURCES: "Bringing the Ford F-150 to Life in Innovative 3D Mobile Ad Experience," Mmaglobal.com, 2015; "Team Detroit and [a•mo•bee] Bring the Ford F-150 to Life with Innovative 3D Mobile Ad Campaign," Amobee.com, 2015; "These 3-D Mobile Ads Are Grabbing Brands' Attention," by Lauren Johnson, Adweek.com, April 13, 2015; "Think Outside the Box: 3-D Mobile Ads Can Boost Engagement," by Yuyu Chen, Clickz.com, October 15, 2014.

results? Or can they be found as in-app ads? What apps are they advertising in? How are they represented on Facebook Mobile? Do they also have a Twitter and/or Pinterest brand page? Do your competitors have an app that users can easily download? You'll want to be able to meet your competitors on each of the platforms they have adopted. Once you've developed an initial vision for your marketing campaign, you can develop a timeline and an action plan of how to meet the milestones identified in your timeline.

Once you have envisioned your marketing campaign and identified your market, it is time to start implementing your mobile campaign. Here are some steps to follow:

- Develop a mobile Web site so mobile consumers can see and buy your products. Make your mobile Web site social by including Facebook, Twitter, Pinterest, and other social site links.
- Develop a Facebook brand page so your social and mobile marketing efforts are integrated.
- Develop a Twitter brand page so customers can follow your posts.
- If you already use a display advertising program like Google's AdWords or a Facebook display ad account, you can create a new campaign using the same ads designed specifically for mobile platforms.
- Consider opening an iAd account and using Apple's iAd network or Google's AdMob in part because these ad networks can publish and track your ads on multiple platforms simultaneously.
- Develop marketing content that is aimed specifically at the mobile user, with videos and high levels of interactivity designed for the mobile screen.
- Measure and manage your campaign. iAd and AdWords, along with many other ad networks, will host and manage your mobile campaigns. In addition, they can provide you with a host of campaign measures that will allow you to see which mobile ads and techniques are attracting the most followers, comments, and social activity concerning your brand. With this basic data you can start to manage the mobile marketing campaign by reducing expenditures on ads that do not work and increasing the budget of ads that do work.

MEASURING MOBILE MARKETING RESULTS

There are many different mobile marketing objectives, and therefore different types of mobile marketing campaigns. Some campaigns are sales-oriented, based on display and search ads, offering coupons or discounts, and taking users directly to a Web site where they can buy something. Measuring the results of these mobile campaigns follows similar campaigns launched on desktops. Other campaigns focus on branding, where the objective is to engage consumers in a conversation, acquire them as fans, and spread the word among their friends. You can use the framework from Figure 7.4 on page 429 to measure the results of these campaigns. The key dimensions to measure for mobile social campaigns are fan acquisition, engagement, amplification, community, brand strength (center of conversation), and sales.

Figure 7.12 illustrates how a brand-oriented marketing campaign utilizing the mobile platform and social marketing might present its effectiveness measures over

FIGURE 7.12	MEASURING THE EFFECTIVENESS OF A MOBILE BRANDING CAMPAIGN

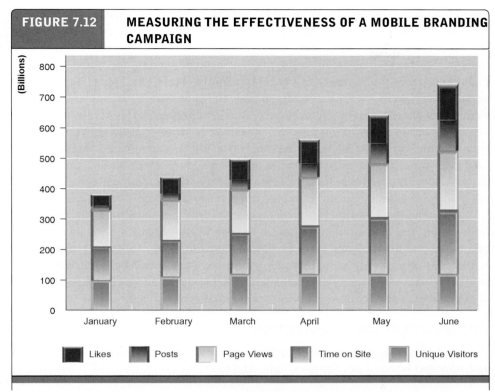

The effectiveness of a branding campaign utilizing the mobile platform and social marketing can be measured by examining the number of Likes, posts, page views, time on site, and unique visitors.

a six-month period. In a branding campaign, the object is not so much sales as it is strengthening consumers' engagement with the brand. In the example provided in Figure 7.12, acquiring fans is measured by the number of unique visitors. Here you can see that over six months, visitors have risen over 60%. Engagement is reflected in the time on-site (in thousands of minutes); amplification is measured by the number of Likes, and this has expanded threefold. Community is measured by the number of posts, suggesting fans are actively engaging with one another and the brand. Posts have risen eightfold in the period. Brand strength is best summarized in this figure as the composite picture of fan acquisition, engagement, amplification, and community measures. Measuring the impacts of this mobile campaign on ultimate sales requires going a step further and measuring which sales can be attributed to this mobile campaign.

7.4 LOCAL AND LOCATION-BASED MOBILE MARKETING

Location-based marketing is one of the fastest growing segments of the digital marketing universe. **Location-based marketing** targets marketing messages to users based on their location. Generally, location-based marketing involves marketing of location-based services. **Location-based services** involve providing services to users based on

location-based marketing
targets marketing messages to users based on their location

location-based services
involve providing services to users based on their location

their location. Examples of location-based services are: personal navigation (How do I get there?), point-of-interest (What's that?), reviews (What's the best restaurant in the neighborhood?), friend-finder (Where are you? Where's the crowd?), and family-tracker services (Where is my child?). There is a connection, of course: the more people use their mobile devices to search for and obtain local services, the more opportunities there are for marketers to target consumers with messages at just the right moment, at just the right location, and in just the right way—not too pushy and annoying, but in a way to improve the consumer experience at the moment of local shopping and buying. This is the ideal in any event. Location-based marketing can take place on a desktop as well because browsers and marketers know your approximate location. But in this section we focus primarily on location-based mobile marketing, which is where the greatest growth and opportunities lie.

Experience and market research suggest that consumers want local ads, offers, information, and content. Consumers have a high likelihood of acting on local ads and purchasing the products and services offered. Because it has evolved so rapidly in the last five years, experience and research with respect to location-based marketing is a work in progress with many different platforms, providers, and techniques. Measures of effectiveness and returns on investment are being developed.

THE GROWTH OF LOCAL MARKETING

Prior to the release of Google Maps in 2005, nearly all local advertising was nondigital and provided by local newspapers, radio and television stations, local yellow pages, and billboards. Of course, some was digital, involving the Web sites of local merchants. Today, total media ad spending in the United States is $187 billion, and approximately $139 billion of this is local media spending by both national and local brands. An estimated 40% of this local advertising (about $55 billion) involves truly local firms like restaurants, grocery stores, theaters, and shoe stores marketing to their local audience. The remaining 60% of local media marketing involves large national firms marketing to local audiences, such as an ad for Coca-Cola in a local newspaper or Web sites created for local auto dealers by national firms. Of the $139 billion of local media spending, about 26% ($36 billion) will be spent on online marketing, and this amount is expected to grow to about $51 billion by (BIA/Kelsey, 2015a).

After the introduction of Google Maps in 2005 and smartphones in 2007, online local marketing began to rapidly expand. Google Maps on desktop computers enabled the targeting of ads to users based on a general sense of their IP address and enabled merchants to display ads to users based on the general location of potential customers, usually within a several square-mile radius. IP addresses can be used to identify a city, and a neighborhood within the city, but not a zip code, street, or building. Google Maps helped users answer the question "Where can I find an Italian restaurant" in a city or section of a city from their desktop. The arrival of smartphones in 2007, and Google's mobile maps app, took this one step further. The GPS receivers in second-generation smartphones introduced in 2008 (Apple's 3G iPhone), along with other techniques, meant that a user's location (latitude and longitude) could be fairly well known by cell phone manufacturers, marketers, service providers, and carriers like AT&T and Verizon. These developments opened an entirely new growth path for local online

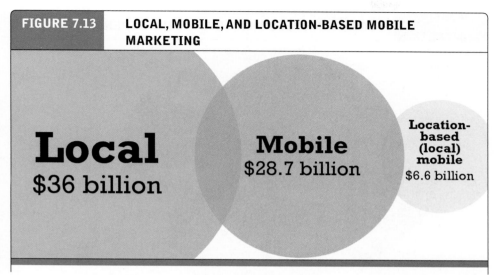

FIGURE 7.13 | **LOCAL, MOBILE, AND LOCATION-BASED MOBILE MARKETING**

Local online marketing will account for $36 billion in marketing expenditures in 2015, with location-based mobile expected to account for $6.6 billion of that amount.

Source: Based on data from eMarketer, 2015a; BIA/Kelsey, 2015a, 2015b.

advertising that heretofore had been confined to the desktop. In this new world, a local food market could shout out to mobile phone users as they walked by the store, offering discounts to responders, and users in turn could search for specific retail stores nearby, even checking their inventory before walking into the store.

THE GROWTH OF LOCATION-BASED (LOCAL) MOBILE MARKETING

Location-based (local) mobile marketing is currently a small part of the online marketing environment, but it is expected to triple over the next 5 years. **Figure 7.13** helps put the location-based mobile market in perspective. In 2015, total online marketing will be about $59 billion and local online marketing is expected to be a healthy and surprisingly large $36 billion. The part of local online that is location-based mobile is expected to generate an estimated $6.6 billion.

The ad formats used in local mobile marketing are familiar—search ads, display, native/social, videos, and SMS text messages. Search ads displayed as a part of user search results comprise the largest location-based mobile ad format, with marketers expected to spend an estimated $7.2 billion in 2015. The local mobile search market is dominated by Google. Display ads are the second largest format, and are expected to account for $4.9 billion in spending in 2015. Social/native ads are the fastest growing format, generating an estimated $3.6 billion in spending in 2015. Here the main players are Facebook and Google. Together, Google and Facebook account for 70% of location-based mobile marketing. Local mobile ads are the fastest growing format with over $3 billion in ads for 2015. The primary platform for video ads today is Google'sYouTube with Facebook and Twitter both developing their video ad platforms. **Figure 7.14** illustrates the relative shares of location-based mobile ad format spending in 2015 (BIA/Kelsey, 2015a).

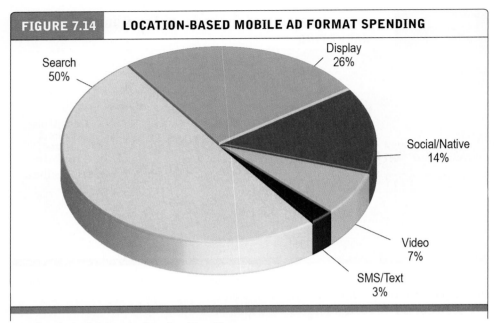

FIGURE 7.14 | **LOCATION-BASED MOBILE AD FORMAT SPENDING**

Search is the leading location-based mobile ad format.
SOURCE: Based on data from BIA/Kelsey, 2015a; eMarketer, Inc., 2015p.

LOCATION-BASED MARKETING PLATFORMS

The key players in location-based mobile marketing are the same giants who dominate the mobile marketing environment described in a previous section, namely, Google, Facebook, Apple, Twitter, YP (formerly Yellow Pages), Pandora, and Millenial. Google is clearly the leading location-based marketer largely because of its widely used Google Maps app on smartphones. When a consumer searches for a location on Google Maps, it is an ideal marketing moment to pop an ad before the consumer's eyes. Google Places is a simple but effective service that provides short business profiles when users search for a specific business. Google's Android operating system has location functionality built into the system, and Google apps, like Google Maps, continuously update the user's location. Google purchased a mobile advertising firm called AdMob in 2009 and claims to be the world's largest mobile advertising firm for both Android and Apple's iOS operating systems. App developers use AdMob to provide their apps with consumer and user location information. Google also sells location information to independent marketing firms. Marketing firms use AdMob to develop full-screen rich media ads. Google's main revenue stream comes from its AdWords service, where marketers bid for keywords on Google's search engine. AdWords used to be the same whether displayed on a desktop computer or a mobile device. Google has upgraded its AdWords service to optimize ads for user contexts and devices, and to provide management of campaigns across all mobile and desktop devices. The new service is called Enhanced AdWords. For instance, if a customer searches for "pizza" on a desktop computer from work at 1 PM, he or she would be shown restaurants nearby and a quick order form. If the customer searched for "pizza" at 8 PM on a smartphone within a half-mile of a pizza restaurant, he or she might be shown a click-to-call phone number and directions to the restaurant. Pizza restaurants pay Google for the chance to show up in these searches.

Google and Apple have advantages in the location-based market: they both have developed extensive maps of Wi-Fi networks throughout the world, allowing them to develop much more precise location information than competitors.

Apple's mobile platform iAd provides location data to iOS app developers and mobile marketing firms. Like AdMob, when users click on an iAd ad, a full-screen ad appears within the app they are using. The ad can be targeted to the user's location.

LOCATION-BASED MOBILE MARKETING: THE TECHNOLOGIES

Location-based services and marketing require marketers and local service providers to have a fairly precise idea of where consumer mobile devices are located. There are two general types of location-based marketing techniques: geo-aware and proximity marketing. **Geo-aware** techniques identify the location of a user's device and then target marketing to the device, recommending actions within reach (which, in itself, requires the marketer to know where relevant things like stores are located). For instance, a marketer may target smartphones within several square city blocks to alert them to available offers from participating merchants. **Proximity marketing** techniques identify a perimeter around a physical location, and then target ads to users within that perimeter, recommending actions possible within the fenced-in area. The perimeter can be from hundreds of feet (in urban areas) to several miles (in suburban locations). For instance, if users walk into the geo-fenced perimeter of a store, restaurant, or retail shop, they will receive ads from these businesses. Both of these techniques utilize the same locating technologies.

Ad networks, local-mobile marketing firms, providers of devices and services like Google and Apple, as well as phone companies use several methods for locating mobile devices, none of which are perfect, and all of which have varying degrees of accuracy. **Table 7.15** describes the major locating technologies used to enable location-based services and marketing.

GPS (Global Positioning System) location is the most accurate positioning method in theory. In practice, the signal can be weak in urban areas, nonexistent inside buildings, signals can be deflected, and it can take a long time (30–60 seconds) for the device to acquire the signal and calculate a position. When a clear signal is obtained, GPS can be accurate to within 3–10 meters under ideal conditions, but more frequently, a cell phone's GPS is accurate only to within 50 meters—half a football field. Also, users have to activate the feature, and many do not for privacy reasons. Assisted GPS (A-GPS) supplements GPS information with other information from the phone network to speed up acquisition. Nearly all smartphones use A-GPS. In Apple's iOS, users can decide whether to turn Location Services on or off. When turned on, the iOS uses GPS, cellular, and Wi-Fi networks to determine the user's approximate location to within 10 meters (30 feet) although in many situations acccuracy can be much higher, around 15 feet. The user's iPhone continuously reports its position and reports to Apple servers.

geo-aware
techniques that identify the location of a user's device and then target marketing to the device

proximity marketing
techniques that identify a perimeter around a physical location, and then target ads to users within that perimeter, recommending actions possible within the fenced-in area

TABLE 7.15	MAJOR LOCATING TECHNOLOGIES
TECHNOLOGY	**DESCRIPTION**
GPS	The user's device downloads GPS data from a GPS satellite. First introduced with the Apple 3G iPhone in 2008. Today, cellphones are required to broadcast their GPS location for emergency assistance purposes.
Wi-Fi	Estimates user's location within a radius of a known Wi-Fi access point.
Bluetooth low energy (BLE)	Used by Apple in iBeacon. Uses less battery power than traditional Bluetooth or GPS and more accurate than targeting through Wi-Fi triangulation.
Geo-search	Uses location information based on the user's search queries.
Cell tower	AT&T, Verizon, and other carriers are in constant contact with their devices, which allows approximation of location by triangulation and refinement of the unit's GPS location. Wireless carriers use a cell phone's MAC address to identify the phone and the location.
Sign in/registration	Estimates users' location when they self-identify their location using sign-in services or social network posts.

Cell tower location is used by wireless telephone carriers to track the location of their devices, which is required to complete phone calls as devices pass from the range of one tower into the range of another. Cell tower location is also the basis of the wireless emergency response system in the United States. The FCC's wireless Enhanced 9-1-1 (E9-1-1) rules require wireless carriers to track cellphone locations whether or not the user has turned on location services in order to assist emergency responders in locating users who make 911 calls.

Wi-Fi location is used in conjunction with GPS signals to more accurately locate a user based on the known location of Wi-Fi transmitters, which are fairly ubiquitous in urban and suburban locations. Apple, Google, and other mobile service providers have developed global databases of wireless access points simply by driving cars around urban areas in much of the world. Google uses Street View cars to build a global database of wireless access points and their geographic location. Android applications can use this database to determine the approximate location of individuals based on the Wi-Fi networks detected by their mobile devices. All Wi-Fi devices continuously monitor the presence of local Wi-Fi networks, and mobile devices report back this data to Apple and Microsoft, along with other device manufacturers, who use similar methods. The goal of these technologies is to provide consumers and marketers with "micro-location data" accurate to within a few feet to support truly real-time, accurate, local marketing at the personal level. For instance, if you are looking at a rack of dress shirts in a retail store, an accurate positioning system could detect this, and direct you to appropriate accessories like socks and ties on surrounding shelves.

WHY IS LOCAL MOBILE ATTRACTIVE TO MARKETERS?

Consumers who seek information about local businesses using mobile devices are much more active and ready to purchase than desktop users. In part this is because desktop searchers for local information are not in as close proximity to merchants as are mobile searchers. A recent Google survey found that over 80% of U.S. consumers use smartphones and tablet computers to conduct local searches on search engines for a variety of local information such as business hours, local store addresses and directions, and availability of products at local stores. The survey found that consumers search for local information through the purchase process, and 50% of smartphone users visited a store within a day of their local search, and 18% made a purchase within a day. The survey also found that over 60% of smartphone users wanted ads customized both to their city/zip code and to their immediate surroundings (Google, 2014a).

LOCATION-BASED MARKETING TOOLS

Location-based digital marketing, like social marketing, presents students of digital marketing with a confusing array of new services, platforms, and firms that provide these services. While some local-based marketing techniques, like placing ads on Google's AdSense platform aimed at mobile customers, are relatively easy to establish for the small business owner, others require the help of mobile marketing provider firms.

A New Lexicon: Location-Based Digital Marketing Features

Location-based services involve providing services to users based on their location. Examples include personal navigation, point-of-interest, reviews, friend-finder, and family-tracker services. **Table 7.16** describes how some of these features can be used for marketing.

Proximity Marketing with Beacons

While all location-based marketing is in some sense proximity marketing, when Apple introduced iBeacon in 2013 with its iOS 7, it made it possible for retail store retailers to communicate directly and quite precisely with customers as they passed within a few feet of in-store beacons. There are many close proximity technologies such as QR codes, Wi-Fi, and NFC (Near Field Communication), but each has drawbacks in terms of precision, cost, and widespread availability. Now that Apple has adopted NFC in its hardware for Apple Pay, NFC will become a good candidate technology for close proximity marketing. Apple's iBeacon uses a different technology called Bluetooth Low Energy (BLE). Android phones also have this capability. BLE is inexpensive to implement, and uses much less power than traditional Bluetooth. Unlike QR codes, BLE has a two-way, push-pull communication capability. Using QR codes, consumers need to show the code to a QR scanner, and then they see information on a product. With iBeacon, consumers can be contacted as soon as they walk into a store and exposed to special offers, and then when browsing the store, contacted as they pass specific areas, like the jewelry department. This all takes place automatically on the user's iPhone. Consumers can respond to these messages as well. For retailers, in-store beacon marketing is aimed at four objectives. The customer can be engaged immediately on entry to the store, and then accompanied electronically from one area to another, somewhat similar to how luxury retail stores assign a salesperson to high-end consumers. Second, beacons can be used to stimulate loyalty programs. Consumers who buy often can be noticed upon entering the store. Third, retailers can engage in flash sales, instant discounts, and other impulse marketing programs inside their

TABLE 7.16	LOCATION-BASED MARKETING TOOLS AND CAMPAIGNS
LOCATION-BASED MARKETING TOOLS	**DESCRIPTION**
Geo-social-based services marketing	Users share their location with friends. Can be used for check-in services like Foursquare; friend finders; transportation services.
Location-based services marketing	Provides services to consumers looking for local services and products.
Mobile-local social network marketing based on users' location	Facebook expands local offerings of deals by local firms, display ads using News Feed. Discount offers from a Gap store when claimed are broadcast to friends.
	Google+ Local. Connecting users with local businesses. Users can conduct searches within a local area and get Zagat reviews.
	Upgraded Foursquare app focuses on social updates but also recommendations and deals.
	Social network monitoring: sends messages within an app based on mentions of interest in products in Facebook and Twitter posts. Used by H&M.
	Intent marketing: scanning social networks for indications of real-time consumer interest in specific products. H&M partnered with LocalResponse to promote clothing inspired by the movie "Girl With the Dragon Tattoo."
Proximity marketing	Send messages to consumers in the area of a store or outlet to generate sales using a virtual fence around a retail location (could also be an airport, train station, or arena). Generally opt in. Miller Coors created a geo-fence around 28 U.S. airports to alert Blue Moon beer fans on where it could be purchased.
In-store messaging	Messaging consumers while entering or browsing in a store. Retailers collect, analyze, and respond to customers' real-time shopping behavior.
Location-based app messaging	American Express My Offers app presents cardholders with personalized deals based on their location.

physical stores. Finally, beacons can be used silently, not pushing offers or goods, but instead just gathering data directly about in-store consumer behavior.

Currently, beacon technology, essentially in-store Bluetooth devices that can communicate with user smartphones entering the store, are stand-alone apps, each following different standards. But several technology firms are trying to build in beacon capabilities to their popular platforms. In 2015, Google announced its Eddystone open-source standard that can work with iOS or Android. Facebook developed a pilot program called Place Tips, offering free Bluetooth devices to merchants. When users are recognized as being close to a merchant, Facebook posts to their News Feed suggesting they visit the merchant or buy a product. Twitter recently invested in Swirl, a beacon platform, but has not yet announced how it will be integrated with Twitter's newsfeed or ad platform.

Reportedly, 20% of mobile marketing firms that use geo-location marketing are using beacons. One analyst claims that over 400 million beacons will be in place in five years although most will be in the non-retail world from museums to parks and tourist sites.

In 2014, Macy's started to deploy iBeacon in many of its retail stores after a successful test of the system in San Francisco and New York. Using an app from Shopkick (a marketing firm) called shopBeacon, Macy's customers who have downloaded the app receive notifications to open the app when they enter a Macy's store. Customers receive promotions, deals, and discounts. The hope is that by using proximity marketing, retail stores will be able to attract more consumers to their stores, and increase purchases from those who come to their stores. While Macy's initially planned to install 4,000 beacons throughout its retail chain, they have not revealed how many are installed, or what the results have been. Target has announced it will be installing beacons in 50 of its stores in 2015 (Marks, 2015).

Despite the claims of proponents of beacon marketing, real-world retailers have only developed a few pilot programs. Consumers do not appear to have much interest in the technology. Beacons require users to have Bluetooth turned on. But only 20% of smartphone users in the United States have Bluetooth turned on, and another 20% claimed their smartphones did not have Bluetooth (even though they likely did have it). Consumers are also concerned about the privacy implications of being tracked through a store or on the streets. Many do not want to be bothered with in-store notifications, and may resent the intrusion. One beacon platform firm found that pushing notices to in-store consumers actually led to a decline in the use of the app, and more than one push notice caused a 300% drop in app usage (eMarketer, Inc., 2015q)

STARTING A LOCATION-BASED MARKETING CAMPAIGN

As with all marketing campaigns, start by identifying your objectives and understand just how a location-based mobile marketing campaign might help your business. Location-based marketing is generally much more action-oriented than other forms of online marketing. A person is in a given location only for a short time, measured in minutes and hours, rarely days or weeks. If you want the consumer to do something, it's now. Does your product or service have this quality? Is there something related to a person's location that fits with your product? Is there something about your products that makes them especially attractive to a mobile audience at a specific location and time? There are very few products and services that don't have a location connection.

Next, consider the target demographic for your campaign and products. Location-aware consumers (those with mobile devices and familiar with location-based services) tend to be a younger, more educated, and wealthier demographic. They have many of the same characteristics as all mobile shoppers.

A strategic analysis of your marketspace is very important. The same questions that you would seek to answer if you were doing a nonlocation-aware mobile marketing campaign apply to a location-based marketing effort, such as examining what your competitors are doing.

Once you have envisioned your marketing campaign and identified your market, it is time to start implementing your mobile campaign. The same steps that you would

TABLE 7.17	MOBILE LOCATION-BASED MARKETING EFFECTIVENESS
SOCIAL MARKETING PROCESS	MEASUREMENT
Acquisition	Impressions; click-through; unique visitors to a mobile or desktop Web site; pages viewed; time on site.
Engagement	Inquire; reserve; visit a physical store; click-to-call; check maps for directions; register; request more information; posts and comments; responders to offers; Likes generated per visitor; click-to-call rate.
Amplification	SMS to friends; notify friends of location; share location or offers with friends.
Community	Content generated by visitors or responders; reviews; posts; positive comments generated.
Sales	Purchases; percentage increase in sales due to local mobile campaign; percentage of customers from local mobile.

follow in implementing a mobile campaign apply to location-based marketing as well. Note that you can't do everything at once—mobile-centric and location-based. Start by doing something simple like local search. Then consider more sophisticated local-based marketing tactics.

MEASURING LOCATION-BASED MARKETING RESULTS

There are a great many ways to measure the success of a mobile location-based campaign, some very sophisticated. The measures of success will vary depending on the objective of the campaign, which might be to raise the awareness of your brand among consumers, to bring customers to your retail store, or a click-to-call campaign where you want people to make reservations for a concert.

Because mobile local campaigns use the same marketing ad formats as both traditional and mobile Web marketing, the basic measures of effectiveness are similar. For instance, the number of impressions (people who see an ad), click-through rate, and unique visitors are basic measures for a mobile local campaign. But mobile location-based marketing is much more personal and social than traditional Web marketing or even simple mobile marketing: it's a marketing message directed to a consumer's personal mobile device based on that person's location. Local mobile marketers hope consumers will take follow-on action almost immediately—inquire, reserve, click-to-call, friend, and ultimately purchase. **Table 7.17** describes some of the basic dimensions and metrics to use when evaluating a mobile marketing campaign. The nature of the location-based campaign makes a difference for how you measure success. For instance, in a click-to-call campaign, you want to measure the volume of calls, duration of call, new versus existing customers, and the number of accidental or hostile calls.

7.5 **CASE STUDY**

ExchangeHunterJumper.com:
Building a Brand with Social Marketing

The Internet and Web have enabled thousands of business ideas to become online realities. The Internet has reduced the costs of starting a small business, and allowed small players to effectively use the same marketing and selling tools as major corporations. Small businesses usually occupy a market niche not occupied by big players or corporations. One such market niche in America, comprising about 10,000 to 30,000 players, is the high-end horse show circuit. These are people who are willing to drop $200,000 on a horse that can jump a five-foot fence with ease. This may be a very small market, but its members are highly motivated to both buy and sell horses, and they are willing to spend in the process. ExchangeHunterJumper.com is one example of how a small business focusing on a tiny niche market was able to successfully build an online brand.

According to Dagny Amber Aslin, founder and owner of ExchangeHunterJumper.com (The Exchange), a Web site created to help owners and professional trainers sell high-end competition horses, it's hard to "get rich" or even make money on the Internet. She adds, "There are a lot of preconceived notions ... I beat down a path

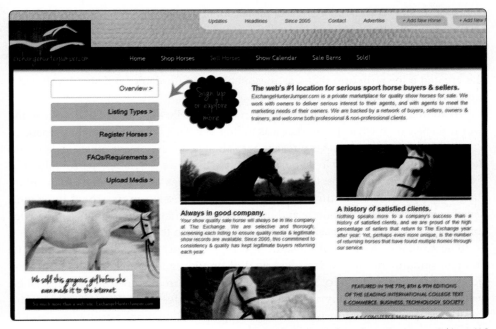

previously unplowed. It cost us a lot of money and we suffered many setbacks from our mistakes." Yet the site is still growing and has succeeded where others failed. How did Aslin break through and develop a site that works for professionals buying and selling alike? How did she build trust? How did she market her services?

Experience helped. Aslin started with applicable experience—in the horse world and in the world of Internet marketing. In addition to riding and competing as a child, Aslin spent several years working as a professional trainer. Working six-day weeks, including weekends, and spending most of her time outdoors riding, teaching, and competing, she saw first-hand the challenges facing professional horsemen, and she gained valuable credibility with those who would become her audience.

While working in the horse business, and learning how difficult it was to make a living, she took a part-time job as an assistant to a top California real estate agent, helping him market and sell high-end real estate in the Santa Barbara area. Among other activities, she helped him develop and expand his Web site. Through that experience, she realized that "selling six-figure horses and seven-figure houses are ridiculously similar—both tend to be overpriced, have emotional strings attached, require vettings and exhaustive negotiations, involve agents, and the list goes on." In 2005, when she moved from California back to the Midwest, where she had spent her childhood, The Exchange was born. Seven years later, the equine marketing model she has built is "a customized copy" of the real estate program she assisted with in Santa Barbara.

Aslin knew that busy horse professionals needed a high-quality, reliable source of suitable mounts for their clients, but their day-to-day business lives left them little time to thoroughly search the market, and they often lacked a good grasp of modern media technology. The same dilemma applied when it came to selling high-end horses. In response, she created an organized, professional process for preparing online horse sale advertisements. It included detailed forms for sellers to fill out, and she insisted that quality photos and video be provided for each horse advertised, enabling her to turn the descriptions into accurate portrayals of each animal and its capabilities. She created a fee structure that was reasonable and affordable, and she developed a multi-channel marketing program.

Aslin understood that her business plan needed to be a living document, evolving over time based on what the market was telling her. This helped her make inroads in a traditional industry that is very resistant to change. Most horse professionals spend their days outside, and tend to do business only with those they know personally—the level of trust is very low. Most existing horse sale Web sites were little more than online classifieds cluttered with unreliable information. Although professional horsemen have been slow to use computers and the Internet, the rise of smartphones and tablet computers has helped increase their comfort level with technology.

The Exchange took all of these things into account, and Aslin went further. In order to remain true to her business goal of providing a *reliable* service to professionals in the horse industry that would become a source of good horses described accurately, Aslin personally reviewed all potential advertisers. In some cases she went back to sellers and insisted on higher quality photographs and video, and in other cases where she determined the horse was not as represented, she turned down their business. The initial business plan process involved strict screening, and it meant turning away money and valuing quality over quantity in every area—horses, buyers, traffic, and ads. It was a hard and expensive premise to adhere to when building a reputation from scratch, but through persistence and dedication it has worked, and today, The Exchange's reputation and "brand" has become one of its most valuable assets.

In discussing some of the obstacles she faced in getting The Exchange up and running, Aslin starts with education—her own or lack thereof, specifically in the areas of graphic design and Web technology. While she knew what professional horsemen needed, she did not know how to translate that into graphic design or onto the Web. She says that looking back on the original logo and print designs is "a painful exercise," but she is happy with the current direction.

The budget was also an initial obstacle, as there wasn't a lot of money to spend up front. However, in hindsight, she believes that gave her an advantage because she had to learn what her market wanted and was able to do so without breaking the bank. Conversely, her main competitor took an opposite track, spent big up front, missed the mark with customers, and is now defunct.

In addition, she faced the negative perception among industry professionals and prospective buyers that equine Internet advertising was "worthless." Further, much of her target audience barely knew how to use a computer, didn't have e-mail addresses, and had been doing business in the same old-school manner for decades. For a few key players this worked very well, but it left a void for those outside that inner circle to move horses. Through a combination of knowledge of the marketplace, on-the-job training, perseverance, and listening to what the market was telling her, The Exchange has successfully begun to fill that void.

Here's how it works. The Exchange handles advertising for sellers and trainers across the country. In 2015, show horses advertised on The Exchange are typically priced from $15,000 to $250,000. The recession caused prices to fall significantly, but the prices in certain parts of the market have rebounded. The Exchange specializes strictly in hunter-jumper show horses, and specifically those suited for high-level competition.

Trainers/sellers who sign up for a premium listing pay a flat $250 fee for the initial advertisement and a subscription fee of $35/month, which includes a listing on The Exchange's Web site featuring the horse's details, photos, show record, lineage, and videos. The Exchange provides copy-writing services and professionally edits all videos supplied by sellers, hosting them on its private server and making them available to download, embed, and share. Each listing typically takes 8–10 hours to prepare. In 2012, The Exchange added a second listing alternative—a Sale Barn listing for $300 a month or $3,000 a year, that allows for listing of up to 10 horses. A three-month commitment is required, but there are no initial or other fees. Aimed at high-volume operations with frequent turnover, the Sale Barn page can link to the seller's Web site, YouTube, Facebook, and Twitter feeds, if available, with the goal of increasing overall brand awareness for the seller's business. Aslin designed the Sale Barn as an affordable option for professionals who might otherwise be reluctant to spend on marketing. International sellers are given a slight additional discount. In 2015, the Sale Program

program has taken off, with 10 different sales barns listed, including one in Germany and one in France.

Statistics show that a horse's first month online is most successful in terms of the number of Web page visits. With the addition of monthly campaign management, The Exchange helps keep each horse's marketing fresh and up to date. Updates can immediately escalate a horse's popularity as much as 30% and attract new potential buyers. Sellers are encouraged to provide updates as frequently as possible. Online videos add to the brand of the horse for sale and are especially important for young horses or those "growing into" their price tags. Updates are added to the Web site and promoted through various media outlets including Facebook and e-mail campaigns.

Sellers currently fill out two separate forms: a credit card registration form and an equine fact sheet. The fact sheet includes a long series of checkboxes from which sellers select preworded traits, coupled with space for additional written descriptions. This saves some production time, although writing the actual copy is still a major part of the value that The Exchange provides. To implement this option, Aslin spent time investigating form-building tools. Custom-built form solutions were likely to be too expensive, so she played with numerous online form generators and ultimately was able to find some that offered great functionality at a relatively low cost. So, for example, a seller can indicate that the horse is a "jumper" and questions specific to jumpers will be displayed.

The Exchange develops a specific marketing strategy for each horse listed. This includes reviewing information submitted, combing through a horse's official show record, considering impartial impressions, and identifying the most likely buyers. If The Exchange thinks that the photos or videos don't help to sell the horse, they advise the seller on how to improve them. This advice stems from experience in marketing all types of horses from coast to coast, and an understanding of varied buyer profiles and geographic trends that exist in the market.

Social marketing forms the core of the Exchange's marketing efforts. Starting in 2009, The Exchange began experimenting with social media including RSS feeds, YouTube, Facebook, Twitter, and now, Instagram. Aslin notes that when she began The Exchange, social media was not yet the phenomenon that it is today, but when its significance started to became apparent, she had no choice but to jump in and begin using it, learning as she went. The Exchange has experienced varying success with social media. For instance, The Exchange runs multiple RSS feeds through the free service, FeedBurner, although thus far, the equestrian set does not appear to be particularly interested in RSS feed subscriptions. The company's YouTube channel has been largely supplanted by a professional video management system from Vzaar that hosts all of its videos, serves to most smartphones, and provides more control, branding, and flexibility than YouTube without any annoying advertisements. Facebook has been the most resounding social media success. The Exchange now has over 11,000 fans on Facebook. In addition, Aslin's personal Facebook friends, which number over 1,400, extend her cumulative Facebook reach to over 12,000 friends and fans, and make her online marketing efforts even more personal. The Exchange's Twitter account has almost 2,000 followers, and links with both The Exchange's Facebook page and its YouTube channel. The YouTube channel has over 300 subscribers, and over 50,000 views. The latest social media platform now in The Exchange's sights is Instagram, which Aslin believes may be very beneficial, because visuals such as photos and video play such an important role in the marketing of show horses. The Exchange's Instagram feed already has almost 2,000 followers. Because every business is different, The Exchange's experience suggests it's important for e-commerce sites to experiment with social media to determine which outlets are most effective in reaching their specific target audiences. The Exchange's successful use of social media in the equestrian industry was recognized when it was named one of 10 finalists for the 2012 PagePlay Equestrian Social Media Awards for best use of social media in North America.

To track the effectiveness of her social marketing efforts, Aslin uses various tracking systems. For instance, Google Analytics allows her to track exactly how many people are on the ExchangeHunterJumper site in real time and how they got there. Aslin has found that focusing solely on Likes is not sufficient. For example, she notes that a photo she posted advertising a horse on Facebook generated only 10 Likes, but that actually almost 150 people followed the link associated with the photo to the ExchangeHunterJumper Web site. She also uses a short URL service, bit.ly, to create unique URLs associated with Facebook and other social media posts that have built-in click trackers. This enables her to quickly see the collective success of her social marketing efforts; in a good month, bit.ly stats show around 5,000 click-throughs to the ExchangeHunterJumper site.

Another challenge is developing the actual social media content, which needs to be presented in such as way as to attract attention, and determining the optimal amount and timing of new content to post each day. Aslin notes that if she posts too many times a day, or posts too much content too close together, the reach of her posts seems to drop off.

Although Facebook is currently the primary social marketing platform for ExchangeHunterJumper, the firm also has loyal followers on Twitter. Although Aslin doubts that many of these followers are actual buyers or sellers at this time, she notes that in the future they probably will be. Her site has grown up along with her clientele, and children who once drooled over ponies on her site are now, 10 years later, soon-to-be adults and, possibly, young professionals.

The firm's Web site is also a key element of its e-commerce presence. Aslin continually reviews the design of the Web site with an eye to making it the most effective marketing tool possible. She built the original site herself in 2005 and updated it almost yearly in response to her target market's needs. In 2012, Aslin relaunched the site for a fifth time, and for the first time ever hired a professional Web development team to convert the static HTML site into a dynamically driven content management system on the Expression Engine platform. While she was able to keep costs low by designing and developing the site's CSS layout, the advanced functionality that was desired, such as the sale horse filter that enables shoppers to sort horses based on price, location, gender, type, and size, still required a hefty five-figure investment. Aslin believes the ability to get to know the market and update the site accordingly has kept The Exchange fresh and innovative. Every iteration of the Web site has been focused on meeting the target market's needs. For instance, she has also spent considerable time and expense to make sure The Exchange's Web site, including video, works just as well on mobile devices as it does on a traditional laptop or desktop computer. Aslin has

SOURCES: Exchangehunterjumper. com, accessed September 21, 2014; Interview with Amber Aslin, founder of ExchangeHunterJumper, September 2014, September 2013, and September 2012.

scrapped plans to create a stand-alone mobile site in favor of using responsive design techniques for The Exchange's site. And possibly on the horizon—browser-friendly 30-inch TV screens! Although potentially representing a whole new environment that would need to be designed for, Aslin believes it would actually be a great tool for her particular industry, given that it is so video reliant.

In addition to the Web site, The Exchange uses a variety of other marketing strategies, including e-mail campaigns, magazine advertising, and word of mouth. It ceased distributing its four-color, printed National Sales List booklet due to its high cost, and now relies almost totally on various types of online marketing. Aslin has found it has been extremely helpful to have the Web development experience she has honed over the years. Here are some of her words of wisdom: She feels that entrepreneurs don't necessarily have to know how to build sites, but do need to be familiar with what is and what is not possible in site construction. It is important to understand which functions are complicated and which are not, so that overly complicated add-ons that don't really add to the user experience can be eliminated from tight budgets. It's also important to know what technology is popular now and what technology is just around the corner. Even if you think you are proficient in all the tasks you will need to launch your business, with the rapid pace of technology, you inevitably spend much of your time learning something totally new, whether you want to or not.

By paying attention to these words of wisdom, as well as to detail at every step of the marketing process, The Exchange has managed to build a successful brand, one the horse community has come to rely upon.

Case Study Questions

1. Find a site on the Web that offers classified ads for horses. Compare this site to exchangehunterjumper.com in terms of the services offered (the customer value proposition). What does The Exchange offer that other sites do not?

2. In what ways were social media effective in promoting The Exchange brand? Which media led to the highest increase in sales and inquiries? Why?

3. Make a list of all the ways The Exchange attempts to personalize its services to both buyers and sellers.

7.6 REVIEW

KEY CONCEPTS

■ **Understand the difference between traditional online marketing and the new social-mobile-local marketing platforms and the relationships between social, mobile, and local marketing.**

- Social, mobile, and local marketing have transformed the online marketing landscape. The major trends and concepts include:
  - The emphasis in online marketing has shifted from exposing consumers to messages toward engaging them in conversations about your brand.
  - Social marketing means all things social: listening, discussing, interacting, empathizing, and engaging the consumer.
  - Social marketing and advertising is not simply a "new ad channel," but a collection of technology-based tools for communicating with shoppers.
  - In the past, businesses could tightly control their brand messaging and lead consumers down a funnel of cues that ended in a purchase. This is no longer the case. Instead, consumer purchase decisions are increasingly driven by the conversations, choices, tastes, and opinions of the consumer's social network.
  - Social, mobile, and local marketing are the fastest growing forms of online marketing.
- Social, mobile, and local digital marketing are self-reinforcing and connected.
- As mobile devices become more powerful, they are more useful for accessing Facebook and other social sites.
- Local and mobile marketing are highly related: local advertisers most often target mobile devices.
- The strong ties among social, mobile, and local marketing have significant implications for managing a marketing campaign in this new environment. When you design a social marketing campaign, you must also consider that your customers will be accessing the campaign using mobile devices, and often they will also be looking for local content.

■ **Understand the social marketing process from fan acquisition to sales and the marketing capabilities of social marketing platforms such as Facebook, Twitter, and Pinterest.**

- In social marketing, the objective is to encourage your potential customers to become fans of your company's products and services and engage with your business by entering into a conversation with it.
- There are five steps in the social marketing process model: fan acquisition, engagement, amplification, community, and brand strength and sales.
- Facebook is a social network with over 1.3 billion members. Facebook is designed to encourage people to reveal as much personal information about themselves as feasible, including activities, behavior, photos, music, movies, and purchases.
- Facebook's features are built to maximize the connections among people in the form of notifications, tagging, messaging, posting, and sharing. In many instances, the movement of personal information is so widespread that it is beyond the understanding of users.
- Social density refers to the number of interactions among members of a group and reflects the "connectedness" of a group, even if these connections are forced on users.
- Facebook has many marketing tools, including the Like button, Brand Pages, News Feed ads, Right-hand sidebar ads, mobile ads, and Facebook Exchange.
- The effectiveness of Facebook ads can be measured using five stages of the social marketing model: fan acquisition, engagement, amplification, community, and ultimately brand strengthening and sales.

- Twitter is a micro-blogging social network site that allows users to send and receive 140-character messages as well as videos, photos, and article previews.
- Twitter marketing tools include Promoted Tweets, Promoted Trends, Promoted Accounts, Enhanced Profile Pages, the Twitter Amplify program, television ad retargeting, Lead Generation Cards, and app install and app engagement ads.
- Measuring the results of Twitter marketing is similar to measuring the results of Facebook and other social marketing platforms, with some minor changes to account for the unique qualities of Twitter.
- Pinterest is the social network site that provides users with an online board to which they can "pin" interesting pictures. The success of Pinterest is based in part on a shift in consumer behavior enabled by new technologies: people talk about brands using pictures rather than words.
- Pinterest marketing tools include Promoted Pins; adding a Pin It logo to your Web site; pinning photos to Pinterest and direct users to your Web site; creating theme-based Pin It boards; placing URLs to stores that you support and receive lead generation fees from; integrating your pins and boards with other social sites; networking with users and followers.
- Pinterest campaigns can be measured using the same procedures as for Facebook and Twitter. The key dimensions to measure are fan (follower) acquisition, engagement, amplification, community, and sales.
- One downside of social marketing is that brands lose a substantial amount of control over where their ads appear in terms of other content and what people say about their brands on social sites.

■ Identify the key elements of a mobile marketing campaign.

- Although still in its infancy, mobile marketing involves the use of mobile devices such as smartphones and tablet computers to display banner ads, rich media, video, games, e-mail, text messaging, in-store messaging, QuickResponse (QR) codes, and couponing.
- Mobile devices represent a radical departure from previous marketing technologies simply because the devices integrate so many human and consumer activities from telephoning or texting friends, to listening to music, watching videos, and using the Web to shop and purchase goods.
- The mobile platform has changed over the past few years, and there are now almost as many tablet users as smartphone users in the United States.
- Mobile users spend over 85% of their mobile minutes using apps, and only 15% using their browsers. Marketers need to place ads in apps where consumers spend most of their time.
- Mobile devices create a multi-screen world: smartphones, tablets, desktops, and television. The reality, and the future, of computing devices is that consumers will be multi-platform: using desktops and laptops at work and home, and smartphones and tablets at home as well as when moving about.
- The implications of the multi-device platform, or screen diversity, environment are that marketing needs to be designed for whatever device the consumer is using, and consistent branding across platforms will be important.
- Unlike social marketing, mobile marketing does not require a great deal of new marketing vocabulary. All the marketing formats available on the desktop are also available on mobile devices. With few exceptions, mobile marketing is very much like desktop marketing—except it is smaller, mobile, and with the user all the time.
- The major marketing opportunities in mobile marketing are search ads, display ads, videos and rich media, messaging (SMS/MMS/PPS), and other familiar formats like e-mail, classified, and lead generation.
- The effectiveness of mobile marketing can be measured using the dimensions of the social marketing process model: fan acquisition, engagement, amplification, community, brand strength, and sales. Traditional Web-browser based metrics also can be used when measuring mobile campaigns.

■ Understand the capabilities of location-based local marketing.

- Location-based marketing is the targeting of marketing messages to users based on their location. Generally, location-based marketing involves marketing of location-based services.

- Examples of location-based services are personal navigation, point-of-interest, reviews, friend-finder, and family-tracker services.
- Location-based marketing is dependent on two technologies: accurate mapping software and mobile device geo-positioning technologies like GPS, Wi-Fi network location data, and Bluetooth low energy (BLE) technology.
- Location-based mobile marketing is currently a small part of the online marketing environment, but is expected to double over the next two years, and is growing far faster than any other form of digital advertising.
- The ad formats used in local mobile marketing are familiar—search ads, display, social/native advertising, video, and SMS text messages. A very large percentage of these local mobile ads will be delivered by search engines such as Google, and social sites such as Facebook.
- The key players in location-based mobile marketing are the same giants of advertising who dominate the mobile marketing environment: Google, Facebook, Apple, Twitter, YP (formerly Yellow Pages), Pandora, and Millenial.
- Geo-aware techniques identify the location of a user's device and then target marketing to the device, recommending actions within reach.
- Geo-targeting of ads involves sending ads based on the user's location.
- Proximity marketing techniques identify a perimeter around a physical location, and then target ads to users within that perimeter, recommending actions possible within the fenced-in area.
- In-store messaging involves messaging consumers while entering and browsing in a retail store. This requires a very precise calculation of location.
- Consumers who seek information about local businesses using mobile devices are much more active and ready to purchase than desktop users.
- Measuring the effectiveness of location-based mobile campaigns involves using the same techniques used for browser-based search and display ads (impressions), but also should include the dimensions of the social marketing process model such as acquisition, engagement, amplification, community, and brand strength and sales.

QUESTIONS

1. Describe the two factors that make social, local, and mobile marketing different from traditional online marketing.
2. Why are social, mobile, and local marketing efforts interconnected?
3. Why is the connection between social, mobile, and local marketing important to marketers?
4. What are the objectives of social marketing?
5. What are the major social network sites?
6. What are the five elements of the social marketing process?
7. What are the three most important features of Facebook for marketers to consider?
8. List and briefly describe the basic Facebook marketing tools.
9. How can you measure the results of a Facebook social marketing campaign?
10. List and briefly describe Twitter marketing tools.
11. How can you measure the results of a Twitter social marketing campaign?
12. In what way are Pinterest postings similar to display ads?
13. List and briefly describe some of Pinterest's marketing tools.
14. Why is mobile marketing different from desktop marketing?
15. What is the fastest growing m-commerce platform and why?
16. Why are in-app ads so important to marketers?
17. What is the multi-screen environment and how does it change marketing?
18. What kinds of ad formats are found on mobile devices?

19. Why is location-based marketing so attractive to marketers?
20. List and describe some basic location-based marketing tools.

PROJECTS

1. Visit the Web sites of at least two different online companies. Make a list of the social, mobile, and local marketing efforts you see on the Web site. Do their pages display Like it! plug-ins, and/or Google +1 logos? Do they have a Facebook page? If so, visit the pages to see how they use their Facebook pages. Is it different from their Web site pages? Can you identify how the firms use mobile marketing? Use your smartphone or tablet to access their Web sites. Are their Web sites designed specifically for each platform? In conclusion, compare and critically contrast these firms, and make recommendations for how you, as a marketing manager, would improve their effectiveness.

2. Visit your Facebook page and examine the ads shown in the right margin. What is being advertised and how do you believe it is relevant to your interests or online behavior? Make a list of ads appearing in your News Feed. Are these ads appropriately targeted to you in terms of your demographics, interests, and past purchases? Go to at least two Web sites, and Like it or Like a product. In the next 24 hours, do you see marketing messages on Facebook related to your Likes?

3. Visit two Web sites of your choice and apply the social marketing process model to both. Critically compare and contrast the effectiveness of these sites in terms of the dimensions of the social marketing process. How well do these sites acquire fans, generate engagement, amplify responses, create a community, and strengthen their brands? What recommendations can you make for these sites to improve their effectiveness?

4. Identify two Pinterest brand pages. Identify how they use Pinterest marketing tools described in this chapter. Are there some tools they are not using? What recommendations can you make for these sites to improve their Pinterest marketing campaigns?

REFERENCES

Aaker, D. A. "Measuring Brand Equity Across Products and Markets." *California Management Review*, Vol 38, No. 3, pp. 102–20. (1996).

AdRoll. "Facebook by the Numbers." AdRoll.com, 2015.

Ailawadi, Kusum L., Donald R. Lehmann, and Scott A. Neslin. "Revenue Premium as an Outcome Measure of Brand Equity." *Journal of Marketing*, 67 (October), 1–17 (October 2003).

AOL/BBDO/Insights Now. "Seven Shades of Mobile: The Hidden Motivations of Mobile Users." (October 2012).

BIA/Kelsey. "U.S. Local Media Forecast 2015 Update." (April 22, 2015a).

BIA/Kelsey. "Mobile Local Discovery: The Next Era of Search." (September 24, 2015b).

Bullas, Jeff. "21 Awesome Facebook Facts and Statistics You Need To Check Out." Jeffbullas.com (accessed October 24, 2015).

comScore. "Which Social Networks Have the Most Engaged Audience?" (April 2, 2015a).

comScore. "comScore Ranks the Top 50 U.S. Digital Media Properties for December 2014." (January 27, 2015b).

comScore. "2015 US Mobile App Report." (2015c).

comScore/Facebook. "The Power of Like: How Brands Reach and Influence Fans Through Social Marketing." White Paper (October 21, 2012).

eMarketer, Inc., "US Mobile Ad Spending, 2013–2019." (March 2015a).

eMarketer, Inc. "US Facebook and Twitter Revenue, by Device." (September 2015b).

eMarketer, Inc. "US Facebook and Twitter Ad Revenue Share, by Device, 2014–2017." (September 2015c).

eMarketer, Inc. "Instagram, Google, and Twitter Net US Mobile Display Ad Revenues, 2015–2017." (July 27, 2015d).

eMarketer, Inc. (Debra Wiliamson). "Instagram Marketing." (July 2015e).

eMarketer, Inc. "US Mobile Phone Internet Users and Penetration, 2013–2019." (February 2015f)

eMarketer, Inc. "US Tablet Users and Penetration, 2013–2019." (February 2015g)

eMarketer, Inc. "US Retail Ecommerce Sales, 2013–2019." (June 2015h).

eMarketer, Inc. "US Digital Travel Metrics, 2013–2019." (May 1, 2015i).

eMarketer, Inc. "US Retail Mcommerce Sales, by Device, 2013–2019." (May 1, 2015j).

eMarketer, Inc. "US Mobile Travel Sales, 2013–2019." (May 2015k).

eMarketer, Inc. "Mobile Website, App or Both." (June 2015l).

eMarketer, Inc. "US Digital Ad Spending, by Device, 2014–2019." (March 2015m).

eMarketer, Inc. "Net US Mobile Ad Revenues, by Company, 2014–2017." (September 2015n).

eMarketer, Inc. "US Mobile Ad Spending by Format, 2014–2019." (March 2015o).

eMarketer, Inc. "US Mobile Local Ad Spending Share, by Format, 2015 & 2019." (September 2015p).

eMarketer, Inc. (Krista Garcia). "Beacons For Retailers." (August 2015q).

eMarketer, Inc. "US Time Spent With Media. Updated Estimates for Fall 2015." (October 2015x).

eMarketer, Inc. "Ways in Which US Smartphone vs. Tablet Owners Plan to Use Their Device When Holiday Shopping." (October 2015y)

Facebook. "Statistics." Newsroom.fb.com (accessed October 26, 2015).

Frommer, Dan. "Vine Is a Sleeping Giant (While Everyone Is Focused on Snapchat)." Qz.com (August 7, 2015).

Google, Inc. "Understanding Consumers' Local Search Behavior." (May 2014).

Google, Inc. "The New Multiscreen World." (August 2012).

IAB (Interactive Advertising Bureau). "Response Design and Ad Creative: An IAB Perspective." (September 2012).

Internet Retailer. "The Mobile 500 2015 Edition." (2014).

Keller, K. L. (1993). "Conceptualizing, Measuring and Managing Customer-Based Brand Equity." *Journal of Marketing*, Vol 57, January, pp 1–22.

Lecher, Colin. "Facebook Says It Tracked People Who Didn't Use Facebook Because of a 'Bug'." Theverge.com (April 9, 2015).

LinkedIn. "Form 10-K LinkedIn Corporation For the fiscal year ended December 31, 2014." Securities and Commission (February 2, 2015).

Macmillan, Douglas, and Evelyn M. Rusli. "Snapchat Is Said to Have More Than 100 Million Monthly Active Users." *Wall Street Journal* (August 26, 2014).

Macy's. "Macy's Outlines New Omnichannel Strategy and Tech." Internetretailer.com (September 18, 2014).

Marks, Gene. "Why Target's Beacon Strategy Is Doomed." *Forbes.* (August 24, 2015).

National Retail Federation (NRF), "2015 Holiday Consumer Spending Survey." (October 20, 2015).

Nielsen. "Smartphones: So Many Apps, So Much Time." Nielsen (July 1, 2015).

Pew Research Center. "U.S. Smartphone Use in 2015." Pew Research Center (April 1, 2015).

Simon, C. J., and M. J. Sullivan. "The Measurement and Determinants of Brand Equity: A Financial Approach," *Marketing Science*, Vol. 12, No 1, pp. 28–52. (1993).

Simply Measured. "The Complete Guide to Analytics on Facebook." (2015).

Statista.com. "Number of Unique U.S. Visitors to Tumblr between July 2012 and July 2015 (in millions)." (accessed October 30, 2015a)

Statista.com. "Number of Monthly Active Instagram Users from January 2013 to September 2015 (in millions)." (accessed October 30, 2015b).

Taylor, Chris. "The Thumb Is Gone: Facebook Like Button Gets a Makeover." Mashable.com (November 6, 2013).

Twitter, Inc. "Report on Form 10-k for the fiscal year ended December 31, 2015 filed with the Securities and Exchange Commission." (March 2, 2015).

UnMetric. "29 Must-Know Terms for Every Social Media Analyst." (2015).

Vega, Tanzina, and Leslie Kaufman. "The Distasteful Side of Social Media Puts Advertisers on Their Guard." *New York Times* (June 3, 2013).

Verdon, Joan. "Beacons Launch Retail Revolution." NorthNewJersey.com. (April 5, 2015).

CHAPTER 8

Ethical, Social, and Political Issues in E-commerce

LEARNING OBJECTIVES

After reading this chapter, you will be able to:

- Understand why e-commerce raises ethical, social, and political issues.
- Understand basic concepts related to privacy and information rights, the practices of e-commerce companies that threaten privacy, and the different methods that can be used to protect online privacy.
- Understand the various forms of intellectual property and the challenges involved in protecting it.
- Understand how the Internet is governed and why taxation of e-commerce raises governance and jurisdiction issues.
- Identify major public safety and welfare issues raised by e-commerce.

The Right to Be Forgotten:
Europe Leads on Internet Privacy

© Lee Avison/Alamy

In June 2014, Google was forced to begin removing certain search engine query results in Europe after a ruling by the Court of Justice of the European Union, Europe's highest court. The ruling gives individuals the right to request that certain links to personal information found through a search of their names be removed. The court's ruling has come to be known as the "right to be forgotten" (sometimes given the acronym RTBF, or sometimes referred to as the "right to delist"). In an age where it seems there are no limits on the ability or willingness of private Internet firms to collect and dissemi-nate personal information, regardless of the user consenting to or knowing of its collection and use, the E.U.'s ruling is possibly the beginning of a new era of digital privacy based on the simple idea that individuals have a right to manage their online personal information and public image. Google, Facebook, Twitter, and many other U.S. Internet-based firms whose business models depend on virtually no limitations on the collection and use of personal information have lobbied strongly against the idea that individuals have a right to manage their personal online information. However, the European Court of Justice's decision is final, and Google, along with Yahoo, Microsoft, and others, have begun to implement the ruling. While simple in concept, the right to be forgotten can be devilishly difficult and expensive to implement in practice.

The court's decision was based on a 2010 lawsuit brought by a Spanish citizen, Mario Costeja Gonzalez, against a Spanish newspaper, and against Google Spain and Google Inc. (the American parent firm), which had linked his name with an auction notice that his house had been repossessed and was being sold in order to pay off debts that appeared in the newspaper. A Google search on Gonzalez' name returned a link to the newspaper notice as the most prominent link. Gonzalez' suit said that issues of his debt and foreclosure had been resolved years ago, and that the reference to this event was ir-relevant and an invasion of his privacy as defined in the European Union Data Protection Directive—Europe's digital era privacy legislation that governs personal information in the 28 countries that make up the European Union. Gonzalez requested that the news-paper remove or alter the pages it posted on the Web, and second, that Google Spain and Google Inc. be required to remove the link between his name and the auction notice in the newspaper. Gonzalez said he was not worried about his Web image as much as the impact on his work and reputation as a lawyer, and the potential of the notice to injure his law business. There had also been thousands of other requests by Europeans asking Google to remove links to their names that they claim are inappropriate, inaccurate, no longer relevant, and interfere with their privacy.

Google and the newspaper argued that because the server providing the results for Google searches in Spain was located outside Europe, the E.U. rules and privacy legislation did not apply. Google also argued that it was a search engine that simply provided links to information stored by others and therefore it was not a repository of personal information. Google also claimed that it was not responsible for the accuracy or relevance of information stored by other organizations, and that it was not subject to the E.U. Data Protection Directive because it pertained to data repositories. Finally, Google argued that under European law, individuals do not have the right to request that their personal data be removed from accessibility via a search engine. In public statements, Google also said it would be difficult or impossible to respond to thousands or millions of requests to eliminate links; granting these rights would allow criminals, fraudsters, sexual predators, and corrupt public officials to rewrite history; and that it would be very expensive to respond to requests and potentially limit innovation in the future.

In May 2014, the Court of Justice ruled that E.U. data protection policies were not limited by territory and apply to search engines no matter where the servers are located. Second, the court found that search engines are "controllers" of individual personal data within the European Union and therefore must comply with E.U. rules. Prior to this ruling, search engines like Google had been considered merely processors of online data, and therefore exempt from data protection rules in Europe. Finally the court found that Europeans do indeed have a right to ask search engines to remove links to personal information about them (the "right to be forgotten") when that information is inaccurate, inadequate, irrelevant, or excessive. The economic interests of the search engine to provide unfettered access to personal information did not justify interfering with the individual's right to be forgotten and personal privacy.

The court also clarified that the right to be forgotten is not absolute, but would have to be balanced against other rights and obligations such as freedom of expression, freedom of the press, and the broader public interest. For instance, the court's ruling did not require the newspaper to change any of the pages in its archives. The original auction notice remains. In other cases, the public has an interest in ensuring that convicted criminals not be allowed to escape their criminal records, which are public records in most jurisdictions. Rather than a blanket right granted to whomever applies to have information removed from search engines, instead the court required a case-by-case assessment that examines the type of information, its potential for harm to the individual's private life, and the interest of the public in having access to that information. Also, for "public figures," those who have thrust themselves into public roles, such as politicians, celebrities, or business leaders, the public interest in knowing may trump the private interest in being forgotten.

As of October 1, 2015, Google said it had received almost 325,000 requests from people who wanted, in aggregate, 1.15 million links to online information about them removed, and that it had removed about 42% of those links based on internal guidelines that they have developed. However, the process has proved to be problematic. Google has been criticized by various European privacy regulators for its practice of informing Web sites that their links are being removed from its search results, noting that this may result in even more attention to the links (this is sometimes known as the Streisand effect, which refers to a lawsuit by Barbra Streisand that sought to have photos of her home removed from an online database, and which ended up publicizing the photos even more). In the United Kingdom, the U.K.'s Information Commissioner's Office has ordered Google to remove links to news stories about the removal of links, on the grounds that the new links defeat the purpose of the original removal. Other critics complain that the decisions should not be left in the hands of a private company. A particularly thorny issue has been the extent to which the right to be forgotten must be applied outside of Europe. Google initially interpreted the ruling as meaning that it must remove links only from its European search results. This interpretation was also adopted by an advisory council convened by Google consisting of prominent European academics, members of the press, and governmental regulators. However, the French privacy regulator, the Commission Nationale de l'Informatique et des Libertés (CNIL) disagrees and has ordered Google to remove search results from all of its sites around the world, or face significant fines. Google will likely attempt to further appeal this decision.

The reactions to the Court of Justice's rulings and France's efforts to extend the right to forget beyond the boundaries of Europe reflect a deep digital divide between Europe and the United States when it comes to privacy and the balance between managing personal information (privacy) and freedom of expression and the press. U.S newspapers like the *New York Times* fear that the ruling may undermine freedom of the press and free speech, leave Europeans less informed in the Internet age, reduce technology innovation, and allow some individuals to hide their crimes of the past. The Wikimedia Foundation, the not-for-profit organization behind Wikipedia, publishes a list of the links to its Web pages that Google has removed from its search engine, so that people will know what information is no longer being made available to them. In Europe, in contrast, many celebrate the ruling as a victory over arrogant U.S. Internet companies who think they can do whatever they want with whatever personal information they can collect and then tell the victims it is all necessary for human progress and innovation, when in fact their sole purpose is to make money selling the same information to advertisers. The German Economics Minister Sigmar Gabriel hailed the ruling, saying that Europe stands against the totalitarian idea of making every detail of human behavior, human emotion, and human thought an object of commercial exploitation. In fact, the right to be forgotten is just the tip of the new European General Data Protection Regulation that, when implemented in 2016, will establish a number of additional data protection rights. Because Europe is the United States' largest trading partner and a very large source of revenues for U.S. Internet firms, there is little doubt that European views on privacy, and the idea that data belongs first and foremost to the individual, will have an impact on U.S. privacy claims and laws, especially if CNIL's requirement that Google remove links from all its sites around the world, not just in Europe, prevails.

SOURCES: "Google Transparency Report," Google.com, October 1, 2015; "France Rejects Google's Effort's to Limit Application of Privacy Ruling," by Mark Scott, *New York Times,* September 21, 2015; "U.K. Wants to Remove Links to Stories About Removing Links to Stories," by Sam Schechner, *Wall Street Journal,* August 20, 2015; "Google Advisory Council: Right to Delist Should Only Apply in EU," by David Meyer, Gigaom.com, February 6, 2015; "A Question Over the Reach of Europe's 'Right to Be Forgotten'," by Mark Scott, *New York Times,* February 1, 2015; "'Right to Be Forgotten' Complaints Streamlined by Data Watchdogs," by Jo Best, Zdnet.com, September 19, 2014; "EU Data Chiefs Meet to Rein in Google Over 'Right to be Forgotten' Approach," by Aoife White, Independent.ie, September 17, 2014; "Discussing Online 'Right to Be Forgotten,' Google Takes European Privacy Tour to Spain," by Mark Scott, *New York Times,* September 9, 2014; "Wikimedia Wants You to Remember the Links Europe Wants You to Forget," by Conor Dougherty, *New York Times,* August 6, 2014; "Google Starts Removing Search Results Under Europe's 'Right to be Forgotten," by Sam Schechner, *Wall Street Journal,* June 26, 2014; "Google Takes Steps to Comply With 'Right to Be Forgotten' Ruling," by Mark Scott, *New York Times,* May 30, 2014; "Google Softens Stance in Europe's Privacy War," by Sam Schechner, *Wall Street Journal,* May 30, 2014; "Right to Be Forgotten? Not That Easy," by Danny Hakim, *New York Times,* May 29, 2014; "EU Court Ruling a Victory for Privacy," by Spiegel Staff, *Der Spiegel,* May 20, 2014; "After European Court Order, Google Works on a Tool to Remove Links," by Mark Scott, *New York Times,* May 15, 2014; "Factsheet on the 'Right to be Forgotten' Ruling," Court of Justice of the European Union, May 14, 2014; "European Court Lets Users Erase Records on Web," by David Streitfeld, *New York Times,* May 13, 2014; "Daily Report: Europe Moves to Reform Rules Protecting Privacy," *New York Times,* March 13, 2014.

Determining how or whether personal information should be retained or deleted on the Internet is just one of many ethical, social, and political issues raised by the rapid evolution of the Internet and e-commerce. For instance, as discussed in the opening case, whether individuals lose control over all personal information once it is placed on the Internet is still up for debate in the United States. In Europe, in contrast, individuals do retain rights to their personal information. These questions are not just ethical questions that we as individuals have to answer; they also involve social institutions such as family, schools, business firms, and in some cases, entire nation-states. And these questions have obvious political dimensions because they involve collective choices about how we should live and what laws we would like to live under.

In this chapter, we discuss the ethical, social, and political issues raised in e-commerce, provide a framework for organizing the issues, and make recommendations for managers who are given the responsibility of operating e-commerce companies within commonly accepted standards of appropriateness.

8.1 UNDERSTANDING ETHICAL, SOCIAL, AND POLITICAL ISSUES IN E-COMMERCE

The Internet and its use in e-commerce have raised pervasive ethical, social, and political issues on a scale unprecedented for computer technology. Entire sections of daily newspapers and weekly magazines are devoted to the social impact of the Internet. But why is this so? Why is the Internet at the root of so many contemporary controversies? Part of the answer lies in the underlying features of Internet technology itself, and the ways in which it has been exploited by business firms. Internet technology and its use in e-commerce disrupt existing social and business relationships and understandings.

Consider for instance Table 1.2 (in Chapter 1), which lists the unique features of Internet technology. Instead of considering the business consequences of each unique feature, **Table 8.1** examines the actual or potential ethical, social, and/or political consequences of the technology.

We live in an "information society," where power and wealth increasingly depend on information and knowledge as central assets. Controversies over information are often disagreements over power, wealth, influence, and other things thought to be valuable. Like other technologies, such as steam, electricity, telephones, and television, the Internet and e-commerce can be used to achieve social progress, and for the most part, this has occurred. However, the same technologies can be used to commit crimes, despoil the environment, and threaten cherished social values. Before automobiles, there was very little interstate crime and very little federal jurisdiction over crime. Likewise with the Internet: before the Internet, there was very little "cybercrime."

Many business firms and individuals are benefiting from the commercial development of the Internet, but this development also exacts a price from individuals, organizations, and societies. These costs and benefits must be carefully considered by those seeking to make ethical and socially responsible decisions in this new envi-

TABLE 8.1	UNIQUE FEATURES OF E-COMMERCE TECHNOLOGY AND THEIR POTENTIAL ETHICAL, SOCIAL, AND/OR POLITICAL IMPLICATIONS
E-COMMERCE TECHNOLOGY DIMENSION	POTENTIAL ETHICAL, SOCIAL, AND POLITICAL SIGNIFICANCE
Ubiquity—Internet/Web technology is available everywhere: at work, at home, and elsewhere via mobile devices, anytime.	Work and shopping can invade family life; shopping can distract workers at work, lowering productivity; use of mobile devices can lead to automobile and industrial accidents. Presents confusing issues of "nexus" to taxation authorities.
Global reach—The technology reaches across national boundaries, around the Earth.	Reduces cultural diversity in products; weakens local small firms while strengthening large global firms; moves manufacturing production to low-wage areas of the world; weakens the ability of all nations—large and small—to control their information destiny.
Universal standards—There is one set of technology standards, namely Internet standards.	Increases vulnerability to viruses and hacking attacks worldwide, affecting millions of people at once. Increases the likelihood of "information" crime, crimes against systems, and deception.
Richness—Video, audio, and text messages are possible.	A "screen technology" that reduces use of text and potentially the ability to read by focusing instead on video and audio messages. Potentially very persuasive messages that may reduce reliance on multiple independent sources of information.
Interactivity—The technology works through interaction with the user.	The nature of interactivity at commercial sites can be shallow and meaningless. Customer e-mails are frequently not read by human beings. Customers do not really "co-produce" the product as much as they "co-produce" the sale. The amount of "customization" of products that occurs is minimal, occurring within predefined platforms and plug-in options.
Information density—The technology reduces information costs, and raises quality.	While the total amount of information available to all parties increases, so does the possibility of false and misleading information, unwanted information, and invasion of solitude. Trust, authenticity, accuracy, completeness, and other quality features of information can be degraded. The ability of individuals and organizations to make sense out of this plethora of information is limited.
Personalization/Customization—The technology allows personalized messages to be delivered to individuals as well as groups.	Opens up the possibility of intensive invasion of privacy for commercial and governmental purposes that is unprecedented.
Social technology—The technology enables user content generation and social networking.	Creates opportunities for cyberbullying, abusive language, and predation; challenges concepts of privacy, fair use, and consent to use posted information; creates new opportunities for surveillance by authorities and corporations into private lives.

ronment. The question is: How can you as a manager make reasoned judgments about what your firm should do in a number of e-commerce areas—from securing the privacy of your customer's clickstream to ensuring the integrity of your company's domain name?

A MODEL FOR ORGANIZING THE ISSUES

E-commerce—and the Internet—have raised so many ethical, social, and political issues that it is difficult to classify them all, and hence, complicated to see their relationship to one another. Clearly, ethical, social, and political issues are interrelated. One way to organize the ethical, social, and political dimensions surrounding e-commerce is shown in **Figure 8.1**. At the individual level, what appears as an ethical issue—"What should I do?"—is reflected at the social and political levels—"What should we as a society and government do?" The ethical dilemmas you face as a manager of a business using the Web reverberate and are reflected in social and political debates. The major ethical, social, and political issues that have developed around e-commerce over the past 10 years can be loosely categorized into four major dimensions: information rights, property rights, governance, and public safety and welfare.

Some of the ethical, social, and political issues raised in each of these areas include the following:

- **Information rights:** What rights to their own personal information do individuals have in a public marketplace, or in their private homes, when Internet technologies make information collection so pervasive and efficient? What rights do individuals have to access information about business firms and other organizations?
- **Property rights:** How can traditional intellectual property rights be enforced in an Internet world where perfect copies of protected works can be made and easily distributed worldwide in seconds?
- **Governance:** Should the Internet and e-commerce be subject to public laws? And if so, what law-making bodies have jurisdiction—state, federal, and/or international?

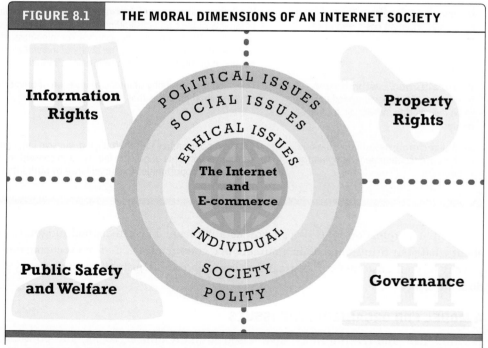

FIGURE 8.1 | **THE MORAL DIMENSIONS OF AN INTERNET SOCIETY**

The introduction of the Internet and e-commerce impacts individuals, societies, and political institutions. These impacts can be classified into four moral dimensions: property rights, information rights, governance, and public safety and welfare.

- **Public safety and welfare:** What efforts should be undertaken to ensure equitable access to the Internet and e-commerce channels? Should governments be responsible for ensuring that schools and colleges have access to the Internet? Are certain online content and activities—such as pornography and gambling—a threat to public safety and welfare? Should mobile commerce be allowed from moving vehicles?

To illustrate, imagine that at any given moment, society and individuals are more or less in an ethical equilibrium brought about by a delicate balancing of individuals, social organizations, and political institutions. Individuals know what is expected of them, social organizations such as business firms know their limits, capabilities, and roles, and political institutions provide a supportive framework of market regulation, banking, and commercial law that provides sanctions against violators.

Now, imagine we drop into the middle of this calm setting a powerful new technology such as the Internet and e-commerce. Suddenly, individuals, business firms, and political institutions are confronted by new possibilities of behavior. For instance, individuals discover that they can download perfect digital copies of music tracks from Web sites without paying anyone, something that, under the old technology of CDs, would have been impossible. This can be done, despite the fact that these music tracks still legally belong to the owners of the copyright—musicians and record label companies. Then, business firms discover that they can make a business out of aggregating these digital musical tracks—or creating a mechanism for sharing musical tracks—even though they do not "own" them in the traditional sense. The record companies, courts, and Congress were not prepared at first to cope with the onslaught of online digital copying. Courts and legislative bodies will have to make new laws and reach new judgments about who owns digital copies of copyrighted works and under what conditions such works can be "shared." It may take years to develop new understandings, laws, and acceptable behavior in just this one area of social impact. In the meantime, as an individual and a manager, you will have to decide what you and your firm should do in legal "gray" areas, where there is conflict between ethical principles but no clear-cut legal or cultural guidelines. How can you make good decisions in this type of situation?

Before examining the four moral dimensions of e-commerce in greater depth, we will briefly review some basic concepts of ethical reasoning that you can use as a guide to ethical decision making, and provide general reasoning principles about the social and political issues of the Internet that you will face in the future.

BASIC ETHICAL CONCEPTS: RESPONSIBILITY, ACCOUNTABILITY, AND LIABILITY

Ethics is at the heart of social and political debates about the Internet. **Ethics** is the study of principles that individuals and organizations can use to determine right and wrong courses of action. It is assumed in ethics that individuals are free moral agents who are in a position to make choices. When faced with alternative courses of action, what is the correct moral choice? Extending ethics from individuals to business firms and even entire societies can be difficult, but it is not impossible. As long as there is a decision-making body or individual (such as a board of directors or CEO in a business firm, or a governmental body in a society), their decisions can be judged against a variety of ethical principles.

ethics
the study of principles that individuals and organizations can use to determine right and wrong courses of action

If you understand some basic ethical principles, your ability to reason about larger social and political debates will be improved. In western culture, there are four basic principles that all ethical schools of thought share: responsibility, accountability, liability, and due process. **Responsibility** means that as free moral agents, individuals, organizations, and societies are responsible for the actions they take. **Accountability** means that individuals, organizations, and societies should be held accountable to others for the consequences of their actions. The third principle—liability—extends the concepts of responsibility and accountability to the area of law. **Liability** is a feature of political systems in which a body of law is in place that permits individuals to recover the damages done to them by other actors, systems, or organizations. **Due process** is a feature of law-governed societies and refers to a process in which laws are known and understood, and there is an ability to appeal to higher authorities to ensure that the laws have been correctly applied.

You can use these concepts immediately to understand some contemporary Internet debates. For instance, consider the 2005 U.S. Supreme Court decision in the case of *Metro-Goldwyn-Mayer Studios v. Grokster, et al.* MGM had sued Grokster and other P2P networks for copyright infringement. The court decided that because the primary and intended use of Internet P2P file-sharing services such as Grokster, StreamCast, and Kazaa was the swapping of copyright-protected music and video files, the file-sharing services should be held accountable and shut down. Although Grokster and the other networks acknowledged that the most common use of the software was for illegal digital music file-swapping, they argued that there were substantial, nontrivial uses of the same networks for legally sharing files. They also argued they should not be held accountable for what individuals do with their software, any more than Sony could be held accountable for how people use VCRs, or Xerox for how people use copying machines. Ultimately, the Supreme Court ruled that Grokster and other P2P networks could be held accountable for the illegal actions of their users if it could be shown that they intended their software to be used for illegal downloading and sharing, and had marketed the software for that purpose. The court relied on copyright laws to arrive at its decisions, but these laws reflect some basic underlying ethical principles of responsibility, accountability, and liability.

Underlying the *Grokster* Supreme Court decision is a fundamental rejection of the notion that the Internet is an ungoverned "Wild West" environment that cannot be controlled. Under certain defined circumstances, the courts will intervene into the uses of the Internet. No organized civilized society has ever accepted the proposition that technology can flaunt basic underlying social and cultural values. Through all of the industrial and technological developments that have taken place, societies have intervened by means of legal and political decisions to ensure that the technology serves socially acceptable ends without stifling the positive consequences of innovation and wealth creation. The Internet in this sense is no different, and we can expect societies around the world to exercise more regulatory control over the Internet and e-commerce in an effort to arrive at a new balance between innovation and wealth creation, on the one hand, and other socially desirable objectives on the other. This is a difficult balancing act, and reasonable people will arrive at different conclusions.

responsibility
as free moral agents, individuals, organizations, and societies are responsible for the actions they take

accountability
individuals, organizations, and societies should be held accountable to others for the consequences of their actions

liability
a feature of political systems in which a body of law is in place that permits individuals to recover the damages done to them by other actors, systems, or organizations

due process
a process in which laws are known and understood and there is an ability to appeal to higher authorities to ensure that the laws have been correctly applied

ANALYZING ETHICAL DILEMMAS

Ethical, social, and political controversies usually present themselves as dilemmas. A **dilemma** is a situation in which there are at least two diametrically opposed actions, each of which supports a desirable outcome. When confronted with a situation that seems to present an ethical dilemma, how can you analyze and reason about the situation? The following is a five-step process that should help:

dilemma
a situation in which there are at least two diametrically opposed actions, each of which supports a desirable outcome

1. **Identify and clearly describe the facts.** Find out who did what to whom, and where, when, and how. In many instances, you will be surprised at the errors in the initially reported facts, and often you will find that simply getting the facts straight helps define the solution. It also helps to get the opposing parties involved in an ethical dilemma to agree on the facts.

2. **Define the conflict or dilemma and identify the higher-order values involved.** Ethical, social, and political issues always reference higher values. Otherwise, there would be no debate. The parties to a dispute all claim to be pursuing higher values (e.g., freedom, privacy, protection of property, and the free enterprise system). For example, supporters of the use of advertising networks such as DoubleClick argue that the tracking of consumer movements on the Web increases market efficiency and the wealth of the entire society. Opponents argue this claimed efficiency comes at the expense of individual privacy, and advertising networks should cease their activities or offer Web users the option of not participating in such tracking.

3. **Identify the stakeholders.** Every ethical, social, and political issue has stakeholders: players in the game who have an interest in the outcome, who have invested in the situation, and usually who have vocal opinions. Find out the identity of these groups and what they want. This will be useful later when designing a solution.

4. **Identify the options that you can reasonably take.** You may find that none of the options satisfies all the interests involved, but that some options do a better job than others. Sometimes, arriving at a "good" or ethical solution may not always be a balancing of consequences to stakeholders.

5. **Identify the potential consequences of your options.** Some options may be ethically correct but disastrous from other points of view. Other options may work in this one instance but not in other similar instances. Always ask yourself, "What if I choose this option consistently over time?"

Once your analysis is complete, you can refer to the following well-established ethical principles to help decide the matter.

CANDIDATE ETHICAL PRINCIPLES

Although you are the only one who can decide which ethical principles you will follow and how you will prioritize them, it is helpful to consider some ethical principles with deep roots in many cultures that have survived throughout recorded history:

- **The Golden Rule:** Do unto others as you would have them do unto you. Putting yourself into the place of others and thinking of yourself as the object of the decision can help you think about fairness in decision making.

- **Universalism:** If an action is not right for all situations, then it is not right for any specific situation (Immanuel Kant's categorical imperative). Ask yourself, "If we adopted this rule in every case, could the organization, or society, survive?"

- **Slippery Slope:** If an action cannot be taken repeatedly, then it is not right to take at all. An action may appear to work in one instance to solve a problem, but if repeated, would result in a negative outcome. In plain English, this rule might be stated as "once started down a slippery path, you may not be able to stop."

- **Collective Utilitarian Principle:** Take the action that achieves the greater value for all of society. This rule assumes you can prioritize values in a rank order and understand the consequences of various courses of action.

- **Risk Aversion:** Take the action that produces the least harm, or the least potential cost. Some actions have extremely high failure costs of very low probability (e.g., building a nuclear generating facility in an urban area) or extremely high failure costs of moderate probability (speeding and automobile accidents). Avoid the high-failure cost actions and choose those actions whose consequences would not be catastrophic, even if there were a failure.

- **No Free Lunch:** Assume that virtually all tangible and intangible objects are owned by someone else unless there is a specific declaration otherwise. (This is the ethical "no free lunch" rule.) If something someone else has created is useful to you, it has value and you should assume the creator wants compensation for this work.

- **The New York Times Test (Perfect Information Rule):** Assume that the results of your decision on a matter will be the subject of the lead article in the *New York Times* the next day. Will the reaction of readers be positive or negative? Would your parents, friends, and children be proud of your decision? Most criminals and unethical actors assume imperfect information, and therefore they assume their decisions and actions will never be revealed. When making decisions involving ethical dilemmas, it is wise to assume perfect information markets.

- **The Social Contract Rule:** Would you like to live in a society where the principle you are supporting would become an organizing principle of the entire society? For instance, you might think it is wonderful to download illegal copies of Hollywood movies, but you might not want to live in a society that does not respect property rights, such as your property rights to the car in your driveway, or your rights to a term paper or original art.

None of these rules is an absolute guide, and there are exceptions and logical difficulties with all of them. Nevertheless, actions that do not easily pass these guidelines deserve some very close attention and a great deal of caution because the appearance of unethical behavior may do as much harm to you and your company as the actual behavior.

Now that you have an understanding of some basic ethical reasoning concepts, let's take a closer look at each of the major types of ethical, social, and political debates that have arisen in e-commerce.

8.2 PRIVACY AND INFORMATION RIGHTS

Privacy is the moral right of individuals to be left alone, free from surveillance or interference from other individuals or organizations, including the state. Privacy is a girder supporting freedom: Without the privacy required to think, write, plan, and associate independently and without fear, social and political freedom is weakened, and perhaps destroyed. **Information privacy** is a subset of privacy. The right to information privacy includes both the claim that certain information should not be collected at all by governments or business firms, and the claim of individuals to control the use of whatever information is collected about them. Individual control over personal information is at the core of the privacy concept. Implicit in the claim to control one's own personal information is the claim to be able to edit and even delete personal information from the Web. This is often called the "**right to be forgotten**," as discussed in the opening case (Rosen, 2012).

Due process also plays an important role in defining privacy. The best statement of due process in record keeping is given by the Fair Information Practices doctrine developed in the early 1970s and extended to the online privacy debate in the late 1990s (described later in this section).

There are two kinds of threats to individual privacy posed by the Internet. One threat originates in the private sector and concerns how much personal information is collected by commercial Web sites and how it will be used. A second threat originates in the public sector and concerns how much personal information federal, state, and local government authorities collect, and how they use it. While these threats are conceptually distinct, in practice they are related as the federal government increasingly relies on Internet companies to provide intelligence on specific individuals and groups, and as Internet records held by search engine companies and others (like Amazon) are sought by legal authorities and attornies.

In 2015, the public discussion of privacy has broadened from a concern about tracking the behavior of individuals while they use the Internet, especially on social networks, to include the impact of mobile devices for tracking the location of people via their smartphones, collecting information on their personal behavior including the shops, churches, political rallies, bars, and other locations they have visited, and collecting a detailed log of their phone calls (Barrett, 2015a; 2015b). There is increasing public attention and criticism of the entire ecosystem of data brokerage firms called data brokers that collect and re-sell this personal information to advertisers. These concerns about tracking and surveilling people throughout their daily lives have been heightened by the revelation that the federal government's National Security Agency has been logging virtually all cell phone calls of all residents for many years. Smartphone apps that tap user information have also received critical attention. In addition, local and state law enforcement agencies have greatly expanded their surveillance technology and capabilities to include mass surveillance of large populations in the search for criminals and terrorists. The falling costs of personal tracking technology like mobile cameras, the ubiquitous use of always-on smartphones fitted out with GPS, and the growth of powerful storage and analytic capabilities, have resulted in a torrent of data, referred to as Big Data, pouring into marketing and law enforcement

privacy
the moral right of individuals to be left alone, free from surveillance or interference from other individuals or organizations, including the state

information privacy
includes both the claim that certain information should not be collected at all by governments or business firms, and the claim of individuals to control the use of whatever information is collected about them

right to be forgotten
the claim of individuals to be able to edit and delete personal information online

databases. Private and government investigations have found both Apple and Google are collecting personal location and behavior data, and sharing this information with marketers and government agencies. The cell phone carriers receive more than a million requests each year from law enforcement agencies for call data (Chen, 2014; Maass and Rajagopalen, 2012). Apart from smartphone surveillance, new wireless cameras mounted on cars (a kind of remote sensing device) have led to a new industry of license plate tracking, resulting in hundreds of millions of license plate photos collected by private firms and police forces, regardless of whether or not the car's owners have done anything wrong (Angwin and Valentino-Devries, 2012). Facial recognition technology employed by Facebook and others simply adds to public anxiety over the loss of personal privacy.

In general, the Internet and the Web provide an ideal environment for both business and government to invade the personal privacy of millions of users on a scale unprecedented in history. Perhaps no other recent issue has raised as much widespread social and political concern as protecting the privacy of 260 million Internet users in the United States alone.

INFORMATION COLLECTED AT E-COMMERCE SITES

personally identifiable information (PII)
any data that can be used to identify, locate, or contact an individual

anonymous information
demographic and behavioral information that does not include any personal identifiers

As you have learned in previous chapters, e-commerce sites routinely collect a variety of information from or about consumers who visit their site and/or make purchases. Some of this data constitutes **personally identifiable information (PII)**, which is defined as any data that can be used to identify, locate, or contact an individual (Federal Trade Commission, 2000a). Other data is **anonymous information**, composed of demographic and behavioral information, such as age, occupation, income, zip code, ethnicity, and other data that characterizes your life such as Web browsing behavior without identifying who you are. **Table 8.2** lists just a few of the personal identifiers routinely collected by online e-commerce sites including mobile sites and apps. This is not an exhaustive list, and in fact many Web sites collect hundreds of different data points on visitors. A study of nine data brokers identified twelve broad categories of information collected by brokers, and 240 data elements from address history, to liens and political leanings, to vehicle and travel data (Federal Trade Commission, 2014).

TABLE 8.2	PERSONAL INFORMATION COLLECTED BY E-COMMERCE SITES	
Name	Gender	Education
Address	Age	Preference data
Phone number	Occupation	Transaction data
E-mail address	Location	Clickstream data
Social security number	Location history	Device used for access
Bank accounts	Likes	Browser type
Credit card accounts	Photograph	

Advertising networks and search engines also track the behavior of consumers across thousands of popular sites, not just at one site, via cookies, Web beacons, tracking software, spyware, and other techniques. For instance, simply clicking a Like button on a Web site enables Facebook to track your movements across the Web.

Table 8.3 illustrates some of the major ways online firms gather information about consumers.

TABLE 8.3	THE INTERNET'S MAJOR INFORMATION-GATHERING TOOLS AND THEIR IMPACT ON PRIVACY
INTERNET CAPABILITY	**IMPACT ON PRIVACY**
Smartphones and apps	Used to track location and share photos, addresses, phone numbers, search, and other behavior to marketers.
Advertising networks	Used to track individuals as they move among thousands of Web sites.
Social networks	Used to gather information on user-provided content such as books, music, friends, and other interests, preferences, and lifestyles.
Cookies and Super Cookies	Used to track individuals at a single site. Super Cookies are nearly impossible to identify or remove.
Third-party cookies (beacons)	Cookies placed by third-party advertising networks. Used to monitor and track online behavior, searches, and sites visited across thousands of sites that belong to the advertising network for the purpose of displaying "relevant" advertising.
Spyware	Can be used to record all the keyboard activity of a user, including Web sites visited and security codes used; also used to display advertisements to users based on their searches or other behavior.
Search engine behavioral targeting (Google and other search engines)	Uses prior search history, demographics, expressed interests, geographic, or other user-entered data to target advertising.
Deep packet inspection	Uses software installed at the ISP level to track all user clickstream behavior.
Shopping carts	Can be used to collect detailed payment and purchase information.
Forms	Online forms that users voluntarily fill out in return for a promised benefit or reward that are linked with clickstream or other behavioral data to create a personal profile.
Site transaction logs	Can be used to collect and analyze detailed information on page content viewed by users.
Search engines	Can be used to trace user statements and views on newsgroups, chat groups, and other public forums on the Web, and profile users' social and political views. Google returns name, address, and links to a map with directions to the address when a phone number is entered.
Digital wallets (single sign-on services)	Client-side wallets and software that reveal personal information to Web sites verifying the identity of the consumer.
Digital Rights Management (DRM)	Software (Windows Media Player) that requires users of online media to identify themselves before viewing copyrighted content.
Trusted Computing Environments	Hardware and software that controls the viewing of copyrighted content and requires users' identification, e.g., Amazon Kindle.

SOCIAL NETWORKS AND PRIVACY

Social networks pose a unique challenge for the maintenance of personal privacy because they encourage people to reveal details about their personal lives (passions, loves, favorites, photos, videos, and personal interests), and to share them with their friends. Social networks have greatly enlarged the depth, scope, and richness of information collected by private corporations. While Google's search engine is a massive database of personal intentions, Facebook has created a massive database of friends, preferences, Likes, posts, and activities. An Austrian researcher was able to obtain his Facebook file (possible under European laws) and received a 1,222-page document of messages, photos, posts, and friends (Sengupta, 2012). Some social networkers share these personal details with everyone on the social network. On the face of it, this would seem to indicate that people who participate in social networks voluntarily give up their rights to personal privacy. How could they claim an expectation of privacy? When everything is shared, what's private?

But the reality is that many adult (18 or over) participants in social networks have a very keen sense of their personal privacy. Facebook is a prime example of senior management pushing the envelope of privacy, and experiencing a number of public relations reversals and growing government concern. For instance, Facebook deployed facial recognition technology without any previous notice, which compromised its users' privacy by allowing them to be tagged in photos without their consent. Researchers at Carnegie Mellon found that it is possible to identify people, even their social security numbers, based on a single Facebook photograph and using facial recognition programs (Angwin, 2011; Acquisti et al., 2011). After consumer uproar and challenges from various state attorneys general, Facebook reversed course and made it easier for users to opt out of the technology. In 2012, Facebook began pushing ads on its users based on their use of apps and offering advertisers the ability to serve ads to Facebook users even while not using Facebook. In 2013, Facebook announced a new privacy policy that it claimed clarified its use of personal information. In the new policy, Facebook claimed it could use any personal information for any purpose it wanted to. After howls of protest from users, privacy groups, and congressmen, the policy was temporarily withdrawn. In 2014, Facebook changed its default privacy settings to reveal information only to friends, and allowed users to see some of the data Facebook collects about them and to edit that data. Actually performing these tasks is quite difficult. In early 2015, Facebook implemented new privacy policies that stipulate that it may share users' personal data with partnered sites for the delivery of targeted ads. For a review of Facebook's various positions on online privacy over the years, and public and congressional reaction to these issues, refer to the *Insight on Society* case, *Facebook and the Age of Privacy,* in Chapter 1.

The result of these public conflicts suggests that social network participants do indeed have a strong expectation of privacy in the sense that they want to control how "their" information is used. People who contribute user-generated content have a strong sense of ownership over the content that is not diminished by posting the information on a social network for one's friends. As for members who post information to everyone, not just friends, these should be seen as "public performances" where the contributors voluntarily publish their performances, just as writers or other artists do. This does not mean they want the entirety of their personal lives thrown open to every Web tracking automaton on the Internet.

MOBILE AND LOCATION-BASED PRIVACY ISSUES

As the mobile platform becomes more and more important, issues about mobile and location-based privacy are also becoming a major concern. In 2012, investigators discovered that iOS and Android apps were funneling location information to mobile advertisers, along with users' address books and photos (Bilton, 2012). As a result, Congress opened an investigation into the privacy policies of smartphone manufacturers, along with Facebook, Pinterest, Yahoo, Google, and 30 others in the app marketplace. Twitter announced that anyone using its "Find Friends" feature on smartphones was also sending every phone number and e-mail address in their address books to the company (Sarno, 2012).

In 2011, a furor erupted over news that Apple iPhones and iPads and Google Android smartphones were able to track and store user location information. In 2012, Facebook launched a new mobile advertising service that tracks what apps people use on their smartphones, and what they do while using the apps. Apple and Google track users' apps also. Apple disclosed that it can target ads based on the apps that a person has downloaded, while Google does not currently do this. For instance, Facebook can target a frequent player of a game such as Words with Friends with ads using the player's Facebook News Feed, which is a major channel for Facebook ads (the other being display ads on the user's page). In 2012, investigators discovered that some cell phone companies had installed tracking devices inside phones to improve customer service. This ignited a flurry of criticism. In 2015, investigators discovered that the U.S. Central Intelligence Agency and the Justice Department had developed an airborne fake cell tower that fools cell phones into revealing their identity and location. Called "Dirtboxes," the devices are located on planes at five airports around the country and can surveil most of the population (Barrett, 2015c). Similar hand-held devices are readily available on the Internet.

In June 2014, the U.S. Supreme Court, in a pathbreaking unanimous decision, ruled that police needed a warrant prior to searching a person's cell phone for information. All mobile devices will likely receive this protection against general, warrantless police searches (Savage, 2014). An earlier decision in 2012 requires police to obtain a warrant prior to attaching GPS tracking devices to a suspect's car. In both cases, the Supreme Court found that cell phones held extensive detailed personal information, retained information for many years, and stored many different types of information. Much of a person's intimate and personal life can be stored on cell phones, making them the modern equivalent of personal papers, which are protected under the Fourth Amendment to the Constitution, which protects the "right of the people to be secure in their persons, houses, papers, and effects, against unreasonable searches and seizures." The U.S. Senate held hearings in June 2014 on the Consumer Location Privacy Protection Act, which requires firms to notify cell phone users and obtain their consent if they want to gather location data. The FTC signed a 20-year consent order with Snapchat after discovering the app was collecting location data contrary to Snapchat's own privacy policy. However, while searching a cell phone for information

TABLE 8.4	INTERNET USERS' EFFORTS TO PRESERVE PRIVACY
ACTION	PERCENTAGE WHO HAVE DONE THIS
Cleared Web browser history or cookies.	59%
Refused to provide information if felt wasn't relevant.	57%
Used Web browser settings to disable or turn off cookies.	34%
Deleted or edited something previously posted online.	29%
Used a temporary e-mail address or user name.	25%
Provided inaccurate or false information about self.	24%
Refused to use Web site that required real name.	23%
Used public computer in order to browse anonymously.	12%
Attempted to get something posted online about them removed.	11%
Encrypted phone calls, text messages, or e-mail.	10%
Used proxy server, Tor, or VPN to browse Web anonymously.	9%

SOURCE: Based on data from Pew Research Center, 2015.

may require a warrant, using a person's cell phone to establish identity or location does not require a warrant.

A backlash against the privacy-invading practices of Internet firms and the online advertising industry is gaining momentum, as reflected in opinion polls. Both attitudes and behavior are changing. Americans have strong feelings about privacy. In a recent survey, over 90% said being in control of who can get personal information, and controlling what information is collected, is "very important." Almost 90% said it is important that others not watch or listen to them without permission. Around 94% of Americans do not believe government agencies, business firms, or other institutions can keep their information private and secure (Pew Research, 2015). While 10% or fewer have taken advanced steps, such as encrypting their communications or using proxy servers to protect their privacy, about 25% or more have used false names, used a temporary e-mail address, or decided not to use a website because it asked for their real name. An estimated 25% of Internet users have ad blocking software (Sloane, 2015) (see **Table 8.4**). Next to hackers, Americans try to avoid advertisers pursuing them while online, and 59% block cookies to make tracking more difficult. Refer to the *Insight on Society* case, *Foursquare: Check Your Privacy at the Door*, in Chapter 2, for more discussion of some of the issues associated with mobile and location-based privacy. The *Insight on Technology* case: *Apple: Champion of Privacy?* discusses the differences in Apple's and Google's approach to privacy in the context of new assistant technology now embedded in their respective smartphones.

PROFILING AND BEHAVIORAL TARGETING

On an average day, around 87% of adult Americans use the Internet, and most of these go online every day (Pew Research Center, 2015). Marketers would like to know who

INSIGHT ON TECHNOLOGY

APPLE: CHAMPION OF PRIVACY?

In June 2015, Tim Cook, CEO of Apple, the world's most valuable corporation, gave a most unusual speech for a Silicon Valley executive. Cook attacked other Internet giants like Google, Facebook, Yahoo, and Microsoft for invading their customers' privacy. Apple, he said, rejects the idea that customers have to make a trade-off between privacy and security. Cook believes people have a fundamental right to privacy. Some of the most prominent firms in Silicon Valley, Cook argued, lull their customers into giving up a treasure of personal information in order to receive some service, like cloud storage, social networking, or photo services for "free." In fact, Cook argued, the trade-off comes at a high cost to the consumer in the form of the loss of privacy and fear about what might become of their personal information. In the end, he said, consumers will regret the trade. These companies, he noted, are gobbling up everything they can learn about consumers and trying to monetize it by selling it to advertisers. Cook's strong statements on the importance of privacy are contrary to the views of Mark Zuckerberg, founder and CEO of Facebook, most famously summarized in his January 2011 interview arguing that the age of privacy is over (see the Chapter 1 *Insight on Society* case, *Facebook and the Age of Privacy*).

The Internet privacy debate has long centered on what information advertisers have about us, how they track people, build profiles, follow us around the Web to retarget ads, and make it impossible to figure out what they do with our personal information, or to do anything about it. The latest polls on consumer attitudes found that people don't want to give up their privacy and personal information, but have become resigned to the situation. They are sharing data, but aren't happy about it. For ordinary people, the privacy issue is not resolved. The Age of Privacy has not ended in the minds of consumers.

But the privacy issue is about to be given a new twist: the evolving technology of personal assistants, built on the latest technology of speech recognition, predictive analytics, and ever faster processors and Internet connections, is behind a new marketing push for Apple iPhones, Android phones, and Microsoft PC and laptop software. These personal assistants are not advertising vehicles, but rather seek to extend the functionality of mobile devices to a new level in which smartphones and tablets play an even greater role in consumers' lives than they do now (if that is imaginable!). The objective is to monitor user activity, use that information to predict future behavior, and then make recommendations and supply information even before users ask for it.

Apple, of course, already has Siri, but with iOS9, Apple introduced Proactive assistant technology. Google has developed Google Now. Microsoft has introduced Cortana to all its devices. All these new assistants aim to anticipate what users want, and when they want it. For Apple, Google, and Microsoft, the assistant-space is turning out to be a major battleground for market share. What's at stake for Apple is more useful services and a better customer experience that will drive sales of it iPhones and tablets. For Google, it's all about collecting information for its advertisers by building attractive, useful services for free. For Microsoft, likewise, a really useful Cortana means more hardware with Windows OS and more software can be sold. A lot is at stake.

While they share objectives, the way each firm goes about collecting the information has important implications for privacy, and whether users will really want these assistants to know so much. The nice thing about human assistants is that you can tell them to stay out of certain areas of your

(continued)

life that are private, just for you, and trusted others. Not so with computer-based assistants.

Apple's Proactive assistant technology aims to collect data on personal behavior from the iPhone itself and do most of the processing on the user's phone. It will collect, for instance, data on which apps you use, where you are, who you talk or text with, and has some limited access to e-mails, using them to identify callers and create calendar events. Using this information, Siri can remind you to call people on their birthday or about meetings, inform you about local businesses, and even find a gas station close to the car rental office at the airport. Listen to music when you exercise in the morning? Siri will start playing your favorite songs without asking.

When it needs to connect to Apple Web servers to, say, let you know there's traffic ahead that may interfere with your doctor's appointment, Apple assigns a random number to your phone, so Apple servers do not know your identity. Your phone will know your health information, but Apple servers will not. Apple makes a distinction between what your phone knows and what the company knows. Although the phone may know a lot, Apple is trying to minimize how much information it itself knows about its users!

Google's approach is, well, so like Google. Google Now aggregates information from Web searches and browsing history, use of other Google services like Google Docs, Gmail, calendar, YouTube, as well as data from the phone such as position, time, app use, and who you communicate with using any phone media. In other words, just about all the data you generate in the process of using the Internet. All this information is stored and processed on Google's cloud servers, which could be anywhere in the United States, Europe, or elsewhere. Google says it will not sell this information to others, but it will use this information to target ads to users. A subtle distinction: Google is not selling data, it's selling access to millions of individuals' screens and it knows a great deal about all of them, perhaps all there is to know about many of its users.

Some believe that Google's more comprehensive approach, while more invasive, will produce a better assistant than what Apple can provide using Proactive assistant technology. Google Now just knows so much more about you. Google plans to introduce a new feature called Google Now on Tap that can understand what users are doing inside apps, and possibly make suggestions about the next step to take in a game. Google Now can display information about local movies and restaurants, movies playing nearby, and remind you that your boss sent an e-mail asking for a spreadsheet by Friday afternoon. Apple's Proactive assistant technology will not be reading your email. Google has been reading user email since Gmail was introduced in 2004.

Apple is making a bet that its privacy regarding assistant technology will be a popular feature at a time in history when public concerns about privacy, invasion of privacy by business and government, and the lack of Internet security are growing, not receding. Google is making a different bet: consumers are primarily interested in utility, functionality, and power, for which they will exchange their privacy.

SOURCES: "iPhone 6s's Hands-Free Siri Is an Omen of the Future," by Farhad Manjoo, *New York Times,* September 22, 2015; "Tech That Hangs on Your Every Word Raises Privacy Questions," by Andrea Peterson, *Washington Post,* September 16, 2015; "What Your iPhone Doesn't Tell Apple," by Geoffrey Fowler, *Wall Street Journal,* September 15, 2015; "Apple Dots Its Privacy 'I's In iOS 9, While Google Appears to Back Pedal," by Allison Schiff, Adexchanger. com, September 1, 2015; "The Tradeoff Fallacy: How Marketers Are Misrepresenting American Consumers and Opening Them Up to Exploitation," by Joseph Turow, Michael Hennessy, and Nora Draper, Annenberg School of Communications, University of Pennsylvania, September 2015; "Apple Privacy May Not Be As Private As You Think," by Theo Priestley, *Forbes,* August 24, 2015; "Apple and Google Know What You Want Before You Do," by Daisuke Wakabayashi, *Wall Street Journal,* August 3, 2015; "Apple Moves to Block iPhone App-Scanning," by Amir Efrati, Information.com, June 24, 2015; "Why Edward Snowden Supports Apple's Stance on Privacy," by Jess Bolluyt, Cheatsheet.com, June 27, 2015; "What Apple's Tim Cook Overlooked in His Defense of Privacy," by Farhad Manjoo, *New York Times,* June 10, 2015; "Tim Cook Says Apple 'Doesn't Want Your Data.' Let's Not Say Things We Can't Take Back," by Lily Hay Newman, Slate.com, June 3, 2015; "Apple's Tim Cook Delivers Blistering Speech on Encryption, Privacy," by Matthew Panzarino, Techcrunch.com, June 2, 2015; "Apple's New Privacy Push Focuses on Data Minimization," by Jedidiah Bracy, Privacy Tech, iapp.org, June, 2015.

these people are, what they are interested in, and what they buy. The more precise the information, the more complete the information, and the more valuable it is as a predictive and marketing tool. Armed with this information, marketers can make their ad campaigns more efficient by targeting specific ads at specific groups or individuals, and they can even adjust the ads for specific groups.

Many Web sites allow third parties—including online advertising networks such as Microsoft Advertising, DoubleClick, and others—to place "third-party" cookies and Web tracking software on a visitor's computer in order to engage in profiling the user's behavior across thousands of Web sites. A third-party cookie is used to track users across hundreds or thousands of other Web sites who are members of the advertising network. **Profiling** is the creation of digital images that characterize online individual and group behavior. **Anonymous profiles** identify people as belonging to highly specific and targeted groups, for example, 20- to 30-year-old males, with college degrees and incomes greater than $30,000 a year, and interested in high-fashion clothing (based on recent search engine use). **Personal profiles** add a personal e-mail address, postal address, and/or phone number to behavioral data. Increasingly, online firms are linking their online profiles to personal offline consumer data collected by database firms tracking credit card purchases, as well as established retail and catalog firms.

The online advertising networks have added several new dimensions to established offline marketing techniques. First, they have the ability to precisely track not just consumer purchases, but all browsing behavior on the Web at thousands of the most popular member sites, including browsing book lists, filling out preference forms, and viewing content pages. Second, they can dynamically adjust what the shopper sees on screen—including prices. Third, they can build and continually refresh high-resolution data images or behavioral profiles of consumers. Other advertising firms have created spyware software that, when placed on a consumer's computer, can report back to the advertiser's server on all consumer Internet use, and is also used to display advertising on the consumer's computer. Most personal computers have hundreds of these programs installed without user consent or understanding.

A different kind of profiling and a more recent form of behavioral targeting is Google's results-based personalization of advertising. Google has a patent on a program that allows advertisers using Google's AdWords program to target ads to users based on their prior search histories and profiles, which Google constructs based on user searches, along with any other information the user submits to Google or that Google can obtain, such as age, demographics, region, and other Web activities (such as blogging). Google also has a second patent on a program that allows Google to help advertisers select keywords and design ads for various market segments based on search histories, such as helping a clothing Web site create and test ads targeted at teenage females. Google uses behavioral targeting to help it display more relevant ads based on keywords. According to Google, the feature is aimed at capturing a more robust understanding of user intent, and thereby delivering a better ad. Google's Gmail, a free e-mail service, offers a powerful interface, and gigabytes of free storage. In return, Google computers read all incoming and outgoing e-mail and place "relevant" advertising in the margins of the mail. Profiles are developed on individual users based on the content in their e-mail.

profiling
the creation of digital images that characterize online individual and group behavior

anonymous profiles
identify people as belonging to highly specific and targeted groups

personal profiles
add a personal e-mail address, postal address, and/or phone number to behavioral data

Both American and European regulators have objected to Google's policy of integrating personal information from all of its services into a single personal profile, and second, failing to let users know what it is doing with their personal information (Charlton, 2013). Google claims that people who send mail to a friend's Gmail account do not have an expectation of privacy, and that anyone who sends information to a third party does not have an expectation of privacy. Privacy groups expressed concerns when Google announced in 2014 that it was purchasing Nest, the maker of digital home thermostats and smoke detection devices that are connected to the Internet. Although Nest says it is run separately from Google and that Nest accounts are not cross-linked with Google accounts, Nest admits that it does share personal information with Google when connected to Google's "Works with Nest integration" system (Gibbs, 2015).

Facial recognition tools add a new dimension to profiling and behavioral targeting. In 2014, several uses of facial recognition are already commonplace. Facebook and Google+ use the software to automatically suggest name tags for members or their friends in photographs. The technology is evolving rapidly: Google has applied for a patent to identify faces in online videos, and Facebook has developed a highly accurate facial recognition system called DeepFace (Singer, 2014a). It is difficult for people to detect if they are being stalked or followed by persons using facial recognition technology, and currently there are no controls over its use.

deep packet inspection

a technology for recording every key stroke at the ISP level

Deep packet inspection is another technology for recording every keystroke at the ISP level of every Internet user (no matter where they ultimately go on the Web), and then using that information to make suggestions, and target ads. While advertising networks are limited, and even Google does not constitute the universe of search, deep packet inspection at the ISP level really does capture the universe of all Internet users. In 2014, deep packet inspection is not used in the United States by advertising firms because it is likely a violation of the Electronic Communications Privacy Act of 1986. However, it is used as a network management and law enforcement tool (Kuehn and Mueller, 2012).

Network advertising firms argue that Web profiling benefits both consumers and businesses. Profiling permits targeting of ads, ensuring that consumers see advertisements mostly for products and services in which they are actually interested. Businesses benefit by not paying for wasted advertising sent to consumers who have no interest in their product or service. The industry argues that by increasing the effectiveness of advertising, more advertising revenues go to the Internet, which in turn subsidizes free content on the Internet. Last, product designers and entrepreneurs benefit by sensing demand for new products and services by examining user searches and profiles.

Critics argue that profiling undermines the expectation of anonymity and privacy that most people have when using the Internet, and changes what should be a private experience into one where an individual's every move is recorded. As people become aware that their every move is being watched, they will be far less likely to explore sensitive topics, browse pages, or read about controversial issues. How can people experience freedom if they believe their every move on the Internet is being watched? In most cases, the profiling is invisible to users, and even hidden. Consumers are not notified that profiling is occurring. Profiling permits data aggregation on hundreds or even thousands of unrelated sites on the Web. Critics debate the economic benefits of profiling because it allows firms to engage in price discrimination, charging more for goods based on, for instance, zip code, gender, and ethnicity (Singer, 2015). The cookies placed by ad networks are persistent, and they can be set to last days, months, years, or even forever. Their tracking occurs over an extended period of time and resumes each time the individual logs on to the Internet. This clickstream data is used to create profiles that can include hundreds of distinct data fields for each consumer. Associating so-called anonymous profiles with personal information is fairly easy, and companies can change policies quickly without informing the consumer. Although the information gathered by network advertisers is often anonymous (non-PII data), in many cases, the profiles derived from tracking consumers' activities on the Web are linked or merged with personally identifiable information. Anonymous behavioral data is far more valuable if it can be linked with offline consumer behavior, e-mail addresses, and postal addresses.

THE INTERNET AND GOVERNMENT INVASIONS OF PRIVACY: E-COMMERCE SURVEILLANCE

Today, the online and mobile behavior, profiles, and transactions of consumers are routinely available to a wide range of government agencies and law enforcement authorities, contributing to rising fears among online consumers, and in some cases, their withdrawal from the online marketplace. The last few years have not been good for advocates of privacy, with revelations that federal government agencies have been routinely gathering cell phone call data on Americans and foreigners in the United States for a period of several years with scant judicial oversight. In June 2013, Edward Snowden, a security contractor for the National Security Agency (NSA), began releasing NSA documents to *The Guardian*, a U.K. newspaper, providing a detailed description of NSA surveillance programs of both U.S. and foreign citizens. These programs were unprecedented in scope and involved wholesale collection of cell phone metadata around the world, tapping communications lines of Google, Yahoo, and other Internet services, and tapping cell phones of foreign leaders. The NSA enlisted the support of the major telecommunications carriers to give it information about Americans' phone calls and e-mail in a program called Prism. These programs were conceived in the aftermath of the terrorist attack on the United States on September 11, 2001, and were envisaged as necessary to protect the country. The programs were authorized by the USA PATRIOT Act of 2001, and subsequent amendments, and were reviewed by relevant Congressional committees. Many in the computer science academic community were aware of these programs, in part because they participated in the development of techniques for discovering patterns in large data sets, as well as so-called machine learning programs. Nevertheless, the revelations alarmed average citizens who previously believed that if they did nothing wrong, surely the government would not be collecting information about them. The revelations also heightened public awareness and criticism of Internet firms like Google and Facebook, and others engaging in extensive tracking and consumer surveillance. Google, Facebook, Microsoft, and others have since tried to resist or prevent warrantless government access to their consumer data (Apuzzo et al., 2015).

Advances in technology for storing, processing, and analyzing unimaginable quantities of personal data, referred to as Big Data and business analytics (data mining and representation software), have further heightened perceptions that privacy is increasingly difficult to define and protect in the age of e-commerce and social networks (Kakutani, 2013; Mayer-Schonberger and Cukier, 2013).

Striking a balance between security and liberty is at the center of the privacy debate (Ford, 2013). While the Internet used to be thought of as impossible for governments to control or monitor, nothing could be actually further from the truth. Law enforcement authorities have long claimed the right under numerous statutes to monitor any form of electronic communication pursuant to a court order and judicial review and based on the reasonable belief that a crime is being committed. This includes the surveillance of consumers engaged in e-commerce. The Communications Assistance for Law Enforcement Act (CALEA), the USA PATRIOT Act, the Cyber Security Enhancement Act, and the Homeland Security Act all strengthen the ability of law enforcement agencies to monitor Internet users without their knowledge and, under certain circumstances when life is purportedly at stake, without judicial oversight. The USA PATRIOT Act, designed to combat terrorism inside the borders of the United States, permits nearly unlimited government surveillance without court oversight, according to several senators (Savage, 2012). However, in June 2015, several provisions of the USA PATRIOT Act expired. In response, Congress passed the USA Freedom Act, which imposes some limits on the bulk collection by the National Security Agency and other U.S. intelligence agencies of U.S. citizens' telecommunications metadata.

Previously, in May 2014, the White House had released a report, *Big Data: Seizing Opportunities and Preserving Values*, that focused on the role of technology, including e-commerce and mobile phones, in expanding the amount and depth of information available and collected on citizens. A supporting report of the President's Council of Advisors on Science and Technology (PCAST) was also released, calling for a consumer privacy bill of rights, a data breach law requiring firms to report losses of consumer data, extension of these privacy rights to non-citizens, use of technologies to enhance privacy, restriction of the use of data that might cause discrimination against various groups in America, and the amendment of the Electronic Communications Privacy Act to strengthen protections against government surveillance of the sort uncovered by Snowden (Executive Office of the President, 2014; PCAST, 2014). In February 2015, the White House issued a draft Consumer Privacy Bill of Rights Act. The draft bill lays out a number of privacy and security requirements for companies that collect consumer data. Firms would be required to disclose their privacy and data use policies in plain language, inform consumers about what data is collected, and provide consumers with greater control over the use of their personal data. Privacy policies would be reviewed and monitored by the Federal Trade Commission, which would have rule-making authority over firms' policies and behavior (Rosenfeld and Hutnick, 2015). The draft has been widely criticized for not going beyond existing laws and practices and for relying on vague criteria, such as "reasonableness" and "context" in data collection and use. The FTC itself has also objected to the proposal.

Other Congressional initiatives in 2015 in this area include the Email Privacy Act, which regulates email providers; the Preserving American Privacy Act, which regulates the collection of information by drones; and the Online Communications and Geolocation Protection Act, which regulates the uses of personal geo-location data. However, at this time, it is not likely that any of these proposed bills will be enacted by Congress.

Taking matters into its own hands, in September 2014, Apple introduced the iPhone 6, which offers the ability for users to encrypt e-mail, photos, and contacts stored on the phone using a strong encryption algorithm. The data can only be decrypted by using a passcode that only the user possesses, and Apple does not retain the key to the code. As a result, the NSA will no longer be able to force Apple and Google to reveal such user data. In September 2015, Apple said it could not comply with a court order to turn over text messages in real time involving an investigation of drug and gun runners. In 2013, Microsoft refused to turn over e-mails from a drug trafficking suspect, saying the records were stored in Ireland (Apuzzo et al., 2015). Not surprisingly, the NSA and law enforcement officials are not happy with this prospect and fear that it will enable criminals and terrorists to evade surveillance. Apple and Google contend that in order for them to compete globally, they must be able to convince consumers that their data is secure, a task made more difficult as a result of the Snowden revelations (Sanger and Chen, 2014).

Government agencies are among the largest users of private sector commercial data brokers, such as Acxiom, Experian, and TransUnion Corporation, that collect a vast amount of information about consumers from various offline and online public sources, such as public records and the telephone directory, and non-public sources, such as "credit header" information from credit bureaus (which typically contains name, aliases, birth date, social security number, current and prior addresses, and phone numbers). Acxiom is the largest private personal database in the world with records on more than 500,000 people and about 1,500 data points per person (Singer, 2012). Information contained in individual reference services' databases ranges from purely identifying information (e.g., name and phone number) to much more extensive data (e.g., driving records, criminal and civil court records, property records, and licensing records). This information can be linked to online behavior information collected from other commercial sources to compile an extensive profile of an individual's online and offline behavior.

When you use a search engine, the IP address of your computer is typically recorded, and cookies are placed on your browser to record the search terms of the current session, time of visit, and links you actually chose. This information is stored in a database where it can be related to previous searches and other personal identifiers that the search engine may have gleaned from those previous searches. Search engine data provides a comprehensive picture of a person's intentions and actions on the Internet. The amount of time such data is retained is not governed by U.S. law, but the European Union has indicated that it should not be retained for more than six months. The three major search engines (Google, Bing, and Yahoo) have varying policies. Recent research has found that the claim that retaining search data for longer periods, such as 18 months, improves the accuracy of searches is not supported by empirical data (Chiou and Tucker, 2014).

LEGAL PROTECTIONS

In the United States, Canada, and Germany, rights to privacy are explicitly granted in, or can be derived from, founding documents such as constitutions, as well as in specific statutes. In England and the United States, there is also protection of privacy in the common law, a body of court decisions involving torts or personal injuries. For instance, in the United States, four privacy-related torts have been defined in court decisions involving claims of injury to individuals caused by other private parties: intrusion on solitude, public disclosure of private facts, publicity placing a person in a false light, and appropriation of a person's name or likeness (mostly concerning celebrities) for a commercial purpose (Laudon, 1996). In the United States, the claim to privacy against government intrusion is protected primarily by the First Amendment guarantees of freedom of speech and association, the Fourth Amendment protections against unreasonable search and seizure of one's personal documents or home, and the Fourteenth Amendment's guarantee of due process. It's important to remember that these protections apply to government intrusions of privacy, not private firms' intrusions.

In addition to common law and the Constitution, there are both federal laws and state laws that protect individuals against government intrusion and in some cases define privacy rights vis-à-vis private organizations such as financial, educational, and media institutions (cable television and video rentals) (see **Table 8.5**).

Informed Consent and Notice

One conceptual basis of American privacy law is notification and consent. It is assumed that consumers can read Terms of Use notices (or privacy policies) concerning how a Web site will use their personal information, and then make a rational choice to either consent to the terms of use, opt out of the data collection (if that is an option), or stop using the site. The concept of **informed consent** (defined as consent given with knowledge of all material facts needed to make a rational decision) also plays an important role in protecting privacy. In the United States, business firms can gather transaction information generated in the marketplace and then use that information for other purposes, without obtaining the explicit affirmative informed consent of the individual. For instance, in the United States, if a shopper purchases books about baseball from an e-commerce company that participates in an advertising network such as DoubleClick, a cookie can be placed on the consumer's hard drive and used by other member companies to sell the shopper sports clothing without the explicit permission or even knowledge of the user. This online preference information may also be linked with personally identifying information. In Europe, this would be illegal. A business in Europe cannot use marketplace transaction information for any purpose other than supporting the current transaction, unless it obtains the individual's consent in writing or by filling out an on-screen form.

There are traditionally two models for informed consent: opt-in and opt-out. The **opt-in** model requires an affirmative action by the consumer to allow collection and use of information. For instance, using opt-in, consumers would first be asked if they approved of the collection and use of information, and then directed to check a selection box if they agreed. Otherwise, the default is not to approve the collection of data. In the **opt-out** model, the default is to collect information unless the consumer takes an affirmative action to prevent the collection of data by checking a box or by filling out a form.

Until recently, many U.S. e-commerce companies rejected the concept of informed consent and instead simply published their information use policy on their site. Nearly all Web sites have Terms of Use policies that users can find if they look carefully. These Terms of Use policies are sometimes called privacy policies, and they describe how the firms will use information collected on their sites. These policies are notices, and as noted above, it is assumed that anyone who uses the site has implicitly agreed

informed consent
consent given with knowledge of all material facts needed to make a rational decision

opt-in
requires an affirmative action by the consumer to allow collection and use of consumer information

opt-out
the default is to collect information unless the consumer takes an affirmative action to prevent the collection of data

TABLE 8.5	FEDERAL AND STATE PRIVACY LAWS
NAME	**DESCRIPTION**

GENERAL FEDERAL PRIVACY LAWS

NAME	DESCRIPTION
Freedom of Information Act of 1966	Gives people the right to inspect information about themselves held in government files; also allows other individuals and organizations the right to request disclosure of government records based on the public's right to know.
Privacy Act of 1974, as amended	Regulates the federal government's collection, use, and disclosure of data collected by federal agencies. Gives individuals a right to inspect and correct records.
Electronic Communications Privacy Act of 1986	Makes conduct that would infringe on the security of electronic communications illegal.
Computer Security Act of 1987	Makes conduct that would infringe on the security of computer-based files illegal.
Computer Matching and Privacy Protection Act of 1988	Regulates computerized matching of files held by different government agencies.
Driver's Privacy Protection Act of 1994	Limits access to personal information maintained by state motor vehicle departments to those with legitimate business purposes. Also gives drivers the option to prevent disclosure of driver's license information to marketers and the general public.
E-Government Act of 2002	Regulates the collection and use of personal information by federal agencies.
USA Freedom Act of 2015	Imposes limits on the bulk collection by federal agencies of U.S. citizens' telecommunication metadata.

FEDERAL PRIVACY LAWS AFFECTING PRIVATE INSTITUTIONS

NAME	DESCRIPTION
Fair Credit Reporting Act of 1970	Regulates the credit investigating and reporting industry. Gives people the right to inspect credit records if they have been denied credit and provides procedures for correcting information.
Family Educational Rights and Privacy Act of 1974	Requires schools and colleges to give students and their parents access to student records and to allow them to challenge and correct information; limits disclosure of such records to third parties.
Right to Financial Privacy Act of 1978	Regulates the financial industry's use of personal financial records; establishes procedures that federal agencies must follow to gain access to such records.
Privacy Protection Act of 1980	Prohibits government agents from conducting unannounced searches of press offices and files if no one in the office is suspected of committing a crime.
Cable Communications Policy Act of 1984	Regulates the cable industry's collection and disclosure of information concerning subscribers.
Video Privacy Protection Act of 1988	Prevents disclosure of a person's video rental records without court order or consent.
Children's Online Privacy Protection Act (1998)	Prohibits deceptive practices in connection with the collection, use, and/or disclosure of personal information from and about children on the Internet.
Health Insurance Portability and Accountability Act of 1996 (HIPAA)	Requires healthcare providers and insurers and other third parties to promulgate privacy policies to consumers and establishes due process procedures.
Financial Modernization Act (Gramm-Leach-Bliley Act) (1999)	Requires financial institutions to inform consumers of their privacy policies and permits consumers some control over their records.

(continued)

TABLE 8.5	FEDERAL AND STATE PRIVACY LAWS (CONT'D)
NAME	DESCRIPTION
SELECTED STATE PRIVACY LAWS	
Online privacy policies	The California Online Privacy Protection Act of 2003 was the first state law in the United States requiring owners of commercial Web sites or online services to post a privacy policy. The policy must, among other things, identify the categories of PII collected about site visitors and categories of third parties with whom the information may be shared. Failure to comply can result in a civil suit for unfair business practices. Nebraska and Pennsylvania prohibit false and misleading statements in online privacy policies. At least 16 states require government Web sites to establish privacy policies or procedures or incorporate machine-readable privacy policies into their Web sites.
Spyware legislation	A number of states, including California, Utah, Arizona, Arkansas, and Virginia, among others, have passed laws that outlaw the installation of spyware on a user's computer without consent.
Disclosure of security breaches	In 2002, California enacted legislation that requires state agencies or businesses that own or license computer data with personal information to notify state residents if they experience a security breach involving that information; today, nearly every state has enacted similar legislation.
Privacy of personal information	Two states, Nevada and Minnesota, require ISPs to keep their customers' PII private unless the customer consents to disclose the information. Minnesota also requires ISPs to get permission from subscribers before disclosing information about subscribers' online surfing habits.
Data encryption	In October 2007, Nevada passed the first law that requires encryption for the transmission of customer personal information. The law took effect October 1, 2008.

to the Terms of Use policy. A recent study reviewed 30 popular social network and community sites and found that it would take the average reader about eight hours to simply read the policy. The longest policy was SoundCloud's, with 7,961 words. Obviously a critical flaw with informed consent as the basis of privacy protections is that it assumes the average user can understand what privacy they may be giving up by using a site (Singer, 2014b; Fiesler and Bruckman, 2014). For instance, Yahoo's privacy policy begins by stating that Yahoo takes the user's privacy seriously and Yahoo does not rent, sell, or share personal information about users with others or non-affiliated companies. However, there are a number of exceptions that significantly weaken this statement. For instance, Yahoo may share the information with "trusted partners," which could be anyone that Yahoo does business with, although perhaps not a company that the user might choose to do business with. In its privacy policy, Yahoo also says it uses cookies, device identifiers, and Web beacons in order to track user clickstream behavior across the Web. To opt-out of interest-based advertising, a user must sign into his or her Yahoo account and allow cookies from Yahoo. U.S. businesses argue that informing consumers about how the information will be used is sufficient to obtain the users' informed consent. Privacy advocates argue that many Terms of Use/privacy policy statements on U.S. Web sites are obscure and difficult to read, and legitimate just about any use of personal information. For instance, in 2014, a furor erupted when it was revealed that both Facebook and OKCupid (a dating site) had conducted undisclosed social experiments involving user behavior on their sites. Facebook secretly manipulated the News Feeds of almost 700,000 users to see if negative posts on users' News Feeds made them more likely to make negative posts as well. Facebook claimed that such research was covered by its Terms of Use; critics argued that conducting such research without explicit informed consent is both unethical and illegal (Storm, 2014). In the United States, most e-commerce companies that offer informed consent use the opt-out model. Unless the consumer checks a box to specifically decline, information is collected. Often, the selection box is at the very bottom of the Web page, where the consumer is unlikely to see it, or located within complex menus.

The Federal Trade Commission's Fair Information Practices Principles

In the United States, the Federal Trade Commission (FTC) has taken the lead in conducting research on online privacy and recommending legislation to Congress. The FTC is a cabinet-level agency charged with promoting the efficient functioning of the marketplace by protecting consumers from unfair or deceptive practices and increasing consumer choice by promoting competition. In addition to reports and recommendations, the FTC enforces existing legislation by suing corporations it believes are in violation of federal fair trade laws.

In 1998, the FTC issued its Fair Information Practice (FIP) principles, on which it has based its assessments and recommendations for online privacy. FIP principles are still the primary basis for privacy legislation. **Table 8.6** describes these principles. Two of the five are designated as basic, "core" principles that must be present to protect privacy, whereas the other practices are less central. The FTC's FIP principles restate and strengthen in a form suitable to deal with online privacy the Fair Information Practices doctrine developed in 1973 by a government study group (U.S. Department of Health, Education and Welfare, 1973).

TABLE 8.6	FEDERAL TRADE COMMISSION'S FAIR INFORMATION PRACTICE PRINCIPLES
Notice/Awareness (core principle)	Sites must disclose their information practices before collecting data. Includes identification of collector, uses of data, other recipients of data, nature of collection (active/inactive), voluntary or required, consequences of refusal, and steps taken to protect confidentiality, integrity, and quality of the data.
Choice/Consent (core principle)	There must be a choice regime in place allowing consumers to choose how their information will be used for secondary purposes other than supporting the transaction, including internal use and transfer to third parties. Opt-in/opt-out must be available.
Access/Participation	Consumers should be able to review and contest the accuracy and completeness of data collected about them in a timely, inexpensive process.
Security	Data collectors must take reasonable steps to assure that consumer information is accurate and secure from unauthorized use.
Enforcement	There must be a mechanism to enforce FIP principles in place. This can involve self-regulation, legislation giving consumers legal remedies for violations, or federal statutes and regulation.

SOURCE: Based on data from Federal Trade Commission, 1998, 2000a.

TABLE 8.7	FTC RECOMMENDATIONS REGARDING ONLINE PROFILING
PRINCIPLE	DESCRIPTION OF RECOMMENDATION
Notice	Complete transparency to user by providing disclosure and choice options on the host Web site. "Robust" notice for PII (time/place of collection; before collection begins). Clear and conspicuous notice for non-PII.
Choice	Opt-in for PII, opt-out for non-PII. No conversion of non-PII to PII without consent. Opt-out from any or all network advertisers from a single page provided by the host Web site.
Access	Reasonable provisions to allow inspection and correction.
Security	Reasonable efforts to secure information from loss, misuse, or improper access.
Enforcement	Done by independent third parties, such as seal programs and accounting firms.
Restricted collection	Advertising networks will not collect information about sensitive financial or medical topics, sexual behavior or sexual orientation, or use social security numbers for profiling.

SOURCE: Based on data from Federal Trade Commission, 2000b.

The FTC's FIP principles set the ground rules for what constitutes due process privacy protection procedures at e-commerce and all other Web sites—including government and nonprofit Web sites—in the United States.

The FTC's FIP principles are guidelines, not laws. They have stimulated private firms and industry associations to develop their own private guidelines (discussed next). However, the FTC's FIP guidelines are often used as the basis of legislation. The most important online privacy legislation to date that has been directly influenced by the FTC's FIP principles is the Children's Online Privacy Protection Act (COPPA) (1998), which requires Web sites to obtain parental permission before collecting information on children under 13 years of age.

In 2000, the FTC recommended legislation to Congress to protect online consumer privacy from the threat posed by advertising networks. **Table 8.7** summarizes the commission's recommendations. The FTC profiling recommendations significantly strengthened the FIP principles of notification and choice, while also including restrictions on information that may be collected.[1] Although the FTC supported industry efforts at self-regulation, it nevertheless recommended legislation to ensure that all Web sites using network advertising and all network advertisers complied.

In the last decade, the FTC has broadened its approach to privacy beyond notice and choice requirements to include a harm-based approach, focusing on practices that are likely to cause harm or unwarranted intrusion in consumers' daily lives. However, in recent years, the FTC has recognized the limitations of both the notice-and-choice and harm-based models. In 2009, the FTC held a series of three public roundtables

---

[1] Much general privacy legislation affecting government, e.g., the Privacy Act of 1974, precludes the government from collecting information on political and social behavior of citizens. The FTC restrictions are significant because they are the FTC's first effort at limiting the collection of certain information.

to explore the effectiveness of these approaches in light of rapidly evolving technology and the market for consumer data. The major concepts that emerged from these roundtables were:

- The increasing collection and use of consumer data
- Consumers' lack of understanding about the collection and use of their personal data, and the resulting inability to make informed choices
- Consumers' interest in and concern about their privacy
- Benefits of data collection and use to both businesses and consumers
- Decreasing relevance of the distinction between PII and non-PII.

As a result of the roundtables, the FTC developed a new framework to address consumer privacy. **Table 8.8** summarizes the important aspects of this framework.

TABLE 8.8	THE FTC'S NEW PRIVACY FRAMEWORK
PRINCIPLE	**APPLICATION**
Scope	Applies to all commercial entities that collect or use consumer data; not limited to those that just collect PII.
Privacy by Design	Companies should promote consumer privacy throughout the organization and at every stage of development of products and services: • Data security • Reasonable collection limits • Reasonable and appropriate data retention policies • Data accuracy • Comprehensive data management procedures
Simplified Choice	Companies should simplify consumer choice. Need not provide choice before collecting and using data for commonly accepted practices: • Product and fulfillment • Internal operations, fraud prevention • Legal compliance • First-party marketing For all other commercial data collection and use, choice is required, and should be clearly and conspicuously offered at a time and in context in which consumer is providing data. Some types of information or practices (children, financial and medical information, deep packet inspection) may require additional protection through enhanced consent. Special choice mechanism for online behavioral advertising: "Do Not Track."
Greater Transparency	Increase transparency of data practices by: • Making privacy notices clearer, shorter, and more standardized to enable better comprehension and comparison • Providing consumers with reasonable access to data about themselves • Providing prominent disclosures and obtaining express affirmative consent before using consumer data in a materially different manner than claimed when data was collected • Educating consumers about commercial data privacy practices

SOURCE: Based on data from Federal Trade Commission, 2010.

Among the most noteworthy is the call for a "Do Not Track" mechanism for online behavioral advertising. The mechanism would involve placing a persistent cookie on a consumer's browser and conveying its setting to sites that the browser visits to signal whether or not the consumer wants to be tracked or receive targeted advertisements. A number of bills have been introduced in Congress to implement Do Not Track, but as yet none have been passed.

In response to growing public and congressional concern with online and mobile privacy violations, the FTC has begun taking a much more aggressive stance based on its new privacy policies developed over several years. In 2011, the FTC reached an agreement with Google concerning charges it used deceptive tactics and violated its own privacy policies when it launched its Google Buzz social network, forcing people to join the network even if they selected not to join. Under the settlement, Google agreed to start a privacy program, permit independent privacy audits for 20 years, and face $16,000 fines for every future privacy misrepresentation. This was the first time the FTC had charged a company with such violations and ordered it to start a privacy program (Federal Trade Commission, 2011). In 2012, the FTC fined Google $22.5 million for violating the agreement and for bypassing privacy settings in Apple's Safari browser in order to track users and show them advertisements. This fine—its largest civil penalty to date—followed on the heels of a concerted crackdown on tech companies for privacy violations and a separate investigation of Google for antitrust violations (Federal Trade Commission, 2012a). In 2012, the FTC also reached a settlement with Facebook resolving charges that Facebook deceived its users by telling them they could keep their information on Facebook private, but then repeatedly allowing it to be shared and made public. The settlement requires Facebook to live up to its promises by giving consumers clear and prominent notice and obtaining their express consent before sharing their information beyond the user's privacy settings. It also requires Facebook to develop a comprehensive privacy program, and obtain independent biennial privacy audits for a period of 20 years (Federal Trade Commission, 2012b).

In 2012, the FTC released a final report based on its work in the previous two years. The report describes industry best practices for protecting the privacy of Americans and focuses on five areas: Do Not Track, mobile privacy, data brokers, large platform providers (advertising networks, operating systems, browsers, and social media companies), and the development of self-regulatory codes. The report called for implementation of an easy to use, persistent, and effective Do Not Track system; improved disclosures for use of mobile data; making it easier for people to see the files about themselves compiled by data brokers; development of a central Web site where data brokers identify themselves; development of a privacy policy by large platform providers to regulate comprehensive tracking across the Internet; and enforcement of self-regulatory rules to ensure firms adhere to industry codes of conduct (Federal Trade Commission, 2012c).

In 2014, the FTC issued a report on the data broker industry, which is at the heart of the online and offline privacy debate in the United States. The report found that data brokers operate without transparency, and most users have no idea how their information is being used. The report found that data brokers collect and store billions of data elements covering nearly every U.S. consumer. One of the nine data brokers studied had information on more than 1.4 billion consumer transactions and 700 billion data elements. Another broker adds more than 3 billion new data points to its database each month. The report called for legislation giving consumers more control over their personal information by creating a centralized portal where data brokers would identify themselves, describe their information collection and use practices, and provide links to access tools and opt-outs; require brokers to give consumers access to their data; provide opportunities to opt-out of data collection; describe where they get information and what inferences they make from the data; and require retailers to notify customers when they share information with data brokers (Federal Trade Commission, 2014). The emphasis in recent FTC privacy reports is not on restricting the collection of information (as in previous eras of privacy regulation), but instead on giving consumers rights with respect to the information collected about them in large databases and its use by various businesses and agencies.

Facing fines, congressional investigations, and public embarrassment over their privacy invading behaviors, with the potential loss of some business and credibility, the major players in the e-commerce industry in the United States are beginning to change some of their policies regarding the treatment of consumer data. Large Internet firms that rely on personal information (Google, Facebook, Microsoft, and many others), along with privacy advocates, are calling on Washington to develop comprehensive consumer privacy protection legislation that would clarify for consumers and business firms the meaning of privacy in the current online commercial environment (Singer, 2013). This represents a change in the meaning of privacy from "leave me alone" to "I want to know and control how my personal information is being used." Invoking a Bill of Rights perspective is shifting the privacy debate toward a rights-based privacy policy, similar to the European model described below.

Measuring Privacy Policies Over Time

While politicians, privacy advocates, and the Internet industry wrangle over what the rules for privacy should be, very little attention has been paid to actually measuring the strength of privacy policies for individual companies, comparing them to other companies, and understanding how privacy policies have changed over time at a specific company. Is Facebook's privacy policy worse, better, or about the same as Apple's, or Google's? Have privacy policies improved after ten years of debate, or have they deteriorated?

A recent research project provides some preliminary answers to these questions. The researchers developed a measure of privacy policies by applying 10 privacy policy principles when reviewing policies (see **Table 8.9**) (Shore and Steinmen, 2015). You will recognize these principles because they derive in primary part from the FTC and Fair Information Practices doctrines previously described. The dimensions themselves were measured on a four-point scale from 0 to 4 (0 meaning the privacy policy fails to meet the criterion and 4 indicating the criterion was fully achieved).

You can use the principles in Table 8.9 as a way to measure the privacy policy of your own online business, or another firm like Facebook, or Google. You can measure a single firm at two points in time to see how its policies changed, or compare two or

TABLE 8.9	CRITERIA TO USE WHEN EXAMINING PRIVACY POLICIES

- Can the privacy policy be easily found, reviewed, and understood by users?
- Does the privacy policy fully disclose how personal information will and will not be used by the organization? Is information about users ever shared or sold without users' explicit permission?
- Can users decide if they want to participate?
- Can users decide and actively indicate that they agree to be profiled, tracked, or targeted?
- Can users decide how and if their sensitive information is shared?
- Are users able to change any information that they input about themselves?
- Can users decide who can access their information?
- Are users notified promptly if their information is lost, stolen, or improperly accessed?
- Can users easily report concerns and get answers?
- Do users receive a copy of all disclosures of their information?

more firms at a single point in time. Shore and Steinman chose to look at Facebook's privacy policies over a ten-year period from 2005 to 2015. They found that Facebook's privacy policies improved from 2005 to 2009, at one point reaching 90% implementation of the criterion, and then steadily declined to 25% in 2015. The areas of notable decline were the amount of information gathered and monitored, informing users about what is shared, clearly identifying data used for profiling, giving users choices in privacy settings, providing information on how Facebook uses cookies, beacons, and weblogs to gather data, and providing an easily understood privacy policy document. The researchers noted that Facebook's privacy policy started out in 2005 with 1,000 words, and by 2015 had ballooned to over 12,000 words!

The European Data Protection Directive

In Europe, privacy protection is much stronger than it is in the United States. In the United States, private organizations and businesses are permitted to use PII gathered in commercial transactions for other business purposes without the prior consent of the consumer (so-called secondary uses of PII). In the United States, there is no federal agency charged with enforcing privacy laws. Instead, privacy laws are enforced largely through self-regulation by businesses, and by individuals who must sue agencies or companies in court to recover damages. This is expensive and rarely done. The European approach to privacy protection is more comprehensive and regulatory in nature. European countries do not allow business firms to use PII without the prior consent of consumers. They enforce their privacy laws by creating data protection agencies to pursue complaints brought by citizens and actively enforce privacy laws.

In 1998, the European Commission's Data Protection Directive went into effect, standardizing and broadening privacy protection in the E.U. nations. The Directive is based on the Fair Information Practices doctrine but extends the control individuals can exercise over their personal information. The Directive requires companies to inform people when they collect information about them and to disclose how it will be stored and used. Customers must provide their informed consent before any company can legally use data about them, and they have the right to access that information, correct it, and request that no further data be collected. Further, the Directive prohibits the transfer of PII to organizations or countries that do not have similarly strong privacy protection policies. This means that data collected in Europe by American business firms cannot be transferred or processed in the United States (which has weaker privacy protection laws). This would potentially interfere with a $6.9 trillion annual trade flow in goods, services, and investment between the United States and Europe.

The U.S. Department of Commerce, working with the European Commission, developed a safe harbor framework that permits U.S. firms to move personal data from Europe to the United States. A **safe harbor** is a private self-regulating policy and enforcement mechanism that meets the objectives of government regulators and legislation but does not involve government regulation or enforcement. The government plays a role in certifying safe harbors, however. Organizations that decide to participate in the safe harbor program must develop policies that meet European standards, and they must publicly sign on to a Web-based register maintained by the Department of Commerce. Enforcement occurs in the United States and relies to a large extent on self-policing and regulation, backed up by government enforcement of fair trade statutes. However, in October 2015, Europe's highest court struck down the safe harbor agreement entirely, in large part due to the revelations by Edward Snowden that Facebook had shared personal information on European citizens with the NSA, and therefore violated the terms of the agreement (Scott, 2015). For the 4,000 or so U.S. companies that rely on the safe harbor agreement to move personal data from Europe to the United States, the court's ruling potentially interferes with their current operations and places them in a legal limbo. Fortunately, other treaties are sufficient to carry on normal operations of businesses until a new agreement is worked out. One possible solution: keep European personal information on cloud servers located in Europe that conform to European data protection laws. However, it is unclear if this solution would meet the business requirements of large technology firms like Google and Facebook who heavily depend on their U.S. data and analytic platforms to process personal information. For more information on the safe harbor, see www.export.gov/safeharbor.

In June 2015, the European Council approved its version of a new proposed E.U. General Data Protection Regulation (GDPR) to replace the existing Data Protection Directive. When it takes effect, the GDPR will apply across all E.U. countries, rather than the current situation in which each member-state regulates privacy matters within its own borders. Facebook and Google, for instance, currently base their European operations in Ireland where privacy protections are minimal. Originally introduced in 2012, the GDPR will apply to any firm operating in any E.U. country, require unambiguous consent to use personal data for purposes like tracking individuals across the Web, limit the ability to use data for purposes other than those for which it was collected (tertiary uses, such as constructing user profiles), and strengthen the right to be forgotten, specifically, by allowing individuals to remove personal data from social platforms like Facebook. The next step is for versions of the GDPR approved by each of the European Council, European Commission, and European Parliament to be reconciled, producing the final version (Evans, 2015; Gibbs, 2015; European Commission, 2014; Pearce and Clarke, 2014; European Commission, 2012).

In 2015, the privacy environment has turned decidedly against American firms like Facebook, Google, and others whose business model requires near unfettered use

safe harbor
a private self-regulating policy and enforcement mechanism that meets the objectives of government regulators and legislation but does not involve government regulation or enforcement

of personal information to support advertising revenues. Five E.U. nations (Netherlands, Germany, France, Spain, and Belgium) have initiated a series of coordinated investigations into these firms' privacy and data policies.

For instance, in 2015 Belgium sued Facebook for collecting and processing data without user consent, or explaining how it would use the information (Schechner and Drozdiak, 2015). France's privacy data-protection regulator ordered Google to expand the right to be forgotten to the entire world, not just to Europeans (Schechner, 2015). Dutch, German, and Belgian authorities are investigating Facebook's combining of data from its services like Instagram and WhatsApp to target advertising, and its use of its Like buttons for tracking browsing habits across the entire Web (Schechner, 2015b).

PRIVATE INDUSTRY SELF-REGULATION

The online industry in the United States has historically opposed online privacy legislation, arguing that industry can do a better job of protecting privacy than government. However, individual firms such as Facebook, Apple, Yahoo, and Google have adopted policies on their own in an effort to address the concerns of the public about personal privacy on the Internet. The online industry formed the Online Privacy Alliance (OPA) in 1998 to encourage self-regulation in part as a reaction to growing public concerns and the threat of legislation being proposed by the FTC and privacy advocacy groups.

The FTC and private industry in the United States has created the idea of safe harbors from government regulation. For instance, COPPA includes a provision enabling industry groups or others to submit for the FTC's approval self-regulatory guidelines that implement the protections of the FIP principles and FTC rules. In May 2001, the FTC approved the TRUSTe Internet privacy protection program under the terms of COPPA as a safe harbor.

OPA has developed a set of privacy guidelines that members are required to implement. The primary focus of industry efforts has been the development of online "seals" that attest to the privacy policies on a site. The Better Business Bureau (BBB), TRUSTe, WebTrust, and major accounting firms—among them PricewaterhouseCoopers' BetterWeb—have established seals for Web sites. To display a seal, Web site operators must conform to certain privacy principles, a complaint resolution process, and monitoring by the seal originator. Nevertheless, online privacy seal programs have had a limited impact on Web privacy practices. Critics argue that seal programs are not particularly effective in safeguarding privacy. In March 2015, for instance, the FTC finalized a settlement in which it fined TRUSTe for failing to annually recertify privacy programs in more than 1,000 instances although claiming that it did so on its Web site (Davis, 2015). For these reasons, the FTC has not deemed the seal programs as "safe harbors" yet (with the exception of TRUSTe's children's privacy seal under COPPA), and the agency continues to push for legislation to enforce privacy protection principles.

The advertising network industry has also formed an industry association, the Network Advertising Initiative (NAI), to develop privacy policies. The NAI policies have two objectives: to offer consumers a chance to opt out of advertising network programs (including e-mail campaigns), and to provide consumers redress from abuses. In order to opt out, the NAI has created a Web site—Networkadvertising.org—where consumers can use a global opt-out feature to prevent network advertising agencies

TABLE 8.10	PRIVACY ADVOCACY GROUPS
ADVOCACY GROUP	FOCUS
Epic.org (Electronic Privacy Information Center)	Washington-based watch-dog group
Privacyinternational.org	Watch-dog organization focused on privacy intrusions by government and businesses
Cdt.org (Center for Democracy and Technology)	Foundation- and business-supported group with a legislative focus
Privacy.org	Clearinghouse sponsored by EPIC and Privacy International
Privacyrights.org	Educational clearinghouse
Privacyalliance.org	Industry-supported clearinghouse

from placing their cookies on a user's computer. If a consumer has a complaint, the NAI has a link to the Truste.org Web site where the complaints can be filed (Network Advertising Initiative, 2010; 2011).

The AdChoices program is an industry-sponsored initiative to encourage Web sites to be more transparent about how they use personal information and to make it more likely that appropriate ads are shown to users by asking users themselves. An AdChoices icon appears next to ads, and clicking on this icon provides more information and the opportunity to provide feedback to the advertiser. There is no data available yet to indicate how well this program is working.

In general, industry efforts at self-regulation in online privacy have not succeeded in reducing American fears of privacy invasion during online transactions, or in reducing the level of privacy invasion. At best, self-regulation has offered consumers notice about whether a privacy policy exists, but usually says little about the actual use of the information, does not offer consumers a chance to see and correct the information or control its use in any significant way, offers no promises for the security of that information, and offers no enforcement mechanism (Hoofnagle, 2005).

PRIVACY ADVOCACY GROUPS

There are a number of privacy advocacy groups on the Web that monitor developments in privacy. Some of these sites are industry-supported, while others rely on private foundations and contributions. Some of the better-known sites are listed in **Table 8.10**.

THE PRIVACY PROTECTION BUSINESS

As Web sites become more invasive and aggressive in their use of personal information, and as public concern grows, a small number of firms have sprung up to sell products that they claim will help people protect their privacy. Venture capital firms have picked up the scent and are investing in small start-up companies based on the premise that people will pay to protect their reputations. For instance, Reputation.com has received over $67 million in funding as of 2015. For as little as $14.95 a month, you can monitor what people are saying about you, or about your children, on social

Web sites. However, these types of firms can succeed only if people are willing to pay out of pocket for privacy protection. Economists studying this issue have found that people are not willing to pay much to protect their privacy (at most about $30), and many are willing to give up their privacy for small discounts (Brustein, 2012; Acquisti et al., 2009). For these reasons the privacy protection business at the retail level has not been successful.

TECHNOLOGICAL SOLUTIONS

A number of privacy-enhancing technologies have been developed for protecting user privacy during interactions with Web sites such as spyware blockers, pop-up blockers, cookie managers, and secure e-mail (see **Table 8.11**). However, the most powerful tools for protecting privacy need to be built into browsers. Responding to pressure from privacy advocates, browsers now have a number of tools that can help users protect their privacy, such as eliminating third-party cookies. One of the most powerful browser-based protections is a built-in Do Not Track capability. Microsoft, Mozilla,

TABLE 8.11	TECHNOLOGICAL PROTECTIONS FOR ONLINE PRIVACY	
TECHNOLOGY	PRODUCTS	PROTECTION
Spyware blockers	Spyware Doctor, ZoneAlarm, Ad-Aware, and Spybot	Detects and removes spyware, adware, keyloggers, and other malware
Pop-up blockers	Browsers: Firefox, IE, Safari, Opera Toolbars: Google, Yahoo, MSN Add-on programs: Adblock, PopupMaster	Prevents calls to ad servers that push pop-up, pop-under, and leave-behind ads; restricts downloading of images at user request
Ad blockers	Adblock Plus; extensions to most browsers; Crystal	Prevents calls to ad servers; interferes with downloading of ad beacons
Secure e-mail	ZL Technologies, SafeMess, Hushmail.com, Pretty Good Privacy (PGP)	E-mail and document encryption
Anonymous remailers	Jack B. Nymble, Java Anonymous Proxy, Mixmaster	Send e-mail without trace
Anonymous surfing	Freedom Websecure, Anonymizer.com, Tor, GhostSurf	Surf without a trace
Cookie managers	Cookie Monster and most browsers	Prevents client computer from accepting cookies
Disk/file erasing programs	Mutilate File Wiper, Eraser, WipeFile	Completely erases hard drive and floppy files
Policy generators	OECD Privacy Policy Generator	Automates the development of an OECD privacy compliance policy
Public Key Encryption	PGP Desktop	Program that encrypts your mail and documents

Google, and Apple have all introduced a default Do Not Track capability. However, refer to the *Insight on Technology* case, *Every Move You Take, Every Click You Make, We'll be Tracking You*, in Chapter 6 for a discussion of the difficulties that have developed in implementing Do Not Track. Most of these tools emphasize security—the ability of individuals to protect their communications and files from illegitimate snoopers.

8.3 INTELLECTUAL PROPERTY RIGHTS

Congress shall have the power to "promote the progress of science and useful arts, by securing for limited times to authors and inventors the exclusive right to their respective writings and discoveries."

—Article I, Section 8, Constitution of the United States, 1788.

Next to privacy, the most controversial ethical, social, and political issue related to e-commerce is the fate of intellectual property rights. Intellectual property encompasses all the tangible and intangible products of the human mind. As a general rule, in the United States, the creator of intellectual property owns it. For instance, if you personally create an e-commerce site, it belongs entirely to you, and you have exclusive rights to use this "property" in any lawful way you see fit. But the Internet potentially changes things. Once intellectual works become digital, it becomes difficult to control access, use, distribution, and copying. These are precisely the areas that intellectual property seeks to control.

Digital media differ from books, periodicals, and other media in terms of ease of replication, transmission, and alteration; difficulty in classifying a software work as a program, book, or even music; compactness—making theft easy; and difficulty in establishing uniqueness. Before widespread use of the Internet, copies of software, books, magazine articles, or films had to be stored on physical media, such as paper, computer disks, or videotape, creating hurdles to distribution, and raising the costs of illegal copies.

The Internet technically permits millions of people to make perfect digital copies of various works—from music to plays, poems, and journal articles—and then to distribute them nearly cost-free to hundreds of millions of Web users. The proliferation of innovation has occurred so rapidly that few entrepreneurs have stopped to consider who owns the patent on a business technique or method that they are using on their site. The spirit of the Web has been so free-wheeling that many entrepreneurs ignored trademark law and registered domain names that could easily be confused with another company's registered trademarks. In short, the Internet has demonstrated the potential to disrupt traditional conceptions and implementations of intellectual property law developed over the last two centuries.

The major ethical issue related to e-commerce and intellectual property concerns how we (both as individuals and as business professionals) should treat property that belongs to others. From a social point of view, the main questions are: Is there continued value in protecting intellectual property in the Internet age? In what ways is society better off, or worse off, for having the concept of property apply to intangible ideas? Should society make certain technology illegal just because it has an adverse impact on some intellectual property owners? From a political perspective, we need to ask how the Internet and e-commerce can be regulated or governed to protect the institution of intellectual property while at the same time encouraging the growth of e-commerce and the Internet.

TYPES OF INTELLECTUAL PROPERTY PROTECTION

There are three main types of intellectual property protection: copyright, patent, and trademark law. In the United States, the development of intellectual property law begins with the U.S. Constitution, which mandated Congress to devise a system of laws to promote "the progress of science and the useful arts." Congress passed the first copyright law in 1790 to protect original written works for a period of 14 years, with a 14-year renewal if the author was still alive. Since then, the idea of copyright has been extended to include music, films, translations, photographs, and most recently the designs of vessels under 200 feet (Fisher, 1999). The copyright law has been amended (mostly extended) 11 times in the last 40 years.

The goal of intellectual property law is to balance two competing interests—the public and the private. The public interest is served by the creation and distribution of inventions, works of art, music, literature, and other forms of intellectual expression. The private interest is served by rewarding people for creating these works through the creation of a time-limited monopoly granting exclusive use to the creator.

Maintaining this balance of interests is always challenged by the invention of new technologies. In general, the information technologies of the last century—from radio and television to CD-ROMs, DVDs, and the Internet—have at first tended to weaken the protections afforded by intellectual property law. Owners of intellectual property have often, but not always, been successful in pressuring Congress and the courts to strengthen the intellectual property laws to compensate for any technological threat, and even to extend protection for longer periods of time and to entirely new areas of expression. In the case of the Internet and e-commerce technologies, once again, intellectual property rights are severely challenged. In the next few sections, we discuss the significant developments in each area: copyright, patent, and trademark.

copyright law

protects original forms of expression such as writings, art, drawings, photographs, music, motion pictures, performances, and computer programs from being copied by others for a minimum of 70 years

COPYRIGHT: THE PROBLEM OF PERFECT COPIES AND ENCRYPTION

In the United States, **copyright law** protects original forms of expression such as writings (books, periodicals, lecture notes), art, drawings, photographs, music, motion pictures, performances, and computer programs from being copied by others for a period of time. Up until 1998, the copyright law protected works of individuals for their lifetime plus 50 years beyond their life, and works created for hire and owned by corporations, such as Mickey Mouse of the Disney Corporation, for 75 years after initial creation. Copyright does not protect ideas—just their expression in a tangible medium such as paper, cassette tape, or handwritten notes.

In 1998, Congress extended the period of copyright protection for an additional 20 years, for a total of 95 years for corporate-owned works, and life plus 70 years of protection for works created by individuals (the Copyright Term Extension Act, also known as CTEA). In *Eldred v. Ashcroft*, the Supreme Court ruled on January 16, 2003, that CTEA was constitutional, over the objections of groups arguing that Congress had given copyright holders a permanent monopoly over the expression of ideas, which ultimately would work to inhibit the flow of ideas and creation of new works by making existing works too expensive (*Eldred v. Ashcroft*, 2003; Greenhouse, 2003a). Librarians, academics, and others who depend on inexpensive access to copyrighted material opposed the legislation.

In the mid-1960s, the Copyright Office began registering software programs, and in 1980, Congress passed the Computer Software Copyright Act, which clearly provides protection for source and object code and for copies of the original sold in commerce, and sets forth the rights of the purchaser to use the software while the creator retains legal title. For instance, the HTML code for a Web page—even though easily available to every browser—cannot be lawfully copied and used for a commercial purpose, say, to create a new Web site that looks identical.

Copyright protection is clear-cut: it protects against copying of entire programs or their parts. Damages and relief are readily obtained for infringement. The drawback to copyright protection is that the underlying ideas behind a work are not protected, only their expression in a work. A competitor can view the source code on your Web site to see how various effects were created and then reuse those techniques to create a different Web site without infringing on your copyright.

Look and Feel

"Look and feel" copyright infringement lawsuits are precisely about the distinction between an idea and its expression. For instance, in 1988, Apple Computer sued Microsoft Corporation and Hewlett-Packard Inc. for infringing Apple's copyright on the Macintosh interface. Among other claims, Apple claimed that the defendants copied the expression of overlapping windows. Apple failed to patent the idea of overlapping windows when it invented this method of presenting information on a computer screen in the late 1960s. The defendants counterclaimed that the idea of overlapping windows could only be expressed in a single way and, therefore, was not protectable under the "merger" doctrine of copyright law. When ideas and their expression merge (i.e., if there is only one way to express an idea), the expression cannot be copyrighted, although the method of producing the expression might be patentable (*Apple Computer, Inc. v. Microsoft*, 1989). In general, courts appear to be following the reasoning of a 1992 case—*Brown Bag Software vs. Symantec Corp.*—in which the court dissected the elements of software alleged to be infringing. There, the Federal Circuit Court of Appeals found that neither similar concept, function, general functional features (e.g., drop-down menus), nor colors were protectable by copyright law (*Brown Bag vs. Symantec Corp.*, 1992).

TABLE 8.12	FAIR USE CONSIDERATIONS TO COPYRIGHT PROTECTIONS
FAIR USE FACTOR	**INTERPRETATION**
Character of use	Nonprofit or educational use versus for-profit use.
Nature of the work	Creative works such as plays or novels receive greater protection than factual accounts, e.g., newspaper accounts.
Amount of work used	A stanza from a poem or a single page from a book would be allowed, but not the entire poem or a book chapter.
Market effect of use	Will the use harm the marketability of the original product? Has it already harmed the product in the marketplace?
Context of use	A last-minute, unplanned use in a classroom versus a planned infringement.

Fair Use Doctrine

doctrine of fair use
under certain circumstances, permits use of copyrighted material without permission

Copyrights, like all rights, are not absolute. There are situations where strict copyright observance could be harmful to society, potentially inhibiting other rights such as the right to freedom of expression and thought. As a result, the doctrine of fair use has been created. The **doctrine of fair use** permits teachers, writers, and others to use copyrighted materials without permission under certain circumstances. **Table 8.12** describes the five factors that courts consider when assessing what constitutes fair use.

The fair use doctrine draws upon the First Amendment's protection of freedom of speech (and writing). Journalists, writers, and academics must be able to refer to, and cite from, copyrighted works in order to criticize, or even discuss them. Professors are allowed to clip a contemporary article just before class, copy it, and hand it out to students as an example of a topic under discussion. However, they are not permitted to add this article to the class syllabus for the next semester without compensating the copyright holder.

What constitutes fair use has been at issue in a number of recent cases. In *Kelly v. Arriba Soft* (2003) and *Perfect 10, Inc. v. Amazon.com, Inc. et al.,* (2007), the Federal Circuit Court of Appeals for the 9th Circuit held that the display of thumbnail images in response to search requests constituted fair use. A similar result was reached by the district court for the District of Nevada with respect to Google's storage and display of Web sites from cache memory, in *Field v. Google, Inc.* (2006). In all of these cases, the courts accepted the argument that caching the material and displaying it in response to a search request was not only a public benefit, but also a form of marketing of the material on behalf of its copyright owner, thereby enhancing the material's commercial value. In what's known as the "dancing baby case," a mother uploaded a 30-second video to YouTube of her baby dancing to a song by Prince called Let's Go Crazy. Universal Music Group, the owner of the copyright to the song, objected. The mother sued, claiming use of the clip was fair use. A federal court agreed that the fair use doctrine permitted the mother to use a 30-second clip of the song (Bergen, 2015).

Fair use is also at issue in a lawsuit filed by the Authors Guild and five major publishing companies against Google. Beginning in 2004, Google announced a project with two parts. A Partner Program would scan books with the permission of publishers, index the books, post snippets of the books on line, and make bibliographic information available on Google's search engine. In the second project, called the Library Project, Google aimed to scan all the books in several university and public libraries, and then make snippets and parts of the book available online without receiving permission from the publishers or paying royalties. Google said it would never show a full page, just relevant portions of a page in response to searches. In 2005, the Authors Guild and the large book publishers filed a lawsuit seeking to prevent Google from implementing the Library Project.

Google argued that the Library Project constituted fair use of publishers' copyrighted works because it only published snippets. Moreover, Google claimed that it was simply helping libraries do what they are intended to do, namely, lend books. Library lending is considered a fair use following an agreement in the late 1930s with publishers, and such lending was codified into the Copyright Act of 1976. Google claimed that helping libraries make books more available to the public was in the broader public interest, and extended existing rights of libraries to encourage book availability.

In 2013, eight years later, following several reversals of opinions, a federal court finally found in favor of Google without reservation by ruling that Google's scanning and making snippets of text available to the public was "fair use" under U.S. copyright law. The judge believed the project had a broad public purpose of making it easier for students, researchers, teachers, and the general public to find books, while also preserving consideration for author and publisher rights. The Google project was "transformative" in the court's view, giving books a new character and purpose, making it easier to discover old books, and leading to increased sales. Two remaining lawsuits are still being decided in 2015 but it appears the fair use judgment will hold. In the meantime, the project itself has stalled, and efforts to scan so-called orphan books in libraries where the copyright holder could not be identified have ended. Google now appears less than enthusiastic about pursuing the project.

The Digital Millennium Copyright Act of 1998

The **Digital Millennium Copyright Act (DMCA)** of 1998 was the first major effort to adjust the copyright laws of the United States to the Internet age, and remains to this day, the primary statue that defines the relationship between copyright owners, Internet service providers (which in this context also includes Web site publishers as well as firms that provide Internet service), and end-users of copyrighted material. The law implements two international treaties of the World Intellectual Property Organization (WIPO), a worldwide body formed by the major nations in North America and Europe, as well as Japan. This is one case where law preceded or at least was contemporaneous with digital technology. **Table 8.13** summarizes the major provisions of the DMCA.

There are a number of different actors and conflicting interests involved in the process of delivering content on the Internet. Obviously, copyright owners do not want

Digital Millennium Copyright Act (DMCA)
the first major effort to adjust the copyright laws to the Internet age

TABLE 8.13	THE DIGITAL MILLENNIUM COPYRIGHT ACT
SECTION	IMPORTANCE
Title I, WIPO Copyright and Performances and Phonograms Treaties Implementation	Makes it illegal to circumvent technological measures to protect works for either access or copying or to circumvent any electronic rights management information.
Title II, Online Copyright Infringement Liability Limitation	Limits liability of ISPs and search engines for copyright infringement if they comply with safe harbors. Requires ISPs to "take down" sites they host if they are infringing copyrights, and requires search engines to block access to infringing sites if they receive proper notice of infringement from the copyright owner.
Title III, Computer Maintenance Competition Assurance	Permits users to make a copy of a computer program for maintenance or repair of the computer.
Title IV, Miscellaneous Provisions	Requires the Copyright Office to report to Congress on the use of copyright materials for distance education; allows libraries to make digital copies of works for internal use only; extends musical copyrights to include "webcasting."

SOURCE: Based on data from United States Copyright Office, 1998.

their work copied and distributed without their consent (and probably compensation), and they do not want their digital rights management software programs broken, compromised, or made ineffectual. ISPs want the freedom to use content within the provisions of "fair use" and do not want to be held liable for content that users may post to their Web sites. ISPs argue that they are similar to telephone transmission lines, merely providing a method of communication, and they should not be required to monitor their users' activities to see if they are posting copyrighted material. Such surveillance, ISPs and civil libertarians argue, would constitute a restriction on freedom of expression. In addition, the economics of the Internet could be compromised if ISPs were unnecessarily restricted. The business model of many Internet firms depends on creating large, even huge, audiences, and the more content that can be displayed, the larger the audience, and the more ads can be sold. ISPs also generate revenue from selling bandwidth, so the greater the bandwidth required to support large audiences, the better it is for them. Restricting content is bad for business. Finally, consumers of Internet content want as much content as possible, at the lowest cost possible, or even free. The more content for users to consume, the more they benefit from the Internet.

The DMCA tries to balance these different interests. Title I of the DMCA implements the WIPO Copyright Treaty of 1996, which makes it illegal to make, distribute, or use devices that circumvent technology-based protections of copyrighted materials, and attaches stiff fines and prison sentences for violations. This makes it illegal, for instance, to break the security software typically found on DVDs, Amazon's Kindle books, and similar devices. There are a number of exceptions to the strong prohibitions against defeating a copyright protection scheme, however, including exceptions for libraries to examine works for adoption, for reverse engineering to achieve interoperability with other software, for encryption research, and for privacy protection purposes.

Title II of the DMCA creates two safe harbors for ISPs. The first safe harbor (the Online Copyright Infringement Liability Limitation Act) provides that ISPs will not be held liable for infringing material that users post to blogs, Web pages, or forums, as long as the ISP did not have knowledge that the content was infringing, did not receive any financial benefit attributable to the infringing activity (assuming they can control this activity), and acts expeditiously to remove infringing content when notified by a notice of infringement. This means that users of, say, YouTube, can post material that infringes a copyright and YouTube cannot be held liable (safe harbor) as long as it does not know the material is infringing, and if it demonstrates that it has in place procedures to take down infringing content once it becomes aware of the matter or receives a proper notice from the copyright owner. Such a notice is called a takedown notice, a claim by the copyright owner that the ISP is hosting infringing content. Copyright owners can also subpoena the personal identities of any infringers using an ISP.

The second safe harbor relates to links to infringing material: ISPs will not be held liable for referring or linking users to a site that contains infringing material or infringing activity. So for example, a search engine that directs users to a Web site that contains pirated songs or movies cannot be held liable. This safe harbor is applicable as long as ISPs did not have knowledge they were linking users to sites containing infringing content, did not receive any financial benefit attributable to the infringing activity (assuming they can control this activity), and acts expeditiously to remove or disable any such link after receiving a proper notice from the copyright owner.

There are a number of administrative requirements for ISPs to be protected by the safe harbor provisions. ISPs must designate an agent to receive takedown notices; adopt and publish a copyright infringement policy (this can be part of a terms of use policy); and comply with takedown notices by removing the content, and/or links to the content. The penalties for willfully violating the DMCA include restitution to the injured parties of any losses due to infringement. Criminal remedies may include fines up to $500,000 or five years imprisonment for a first offense, and up to $1 million in fines and 10 years in prison for repeat offenders. These are serious penalties, but they have rarely been imposed.

The DMCA relieves ISPs of any liability for posting or linking to copyrighted material, if they can meet the safe harbors' conditions. This means users of YouTube can post what they want, and YouTube will not be held liable for infringing content even if it violates YouTube's terms of use policy, which states that users shall not post infringing content. However, it does require YouTube to remove content or links that are infringing once it receives a valid takedown notice. With respect to receiving financial benefits, ISPs may indeed receive financial benefits from posting infringing content if they can show that they can't control the behavior of their users, or that there is no way of knowing prior to the posting that the material is infringing. For instance, how can YouTube be held responsible for users who post copyrighted songs or movies? How could YouTube know, at the time of posting, that the content is infringing?

ISPs and individuals who post content are also protected from frivolous takedown notices. For instance, the ruling in the "dancing baby" case discussed on page 530 put copyright owners on notice that they needed to be careful issuing takedown notices if use of the copyrighted material might constitute fair use and that the DMCA does not supersede the doctrine of fair use.

Safe harbor provisions of the DMCA were also at the heart of a $1 billion lawsuit originally brought by Viacom in 2007 against Google and YouTube for willful copyright infringement. In the Viacom case, Viacom alleged that YouTube and Google engaged in massive copyright infringement by deliberately and knowingly building up a library of infringing works to draw traffic to the YouTube site and enhance its commercial value. Entire episodes of shows like SpongeBob SquarePants and the Jon Stewart show were appearing on YouTube without permission or payment. In response, Google and YouTube claimed that they are protected by the DMCA's safe harbor provisions and that it is impossible to know whether a video is infringing or not. YouTube also does not display ads on pages where consumers can view videos unless it has an agreement with the content owner. In 2007, Google announced a filtering system (Content ID) aimed at addressing the problem. It requires content owners to give Google a copy of their content so Google can load it into an auto-identification system. Then after a video is uploaded to YouTube, the system attempts to match it with its database of copyrighted material and removes any unauthorized material. The copyright owner has several options: it can mute the audio; block a whole video; monetize the video by running ads against it; and track the video's viewer statistics. In March 2014, seven years after the billion dollar suit was filed, and multiple court room appearances, Google and Viacom settled out of court. Google's ability to take down copyrighted material using Content ID had become very effective, and Google agreed to rent hundreds of Viacom shows (Kaufman, 2014). Both parties recognized in a joint statement that they could achieve their objectives by collaborating rather than continuing the lawsuit.

The entertainment industry continues to be aggressive in pursuing online copyright infringement. In 2012, the U.S. Department of Justice seized the domain Megaupload.com, one of the largest cyberlockers on the Internet dedicated to storing and sharing copyrighted movies and music. A **cyberlocker** is an online file storage service dedicated to sharing copyrighted material (often movies) illegally. Megaupload's founder, Kim Dotcom, was arrested in New Zealand at his home, and $17 million in assets, and later, $37 million in cash in Hong Kong, was confiscated. Mr. Dotcom is currently back in court, and fighting efforts by the United States to extradite him from New Zealand to face copyright, racketeering, and money laundering charges (Reuters, 2015).

Since the Megaupload case, other cyberlockers have restricted their activities to avoid a similar fate as Megaupload. In 2013, the Center for Copyright Information (CCI), along with 5 of the largest ISPs, major entertainment industry companies, and the Consumer Advisory Board launched the Copyright Alert System (CAS)—a tiered notice and response system aimed at reducing copyright infringement over P2P networks. During its first 10 months of operation, the CAS sent out over 1.3 million alerts to 720,000 ISP account holders of alleged copyright infringement. If the account holder ignores repeated alerts, their ISP may impose consequences, such as a downgrade of

cyberlocker
an online file storage service dedicated to sharing copyrighted material illegally

the customer's Internet service. The CCI believes that the CAS has great promise for its ability to move user behavior away from copyright infringement and toward legal sources of content (Center for Copyright Information, 2014). Refer to the chapter-ending case study on The Pirate Bay.

While there has been some progress in limiting infringing content on the Internet, new mobile apps such as Periscope and Meerkat make it easy for people to capture live video and stream it to these apps on mobile devices, making it extremely difficult for content owners to protect the value of their live products. Periscope is owned by Twitter and users can post live videos to Twitter. Meerkat can post live video streams to most social network sites, including Facebook. In 2015, Periscope and Meerkat were used by thousands to watch the pay-per-view broadcast of the welterweight fight between Floyd Mayweather and Manny Pacquiao for free. The pay-per-view price on cable networks was $100. Other users have streamed live TV series such as HBO's Game of Thrones. Periscope received 1,400 DMCA takedown requests in the first three months of its existence. Twitter says it has complied with 71% of these (Harrison, 2015). But the DMCA takedown notices do not help a unique live event such as a championship boxing match retain its value. The value of the event is largely in attracting viewers willing to pay to see it as it happens, and once a free alternative is available, that value is destroyed.

PATENTS: BUSINESS METHODS AND PROCESSES

"Whoever invents or discovers any new and useful process, machine, manufacture, or composition of matter, or any new and useful improvement thereof, may obtain a patent therefore, subject to the conditions and requirements of this title."

—Section 101, U.S. Patent Act

A **patent** grants the owner a 20-year exclusive monopoly on the ideas behind an invention. The congressional intent behind patent law was to ensure that inventors of new machines, devices, or industrial methods would receive the full financial and other rewards of their labor and still make widespread use of the invention possible by providing detailed diagrams for those wishing to use the idea under license from the patent's owner. Patents are obtained from the United States Patent and Trademark Office (USPTO), which was created in 1812. Obtaining a patent is much more difficult and time-consuming than obtaining copyright protection (which is automatic with the creation of the work). Patents must be formally applied for, and the granting of a patent is determined by Patent Office examiners who follow a set of rigorous rules. Ultimately, federal courts decide when patents are valid and when infringement occurs.

Patents are very different from copyrights because patents protect the ideas themselves and not merely the expression of ideas. There are four types of inventions for which patents are granted under patent law: machines, man-made products, compositions of matter, and processing methods. The Supreme Court has determined that patents extend to "anything under the sun that is made by man" (*Diamond v. Chakrabarty*, 1980)

patent
grants the owner an exclusive monopoly on the ideas behind an invention for 20 years

as long as the other requirements of the Patent Act are met. There are three things that cannot be patented: laws of nature, natural phenomena, and abstract ideas. For instance, a mathematical algorithm cannot be patented unless it is realized in a tangible machine or process that has a "useful" result (the mathematical algorithm exception).

In order to be granted a patent, the applicant must show that the invention is new, original, novel, nonobvious, and not evident in prior arts and practice. As with copyrights, the granting of patents has moved far beyond the original intent of Congress's first patent statute, which sought to protect industrial designs and machines. Patent protection has been extended to articles of manufacture (1842), plants (1930), surgical and medical procedures (1950), and software (1981). The Patent Office did not accept applications for software patents until a 1981 Supreme Court decision that held that computer programs could be a part of a patentable process. Since that time, thousands of software patents have been granted. Virtually any software program can be patented as long as it is novel and not obvious.

Essentially, as technology and industrial arts progress, patents have been extended to both encourage entrepreneurs to invent useful devices and promote widespread dissemination of the new techniques through licensing and artful imitation of the published patents (the creation of devices that provide the same functionality as the invention but use different methods) (Winston, 1998). Patents encourage inventors to come up with unique ways of achieving the same functionality as existing patents. For instance, Amazon's patent on one-click purchasing caused Barnesandnoble.com to invent a simplified two-click method of purchasing.

The danger of patents is that they stifle competition by raising barriers to entry into an industry. Patents force new entrants to pay licensing fees to incumbents, and thus slow down the development of technical applications of new ideas by creating lengthy licensing applications and delays. Nowhere is the tradeoff between encouraging innovation and yet avoiding raising barriers to market entry (and thereby discouraging innovation) more evident than in the patent battle that has raged between Apple and Samsung in the smartphone market.

In April 2011, Apple filed suit in the United States against Samsung alleging that Samsung's Galaxy smartphones violated Apple patents on its iPhone and iPad computer. By 2012, Apple and Samsung were involved in over 50 different patent lawsuits throughout the world. See **Table 8.14** for a brief history of the Apple/Samsung smartphone patent wars.

The history of the patent battle is quite complex, and lengthy, lasting over five years. There are three questions raised in this litigation. First, does Apple have valid patents on iPhone and iPad hardware and software? Second, did Samsung's phones and tablets infringe on these Apple patents? And third, if Samsung did infringe, what should the penalty be? There are two possibilities: Samsung pays a fine for damages and/or Samsung removes its infringing products from the market. A fourth question is separate from the lawsuits per se and concerns society, the rest of us: what is the best outcome for society?

After five years and two jury trials, the courts have decided that Apple does have valid patents on the physical iPhone, as well as the operating system, including the user interface and screen functionality. Second, the courts did find that Samsung

TABLE 8.14	APPLE/SAMSUNG SMARTPHONE PATENT WARS
YEAR	DESCRIPTION
2011–2012	In April 2011 Apple filed suit in the United States charging Samsung devices violated Apple patents, and Samsung claimed similar infringement by Apple. The smartphone patent wars begin. Apple's patents had been filed in January 2007 shortly after the introduction of the iPhone. The design patents covered the basic shape of the phone, software features (slide-to-unlock, autocorrect, bounce-back effect, and quicklinks), trade dress features, and user interface—home button, icons with rounded and tapered edges). In short, everything that made the iPhone a unique product. By 2012, Apple and Samsung are involved in 50 different lawsuits around the world involving the design of tablets and smartphones.
August 2012	First jury verdict mostly favorable to Apple. Found Samsung had infringed on design and utility patents, and Apple's trade dress features. Awarded Apple $1.049 billion. An injunction preventing Samsung from selling infringing products was at first denied, but later granted.
November 2013	A retrial of the first jury trial. Samsung admitted to infringing on Apple patents, but argued the penalty was too high. The jury reduced the damages to $290 million.
May 2014	Another jury trial. Apple wins jury verdict of $119.6 million against Samsung, finding that Samsung infringed on patents for slide-to-unlock, autocorrect, and quicklinks features. Judge declines to force removal of devices from market, instead argues for damages as penalty.
September 2015	Apple and Samsung announced an agreement to participate in court-supervised mediation of their five-year dispute. This is the third effort at mediation (the first two failed).
March/April 2016	A second damages re-trial is scheduled should mediation fail.

infringed on some of Apple's patents, and even Samsung admits as much. Third, the courts have generally avoided forcing Samsung to remove its infringing devices from the market, and instead have focused on damages with some exceptions for older phones (Decker, 2015). However, in September 2015, Apple finally won a U.S. appeals court judgment that enjoins Samsung from selling smartphones with Apple's patented slide-to-unlock, autocorrect, and quicklinks features. This was a major victory in principle that Apple can use in the future against other copycat firms (Chen, 2015; Kendall and Wakabayashi, 2015). But Samsung had already designed around these features and came up with its own user interface that accomplishes the same tasks. Hence, the ruling is not likely to have a notable impact on Samsung's sales revenues. The original jury award of $1 billion has been whittled down over the years. Analysts believe the cost to Apple of this litigation is at least equal to the damage award it may ultimately be paid. Over the last five years of litigation, Samsung has changed its interface and functionality to greatly reduce its infringement. Software features can always be designed around. The final chapter may not be written until 2016.

An answer to the fourth question, what is the best outcome for society, is more difficult to determine. Apple's forceful defense has put copycat firms on notice that if they infringe on patents owned by large firms such as Apple, it could be harmful to their brands and possibly result in significant damages. Samsung has been pushed into the lower end of the market where it competes with less expensive, copycat smartphones from China. Samsung has a very large chunk of the smartphone market worldwide, but it has been denied pricing power and resulting profits. The litigation may have strengthened Apple's claim that its computers and smartphones are truly unique, and original. Apple today is the largest corporation in the United States by market capitalization and also the most profitable in the world. Samsung's copying of Apple designs and features may only have strengthened Apple's claims to be a superior product.

E-commerce Patents

Much of the Internet's infrastructure and software was developed under the auspices of publicly funded scientific and military programs in the United States and Europe. Unlike Samuel F. B. Morse, who patented the idea of Morse code and made the telegraph useful, most of the inventions that make the Internet and e-commerce possible were not patented by their inventors. The early Internet was characterized by a spirit of worldwide community development and sharing of ideas without consideration of personal wealth (Winston, 1998). This early Internet spirit changed in the mid-1990s with the commercial development of the World Wide Web.

In 1998, a landmark legal decision, *State Street Bank & Trust v. Signature Financial Group, Inc.*, paved the way for business firms to begin applying for "business methods" patents. In this case, a Federal Circuit Court of Appeals upheld the claims of Signature Financial to a valid patent for a business method that allows managers to monitor and record financial information flows generated by a partner fund. Previously, it was thought business methods could not be patented. However, the court ruled there was no reason to disallow business methods from patent protection, or any "step by step process, be it electronic or chemical or mechanical, [that] involves an algorithm in the broad sense of the term" (*State Street Bank & Trust Co. v. Signature Financial Group*, 1998). The State Street decision led to an explosion in applications for e-commerce "business methods" patents. In June 2010, the U.S. Supreme Court issued a divided opinion on business methods patents in the *Bilski et al. v. Kappos* case (*Bilski et al. v. Kappos*, 2010). The majority argued that business methods patents were allowable even though they did not meet the traditional "machine or transformation test," in which patents are granted to devices that are tied to a particular machine, are a machine, or transform articles from one state to another. The minority wanted to flatly declare that business methods are not patentable in part because any series of steps could be considered a business method (Schwartz, 2010). The Supreme Court struck another blow against business method patents in 2014, with its decision in *Alice Corporation vs. CLS Bank International*. The Court ruled that basic business methods cannot be patented and that while software can be patented, implementing an abstract idea that otherwise could not be patented by using software does not transform the idea into a patentable innovation (*Alice Corporation Pty. Ltd. v. CLS Bank International*, 2014).

Table 8.15 lists some of the better-known e-commerce patents. Some are controversial. Reviewing these, you can understand the concerns of commentators and corporations. Some of the patent claims are very broad (for example, "name your price" sales methods), have historical precedents in the pre-Internet era (shopping

TABLE 8.15	SELECTED E-COMMERCE PATENTS	
COMPANY	SUBJECT	UPDATE
Amazon	One-click purchasing	Amazon attempted to use patent originally granted to it in 1999 to force changes to Barnes & Noble's Web site, but a federal court overturned a previously issued injunction. Eventually settled out of court. In 2007, a USPTO panel rejected some of the patent because of evidence another patent predated it. Amazon amended the patent, and the revised version was confirmed in 2010.
Priceline	Buyer-driven "name your price" sales	Originally filed by Walker Digital, an intellectual property laboratory, and then assigned to Priceline. Granted by the USPTO in 1999. Shortly thereafter, Priceline sued Microsoft and Expedia for copying its patented business method.
Sightsound	Music downloads	Sightsound won a settlement in 2004 against Bertelsmann subsidiaries CDNow and N2K music sites for infringing its patent.
Akamai	Internet content delivery global hosting system	A broad patent granted in 2000 covering techniques for expediting the flow of information over the Internet. Akamai sued Digital Island for violating the patent and, in 2001, a jury found in its favor.
DoubleClick	Dynamic delivery of online advertising	The patent underlying DoubleClick's business of online banner ad delivery, originally granted in 2000. DoubleClick sued competitors 24/7 Media and L90 for violating the patent and ultimately reached a settlement with them.
Overture	Pay for performance search	System and method for influencing position on search result list generated by computer search engine, granted in 2001. Competitor FindWhat sued Overture, charging that patent was obtained illegally; Overture countered by suing both FindWhat and Google for violating patent. Google agreed to pay a license fee to Overture in 2004 to settle.
Acacia Technologies	Streaming video media transmission	Patents for the receipt and transmission of streaming digital audio and or video content originally granted to founders of Greenwich Information Technologies in 1990s. Patents were purchased by Acacia, a firm founded solely to enforce the patents, in 2001.
Soverain Software	Purchase technology	The so-called "shopping cart" patent for network-based systems, which involves any transaction over a network involving a seller, buyer, and payment system. In other words, e-commerce! Soverain filed suit against Amazon for patent infringement, which Amazon paid $40 million to settle. In 2013 a federal district court ruled Soverain's claims against Newegg in part invalid.
MercExchange (Thomas Woolston)	Auction technology	Patents on person-to-person auctions and database search, originally granted in 1995. eBay ordered to pay $25 million in 2003 for infringing on patent. In July 2007, a motion for permanent patent injunction against eBay was denied. MercExchange and eBay settled the dispute in 2008 on confidential terms.
Google	Search technology	Google PageRank patent filed in 1998 and granted in 2001. Became non-exclusive in 2011 and expires in 2017.
Google	Location technology	Patent for a method of using location information in an advertising system issued to Google in 2010.
Apple	Social technology	Apple applied for a patent in 2010 that allows groups of friends attending events to stay in communication with each other and share reactions to live events as they are occurring.
PersonalWeb	Cloud computing, distributed search engine file systems, storage systems	Claims patents are being infringed by Facebook, Yahoo, Google, Apple, Microsoft, and others.

carts), and seem "obvious" (one-click purchasing). Critics of online business methods patents argue that the Patent Office has been too lenient in granting such patents, and that in most instances, the supposed inventions merely copy pre-Internet business methods and thus do not constitute "inventions" (Harmon, 2003; Thurm, 2000; Chiappetta, 2001). The Patent Office argues, on the contrary, that its Internet inventions staff is composed of engineers, lawyers, and specialists with many years of experience with Internet and network technologies, and that it consults with outside technology experts before granting patents. To complicate matters, the European Patent Convention and the patent laws of most European countries do not recognize business methods per se unless the method is implemented through some technology (Takenaka, 2001).

TRADEMARKS: ONLINE INFRINGEMENT AND DILUTION

> A trademark is "any word, name, symbol, or device, or any combination thereof ... used in commerce ... to identify and distinguish ... goods ... from those manufactured or sold by others and to indicate the source of the goods."
>
> —The Trademark Act, 1946

trademark
a mark used to identify and distinguish goods and indicate their source

Trademark law is a form of intellectual property protection for **trademarks**—a mark used to identify and distinguish goods and indicate their source. Trademark protections exist at both the federal and state levels in the United States. The purpose of trademark law is twofold. First, trademark law protects the public in the marketplace by ensuring that it gets what it pays for and wants to receive. Second, trademark law protects the owner—who has spent time, money, and energy bringing the product to the marketplace—against piracy and misappropriation. Trademarks have been extended from single words to pictures, shapes, packaging, and colors. Some things may not be trademarked such as common words that are merely descriptive ("clock"). Federal trademarks are obtained, first, by use in interstate commerce, and second, by registration with the U.S. Patent and Trademark Office (USPTO). Federal trademarks are granted for a period of 10 years and can be renewed indefinitely.

Disputes over federal trademarks involve establishing infringement. The test for infringement is twofold: market confusion and bad faith. Use of a trademark that creates confusion with existing trademarks, causes consumers to make market mistakes, or misrepresents the origins of goods is an infringement. For instance, in July 2015, Multi Time Machine (MTM) sued Amazon for violation of its trademarks and confusing consumers looking to buy MTM watches. MTM makes military style watches that are not sold on Amazon. If a user searches on Amazon for an MTM watch, the search results shows watches being offered by MTM competitors that are similar in style to MTM's. MTM argued that this could confuse customers and the court agreed, allowing the case to proceed to trial (Levine, 2015). In addition, the intentional misuse of words and symbols in the marketplace to extort revenue from legitimate trademark owners ("bad faith") is proscribed.

In 1995, Congress passed the Federal Trademark Dilution Act (FTDA), which created a federal cause of action for dilution of famous marks. This legislation dispenses with the test of market confusion (although that is still required to claim infringement), and extends protection to owners of famous trademarks against **dilution**, which is defined as any behavior that would weaken the connection between the trademark and the product. In 2006, the FTDA was amended by the Trademark Dilution Revision Act (TDRA), which allows a trademark owner to file a claim based on a "likelihood of dilution" standard, rather than having to provide evidence of actual dilution. The TDRA also expressly provides that dilution may occur through blurring (weakening the connection between the trademark and the goods) and tarnishment (using the trademark in a way that makes the underlying products appear unsavory or unwholesome). Internationally, WIPO handles many cybersquatting cases under its Uniform Dispute Resolution Procedures. In 2014, WIPO warned that the expansion of generic top-level domains authorized by ICANN is likely to be very disruptive in terms of trademark protection (New, 2014). Although the cost of obtaining a new gTLD is not unsubstantial (it is estimated to be more than $180,000), by May 2015, 583 new gTLDs had been approved. Successful applicants become owners of these gTLDs, and can create and sell new domains with the gTLD suffix, such as Avenger.movie. Many of these new domains may potentially conflict with the established trademarks of others.

To deal with these trademark conflicts, ICANN developed a set of procedures to rapidly resolve disputes called the Uniform Rapid Suspension System (URS), a domain name dispute procedure that allows a trademark owner to seek suspension of a domain name in a new generic top-level domain (gTLD). ICANN also established a Trademark Clearing house as a repository of data on registered, court-validated, or statute-protected trademarks. Trademark owners register their marks for a fee.

One successful applicant for a new gTLD is Vox Populi Registry Ltd. Based in the U.K., Vox purchased the gTLD .sucks, and began selling domains such as Apple.sucks and CitiGroup.sucks exclusively to corporations who did not want their brand name associated with .sucks. At some point, .sucks domains will be available to the general public, at which point anyone would be able to create a new domain that potentially embarrasses a major brand name or casts it in a negative light (Bloomberg, 2015). ICANN has said it may seek remedies and has alerted the Federal Trade Commission and asked for an opinion on the legality of Vox Populi's behavior. ICANN is not a regulatory agency with enforcement powers, and its agreements with new domain owners does not discuss their business models (Fung, 2015).

dilution
any behavior that would weaken the connection between the trademark and the product

Trademarks and the Internet

The rapid growth and commercialization of the Internet have provided unusual opportunities for existing firms with distinctive and famous trademarks to extend their brands to the Internet. These same developments have provided malicious individuals and firms the opportunity to squat on Internet domain names built upon famous marks, as well as attempt to confuse consumers and dilute famous or distinctive marks (including your personal name or a movie star's name). The conflict between legitimate trademark owners and malicious firms was allowed to fester and grow because

Network Solutions Inc. (NSI), originally the Internet's sole agency for domain name registration for many years, had a policy of "first come, first served." This meant anyone could register any domain name that had not already been registered, regardless of the trademark status of the domain name. NSI was not authorized to decide trademark issues (Nash, 1997).

In response to a growing number of complaints from owners of famous trademarks who found their trademark names being appropriated by Web entrepreneurs, Congress passed the **Anticybersquatting Consumer Protection Act (ACPA)** in November 1999. The ACPA creates civil liabilities for anyone who attempts in bad faith to profit from an existing famous or distinctive trademark by registering an Internet domain name that is identical or confusingly similar to, or "dilutive" of, that trademark. The act does not establish criminal sanctions. It proscribes using "bad-faith" domain names to extort money from the owners of the existing trademark **(cybersquatting)**, or using the bad-faith domain to divert Web traffic to the bad-faith domain that could harm the good will represented by the trademark, create market confusion, or tarnish or disparage the mark **(cyberpiracy)**. It is conceivable that domains such as the previously described Apple.sucks might be seen as a kind of cybersquatting and a violation of the ACPA. The act also proscribes the use of a domain name that consists of the name of a living person, or a name confusingly similar to an existing personal name, without that person's consent, if the registrant is registering the name with the intent to profit by selling the domain name to that person.

Trademark abuse can take many forms on the Web. **Table 8.16** lists the major behaviors on the Internet that have run afoul of trademark law and some of the court cases that resulted.

Cybersquatting and Brandjacking

In one of the first cases involving the ACPA, E. & J. Gallo Winery, owner of the registered mark "Ernest and Julio Gallo" for alcoholic beverages, sued Spider Webs Ltd. for using the domain name Ernestandjuliogallo.com. Spider Webs Ltd. was a domain name speculator that owned numerous domain names consisting of famous company names. The Ernestandjuliogallo.com Web site contained information on the risks of alcohol use, anti-corporate articles about E. & J. Gallo Winery, and was poorly constructed. The court concluded that Spider Webs Ltd. was in violation of the ACPA and that its actions constituted dilution by blurring because the Ernestandjuliogallo.com domain name appeared on every page printed off the Web site accessed by that name, and that Spider Webs Ltd. was not free to use this particular mark as a domain name (*E. & J. Gallo Winery v. Spider Webs Ltd.*, 2001). In August 2009, a court upheld the largest cybersquatting judgment to date: a $33 million verdict in favor of Verizon against OnlineNIC, an Internet domain registration company that had used over 660 names that could easily be confused with legitimate Verizon domain names. Although there have not been many cases decided under the ACPA, that does not mean the problem has gone away. Impersonation of individuals and brands on social network sites adds another dimension to the problem. Both Twitter and Facebook make cybersquatting and impersonation a violation of their terms of service.

Anticybersquatting Consumer Protection Act (ACPA)

creates civil liabilities for anyone who attempts in bad faith to profit from an existing famous or distinctive trademark by registering an Internet domain name that is identical or confusingly similar to, or "dilutive" of, that trademark

cybersquatting

involves the registration of an infringing domain name, or other Internet use of an existing trademark, for the purpose of extorting payments from the legitimate owners

cyberpiracy

involves the same behavior as cybersquatting, but with the intent of diverting traffic from the legitimate site to an infringing site

TABLE 8.16	INTERNET AND TRADEMARK LAW EXAMPLES	
ACTIVITY	DESCRIPTION	EXAMPLE CASE
Cybersquatting	Registering domain names similar or identical to trademarks of others to extort profits from legitimate holders	*E. & J. Gallo Winery v. Spider Webs Ltd.*, 129 F. Supp. 2d 1033 (S.D. Tex., 2001) aff'd 286 F. 3d 270 (5th Cir., 2002)
Cyberpiracy	Registering domain names similar or identical to trademarks of others to divert Web traffic to their own sites	*Ford Motor Co. v. Lapertosa*, 2001 U.S. Dist. LEXIS 253 (E.D. Mich., 2001); *PaineWebber Inc. v. Fortuny*, Civ. A. No. 99-0456-A (E.D. Va., 1999); *Playboy Enterprises, Inc. v. Global Site Designs, Inc.*, 1999 WL 311707 (S.D. Fla., 1999); *Audi AG and Volkswagen of America Inc. v. Bob D'Amato* (No. 05-2359; 6th Cir., November 27, 2006)
Metatagging	Using trademarked words in a site's metatags	*Bernina of America, Inc. v. Fashion Fabrics Int'l, Inc.*, 2001 U.S. Dist. LEXIS 1211 (N.D. Ill., 2001); *Nissan Motor Co., Ltd. v. Nissan Computer Corp.*, 289 F. Supp. 2d 1154 (C.D. Cal., 2000), aff'd, 246 F. 3rd 675 (9th Cir., 2000)
Keywording	Placing trademarked keywords on Web pages, either visible or invisible	*Playboy Enterprises, Inc. v. Netscape Communications, Inc.*, 354 F. 3rd 1020 (9th Cir., 2004); *Nettis Environment Ltd. v. IWI, Inc.*, 46 F. Supp. 2d 722 (N.D. Ohio, 1999); *Government Employees Insurance Company v. Google, Inc.*, Civ. Action No. 1:04cv507 (E.D. VA, 2004); *Google, Inc. v. American Blind & Wallpaper Factory, Inc.*, Case No. 03-5340 JF (RS) (N.D. Cal., April 18, 2007)
Linking	Linking to content pages on other sites, bypassing the home page	*Ticketmaster Corp. v. Tickets.com*, 2000 U.S. Dist. Lexis 4553 (C.D. Cal., 2000)
Framing	Placing the content of other sites in a frame on the infringer's site	*The Washington Post, et al. v. TotalNews, Inc., et al.*, (S.D.N.Y., Civil Action Number 97-1190)

However, it is not always easy for a firm to prevent trademark infringement by cybersquatters, or to prevent squatters from profiting from their infringing activities. In 2015, for instance, the Academy of Motion Picture Arts and Sciences (AMPAS) accused domain registrar GoDaddy of cybersquatting (*Academy of Motion Picture Arts and Sciences v. GoDaddy.com Inc et al.*, 2015). AMPAS claimed GoDaddy acted in bad faith by allowing customers to purchase 293 domain names such as Academyawards.net, Oscarsredacademyawards.net, Oscarsredcarpet.com, Billycrystal2012oscars.com, and Theoscargoestothehangover.com, and then sharing in the advertising revenues those pages generated. The court ruled that GoDaddy relied on representations of their users that their domain registrations did not infringe any trademarks, and that it took down domains after receiving takedown requests. AMPAS failed to prove intent to profit from AMPAS marks, according to the court. This suit demonstrates that trademark owners need to be vigilant in detecting infringement, sending takedown notices immediately, and following up to make sure the infringing sites are taken down. The burden is clearly on the trademark owner. The suit also demonstrates that cybersquatters have little incentive to stop trying to defraud and confuse consumers. If they are caught, their sites are taken down, but there is no penalty for trying (Stempel, 2015).

Cyberpiracy

Cyberpiracy involves the same behavior as cybersquatting, but with the intent of diverting traffic from the legitimate site to an infringing site. In *Ford Motor Co. v. Lapertosa*, Lapertosa had registered and used a Web site called Fordrecalls.com as an adult entertainment Web site. The court ruled that Fordrecalls.com was in violation of the ACPA in that it was a bad-faith attempt to divert traffic to the Lapertosa site and diluted Ford's wholesome trademark (*Ford Motor Co. v. Lapertosa*, 2001).

The Ford decision reflects two other famous cases of cyberpiracy. In the *Paine Webber Inc. v. Fortuny* case, the court enjoined Fortuny from using the domain name www.painewebber.com—a site that specialized in pornographic materials—because it diluted and tarnished Paine Webber's trademark and diverted Web traffic from Paine Webber's legitimate site—Painewebber.com (*Paine Webber Inc. v. Fortuny*, 1999). In the *Playboy Enterprises, Inc. v. Global Site Designs, Inc.* case, the court enjoined the defendants from using the Playboy and Playmate marks in their domain names Playboyonline.net and Playmatesearch.net and from including the Playboy trademark in their metatags. In these cases, the defendants' intention was diversion for financial gain (*Playboy Enterprises, Inc. v. Global Site Designs, Inc.*, 1999).

Typosquatting is a form of cyberpiracy in which a domain name contains a common misspelling of another site's name. These domains are sometimes referred to as "doppelganger" domains. Often the user ends up at a site very different from one they intended to visit. For instance, John Zuccarini is an infamous typosquatter who was jailed in 2002 for setting up pornographic Web sites with URLs based on misspellings of popular children's brands, such as Bob the Builder and Teletubbies. The FTC fined him again in October 2007 for engaging in similar practices (McMillan, 2007). Harvard Business School professor Ben Edelman conducted a study that found that there were at least 938,000 domains typosquatting on the top 3,264 ".com" Web sites, and that 57% of these domains included Google pay-per click ads. In July 2011, Facebook filed a lawsuit against 25 typosquatters who established Web sites with such domain names as Faceboook, Facemook, Faceboik, and Facebooki. In 2013, Facebook was awarded $2.8 milion in damages.

Metatagging

The legal status of using famous or distinctive marks as metatags is more complex and subtle. The use of trademarks in metatags is permitted if the use does not mislead or confuse consumers. Usually this depends on the content of the site. A car dealer would be permitted to use a famous automobile trademark in its metatags if the dealer sold this brand of automobiles, but a pornography site could not use the same trademark, nor a dealer for a rival manufacturer. A Ford dealer would most likely be infringing if it used "Honda" in its metatags, but would not be infringing if it used "Ford" in its metatags. (Ford Motor Company would be unlikely to seek an injunction against one of its dealers.)

In the *Bernina of America, Inc. v. Fashion Fabrics Int'l, Inc.* case, the court enjoined Fashion Fabrics, an independent dealer of sewing machines, from using the trademarks "Bernina" and "Bernette," which belonged to the manufacturer Bernina, as metatags. The court found the defendant's site contained misleading claims about Fashion Fabrics' knowledge of Bernina products that were likely to confuse customers. The use of the Bernina trademarks as metatags per se was not a violation of ACPA, according to the court, but in combination with the misleading claims on the site would cause confusion and hence infringement (*Bernina of America, Inc. v. Fashion Fabrics Int'l, Inc.*, 2001).

In the *Nissan Motor Co., Ltd. v. Nissan Computer Corp.* case, Uzi Nissan had used his surname "Nissan" as a trade name for various businesses since 1980, including Nissan Computer Corp. Nissan.com had no relationship with Nissan Motor, but over the years began selling auto parts that competed with Nissan Motor. The court ruled that Nissan Computer's behavior did indeed infringe on Nissan Motor's trademarks, but it refused to shut the site down. Instead, the court ruled Nissan Computer could continue to use the Nissan name and metatags, but must post notices on its site that it was not affiliated with Nissan Motor (*Nissan Motor Co., Ltd. v. Nissan Computer Corp.*, 2000).

Keywording

The permissibility of using trademarks as keywords on search engines is also subtle and depends (1) on the extent to which such use is considered to be a "use in commerce" and causes "initial customer confusion" and (2) on the content of the search results.

In *Playboy Enterprises, Inc. v. Netscape Communications, Inc.*, Playboy objected to the practice of Netscape's and Excite's search engines displaying banner ads unrelated to *Playboy Magazine* when users entered search arguments such as "playboy," "playmate," and "playgirl." The Ninth Circuit Court of Appeals denied the defendant's motion for a summary judgment and held that when an advertiser's banner ad is not labeled so as to identify its source, the practice could result in trademark infringement due to consumer confusion (*Playboy Enterprises, Inc. v. Netscape Communications, Inc.*, 2004).

Google has also faced lawsuits alleging that its advertising network illegally exploits others' trademarks. For instance, insurance company GEICO challenged Google's practice of allowing competitors' ads to appear when a searcher types "Geico" as the search query. A U.S. district court ruled that this practice did not violate federal trademark laws as long as the word "Geico" was not used in the ads' text (*Government Employees Insurance Company v. Google, Inc.*, 2004). Google quickly discontinued allowing the latter, and settled the case (Associated Press, 2005). In July 2009, Rosetta Stone, the language-learning software firm, filed a lawsuit against Google for trademark infringement, alleging its AdWords program allowed other companies to use Rosetta Stone's trademarks for online advertisements without permission. In April 2012, the 4th Circuit Court of Appeals held that a jury might hold Google liable for trademark infringement, pointing to evidence that an internal Google study found that even sophisticated users were sometimes unaware that sponsored links were advertisements. In November 2012, Rosetta Stone and Google settled, which was seen as a strategic win for Google because it eliminated one of the last major cases challenging the legitimacy of its AdWords program. Currently Google allows anyone to buy anyone else's trademark as a keyword. In 2011, Microsoft decided to follow this practice as well with Bing and Yahoo Search.

Linking

linking
building hypertext links from one site to another site

deep linking
involves bypassing the target site's home page, and going directly to a content page

Linking refers to building hypertext links from one site to another site. This is obviously a major design feature and benefit of the Web. **Deep linking** involves bypassing the target site's home page and going directly to a content page. In *Ticketmaster Corp. v. Tickets.com*, Tickets.com—owned by Microsoft—competed directly against Ticketmaster in the events ticket market. When Tickets.com did not have tickets for an event, it would direct users to Ticketmaster's internal pages, bypassing the Ticketmaster home page. Even though its logo was displayed on the internal pages, Ticketmaster objected on the grounds that such "deep linking" violated the terms and conditions of use for its site (stated on a separate page altogether and construed by Ticketmaster as equivalent to a shrink-wrap license), and constituted false advertising, as well as the violation of copyright. The court found, however, that deep linking per se is not illegal, no violation of copyright occurred because no copies were made, the terms and conditions of use were not obvious to users, and users were not required to read the page on which the terms and conditions of use appeared in any event. The court refused to rule in favor of Ticketmaster, but left open further argument on the licensing issue. In an out-of-court settlement, Tickets.com nevertheless agreed to stop the practice of deep linking (*Ticketmaster v. Tickets.com*, 2000).

Framing

framing
involves displaying the content of another Web site inside your own Web site within a frame or window

Framing involves displaying the content of another Web site inside your own Web site within a frame or window. The user never leaves the framer's site and can be exposed to advertising while the target site's advertising is distorted or eliminated. Framers may or may not acknowledge the source of the content. In *The Washington Post, et al. v. TotalNews, Inc.* case, The Washington Post Company, CNN, Reuters, and several other news organizations filed suit against TotalNews, Inc., claiming that TotalNews's use of frames on its Web site, TotalNews.com, infringed upon the respective plaintiffs' copyrights and trademarks, and diluted the content of their individual Web sites. The plaintiffs claimed additionally that TotalNews's framing practice effectively deprived the plaintiffs' Web sites of advertising revenue.

TotalNews's Web site employed four frames. The TotalNews logo appeared in the lower left frame, various links were located in a vertical frame on the left side of the screen, TotalNews's advertising was framed across the screen bottom, and the "news frame," the largest frame, appeared in the center and right. Clicking on a specific news organization's link allowed the reader to view the content of that particular organization's Web site, including any related advertising, within the context of the "news frame." In some instances, the framing distorted or modified the appearance of the linked Web site, including the advertisements, while the appearance of Total-News's advertisements, in a separate frame, remained unchanged. In addition, the URL remained fixed on the TotalNews address, even though the content in the largest frame on the Web site was from the linked Web site. The "news frame" did not, however, eliminate the linked Web site's identifying features.

The case was settled out of court. The news organizations allowed TotalNews to link to their Web sites, but prohibited framing and any attempt to imply affiliation with the news organizations (*The Washington Post, et al. v. TotalNews, Inc.*, 1997).

CHALLENGE: BALANCING THE PROTECTION OF PROPERTY WITH OTHER VALUES

The challenge in intellectual property ethics and law is to ensure that creators of intellectual property can receive the benefits of their inventions and works, while also making it possible for their works and designs to be disseminated and used by the widest possible audience. Protections from rampant theft of intellectual property inevitably lead to restrictions on distribution, and the payments to creators for the use of their works—which in itself can slow down the distribution process. Without these protections, however, and without the benefits that flow to creators of intellectual property, the pace of innovation could decline. In the early years of e-commerce, up to 2005, the balance has been struck more toward Internet distributors and their claim to be free from restrictions on intellectual content, particularly music. Since the development of the iTunes store, smartphones, and tablets, after 2005, the balance has swung back toward content owners, largely because Internet distributors depend on high-quality content to attract audiences, but also partly due to the effectiveness of lawsuits in raising the costs to Internet firms that fail to protect intellectual property.

8.4 GOVERNANCE

Governance has to do with social control: Who will control the Internet? Who will control the processes of e-commerce, the content, and the activities? What elements will be controlled, and how will the controls be implemented? A natural question arises and needs to be answered: Why do we as a society need to "control" e-commerce? Because e-commerce and the Internet are so closely intertwined (though not identical), controlling e-commerce also involves regulating the Internet.

governance
has to do with social control: who will control e-commerce, what elements will be controlled, and how will the controls be implemented

CAN THE INTERNET BE CONTROLLED?

Early Internet advocates argued that the Internet was different from all previous technologies. They contended that the Internet could not be controlled, given its inherent decentralized design, its ability to cross borders, and its underlying packet-switching technology that made monitoring and controlling message content impossible. Many still believe this to be true today. The implication is that the content and behavior of e-commerce sites—indeed Internet sites of any kind—cannot be "controlled" in the same way. Content issues such as pornography, gambling, and offensive written expressions and graphics, along with commercial issue of intellectual property protection, ushered in the current era of growing governmental regulation of the Internet and e-commerce throughout the world. Currently, we are in a mixed-mode policy environment where self-regulation through a variety of Internet policy and technical bodies co-exists with limited government regulation (Stone, 2010). See Chapter 3 for a review of the different governing bodies involved in overseeing the Internet, including ICANN and IANA, and proposed changes in the United States' authority over IANA (see pages 136–137).

In fact, as you learned in the Chapter 3 *Insight on Society* case, *Government Regulation and Surveillance of the Internet*, the Internet is technically very easily controlled, monitored, and regulated from central locations (such as network access points, telecommunication firm or agency fiber trunk lines, as well as servers and routers throughout the network). For instance, in China, Saudi Arabia, Iran, North Korea, Thailand, Singapore, and many other countries, access to the Web is controlled from government-owned centralized routers that direct traffic across their borders and within the country (such as China's "Great Firewall of China," which permits the government to block access to certain U.S. or European Web sites), or via tightly regulated ISPs operating within the countries. In China, for instance, all ISPs need a license from the Ministry of Information Industry (MII), and are prohibited from disseminating any information that may harm the state or permit pornography, gambling, or the advocacy of cults. In addition, ISPs and search engines such as Google, Yahoo, and Bing typically self-censor their Asian content by using only government-approved news sources or, in the case of Google, exit the country altogether. Twitter is not planning any Chinese presence. China has also instituted regulations that require cafes, restaurants, hotels, and bookstores to install Web monitoring software that identifies those using wireless services and monitors Web activity. Because of the design of the Internet, a substantial part of global Internet traffic flows through U.S. telecommunication facilities.

Following the outbreak of street demonstrations in 2009 protesting a rigged election, the Iranian government unleashed one of the world's most sophisticated mechanisms for controlling and censoring the Web. Built with the assistance of Western companies like Siemens and Nokia, the system uses deep packet inspection to open every packet, look for keywords, reseal it, and send it on the network. In Great Britain, Prime Minister David Cameron suggested that he might temporarily block social network sites such as Facebook and Twitter during periods of social unrest such as the rioting that hit the country in 2011.

In the United States, as we have seen in our discussion of intellectual property, e-commerce sites can be put out of business for violating existing laws, and ISPs can be forced to "take down" offending or stolen content. Government security agencies such as the NSA and the FBI can obtain court orders to monitor ISP traffic and engage in widespread monitoring of millions of e-mail messages. Under the USA PATRIOT Act, American intelligence authorities are permitted to tap into whatever Internet traffic they believe is relevant to the campaign against terrorism, in some circumstances without judicial review. Working with the large ISP firms such as AT&T, Verizon, and others, U.S. security agencies have access to nearly all Internet communications throughout the country. And many American corporations are developing restrictions on their employees' at-work use of the Web to prevent gambling, shopping, and other activities not related to a business purpose.

In the United States, efforts to control media content on the Web have run up against equally powerful social and political values that protect freedom of expression, including several rulings by the Supreme Court that have struck down laws attempting to limit Web content in the United States. The U.S. Constitution's First Amendment says, "Congress shall make no law ... abridging the freedom of speech, or of the press." As it turns out, the 200-year-old Bill of Rights has been a powerful brake on efforts to control twenty-first-century online content.

TAXATION

Few questions illustrate the complexity of governance and jurisdiction more potently than taxation of e-commerce sales. In both Europe and the United States, governments rely on sales taxes based on the type and value of goods sold. In Europe, these taxes are collected along the entire value chain, including the final sale to the consumer, and are called "value-added taxes" (VAT), whereas in the United States, taxes are collected by states and localities on final sales to consumers and are called consumption and use taxes. In the United States, there are 50 states, 3,000 counties, and 12,000 municipalities, each with unique tax rates and policies. Cheese may be taxable in one state as a "snack food" but not taxable in another state (such as Wisconsin), where it is considered a basic food. Consumption taxes are generally recognized to be regressive because they disproportionately tax poorer people, for whom consumption is a larger part of total income.

Sales taxes were first implemented in the United States in the late 1930s as a Depression-era method of raising money for localities. Ostensibly, the money was to be used to build infrastructure such as roads, schools, and utilities to support business development, but over the years the funds have been used for general government purposes of the states and localities. In most states, there is a state-based sales tax, and a smaller local sales tax. The total sales tax ranges from zero in some states (North Dakota) to as much as 13% in New York City.

The development of "remote sales" such as mail order/telephone order (MOTO) retail in the United States in the 1970s broke the relationship between physical presence and commerce, complicating the plans of state and local tax authorities to tax all retail commerce. States sought to force MOTO retailers to collect sales taxes for them based on the address of the recipient, but Supreme Court decisions in 1967 and 1992 established that states had no authority to force MOTO retailers to collect state taxes unless the businesses had a "nexus" of operations (physical presence) in the state. In 2015, the Supreme Court upheld a challenge to a Colorado law that would have required firms to report online sales to state residents as one step to ensure the residents paid taxes on Internet sales in Colorado, which is required by state law. But the court also stated that the premise of allowing Internet sales by out-of-state firms like Amazon to go untaxed in order to support Internet sales was no longer appropriate when e-commerce has exploded to a $531 billion market place (Liptakmarch, 2015).

The explosive growth of e-commerce, the latest type of "remote sales," has once again raised the issue of how—and if—to tax remote sales. Since its inception, e-commerce has benefited from a tax subsidy of up to 13% for goods shipped to high sales-tax areas. Local retail merchants have complained bitterly about the e-commerce tax subsidy. E-commerce merchants have argued that this form of commerce needs to be nurtured and encouraged, and that in any event, the crazy quilt of sales and use tax regimes would be difficult to administer for Internet merchants. Online giants like Amazon claim they should not have to pay taxes in states where they have no operations because they do not benefit from local schools, police, fire, and other governmental services. State and local governments meanwhile see billions of tax dollars slipping from their reach. As Amazon's business model has changed with its building of large distribution centers close to urban areas to enable next-day delivery, so has its opposition to paying sales taxes softened. The *Insight on Business* case, *Internet Sales Tax Battle*, provides further insight into the fight over e-commerce sales taxes.

In 1998, Congress passed the Internet Tax Freedom Act, which placed a moratorium on "multiple or discriminatory taxes on electronic commerce," as well as on taxes on Internet access, for three years until October 2001. Since that time, the moratorium has been extended several times, most currently until December 11, 2015. In 2015, the House of Representatives passed a bill to permanently ban taxes on Internet access, but the legislation has not yet passed the Senate (Shrum, 2015).

The taxation situation in Europe, and trade between Europe and the United States, is similarly complex. The Organization for Economic Cooperation and Development (OECD), the economic policy coordinating body of European, American, and Japanese governments, is currently investigating different schemes for applying consumption and business profit taxes for digitally downloaded goods. The European Union began collecting a VAT on digital goods such as music and software delivered to consumers by foreign companies in 2003. Previously, E.U. companies were required to collect the VAT on sales to E.U. customers, but U.S. companies were not. This gave American companies a huge tax edge. European countries have other tax issues with Internet companies like Google, Apple, Yahoo, and others, that sell goods to consumers in one country, but book the sales in a low-tax country like Ireland.

NET NEUTRALITY

net neutrality
the concept that Internet service providers should treat all Internet traffic equally (or "neutrally")

Net neutrality refers to the idea that Internet service providers (ISPs), including cable Internet and wireless carriers, should treat all data on the Internet in the same manner, and not discriminate or price differentially by content, protocol, platform, hardware, or application. Prior to February 2015, ISPs could discriminate against certain users on the basis of protocol or amount of usage. For instance, users of illegal downloading sites that utilize the BitTorrent protocol were blocked or throttled back (Internet speeds were slowed). Users who watched large volumes of movies on Netflix or other services were occasionally throttled back; wireless cellphone carriers choked off data speeds for heavy users when their networks became clogged; and large Internet services like Netflix and YouTube, that together consume an estimated 50% of the Internet's bandwidth in the United States, were encouraged to strike deals with ISPs and pay a higher fee than ordinary business or home users (Gryta, 2015a).

INSIGHT ON BUSINESS

INTERNET SALES TAX BATTLE

Most people are happy when they discover they don't have to pay any sales tax on a purchase they make online. However, few stop to consider the implications of their tax-free purchases. Constitutionally bound to balance their budgets, starved for revenue, and simultaneously facing increased demand for public services, states have been suffering a persistent budget crunch. Many of the 45 states that levy sales taxes have been eyeing the lost revenue from e-commerce sales, estimated at nearly $14 billion nationwide in 2013 and steadily growing as more and more commerce shifts to the Web and the mobile platform at the expense of bricks-and-mortar stores. Economists point out that the lost revenue from out-of-state e-commerce sales affects not only state and local sales tax collections, but also jobs and ultimately, state income tax collections as well.

Internet sales tax policy has been dictated by the Supreme Court decision in *Quill v. North Dakota*, which held that retailers without a store or other physical presence (nexus) in a state could not be forced to collect state sales taxes. Citizens were supposed to be responsible for remitting unpaid sales tax along with their state income tax returns. This unsurprisingly proved to be unworkable, with nearly universal noncompliance. The rationale for not closing this loophole, which resulted from a MOTO (Mail Order/Telephone Order) case, was to provide protection for a nascent market. With total 2015 B2C e-commerce sales expected to top $530 million in the United States, this argument had lost its punch. A recent Supreme Court decision on a slightly different issue has also raised the possibility that the Supreme Court might be willing to reconsider its previous decision in the *Quill* case, with Supreme Court Justice Anthony Kennedy writing that the

Quill decision harms states to a much greater degree than anticipated.

Internet retail kingpin Amazon has been at the center of the political battle. Multiple states, frustrated by the lost revenue that could have been used to balance their budgets and prevent further layoffs, have taken Amazon on. Texas, Illinois, New York, Rhode Island, and North Carolina were some of the first states to take aim at Amazon via tax bills and legislation intended to get the e-tailer to pay its share of sales taxes. These efforts prompted Amazon to withdraw its physical presence from and terminate its affiliate relationships in those states. California, which estimated that it lost $1.1 billion per year in uncollected sales tax, passed legislation expanding the definition of nexus in 2011, but delayed tax collection until 2012.

Facing a continuing state-by-state assault, Amazon recognized that its former competitive advantage was ultimately going to come to an end. It devised a dual-pronged strategy. In the short term, it negotiated deals with states in which it planned to open distribution centers. These distribution centers were strategically located to support its long-term goal and what it hopes will become its new competitive advantage—same day delivery.

For example, in 2012, Amazon settled its dispute with Texas when it agreed to create 2,500 local jobs over four years' time, pay an undisclosed amount to resolve its tax bill, and begin collecting sales tax from Texas residents. Similarly, in 2012, Amazon reached an agreement with New Jersey that allowed it to build two distribution centers in the state. Amazon will also receive yet to be determined tax incentives from the state Economic Development Authority. In California, in exchange for the one-year tax reprieve, Amazon agreed to spend $500 million building new facilities, which also positioned it for same-day delivery in two major metropolitan areas.

(continued)

In 2015, Amazon withdrew requests for tax breaks in Minnesota as it made plans to build a new distribution center there.

Rather than continuing to make agreements with states individually, Amazon hopes that the federal government will step in soon. In 2011, Amazon threw its support behind a new bill called the Main Street Fairness Act. Under the terms of the bill, businesses with less than $1 million in annual sales would not have had to remit sales taxes. States would have had to agree to the Streamlined Sales and Use Tax Agreement, which simplifies their tax policies so that it will be easier for Internet retailers to conform. Now known as the Marketplace Fairness Act (MFA), the bill cleared the Senate in 2013 but has struggled to pass in the House of Representatives, where lawmakers are concerned that the MFA (now renamed the Remote Transaction Parity Act) would force small businesses to manage over 9,000 state and local tax codes, and that supporting a new law that looks and sounds like a new tax would be unpopular. The bill would create a uniform set of rules for collecting taxes from e-commerce sales. The states that don't collect any sales tax (Alaska, Oregon, New Hampshire, Montana, and Delaware) are also opponents of the bill, as it would force them to levy taxes that would otherwise not be part of their own tax code.

It's no surprise that Amazon, Walmart, Best Buy, and other retailers are all lobbying hard in favor of the bill, which would eliminate a major advantage for many of their smaller competi-

tors. Amazon believes that a nationwide online sales tax would improve its competitive prospects against rivals who don't have affiliates in each state. Perhaps hedging its bets in case the bill does not pass, Amazon has continued to battle individual states on their rights to collect sales tax on e-commerce purchases. But increasingly, the company is accepting that it is fighting a losing battle. Residents in Indiana, Nevada, and Tennessee began paying sales taxes in 2014, and in 2015, Illinois and Michigan joined the ranks of states where Amazon collects sales taxes. In 2016 South Carolinians will pay sales tax on their Amazon purchases as well. Because many of these states are the most populated, Amazon now collects sales tax from approximately 75% of all U.S. consumers. Amazon's profits have suffered as a result of the change but many analysts believe that the additional taxes are unlikely to materially impact Amazon's revenue in many states.

Grassroots campaigns against the MFA, such as the "Stop Internet Sales Tax" campaign, have sprung up, protesting that the MFA is a bill created with the interests of major retailers in mind, without consideration for small and local businesses or consumers. Still, Amazon and other e-tailers have legitimate points regarding fairness and civic responsibility. We have all enjoyed purchasing online goods from out-of-state sellers and evading the sales tax, but this is not a new tax. It is a tax that we have enjoyed evading, and one that the states desperately need to pay for the services and professions we rely on every day.

SOURCES: "Internet Sales Tax Bill Looms Again, What Entrepeneurs Need to Know," by Erica Nicole, Yfsmagazine.com, June 16, 2015; "Strategies: The End May (Finally) Be Near for the Online Sales Tax Loophole," by David Schachter, Bizjournals.com, May 15, 2015; "Bid to Collect Online Sales Taxes Is Stalled in Congress," by Lindsay Wise, Thenewstribune.com, May 7, 2015; "Michigan Passes New "Amazon Tax" Law Requiring Internet Sales Tax Collection," by Joel C. Farrar, Lexology.com, April 21, 2015; "Upholding Internet Sales Tax Law, a Justice Invites a New Case," by Adam Liptak, *New York Times,* March 3, 2015; "Amazon Will Soon Collect Sales Tax From 74% of U.S. Consumers," by Matt Lindner, Internetretailer.com, January 26, 2015; "Tax Collections on Online Retail Sales: The Rest of the Story," by Robert A. Robicheaux, *State Tax Notes,* September 15, 2014; "Amazon's Loathsome Tax Scheme: How Behemoths Defeat Main Street – And How We Can Stop Them," by Kathleen Sharp, Salon.com, July 12, 2014; "'Stop Internet Sales Tax' Grassroots Campaign Challenges Marketplace Fairness Act," *Digital Journal,* July 1, 2014; "Amazon Takes Sales Hit in States with Online Tax, Study Finds," *Seattle Times,* April 22, 2014; "New Year Rings in Sales Tax for Amazon Shoppers in Three States," by Greg Bensinger, *Wall Street Journal,* January 1, 2014; "Supreme Court Declines Case on Making Online Retailers Collect Sales Taxes," by Robert Barnes, *Washington Post,* December 2, 2013; "Amazon Lobbies Heavily for Internet Sales Tax," by Kyung M. Song, *Seattle Times,* September 7, 2013; "Impact of Marketplace Fairness on Select Jurisdictions," *IHS Global Insight,* May 2013; "Small E-retailers Mobilize to Lobby Against Online Sales Tax Collection," by Paul Demery, *Internet Retailer,* September, 14, 2012; "Coalition Launched to Oppose Internet Sales Tax Legislation," by Juliana Gruenwald, *NextGov Newsletter,* September 13, 2012; "Amazon, Forced to Collect a Tax, Is Adding Roots," by David Streitfeld, *New York Times,* September 11, 2012; "10 Surprising Facts About Online Sales Taxes," by Robert W. Wood, *Forbes,* September 11, 2012; "Amazon.com to Begin Collecting Sales Tax on N.J. Orders Next Year," by Matt Friedman and Jarrett Renshaw, NJ.com, May 30, 2012.

ISPs had long opposed the idea of net neutrality. ISPs claimed they needed to be able to manage the loads on their networks to ensure stable service, without blackouts or slow downs. Throttling back heavy users was necessary to manage network load. They also argued that heavy individual or business users should pay more than the average user at home who uses the Web for e-mail, Web surfing, and e-commerce, all of which do not require a lot of bandwidth. More to the point, the ISPs claimed the Federal Communications Commission (FCC) did not have the authority to regulate ISPs because ISPs were not defined by the FCC as common carriers like traditional telephone companies. ISPs instead were classified in FCC regulations of the 1990s as information services in large part because the Internet, at that time, was considered to be a innovative provider of information that should be nurtured and not interfered with or regulated by the FCC. The Internet then was just not that important to the operation of society.

This view ended on February 15, 2015, when the FCC ruled that Internet broadband service providers really should be viewed as public utilities similar to telephone companies, and therefore should be regulated by the FCC in order to ensure fair access to all, deployment of acceptable broadband service levels, and competition among providers. This change reflected the fact that the Internet had evolved by 2015 into one of the primary telecommunications services in the country, and world, necessary to the everyday life of millions of people, businesses, and governments, and therefore a common carrier vital to the operation of society (just like a railroad service). The FCC was created by the Communications Act of 1934 to regulate telegraph and radio, and then later added regulation of television, satellite, and cable in all states. The FCC also overruled state laws that made it difficult for cities to operate their own broadband networks. In this way, a decades-long debate over net neutrality moved a step towards resolution. The ruling does not provide for regulation of ISP pricing, which remains in the hands of the ISPs (Gryta, 2015b).

However, the debate over net neutrality is not totally yet over. The large telecommunications carriers are preparing legal challenges to the FCC ruling. In the past, the courts themselves have not agreed on the idea that ISPs should be regulated as common carriers, or that the FCC should interfere with the management of provider networks. Yet there is strong public support for regulation of ISPs to ensure faster broadband deployment, more competition to reduce prices, and service level improvements. Popular services like Netflix publicly supported the FCC decision as a win for consumers (Ruiz, 2015)

8.5 PUBLIC SAFETY AND WELFARE

Governments everywhere claim to pursue public safety, health, and welfare. This effort produces laws governing everything from weights and measures to national highways, to the content of radio and television programs. Electronic media of all kinds (telegraph, telephone, radio, and television) have historically been regulated by governments seeking to develop a rational commercial telecommunications environment and to control the content of the media—which may be critical of government or offensive to powerful groups in a society. Historically, in the United States, newspapers and print media have been beyond government controls because of constitutional guarantees of freedom of speech. Electronic media such as radio and television have, on the other hand, always been subject to content regulation because they use the publicly owned frequency spectrum. Telephones have also been regulated as public utilities and "common carriers," with special social burdens to provide service and access, but with no limitations on content.

In the United States, critical issues in e-commerce center around the protection of children, strong sentiments against pornography in any public media, efforts to control gambling, and the protection of public health through restricting sales of drugs and cigarettes.

PROTECTING CHILDREN

Pornography is an immensely successful Internet business. Statistics with respect to revenues generated by online pornography range widely. Reports of Web traffic to pornography sites constituting 30% of all Web traffic are likely not true and have no solid foundation. A sample of the million most-visited sites in the world found that 4% of the Web sites contained pornographic material, and 14% of Web searches involved sexual content (Ward, 2013). Online pornography is estimated to generate $10 to $12 billion annually in the United States, and the global revenue is estimated to be $97 billion. Traditional DVD porn revenues have fallen off by 80% as so-called tube sites (YouTube for porn) have rapidly expanded with free and freemium content online. Piracy is rampant as with traditional video content. Revenues are now primarily derived from premium subscriptions and advertising.

To control the Web as a distribution medium for pornography, in 1996, Congress passed the Communications Decency Act (CDA). This act made it a felony criminal offense to use any telecommunications device to transmit "any comment, request, suggestion, proposal, image, or other communications which is obscene, lewd, lascivious, filthy, or indecent" to anyone, and in particular, to persons under 18 years of age (Section 502, Communications Decency Act of 1996). In 1997, the Supreme Court struck down most of the CDA as an unconstitutional abridgement of freedom of speech protected by the First Amendment. While the government argued the CDA was like a zoning ordinance designed to allow "adult" Web sites for people 18 years of age or over, the Court found the CDA was a blanket proscription on content and rejected the "cyberzoning" argument as impossible to administer. One section of the CDA that did survive scrutiny, Section 230, provides immunity for providers and users of interactive computer services (such as ISPs and Web sites) from being considered a publisher that might be liable for harmful content posted by others. This is the law that allows social networks, blogs, and online bulletin boards to operate without fear of being held liable for online defamation or libel. In 2002, the Supreme Court struck down another law, the Child Pornography Prevention Act of 1996, which made it a crime to create, distribute, or possess "virtual" child pornography that uses computer-generated images or young adults rather than real children, as overly broad (*Ashcroft v. Free Speech Coalition*). The Children's Online Protection Act (COPA) of 1998 met with a similar fate.

In 2001, Congress passed the Children's Internet Protection Act (CIPA), which requires schools and libraries in the United States to install "technology protection measures" (filtering software) in an effort to shield children from pornography. In June 2003, the Supreme Court upheld CIPA, overturning a federal district court that found the law interfered with the First Amendment guarantee of freedom of expression. The Supreme Court, in a 6–3 opinion, held that the law's limitations on access to the Internet posed no more a threat to freedom of expression than limitations on access to books that librarians choose for whatever reason not to acquire. The dissenting justices found this analogy inappropriate and instead argued the proper analogy was if librarians were to purchase encyclopedias and then rip out pages they thought were or might be offensive to patrons. All the justices agreed that existing blocking software was overly blunt, unable to distinguish child pornography from sexually explicit material (which is protected by the First Amendment), and generally unreliable (Greenhouse, 2003b). Other legislation such as the 2002 Domain Names Act seeks to prevent unscrupulous Web site operators from luring children to pornography using misleading domain names or characters known to children. A plan to create an .xxx domain for adult Web site content was approved by ICANN in June 2010, and in September 2011, limited registration for .xxx domains began. Trademark holders who do not wish their brand to be associated with an .xxx domain can block requests by other companies for domain names that include their brand name. The 2003 Protect Act is an omnibus law intended to prevent child abuse that includes prohibitions against computer-generated child pornography. Part of that statute was previously held to be unconstitutional by the Eleventh Circuit Court of Appeals, but in May 2008, the Supreme Court reversed the circuit court and upheld the provision (Greenhouse, 2008).

The Children's Online Privacy Protection Act (COPPA) (1998) prohibits Web sites from collecting information on children under the age of 13. It does permit such data collection if parental consent is obtained. Because COPPA does not interfere with speech or expression, it has not been challenged in the courts. However, since 1998, entirely new technologies like social networks, online tracking, advertising networks, online gaming, and mobile apps have appeared that are now being used to gather data on children and which were not specifically addressed in COPPA or FTC regulations. Responding to these changes in technology and public pressure, the FTC announced a new set of rules that are now in effect. The new rules prohibit online tracking of children across the Web with cookies or any other technology such as persistent identifiers; prohibit ad networks from following children across the Web and advertising to them without parental consent; make clear that mobile devices are subject to COPPA, including games and software apps; and make clear that third-party data collection firms that collect data on Web sites are responsible for any unlawful data collection. Search engines and ISPs also have a role to play in eliminating child pornography from the Web. The Internet Watch Foundation is a private non-profit organization based in the United Kingdom whose mission is to eliminate child pornography from the Web, and has over 200 corporate members from the Internet technology community (IWF.org, 2015). In 2015, Google, Facebook, Microsoft, and Twitter joined together and are using the Internet Watch Foundation's hash list to remove abusive child images from their services. Other companies working with the Internet Watch Foundation include Cisco, Blackberry, Dropbox, and PayPal (Lien, 2015). See the

Chapter 7 *Insight on Society* case, *Marketing to Children of the Web in the Age of Social Networks*, for more information.

CIGARETTES, GAMBLING, AND DRUGS: IS THE WEB REALLY BORDERLESS?

In the United States, both the states and the federal government have adopted legislation to control certain activities and products in order to protect public health and welfare. Cigarettes, gambling, medical drugs, and of course addictive recreational drugs, are either banned or tightly regulated by federal and state laws (see *Insight on Society: The Internet Drug Bazaar*). Yet these products and services are ideal for distribution over the Internet through e-commerce sites. Because the sites can be located offshore, they can operate beyond the jurisdiction of state and federal prosecutors. Or so it seemed until recently. In the case of cigarettes, state and federal authorities have been quite successful in shutting down tax-free cigarette Web sites within the United States by pressuring PayPal and credit card firms to drop cigarette merchants from their systems. The major shipping companies—UPS, FedEx, and DHL—have been pressured into refusing shipment of untaxed cigarettes. Philip Morris has also agreed not to ship cigarettes to any resellers that have been found to be engaging in illegal Internet and mail order sales. However, a few off-shore Web sites continue to operate using checks and money orders as payments and the postal system as a logistics partner, but their level of business has plummeted as consumers fear state tax authorities will present them with huge tax bills if they are discovered using these sites. In 2010, President Obama signed the Prevent All Cigarette Trafficking Act. The law restricts the sale of untaxed cigarettes and other tobacco products over the Internet and bans the delivery of tobacco products through the U.S. mail.

Gambling also provides an interesting example of the clash between traditional jurisdictional boundaries and claims to a borderless, uncontrollable Web. The online gambling market, based almost entirely offshore—primarily in the United Kingdom and various Caribbean Islands—grew by leaps and bounds between 2000 and 2006, with much of the action (some estimate up to 50%) coming from customers based in the United States. Online gambling is still banned in most of the United States even though the global market is now a $25 billion dollar business, almost entirely offshore, and roughly one-third the size of the entire U.S. gambling business (about $69 billion, including lotteries and public gambling) (O'Keefe, 2014). U.S. casino gambling in 2014 generated an estimated $38 billion. Congress initially outlawed online gambling and the payment systems including credit cards used to support it in 2006 (the Unlawful Internet Gambling Enforcement Act of 2006 and the Wire Act) and the U.S. Department of Justice enforced the law vigorously, denying offshore operators access to American payment systems, crippling their U.S. business, and arresting several executives. However, the mood has changed in the last five years. State revenue needs have grown, and many in the casino gambling industry have switched sides and now support online gambling, seeing it as a revenue growth opportunity. The federal government has also changed its position and reversed its stance against Internet gambling, removing a major obstacle for states (Wyatt, 2011). The ethical issues surrounding online gambling may have less influence on the public debate than the need for new tax revenues, and for firms, the hope for additional revenues.

INSIGHT ON SOCIETY

THE INTERNET DRUG BAZAAR

In June 2015, Interpol announced the results of its eighth-annual Operation Pangea effort to combat sales of illegal drugs online. The operation shut down 2,414 Web sites and resulted in the arrest of 156 people and the seizure of 20.7 million doses of illegal drugs worth $81 million. Despite successes such as this, however, the Internet drug bazaar operated by rogue Internet drug outlets remains a continuing public health and safety issue.

The International Narcotics Control Board, a U.N. narcotics watchdog agency, has provided guidelines and a framework for governments struggling to contain growing abuse of prescription drugs on the Internet. A Google search for drugs "no prescription" in 2015, for instance, returns more than 39 million results. In many countries, trafficking in illegal prescription drugs now equals or exceeds the sale of heroin, cocaine, and amphetamines. While properly regulated Internet pharmacies offer a valuable service by increasing competition and access to treatments in underserved regions, online pharmacies are a long way from proper regulation.

The sale of drugs without a prescription is not the only danger posed by the Internet drug bazaar. Rogue online pharmacy sites may be selling counterfeit drugs or unapproved drugs. For instance, in the past, the FDA has issued warnings that consumers who had purchased Ambien, Xanax, and Lexapro online had instead received a product containing haloperial, a powerful antipsychotic drug. Google and other search engines have come under fire for their relationships with purveyors of illegal drugs and other unlawful products like stolen credit cards and fake IDs. In 2014, Google announced a settlement in a shareholder lawsuit over accusations that it had allowed advertising from illegal drug sellers outside the United States. As part of the settlement, Google agreed to allocate $50 million per year to an internal effort to sever ties with and disrupt the operations of illegal online pharmacies. FedEx was also indicted in 2014 for knowingly shipping packages from illegal online pharmacies. In 2015, FedEx failed in its attempts to have drug-trafficking and money-laundering charges against it dismissed. UPS has also paid over $40 million in fines for similar infractions.

Despite these dangers, online pharmacies remain alluring and are one of the fastest growing business models, with, oddly, senior citizens— usually some of the most law-abiding citizens— leading the charge for cheaper drugs. The main attraction of online drug sites is price. Typically, online pharmacies are located in countries where prescription drugs are price-controlled, or where the price structure is much lower, such as Canada, the United Kingdom, and European countries, as well as India and Mexico. U.S. citizens can often save 50%–75% by purchasing from online pharmacies located in other countries.

Currently, a patchwork regulatory structure governs the sale of drugs online. At the federal level, the 1938 Food, Drug, and Cosmetic Act (FDCA) requires that certain drugs may only be purchased with a valid doctor's prescription and must be dispensed by a state-licensed pharmacy. To get around this requirement, some online pharmacies use questionnaires to diagnose disease and have these questionnaires reviewed by doctors who write the prescription. The Ryan Haight Online Pharmacy Consumer Act, which took effect in 2009, bans the sale of prescription drugs over the Internet without a legitimate prescription issued by a medical practitioner who has examined the patient in person at least once, and requires online

(continued)

pharmacies to comply with pharmacy licensing laws in every state where they do business, and to register with the FDA before beginning to sell drugs online. This requirement is virtually unenforceable because foreign online pharmacies can easily run their Web sites from an offshore location, making it difficult for federal and state authorities to exercise jurisdiction over them. For example, in 2015, many of the rogue pharmacies identified by the FDA are registered overseas, and not even ICANN, the Internet's central administrator, currently has the power to shut those sites down.

Another haven for online purveyors of illegal drugs is the "Dark" or "Deep" Web, which consists of sites that are not accessible by search engines and often feature security measures designed to allow complete anonymity or to mask illegal activity. In 2013, the most prominent online drug marketplace on the Deep Web was the Silk Road, which was estimated to attract as much as $45 million a year in illegal drug purchases and $1.2 billion worth of total transactions. The Silk Road required users to run Tor anonymity software and accepted the virtual currency Bitcoin (see the *Insight on Society* case *Bitcoin in Chapter 5*), allowing online drug buyers an unprecedented level of protection. The Silk Road was not so much a pharmacy as it was a sort of eBay for illegal drugs. But in 2013, the Silk Road's founder and chief operator, a shadowy figure known as "Dread Pirate Roberts," was revealed to be a former Eagle Scout named Ross Ulbricht, who was arrested, charged with drug trafficking and money laundering, and eventually sentenced to life in prison in 2015. Federal agents also seized $33.6 million in Bitcoins from Ulbricht. Although the arrest was a major blow, it it still very easy to purchase illegal drugs on the Deep Web. According to researchers at Carnegie Mellon University, more than 50% of the Deep Web drug marketplaces (which they call darknet markets) have Web sites directly derived from the template used by Silk Road. As one market is closed, or closes, another pops up to take its place. According to the research, these darknet markets average $300,000 to $500,000 a day, with marijuana accounting for about 25% of sales, followed by MDMA, stimulants, psychedelic drugs, prescription drugs, and opioids. And though many Bitcoin exchanges are forcing users to provide their identities, law enforcement agencies have not developed reliable methods for tracking virtual currencies. While law enforcement agencies grapple with such sites, traditional illegal pharmacies continue to proliferate. The FDA recommends that consumers look for the NABP Verified Internet Pharmacy Practices Sites (VIPPS) seal, which verifies that the site is legitimate with respect to conformance with state laws, and requires a prescription for controlled drugs. So far, 40 major Internet pharmacies have signed on, including Drugstore.com, Caremark.com, Walgreens.com, and many other U.S. online pharmacies.

SOURCES: "Find a VIPPS Online Pharmacy," Nabp.net, accesssed October 4, 2015; "Buying Drugs Online Remains Easy, 2 Years After FBI Killed Silk Road," by Steven Nelson, Usnews.com, October 2, 2015; "Measuring the Longitudinal Evolution of the Online Anonymous Marketplace," by Kyle Sosa and Nicolas Christin, Proceedings of the 24th USENIX Security Symposium, August 12–15, 2015; "Interpol-coordinated Operation Strikes at Organized Crime with Seizure of 20 Million Illicit Medicines," Interpol.int, June 18, 2015; "Ross Ulbricht, Creator of Silk Road Website, Is Sentenced to Life in Prison," by Benjamin Weiser, *New York Times*, May 29, 2015; "FedEx Seeks to Show It's Good Guy in Internet Drug Crackdown," by Joel Rosenblatt, Bloomberg.com, May 14, 2015; "Icann, Regulators Clash Over Illegal Online Drug Sales," by Jeff Elder, *Wall Street Journal*, October 27, 2014; "Silk Road's Alleged Mastermind Faces More U.S. Charges," by Erik Larson and Bob Van Voris, Bloomberg.com, August 22, 2014; "Google Settles Shareholder Suit Over Online Drug Ads," Dan Levine, Reuters.com, August 8, 2014; "FedEx Indicted for Shipping Drugs Sold Online," by Katie Lobosco, Money.cnn.com, July 17, 2014; "Digital Citizens Alliance Report Strongly Critical of Google," Stevenimmons.org, March 12, 2014; "Eagle Scout. Idealist. Drug Trafficker?," by David Segal, *New York Times*, January 18, 2014; "Meet the Dread Pirate Roberts, The Man Behind Booming Black Market Drug Website Silk Road," by Andy Greenberg, *Forbes*, September 2, 2013; "In Whom We Trust: The Role of Certification Agencies in Online Drug Markets," by Roger Bate et al., *NBER Working Paper*, March 2012; "UN Cracks Down on International Drug Fraudsters," by Natalie Morrison, In-pharmatechnologist.com, March 1, 2012; "Ryan Haight Online Pharmacy Consumer Protection Act," H.R. 6353, 110th Congress, 2008.

In June 2012, Delaware became the first state to legalize online gambling in all its forms (Berzo, 2012), and three others have followed: Nevada, New Jersey and the U.S. Virgin Islands. In 2015, seven states are considering bills that would legalize online gambling: California, Illinois, Massachusetts, Mississippi, New York, Pennsylvania, and Washington (National Conference of State Legislators, 2015).

In 2013, Station Casinos, a local Las Vegas company, opened the nation's first legal, pay-to-play poker Web site. The site claims it can use geo-location technology to ensure that the players are in the State of Nevada and over the age of 21, a condition of its operation insofar as the federal government does not yet permit online poker whereas it is legal in Nevada and supported by the large casinos as an extension of their brands.

However, so far, legal online gambling has disappointed expectations: New Jersey expected to make $160 million in state revenue from online gambling in 2014, but had collected only $9 million by June 2014, in part because of the recession. While online gambling sputters along in a slow-growth economy, fantasy sports and betting is exploding. Two firms dominate the online fantasy sports market: DraftKings and FanDuel. Both firms advertise heavily during college and professional sports games. In fantasy sports, players assemble their ideal fantasy teams, drafting real-life athletes to their team, and then, based on the performance of those players in real games, they can win significant prizes. The most popular sports are college football and basketball, and professional football and baseball. Players are given a budget that they can use to draft players, and some of the combined fees for each game make up the pool for which players compete. Entry fees range widely from less than a dollar, to over $1,000 (Belson, 2015). DraftKings claims that several winner prizes have exceeded $1 million although none of the sites publish a list of winners.

Fantasy sports games are permitted in 45 states. Fantasy sports were exempted from the Unlawful Internet Gambling Enforcement Act of 2006 (UIGEA) under industry pressure from the then much smaller fantasy sports business. The industry argued that fantasy sports are not gambling, but instead games of skill like chess or Scrabble. As the industry has grown to billion-dollar venture capital valuations, however, and with allegations of cheating customers, deceptive practices, lack of transparency, and insider irregularities, state and federal legislators are holding hearings and considering regulations (Russo, 2015; Drape, 2015). In November 2015, New York State attorney general Eric Schneiderman told both DraftKings and FanDuel to stop taking entries from New York State residents because, in the state's opinion, their operations constitute illegal gambling.

8.6   **CASE STUDY**

The Pirate Bay:
Searching for a Safe Haven

T he Pirate Bay (TPB), for years, has been one of the world's best-known and most popular pirated music and content sites, offering free access to millions of copyrighted songs and thousands of copyrighted Hollywood movies, television shows, and video games. This despite the fact that TPB has been subjected to repeated legal efforts to shut it down. In fact, the authorities pursuing TPB must feel as if they are engaged in a never-ending game of Whack-a-mole, as each time they "whack" TPB, it somehow manages to reappear. But the battle is far from over, and for the first time, it appears possible that the "good guys" are actually winning. The Internet is becoming a tough place for music and video pirates to make a living in part because of enforcement actions, but more importantly because of new mobile and wireless technologies that enable high-quality content to be streamed for just a small fee.

TPB is part of a European social and political movement that opposes copyrighted content and demands that music, videos, TV shows, and other digital content be free and unrestricted. TPB does not operate a database of copyrighted content. Neither

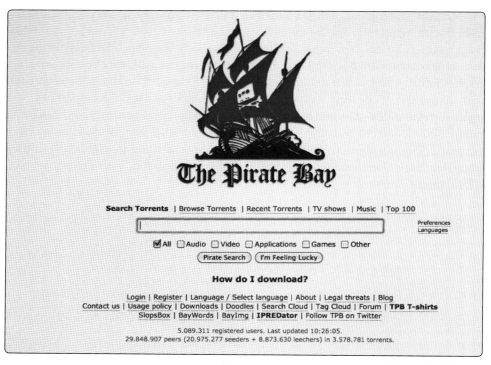

© Tommy (Louth) / Alamy

does it operate a network of computers owned by "members" who store the content, nor does it create, own, or distribute software (like BitTorrent and most other so-called P2P networks) that permits such networks to exist in the first place. Instead, TPB simply provides a search engine that responds to user queries for music tracks, or specific movie titles, and generates a list of search results that include P2P networks around the world where the titles can be found. By clicking on a selected link, users gain access to the copyrighted content, but only after downloading software and other files from that P2P network.

TPB claims it is merely a search engine providing pointers to existing P2P networks that it does not itself control. It says that it cannot control what content users ultimately find on those P2P networks, and that it is no different from any other search engine, such as Google or Bing, which are not held responsible for the content found on sites listed in search results. From a broader standpoint, TPB's founders also claim that copyright laws in general unjustly interfere with the free flow of information on the Internet, and that in any event, they were not violating Swedish copyright law, which they felt should be the only law that applied. And they further claimed they did not encourage, incite, or enable illegal downloading. Nevertheless, the defendants have never denied that theirs was a commercial enterprise. Despite all the talk calling for the free, unfettered spread of culture, TPB was a money-making operation from the beginning, designed to produce profits for its founders, with advertising as the primary source of revenue.

However, the First Swedish Court in Stockholm declared TPB's four founders guilty of violating Swedish copyright law, and sentenced each to one year in prison and payment of $3.5 million in restitution to the plaintiffs, all Swedish divisions of the major record firms (Warner Music, Sony, and EMI Group among them). The court found that the defendants had incited copyright infringement by providing a Web site with search functions, easy uploading and storage possibilities, and a tracker. The court also said that the four defendants had been aware of the fact that copyrighted material was shared with the help of their site and that the defendants were engaged in a commercial enterprise, the basis of which was encouraging visitors to violate the copyrights of owners. In fact, the primary purpose of TPB was to violate copyrights in order to make money for the owners (commercial intent).

Meanwhile, the U.S. government pressured the Swedish government to strengthen its copyright laws to discourage rampant downloading. In Sweden, downloading music and videos from illegal sites was very popular, engaged in by 43% of the Swedish Internet population. To strengthen its laws, Sweden adopted the European Union convention on copyrights, which allows content owners to receive from Internet providers the names and addresses of people suspected of sharing pirated files. In France, participating in these pirate sites will result in banishment from the Internet for up to three years. As a result, Internet traffic in Sweden declined by 40%, and has stayed there.

TPB has appealed the court judgment and has not paid any fines. That doesn't mean that TPB has not been affected by the lawsuits, however. In 2011, the firm moved its servers into caves in Sweden, and dispersed multiple copies of its program to other countries. In response to the lawsuits, police raids, and confiscation of servers, TPB has had stints in France, Finland, Italy, Germany, Denmark, Ireland, the U.K., and Greece

SOURCES: "Don't Trust The Pirate Bay: Movie Torrent Site Down Again, Amid Growing Skepticism and More Malware," by Jeff Stone, Ibtimes.com, October 2, 2015; "Last Pirate Bay Co-Founder Released from Prison," by Alex Hern, Theguardian.com, September 29, 2015; "Peter Sunde: The Pirate Bay Should Stay Down," by Ernesto, Torrentfreak.com, December 14, 2014; "Pirate Bay Co-Founder Peter Sunde Arrested Years After Conviction," by Natasha Lomas, Techcrunch.com, June 1, 2014; "The Pirate Bay and the Business of Piracy," by Leo Sun, Fool.com, May 21, 2014; "Google Asked to Censor Two Million Pirate Bay URLs," by Ernesto, Torrentfreak.com, April 20, 2014; "Singapore Proposes Law to Block Sites Such as Pirate Bay," by Aloysius Low, Cnet.com, April 7, 2014; "MPAA Still Hunting for Cash as Pirate Bay Financier Set to Go Bankrupt," by Andy, Torrentfreak.com, June 10, 2013; "Pirate Bay Founder Submits Emotional Plea for Pardon," by Ernesto, Torrentfreak.com, July 7, 2012; "The Pirate Bay Evades ISP Blockade with IPv6, Can Do It 18 Quintillion More Times," by Sebastian Anthony, Extremetech.com, June 8, 2012; "World's Biggest Ad Agency Keelhauls 2,000 Pirate Sites," by Natalie Apostolou, *The Register,* June 14, 2011; "Internet Piracy and How to Stop It," *New York Times,* June 8, 2011; "The Pirate Bay: Five Years After the Raid," by Ernesto, Torrentfreak.com, May 31, 2011; "The Protect IP Act: COICA Redux," by Abigail Phillips, Electronic Frontier Foundation, May 12, 2011; "Pirate Bay Keeps Sinking: Another Lawsuit Coming," by Stan Schroeder, Mashable.com, June 22, 2010; "Pirate Bay Sunk by Hollywood Injunction for Now," by Charles Arthur, *The Guardian,* May 17, 2010; "British Put Teeth in Anti-Piracy Proposal," by Eric Pfanner, *New York Times,* March 14, 2010.

within the last few years. These countries have in some cases refused to allow Internet service providers in their countries to host or link to TPB, no matter where in the world its servers are located. In 2013, authorities shut down TPB's top-level domains in Sweden, Greenland, and Iceland, but TPB has continued to try to operate by hopping from country to country, moving to Sint Maarten, to tiny Ascension Island, to Peru, and back again to Sweden. In 2014, TPB proved as elusive as ever for law enforcement, although co-founder Gottfrid Svartholm Warg began serving a 42-month term in prison in Denmark for both copyright infringement and computer crimes unrelated to TPB, co-founder Peter Sunde was arrested after years on the run, and served a five-month prison term for copyright violation, and Fredrik Neij, another co-founder, was arrested in Thailand, then transferred to Swedish custody to serve a 10-month prison sentence. In 2014, the company's financial resources also began to run dry. As interest continued to accrue on financial penalties previously levied on TPB, Carl Lundstrom, the site's primary financial backer, declared bankruptcy.

However, TPB continued to operate in 2014, until December 9th, when Swedish police again raided the site and shut it down. The site remained offline for seven weeks, until January 2015, the longest period of time it had ever been shut down. Members of the hacker group Anonymous claim it is now in fact an FBI honeypot designed to trap the unwary, and its number of visitors has dropped precipitously. Even if rumors about the FBI are not true, many believe that it is not a good idea to use TPB anymore for other reasons: the site is now riddled with ads containing malware and it frequently goes offline. Even one of its original co-founders, Peter Sunde, has recommended that the site shut down once and for all. Nonetheless, TPB lives on.

TPB has caused a number of countries, including England, France, Malaysia, Finland, and the United States, to consider strong intellectual property protection laws that will prevent domestic search engines and ISPs from linking to infringing sites, or resolving their domain names. In addition, the world's largest advertising agency, GroupM, has put TPB and 2,000 other sites on its blacklist of copyright infringing sites on which it will not buy advertising space.

The record industry's struggle against TPB is just part of the battle that it has been waging for some time. In 2005, the Supreme Court ruled in the ground-breaking *Metro-Goldwyn Mayer v. Grokster, et al.* case that the original peer-to-peer file sharing services, such as Grokster, Kazaa, and StreamCast, could be held liable for copyright infringement, because they had intentionally sought to encourage users to share copyrighted material. All of these services have since gone out of business. But these legal victories, and stronger government enforcement of copyright laws, have not proven to be the magic bullet that miraculously solves all the problems facing the music industry. The music industry has had to drastically change its business model and decisively move toward digital distribution platforms. They have made striking progress, and sales of music in a purely digital format now account for more revenue than sales of music in a physical format. To do so, the music industry has employed a number of different business models and online delivery platforms, including Apple's iTunes pay-per-download model, subscription models, and cloud-based streaming models.

In each of these new media delivery platforms, the copyright owners—record companies, artists, and Hollywood studios—have struck licensing deals with the technology platform owners and distributors (Apple, Amazon, and Google). These new platforms offer a win-win solution. Consumers benefit by having near instant access to high-quality music tracks and videos without the hassle of P2P software downloads. Content owners get a growing revenue stream and protection for their copyrighted content. And the pirates? TPB and other pirate sites may not be able to compete with new and better ways to listen to music and view videos. Like the real pirates of the Caribbean, who are now just a footnote in history books, technology and consumer preference for ease of use may leave them behind.

Case Study Questions

1. Why did TPB believe it was not violating copyright laws? What did the Swedish court rule?

2. How has TPB managed to continue operating despite being found in violation of copyright laws?

3. How has the music industry reacted to the problems created by pirates like TPB?

8.7 REVIEW

KEY CONCEPTS

■ **Understand why e-commerce raises ethical, social, and political issues.**

- Internet technology and its use in e-commerce disrupts existing social and business relationships and understandings. Suddenly, individuals, business firms, and political institutions are confronted by new possibilities of behavior for which understandings, laws, and rules of acceptable behavior have not yet been developed. Many business firms and individuals are benefiting from the commercial development of the Internet, but this development also has costs for individuals, organizations, and societies. These costs and benefits must be carefully considered by those seeking to make ethical and socially responsible decisions in this new environment, particularly where there are as yet no clear-cut legal or cultural guidelines.
- The major issues raised by e-commerce can be loosely categorized into four major dimensions:
  - *Information rights*—What rights do individuals have to control their own personal information when Internet technologies make information collection so pervasive and efficient?
  - *Property rights*—How can traditional intellectual property rights be enforced when perfect copies of protected works can be made and easily distributed worldwide via the Internet?
  - *Governance*—Should the Internet and e-commerce be subject to public laws? If so, what law-making bodies have jurisdiction—state, federal, and/or international?
  - *Public safety and welfare*—What efforts should be undertaken to ensure equitable access to the Internet and e-commerce channels? Do certain online content and activities pose a threat to public safety and welfare?
- Ethical, social, and political controversies usually present themselves as dilemmas. Ethical dilemmas can be analyzed via the following process:
  - Identify and clearly describe the facts.
  - Define the conflict or dilemma and identify the higher-order values involved.

- Identify the stakeholders.
- Identify the options that you can reasonably take.
- Identify the potential consequences of your options.
- Refer to well-established ethical principles, such as the Golden Rule, Universalism, the Slippery Slope, the Collective Utilitarian Principle, Risk Aversion, the No Free Lunch Rule, the *New York Times* Test, and the Social Contract Rule to help you decide the matter.

■ **Understand basic concepts related to privacy and information rights, the practices of e-commerce companies that threaten privacy, and the different methods that can be used to protect online privacy.**

- To understand the issues concerning online privacy, you must first understand some basic concepts:
    - *Privacy* is the moral right of individuals to be left alone, free from surveillance or interference from others.
    - *Information privacy* includes both the claim that certain information should not be collected at all by governments or business firms, and the claim of individuals to control the use of information about themselves.
    - *Due process* as embodied by the Fair Information Practices doctrine, informed consent, and opt-in/opt-out policies also plays an important role in privacy.
- Almost all e-commerce companies collect some personally identifiable information in addition to anonymous information and use cookies to track clickstream behavior of visitors. Advertising networks and search engines also track the behavior of consumers across thousands of popular sites, not just at one site, via cookies, spyware, search engine behavioral targeting, and other techniques.
- There are a number of different methods used to protect online privacy. They include:
    - Legal protections deriving from constitutions, common law, federal law, state laws, and government regulations. In the United States, rights to online privacy may be derived from the U.S. Constitution, tort law, federal laws such as the Children's Online Privacy Protection Act (COPPA), the Federal Trade Commission's Fair Information Practice principles, and a variety of state laws. In Europe, the European Commission's Data Protection Directive has standardized and broadened privacy protection in the European Union nations.
    - Industry self-regulation via industry alliances, such as the Online Privacy Alliance and the Network Advertising Initiative, that seek to gain voluntary adherence to industry privacy guidelines and safe harbors. Some firms also hire chief privacy officers.
    - Privacy-enhancing technological solutions include spyware and pop-up blockers, secure e-mail, anonymous remailers, anonymous surfing, cookie managers, disk file-erasing programs, policy generators, and public key encryption programs.

■ **Understand the various forms of intellectual property and the challenges involved in protecting it.**

- *Copyright law* protects original forms of expression such as writings, drawings, and computer programs from being copied by others for a minimum of 70 years. It does not protect ideas—just their expression in a tangible medium. Copyrights, like all rights, are not absolute. The doctrine of fair use permits certain parties under certain circumstances to use copyrighted material without permission. The Digital Millennium Copyright Act (DMCA) was the first major effort to adjust copyright law to the Internet age. The DMCA implements a World Intellectual Property Organization treaty, which declares it illegal to make, distribute, or use devices that circumvent technology-based protections of copyrighted materials, and attaches stiff fines and prison sentences for violations.
- *Patent law* grants the owner of a patent an exclusive monopoly to the ideas behind an invention for 20 years. Patents are very different from copyrights in that they protect the ideas themselves and not merely the expression of ideas. There are four types of inventions for which patents are granted under patent

law: machines, man-made products, compositions of matter, and processing methods. In order to be granted a patent, the applicant must show that the invention is new, original, novel, nonobvious, and not evident in prior arts and practice. Most of the inventions that make the Internet and e-commerce possible were not patented by their inventors. This changed in the mid-1990s with the commercial development of the World Wide Web. Business firms began applying for "business methods" and software patents.

- *Trademark protections* exist at both the federal and state levels in the United States. The purpose of trademark law is twofold. First, trademark law protects the public in the marketplace by ensuring that it gets what it pays for and wants to receive. Second, trademark law protects the owner who has spent time, money, and energy bringing the product to market against piracy and misappropriation. Federal trademarks are obtained, first, by use in interstate commerce, and second, by registration with the U.S. Patent and Trademark Office (USPTO). Trademarks are granted for a period of 10 years and can be renewed indefinitely. Use of a trademark that creates confusion with existing trademarks, causes consumers to make market mistakes, or misrepresents the origins of goods is an infringement. In addition, the intentional misuse of words and symbols in the marketplace to extort revenue from legitimate trademark owners ("bad faith") is proscribed. The Anticybersquatting Consumer Protection Act (ACPA) creates civil liabilities for anyone who attempts in bad faith to profit from an existing famous or distinctive trademark by registering an Internet domain name that is identical or confusingly similar to, or "dilutive" of, that trademark. The major behaviors on the Internet that have run afoul of trademark law include cybersquatting, cyberpiracy, metatagging, keywording, linking, and framing.

■ **Understand how the Internet is governed and why taxation of e-commerce raises governance and jurisdiction issues.**

- Governance has to do with social control: who will control e-commerce, what elements will be controlled, and how will those controls be implemented. We are currently in a mixed-mode policy environment where self-regulation, through a variety of Internet policy and technical bodies, co-exists with limited government regulation.

- E-commerce raises the issue of how—and if—to tax remote sales. The national and international character of Internet sales has wreaked havoc on taxation schemes in the United States that were built in the 1930s and based on local commerce and local jurisdictions. E-commerce has benefited from a tax subsidy since its inception. E-commerce merchants have argued that this new form of commerce needs to be nurtured and encouraged, and that in any event, the crazy quilt of sales and use tax regimes would be difficult to administer for Internet merchants. In 1998, Congress passed the Internet Tax Freedom Act, which placed a moratorium on multiple or discriminatory taxes on electronic commerce, and any taxation of Internet access, and since that time has extended the moratorium several times, most recently until December 2015. Federal legislation to implement a uniform set of rules for collecting taxes on e-commerce sales is currently pending in Congress.

■ **Identify major public safety and welfare issues raised by e-commerce.**

- Critical public safety and welfare issues in e-commerce include:
  - The protection of children and strong sentiments against pornography. Several attempts by Congress to legislate in this area have been struck down as unconstitutional. The Children's Internet Protection Act (CIPA), which requires schools and libraries in the United States to install "technology protection measures" (filtering software) in an effort to shield children from pornography, has, however, been upheld by the Supreme Court.
  - Efforts to control gambling and restrict sales of cigarettes and drugs. In the United States, cigarettes, gambling, medical drugs, and addictive recreational drugs are either banned or tightly regulated by federal and state laws. Many offshore sites for these products and services have been shut down following government pressure. Online gambling is growing, but slower than anticipated. Online fantasy sports betting is growing rapidly.

QUESTIONS

1. What basic assumption does the study of ethics make about individuals?
2. What are the basic principles of ethics?
3. Explain Google's position that YouTube does not violate the intellectual property rights of copyright owners.
4. Define universalism, slippery slope, the *New York Times* test, and the social contract rule as they apply to ethics.
5. Explain why someone with a serious medical condition might be concerned about researching his or her condition online, through medical search engines or pharmaceutical sites, for example. What is one technology that could prevent one's identity from being revealed?
6. Name some of the personal information collected by Web sites about their visitors.
7. How does information collected through online forms differ from site transaction logs? Which potentially provides a more complete consumer profile?
8. How is the opt-in model of informed consent different from opt-out? In which type of model does the consumer retain more control?
9. What are the two core principles of the FTC's Fair Information Practice principles?
10. How do safe harbors work? What is the government's role in them?
11. Name three ways online advertising networks have improved on, or added to, traditional offline marketing techniques.
12. Explain how behavioral targeting is supposed to benefit both consumers and businesses.
13. How could the Internet potentially change protection given to intellectual property? What capabilities make it more difficult to enforce intellectual property law?
14. What does the Digital Millennium Copyright Act (DMCA) attempt to do? Why was it enacted? What types of violations does it try to prevent?
15. Define cybersquatting. How is it different from cyberpiracy? What type of intellectual property violation does cybersquatting entail?
16. What is deep linking and why is it a trademark issue? Compare it to framing—how is it similar and different?
17. What are some of the tactics businesses that are illegal in the United States use to operate outside the law on the Internet?
18. Why can't pornographic sites simply be banned in the United States? Why has the Supreme Court struck down legislation intended to protect children from pornography?
19. What is the "right to be forgotten"? What are some of the risks and benefits of establishing this right?
20. What is the doctrine of "fair use"? Why did the courts decide that Google's scanning of copyrighted books was a "fair use"?

PROJECTS

1. Go to Google and find the Advanced Search link. Examine its SafeSearch filtering options. Surf the Web in search of content that could be considered objectionable for children using each of the options. What are the pros and cons of such restrictions? Are there terms that could be considered inappropriate to the filtering software but be approved by parents? Name five questionable terms. Prepare a brief presentation to report on your experiences and to explain the positive and negative aspects of such filtering software.

2. Develop a list of privacy protection features that should be present if a Web site is serious about protecting privacy. Then, visit at least four well-known Web sites and examine their privacy policies. Write a report that rates each of the Web sites on the criteria you have developed.

3. Review the provisions of the Digital Millennium Copyright Act of 1998. Examine each of the major sections of the legislation and make a list of the protections afforded property owners and users of copyrighted materials. Do you believe this legislation balances the interests of owners and users appropriately? Do you have suggestions for strengthening "fair use" provisions in this legislation?

4. Visit at least four Web sites that take a position on e-commerce taxation, beginning with the National Conference of State Legislatures (Ncsl.org) and the National Governors Association (Nga.org). You might also include national associations of local businesses or citizen groups opposed to e-commerce taxation. Develop a reasoned argument for, or against, taxation of e-commerce.

REFERENCES

Academy of Motion Picture Arts and Sciences v. GoDaddy. com Inc et al. U.S. District Court, Central District of California, No. 10-03738 (2015).

Acquisti, Alessandro, Ralph Gross, and Fred Stutzman. "Faces of Facebook: Privacy in the Age of Augmented Reality," Heinz College & CyLab Carnegie Mellon University (August 4, 2011).

Acquisti, Alessandro, Leslie John, and George Loewenstein. "What Is Privacy Worth?" Twenty First Workshop on Information Systems and Economics (WISE) (December 14–15, 2009).

Alice Corporation Pty. Ltd. v. CLS Bank International, et al., Supreme Court of the United States, No. 13-298. June 19, 2014.

Angwin, Julia, and Jennifer Valentino-DeVries. "New Tracking Frontier: Your License Plates." *Wall Street Journal* (September 28, 2012).

Angwin, Julia. "Face-ID Tools Pose New Risk." *Wall Street Journal* (August 1, 2011).

Apple Computer, Inc. v. Microsoft Corp. 709 F. Supp. 925, 926 (N. D. Cal. 1989); 799 F. Supp. 1006, 1017 (N. D. Cal., 1992); 35 F. 3d 1435 (9th Cir.); cert. denied, 63 U. S. L. W. 3518 (U.S., Feb. 21, 1995) (No. 94-1121).

Apuzzo, Matt, David Sanger, and Michael Schmidt. "Apple and Other Tech Companies Tangle With U.S. Over Data Access." *New York Times,* September 7, 2015.

Ashcroft v. Free Speech Coalition, 535 U.S. 234 (2002).

Associated Press. "Google Settles Final Piece of Geico Case." BizReport.com (September 8, 2005).

Barrett, Devlin. "U.S. Will Change Stance on Secret Phone Tracking." *Wall Street Journal,* May 3, 2015a.

Barrett, Devlin. "Sen. Markey Presses Cellphone Companies on Surveillance." *Wall Street Journal,* May 21, 2015b.

Barrett, Devlin. "CIA Aided Program to Spy on U.S. Cellphones," *Wall Street Journal,* March 10, 2015c.

Belson, Ken. "A Primer on Daily Fantasy Football Sites." *New York Times* (October 6, 2015).

Bernina of America, Inc. v. Fashion Fabrics Int'l., Inc. 2001 U. S. Dist. LEXIS 1211 (N. D. Ill., Feb. 8, 2001).

Berzo, Alexandra. "Delaware Lawmakers Clear Online Gambling." *Wall Street Journal* (June 27, 2012).

Billboard. "Music Piracy Site Sharebeast Shut Down By Justice Department." Billboard.com (September 14, 2015).

Bilski et al. v. Kappos, 177 L. Ed. 2d 792, 130 S. Ct. 3218, 561 U.S. 593 (2010).

Bilton, Nick. "Apple Loophole Gives Developers Access to Photos." *New York Times* (February 28, 2012).

Bloomberg News. "Master of Your Domain? Maybe in .Com But Not in .Sucks." (May 13, 2015).

Brown Bag vs. Symantec Corp., 960 F. 2d 1465 (9th Cir. 1992).

Brustein, Joshua. "Start-Ups Seek to Help Users Put a Price on Their Personal Data." *New York Times* (February 12, 2012).

Center for Copyright Information. "The Copyright Alert System: Phase One and Beyond." (May 28, 2014).

Charlton, Angela. "France Threatens Google with Privacy Fines." *New York Times* (June 20, 2013).

Chen, Brian. "Verizon Publishes First Transparency Report on Data Requests." *Wall Street Journal,* January 22, 2014.

Chen, Brian. "Appeals Court Upholds Apple's Patent Victory Over Samsung." *New York Times* (May 18, 2015).

Chiappetta, Vincent. "Defining the Proper Scope of Internet Patents: If We Don't Know Where We Want to Go, We're Unlikely to Get There." *Michigan Telecommunications Technology Law Review* (May 2001).

Davis, Wendy. "TRUSTe Finalizes Settlement with FTC." Mediapost.com (March 18, 2015).

Decker, Susan. "Apple Wins Ruling to Force Samsung to Change Phones, Tablets." Bloomberg.com (September 17, 2015).

Diamond v. Chakrabarty, 447 US 303 (1980).

Drape, Joe, and Jacqueline Williams, "FanDuel Makes Changes." *New York Times* (October 8, 2015).

E. & J. Gallo Winery v. Spider Webs Ltd. 129 F. Supp. 2d 1033 (S.D. Tex., 2001) aff'd 286 F. 3d 270 (5th Cir., 2002).

Eldred v. Ashcroft, 537 U.S. 186 (2003).

European Commission. "Progress on EU Data Protection Reform Now Irreversible Following European Parliament Vote." (March 12, 2014).

European Commission. "Commission Proposes a Comprehensive Reform of the Data Protection Rules." (January 26, 2012).

Evans, Marcus. "European Council Approves EU General Data Protection Regulation Draft; Final Approval May Come by End of 2015. Dataprotectionreport.com (June 15, 2015).

Executive Office of the President. "Big Data: Seizing Opportunities, Preserving Values." (May 1, 2014).

Federal Trade Commission. "Data Brokers: A Call for Transparency and Accountability." (May 27, 2014).

Federal Trade Commission. "Google Will Pay $22.5 Million to Settle FTC Charges It Misrepresented Privacy Assurance to Users of Apple's Safari Internet Browser." (August 9, 2012a).

Federal Trade Commission. "Facebook Must Obtain Consumers' Consent Before Sharing Their Information Beyond Established Privacy Settings." (August 10, 2012b).

Federal Trade Commission. "Protecting Consumer Privacy in an Era of Rapid Change." (March 26, 2012c).

Federal Trade Commission. "FTC Charges Deceptive Privacy Practices in Google's Rollout of Its Buzz Network." (March 3, 2011).

Federal Trade Commission. "Protecting Consumer Privacy in an Era of Rapid Change." (December 2010).

Federal Trade Commission. "Privacy Online: Fair Information Practices in the Electronic Marketplace." (May 2000a).

Federal Trade Commission. "Online Profiling: A Report to Congress." (June 2000b).

Federal Trade Commission. "Privacy Online: A Report to Congress." (June 1998).

Field v. Google, Inc. 412 F.Supp. 2nd 1106 (D. Nev., 2006).

Fiesler, Casey, Jessica L. Feuston, and Amy Bruckman. "Copyright Terms in Online Creative Communities." Georgia Institute of Technology, Working Paper (April 26, 2014).

Fisher, William W. III. "The Growth of Intellectual Property: A History of the Ownership of Ideas in the United States." Law.harvard.edu/Academic_Affairs/coursepages/tfisher/iphistory.html (1999).

Ford, Paul. "Balancing Security and Liberty in the Age of Big Data." Businessweek.com (June 13, 2013).

Ford Motor Co. v. Lapertosa 2001 U.S. Dist. LEXIS 253 (E. D. Mich. Jan. 3, 2001).

Fung, Brian. "The Group That Created '.sucks' Now Wants Government to Keep It From Spinning Out of Control." *Washington Post* (April 9, 2015).

Gibbs, Samuel. "Google's New Nest Cam Is Always Watching, If You Let It into Your Home," *The Guardian,* June 18, 2014.

Gibbs, Samuel. "EU States Agree on Framework for Pan-European Data Privacy Rules." *The Guardian,* June 15, 2015.

Government Employees Insurance Company v. Google, Inc. Civ. Action No. 1:04cv507 (E.D. VA, December 15, 2004).

Greenhouse, Linda. "Supreme Court Upholds Child Pornography Law." *New York Times* (May 20, 2008).

Greenhouse, Linda. "20 Year Extension of Existing Copyrights Is Upheld." *New York Times* (January 16, 2003a).

Greenhouse, Linda. "Justices Back Law to Make Libraries Use Internet Filters." *New York Times* (June 24, 2003b).

Gryta, Thomas. "An Early Net-Neutrality Win: Rules Prompt Sprint to Stop Throttling." *Wall Street Journal* (June 17, 2015a).

Gryta, Thomas. "FCC Approves Net Neutrality Rules, Setting Stage for Legal Battle." *Wall Street Journal* (February 26, 2015b).

Harmon, Amy. "Pondering Value of Copyright vs. Innovation." *New York Times* (March 3, 2003).

Hartline, Devlin. "The MovieTube Litigation Part I: Who Needs SOPA." Lawtheories.com (August 31, 2015).

Hoofnagle, Chris Jay. "Privacy Self-Regulation: A Decade of Disappointment." Electronic Privacy Information Center (Epic.org) (March 4, 2005).

ICANN. "Applicant Guidebook gTLD." Newgtlds.icann.org (2015).

Internet Watch Foundation. "Our Mission." IWF.org (accessed October 10, 2015).

Kakutani, Michiko. "Watched by the Web: Surveillance Is Reborn." *New York Times* (June 10, 2013).

Kaufman, Leslie. "Viacom and YouTube Settle Suit Over Copyright Violations." *New York Times* (March 18, 2014).

Kelly v. ArribaSoft. 336 F3rd 811 (CA 9th, 2003).

Kendall, Brent, and Daisuke Wakabayashi, "Apple Wins Ruling in Patent Case Against Samsung." *Wall Street Journal* (September 17, 2015).

Kuehn, Andreas, and Milton Mueller. "Profiling the Profilers: Deep Packet Inspection and Behavioral Advertising in Europe and the United States." Available at SSRN: http://ssrn.com/abstract=2014181 (September 1, 2012).

Laudon, Kenneth. "Markets and Privacy." *Communications of the ACM* (September 1996).

Levine, Dan. "Amazon Must Face Trademark Lawsuit Over Search Results." Reuters.com (July 6, 2015).

Lien, Tracy. "Google, Facebook, Twitter Join Crackdown On Child Porn." *Los Angeles Times* (August 10, 2015).

Lowe, Kinsey. "Studios Sue MovieTube Websites for Illegal Streaming and Downloads." Hollywoodreporter.com (August 17, 2015).

Maass, Peter, and Megha Rajagopalan. "That's No Phone. That's My Tracker." *New York Times* (July 13, 2012).

Mayer-Schonberger, Viktor, and Kenneth Cukier. *Big Data: A Revolution That Will Transform How We Live, Work, and Think.* Eamon Dolan/Houghton Mifflin Harcourt (2013).

McMillan, Robert. "Porn Typosquatter Fined Again by FTC." *InfoWorld* (October 16, 2007).

Nash, David B. "Orderly Expansion of the International Top-Level Domains: Concurrent Trademark Users Need a Way Out of the Internet Trademark Quagmire." *The John Marshall Journal of Computer and Information Law,* Vol. 15, No. 3 (1997).

National Conference of State Legislators. "2015 Internet Gambling Legislation." (August 21, 2015).

Network Advertising Initiative. "Network Advertising Initiative Releases 2010 Compliance Report." Networkadvertising.org (February 18, 2011).

Network Advertising Initiative. "Major Marketing/Media Trade Groups Launch Program to Give Consumers Enhanced Control over Collection and Use of Web Viewing Data for Online Behavioral Advertising." (October 4, 2010).

New, William. "WIPO: Internet Domain Expansion Disruptive to Trademark Strategies." Ip-watch.com (March 17, 2014).

Nissan Motor Co., Ltd. v. Nissan Computer Corp. 289 F. Supp. 2d 1154 (C. D. Cal.), aff'd, 2000 U. S. App. LEXIS 33937 (9th Cir. Dec. 26, 2000).

PaineWebber Inc. v. Fortuny, Civ. A. No. 99-0456-A (E. D. Va. Apr. 9, 1999).

Patient Privacy Rights. Patient Privacy Rights Trust Framework. 2013. https://patientprivacyrights.org/trust-framework/.

Pearce, Sarah, and Annie Clarke. "EU: European Commission Commits to Finalising Negotiations on the EU Data Protection Regulation in 2015." Lexology.com (September 15, 2014).

Perfect 10, Inc. v. Amazon.com, Inc. 487 F3rd 701 (CA 9th, 2007).

Pew Research Center (Mary Madden and Lee Rainie). "Americans' Attitudes About Privacy, Security, and Surveillance." May 20, 2015.

Pew Research Center (Susannah Fox and Lee Rainie). "The Web at 25 in the U.S." February 27, 2014.

Playboy Enterprises, Inc. v. Global Site Designs, Inc. 1999 WL 311707 (S. D. Fla. May 15, 1999).

Playboy Enterprises, Inc. v. Netscape Communications, Inc. 354 F. 3rd 1020 (9th Cir., 2004).

Presidents Council of Advisors on Science and Technology. "PCAST Report on Big Data and Privacy: A Technological Perspective" (May 1, 2014).

Reuters. "Megaupload Founder Kim Dotcom Appears in Court to Fight U.S. Extradition." Reuters.com (September 21, 2015).

Rosen, Jeffrey. "The Right to be Forgotten." *Stanford Law Review,* 64. Stan. L. Rev. Online 88 (February 13, 2012).

Ruiz, Rebecca. "Publication of New Internet Rules to Prompt Cheers and Challenges." *New York Times* (April 5, 2015).

Russo, Ralph. "Daily Fantasy Football Draws Attention, Ire of NCAA." *Associated Press* (October 8, 2015).

Sarno, David. "SmartPhone Apps Dial Up Privacy Worries." *Los Angeles Times* (February 16, 2012).

Savage, Charlie. "Between the Lines of the Cellphone Privacy Ruling." *New York Times* (June 25, 2014).

Savage, Charlie. "Democratic Senators Issue Strong Warning About Use of the Patriot Act." *New York Times* (March 16, 2012).

Schechner, Sam. "French Privacy Watchdog Orders Google to Expand Right to Be Forgotten." *Wall Street Journal,* June 12, 2015a.

Schechner, Sam, and Natalia Drozdiak. "Belgium Takes Facebook to Court Over Privacy, User Tracking." *Wall Street Journal,* June 16, 2015.

Schwartz, John. "Justices Take Broad View of Business Methods Patents." *New York Times* (June 28, 2010).

Schwartzel, Erich. "Hollywood Studio Sues Over Alleged Online Piracy." *Wall Street Journal* (September 1, 2015).

Scott, Mark. "European Court Adviser Calls Trans-Atlantic Data-Sharing Pact Insufficient." *New York Times,* September 23, 2015.

Sengupta, Somini. "Europe Weighs Tough Law on Online Privacy." *New York Times* (January 23, 2012).

Shore, Jennifer and Jill Steinman. "Did You Really Agree to That? The Evolution of Facebook's Privacy Policy." Harvard Dataverse. August 6, 2011. http://dx.doi.org/10.7910/DVN/JROUKG.

Shrum, Rob. "Congress Temporarily Extends Internet Access Tax Ban." Mywireless.org (October 1, 2015).

Singer, Natasha. "The Government's Consumer Data Watchdog." *New York Times,* May 23, 2015.

Singer, Natasha. "Never Forgetting a Face." *New York Times* (May 17, 2014a).

Singer, Natasha. "Didn't Read Those Terms of Service? Here's What You Agreed to Give Up." *New York Times* (April 28, 2014b).

Singer, Natasha. "An American Quilt of Privacy Laws, Incomplete." *New York Times* (March 30, 2013).

Singer, Natasha. "Consumer Data, But Not For Consumers." *New York Times* (July 21, 2012).

Sloane, Garrett. "As Ad Blocker Usage Explodes, Can YouTube Win Back Scofflaws With a Subscription Model?" *Ad Week* (April 9, 2015).

State Street Bank & Trust Co. v. Signature Financial Group, 149 F. 3d 1368 (1998).

Stempel, Jonathan. "GoDaddy Prevails in Lawsuit over Oscar Trademarks." Reuters, September 11, 2015.

Stone, Brad. "Scaling the Digital Wall in China." *New York Times* (January 15, 2010).

Takenaka, Toshiko. "International and Comparative Law Perspective on Internet Patents." *Michigan Telecommunications Technology Law Review* (May 15, 2001).

Thurm, Scott. "The Ultimate Weapon: It's the Patent." *Wall Street Journal* (April 17, 2000).

Ticketmaster v. Tickets.com. 2000 U.S. Dist. Lexis 4553 (C.D. Cal., August 2000).

United States Copyright Office. "Digital Millennium Copyright Act of 1998: U.S. Copyright Office Summary." (December 1998).

Washington Post Co., et al v. TotalNews, Inc., et al., S.D.N.Y., Civil Action Number 97-1190 (February 1997).

Weber, Harrison. "Periscope Has Received 1,391 Copyright Takedown Requests So Far — Twitter Complied with 71% of Them." Venturebeat.com (August 11, 2015).

Winston, Brian. *Media Technology and Society: A History From the Telegraph to the Internet.* Routledge (1998).

Wyatt, Edward. "Ruling by Justice Department Opens a Door on Online Gambling." *New York Times* (December 24, 2011).

E-commerce in Action

Online Retail and Services

After reading this chapter, you will be able to:

- Understand the environment in which the online retail sector operates today.
- Explain how to analyze the economic viability of an online firm.
- Identify the challenges faced by the different types of online retailers.
- Describe the major features of the online service sector.
- Discuss the trends taking place in the online financial services industry.
- Describe the major trends in the online travel services industry today.
- Identify current trends in the online career services industry.
- Understand the business models of on-demand service companies.

Blue Nile Sparkles

for Your Cleopatra

Men: looking for that special gift for your Cleopatra but don't want to spend a lot of time shopping? Want to give the "Big Rock" without spending a mountain of cash for the engagement experience? Not sure about the future value of diamonds? Then how about pearls, gold, or platinum?

Your answer has arrived: BlueNile offers you an online selection of almost 230,000 diamonds for that special someone. You can buy them cut and polished or put them into settings like rings, bracelets, earrings, necklaces, pendants, watches, and brooches that you choose online. All the dia-

© Ken Gillespie Photography / Alamy

monds are graded by the 4Cs: carats (size), cut, color, and clarity, and a report for each diamond prepared by the Gemological Institute of America is available online. To make it easier, the carats are translated into milligrams, and one carat is exactly 200 milligrams of mass (if that helps). Just ask her what size she wants, and then look in your wallet.

BlueNile.com started out as RockShop.com in March 1999 in Seattle, Washington. In November 1999, the company launched the Blue Nile brand and changed its name to Blue Nile Inc., opening up its Web site, BlueNile.com, in December 1999. In 2004, it went public. In 2007, Blue Nile sold the biggest item in Internet history, a $1.5 million single diamond of around 10 carats, a size that would cover your finger with a penny-size rock. In 2010, another diamond sold for $500,000.

Back in the early days of e-commerce, no one ever thought that the Internet would be a place where fine jewelry was sold. Typically, gifts of jewelry such as diamonds are associated with a significant emotional event, such as an engagement, marriage, or anniversary. Generally, the event is shared with a significant other and often involves shopping together for the gem. Shopping online hardly matches the emotional impact of walking into Tiffany's or another established retail store, with clear glass cases filled with brilliantly shining baubles, attended by a small army of sales clerks that make you feel oh so special. Diamonds represent a significant cost, and there is significant uncertainty about their value and pricing. Surveys show that most shoppers believe jewelry is highly overpriced, but they lack the knowledge and information to negotiate a better price or even to judge the quality of what they are buying. Most experts thought that, given the emotional significance and uncertainty involved in purchasing diamonds, few consumers would heighten the built-in anxiety by going to a strange Web site and plunking down $5,000 or more for a diamond they could not see or touch for several days.

But jewelry and high-fashion retailers are leading the second act of online retailing, bursting on the scene with high-growth rates and spectacular average sales transaction levels. As it turns out, the retail jewelry industry is an ideal candidate for Web sales. Here's why.

The $69 billion fine jewelry industry in the United States is a byzantine, fragmented collection of about 21,500 specialty jewelry stores and another 100,000-plus that sell jewelry along with other products. Diamond jewelry and loose diamonds together constitute more than 50% of retailers' sales. To supply this fragmented market, several layers of wholesalers and middlemen intervene, from rough diamond brokers to diamond cutters, diamond wholesalers, jewelry manufacturers, jewelry wholesalers, and finally, regional distributors. Oddly, the source of raw mined diamonds is monopolized by a single company, De Beers, which controls around half of the world market. The fragmented supply and distribution chains add to huge markups based on monopoly-set prices for raw diamonds. Currently, the typical retail store markup for diamonds is between 50% and 100%. Blue Nile's markup is around 30%.

Blue Nile's 2014 revenues were $473.5 million, up around 5% from $450 million in 2013. International sales (in more than 40 countries worldwide) grew from $73 million in 2013 to $81 million in 2014. However, net income declined slightly, by 11%, to $9.7 million from $10.9 million in 2013. As Blue Nile continues to grow into new regions, including the lucrative China market, it expects its revenues to hold mostly steady. Through the first quarter of 2015, its net sales and net income grew slightly from 2014 levels.

Blue Nile's online competitors include Tiffany, Ice, and even Amazon. Together, these companies are transforming the jewelry business. Blue Nile, for instance, has simplified the supply side of diamonds by cutting out several layers of middlemen and instead dealing directly with wholesale diamond owners and jewelry manufacturers.

Blue Nile minimizes its inventory costs and limits its risk of inventory markdowns. On the sell side of distribution, Blue Nile has eliminated the expensive stores, sales clerks, and beautiful, but expensive, glass cases. Instead, Blue Nile offers a Web site at which it can aggregate the demand of thousands of unique visitors for diamonds and present them with a more attractive shopping experience than a typical retail store. The result of rationalizing the supply and distribution chain is much lower markups. For example, Blue Nile will purchase a pair of oval emerald and diamond earrings from a supplier for $850 and charge the consumer $1,020. A traditional retailer would charge the consumer $1,258.

Blue Nile has improved the shopping experience primarily by creating a trust- and knowledge-based environment that reduces consumer anxiety about the value of diamonds. In essence, Blue Nile and the other online retailers give the consumer as much information as a professional gemologist would provide. The Web site contains educational guides to diamonds and diamond grading systems, and each diamond receives an independent quality rating from a nonprofit industry association. There's a 30-day, money-back, no-questions-asked guarantee. The company's focus is "empowering the customer with information." And empower they do. The average customer visits the Web site repeatedly over several weeks, views at least 200 pages, and typically calls Blue Nile's live customer service line at least once. Repeat business accounts for around 25% of revenue.

SOURCES: "Blue Nile Opening 3 or 4 Stores Next Year," by Rob Bates, Jckonline.com, September 17, 2015; "U.S. Engagement Sales Account for 57.6% of Blue Nile's Sales," by Matt Lindner, Internetretailer.com, August 10, 2015; "Leading Jewelry E-retailer Blue Nile Opens Its First Physical Showroom," by Matt Lindner, Internetretailer.com, June 5, 2015;

In 2009, Blue Nile rebuilt its Web site, strengthening its appeal to its mostly male customer base while attempting to draw more women to the site. In 2010, it introduced a mobile Web site and iPhone/iPad app. The iPhone app provides users with a quick way to set specifications for a diamond and see the price as well as a Call button that provides a direct link to the Blue Nile call center for phone orders. In 2013, Blue Nile's mobile revenues were about $22 million, almost 2.5 times what they were in 2012. In 2014, mobile revenues continued to soar, almost doubling to approximately $42 million. The majority of its mobile revenue is generated from its mobile Web site, accessed via tablet computers. The biggest mobile sale to date: a $300,000 engagement ring! Blue Nile has also dived into social media marketing, with a Facebook page that has over 1.2 million Likes, a YouTube channel with 2.5 million views, a Pinterest page with over 85,000 followers, an Instagram feed with 43,500 followers, and a Twitter feed with over 14,000 followers. Users attracted to an image of jewelry posted on these sites can click links that take them directly to a purchase page for the item.

In 2012, Blue Nile began a shift in its strategy driven by the possibility that online retailers will have to begin collecting Internet sales taxes in most jurisdictions (see the *Insight on Business* case, *Internet Sales Tax Battle*, in Chapter 8). The company is moving toward fashion jewelry and higher price points and away from simply offering the lowest prices. Blue Nile has begun offering a proprietary line of high-end jewelry, and has added a design director and a new chief merchant to retool its product offerings. Still, even with additional sales taxes, Blue Nile's Internet-based distribution methods and lack of overhead from physical stores will allow them to continue to offer competitive prices.

In 2013, Blue Nile announced a partnership with Nordstrom that allows prospective customers to see rings before they buy them online. Rings in the Nordstrom outlets are for display only, but using iPads, Nordstrom jewelry experts can help customers to purchase rings that appeal to them from the Blue Nile site while in the store. As of early 2014, Blue Nile reported that the early response was positive, with a $95,000 purchase representing the largest transaction yet at an in-store display case. Over 90% of visitors to the Nordstrom displays came specifically for Blue Nile products. Buoyed by this success, Blue Nile announced that it would open its first physical store, which it calls a webroom, in 2015 in Long Island, New York. The webroom allows customers to see and try on products before actually purchasing them online. Initial results have been so promising that Blue Nile plans to open three or four physical locations in 2016.

So far, the "Blue Nile" effect of lower margins and Internet efficiency has mainly impacted the small mom-and-pop jewelry stores. Many small retailers have disappeared in the last few years due to rising diamond prices and pressure from larger companies. The big retailers, such as Tiffany, Zales, and others, sell more than Blue Nile, and continue to benefit from consumer interest in diamond engagement and wedding rings. But Blue Nile has grown more in the past three years than its closest online-only jewelry competitors. However, Blue Nile will still have to keep a keen watch on its competitors to keep its edge online.

"An Engaging Q4 for Blue Nile: Revenue Increases Nearly 8%," by Thad Rueter, Internetretailer.com, February 10, 2015; "The 2014 US Jewelry State of the Market Report," by Edahn Golan Diamond Research, 2015; "Internet Retailer Top 500 Guide 2015 Edition," by Internet Retailer, 2015; "As Smartphones Spread, Retailers Scramble to Ring Up Sales," by Angel Gonzalez, *Seattle Times*, April 12, 2014; "Blue Nile CEO Says Click-and-brick Jewelry Experiment with Nordstrom Is Working Well," by John Cook, Geekwire.com, March 26, 2014; "Why Blue Nile Seems Stuck," by Rob Bates, Jckonline.com, August 15, 2014; "Internet Retailer Mobile 500 2015 Edition," Internet Retailer, 2015; "Nordstrom and Blue Nile Tie the Knot in a Store-to-Web Partnership," by Katie Evans, Internetretailer.com, December 9, 2013; "Blue Nile's New Direction, and What It Says about Our Industry," by Rob Bates, Jckonline. com, September 7, 2012; "Customer Says 'I Do' To a $300,000 Mobile Transaction," by Bill Siwicki, Internetretailer.com, September 15, 2011; "Blue Nile CEO: More Shoppers Saying 'I Do,'" by Christina Berk, Cnbc.com, November 29, 2010; "Shopping on a Phone Finds Its Customer," by Geoffrey Fowler, *Wall Street Journal*, November 26, 2010; "Blue Nile's App Is a Girl's Best Friend (And Maybe a Boy's Too)," by Christina Berk, Cnbc.com, September 16, 2010; "Selling Information, Not Diamonds," by Kaihan Krippendorf, Fastcompany.com, September 1, 2010; "Blue Nile Sparkles," by Kaihan Krippendorf, Fastcompany.com, August 30, 2010; "Digital Bling: Diamonds for Sale Online," by Wendy Kaufman, NPR.org, February 14, 2010; "New Blue Nile Site Hits Web," *New York Times*, September 1, 2009; "Blue Nile Aims to Sparkle With Re-designed Web Site," Internet Retailer, September 1, 2009; "Blue Nile: A Guy's Best Friend," by Jay Greene, *Business Week*, May 29, 2008.

The Blue Nile case illustrates some of the advantages that an online retail company has over traditional offline retailers—and some of the disadvantages. An online company can radically simplify the existing industry supply chain and develop an entirely new Web-based distribution system that is far more efficient than traditional retail outlets. At the same time, an online retailer can create a better value proposition for the customer, improving customer service and satisfaction in the process. On the other hand, online companies often have razor-thin profit margins, lack a physical store network to bolster sales to the non-Internet audience, and are sometimes based on unproven business assumptions that, in the long term, may not pan out. In contrast, large offline retailers such as Walmart, JCPenney, Sears, and Target have established brand names, a huge real estate investment, a loyal customer base, and extraordinarily efficient inventory control and fulfillment systems. As we shall see in this chapter, traditional offline catalog merchants are also advantaged. We will also see that, in order to leverage their assets and core competencies, established offline retailers need to cultivate new competencies and a carefully developed business plan to succeed online.

As with retail goods, the promise of online service providers is that they can deliver superior-quality service and greater convenience to millions of consumers at a lower cost than established bricks-and-mortar service providers and still make a respectable return on invested capital. The service sector is one of the most natural avenues for e-commerce because so much of the value in services is based on collecting, storing, and exchanging information—something for which the Web is ideally suited. And, in fact, online services have been extraordinarily successful in attracting banking, brokerage, travel, and job-hunting customers. The quality and amount of information online to support consumer decisions in finance, travel, and career placement is extraordinary, especially when compared to what was available to consumers before e-commerce. The online service sector—like online retail—has established a significant beachhead and now plays a large role in consumer time on the Internet. In areas such as brokerage, banking, and travel, online services are an extraordinary success story and have transformed their industries. In Sections 9.5–9.7 of this chapter, we take a close look at three of the most successful online services: financial services (including insurance and real estate), travel services, and career services. In Section 9.8, we examine the new on-demand services companies, such as Uber, Airbnb, and a whole host of others, that have rocketed to prominence in the last several years. Using a business model that is both local and mobile, this new type of service company provides a platform for consumers to connect with providers who can provide on-demand services, such as transportation, short-term room rental, grocery shopping, and more.

9.1   THE ONLINE RETAIL SECTOR

Table 9.1 summarizes some of these leading trends in online retailing for 2015–2016. Perhaps the most important theme in online retailing is the effort by retailers—both

TABLE 9.1	**WHAT'S NEW IN ONLINE RETAIL 2015–2016**

- Retail mobile e-commerce is exploding, increasing from around $58 billion In 2014 to an expected $77 billion in 2015.
- Social networks such as Facebook, Twitter, Pinterest, and Instagram, together with online retailers, continue to try to understand how best to facilitate social e-commerce, with the introduction of Buy buttons on Facebook, Twitter, and Pinterest.
- Local e-commerce, headlined by new local on-demand service companies such as Uber, skyrockets to an estimated $25 billion.
- The number of online buyers continues to increase, to over 170 million in 2015, and the average annual purchase also continues to increase, up by about 10% in 2015 to $1,983.
- Online retailers remain generally profitable by focusing on revenue growth, increasing the size of average purchase amounts, and improving efficiency of operations.
- Online retail remains the fastest growing retail channel.
- Buying online has become a normal, mainstream, everyday experience. Almost 90% of Internet users in the United States are now online shoppers.
- The selection of goods for purchase online continues to increase to include luxury goods, such as jewelry, gourmet groceries, furniture, and wine, as customer trust and experience increase.
- Informational shopping for big-ticket items such as cars and appliances continues to expand rapidly to include nearly all retail goods (both durables and non-durables).
- Specialty retail sites show rapid growth in online retail as they develop customized retail goods and customer online configuration of goods.
- Online retailers place an increased emphasis on providing an improved "shopping experience," including ease of navigation and use, online inventory updates, interactive tools, customer feedback and ratings, and social shopping opportunities.
- Online retailers increase the use of interactive marketing technologies and techniques such as blogs, user-generated content, and video that exploit the dominance of broadband connections and offer features such as zoom, color switch, product configuration, and virtual simulations of households and businesses.
- Retailers are increasingly becoming omni-channel retailers, integrating the multiple retail channels provided by physical stores, the Web, and the mobile platform.
- New virtual merchants such as Birchbox, Naturebox, and others emerge that are using a new subscription-based revenue model for retail.
- Big Data and powerful analytic programs begin to be used for predictive marketing by both large and small retailers.

offline and online—to integrate their operations so they can serve customers in the various ways they want to be served.

By any measure, the size of the U.S. retail market is huge. In a $17.8 trillion economy, personal consumption of retail goods and services accounts for about $12.2 trillion (about 68%) of the total gross domestic product (GDP) (Bureau of Economic Analysis, U.S. Department of Commerce, 2015).

THE RETAIL INDUSTRY

The retail industry is composed of many different types of firms. **Figure 9.1** illustrates the major segments: durable goods, general merchandise, food and beverage, specialty stores, gasoline and fuel, mail order/telephone order (MOTO), and online retail firms. Each of these segments offers opportunities for online retail, and yet in each segment,

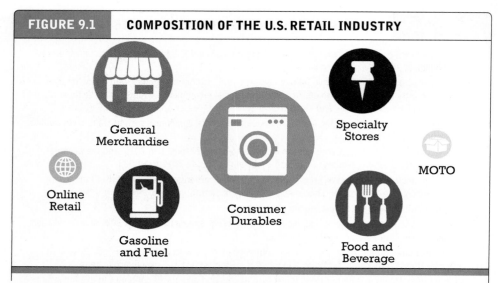

FIGURE 9.1 **COMPOSITION OF THE U.S. RETAIL INDUSTRY**

General Merchandise

Specialty Stores

Online Retail

MOTO

Consumer Durables

Gasoline and Fuel

Food and Beverage

The retail industry can be grouped into seven major segments.
SOURCE: Based on data from U.S. Census Bureau, 2012.

the uses of the Internet may differ. Some eating and drinking establishments use the Web and mobile apps to inform people of their physical locations and menus, while others offer delivery via online orders. Retailers of durable goods typically use the online channel primarily as an informational tool rather than as a direct purchasing tool, although this has begun to change.

The MOTO sector is the most similar to the online retail sales sector. In the absence of physical stores, MOTO retailers distribute millions of physical catalogs (their largest expense) and operate large telephone call centers to accept orders. They have developed extraordinarily efficient order fulfillment centers that generally ship customer orders within 24 hours of receipt. MOTO was the fastest growing retail segment throughout the 1970s and 1980s. It grew as a direct result of improvements in the national toll-free call system, the implementation of digital switching in telephone systems, falling long distance telecommunications prices, and of course, the expansion of the credit card industry and associated technologies, without which neither MOTO nor e-commerce would be possible on a large national scale. MOTO was the last "technological" retailing revolution that preceded e-commerce. Because of their experience in fulfilling small orders rapidly, the transition to e-commerce was not difficult for these firms.

ONLINE RETAILING

Online retail is perhaps the most high-profile e-commerce sector. Over the past decade, this sector has experienced both explosive growth and spectacular failures. Many of the early pure-play online-only firms that pioneered the retail marketspace failed. Entrepreneurs and their investors seriously misjudged the factors needed to succeed in this market. But the survivors of this early period emerged much stronger, and along with traditional offline general and specialty merchants, as well as new start-ups, the e-tail space is growing very rapidly and is increasing its reach and size.

E-commerce Retail: The Vision

In the early years of e-commerce, literally thousands of entrepreneurial Web-based retailers were drawn to the marketplace for retail goods, simply because it was one of the largest market opportunities in the U.S. economy. Many entrepreneurs initially believed it was easy to enter the retail market. Early writers predicted that the retail industry would be revolutionized, literally "blown to bits"—as prophesized by two consultants in a famous Harvard Business School book (Evans and Wurster, 2000). The basis of this revolution would be fourfold. First, because the Internet greatly reduced both search costs and transaction costs, consumers would use the Web to find the lowest-cost products. Several results would follow. Consumers would increasingly drift to the Web for shopping and purchasing, and only low-cost, high-service, quality online retail merchants would survive. Economists assumed that the Web consumer was rational and cost-driven—not driven by perceived value or brand, both of which are nonrational factors.

Second, it was assumed that the entry costs to the online retail market were much less than those needed to establish physical storefronts, and that online merchants were inherently more efficient at marketing and order fulfillment than offline stores. The costs of establishing a powerful Web site were thought to be minuscule compared to the costs of warehouses, fulfillment centers, and physical stores. There would be no difficulty building sophisticated order entry, shopping cart, and fulfillment systems because this technology was well known, and the cost of technology was falling by 50% each year. Even the cost of acquiring consumers was thought to be much lower because of search engines that could almost instantly connect customers to online vendors.

Third, as prices fell, traditional offline physical store merchants would be forced out of business. New entrepreneurial companies—such as Amazon—would replace the traditional stores. It was thought that if online merchants grew very quickly, they would have first-mover advantages and lock out the older traditional firms that were too slow to enter the online market.

Fourth, in some industries—such as electronics, apparel, and digital content—the market would be disintermediated as manufacturers or their distributors entered to build a direct relationship with the consumer, destroying the retail intermediaries or middlemen. In this scenario, traditional retail channels—such as physical stores, sales clerks, and sales forces—would be replaced by a single dominant channel: the Web.

Many predicted, on the other hand, a kind of hypermediation based on the concept of a virtual firm in which online retailers would gain advantage over established offline merchants by building an online brand name that attracted millions of customers, and outsourcing the expensive warehousing and order fulfillment functions—the original concept of Amazon and Drugstore.com.

As it turned out, few of these assumptions and visions were correct, and the structure of the retail marketplace in the United States, with some notable exceptions, has not been blown to bits, disintermediated, or revolutionized in the traditional meaning of the word "revolution." With several notable exceptions, online retail has often not been successful as an independent platform on which to build a successful "pure-play" Web-only business. As it turns out, the consumer is not primarily price-driven when shopping on the Internet but instead considers brand name, trust, reliability, delivery time, convenience, ease of use, and above all "the experience," as at least as important as price (Brynjolfsson, Dick, and Smith, 2004).

However, the Internet has created an entirely new venue for **omni-channel** firms (those that sell products through a variety of channels and integrate their physical stores with their Web sites and mobile platform), and in some cases, the Internet has supported the development of pure-play online-only merchants, both general merchandisers as well as specialty retailers. As predicted, online retail has indeed become the fastest growing and most dynamic retail channel in the sense of channel innovation. The Web has created a new marketplace for millions of consumers to conveniently shop. The Internet and Web have continued to provide new opportunities for entirely new firms using new business models and new online products—such as Blue Nile, as previously described. The online channel can conflict with a merchant's other channels, such as direct sales forces, physical stores, and mail order, but this multi-channel conflict can be managed and turned into a strength.

omni-channel

retailers that sell products through a variety of channels and integrate their physical stores with their Web site and mobile platform

The Online Retail Sector Today

Although online retailing is one of the smallest segments of the retail industry, constituting about 6% of the total retail market today, it is growing at a faster rate than its offline counterparts, with new functionality and product lines being added every day (see **Figure 9.2**). The apparel and accessories category generates the highest percentage of revenue, estimated to be at around $63 billion in 2015. Consumers have a wide choice of online shopping options in this category, such as omni-channel department store chains like Macy's, Nordstrom, Target, and Walmart and specialty retailers like Gap, Zulily, J.Crew, Urban Outfitters, Abercrombie & Fitch, and Ralph Lauren. This is one category where Amazon does not dominate, in part because clothing shoppers tend to identify more strongly with a specific brand than they do with products that are more of a commodity, such as consumer electronics.

The computers and consumer electronics category generates the second-highest percentage of revenue, estimated at around $58 billion in 2015. Online shopping options for this category include Amazon, direct-manufacturers such as Apple, Dell, HP, and Lenovo, omni-channel chains such as Best Buy, and catalog merchants such as CDW and PC Connection.

The automobile and automobile parts and accessories category is in third place, generating an estimated $36 billion in 2015, primarily from auto parts and accessories. Currently, U.S. franchising law prohibits automobile manufacturers from selling cars directly to consumers, so automobile retailing is dominated by dealership networks. Automobile manufacturers use the Internet to deliver branding advertising, while dealers focus on generating leads. Consumers typically focus on product and pricing research, which they then use to negotiate with dealers. Direct online automobile sales are currently not common due to the complexity of the vehicle purchasing process, but they are likely to become more commonplace in the future. For example, start-up

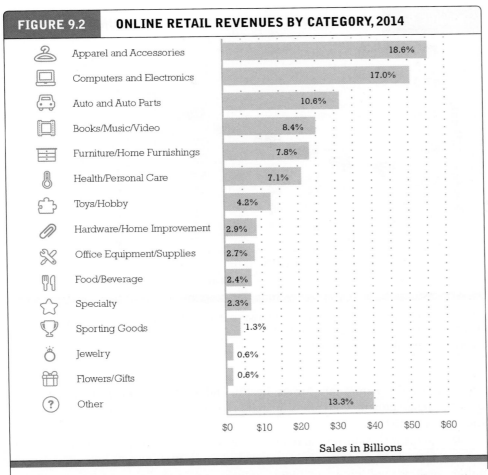

FIGURE 9.2   ONLINE RETAIL REVENUES BY CATEGORY, 2014

Category	Percentage
Apparel and Accessories	18.6%
Computers and Electronics	17.0%
Auto and Auto Parts	10.6%
Books/Music/Video	8.4%
Furniture/Home Furnishings	7.8%
Health/Personal Care	7.1%
Toys/Hobby	4.2%
Hardware/Home Improvement	2.9%
Office Equipment/Supplies	2.7%
Food/Beverage	2.4%
Specialty	2.3%
Sporting Goods	1.3%
Jewelry	0.6%
Flowers/Gifts	0.6%
Other	13.3%

Sales in Billions

Apparel and accessories is the leading online purchase category in terms of revenue generated, accounting for over 18% of all online retail revenues.

SOURCES: Based on data from Internet Retailer, 2015; eMarketer, Inc., 2015y.

Beepi, has developed a business model based on eliminating dealers and sells used cars directly to consumers via a mobile app.

Books, music, and video are among the original items sold successfully online. This still popular online category is expected to generate an estimated $29 billion in 2015. Leading retailers in this category include Amazon, Apple, Netflix, Google Play, Barnes & Noble, and Hulu.

The furniture and home furnishing category is expected to generate an estimated $30 billion in 2015. In the past, the expense of shipping large items such as furniture, mattresses, and rugs was a deterrent to online sales, but that is beginning to change. In addition to Amazon, leading online retailers in this category include other purely online companies such as Wayfair and Overstock, as well as omni-channel retailers such as William-Sonoma, Restoration Hardware, Bed Bath & Beyond, and Crate and Barrel.

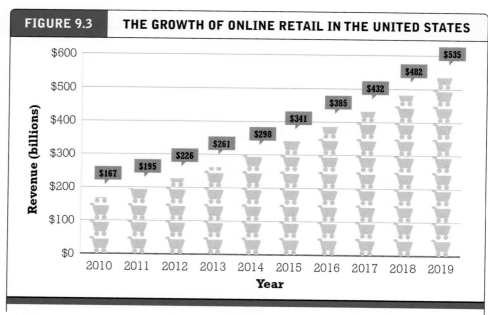

FIGURE 9.3   **THE GROWTH OF ONLINE RETAIL IN THE UNITED STATES**

Online retail revenues will be an estimated $340 billion in 2015, and are expected to increase to $535 billion by 2019, more than doubling since 2013.

SOURCES: Based on data from eMarketer, 2015a.

The health and personal care (drugs, health, and beauty supplies) category has also enjoyed steady growth, with an estimated $24 billion in revenue in 2015 (eMarketer, Inc., 2015x; 2015y).

Due to the recession, online retail revenues were basically flat from 2008 to 2009, but they since have resumed their upward trajectory (**Figure 9.3**). When we refer to online retail, we will not be including online services revenues such as travel, job-hunting, or the purchase of digital downloads such as software applications and music. Instead, for the purposes of this chapter, online retail refers solely to sales of physical goods over the Internet. The Internet provides a number of unique advantages and challenges to online retailers. **Table 9.2** summarizes these advantages and challenges.

Despite the high failure rate of online retailers in the early years, more consumers than ever are shopping online. For most consumers, the advantages of online shopping overcome the disadvantages. In 2015, it is estimated that over 75% of Internet users over the age of 14 (around 170 million people) will buy at an online retail store, generating about $340 billion in online retail sales. While the number of new Internet users in the United States is not growing as rapidly at it was, with over 80% of the U.S. population already on the Internet, this slowdown will not necessarily reduce the growth in online retail e-commerce because the average shopper is spending more on the Internet each year and finding many new categories of items to buy. For instance, in 2003, the average annual amount spent online by users was $675, but by 2015, it had jumped to almost $2,000 (eMarketer, Inc., 2015a, 2005). Also, as noted in Chapter 6, millions of additional consumers research products online and are influenced in their purchase decisions at offline stores.

TABLE 9.2	ONLINE RETAIL: ADVANTAGES AND CHALLENGES
ADVANTAGES	**CHALLENGES**
Lower supply chain costs by aggregating demand at a single site and increasing purchasing power	Consumer concerns about the security of transactions
Lower cost of distribution using Web sites rather than physical stores	Consumer concerns about the privacy of personal information given to Web sites
Ability to reach and serve a much larger geographically distributed group of customers	Delays in delivery of goods when compared to store shopping
Ability to react quickly to customer tastes and demand	Inconvenience associated with return of damaged or exchange goods
Ability to change prices nearly instantly	Overcoming lack of consumer trust in online brand names
Ability to rapidly change visual presentation of goods	Added expenses for online photography, video, and animated presentations
Avoidance of direct marketing costs of catalogs and physical mail	Online marketing costs for search, e-mail, and displays
Increased opportunities for personalization, customization	Added complexity to product offerings and customer service
Ability to greatly improve information and knowledge delivered to consumer	Greater customer information can translate into price competition and lower profits
Ability to lower consumers' overall market transaction costs	

The primary beneficiaries of this growing consumer support are not only the pure online companies but also the established offline retailers who have the brand-name recognition, supportive infrastructure, and financial resources to enter the online marketplace successfully. **Table 9.3** lists the top online retail firms ranked by online sales. The list contains pure-play online retailers for whom the Internet is the only sales channel, such as Amazon (in first place) and Newegg; omni-channel firms that have established brand names and for whom e-commerce still plays a relatively small role when compared to their offline physical store channels, such as Walmart, Sears, Macy's, Home Depot, Costco, BestBuy, and Target; and manufacturers of computer and electronic equipment, such as Apple and Dell. In 2014, the top 10 retailers accounted for about 50% of all online retail, while the top 500 retailers accounted for about 85%. The next 500 accounted for an additional 5%, so just 1,000 retailers generated approximately 90% of all retail e-commerce sales. Many of the fastest growing firms are mid-size merchants, particularly newcomers that focus on a particular niche, such as Blue Apron, which uses a subscription-based sales model for make-at-home meals, and Dollar Shave Club, another company that uses a subscription-based sales model for inexpensive razors. Conversely, companies that can't show consumers that they can offer them something of value not available elsewhere are likely to have a difficult time surviving. For pure-play firms, the challenge is to turn visitors into customers, and to develop efficient operations that permit them to achieve long-term profitability.

TABLE 9.3	THE TOP 15 U.S. RETAILERS RANKED BY ONLINE SALES	
RETAILER	**ONLINE SALES (2014)** (in billions)	**TYPE**
Amazon	$79.48	Online only
Walmart	$12.14	Omni-channel bricks-and-clicks
Staples	$11.23	Omni-channel bricks-and-clicks
Apple*	$10.42	Manufacturer-direct
Sears	$5.70	Omni-channel bricks-and-clicks
Macy's	$5.40	Omni-channel bricks-and-clicks
Office Depot	$4.30	Omni-channel bricks-and-clicks
CDW	$3.80	Catalog
Home Depot	$3.76	Omni-channel bricks-and-clicks
Costco	$3.74	Omni-channel bricks-and-clicks
Dell	$3.65	Manufacturer-direct
Best Buy	$3.54	Omni-channel bricks-and-clicks
QVC	$3.53	Catalog
Target	$2.99	Omni-channel bricks-and-clicks
Newegg	$2.83	Online only

*Does not include revenues derived from iTunes, iBooks, or the App Store

SOURCES: Based on data from Internet Retailer, 2015a; company reports on Form 10-K filed with the Securities and Exchange Commission.

Profitability remains a key issue for online-only retailers. Not many of these companies are public and therefore required to report their financial results, but of the few that are, only a handful were profitable in 2014. Even Amazon reported a net loss. One that was profitable was Zulily, a children's and women's clothing retailer that uses a flash sales model. Zulily's revenues grew by over 70% in 2014, reaching $1.2 billion, and it recorded a profit of about $15 million. For traditional firms that are less dependent on e-commerce sales, the challenge is to integrate the offline and online channels so customers can move seamlessly from one environment to another.

Clearly one of the most important e-commerce retail themes of 2015–2016, and into the future, is the ability of offline traditional firms such as Walmart, Target, Macy's, and others to continue to integrate their Web and mobile operations with their physical store operations in order to provide an "integrated shopping customer experience" and leverage the value of their physical stores. **Table 9.4** illustrates some of the various ways in which traditional retailers have integrated the Web, the mobile platform, and store operations to develop nearly seamless omni-channel shopping. This list is not exclusive, and retailers continue to develop new links between channels.

Rather than demonstrate disintermediation, online retailing provides an example of the powerful role that intermediaries continue to play in retail trade. Established offline retailers have rapidly gained online market share. Increasingly, consumers are

TABLE 9.4	RETAIL E-COMMERCE: OMNI-CHANNEL INTEGRATION METHODS
INTEGRATION TYPE	**DESCRIPTION**
Online order, in-store pickup	Probably one of the first types of integration.
Online order, store directory, and inventory	When items are out of stock online, customer is directed to physical store network inventory and store location.
In-store kiosk Web order, home delivery	When retail store is out of stock, customer orders in store and receives at home. Presumes customer is Web familiar.
In-store retail clerk Web order, home delivery	Similar to above, but the retail clerk searches Web inventory if local store is out of stock as a normal part of the in-store checkout process.
Order online, in-store returns, and adjustments	Defective or rejected products ordered online can be returned to any store location.
Online catalog	Online catalog supplements offline physical catalog and often the online catalog has substantially more product on display.
Manufacturers use online promotions to drive customers to their distributors' retail stores	Consumer product manufacturers such as Colgate-Palmolive and Procter & Gamble use online channels to design new products and promote existing product retail sales.
Gift card, loyalty program points can be used in any channel	Recipient of gift card, loyalty program points can use them to purchase in-store, online, or via catalog, if offered by merchant.
Mobile order, Web site and physical store sales	Apps take users directly to specially formatted Web site for ordering, or to in-store bargains.
Geo-fencing mobile notification, in-store sales	Use of smartphone geo-location technology to target ads for nearby stores and restaurants.

attracted to stable, well-known, trusted retail brands and retailers. The online audience is very sensitive to brand names and is not primarily cost-driven. Other factors such as reliability, trust, fulfillment, and customer service are equally important.

The most significant changes in retail e-commerce in 2015 are the explosive growth in social e-commerce, the growing ability of firms to market local services and products through the use of location-based marketing, and not least, the rapidly growing mobile platform composed of smartphones and tablet computers. In retail circles, tablets are being called "the ultimate shopping machine," enabling consumers to browse media-rich online catalogs just like they used to do with physical catalogs, and then buy when they feel the urge.

Social e-commerce refers to marketing and purchasing on social network sites like Facebook, Twitter, Pinterest, Instagram, Tumblr, and others. All of these sites have developed into major marketing and advertising platforms that help direct consumers to external Web sites to purchase products. And, after trials in 2014, Facebook, Twitter, Pinterest, and Instagram have all introduced Buy buttons that allow consumers to more easily purchase goods on a much wider scale. In 2014, the top 500 retailers in Internet Retailer's Social Media 500 earned about $3.3 billion from social commerce, a 26% increase over 2013.

Whereas in the past only large firms could afford to run online marketing and ad campaigns, this has changed with the development of local marketing firms like Groupon, LivingSocial, and dozens of others, as well as Amazon Local, which make it possible for consumers to receive discount deals and coupons from local merchants based on their geographic location. Using billions of daily e-mails, these so-called daily deal sites have sold millions of coupons to purchase local goods and services at steep discounts. For the first time, local merchants can advertise their products and services online at a relatively inexpensive cost.

Social and local e-commerce are enabled by the tremendous growth in mobile Internet devices, both smartphones and tablet computers. In 2015, U.S. retail m-commerce is expected to generate around $77 billion overall. In 2015, over 70% of online buyers are expected to make a purchase using a mobile device, and it is estimated that this percentage will grow to over 80% by 2018 (eMarketer, Inc., 2015b, 2015c).

9.2   ANALYZING THE VIABILITY OF ONLINE FIRMS

In this and the following chapters, we analyze the viability of a number of online companies that exemplify specific e-commerce models. We are primarily interested in understanding the near-to-medium term (1–3 years) economic viability of these firms and their business models. **Economic viability** refers to the ability of firms to survive as profitable business firms during the specified period. To answer the question of economic viability, we take two business analysis approaches: strategic analysis and financial analysis.

economic viability
refers to the ability of firms to survive as profitable business firms during a specified period

STRATEGIC ANALYSIS

Strategic approaches to economic viability focus on both the industry in which a firm operates and the firm itself (see Chapter 2, Sections 2.2 and 2.5). The key industry strategic factors are:

- *Barriers to entry*: Can new entrants be barred from entering the industry through high capital costs or intellectual property barriers (such as patents and copyrights)?

- *Power of suppliers*: Can suppliers dictate high prices to the industry or can vendors choose from among many suppliers? Have firms achieved sufficient scale to bargain effectively for lower prices from suppliers?

- *Power of customers*: Can customers choose from many competing suppliers and hence challenge high prices and high margins?

- *Existence of substitute products*: Can the functionality of the product or service be obtained from alternative channels or competing products in different industries? Are substitute products and services likely to emerge in the near future?

- *Industry value chain*: Is the chain of production and distribution in the industry changing in ways that benefit or harm the firm?

- *Nature of intra-industry competition*: Is the basis of competition within the industry based on differentiated products and services, price, scope of offerings, or focus of offerings? How is the nature of competition changing? Will these changes benefit the firm?

The strategic factors that pertain specifically to the firm and its related businesses include:

- *Firm value chain*: Has the firm adopted business processes and methods of operation that allow it to achieve the most efficient operations in its industry? Will changes in technology force the firm to realign its business processes?

- *Core competencies*: Does the firm have unique competencies and skills that cannot be easily duplicated by other firms? Will changes in technology invalidate the firm's competencies or strengthen them?

- *Synergies*: Does the firm have access to the competencies and assets of related firms either owned outright or through strategic partnerships and alliances?

- *Technology*: Has the firm developed proprietary technologies that allow it to scale with demand? Has the firm developed the operational technologies (e.g., customer relationship management, fulfillment, supply chain management, inventory control, and human resource systems) to survive?

- *Social and legal challenges*: Has the firm put in place policies to address consumer trust issues (privacy and security of personal information)? Is the firm the subject of lawsuits challenging its business model, such as intellectual property ownership issues? Will the firm be affected by changes in Internet taxation laws or other foreseeable statutory developments?

FINANCIAL ANALYSIS

Strategic analysis helps us comprehend the competitive situation of the firm. Financial analysis helps us understand how in fact the firm is performing. There are two parts to a financial analysis: the statement of operations and the balance sheet. The statement of operations tells us how much money (or loss) the firm is achieving based on current sales and costs. The balance sheet tells us how many assets the firm has to support its current and future operations.

Here are some of the key factors to look for in a firm's statement of operations:

- *Revenues*: Are revenues growing and at what rate? Many e-commerce companies have experienced impressive, even explosive, revenue growth as an entirely new channel is created.

- *Cost of sales*: What is the cost of sales compared to revenues? Cost of sales typically includes the cost of the products sold and related costs. The lower the cost of sales compared to revenue, the higher the gross profit.

- *Gross margin*: What is the firm's gross margin, and is it increasing or decreasing? **Gross margin** is calculated by dividing gross profit by net sales revenues. Gross margin can tell you if the firm is gaining or losing market power vis-à-vis its key suppliers.

gross margin
gross profit divided by net sales

- *Operating expenses*: What are the firm's operating expenses, and are they increasing or decreasing? Operating expenses typically include the cost of marketing, technology, and administrative overhead. They also include, in accordance with professional accounting standards (see below), stock-based compensation to employees and executives, amortization of goodwill and other intangibles, and impairment of investments. In e-commerce companies, these turn out to be very important expenses. Many e-commerce firms compensated their employees with stock shares (or options), and many e-commerce firms purchased other e-commerce firms as a part of their growth strategy. Many of the companies were purchased at extremely high values using company stock rather than cash; in numerous instances, the purchased companies fell dramatically in market value. All these items are counted as normal operating expenses.

- *Operating margin*: What did the firm earn from its current operations? **Operating margin** is calculated by dividing operating income or loss by net sales revenue. Operating margin is an indication of a company's ability to turn sales into pre-tax profit after operating expenses have been deducted. Operating margin tells us if the firm's current operations are covering its operating expenses, not including interest expenses and other non-operating expenses.

- *Net margin*: **Net margin** tells us the percentage of its gross sales revenue the firm was able to retain after all expenses are deducted. Net margin is calculated by dividing net income or loss by net sales revenue. Net margin sums up in one number how successful a company has been at the business of making a profit on each dollar of sales revenues. Net margin also tells us something about the efficiency of the firm by measuring the percentage of sales revenue it is able to retain after all expenses are deducted from gross revenues, and, within a single industry, it can be used to measure the relative efficiency of competing firms. Net margin takes into account many non-operating expenses such as interest and stock compensation plans.

When examining the financial announcements of e-commerce companies, it is important to realize that online firms often choose not to announce their net income according to generally accepted accounting principles (GAAP). These principles have been promulgated by the Financial Accounting Standards Board (FASB), a board of professional accountants that establishes accounting rules for the profession, and which has played a vital role since the 1934 Securities Act, which sought to improve financial accounting during the Great Depression. Many e-commerce firms in the early years instead reported an entirely new calculation called *pro forma earnings* (also called EBITDA—earnings before income taxes, depreciation, and amortization). Pro forma earnings generally do not deduct stock-based compensation, depreciation, or amortization. The result is that pro forma earnings are always better than GAAP earnings. The firms that report in this manner typically claim these expenses are non-recurring and special and "unusual." In 2002 and 2003, the SEC issued new guidelines (Regulation G) that prohibit firms from reporting pro forma earnings in official reports to the SEC, but still allow firms to announce pro forma earnings in public statements (Weil, 2003). Throughout this book, we consider a firm's income or loss based on GAAP accounting standards only.

A **balance sheet** provides a financial snapshot of a company's assets and liabilities (debts) on a given date. **Assets** refer to stored value. **Current assets** are those assets such as cash, securities, accounts receivable, inventory, or other investments that are likely to be able to be converted to cash within one year. **Liabilities** are outstanding obligations of the firm. **Current liabilities** are debts of the firm that will be due within one year. Liabilities that are not due until the passage of a year or more are characterized as **long-term debt**. For a quick check of a firm's short-term financial health, examine its **working capital** (the firm's current assets minus current liabilities). If

operating margin
calculated by dividing operating income or loss by net sales revenue

net margin
the percentage of its gross sales revenue the firm is able to retain after all expenses are deducted; calculated by dividing net income or loss by net sales revenue

balance sheet
provides a financial snapshot of a company on a given date and shows its financial assets and liabilities

assets
refers to stored value

current assets
assets such as cash, securities, accounts receivable, inventory, or other investments that are likely to be able to be converted to cash within one year

liabilities
outstanding obligations of the firm

current liabilities
debts of the firm that will be due within one year

long-term debt
liabilities that are not due until the passage of a year or more

working capital
firm's current assets minus current liabilities

working capital is only marginally positive, or negative, the firm will likely have trouble meeting its short-term obligations. Alternatively, if a firm has a large amount of current assets, it can sustain operational losses for a period of time.

<h2>9.3   E-COMMERCE IN ACTION: E-TAILING BUSINESS MODELS</h2>

So far, we have been discussing online retail as if it were a single entity. In fact, as we briefly discussed in Chapter 2, there are four main types of online retail business models: virtual merchants, omni-channel merchandisers (sometimes referred to as bricks-and-clicks or clicks-and-bricks), catalog merchants, and manufacturer-direct firms. **Figure 9.4** illustrates the respective shares of 2014 online retail sales for each of these categories of firms. In addition, there are small mom-and-pop retailers that use the eBay, Amazon, and Yahoo Stores sales platforms, as well as affiliate merchants whose primary revenue derives from sending traffic to their "mother" sites. Each of these different types of online retailers faces a different strategic environment, as well as different industry and firm economics.

VIRTUAL MERCHANTS

Virtual merchants are single-channel e-commerce firms that generate almost all their revenue from online sales. Virtual merchants face extraordinary strategic chal-

virtual merchants
single-channel Web firms that generate almost all of their revenue from online sales

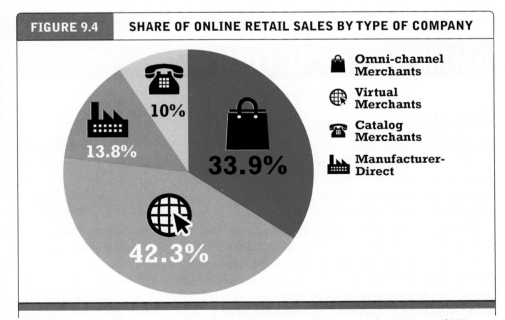

FIGURE 9.4   SHARE OF ONLINE RETAIL SALES BY TYPE OF COMPANY

- Omni-channel Merchants
- Virtual Merchants
- Catalog Merchants
- Manufacturer-Direct

10%
13.8%
33.9%
42.3%

Online retail revenues will be an estimated $340 billion in 2015, and are expected to increase to $535 billion by 2019, more than doubling since 2013.
SOURCES: Based on data from eMarketer, 2015a.

lenges. They must build a business and brand name from scratch, quickly, in an entirely new channel and confront many virtual merchant competitors (especially in smaller niche areas). Because these firms typically do not have any physical stores, they do not have to bear the costs associated with developing and maintaining physical stores but they face large costs in building and maintaining an e-commerce presence, building an order fulfillment infrastructure, and developing a brand name. Customer acquisition costs are high, and the learning curve is steep. Like all retail firms, their gross margins (the difference between the retail price of goods sold and the cost of goods to the retailer) are low. Therefore, virtual merchants must achieve highly efficient operations in order to preserve a profit, while building a brand name as quickly as possible in order to attract sufficient customers to cover their costs of operations. Most merchants in this category adopt low-cost and convenience strategies, coupled with extremely effective and efficient fulfillment processes to ensure customers receive what they ordered as fast as possible. In the following *E-commerce in Action* section, we take an in-depth look at the strategic and financial situation of Amazon, the leading online virtual merchant. In addition to Amazon, other successful virtual merchants include Newegg, Overstock, Rakuten (Buy.com), Gilt Groupe, Zulily, Wayfair, Rue La La, Blue Nile (profiled in the opening case), Bluefly, Hayneedle, Net-a-Porter, and Shoebuy. Recently, a new group of virtual merchants have emerged that use a subscription revenue model. Examples include Birchbox (personalized beauty samples delivered monthly), Stitch Fix (clothing selected by a personal stylist) (see the *Insight on Technology* case, *Big Data and Predictive Marketing,* on pages 594–595 for more on Birchbox and Stitch Fix), Barkbox (pet supplies), Naturebox (healthy snacks), Bulu Box (supplements and vitamins), and hundreds more. According to Internet Retailer, overall, virtual merchants accounted for $125 billion (about 42%) of online retail sales by the Internet Retailer Top 500 merchants in 2014 (Internet Retailer, 2015).

E-COMMERCE IN ACTION

AMAZON

Amazon, the Seattle-based virtual merchant, is one of the most well-known names in the world. As stated in its annual report filed with the U.S. Securities and Exchange Commission, Amazon's objective is to be Earth's most customer-centric company. Exactly what this means, and how it might be possible to achieve it, is a matter of speculation for both customers and investors. Yet this has not stopped Amazon's founder, Jeff Bezos, and his team from becoming the world's most successful and innovative online retailer.

Few business enterprises have experienced the roller-coaster ride from explosive early growth, to huge losses, and then on to profitability that Amazon has. No Internet business has been both so widely reviled and so hotly praised throughout its development. Its stock reflects these changing fortunes, fluctuating over the past 15 years, from an early high of $106 in 1999, to a low of $6 a share in 2001, then bouncing back and forth between $50–$90 in 2003–2009, and then climbing again to high of over $580 in 2015. While controversial, Amazon has also been one of the most innovative online retailing stories in the history of e-commerce. From the earliest days of e-commerce, Amazon has continuously adapted its business model based on both its market experience and its insight into the online consumer.

The Vision

The original vision of founder Jeff Bezos and his friends was that the Internet was a revolutionary new form of commerce and that only companies that became really big early on (ignoring profitability) would survive. The path to success, according to founder Bezos, was to offer consumers three things: the lowest prices, the best selection, and convenience (which translates into feature-rich content, user-generated reviews of books and products, fast and reliable fulfillment, and ease of use). Currently, Amazon offers consumers millions of unique new, used, and collectible items in a variety of different categories, both physical and digital. Its physical goods include books, movies, music, and games; electronics and computers; home, garden, and tools; grocery; health and beauty; toys, kids, and baby; clothing, shoes, and jewelry; sports and outdoors; and auto and industrial. Its digital products include unlimited instant videos, digital games and software, MP3s and Cloud Player, Audible audiobooks, and Kindle e-book reader products. And if Amazon does not carry it, it will help you find it at online merchants who "rent space" from Amazon, or even at an external online vendor. In short, Amazon has become the largest, one-stop online merchant, a kind of combined "shopping portal" and "product search portal" that puts it in direct competition with other large online general merchants, eBay, and general portals such as Yahoo, MSN, and even Google. As Amazon succeeded in becoming the world's largest online store, it also expanded its original vision to become one of the largest suppliers of online merchant and search services.

Business Model

Amazon's business is currently organized into two basic segments: North American and International. Within those segments, it serves not only retail customers but also merchants and developers. The retail component of the business sells physical and digital products that Amazon has purchased and then resells to consumers just like a traditional retailer. It also manufactures and sells a variety of versions of its Kindle e-reader and Kindle Fire series of devices, including tablet computers and smart TVs. The Fire smartphone has been less successful, due to a lack of available apps.

Another major component of Amazon's business is its third-party merchant segment. Amazon Services enables third parties to integrate their products into Amazon's Web site, and use Amazon's customer technologies. In the early years of its business, Amazon entered into partnerships with large merchants such as Toys"R"Us, Borders, and Target, and created storefronts for these companies within the larger Amazon site. Today, Amazon has increasingly left the enterprise-level business to competitors and instead focused its efforts on small and medium-sized retail merchants.

Thousands of these types of merchants have signed on with Amazon, offering products that in some instances even compete with those that Amazon itself sells. For instance, a single product on the Amazon Web site may be listed for sale simultaneously by Amazon, by a large branded merchant participant such as Target, and by a business or individual selling a new, used, or collectible version of the product through Amazon Marketplace. For these types of merchants, Amazon is not the seller of record, does not own these products, and the shipping of products is usually handled by the third party (although in some instances, Amazon provides fulfillment services as well). Amazon collects a monthly fixed fee, sales commission (generally estimated to be between 10% and 20% of the sale), per-unit activity fee, or some combination thereof from the third party. In this segment, Amazon acts as an online shopping mall, collecting "rents" from other merchants and providing "site" services such as order entry and payment.

In many respects, Amazon's third-party seller segment is an effort to compete directly with eBay, the Web's most successful third-party merchant sales platform. eBay has a registered trading community of over 157 million active buyers and sellers. Amazon has even developed its own version of PayPal, Checkout by Amazon, designed for use at the point of sale. At the same time, eBay itself has moved closer to Amazon's business model by encouraging merchants to sell rather than auction goods on its site.

Another major part of Amazon's business is Amazon Web Services (AWS). Through this segment, Amazon offers a variety of Web services that provide developers with direct access to Amazon's technology platform and allow them to build their own applications based on that platform. In 2014, AWS accounts for $4.6 billion of Amazon's revenues and is on track to generate over $6 billion in 2015. Refer to Chapter 3 for a more detailed examination of AWS.

Despite the success of AWS, Amazon still generates revenue primarily by selling products. While Amazon started out as an online merchant of books, CDs, and DVDs, since 2002, it has diversified into becoming a general merchandiser of millions of other products. Amazon has turned itself into a major online media and content firm and, following its success with Kindle e-books, has also made a strong move into the music and streaming video business, with Amazon Music and Amazon Instant Video. In 2014, 25% of its revenue came from media sales while electronics and general merchandise accounted for 68%. In addition to Amazon.com in the United States, Amazon also operates a number of localized sites in Europe, Asia, and Canada. Although Amazon derives 37% of its gross revenue offshore, its international revenue growth decreased to only 12% in 2014, while North American revenue grew by 25%.

Financial Analysis

Amazon's revenues have increased from about $600 million in 1998 to an astounding $89 billion in 2014 (see **Table 9.5**). From 2011 to 2014, Amazon's revenues have more than doubled. This is very impressive, explosive revenue growth. However, Amazon's growth strategies have made it difficult for the company to maintain consistent profits. Although it showed a profit of $631 million in 2011, in 2012, Amazon experienced a net loss of $39 million. In 2013, it reversed that loss and reported net income of $274 million but fell short of analysts' estimates. In 2014, Amazon once again reported a net loss of $241 million, due in large part to operating expenses that rose from $19 billion in 2013 to $26 billion in 2014. Even though investors are generally unhappy with Amazon's poor earnings record, they have driven the price of the stock to as high as

TABLE 9.5	AMAZON'S CONSOLIDATED STATEMENTS OF OPERATIONS AND SUMMARY BALANCE SHEET DATA 2012–2014

CONSOLIDATED STATEMENTS OF OPERATIONS (in millions)

For the fiscal year ended December 31,	2014	2013	2012
Revenue			
Net sales/products.	$70,080	$ 60,903	$ 51,733
Net sales/services	18,908	13,549	9,360
Cost of sales	$62,752	$ 54,181	$ 45,971
Gross profit	26,236	20,271	15,122
Gross margin	29.5%	27.2%	24.8%
Operating expenses			
Marketing	4,332	3,133	2,408
Fulfillment.	10,766	8,585	6,419
Technology and content.	9,275	6,565	4,564
General and administrative	1,552	1,129	896
Other operating expense (income), net. . .	133	114	159
Total operating expenses.	26,058	19,526	14,446
Income from operations	178	745	676
Operating margin	0.2%	1%	1.1%
Total non-operating income (expense) . .	(289)	(239)	(132)
Income before income taxes	(111)	506	544
Provision for income taxes.	(167)	(161)	(428)
Equity-method investment activity, net of tax	37	(71)	(155)
Net income (loss).	**(241)**	**274**	**(39)**
Net margin	**−0.3%**	**0.03%**	**−0.06%**

SUMMARY BALANCE SHEET DATA (in millions)

At December 31,	2014	2013	2012
Assets			
Cash, cash equivalents, and marketable securities.	17,416	12,447	11,448
Total current assets	31,327	24,625	21,296
Total assets.	54,505	40,159	32,555
Liabilities			
Total current liabilities	28,089	22,980	19,002
Long-term liabilities.	15,675	7,433	5,361
Working capital.	3,238	1,645	2,294
Stockholders' Equity (Deficit)	10,741	9,746	8,192

SOURCE: Amazon.com, Inc., 2015.

$580 a share in 2015. What this means is that investors are still betting that Amazon will keep growing for a long time and that ultimately, it will be able to consistently earn significant profits.

At the end of December 2014, Amazon had about $17.4 billion in cash and marketable securities. These liquid assets were obtained from sales, sales of stock and notes to the public, venture capital investors, and institutional investors in return for equity (shares) in the company or debt securities. Total assets are about $54 billion. The company emphasizes the strength of its "free cash flow" as a sign of financial strength, suggesting it has more than enough cash available to cover short-term liabilities (such as financing holiday season purchasing). Amazon's current assets should certainly be enough to cover future short-term deficits should they occur.

Strategic Analysis—Business Strategy

Amazon engages in a number of business strategies that seek to maximize growth in sales volume, while cutting prices to the bare bones. Its revenue growth strategies include driving the growth of e-book sales by offering continuing enhancements of its Kindle e-reader and Kindle Fire tablet computer, both in the United States and internationally, as well as new e-book publishing initiatives; expanding further into the device manufacturing business; expanding its music and streaming video business, with its Amazon Music and Instant Video services; expanding its Amazon Web Services offerings and extending their geographic reach; moving toward a broader trading platform by expanding the third-party seller segment; and moving toward greater product focus by grouping its offerings into major categories called stores. Amazon is still following Walmart's and eBay's examples by attempting to be a mass-market, low-price, high-volume online supermarket where you can get just about anything. To achieve profitability in this environment, Amazon has invested heavily in supply chain management and fulfillment strategies to reduce its costs to the bare minimum while providing excellent customer service and even free shipping.

Specific programs to increase retail revenues are the continuation of free shipping from Amazon Retail (a strategy that has increased order sizes by 25%), Amazon Prime (which for $99 a year provides free two-day shipping and one-day delivery upgrades for $3.99, as well as free access to Prime Music and Prime Video), greater product selection, and shorter order fulfillment times. Amazon offers customers same-day shipping in 14 markets in the United States and now offers its Prime Now one-hour delivery service in nine cities. A ticking clock can be seen next to some Amazon sale items indicating the hours remaining for an order to make it to the customer by the next day.

Amazon has moved strongly into the mobile shopping space as well, with shopping apps for the iPhone, BlackBerry, Android, Windows Phone, and iPad. It also has Deals, Price Check, and Student apps for the iPhone and has opened an Appstore for Android applications. In 2015, it rolled out the initial version of its Amazon Prime Now mobile app, which is quickly expanding across the United States and offers delivery speeds as fast as one hour. In 2014, Amazon earned around $16.8 billion from mobile commerce, and analyts expect that amount to increase signficantly in 2015. Amazon has not been as successful in developing its own smartphone, however. In 2015, it withdrew its resources from the continued development of the Amazon Fire phone, which had opened to underwhelming sales in 2014 and never developed an audience.

Amazon has continued to build on the rousing success of its Kindle e-book reader platform, which it has touted as the best-selling product in its history. It has continued to release iterations of the Kindle e-book reader and Fire. According to Amazon, it now sells more Kindle books than all print books combined.

In 2012, Amazon increased its efforts in the entertainment business, adding content to its Instant Video library through an expanded content licensing agreement with NBC Universal and similar arrangements with CBS, Viacom, and nearly every major Hollywood studio. Further agreements were inked with Viacom, PBS, A + E, Scripps Networks, and FX in 2013. In 2014, it added HBO and developed a series of original shows to keep pace with closest competitor NetFlix. In 2015, Amazon announced that its content creation arm, Amazon Studios, would begin to develop original movies for theatrical release. These films will move to Amazon Prime within just a month or two of their debut.

On the cost side, Amazon increasingly uses "postal injection" for shipping, in which Amazon trucks deliver pre-posted packages to U.S. Postal System centers. In 2012, Amazon began an aggressive strategy to build warehouses all across the country to improve its delivery speeds. This has continued through 2015, with new fulfillment centers opening in New Jersey, Texas, and North Carolina. Many of Amazon's customers who had previously been exempt must now pay sales tax due to legislation in a number of states. With this competitive advantage evaporating, Amazon is seeking to trump all competitors on delivery speed. The ultimate goal for Bezos and Amazon: same-day delivery in many areas of the country, perhaps even via airborne delivery drones, in the near future, as part of a project called Amazon Prime Air.

Strategic Analysis—Competition

Amazon has both offline and online competition. Major competitors includes eBay (its primary online competitor) and omni-channel retailers such as Walmart, Sears, and JCPenney. Amazon also competes in a number of product areas with catalog merchants such as L.L.Bean and Lands' End and with other online bookstores such as Barnesandnoble.com. Insofar as portal sites such as MSN and Yahoo operate online stores, they are also competitors. Another growing rival is China-based Alibaba, which handles more business worldwide than eBay and Amazon combined and which went public in 2014. Amazon also competes with Web services firms that provide hosting, shopping cart, and fulfillment services. What's more, it has fully engaged iTunes and Netflix in competition by offering video and audio downloads. Amazon Music allows users to store and play music online, offers over 35 million DRM-free MP3 songs from both major music labels and thousands of independent labels, and can be played on virtually any hardware device and managed with any music software. Amazon Instant Video offers over 100,000 movies and TV shows to rent or buy, and

Amazon Prime Music, launched in 2014, offers over 1 million tracks that users can stream for free.

Strategic Analysis—Technology

Anyone who believes that information technology doesn't make a difference clearly does not know much about Amazon. Amazon arguably has the largest and most sophisticated collection of online retailing technologies available at any single online site. It has implemented numerous Web site management, search, customer interaction, recommendation, transaction processing, and fulfillment services and systems using a combination of its own proprietary technologies and commercially available, licensed technologies. Amazon's transaction-processing systems handle millions of items, numerous status inquiries, gift-wrapping requests, and multiple shipment methods. Customers can receive orders in single or multiple shipments, based on availability, and track the progress of each order. On the fulfillment side, every warehouse employee carries a shoehorn-sized device that combines a bar code scanner, a display screen, and a two-way data transmitter. It continues to invest heavily in AWS, new versions of the Kindle e-reader, and consumer electronics such as the Kindle Fire devices. In 2014, Amazon spent over $9.2 billion on technology and new content and is on track to spend even more in 2015.

Strategic Analysis—Social and Legal Challenges

Amazon continually faces lawsuits concerning various aspects of its business. Most common are patent infringement suits, largely settled out of court. Currently, there are a number of pending patent suits, including some involving the Kindle.

In recent years, Amazon has faced increased challenges from states eager to begin collecting sales taxes from online purchases. Until 2011, only customers in five states were required to pay sales taxes. Between distribution center expansion and state legislation requiring large online sellers to collect sales tax even in the absence of a physical presence, that number has ballooned to 26 in 2015. Although Amazon lost several legal battles involving the imposition of sales taxes, early on, many states had offered it sweet tax break deals to lure its business, perhaps not expecting that untaxed sales would become billions of dollars in lost tax revenue. As many of those deals expire, Amazon has already begun, as mentioned previously, an aggressive (and costly) expansion of its warehousing infrastructure across the United States to support same-day delivery.

Future Prospects

In 2015, Amazon finally began to show investors and analysts what they had been waiting years to see—signs of long-term profitability. The company reported a $92 million profit in the second quarter of 2015, up from a $126 million loss over the same period in 2014. North American sales, particularly in electronics and general merchandise, spurred the strong quarter, and Amazon's projections indicate that this growth is likely to continue throughout the year and beyond. The profitability of its AWS unit is also a major positive for Amazon, and that segment showed continued rapid growth.

Amazon Prime is also a key component of the company's strong performance. Overall, over the first six months of 2015, Amazon registered over $45 billion in sales, up over 17% from the $39 billion logged during the same period the previous year. While the company continues to spend heavily on future products and services, Amazon at last appears to have turned the corner to profitability (Amazon, 2015a, 2015b; Golden, 2015; D'Onfro, 2015; Bensinger, 2015; Silbert, 2015; Asay, 2015; Lindner, 2015; Del Ray, 2015; Singleton, 2015; Somaiya, 2014; Portillo, 2014; McIntyre, 2014; Ovide, 2014; Demos and Jarzemsky, 2014).

OMNI-CHANNEL MERCHANTS: BRICKS-AND-CLICKS

Also called omni-channel merchants, **bricks-and-clicks** companies have a network of physical stores as their primary retail channel, but also have online offerings. Omni-channel firms include Walmart, Macy's, Sears, JCPenney, Staples, OfficeMax, Costco, Target, and other brand-name merchants. While bricks-and-clicks merchants face high costs of physical buildings and large sales staffs, they also have many advantages such as a brand name, a national customer base, warehouses, large scale (giving them leverage with suppliers), and a trained staff. Acquiring customers is less expensive because of their brand names, but these firms face challenges in coordinating prices across channels and handling returns of Web purchases at their retail outlets. However, these retail players are used to operating on very thin margins and have invested heavily in purchasing and inventory control systems to control costs, and in coordinating returns from multiple locations. Bricks-and-clicks companies face the challenge of leveraging their strengths and assets to the Web, building a credible Web site, hiring new skilled staff, and building rapid-response order entry and fulfillment systems. According to Internet Retailer, in 2014, the chain retailers accounted for around $100 billion (around 34%) of all the Internet Retailer Top 500's online retail sales (Internet Retailer, 2015).

> **bricks-and-clicks**
> companies that have a network of physical stores as their primary retail channel, but have also introduced online offerings

Macy's is a prime example of a traditional merchant based on physical stores moving successfully to become an omni-channel retailer. Rowland H. Macy opened the first R.H. Macy & Co. store in New York City in 1858, and moved the flagship store (now the site of the famous Macy's Thanksgiving parade) to Herald Square at 34th Street and Broadway in 1902. Today, Macy's is one of the largest national department store chains, with around 775 Macy's department stores throughout the United States.

Like many traditional retailers, Macy's has had to change its business model to accommodate the Internet. Macy's (then called Federated Department Stores Inc.) jumped into e-commerce in 1995 with the creation of the Macys.com Web site. In 1999, Federated bought Fingerhut, at that time a leading catalog and direct marketer, in part for its expertise in e-commerce fulfillment and database management. Although the Fingerhut acquisition did not prove to be a financial success, Macy's e-commerce efforts benefitted from the acquisition.

In 2015, Macy's ranked 7th on Internet Retailer's list of the top 500 retail Web sites ranked by annual sales, with about $5.4 billion in online sales, representing over 30%

growth over 2013, and more than tripling since 2010. Growth of its physical store sales pales by comparison, and in 2015, it announced that it might close as many as 40 of its physical stores in 2016 as it focuses more and more on its e-commerce operations.

The Macy's Web site receives around 13 million monthly unique visitors. Web site features and functions include an interactive catalog, enlarged product views, ability to see products in different colors and from alternate views, including via zoom and videos. It also offers product comparisons, product ratings, and product recommendations, as well as a real-time inventory check system. Macy's ranked 6th in the 2015 National Retail Federation Favorite Retail Stores survey of companies with respect to the best e-commerce sites for convenience, safety, and customer service.

Macy's has jumped into social media as well, with a Facebook page that has over 14 million Likes, a Twitter feed with over 870,000 followers, a Pinterest page with 48 different boards, over 670,000 pins, and 116,000 followers, and a YouTube channel with over 6 million views. Macy's is also an early adopter of Buyable Pins recently introduced by Pinterest.

Mobile sales at Macy's are booming, and reached an estimated $790 million in 2014, according to Internet Retailer, 13th on their list of the top 500 mobile retailers for 2014. It has iPhone and Android apps, new versions of which it launched in 2014, and an HMTL5 mobile Web site powered by Usablenet. It currently gets most of its mobile sales from tablets (65%) and via its mobile Web site (also 65%). It has also tried QR codes, SMS marketing, and augmented reality. In a trial run into mobile game advertising, Macy's ran an ad in the Pandora iPhone application that encouraged users to play a game while listening to music. The top of the ad promoted a one-day sale, and after playing the game, users could click through to visit the Macy's mobile site, where the sale was promoted. Previously, Macy's had partnered with Spotify as one of Spotify's first mobile advertisers. Macy's ran audio ads inside Spotify's iPhone app to promote its MStyleLab, targeted at Millennials. In 2015, Macy's continues to focus on refining its omni-channel approach, encompassing its physical stores, its Web site, and the mobile platform. It was among the first retailers to support Apple Pay, Apple's mobile payment system, offering it in addition to Macy's own mobile wallet that allows shoppers to virtually store and access offers and coupons. It is piloting same-day delivery of products ordered online in 8 major U.S. markets, using Deliv, a crowd-sourced delivery provider. Its Buy Online Pickup In Store program, piloted in 2013, also rolled out to all Macy's stores nationwide. It is also piloting new point-of-sale technology that will enable shoppers to purchase with mobile devices while in the store, as well as iBeacon technology (see Chapter 7) (Macy's, 2015; Internet Retailer, 2015a; Bloomberg News, 2015; Smith, 2015; Kats, 2013; Love, 2013; Johnson, 2012).

CATALOG MERCHANTS

catalog merchants
established companies that have a national offline catalog operation that is their largest retail channel, but who have recently developed online capabilities

Catalog merchants such as Lands' End, L.L.Bean, CDW Corp., PC Connection, and Cabela's are established companies that have a national offline catalog operation, but who have also developed online capabilities. Catalog merchants face very high costs for printing and mailing millions of catalogs each year—many of which have a half-life of 30 seconds after the customer receives them. Catalog merchants typically have developed centralized fulfillment and call centers, extraordinary service, and excellent fulfillment in partnership with package delivery firms such as FedEx and UPS. Catalog firms have suffered in recent years as catalog sales growth rates have fallen. As a result, catalog merchants have had to diversify their channels either by building stores (L.L.Bean), being bought by store-based firms (Sears purchased Lands' End), or by building a strong Web presence.

Catalog firms are uniquely advantaged because they already possess very efficient order entry and fulfillment systems. However, they face many of the same challenges as bricks-and-mortar stores—they must leverage their existing assets and competencies to a new technology environment, build a credible Web presence, and hire new staff. Nevertheless, according to Internet Retailer, in 2014, its Internet Retailer Top 500 catalog merchants generated combined Web sales of about $29.6 billion (Internet Retailer, 2015).

Arguably one of the most successful online catalog merchants is LandsEnd.com. Lands' End started out in 1963 in a basement of Chicago's tannery district selling sailboat equipment and clothing, handling 15 orders on a good day. Since then it expanded into a direct catalog merchant, distributing over 200 million catalogs annually and selling a much expanded line of "traditionally" styled sport clothing, soft luggage, and products for the home. Lands' End was the first apparel retailer to have an e-commerce-enabled Web site, launching in 1995 with 100 products and travelogue essays. Located in Dodgeville, Wisconsin, it has since grown into one of the Web's most successful apparel sites.

Lands' End has always been on the leading edge of online retailing technologies, most of which emphasize personal marketing and customized products. Lands' End was the first e-commerce Web site to allow customers to create a 3-D model of themselves to "try on" clothing. Lands' End "Get Live Help" enables customers to chat online with customer service representatives; Lands' End Custom allows customers to create custom-crafted clothing built for their personal measurements. While customized clothing built online was thought to be a gimmick in the early years of online retailing, today, 40% of Lands' End clothing sold online is customized. In 2003, Lands' End was purchased by Sears (which itself was purchased by Kmart in 2004) and then was spun off as an independent company again in 2014, with 2014 online revenues of about $1.2 billion. In 2015, Lands' End was 15th on the National Retail Foundation's Favorite 50 survey (Smith, 2015). Features that garner praise include live video chat, product recommendations that reflect a shopper's preferences, content display based on the shopper's location and referral source, and iPhone and iPad apps that deliver Lands' End catalogs to mobile users. The digital catalogs contain exclusive content, including stories written by Lands' End employees. Shoppers can also visit Lands' End on Facebook, where it has over 1.2 million Likes. Lands' End also has a Twitter presence, where it has about 65,000 followers, and 38 different Pinterest boards with 12,500 followers (Landsend.com, 2015).

MANUFACTURER-DIRECT

Manufacturer-direct firms are either single- or multi-channel manufacturers that sell directly online to consumers without the intervention of retailers. Manufacturer-direct firms were predicted to play a very large role in e-commerce manufacturers,

manufacturer-direct
single- or multi-channel manufacturers who sell directly online to consumers without the intervention of retailers

but this has generally not happened. The primary exceptions are computer hardware, such as Apple, Dell, and Hewlett-Packard, and apparel manufacturers, such as Ralph Lauren, Nike, Under Armour, Carter's, Tory Burch, Deckers, Kate Spade, Jones Retail, and Vera Bradley. Most consumer products manufacturers do not sell directly online, although this has started to change. For instance, Procter & Gamble offers PGeStore, which carries over 50 different Procter & Gamble brands. Overall, according to Internet Retailer, consumer brand manufacturers account for about $41 billion (14%) of its Internet Retailer Top 500 online retail sales (Internet Retailer, 2015a).

channel conflict

occurs when retailers of products must compete on price and currency of inventory directly against the manufacturers

Manufacturer-direct firms sometimes face channel conflict challenges. **Channel conflict** occurs when retailers of products must compete on price and currency of inventory directly against the manufacturer, who does not face the cost of maintaining inventory, physical stores, or sales staffs. Firms with no prior direct marketing experience face the additional challenges of developing a fast-response online order and fulfillment system, acquiring customers, and coordinating their supply chains with market demand. Switching from a **supply-push model** (where products are made prior to orders received based on estimated demand and then stored in warehouses awaiting sale) to a **demand-pull model** (where products are not built until an order is received) has proved extremely difficult for traditional manufacturers. Yet for many products, manufacturer-direct firms have the advantage of an established national brand name, an existing large customer base, and a lower cost structure than even catalog merchants because they are the manufacturer of the goods and thus do not pay profits to anyone else. Therefore, manufacturer-direct firms should have higher margins.

supply-push model

products are made prior to orders received based on estimated demand

demand-pull model

products are not built until an order is received

One of the most frequently cited manufacturer-direct retailers is Dell Inc., the world's largest direct computer systems supplier, providing corporations, government agencies, small-to-medium businesses, and individuals with computer products and services ordered straight from the manufacturer's headquarters in Austin, Texas. Although sales representatives support corporate customers, individuals and smaller businesses buy direct from Dell by phone, fax, and via the Internet, with about $3.6 billion in sales generated online in 2014 (ranking 2nd only to Apple among consumer brand manufacturers and 12th on Internet Retailer's Top 500 list of online retailers) (Internet Retailer, 2015).

When Michael Dell started the company in 1984 in his college dorm room, his idea was to custom-build computers for customers, to eliminate the middleman, and more effectively meet the technology needs of his customers. Today, the company sells much more than individual computer systems; it also offers enterprise systems, desktop, and laptop computers, as well as installation, financing, repair, and management services. By relying on a build-to-order manufacturing process, the company achieves faster inventory turnover (five days), and reduced component and finished goods inventory levels; this strategy virtually eliminates the chance of product obsolescence.

The direct model simplifies the company's operations, eliminating the need to support a wholesale and retail sales network, as well as cutting out the costly associated markup, and gives Dell complete control over its customer database. In addition, Dell can build and ship custom computers nearly as fast as a mail-order supplier can pull a computer out of inventory and ship it to the customer.

To extend the benefits of its direct sales model, Dell has aggressively moved sales, service, and support online. Each month, the company typically has about 6 million unique visitors at the Dell Web site, where it maintains an estimated 80 country-specific Web sites. Dell's Premier service enables companies to investigate product offerings, complete order forms and purchase orders, track orders in real time, and review order histories all online. For its small business customers, it has created an online virtual account executive, as well as a spare-parts ordering system and virtual help desk with direct access to technical support data. Dell has also continued to broaden its offerings beyond pure hardware product sales, adding warranty services, product integration and installation services, Internet access, software, and technology consulting, referring to them as "beyond the box" offerings. These include nearly 30,000 software and peripheral products from leading manufacturers that can be bundled with Dell products. Dell has also embraced social media. It has a corporate blog, called Direct2Dell, and a presence on Facebook (with over 8.5 million Likes), Pinterest (with 15 boards, including boards on entrepreneurship, infographics, and tech tips), and Twitter (with almost 525,000 followers). It posts Twitter-exclusive sales for those who follow Dell Outlet. It also has a channel on YouTube that it calls the Dell Vlog Channel, with over 55,000 subscribers. In 2011, it released mobile apps for the iPhone and Android that featured in-app purchasing, customer ratings and reviews, product comparison, order tracking, a Shopping Advisor, and easy access to various customer support options. Dell promoted the release of the app via both a standard e-mail campaign and one optimized for mobile viewing, and discovered that the open rate for the mobile e-mail was twice that of the standard version, and the clickthrough rate was more than five times higher. In 2012, Dell redesigned its two-year-old mobile site, with a new layout, updated HTML5 navigation, and a host of new functionalities, including shopping assistance, Dell's full product image gallery, social sharing, mobile live chat, a product comparison tool, and simpler, more intuitive purchase process, as well as a more robust set of mobile analytics tools. By 2014, it was reaping the benefits, with mobile revenue triple what it was in 2012 (Dell, Inc.; Internet Retailer, 2015, 2014; Dusto, 2012).

COMMON THEMES IN ONLINE RETAILING

We have looked at some very different companies in the preceding section, from entrepreneurial virtual merchants to established offline giants. Online retail is the fastest growing channel in retail commerce, has the fastest growing consumer base, and has growing penetration across many categories of goods. On the other hand, profits for many start-up ventures have been difficult to achieve, and it took even Amazon eight years to show its first profit.

The reasons for the difficulties experienced by many online retailers in achieving profits are also now clear. The path to success in any form of retail involves having a central location in order to attract a larger number of shoppers, charging high enough prices to cover the costs of goods as well as marketing, and developing highly efficient inventory and fulfillment systems so that the company can offer goods at lower costs than competitors and still make a profit. Many online merchants failed to follow these fundamental ideas, lowering prices below the total costs of goods and operations, failing to develop efficient business processes, failing to attract a large enough audience to their Web sites, and spending far too much on customer acquisition and marketing. By 2015, the lessons of the past have been learned, and far fewer online merchants are selling below cost, especially if they are start-up companies. There's also been a change in consumer culture and attitudes. Whereas in the past consumers looked to the Web for really cheap prices, in 2015, they look to online purchasing for convenience, time savings, and time shifting (buying retail goods at night from the sofa). Consumers have been willing to accept higher prices in return for the convenience of shopping online and avoiding the inconvenience of shopping at stores and malls. This allows online merchants more pricing freedom.

A second common theme in retail e-commerce is that, for the most part, disintermediation has not occurred and the retail middleman has not disappeared. Indeed, virtual merchants, along with powerful offline merchants who moved online, have maintained their powerful grip on the retail customer, with some notable exceptions in electronics and software. Manufacturers—with the exception of electronic goods—have used the Web primarily as an informational resource, driving consumers to the traditional retail channels for transactions. Leaving Amazon aside, the most significant online growth has been that of offline general merchandiser giant intermediaries such as Walmart, Sears, Costco, JCPenney, Macy's, Target, and Nordstrom. Many of the first-mover, Web pure-play merchants (online intermediaries) failed to achieve profitability and closed their doors en masse as their venture capital funds were depleted. Traditional retailers have been the fast followers (although many of them cannot be characterized as particularly "fast") and are most likely to succeed online by extending their traditional brands, competencies, and assets. In this sense, e-commerce technological innovation is following the historical pattern of other technology-driven commercial changes, from automobiles to radio and television, where an explosion of start-up firms attracts significant investment, but quickly fail, and are consolidated into larger existing firms.

A third theme is that in order to succeed online, established merchants need to create an integrated shopping environment that combines their catalog, store, and online experiences into one. Customers want to shop wherever they want, using any device, and at any time. Established retailers have significant fulfillment, inventory management, supply chain management, and other competencies that apply directly to the online channel. To succeed online, established retailers need to extend their brands, provide incentives to consumers to use the online channel (which given the same prices for goods is more efficient to operate than a physical store), avoid channel conflict, and build advertising campaigns using online search engines such as Google, Yahoo, and Bing, and shopping comparison sites.

A fourth theme is the growth of online specialty merchants selling high-end, fashionable and luxury goods such as diamonds (Blue Nile), jewelry (Tiffany), and high fashion (Emporio Armani and Gilt) or selling discounted electronics (BestBuy), apparel (Gap), or office products (OfficeDepot). These firms are demonstrating the vitality and openness of the Internet for innovation and extending the range of products available online. Many virtual merchants have developed large, online customer bases, as well as the online tools required to market to their customer base. These online brands can be strengthened further through alliances and partnerships that add the required competencies in inventory management and fulfillment services. Virtual merchants need to build operational strength and efficiency before they can become profitable.

Another theme in 2015 is the continuing extraordinary growth in social commerce, local marketing and commerce, and mobile commerce. In the space of eight years since the first iPhone appeared, the mobile platform has emerged as a retail marketing and shopping tool, which will greatly expand e-commerce, potentially driving e-commerce to 20% of all commerce in the next five years. Local merchants will be a major benefactor of the growing mobile commerce platform. In an equally short time, Americans have begun to spend an increasing amount of their Internet time on social network sites where they share attitudes and experiences about business firms, products, and services. In a few years, social sites may turn into large purchasing venues.

A final theme in 2015 is the increasing use by retailers, large and small, of Big Data in their marketing efforts. The *Insight on Technology* case, *Big Data and Predictive Marketing*, examines this development.

9.4 THE SERVICE SECTOR: OFFLINE AND ONLINE

The service sector is typically the largest and most rapidly expanding part of the economies in advanced industrial nations such as the United States, and many European and some Asian countries. In the United States, the service sector (broadly defined) employs about four out of every five workers and accounts for about 80% of the United State's gross domestic product (GDP) (U.S. Department of Labor, Bureau of Labor Statistics, 2013; Bardhan, 2014). E-commerce in the service sector offers extraordinary opportunities to deliver information, knowledge, and transaction efficiencies.

The major service industry groups are finance, insurance, real estate, travel, professional services such as legal and accounting, business services, health services, and educational services. Business services include activities such as consulting, advertising and marketing, and information processing. Within these service industry groups, companies can be further categorized into those that involve **transaction brokering** (acting as an intermediary to facilitate a transaction) and those that involve providing a "hands-on" service. For instance, one type of financial service involves stockbrokers who act as the middle person in a transaction between buyers and sellers. Online mortgage companies such as LendingTree refer customers to mortgage companies that actually issue the mortgage. Employment agencies put a seller of labor in contact with a buyer of labor. The service involved in all these examples is brokering a transaction.

transaction brokering
acting as an intermediary to facilitate a transaction

In contrast, some industries perform specific hands-on activities for consumers. In order to provide their service, these professionals need to interact directly and personally with the "client." For these service industries, the opportunities for e-commerce are somewhat different. Currently, doctors and dentists cannot treat patients over the Internet. However, the Internet can assist their services by providing consumers with information, knowledge, and communication.

With some exceptions (for example, providers of physical services, such as cleaning, gardening, and so on), perhaps the most important feature of service industries (and occupations) is that they are knowledge- and information-intense. In order to provide value, service industries process a great deal of information and employ a

INSIGHT ON TECHNOLOGY

BIG DATA AND PREDICTIVE MARKETING

Big Data is a phrase that refers to the deluge of digital data that is being produced by 3.1 billion people using the Internet, 1.8 billion using smartphones, over 1.5 billion people on social networks, and an explosion of data sensors from home thermostats, RFID tags on goods in stores, wearable computing devices like Apple Watch, to retail store cameras and traffic counters. Estimates vary, but an IBM report claimed Big Data amounts to 2.5 billion gigabytes a day. It is estimated that 80% of the world's digital data has been created in the last two years. But Big Data is more than about volume, It is also about velocity: data comes in real time torrents, loses value quickly, and requires rapid responses; variety: the data deluge contains both structured numeric data and unstructured text documents, e-mail, video, audio, stock ticker data and financial transactions; variability: the flow of data is event driven and leads to peak loads, followed by relative calm; and complexity: the data comes from different sources and requires cleansing, matching, and reformatting in order to be useful. Storing all this data requires new kinds of database technologies, and analyzing all this data involves software called business analytics.

Big Data is important for business because it can lead to better decisions and competitive advantages for firms that get it right. Nowhere is this more true than retailing where a great deal of consumer information is now being generated, new products are continually arriving on the scene, and customers have a lot of choices about where to buy. Big Data is influencing the design and marketing of retail products and in-store sales efforts. Big Data and powerful analytics programs make possible predictive marketing, the ability to send personalized messages to customers recommending products before they ask. The hope for retail

firms is that Big Data will make us all into big spenders.

Predictive marketing is not entirely new. Skilled salespeople have always been able to size up a customer and predict how much a customer is willing to spend, informing what they decide to show a customer. It's called salesmanship. Predictive marketing is different because it is not based on traditional sales skills but instead on the collection of data and the use of software programs to maximize the likelihood of a sale. Predictive marketing can scale to millions of customers and make decisions in milliseconds.

Big Data and predictive marketing are not just for huge national retailers, but now can be used by much smaller firms as well. One such firm is Stitch Fix, a women's clothing retailer who is using the monthly subscription revenue model popularized by Birchbox (discussed below). Stitch Fix blends expert styling advice, software, and unique products to deliver a personalized shopping experience. Customers fill out a Style Profile online, which is then analyzed by the firm's proprietary software to identify products that the customer is likely to purchase. Personal stylists interpret the output of the system and then handpick five clothing items and accessories each month that are unique to the customer's taste, budget, and life style. The customer is not required to purchase the items until they have been received and accepted; they can be returned if they do not suit. Over time, the software it uses keeps track of what the customer purchased, and learns to make better predictions in the future based on what customers actually keep (as opposed to what they say they want, a key difference). The better Stitch Fix can make the right choices about what its customers will likely buy, the more revenue it generates. The key to the success of this system is the data collected in the Style Profile online questionnaire that has about 20 questions involving basic demographic information, plus a photo section that depicts seven different styles. Customers can respond to each style suggestion to anchor themselves in the Stitch Fix software. Based on the customer's demographic information and selections of preferred styles, the software predicts which of several thousand products the customer would like. Stitch Fix is growing explosively, with industry analysts projecting that it will take in more than $200 million in revenue in 2015 without having to resort to much paid marketing. Stitch Fix already has three distribution centers, with plans to open a fourth in November 2015.

Birchbox is another subscription-based retailer using predictive marketing and Big Data. Birchbox calls itself a discovery commerce platform and claims to be redefining the retail process by offering consumers a unique and personalized way to discover, learn about, and shop for the best beauty, grooming, and lifestyle products. Headquartered in New York City, Birchbox launched in 2010 and extended into men's products in 2012 with Birchbox Man. Customers fill out a survey telling the company their skin color, hair type, age, and favorite grooming products. The company uses software to match that personal information with profiles of other customers, observes what these other customers have purchased, and makes an educated guess about the beauty products new customers will purchase. The software program analyzes a 15-page profile of each customer, with over 66 characteristics tracked. For each product in inventory, a predictive heat score is produced that is, in essence, the probability that the customer will purchase a product. Birchbox then fills a box each month with beauty samples that match the customer's profile. Birchbox has raised over $70 million in funding over the past five years, operates in six countries, and has over 800 brand partners and more than 1 million subscribers. Its revenue is estimated to be in the $150 million range.

At the other end of the spectrum Walmart, the world's largest retailer with over $485 billion in revenue, is using Big Data and predictive marketing both online and in its stores. Over 50% of Walmart's Web traffic comes from mobile devices. Walmart's strategy is to turn mobile devices into shopping instruments for both online and offline shopping. Its mobile app generates shopping lists automatically for customers based on what they and other customers purchase each week. When the customer is in the store, a proximity marketing feature prompts the user to switch into store mode, and then customers are sent discounts and loyalty offers.

Experience with Big Data and predictive marketing in retail is still somewhat limited in 2015. There are many pilot projects, but little information on how well these systems really work for online or offline retail firms. The ability of Big Data to reverse the reduction in shoppers at physical retail stores that has occurred in the last few years is not certain. So far, there appears to be more data than there is analysis and strategy in predictive marketing. In opinion surveys, firms identify getting value from the data they have as the most challenging aspect of predictive marketing. A key limitation is the scarcity of data scientists who can bring meaning to the data, and managers who can translate these results into sales tactics and strategies.

SOURCES: "Key to Success: Beauty Box Company Birchbox Says It's Not Just About the Box," by Esha Chhabra, Forbes.com, September 23, 2015; "Stitch Fix Opening Distribution Center in Arizona," Tucson.com, September 10, 2015; "What Stitch Fix Figured Out About Mass Customization," by Simone Ahuja, Hbr.org, May 26, 2015; "Why Sephora's Digital Boss Joined Stitch Fix, the Personal Stylist Startup That's Growing Like Mad," by Jason Del Ray, Recode.net, March 22, 2015; "How America's E-commerce Giants Compare Across the Desktop, Mobile Web, and Mobile App Arenas," by Ariel Rosenstein, Thenextweb.com, January 14, 2015; "A New Kind of E-Commerce Adds a Personal Touch," by Molly Wood, *New York Times,* August 13, 2014; "Big Data's High-Priests of Algorithms," by Elizabeth Dwoskin, *Wall Street Journal,* August 8, 2014; "Shoppers Are Fleeing Physical Stores," by Shelly Banjo and Paul Ziobro, *Wall Street Journal,* August 5, 2014; "Retailers Use Big Data to Turn You into a Big Spender," by Mark Milian, Bloomberg.com, June 3, 2014; "How Big Data Helps Stores Like Macy's and Kohl's Track You Like Never Before," by Barbara Thau, *Forbes,* January 24, 2014; "The Risks of Big Data for Companies," by John Jordan, *Wall Street Journal,* October 20, 2013; "Fashion Industry Meets Big Data," by Kathy Gordon, *Wall Street Journal,* September 8, 2013; "Wal-Mart Puts Its Faith in Big Data for Mobile Strategy," by Cadie Thompson, Cnbc.com, May 22, 2013.

highly skilled, educated workforce. For instance, to provide legal services, you need lawyers with law degrees. Law firms are required to process enormous amounts of textual information. Likewise with medical services. Financial services are not so knowledge-intensive, but require much larger investments in information processing just to keep track of transactions and investments. In fact, the financial services sector is the largest investor in information technology, with over 80% of invested capital going to information technology equipment and services.

Services differ in the amount of personalization and customization required, although just about all services entail some personalization or customization. Some services, such as legal, medical, and accounting services, require extensive personalization—the adjustment of a service to the precise needs of a single individual or object. Others, such as financial services, benefit from customization by allowing individuals to choose from a restricted menu. The ability of Internet and e-commerce technology to personalize and customize service, or components of service, is a major factor undergirding the extremely rapid growth of e-commerce services. Future expansion of e-services will depend in part on the ability of e-commerce firms to transform their customized services—choosing from a list—into truly personalized services, such as providing unique advice and consultation based on a digital yet intimate understanding of the client (at least as intimate as professional service providers).

9.5   ONLINE FINANCIAL SERVICES

The online financial services sector is a shining example of an e-commerce success story, but one with many twists and turns. While the innovative online firms such as E*Trade have been instrumental in transforming the brokerage industry, the impacts of e-commerce on the large, powerful banking, insurance, and real estate firms have been delayed by consumer resistance and the lack of industry innovation. For instance, online-only banks have not displaced or transformed the large national banks or even regional and local banks. But e-commerce has nevertheless transformed the banking and financial industries, as the major institutions have deployed their own online applications to service an increasingly connected online customer base. Insurance has become more standardized and easier to purchase online. Although security is still a concern, consumers are much more willing to trust online sites with their financial information than in the past. Firms such as Mint (now owned by Quicken), SmartyPig, Credit Karma, Moven, and Simple (now owned by Spanish banking giant BBVA) continue to show growth. Multi-channel, established financial services firms—the slow followers—also continue to show modest gains in online transactions.

ONLINE FINANCIAL CONSUMER BEHAVIOR

Surveys show that consumers are attracted to financial sites because of their desire to save time and access information rather than save money, although saving money is an important goal among the most sophisticated online financial households. Most online consumers use financial services sites for mundane financial management, such as checking balances of existing accounts, and paying bills, most of which were established offline. Once accustomed to performing mundane financial management activities, consumers move on to more sophisticated capabilities such as using personal financial management tools, making loan payments, and considering offers from online institutions.

ONLINE BANKING AND BROKERAGE

NetBank and Wingspan Bank pioneered online banking in the United States in 1996 and 1997, respectively. Although late by a year or two, the established brand-name national banks have taken a substantial lead in market share as the percentage of their customers who bank online has grown rapidly. The top banks are all large, national banks that also offer online banking: Bank of America, JPMorgan Chase, Citigroup, Wells Fargo, and Capital One. The major direct banks (those that operate without a network of branches or branded ATMs) include Ally, Discover, Capital One 360, State Farm, and USAA. These direct banks have seen customer deposits grow faster than regular banks, indicating their growing popularity, particularly with younger customers. Several start-ups have also moved into the online banking and financial services spaces. For instance, Moven offers debit account services linked with online and mobile financial management tools. Simple, owned by Spanish bank BBVA, provides checking accounts linked to debit cards in addition to financial management tools.

In 2015, about 140 million American adults (over 55% of the adult U.S. population) are expected to use online banking, and this number is projected to grow to 162 million (over 60%) by 2019. Over 104 million use mobile devices, with 93 million using a mobile phone, and 56 million using a tablet computer. While online banking has become a primary banking channel for age groups, Millennials (those in the 18- to 34-year-old group) are adopting mobile banking at a much higher rate than those who are older. Top mobile banking activities include checking balances and bank statements, viewing recent transactions, transferring money from one account to another, paying bills, making bill payments, and depositing checks using smartphone apps that snap a photo of the check. Security issues still deter some. A survey by Javelin Strategy & Research found that about 45% of those surveyed cited security concerns as the reason why they did not use mobile banking services (eMarketer, 2015d, 2015e; Chaudhuri, 2014).

From the bank's perspective, online and mobile banking can provide significant cost savings. According to Javelin Strategy & Research, the average in-person transaction at a bank branch costs $4.25, while an online transaction costs 19 cents, and a mobile transaction, just 10 cents (Javelin Strategy & Research, 2013).

The history of online brokerage has been similar to that of online banking. Early innovators such as E*Trade have been displaced from their leadership positions in terms of numbers of online accounts by discount broker pioneer Charles Schwab and financial industry giant Fidelity (which has more mutual fund customers and more funds under management than any other U.S. firm).

According to comScore, almost 50 million U.S. Internet users have access to an online brokerage account and online trading sites averaged about 10.8 million visitors a month. Over 33% of visitors use a mobile device, or both a mobile device and a computer (comScore, 2014a, 2014b). The most frequent activities conducted on mobile devices include monitoring one's portfolio and the market, getting stock quotes, placing

TABLE 9.6	TOP ONLINE BROKERAGES, 2015
FIRM	NUMBER OF UNIQUE VISITORS (IN MILLIONS)
Fidelity	6.37
Vanguard	3.35
Schwab	2.72
E*Trade	1.63
ML (Merrill Lynch)	1.39
TD Ameritrade	1.36
Scottrade	1.33

SOURCES: Based on data from Compete.com, 2015

and checking on orders, and doing general financial research. The top trading Web site among U.S. Internet users in 2015 is Fidelity Investments, with around 6.3 million monthly unique visitors (see **Table 9.6**). The major online brokerage firms are investing significantly in search engine marketing, and are among the biggest spenders in the paid search market. They are also increasingly using social media to engage with customers, although they must be careful to comply with all regulations and rules as they do so. For instance, some brokerage firms use Twitter to deliver commentary, company information, marketing, and customer service. As with banking, Millennials use mobile devices for investment services with much greater frequency than older investors (eMarketer, 2015f).

Multi-Channel vs. Pure Online Financial Services Firms

Online consumers prefer to visit financial services sites that have physical outlets or branches. In general, multi-channel financial services firms that have both physical branches or offices and solid online offerings are growing faster than pure-online firms that have no physical presence, and they are assuming market leadership as well. Traditional banking firms have literally thousands of branches where customers can open accounts, deposit money, take out loans, find home mortgages, and rent a safety deposit box. Top online brokerage firms do not have the same physical footprint as the banks do, but each has a strong physical presence or telephone presence to strengthen its online presence. Fidelity has walk-in service center branches, but it relies primarily on the telephone for interacting with investors. Charles Schwab has investment centers around the country as an integral part of its online strategy. Pure-online banks and brokerages cannot provide customers with some services that still require a face-to-face interaction.

Financial Portals and Account Aggregators

financial portals
sites that provide consumers with comparison shopping services, independent financial advice, and financial planning

Financial portals are sites that provide consumers with comparison shopping services, independent financial advice, and financial planning. Independent portals do not themselves offer financial services, but act as steering mechanisms to online providers. They generate revenue from advertising, referral fees, and subscription fees. For example, Yahoo's financial portal, Yahoo Finance, offers consumers the ability to track their stock portfolio, market overviews, real-time stock quotes, news, financial advice, and streaming video interviews with financial leaders. Other independent financial portals include Intuit's Quicken, MSN's MSN Money, and CNNMoney. A host of financial portal sites have sprung up to help consumers with financial management and planning such as Mint (owned by Quicken), SmartPiggy, and Credit Karma.

Account aggregation is the process of pulling together all of a customer's financial (and even nonfinancial) data at a single personalized Web site, including brokerage, banking, insurance, loans, frequent flyer miles, personalized news, and much more. For example, a consumer can see his or her TD Ameritrade brokerage account, Fidelity 401(k) account, Travelers Insurance annuity account, and American Airlines frequent flyer miles all displayed on a single site. The idea is to provide consumers with a holistic view of their entire portfolio of assets, no matter what financial institution actually holds those assets.

> **account aggregation**
> the process of pulling together all of a customer's financial (and even nonfinancial) data at a single personalized Web site

The leading provider of account aggregation technology is Yodlee. It uses screen-scraping and other techniques to pull information from 14,000 different data sources. A smart-mapping technology is also used so that if the underlying Web sites change, the scraping software can adapt and still find the relevant information. Today, Yodlee is used by 800 leading financial institutions and companies, including 9 of the 15 largest U.S. banks, and this network reaches more than 100 million end users (Yodlee, 2015).

ONLINE MORTGAGE AND LENDING SERVICES

During the early days of e-commerce, hundreds of firms launched pure-play online mortgage sites to capture the U.S. home mortgage market. Early entrants hoped to radically simplify and transform the traditional mortgage value chain process, dramatically speed up the loan closing process, and share the economies with consumers by offering lower rates.

By 2003, over half of these early-entry, pure-online firms had failed. Early pure-play online mortgage institutions had difficulties developing a brand name at an affordable price and failed to simplify the mortgage generation process. They ended up suffering from high start-up and administrative costs, high customer acquisition costs, rising interest rates, and poor execution of their strategies.

Despite this rocky start, the online mortgage market is slowly growing; it is dominated by established online banks and other online financial services firms, traditional mortgage vendors, and a few successful online mortgage firms.

Many mortgage shoppers research mortgages online, but few actually apply online because of the complexity of mortgages. Most mortgages today are written by intermediary mortgage brokers, with banks still playing an important origination role but generally not servicing mortgages they originate.

Although online mortgage originations currently represent a small percentage of all mortgages, their number is expected to continue to grow slowly but surely over the next several years.

Consumer benefits from online mortgages include reduced application times, market interest rate intelligence, and process simplification that occurs when participants in the mortgage process (title, insurance, and lending companies) share a common information base. Mortgage lenders benefit from the cost reduction involved in online processing of applications, while charging rates marginally lower than traditional bricks-and-mortar institutions.

Nevertheless, the online mortgage industry has not transformed the process of obtaining a mortgage. A significant brake on market expansion is the complexity of the mortgage process, which requires physical signatures and documents, multiple institutions, and complex financing details—such as closing costs and points—that are difficult for shoppers to compare across vendors. Nevertheless, as in other areas, the ability of shoppers to find low mortgage rates online has helped reduce the fees and interest rates charged by traditional mortgage lenders.

ONLINE INSURANCE SERVICES

In 1995, the price of a $500,000 20-year term life policy for a healthy 40-year-old male was $995 a year. In 2015, the same policy could be had for around $345—a decline of about 65%—while other prices have risen 15% in the same period. In a study of the term life insurance business, Brown and Goolsbee discovered that Internet usage led to an 8%–15% decline in term life insurance prices industry-wide (both offline and online), and increased consumer surplus by about $115 million per year (and hence reduced industry profits by the same amount) (Brown and Goolsbee, 2000). Price dispersion for term life policies initially increased, but then fell as more and more people began using the Internet to obtain insurance quotes.

Unlike books and CDs, where online price dispersion is higher than offline, and in many cases online prices are higher than offline, term life insurance stands out as one product group supporting the conventional wisdom that the Internet will lower search costs, increase price comparison, and lower prices to consumers. Term life insurance is a commodity product, however, and in other insurance product lines, the Web offers insurance companies new opportunities for product and service differentiation and price discrimination.

The insurance industry forms a major part of the financial services sector. It has four major segments: automobile, life, health, and property and casualty. Insurance products can be very complex. For example, there are many different types of non-automotive property and casualty insurance: liability, fire, homeowners, commercial, workers' compensation, marine, accident, and other lines such as vacation insurance. Writing an insurance policy in any of these areas is very information-intense, often necessitating personal inspection of the properties, and it requires considerable actuarial experience and data. The life insurance industry has also developed life insurance policies that defy easy comparison and can only be explained and sold by an experienced sales agent. Historically, the insurance industry has relied on thousands of local insurance offices and agents to sell complex products uniquely suited to the circumstances of the insured person and the property. Complicating the insurance marketplace is the fact that the insurance industry is not federally regulated, but rather is regulated by 50 different state insurance commissions that are strongly influenced by local insurance agents. Before a Web site can offer quotations on insurance, it must obtain a license to enter the insurance business in all the states where it provides quotation services or sells insurance.

Like the online mortgage industry, the online insurance industry has been very successful in attracting visitors who are looking to obtain prices and terms of insurance policies. While many national insurance underwriting companies initially did not offer competitive products directly online because it might injure the business operations of their traditional local agents, the Web sites of almost all of the major firms now provide the ability to obtain an online quote. Even if consumers do not actually purchase insurance policies online, the Internet has proven to have a powerful influence on consumer insurance decisions by dramatically reducing search costs and changing the price discovery process. According to a 2015 survey, over 70% of American consumers looked for life insurance information online, with 30% indicating that the Internet was their most valuable source of information. However, consumers also continue to rely on financial advisors as well for advice, with over half seeking information from both sources (LIMRA, 2015). Another survey found that nearly 2 in 3 consumers who own a mobile device said they already have or plan to use those devices to access services to their life insurance policies, although currently only about 30% of life insurance services have such capabilities (LIMRA, 2014a). Other forms of insurance are more likely to be purchased online. For instance, according to a 2014 comScore study, the online channel continues to be consumers' preferred method for shopping for auto insurance policies, with over 70% of shoppers getting an online quote. Over 35% indicated that they would likely purchase auto insurance online in the future, up 5% from 2011 (comScore, 2014c). Insurance companies are also making increased use of social media. For instance, a LIMRA survey found that over 90% of life insurance companies had social media programs, up from 60% in 2010. Facebook and LinkedIn are the most popular platforms, both used by over 90% (LIMRA, 2014b). All of the major insurers, such as GEICO, Allstate, State Farm, Progressive, and Travelers, have a significant online presence. Some of the leading online insurance services companies include InsWeb, Insure.com, Insurance.com, QuickQuote, and NetQuote.

ONLINE REAL ESTATE SERVICES

During the early days of e-commerce, real estate seemed ripe for an Internet revolution that would rationalize this historically local, complex, and local agent-driven industry that monopolized the flow of consumer information. Potentially, the Internet and e-commerce might have disintermediated this huge marketspace, allowing buyers and sellers, renters and owners, to transact directly, lower search costs to near zero, and dramatically reduce prices. However, this did not happen. What did happen is extremely beneficial to buyers and sellers, as well as to real estate agents. At one point, there were an estimated 100,000 real estate sites on the Internet worldwide. Many of these sites have disappeared. However, the remaining online sites have started to make headway toward transforming the industry. In addition, most local real estate brokers in the United States have their own agency Web sites to deal with clients, in addition to participating with thousands of other agencies in multiple listing services that list homes online. Some of the major online real estate sites are Realtor.com and its parent, Move.com (now owned by global media giant News Corp.), Zillow and Trulia (now owned by the same company), HomeGain, ZipRealty, Craigslist, and Redfin. Zillow and Trulia together account for about 30% of all desktop and mobile visits to real estate sites in 2015, while Realtor.com attracts about 11% of traffic (Hagey, 2015).

Real estate differs from other types of online financial services because it is impossible to complete a property transaction online. Clearly, the major impact of Internet real estate sites is in influencing offline decisions. The Internet has become a compelling method for real estate professionals, homebuilders, property managers and owners, and ancillary service providers to communicate with and provide information to consumers. According to the National Association of Realtors, 93% use the Internet to search for a home, with 50% using a mobile Website or app as part of the search. For many of these (43%), looking online was the first step in the process. At the same time, 88% used the services of a real estate agent to complete the purchase (National Association of Realtors, 2014).

The primary service offered by real estate sites is a listing of houses available. In August 2015, Realtor.com, the official site of the National Association of Realtors, listed over 4 million homes and had over 11 million unique visitors. Listings typically feature detailed property descriptions, multiple photographs, and virtual 360-degree tours. Consumers can link to mortgage lenders, credit reporting agencies, house inspectors, and surveyors. There are also online loan calculators, appraisal reports, sales price histories by neighborhood, school district data, crime reports, and social and historical information on neighborhoods. Some online real estate brokers now charge substantially less than traditional offline brokers who typically charge 6% of the sale price. They can do this because the buyers (and in some cases, the sellers) do much of the work of traditional real estate agents, such as prospecting, choosing neighborhoods, and identifying houses of interest prior to contacting an online agent. For instance, Move (the parent company of Realtor.com) also offers a "Find a Neighborhood" feature that allows users to choose the type of neighborhood they want to live in by weighing factors such as the quality (and tax costs) of schools, age of the population, number of families with children nearby, and available social and recreational services. Move also offers mobile apps for the iPad and iPhone, Android, and Windows phones. For instance, the Area Scout function allows users to see the list prices of all homes in a neighborhood on the street level.

Despite the revolution in available information, there has not been a revolution in the industry value chain. The listings available on Web sites are provided by local multiple listing services supported by local real estate agents. Sometimes, addresses of the houses are not available, and online users are directed to the local listing agent who is hired by the seller. Traditional hands-on real estate brokers will show the house and handle all transactions with the owner to preserve their fees, typically ranging from 5% to 6% of the transaction.

9.6 ONLINE TRAVEL SERVICES

Online travel is one of the most successful B2C e-commerce segments, and accounts for almost one-third of all U.S. B2C ecommerce revenues in 2015. The Internet has become the most common channel used by consumers to research travel options, seek the best possible prices, and book reservations for airline tickets, hotel rooms, rental cars, cruises, and tours. Today, more travel is booked online than offline. In 2015, about 134 million (over 63% of all U.S. Internet users) are expected to research travel and over 110 million will book travel online. Online travel services revenues are expected to reach almost $170 billion in 2015, and continue growing to over $200 billion by 2019 (see **Figure 9.5**) (eMarketer, Inc., 2015g).

FIGURE 9.5	ONLINE TRAVEL SERVICES REVENUES

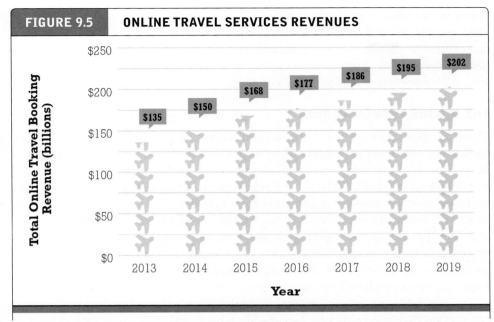

U.S. online leisure/unmanaged business travel service revenues has resumed growing and is expected to reach over $200 billion by 2019.

SOURCE: Based on data from eMarketer, Inc., 2015g.

WHY ARE ONLINE TRAVEL SERVICES SO POPULAR?

Online travel sites offer consumers a one-stop, convenient, leisure and business travel experience where travelers can find content (descriptions of vacations and facilities), community (chat groups and bulletin boards), commerce (purchase of all travel elements), and customer service (usually through call centers). Online sites offer much more information and many more travel options than traditional travel agents. For suppliers—the owners of hotels, rental cars, and airlines—the online sites aggregate millions of consumers into singular, focused customer pools that can be efficiently reached through on-site advertising and promotions. Online sites create a much more efficient marketplace, bringing consumers and suppliers together in a low-transaction cost environment.

Travel services are an ideal service for the Internet, and therefore e-commerce business models work well for this product. Travel is an information-intensive product requiring significant consumer research. It is a digital product in the sense that travel requirements—planning, researching, comparison shopping, reserving, and payment—can be accomplished for the most part online in a digital environment. On the travel reservation side, travel does not require any "inventory": there are no physical assets. And the suppliers of the product—owners of hotels, airlines, rental cars, vacation rooms, and tour guides—are highly fragmented and often have excess capacity. Always looking for customers to fill vacant rooms and rent idle cars, suppliers will be anxious to lower prices and willing to advertise on Web sites that can attract millions of consumers. The online intermediaries—such as Travelocity, Expedia, and others—do not have to deploy thousands of travel agents in physical offices across the country but can instead concentrate on a single interface with a national consumer audience.

Travel services do not require the kind of expensive multi-channel "physical presence" strategy required of financial services (although they generally operate centralized call centers to provide personal customer service). Therefore, travel services "scale" better, permitting earnings to grow faster than costs. But these efficiencies also make it hard for reservation sites to make a profit.

THE ONLINE TRAVEL MARKET

There are four major sectors in the travel market: airline tickets, hotel reservations, car rentals, and travel packages. Airline tickets are the source of the greatest amount of revenue in online travel. Airline reservations are largely a commodity. They can be easily described online. The same is true with car rentals; most people can reliably rent a car over the phone or online and expect to obtain what they ordered. Although hotels are somewhat more difficult to describe, hotel branding, supplemented by Web sites that include descriptions, photographs, and virtual tours, typically provides enough information to most consumers to allow them to feel as if they know what they are purchasing, making them comfortable enough to make hotel reservations online. Travel packages purchased online constituted the smallest percentage of travel sales.

Increasingly, corporations are outsourcing their travel offices entirely to vendors who can provide Web-based solutions, high-quality service, and lower costs. Online vendors to corporations provide **corporate online booking solutions (COBS)** that provide integrated airline, hotel, conference center, and auto rental services at a single site.

corporate online booking solutions (COBS)

provide integrated airline, hotel, conference center, and auto rental services at a single site

ONLINE TRAVEL INDUSTRY DYNAMICS

Because much of what travel agency sites offer is a commodity, and thus they face the same costs, competition among online providers is intense. Price competition is difficult because shoppers, as well as online site managers, can comparison shop easily. Therefore, competition among sites tends to focus on scope of offerings, ease of use, payment options, and personalization. Some well-known travel sites are listed in **Table 9.7**.

The online travel services industry has gone through a period of intense consolidation. Expedia now owns Travelocity, Orbitz, CheapTickets, Hotels.com, Hotwire, and meta-search engine Trivago, giving it a 75% market share among U.S. online travel agencies. Its primary competition consists of Priceline, which owns Booking.com, Lowestfare.com, and Kayak. Together, Expedia and Priceline control a whopping 95% of the online travel agency booking market. However, Google is also poised to become a player in the market, with its Google Flights and Google Hotel Finder that also provides booking functionality. The U.S. Department of Justice also cited the TripAdvisor's introduction of an Instant Booking service as a factor in its approval of Expedia's acquisition of Orbitz.

In addition to industry consolidation, the online travel industry has been roiled by meta-search engines that scour the Web for the best prices on travel and lodging, and then collect finder or affiliate fees for sending consumers to the lowest-price sites. Travel aggregator sites include Trivago, Kayak, Fly.com, and Mobissimo. These sites, in the eyes of many industry leaders, commoditize the online travel industry even further, cause excessive price competition, and divert revenues from the leading, branded firms who have made extensive investments in inventory and systems.

TABLE 9.7	**MAJOR ONLINE TRAVEL SITES**
NAME	**DESCRIPTION**
LEISURE/UNMANAGED BUSINESS TRAVEL	
Expedia	Largest online travel service; leisure focus. Now also owns Orbitz, Travelocity, CheapTickets, Hotels.com, and Hotwire.
Orbitz	Began as supplier-owned reservation system; now owned by Expedia.
Travelocity	Leisure focus. Owned by Expedia.
Priceline	Name Your Price model; leisure focus. Also owns Booking.com, and Lowestfare.com, Expedia's primary competitor.
TripAdvisor	Travel review site that also allows you to compare prices and book reservations.
CheapTickets	Discount airline tickets, hotel reservations, and auto rentals. Acquired by Expedia when it purchased Orbitz.
Hotels.com	Hotel reservation network; leisure and corporate focus. Owned by Expedia.
Hotwire	Discount fares based on airline excess inventory. Owned by Expedia.
MANAGED BUSINESS TRAVEL	
GetThere	Corporate online booking solution (COBS). Owned by Sabre Corporation.
BCD Travel	Full-service corporate travel agency.

Mobile devices and apps used for pre-trip planning, booking, check-in, and context and location-based destination information are also transforming the online travel industry (see also the case study on Orbitz's mobile strategy in Chapter 4). For instance, in 2015, about 75 million people are expected to use a mobile device to research travel, and that number is estimated to increase to 113 million by 2013. Around 45 million are expected to actually book travel using a mobile device in 2015, and that number is expected to increase to over 75 million people by 2019. Smartphones are used slightly more than tablets to both research and book travel (eMarketer, Inc., 2015h, 2015i, 2015j, 2015k). Most of the major airlines now have apps for a variety of mobile platforms to enable flight research, booking, and management. Apps from hotels and car rental companies are available from most of the major players such as Hertz and Avis for car rentals, and Best Western, Choice Hotels, Hilton, and Starwood for hotels. Apps may sometimes target specific consumer behavior. For instance, Expedia reports that 25% of its mobile hotel sales are made at properties within 10 miles of the user's current location, indicating that they are searching for and booking rooms on-the-go, as they travel. Mobile devices are also proving to be quite popular for booking at the last minute. Marriott says that 35% of its smartphone bookings are for same-day travel (eMarketer, Inc., 2014).

Social media is also having a big impact on the online travel industry. User-generated content and online reviews are having an increasing influence on travel-buying decisions. The *Insight on Society* story, *Phony Reviews,* examines some of the issues this presents for the industry.

INSIGHT ON SOCIETY

PHONY REVIEWS

People used to rely on travel agents for professional recommendations about travel destinations, hotels, and restaurants to choose while on vacation. Today, however, sites like TripAdvisor and Yelp have taken over that function. TripAdvisor has been a smashing success, with more than 100 million user-generated reviews, $1 billion in revenue, and 60 million members. Yelp has 70 million reviews of restaurants and other services, and a market capitalization of $4 billion. The sites have become trusted sources for travelers as they try to decide where to travel, what hotels to book, and where to eat. A good rating can be worth thousands of dollars in bookings. But are all those reviews for real? Can they be trusted?

Although the majority of reviews on TripAdvisor, Yelp, and related sites are probably trustworthy and 88% of users trust online reviews, fraudulent reviews are commonplace. Hotels pay people to create false identities and post favorable reviews on their properties, a practice known as "astroturfing," and also to slam competing venues. In 2013, astroturfing began to draw attention from the legal system, including the New York State Attorney General's office, which began cracking down on astroturfing by businesses giving themselves or paying for positive reviews, and a Virginia court, which ruled in 2014 that anonymous reviews aren't protected by the First Amendment unless the reviewer was a customer.

Astroturfing is just one of several types of problems with online reviews. A disgruntled consumer with an axe to grind can do a lot of damage on online review sites. For instance, Dancing Deer Mountain, a small wedding venue in Junction City, Oregon, had steady business until one wedding went horribly wrong. The proprietors said that rules about bringing in outside alcohol were broken; the situation with the wedding-goers purportedly became combative as a result. Afterwards, scathing online reviews were posted. As a result, business dropped off precipitously. The owners tried suing the reviewers but lost under Oregon law that protects free speech.

Businesses can also damage their reputations by mishandling bad reviews, phony or otherwise. An Arizona bakery went viral in 2013 after an unflattering appearance on a reality show drew negative social media attention. The bakery's owners used Facebook, Yelp, and Reddit to make personal attacks against anyone who had posted a negative review and quickly gained unwanted notoriety. In 2014, a British hotel fined two guests after they made a scathing review on TripAdvisor, but after local media scrutiny, the hotel refunded the money and vowed to improve its services.

For sites such as TripAdvisor and Yelp, the growth in phony reviews presents a considerable challenge. The authenticity and accuracy of reviews are critically important to their success, but garnering a high review score is equally important to the businesses listed on the site. Studies have found that if a business can increase its Yelp rating by one star, its revenues will increase anywhere from 5% to 9%, and in March 2014, an industry study found that small businesses using Yelp experienced annual revenue increases of $8,000. This gives businesses ample incentive to post phony reviews praising their own business and slamming their competitors. A 2013 study concluded that approximately 16% of Yelp reviews are fraudulent. With this in mind, Yelp continues to develop ways to remove suspect reviews, including those from rings of businesses who work together to fraudulently increase the ratings of each business in the group. Yelp has also developed its own filtering algorithms, which are intended to detect phony reviews.

To help business battle phony reviews, Yelp has also introduced Consumer Alerts, which inform readers when a review is likely to be fraudulent. The alerts are generated via an algorithm that monitors the site for suspicious posting patterns. While this helps to combat phony reviews, it also increases the risk that legitimate positive reviews will be flagged and removed, hurting both the reputation of the business and the reputation of the review. Since then, Yelp has released additional rounds of Consumer Alerts for over 150 businesses. Still, this is only a fraction of the total number of businesses likely committing fraud on Yelp.

TripAdvisor also claims it uses an algorithm to help filter out false reviews, although it rejects requiring would-be reviewers to supply a reservation number in order to prove that they have actually stayed at the property that they are reviewing. According to TripAdvisor, it takes the authenticity of its reviews very seriously, and has numerous methods to ensure their legitimacy, including automated site tools and a team of review integrity experts. It also relies on the review community itself to identify suspicious content and trolls the sites where businesses advertise for fake reviewers. But TripAdvisor has been fined multiple times by regulatory agencies for misrepresenting the authenticity of its reviews, including $610,000 in Italy in 2014 and $484,000 in France in 2011.

In 2015, researchers from Harvard Business School have mined and analyzed reviews from these sites to get a better understanding of what makes a review suspicious. Truthful reviewers tend to talk about specific details, while the fraudulent reviewers, not surprisingly, tended to talk more about themselves, reasons for the trip, and travel- ing companions, lacking actual experience with the venue. Positive review fraud is driven by sudden dips in reputation, and negative review fraud is driven by changing patterns in competition, like a new restaurant in the area. Most fraudulent reviews are either one or five stars, with very few in between, and fraudulent reviews of chain restaurants are very rare, since these companies are likelier to have sophisticated marketing and branding efforts that go well beyond online review sites.

Will this improved understanding of fraudulent reviews clean up TripAdvisor and Yelp once and for all? Probably not. But review sites and regulators are cracking down on phony reviews with increasing vigor. In 2013, for instance, 19 companies received fines from New York regulators totaling $350,000 for buying and selling fraudulent reviews, and in 2015 Yelp sued a company operating multiple businesses involved in selling fraudulent reviews to restaurants. To complicate matters further, a new competitor named TripExpert has also entered the fray, using aggregated scores from a variety of sources instead of customer reviews. The site claims that this will avoid many of the pitfalls of fraudulent user reviews. However, it might be the case that TripAdvisor and Yelp are actually improving service at hotels and restaurants. In Ireland, for example, reviews of hotels improved from 3.6 to 3.8 in 2014, but this was attributable to corresponding improvements in service, not fraud. The best approach is still to take what you read with a grain of salt, discarding both the overwhelmingly positive and the unrelentingly negative reviews.

SOURCES: "Fake It Till You Make It: Reputation, Competition, and Yelp Review Fraud," by Michael Luca and Georgios Zervas, Harvard Business School, July 2015; "Vacation Season Is Coming and Luckily This NYC Startup Is Here," Alleywatch.com, April 28, 2015; "TripAdvisor Reviews Are Now So Powerful They Impact the Tourist Industry of Entire Countries," by Joshua Barrie, Businessinsider.com, March 16, 2015; "Yelp Is Suing a Company for Allegedly Selling Fake Positive Reviews to Restaurants," by Lizzie Plaugic, Theverge.com, February 20, 2015; "Online Reviews: Fakes, Linguistic Analysis & Protecting Children," by Thomas A. Dickerson, Eturbonews.com, February 11, 2015; "How to Spot Fake Online Travel Reviews," by Ismat Sarah Mangla, Ibtimes.com, December 23, 2014; "The Art of the Amateur Online Review," by Michael Erard, New York Times, November 29, 2014; "Trip Advisor Bad Review 'Fine' to Be Refunded by Blackpool Hotel," Bbcnews.com, November 19, 2014; "How TripExpert, a New Review Site, Is Doing Things Differently Than TripAdvisor," Hotelchatter.com, June 12, 2014; "A Virginia Court Slams Phony Reviews," by Jill Krasny, Inc.com, January 10, 2014; "Leaving Negative Reviews Online Is Not as Safe as It Used to Be," by Alex Goldman, Onthemedia.org, January 9, 2014; "Fake Yelp Reviews: Anatomy of an 'Astroturfing' Post," by Dhiya Kuriakose, The Guardian, September 25, 2013; "Amy's Baking Co. Meltdown Begs the Question: Is Yelp Bad for Small Business?" by Caitlin Dewey, Washington Post, May 17, 2013; "Companies To Pay $350,000 Fine Over Fake Online Reviews," by Lance Whitney, Cnetnews.com, September 23, 2013; "Give Yourself 5 Stars? Online, It Might Cost You," by David Streitfeld, New York Times, September 22, 2013; "TripAdvisor: Can Users Be Sued for Bad Reviews?" by Natalie Paris, Telegraph.co.uk, September 12, 2013; "Why Yelp Will Never Be Rid of Phony Reviews," by Joshua Brustein, Businessweek.com, August 13, 2013; "Yelp Consumer Alerts: Letting You Know Before You Spend Your Dough," Yelp Official Blog, August 12, 2013; "Deceptive Reviews: The Influential Tail," Eric Anderson and Duncan Simester, MIT, May 2013.

9.7 ONLINE CAREER SERVICES

Next to travel services, one of the Internet's most successful online services has been job services (recruitment sites) that provide a free posting of individual resumes, plus many other related career services; for a fee, they also list job openings posted by companies. Career services sites collect revenue from other sources as well, by providing value-added services to users and collecting fees from related service providers.

The online job market is dominated by two large players: Monster, with about 9 million unique monthly visitors, and CareerBuilder, with about 5 million. Job listing aggregators, such as Indeed (22 million unique visitors), Glassdoor (12 million), and and SimplyHired (4 million) are also very popular. The social network site LinkedIn has also become an increasingly important player in this market (see the opening case in Chapter 11).

Traditionally, companies have relied on five employee recruitment tools: classified and print advertising, career expos (or trade shows), on-campus recruiting, private employment agencies (now called "staffing firms"), and internal referral programs. In comparison to online recruiting, these tools have severe limitations. Print advertising usually includes a per-word charge that limits the amount of detail employers provide about a job opening, as well as a limited time period within which the job is posted. Career expos do not allow for pre-screening of attendees and are limited by the amount of time a recruiter can spend with each candidate. Staffing firms charge high fees and have a limited, usually local, selection of job hunters. On-campus recruiting also restricts the number of candidates a recruiter can speak with during a normal visit and requires that employers visit numerous campuses. And internal referral programs may encourage employees to propose unqualified candidates for openings in order to qualify for rewards or incentives offered.

Online recruiting overcomes these limitations, providing a more efficient and cost-effective means of linking employers and potential employees, while reducing the total time to hire. Online recruiting enables job hunters to more easily build, update, and distribute their resumes while gathering information about prospective employers and conducting job searches.

IT'S JUST INFORMATION: THE IDEAL WEB BUSINESS?

Online recruitment is ideally suited for the Web. The hiring process is an information-intense business process that involves discovering the skills and salary requirements of individuals and matching them with available jobs. In order to accomplish this matchup, there does not initially need to be face-to-face interaction, or a great deal of personalization. Prior to the Internet, this information sharing was accomplished locally by human networks of friends, acquaintances, former employers, and relatives, in addition to employment agencies that developed paper files on job hunters. The Internet can clearly automate this flow of information, reducing search time and costs for all parties.

Table 9.8 lists some of the most popular recruitment sites.

Why are so many job hunters and employers using Internet job sites? Recruitment sites are popular largely because they save time and money for both job hunters and

TABLE 9.8	POPULAR ONLINE RECRUITMENT SITES	
RECRUITMENT SITE	**BRIEF DESCRIPTION**	
GENERAL RECRUITMENT SITES		
Monster	One of the first commercial online sites in 1994. Today, a public company offering general job searches in 50 countries.	
CareerBuilder	Owned by Tegna (formerly Gannett), Tribune, and McClatchy (all newspaper companies). Provides job search for more than 10,000 Web sites, including AOL, and 140 newspapers; over 1 million jobs listed.	
Indeed	Job site aggregator	
SimplyHired	Job site aggregator	
Craigslist	Popular classified listing service focused on local recruiting	
Glassdoor	Best known for anonymous reviews of companies and management posted by current and former employees, but also has listings for millions of jobs.	
EXECUTIVE SEARCH SITES		
Futurestep	Korn/Ferry site, low-end executive recruiting	
Spencerstuart	Middle-level executive recruiting	
ExecuNet	Executive search firm	
NICHE JOB SITES		
SnagAJob	Part-time and hourly jobs	
USAJobs	Federal government jobs	
HigherEdJobs	Education industry	
EngineerJobs	Engineering jobs	
Medzilla	Biotechnology, pharmaceutical, medical, and healthcare industry	
Showbizjobs	Entertainment industry	
Salesjobs	Sales and marketing	
Dice	Information technology jobs	
MBAGlobalNet	MBA-oriented community site	

employers seeking recruits. For employers, the job boards expand the geographical reach of their searches, lower costs, and result in faster hiring decisions.

For job seekers, online sites are popular not only because their resumes can be made widely available to recruiters but also because of a variety of other related job-hunting services. The services delivered by online recruitment sites have greatly expanded since their emergence in 1996. Originally, online recruitment sites just provided a digital version of newspaper classified ads. Today's sites offer many other services, including skills assessment, personality assessment questionnaires, personalized account management for job hunters, organizational culture assessments, job search tools, employer blocking (prevents your employer from seeing your posting), employee blocking (prevents your employees from seeing your listings if you are their employer), and e-mail notification. Online sites also provide a number of educational services such as resume writing advice, software skills preparation, and interview tips.

For the most part, online recruitment sites work, in the sense of linking job hunters with jobs, but they are just one of many ways people actually find jobs. A survey by The Conference Board found that the majority (70%) of job seekers rely equally on both the Internet and newspapers to look for jobs, with about half relying on word-of-mouth leads, and about a quarter on employment agencies. Given that the cost of posting a resume online is zero, the marginal returns are very high.

The ease with which resumes can be posted online has also raised new issues for both job recruiters and job seekers. If you are an employer, how do you sort through the thousands of resumes you may receive when posting an open job? If you are a job seeker, how do you stand out among the thousands or even millions of others? Perhaps one way is to post a video resume. In a survey by Vault, nearly nine in 10 employers said they would watch a video resume if it were submitted to them, in part because it would help them better assess a candidate's professional presentation and demeanor, and over half said they believed video would become a common addition to future job applications. CareerBuilder became the first major online job site to implement a video resume tool for job candidates, following a previous launch for an online video brand-building tool for employers.

Perhaps one of the most important functions of online recruitment sites is not so much their capacity to actually match employers with job hunters but their ability to establish market prices and terms, as well as trends in the labor market. Online recruitment sites identify salary levels for both employers and job hunters and categorize the skill sets required to achieve those salary levels. In this sense, online recruitment sites are online national marketplaces that establish the terms of trade in labor markets. The existence of online national job sites should lead to a rationalization of wages, greater labor mobility, and higher efficiency in recruitment and operations because employers will be able to quickly find the people they need.

ONLINE RECRUITMENT INDUSTRY TRENDS

Trends for 2015–2016 in the online recruitment services industry include the following:

- **Social recruiting:** According to a recent survey of over 1,400 recruiters and human resource professionals, 92% use social recruiting, with LinkedIn being a primary resource (Jobvite, 2015). LinkedIn, probably the most well-known business-oriented social network, has grown significantly to over 380 million members representing over 170 different industries in over 200 countries as of September 2015. LinkedIn's corporate hiring solutions are used by over 90 of the Fortune 100 companies, and more than 3 million companies have a LinkedIn page. Consumers are using sites such as LinkedIn to establish business contacts and networks. For instance, according to LinkedIn, its members do almost 6 billion professionally-oriented searches on LinkedIn a year. Employers are also using LinkedIn to conduct searches to find potential job candidates that may not be actively job hunting. For instance, LinkedIn offers companies a feature called LinkedIn Talent Solutions that includes tools that help corporate recruiters find "passive talent" (people who are not actively looking for a new job), as well as custom company profiles that are specifically designed for recruitment. According to LinkedIn Talent Solutions, U.S. company reliance on social recruiting to find quality employees has increased by over 50% since 2011, with 46% of those surveyed indicating that social recruiting was the most important source for key positions (LinkedIn Talent Solutions, 2015). Social network sites are also being used by employers to "check up" on the background of job candidates. A study by Harris Interactive of over 2,000 managers and human resource employees found that over 50% are using social networks to screen job candidates, and almost 50% have rejected candidates because of content on a social site. Employers typically search Facebook, Twitter, and LinkedIn. Provocative or inappropriate photos were the biggest negative factor followed by drinking and drug references. However, on the flip side, recruiters also noted that not having any online presence at all also hurts candidates, with more than a third indicating that they would be less likely to interview a job candidate if they cannot find information about that person online (Careerbuilder, 2015).

- **Mobile:** As with other forms of services, career services firms have also moved onto the mobile platform. A recent survey found that mobile devices were the primary devices used by Millennials and Gen X to search for jobs (eMarketer, Inc., 2015x). To reach this audience, CareerBuilder, Monster, LinkedIn, and most of the other major sites all have a mobile Web site, as well as apps that allow job seekers to create and upload resumes, search jobs by keyword, location, and company, e-mail jobs, browse and apply, and more. LinkedIn's app, for instance, can also recommend jobs based on data you provide on your profile page. In 2015, mobile accounts for 52% of the unique members visiting LinkedIn.

- **Job search engines/aggregators:** As with travel services, search engines that focus specifically on jobs are posing a new threat to established online career sites. For instance, Indeed, SimplyHired, and Us.jobs "scrape" listings from thousands of online job sites such as Monster, CareerBuilder, specialty recruiting services, and the sites of individual employers to provide a free, searchable index of thousands of job listings in one spot. Because these firms do not charge employers a listing fee, they are currently using a pay-per-click or other advertising revenue model.

- **Data analytics and algorithms:** Companies are increasingly using Big Data technologies in the hiring process, as well as adaptive algorithms that help them match job seekers to job openings.

- **Hiring by algorithm:** Companies are increasingly using algorithms to sift online job applications, focusing on key words to match job seekers with jobs.

9.8 ON-DEMAND SERVICE COMPANIES

On-demand service companies provide a platform that enables the on-demand delivery of various services, by connecting providers ("sellers") who wish to exploit their "spare" resources, such as cars, rooms with beds, and ability to perform various services

TABLE 9.9	EXAMPLES OF ON-DEMAND SERVICE FIRMS
FIRM	SERVICES ENABLED
Airbnb	Lodging
Uber	Transportation
Lyft	Transportation
Task Rabbit	Errand and household tasks
Instacart	Grocery shopping
GrubHub	Restaurant food delivery
Homejoy	Household tasks
Washio	Laundry
Postmates	Courier
Zeel	Massages

via their personal labor, with consumers ("buyers") who would like to utilize those resources and services. Other common phrases sometimes used to describe these online businesses are "sharing economy," "collaborative commerce," "peer to peer consumption," "mesh economy," and "we-commerce." However, unlike traditional sharing where there is no fee charged in the transaction, these firms collect a fee from both sellers and buyers for using their platforms (Rosenberg, 2013). In the last few years, hundreds of startups, funded by over $26 billion in venture capital, have created a plethora of such platforms that allow owners of resources that are underutilized to sell access to those resources to consumers who would prefer not to, or are unable to, buy those resources themselves (Needleman and Loten, 2014; Friedman, 2014).

A number of these on-demand service firms have grown exponentially over the last five years. **Table 9.9** describes just a few of the hundreds of firms whose business model is to provide transaction platforms that enable the on-demand delivery of various services. See the *Insight on Business* case, *Food on Demand: Instacart and GrubHub,* for a look at two of these companies focused on the delivery of food on demand.

Collaborative commerce, trading platforms, and peer-to-peer commerce are not new. While eBay involves the sale of items at auction or for fixed prices, on-demand service firms provide sell access to cars, room, spaces, and even skilled people. What is new about these firms is their use of mobile and Internet technology to enable transactions on their platforms. This is especially true of the car and lodging services where transactions are local and mobile. Second, the growth of these firms is supported by the use of online reputation systems based on peer review, to establish a trusted environment where sellers and consumers can feel confident transacting with one another. Online peer review of both the providers and the consumers helps to ensure that both parties have acceptable reputations, and that a high quality of service is provided. These firms have learned from eBay and Netflix the importance of peer reviews

INSIGHT ON BUSINESS

FOOD ON DEMAND: INSTACART AND GRUBHUB

It seems as if, every day, a new on-demand service company pops up that describes itself as the "Uber" of something. For example, Zeel is the Uber of massages, allowing users to bring a massage therapist directly to their location. Buddytruk is the Uber for pickup trucks, allowing users to quickly get help with moving goods from place to place. These types of businesses are relatively easy to create, requiring only a robust and easy-to-use app platform where customers can seek out these services, and a team of freelancers willing to provide these services, whether they be drivers, massage therapists, or anything else.

It's no surprise, then, that a host of companies have launched on-demand services for the $638 billion grocery and convenience goods market, as well as for the nearly $700 billion restaurant market. In the past, services like Webvan and Kozmo attempted to popularize this model of buying groceries, but failed. Online food services have remained a relatively untapped area of potential e-commerce growth. However, the time may now be right for online grocery and restaurant delivery to take off. Instacart, one of the leaders in on-demand grocery delivery, and GrubHub, a fast growing on-demand restaurant delivery service, are two of the biggest companies in this emerging market.

Instacart is a service that allows users to order groceries on the Web or via the Instacart app. Instacart then connects you with dedicated shoppers nearby who buy and deliver the groceries from local stores. The company has 300 full-time employees, as well as 1,200 part-time employees and 7,000 contract workers, most of whom are dedicated shoppers. Instacart serves 18 cities in the United States and is growing quickly into new cities. Instacart's key demographics are Millennials, office workers, and urbanites, as well as senior citizens. The prospect of ordering groceries from their favorite stores without the hassle of driving and standing in line is attractive to many users, especially those without a car.

For a company like Instacart, the online experience is critical, whether it be on the Web or via app. Instacart's app for its dedicated shoppers has been optimized for the fastest possible shopping experience. The app allows shoppers to determine exactly where requested items are located using aisle navigation. It updates shoppers in real time when products aren't available, and provides highly customizable options to replace them from a catalog of 4 million products. In-app chat allows shoppers to communicate with customers. A barcode scanning feature allows shoppers to verify that they've picked the correct item for customers.

Instacart is growing quickly, with $100 million in revenue in 2014, a tenfold increase over its 2013 revenue. Many stores, such as Whole Foods, have reported noticeable increases in sales since entering into agreements with Instacart. In 2014, Instacart obtained $200 million in venture capital at a $2 billion valuation, and investors haven't been shy about supporting Instacart as it expands its grocery delivery platform and eventually seeks to grow that platform into other areas, like restaurants. Instacart expects to use that money to grow organically as well as via key acquisitions.

The on-demand restaurant delivery market already has a host of companies jockeying for position, however, and the most prominent of these in

(continued)

the United States is GrubHub. GrubHub is a service that allows users to buy food from local restaurants and have it delivered. Using the GrubHub app, users can type in their address and see a map of all of the local restaurants that deliver in the area, as well as restaurants that offer food for pickup. Filters allow app users to narrow options by name, menu item, or style of cuisine, and users can order by phone or online. GrubHub also offers special deals, reviews, and other perks for diners. For restaurants that aren't big enough to have their own mobile app, partnering with GrubHub is a great way to increase their exposure and bring in more customers from mobile users. GrubHub currently works with approximately 35,000 restaurants.

GrubHub went public in 2014, and its 2015 share price reflects its solid growth. GrubHub posted a 46% increase in active diners over that span, reading over five million active diners. The average number of meals ordered per day rose 30%. And most importantly, the company is profitable even while it works to continue its growth via acquisitions. GrubHub purchased two meal delivery services in 2015, Boston-based DiningIn and California-based Restaurants on the Run, for a combined $80 million, and GrubHub is working to expand its service even to restaurants that don't normally have the capability to deliver food.

However, GrubHub's future as a dominant service in on-demand restaurant delivery is far from guaranteed. Bigger rivals with cash to burn have entered the fray, such as Yelp, which purchased an online ordering and delivery platform in 2015, signaling a desire to compete with GrubHub. Amazon is testing a similar service to Instacart, AmazonFresh, in Seattle, New York, and Los Angeles, and could represent an eventual threat to GrubHub as well, as does Uber, which launched UberEats, a restaurant delivery service in a number of cities, in 2015. Square, the online payment services company that purchased high-end food delivery company Caviar for $90 million in 2014, may also be a potential competitor. Even Google is considering entering this arena, potentially using its commanding position in search to offer an option to deliver food when users search for restaurants on their mobile phones. And in Europe and other areas outside the United States, Rocket Internet operates on-demand restaurant delivery services in 71 countries and is the market leader in 59 of these, including in China, India, Mexico, Indonesia, and Nigeria, areas with low Internet penetration and good growth potential. GrubHub currently operates only in the United States and London, which are much closer to saturated areas of growth.

Despite the risks and challenges on the horizon, Instacart and GrubHub are well positioned going forward. Both have posted solid growth rates, which should increase their efficiency by reducing cost per delivery and allowing both companies to bundle deliveries from multiple grocery stores or restaurants. And both have robust, highly customizable app platforms both for users and the dedicated shoppers and drivers. This time around, on-demand grocery and food delivery looks like it's here to stay.

SOURCES: "Lyft vs. Uber," Lyftvsuber.com, accessed September 25, 2014; "Uber Reaches Deal with New York on Surge Pricing in Emergencies," by Mike Isaac, *New York Times,* July 8, 2014; "Police to Start Ticketing Uber Drives in Orlando," by Amanda Ober, Wesh.com, June 24, 2014; "What It Takes to Build the Next Uber," by Ellen Huet, *Forbes,* June 23, 2014; "Uber's $18.2B Valuation Is a Head Scratcher," Christopher Mims, *Wall Street Journal,* June 6, 2014; "Lessons from Uber: Why Innovation and Regulation Don't Mix," Larry Downes, *Forbes,* February 6, 2014.

and ratings. A third factor is that successful firms lower the cost of services like urban transportation, lodging, office space, and personal errand services. Firms that can do this are highly disruptive of existing firms and business models.

Uber and Airbnb are among the most successful and well-known on-demand service companies. See the opening case in Chapter 1 for a description of Uber and an in-depth discussion of the issues that this business model raises.

Airbnb was founded in 2008 as a way to find lodging for attendees at a business convention. Since then, Airbnb has expanded to the entire lodging marketplace, and has grown exponentially. Airbnb now operates in more than 34,000 cities in 190 countries, and lists over 1.5 million properties for rent, including 1,400 castles and dozens of yurts in Mongolia. In the seven years since its founding, Airbnb has grown to be larger than the Intercontinental, the world's largest private hotel chain, which has about 4,900 hotels, and about 725,000 rooms around the world.

Through October 2015, Airbnb has raised $2.29 billion and has a current valuation of over $25 billion. People with spaces to rent, which can range from a single sofa to an entire apartment or house, create an account and a profile, and then list their properties on the site. The amount charged depends on the host and is usually based on the host's assessment of similar listings nearby and market demand. Travelers seeking to rent spaces register and create an account, which includes a profile. They then consult the Web site listings, read reviews of the host, and contact the host to arrange for the rental. After the rental period, hosts rate their renters, and vice versa. Renters pay through their Airbnb account, which must be funded by a credit card. Airbnb charges guests a sliding fee of 6% to 12%, depending on the price of the booking, and charges the host 3%. The hosts are issued a 1099 form at the end of the year to report taxes due on the income.

Uber and Airbnb stand out not only as the most successful of on-demand service firms, but also as the most disruptive and controversial. For instance, with Airbnb, property renters do not have the regulatory or tax burdens that hotel owners have. It is possible that the success of Airbnb could greatly reduce the demand for regulated hotels. There is little research on this topic, but an early paper found that Airbnb had a small impact on rental income at lower-end tourist hotels, but little empirical impact on business traveler hotels (Zervas et al., 2015). The possibility of negative outcomes from transactions on these sharing economy sites (e.g., a driver robs or harms a passenger, or an apartment is destroyed by renters) is leading both firms to require liability insurance, or to offer such insurance for free. It is unlikely that on-demand service firms will escape regulation altogether, but due to their popularity and success, it is likely that regulation will be minimal.

CASE STUDY

OpenTable:
Your Reservation Is Waiting

OpenTable is the leading supplier of reservation, table management, and guest management software for restaurants. In addition, the company operates OpenTable.com, the world's most popular Web site for making restaurant reservations online. In just over 15 years, OpenTable has gone from a start-up to a successful and growing public company that counts around two-thirds of the nation's reservation-taking restaurants as clients.

Today, more than 32,000 restaurants in the United States, Canada, Mexico, the United Kingdom, Germany, and Japan use the OpenTable hardware and software system. This system automates the reservation-taking and table management process, while allowing restaurants to build diner databases for improved guest recognition and targeted e-mail marketing. The OpenTable Web site, mobile site, and mobile app provide a fast, efficient way for diners to find available tables in real time. The Web sites and app connect directly to the thousands of computerized reservation systems at OpenTable restaurants, and reservations are immediately recorded in a restaurant's electronic reservation book.

© Justin Sullivan/Getty Images

Restaurants subscribe to the OpenTable Electronic Reservation Book (ERB), the company's proprietary software, which is installed on a touch-screen computer system and supported by asset-protection and security tools. The ERB software provides a real-time map of the restaurant floor and enables the restaurant to retain meal patterns of all parties, serving as a customer relationship management (CRM) system for restaurants. The software is upgraded periodically, and the latest version is designed to provide increased ease of use and a more thorough view of table availability to help turn more tables, enhance guest service, personalize responses to diners, coordinate the seating process, and maximize guest seating. The ERBs at OpenTable's customer restaurants connect via the Internet to form an online network of restaurant reservation books.

OpenTable's revenue comes from two sources. Restaurants pay a one-time fee for on-site installation and training, a monthly subscription fee for software and hardware, and a transaction fee for each restaurant guest seated through online reservations. The online reservation service is free to diners. The business model encourages diners to assist in viral marketing. When an individual makes a reservation, the site "suggests" that they send invites to their dinner companions directly from OpenTable that include a link back to the OpenTable site.

OpenTable is a service-based (software as service, or SaaS) e-commerce company. In other words, customers don't buy software and install it on their computers, but instead go online and get the software functionality through subscriptions. OpenTable is also an online service that does not sell goods, but instead enables diners to make reservations, like social networking sites provide services.

The restaurant industry was slow to leverage the power of the Internet. This was in part because the industry was, and continues to be, highly fragmented and local—made up of more than 30,000 small, independent businesses or local restaurant-owning groups.

The founders of OpenTable knew that dealing with these restaurants as a single market would be difficult. They also realized that the Internet was changing things for diners by providing them with instant access to reviews, menus, and other information about dining options. And there was no method for making reservations online—we all know reserving by phone is time-consuming, inefficient, and prone to errors. In order to make the system work, reach and scale were very important. For diners to use an online reservation system, they would need real-time access to a number of local restaurants, and the ability to instantly book confirmed reservations around the clock. If customers were planning a trip to another city, OpenTable would need participating restaurants in those cities.

The company was originally incorporated in San Francisco in 1998 as Easy-eats.com, morphing into OpenTable.com, Inc. a year later. When the company was founded, most restaurants did not have computers, let alone systems that would allow online reservations made through a central Web site. OpenTable's initial strategy was to pay online restaurant reviewers for links to its Web site and target national chains in order to quickly expand its reach. This got the company into 50 cities, but it was spending $1 million a month and bringing in only $100,000 in revenue. Not exactly a formula for success. The original investors still felt there was a viable business to be built, and they made a number of management changes, including installing investor and board member Thomas Layton, founder of CitySearch.com, as OpenTable's CEO. Layton cut staff, shut down marketing efforts, and got the company out of all but four cities: Chicago, New York, San Francisco, and Washington, D.C.

The company retooled its hardware and software to create the user-friendly ERB system and deployed a door-to-door sales force to solicit subscriptions from high-end restaurants. The combination of e-commerce, user-friendly technology, and the personal touch worked. The four markets OpenTable targeted initially developed into active, local networks of restaurants and diners that continue to grow. OpenTable has implemented the same strategy across the country, and now includes approximately 32,000 OpenTable restaurant customers. In 17 years, the company has seated approximately 885 million diners, including 245 million via its mobile solutions, and it is currently averaging 17 million diners per month. In the second quarter of 2015, half of its seating requests in North America originated from a mobile device.

As the company grew, investors began making plans for it to go public. Layton stepped down from his position as CEO in 2007, though he remained a board member. He was replaced by Jeffrey Jordan, former president of PayPal. Jordan had some experience with public companies from working with eBay on its acquisition of PayPal. In 2009, he chose an aggressive strategy—going ahead with an initial public offering (IPO) despite a terrible economy and worse financial markets. The gamble paid off. On its first day of trading, OpenTable's shares climbed 59% and the share price climbed to over $100 in 2013, more than five times the $20 IPO price.

Despite the challenging economy, OpenTable's numbers at the time of the IPO were strong, and since then, it has continued to grow. In 2014, Priceline announced that it would acquire OpenTable for $2.6 billion. Priceline had long been rumored to be interested in OpenTable. OpenTable will benefit from Priceline's global reach as it continues to expand its business beyond the United States, which has thus far accounted for about 80% of its revenues. Priceline has a strong track record of successful acquisitions, including Booking.com, which propelled Priceline's revenue from the millions to the billions. Clearly, Priceline believes OpenTable can help it grow even further, this time into restaurant reservations. They might be right: OpenTable is well-positioned for future growth. Its size, track record of growth, and high customer satisfaction rates should continue to work in its favor. Priceline plans to allow OpenTable to operate autonomously.

The company has benefited from having e-commerce revenue streams from subscription fees and per-transaction charges, rather than depending on advertising. Further, more than 50% of OpenTable's revenue comes from B2B subscriptions, which are typically part of long-term contracts. Restaurants that have invested in OpenTable's software package are less likely to want to incur the switching costs associated with changing to a different reservation management package.

Another reason for its success is that OpenTable has a large number of satisfied customers. Restaurant owners report that they and their staff members find the software easy to use, and it helps them manage their business better. Specifically, it streamlines operations, helps fill additional seats, and improves quality of service, providing a concrete return on investment. This has led to both high customer satisfaction and high retention rates.

OpenTable has also taken advantage of the interconnected needs of restaurants and diners. Restaurants want cost-effective ways to attract guests and manage their reservations, while diners want convenient ways to find available restaurants, choose among them, and make reservations. By creating an online network of restaurants and diners that transact with each other through real-time reservations, OpenTable has figured out how to successfully address the needs of both.

OpenTable's market exhibits network effects: the more people use it, the more utility the system delivers. More diners discover the benefits of using the online reservation system, which in turn delivers value to restaurant customers, and helps attract more restaurants to the network.

While OpenTable is the biggest, most successful online player in the restaurant reservations market, it does have competitors. MenuPages offers access to restaurant menus and reviews, but visitors to the site can't make reservations, and the site covers only eight U.S. cities. In 2012, OpenTable partnered with onetime competitor Urbanspoon, acquiring its reservation management system, Rezbook, and becoming Urbanspoon's reservation provider. Looming on the horizon is Google, which purchased online restaurant guide Zagat in September 2011, raising the specter that it might try to compete with OpenTable, although Zagat does not yet possess that functionality. Competitors in other countries where OpenTable does not yet operate, such as Restalo in Spain and Italy, and in markets like casual dining, such as NoWait, represent challenges to OpenTable. India-based startup Zomato acquired U.S.-based NexTable in 2015, adding another challenger to the mix.

The company is committed to shrewd technological investments to advance its position. It has a mobile Web site, mobile applications that work on just about every smartphone platform, and an iPad app that fully integrates with its ERB software. GPS enables mobile users to locate and make reservations at nearby venues. In 2015, OpenTable launched a version of its app for Apple Watch that reminds diners of their reservations, provides directions, and shows a countdown. It is also testing a premium service that involves paying for an additional fee for last-minute, prime-time reservations at popular restaurants, using a surge pricing algorithm similar to that used by Uber.

OpenTable is attempting to shift its relationship with both diners and restaurants from a "transactional" relationship to an "experiential" relationship, which focuses on the experience of dining. OpenTable launched a payments feature that allows users to pay for meals completely within the OpenTable app on the iPhone, and in 2015 made this feature available for Android phones as well. Although a small number of restaurants currently offer the service, OpenTable is partnering with other mobile payment systems like Aloha to widen their mobile payment availability. OpenTable also redesigned its flagship Web site in 2014 to improve visual appeal and speed, and continued to update its image in 2015 with a complete rebranding, including a new logo and tagline and a marketing campaign, 100 Open Tables, featuring giveaways of iconic dining experiences around the world.

SOURCES: "Fast Facts," Opentable.com, accessed October 1, 2015; "OpenTable Experiments with Surge Pricing for Restaurant Reservations," by David Kaplan, Skift.com, September 29, 2015; "OpenTable Integrates with Aloha POS Systems, Ramps Up Mobile Payments," by Paolo Lucchesi, Insidescoopsf.com, May 19, 2015; "OpenTable App for Apple Watch Now Available," Opentable.com, April 24, 2015; "Zomato Buys NexTable to Rival OpenTable and Yelp in Reservations," Ingrid Lunden, Techcrunch.com, April 22, 2015; "OpenTable Unveils Rebrand to Deepen Connection with Diners and Restaurants," Opentable.com, March 3, 2015; "OpenTable Seats a Record Two Million Diners in a Single Day," Opentable.com, February 19 , 2015; "Priceline Agrees to Buy OpenTable for $2.6 Billion," by Drew FitzGerald, Wall Street Journal, June 13, 2014; "OpenTable Is Moving from 'Transactional' to 'Experiential'," by Ava Seave, Forbes.com, April 22, 2014; "OpenTable's Media Play: Before, During and After Dining," by Ava Seave, Forbes.com, April 21, 2014; "OpenTable Launches Pilot Mobile Payment Program in San Francisco," by Emily Price, Engadget.com, February 7th, 2014; "OpenTable, Inc. Announces 4Q and Full Year 2013 Financial Results," Opentable.com, February 6, 2014; "European OpenTable Competitor Restalo Raises $10M Series B Led By Seaya Ventures," by Steve O'Hear, Techcrunch.com, September 17, 2013; "Pittsburg Startup NoWait Could Overtake OpenTable's Volume in 2014," by Louis Bedigan, Benzinga.com, August 20, 2013; "Forget Flagging the Waiter: OpenTable Testing App That Lets You Pay," by Teresa Novellino, Upstart.bizjournals.com, July 31, 2013; "OpenTable Partners with Urbanspoon; Acquires Rezbook," Opentable.com, July 31, 2013; "OpenTable Releases New Electronic Reservation Book and iPad App for Restaurants," Opentable.com, April 4, 2012; "Google Buys Zagat to View the OpenTable, Yelp," by Alexei Oreskovic, Reuters, September 8, 2011; "Behind OpenTable's

Success," Kevin Kelleher, Cnnmoney.com, September 23, 2010; "OpenTable Introduces the Next Generation of Its Electronic Reservation Book Software," Restaurantnews.com, August 17, 2010; "OpenTable Unveils Version 2.0 of its iPhone App," AppScout.com, August 14, 2009; Open Table S-1/A Amendment #6, filed with the Securities and Exchange Commission, May 19, 2009.

OpenTable's growth is projected to continue in the United States, Canada, and Mexico despite considerable market penetration. Selective international expansion is planned beyond its current operations in Germany, Japan, and the United Kingdom. OpenTable supports each of these locations with a direct sales force servicing approximately 1,000 restaurants.

The company's international strategy is to replicate the successful U.S. model by focusing initially on building a restaurant customer base. OpenTable believes the localized versions of its software will compare favorably against competitive software offerings, enabling them to expand across a broad selection of local restaurants.

Case Study Questions

1. Why have OpenTable competitors had a difficult time competing against Open-Table?

2. What characteristics of the restaurant market make it difficult for a reservation system to work?

3. How did OpenTable change its marketing strategy to succeed?

4. Why would restaurants find the SaaS model very attractive?

9.10 REVIEW

KEY CONCEPTS

■ **Understand the environment in which the online retail sector operates today.**

- Personal consumption of retail goods and services comprise about 68% and account for about $12.2 trillion of total GDP.
- The retail industry can be divided into seven major firm types: general merchandise, durable goods, specialty stores, food and beverage, gasoline and fuel, MOTO, and online retail firms. Each type offers opportunities for online retail. The MOTO sector is the most similar to the online retail sales sector.
- During the early days of e-commerce, some predicted that the retail industry would be revolutionized, based on reduced search costs, lower marketing entry costs, the replacement of physical store merchants by online companies, elimination of middlemen (distintermediation), and hypermediation.
- Today, it has become clear that few of the initial assumptions about the future of online retail were correct. Also, the structure of the retail marketplace in the United States has not been revolutionized. The reality is that:
  - Online consumers are not primarily cost-driven—instead, they are as brand-driven and influenced by perceived value as their offline counterparts.
  - Online market entry costs were underestimated, as was the cost of acquiring new customers.
  - Older traditional firms, such as the general merchandising giants and the established catalog-based retailers, are taking over as the top online retail sites.

- Disintermediation did not occur. On the contrary, online retailing has become an example of the powerful role that intermediaries play in retail trade.

■ Explain how to analyze the economic viability of an online firm.

- The economic viability, or ability of a firm to survive during a specified time period, can be analyzed by examining the key industry strategic factors, the strategic factors that pertain specifically to the firm, and the financial statements for the firm.
- The key industry strategic factors include barriers to entry, the power of suppliers, the power of customers, the existence of substitute products, the industry value chain, and the nature of intra-industry competition.
- The key firm strategic factors include the firm value chain, core competencies, synergies, the firm's current technology, and the social and legal challenges facing the firm.
- The key financial factors include revenues, cost of sales, gross margin, operating expenses, operating margin, net margin, and the firm's balance sheet.

■ Identify the challenges faced by the different types of online retailers.

- *Virtual merchants* are single-channel Web firms that generate all of their revenues from online sales. Their challenges include building a business and a brand name quickly, many competitors in the virtual marketplace, substantial costs to build and maintain an e-commerce presence, considerable marketing expenses, large customer acquisition costs, a steep learning curve, and the need to quickly achieve operating efficiencies in order to preserve a profit. Amazon is the most well-known example of a virtual merchant.
- *Omni-channel merchants* (bricks-and-clicks) have a network of physical stores as their primary retail channel, but also have online operations. Their challenges include high cost of physical buildings, high cost of large sales staffs, the need to coordinate prices across channels, the need to develop methods of handling cross-channel returns from multiple locations, building a credible e-commerce presence, hiring new skilled staff, and building rapid-response order entry and fulfillment systems. Macy's is an example of a bricks-and-clicks company.
- *Catalog merchants* are established companies that have a national offline catalog operation as their largest retail channel, but who also have online capabilities. Their challenges include high costs for printing and mailing, the need to leverage their existing assets and competencies to the new technology environment, the need to develop methods of handling cross-channel returns, building a e-commerce presence, and hiring new skilled staff. Lands' End is an example of a catalog merchant.
- *Manufacturer-direct merchants* are either single- or multi-channel manufacturers who sell to consumers directly online without the intervention of retailers. Their challenges include channel conflict, quickly developing a rapid-response online order and fulfillment system; switching from a supply-push (products are made prior to orders being received based on estimated demand) to a demand-pull model (products are not built until an order is received); and creating sales, service, and support operations online. Dell is an example of a manufacturer-direct merchant.

■ Describe the major features of the online service sector.

- The service sector is the largest and most rapidly expanding part of the economy of advanced industrial nations.
- The major service industry groups are financial services, insurance, real estate, business services, and health services.
- Within these service industry groups, companies can be further categorized into those that involve transaction brokering and those that involve providing a "hands-on" service.

- With some exceptions, the service sector is by and large a knowledge- and information-intense industry. For this reason, many services are uniquely suited to e-commerce and the strengths of the Internet.
- E-commerce offers extraordinary opportunities to improve transaction efficiencies and thus productivity in a sector where productivity has so far not been markedly affected by the explosion in information technology.

■ **Discuss the trends taking place in the online financial services industry.**

- The online financial services sector is a good example of an e-commerce success story, but the success is somewhat different than what had been predicted in the early days of e-commerce. Today, the multi-channel established financial firms are growing the most rapidly and have the best prospects for long-term viability.
- Multi-channel firms that have both physical branches and solid online offerings have assumed market leadership over pure-online firms.
- Financial portals provide comparison shopping services and steer consumers to online providers for independent financial advice and financial planning.
- Account aggregation is another rapidly growing online financial service, which pulls together all of a customer's financial data on a single personalized Web site.
- Despite a rocky start, the online mortgage market is slowly growing; it is dominated by established online banks and other online financial services firms, traditional mortgage vendors, and a few successful online mortgage firms.
- Term life insurance stands out as one product group supporting the early visions of lower search costs, increased price transparency, and the resulting consumer savings. However, in other insurance product lines, the Web offers insurance companies new opportunities for product and service differentiation and price discrimination.
- The early vision that the historically local, complex, and agent-driven real estate industry would be transformed into a disintermediated marketplace where buyers and sellers could transact directly has not been realized.
- The major impact of the online real estate industry is in influencing offline purchases and the primary service is a listing of available houses, with secondary links to mortgage lenders, credit reporting agencies, neighborhood information, loan calculators, appraisal reports, sales price histories by neighborhood, school district data, and crime reports.

■ **Describe the major trends in the online travel services industry today.**

- The Internet has become the most common channel used by consumers to research travel options and book reservations for airline tickets, rental cars, hotel rooms, and tours.
- The major trends in online travel services include consolidation, the rise of meta-search engines, mobile devices, and social media.

■ **Identify current trends in the online career services industry.**

- Next to travel services, job-hunting services have been one of the Internet's most successful online services because they save money for both job hunters and employers.
- Online recruiting can also serve to establish market prices and terms, thereby identifying both the salary levels for specific jobs and the skill sets required to achieve those salary levels.
- The major trends in the online career services industry are social networking, mobile, job search engines, consolidation, diversification, and localization.

■ **Understand the business models of on-demand service companies.**

- On-demand service companies provide a platform that enables the on-demand delivery of various services, by connecting providers ("sellers") who wish to exploit their "spare" resources, such as cars, rooms with beds, and ability to perform various services via their personal labor, with consumers ("buyers") who would like to utilize those resources and services. The companies collect a fee both from sellers and buyers for using the platform.

- Uber, a car rental service, and Airbnb, a room rental service, are the most well-known on-demand services companies. They are also among the most disruptive and controversial.

QUESTIONS

1. Why were so many entrepreneurs drawn to start businesses in the online retail sector initially?
2. What frequently makes the difference between profitable and unprofitable online businesses today?
3. Which segment of the offline retail business is most like online retailing? Why?
4. Describe the technological retail revolution that preceded the growth of e-commerce. What were some of the innovations that made later online retailing possible?
5. Name two assumptions e-commerce analysts made early on about consumers and their buying behavior that turned out to be false.
6. Explain the distinction between disintermediation and hypermediation as it relates to online retailing.
7. Compare and contrast virtual merchants and bricks-and-clicks firms. What other type of online retailer is most like the virtual merchant?
8. What is the difference between a supply-push and a demand-pull sales model? Why do most manufacturer-direct firms have difficulty switching from the former to the latter?
9. What are five strategic issues specifically related to a firm's capabilities? How are they different from industry-related strategic issues?
10. Which is a better measure of a firm's financial health: revenues, gross margin, or net margin? Why?
11. What are some of the difficulties in providing services in an online environment? What factors differentiate the services sector from the retail sector, for example?
12. Compare and contrast the two major types of online services industries. What two major features differentiate services from other industries?
13. What is the biggest deterrent to growth of the online insurance industry nationally?
14. Define channel conflict and explain how it applies to the retail industry.
15. What is the most common use of real estate Web sites? What do most consumers do when they go to them?
16. How have travel services suppliers benefited from consumer use of travel Web sites?
17. Name and describe five traditional recruitment tools companies have used to identify and attract employees. What are the disadvantages of such tools compared to online career sites?
18. In addition to matching job applicants with available positions, what larger function do online job sites fill? Explain how such sites can affect salaries and going rates.
19. Describe the business model of sharing economy companies.
20. Why are on-demand service companies viewed as being disruptive and controversial?

PROJECTS

1. Access the EDGAR archives at Sec.gov, where you can review 10-K filings for all public companies. Search for the 10-K report for the most recent completed fiscal year for two online retail companies of your choice (preferably ones operating in the same industry, such as Staples Inc. and Office Depot Inc., Amazon and Walmart, etc.). Prepare a presentation that compares the financial stability and prospects of the two businesses, focusing specifically on the performance of their respective e-commerce operations.

2. Find an example not mentioned in the text of each of the four types of online retailing business models. Prepare a short report describing each firm and why it is an example of the particular business model.

3. Drawing on material in the chapter and your own research, prepare a short paper describing your views on the major social and legal issues facing online retailers.

4. Choose a services industry not discussed in the chapter (such as legal services, medical services, accounting services, or another of your choosing). Prepare a 3- to 5-page report discussing recent trends affecting online provision of these services.

5. Together with a teammate, investigate the use of mobile apps in the online retail or financial services industries. Prepare a short joint presentation on your findings.

REFERENCES

Amazon.com, Inc. Form 10-K for the fiscal year ended December 31, 2015, filed with the Securities and Exchange Commission (January 30, 2015a).

Amazon.com, Inc. Form 10-Q for the quarterly period ended June 30, 2015, filed with the Securities and Exchange Commission (July 24, 2015b).

Asay, Matt. "AWS Now 10X The Size of Its Competitors: Is The Cloud Arms Race Over?" Techrepublic.com (May 20, 2015).

Bardhan, Ashok. "The US Economy Grows, But Jobs Don't." Yale Global Online (March 13, 2014).

Bensinger, Greg. "Amazon Delivers Bigger-Than-Expected Profit." *Wall Street Journal* (January 29, 2015).

Bloomberg News. "Macy's May Close Up to 40 Stores as It Ramps Up E-commerce Efforts." Internetretailer.com (September 9, 2015)

Brown, Jeffrey, and Austan Goolsbee. "Does the Internet Make Markets More Competitive? Evidence from the Life Insurance Industry." John F. Kennedy School of Government, Harvard University. Research Working Paper RWP00-007 (2000).

Brynjolfsson, Erik, Astrid Andrea Dick, and Michael D. Smith. "Search and Product Differentiation at an Internet Shopbot," Center for eBusiness@MIT (December, 2004).

Bureau of Economic Analysis, U.S. Department of Commerce. "Table 3: Gross Domestic Product and Related Measures: Level and Change from Preceding Period." www.bea.gov (accessed August 20, 2015).

Careerbuilder. "35 Percent of Employers Less Likely to Interview Applicants They Can't Find Online, According to Annual CareerBuilder Social Media Recruitment Survey." (May 14, 2015).

Chaudhuri, Saabira. "Lenders Place Their Bets on Mobile Banking." *Wall Street Journal* (April 9, 2014).

Compete.com. "Site Profiles: Fidelity.com, Scottrade, TDAmeritrade, E-Trade, Vanguard, Charles Schwab, and Merrill Lynch." accessed October 5, 2015.

comScore. "Brokerage Trends." (January 24, 2014a).

comScore. "Digital Banking Trends and Observations." (2014b).

comScore. "2014 Online Auto Insurance Shopping Report." (November 13, 2014c).

Del Rey, Jason. "Amazon Will Shut Down Amazon Webstore, Its Competitor to Shopify and Bigcommerce." Recode.net (March 18, 2015).

Demos, Telis, and Matt Jarzemsky. "Alibaba IPO: A Big Deal, and, Backers Argue, a Real Steal." *Wall Street Journal* (September 11, 2014).

D'Onfro, Jillian. "The Biggest Mystery About Amazon's Business Right Now." Businessinsider.com (February 4, 2015).

Dusto, Amy. "Dell Revamps Its Mobile Site." Internetretailer.com (September 19, 2012).

eMarketer, Inc. "US Retail Ecommerce Sales, 2013–2019." (June 2015a).

eMarketer, Inc. "US Retail Mcommerce Sales, 2013–2019." (May 2015b).

eMarketer, Inc. "US Mobile Buyers, by Device, 2013–2019." (June 2015c).

eMarketer, Inc. "Many US Mobile Phone Users Hesitant About Banking on Mobile Devices." (August 24, 2015d).

eMarketer, Inc. "Millennials Embrace Mobile Banking." (August 18, 2015e).

eMarketer, Inc. "Mobile Tools are Helpful to Investors, but Humans Still Matter." (July 17, 2015f).

eMarketer, Inc. (Cindy Liu). "Worldwide Digital Travel Sales: The eMarketer Forecast for 2015." (July 2015g).

eMarketer, Inc. "US Digital Travel Researchers and Bookers, 2013–2019." (May 2015h).

eMarketer, Inc. "US Mobile Travel Researchers, 2013–2019." (May 2015i).

eMarketer, Inc. "US Mobile Travel Bookers, 2013–2019." (May 2015j).

eMarketer, Inc. "US Mobile Travel Bookers, by Device, 2013–2019 (May 2015k).

eMarketer, Inc. (Krista Garcia). "Retailers and Digital Commerce: Trends and Benchmarks for Five Sectors." (June 2015x).

eMarketer, Inc. "US Retail Ecommerce Sales, by Product Category. 2103–2019." (June 2015y).

eMarketer, Inc. (Jeremy Kressman). "Travel Purchases on the Go." (June 2014).

eMarketer, Inc. "Recruiters Rely More on Social Media for Talent." (February 26, 2013).

eMarketer, Inc. (Jeffrey Grau). "E-commerce in the US: Retail Trends." (May 2005)

Evans, Philip, and Thomas S. Wurster. *Blown to Bits: How the New Economics of Information Transforms Strategy.* Cambridge, MA: Harvard Business School Press (2000).

Friedman, Thomas L. "And Now for a Bit of Good News..." *New York Times* (July 19, 2014).

Golden, Bernard. "Amazon Opens Up About AWS Revenues." CIO.com (May 12, 2015).

Hagey, Paul. "Zillow Extends Its Web Traffic Lead in May." Inman.com (June 3, 2015).

Internet Retailer. "Top 500 Guide 2015 Edition." (2015).

Internet Retailer. "The Mobile 500 2015 Edition." (2014).

Javelin Strategy & Research. "Javelin Identifies $1.5B in Mobile Banking Cost Savings by Leveraging Omnichannel Approach." (July 8, 2013).

Jobvite. "The Jobvite Recruiter Nation Survey 2015." (2015).

Johnson, Lauren. "Macy's Partners with Spotify to Further Mobile Advertising Stride." Mobilecommercedaily.com (August 1, 2012).

Kats, Rimma. "Macy's Exec: Mobile Amplifies Multichannel, Multiscreen Marketing." Mobilecommercedaily.com (May 13, 2013).

Lands' End, Inc. "About Lands' End." Landsend.com (accessed October 1, 2015).

LIMRA. "Information Seeking in the U.S.: Consumer Internet Use for Retail Insurance in 2015." (2015).

LIMRA. "Disruptive Consumers Want More Mobile Services." (July 9, 2014a).

LIMRA. "Insurers' Use of Social Media Has Jumped More than 50 Percent Since 2010." (July 22, 2014b).

Lindner, Matt. "Amazon's Q2 North America Sales Surge 25.5%." Internetretailer.com (July 23, 2015).

LinkedIn Talent Solutions. "US Recruiting Trends: 3 Must-Know Talent Acquisition Trends for 2015 4th Annual Report." (2015).

Love, Jack. "News Analysis: Big Store Sales Are a Tale of Two Channels." Internetretailer.com (August 19, 2013).

Macy's. "Macy's Outlines New Omnichannel Strategy and Tech." Internetretailer.com (September 18, 2014).

McIntyre, Hugh. "Amazon's New Music Streaming Service Not Exactly Ready For 'Prime' Time." *Forbes* (June 13, 2014).

National Association of Realtors. "2014 Profile of Home Buyers and Sellers." (November 3, 2014).

Needleman, Sarah, and Angus Loten. "Startups Want to Be the Next Airbnb, Uber." *Wall Street Journal* (May 7, 2014).

Ovide, Shira. "Google, Amazon and Microsoft's Costly Spending War." Blogs.wsj.com (April 28, 2014).

Portillo, Ely. "Amazon to Open Distribution Center Near Concord Airport." *Charlotte Observer* (September 9, 2014).

Silbert, Sarah. "Why Amazon is Going to Stop Making Its Own Stuff." *Fortune* (September 1, 2015).

Singleton, Micah. "Amazon Kills Amazon Wallet Six Months After Launch." Theverge.com (January 21, 2015).

Smith, Sandy. "The Favorite 50 2015." Nrf.com (September 1, 2015).

Somaiya, Ravi. "Amazon to Stream Original HBO Content." *New York Times* (April 23, 2014).

U.S. Census Bureau. *Statistical Abstract of the United States 2012* (2012).

U.S. Department of Labor Bureau of Labor Statistics. "Industry Employment and Output Projections to 2022." *Monthly Labor Review* (December 2013).

Weil, Jonathon. "Securities Rules Help to Close the Earning Reports GAAP." *Wall Street Journal* (April 24, 2003).

Yodlee, Inc. "Form 10-K for the fiscal year ended December 31, 2014." (March 4, 2015).

Zervas, Georgios, Davide Proserpio, and John W. Byers. "The Rise of the Sharing Economy: Estimating the Impact of Airbnb on the Hotel Industry." Working Paper. SSRN (May 7, 2015).

CHAPTER 10

Online Content and Media

After reading this chapter, you will be able to:

- Understand the major trends in the consumption of media and online content, the major revenue models for digital content delivery, digital rights management, and the concept of media convergence.
- Understand the key factors affecting the online publishing industry.
- Understand the key factors affecting the online entertainment industry.

Cord Cutters and Cord Shavers:

The Emerging Internet Broadcasting System (IBS)

© NetPhotos / Alamy

Cable and satellite television providers like to boast that they offer hundreds, if not thousands, of channels. But who really watches that many channels? Do you really even need cable or satellite TV? An estimated 7% of U.S. households (8.6 million homes) have already said no. These homes have a broadband Internet connection, but have chosen not to have cable or satellite TV. They are called cord cutters (even though they still have an Internet broadband "cord") and while they represent a small, growing band of pay TV resistors, they still account for just a small part of the 94 million cable and satellite TV subscribers. Nevertheless, cord cutters and cord shavers (people who reduce their pay TV subscriptions to a minimum) are shrinking the number of pay TV households at about 1% annually. Not exactly a collapsing market, but not one that is expanding either. Instead of signing up for cable or satellite TV (which typically costs over $100 a month), cord cutters are choosing online providers such as Hulu (which can be had for only about $7.99 a month, and which allows viewers to stream current and past TV series on a schedule of their choice). More worrisome to the cable industry is that people who subscribe to so-called over-the-top (OTT) video services such as Hulu and Netflix are twice as likely to kick out cable TV. Likewise with millennial households: 24% of those under 35 and who use Hulu or Netflix don't pay for cable TV.

Yet some sort of paid cable, satellite, or telecommunications (Verizon FiOS or AT&T U-verse) TV service can be found in 103 million out of the 115 million TV households. As subscribers slowly leave pay TV (or never sign up in the first place), cable and satellite providers have increased monthly fees faster than the rate of inflation. The average cable TV bill across the country is now $123 a month, and has risen about 8% annually for the last decade. But this world of pay TV service now faces challenges as tech-based Internet giants move into original television programming and use their Internet skills and brands to create, promote, and distribute television content.

A new Internet-based broadcasting system has begun to challenge the existing cable TV distribution and production system. More original content designed for Internet distribution is coming from non-traditional sources such as Netflix, Hulu, and even Amazon, not to mention Google. For instance, Amazon has created Amazon Studios to produce made-for-Web original series, with 11 to 26 episodes each year. Amazon Prime customers can stream these

SOURCES: "Cord-cutting Headaches for Pay TV Have Now Progressed Beyond Just a Dull, Throbbing Pain," by Todd Spangler, *Variety*, August 8, 2015; "US Cable TV Companies Shares Crushed After Disney Disappoints," by Lisa Richwein, Reuters, August 5, 2015; "Shifting Video and TV Audiences," by David Hallerman, eMarketer, Inc., August 2015; "Why Cord Cutting is a Myth," by Leigh Gallagher, *Fortune*, July 22, 2015; "Hulu Explores Adding Ad-Free Option to Its Service," by Mike Shields and Shalini Ramachandran, *Wall Street Journal*, July 16, 2015; "Showtime to Introduce Net Streaming Service in July," by Emily Steel, *New York Times*, June 3, 2015; "US Time Spent With Media," eMarketer, May 2015; "At the Head of the Pack, HBO Shows the Way Forward," by John Koblin and Emily Steel, *New York Times*, April 12, 2015; "HBO's Streaming Service Will Start in April, Initially on Apple Devices Only," by Emily Steel, *New York Times*, March 9, 2015; "CBS Becomes First Major Network to Launch Internet TV Service: You Can Watch 'The Good Wife,' But Not the NFL," by Jacob Kastrenakes, The Verge.com, October 16, 2014; "The Rise of the YouTube Musical," by John Jurgenson, *Wall Street Journal*, June 5, 2014; "With Online Video Offerings, the Establishment Plays the Upstart," by Stuart Elliott, *New York Times*, May 1, 2014; "Famous Faces Cross Over to Online Video," by Stuart Elliot, *New York Times*, April 30, 2014; "Yahoo to Offer TV-Style Comedy Series on the Web," by Vindu Goel and Bill Carter, *New York Times*, April 28, 2014; "Amazon to Stream Original HBO Content," by Ravi Somaiya, *New York Times*, April 23, 2014; "Made-for-Web Video Content," by Paul Verna, eMarketer, Inc., August 2013; "Hulu to Create More Original Shows," by Sam Schechner and Christopher Stewart, *Wall Street Journal*, January 17, 2012.

series without any additional cost. Amazon has also struck a deal with HBO to give Amazon Prime members free access to older HBO series such as *The Sopranos, The Wire,* and *Band of Brothers.* This is the first time HBO has licensed its content to online viewers outside of its traditional pay TV business. The HBO content will also be available on Amazon's set-top box, Fire TV. Netflix, the most successful video-on-demand streaming service to date, began producing original series in 2010. Netflix's first effort was *Arrested Development.* Subsequent series have included *House of Cards* and *Orange is the New Black,* both of which have won Emmy awards. Hulu produced *Battleground,* its first scripted original show in 2012, and it is now in its fourth season. Hulu has since gone on to produce four more TV series.

Producers of content in Hollywood and New York also benefit from the new Internet broadcasting system because they no longer need to depend on cable providers to distribute their content. The Internet has become a substitute distribution system for high quality content. Consumers increasingly want to take control of the programming and scheduling of the TV shows they watch. On the Internet, consumers can binge watch an entire year's worth of a series, something cable TV doesn't provide. And consumers don't want to be forced to buy a bundle of channels or pay for content they never watch. The new Internet broadcasting system offers freedom of choice, a la carte TV, and consumer control.

Also troubling for the cable industry is that it is no longer the financial sure bet it once was for investors. In the past, cable systems were a cash cow utility business: add new customers by the millions, charge what you want, and pay good dividends. Stock goes up. Today cable systems are adding just enough new subscribers to replace the cord cutters. Soon they may not be able to do even that. Investors see the end of growth, disaggregation of the cable bundle, and potentially an increase in the cord-cutting rate. In the summer of 2015, cable and satellite provider stocks sank, major players consolidated and the industry became even more concentrated and oligopolistic, which usually translates to rising prices and poor service.

Content producers also face many new opportunities and risks in the Internet broadcasting system. In the past, broadcast networks CBS, NBC, ABC, and Fox were the major primetime content producers. They have since been joined by the top cable content providers, such as USA, TNT, History Channel, TBS, and FX, all of which create their own original content. These content producers earn money by charging cable and satellite providers for the right to distribute their content. However, the cable provider system is highly concentrated, and a few firms (Comcast, Time Warner Cable, Charter, and Cablevision) control access to over 90% of American homes. In the past, content producers were in a weak bargaining position.

In the new Internet distribution system, content producers now have a number of alternatives, such as licensing their content to Hulu, Netflix, Apple, or other pay-for-content Internet channels, or even streaming it themselves. For instance, CBS launched its own streaming, a la carte television service in 2015, providing access to over 6,000 on-demand episodes of its current and past shows. HBO quickly followed suit with its own streaming service, HBO Now, as did Showtime, a premium cable channel, with unlimited access to hundreds of series, documentaries, and movies. Who needs cable or satellite TV?

The Internet broadcasting system is in its infancy, and there is still a long way to go before the 103 million households with paid TV service cut the cable. Yet the process has begun, and the television industry is in the beginning of a digitally inspired disruption.

T he opening case illustrates how online content distributors like Hulu, Netflix, Amazon, Google (YouTube), and others are moving into premium content production and sales, and also becoming alternative providers of traditional television and movie content, rivaling existing cable and satellite distributors. If consumers can find their favorite television shows and movies online, then why should they pay for cable or satellite TV, especially when a variety of devices enable users to display their computer and phone screens on a home TV set? If consumers can watch their favorite shows on a smartphone or tablet, why should they buy a TV? As Internet users increasingly change their reading and viewing habits, spurred on by the growth of mobile devices, they are challenging existing business models that worked for decades to support newspapers, books, magazines, television, and Hollywood movies. Clearly, the future of content—news, music, and video—is online. Today, the print industry, including newspapers, books, and magazines, is having a difficult time coping with the movement of their readership to digital alternatives. Broadcast and cable television, along with Hollywood and the music industry, are also wrestling with outdated business models based on physical media. Established media giants are continuing to make extraordinary investments in unique online content, new technology, new digital distribution channels, and entirely new business models. Internet giants like Apple, Google, Amazon, and Facebook are competing to dominate online content distribution.

10.1   ONLINE CONTENT

No other sector of the American economy has been so challenged by the Internet and the Web than the content industries. The online content industries are organized into two major categories: the print industries (newspapers, magazines, and books), and the entertainment industries, which includes television, movies, music (including radio), and games. Together, the online content industries are expected to generate revenues of about $22 billion in 2015.

In this chapter, we will look closely at publishing (newspapers, magazines, and books) and entertainment (television and movies, music and radio, and games) as they attempt to transform their traditional media into digitally deliverable forms and experiences for consumers, while at the same time earning profits. These industries make up the largest share of the commercial content marketplace, both offline and online. In each of these industries, there are powerful offline brands, significant new pure-play online providers and distributors, consumer constraints and opportunities, a variety of legal issues, and new mobile technology platforms that offer an entirely new content distribution system in the form of smartphones and tablet computers.

Table 10.1 describes the most recent trends in online content and media for 2015–2016.

TABLE 10.1	WHAT'S NEW IN ONLINE CONTENT AND MEDIA, 2015–2016

BUSINESS

- Explosive growth of the mobile platform of smartphones and tablets accelerates the transition to digital content.
- Vertical integration: Amazon, Google (YouTube), Hulu, and Netflix (owners of the distribution channel) enter the content production business for video, books, and online TV-like video channels.
- The cable industry is disrupted by growth of Internet content distributors.
- Apple enters the music streaming business.
- The percentage of Internet users who watch digital video continues to increase, to around 200 million people, about 87% of Internet users.
- Music: digital music sales top physical sales; streaming surpasses downloading.
- TV: the number of Americans watching TV online continues to grow, to over 153 million (about 73% of the U.S. Internet population).
- E-book sales growth slows but represents one-third of all book revenues.
- Movies: Americans continue to spend more on online movies than for DVDs.
- Newspapers: online readership exceeds print readership. Online ad revenues grow but not enough to offset declining print ad revenues.
- Gaming market: console game sales stagnate as mobile gaming soars.
- The four Internet Titans compete: Apple, Google, Amazon, and Facebook vie for ownership of the online entertainment and content ecosystem, selling experiences as well as content.
- Cable and satellite companies seek to consolidate: Comcast made an unsuccessful $45 bid for Time Warner; Charter Communicatons is preparing its own offer.

TECHNOLOGY

- Smartphones, tablet computers, and e-readers together create a rich mobile multimedia entertainment environment.
- Netflix remains the largest consumer of bandwidth, consuming about 37% of Internet traffic.
- Apps become the foundation for an app economy as they morph into content-distribution platforms that are proprietary, where users can be charged for content.
- Cloud storage services grow to serve the huge market for mobile device content. Apple launches iCloud video service that allows users to watch purchased videos on multiple Apple devices (iPhones, iPads, and Macs). Amazon and Google develop similar cloud services.

SOCIETY

- Media consumption: Americans spend around 4,200 hours a year consuming various types of media, more than twice as many hours as they work.
- Time spent using digital media exceeds time spent with television; time spent on mobile devices exceeds time spent on desktops.
- The Federal Communications Commission issues new net neutrality rules that prohibit broadband providers from blocking, slowing down, or speeding up access to specific websites.

CONTENT AUDIENCE AND MARKET: WHERE ARE THE EYEBALLS AND THE MONEY?

The average American adult spends around 4,300 hours each year consuming various media, twice the amount of time spent at work (2,000 hours/year) (see **Figure 10.1**). U.S. entertainment and media revenues (both online and offline) in 2014 were estimated to be $264 billion, and they are expected to grow at a compound rate of 6% annually to 2019. Sales of tablets and smartphones have created new revenue streams for entertainment and media firms as consumer behavior changes in response to the new technologies. Content is no longer tied to physical products and can be delivered over the Internet from cloud servers to multiple mobile devices, reducing costs for consumers. Currently, online digital entertainment and media revenue is 8% of total entertainment and media revenue, or an estimated $21 billion. Millennials, the generation of people born between 1980 and 2000 (sometimes referred to as Digital Natives), are often thought to consume media very differently from their parents and older Baby Boomers. For a discussion of how Millennials differ in media consumption, see *Insight on Society: Are Millennials Really All That Different?*

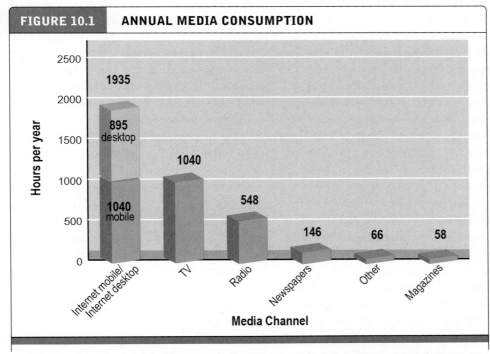

FIGURE 10.1   ANNUAL MEDIA CONSUMPTION

Each American spends around 4,300 hours annually on various types of media. Time spent on the Internet (both mobile and desktop) is expected to exceed time spent on traditional television.

SOURCES: Based on data from eMarketer, Inc., 2015a; authors' estimates.

INSIGHT ON SOCIETY

ARE MILLENIALS REALLY ALL THAT DIFFERENT?

If you were born between 1981 and 2000, congratulations! You are a Millennial and the subject of Millennial mania, which is now gripping the advertising, retailing, educational, and journalistic worlds. Not since the Baby Boomers has so much coverage been given to a single generation.

Some people believe that Millennials are so different from previous generations that they require new kinds of products, new types of marketing and advertising techniques to persuade them to buy, and entirely new educational techniques. For instance, TicTac is coming to market with a Millennial product that changes flavors as it melts, from cherry, to peach, to lemonade. The company believes Millennials are bored with its old product. Millennials drink more specialty coffee, so coffee makers are responding with multiple new specialty coffee drinks. How about an orange-pineapple latte? Whole Foods is opening a line of stores geared to Millennial shoppers that has curated selections, innovative technology, and streamlined design. And there's a hint of lower prices geared to the fact that Millennials are earning less, have higher rates of unemployment, and extraordinary student debt. There's a lot of money at stake getting the pulse of Millennials and figuring out how to market to them. Millennials now make up the largest generation in the United States, constituting about 80 million consumers, and over 30% of the labor force.

Millennials are just the latest in a long line of generalizations about people who grew up in specific time periods that are believed to have shaped the character of their entire generation. The Greatest Generation (1901–1924) came of age during the Great Depression and served in World War II. The Baby Boomers (1946–1964) grew up with the civil rights movement, political unrest, and rock and roll. Generation X (1965–1980) continued the trends of the Baby Boomers except more so. Generation Xers were the first to experience a slowdown in living standards, and a growing sense that they might not earn as much as their parents. The Millennials are continuing many of the trends of previous generations, including an alienation from cultural and political institutions, a decline in religious belief and marriage rates, higher levels of student loan debt, poverty, and unemployment, and the reality—not just the fear—that they will earn less than their parents at a similar age. The Millennials are much more ethnically diverse as well: nearly half of the Millennial generation were not born in the United States.

But perhaps more important according to some is that Millennials are digital natives: they are first generation to be born into the digital revolution of the 20th century. They grew up with the commercial Internet. According to Marc Prensky, an author and promoter of educational games, Millennials' brains are physically different because of long-term exposure to interactive video games, console controllers (the "twitch" effect), graphical interfaces, and non-linear hypertext experiences on the Internet. Today's digital natives, in his view, cannot learn from books, newspapers, or linear stories even if they are video-based. They are bored by these old-school learning tools. The implications for education are, according to Prensky, to throw out traditional, old-style, linear thinking found in books and school curricula, and replace these with video games and link-clicking for nearly all subjects. This is called "gamification" of education.

But real-world Millennials don't seem to fit the Prensky mold. In fact, there is no evidence that Millennials think differently from other generations, have physically different brains, or can learn only by using games. More Millennials have a college degree and more graduate school attendance than other generations. They apparently do learn in traditional environments, and they didn't get through all this education by playing games! Academic researchers have dismissed much of the digital native thesis, finding that while digital natives use more technology tools to learn in college, they do not use radically different digital tools such as virtual worlds, games, or social collaboration tools. The research does not find support for claims that Millennials have adopted learning styles that are radically different from those of their parents.

But clearly Millennials have had a very different experience growing up with technology than their parents, given the incredible advancement of digital technologies in the last three decades that have created entirely new platforms like smartphones, tablets, digital photography, highly interactive console and PC games, all of which have changed how content—books, newspapers, magazines, TV, and Hollywood movies—is created, distributed, and consumed. Millennials probably think like everyone else (let's hope so), but they do have different patterns of content consumption. Let's look at the data.

Given their intense use of the Internet, and absorption in digital experiences, including games, one would think Millennials would read few books (too boring and not twitchy or interactive enough), and that they would believe the Internet contained just about all the content and knowledge worth knowing about. Not so, according to a large study by Pew Research: Millennials are more likely to have read a book in the past 12 months than older adults, 88% vs. 79%. Almost 40% report having read an e-book in the past year, about the same as older adults. They are more likely to use a smartphone to read e-books than a Kindle. And they are more likely to think that there's a lot of useful information that is not on the Internet, more so than older adults. They are just as likely to have used a library in the past twelve months, and more likely to have used a library Web site. Even more unexpected: a study of 2,000 American and U.K. Millennials found this group overwhelmingly preferred printed books to e-books, and preferred buying them at bookstores rather than online stores like Amazon. Apparently, 600 years of reading printed books has created a print habit that might survive the Internet!

Millennials are only half as likely to subscribe to a print newspaper (13% vs. 26% for elders), but they are more likely to read news on digital news sites or get news (or links to news stories) from social sites, and to use their cell phones to follow news stories. Millennials are not news-less: 69% read news stories every day, some in print and even more online.

Given Millennials' intense exposure to high speed, interactive, "twitch"-oriented video and video games, surely they are not about to watch passive TV series online or offline, like regular cable television, or stream feature-length movies that require concentration. Surely they would not sit for thirty hours to binge watch a TV series already ten years old. Here too, the evidence does not fit the stereotype, although there are some differences. Contrary to the stereotype, Millennials watch 100–130 hours of regular cable TV per month, about the same as older adults. Marketers believe Millennial interest in TV is greater than any generation. Over 70% watch television live, without digital delays or streaming, slightly less than older adults. They

(continued)

like comedy and sitcoms more than older adults, and are more likely to watch TV on a smartphone or tablet. They also adore older TV series that they may have watched as children. In fact, they seem to have transformed the Internet from a media that involves reading to one that involves viewing. About 55% of binge viewers are Millennials.

Millennials are more involved with online video: they watch 200 more videos per month than older adults, mostly on YouTube, in large part because they are more likely to have and use smartphones. Millennials are nearly twice as likely to use streaming services like Netflix, Hulu, and Amazon, and are less likely to have cable or satellite TV service than older adults (60% vs. 80%). About 13% of Millennials have no pay TV service, not that different from 9% of older adults. Millennials are not cutting the cord in large numbers. They are using their smartphones and tablets as TV substitutes, viewing TV shows wherever and whenever they want. Almost 20% of Millennials use only a mobile device for Internet access, compared to 5% for older adults. Millennials are driving a surge in YouTube action sports videos (surfing, skateboarding, and snowboarding). Red Bull, the energy drink company, has over 4.5 million views of its action sports YouTube channel. When it comes to finding interesting TV shows and videos, Millennials rely much more than other adults on their Facebook friends and newsfeeds. Finally, Millennials play a more active role in creating video content than older adults by posting photos and videos to social sites.

Millennials really do consume content differently than older adults of previous generations, although the differences appear to be far less and more commonsensical than journalists portray. For instance, Millennials take more advantage of the latest technologies from smartphones to access streaming music and TV services than, say, Baby Boomers, although Baby Boomers, the generation that created the digital revolution, have adopted the new technologies nearly as much. Millennials have not lost interest in society or news about society, they just access it online somewhat more than older adults. Millennials do indeed create and share more content than elders, and control their TV schedules more often, including binge viewing, even though they are watching hundreds of hours of cable TV every month.

Millennials are different, but not so different that we don't recognize them as our children, inheritors of very powerful digital technologies, to be sure, but inheritors also of several thousand years of literature, history, and culture, which they continue to find of enduring value.

SOURCES: "For Online Sports Videos, the Action Is Off the Field," by Conor Dougherty, *New York Times*, September 11, 2015; "The Rise of Phone Reading," by Jennifer Maloney, *Wall Street Journal*, August 14, 2015; "Millennials: Seven Insights into Their Evolving Screen Choices and Viewing Habits," by Jeremy Kressman, eMarketer, Inc., August 2015; "State of the News Media 2015," by Amy Mitchell, Pew Research Center, Journalism and Media, April 29, 2015; "Millennials' Media Usage," by Mark Doliver, eMarketer, Inc., April 2015; "New Research Reveals Print Habits Die Hard With Millennial Readers," Publishingtechnology.com, March 26, 2015; "How Millennials Get News: Inside the Habits of America's First Digital Generation," by The Media Insight Project, American Press Institute, March 16, 2015; "15 Economic Facts About Millennials," by The Council of Economic Advisers, The White House, October 2014; "Younger Americans and Public Libraries: How Those Under 30 Engage With Libraries and Think About Libraries' Role in Their Lives and Communities," by Kathryn and Lee Ranie, Pew Research Center, September 10, 2014; "Millennials in Adulthood: Detached From Institutions, Networked With Friends," Pew Research Center, March, 2014; "A Generation in Transition: Religion, Values, and Politics Among College-Age Millennials. Findings from the 2012 Millennial Values Survey," by Robert P. Jones, Daniel Cox, and Thomas Banchoff, Public Religion Research Institute, Berkeley Center, Georgetown University, 2013; "Younger Americans' Reading and Library Habits," by Kathryn Zickuhr, et al., Pew Research Center, October 23, 2012; "Are Digital Natives a Myth or Reality? University Students' Use of Digital Technologies," by Anoush Margaryana, Allison Littlejohna, and Gabrielle Vojtb, *Computers & Education*, Volume 56, Issue 2, February 2011; "Digital Natives, Digital Immigrants," by Marc Prensky, in *On the Horizon* (MCB University Press, Vol. 9 No. 5, October 2001; "Digital Natives, Digital Immigrants, Part II" by Marc Prensky, in *On the Horizon* (MCB University Press, Vol. 9 No. 6, October 2001); "Millennials Rising: The Next Great Generation," by Neil Howe, William Strauss, and R.J. Matson, *Vintage*, September 2000.

Media Utilization: A Converging Digital Stream

The proliferation of mobile devices—tablets and smartphones—has led to an increase in the total amount of time spent listening to radio, watching TV and movies, and reading books, newspapers, and even magazines. Internet mobile and desktop account for over 60% of total media time spent. While the number of hours of TV viewing used to be far larger than Internet usage, since the development of mobile devices, time spent on desktops plus the mobile Internet is now expected to consume 5.4 hours compared to 4.15 hours spent watching television on a TV in 2015. On the other hand, a great deal of Internet usage is watching time-shifted television shows! In 2015, an estimated 153 million people will use their computers and mobile devices to watch television shows, about 50% of the general population. Therefore, the distinction between Internet usage and television usage is not easy to make. The method of transmission is just different: cable TV versus the Internet. The Internet, television, and movies are converging into a single digital stream. This convergence is described later in the chapter. Well over 60% of television viewers multitask while watching television, usually using a smartphone or tablet computer, texting with friends, reading e-mail, searching the Web, or visiting social network sites (eMarketer, Inc., 2014a).

Internet and Traditional Media: Cannibalization versus Complementarity

Several studies reveal that time spent on the Internet reduces consumer time available for other media (Pew Research Center, 2013). This is referred to as cannibalization. The alternative argument is that the Internet and traditional media are complementary and mutually supportive rather than substitutive. True, there has been a massive shift of the general audience to the Web, tablets, and smartphones, and once there, a large percentage of time is spent on viewing content. Yet, more recent data finds a more complex picture. Despite the availability of the Internet on high-resolution tablet computers, television viewing remains strong, video viewing on all devices has increased, and the reading of all kinds of books, including physical books, has increased. New television sets are Internet-enabled, allowing consumers to use the Internet to view TV shows on their traditional TVs. Total music consumption measured in hours a day listening to music has increased even as sales of CDs have drastically declined; likewise, movie consumption has increased even as DVD sales also decline markedly. Music streaming is growing at 30% a year. The impact of the Internet on media appears to be increasing the total demand for media, including stimulating demand for products like books. The overall pattern is that physical products like CDs and DVDs are being replaced by digital versions delivered on computers, tablets, and smartphones either as downloaded content or as streaming services.

Media Revenues

An examination of entertainment and media industry revenues reveals a somewhat different pattern when compared to media consumption (see **Figure 10.2**). In 2014, media of all kinds generated $264 billion in revenue (not including transmission fees

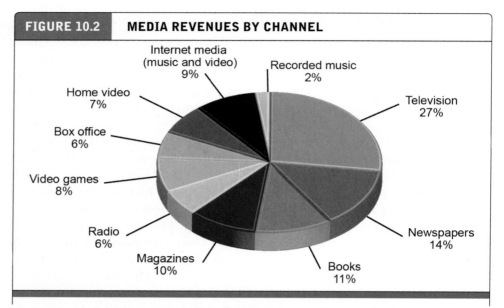

FIGURE 10.2 | **MEDIA REVENUES BY CHANNEL**

Internet media (music and video) 9%
Recorded music 2%
Television 27%
Home video 7%
Box office 6%
Video games 8%
Radio 6%
Magazines 10%
Books 11%
Newspapers 14%

Traditional media (television, print, and radio) still dominate the entertainment and media market, but Internet media (streaming videos, music, and content) is the fastest growing segment.

SOURCES: Based on data from industry sources; authors' estimates.

for content such as cable TV subscription fees). Television and home video accounted for about 34% of media revenues, print media (books, newspapers, and magazines) for 34%, Internet media (online music and video), 8.7%, music media (radio and recorded music), 8.4%, box office, 6.5%, and video games, 8.5%. Internet media, while relatively small now, is growing at 12% annually, far faster than traditional media revenues.

Three Revenue Models for Digital Content Delivery: Subscription, A La Carte, and Advertising-Supported (Free and Freemium)

There are three revenue models for delivering content on the Internet. The two pay models are subscriptions (usually "all you can eat") and a la carte (pay for what you use). The third model uses advertising revenue to provide content for free, usually with a freemium (higher price) option. There is also completely free, user-generated content, which we will discuss later. Contrary to early analysts' projections that "free" would drive "paid" out of business, it turns out that both models are viable now and in the near future. Consumers increasingly choose to pay for high-quality, convenient, and unique content, and they have gladly accepted free advertiser-supported content when that content is deemed not worth paying for but entertaining nevertheless. There's nothing contradictory about all three models working in tandem and cooperatively: free content can drive customers to paid content, as streaming services like Pandora and Spotify have discovered.

Online Content Consumption

Now let's look at what kinds of online content Internet users purchase or view online (**Figure 10.3**). It's not a surprise that 78% of Internet users watch online videos of many kinds, but it is a surprise that 67% of Internet users read newspapers. Listening to online radio and watching TV shows and movies online are the next most popular, followed by playing online games and listening to music on mobile devices. E-book consumption (32%) has grown at triple-digit rates since the Kindle was introduced in 2007 and the iPad in 2010 but has slowed to around 12% annual growth in 2015. What this reveals is that Internet users retain their affinity to traditional formats—newspapers, radio, TV shows, books, and music tracks and albums—and bring these tastes to the Internet and their mobile phones and tablets.

Figure 10.4 shows the estimated revenues from the online entertainment and media industries, projected to 2018. In 2015, total paid online entertainment content is estimated to be nearly $18 billion, and is expected to reach $26 billion by 2018. Online TV and movies is the largest and fastest growing online entertainment form, growing at 16% in 2015. Online music sales are no longer growing at double digits in 2015, but music remains the second largest revenue generator of online entertainment content.

The online video audience (both television and movies) is huge, estimated at around 204 million Americans who watch over 50 billion videos monthly in 2015.

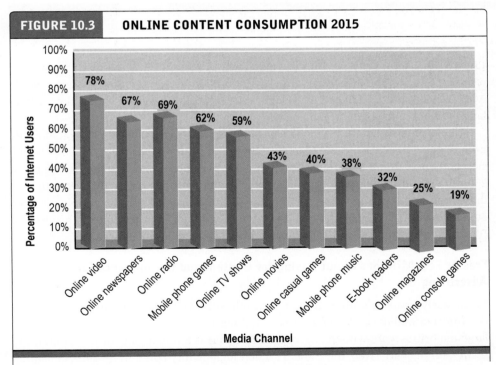

FIGURE 10.3 — ONLINE CONTENT CONSUMPTION 2015

SOURCES: Based on data from eMarketer, Inc., 2015b; industry sources; authors' estimates.

| FIGURE 10.4 | PAID ONLINE ENTERTAINMENT CONTENT REVENUES IN THE UNITED STATES, 2013–2018 |

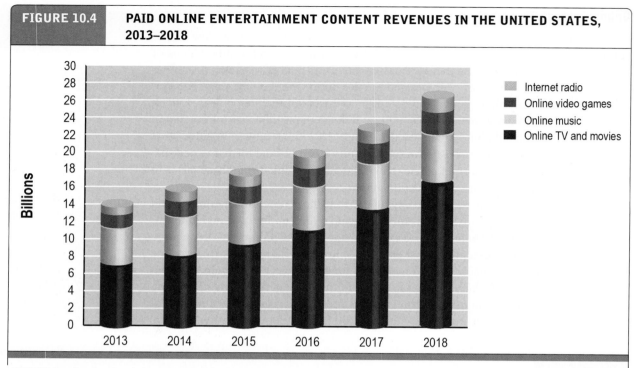

SOURCES: Based on data from industry sources; authors' estimates.

Figure 10.5 shows the top online video sites in May 2015. The most popular site remains Google (YouTube) with around 159 million viewers, followed by Facebook, AOL, Yahoo, and VEVO. The monetary value of all these videos is that they attract large audiences that can be shown ads.

The overall size of the online video audience (with more than 200 million monthly unique viewers in the United States) is about the same size as the traditional television audience. There are 116 million households with televisions, representing about 200 million individuals who tune in every month. However, major TV events tend to draw a much higher one-time viewership. For instance, 111 million people watched Super Bowl XLIX in 2015, the most widely viewed television program in history. No Internet video draws such large audiences during a single time period.

Free or Fee: Attitudes About Paying for Content and the Tolerance for Advertising

In the early years of online content, multiple surveys found that large majorities of the Internet audience expected to pay nothing for online content although equally large majorities were willing to accept advertising as a way to pay for free content. In reality, on the early Web, there wasn't much high-quality content. By 2015, consumer behavior and attitudes toward paying for content had greatly changed. Until Internet services such as iTunes arrived in 2007, few thought the "fee" model could compete with the "free" model, and most Internet aficionados and experts concluded that

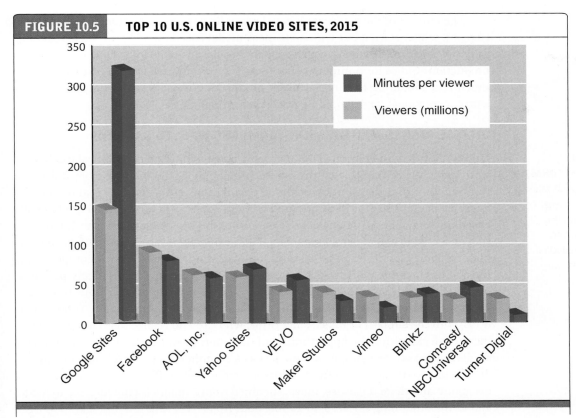

FIGURE 10.5 **TOP 10 U.S. ONLINE VIDEO SITES, 2015**

Legend:
- Minutes per viewer
- Viewers (millions)

Categories: Google Sites, Facebook, AOL, Inc., Yahoo Sites, VEVO, Maker Studios, Vimeo, Blinkz, Comcast/NBCUniversal, Turner Digial

SOURCE: Based on data from comScore, 2015a.

information on the Internet wants to be free. Cable TV systems and cable content providers like ESPN offer a totally different history: they always charged for service and content, and cable executives, investors, and TV experts never thought information wanted to be free. Neither did the Hollywood and New York media companies that paid for and provided the content to television and movie theaters. In 2015, millions of Internet users pay for high-quality content delivered on a convenient device such as a smartphone, tablet computer, or e-reader or using Internet TV services like Netflix, Apple TV, or Amazon. Like cable TV, Apple iTunes charges for service and content as well. In a demonstration of just how much quality online content is worth paying for, by 2015, Apple had sold over 35 billion songs, over 700 million TV shows, and more than 200 million movies. Worldwide, iTunes has more than 800 million credit cards on file. Pandora, the second largest source of Internet music with about 250 million subscribers, and the largest streaming service, has 80 million monthly active listeners. While an estimated 21 million Internet users in the United States still download songs from illegal P2P sites (down from 33 million in 2005), over 100 million people stream music to various devices both from the Internet and satellite services that are paid for by advertisers, and about 8 million pay for the stream as subscribers on a monthly basis (Sisario, 2015).

The culture of the Internet changed when firms such as YouTube (and its parent Google), which started out with a business model based on amateur videos and illegally uploaded music videos, began cooperating closely with Hollywood and New York production studios for premium content. As it turns out, free content isn't worth very much and should be free, especially if producers give it away. Premium content is worth a great deal, and should be priced accordingly.

DIGITAL RIGHTS MANAGEMENT (DRM) AND WALLED GARDENS

digital rights management (DRM)
refers to the combination of technical and legal means for protecting digital content from unlimited reproduction without permission

Digital rights management (DRM) refers to a combination of technical (both hardware and software) and legal means for protecting digital content from unlimited reproduction and distribution without permission. DRM hardware and software encrypts content so that it cannot used without some form of authorization typically based on a payment. The objective is to control the uses of content after it has been sold or rented to consumers. Essentially, DRM can prevent users from purchasing and making copies for widespread distribution over the Internet without compensating the content owners. While music tracks in the iTunes Store were originally protected by DRM, in 2009, Apple abandoned the practice because of user objections, and because Amazon had opened an online music store in 2007 without any DRM protections, with the support of music label firms, who came to realize that DRM prevented them from exploiting the opportunities of the Internet and perhaps even encouraged an illegal market. Streaming content services are inherently difficult to copy and redistribute. Movies streamed from Netflix are technically difficult for the average user to capture and share. Likewise, music streamed from Pandora is cumbersome to record and share. Streaming services, including both Apple and Amazon, use a kind of DRM

walled garden
refers to a kind of DRM that uses proprietary file formats, operating systems, and hardware to control the use of content after initial sale

called a **walled garden** to restrict the widespread sharing of content. They do this by tying the content to the hardware, operating system, or streaming environment. E-books purchased from Amazon can only be read on Kindles or Kindle apps and Kindle books cannot be converted to other formats. By locking the content to a physical device, or a digital stream with no local storage, the appliance makers derive additional revenues and profits by locking customers into their service or device and satisfy the demands of content producers to be fairly compensated for their work.

MEDIA INDUSTRY STRUCTURE

The media content industry prior to 1990 was composed of many smaller independent corporations specializing in content creation and distribution in the separate industries of film, television, book and magazine publishing, and newspaper publishing. During the 1990s and into this century, after an extensive period of consolidation, huge entertainment and publishing media conglomerates emerged.

The media industry is still organized largely into three separate vertical stovepipes: print, movies, and music. Each segment is dominated by a few key players. We do not include the delivery platform firms here, such as Comcast, Time Warner Cable, AT&T, Verizon, Sprint, and Dish Network, because in general they do not create content but instead move content across cable, satellite, and telephone lines. The transmission industry is itself highly oligopolistic, with two dominant players in each distribution market. In telephony and wireless distribution, AT&T and Verizon dominate. In cable distribution, Comcast and Time Warner dominate. Generally, there is very little crossover from one segment to another. Newspapers do not also produce Hollywood films, and publishing firms do not own newspapers or film production studios. The purchase of the *Washington Post* in 2013 by Jeff Bezos, the founder of Amazon, and an Internet mogul in his own right, was an anomaly. Even within media conglomerates that span several different media segments, separate divisions control each media segment. The competition between corporate divisions in mega-sized corporations is often more severe than with marketplace competitors.

MEDIA CONVERGENCE: TECHNOLOGY, CONTENT, AND INDUSTRY STRUCTURE

Media convergence is a much used but poorly defined term. There are at least three dimensions of media where the term convergence has been applied: technology, content (artistic design, production, and distribution), and the industry's structure as a whole. Ultimately for the consumer, convergence means being able to get any content you want, when you want it, on whatever platform you want it—from an iPod to an iPad, Android phone, or home PC, or set-top device like Apple TV.

Technological Convergence

Convergence from a technology perspective **(technological convergence)** has to do with the development of hybrid devices that can combine the functionality of two or more existing media platforms, such as books, newspapers, television, movies, radio, and games, into a single device. Examples of technological convergence include the iPad, iPhone, and Android ("smartphones") that combine print, music, pictures, and video in a single device.

technological convergence
development of hybrid devices that can combine the functionality of two or more existing media platforms into a single device

Content Convergence

A second dimension of convergence is **content convergence**. There are three aspects to content convergence: design, production, and distribution.

content convergence
convergence in the design, production, and distribution of content

There is a historical pattern in which content created in an older media technology migrates to the new technology largely intact, with little artistic change. Slowly, the different media are integrated so that consumers can move seamlessly back and forth among them, and artists (and producers) learn more about how to deliver content in the new media. Later, the content itself is transformed by the new media as artists learn how to fully exploit the capabilities in the creation process. At this point, content convergence and transformation has occurred—the art is different because of the new capabilities inherent to new tools. For instance, European master painters of the fifteenth century in Italy, France, and the Netherlands (such as van Eyck, Caravaggio, Lotto, and Vermeer) quickly adopted new optical devices such as lenses, mirrors, and early projectors called *camera obscura* that could cast near-photographic quality images on canvases, and in the process they developed new theories of perspective and new techniques of painting landscapes and portraits. Suddenly, paintings took on the qualities of precision, detail, and realism found later in photographs (Boxer, 2001). A similar process is occurring today as artists and writers assimilate new digital and Internet tools into their toolkits. For instance, GarageBand from Apple enables low-budget independent bands (literally working in garages) to mix and control eight different digital music tracks to produce professional sounding recordings on a shoestring budget. Writers of books are beginning to think about video and interactive versions of their books. Online newspapers are changing the news cycle to a 24-hour stream, producing their own video channels, and expanding user comment opportunities on their Web sites.

On the production side, tools for digital editing and processing (for film and television) are driving content convergence. Given that the most significant cost of content is its creation, if there is a wide diversity of target delivery platforms, then it is wise to develop and produce only once using technology that can deliver to multiple platforms. Generally, this means creating content on digital devices (hardware and software) so that it can be delivered on multiple digital platforms.

Figure 10.6 depicts the process of media convergence and transformation using the example of books. For example, consider this book. In 2015, this book was written with a view to appearing on iPads and Kindle e-book readers, and is moving closer to the media maturity stage, in which the book will be available mostly as a purely

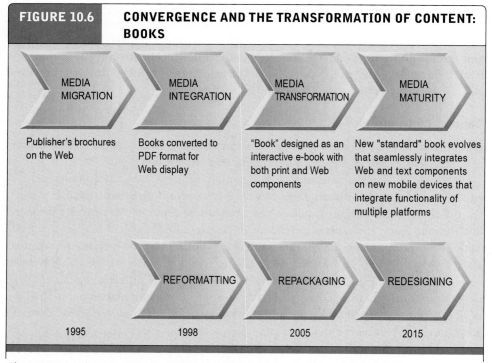

FIGURE 10.6 — **CONVERGENCE AND THE TRANSFORMATION OF CONTENT: BOOKS**

The Internet is making it possible for publishers and writers to transform the standard "book" into a new form that integrates features of both text and the Internet, and also transforms the content of the book itself.

digital product with substantial visual and aural content that can be displayed on many different digital devices. By that time, the learning experience will be transformed by greater use of interactive graphics, videos, as well as an integrated testing system that monitors student performance during the semester. Even the number of pages read by students, and the time on page, will be accounted for by this near-future digital learning system. Traditional bound books will probably still be available (books have many advantages), but most likely, print editions will be printed on demand by customers using their own print facilities.

Industry Structure Convergence

A third dimension of convergence is the structure of the various media industries. **Industry convergence** refers to the merger of media enterprises into powerful, synergistic combinations that can cross-market content on many different platforms and create new works that use multiple platforms. This can take place either through purchases or through strategic alliances. Traditionally, each type of media—film, text, music, television—had its own separate industry, typically composed of very large players. For instance, the entertainment film industry has been dominated by a few large Hollywood-based production studios, book publication is dominated by a few large book publishers, and music production is dominated by four global record label firms.

> **industry convergence**
> merger of media enterprises into synergistic combinations that create and cross-market content on different platforms

However, the Internet has created forces that make mergers and partnerships among media and Internet firms a necessary business proposition. Media industry convergence may be necessary to finance the substantial changes in both the technology platform and the content. Traditional media firms who create the content generally do not possess the core competencies or financial heft to distribute it on the Internet. Technology companies that dominate the Internet (Google, Apple, Amazon, and Facebook) have the competency and wealth to pursue Internet channel strategies, but do not currently have the competencies needed to create content. Business combinations and partnerships are made to solve these issues.

While traditional media companies have not done well in purchases of Internet platform companies, the technology owners such as Apple, Amazon, Facebook, Microsoft, and Google have generally avoided merging with media companies, and instead rely on contractual arrangements with media companies to protect intellectual property rights and to create a business pricing model that both parties can accept. However, this pattern may be changing. For instance, CBS Inc., a movie and television content producer, produces television shows for Netflix; Netflix and Hulu have begun production and distribution of their own original TV shows; Google is producing original content designed for Internet distribution on YouTube. Amazon created its own book imprint, Amazon Books Publishing, and entered the book publishing business. In this sense, the Internet is changing greatly the media industry from what it was in the recent past.

In the end, consumers' demands for content anywhere, anytime, and on any device is pushing the technology and content companies toward both strategic alliances and strategic conflicts in their search for advantage.

10.2 THE ONLINE PUBLISHING INDUSTRY

Nothing is quite so fundamental to a civilized society as reading text. Text is the way we record our history, current events, thoughts, and aspirations, and transmit them to all others in the civilization who can read. Even television shows and movies require scripts. Today, the publishing industry (composed of books, newspapers, magazines, and periodicals) is a $103 billion media sector based originally on print, and now moving rapidly to the Internet and mobile delivery. The Internet offers the text publishing industry an opportunity to move toward a new generation of newspapers, magazines, and books that are produced, processed, stored, distributed, and sold over the Web, available anytime, anywhere, and on any device. The same Internet offers the possibility of destroying many existing print-based businesses that may not be able to make this transition and remain profitable.

ONLINE NEWSPAPERS

Newspapers in 2015 are the most troubled segment of the print publishing industry. A free fall in revenues that accelerated with the recession of 2008–2010 has stabilized. Newspaper industry revenues have shrunk from their high of $60 billion in 2000 to about $31 billion in 2014. See **Figure 10.7**. The newspaper labor force has roughly been cut in half over this period. The newspaper industry has been in an extended period of digital disruption since the rise of the Web in 2000 and the emergence of powerful search engines like Google, which allow consumers to search for news on any subject without having to browse a physical newspaper or an online edition. Social media sites have become a major source of unique visitors, who, unfortunately, do not browse for news and usually stay on the newspaper's site for only a few moments to read a single article. These fleeting visitors typically do not engage with the newspaper as a whole or with its online ads. Even before the Internet and Web, newspaper revenue was falling due to the influence of earlier technologies like broadcast and cable television. In 2014, three of the largest newspaper organizations (Gannett, Tribune Company, and E.W. Scripps) span off their newspaper operations as independent firms so they could focus on television and other media assets, including in some cases, successful digital properties. Newspapers will now be pure-play print and online enterprises and will have to make it on their own without the protection of television or other media assets (Carr, 2014).

The striking growth of alternative pure digital news sources in the last five years, from Twitter and Facebook, to BuzzFeed, Reddit, and Huffington Post, poses additional challenges in 2015. Online news sources like Yahoo and Google News, and many others, are attracting millions of consumers everyday, and steer potential newspaper readers—both online and offline—away from the most valuable front page of print and digital edition newspapers. The shift of consumers toward the mobile platform and social media deepens the potential for disruption in the newspaper industry. Social media sites are playing a significant factor in directing traffic directly to specific newspaper articles, bypassing the newspaper's valuable front page, and increasingly, are

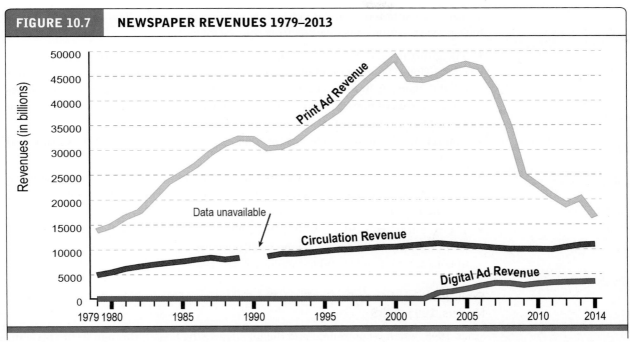

| FIGURE 10.7 | **NEWSPAPER REVENUES 1979–2013** |

Newspaper ad revenues have declined by 50% since 1980. As a percentage of total revenues, circulation subscription revenues have become more important. Digital is a small source of revenue but growing up until recently.

SOURCE: Based on data from Newspaper Association of America, 2014, Pew Research Center, 2015.

providing their own original reporting and commentary by hiring professional journalists away from troubled newspapers. In 2015, the *New York Times,* along with nine other news media outlets, agreed as an experiment to embed a few of its articles directly into Facebook's News Feed as a way to attract millions of new readers, and hopefully convert them from free readers to paid digital subscribers. Facebook calls these news stories **Instant Articles**. Other news publishers are considering a similar move. The downside is that readers might not ever return to the newspaper Web sites, which are the most lucrative for digital newspapers. Newspaper survival will depend on how fast newspaper organizations can transform themselves from print to digital, and how fast they can monetize the expanding audience for news all the time, anywhere, on all devices.

Instant Articles
a new Facebook feature that inserts selected articles from mainstream news outlets in a user's Newsfeed

As can be seen from Figure 10.7, while newspaper circulation revenues (subscriptions plus newsstand sales) have declined 10% since 2000 to around $11 billion, print advertising, which includes display ads, classified ads, and legal notices, has fallen precipitously from a high of $48 billion in 2000 to $16 billion in 2014. Online advertising in newspapers in the last year has shown weak growth, accounting for about $3.5 billion in revenue, and newspapers' revenues from online ads are still only 15% of print ad revenue, and only 10% of total revenue. The gains in online digital ad revenue are not large enough to compensate for the loss of print revenue. Only the music industry has suffered a similar devastating decline in revenue. The 15-year decline in newspaper revenues has resulted from four factors:

- The growth of the Web and mobile devices as an alternative medium for news and advertising. The movement of consumers to an online life style has drained billions of ad dollars (including classified ads) from the printed newspaper. The same has not been true of television advertising as we will discuss later in the chapter. Even radio advertising has stood up well to the digital revolution.

- The rise of alternative digital sources for news, commentary, feature stories, and articles.

- The difficulty of traditional newspaper firms and their managers to develop suitable business and revenue models that could survive and even prosper on the Internet, and the mobile/social platform.

- The rise of social media, and its role in directing traffic to newspaper content, has challenged newspapers to change their business model to accommodate changes in consumer behavior and technology.

From Print-centric to Digital First: The Evolution of Newspaper Online Business Models, 1995–2015

Since 1995, when e-commerce and digital advertising began, through to the present, newspapers have developed three distinct business models in an effort to adapt to the Internet, and more recently, the mobile and social platform (see **Figure 10.8**). The three models are: Print-centric (1995–2000), Integrated Print/Web (2000–2010), and the most current model, Digital First (2010–present). You can compare these models on four dimensions:

- **Search and discovery:** How do readers find the news?
- **Awareness:** How are potential readers made aware of news?
- **Engagement:** How are readers engaged with the news and journalists?
- **Technology platform:** How, when, and where is the news delivered to readers? (New York Times, 2014).

The milestones reflect important dates in the evolution of the Web and the mobile-social platform. In 1998 to 2000, Google launched its search engine with 60 million pages indexed, and introduced search engine paid advertising based on its Page Rank algorithm. In 2007, Apple introduced its iPhone, creating a truly mobile and universal Web device, and Facebook opened its site to the public, and in 2008 signed up over 100 million users, creating the first large-scale, online social network.

Prior to the development of the Web, search engines, mobile devices, and social media platforms, readers discovered the news by browsing (a form of searching) the printed paper. They became aware of stories by reading the front page, section pages, and article titles. Readers did not engage with journalists, editors, or other contributors, except for the few who wrote letters to the editor (less than 1% of all readers). Journalism was considered a profession, and readers were not expected to do much more than read and be fascinated, enlightened, and entertained by people who obvi-

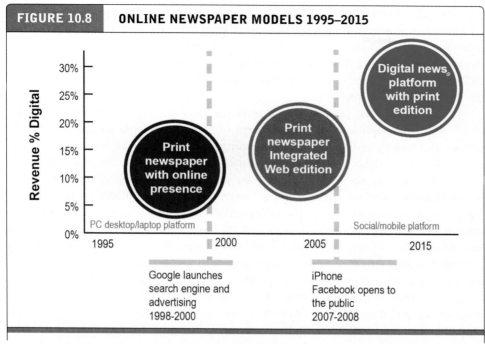

FIGURE 10.8 **ONLINE NEWSPAPER MODELS 1995–2015**

Newspapers have gone through three different business models as they adapt to the Internet.

ously were more informed than they. Journalists worked all day on their articles and filed them at 5 PM; professional editors revised the copy, and compositors put it on the page for the presses, which ran after midnight. The news stream ended at 5 PM. The technology platform was print, sometimes with color (a major innovation and expense in this period).

With the introduction of the Web and its growing popularity, newspapers retained their existing print-centric strategy and culture. In the Print-centric period from 1995 to 2000, newspapers created digital copies of their print editions and posted them online. Readers discovered stories as they did before, by reading the front page online, following links to stories, and clicking on topic areas or sections (e.g., Sports or Technology). Stories were promoted by a business department that sought to enlarge the print audience and to attract advertisers based on readership and online visitors. Digital advertising was very limited, in part because advertisers did not believe it was effective. Readers were not engaged with journalists except insofar as they read the stories and could identify with the subjects of stories. The business process of creating journalism did not change: articles were filed at 5 PM and went to print editors, and then were sent to the Web team and the print group. There was little difference, if any, between the print and online versions. The technology platform for the digital edition was the desktop or laptop, and news was consumed at home and work.

In the Integrated Print/Web period, from 2000 to 2010, newspapers adopted multimedia elements such as video, added more interactive elements like crossword puzzles and contests, and provided more reader feedback opportunities, especially on opinion and editorial pages. There were opportunities to personalize the news using RSS feeds and push news to the reader. Nevertheless, news was discovered by the reader visiting the Web site; promoting content online was limited, primarily to RSS feeds. Readers were somewhat more engaged. The technology platform remained the desktop or laptop platform.

In the Digital First period, from 2008 to the present, three developments in the technology and popular audience platform occurred: the rapid adoption of smartphones and tablets, and the equally astounding growth of social media sites like Facebook and Twitter, which have come to dominate consumer time on the Web and mobile devices. In addition, the rise of start-up news sites specifically focused on using the new technology and platforms has spurred newspapers to radically transform their business—or go out of business. The new platform is not based on personal computers using a browser, but on mobile devices and apps, with desktops and laptops now just one pillar of the delivery platform. In this new environment, the news does not stop at 5 PM, but goes on 24×7. Stories might start with a tweet, or from a Facebook post, followed by thousands of tweets, then millions of shares on multiple social sites and finally an article in the online newspaper, and perhaps in the print edition as well. Often amateurs on scene know more about the news in the first hours of a story than any collection of journalists in their offices. Amateurs provide video feeds, commentary, and opinion.

The Digital First business model inverts previous models: the top priority is producing the most engaging, continually updated digital edition, and then producing a print product based on the news developed in the digital edition. In the case of pure digital start-ups, there is no print edition, and the news is just a continuous stream of updates, blogs, tweets, and posts, rather than a fixed article. News articles are time-stamped, indicating an update is on the way and the reader should return to follow the story. Instead of waiting for readers to discover the news, or search for the news on a search engine, the news is pushed to readers on any of a variety of venues where they happen to be—social media sites, mobile news feeds, Twitter, or Yahoo or Google News. Journalists remain paid professionals, but they follow Twitter feeds and social media sites, and promote their stories and personas on social media sites. Their job is no longer simply reporting and writing, and getting the facts right, but promoting and engaging readers on a personal level through their own efforts. Superior reporting and writing is no longer the sole criterion for hiring and advancement. More emphasis is put on reporters' abilities to attract audiences on their own social media pages and Twitter feeds.

The Digital First business model is not yet a reality for traditional newspapers. The largest print newspaper organizations, such as the *Wall Street Journal*, *New York Times*, *Washington Post*, and others, have begun the journey towards becoming Digital First news organizations. In 2014 the *Wall Street Journal* launched its Real-Time news desk, a headquarters group of 60 editors aiming to produce a continuous and lively flow of digital news and commentary to social media sites, mobile followers, and its online sites (Romenesko, 2014). The *New York Times* also initiated a Digital First model in

FIGURE 10.9	UNIQUE MONTHLY VISITORS AT ONLINE NEWSPAPERS

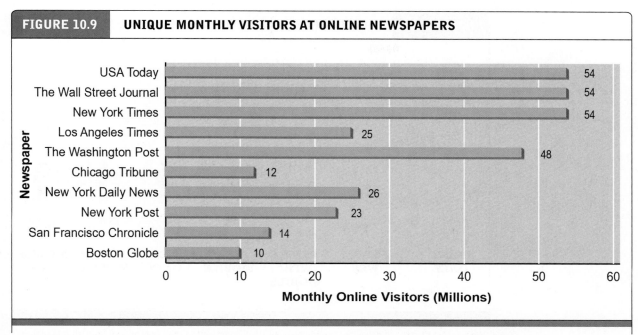

Online newspaper readership is expanding rapidly as consumers shift to mobile devices and participate in social networks.
SOURCES: Based on data from Pew Research Center, 2015.

January 2014. In 2015, the *Wall Street Journal* launched a new digital first Web site, with redesigned Web and video pages, iPad and Android apps, and a greater emphasis on breaking news stories that are refined in the course of a 24-hour news cycle (see the opening case in Chapter 4). In the past two years, the *New York Times*, the *Washington Post*, *USA Today*, and Bloomberg News have all made similar changes to succeed in a mobile-tablet-desktop digital market place.

Online Newspaper Industry: Strengths and Challenges

The newspaper industry still has some major strengths, which it will need to draw upon as it faces the challenges of the future. In the following section, we review those strengths and challenges.

Strength: Newspaper Audience Size and Growth. Online readership of newspapers is growing at more than 10% a year. About 67% of Internet users (about 176 million people) read newspaper content online, making it the second most popular online activity behind watching video, and is about 10% higher than 2014. See **Figure 10.9** for a list of the top ten online newspapers in the United States. The online newspaper is one of the most successful of all online media in terms of audience size. Mobile newspaper readership is especially strong among young persons due to their greater usage of smartphones and tablet computers.

Newspapers have responded to the changing audience by providing access to their content on all digital platforms (see **Figure 10.10**). With 59% of Americans having a

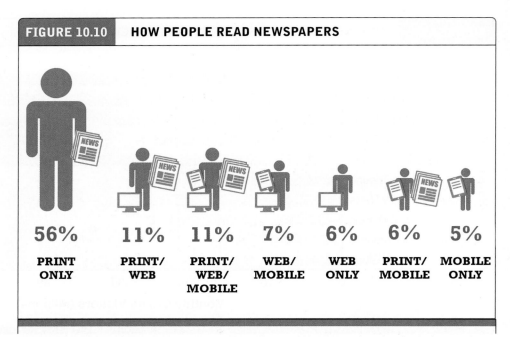

| FIGURE 10.10 | **HOW PEOPLE READ NEWSPAPERS** |

56%
PRINT ONLY

11%
PRINT/ WEB

11%
PRINT/ WEB/ MOBILE

7%
WEB/ MOBILE

6%
WEB ONLY

6%
PRINT/ MOBILE

5%
MOBILE ONLY

Web-only readership of newspapers remains quite small compared to print only and multi-platform reading.
SOURCE: Based on data from Journalism.org, 2015.

smartphone, 49% a tablet, and 75% accessing the Internet through mobile devices, in a few short years newspapers have become truly multi-platform by developing apps and Web sites optimized for mobile devices (eMarketer, Inc., 2015b; Pew Research Center, 2014a). Only 56% of newspaper readers are exclusively print readers, 45% use a combination of Web, print, or mobile. Mobile and tablet engagement is growing at more than 70% annually, especially among 18- to 34-year olds (Newspaper Association of America, 2014c).

Online newspapers also attract a wealthy and consumer-intense demographic, reaching 64% of 25- to 34-year-olds and 75% of individuals in households earning more than $100,000 a year on average throughout the quarter. Given the large online newspaper audience, it is clear that the future of newspapers lies in the online and mobile market even as readership and subscriptions to the traditional print newspapers continue to decline at a steady pace.

Challenge: Digital Ad Revenue. Newspapers hope that the digital ad revolution and revenue will hit their shores, and lift total ad revenues. But here's the problem: while unique visitors to newspaper Web sites are expanding, increasingly this traffic is less valuable for two reasons. First, the audience is increasingly coming from social media sites and search engines in order to find specific articles, rather than coming directly to the newspaper's home page (so-called side-door entry). Second, these visitors from social sites are less engaged, and less valuable (see **Figure 10.11**).

FIGURE 10.11 | **ROUTES AND ENGAGEMENT IN NEWSPAPERS**

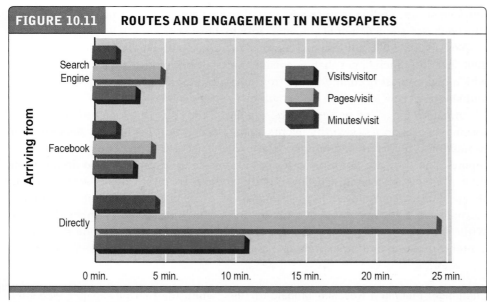

Newspaper visitors who come to newspaper Web sites directly in search of news are far more engaged and generate more digital ad revenue.
SOURCE: Based on data from Pew Research Center, 2014b.

The less engaged visitors are in terms of pages viewed, minutes on site, and return visits, the less time there is to show them ads and earn revenue. Direct visitors are therefore much more valuable and newspapers are hoping re-designed Web sites and apps will increase the number of home page visitors. As a result, growth in digital ad revenues at online newspapers has been tepid despite increasing unique visitors. While print ad revenue continued to decline in 2014 by an estimated 10%, newspaper digital ad revenue grew only 1.5%. In comparison, total Internet digital ad revenue (search, social, and display ads) grew at a robust 31% (eMarketer , Inc., 2015c). If current trends continue, it is unlikely newspapers can rely on growing unique visitors from social sites, or growing digital ad revenues, to reverse the revenue declines of the past decade. Instead they will need to build on their expanding digital subscription market composed of loyal readers who visit the paper everyday for curation and opinion.

Strength: Content Is King. Why do people continue to buy newspapers and pay for newspaper content online? The oft-repeated bon mot that "content is king" appears to be true in the case of print as well as online content of all kinds, including news and pure digital news sites. As in competitive sports, in general, quality counts. The reason why online newspapers attract exceptionally large and loyal audiences who are deeply engaged is simple: quality of content. Compared to other media, newspapers are the most trusted source of news and commentary on local, national, and international stories (Nielsen, 2013). Local newspapers produce the highest levels of ad engagement: 35% of consumers report making purchases on the basis of local newspaper ads. Online banner ads, e-mail campaigns, and fleeting mobile ads in a Facebook Newsfeed do not even come close to these engagement levels. Newspapers employ about 40,000 full-time professional editorial staff, down from about 60,000 in 2000, but still much larger than television, radio, or newer pure digital news sources, which obtain most of their content from unpaid bloggers, cellphone photographers, and bloggers (Pew Research Center, 2014c).

Amateur blogs and tweets may be wonderful for expressing opinions, or making instant reports on newsworthy events as they occur, but they are no substitute for professional reporters and editors, who make sense out of the constant stream of reports, and they are not a place for brand-conscious advertisers who do not want their products associated with low-quality content. In 2014, Google began offering Google Journalism Fellowships to journalism students in the stated belief that quality journalism is a key ingredient of a vibrant and functioning society (Wingfield, 2013a). While Internet news giants are dependent on newspapers to provide them with content to search and index, newspapers are equally dependent on Internet giants for visitors.

Challenge: Finding a Revenue Model. In 1995, when the first newspaper Web sites appeared, newspapers offered their content for free, with registration. The hope was that advertising would support the Web site's operation and provide a new revenue stream for the print edition content. In some cases, free content was limited to the most popular articles and did not include the classified ads, a lucrative newspaper franchise. At that time, print advertising provided over 75% of revenues and subscription revenue generated about 25%.

Charging for general newspaper content was an obvious answer, but publications that tried this during the 1995–2005 period were punished by an Internet culture that expected online content such as music and news to be free. For instance, in 1998, Slate, an online magazine owned by Microsoft, began charging its 140,000 readers a $19.95 annual subscription fee (a so-called **paywall**). There was a free Front Porch section with a few articles. In 1999, Slate dropped its subscription fee after only 20,000 readers signed up. Some specialized content newspapers, like the *Wall Street Journal*, were able to charge an annual subscription fee ($50 annually) and survive. In a year the *Journal* had 200,000 paid subscribers. Similarly, the *Financial Times* (London) introduced a subscription service in 2001, and in 2007 adopted a **metered subscription** model where readers got ten free articles but were asked to pay a $395 subscription fee after that. Both the *Journal* and *Financial Times* were exceptions to consumer resistance to paying for news, and based on a wealthy, focused readership interested in high-value information.

The introduction of the iTunes store in 2003, and the iPhone in 2007 changed the public perception of paid content. While plenty of pirated music was available, Apple devices (iPods and later iPhones and iPads) and iTunes provided a high-quality, convenient, and legal alternative that users were willing to pay for. In 2014, paying a subscription fee for content is the foundation of streaming video and music services from Netflix to Pandora.

paywall
paid subscription service

metered subscription
paid subscription service where some content is offered for free, similar to a freemium revenue model

Newspapers and online magazines have benefited from this change in popular culture. An estimated 450 of the country's 1,380 daily newspapers now charge for online access (Edmunds, 2013). These plans have three key elements: a paywall for heavy users; considerable free content for casual or link traffic (visitors from social media sites, for instance, who stay for a few moments and then move on); and a bundled price for both print and digital subscriptions, in some cases offering the digital version free with a print subscription, allowing users to read the paper on any digital device.

In 2011, the *New York Times* introduced a metered subscription model where casual readers could read 20 articles for free, and unlimited reading of current archived content for $35 annually. Print subscribers received the digital subscription for free. The free-to-print subscribers policy put the emphasis on subscription to the *Times* content, and not to any particular platform. This is important because today's newspaper readers are multi-platform: they read the content with a variety of devices depending on the context. A metered subscription model is identical to a freemium model: some content is free but ad-supported, while unlimited content is only through a subscription. In 2013, the number of free articles was reduced to 10, given the success of the metered model. In 2013, the *New York Times* subscription revenue exceeded ad revenue for the first time. In 2015, the *Times* has over 900,000 digital subscribers. In 2014, the *Times* introduced its NYT Now app for a subscription fee. It failed to attract more than 20,000 subscribers, and in 2015 the Times made NYT Now free, in the hope that many app users would eventually pay for a full priced digital subscription (Alpert, 2015). With 57 million online visitors and 20 million mobile readers, there's plenty of room for the *Times* to grow its subscriber base. Fortunately, for newspaper firms, the public has accepted the notion of paying for high quality content available nowhere else.

Challenge: Growth of Pure Digital Competitors. The Web has provided an opportunity for newspapers to extend their print brands, but at the same time it has given digital entrepreneurs the opportunity to disaggregate newspaper content by creating specialized Web sites for popular content such as weather, classified ads (Craigslist), restaurant and product reviews (Yelp), as well as topical national and international news sites and apps that compete with online newspapers. Despite the declining revenues of the traditional print newspaper industry, entrepreneurs have poured money into news sites, and even newspapers. Since 2011, Warren Buffett has purchased 28 newspapers for an estimated $344 million in a belief that newspapers delivering comprehensive and reliable information to small tightly bound communities, and that have a reasonable Internet strategy, will be viable for a long time (Berkshire Hathaway, 2013). In August 2013, Jeffrey Bezos purchased the iconic *Washington Post* for $250 million in the belief that newspapers are not just papers but news gathering and distribution businesses independent of any technology or platform (Hagey and Bensinger, 2013).

While actual print newspapers are attracting wealthy individual investors, venture capital investors have poured over $1 billion dollars into purely digital online news

TABLE 10.2	START-UP DIGITAL NEWS SITES
START UP	**DESCRIPTION**
Huffington Post	Founded in 2005, sold to AOL for $350 million in 2011. Aggregates content from traditional news outlets, invited paid bloggers, legions of unpaid bloggers, and original reporting.
Buzzfeed	Founded in 2006. Focus on using social media to generate viral stories. Buzzfeed focuses on shareable content like quizzes and listicles ("The five most important people"), and photos and gifs. This Digital First media organization also includes more traditional news topics like politics, business, and technology. Originally a news aggregator but now hiring journalists for traditional news reporting. In the top 50 Web sites in terms of traffic, exceeding *Wall Street Journal* and *Forbes*. Has raised $50 million in venture funding since 2012, with an estimated valuation of $850 million.
Flipboard	Founded in 2010. News aggregator app organizes stories in a magazine format that user flips through. Content drawn from traditional media and social sites, such as Twitter and Facebook datastreams, and then reassembled in an easy-to-navigate, personalized format in a mobile—and now a desktop—touchscreen environment. Apple's app of the year. *Time, New York Times*, and book publishers joining up to push content. Over 50 million readers. Has raised $110 million in venture funding since 2011 and is now valued at $800 million in 2015.
Vox	Founded in 2014. A property of Vox Media (2008) along with six other specialty brands, 300 Web sites, and 400 unpaid bloggers. The brands are deep verticals including SBNation (sports), The Verge (tech), Polygon (games), Curbed (real estate), Eater (food), and Racked (retail shopping). Vox covers politics and general news. Hired Ezra Klein (ex-*Washington Post* writer) to be editor-in-chief. Eschews banner ads for sponsored videos and stories. Vox Media has raised over $100 million, and is now valued at $380 million.
Reddit	Founded in 2005. Purchased by Conde Nast in 2006 and operated as an independent company. A bulletin board of user generated posts made up of 185,000 forums from science trivia, politics, videogames, humor, and photos. Registered community members can submit content, such as text posts or direct links. Mostly male, college-educated members contribute content. Limited advertising on the main pages. Unprofitable, but with 160 million unique visitors. Estimated market value $400 million.
Vice	Founded as a magazine in 1994 and moved on to Web sites in 2000 as Vice Media. Vice is a bulletin board of user generated articles, aggregated content, and photos. Focuses on irreverent content appealing to young readers, and reporting from dangerous locations. Vice's YouTube channel is a video-based news site. Reportedly valued by investors at $2.5 billion in 2015. Vice has 35 million unique visitors, and reportedly will generate over $900 million in revenue in 2015. Earnings are unknown.

sites. **Table 10.2** describes the leading native digital start-up news sites and their investment profile. Huffington Post and Buzzfeed were growing at over 100% a year although this growth is expected to slow in coming years (Fischer, 2014; Isaac, 2014). Within the last five years, both sites have surpassed the *New York Times* in terms of unique visitors, and currently BuzzFeed has 78 million unique visitors a month. Other more traditional pure online news sites like Yahoo, Google, ESPN, and CNN have also shown extraordinary growth (see **Figure 10.12**).

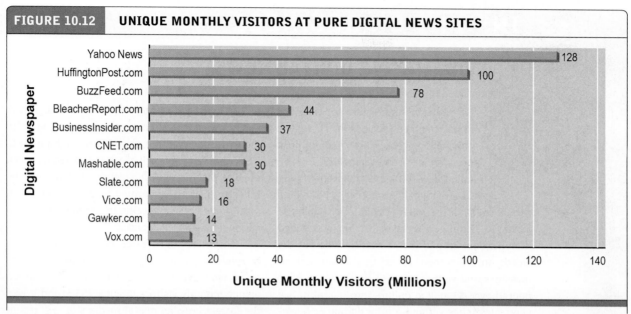

FIGURE 10.12   UNIQUE MONTHLY VISITORS AT PURE DIGITAL NEWS SITES

Native digital news sites have greatly expanded their unique visitor count and are direct competitors of established newspapers and their online editions.

SOURCE: Based on data from Pew Research Center, Journalism and Media. Newspapers: Fact Sheet, April 29, 2015.

Not all digital news services succeed, and none are profitable so far. For instance, Digg, a news aggregator site, failed in 2011 despite having 230 million unique visitors at one point.

Challenge: Can Newspapers Survive Digital Disruption. The newspaper industry would appear at first glance to be a classic case of a disruptive technology—the Internet, mobile devices, and apps—destroying a traditional business model based on physical products and physical distribution. Incumbents (the existing print newspapers) slowly and incrementally improve their products over time. New firms—disruptors—introduce new products (Huffington Post, Buzzfeed, Vox), which are not as good as the incumbents' products, but are based on newer and more powerful technologies. The new products are less expensive, or free, and target underserved or entirely new markets. They often are founded and promoted by people new to the industry. Eventually the disruptor's products are improved and become more acceptable, or good enough. At this point, the new products and the disruptors start draining significant market share from the incumbents who eventually fail. Incumbents fail for a variety of reasons, from an expensive legacy production process, large human capital investments, a contrary culture, and an inability to perceive rapid changes in the business and technology environment. For a description of a news industry start-up that may have a disruptive impact on traditional newspapers, see the *Insight on Business* case, *Vox: Native Digital News.*

INSIGHT ON BUSINESS

VOX: NATIVE DIGITAL NEWS

Despite the unprecedented array of entertainment options in the smartphone era, people are reading more news online than ever before. In fact, reading news online is the second most popular activity online with over 176 million people (67% of the Internet population) doing so in 2015. Digital news readers are highly engaged with the content and the journalists who put the words on the screen. All of this is not lost on investors and venture capital firms, which have poured over $1 billion dollars into digital native news sites (sites without a print edition or television franchise) in the last few years.

Vox Media is a prime example of a startup media firm grounded in the digital news stream that originated on the Internet and has since moved to a mobile social platform as well. Founded in 2003, Vox Media is a privately held company based in Washington D.C. with 400 employees. Vox Media does not reveal revenue figures although the company claimed it was profitable in 2014. The real money comes from venture capital, with the latest investment of $200 million in August 2015 from Comcast's NBC Universal division, valuing the company at a whopping $1 billion. Gaining access to NBCUniversal's content distribution and production capabilities will help Vox Media to branch out into other forms of multimedia.

Vox Media has pursued a unique strategy from the beginning. Rather than creating a single digital news site, as, say, traditional newspapers have done, and showing tabs for various areas of interest (sports, business, or entertainment), it instead has unbundled the general news site into a number of focused news sites, populating them with content from hundreds of different blogs that it has created or purchased. It started with SBNation (SportsBlogNation), a sports news site that is a collection of 308 blogs, each with its own name, URL, brand, and writer/bloggers. For instance, when you go to the SBNation Web site, you will see a tab for NFL. Click that, and you will see a list of teams. Click on, say, the Pittsburgh Steelers, and you will be taken to a Web site devoted to the Steelers, with much more content specific to the Steelers than a national newspaper provides.

These niche sites foster much greater intensity of reader engagement, and the approach seems to be working: Vox Media reached 54 million unique monthly visitors in June 2015, and it was the fastest growing digital media site in a recent report, with the typical visitor being an individual under 35 with income over $100,000 a year. Over 40% of its readership belongs to the coveted age 18-to-34 demographic.

Vox Media has built on the success of SBNation and currently owns eight specialty sites, which themselves are often collections of blogs or Web sites. Vox verticals include Eater (food), Curbed (real estate), Verge (culture), Polygon (game), Racked (fashion), Re/code (tech), and most recently, a general news and commentary site, Vox.com.

Vox.com was created in January 2014 when Vox hired respected political reporter Ezra Klein from the Washington Post, in large part because of Vox Media's technology for delivering online news and its commitment to digital news. Vox.com launched in April 2014. At Vox, Klein is aiming to create a new kind of digital journalism that will keep readers up to date with the news, but also provide background understanding and context to the news stream.

Vox Media is often regarded as the future of digital news publishing because of its technology, culture, and business organization. Traditional newspaper firms typically have a melange of technologies, built at different times, to coordinate the flow of news with both print and Web versions. At Vox, millions of dollars were invested in a content management system (CMS) called Chorus from the very beginning of the firm. A traditional CMS allows content creators to create text products that seamlessly integrate other types of media. Chorus goes beyond content creation and management because it provides the publishing environment as well. When reporters and editors are done, they can use Chorus to publish formatted content to various Web sites and social media. They can also read comments back from readers and eliminate inappropriate comments in real time. Chorus also features tools to help police reader comments more efficiently, as well as the Story Stream tool, which allows journalists to click and drag content from other stories and assemble it into a coherent document. Chorus is an extraordinary technological achievement.

Vox also has a unique organizational structure when compared to traditional newspapers. At Vox, the organization is flat, with fewer middle and senior managers. This gives extraordinary discretion to reporters compared to the lengthy editorial review process that can take hours at a traditional paper.

The journalistic process at digital news sites is also different from traditional newspapers. The discrete stages of a traditional print news site move in serial order (research, first draft, copyedit, fact check, second draft, proofread, composite, print). In a pure digital environment these steps are greatly compressed into a continuous process, with some stages running in parallel. For instance, research and drafting takes place with light editing, using a collaborative software environment that allows these steps to occur nearly simultaneously. Later, more in-depth editing and fact checking, re-drafting, and proofing all occur together, with publishing the last step.

Whether or not Vox will ultimately succeed depends on whether it is able to attract a large audience and enough advertisers to the site. Unbundling news into more focused, vertical Web sites and harnessing technology to reduce the cost and improve the speed of content creation has been a good start. But there still is one missing ingredient that traditional journalists point to: quality reporting. Critics worry that without interviewing newsmakers, doing background research, and taking the time to write an original article, news gains immediacy, but suffers in quality. Aggregating existing content adds no real economic value to the news stream. Business analysts also point out that few of the digital news sites, even Huffington Post, have generated profits. They are all money losers at the moment. Most of the digital news sites are private and do not report revenues or profits. Among the few that do, Yahoo reported 7% declines in ad revenue for 2014 and those losses have continued into 2015, with Yahoo losing another 7% in ad revenue. The pure digital news sites face the same problems online as traditional newspapers do, namely, the declining revenues from digital advertising. However, internal documents at Buzzfeed, the second most heavily trafficked "new media" company behind Huffington Post, show that the company has been profitable since 2013 and that its revenue tripled from 2012 to 2013 and was on track to grow another 140 percent in 2014. While the cost of generating traffic to these sites is substantial, Vox and its peers are continuing their push toward profitability.

■■■ **SOURCES:** "Internal Documents Show BuzzFeed's Skyrocketing Investment in Editorial," by J.K. Trotter, Gawker.com, August 12, 2015; "NBCU Ups Its Share of Vox Media," by Lukas I. Alpert, *Wall Street Journal*, August 12, 2015; "Vox Media Network," Quantcast.com, accessed August 12, 2015; "The Agency View on Vox Media: The Modern-Day Conde Nast," by Lucia Moses, Digiday.com, August 3, 2015; "Yahoo's Display Ad Revenue Falls Again," by Douglas Macmillan, *Wall Street Journal*, April 21, 2015; "Vox Takes $46.5 Million in Funding as Media Investments Stay Hot," by Jason Abbruzzese, Mashable.com, November 30, 2014; "Vox Media Ventures into General News and News Analysis With Vox.com," by Paul Farhi, *Washington Post*, April 7, 2014; "Vox Takes Melding of Journalism and Technology to a New Level," by Leslie Kaufman, *New York Times*, April 6, 2014; "Putting Journalism Cart Before Advertising Horse," by Michael Wolf, Usatoday.com, February 26, 2014; "Telling Stories About the Future of Journalism," by George Packer, *New York Magazine*, January 27, 2014; "Ezra Klein Is Joining Vox Media as Web Journalism Asserts Itself," *New York Times*, January 26, 2014.

Pure digital news sites have many advantages over print newspapers. They don't have the cost of printing papers; they can create new work flows and business processes that are more efficient and timely; they have a lower cost structure, often relying on user generated content and minimal payments to reporters and bloggers, with lower pension costs; and they can take advantage of newer technologies for producing the news. While the quality of journalism on these pure digital sites is not as good as traditional print newspapers, this situation is changing rapidly as the pure digital sites hire talented journalists and editors from print newspapers that are experiencing financial difficulties.

What online news sites often do not have is credibility and trust. For instance, Buzzfeed has been the subject of many lawsuits accusing it of copying content from competing newspapers and sites without attribution, claiming the content as its own. Without trust and quality, online news sites are simply distractions filled with celebrity photos, and there is significant competition for this kind of content.

If the newspaper industry has a future, it will be online and multiplatform. The challenge for newspapers is to create value by focusing on differentiated, timely, and exclusive content available nowhere else; to transform its culture of journalism to provide a continuous news stream just as its pure digital competitors; and to make this content available anywhere, anytime, anyplace, on any device. In short, newspapers will have to become Digital First publications, while maintaining their historic quality edge, and meeting the challenge from their pure digital competitors.

MAGAZINES REBOUND ON THE TABLET PLATFORM

Magazines in the United States reached their peak circulation in the early 1980s, with more than 40 million people reading some kind of weekly or monthly magazine. Most Americans at that time got their national and international news from the three weekly news magazines, *Time, Newsweek,* and *U.S. News and World Report.* The "glossies," as general-interest magazines were known, attracted readers with superb writing, short-form articles, and stunning photography brought to life by very high-resolution color printing (Vega, 2012).

Circulation fell after 2000 in part because of the Internet. At first, the Internet and the Web did not have much impact on magazine sales, in part because the PC was no match for the high-resolution, large-format pictures found in, say, *Life* or *Time.* Eventually, as screens improved, as video on the Web became common, and the economics of color publishing changed, magazine circulation began to plummet and advertisers turned their attention to the digital platform on the Web, where readers were increasingly getting their news, general-interest journalism, and photographic accounts of events (Pew Research Center, 2014c). Overall circulation declined by 2.2% in 2014.

Magazine newsstand sales have declined significantly since 2001. Yet special-interest, celebrity, homemaking, and automobile magazines remained stable. The largest monthly subscription magazine for several decades has been the *AARP* (American Association of Retired Persons) magazine, with a paid circulation of over 20 million readers. News magazines like *Time, Newsweek,* and *U.S. News and World Report* have done less well than picture-oriented magazines in fashion, celebrity, and lifestyle (Trachtenberg, 2015).

While newstand sales are falling at about 10% a year, and subscription sales are flat, magazines have responded by developing digital replica magazines—fairly close copies of the physical magazine. Currently, there are about 300 digital replica magazines, and about 8 million units are sold each year. Total revenues from subscriptions and newstand sales of magazine are expected to be around $25 billion in 2015, about the same as 2014, and revenues are expected to remain flat through 2020. Ad revenues will constitute $15 billion of the total. The good news for magazines is that digital revenues are climbing at 22% a year, amounting to nearly $4 billion in 2015. Unfortunately, print advertising (about $13 billion) is declining at 4% a year (Sebastian, 2014). The increasing digital revenue is not quite enough to compensate for the decline in print ad revenue (eMarketer, Inc., 2014c). The magazine industry parallels closely the newspaper industry: newstand sales are down, circulation and subscription revenues are flat, print ads are down, digital ads are up (Magazine Publishers Association, 2014). One possible solution is to begin charging a subscription fee for access to the digital editions, which currently are often free. The *New Yorker*, perhaps the most prestigious magazine in the country, is also one of the most widely read, with 1 million print subscribers and 12 million unique visitors to its Web site. In 2014, the magazine introduced a metered paywall. Some articles are free, but frequent readers will be charged an annual subscription fee (Somaiya, 2014). Like newspapers, magazines are experimenting with different revenue models in an effort to monetize the rapidly growing tablet audience. Most magazines participate in Apple's iPad Subscription Service, which allows magazines to offer subscriptions from within their app and have the transaction processed by the App Store billing system. Publishers set the price, and customers can subscribe with one click. Apple keeps 30% of the transaction. Publishers can also direct app readers to their Web site for a subscription, in which case Apple does not make any fee. Virtual storefronts such as Google Play have helped publishers grow their digital subscriber base. In 2015, Apple introduced its News app. Magazines such as *Time* and 75 others will publish articles in an effort to capture a younger, mobile audience (Trachtenberg, 2015).

Despite the shrinkage of print subscription and newsstand sales in the past few years, the growth of digital magazine sales has been extraordinary. The total magazine audience size increased over 10% in 2015, due entirely to growth of digital magazines, especially mobile Web editions, and the percentage of online readers of magazines tripled in the last three years (Magazine Publishers Association, 2015). Almost one-third of the Internet population in the United States (about 65 million people) read magazines online. More than 35% of tablet computer owners read magazine content once a week, and there are an estimated 1,200 magazine apps for mobile readers.

Popular Web sites like Pinterest, an image-collecting site that attracts millions of women, and Facebook, Yahoo, and Twitter are among the largest drivers of traffic to digital magazines. The widespread adoption of tablet computers has helped create the visual Internet, where glossy magazine publishers, who are inherently oriented to richly detailed color photography, can display their works and advertisements to great advantage.

With hundreds of popular online magazines to choose from, magazine aggregators like Zinio, Next Issue Media, Magzter, Flipboard, and Pulse make it possible for customers to find their favorite magazines using a single app. A **magazine aggregator** is a Web site or app that offers users online subscriptions and sales of many digital magazines.

magazine aggregator
a Web site or app that provides subscriptions and sales of many digital magazines

E-BOOKS AND ONLINE BOOK PUBLISHING

In April 2000, Stephen King, one of America's most popular writers, published a novella called *Riding the Bullet*. This novella was only available as an e-book. King was the first major fiction writer to create an e-book-only volume of a new work. King's publisher, Simon & Schuster, arranged for sales online through online retailers such as Amazon. In the first day, there were 400,000 downloads, so many that Amazon's servers crashed several times. More than 600,000 downloads occurred in the first week. While Amazon gave the book away for free in the first two weeks, when it began charging $2.50 for a 66-page novella—about the same price per page as a standard King hardcover novel—sales continued to be brisk. This experiment showed Simon & Schuster, and Amazon, that there was a mass market for e-book popular fiction. Previous efforts to create a popular e-book had all failed. For publishers, it meant their entire back list of older books suddenly had monetary value if they could be sold as e-book editions.

Ten years later, on April 15, 2010, Amanda Hocking, an unknown and unpublished writer from Austin, Minnesota, uploaded one of her vampire novels, *My Blood Approves*, to Amazon's self-publishing site, and later to the Barnes & Noble e-book store. Her novels had been rejected by many of the publishing houses in New York. By March 2011, she had sold more than 1 million copies of her e-books, which generally sell for 99 cents to $2.99, and earned more than $2 million. In 2012, Hocking was listed as one of the Amazon 99 cent millionaires. In 2013, Hugh Howey's self-published science fiction e-book *Wool* sold more than 500,000 copies and earned him more than $1 million dollars in royalties and film rights. Around 25% of Amazon's top 100 selling books are now self published. Twenty-three so-called Indie (independently published) books have sold more than 250,000 copies, and four Indie authors have sold more than 1 million copies of their books, according to Amazon (Alter, 2013). Admittedly these success stories are rare, and the vast majority of Indie authors in 2015 are unable to make a living, let alone $1 million.

The book publishing industry's experience with the Internet is very different from the newspaper and magazine industries. E-book editions of fiction and non-fiction books (so-called trade books) have been very successful, yet printed book sales have not collapsed and have remained about the same over time. Professional books, which includes college textbooks, remain almost entirely printed for a variety of reasons. Book publishing revenues have been stable over the last five years. In 2014, the book publishing industry generated $28 billion in revenue and sold 2.7 billion books (both e-books and printed books). Trade books (general fiction and non-fiction) generated

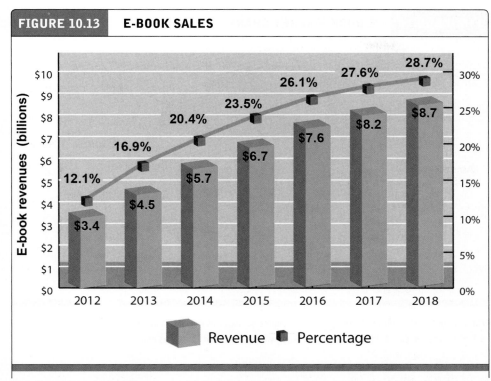

| FIGURE 10.13 | E-BOOK SALES |

This figure shows both total revenues and the percentage that e-books sales constitute of total book sales revenues. The growth rate of e-books has markedly slowed since 2013. E-books account for about 23% of all book sales.

SOURCE: Based on data from Association of American Publishers, 2015a; 2015b; authors' estimates.

$14.6 billion in revenue on sales of 2.3 billion books (AAP, 2015). These numbers are 1% higher than 2013.

In the space of a decade, e-books have gone from an unusual experiment by a major author, to an everyday experience for millions of Americans, and an exciting new market for authors. Sales of e-books have exploded in a few short years, and the process of writing, selling, and distributing books has changed. E-book sales in 2015 are expected to be $6.7 billion dollars, 23% of all consumer book sales. By 2018, this percentage is expected to grow to 29% (see **Figure 10.13**). Accounting for e-book sales in the mix of total book sales is difficult because 30% of the books sold on Amazon do not have ISBNs (International Standard Book Numbers), and therefore, are not counted by the publishing industry, whose books always have ISBN identifying numbers. Industry-based reports on e-book sales only include those published with ISBNs, and Indie books generally do not have ISBNs. (Author Earnings Report, 2015). Analysts estimate that 25% of Amazon's e-book sales result from Indie written e-books. The industry estimates presented here likely underestimate e-book sales. An entire new channel for self-published authors now exists, a channel not controlled by the major

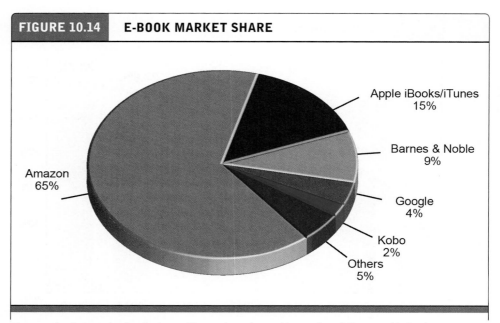

| FIGURE 10.14 | **E-BOOK MARKET SHARE** |

Amazon dominates e-book sales by a wide margin and uses this margin to influence e-book prices.

SOURCE: Based on data from various company filings with Securities and Exchange Commission.

New York publishing companies and their professional editors. In the process, the number of independent book sellers—the local book stores—has dropped significantly, from 40,000 to only 20,000 in 2015. The book distribution market was disrupted and yet in 2015 it is apparent that the major publishing firms have maintained their positions as the dominant source of book content.

But traditional book sales have remained stable in 2015. Paperback sales are up 5% while hard cover book sales are stable (AAP, 2015). The triple-digit growth of e-books five years ago has slowed to less than 10% on a unit basis. While the Kindle platform unleashed a torrent of indie manuscripts from thousands of would-be writers, only a few well-publicized authors have achieved popular success and a living income. Therefore, unlike the newspaper business, it's too soon to declare that the book industry has been digitally destroyed or wounded, and some reason to believe that printed books will continue to be with us long into the future. The e-book market in the United States is dominated by three players: Amazon, Apple, and Barnes & Noble (see **Figure 10.14**).

Amazon and Apple: The New Digital Media Ecosystems

Although precursors of e-books and e-book readers began to be introduced in the 1990s and early 2000s, it was not until 2007 that the future of e-books was firmly established. In that year, Apple released the first iPhone and Amazon introduced the Kindle, which allowed users to download books from the Kindle store using AT&T's cell network. Amazon's bookstore is the largest online bookstore on the Internet.

In 2015, Amazon's e-book and media store contains more than 1 million e-book titles and there are about 80 million adults who use e-readers like the Kindle and tablet computers like the iPad. One-quarter of all books sold in the United States are Kindle e-books, and Amazon in 2015 has about 65% of the total e-book market. Prior to the introduction of the iPad tablet computers, Amazon accounted for 90% of the e-book market. This did not last long: Apple's entry into the e-book marketspace temporarily reduced this share to 60% up until recently, when Amazon's share of the e-book market returned to near 65%.

E-books received another large boost in 2010 when Apple introduced its first iPad tablet computer. With its large screen and access to the iTunes Store of online music, video, TV, and books, the iPad was an ideal media entertainment device. And with its high-resolution screen, the iPad was an even better e-book reader than the Kindle, albeit not easily slipped into a purse. While Amazon got the jump on Apple in dedicated e-book readers, Apple's approach from the beginning was a multipurpose device that could handle movies, music, magazines, and books, as well having a Wi-Fi connection to the Internet. Apple's iBooks Store at launch in 2010 had 60,000 titles, and is estimated to have about 2 million titles in 2015. Apple has an estimated 20% of the e-book market, although it is gaining ground on Amazon's market share.

The result of the Amazon and Apple ecosystems, combining hardware, software, and online mega stores, is an explosion in online book content, readership, authorship, marketing, and at least a partial upending of the traditional book publishing and marketing channels. Traditional book publishing has similarly been altered. In the traditional process, authors worked with agents, who sold book manuscripts to editors and publishers, who sold books through bookstores, at prices determined largely by the publishers. Because bookstores had a vested interest in selling books at a profit, there was only limited discounting during clearance sales. In the new publishing model, authors still write books, but then bypass traditional agent and publisher channels and instead publish digital books that are sold on Amazon or the iTunes Store. Prices are determined by the author, usually much lower than traditional books depending on the popularity of the author, and the digital distributor takes a percentage of the sale (usually 30%). New self-published authors typically give away their early works to develop an audience, and then, when an audience appears, charge a small amount for their books, typically 99 cents to $2.99. Marketing occurs by word of mouth on social networks, author blogs, and public readings. While a small percentage of all books are produced this way, it is a growing and popular form of publishing and some authors are able to strike it rich. They're called "99 cent millionaires," and there's enough around to arouse the passions of thousands of potential writers of the great American novel, as well as lesser genres from police procedurals to paranormal romance writers.

E-Book Business Models

The e-book industry is composed of intermediary retailers (both brick-and-mortar stores and online merchants), traditional publishers, technology developers, device makers (e-readers), and vanity presses (self-publishing service companies). Together, these players have pursued a wide variety of business models and developed many alliances in an effort to move text onto the computer screen.

There are five large publishers that dominate trade book, education, and religious book publishing. These traditional publishers have the largest content libraries for conversion to e-books and they produce over 80% of new book titles in a year. In the e-book marketplace, the large publishers started out using a **wholesale model** of distribution and pricing, in part because this is the same model they used with hard cover books. In this model, the retail store pays a wholesale price for the book and then decides at what price to sell it to the consumer. The retailer sets the price with, of course, some kind of understanding with the publisher that the book will not be given away for free. In the past, the wholesale price was 50% of the retail price. A retailer would pay the publisher a $10 wholesale price and mark it up to a $20 retail price. However, retailers could also determine to sell the book at a much lower sale price, say $5, as a way to attract readers to the store or as a close-out sale. Brick-and-mortar stores had a vested interest in selling most books above their wholesale cost. With e-books, publishers discovered that some online retailers like Amazon and Apple might sell books below cost in order to encourage customers to purchase their e-book reader devices or to sell them other goods.

In the case of e-books, publishers sought to keep their prices high enough so as not to discourage sales of hard cover books, which typically sell for $26. Generally, this meant publishers wanted e-books to sell at a retail price of $12.99 to $14.99, depending on the popularity of the book and the stage in the product life cycle (months since first publication). E-book distributors like Amazon were charged a wholesale price of about $9 and were expected to mark up the product to around $12.99 to $14.99 or more. Instead, Amazon chose to sell e-books for $9.99, at or below cost, in order to attract buyers to its content store to buy Kindles, and to attract new customers to its online retail store. Amazon lost $1 to $3 on every e-book sold, but recouped the money by selling Kindles for hundreds of dollars, and from additional sales of other products. With Amazon selling e-books at $9.99, the lowest prices on the Web, publishers were forced to sell their e-books on all other Web sites at the $9.99 Amazon price. Using this strategy, Amazon not only sold millions of Kindles but also sold 90% of all e-book titles on the Web in 2010 and 2011. Amazon had a near monopoly on e-books.

Publishers opposed Amazon's policy as debasing the perceived value of both physical and digital books, and as a mortal threat to the publishers who could not survive if their e-books were priced at $9.99 across the Web. They claimed Amazon was engaging in predatory pricing, designed to destroy traditional book publishers. In 2010, five of the largest publishers secretly met with Steve Jobs and Apple. They agreed to a new pricing model called the agency model. In the **agency model**, the distributor is an agent of the publisher, and can be directed to sell e-books at a price determined by the publisher, around $14.99 and higher for certain titles. In return for a 30% commission, Apple agreed to support this model, as did Google, neither of whom were comfortable watching as Amazon dominated one of the hottest areas of

wholesale model
prices are determined by the retailer

agency model
the retailer is an agent and prices are set by the manufacturer

Web content sales. In these meetings, publishing executives discussed a common pricing strategy.

The agency model temporarily turned the tables on Amazon: it now had to charge whatever price the publishers wanted or the publishers would not sell Amazon any books (they would not choose Amazon as an agent for their products). A result of the agency model was that Amazon's prices on e-books rose to the publisher desired levels, and its market share fell to 60% in 2012. Apple, Google, Barnes & Noble, and the five major publishers were delighted. The Justice Department was not delighted: it sued the five publishers and Apple for price fixing in violation of antitrust laws. All five of the publishers settled, but Apple refused to settle and asked for a trial before a judge. In 2013, the United States District Court found that Apple had engaged in price fixing, not because of its agency pricing model, which is quite common throughout retail trade, but because of its "most favored seller" clause in its agreements with publishers, which had the effect of discouraging other sites (like Amazon) from selling e-books for less than Apple's iBooks Store price. In addition, the publishers and Apple conspired to act in concert, rather than as individual publishers. Under the agreements, the publishers, not Amazon, would determine prices on Amazon. If publishers sold their books on Amazon for $9.95, then publishers would have to sell their e-books at the iBooks Store for $9.95. The court found that Apple and the book publishers' plan would result in less price competition, and higher prices, by enforcing a single higher price on all online distributors and e-books. In the field of antitrust, less competition and higher prices for all is considered a cardinal violation of the law. After the ruling, e-book prices on Amazon have fallen to an average of $9.99, with some older titles far less, with limited discounting, and its market share rose to 65%. In August 2014, Apple agreed to pay a $450 million fine to compensate consumers for its price fixing behavior. While the ruling prevents Apple from fixing prices of e-books, it does nothing to solve the issues surrounding Amazon's dominance of the e-book marketplace. Publishers will need to each reach independent marketing agreements with Amazon, one by one. Critics of the court case believe Amazon's market power will force publishers to submit to Amazon's price terms.

In May 2014, following court rulings against the publishers, Amazon and the Hachette group tried to negotiate an agreement on pricing. To demonstrate its market power and strengthen its negotiating position, Amazon withdrew all Hachette books from its Web site, leading to author-organized protests. In November 2014, Hachette and Simon & Schuster (one of the largest publishers in the United States) agreed on terms with Amazon that allow the publishers to set the prices of their books (the agency model) but allow Amazon to offer incentives to publishers to reduce prices on selected books, and provide for publisher payments to Amazon for listing their books (Streitfield, 2014a; 2014b). Prices on e-books as a result are highly variable, ranging from $9.95 to $16.95.

The Challenges of the Digital E-Book Platform

Because of the rapid growth in e-books, the book publishing industry is in stable condition. Yet the industry faces a number of challenges. The early fear of cannibalization, namely inexpensive and less profitable e-books replacing more expensive and profitable print books, has mostly been put to rest. Unlike the newspaper and magazine industries, printed books are surviving in large part because purchasers of e-book readers continue to purchase printed books, and switch back and forth from digital to print as circumstances merit, and because more than 50% of book readers continue to prefer the physical format, while only 6% of book readers use e-books exclusively (eMarketer, 2014d). In the professional and educational book markets, e-books have not yet made substantial inroads. In an Hewlett-Packard sponsored study, 57% of college students preferred physical books and only 21% preferred e-books (Tan, 2014). Several other studies have found more than 70% of college students prefer physical books because they find it easier to concentrate when using a physical book, there are fewer distractions, and comprehension and retention is better (Student Monitor, 2014; Marques, 2012). Students find the user interface of e-books more difficult to use compared to printed books. E-books may be like audio books, a useful alternative but not a substitute. The falling growth rate of e-books from double-digit to single-digit growth in the last few years may reflect this market reality.

The biggest challenge facing the book publishing industry is control over pricing on the digital e-book platforms of Amazon, Apple, and others. Currently, Amazon controls the largest market share, about 65%, which, while not a monopoly, nevertheless gives Amazon extraordinary market power (refer back to Figure 10.14 on page 672).

For critics, Amazon threatens to decimate the traditional book publishing industry, replacing the old print world of a small number of publishers, limited numbers of titles, several thousand independent bookstores, elitist editors in New York, and newspaper book critics, with a new digital world of publishing where content is shaped by algorithms identifying what the consumer wants to read about, writers are their own editors, critics are replaced by reader comments, and distribution is controlled by one or a few online stores (Packer, 2014). Efforts by Amazon to create its own book publishing brand, circumventing the traditional book publishers, have only worsened relations between the world's largest book store and the world's largest publishers (Streitfield, 2014).

Amazon, as the largest player in the e-book market, offers the biggest challenge. This is ironic because Amazon, through its online store and Kindle e-book marketplace and reader, has helped the publishing industry to survive the transition to a digital marketplace, both by providing the largest book store on earth, and by creating the Kindle e-book platform. While the expansion of e-book revenues has offset a small decline in print sales, the industry has lost pricing power vis-à-vis its largest distribution partner, Amazon. Amazon, if not a monopoly, nevertheless exercises extraordinary market power over the publishers.

A second serious challenge is the further evolution of the digital distribution platform. In July 2014, Amazon announced Kindle Unlimited, a subscription service where for $9.95 a month, customers can read all the books they want. Over 600,000 titles are available, according to Amazon, but this Netflix for books does not include any books from the big five publishers—Hachette, HarperCollins, Simon & Schuster, Macmillan, and Penguin Random House. How the revenue of e-book subscriptions is split up has not been announced, but publishing firms (and authors) would surely want a substantial part of that revenue before signing up. Major publishers believe subscription e-book services would negatively impact book publisher and author revenues. Control over pricing is again the key issue.

While the book publishing industry has survived, even prospered, in the first era of e-books and the digital distribution platform provided by Amazon, Apple, and others, the long-term prospects for book publishing revenues and profits remain an open question.

Interactive Books: Converging Technologies

The future of e-books may depend in part on changes in the concept and design of a book. The modern e-book is not really very different from the first two-facing page, bound books that began to appear in seventeenth-century Europe and had already appeared in the fourth century BCE in ancient China. The traditional Western book has a very simple, nondigital operating system: text appears left to right, pages are numbered, there is a front and a back cover, and text pages are bound together by stitching or glue. In educational and reference books, there is an alphabetical index in the back of the book that permits direct access to the book's content. While these traditional books will be with us for many years given their portability, ease of use, and flexibility, a parallel new world of interactive e-books is expected to emerge in the next five years. Interactive books combine audio, video, and photography with text, providing the reader with a multimedia experience thought to be more powerful than simply reading a book. In 2012, Apple released iBook Author, an app to help authors create interactive books. Hundreds of children's books are already built as interactive books. In 2012, Apple also introduced iBook Textbooks, a line of interactive textbooks created by several of the largest textbook publishing firms. Some experts believe that traditional print books will be curiosities by 2020. Yet as of 2015 these newer multimedia textbooks have not yet been successful in the marketplace (Streitfield, 2013b). Among the failures are Social Books, Push Pop Press, Copia, Small Demons, and Vook, which promised to combine video with traditional print.

10.3 THE ONLINE ENTERTAINMENT INDUSTRY

The entertainment industry is generally considered to be composed of four traditional, commercial players and one new arrival: television, radio broadcasting, Hollywood films, music, and games (the new arrival). Together, these largely separate entertainment players generate $143 billion in annual revenue. This includes both digital and traditional format revenues. **Figure 10.15** illustrates the relative sizes of these commercial entertainment markets as of 2014. By far, the largest entertainment producer is television (broadcast, satellite, and cable), and then motion pictures, followed by music, radio, and games (both stand-alone and online games). While online, computer,

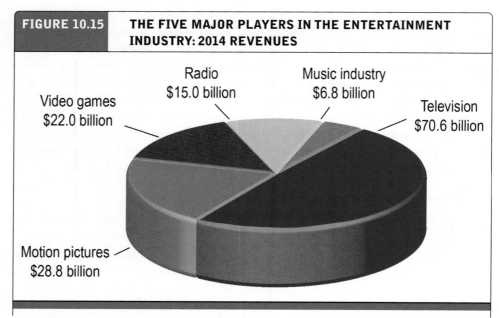

| FIGURE 10.15 | THE FIVE MAJOR PLAYERS IN THE ENTERTAINMENT INDUSTRY: 2014 REVENUES |

Radio $15.0 billion

Music industry $6.8 billion

Video games $22.0 billion

Television $70.6 billion

Motion pictures $28.8 billion

SOURCES: Based on data from industry sources; authors' estimates.

and console games have grown to be larger than film box office revenues (about $10 billion), total Hollywood film revenues dwarf the game industry when other sources of movie revenue are added such as streaming, DVD rental and sales, and licensing. Radio remains a strong revenue producer aided in part by the growth of Internet radio services like Spotify and Pandora, but is still largely reliant on FM and AM broadcast technologies, especially in automobiles. Recorded music is the smallest of the major players at $12 billion, half of its size ten years ago.

Along with the other content industries, the entertainment segment is undergoing a transformation brought about by the Internet and the extraordinary growth of mobile devices. Several forces are at work. Accelerated platform development such as the iPhone/iPad video and music platform, other smartphones and tablets, the Amazon music and video platform, not to mention the Netflix streaming platform, have changed consumer preferences and increased demand for music, video, television, and game entertainment delivered over Internet devices, whether in subscription or a la carte pay-per-view forms. Social network platforms are also spurring the delivery of entertainment content to desktop and mobile devices. Social network sites are rapidly adding video to their services, as well as providing a platform for sharing TV and movie experiences. The iTunes store and Amazon have demonstrated successful download music services where users pay for tracks and albums. Music subscription services like Pandora, Spotify, and Rhapsody have never made a profit and bleed cash despite having millions of subscribers. Both kinds of services—download and streaming—have demonstrated that millions of consumers are willing to pay reasonable prices for high-quality content, portability, and convenience. The growth in broadband has obviously made possible both wired and wireless delivery of all forms of entertainment over the Internet, potentially displacing cable and broadcast television networks. Closed platforms, like the Kindle and streaming services like Netflix, also work to reduce the need for DRM. Streaming music and video are inherently copyright-protected because the content is never downloaded to a computer (similar to cable TV). All of these forces have combined in 2015 to bring about a transformation in the entertainment industries.

In an ideal world, consumers would be able to watch any movie, listen to any music, watch any TV show, and play any game, when they want, and where they want, using whatever Internet-connected device is convenient. Consumers would be billed monthly for these services by a single provider of Internet service. This idealized version of a convergent media world is many years away, but clearly this is the direction of the Internet-enabled entertainment industry, in part because technology will enable this outcome, but also because of the emergence of very large-scale, integrated technology media companies like Amazon, Google, Apple, and Netflix. Many analysts believe the large entertainment media giants of the future will be technology companies that have moved into the production of content.

When we think of the producers of entertainment in the offline world, we tend to think about television networks such as ABC, Fox, NBC, HBO, or CBS; Hollywood film studios such as MGM, Disney, Paramount, and Twenty-First Century Fox; and music labels such as Sony BMG, Atlantic Records, Columbia Records, and Warner Records. Interestingly, none of these international brand names have a significant entertainment presence on the Internet. Although traditional forms of entertainment such as television shows and Hollywood movies are now commonplace on the Web, neither the television nor film industries have built an industry-wide delivery system. Instead, they are building relationships with tech-based Internet distributors like Netflix, Yahoo, Google, Amazon, Facebook, MSN, and Apple, all of whom have become significant players in media distribution.

ONLINE ENTERTAINMENT AUDIENCE SIZE AND GROWTH

Measuring the size and growth of the Internet content audience is far less precise than measuring a television audience. In fact, one of the issues facing television producers is an inability to count Internet viewing, or time-delayed viewing. Recognizing the difficulties of measuring an Internet audience, let's first examine the use of traditional entertainment content, such as feature-length movies, music, online TV, online radio, and games. **Figure 10.16** shows the current and projected growth for commercial online entertainment revenues for the major players: music, Internet radio, online TV, online games, and online video. Most noticeable is the extraordinary growth of online TV and movies, driven in large part by adoption of mobile devices, as well as the success of TV and movie streaming sites. Other forms of online entertainment will also continue to grow, but at single-digit rates. As the Internet takes on the distribution of TV shows and movies, the role (and revenue) of cable television delivery systems declines.

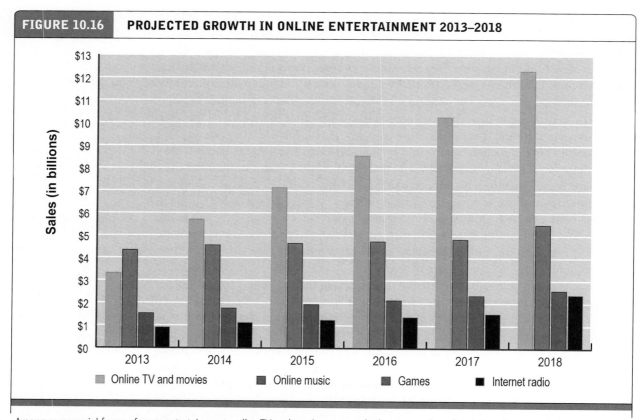

FIGURE 10.16 **PROJECTED GROWTH IN ONLINE ENTERTAINMENT 2013–2018**

Among commercial forms of mass entertainment, online TV and movies engage the largest number of people and generate the largest online revenues in 2015. By 2017, TV and movies will engage more people and generate more revenue than all other forms of digital media, including music.

SOURCES: Based on data from industry sources; authors' estimates.

There will be some interesting changes by 2018. Movies will surpass music as the largest form of online entertainment. Online TV will grow very rapidly (by more than 15% annually), while online games and radio remain relatively smaller generators of revenue, declining in significance when compared to movies, music, and TV.

TELEVISION AND PREMIUM VIDEO

In the television industry in 2015, viewers have gone mobile, Internet streaming and downloading distributors like Netflix and Apple have gained market power vis-à-vis TV and movie production firms, and cable television systems are losing ground to Internet and mobile app delivery of content. New streaming services provided by firms like Netflix, Hulu, and Amazon, and convenient downloading of movies and entire TV series, have created powerful alternatives to traditional cable television delivery systems. Cable distribution systems are challenged as the Internet offers alternative, unbundled, a la carte access to TV programs. **Linear TV**—watching a TV

linear TV

watching a television series in installments over an entire season

series over an entire season as installments—is being supplanted by **binge watching** of entire seasons online over a few days . This is not possible with linear TV on cable or broadcast platforms. Contrary to expectations, the big TV screen in the home is as popular as ever, supported by social networks that buzz with chat about what's on TV right now. In 2015, over 153 million Americans watch TV online, about 60% of the Internet population (eMarketer, Inc., 2015b). Increasingly, the TV household is a cross-platform phenomenon. Every day, Americans watch about 4½ hours of TV on tradi-tional TV sets, but 5¾ hours online using a computer or mobile device. While teens continue to spend more time texting than ever, over 90% of millennials (ages 16–34 in 2015) report watching streamed television shows and movies (eMarketer, Inc., 2015c). The largest online TV and movie download distributor is Apple's iTunes (which provides downloads or cloud storage and rentals, but not until recently a streaming service). iTunes has 67% of the digital TV download market and 65% of the movie download market. No competitor comes close to producing Apple's combined TV plus movie download 2014 revenue of $2.1 billion annually. It's a different story with streaming video: Netflix is the market leader in streaming movies and TV shows, producing $3.4 billion in revenue in 2014. Streaming has replaced downloading as the leading consumer video viewing platform.

The television industry, the major source of premium video on the Internet, is beginning a transition to a new delivery platform—the Internet and mobile smart-phones and tablet computers. As a result, the cable and satellite TV distribution model is challenged by new Internet competitors. Over 107 million consumers use a mobile phone to watch movies and television (eMarketer, Inc., 2015d). This transition closely follows an earlier but related transition to DVRs and time-shifting by consumers who no longer were constrained by television executives' programming and scheduling decisions. The current transition to Internet and especially mobile delivery of televi-sion is not leading to a decline in traditional television viewing, which has in fact increased slightly. The new platform is changing how, when, and where consumers can watch TV. Cloud computing, the storage and streaming of content from large Internet datacenters rather than on individual personal devices, has created a large shift away from ownership of content, and a focus instead on access to content any-where, anytime, from any device as a streaming service. Streaming of movies from subscription services has expanded more rapidly than buying and downloading of movies. Social networks have enabled a new kind of **social TV**, where consumers share comments while viewing television shows. The most important activity in today's television household may not be what's on screen, but instead what's being said about what's on screen. Television rating agencies today do not have a methodol-ogy for measuring this kind of engagement.

Expansion of broadband networks, especially those serving mobile devices such as Wi-Fi and high-speed cellular networks, and the growth of cloud servers, has enabled the growth of a whole new class of television distributors. Cloud distributors, like Apple's iCloud service and Walmart's Vudu service, allow users to purchase video and movies, store them in iCloud, and view the entertainment from any device, anywhere. Whereas the dominant way consumers obtained a TV signal in the past was from over-

binge watching
watching a television series in its entirety in single or multiple sittings in a brief period of time

social TV
involves consumers sharing comments via social networks while viewing television

TABLE 10.3	NEW DIGITAL TV SUBSCRIPTION SERVICES
DIGITAL SERVICE	**PROVIDER**
LIVE AND ON-DEMAND SERVICE	
Dish Sling TV	Dish Network (satellite provider) digital mini-package of eight channels. $20/month. $5 additional for access to film libraries, and other networks.
Sony PlayStation Vue	Videos from four TV/movie studios. Available on PlayStation and Apple iPhones and iPads. $50/month.
Comcast Stream	Comcast's online live and on-demand service of broadcast networks and HBO premium cable shows. $15/month.
Apple TV	Apple's proposed new offering will broadcast networks ABC, CBS, and Fox, and some cable networks like ESPN. Will stream to mobile and home Apple TV boxes. Suggested pricing $20–$40/month.
AT&T Direct TV	AT&T's bundle of wireless and on-demand TV and movies based on its purchase in 2015 of DirectTV for $49 billion.
ON-DEMAND ONLY	
Netflix	Thousands of movies and TV episodes along with original series like *House of Cards*, and *Unbreakable Kimmy Schmidt*. $8/month.
Amazon Prime	Thousands of movies and TV episodes, free to Amazon Prime subscribers, with some original programming. $99/year.
Hulu Plus	TV shows from broadcasting and cable networks, as well as original HBO shows. $8/month.
Noggin	Video app by Viacom. Aimed at preschool children. Offers access to archive of past shows. $5.99/month.
A LA CARTE NETWORKS*	
Showtime	Premiere cable network original programming available on Apple, Roku, Hulu, and Vue. $11/month.
HBO Now	HBO programming, films, and documentaries available on PlayStation and Apple mobile devices. $15/month.
CBS All Access	Live TV in selected cities and on-demand streaming of past shows in CBS archives. $6/month.

*Current and past shows (original content) from premiere content networks

over-the-top (OTT)
use of the Internet to deliver entertainment services to the home on cable TV or FiOS networks

the-air broadcasters, cable TV, or satellite distributors (so-called linear TV), a new "over-the-top" (OTT) channel has developed led by powerful technology companies such as Apple, Google, Hulu, Vudu, Netflix, and many others, all of whom offer consumers access to television shows and some full-length feature movies using the household Internet service rather than the cable TV service. See **Table 10.3**. **Over-the-top (OTT)** entertainment services refers to the use of the Internet to deliver online entertainment services to the home. "Over-the-top" refers to the fact that the entertainment service rides "on top" of other network services like cable TV and telephone service. It's as if we have a new Internet Broadcasting System with many new players. With OTT entertainment, TV does not have to be linear, and consumers do not have to purchase a bundle of channels, most of which they never watch. This new network is obviously a threat to cable television and the other distributors, who have their own on-demand services for television series and movies. If customers switch to Internet delivery of TV shows and movies, they have less incentive to continue paying for cable TV service.

The Internet and the mobile platform have also changed the viewing experience. The best screen when commuting or traveling is the smartphone and tablet. More importantly, Internet-enabled social networks like Facebook and Twitter have made TV viewing a social experience shared among neighbors, friends, and colleagues. In the past, television was often a social event involving family and friends in the same room watching a single TV show. In 2015, the social circle has expanded to include Facebook and Twitter friends in different locations, changing television from a "lean back and enjoy" experience into a "lean forward and engage" experience. Many viewers are multitasking: co-viewing shows while texting, commenting, and chatting online while the show unfolds.

While the Internet so far has had an expansive and positive impact on the television industry, challenges lie ahead. The largest providers of television in virtually all countries are cable television systems that charge consumers a monthly service fee for providing service, often accompanied by Internet and/or telephone service. This service in the United States costs, on average, about $125 per month per household. Cable systems also generate advertising revenues from local and national advertisers. The revenues generated are used to maintain the physical cable network, and pay program producers (often called cable networks) for their content. For instance, HBO (Home Box Office network) creates a variety of television shows for the nearly 11,000 local cable systems in the United States, and collects fees from local and national cable systems like Time Warner and their subscribers. ESPN, the largest sports network on TV and the Internet, charges local and national cable systems per-viewer fees. But with so much video available online from many different distributors, many users are thinking about "cutting the cable cord" and just relying on the Internet for their video entertainment. Other viewers are "cord shavers," who have reduced their subscriptions to digital channels. Likewise, the improvement in over-the-air digital broadcasting of television signals has resulted in a slight increase in over-the-air viewers (about 15% of all television viewers). So far, cord cutting and shaving has been very limited and has been exaggerated. There are 95 million pay TV consumers, and an estimated 100,000 have cut the cord. Millenials are somewhat less likely to have pay TV cable service, and spend more time watching TV online than older consumers. But these differences also reflect differences in income. The vast majority of millenials watch TV like their parents by watching ordinary cable television (eMarketer, 2015; 2014). Nevertheless, the high service fees for cable television service, and expanding Internet capabilities, suggest that cable television growth is over, and subscriptions will fall. In August 2015, the stock price of media firms connected to cable television took a large loss in market value because of investor concerns about declining growth in traditional pay TV, both cable and satellite (Flint, 2015).

FEATURE-LENGTH MOVIES

In Hollywood, the transition to a digital delivery platform is well underway, and the industry is poised to maintain its revenue stream based on new digital platforms. As consumers have become fully connected to broadband networks on mobile, desktop, and home TVs, Hollywood has responded with a host of new viewing options. As a result, consumer spending on movie entertainment, whether physical or digital, has been stable, with significant growth in several digital platforms (Arnold, 2014).

The key to the success of Hollywood studios in the digital era is their control over original, full-length feature production, and control over who will distribute their movies, when, and how. Distributors—whether Internet providers or cable systems—need to meet the terms of Hollywood studios. The dominance of Hollywood studios in content creation is being challenged, but for now still seems secure. An estimated 113 million Americans will watch movies online in 2015, growing to 138 million in 2019 (see **Figure 10.17**).

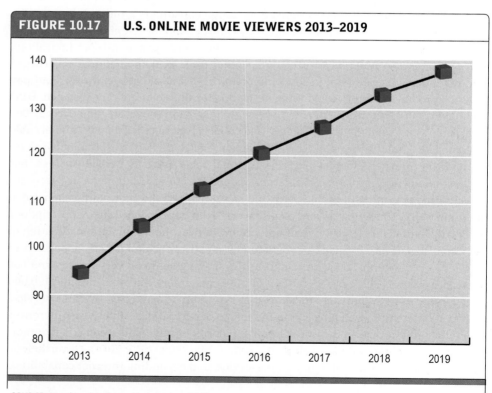

FIGURE 10.17 | **U.S. ONLINE MOVIE VIEWERS 2013–2019**

SOURCE: Based on data from eMarketer, Inc., 2015e.

FIGURE 10.18	HOME MOVIE ENTERTAINMENT REVENUE BY FORMAT

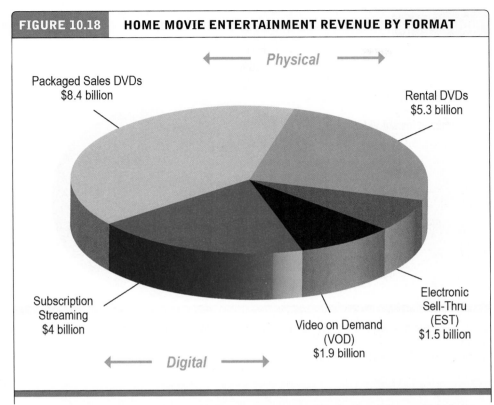

Physical formats make up 65% of home movie revenue, but they are shrinking at 15% annually. Digital formats are growing at 16% annually.

SOURCE: Based on data from Digital Entertainment Group, 2015.

Aside from box office theater revenues, the movie industry derives revenue from both physical formats (mostly DVDs) and digital formats like selling movies for download (called Electronic Sell Through or EST), selling access on cable or the Internet to specific movies a la carte (called Internet Video On Demand (iVOD)), and subscription streaming over the Internet (see **Figure 10.18**).

Each of these digital formats has a leading player. The EST download leader is Apple's iTunes store with about 68% of the download market and $2 billion in annual sales. Consumers purchase and own the downloaded movie. Apple is also the leader in iVOD a la carte rentals, but other major players include Amazon, Hulu, and cable systems, which also rent movies on demand (usually referred to as VOD without the 'i' of online video). Netflix is, of course, the leading subscription streaming service, with about 60% of the streaming movie audience, generating an estimated $3.5 billion in revenue annually. Streaming has grown faster and larger than iVOD, and this is reflected in the market share of Netflix and Apple (see **Figure 10.19**). New entrants of significant size include Hulu, premium cable television networks such as HBO and Showtime, and Amazon.

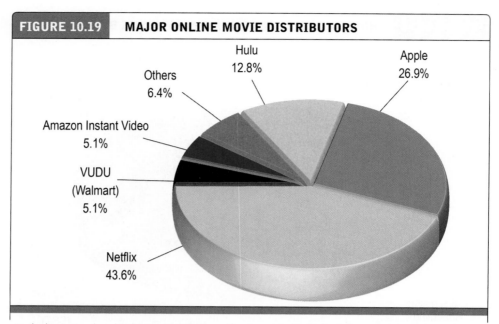

| FIGURE 10.19 | **MAJOR ONLINE MOVIE DISTRIBUTORS** |

Apple dominates downloading and purchasing of movies, while Netflix leads in streaming movies and TV shows.

SOURCE: Based on data from industry sources.

Hybrid services such as Walmart's Vudu service allow consumers to purchase a DVD and then also stream it later from any device. Vudu is enabled by a distribution channel called UltraViolet. UltraViolet is an industry-sponsored cloud-based storage and proof-of-purchase system. Users enter a code into their UltraViolet online account, which gives them access to a movie they have purchased from any device, including Android and Apple smartphones. There are an estimated 15 million subscribers using UltraViolet.

Revenue from sale and rental of DVDs has been declining since 2006, sometimes at double-digit rates. In 2014, DVD revenue was $13.7 billion, down a whopping 15% compared to 2013. Unit sales are one-half of their 2006 levels. But also notice that DVD revenues are still a substantial 43% of total movie revenues. DVDs remain very profitable. The decline in DVD revenues is partially offset by the stunning growth of digital formats, especially subscription streaming, which grew 16% in 2014 to $7.4 billion. Box office theater display of movies generated about $10.4 billion, one-third of total movie revenues, essentially the same as the previous year. The net result is that Hollywood revenues were flat, at around $31.5 billion in 2014. Of all the content industries, the movie industry has been able to maintain its revenue stream and not be digitally destroyed by new technologies, at least for now.

Hollywood faces a number of challenges as it tries to keep up with a rapidly changing distribution platform, increasingly digital, streaming, and even mobile. The fastest growing digital streaming format does not produce much revenue on a per unit basis. Studios make about $4.50 on each DVD, but only $2.00 for each VOD downloaded movie sale, and only 50 cents for each streamed movie. This means the studios are under pressure to keep their new movies in the physical format of DVDs, digital theater display, or video downloads, and use the streaming channel (Netflix) for older movies that might not sell at any price without the Internet, or have already been seen by millions of customers. Hollywood achieves this market segmentation by controlling the "release window" of movies, staggering market release. This is a form of price discrimination: those who really want to see the movie as soon as possible are willing to pay a higher price. The first tier is the theater box office, followed by DVDs, cable video-on-demand, then Internet video-on-demand, and finally subscription streaming services. Of course, the longer the studios hold a first-rate movie off the Internet, the greater the likelihood it will be pirated. The **release window** is changing under pressure from consumers to release films earlier to streaming and VOD services. Release windows are shrinking from nine months to four months, especially for poorly performing movies where DVD and box office sales are weak.

release window
Staging the release of new movies across different distribution channels with different prices

A second challenge involves the growing strength of online movie distributors, which may become competitors. Prior to the Internet, distributors such as movie theater chains and DVD rental and sales stores were never in a position to create their own movies and enter the movie production business. But in the digital era, it is conceivable that distributors like Netflix, Amazon, Hulu, and Google have the financial strength to attempt to make feature-length movies, and reduce their licensing costs. Netflix, Hulu, and Amazon have already demonstrated their ability to create popular TV series. Firms based on streaming are incentivized to produce their own content to avoid steep licensing fees demanded by Hollywood studios. For instance, in 2015, Netflix has an estimated $9 billion obligation to pay studios for content, and this accounts for 70% of its operating costs. Therefore, Netflix is investing heavily in original content production.

Piracy also remains a threat to the movie and television industry, despite years of effort by the industry and government to reduce piracy. Nevertheless, industry studies find that 24% of Internet traffic worldwide involves infringing content (illegal copies of movies and music), and about half of this involves bit torrent traffic (Envisional, 2013). In the United Kingdom, 30% of the Internet population has watched a pirated movie, either a pirated DVD or Internet download. In the United States, only 17% of Internet content is infringing. These numbers have declined in the last five years. BitTorrent is the most common illegal file transfer system. Other forms on Internet piracy include cyberlockers/file hosting sites (like Megaupload, now shut down), and third-party portals like MovieWatch and Movie2k, which link users to illegitimate streaming video and movie sites.

In the past, the movie industry estimated that it lost over $6 billion a year in pirated movies distributed over the Internet, copied from DVDs, early production copies, and in-theater videoing (Bialik, 2013). More recent academic research now estimates the loss is closer to $2 to $3 billion in the United States, roughly 10% of the $30 billion movie industry in the United States (Danaher et al., 2013). Critics argue the industry has exaggerated the losses. The emergence of multiple legitimate sources for streaming and downloading movies in a convenient and safe manner appears to have reduced the overall amount of piracy, both for movies and music. A Google research paper found that searches for pirated movies peaked in 2008, and have been dropping steadily, while searches for online rentals and streaming are up (Google, 2011). As Google has moved into a closer relationship with TV and movie studios, and has its own ambitions to create original content, it has strengthened its efforts to reduce access to pirate sites. Insofar as searches are an indicator of consumer interest and intent, the public interest in pirated movies is declining. Services like Netflix and iTunes that permit access to streams of movies for $8 a month, or download rentals for a few dollars, have arguably reduced the motivation to pirate movies for many potential pirates. However, the extended release window of Hollywood increases the incentive and rewards for pirating recent releases.

In countries like France, which has passed strong laws to protect artists and discourage illegal downloading (the HADOPI laws), once the laws were implemented, sales of movies on DVDs and legitimate downloading sites increased by 25% in the following twelve months (Danaher et al., 2013).

Government actions to close down cyberlockers also can have a powerful impact on movie sales. In January 2012, the U.S. government, along with other governments, closed down the world's largest cyberlocker, Megaupload. In a few days, 25 petabytes of music and movies disappeared from the Internet. In 12 countries where Megaupload was the most widely used, digital revenues for two movie studios in the study were 6–12% higher in the 18 weeks following the shutdown (Danaher and Smith, 2014; Fritz, 2013). With few exceptions, the academic literature produced since 2000 shows that piracy causes a significant reduction in sales of legitimate movies (Danaher et al., 2013).

While piracy of movies persists, the industry has reduced efforts to fight it through legislation, or prosecution of individuals who purchase pirated movies (large piracy operations are still a target for the movie industry). In large part this is due to the expansion of digital movie platforms that make paying an $8 monthly fee to Netflix for thousands of hours of movies, or subscribing to Amazon Instant Video, a much more convenient and less risky activity than downloading virus-laden BitTorrent files. In essence, Hollywood and the Internet have begun to put piracy out of business by providing superior products and service at a very low price (Tassi, 2014).

Insight on Technology: Hollywood and the Internet: Let's Cut a Deal describes how Hollywood studios and Internet distributors are cutting deals to provide more video and movie content online.

MUSIC

Perhaps no other content industry has been so severely disrupted by the Internet and new business models as the recorded music industry. Revenues for the industry have been cut in half since 1999. By 2010, revenues stabilized and since then, have

INSIGHT ON TECHNOLOGY

HOLLYWOOD AND THE INTERNET: LET'S CUT A DEAL

In tough times, people go to the movies. All things considered, 2014 was a good year for the movie industry. Despite the continuing effects of the recession, or because of them, box office receipts were $10.4 billion in North America, about the same from the previous year. Global box office sales were also up, to $36.4 billion in 2014, a record, and 3% higher than the previous year. Admissions were actually down slightly, with 1.3 billion tickets sold in the United States, but ticket prices were up slightly, making up for the decrease in the number of tickets sold. The number of films released in 2014 increased by 7% to 136. And online revenues from downloading and streaming exploded to $7.4 billion (about 35% of the home movie market). In 2014, users downloaded over 350,000 movies from iTunes every day. By any measure, the Hollywood money machine has been transformed by the Internet as DVD physical unit sales declined to half of what they were in 2005. But, so far the movie business has avoided the kind of disruption that has occurred in the music business. People still crowd into theaters to see the latest movies, and while many still rent or purchase DVDs, many have learned to live with streamed movies even if they are older than what they can see in the theater. The reasons why Hollywood has survived the disruptive potential of the Internet are complex.

The Internet has made older movies more valuable simply because they can be inexpensively stored on cloud servers, are easily discovered by consumers, and can be streamed for nearly zero cost, producing a new revenue stream. Continuing sales of DVDs, and revenues from online streaming services and download

sales at the iTunes Store, drive revenues higher for even older movies. *Avatar*, originally released in 2009, now has grossed over $760 million; *Titanic*, released in 1997, $658 million. More recent blockbusters include *The Avengers* (2012), generating $623 million, and *Frozen* (2013), which hit $1.2 billion in its first year. If only all movies could produce results like these, Hollywood would be golden again. The Internet has made Hollywood's backlist much more valuable.

But all is not totally well in Tinseltown. Once movies are shown in theaters, where Hollywood generates 30% of its revenue, they move on to less-profitable venues, from DVDs (which are very profitable) to cable television video-on-demand services, and then to Internet distributors like Netflix and Apple for either purchase, rental download, or streaming. Internet streaming services like Netflix are low on the Hollywood food chain in part because they don't have the revenues to pay for the latest movies. Hollywood prefers to deal with Amazon, which sells and rents millions of DVDs, or Apple, which charges its customers $5–$12 for recently released movies for download, compared to Netflix, which charges only $8 a month for access to thousands of movies. Next in line are cable network video-on-demand services, which charge anywhere from $5 to $12 a view. Eventually, movies end up with cable networks and broadcast television stations years after they were released. Even cable networks have greatly reduced their distribution of feature-length movies and replaced them with much less expensive unscripted reality shows. This "release window" differs for various films based on the studio's estimate of the revenue potential for each film. A very popular film will be delayed all along the release window.

(continued)

Hollywood is facing several problems moving forward to a world where most people will be watching movies on the Internet, either at home, or on the go, using tablet computers and smartphones. One problem is that the fastest growing segment of its business, the Internet, is also the least profitable. A second problem is that Hollywood does not control its own Internet distribution network, but instead is forced to rely on the likes of Netflix, Apple, Amazon, and Google, each of which attract large online audiences. Likewise, the big Internet distributors face a content problem: they cannot attract large audiences unless they can access recently made movies. Old movies and movie libraries on Netflix have limited appeal; consumers are looking for the latest releases. But Hollywood charges a very high premium for recent movies, reducing profits at Netflix, which are already very low.

Initially, Hollywood was highly dependent on Amazon's sales of DVDs as rental revenue from physical stores declined. iTunes is still the largest downloading service of movies a la carte (so-called electronic sell-through, or EST). In the last two years, the market dynamics have changed, in large part because of Netflix's success with its streaming video model. Why download to own when you can subscribe to a steady stream of movies? Hollywood is in the enviable position of being pursued by Internet distributors who are short of high-quality content. This is very different from what happened in the music business over the last decade. Multiple buyers of movies have appeared, not just Amazon or iTunes. Google has developed its own home TV device (like Apple TV) that is a platform for movie streaming. Hulu is also ramping up again as a distribution platform.

Netflix continues to dominate online movie revenues, with a 44% market share compared to Apple's 27%. At one time, Apple had a 70% share of Internet movie revenue, and Hollywood studios feared Apple would be able to dominate Internet distribution and dictate prices. Now with Netflix dominating the streaming market, Hollywood fears it will be forced to sell its product for a pittance compared to DVD prices. For this reason, Hollywood has been restricting the release of movies to Netflix, doling out access to recent movies very carefully. Hollywood would much prefer that fans download movies from Apple rather than wait to rent or stream them. To encourage this, Hollywood has created a new product called Digital HD that allows fans to download high definition copies of movies three weeks prior to their release on DVD or video-on-demand services. There are different versions of Digital HD. For example, Disney Movies Anywhere allows consumers to pay for recent HD movies stored on a cloud server, and play them anywhere, anytime. Vudu (owned by Walmart) enables downloading of HD movies and digital locker storage for play later. Another service, UltraViolet, allows consumers to buy a digital copy once, store it in the cloud, and view anytime. Amazon's Digital Copy service enables the purchase of a digital-only movie, as well as a DVD with digital copy access. In these ways Hollywood can afford to release new movies into digital distribution channels because consumers are willing to pay a premium, or buy the DVD for full price and receive a digital cloud copy for "free."

Digital HD movies are priced so that they produce as much revenue as traditional DVDs. This is the first time Hollywood has changed its release window strategy in order to drive digital download sales. The studios can charge a premium price for new movie digital downloads, making this outlet more valuable than either the DVD channel or the video-on-demand channel offered by cable networks. In some cases, movie producers such as Disney and Sony have opened up their own online stores for selling recent releases directly to consumers. This opens the possibility that Hollywood studios can circumvent

Internet distributors entirely. Who needs Apple or Netflix or Amazon?

More and more, large firms are entering the premium video downloading and streaming market, and competing with one another for Hollywood movies, driving up prices. Amazon is seeking to strike deals with the studios for digital a la carte purchases and streaming of recent movies. Amazon has struck a deal with Viacom to purchase TV episodes and movies to stock its streaming service. In 2014, Amazon announced it would produce five original TV series for streaming to its Amazon Prime subscribers for no additional cost. By 2015, Amazon had a total of 31 original series. No one knows who watches these series because Amazon does not release the figures, just like Netflix refuses to do. But Amazon series have received critical acclaim and an Emmy nomination for its comedy *Transparent*. It has hired Woody Allen to write and direct his own series. Hulu has begun streaming HBO and Showtime series and movies for an additional monthly charge. Netflix is clearly not the only game in town for Internet movie distribution.

In the end, Hollywood and the Internet need each other, and the only question is how to find the price, define the terms of trade, and cut a deal where both parties come out winners. The flurry of deals in 2014 and 2015 bodes well for consumers, and probably for both Internet distributors and Hollywood studios. Consumers are finding multiple services that allow them to watch movies on whatever device is convenient, and move from one device to another with a lot less effort than in the past. Given the shift of eyeballs to online entertainment, Hollywood is expanding its audience, maintaining and even enhancing its prices. With lots of Internet distributors competing, Hollywood gains in power from the competition among alternative distributors. Netflix will not have a stranglehold over the Hollywood studios. And Internet companies are coming up with even more reasons why consumers should forget about cable TV and watch the Internet, which means more ad revenues for Internet distributors. How all these calculations will work out remains to be seen. Tune in next year on the same channel.

SOURCES: "Amazon Pushes to Deliver More Prime Time," by Emily Steel, *New York Times,* July 31, 2015; "Hulu Will Offer Showtime for Extra $8.99 a Month, Differentiating Itself From Netflix," by Keach Hagey, *New York Times,* June 23, 2015; "2014 Analysis: Home Entertainment Steps Up to Keep Up With Connected Consumer," by Thomas Arnold, *Variety,* December 26, 2014; "NPD Reports Movies Drive EST Growth with Strong Revenue Increases Continuing," NPD.com, June 3, 2014; "Sales of Digital Movies Surge," by Ben Fritz, *Wall Street Journal,* January 7, 2014; "Electronic Sell Through Spending Soars 50%," Digital Entertainment Group, January 7, 2014; "How the New iPhone Helps Hollywood," by Andy Lewis, *Hollywood Reporter,* September 6, 2013; "Amazon Invests Millions in Original TV Shows to Get You to Buy More Diapers," by Timothy Senovac, *Huffington Post,* May 31, 2013; "Google Goes Hollywood with the Internship," by Ronald Grover and Alexei Oreskovic, Reuters.com, May 28, 2013; "Netflix Passes Apple to Take Lead in Online Movie Business," by Dan Graziano, BGR.com, June 6, 2012; "Hollywood Studios Warm to Apple's iCloud Effort," by Jessica Vascellaro and Erica Ordern, *Wall Street Journal,* March 12, 2012; "Web Deals Cheer Hollywood, Despite Drop in Moviegoers," by Brooks Barnes, *New York Times,* February 24, 2012; Netflix Secures Streaming Deal With DreamWorks," by Brooks Barnes and Brian Stelter, *New York Times*, September 25, 2011.

remained flat. Total revenues were about $7 billion in 2014, roughly half of their level in 2000. Global sales of music fell less than one percent in 2014, down to $15 billion, compared to $27 billion in 1999 (IFPI, 2015).

Digital revenues now make up about 65% of all music revenues (about $4.5 billion), and are expected to rise slowly to $5.4 billion by 2016 (see **Figure 10.20**). Revenues from CDs are declining but are still a strong performer, accounting for 27% of the industry's revenue (about $1.9 billion). Streaming music sales from ad

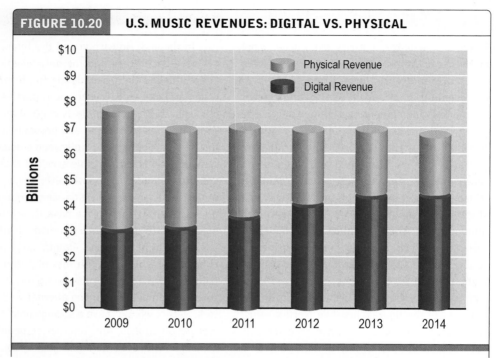

FIGURE 10.20   U.S. MUSIC REVENUES: DIGITAL VS. PHYSICAL

Music industry revenues have fallen by 50% since 2000, and have only recently stabilized at around $7 billion. Digital music now makes up about 65% of all music revenues.
SOURCE: Based on data from Recording Industry of America (RIAA), 2015; industry sources.

supported streaming and subscription streaming sites now total $1.1 billion, or about 16% of industry revenue. Digital revenues have obviously not made up for the loss of revenue caused by the drastic decline in CD sales. While CD sales declined 13% last year, vinyl sales grew around 50% from 6.1 million units sold in 2013 to 9.2 million in 2014 (RIAA, 2015). Vinyl is escaping the niche market of hobbyists, in part due to its superior sound reproduction when compared to digital tracks, and a growing number of groups are issuing vinyl editions alongside CD editions although these are only 2% of industry revenues.

For most of its history, the music industry depended on a variety of physical media to distribute music—acetate records, vinyl recordings, cassette tapes, and finally CD-ROMs. At the core of its revenue was a physical product. Since the 1950s, that physical product was an album—a collection of bundled songs that sold for a much higher price than singles. The Internet changed all that when, in 2000, a music service called Napster begin distributing pirated music tracks over the Internet to consumers using their PCs as record players. Despite the collapse of Napster due to legal challenges, hundreds of other illegal sites showed up, resulting in music industry revenues falling from $14 billion in 1999 to an estimated $7 billion in 2014. The appearance of powerful mobile media players beginning in 2001 that could be connected to the Internet, like Apple's iPod, and later iPhone and iPad, and then the stunning growth of music streaming sites, further eroded sales of CD albums. Streaming has fundamentally altered the sale of physical music formats because it is no longer necessary to "own" a physical unit in order to hear the music consumers want.

The music industry initially resisted the development of legal digital channels of distribution, but ultimately and reluctantly struck deals with Apple's new iTunes Store in 2003, as well as with several small subscription music services, for online distribution. By the time streaming music services appeared on the scene in 2006, the music industry had dropped its opposition to digital formats, and quickly reached agreements with Pandora, Spotify, and others to stream music on their subscription and "free" ad-supported services in return for fees. Today, digital downloads of tracks and albums are widely perceived as the savior of the music industry, which was losing sales to piracy and file sharing. Nevertheless, revenues from the sales of digital downloads of individual songs from iTunes selling for 99 cents pale in comparison to revenues produced by CD albums. **Figure 10.21** shows consumer spending on digital music in four different formats: single songs, albums, streaming, and ringtones.

While some have argued that Apple's iTunes music service offering single tracks for 99 cents destroyed the sales of albums, this clearly is not the case. Album downloads have held up well against single downloads, and actually have grown faster

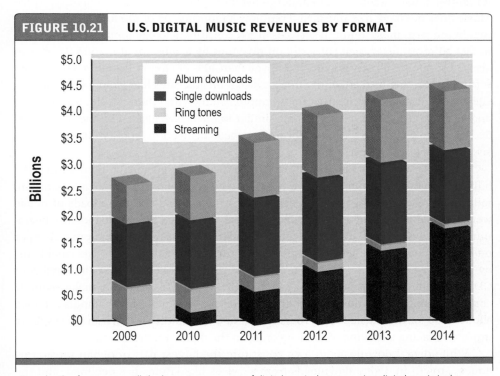

FIGURE 10.21   U.S. DIGITAL MUSIC REVENUES BY FORMAT

Downloads of songs are still the largest component of digital music, but streaming digital music is the fastest growing format.

SOURCE: Based on data from Recording Industry of America (RIAA), 2015; eMarketer, Inc., 2015f.

than single downloads. For instance, in 2014, Adele's *21* sold a record 11 million CDs and 3 million digital albums, becoming one of the most popular albums in history. This performance will likely be surpassed by Taylor Swift's *1989* album, which sold over 4 million units (both CDs and downloads) by March 2015, just six months after its release. Sales of digital or CD albums appear to be a function more of the music quality and popularity than the format.

There are two kinds of digital music services, each with a different business model: digital download and streaming subscription services. Digital download services (also known as download to own) are exemplified by iTunes, Amazon, and Google Play, where users download tracks and albums a la carte and pay a fee for each song. Increasingly, the songs are stored on a cloud server so users can listen to the music from any of several personal devices. All revenue derives from the sale of music albums or single tracks. Streaming subscription services (also known as Internet radio) like Pandora, Last.fm, iHeart, and Spotify have two revenue streams: ad supported and subscription service. Ad supported streaming is a fremium model that allows users access to free streamed music for a limited number of hours per month and relies on advertising to generate revenue for the free streams. Streaming digital music generates about 30% of all digital music sales. The music is delivered to users from a cloud server and is not stored on user devices. Subscription services charge a monthly fee for ad-free music. About 5% of Pandora's listeners pay a fee, similar to Spotify. Apple Music does not have free music and requires a monthly fee of $10 for ad-free streaming. In the past, most fremium services urged consumers to pay for subscriptions, but in fact ad revenues exceed subscription revenues by a substantial margin. Users can also subscribe for a monthly fee, but fewer than 10% of stream listeners pay for subscriptions, relying instead on the free service with ads. Sites like Pandora are curated sites where users select an artist they want to listen to, and then the site uses experts and algorithms to build a list of artists similar to the artist selected by the user. Users do not control what they hear and cannot repeat a selection. Spotify allows users to specify artists and songs.

Digital download is the biggest part of the digital music industry, generating $2.5 billion or 35% of the industry's revenue. The largest players are iTunes and Amazon, followed by Google Play. While illegal pirated file sharing and downloads of music were the leading edge of a digital tide that deeply disrupted the music industry beginning in the 1990s, legal digital download and streaming services have put a damper on illegal music piracy. Legal digital music sources have saved the music label firms by generating solid revenues and profits, albeit not as generous as in the heyday of CDs. While music labels might make $7 on a CD sold at $16, they only make about 32 cents for a single track downloaded from iTunes for 99 cents. Digital albums produce about $3.00 for the music labels, roughly half of a CD album sale. Artists are similarly impacted, facing a halving of their incomes in the digital environment.

While digital downloads to own constitute the largest part of digital music revenues, growth in digital downloads from services like iTunes has declined, and the fastest growing segment is the streaming music services. It appears that the success of music streaming services is cannibalizing the sales of downloads, and in 2014 the sales of downloads declined by 10%, a trend that started in 2012. The leading players in streaming are Pandora, Yahoo Music, Last.fm, and Spotify. With the growth of cloud computing and cloud-based music services, the very concept of owning music began to shift instead to accessing music from any device, anywhere. Streaming music services are adding new listeners at a growth rate of 47.5% in 2014. Unfortunately, while streaming services are growing listeners at a torrid pace, they have not managed to earn a profit because of infrastructure costs, the costs of acquiring music content from the music labels, and freemium revenue models supported by advertising revenues. For artists and music label firms, streaming services have little to offer. While music labels might receive 32 cents for every iTunes track they sell, they receive only .63 of a penny on a streamed version of the same song. This revenue is split with the artists, who receive .32 of a penny. *Rolling Stone* calculated that a very popular song selling 1 million streams would produce revenue of $3,166 for the artist and a similar amount for the music label. For this reason, many artists and groups refuse to allow streaming of their music.

In 2014, Taylor Swift, the world's most popular singer, pulled her music from Spotify's free service because it pays such a low royalty rate. In 2015, she similarly pulled her album 1989 from Apple's newly announced Apple Music service because Apple was planning to not charge for the first three months of the service. Many other singers have withdrawn their performances from free streaming services, and there is a growing movement among musicians to seeking higher compensation from streaming sites.

None of the streaming subscription services has ever shown a profit. It is unclear if streaming music is a viable business model. Pandora and the other streaming services demonstrate negative scale: the bigger they become, the more money they lose. Nevertheless, investors have nevertheless poured money into Pandora and Spotify hoping that their large audiences can be monetized. The reason for investor optimism is growth. Pandora's audience grew by 7% in 2014 to 81 million listeners, and its revenue by 47%, almost entirely from advertising on its free service. In 2015, Apple also launched its Apple Music streaming service, which competes with Pandora and Spotify. The music never stops.

GAMES

No Internet media content form has grown as explosively as online games. In the last few years, online gaming has grown faster than console gaming. Today online gaming is going through a significant transition, from consoles to PCs, smartphones, and to professional gaming as a stadium sport. In August 2015, for instance, 11,000 fans packed into Madison Square Garden in New York to watch 10 professional players play the online game *League of Legends* (Needleman, 2015). Console gaming used to be the heart of the digital gaming industry, and still is from a revenue perspective. But this has begun to change with the introduction of smartphones and tablets, as well as social and casual gaming, which do not require users to purchase an expensive console or packaged software. Smartphones and tablets have ushered in an era of free-to-play and $1.99 game apps and much simpler game scenarios that do not require millions of investment dollars. Well over 200 million Internet users play some kind of game online in the United States, and that number swells to over 400 million worldwide. In 2015, over 164 million people play games on mobile devices (smartphones and tablets), over three times as many who play games on game consoles. Casual PC gamers are twice as common as console gamers (about 50 million) (eMarketer, Inc., 2015g; Price-WaterhouseCoopers, 2015b).

In the United States, revenue from digital games in all formats (mobile, PC based, massive multiplayer, social, and console) in 2014 was estimated at nearly $12 billion (Superdataresearch.com, 2015a). Other consulting firms put the total at $15 billion, with 30% growth to $19.5 billion by 2019 (PriceWaterhouseCoopers, 2015b). To put this in perspective, the $12 to $15 billion game sector is about one-half of the total Hollywood movie sector, and about twice the size of all digital music revenue in 2014. Online gaming alone generates a significant part of all online entertainment revenues, and engages nearly 60% of Internet users.

There are five types of digital gamers. Casual gamers play games on a desktop or laptop computer. They are called casual gamers because they play games for a few minutes at a time, stop and start games, and are not intensively involved. Social gamers are those who play games using a Web browser or app on a social network like Facebook, often with friends. Mobile gamers play games using their smartphones or tablet computers. Mobile gamers are social gamers as well, with fleeting involvement. Massively multiplayer online gamers (MMO) use their computers to play with a large number of players around the globe. Console gamers play games online (or offline) using a dedicated console like Xbox, PlayStation, or Wii. Often, console gamers are connected over the Internet to enable group play (see Figure 10.22).

While many more people play mobile and desktop games online, more than half of online gaming revenue is generated by console gamers, largely through the purchase of expensive physical games on DVDs or online digital downloads of the games. In 2015, however, sales of console software on DVDs, and consoles themselves, hit a soft spot, and fell 25% (see **Figure 10.22**). In 2015, total online game revenues are estimated to be $15.8 billion, and $9.2 billion of that will come from sales of console games (not including the cost of the console itself). PC games come in second at $3.5 billion, about one-third of total online revenues. Mobile games will generate an estimated $2 billion (eMarketer, Inc., 2015h). In terms of the future, overall game revenues are expected to grow by 30% to 2019, led by growth on console and PC game revenues (Takahashi, 2015). Mobile game revenues are the slowest growing segment in terms of revenue. The possibilities of selling virtual goods or displaying ads on mobile games apps are very limited and therefore mobile game companies need to rely on in-app advertising and sales of virtual goods to make their revenue targets. While casual and social gaming rapidly grows, most online and mobile games are free or nearly so, and users do not stay in the games very long. These two features make it difficult for gaming firms to monetize their user base by showing advertisements and charging for services. What gamer wants the game interrupted by an important message from the sponsor? The business model of social and casual gaming is still not settled. Marketers have just recently begun to build video marketing campaigns that increase a brand's engagement and interaction with customers who are playing at social mobile gaming sites.

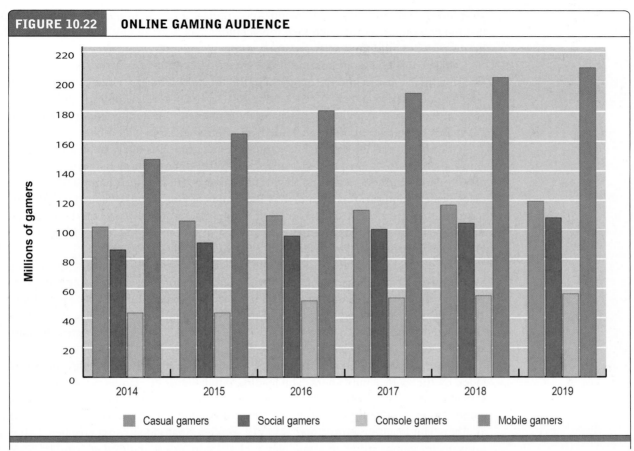

FIGURE 10.22 **ONLINE GAMING AUDIENCE**

SOURCE: Based on data from eMarketer, 2015g.

The rapid growth of mobile game players based on tablets and smartphones is a sea change for the gaming industry that was previously dominated by closed-platform console games and hardware firms like Microsoft, Nintendo, and Sony, and software firms like Activision and Electronic Arts. The growth of smartphones, tablets, and mobile games has catapulted Apple's App Store and the Google Play store into the leading merchants of digital games, which, of course, use Apple and Google Android hardware and software. Apple and Google take 30% of game sales and also benefit from the sales of the hardware and software needed to play the games. Mobile games appeal to a younger demographic, offer lower prices, and initially are often free. You can play mobile games anywhere you can use a phone, which is nearly everywhere. Console games take much longer to develop, have very large budgets, and are expensive to purchase.

The mobile platform is a more open platform that allows thousands of developers to create entertaining games on much smaller budgets, as well as new and innovative games on a faster schedule. In contrast, the console platform has evolved much more slowly than mobile computing. In 2014, a new Sony PlayStation replaced a seven-year-old model, and a new Microsoft Xbox replaced an eight-year-old model. In a fast-moving online world, such long replacement cycles inevitably lead to declines in hardware sales, and limit software innovation.

While console, PC, and online social games will continue to grow their audience size slowly, the fastest audience growth in the future will be in mobile games that can be played anywhere and anytime (Gaudiosi, 2015). In 2014, half of smartphone owners, 46% of the population, played games on their phones. The challenge for mobile and PC games is to generate more revenue from their very large player base.

One solution to PC and mobile game revenue growth is likely to be professional gaming, otherwise known as e-sports. E-sports, like other professional sports, is based on competition among teams of players. The competition at the championship level takes place in auditoriums attended by thousands of fans, and is watched by millions more on the Internet. In 2015, over 70 million people watch e-sports on the Internet. A single championship tournament streamed around the world attracted 8.5 million viewers at peak times (Plambeck, 2015; Wingfield, 2014a).

The games are broadcast over cable television channels, but more commonly over Internet channels like Twitch.tv. Twitch accounts for over 80% of online e-sports viewing in the United States, and was purchased by Amazon in 2015 for $1.1 billion. Twitch.tv draws peak-time audiences of nearly 1 million viewers in 2015, as many as MTV, TruTV, and MSNBC, to name a few cable networks. Other broadcasters include YouTube and Dailymotion.

The organization of the tournaments, and the prize money for the players, is provided by the games' publishers. The leading publisher of PC games played at professional levels is Riot Games, publisher of *League of Legends,* a multiplayer online battle game. There are twenty *League of Legends* professional teams that compete with one another. The league requires teams to hire professional video game coaches. Other multiplayer games suited to arena play include *StarCraft II* and *Call of Duty.* In 2015, Twitch.tv is the fourth largest consumer of peak-time Internet traffic (Needleman, 2015).

E-sports has been growing at over 50% a year in the last few years, and is expected to generate over $600 million in global revenue, $140 million of that in the United States. The e-sports leagues make money from selling tickets to arena championship games, merchandise sales, corporate sponsorships, and selling ad space during the broadcasts (Superdataresearch.com, 2015b). Advertisers are attracted to e-sports because the audience is predominantly composed of young males between the ages of 21 and 34, who are hard to reach using traditional media. Coca Cola, Nissan, Ford, and Google are among the largest sponsors of e-sports. College teams have sprung up across the country, including Harvard and Princeton, and Robert Morris University in Chicago now offers several scholarships for students who will play on its video game team (Wingfield, 2014b). At current rates of growth, e-sports will approach Hollywood in terms of global revenues, and eclipse console game revenue by 2020, transforming online gaming into a popular sport.

CASE STUDY

Netflix:
How Does This Movie End?

I n the Netflix online television comedy-drama series, *Orange is the New Black*, the lead character is Piper Chapman (Taylor Schilling), a recently engaged blond New Yorker sent to a federal prison for a crime committed years before. Critically acclaimed, and widely followed, *Orange* follows in the footsteps of Netflix's earlier successful online TV series *House of Cards*, a political insider's tale of Washington politics starring Kevin Spacey. *House of Cards* was the first-ever online television series to win an Emmy award (for best director). *Orange* won three Emmy creative awards in 2014. In 2014, Netflix racked up 31 nominations, and in 2015, 34 nominations. By producing its own content, Netflix is able to differentiate itself from cable TV shows, as well as obtain content for a lower price, and attract new subscribers.

While Netflix does not release the number of viewers for any of its original TV shows, executives do credit these two shows with driving the streaming service to a record 62 million worldwide subscribers by the second quarter of 2015 (42 million in the United States), with growth running at a blistering pace of 2.5 million new subscribers each quarter. For Netflix, orange is indeed the new "black," as in a positive top line revenue. Netflix shares doubled in 2015 and soared to over $700 a share (from its $15 offering price in 2002). It is currently selling at over 220 times its projected earnings, much more expensive than Google, Facebook, or other tech companies. Revenues in 2014 were $5.5 billion, up 28% from 2013, but profits were a paltry $226 million.

© Digitallife/Alamy

Netflix got its start as a mail order company renting DVDs of older Hollywood movies using the postal system. Founded by two Silicon Valley entrepreneurs, Marc Randolph and Reed Hastings, in 1997, the company started by renting individual copies of 900 DVD movie titles and delivering them to customers by postal mail. In 2000, it switched to a subscription model where customers could receive DVDs on a regular basis for a monthly fee. By 2006, it had delivered its billionth DVD and became the largest subscription provider of DVDs. In 2007, Netflix began a video-on-demand streaming service of movies although it still retains a DVD subscription business. In 2015, Netflix is the largest player in the movie and TV series streaming market, and consumes over 37% of the U.S. Internet bandwidth to serve its customers.

Netflix is one of those Silicon Valley stories that might make a good movie, or even a television series, because of its potential for disrupting the American television and movie landscape (or what's called premium video). It's a dream-come-true story of accomplishment, pluck, innovation, and Internet technology. In a few short years Netflix created the largest DVD rental business in the country, then created the largest streaming video service. Today Netflix accounts for over 90% of digital movie streaming, while its chief streaming competitors, Amazon and Hulu, make up the remaining market; Netflix has created the largest database on consumer video preferences and built a recommendation system that encourages consumers to see more movies; Netflix discovered that older TV series had strong niche followings and built a new model of "binge watching" where consumers could watch all the episodes of a series in several sittings. Finally, Netflix has entered the content creation business by developing original TV series.

In the movie and TV business there are only two ways to make money: either own the content or own the pipes that deliver the content. All the better if you can do both. Netflix has turned itself into a major pipeline to 42 million Internet users in the United States and is increasingly recognized as an important pipeline to large audiences. For instance, in 2013, Netflix announced a deal with the Weinstein Company, a major American film studio and producer of ten Academy Award films, to become the exclusive subscription TV home for the film studio's content, beginning in 2016. This move puts Netflix into the same league of premium channel distributors and in direct competition with other cable networks like HBO, Starz, Showtime, and A&E for the rights to show movies about eight months after their theater run is complete. In 2014, Netflix and Warner Brothers agreed to have Netflix become the exclusive Internet distributor of the *Batman* series prequel *Gotham*.

In one possible ending scenario for the Netflix movie, the company challenges the much larger cable television industry, which is based on an entirely different technology and business model, namely, selling expensive bundles of hundreds of TV channels that few people watch, then raising monthly fees faster than the rate of inflation. Given Netflix's large national audience of streamers, the company makes new friends in Hollywood and New York that are looking for ways to distribute their shows to a new online, mobile, and social world; Hollywood stretches the distribution window so that Internet distributors like Netflix get the same treatment as cable systems by allowing them to show the latest movies and shows at about the same time as cable systems. And the cable television industry is forced to retreat from its bundling practices and offer customers the ability to select just those channels they actually watch. Cable industry revenues plunge as a result. In this dream scenario, Netflix goes on to challenge the cable networks by producing its own original TV dramas, and adds comedy and documentaries to the mix. A story with a happy ending for Netflix! But happy endings happen mostly in Hollywood.

The outcome of this movie depends on how well Netflix can deal with some considerable challenges. For instance, one source of Netflix's poor profitability is that the costs of content are very high, both purchased older series as well as new content, which is far more risky. The owners of older cable TV series and Hollywood movies charge Netflix for the privilege of distributing their content as much as they do established cable TV networks. In 2014 Netflix reported streaming content obligations to content producers of $9.4 billion! With $5.5 billion in gross revenue, it paid out $5 billion in expenses, almost entirely payments to content producers (about $4.5 billion), and some marketing. Netflix barely makes any profit on its $5.5 billion in revenue (about $266 million, a profit margin of about 5%). Netflix is, after all, just a delivery platform, and the company is in a constant bidding war with both cable and Internet giants all looking for the same thing—popular TV series with a built-in audience, on the cheap. But content owners have wised up to the value of their backlist TV series and have raised their prices accordingly. Series just a year old are very expensive or non-existent. For instance, in 2008, Netflix reached a $30 million deal with the Starz cable network for several popular TV series and movies. When the deal came up for renewal in 2012, Starz wanted $300 million. Netflix is paying hundreds of millions to Disney, Paramount, Lionsgate, and MGM to license hit shows and movies. As a result of content owners charging more, the costs of its large and frequently updated content library are rising more quickly than its revenues. In an effort to reduce the cost of licensing, Netflix began production of its own content. But this is very expensive as well. The critically acclaimed *House of Cards* cost Netflix $100 million for 26 episodes, $4 million an episode. Older content like *Madmen* runs about $1 million an episode. It's possible that Netflix does not scale, and that the more subscribers it has, the less profit it makes because the cost of doing business rises faster than revenue.

A second challenge Netflix faces is the risk of creating new content. It's not as if wealthy Silicon Valley entrepreneurs can fly to Hollywood or New York with lots of cash and simply purchase new content. As one pundit noted, this might lead to a mugging, but not a successful TV series or movie. Silicon Valley is generally not the place to go if you're looking for story tellers, writers, producers, directors, talent agents, and cinematographers. Algorithms don't come up with new ideas for novels, plays, movies, or TV series. Netflix started out as a recycler of old TV and movie content, and like HBO in the cable world, is trying to expand into original content production both to reduce costs and to build a brand name as a content creator, not just a middle man. Content can be sold and re-sold to cable networks, or other Internet distributors. But there is considerable risk in original content, long-form TV or Hollywood quality video. Older series are proven series, and Netflix can identify which of its customers watched the series in previous years, and estimate the audience size, and whether new subscribers will be attracted by the re-plays. But when it comes to new TV series, Netflix has tried to use its algorithms to predict what new series its customers might

SOURCES: "Verizon to Offer Free Mobile TV Serfvice, Hoping to Draw Millennials," by Emily Steel, *New York Times*, September 8, 2015; "Netflix Viewership Finally Gets a Yardstick," by Joe Flint and Ben Fritz, *Wall Street Journal*, August 26, 2015; "Here Are the Original Shows Netflix Viewers Say They're Watching," by Peter Kafka, Recode.net, August 26, 2015; "Netflix, Amazon Rack Up Emmy Nominations," by Daniel Bukszpan, *Fortune*, July 16, 2015; "Netflix Soars to All-Time High as Customers Top 62 Million," by Lucas Shaw, Bloomberg News, April 16, 2015; Netflix, "Form 10k for the Fiscal Year Ended December 31, 2014," filed with Securities and Exchange Commission January 29, 2015; Apple Inc., "Form 10-K for the Fiscal Year Ended September 27, 2014," filed with Securities and Exchange Commission October, 27, 2014; "Video Streaming Beats DVR and Video On Demand Viewing," eMarketer, Inc., September 6, 2013; "The Comedy Lineup Expands on Netflix," by Brian Stelter, *New York Times*, August 29, 2013; "Netflix Insiders Take the Money and Run," by Adam Levin-Weinberg, Motley Fool, August 29, 2013; "Netflix Expands Content Deal with Weinstein Co.," Amol Sharma and Ben Fritz, *Wall Street Journal*, August 20, 2013; "Form 10-Q Netflix Inc.," United States Securities and Exchange Commission, July 25, 2013; "Media Journal: Netflix Profit, Subscribers Rise, but Wall Street Underwhelmed," by William Launder, *Wall Street Journal*, July 23, 2013; "The State of Streaming TV, According to Netflix," by Tom Gara, *Wall Street Journal*, July 22, 2013; "Original Content Ever More Important to Netflix," Brian Fitzgerald, *Wall Street Journal*, July 22, 2013; "Inside Netflix's Historic 'House of Cards' Emmy Nods," by Maria LaMagna, July 18, 2013; "How Netflix Is Shaking Up Hollywood," by Amol Sharma, *Wall Street Journal*, July 7, 2013; "Apple and Netflix Dominate Online Video," by Brian Chen, *New York Times*, June 19, 2013; "DreamWorks and Netflix in Deal for New TV Shows," by Brooks Barnes, *New York Times*, June 17, 2013; "Once Film Focused, Netflix Transitions to TV Shows," by Brian Stelter, February 27, 2012; "Amazon Adds Streaming-Video Service For Prime Members," by Nat Worden and Stu Woo, *Wall Street Journal*, February 23, 2011.

be interested in with mixed results. Netflix has produced some real winners according to critics, but it has also produced some real losers that did not get critical acclaim like *Lillyhammer*, *Hemlock Grove*, and *Bad Samaritans*. While Netflix's *House of Cards* and *Orange Is the New Black* have garnered half a dozen Emmies, HBO (the cable-based network in business since 1972) has over 400 Emmies. There has been only one tech company in history that was successful with video content production for movies or television, and that is Pixar, Steve Job's firm, which pioneered animated feature length movies. It is impossible to know how well Netflix's original content is performing because the company refuses to release this data. In 2015, Nielsen has begun a rating service for Netflix shows. This service is paid for by the content producers who will base their charges in part on how many Netflix subscribers stream their shows.

While Netflix stands out as a powerful Internet brand today, Netflix has many powerful competitors. Netflix does not have unique technology. In fact, streaming technology is widespread and well understood. The success of Netflix's streaming model has attracted Amazon, Apple, Yahoo, Google, and content producers like Hulu and HBO to the fray. In September 2015, Verizon announced a free, ad-supported mobile streaming service call Go90, aimed at Millennials who routinely watch video on their smartphones. Some of these firms are tech firms with very large Internet audiences, strong brand names, and a good understanding of what their millions of online customers want.

Apple is the leader in downloaded movies where customers own or rent movies, and of course, it does own iTunes, the world's largest online media store for the purchase of music, videos, and TV series. HBO, founded in 1972, is the oldest and most successful pay television service in the United States with over 35 million cable TV subscribers, and the originator of a long list of highly successful original TV series and movies such as *Sex and the City*, *The Sopranos*, *The Wire*, *Game of Thrones*, and *True Blood*. If Netflix has a direct competitor on the creative front, it is HBO, a more traditional programmer that does not use computer algorithms to design its content, but instead relies on the hunches and gifts of editors, producers, and directors to produce its content.

Netflix's competitors have very deep pockets. This means Netflix also has competitors for talent and the production of new content, and perhaps price pressure as well. For instance, Amazon offers free streaming to Amazon Prime customers, and in 2014 has taken on HBO TV series to stream to Prime customers without additional fees. Google is actively pursuing long-form content creators for its video channel program. There is no cost to Google users because the service is ad supported.

So another possible ending for the Netflix movie is that ultimately it can't compete with Apple, Google, Yahoo, Hulu, and Amazon, or the content producers like CBS and HBO Now, which have started their own streaming services. Netflix can be imitated by its competitors, and its profitability reduced to less than shareholders can tolerate. Apple's 2014 revenue was a staggering $182 billion, 33 times larger than Netflix, and it has a cash reserve of $155 billion. It is entirely within Apple's capabilities, or Amazon's or Google's, and many others' to develop a competing streaming video service. In August 2015 Wall Street finally got the message that Netflix was facing a slew of streaming competitors, and its stock fell over 20%. This show is not over until the last episode is finished. Stay tuned.

Case Study Questions

1. What are three challenges that Netflix faces?

2. What are the key elements of Netflix's strategy in 2014?

3. What are the implications of Netflix's new strategy for the cable television systems like Comcast and TimeWarner?

4. Why is Netflix in competition with Apple, Amazon, and Google, and what strengths does Netflix bring to the market?

10.5 REVIEW

KEY CONCEPTS

- **Understand the major trends in the consumption of media and online content, the major revenue models for digital content delivery, digital rights management, and the concept of media convergence.**
- Major trends in the consumption of media and online content include the following:
  - The average American adult spends around 4,300 hours per year consuming various media. The most hours are spent online, using a desktop or mobile device, followed by watching television and listening to the radio.
  - Although several studies indicate that time spent on the Internet reduces consumer time available for other media, recent data reveals a more complex picture, as Internet users multitask and consume more media of all types than do non-Internet users.
  - In terms of all media revenue, print media (newspapers, books, and magazines) and television/home video each account for about the same amount of revenue (about 34%). Internet media (music and video) currently accounts for only 8.7% of all media revenue.
  - The three major revenue models for digital content delivery are the subscription, a la carte, and advertising-supported (free and freemium) models.
  - In terms of paid online content, online TV and movies is the largest and fastest growing form of online entertainment.
  - Digital rights management (DRM) refers to the combination of technical and legal means for protecting digital content from reproduction without permission. Walled gardens are a kind of DRM that restrict the widespread sharing of content.
- The concept of media convergence has three dimensions:
  - Technological convergence, which refers to the development of hybrid devices that can combine the functionality of two or more media platforms, such as books, newspapers, television, radio, and stereo equipment, into a single device.
  - Content convergence, with respect to content design, production, and distribution.
  - Industry convergence, which refers to the merger of media enterprises into powerful, synergistic combinations that can cross-market content on many different platforms and create works that use multiple platforms.
  - In the early years of e-commerce, many believed that media convergence would occur quickly. However, many early efforts failed, and new efforts are just now appearing.

- ■ Understand the key factors affecting the online publishing industry.

- Key factors affecting online newspapers include:
    - *Audience size and growth.* Although the newspaper industry as a whole is the most troubled part of the publishing industry, online readership of newspapers is growing, fueled by smartphones, e-readers, and tablet computers.
    - *Revenue models and results.* Online newspapers predominantly rely on both advertising and subscription revenues. Digital ad revenues are not sufficient to cover losses in print advertising.
- Key factors affecting online magazines include:
    - *Online audience and growth:* Digital magazine sales have soared, with almost a third of the Internet population now reading magazines online.
    - *Magazine aggregation:* Magazine aggregators (Web sites or apps) offer users online subscriptions and sales of many digital magazines.
- Key factors affecting e-books and online book publishing include:
    - *Audience size and growth.* E-book sales growth has leveled off following an explosive growth period. Growth today is fueled by the Amazon Kindle, Apple iPad, and smartphones. The mobile platform of smartphones and tablets has made millions of books available online at a lower price than print books. The future of the book will be digital although printed books will not disappear for many years.
    - *Challenges.* The two primary challenges facing e-book publishing are control over pricing and the continued evolution of the e-book model, including rentals and subscription services.
    - *Competing business models.* E-book business models include the wholesale model and the agency model.
    - *Convergence.* The publishing industry is making steady progress toward media convergence. Newly authored e-books are appearing with interactive rich media, which allow the user to click on icons for videos or other material.

- ■ Understand the key factors affecting the online entertainment industry.

- There are five main players in the entertainment sector: television, motion pictures, music, games, and radio broadcasting. The entertainment segment is currently undergoing great change, brought about by the Internet and the mobile platform. Consumers have begun to accept paying for content and also to expect to be able to access online entertainment from any device at any time.
- Key factors include the following:
    - *Audience size and growth.* The audience for online movies and television is growing dramatically.
    - *The emergence of streaming services and the mobile platform.* In the movie and television industries, two major trends are the move to streaming services, from Amazon, Apple, to Hulu and other channels, and the continued increase in online purchases and downloads. Although physical sales of products (DVDs) are dropping significantly, more and more consumers are purchasing movies and television episodes on mobile devices.
    - The music industry is experiencing similar trends as the movie industry: the growth of streaming services, or Internet radio, the continued expansion of online purchases, and increased downloads on mobile devices. However, the unbundling of a traditional music product, the album, into individual songs, has decimated music industry revenues.
    - Of the four types of gamers—casual, social, mobile, and console—the greatest growth is anticipated for mobile gamers, as the mobile market is rapidly expanding along all e-commerce fronts.

QUESTIONS

1. What are the three dimensions in which the term "convergence" has been applied? What does each of these areas of convergence entail?

2. What are the basic revenue models for online content, and what is their major challenge?
3. What are the two primary e-book business models?
4. What effect is the growth of tablet computing having on online entertainment and content?
5. What techniques do music subscription services use to enforce DRM?
6. What type of convergence does the Kindle Fire represent?
7. What are the three different business models that newspapers have used to try to adapt to the Internet?
8. What are the different revenue models that newspapers have used?
9. What advantages do pure digital news sites have over print newspapers? What advantages do traditional newspapers have over pure digital sites?
10. How has the book publishing industry's experience with the Internet differed from the newspaper and magazine industries' experience?
11. How has the Internet changed the packaging, distribution, marketing, and sale of traditional music tracks?
12. How has streaming technology impacted the television industry?
13. Why is the growth of cloud storage services important to the growth of mobile content delivery?
14. Has the average consumer become more receptive to advertising-supported Internet content? What developments support this?
15. What factors are needed to support successfully charging the consumer for online content?
16. Why are apps helping the newspaper and magazine industries where Web sites failed?
17. What alternatives do magazine publishers have to using Apple and Google newsstands as distribution channels?
18. Why did the Justice Department sue major publishing firms and Apple?
19. What are some of the challenges currently facing the book publishing industry?
20. Name and describe the four types of Internet gamers. Which type attracts the most gamers?

PROJECTS

1. Research the issue of media convergence in the newspaper industry. Do you believe that convergence will be good for the practice of journalism? Develop a reasoned argument on either side of the issue and write a 3- to 5-page report on the topic. Include in your discussion the barriers to convergence and whether these restrictions should be eased.

2. Go to Amazon and explore the different digital media products that are available. For each kind of digital media product, describe how Amazon's presence has altered the industry that creates, produces, and distributes this content. Prepare a presentation to convey your findings to the class.

3. Identify three online sources of content that exemplify one of the three digital content revenue models (subscription, a la carte, and advertising-supported) discussed in the chapter. Describe how each site works, and how it generates revenue. Describe how each site provides value to the consumer. Which type of revenue model do you prefer, and why?

4. Identify a popular online magazine that also has an offline subscription or newsstand edition. What advantages (and disadvantages) does the online edition have when compared to the offline physical edition? Has technology platform, content design, or industry structure convergence occurred in the online magazine industry? Prepare a short report discussing this issue.

5. In August 2014, Amazon purchased Twitch, which lets users stream their video game sessions, for almost $1 billion. Why would Amazon spend so much money on Twitch? Create a short presentation either defending the purchase or explaining why you think it was a bad idea.

REFERENCES

Alpert, Lukas. "For New York Times, a Gamble on Give-aways." *Wall Street Journal* (August 2, 2015).

Alter, Alexandra. "Sci-Fi's Underground Hit." *Wall Street Journal* (March 14, 2013).

Arnold, Thomas. "2014 Analysis: Home Entertainment Steps Up to Keep Up With Connected Customer." *Variety* (December 26, 2014).

Association of American Publishers. "US Publishing Industry Annual Survey Reports $28 Billion in Revenue." (June 10, 2015).

Association of American Publishers. "Monthly StatShot." (June 2015b).

Berkshire Hathaway Corporation. "Annual Report 2013." (March 1, 2013).

Bialik, Carl. "Studios Struggle for Focus on Film Pirates Booty." *Wall Street Journal* (April 5, 2013).

Boxer, Sarah. "Paintings Too Perfect? The Great Optics Debate." *New York Times* (December 4, 2001).

Carr, David. "Print Is Down, and Now Out." *New York Times* (August 10, 2014).

comScore. "comScore Releases May 2015 U.S. Online Video Rankings." (May 2015).

Danaher, Brett, and Michael D. Smith. "Gone in 60 Seconds: The Impact of the Megaupload Shutdown on Movie Sales." *International Journal of Industrial Organization* (March 2014).

Danaher, Brett, Michael D. Smith, and Rahul Tang. "Piracy and Copyright Enforcement Mechanisms," *Innovation Policy and the Economy*, Vol. 14 (May 3, 2013).

Edmunds, Rick. "Newspapers Stabilizing, but Still Threatened." Poynter Institute and Pew Research Center. (July 18, 2013).

eMarketer, Inc. "US Time Spent with Media: eMarketer's Updated Estimates for Spring 2015." (May 2015a).

eMarketer, Inc. (Alison McCarthy) "US Digital Users: Q1 2015 Complete Forecast." (February 2015b).

eMarketer, Inc. "US Digital TV Viewers, 2013-2019." (February 2015c).

eMarketer, Inc., "US Mobile Phone Video Viewers 2013–2019." (February 2015d).

eMarketer, Inc. (Paul Verna). "Q1 2015 State of Video." (March 2015e).

eMarketer, Inc. "US Digital Music Shipments and Revenues, by Format, 2013 & 2014." (March 18, 2015f)

eMarketer, Inc. "US Online Gaming Audience: Mobile, Social, Casual, and Console." (July 2015g).

eMarketer, Inc. "Mobile Game Revenues to Grow 16.5% in 2015 Surpassing $3 Billion." (July 2015h).

eMarketer, Inc. (Paul Verna). "Simultaneous Media Use: Screen Fragmentation Complements Traditional Channels." (October 2014a).

eMarketer, Inc. (David Hallerman) "Shifting Video and TV Audiences." (August 2014b).

eMarketer, Inc. "Magazine Ad Spending, United States, 2012–2018." (June 2014c).

eMarketer, Inc., "Ebook Readers Use Devices to Supplement, Not Replace, Printed Media." (January 30, 2014d).

Envisional, Inc. "An Estimate of Infringing Use of the Internet." (2013).

Fischer, Mary. "BuzzFeed and the Huffington Post Crush Legacy Outlets in Traffic Growth." *American Journalism Review* (May 21, 2014).

Flint, Joe. "Cord Cutting Weighs on Cable TV." *Wall Street Journal* (August 9, 2015).

Fritz, Ben. "Movie Sales Increase With Shutdown of Piracy Site." *Wall Street Journal* (March 7, 2013).

Gaudiosi, John. "Mobile Game Revenues Set to Overtake Console Games in 2015," *Fortune* (January 2015).

Google. (Deborah Schwartz) "A Window Into Film." (April 2011).

Hagey, Keach and Greg Bensinger. "Jeff Bezo's Tool Kit for the Post." *Wall Street Journal* (August 6, 2013).

IFPI. "Global Statistics." (April 14, 2015).

Isaac, Mike. "A Push to Go Beyond Lists for Content at BuzzFeed." *New York Times* (August 11, 2014).

Journalism.org. "Newspapers: Audience by Platform." Journalism.org (July 2015).

Magazine Publishers Association. Magazine Publishers Association. "Magazine Media Fact Book 2015." (March 2015).

Marques, Silas. "E-Textbooks Usage by Students at Andrews University: A Study of Attitudes, Perceptions, and Behaviors." Proceedings of the IATUL Conferences 2012 Andrews University (2012).

Needleman, Sarah. "Inside the 'League of Legends." *Wall Street Journal* (August 23, 2015).

Needleman, Sarah. "The Newest Job in Sports: Video-game Coach," *Wall Street Journal*, July 29, 2015.

New York Times. "Innovation." (May 2014).

Newspaper Association of America. "NAA Media Revenue 2013: Dollars Grow in Several Categories." (April 18, 2014a).

Newspaper Association of America. "Annual Daily and Sunday Newspaper Circulation Expenditures." (April 18, 2014b).

Newspaper Association of America. "Newspaper Web Audience." (July 7, 2014c).

Nielsen. "2013 Nielsen National Cross Media Engagement Study." (April 16, 2013).

Packer, George. "Cheap Words: Amazon Is Good for Customers. But Is It Good for Books?" *New Yorker* (February 17, 2014).

Pew Research Center. "Journalism and Media. Newspapers: Fact Sheet." (April 29, 2015).

Pew Research Center (Kenneth Olmstead). "5 Key Findings About Digital News Audiences." (March 17, 2014a).

Pew Research Center (Amy Mitchell, Mark Jurkowitz, and Kenneth Olmstead). "Audience Routes: Direct, Search, and Facebook." (March 12, 2014b.)

Pew Research Center. "State of the News Media 2014." (2014c).

Plambeck, Joseph. "Daily Report: E-Sports Continues to Reshape Gaming Landscape." *New York Times* (August 5, 2015).

PriceWaterhouseCooper (PWC). "Global Entertainment and Media Outlook 2015–2019." (2015a).

PriceWaterhouseCoopers (PWC). "Global Video Games Report: Key Insights At A Glance." Pwc.com (2015b).

Recording Industry Association of America (RIAA). "News and Notes on 2014 RIAA Music Industry Shipments and Revenue Statistics 2014." (2015).

Romenesko, Jim. "Wall Street Journal Memo: Newsroom Changes Mean a Faster-moving, Digital First News Operation." Jimromenesko.com. (January 21, 2014.)

Sisario, Ben. "Apple Takes On a Market Full of Streaming Services." *New York Times* (June 3, 2015).

Somaiya, Ravi. "The New Yorker Alters Its Online Strategy." *New York Times* (July 8, 2014).

Steel, Emily. "Suddenly, Plenty of Options for Cord Cutters." *New York Times* (July 15, 2015).

Streitfield, David. "Amazon, a Friendly Giant As Long As It's Fed." *New York Times* (July 12, 2014).

Streitfield, David. "Out of Print, but Not Out of Mind." *New York Times* (December 1, 2013b).

Streitfield, David. "Writers Feel an Amazon-Hachette Spat." *New York Times* (May 14, 2014a).

Streitfield, David. "Amazon and Hachette Resolve Dispute." *New York Times* (November 13, 2014b).

Studentmonitor.com. "American College Students Say They Would Rather Study With Real Books, Not Laptops." (September 2014).

Superdataresearch.com. "North America Digital Games Report, 2014." (2015a).

Superdataresearch.com. "Worldwide E-sports Market Reaches 134 Million Viewers." (May 4, 2015b).

Takahashi, Dean. "US Games Industry Forecast to Grow 30 Percent to $19.6 Billion by 2019." Venturebeat.com (June 2,2015).

Tassi, Paul. "Whatever Happened to the War on Piracy." *Forbes* (January 24, 2014).

Trachtenberg, Jeffrey. "Clock is Ticking for Time Inc.'s CEO." *Wall Street Journal* (July 27, 2015).

USnewspapersonline.com. "Top Twenty Online Newspapers." (July 2015).

Vega, Tanzina. "Marketers Find a Friend in Pinterest." *New York Times* (April 17, 2012).

Wingfield, Nick. "In E-Sports, Video Gamers Draw Real Crowds and Big Money." *New York Times* (August 30, 2014a).

Wingfield, Nick. "E-Sports at College, With Stars and Scholarships." *New York Times* (December 8, 2014b).

Wingfield, Nick. "Technology Industry Extends a Hand to Struggling Print Media." *New York Times* (August 11, 2013).

CHAPTER 11

Social Networks, Auctions, and Portals

LEARNING OBJECTIVES

After reading this chapter, you will be able to:

- Describe the different types of social networks and online communities and their business models.
- Describe the major types of auctions, their benefits and costs, how they operate, when to use them, and the potential for auction abuse and fraud.
- Describe the major types of Internet portals and their business models.

Social Network Fever

Spreads to the Professions

When social networks first appeared a decade ago, it was widely believed the phenomenon would be limited to crazed teenagers already captive to online games and video game consoles. Most of the technorati in Silicon Valley and Wall Street felt this was a blip on the horizon, and their full attention was occupied by search engines, search engine marketing, and ad placement. But when the population of social network participants pushed into the hundreds of millions, even the technical elite woke up to the fact that these huge audiences were not just a bunch of teenagers. Instead, a wide slice of American society was participating. Steve Ballmer, CEO of Microsoft, expressed the conviction as early as 2007 that social networks would have some staying power, although he tempered that outlook with reservations about just how long that would be, given their youthful appeal and faddish nature. This was just before Microsoft paid $250 million for a small stake in Facebook, which valued the company at $15 billion. Trying to sound convincing, the month before his company spent $1.65 billion for YouTube, Google CEO Eric Schmidt asserted his belief that despite prevailing opinion, social networks were a bona fide business opportunity.

Courtesy of Carol Traver

By October 2015, Facebook had grown to over 1.5 billion active monthly users worldwide. The social network craze obviously has awakened the technology giants, but they focus mostly on the really huge audiences attracted to general social networks such as Facebook, Twitter, Instagram, and YouTube. However, in the background there is a fast-growing collection of social networks that are aimed at communities of practitioners or specific interest groups.

Take LinkedIn, for example, probably the best-known and most popular business network site. LinkedIn is an online network with more than 380 million worldwide members in over 200 countries, representing 170 different industries. In 2015, according to LinkedIn, it typically has around 97 million monthly unique visiting members, including about 50 million who visit using a mobile device. In May 2011, LinkedIn went public in what was, at the time, the biggest Internet IPO since Google, raising more than $350 million and giving it a company valuation of $8.9 billion. The company priced its IPO at $45 per share. As of October 2015 its stock was priced at around $207 per share, making its market capitalization about $26.4 billion. LinkedIn allows a member to create a profile, including a photo, to summarize his or her professional accomplishments. Members' networks include their connections, their connections' connections, as well as people they know, potentially linking them to thousands of others. How members use LinkedIn depends somewhat on

SOURCES: "About Us," LinkedIn.com Press Center, accessed October 21, 2015; "LinkedIn Corporation Market Cap," YCharts.com, accessed October 21, 2015; "Welcome to The CAPS Community," Caps.fool.com, accessed October 21, 2015; "New Social Network Aims to Find News Tech Pros Really Care About," by Kristin Burnham, Computerworld.com, September 21, 2015; LinkedIn Form 10-Q for the quarterly period ended June 30, 2015, filed with the U.S. Securities and Exchange Commission, July 31, 2015; "35 Percent of Employers Less Likely to Interview Applicants They Can't Find Online, According to Annual CareerBuilder Social Media Recruitment Survey," Careerbuilder.com, May 14, 2015; "The Top 100 Websites of 2013," by Eric Griffith, Pcmag.com, January 2, 2014; "Marketing on LinkedIn: New Opportunities, But Old Issues Remain," eMarketer, Inc., August 23, 2013; "LinkedIn Builds Its Publishing Presence," by Leslie Kaufman, *New York Times*, June 16, 2013; "How Professionals Use LinkedIn," eMarketer, August 5, 2011.

their position. Top executives use the site mainly for industry networking and promoting their businesses. Middle managers use LinkedIn primarily to keep in touch with others and also for industry networking. Lower-level employees typically use the site for job searching and networking with co-workers.

Those with a particular interest in the stock market can choose from a crop of Web sites aimed at stock investors who want to share their ideas with other investors. These social networks are not just bulletin boards with anonymous comments, but active communities where users are identified and ranked according to the performance of their stock picks. One network is Stockr, chosen as one of PC Magazine's top 100 Web sites in 2013. Stockr is a community where stock investors exchange ideas and track the performance of financial bloggers. Like the larger social networks, financial social networks allow users to connect with other investors, discuss issues focused on the stock market, and sometimes just show off investing prowess. The Motley Fool, one of the best-known online stock investment services, started its CAPS stock-rating social network in 2006 and has over 180,000 members.

You can find similar social networks for a variety of specific professional groups such as health care (DailyStrength), law (LawLink), physicians (Sermo), human resources (Hr.com), and Quibb (technology professionals). These social networks encourage members to discuss the realities of their professions and practices, sharing successes and failures. The rapid growth of professional social networks, linked to industry and careers, demonstrates how widespread and nearly universal the appeal of social networks is. What explains the very broad attraction to social networks? E-mail is excellent for communicating with other individuals, or even a small group. But e-mail is not very good at getting a sense of what others in the group are thinking, especially if the group numbers more than a dozen people. The strength of social networks lies in their ability to reveal group attitudes and opinions, values, and practices.

Professionals who join social networks need to be careful about the content they provide, and the distribution of this content. As business social networks have grown, and as the number of participants expands, employers are finding them a great place to discover the "inner" person who applies for a job. A 2015 survey by CareerBuilder, the most widely used employment site in the United States, found that 52% of employers use social networks to screen job candidates. The survey found that 48% of hiring managers who use social media to vet candidates discovered information that led them not to hire an applicant, such as provocative material posted by the candidate, information about the candidate drinking or using drugs, or criticism by the candidate of former employers. On the other hand, 32% of managers found information that led them to hire someone, such as evidence of a professional image, well-rounded personality, creativity, and good communication skills. Based on this survey, it's wise to use social networks' maximum privacy settings and release to the public only the most innocuous content. Likewise, be cautious of social networks that do not provide "take down" policies, which allow users to remove embarrassing materials from their pages.

I n this chapter, we discuss social networks, auctions, and portals. What do social networks, auctions, and portals have in common? They are all based on feelings of shared interest and self-identification—in short, a sense of community. Social networks and online communities explicitly attract people with shared affinities, such as ethnicity, gender, religion, and political views, or shared interests, such as hobbies, sports, and vacations. The auction site eBay started as a community of people interested in trading unwanted but functional items for which there was no ready commercial market. That community turned out to be huge—much larger than anyone expected. Portals also contain strong elements of community by providing access to community-fostering technologies such as e-mail, chat groups, bulletin boards, and discussion forums.

11.1 SOCIAL NETWORKS AND ONLINE COMMUNITIES

The Internet was designed originally as a communications medium to connect scientists in computer science departments around the continental United States. From the beginning, the Internet was intended, in part, as a community-building technology that would allow scientists to share data, knowledge, and opinions in a real-time online environment (see Chapter 3) (Hiltzik, 1999). The result of this early Internet was the first "virtual communities" (Rheingold, 1993). As the Internet grew in the late 1980s to include scientists from many disciplines and university campuses, thousands of virtual communities sprang up among small groups of scientists in very different disciplines that communicated regularly using Internet e-mail, listservs, and bulletin boards. The first articles and books on the new electronic communities began appearing in the mid- to late 1980s (Kiesler et al., 1984; Kiesler, 1986). One of the earliest online communities, The Well (Whole Earth 'Lectronic Link), was formed in San Francisco in 1985 by a small group of people who once shared an 1,800-acre commune in Tennessee. The Well continues to have thousands of members devoted to discussion, debate, advice, and help (Hafner, 1997; Rheingold, 1998). With the development of the Web in the early 1990s, millions of people began obtaining Internet accounts and Web e-mail, and the community-building impact of the Internet strengthened. By the late 1990s, the commercial value of online communities was recognized as a potential new business model (Hagel and Armstrong, 1997).

The early online communities involved a relatively small number of Web aficionados, and users with intense interests in technology, politics, literature, and ideas. The technology was largely limited to posting text messages on bulletin boards sponsored by the community, and one-to-one or one-to-many e-mails. In addition to The Well, early networks included GeoCities, a Web site hosting service based on neighborhoods. By 2002, however, the nature of online communities had begun to change. User-created Web sites called blogs became inexpensive and easy to set up without any technical expertise. Photo sites enabled convenient sharing of photos. Beginning in 2007, the growth of mobile devices like smartphones, tablet computers, digital cameras, and portable media devices enabled sharing of rich media such as photos, music, and videos. Suddenly there was a much wider audience for sharing interests and activities, and much more to share.

A new culture emerged as well. The broad democratization of the technology and its spread to the larger population meant that online social networks were no longer limited to a small group but instead broadened to include a much wider set of people and tastes, especially pre-teens, teens, and college students who were the fastest to adopt many of these new technologies. Entire families and friendship networks soon joined. The new social network culture is very personal and "me" centered, displaying photos and broadcasting personal activities, interests, hobbies, and relationships on social network profiles. In an online social network, the "news" is not something that happened somewhere else to other people; instead, the news is what happened to you today, and what's going on with your friends and colleagues. Today's social networks are as much a sociological phenomenon as they are a technology phenomenon.

Currently, social network participation is one of the most common usages of the Internet. Over three-quarters of all Internet users and about 65% of the total U.S. population—about 180 million Americans—use social networks (eMarketer, Inc., 2015a). Facebook has over 1.5 billion active users of its Web site (with about 164 million in North America) and a little over 1.3 billion mobile monthly users (Facebook, 2015). There is obviously an overlap between these two sets of users. In the United States, Facebook typically has around 160 million monthly unique visitors to its Web site and over 125 million users of its smartphone app (again, with many of these being overlapping) (comScore, 2015b). Google + is included here as a social network, but in 2015, Google has been downplaying Google +, and cutting the link between Google + and its other services such as YouTube. In the past, a Google + account was required in order to be able to fully use any of Google's other services as a subscriber. As a result, Google + subscriber numbers included many people who were using some other Google service. Google + has never achieved the success of other social networks such as Facebook or Instagram (Miners, 2015d). Other large social networks include LinkedIn (profiled in the opening case), Twitter, Pinterest, Instagram, and Tumblr. While Facebook is the most popular social network, it is also the slowest growing, up just a few percentage points since 2012. Facebook appears to have hit a plateau in the United States, and its real hope for growth is offshore, where it is pushing to create basic Internet access so more people will join the network. Newer social networks, such as Pinterest and Instagram, have doubled in the past three years to 31% and 28% of Internet users (Pew Research, 2015).

Worldwide, the social network phenomena is even stronger with nearly 2 billion users worldwide, 27% of the world's population, and still growing at 9% annually. Social networks are a top online destination in every country, accounting for the majority of time spent online, and reaching over 60% of active Internet users. Asia-Pacific has the largest social network audience, followed by the Middle East and Africa, and Latin America, while North America has the highest penetration of social network usage among the general population (eMarketer, Inc., 2015a). Although Facebook dominates the global social network marketspace, in some countries, localized social networks are signficant, such as Orkut (owned by Google) in Brazil, Mixi and social messaging app LINE in Japan, Qzone, QQ, Sina Weibo, and RenRen in China, XING in Germany, Tuenti in Spain, and VK in Russia. There is an online social network for you to join almost anywhere you go! Unfortunately, there's very little, if any, communication across social networks.

WHAT IS AN ONLINE SOCIAL NETWORK?

So exactly how do we define an online social network, and how is it any different from, say, an offline social network? Sociologists, who frequently criticize modern society for having destroyed traditional communities, unfortunately have not given us very good definitions of social networks and community. One study examined 94 different sociological definitions of community and found four areas of agreement. **Social networks** involve (a) a group of people, (b) shared social interaction, (c) common ties among members, and (d) people who share an area for some period of time (Hillery, 1955). This will be our working definition of a social network. Social networks do not necessarily have shared goals, purposes, or intentions. Indeed, social networks can be places where people just "hang out," share space, and communicate.

It's a short step to defining an **online social network** as an area online where people who share common ties can interact with one another. This definition is very close to that of Howard Rheingold's—one of The Well's early participants—who coined the term *virtual communities* as "cultural aggregations that emerge when enough people bump into each other often enough in cyberspace." It is a group of people who may or may not meet one another face to face, and who exchange words and ideas through the mediation of an online social meeting space. The Internet removes the geographic and time limitations of offline social networks. To be in an online network, you don't need to meet face to face, in a common room, at a common time.

THE GROWTH OF SOCIAL NETWORKS AND ONLINE COMMUNITIES

Figure 11.1 shows the top social networks, which together account for well over 90% of the Internet's social network activity.

While those between the ages of 12 and 34 still have the highest rates of Facebook usage, ranging from 78% to 88%, two-thirds of those between 35 and 44 use Facebook, as do half of 45- to 64-year-olds. Surprisingly, adults over 65 comprise the fastest growing group on Facebook. Similar patterns are observed worldwide as older populations use social networks to stay in touch with children and relatives (eMarketer, Inc., 2015a). Facebook is the most popular social network among teens (71% use Facebook), with Instagram and Snapchat not far behind (Miners, 2015a).

More so than Facebook, Twitter is predominantly used by young adults (18–34). Only about 16% of 35- to 44-year-olds report using Twitter. Newer social networks tend to follow this same pattern, with young people being the first adopters.

While Facebook and Twitter still tend to dominate the news, a new kind of social network is appearing and growing much faster than Facebook with respect to unique

social network
involves a group of people, shared social interaction, common ties among members, and people who share an area for some period of time

online social network
an area online, where people who share common ties can interact with one another

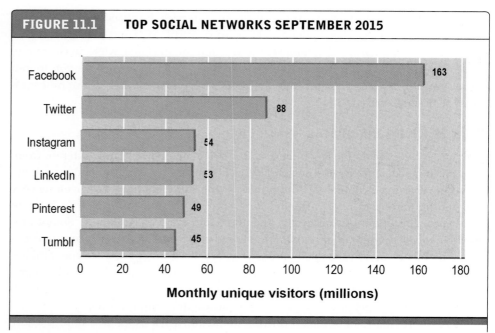

FIGURE 11.1 | **TOP SOCIAL NETWORKS SEPTEMBER 2015**

Facebook is by far and away the dominant social network in the United States in terms of monthly unique visitors.

SOURCES: Based on data from Compete, Inc., 2015.

visitors and subscribers. These new social networks are attracting marketers and advertisers as well. For instance, Pinterest, described in the closing case in Chapter 1, is a visually oriented site that allows users to curate their tastes and preferences, expressed in visual arts. You can think of Pinterest as a visual blog. Users post images to an online "pinboard." The images can come from any source. Users can also "re-pin" images they see on Pinterest. Pinterest's membership has skyrocketed since its launch, accumulating more than 100 million active members worldwide as of September 2015. Instagram is another social network that focuses on video and photo sharing. A mobile app that enables a user to easily share images to social networks, Instagram was acquired by Facebook for $1 billion in 2012 and has over 400 million members in September 2015. Tumblr is an easy-to-use blogging site with tools for visual and text curating, sharing with others, and reblogging contents. Tumblr started in 2007, was acquired by Yahoo in 2013, and has around 20 million users in 2015.

Other social networks are not necessarily competing with Facebook, but adding to the social network mix and enlarging the total social network audience. **Table 11.1** describes some other popular social networks.

Contributing to the continued growth and commercial success of networks is the rapid adoption and intense use of mobile devices. About 82% of Facebook's users are mobile users although not exclusively. Several of the largest newer social networks like Instagram, Snapchat, and Vine are almost entirely mobile. In 2015, over 76% of

TABLE 11.1	OTHER SOCIAL NETWORKS
SOCIAL NETWORK	**DESCRIPTION**
Myspace	Early leader in social networking was overtaken by Facebook; being reinvented as a music-oriented social network by pop star Justin Timberlake.
Meetup	Helps groups of people with shared interests plan events and meet offline.
Tagged	A network aimed at introducing members to one another through games, shared interests, friend suggestions, and browsing profiles.
MeetMe	Another social network aimed at meeting new people.
Polyvore	Topic-focused social network (fashion).
deviantART	Web site focused on art, sharing of images.
Vevo	Video and music sharing site.

Facebook's revenue comes from mobile users. See the *Insight on Technology* case, *The Appification of Facebook*, for more on the way apps are transforming Facebook.

A new crop of social networks launched since 2008 focuses on messaging, either sending of text or photos. Snapchat (2009) lets users send photos to friends that self-extinguish in ten seconds. Slingshot (2014) lets Facebook users instant message photos and video to their Facebook friends. WhatsApp (2009; acquired by Facebook in 2014) is a messaging service that, for $1, lets users send text, photos, and videos to their friends' cellphones using the Internet and without having to pay telecommunications companies for cellphone SMS messaging services. Six of the world's most-used apps are messaging services. At Facebook, users reportedly use WhatsApp and Messenger over 25 times a day but visit their Facebook News Feed only fifteen times a day (Seetharaman, 2015). It is unclear if these social networks based on messaging are economically viable on their own or if they will only flourish as within more successful social networks like Facebook.

The number of unique visitors is just one way to measure the influence of a site. Time on site is another important metric. The more time people spend on a site, called engagement, the more time to display ads and generate revenue. In this sense, Facebook is much more addictive and immersive than the other top social networks. Over time, Facebook has tweaked its content and algorithms in order to keep users on the site longer. In 2014, Facebook added videos (both ads and user-contributed), and in 2015 is now displaying around 4 billion videos a day. It tries to show videos that reflect the user's interests and friends and also plays them automatically in the News Feed, forcing users to turn them off but also ensuring that they are seen for at least a few

INSIGHT ON TECHNOLOGY

THE APPIFICATION OF FACEBOOK

Facebook founder Mark Zuckerberg first envisioned Facebook as a unitary experience, a place where all your social needs could be addressed. This approach fit with the branding strategy of Facebook connecting people all around the world and the Facebook mobile app used a similar all-in-one interface for many years. However, in an effort to create a more mobile-friendly experience, Facebook is moving from a single do-it-all app to a collection of apps that stand alone and compete with other apps in specific categories. This will allow the main Facebook app to focus on what it does best—posting updates and displaying the News Feed and Timelines of users while other functions of Facebook will operate separately. It's a risky strategy that worried investors at first and has met with mixed results, including some major successes.

The first app split off was Messenger, previously a functionality within Facebook that is used by hundreds of millions around the world. The Messenger function within Facebook's app was turned off and replaced by an icon. When users press the icon, the Messenger app launches. The Messenger app is faster and leaner than its predecessor, and can be more easily customized by the user. As a result, messages can be delivered 20% faster than before. Other new features include the ability to set up groups of contacts based on the user's cell phone contacts, create groups of contacts for different purposes (such as a party or trip), and deliver quick voice messages and photos. Privacy advocates have balked at Messenger's ability to automatically attach the user's location to each message, which is very appealing to advertisers offering location-based ads.

To further the long-term strategy of developing Facebook as a collection of stand-alone apps,

Facebook created a new unit called Creative Labs to build apps free of the burden of integration with the main Facebook app. The idea is that single function apps can have a simpler interface, run faster, and be more intuitive. Creative Labs programmers report greater freedom to develop new products.

Facebook's track record with apps is mostly disappointing. Skeptical investors and critics point out that the most innovative and popular products coming out of Facebook are those that it recently purchased rather than any developed in-house. Facebook has launched a number of ho-hum apps that few people use. Home was an Android feature that locked your smartphone screen to your Facebook. Few adopted it, as most found it redundant. Seeing the rapid growth of Instagram, the photo-based social network, Facebook developed a copycat app called Camera. Sensing another flop, it bought Instagram in April 2012 for $1 billion, hoping to appeal to younger users. Camera has since been discontinued while Instagram has grown from 40 to over 400 million users; however, it does not yet generate any revenue. Paper, the first new app to emerge from Creative Labs, allows users to navigate the News Feed using touch gestures. It has yet to find significant support.

On the other hand, in 2015, it appears the spinoff of Messenger has worked—it's now the second most popular app in the United States, ahead of YouTube and behind only the flagship Facebook app. New features such as Businesses on Messenger and Facebook Video Messenger have broadened the appeal to different types of users, making it a much more compelling experience than the integrated app. By opening Messenger to users without Facebook accounts and third-party developers, Facebook has signaled that it wants Messenger to be a fully autonomous platform. Facebook has been seeking a platform like this for several years. It may now have two.

In 2012, Facebook was rebuffed when it tried to buy SnapChat, the self-deleting messaging app, for $3 billion. Snapchat is one of several mobile messaging services that have become wildly popular, with twice as many messages sent over the mobile Internet than via traditional texts, according to Deloitte Research. In December 2012, Facebook cloned Snapchat with an app called Poke. However, like Camera and Paper, Poke did not take off. Instead, in 2014 Facebook bought the world's largest messaging service, WhatsApp, for a stunning $22 billion. Yes, that's right: $22 billion, possibly the largest acquisition in dot-com history! With 900 million users, and adding 1 million users a day, WhatsApp has become the fastest growing app in history. WhatsApp charges users $1 a year after their second year (the first year is free) to send text messages to cell phone numbers using the Internet rather than the more expensive mobile cell networks. For Facebook, the purchase solidifies its status as the unquestioned leader in Internet messaging and helps it to attract a younger demographic, while eliminating its largest competitor. Facebook has also incorporated many of WhatsApp's most useful features into Messenger. Still, like Instagram, WhatsApp will function as an autonomous unit within Facebook. WhatsApp is lighter-weight and simpler than Messenger, works on a wider variety of devices, and is free to users in developing markets.

Optimistic analysts argue that while the prices paid by Facebook for Instagram and WhatsApp cannot be justified by any current measures of revenue and earnings, they may be the foundation for a much larger social platform that could include retail and media sales, payment processing, and additional functionality that cannot yet be foreseen. According to Zuckerberg, advertising will be phased in gradually to both Messenger and WhatsApp just as it was on Facebook and in the Pages API so that neither the user experience nor app growth will be compromised.

The formation of Creative Labs and acquisitions of Instagram and WhatsApp were designed to address looming, and possibly long-term, challenges. Facebook's growth has flatlined in the United States and slowed markedly around the world. Engagement is faltering, with an 8% drop in active usage in 2014. Facebook demographics are going in the wrong direction: young teens and 18–24-year-olds appear to be losing interest, spending more time on niche social networks. Creative Labs and the strategy of developing stand-alone apps that are linked to Facebook, but not integrated into its mobile app, may be a solution. In 2014, Facebook also spun off its Groups functionality into a stand-alone app, and in 2015, Creative Labs released a host of new apps, including Mentions, an app for celebrities and other public figures with verified profiles or pages; Moments, which allows users to organize photos from events; and Riff, which allows users to create brief videos with friends in the hopes that they'll go viral. However, recent experience suggests that if and when its in-house solutions falter, Facebook will likely wield its considerable financial heft in the app marketplace.

SOURCES: "Facebook's Messenger Topples YouTube, Second Most Popular App in the U.S.," by Shubhomita Bose, Smallbiztrends.com, September 11, 2015; "Facebook Gives Verified Profiles Its Mentions App With 'Live' Streaming and Posts Just To Followers," by Josh Constine, Techcrunch.com, September 10, 2015; "Facebook's Playbook for Monetizing Messenger and WhatsApp," by Josh Constine, Techcrunch.com, July 29, 2015; "Facebook Inc's Ultimate Unbundling: Messenger," by Evan Niu, Fool.com, June 25, 2015; "We're Starting to See the Fruits of Facebook's $22 Billion WhatsApp Deal," by Hope King, Cnnmoney.com, June 24, 2015; "Facebook Moments App Helps Users Swap and Organize Photos," by David Cohen, Adweek.com, June 15, 2015; "Are We Entering the Age of Facebook Fatigue?" by Davina Harwood-Smart, LinkedIn.com, May 27, 2015; "Facebook Launches Groups App to Streamline Online Gatherings on Mobile," by Roberto Baldwin, Thenextweb.com, November 18, 2014; "Can Facebook Innovate? A Conversation With Mark Zuckerberg," by Farhad Manjoo, *New York Times*, April 16, 2014; "The Future of Facebook May Not Say 'Facebook,'" by Farhad Manjoo, *New York Times*, April 16, 2014; "Facebook Requires Users to Install Separate Messaging App," by Vindu Goel, *New York Times*, April 15, 2014; "I Thought Facebook's WhatsApp Deal Was Crazy. Then I Did Some Math," by Dennis Berman, *Wall Street Journal*, February 24, 2014; "Facebook's Plot to Conquer Mobile: Shatter Itself Into Pieces," by Josh Constine, Techcrunch.com, January 29, 2014.

TABLE 11.2	TIME SPENT ON TOP SOCIAL NETWORKS
WEB SITE	MINUTES/MONTH (IN BILLIONS)
Facebook	230
Instagram	12.2
Twitter	6.6
Pinterest	6.5
Snapchat	6.4
Tumblr	5.0
LinkedIn	1.7
Vine	1.5

SOURCES: Based on data from comScore, 2015b.

moments (Miner, 2015). Facebook also made three changes to its News Feed algorithm in 2015 to capture more user attention: increasing content from users' favorite friends; decreasing content from friends of users' friends; and showing multiple posts in a row from the same source for users with few friends (Gaudin, 2015).

Table 11.2 illustrates the different levels of engagement with the top social networks.

The amount of revenue generated is the ultimate metric for measuring a company's business potential. The top three search engine companies (Google, Yahoo, and Microsoft) are expected to generate about $27 billion in U.S. search and display advertising revenue in 2015 (eMarketer, Inc., 2015b). In contrast, social networks in the United States in 2015 are expected to generate about $9.6 billion in advertising revenue. Social networks are the fastest growing form of Internet usage and advertising revenue, but they are not yet as lucrative as traditional search engines/portals in terms of ad dollars generated. A part of the problem is that subscribers do not go to social networks to seek ads for relevant products, nor pay attention to the ads that are flashed before their eyes (see Chapters 6 and 7). In addition, the small screen of the smartphone, the dominant social network platform, is not ideal for display advertising.

TURNING SOCIAL NETWORKS INTO BUSINESSES

While the early social networks had a difficult time raising capital and revenues, today's top social networks are now monetizing their huge audiences. Early social networks relied on subscriptions, but today, most social networks rely on advertising or the investments of venture capitalists. Users of portals and search engines have come to accept advertising as the preferred means of supporting Web experiences rather than paying for it. One important exception is LinkedIn, which offers basic free memberships for individuals but charges for premium services. **Figure 11.2** shows the comparative amount of ad spending on various social networks. Facebook, with almost $7 billion in ad revenue, towers over the other sites.

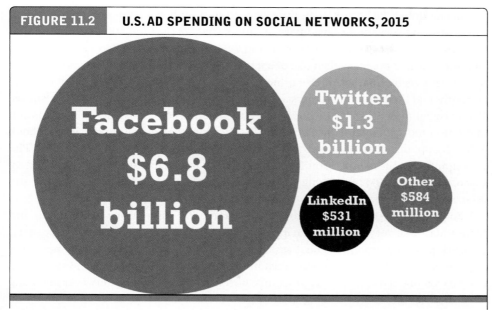

FIGURE 11.2 **U.S. AD SPENDING ON SOCIAL NETWORKS, 2015**

Facebook $6.8 billion

Twitter $1.3 billion

Other $584 million

LinkedIn $531 million

SOURCE: Based on data from eMarketer, 2015c.

Social networks do not always succeed as businesses. For instance, Twitter began as a social messaging service on which users could communicate with followers. It quickly turned into an Internet broadcasting network for millions of on-scene observers acting as citizen reporters, political organizers, celebrities, and politicians. In 2015, it has just over 300 million users, growing at 20% annually. But Twitter's meteoric growth has slowed from its earlier years, and in 2014, it lost $577 million, disappointing investors who expect more advertising dollars and real revenue. Twitter has never shown a profit. In 2015, Twitter is turning its home page into a portal for streaming news and essays, organized by content area, curated topics, and perhaps authored essays. It is trying to make Twitter more accessible to non-subscribers by offering free content, but, as before, to re-tweet or reply to a tweet, a subscription is necessary (Miner, 2015). Executives are hoping these changes will attract more subscribers, more tweets, more ads, and hence more revenue.

The rapid adoption of mobile devices initially posed a challenge to social networks like Facebook, as well as Google's search engine, because they were largely based on the desktop platform. Google dominated mobile ad revenues up until 2013 because its search engine and Google Maps were among the most popular apps. Facebook quickly developed its own mobile app, and purchased others, and within the space of four years has been able to capture a significant part of the mobile ad market, using its mobile News Feed to provide users a continual stream of ads. The top six apps, and eight of the top nine, are owned by either Google or Facebook. For Facebook, that includes the main Facebook app, Facebook Messenger, Instagram, and WhatsApp. Today, over 75% of Facebook's revenue ($2.2 billion) comes from mobile advertising. For Google, 20% of its ad revenue comes from mobile, a whopping $12 billion in mobile ads. Together, Facebook and Google command about one-half of the global mobile ad market (Seetharaman, 2015).

Social networks have had an important impact on how businesses operate, communicate, and serve their customers. A 2015 survey of Fortune 500 firms found that 93% used LinkedIn, 78% used Twitter, and 74% used Facebook (Barnes et al., 2015). The most visible business firm use of social networks is as a marketing and branding tool. A less visible marketing use of networks is as a powerful listening tool that has strengthened the role of customers and customer feedback systems inside a business. Public social networks like Facebook have not been used extensively in firms as collaboration tools thus far. However, in 2015, Facebook began rolling out its Facebook at Work app, designed to spur collaboration and networking inside large firms. The new app faces stiff competition from a wide array of collaboration tools provided by Cisco, Microsoft, IBM, and along with other technologies like instant messaging and teleconferencing (Gaudin, 2015).

Social networks are where corporate brands and reputations are formed, and firms today take very seriously the topic of "online reputation," as evidenced by social network posts, commentary, chat sessions, and Likes. In this sense, social networks become an extension of corporate customer relationship management systems and extend existing market research programs. Beyond branding, social networks are being used increasingly as advertising platforms to contact a younger audience than Web sites and e-mail, and as customers increasingly shift their eyeballs to social networks. Rosetta Stone, for instance, uses its Facebook page to display videos of its learning technology, encourage discussions and reviews, and post changes in its learning tools. Yet the business use of social networks does not always go well. The *Insight on Society* case, *The Dark Side of Social Networks*, discusses some of the risks associated with social networks.

TYPES OF SOCIAL NETWORKS AND THEIR BUSINESS MODELS

There are many types and many ways of classifying social networks and online communities. While the most popular general social networks have adopted an advertising model, other kinds of networks have different revenue sources. Social networks have different types of sponsors and different kinds of members. For instance, some are created by firms such as IBM for the exclusive use of their sales force or other employees (intra-firm communities or B2E [business-to-employee] communities); others are built for suppliers and resellers (inter-organizational or B2B communities); and others are built by dedicated individuals for other similar persons with shared interests (P2P [people-to-people] communities). In this chapter, we will discuss B2C communities for the most part, although we also discuss briefly P2P communities of practice.

Table 11.3 on page 724 describes in greater detail the five generic types of social networks and online communities: general, practice, interest, affinity, and sponsored. Each type of community can have a commercial intent or commercial consequence. We use this schema to explore the business models of commercial communities.

general communities

offer members opportunities to interact with a general audience organized into general topics

General communities offer members opportunities to interact with a general audience organized into general topics. Within the topics, members can find hundreds of specific discussion groups attended by thousands of like-minded members who share an interest in that topic. The purpose of the general community is to attract enough members to populate a wide range of topics and discussion groups. The busi-

INSIGHT ON SOCIETY

THE DARK SIDE OF SOCIAL NETWORKS

ChapStick thought it had a great marketing idea when it decided to launch a new Facebook ad—a mildly provocative picture of a young woman on her disheveled sofa—derriere in the air—rummaging behind the couch. The ad proclaimed: WHERE DO LOST CHAPSTICKS GO? The subtitle invited user comment on Facebook's page. ChapStick was completely unprepared for what came next. Little did ChapStick realize that it was about to endure a social network advertising fiasco.

First, a blogger cited the ad in a post about the pervasiveness of sexist advertising. When she posted to ChapStick's Facebook page, her comment was deleted. Other Facebook posters followed suit. Their comments were also deleted. It wasn't long before a stream of comments mocking the "Be Heard" subtitle ensued.

ChapStick had an opportunity to begin a conversation with its customers that would have demonstrated its cognizance of and sensitivity to sexist advertising. Rather than a public relations nightmare, it could have created a public relations coup, stamping itself as a company that cares about its most loyal fans. Instead, ChapStick remained silent and deleted dissenting posts. On traditional media platforms that might have been sufficient, but social networks are interactive, and campaigns don't always go as planned.

Finally, when it could no longer delete the negative posts quickly enough, ChapStick pulled the ad and responded. However, ChapStick never owned up to the mass deletions it had perpetrated in its anemic response, instead offering regret if fans "felt" this had happened and essentially blaming posters for being uncivil or posting "menacing" comments.

When ChapStick finally tried to assure its fans that it valued them and was listening, it was hardly credible. In short, ChapStick presented us with a textbook case in how not to conduct social network advertising!

Attempts to control social media response on Twitter can be equally misguided. MasterCard's PR firm, House PR, was in charge of organizing a social media campaign to promote the 2014 Brit Awards event for British music. House demanded that journalists agree to very specific terms to obtain accreditation for the event, including guarantees from the journalists to use both official and personal accounts to live tweet the awards, to provide links to specific videos determined by House, and to use the #PricelessSurprises hashtag in these tweets. Journalists chafed at the attempts to micromanage their social media participation, with many tweeting their outrage at the terms. Forcing social media participants to respond in a predetermined way might work sometimes, but when it doesn't, as it didn't for MasterCard, it can be embarrassing and damaging to the company's brand.

Fast food giant McDonald's also confronted the dark side of social networks when it began a public relations campaign on Twitter. Using the hashtag #meetthefarmers, it inserted promotional tweets into the streams of Twitter users and paid for premium search engine results. The Supplier Stories campaign encouraged users to share stories about the farmers who sold their meat and produce to McDonald's. All was proceeding nicely until McDonald's replaced the hashtag with #McDStories. Now encouraging users to share their general consumer stories, McDonald's almost immediately lost control of its advertising campaign. The Twittersphere exploded with tweets

(continued)

comparing McDonald's fare to dog food, sprinkled with barbs about Type II diabetes, obesity, and food poisoning. The best that can be said for McDonald's is that it was prepared to pull the plug on the campaign should anything go awry. Within two hours, the promotion was halted. In 2014, McDonald's continued to struggle with social media, misspelling words in an Instagram advertising campaign and aggravating users with excessive advertising, as well as struggling with negative feedback to its #RonaldMcDonald mascot relaunch and accompanying hashtag.

The ChapStick, MasterCard, and McDonald's fiascos are instructive. ChapStick had no policies in place for how to respond to an ad campaign gone wrong. MasterCard attempted to exert corporate control over a medium that users value for its ability to provide honest, unfiltered individual feedback. McDonald's failed to fully recognize the polarizing nature of its product, making soliciting general comments a risky proposition. Companies with controversial products need to tread carefully, and companies need to be prepared to handle negative comments appropriately and take responsibility for mistakes.

Not all companies are learning from the experience of other firms. In 2014, homemade pizza maker DiGiorno's blundered when it used a hashtag meant to bring awareness to domestic violence, #WhyIStayed, in a tweet promoting its pizza. Outrage came swiftly and DiGiorno's took the tweet down amid a storm of criticism. The New England Patriots football team ran a campaign that automatically retweeted users' Twitter account names superimposed on team jerseys when users tweeted the #1MillionPatriots hashtag. Users seized the opportunity to wreak havoc, creating offensive Twitter handles that embarrassed the Patriots. And US Airways inadvertently tweeted a graphic pornographic image in response to a customer service complaint. Perhaps most surprisingly of all, Twitter's own chief financial officer accidentally publicly tweeted a message about an acquisition the company was still considering.

But in 2014, KFC set a good example when the news broke that a 3-year-old girl from Mississippi who had been mauled by her grandfather's dogs had subsequently been asked to leave a local KFC because she reportedly was scaring the other patrons. The visit to the restaurant had been a special treat for the girl from her family after a doctor's visit. When the news hit social media, KFC was caught in a firestorm of enraged customers. The company took the next several days to respond to as many individual comments as it could, posted a personal apology to the girl's Facebook page, and pledged $30,000 toward her medical bills.

Marketing is not the only social media hazard. For employees, privacy protection for Facebook posts is still being determined in the courts. For example, Danielle Mailhoit was the manager of a Home Depot store in Burbank, California. After she was fired, she filed suit claiming gender and disability discrimination due to her vertigo. The defense attorney filed a broad request for all of Mailhoit's social media activity. In September 2012, a federal judge ruled this request overly broad and limited discovery to only communications between the plaintiff and current or former Home Depot employees. Stating that they were unlikely to be relevant unless they were directly related to the lawsuit or her former employment, she also denied Home Depot's request for photos.

Employers must be careful with personal information gleaned from social networks. If it can be proven that membership in a protected group was discovered during the hiring process and used to reject a candidate or later used to terminate an employee, a claim can be filed under one of the Federal Equal Employment Opportunity (EEO) laws. These include Title VII of the Civil Rights Act of 1964, the Age Discrimination in Employment Act of 1967 (ADEA), Title I and Title V of the Americans with Disabilities Act of 1990 (ADA), and

Title II of the Genetic Information Nondiscrimination Act of 2008 (GINA), which prohibits employment discrimination based on genetic information about an applicant, employee, or former employee. GINA's regulations provide a distinction between whether genetic information is acquired purposefully or inadvertently. Inadvertent acquisition includes acquisition through social networks, equating it to accidentally overhearing a conversation at work.

However, data on a social media site protected by privacy controls should not be able to be "inadvertently" acquired. The Stored Communications Act (SCA) covers privacy protection for e-mail and digital communications. The latest court rulings on its application to social network communications have held that Facebook wall postings and other social media comments are protected as long as they have not been made public.

Facebook, to protect its business model, is speaking out against recent hiring practices that have come to its attention—and threatening legal action. According to both Facebook and the American Civil Liberties Union (ACLU), some companies have been asking new hires either to friend the hiring manager or to submit their password. Facebook's Privacy Page condemns this practice, stating that it violates both individual users' and their friends' expectations of privacy, jeopardizes security, and could reveal a user's membership in a protected group.

Legislators in a growing number of states have decided to be proactive. In 2012, California banned employers from asking prospective employees for their social media user names and passwords. In 2013, New Jersey became the 12th state to restrict employer access to employee social media accounts, although New Jersey–based employers are still granted some rights in the cases of companies dealing with public safety and workplace investigations. In 2014, Rhode Island passed its own legislation making it illegal for an employer or school to demand login information for social media accounts for prospective employees or students, and other states are expected to follow suit, including Louisiana, Wisconsin, and Virginia, which passed its version of the law in 2015.

Carefully crafted policies can help companies to avoid the dark side of social networking. Advertising and hiring are but two of the areas that must be monitored. The Human Resources department must also develop policies regarding employee use of social networks. Employee education programs must be implemented to apprise employees of infractions that can be grounds for disciplinary action. IT departments must develop stringent policies to protect proprietary data and defend company networks from cyberscams. Social networking is an exciting new tool, but one that requires safeguards.

SOURCES: "Virginia's New Social Media Law Protects Employees," Troutmansanders.com, July 1, 2015; "The 5 Worst Twitter Marketing Fails of 2014," by Kim Lachance Shandrow, Entrepreneur.com, December 18, 2014; "10 Worst Social Media Fails of 2014," by Emily Alford, Clickz.com, December 18, 2014; "The Top 10 Social Media Fails of 2014," by Rebecca Borison, Inc.com, December 10, 2014; "McDonalds Instagram Fail: How Brands Can Avoid Advertising Disasters on Social Media Networks," Theweemarketingagency.com, August 6, 2014; "RI Passes Social Media Privacy Law," by Bill Tomison, Wpri.com, July 3, 2014; "Facebook's Facing a Losing Battle to Protect Users' Privacy," by Lisa Vaas, Nakedsecurity.sophos.com, June 30, 2014; "KFC Shows How to Handle a Social Media Disaster," by Mary Elizabeth Williams, Salon.com, June 17, 2014; "19 Horrific Social Media Fails from the First Half of 2014," by Christopher Ratcliff, Econsultancy.com, June 16, 2014; "States Continue Banning Employer Access to Social Media," by Brian Heaton, Govtech.com, May 21, 2014; "Brit Awards Sponsors in Priceless Twitter PR Fail," Theguardian.com, February 19, 2014; "NJ Passes a Business-Friendly Workplace Social Media Privacy Law," by Eric B. Meyer, Theemployerhandbook.com, September 3, 2013; "Judge: Home Depot Went Too Far in Seeking Worker's Social Posts," by Declan McCullagh, News.cnet.com, September 17, 2012; "California May Ban Employers from Asking for Facebook Passwords," by Jessica Guynn, *Los Angeles Times,* May 11, 2012; "Facebook Speaks Out Against Employers Asking for Passwords," by Doug Gross, Cnn.com, March 23, 2012; "Why McDonald's Should Have Known Better," by Shelley DuBois, Cnnmoney. com, January 31, 2012; "McDonald's Social Media Director Explains Twitter Fiasco," by Jeff John Roberts, Paidcontent. org, January 24, 2012; "Lessons from the ChapStick Social Media Fiasco," by Ted Rubin, Tedrubin.com, December 3, 2011; "ChapStick Gets Itself in a Social Media Death Spiral: A Brand's Silent War Against Its Facebook Fans," by Tim Nudd, *Adweek,* October 26, 2011; "The Dangers of Using Social Media Data in Hiring," by Gregg Skall, *Radio Business Report,* June 6, 2011; "Stored Communications Act Protects Facebook and MySpace Users' Private Communication," by Kathryn Freund, Jolt.law.harvard.edu, June 11, 2010.

TABLE 11.3	TYPES OF SOCIAL NETWORKS AND ONLINE COMMUNITIES
TYPE OF SOCIAL NETWORK / COMMUNITY	**DESCRIPTION**
General	Online social gathering place to meet and socialize with friends, share content, schedules, and interests. Examples: Facebook, Pinterest, Instagram, Tumblr, and Twitter.
Practice	Social network of professionals and practitioners, creators of artifacts such as computer code or music. Examples: Just Plain Folks (musicians' community), LinkedIn (business), and Doximity (physicians and health care professionals).
Interest	Community built around a common interest, such as games, sports, music, stock markets, politics, health, finance, foreign affairs, or lifestyle. Examples: Debatepolitics.com (political discussion group) and PredictWallStreet (stock market site).
Affinity	Community of members who self-identify with a demographic or geographic category, such as women, African Americans, or Arab Americans. Examples: BlackPlanet (African American community and social network site) and Healthboards.com (focusing on women's health issues).
Sponsored	Network created by commercial, government, and nonprofit organizations for a variety of purposes. Examples: Nike, IBM, Cisco, and political candidates.

ness model of general communities is typically advertising supported by selling ad space on pages and videos.

practice networks
offer members focused discussion groups, help, information, and knowledge relating to an area of shared practice

Practice networks offer members focused discussion groups, help, information, and knowledge relating to an area of shared practice. For instance, Linux.org is a nonprofit community for the open source movement, a worldwide global effort involving thousands of programmers who develop computer code for the Linux operating system and share the results freely with all. Other online communities involve artists, educators, art dealers, photographers, and nurses. Practice networks can be either profit-based or nonprofit, and support themselves by advertising or user donations.

interest-based social networks
offer members focused discussion groups based on a shared interest in some specific topic

Interest-based social networks offer members focused discussion groups based on a shared interest in some specific subject, such as business careers, boats, horses, health, skiing, and thousands of other topics. Because the audience for interest communities is necessarily much smaller and more targeted, these communities have usually relied on advertising and tenancy/sponsorship deals. Social networks such as Fool.com, Military.com, Sailing Anarchy, and Chronicle Forums all are examples of social networks that attract people who share a common pursuit. Job markets and forums such as LinkedIn can be considered interest-based social networks as well.

affinity communities
offer members focused discussions and interaction with other people who share the same affinity

Affinity communities offer members focused discussions and interaction with other people who share the same affinity. "Affinity" refers to self- and group identification. For instance, people can self-identify themselves on the basis of religion, ethnicity, gender, sexual orientation, political beliefs, geographical location, and hundreds of other categories. For instance, Oxygen and NaturallyCurly are affinity communities

TABLE 11.4	SOCIAL NETWORK FEATURES AND TECHNOLOGIES
FEATURE	**DESCRIPTION**
Profiles	User-created Web pages that describe the owner on a variety of dimensions
Newsfeed	A listing of updates from friends, advertisements, and notifications in chronological order
Timeline	A history of updates, posts from friends, photos, and other objects in chronological order
Friends networks	Ability to create a linked group of friends, a social community
Network discovery	Ability to find other social networks, find new groups and friends, and discover friends of friends
Favorites (Like)	Ability to communicate favorite sites, bookmarks, content, and destinations
Games and apps	Games developed for the social network, and apps that extend its functionality
Instant messaging	Instant messaging, chat
Storage	Storage for photos, videos, text
Message boards	Ability to post updates to friends, e.g. Wall
Groups	Discussion groups, forums, and consumer groups organized by interest, e.g., For Sale Groups

designed to attract women by offering discussion and services that focus on topics such as babies, beauty, books, diet and fitness, entertainment, health, and home and garden. These social networks are supported by advertising along with revenues from sales of products.

Sponsored communities are online communities created by government, non-profit, or for-profit organizations for the purpose of pursuing organizational goals. These goals can be diverse, from increasing the information available to citizens; for instance, a local county government site such as Westchestergov.com, the Web site for Westchester County (New York) government; to an online auction site such as eBay; to a product site such as Tide.com, which is sponsored by an offline branded product company (Procter & Gamble). Cisco, IBM, HP, and hundreds of other companies have developed their internal corporate social networks as a way of sharing knowledge.

sponsored communities
online communities created for the purpose of pursuing organizational (and often commercial) goals

SOCIAL NETWORK FEATURES AND TECHNOLOGIES

Social networks have developed software applications that allow users to engage in a number of activities. Not all social networks have the same features, but there is an emerging feature set among the larger communities. Some of these software tools are built into the site, while others can be added by users to their profile pages as widgets (described in earlier chapters). **Table 11.4** describes several social network functionalities.

| 11.2 | **ONLINE AUCTIONS** |

consumer-to-consumer (C2C) auctions

auction house acts as an intermediary market maker, providing a forum where consumers can discover prices and trade

Auctions are used throughout the e-commerce landscape. The most widely known auctions are **consumer-to-consumer (C2C) auctions**, in which the auction house is simply an intermediary market maker, providing a forum where consumers—buyers and sellers—can discover prices and trade. The market leader in C2C auctions is eBay, which, as of June 2015, had around 157 million active users in the United States and over 550 million items listed on any given day within thousands of different categories. In August 2015, eBay had around 98 million unique visitors, placing it 17th on the list of top 50 digital media (both desktop and mobile) properties (comScore, 2015a). In 2014, eBay had about $7 billion in net revenues from its Marketplaces segment, a 6% increase from 2013, and the total worth of goods sold or auctioned was around $83 billion (Gross Merchandise Value) (eBay, 2015). eBay is further discussed in the case study at the end of this chapter. In the United States alone, there are several hundred auction sites, some specializing in unique collectible products such as stamps and coins, others adopting a more generalist approach in which almost any good can be found for sale.

business-to-consumer (B2C) auctions

business sells goods it owns, or controls, using various dynamic pricing models

Less well known are **business-to-consumer (B2C) auctions**, where a business owns or controls assets and uses dynamic pricing to establish the price. Increasingly, online retail sites, such as Sam's Club, are adding auctions to their sites. Auctions also constitute a significant part of B2B e-commerce in 2015, and more than a third of procurement officers use auctions to procure goods.

Some leading online auction sites are listed in **Table 11.5**. Auctions are not limited to goods and services. They can also be used to allocate resources, and bundles of resources, among any group of bidders. For instance, if you wanted to establish an optimal schedule for assigned tasks in an office among a group of clerical workers, an auction in which workers bid for assignments would come close to producing a nearly optimal solution in a short amount of time (Parkes and Ungar, 2000). In short, auctions—like all markets—are ways of allocating resources among independent agents (bidders).

BENEFITS AND COSTS OF AUCTIONS

The Internet is primarily responsible for the resurgence in auctions. The Internet provides a global environment and very low fixed and operational costs for the aggregation of huge buyer audiences, composed of millions of consumers worldwide, who can use a universally available technology (Internet browsers) to shop for goods.

Benefits of Auctions

Aside from the sheer game-like fun of participating in auctions, consumers, merchants, and society as a whole derive a number of economic benefits from participating in Internet auctions. These benefits include:

- **Liquidity:** Sellers can find willing buyers, and buyers can find sellers. Sellers and buyers can be located anywhere around the globe. Just as important, buyers and sellers can find a global market for rare items that would not have existed before the Internet.

- **Price discovery:** Buyers and sellers can quickly and efficiently develop prices for items that are difficult to assess, where the price depends on demand and supply, and where the product is rare.

- **Price transparency:** Public Internet auctions allow everyone in the world to see the asking and bidding prices for items.

- **Market efficiency:** Auctions can, and often do, lead to reduced prices, and hence reduced profits for merchants, leading to an increase in consumer welfare—one measure of market efficiency.

- **Lower transaction costs:** Online auctions can lower the cost of selling and purchasing products, benefiting both merchants and consumers. Like other Internet markets, such as retail markets, Internet auctions have very low (but not zero) transaction costs.

- **Consumer aggregation:** Sellers benefit from large auction sites' ability to aggregate a large number of consumers who are motivated to purchase something in one marketspace.

- **Network effects:** The larger an auction site becomes in terms of visitors and products for sale, the more valuable it becomes as a marketplace for everyone by providing

TABLE 11.5	LEADING ONLINE AUCTION SITES
GENERAL	
eBay	The world market leader in auctions: 98 million visitors a month and hundreds of millions of products.
eBid	In business since 1998. Operates in 23 countries, including the United States. Currently, one of the top competitors to eBay. Offers much lower fees.
uBid	Marketplace for excess inventory from pre-approved merchants.
OnlineAuction	Allows sellers to list for a low monthly fee, without a per-item listing or additional fees when the item sells.
SPECIALIZED	
Racersauction	Specialized site for automobile racing parts.
Philatelicphantasies	Stamp site for professionals, monthly online stamp auction.
Stacksbowers	America's largest fully automated auction company of certified coins including ancient gold, silver, and copper coins. Also offers sports cards.
Bid4Assets	Liquidation of distressed real estate assets from government and the public sector, corporations, restructurings, and bankruptcies.
Oldandsold	Online auction service specializing in quality antiques. Dealers pay a 3% commission on merchandise sold.
B2C AUCTIONS	
Auctions.samsclub	Merchandise from Sam's Club in a variety of categories.
Shopgoodwill	Goodwill's online auction site. Offers a wide variety of collectibles, books, and antiques chosen from the goods donated to Goodwill.

liquidity and several other benefits listed previously, such as lower transaction costs, higher efficiency, and better price transparency.

Risks and Costs of Auctions

There are a number of risks and costs involved in participating in auctions. In some cases, auction markets can fail—like all markets at times. (We describe auction market failure in more detail later.) Some of the more important risks and costs to keep in mind are:

- **Delayed consumption costs:** Internet auctions can go on for days, and shipping will take additional time.
- **Monitoring costs:** Participation in auctions requires your time to monitor bidding.
- **Equipment costs:** Internet auctions require you to purchase a computer system and pay for Internet access.
- **Trust risks:** Online auctions are a significant source of Internet fraud. Using auctions increases the risk of experiencing a loss.
- **Fulfillment costs:** Typically, the buyer pays fulfillment costs of packing, shipping, and insurance, whereas at a physical store these costs are included in the retail price.

Auction sites such as eBay have taken a number of steps to reduce consumer participation costs and trust risk. For instance, auction sites attempt to solve the trust problem by providing a rating system in which previous customers rate sellers based on their overall experience with the merchant. Although helpful, this solution does not always work. Auction fraud is a leading source of e-commerce complaints to federal law enforcement officials. Another partial solution to high monitoring costs is, ironically, fixed pricing. At eBay, consumers can reduce the cost of monitoring and waiting for auctions to end by simply clicking on the Buy It Now! button and paying a premium price. The difference between the Buy It Now price and the auction price is the cost of monitoring.

Nevertheless, given the costs of participating in online auctions, the generally lower cost of goods on Internet auctions is in part a compensation for the other additional costs consumers experience. On the other hand, consumers experience lower search costs and transaction costs because there usually are no intermediaries (unless, of course, the seller is an online business operating on an auction site, in which case there is a middleman cost), and usually there are no local or state taxes.

Merchants face considerable risks and costs as well. At auctions, merchants may end up selling goods for prices far below what they might have achieved in conventional markets. Merchants also face risks of nonpayment, false bidding, bid rigging, monitoring, transaction fees charged by the auction site, credit card transaction processing fees, and the administration costs of entering price and product information.

AUCTIONS AS AN E-COMMERCE BUSINESS MODEL

Online auctions have been among the most successful business models in retail and B2B commerce. eBay, the Internet's most lucrative auction site, has been profitable nearly since its inception. The strategy for eBay has been to make money off every stage in the auction cycle. eBay earns revenue from auctions in several ways: transaction fees based on the amount of the sale, listing fees for display of goods, financial service fees from payment systems such as PayPal, and advertising or placement fees where sellers pay extra for special services such as particular display or listing services. PayPal has been faster growing and more profitable than eBay's markets, growing to more than half of eBay's revenue. In 2015 eBay spun off PayPal into a separate company, and going forward will have to make its profits from its markets operation.

However, it is on the cost side that online auctions have extraordinary advantages over ordinary retail or catalog sites. Auction sites carry no inventory and do not perform any fulfillment activities—they need no warehouses, shipping, or logistical facilities. Sellers and consumers provide these services and bear these costs. In this sense, online auctions are an ideal digital business because they involve simply the transfer of information.

Even though eBay has been extraordinarily successful, the success of online auctions is qualified by the fact that the marketplace for online auctions is highly concentrated. eBay dominates the online auction market, followed by eBid and uBid. In the last several years eBay's growth has slowed considerably as consumers shift toward Buy It Now purchases rather than auctions. Many of the smaller auction sites are not profitable because they lack sufficient sellers and buyers to achieve liquidity. In auctions, network effects are highly influential, and the tendency is for one or two very large auction sites to dominate, with hundreds of smaller specialty auction sites (sites that sell specialized goods such as stamps) being barely profitable.

TYPES AND EXAMPLES OF AUCTIONS

The primary types of auctions found on the Internet are English auctions, Dutch Internet auctions, Name Your Own Price auctions, and so-called penny auctions.

The **English auction** is the easiest to understand and the most common form of auction on eBay. Typically, there is a single item up for sale from a single seller. There is a time limit when the auction ends, a reserve price below which the seller will not sell (usually secret), and a minimum incremental bid set. Multiple buyers bid against one another until the auction time limit is reached. The highest bidder wins the item (if the reserve price of the seller has been met or exceeded). English auctions are considered to be seller-biased because multiple buyers compete against one another—usually anonymously.

The **Dutch Internet auction** format is perfect for sellers that have many identical items to sell. Sellers start by listing a minimum price, or a starting bid for one item, and the number of items for sale. Bidders specify both a bid price and the quantity they want to buy. The uniform price reigns. Winning bidders pay the same price per item, which is the lowest successful bid. This market clearing price can be less than some bids. If there are more buyers than items, the earliest successful bids get the goods. In general, high bidders get the quantity they want at the lowest successful price, whereas low successful bidders might not get the quantity they want (but they will get something).

The **Name Your Own Price auction** was pioneered by Priceline, and is the second most-popular auction format on the Web. Although Priceline also acts as an intermediary, buying blocks of airline tickets, hotel rooms, and vacation packages at a discount and selling them at a reduced retail price or matching its inventory to bidders, it is best known for its Name Your Own Price auctions, in which users specify

English auction
most common form of auction; the highest bidder wins

Dutch Internet auction
public ascending price, multiple unit auction. Final price is lowest successful bid, which sets price for all higher bidders

Name Your Own Price auction
auction where users specify what they are willing to pay for goods or services

what they are willing to pay for goods or services, and multiple providers bid for their business. Prices do not descend and are fixed: the initial consumer offer is a commitment to purchase at that price. In 2014, Priceline had more than $8.4 billion in revenues, and in 2015, it attracts around 31 million unique visitors a month. It is one of the top-ranked travel sites in the United States.

But how can Priceline offer such steep discounts off prices for services provided by major brand-name providers? There are several answers. First, Priceline "shields the brand" by not publicizing the prices at which major brands sell. This reduces conflict with traditional channels, including direct sales. Second, the services being sold are perishable: if a Priceline customer did not pay something for the empty airline seat, rental car, or hotel room, sellers would not receive any revenue. Hence, sellers are highly motivated to at least cover the costs of their services by selling in a spot market at very low prices. The strategy for sellers is to sell as much as possible through more profitable channels and then unload excess capacity on spot markets such as Priceline. This works to the advantage of consumers, sellers, and Priceline, which charges a transaction fee to sellers.

penny (bidding fee) auction

bidder must pay a non-refundable fee to purchase bids

So-called penny auctions are really anything but. To participate in a **penny auction** (also known as a **bidding fee auction**), you typically must pay the penny auction site for bids ahead of time, typically 50 cents to $1 dollar, usually in packs costing $25-$50. Once you have purchased the bids, you can use them to bid on items listed by the penny auction site (unlike traditional auctions, items are owned by the site, not third parties). Items typically start at or near $0 and each bid raises the price by a fixed amount, usually just a penny. Auctions are timed, and when the time runs out, the last and highest bidder wins the item. Although the price of the item itself may not be that high, the successful bidder will typically have spent much more than that. Unlike a traditional auction, it costs money to bid and that money is gone even if the bidder does not win the auction. The bidder's cumulative cost of bidding must be added to the final price of a successful bid to determine the true cost of the item. The Federal Trade Commission has issued an alert about penny auctions, warning that bidders may find that they spend far more than they intended (Consumer Reports.org, 2013). Examples of penny auction sites include QuiBids, Beezid, and HappyBidDay.

WHEN TO USE AUCTIONS (AND FOR WHAT) IN BUSINESS

There are many different situations in which auctions are an appropriate channel for businesses to consider. For much of this chapter, we have looked at auctions from a consumer point of view. The objective of consumers is to receive the greatest value for the lowest cost. Now, switch your perspective to that of a business. Remember that the objective of businesses using auctions is to maximize their revenue (their share of consumer surplus) by finding the true market value of products and services, a market value that hopefully is higher in the auction channel than in fixed-price channels. **Table 11.6** provides an overview of factors to consider.

The factors are described as follows:

• **Type of product:** Online auctions are most commonly used for rare and unique products for which prices are difficult to discover, and there may have been no market for the goods. However, Priceline has succeeded in developing auctions for

TABLE 11.6	FACTORS TO CONSIDER WHEN CHOOSING AUCTIONS
CONSIDERATIONS	**DESCRIPTION**
Type of product	Rare, unique, commodity, perishable
Stage of product life cycle	Early, mature, late
Channel-management issues	Conflict with retail distributors; differentiation
Type of auction	Seller vs. buyer bias
Initial pricing	Low vs. high
Bid increment amounts	Low vs. high
Auction length	Short vs. long
Number of items	Single vs. multiple
Price-allocation rule	Uniform vs. discriminatory
Information sharing	Closed vs. open bidding

perishable commodities (such as airline seats) for which retail prices have already been established, and some B2B auctions involve commodities such as steel (often sold at distress prices). New clothing items, new digital cameras, and new computers are generally not sold at auction because their prices are easy to discover, catalog prices are high, sustainable, and profitable, they are not perishable, and there exists an efficient market channel in the form of retail stores (online and offline).

- **Product life cycle:** For the most part, businesses have traditionally used auctions for goods at the end of their product life cycle and for products where auctions yield a higher price than fixed-price liquidation sales. However, products at the beginning of their life cycle are increasingly being sold at auction. Early releases of music, books, videos, games, and digital appliances can be sold to highly motivated early adopters who want to be the first in their neighborhood with new products. Online sales of event tickets from music concerts to sports events now account for upwards of 25% of all event ticket sales in the United States.

- **Channel management:** Established retailers such as JCPenney and Walmart, and manufacturers in general, must be careful not to allow their auction activity to interfere with their existing profitable channels. For this reason, items found on established retail-site auctions tend to be late in their product life cycle or have quantity purchase requirements.

- **Type of auction:** Sellers obviously should choose auctions where there are many buyers and only a few, or even one, seller. English ascending-price auctions such as those at eBay are best for sellers because as the number of bidders increases, the price tends to move higher.

- **Initial pricing:** Research suggests that auction items should start out with low initial bid prices in order to encourage more bidders to bid (see "Bid increments" below). The lower the price, the larger the number of bidders will appear. The larger the number of bidders, the higher the prices move.

- **Bid increments:** It is generally safest to keep bid increments low so as to increase the number of bidders and the frequency of their bids. If bidders can be convinced that, for just a few more dollars, they can win the auction, then they will tend to make the higher bid and forget about the total amount they are bidding.

- **Auction length:** In general, the longer auctions are scheduled, the larger the number of bidders and the higher the prices can go. However, once the new bid arrival rate drops off and approaches zero, bid prices stabilize. Most eBay auctions are scheduled for seven days.

- **Number of items:** When a business has a number of items to sell, buyers usually expect a "volume discount," and this expectation can cause lower bids in return. Therefore, sellers should consider breaking up very large bundles into smaller bundles auctioned at different times.

- **Price allocation rule:** Most buyers believe it is "fair" that everyone pay the same price in a multi-unit auction, and a uniform pricing rule is recommended. eBay Dutch Internet auctions encourage this expectation. The idea that some buyers should pay more based on their differential need for the product is not widely supported. Therefore, sellers who want to price discriminate should do so by holding auctions for the same goods on different auction markets, or at different times, to prevent direct price comparison.

- **Closed vs. open bidding:** Closed bidding has many advantages for the seller, and sellers should use this approach whenever possible because it permits price discrimination without offending buyers. However, open bidding carries the advantage of "herd effects" and "winning effects" (described later in the chapter) in which consumers' competitive instincts to "win" drive prices higher than even secret bidding would achieve.

AUCTION PRICES: ARE THEY THE LOWEST?

It is widely assumed that auction prices are lower than prices in other fixed-price markets. Empirical evidence is mixed on this assumption. There are many reasons why auction prices might be higher than those in fixed-price markets for items of identical quality, and why auction prices in one auction market may be higher than those in other auction markets. Consumers are not driven solely by value maximization but instead are influenced by many situational factors, irrelevant and wrong information, and misperceptions when they make market decisions (Simonson and Tversky, 1992). Auctions are social events—shared social environments, in which bidders adjust to one another (Hanson and Putler, 1996). Briefly, bidders base their bids on what others have previously bid, and this can lead to an upward cascading effect (Arkes and Hutzel, 2000). In a study of hundreds of eBay auctions for Sony PlayStations, CD players, Mexican pottery, and Italian silk ties, Dholakia and Soltysinski (2001) found that bidders exhibited **herd behavior** (the tendency to gravitate toward, and bid for, auction listings with one or more existing bids) by making multiple bids on some auctions (coveted comparables), and making no bids at auctions for comparable items (overlooked comparables). Herd behavior resulted in consumers

herd behavior
the tendency to gravitate toward, and bid for, auction listings with one or more existing bids

paying higher prices than necessary for reasons having no foundation in economic reality (Liu and Sutanto, 2012).

The behavioral reality of participating in auctions can produce many unintended results. Winners can suffer **winner's regret**, the feeling after winning an auction that they paid too much for an item, which indicates that their winning bid does not reflect what they thought the item was worth but rather what the second bidder thought the item was worth. Sellers can experience **seller's lament**, reflecting the fact that they sold an item at a price just above the second place bidder, never knowing how much the ultimate winner might have paid or the true value to the final winner. Auction losers can experience **loser's lament**, the feeling of having been too cheap in bidding and failing to win. In summary, auctions can lead to both winners paying too much and sellers receiving too little. Both of these outcomes can be minimized when sellers and buyers have a very clear understanding of the prices for items in a variety of different online and offline markets.

CONSUMER TRUST IN AUCTIONS

Auction sites have the same difficulties creating a sense of consumer trust as all other e-commerce Web sites, although in the case of auction sites, the operators of the marketplace do not directly control the quality of goods being offered and cannot directly vouch for the integrity of the buyers or the sellers. This opens the possibility for criminal or unreliable actors to appear as either sellers or buyers. Several studies have found that trust and credibility increase as users gain more experience, if trusted third-party seals are present, and if the site has a wide variety of consumer services for tracking purchases (or fraud), thus giving the user a sense of control (Krishnamurthy, 2001; Stanford-Makovsky, 2002; Nikander and Karvonen, 2002; Bailey et al., 2002; Kollock, 1999). Because of the powerful role that trust plays in online consumer behavior, eBay and most auction sites make considerable efforts to develop automated trust-enhancing mechanisms such as seller and buyer ratings, escrow services, buyer and seller insurance, guaranteed money back features, and authenticity guarantees (see the next section).

WHEN AUCTION MARKETS FAIL: FRAUD AND ABUSE IN AUCTIONS

Online and offline auction markets can be prone to fraud, which produces information asymmetries between sellers and buyers and among buyers, which in turn causes auction markets to fail. Some of the possible abuses and frauds include:

- **Bid rigging:** Agreeing offline to limit bids or using shills to submit false bids that drive prices up.
- **Price matching:** Agreeing informally or formally to set floor prices on auction items below which sellers will not sell in open markets.
- **Shill feedback, defensive:** Using secondary IDs or other auction members to inflate seller ratings.
- **Shill feedback, offensive:** Using secondary IDs or other auction members to deflate ratings for another user (feedback bombs).
- **Feedback extortion:** Threatening negative feedback in return for a benefit.

winner's regret
the winner's feeling after an auction that he or she paid too much for an item

seller's lament
concern that one will never know how much the ultimate winner might have paid, or the true value to the final winner

loser's lament
the feeling of having been too cheap in bidding and failing to win

- **Transaction interference:** E-mailing buyers to warn them away from a seller.
- **Bid manipulation:** Using the retraction option to make high bids, discovering the maximum bid of the current high bidder, and then retracting the bid.
- **Non-payment after winning:** Blocking legitimate buyers by bidding high, then not paying.
- **Shill bidding:** Using secondary user IDs or other auction members to artificially raise the price of an item.
- **Transaction non-performance:** Accepting payment and failing to deliver.
- **Non-selling seller:** Refusing payment or failing to deliver after a successful auction.
- **Bid siphoning:** E-mailing another seller's bidders and offering the same product for less.

Auction sites have sought to reduce these risks through various methods including:

- **Rating systems:** Previous customers rate sellers based on their experience with them and post them on the site for other buyers to see.
- **Watch lists:** These allow buyers to monitor specific auctions as they proceed over a number of days and only pay close attention in the last few minutes of bidding.
- **Proxy bidding:** Buyers can enter a maximum price they are willing to pay, and the auction software will automatically place incremental bids as their original bid is surpassed.

eBay and many other auction sites have investigation units that receive complaints from consumers and investigate reported abuses. Nevertheless, with millions of visitors per week and hundreds of thousands of auctions to monitor, eBay is highly dependent on the good faith of sellers and consumers to follow the rules.

11.3 E-COMMERCE PORTALS

Port: From the Latin porta, an entrance or gateway to a locality.

Portals are among the most frequently visited sites on the Web if only because they often are the first page to which many users point their browser on startup. The top portals such as Yahoo, MSN, and AOL have hundreds of millions of unique visitors worldwide each month. Web portal sites are gateways to the billions of Web pages available on the Internet. Millions of users have set Facebook as their home page, choosing to start their sessions with news from their friends, and many stay on Facebook for several hours a day. We have already discussed Facebook in Section 11.1. Perhaps the most important service provided by portals is to help people find the information they are looking for on the Web and, like newspapers, to expose people to information they were not looking for but which they nonetheless find entertaining or interesting. The original portals in the early days of e-commerce were search engines. Consumers would pass through search engine portals on their way to rich, detailed, in-depth content on the Web. But portals evolved into much more complex Web sites that provide news, entertainment, maps, images, social networks, in-depth information, and education on a growing variety of topics all contained at the portal site. Portals today seek to be a sticky destination site, not merely a gateway through which visitors pass. In this respect, Web portals are very much like television networks: destination sites for content supported by advertising revenues. Portals today want visitors to stay a long time—the longer the better to expose visitors to ads. For the most part they succeed: portals are places where people linger for a long time.

Portals also serve important functions within a business or organization. Most corporations, universities, churches, and other formal organizations have **enterprise portals** that help employees or members navigate to important content, such as human resources information, corporate news, or organizational announcements. For instance, your university has a portal through which you can register for courses, find classroom assignments, and perform a host of other important student activities. Increasingly, these enterprise portals also provide general-purpose news and real-time financial feeds provided by content providers outside the organization. Corporate portals and intranets are the subject of other textbooks focused on the corporate uses of Web technology and are beyond the scope of this book (see Laudon and Laudon, 2012). Our focus here is on e-commerce portals.

enterprise portals
help employees navigate to the enterprise's human resource and corporate content

THE GROWTH AND EVOLUTION OF PORTALS

Web portals have changed a great deal from their initial function and role. As noted above, most of today's well-known portals, such as Yahoo, MSN, and AOL, began as search engines. The initial function provided by portals was to index Web page content and make this content available to users in a convenient form. Early portals expected visitors to stay only a few minutes at the site. As millions of people signed on to the Internet in the early 2000s, the number of visitors to basic search engine sites exploded commensurately. At first, few people understood how a Web search site could make money by passing customers on to other destinations. But search sites attracted huge audiences, and therein lay the foundation for their success as vehicles for marketing and advertising. Search sites, recognizing the potential for commerce, expanded their offerings from simple navigation to include commerce (the sale of items directly from the Web site as well as advertising for other retail sites), content (in the form of news at first, and later in the form of weather, investments, games, health, and other subject matter), and distribution of others' content. These three characteristics have become the basic definition of portal sites, namely, sites that provide three functions: navigation of the Web (search), commerce, and content.

Because the value of portals to advertisers and content owners is largely a function of the size of the audience each portal reaches, and the length of time visitors stay on site, portals compete with one another on reach and unique visitors. *Reach* is defined as the percentage of the Web audience that visits the site in a month (or some other time period), and *unique visitors* is defined as the number of uniquely identified individuals who visit in a month. Portals are inevitably subject to network effects: The value of the portal to advertisers and consumers increases geometrically as reach increases, which, in turn, attracts still more customers. These effects have resulted in the differentiation of the portal marketspace into three tiers: a few general-purpose mega portal sites that garner 60%–80% of the Web audience, second-tier general-purpose sites that hover around 20%–30% reach, and third-tier specialized vertical market portals that attract 2%–10% of the audience. As described in Chapter 3, the top five portals/search engines (Google, Yahoo, MSN/Bing, AOL, and Ask) account for more than 95% of online searches. A similar pattern of concentration is observed when considering the audience share of portals/search engines (including both desktop and mobile) as illustrated in **Figure 11.3**. However, this picture is changing as large audiences move to social network sites, and millions of users make these sites their opening or home pages and the place where they spend most of their digital time. Social network sites like Facebook are broadening their content with videos, movies, and news, transforming themselves into a hybrid social network and portal. Web sites of companies that provide ISP services, such as Verizon, Comcast (Xfinity), Cablevision (Optimum Online), and others are also common portal/home pages for millions of users.

For more insight into the nature of the competition and change among the top portals, read *Insight on Business: The Transformation of AOL*.

TYPES OF PORTALS: GENERAL-PURPOSE AND VERTICAL MARKET

general-purpose portals

attempt to attract a very large general audience and then retain the audience on-site by providing in-depth vertical content

There are two primary types of portals: general-purpose portals and vertical market portals. **General-purpose portals** attempt to attract a very large general audience and then retain the audience on-site by providing in-depth vertical content channels, such as information on news, finance, autos, movies, and weather. General-purpose portals typically offer Web search engines, free e-mail, personal home pages, chat rooms, community-building software, and bulletin boards. Vertical content channels on general-purpose portal sites offer content such as sports scores, stock tickers, health tips, instant messaging, automobile information, and auctions.

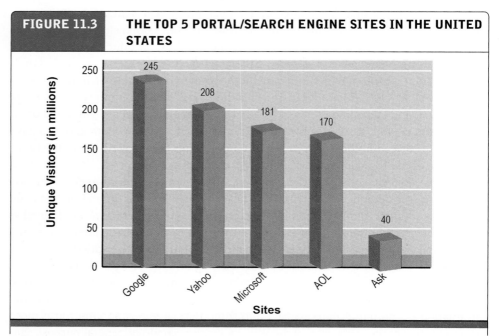

FIGURE 11.3 | **THE TOP 5 PORTAL/SEARCH ENGINE SITES IN THE UNITED STATES**

SOURCE: Based on data from comScore, 2015.

INSIGHT ON BUSINESS

THE TRANSFORMATION OF AOL

You have to hand it to AOL; its corporate DNA must include a gene for tenacity. From its inauspicious beginnings as an online game server for the Atari 2600 video game console to its dizzying heights as the leading ISP in the United States—a time that even spawned a Meg Ryan/Tom Hanks movie entitled *You've Got Mail* after the ubiquitous greeting AOL users heard each time they signed on—to its equally staggering decline after its failed merger with Time Warner—somehow AOL has found a way to survive.

Started in the early 1980s as Control Video Corporation, it provided an online service called Gameline for the Atari 2600. The company didn't make enough money, and in 1983, it was reorganized as Quantum Computer Services, providing a dedicated online service for Commodore 64 and 128 computers called Quantum Link. In 1988, the company added online services called Apple Link and PC Link, and in 1989, its name was changed to America Online.

In 1991, AOL launched an online program for the DOS operating system (the early Microsoft operating system that used text commands) and one for Windows the following year. AOL positioned itself as the online service for people who weren't comfortable with technology, a shrewd move at the time. Initially, it provided proprietary software and charged users hefty hourly fees. In 1996, it switched to a subscription-based model, charging $19.99 per month. Mass distribution of AOL CD-ROMs through the mail spurred adoption—AOL was everywhere, giving over 10 million people their first exposure to the Web, e-mail, instant messaging, and chat rooms. However, the company was slow to provide access to the open Internet, and complaints erupted, in particular, about dropped connections and busy signals. Still,

it continued to grow. In 1996, in another boon to its brand, AOL signed a five-year agreement that it would be bundled with Windows on new PCs. The first major Web portal for the general public was on its way.

In 2000, before the company's spectacular fall began, Time Warner bought AOL for $165 billion. Despite the media fanfare, there were problems from the start with what is now acknowledged by current CEO Tim Armstrong to be the worst merger in corporate history. In the first year, the merged company already had difficulty reaching growth targets, possibly because AOL had improperly inflated its pre-merger revenue. In 2002, advertising revenue declined sharply. The number of AOL ISP subscribers peaked that year at 26.7 million and has been declining ever since. AOL underestimated the growth of broadband, doing little to develop a competitive offering, while Google's search engine gained popularity, siphoning away advertising dollars. Today, there are only around 2.2 million ISP subscribers. However, these subscribers still generated $606 million in 2014, almost 25% of the company's revenue. Incredibly, these core dial-up holdouts have kept the company afloat.

Between 2002 and 2007 the company occupied various positions on the continuum between misstep and turmoil. Its stock price plummeted, it was investigated by the SEC for several unorthodox advertising deals, the Justice Department conducted a criminal probe, financial reports had to be revised downward, and the positions of CEO and VP of Marketing became revolving doors.

In 2007, AOL began pursuing a new strategy, creating more than a dozen niche content sites. The following year, Time Warner negotiated with both Microsoft and Google in an attempt to sell AOL. When this was unsuccessful, it decided to spin off the company instead. First, it repurchased Google's

(continued)

5% stake for $283 million. Google's purchase price in 2005 had been $1 billion.

When Tim Armstrong came on board in 2009, he added senior staff members from Google and Yahoo with an eye toward turning the company into the biggest creator of premium content on the Web and the largest seller of online display ads. Positioning AOL to be ready when the line between online and broadcast programming permanently blurred, he began assembling the infrastructure, acquiring a number of companies specializing in the delivery of online content. The real blockbuster acquisition was the Huffington Post in 2011 for $315 million. Armstrong appeared to be betting big on its charismatic leader, Arianna Huffington, and its 25 million unique monthly visitors. Around 20% of AOL's workforce was eliminated following the purchase.

It soon became clear that the big bet was actually on online video, with HuffPost Live as one significant part of the wager. Launched in 2012, HuffPost Live features live discussions on current events 12 hours a day, five days a week. The unique twist and perceived draw is user interaction. Viewers submit chat comments as programs are airing and can also tweet and submit their own videos. Viewers will also increasingly be included in programming, so that they can engage with the host and his or her guest, creating a "social video" experience. Rather than scheduling specific programs at specific times of the day, or even for a set period of time, topics are conversational, not bound by timeframe, and not bound by the hot topic of the day—a sort of freeform television. To which Armstrong is of course hoping to add live advertising. Cadillac and Verizon are two of the main investors in the venture.

AOL also has teams of video producers in both New York and Los Angeles that are creating branded entertainment video. Sometimes working with celebrities, these teams, as well as video partners from around the world, are producing hundreds of videos a day of an informational, how-to, or entertainment nature. Sources include wholly owned properties such as TechCrunch, one of the most popular tech blogs on the Internet. These videos will attempt to tread the line between branded infomercial and useful and sought-after information. AOL has continued its efforts to develop original programming, primarily via its AOL On Channel. AOL is also not just relying on developing its own premium content. It recently reached a deal with Miramax to stream films on AOL On for free, supported by advertising, and it hopes to continue acquiring the rights to premium content from other studios as well. Some of AOL's video productions have attracted as many as 15 million viewers.

AOL has also focused on programmatic advertising, an automated form of ad buying that promises to cut out advertising middlemen and allow both content providers and advertisers to make more money. AOL announced that it had already struck deals with major ad agencies to participate in these automated ad exchanges, which it believes will begin a seismic shift of TV advertising dollars to online video. To that end, the company also bought video ad company Adap.tv to bolster its position in online video. In 2014, AOL unveiled its new automated advertising platform, named One, which it hopes will become the standard for automated purchases of digital media. However, other companies including Google and Adobe are challenging One with their own offerings. AOL also rolled out a mobile native ad product across all of its sites that featured six times the conversion rate of traditional mobile banner ads and the participation of over 50 major brand advertisers. To improve user engagement, AOL purchased the advertising company Gravity, which personalizes sites based on users' interests across Internet and social site searches, making them more engaging.

Many companies are opting to use AOL for their advertising services, none more prominent than Microsoft, which announced a partnership with AOL in 2015. AOL will handle advertising on Xbox, Skype, and other Microsoft products in the United States and many other significant markets.

In return, AOL Web sites will use Microsoft's Bing search engine. The partnership strengthens AOL's position in the online advertising sphere.

AOL's burgeoning advertising business had made it an increasingly appealing acquisition target even before the Microsoft deal. Fifteen years after it was first purchased by Time Warner, AOL was once again acquired in 2015 as part of a $4.4 billion deal, this time by Verizon. For Verizon, the most intriguing piece of AOL's business was its digital advertising and video capability. As a mobile carrier, Verizon makes money when its customers stream videos on their mobile devices, making the two companies a good match. Verizon sees a future where it uses its mobile network and AOL's content delivery platform to successfully launch a content streaming business. However, the future of AOL's current content properties isn't as clear. Verizon's own attempts to generate content have been mostly unsuccessful, so acquiring AOL provides it with an established foothold in that area. But regulators are on guard against Internet providers also becoming major content providers, given the tools for censorship at their disposal. Verizon may elect to spin off entities like The Huffington Post, which is now valued at over $1 billion.

▬▬ **SOURCES:** "AOL in Deal With Microsoft to Take Over Display Ad Business," by Dino Grandoni, *New York Times,* June 29, 2015; "The Real Reason Verizon Bought AOL," by Kevin Fitchard, *Fortune,* June 24, 2015; "Will Huffington Post Lose Arianna Huffington?" by Brian Stelter, Cnnmoney.com, June 3, 2015; "Verizon Buys AOL for $4.4 Billion," by Ben Rooney, Cnnmoney.com, May 12, 2015; "AOL Still Has 2.2 Million Dialup Subscribers, and They're Paying More," by Dan Frommer, Qz.com, February 11, 2015; "AOL Earnings: Programmatic Platform Boosts Ad Revenues Yet Again," by Trefis Team, Forbes.com, August 8, 2014; "AOL, Yahoo, YouTube, Each Take Unique Road to Video," by Steve Rosenbaum, HuffingtonPost, May 5, 2014; "AOL Claims Huge Conversion Rates in Test Campaigns," by Christopher Heine, Adweek.com, April 24, 2014; "AOL, Microsoft Lure Advertisers with TV-Style Shows," by Jennifer Saba and Lisa Richwine, Reuters, April 23, 2014; "AOL Rolls out New Platform in Bid to Become Digital Ad Hub," by Jennifer Saba, Reuters, March 26, 2014; "AOL Buys Gravity, a Firm That Personalizes Web Searches," by Leslie Kaufman, *New York Times,* January 23, 2014; "AOL CEO Leads Charge to Pry Ad Dollars From TV," by Keach Hagey, *Wall Street Journal,* September 24, 2013; "AOL Urges Industry to Embrace Programmatic Buying," by Mike Shields, *Adweek,* September 23, 2013; "AOL to Launch Programmatic Upfront During Advertising Week," by Mike Shields, *Adweek,* July 24, 2013; "AOL CEO Tim Armstrong: 'We Haven't Won Yet'," by Daniel Terdiman, News.cnet.com, September 11, 2012; "AOL's Ad Revenue Up; Armstrong Bullish on Video," by Tanzina Vega, *New York Times,* July 25, 2012; "AOL Buys TechCrunch, 5Min and Thing Labs," by Jessica E. Vascellaro and Emily Steel, *New York Times,* September 29, 2010; "Eleven Years of Ambition and Failure at AOL," by Saul Hansell, *New York Times,* July 24, 2009; "Daring to Dream of a Resurgent AOL," by Saul Hansell, *New York Times,* July 23, 2009; "Before Spin-off, AOL Tries for That Start-up Feeling," *New York Times,* July 20, 2009.

Vertical market portals (sometimes also referred to as destination sites or vortals) attempt to attract highly focused, loyal audiences with a deep interest in either community or specialized content—from sports to the weather. In addition to their focused content, vertical market portals have recently begun adding many of the features found in general-purpose portals. For instance, in addition to being a social network, you can also think of Facebook as a portal—the home page for millions of users, and a gateway to the Internet. Facebook is an affinity group portal because it is based on friendships among people. Facebook offers e-mail, search, games, and apps.

The concentration of audience share in the portal market reflects (in addition to network effects) the limited time budget of consumers. This limited time budget works to the advantage of general-purpose portals. Consumers have a finite amount of time to spend on the Web, and as a result, most consumers visit fewer than 30 unique domains each month. Facing limited time, consumers concentrate their visits at sites that can satisfy a broad range of interests, from weather and travel information, to stocks, sports, and entertainment content.

General-purpose sites such as Yahoo try to be all things to all people and attract a broad audience with both generalized navigation services and in-depth content and community efforts. For instance, Yahoo has become the Web's largest source of news:

vertical market portals
attempt to attract highly focused, loyal audiences with a deep interest in either community or specialized content

more people visit Yahoo News than any other news site including online newspapers. Yet recent changes in consumer behavior on the Web show that consumers are spending less time "surfing the Web" and on general browsing, and more time doing focused searches, research, and participating in social networks. These trends will advantage special-purpose, vertical market sites that can provide focused, in-depth community and content.

As a general matter, the general-purpose portals are very well-known brands, while the vertical content and affinity group portals tend to have less well-known brands. **Figure 11.4** lists examples of general-purpose portals and the two main types of vertical market portals.

PORTAL BUSINESS MODELS

Portals receive income from a number of different sources. The revenue base of portals is changing and dynamic, with some of the largest sources of revenue declining. **Table 11.7** summarizes the major portal revenue sources.

The business strategies of both general-purpose and vertical portals have changed greatly because of the rapid growth in search engine advertising and intelligent ad placement networks such as Google's AdSense, which can place ads on thousands of Web sites based on content. General portal sites such as AOL and Yahoo did not have well-developed search engines, and hence have not grown as fast as Google, which has a powerful search engine. Microsoft, for instance, has invested billions of dollars in its Bing search engine to catch up with Google. On the other hand, general portals have content, which Google did not originally have, although it added to its content by purchasing YouTube and adding Google sites devoted to news, financial information, images, and maps. Facebook users stay on-site and linger three times as long as visitors to traditional portals like Yahoo. For this reason social network sites, Facebook in particular, are direct competitors of Yahoo, Google, and the other portals. Yahoo has

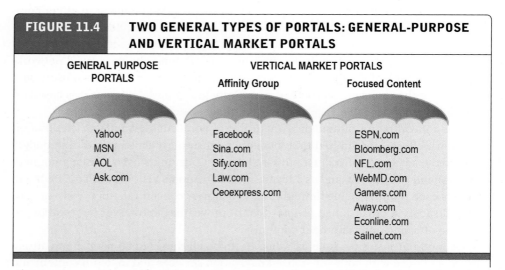

FIGURE 11.4 TWO GENERAL TYPES OF PORTALS: GENERAL-PURPOSE AND VERTICAL MARKET PORTALS

GENERAL PURPOSE PORTALS

Yahoo!
MSN
AOL
Ask.com

VERTICAL MARKET PORTALS

Affinity Group

Facebook
Sina.com
Sify.com
Law.com
Ceoexpress.com

Focused Content

ESPN.com
Bloomberg.com
NFL.com
WebMD.com
Gamers.com
Away.com
Econline.com
Sailnet.com

There are two general types of portals: general-purpose and vertical market. Vertical market portals may be based on affinity groups or on focused content.

TABLE 11.7	TYPICAL PORTAL REVENUE SOURCES
PORTAL REVENUE SOURCE	DESCRIPTION
General advertising	Charging for impressions delivered
Tenancy deals	Fixed charge for guaranteed number of impressions, exclusive partnerships, "sole providers"
Commissions on sales	Revenue based on sales at the site by independent providers
Subscription fees	Charging for premium content
Applications and games	Games and apps are sold to users; advertising is placed within apps

struggled in the last three years to grow revenues and earnings despite the fact that its unique visitor count has held steady with Google's. One part of the problem is the falling price of display ads, which are the mainstay of Yahoo's ad platform. Another key issue is declining user engagement with materials on the site and the amount of time spent on the site. To address these issues, Yahoo has made a number of acquisitions including Aviate, Tumblr, and Flickr, and launched digital magazines like Yahoo Food and Yahoo Tech that curate content from around the Web. The key to display ad revenue is content and engagement: the more you can show users, the longer they stay on your site, the more ad revenue can be generated. So far, Yahoo and the other general portal sites have not been able to compete with social network sites on these dimensions of engagement and time on site.

The survival strategy for general-purpose portals in the future is therefore to develop deep, rich vertical content in order to reach and engage customers at the site. This involves hiring professional journalists rather than rely on bloggers who write listicle articles, and offering more quality entertainment in the forms of movies, TV series, and music. The strategy for much smaller vertical market portals is to put together a collection of vertical portals to form a vertical portal network, a collection of deep, rich content sites. The strategy for search engine sites such as Google is to obtain more content to attract users for a long time and expose them to more ad pages (or screens).

11.4 CASE STUDY

eBay Evolves

When you hear someone mention online auctions, the first site that comes to mind is likely eBay. Founded in 1995 as an offbeat, quirky place to buy and sell almost anything via auctions, eBay now derives the majority of its revenue from traditional e-commerce. As the company continues to model its business after competitors such as Amazon and Alibaba, eBay has banned the sales of quirkier services like tarot card readings and magic spells, and has instituted a rewards program with prominent retail chains like Dick's Sporting Goods and Toys "R" Us.

The transformation began in November 2007, when former CEO Meg Whitman exited and was replaced by former Bain & Company managing director, John Donahoe. The company had already begun to stall, and the trend continued through 2009. For many buyers, the novelty of online auctions had worn off, and they were returning to easier and simpler methods of buying fixed-price goods from retailers such as Amazon, which, by comparison, had steady growth during the same time period. Search engines and comparison shopping sites were also taking away some of eBay's auction business by making items easier to find on the Web.

Donahoe quickly found that dramatically altering the business model of an Internet company is never easy, particularly one that is one of the most recognizable sites on

© Iain Masterton / Alamy

the Web. His three-year revival plan moved eBay away from its origins as an online flea market, and at first it began to resemble an outlet mall where retailers sold out-of-season, overstocked, refurbished, or discontinued merchandise. From there it was a straightforward progression to partnering with retail chains to simply serve as another channel for current merchandise.

Small sellers were encouraged to shift away from the auction format and move toward the fixed-price sales model. The fee structure was adjusted, listing fees for fixed-price sales were lowered, improvements were made to the search engine, and rather than displaying ending auctions first, a formula was devised that took into account price and seller reputation so that highly rated merchants appeared first and received more exposure.

Unsurprisingly, the growing pains during this period included increasing complaints from sellers about excessive fees and eBay's favoritism toward big retailers. The hundreds of thousands of people who supported themselves by selling on eBay and many millions more who used eBay to supplement their income often felt slighted. With its stock continuing to drop, analysts' faith that Donahoe could turn things around dwindled. This pessimism discounted eBay's history of sensible growth marked by a number of canny purchases.

Its signature purchase was, of course, PayPal, whose payment services enable the exchange of money between individuals over the Internet. This acquisition was the key to eBay's endurance through the lean years, protecting it from weakness in its auction business, and the propeller that pushed it towards the future. PayPal has accounted for over 40% of eBay's revenues for some time, and has been a significant factor in eBay's growth. In 2014, PayPal had over 152 million active accounts and continues to grow at a steady pace.

PayPal's success gave eBay's Marketplaces segment time to rebound. Strong results were at last realized between 2012 and 2014. eBay's investments in mobile technology were also an important factor in its resurgence. eBay's mobile investments began in 2010 with RedLaser, a barcode-scanning mobile application. This was followed by Critical Path, an industry leading mobile app developer, doubling the size of eBay's mobile team. eBay also purchased WHERE, a location-based media and advertising company with a local discovery mobile application, and Zong, a provider of mobile payments through mobile carrier billing. PayPal was used to purchase Fig Card, a small mobile payment startup. These outlays have borne fruit, supporting $47 billion in mobile transactions in 2013. Approximately 45% ($22 billion) of these transactions were mobile Marketplaces sales, while the other 55% ($27 billion) represented mobile PayPal transactions.

eBay recognized the coming mobile revolution even before the first iPhone or the establishment of the App Store, according to Olivier Ropars, senior director of Mobile Commerce. This prescience resulted in eBay achieving its 100 millionth app download and 100 millionth mobile listing relatively early on, in 2012. In 2013, eBay encountered increased competition in mobile commerce, and moved quickly to acquire mobile payment gateway Braintree for $800 million. Braintree's technology allows eBay consumers to more easily make payments on smartphones and tablets, and the acquisition also eliminates a major competitor in that space for PayPal. In 2015, eBay remains on the cutting edge, introducing an app for the Apple Watch that allows users

SOURCES: "PayPal Introduces an SDK for PayPal Here, Its Square-like Credit Card Reader," by Roberto Baldwin, Thenextweb.com, September 4, 2014; "eBay's 900 Million Dollar Question," by Chad Henage, Motley Fool, June 17, 2014; "Alibaba Takes on eBay, Etsy with U.S.-based Shopping Site," by Gail Sullivan, Washington Post, June 11, 2014; "Web? Store? Mobile? Shoppers Want It All," by Don Davis, Internetretailer.com, June 11, 2014; "Did Panda Really Beat Up On eBay?" by Thad Rueter, Interneretailer.com, June 9, 2014; "eBay Plays the Field," by Katie Evans, Internetretailer.com, June 2, 2014; "How the Once Impregnable eBay Fell Victim to Hackers (and You Can Too)," by Jeremy Quittner, Inc.com, May 30, 2014; "eBay Reports 13% Sales Growth and Rejects PayPal Spinoff," by Katie

Evans, Internetretailer.com, January 22, 2014; "Behind eBay's $800M Buy: Braintree will Replace PayPal's Developer Platform," by Kevin Fitchard, Gigaom.com, September 26, 2013; "Amazon, eBay Lead Way as E-Commerce Sales Still Surge," by Brian Deagon, *Investor's Business Daily*, July 2, 2013; "eBay Hits 100m Mobile App Download Mark," by Dervedia Thomas, Dailydealmedia.com, September 29, 2012; "eBay: We Need to Behave More Like a Retailer," by Sarah Shearman, Tameday.com, September 25, 2012; "eBay Logo Gets a Refresh; The Time Felt Right After 17 Years," by Mark Tyson, Hexus.com, September 14, 2012; "eBay Bans Magic Spells and Potions," by Katy Waldman, Slate.com, August 17, 2012; "Behind eBay's Comeback," by James B. Stewart, *New York Times*, July 27, 2012; "Bill Me Later, eBay's Credit Version of PayPal, Helps Company's Profits but Exposes It to Risk," by Alistair Barr, MercuryNews.com, July 12, 2012; "PayPal Strength Helps eBay Exceed Forecasts," by Somini Sengupta, *New York Times*, April 18, 2012; "eBay Favors Big-Box Retailers in Holiday Promotions," by Ina Steiner, eCommerce-Bytes.com, December, 16, 2011; "How Jack Abraham Is Reinventing eBay," by Danielle Sacks, *Fast Company*, June 22, 2011; "Connecting the Dots on eBay's Local Shopping Strategy," by Leena Rao, Techcrunch.com, May 15, 2011; "eBay CEO Sees Opportunities in Online and Offline Commerce," by Scott Morrison, *Wall Street Journal*, February 10, 2011.

to see an overview of their notifications and bid statuses, as well as rolling out more updates for their iOS and Android apps that improve search results.

While many other acquisitions through the years have also helped to transform eBay from an online garage sale to a mainstream competitor with Amazon, its adoption of the "social, mobile, local" driving theme has been central to its survival. Positioning itself at the center of the online—offline—mobile triangle by offering a wide variety of services that enable merchants to more easily integrate their cross-channel retailing has been the key to eBay's resurgence and to its continued success.

However, eBay's return to prominence is not without continuing challenges. In 2014, eBay was the victim of a hacking attack that compromised the information of nearly 150 million of its customers. Paypal was unaffected, and the company doesn't believe that any financial information was stolen, but the incident underscored the need for eBay to remain vigilant with its security measures. eBay sales decreased steeply in the wake of the breach, dropping 5.4% in 10 days. Competitors are also ramping up their efforts to battle eBay, with Amazon continuing to focus on third-party sales and Alibaba announcing a U.S.-based site to compete with eBay called 11 Main. What's more, Google rolled out an update to its search algorithm, reducing eBay's search traffic by as much as 33%.

In 2015, eBay elected to spin off PayPal as its own separate company, leaving eBay with its Marketplaces segment, its StubHub ticket sales segment, and a handful of other business units. Although Donahoe and the rest of eBay's leadership had resisted a spinoff for years, the move was prompted by a desire for PayPal to distinguish itself from eBay and become more agile within the rapidly-developing marketplace of online payments. As part of the split, eBay has agreed to route 80% of its sales through PayPal, but PayPal is free to pursue deals with other merchants, potentially boosting its market share even further. However, the move will surely decrease the attractiveness of what's left of eBay from an investment perspective. Many investors believe PayPal has been the true driver of eBay's bottom line. Analysts are already bracing for disappointing earnings, with shares falling in 2015 on gloomy 2016 sales projections. Nevertheless, eBay remains one of the most trusted online brands and e-commerce leaders, and it has worked hard to improve its marketplace design and offerings, including eBay Now, its new same-day delivery program. Will eBay be able to respond to these new challenges as well as it has to those in the past without PayPal to bolster it?

Case Study Questions

1. Contrast eBay's original business model with its current business model.

2. What are the problems that eBay is currently facing? How is eBay trying to solve these problems?

3. Are the solutions eBay is seeking to implement good solutions? Why or why not? Are there any other solutions that eBay should consider?

4. Who are eBay's top three competitors online, and how will eBay's strategy help it compete? Will eBay be providing a differentiated service to customers?

11.5 REVIEW

KEY CONCEPTS

- **Describe the different types of social networks and online communities and their business models.**

- Social networks involve a group of people, shared social interaction, common times among members, and a shared area for some period of time. An online social network is one where people who share common ties can interact with one another online.
- The different types of social networks and communities and their business models include:
  - *General communities:* Members can interact with a general audience segmented into numerous different groups. Most general communities began as non-commercial subscription-based endeavors, but many have been purchased by larger community portal sites.
  - *Practice networks:* Members can participate in discussion groups and get help or information relating to an area of shared practice, such as art, education, or medicine. These generally have a nonprofit business model in which they simply attempt to collect enough in subscription fees, sales commissions, and limited advertising to cover the cost of operations.
  - *Interest-based communities:* Members can participate in focused discussion groups on a shared interest. The advertising business model has worked because the targeted audience is attractive to marketers. Tenancy and sponsorship deals provide another similar revenue stream.
  - *Affinity communities:* Members can participate in focused discussions with others who share the same affinity or group identification. The business model is a mixture of subscription revenue from premium content and services, advertising, tenancy/sponsorships, and distribution agreements.
  - *Sponsored communities:* Members can participate in online communities created by government, nonprofit, or for-profit organizations for the purpose of pursuing organizational goals. They use community technologies and techniques to distribute information or extend brand influence. The goal of a branded product site is to increase offline product sales. These sites do not seek to make a profit and are often cost centers.

- **Describe the major types of auctions, their benefits and costs, how they operate, when to use them, and the potential for auction abuse and fraud.**

- Auctions are markets where prices vary (dynamic pricing) depending on the competition among the participants who are buying or selling products or services. They can be classified broadly as C2C or B2C, although generally the term C2C auction refers to the venue in which the sale takes place, for example, a consumer-oriented Web site such as eBay, which also auctions items from established merchants. A B2C *auction* refers to an established online merchant that offers its own auctions. There are also numerous B2B online auctions for buyers of industrial parts, raw materials, commodities, and services. Within these three broad categories of auctions are several major auction types classified based upon how the bidding mechanisms work in each system:
  - *English auctions:* A single item is up for sale from a single seller. Multiple buyers bid against one another within a specific time frame with the highest bidder winning the object as long as the high bid has exceeded the reserve bid set by the seller, below which he or she refuses to sell.
  - *Dutch Internet auctions:* Sellers with many identical items for sale list a minimum price or starting bid, and buyers indicate both a bid price and a quantity desired. The lowest winning bid that clears the available quantity is paid by all winning bidders. Those with the highest bid are assured of receiving the quantity they desire but only pay the amount of the lowest successful bid (uniform pricing rule).

- *Name Your Own Price or reverse auctions:* Buyers specify the price they are willing to pay for an item, and multiple sellers bid for their business. This is one example of discriminatory pricing in which winners may pay different amounts for the same product or service depending on how much they have bid.
  - *Penny (bidding fee) auctions:* Bidder pay a non-refundable fee to purchase bids.
- Benefits of auctions include: liquidity, price discovery, price transparency, market efficiency, lower transaction costs, consumer aggregation, network effects, and market-maker benefits.
- Costs of auctions include: delayed consumption, monitoring costs, equipment costs, trust risks, and fulfillment costs.
- Auction sites have sought to reduce these risks through various methods including rating systems, watch lists, and proxy bidding.
- Auctions can be an appropriate channel for businesses to sell items in a variety of situations. The factors for businesses to consider include the type of product, the product life cycle, channel management, the type of auction, initial pricing, bid increments, auction length, number of items, price allocation, and closed versus open bidding.
- Auctions are particularly prone to fraud, which produces information asymmetries between buyers and sellers. Some of the possible abuses and frauds include bid rigging, price matching, defensive shill feedback, offensive shill feedback, feedback extortion, transaction interference, bid manipulation, non-payment after winning, shill bidding, transaction non-performance, non-selling sellers, and bid siphoning.

■ **Describe the major types of Internet portals and their business models.**

- Portals are gateways to billions of Web pages available on the Internet. Originally, their primary purpose was to help users find information on the Web, but they evolved into destination sites that provided a myriad of content from news to entertainment. Today, portals serve three main purposes: navigation of the Web (search), content, and commerce.
- Among the major portal types are:
  - *Enterprise portals:* Corporations, universities, churches, and other organizations create these sites to help employees or members navigate to important content such as corporate news or organizational announcements.
  - *General-purpose portals:* Examples are AOL, Yahoo, and MSN, which try to attract a very large general audience by providing many in-depth vertical content channels. Some also offer ISP services on a subscription basis, search engines, e-mail, chat, bulletin boards, and personal home pages.
  - *Vertical market portals:* Also called destination sites, they attempt to attract a highly focused, loyal audience with an intense interest in either a community they belong to or an interest they hold. Vertical market portals can be divided into two main classifications, although hybrids that overlap the two classifications also exist.
  - *Affinity groups:* Designed to serve aggregates of people who identify themselves by their attitudes, values, beliefs, and behavior.
  - *Focused content portals:* These sites contain in-depth information on a particular topic that all members are interested in. They can provide content on such broad topics as sports, news, weather, entertainment, finance, or business, or they can appeal to a much more focused interest group such as boat, horse, or video game enthusiasts.
- Portals receive revenue from a number of different sources. The business model is presently changing and adapting to declines in certain revenue streams, particularly advertising revenues. Revenue sources can include general advertising, tenancy deals, subscription fees, and commissions on sales.
- The survival strategy for general-purpose portals is to develop deep, rich vertical content in order to attract advertisers to various niche groups that they can target with focused ads. The strategy for the

small vertical market portals is to build a collection of vertical portals, thereby creating a network of deep, rich content sites for the same reason.

QUESTIONS

1. What do social networks, auctions, and portals have in common?
2. What are the four defining elements of a social network—online or offline?
3. Why is Pinterest considered a social network, and how does it differ from Facebook?
4. What are three mobile social networks?
5. Why are mobile social networks growing so fast?
6. What are two measures that can be used to understand the importance of social networks and to compare them to other Internet experiences?
7. What is an affinity community, and what is its business model?
8. List and describe four different types of auctions.
9. What is the difference between a C2C and a B2C auction?
10. How does a Name Your Own Price auction, such as Priceline's, work?
11. List and briefly explain three of the benefits of auction markets.
12. What are the four major costs to consumers of participating in an auction?
13. Why has the FTC warned consumers about penny (bidding fee) auctions?
14. What is herd behavior and how does it impact auctions?
15. Name and describe five types of possible abuses and frauds that may occur with auctions.
16. What types of products are well suited for an auction market? At what points in the product life cycle can auction markets prove beneficial for marketers?
17. What three characteristics define a portal site today?
18. What are the two main types of vertical market portals, and how are they distinguished from one another?
19. List and briefly explain the main revenue sources for the portal business model.
20. Why has Yahoo struggled in the last three years?

PROJECTS

1. Find two examples of an affinity portal and two examples of a focused-content portal. Prepare a presentation explaining why each of your examples should be categorized as an affinity portal or a focused-content portal. For each example, surf the site and describe the services each site provides. Try to determine what revenue model each of your examples is using and, if possible, how many members or registered visitors the site has attracted.

2. Examine the use of auctions by businesses. Go to any auction site of your choosing and look for outlet auctions or auctions directly from merchants. Research at least three products for sale. What stage in the product life cycle do these products fall into? Are there quantity purchasing requirements? What was the opening bid price? What are the bid increments? What is the auction duration? Analyze why these firms have used the auction channel to sell these goods and prepare a short report on your findings.

3. Visit one for-profit-sponsored and one nonprofit-sponsored social network. Create a presentation to describe and demonstrate the offering at each site. What organizational objectives is each pursuing? How is the for-profit company using community-building technologies as a customer relations management tool?

4. Visit one of the social networks listed in Table 11.1 and compare it to Facebook. In what ways is it similar to Facebook, and in what ways is it different? Which do you prefer, and why?

REFERENCES

Arkes, H. R., and L. Hutzel. "The Role of Probability of Success Estimates in the Sunk Cost Effect." *Journal of Behavioral Decisionmaking* (2000).

Bailey, Brian P., Laura J. Gurak, and Joseph Konstan. "Do You Trust Me? An Examination of Trust in Computer-Mediated Exchange," In *Human Factors and Web Development*, 2nd Edition. Mahwah, NJ: Lawrence Erlbaum (2002).

Barnes, Nora, Ava Lescault, and Glenn Holmes. "The 2015 Fortune 500 and Social Media: Instagram Gains, Blogs Lose." University of Massachusetts (Dartmouth) (2015).

comScore, Inc.,"comScore Ranks the Top 50 U.S. Digital Media Properties for August 2015." (September 2015a).

comScore, Inc. "The 2015 U.S. Mobile App Report." (2015b).

Consumerreports.org. "With Penny Auctions, You Can Spend a Bundle But Still Leave Empty-Handed." (June 30, 2014).

Dholakia, Utpal, and Kerry Soltysinski. "Coveted or Overlooked? The Psychology of Bidding for Comparable Listings in Digital Auctions." *Marketing Letters* (2001).

eBay, Inc. "Form 10-K for the Fiscal Year Ended December 31, 2014." Filed with the Securities and Exchange Commission. (January 31, 2015).

eMarketer, Inc. (Alison McCarthy). "Worldwide Social Network Users." (May 2015a).

eMarketer, Inc. (Cindy Liu). "US Ad Spending: Q1 2015 Complete Forecast." (March 2015b).

eMarketer, Inc. "US Social Network Ad Revenues, by Venue, 2013–2017 (millions, % change and % of total)." (March 2015c).

Facebook. "Newsroom/Company Info." (accessed October 21, 2015).

Gaudin, Sharon. "Facebook at Work Should Be Ready by Year's End." Computerworld.com (September 17, 2015).

Hafner, Katie. "The Epic Saga of The Well: The World's Most Influential Online Community (and It's Not AOL)." Wired (May 1997).

Hagel, John III, and Arthur G. Armstrong. *Net Gain: Expanding Markets Through Virtual Communities*. Cambridge, MA: Harvard Business School Press (1997).

Hanson, Ward, and D. S. Putler. "Hits and Misses: Herd Behavior and Online Product Popularity." Marketing Letters (1996).

Hillery, George A. "Definitions of Community: Areas of Agreement." *Rural Sociology* (1955).

Hiltzik, Michael. *Dealers of Lightning: Xerox PARC and the Dawn of the Computer Age*. New York: Harper Collins (1999).

Kiesler, Sara. "The Hidden Messages in Computer Networks." *Harvard Business Review* (January–February 1986).

Kiesler, Sara, Jane Siegel, and Timothy W. McGuire. "Social Psychological Aspects of Computer-Mediated Communication." *American Psychologist* (October 1984).

Kollock, Peter. "The Production of Trust in Online Markets." In *Advances in Group Processes* (Vol 16) edited by E. J. Lawler, M. Macy, S. Thyne, and H. A. Walker. Greenwich, CT: JAI Press (1999).

Krishnamurthy, Sandeep. "An Empirical Study of the Causal Antecedents of Customer Confidence in ETailers." *First Monday* (January 2001).

Laudon, Kenneth C., and Jane P. Laudon. *Management Information Systems: Managing the Digital Firm. 14th edition.* Upper Saddle River, NJ, Prentice Hall (2014).

Liu, Yi, and Juliana Sutanto. "Buyers' Purchasing Time and Herd Behavior on Deal-of-the-Day Group-buying Websites." *Electronic Markets* (June 2012).

Miners, Zach. "Facebook Is Still King of Social Media Among Teens." Computerworld.com (April 8, 2015a).

Miners, Zach. "Facebook Video is Booming, with 4B Views Per Day." Computerworld.com (April 22, 2015b).

Miners, Zach. "Twitter Turns Its Home Page into a News and Information Hub." Computerworld.com (April 15, 2015c).

Miners, Zach. "Google Severs Google+ From Some of Its Sites." Computerworld.com (July 27, 2015d).

Nanji, Ayaz. "Blogs and Social Media Usage by Fortune 500 Companies." Marketingprofs.com (September 12, 2014).

Nikander, Pekka, and Kristina Karvonen. "Users and Trust in Cyberspace." In the Proceedings of Cambridge Security Protocols Workshop 2000, April 3–5, 2000, Cambridge University (2002).

Parkes, David C., and Lyle Ungar. "Iterative Combinatorial Auctions: Theory and Practice." *Proceedings of the 17th National Conference on Artificial Intelligence* (AAAI-00) (2000).

Pew Research Center. "Mobile Messaging and Social Media 2015." (Maeve Duggan) (August 19, 2015).

Rheingold, Howard. *Hosting Web Communities.* New York: John Wiley and Sons (1998). Also see Rheingold.com for more recent articles by Rheingold.

Rheingold, Howard. *The Virtual Community.* Cambridge MA: MIT Press (1993).

Rosenbloom, Stephanie. "For the Plugged-In, Too Many Choices." *New York Times* (August 10, 2011).

Seetharaman, Deepa. "Chat Apps Take a Swipe at Facebook." *Wall Street Journal* (July 8, 2015).

Simonson, Itamar, and Amos Tversky. "Choice in Context: Tradeoff Contrast and Extremeness Aversion." *Journal of Marketing Research,* Vol. 20, 281–287 (1992).

Stanford Persuasive Technology Lab and Makovsky & Company. "Stanford-Makovsky Web Credibility Study 2002." Stanford Persuasive Technology Lab. (Spring 2002).

CHAPTER

12

B2B E-commerce: Supply Chain Management and Collaborative Commerce

LEARNING OBJECTIVES

After reading this chapter, you will be able to:

- Discuss the evolution and growth of B2B e-commerce, as well as its potential benefits and challenges.
- Understand how procurement and supply chains relate to B2B e-commerce.
- Identify major trends in supply chain management and collaborative commerce.
- Understand the different characteristics and types of Net marketplaces.
- Understand the objectives of private industrial networks, their role in supporting collaborative commerce, and the barriers to their implementation.

Volkswagen

Builds Its B2B Platform

Volkswagen AG is the world's third largest vehicle manufacturer, producing 10.1 million cars, trucks, and vans in 2014, and generating approximately $227 billion in revenue, and a record $14.25 billion in profit. In addition to the Volkswagen brand, the Volkswagen Group also owns luxury carmakers such as Porsche, Audi, Bentley, Bugatti, and Lamborghini, commercial vehicle brands such as Scania and MAN, and family carmakers SEAT in Spain and SKODA in the Czech Republic. The company has over 590,000 employees and operates 119 plants in Europe, Africa, the Asian/Pacific rim, and the Americas, and it sells vehicles in 153 countries. Volkswagen's share of the global passenger car market in 2014 was 12.9%, making it the third largest producer in the world, behind Toyota and General Motors. In Western Europe, about 25% of all new cars are made by the Volkswagen Group. China is the company's largest

© Julian Clune / Alamy

market with sales of 3.67 million vehicles, constituting about 22% of the Chinese passenger car market.

The various companies and production plants in the Volkswagen Group annually purchase components, automotive parts, and indirect materials worth about $164 billion (which constitutes about 72% of Volkswagen's annual revenue). Obviously, the procurement process and relationships with suppliers are absolutely critical for Volkswagen's success.

Today, the Volkswagen Group manages almost all of its procurement needs via the Internet. It began building its Internet-based VWGroupSupply platform in 2000. The Volkswagen Group was looking for ways to create more efficient relationships with its suppliers and reduce the cost of paper-based procurement processes. However, the company did not want to automate procurement using a public independent exchange or an industry consortium because it would have had to adapt its own business processes to a common framework that could be used by many different organizations. Volkswagen hoped that by building its own B2B network, it could compete more effectively against other automakers.

Instead, Volkswagen opted for a private platform that would allow it to integrate its suppliers more tightly with its own business processes, and where it could control more precisely who was invited to participate. VWGroupSupply now handles over 90% of all global purchasing for the Volkswagen Group, including all automotive and parts components. It is one of the most comprehensive e-procurement systems in the global

SOURCES: "Volkswagen Group Annual Report 2014," Volkswagen Group, March 16, 2015; "VW Ready to Transform Automotive Supply Chains," Supplychain247.com, March 3, 2015; "VW Says 2014 Profit Rose to Record on Sales Gains at Audi, Porsche," Autonews.com, February 27, 2015; "Germany: Volkswagen Begins Future Automotive Supply Chain Tracks," by Graeme Roberts, Just-auto.com, February 27, 2015; "Automotive Industry Guiding Principles to Enhance Sustainability Performance in the Supply Chain," Aiag.org, May 8, 2014; "Volkswagen: Sharing the Challenge. Sustainability in Supplier Relations," Volkswagen AG, May 2014; "Registration of Your Company on the Group Business Platform (GBP)," Volkswagen, April 9, 2014; "Automakers Adopt Supply Chain Standards," by Ben Dipietro, *Wall Street Journal*, April 1, 2014; "VW Conquers the World: Germany's Biggest Carmaker Is Leaving Rivals in the Dust," *The Economist*, July 7, 2012; "e-Procurement within the Volkswagen Group," by Alex Smith, Littleknowhow.com, September 25, 2011; "Customer Specific Quality Requirements of the Volkswagen Group," IATF Global Certification Body Conference, February 10, 2011; "Automotive B2B Developments at Odette25," GXS.com, June 22, 2010; "Best Practices: VW Revs Up its B2B Engine," by Martin Hoffman, *Optimize*, March 2004.

automotive industry, and Volkswagen claims that it is the world's largest B2B supplier platform. Volkswagen also refers to it as the Group Business Platform. From an initial seven applications in 2003, the platform now offers over 60 different online applications, such as requests for quotations (RFQs), contract negotiations, catalog purchases, purchase order management, engineering change management, vehicle program management, and payments, among others. The Volkswagen Group developed the platform using technology from a number of vendors, including Ariba, IBM, and i2 Technologies.

Suppliers of all sizes can access the Group Business Platform with standard Web browser software. It can also be accessed via mobile devices. The Platform is limited to suppliers who have done business with one or more companies in the Volkswagen Group and potential new suppliers who go through an authorization process. Currently, over 45,000 suppliers are registered, and there are over 200,000 users every day. The system maintains a common data repository with details on each supplier concerning procurement, logistics, production, quality, technical design, and finance.

The Platform also provides suppliers with a variety of information, such as Volkwagen's Sustainability in Supplier Relations Policy, Environmental Policy, Occupational Safety Policy, and Declaration on Social Rights and Industrial Relationships. In 2013, Volkswagen's Group Supply Platform made a major effort to strengthen its sustainable supply chain initiative by requiring suppliers to meet VW sustainability requirements covering environment and social standards. For instance, suppliers must demonstrate they meet recycling and prohibited materials requirements. Volkswagen also requires suppliers to make a clear commitment to internationally accepted standards prohibiting discrimination, working conditions, and child labor.

VWGroupSupply's online catalog contains over 2.5 million items. The catalog uses the eCl@ss standard for classifying its contents. All suppliers who participate in the catalog ordering process classify their products using this standard.

Online negotiations involve multiple bids by suppliers for various purchasing contracts. VWGroupSupply ensures that all participants meet its technical and commercial qualifications. Before an online solicitation begins, the system informs vendors about the data and precise rules governing negotiations. Over 13,000 different vendors have taken part in online negotiations.

However, being the world's largest B2B automotive procurement system has its drawbacks in terms of speed, complexity, and innovation. The automotive world has changed drastically since VWGroupSupply platform launched in 2003. New technologies, shorter product cycles, and a greater emphasis on innovation mean that suppliers need to be much more involved in product design and development. Likewise, in order for it to move quickly, Volkswagen needs the innovation and scale of its suppliers. In 2015, the Volkswagen Group introduced the Future Automotive Supply Tracks (FAST) program to meet these challenges. FAST will start by reducing the number of suppliers, selecting those with best track records, and then involving these suppliers much earlier in the pre-series development of vehicles. The hope is to harmonize the contributions of both suppliers and Volkswagen Group to produce new, more innovative vehicles, at an ever faster pace.

The Volkswagen case illustrates the exciting potential for B2B e-commerce to lower production costs, increase collaboration among firms, speed up new product delivery, and ultimately revolutionize both the manufacturing process inherited from the early twentieth century and the way industrial products are designed and manufactured. This case also introduces new themes in B2B commerce: sustainability, environmental impacts, and social justice. Volkswagen's Group Business Platform is an example of just one type of B2B e-commerce, but there are many other equally promising efforts to use the Internet to change the relationships among manufacturers and their suppliers. In the fashion industry, the combination of high-speed value chains coupled with equally high-speed trendy design not only clears shelves (and reduces the likelihood of clearance sales), but increases profits by increasing value to consumers (Zarroli, 2013; Cachon and Swinney, 2011). The success of Volkswagen's Group Business Platform and similar networks operated by the major automobile firms in the world stands in contrast to an earlier industry-sponsored marketplace called Covisint. Founded in 1999 by five of the world's largest automakers (General Motors, Ford, Chrysler, Nissan, and Peugeot), Covisint hoped to provide a digital marketplace connecting thousands of suppliers to a few huge buyers using auctions and procurement services. While initially successful, Covisint was sold in June 2004, although it continues as a B2B services firm in a number of industries. Its auction business was sold to FreeMarkets, an early B2B auction company, which itself was sold to another B2B e-commerce firm called Ariba later in 2004. In 2014, Ariba survives as a successful software firm (now owned by SAP AG) focusing on the procurement process and the operation of a successful supplier trading platform and network.

The failure of Covisint (as well as Ford's AutoExchange) and the simultaneous growth in B2B e-commerce efforts such as Volkswagen's Group Business Platform illustrate the difficulties of achieving the broad visions established during the early days of e-commerce. Like B2C commerce, the B2B marketplace has consolidated, evolved, and moved on to more attainable visions. Changes in information technology, from smartphones to cloud computing, have greatly reduced the cost of B2B trading systems. In the process, many B2B efforts have experienced extraordinary success. There are many failed efforts to consider as well; these provide important lessons to all managers.

In this chapter, we examine three major B2B e-commerce themes: procurement, supply chain management, and collaborative commerce. Each of these business processes has changed greatly with the evolution of B2B e-commerce systems. In Sections 12.1 and 12.2, we provide an overview of B2B e-commerce, the procurement process, and supply chains. In Section 12.3, we place B2B e-commerce in the context of trends in procurement, supply chain management, and collaborative commerce. The final two sections describe the two fundamental types of B2B e-commerce: Net marketplaces and private industrial networks.

Table 12.1 summarizes the leading trends in B2B e-commerce in the 2015–2016 period. Perhaps the most important themes are growing industry concern with supply chain risk and environmental impact, along with a growing public concern with the accountability of supply chains—in particular, violations of developed-world expectations

TABLE 12.1	MAJOR TRENDS IN B2B E-COMMERCE, 2015–2016

BUSINESS

- B2B e-commerce growth continues to accelerate in 2015 to pre-recession levels as the global economy continues to recover from recession.
- B2B e-distributors adopt the the same marketing and sales techniques as successful consumer e-commerce companies such as Amazon.
- Risk management: companies heighten their focus on risks in supply chains after being blindsided in recent years by a number of natural and man-made disasters.
- Regional manufacturing: risks of far-flung global networks lead to an increase in regional manufacturing and supply chains, moving production closer to market demand.
- Flexibility: growing emphasis on rapid-response and adaptive supply chains rather than lowest cost supply chains, which typically carry great risks.
- Supply chain visibility: growing calls for more real-time data that would allow managers to see across not only their production, but also see into the production and financial condition of their key suppliers.
- Social and mobile commerce and customer intimacy: B2B buyers, like consumers, are tapping into tablets, smartphones, and social networks for purchasing, scheduling, exception handling, and coordinating with their suppliers in order to manage supply chain risk.

TECHNOLOGY

- Big Data: global trade and logistics systems are generating huge repositories of B2B data, swamping management understanding and controls.
- Business analytics: growing emphasis on use of business analytics software (business intelligence) to understand very large data sets.
- Cloud: migration of B2B hardware and software to cloud computing and cloud apps, away from individual corporate data centers, as a means of slowing rising technology costs. B2B systems move to cloud computing providers like IBM, Oracle, Amazon, Google, and HP as their core technology.
- Mobile platform: growing use of mobile platform for B2B systems (CRM, SCM, and enterprise), putting B2B commerce into managers' palms.
- Social networks: increasing use of social network platforms for feedback from customers, strengthening customer and supplier relationships, adjusting prices and orders, and enhancing decision making.
- Internet of Things: The number of Internet-connected sensors and other intelligent devices that measure and monitor data continues to grow exponentially and begins to impact how supply chains operate.

SOCIETY

- Accountability: growing demands for supply chain accountability and monitoring in developed countries driven by reports of poor working conditions in Asian factories.
- Sustainable supply chains: growing public demand for businesses to mitigate their environmental impact leads from local environmental optimization to consideration of the entire supply chain from design, production, customer service, and post-use disposal.
- Acceptance and growth of B2B platforms: Ariba, one of the largest Net marketplaces, has over 1.7 million connected businesses, including two-thirds of the Forbes Global 2000 largest companies, that participate in transactions with a value of over $700 billion a year.

of working conditions in third-world factories that play a key role in the production of goods sold in more developed countries. What many firms have learned in the last decade is that supply chains can strengthen or weaken a company depending on a number of factors related to supply chain efficiency such as community engagement, labor relations, environmental protection, and sustainability. Yet many believe that all of these related factors are important to the long profitability of firms (Beard and Hornik, 2011). At the same time, in part because of the globalization of supply chains, B2B e-commerce systems are now used by nearly all of the American S&P 500 firms, where over half of all revenues are produced offshore. Thousands of smaller firms are now able to participate in B2B systems as low-cost cloud-based computing and software-as-a-service (SaaS) become widely available. The cost of participating in B2B e-commerce systems has fallen significantly, allowing smaller firms to participate along with giant firms. Taking advantage of the exploding mobile platform, more companies are using smartphones and tablet computers to run their businesses from any location. There are thousands of iPhone and Android apps available from enterprise B2B vendors like SAP, IBM, Oracle, and others that link to supply chain management systems (Enright, 2013; Bolukbasi, 2011; Melnyk, 2010). Social network tools are pushing into the B2B world as well as the consumer world. B2B managers are increasingly using public and private social network sites and technologies to enable long-term conversations with their customers and suppliers. Executives at firms large and small are coming to realize that they are competing not just with other firms but with those firms' supply chains as well. **Supply chain competition** refers to the fact that in some industries firms are able to differentiate their product or pricing, and achieve a competitive advantage, due to superior supply chain management. Arguably, firms with superior supply chains can produce better products, more quickly, and at a lower cost than those with simply adequate supply chains (Antai, 2011).

supply chain competition
differentiating a firm's products or prices on the basis of superior supply chain management

12.1 AN OVERVIEW OF B2B E-COMMERCE

The trade between business firms represents a huge marketplace. The total amount of B2B trade in the United States in 2015 is expected to be about $14.6 trillion, with B2B e-commerce contributing about $6.3 trillion of that amount (U.S. Census Bureau, 2015; authors' estimates). By 2019, B2B e-commerce is expected to grow to about $8.6 trillion in the United States.

The process of conducting trade among business firms is complex and requires significant human intervention, and therefore, consumes significant resources. Some firms estimate that each corporate purchase order for support products costs them, on average, at least $100 in administrative overhead. Administrative overhead includes processing paper, approving purchase decisions, spending time using the telephone and fax machines to search for products and arrange for purchases, arranging for shipping, and receiving the goods. Across the economy, this adds up to trillions of dollars annually being spent for procurement processes that could potentially be automated. If even just a portion of inter-firm trade were automated, and parts of the entire procurement process assisted by the Internet, then literally trillions of dollars might be released for more productive uses, consumer prices potentially would fall, productivity would increase, and the economic wealth of the nation would expand. This is the promise of B2B e-commerce. The challenge of B2B e-commerce is changing existing patterns and systems of procurement, and designing and implementing new digital B2B solutions.

SOME BASIC DEFINITIONS

B2B commerce
all types of inter-firm trade

B2B e-commerce (B2B digital commerce)
that portion of B2B commerce that is enabled by the Internet and mobile apps

supply chain
the links that connect business firms with one another to coordinate production

automated order entry systems
involve the use of telephone modems to send digital orders

seller-side solutions
seller-biased markets that are owned by, and show only goods from, a single seller

electronic data interchange (EDI)
a communications standard for sharing business documents and settlement information among a small number of firms

buyer-side solutions
buyer-biased markets that are owned by buyers and that aim to reduce the procurement costs of supplies for buyers

Before the Internet, business-to-business transactions were referred to simply as *trade* or the *procurement process*. We use the term **B2B commerce** to describe all types of inter-firm trade to exchange value across organizational boundaries. B2B commerce includes the following business processes: customer relationship management, demand management, order fulfillment, manufacturing management, procurement, product development, returns, logistics/transportation, and inventory management (Barlow, 2011). This definition of B2B commerce does not include transactions that occur within the boundaries of a single firm—for instance, the transfer of goods and value from one subsidiary to another, or the use of corporate intranets to manage the firm. We use the term **B2B e-commerce** (or **B2B digital commerce**) to describe specifically that portion of B2B commerce that is enabled by the Internet (including mobile apps) (Fauska, et al., 2013). The links that connect business firms in the production of goods and services are referred to as the supply chain. **Supply chains** are a complex system of organizations, people, business processes, technology, and information, all of which need to work together to produce products efficiently. Today's supply chains are often global, connecting the smartphones in New York to the shipyards in Los Angeles and Quindow, and to the Foxconn factories that produce the phones. They are also local and national in scope.

THE EVOLUTION OF B2B E-COMMERCE

B2B e-commerce has evolved over a 35-year period through several technology-driven stages (see **Figure 12.1**). The first step in the development of B2B e-commerce in the mid-1970s was **automated order entry systems** that involved the use of telephone modems to send digital orders to health care products companies such as Baxter Healthcare. Baxter, a diversified supplier of hospital supplies, placed telephone modems in its customers' procurement offices to automate reordering from Baxter's computerized inventory database (and to discourage reordering from competitors). This early technology was replaced by personal computers using private networks in the late 1980s, and by Internet workstations accessing electronic online catalogs in the late 1990s. Automated order entry systems are **seller-side solutions**. They are owned by the suppliers and are seller-biased markets—they show only goods from a single seller. Customers benefited from these systems because they reduced the costs of inventory replenishment and were paid for largely by the suppliers. Automated order entry systems continue to play an important role in B2B commerce.

By the late 1970s, a new form of computer-to-computer communication called **electronic data interchange (EDI)** emerged. We describe EDI in greater detail later in this chapter, but at this point, it is necessary only to know that EDI is a communications standard for sharing business documents such as invoices, purchase orders, shipping bills, product stocking numbers (SKUs), and settlement information among a small number of firms. Virtually all large firms have EDI systems, and most industry groups have industry standards for defining documents in that industry. EDI systems are owned by the buyers, hence they are **buyer-side solutions** and buyer-biased because they aim to reduce the procurement costs of supplies for the buyer. Of course,

---

FIGURE 12.1	**THE EVOLUTION OF THE USE OF TECHNOLOGY PLATFORMS IN B2B E-COMMERCE**

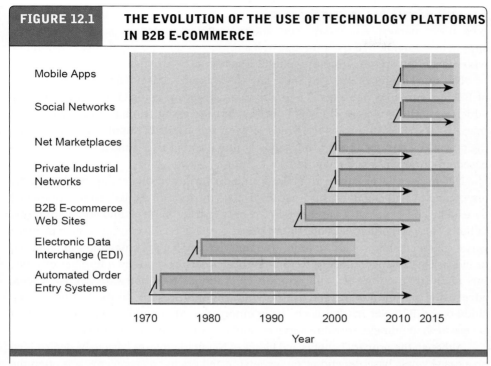

B2B e-commerce has gone through many stages of development since the 1970s. Each stage reflects a major change in technology platforms from mainframes to private dedicated networks, and finally to the Internet, mobile apps and social networks.

---

by automating the transaction, EDI systems also benefit the sellers through customer cost reduction. The topology of EDI systems is often referred to as a **hub-and-spoke system**, with the buyers in the center and the suppliers connected to the central hub via private dedicated networks.

EDI systems generally serve vertical markets. A **vertical market** is one that provides expertise and products for a specific industry, such as automobiles. In contrast, **horizontal markets** serve many different industries.

B2B e-commerce Web sites emerged in the mid-1990s along with the commercialization of the Internet. **B2B e-commerce Web sites** are perhaps the simplest and easiest form of B2B e-commerce to understand, because they are just online catalogs of products made available to the public marketplace by a single supplier. In this sense, they mimic the functionality of B2C e-commerce Web sites. Owned by the supplier, they are seller-side solutions and seller-biased because they show only the products offered by a single supplier.

B2B e-commerce Web sites are a natural descendant of automated order entry systems, but there are two important differences: (1) the far less expensive and more universal Internet becomes the communication media and displaces private networks, and (2) B2B e-commerce Web sites tend to serve horizontal markets—they carry products that serve a wide variety of industries. Although B2B e-commerce Web sites

hub-and-spoke system
suppliers connected to a central hub of buyers via private dedicated networks

vertical market
one that provides expertise and products for a specific industry

horizontal market
market that serves many different industries

B2B e-commerce Web site
online catalog of products made available to the public marketplace by a single supplier

emerged prior to Net marketplaces (described next), they are usually considered a type of Net marketplace. Today, more and more B2B manufacturers, distributors, and suppliers are using B2B e-commerce Web sites to sell directly to business customers, who most often are procurement/purchasing agents, as discussed in Section 12.2.

Net marketplace
brings hundreds to thousands of suppliers and buyers into a single Internet-based environment to conduct trade

Net marketplaces emerged in the late 1990s as a natural extension and scaling-up of B2B e-commerce Web sites. There are many different kinds of Net marketplaces, which we describe in detail in Section 12.4, but the essential characteristic of a Net marketplace is that it brings hundreds or even thousands of suppliers—each with a digital catalog and potentially thousands of purchasing firms—into a single Internet-based environment to conduct trade.

Net marketplaces can be organized under a variety of ownership models. Some are owned by independent third parties backed by venture capital, some are owned by established firms who are the main or only market players, and some are a mix of both. Net marketplaces establish the prices of the goods they offer in four primary ways—fixed catalog prices, or more dynamic pricing, such as negotiation, auction, or bid/ask ("exchange" model). Net marketplaces earn revenue in a number of ways, including transaction fees, subscription fees, service fees, software licensing fees, advertising and marketing, and sales of data and information. In the last few years, cloud-based B2B Net marketplaces have emerged, and generate revenue by selling access to their storage, software services, and communications facilities.

Although the primary benefits and biases of Net marketplaces have to be determined on a case-by-case basis depending on ownership and pricing mechanisms, it is often the case that Net marketplaces are biased against suppliers because they can force suppliers to reveal their prices and terms to other suppliers in the marketplace. Net marketplaces can also significantly extend the benefits of simple electronic storefronts by seeking to automate the procurement value chain of both selling and buying firms.

private industrial networks (private trading exchange, PTX)
Internet-based communication environments that extend far beyond procurement to encompass truly collaborative commerce

Private industrial networks also emerged in the last decade as natural extensions of EDI systems and the existing close relationships that developed between large industrial firms and their trusted suppliers. Described in more detail in Section 12.5, **private industrial networks** (sometimes also referred to as a *private trading exchange*, or *PTX*) are Internet-based communication environments that extend far beyond procurement to encompass supply chain efficiency enhancements and truly collaborative commerce. The VWGroupSupply platform described in the opening case is an excellent example of a private industrial network. Private industrial networks permit buyer firms and their principal suppliers to share product design and development, marketing, inventory, production scheduling, and unstructured communications. Like EDI, private industrial networks are owned by the buyers and are buyer-side solutions with buyer biases. These systems are directly intended to improve the cost position and flexibility of large industrial firms (Yoo et al., 2011; Kumaran, 2002). These private industrial networks have a much higher survival rate than other Net marketplaces (Rosenzweig, 2011).

Naturally, private industrial networks have significant benefits for suppliers as well. Inclusion in the direct supply chain for a major industrial purchasing company can allow a supplier to increase both revenue and margins because the environment is not competitive—only a few suppliers are included in the private industrial network. These networks are the most prevalent form of B2B e-commerce, and this will continue into the foreseeable future.

FIGURE 12.2	**GROWTH OF B2B E-COMMERCE 2010–2019**

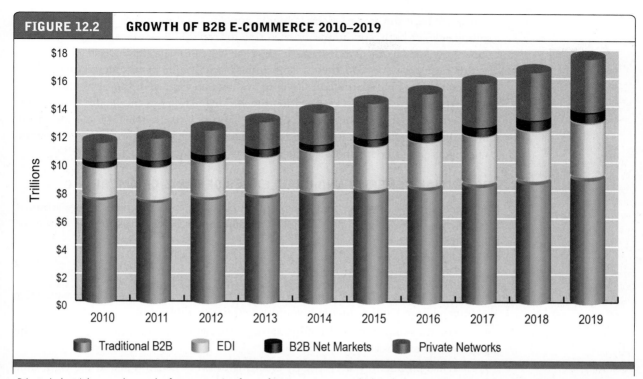

Traditional B2B   EDI   B2B Net Markets   Private Networks

Private industrial networks are the fastest growing form of B2B e-commerce, which includes EDI, B2B Net marketplaces, and private industrial markets.

SOURCES: Based on data from U.S. Census Bureau, 2015; authors' estimates.

THE GROWTH OF B2B E-COMMERCE

Figure 12.2 illustrates the growth of B2B e-commerce, as well that of traditional B2B commerce, during the period 2010–2019. However, let's focus on the growth of B2B e-commerce during the period 2015–2019. During this time, B2B e-commerce is projected to grow from about $6.3 trillion in 2014 (about 43% of total B2B commerce in the United States) to $8.6 trillion (48% of total B2B commerce) in 2019. Several observations are important to note with respect to Figure 12.2. First, it shows that the initial belief that online marketplaces would become the dominant form of B2B e-commerce is not supported. Second, private industrial networks play a dominant role in B2B e-commerce, both now and in the future. Third, non-EDI B2B e-commerce is the most rapidly growing type of B2B e-commerce. However, EDI remains quite common and continues to be a workhorse of B2B commerce.

Not all industries will be similarly affected by B2B e-commerce, nor will all industries similarly benefit from B2B. Several factors influence the speed with which industries migrate to B2B e-commerce and the volume of transactions. Those industries in which there is already significant utilization of EDI (indicating concentration of buyers and suppliers) and large investments in information technology and Internet infrastructure can be expected to move first and fastest to B2B e-commerce utilization. The aerospace and defense, computer, and industrial equipment industries meet these criteria. Where the marketplace is highly concentrated on either the purchasing or selling side, or both, conditions are also ripe for rapid B2B e-commerce growth, as in the energy and chemical industries. In the case of health care, the federal government, health care providers (doctors and hospitals), and major insurance companies are moving toward a national medical record system and the use of the Internet for managing medical payments. Coordinating the various players in the health care system is an extraordinary B2B challenge. Computer service firms like IBM and Microsoft, and B2B service firms like Covisint, are expanding the use of information ecosystems where health providers and insurers can share information.

POTENTIAL BENEFITS AND CHALLENGES OF B2B E-COMMERCE

Regardless of the specific type, B2B commerce as a whole promises many strategic benefits to firms—both buyers and sellers—and impressive gains for the economy. B2B e-commerce can:

- Lower administrative costs
- Lower search costs for buyers
- Reduce inventory costs by increasing competition among suppliers (increasing price transparency) and reducing inventory to the bare minimum
- Lower transaction costs by eliminating paperwork and automating parts of the procurement process
- Increase production flexibility by ensuring delivery of parts just at the right time (known as just-in-time production)
- Improve quality of products by increasing cooperation among buyers and sellers and reducing quality issues
- Decrease product cycle time by sharing designs and production schedules with suppliers
- Increase opportunities for collaborating with suppliers and distributors
- Create greater price transparency—the ability to see the actual buy and sell prices in a market
- Increase the visibility and real-time information sharing among all participants in the supply chain network.

B2B e-commerce offers potential first-mover strategic benefits for individual firms as well. Firms that move their procurement processes online first will experience impressive gains in productivity, cost reduction, and potentially much faster introduction of new, higher-quality products. While these gains may be imitated by other competing firms, it is also clear from the history of B2B e-commerce that firms making sustained investments in information technology and B2B e-commerce can adapt much faster to new technologies as they emerge, creating a string of first-mover advantages.

While there are many potential benefits to B2B e-commerce, there are also considerable risks and challenges. Often real-world supply chains fail to provide visibility into the supply chain because they lack real-time demand, production, and logistics data, and have inadequate financial data on suppliers. The result is unexpected supplier failure and disruption to the supply chain. Builders of B2B supply chains often had little concern for the environmental impacts of supply chains, the sensitivity of supply chains to natural events, fluctuating fuel and labor costs, or the impact of public values involving labor and environmental policies. The result in 2015 is that many Fortune 1000 supply chains are risky, vulnerable, and socially and environmentally unsustainable. Read *Insight on Society: Where's My iPad? Apple's Supply Chain Risks and Vulnerabilities* for a look at the impact the Tohoku earthquake in the prefecture of Fukushima, Japan, had on global supply chains, as well as the reputational risk posed by supply chains.

12.2 THE PROCUREMENT PROCESS AND SUPPLY CHAINS

The subject of B2B e-commerce can be complex because there are so many ways the Internet can be used to support the exchange of goods and payments among organizations, efficient supply chains, and collaboration. At the most basic level, B2B e-commerce is about changing the **procurement process** (how business firms purchase goods they need to produce goods they will ultimately sell to consumers) of thousands of firms across the United States and the world. In the procurement process, firms purchase goods from a set of suppliers, and they in turn purchase their inputs from a set of suppliers. The supply chain includes not just the firms themselves, but also the relationships among them and the processes that connect them.

procurement process
how firms purchase goods they need to produce goods for consumers

STEPS IN THE PROCUREMENT PROCESS

There are seven separate steps in the procurement process (see **Figure 12.3**). The first three steps involve the decision of who to buy from and what to pay: searching for suppliers of specific products; qualifying both sellers and the products they sell;

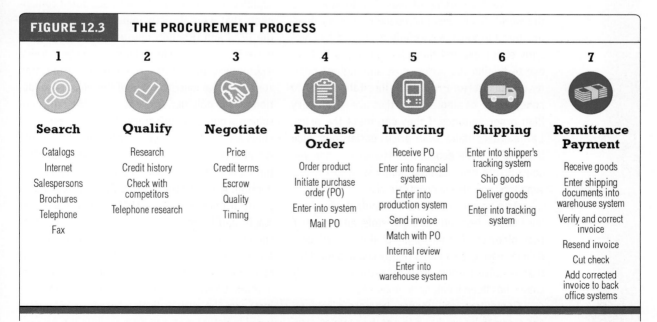

FIGURE 12.3	**THE PROCUREMENT PROCESS**

1	2	3	4	5	6	7
Search	**Qualify**	**Negotiate**	**Purchase Order**	**Invoicing**	**Shipping**	**Remittance Payment**
Catalogs	Research	Price		Receive PO	Enter into shipper's tracking system	
Internet	Credit history	Credit terms	Order product	Enter into financial system	Ship goods	Receive goods
Salespersons	Check with competitors	Escrow	Initiate purchase order (PO)	Enter into production system	Deliver goods	Enter shipping documents into warehouse system
Brochures	Telephone research	Quality	Enter into system	Send invoice	Enter into tracking system	Verify and correct invoice
Telephone		Timing	Mail PO	Match with PO		Resend invoice
Fax				Internal review		Cut check
				Enter into warehouse system		Add corrected invoice to back office systems

The procurement process is a lengthy and complicated series of steps that involves the seller, buyer, and shipping companies in a series of connected transactions.

INSIGHT ON SOCIETY

WHERE'S MY IPAD? SUPPLY CHAIN RISK AND VULNERABILITY

In 2011, a magnitude 9.0 earthquake occurred offshore of northern Japan. The Tohoku earthquake was the largest in recorded history and immediately created a number of tsunami waves, some of which exceeded 100 feet in height and penetrated up to six miles inland. In their path were six coastal nuclear reactors in the Fukushima Prefecture near the town of Okuma, the largest nuclear power site in the world. Several of the nuclear reactors exploded and began leaking dangerous levels of radiation as fuel rods melted at temperatures exceeding 5,000 degrees.

The Tohoku earthquake exposed significant weaknesses and vulnerabilities in today's modern B2B supply chains. Technology, globalization of trade, and high levels of wage disparity between the developed and undeveloped worlds have led to a massive outsourcing of manufacturing around the world. Today, every component of every manufactured product is carefully examined by company engineers and financial managers with an eye to finding the lowest cost and highest quality manufacturer. Production inevitably tends to concentrate at single firms that are given very high order volumes if they can meet the price. Large orders make lower prices easier to provide because of scale economies. However, when you concentrate production globally with just a few suppliers, you also concentrate risk.

As a result, the world's manufacturing base has become less redundant, flexible, and adaptive than older traditional supply chains. Interdependencies have grown into a tightly coupled machine that is quite fragile. Risk assessment in supply chains has been weak or nonexistent.

Computers, cell phones, tractors, airplanes, and automobiles are just a few of the complex manufactured goods that rely on parts and subassemblies made thousands of miles away from their final assembly plants. Most of these manufacturers know who their first-tier suppliers are but may be less aware about who supplies their suppliers, and so on down the line of the industrial spider's web that constitutes the real world of supply chains. Few firms had considered the impact of an earthquake on their supply chains, or a nuclear meltdown, or even a financial collapse in the global banking system—all typical risks found in the real world.

Take the Apple iPad. In a teardown of an iPad after the earthquake, IHS iSuppli, a market research firm, identified at least five major components sourced from Japanese suppliers, some of whom were located in northern Japan. Not all of these suppliers were directly impacted by the earthquake, but some were, and many had sub-suppliers of various hard-to-replace small components that were directly impacted. For instance, the iPad and iPhone's unusually shaped lithium batteries used a crucial polymer made by Kureha, a Japanese firm in the nuclear contamination zone. Kureha controls 70% of the global production of this polymer. Apple was not the only consumer product manufacturer hit hard: computer chips are built on silicon wafers, and 25% of the world's supply is made by two Japanese manufacturers, both of which had to shut down wafer production. A few years later, in 2015, a tear-down of the iPhone 6 Plus by IHS iSuppli found that Apple had learned its lesson and diversified its supply chain by often having two manufacturers for the same components sourced from different countries, and also having various components manufactured in different parts of the globe. For instance, the retina display screen is manufactured in both Japan and Korea, while the A8 processor is manufactured in both Taiwan and Korea; the NFC chips are made in Holland and Austria, while the audio chip is from United States and the accelerometer chip is from Germany.

Apple was not the only manufacturer that learned a lesson in supply chain risk from the Japanese earthquake: Boeing was without carbon fiber airframe assemblies made in Japan; Ford and GM closed factories for lack of Japanese transmissions; and Caterpillar reduced production at its factories worldwide as it attempted to secure alternative suppliers.

Supply chain risk involves more than disruptions in production, as Apple and many other companies have discovered. Supply chains can produce reputational risks when key suppliers engage in labor and environmental policies and practices that are unacceptable to developed world audiences. For instance, for much of 2012, Apple was under attack in the United States and Europe after an audit by the Fair Labor Association found that workers at several assembly plants operated by Apple contractor Foxconn were exposed to toxic chemicals and forced to work over 60 hours a week under dangerous work conditions.

Also in 2012, a fire in a clothing factory in Dhaka, Bangladesh, killed 117 workers, mostly women and children. Well-known brands from Europe and the United States, among them Walmart and Spanish giant Inditex, were producing clothing in this factory. Walmart claimed a subcontractor was using this factory without Walmart's knowledge. The fire created a worldwide protest, and has led to government and industry efforts to certify factory safety in Bangladesh and hold firms responsible for working conditions.

It also isn't just natural disasters and fires that can disrupt supply lines. In 2015, supply lines from Asia to the United States were shut down for nearly a month by a longshoreman's dock strike that resulted in a slowdown of automobile production throughout the United States. This in turn backed up production in Asia of car parts. Thailand, the world's third largest fish exporter, was discovered to be using slave labor to harvest fish, and its product was banned by the European Union. Many American companies had their supplies disrupted, and needed to find other suppliers. Finally a new class of supply chain risk is becoming apparent: cybersecurity risks. With hundreds of suppliers, it is very difficult for any single purchasing firm to assess the security of its suppliers' systems. Reducing the number of suppliers is one method. Working only with trusted partners is another. Yet there remains a large opportunity for cybercriminals and rogue governments to disrupt global supply chains.

One might think that in the so-called global and Internet economy, computer-based supply chains could quickly and effortlessly adjust to find new suppliers for just about any component or industrial material in a matter of minutes. Think again. New supply chains will need to be built that optimize not just cost but also survivability in the event of disasters, as well as meet the ethical demands of the major consuming countries in Europe and the United States.

SOURCES: "Financial Firms Grapple With Cyber Risk in the Supply Chain," by Rachael King, *Wall Street Journal*, May 25, 2015; "Supply Chain Slavery Comes Into Focus for Companies," by Ben DiPietro, *Wall Street Journal*, March 30, 2015; "Asian Supply Lines Hit by West Coast Ports," *Reuters*, February 16, 2015; "Teardown Shows Apple's iPhone 6 Cost at Least $200 to Build" by Arik Hesseldahl, Recode.net, September 23, 2014; "Apple Goes on Hiring Binge in Asia to Speed Product Releases," by Eva Dou, *Wall Street Journal*, March 3, 2014; "Teardown: Apple's Latest iPhones Are Not as Green as the Company Claims," by Roger Chang, Wired.com, September 20, 2013; "Gold iPhone 5S Backordered Online in US, Elsewhere," by Josh Lowensohn, Cnetnews.com, September 20, 2013; "Infographic Breaks Down Apple's iPhone Supply Chain," by Bryan Chaffin, MacObserver.com, August 6, 2013; "Bangladesh Factory, Site of Fire That Trapped and Killed 7, Made European Brands," by Julfikar Ali Manik and Jim Yardley, *New York Times*, January 27, 2013; "Disruptions: Too Much Silence on Working Conditions," by Nick Bilton, *New York Times*, April 8, 2012; "Audit Faults Apple Supplier," by Jessica Vascellaro, *Wall Street Journal*, March 30, 2012; "Under the Hood of Apple's Tablet," by Don Clark, *Wall Street Journal*, March 16, 2012; "In China, Human Costs Are Built Into an iPad," by Charles Duhigg and David Barboza, *New York Times*, January 25, 2012; "Japan: The Business After Shocks," by Andrew Dowell, *Wall Street Journal*, March 25, 2011; "Some Worry the Success of Apple Is Tied to Japan," by Miguel Helft, *New York Times*, March 22, 2011; "Crisis Tests Supply Chain's Weak Links," by James Hookway and Aries Poon, *Wall Street Journal*, March 18, 2011; "Caterpillar Warns of Supply Problems From Quake," by Bob Tita, *Wall Street Journal*, March 18, 2011; "Lacking Parts, G.M. Will Close Plant," by Nick Bunkley, *New York Times*, March 17, 2011.

direct goods
goods directly involved in the production process

indirect goods
all other goods not directly involved in the production process

MRO goods
products for maintenance, repair, and operations

contract purchasing
involves long-term written agreements to purchase specified products, under agreed-upon terms and quality, for an extended period of time

spot purchasing
involves the purchase of goods based on immediate needs in larger marketplaces that involve many suppliers

and negotiating prices, credit terms, escrow requirements, quality, and scheduling of delivery. Once a supplier is identified, purchase orders are issued, the buyer is sent an invoice, the goods are shipped, and the buyer sends a payment. Each of these steps in the procurement process is composed of many separate business processes and subactivities. Each of these activities must be recorded in the information systems of the seller, buyer, and shipper. Often, this data entry is not automatic and involves a great deal of manual labor, telephone calls, faxes, and e-mails.

TYPES OF PROCUREMENT

Two distinctions are important for understanding how B2B e-commerce can improve the procurement process. First, firms make purchases of two kinds of goods from suppliers: direct goods and indirect goods. **Direct goods** are goods integrally involved in the production process; for instance, when an automobile manufacturer purchases sheet steel for auto body production. **Indirect goods** are all other goods not directly involved in the production process, such as office supplies and maintenance products. Often these goods are called **MRO goods**—products for maintenance, repair, and operations.

Second, firms use two different methods for purchasing goods: contract purchasing and spot purchasing. **Contract purchasing** involves long-term written agreements to purchase specified products, with agreed-upon terms and quality, for an extended period of time. Generally, firms purchase direct goods using long-term contracts. **Spot purchasing** involves the purchase of goods based on immediate needs in larger marketplaces that involve many suppliers. Generally, firms use spot purchasing for indirect goods, although in some cases, firms also use spot purchasing for direct goods.

According to some estimates, about 65% of inter-firm trade involves contract purchasing of direct goods, and 35% involves spot purchasing of indirect goods (Ariba, 2014; Kaplan and Sawhney, 2000). There are, of course, differences among industries. Purchases of direct goods play a dominant role in the extraction and metal industries, for instance. This finding is significant for understanding B2B e-commerce.

Although the procurement process involves the purchasing of goods, it is extraordinarily information-intense, involving the movement of information among many existing corporate systems. The procurement process today is also very labor-intensive, directly involving over 1 million employees in the United States, not including those engaged in transportation, finance, insurance, or general office administration related to the process. The key players in the procurement process are the purchasing managers. They ultimately decide who to buy from, what to buy, and on what terms. Purchasing managers ("procurement managers" in the business press) are also the key decision makers for the adoption of B2B e-commerce solutions. As purchasing managers have become more familiar and comfortable with B2C e-commerce in their personal lives, they are increasingly coming to expect the same type of purchasing experience in the B2B arena. As a result, B2B manufacturers, suppliers, and distributors are finding that in order to effectively compete, they must pay more attention to the online customer experience, just as their B2C counterparts do. Features that B2B customers now expect include enhanced search functionality, up-to-date product pricing and availability information, product configurators, mobile support, apps along with Web sites, online support forums, live customer service reps, and a database that contains their corporate purchasing history, shipping preferences, and payment data, and provides support for repeat orders.

MULTI-TIER SUPPLY CHAINS

Although Figure 12.3 captures some of the complexity of the procurement process, it is important to realize that firms purchase thousands of goods from thousands of suppliers. The suppliers, in turn, must purchase their inputs from their suppliers. Large manufacturers such as Ford Motor Company have over 20,000 suppliers of parts, packaging, and technology. The number of secondary and tertiary suppliers is at least as large. Together, this extended **multi-tier supply chain** (the chain of primary, secondary, and tertiary suppliers) constitutes a crucial aspect of the industrial infrastructure of the economy. **Figure 12.4** depicts a firm's multi-tier supply chain.

multi-tier supply chain
the chain of primary, secondary, and tertiary suppliers

The supply chain depicted in Figure 12.4 is a three-tier chain simplified for the sake of illustration. In fact, large Fortune 1000 firms have thousands of suppliers, who in turn have thousands of smaller suppliers. The complexity of the supply chain suggests a combinatorial explosion. Assuming a manufacturer has four primary suppliers and each one has three primary suppliers, and each of these has three primary suppliers, then the total number of suppliers in the chain (including the buying firm) rises to 53. This figure does not include the shippers, insurers, and financiers involved in the transactions.

FIGURE 12.4 **THE MULTI-TIER SUPPLY CHAIN**

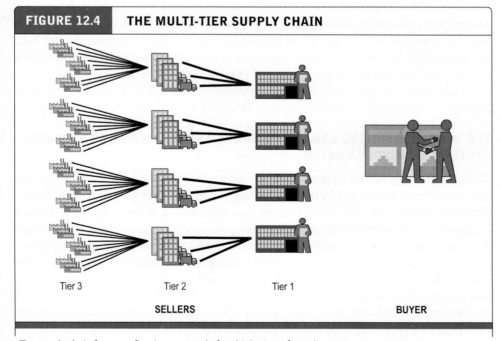

Tier 3   Tier 2   Tier 1

SELLERS   BUYER

The supply chain for every firm is composed of multiple tiers of suppliers.

TABLE 12.2	CONCEPTS AND CHALLENGES IN SUPPLY CHAIN MANAGEMENT
CONCEPT/CHALLENGE	DESCRIPTION
Visibility	Ability to monitor suppliers, orders, and logistics
Demand forecasting	Informing your suppliers of future demand
Production scheduling	Informing your suppliers of the production schedule
Order management	Keeping track of orders to your suppliers
Logistics management	Managing your logistics partners based on your production schedule

Immediately, you can see from Figure 12.4 that the procurement process involves a very large number of suppliers, each of whom must be coordinated with the production needs of the ultimate purchaser—the buying firm. You can also understand how difficult it is to manage the supply chain, or obtain visibility into the supply chain simply because of its size and scope.

VISIBILITY AND OTHER CONCEPTS IN SUPPLY CHAIN MANAGEMENT

supply chain visibility
the extent to which purchasing firms can monitor second- and third-tier suppliers' activities

The global, multi-tier nature of supply chains produces a number of challenges for supply chain managers. A central concept of supply chains is **supply chain visibility**, which refers to the ability of a firm to monitor the output of its first- and second-tier suppliers, track and manage supplier orders, and manage transportation and logistics providers who are moving the products. A supply chain is visible when you know exactly what you have ordered from your suppliers and what their production schedule is, and when you can track the goods through shipping and trucking firms to your in-bound warehouse. With this knowledge, the firm's internal enterprise systems can produce production schedules and develop financial forecasts (Long, 2014; Cecere, 2014; Cecere, 2013.)

Other key concepts in supply chain management, and which are also central management challenges, are described in **Table 12.2**.

THE ROLE OF EXISTING LEGACY COMPUTER SYSTEMS AND ENTERPRISE SYSTEMS IN SUPPLY CHAINS

legacy computer systems
older mainframe systems used to manage key business processes within a firm in a variety of functional areas

enterprise systems
corporate-wide systems that relate to all aspects of production, including finance, human resources, and procurement

Complicating any efforts to coordinate the many firms in a supply chain is the fact that each firm generally has its own set of legacy computer systems, sometimes home-grown or customized, that cannot easily pass information to other systems. **Legacy computer systems** generally are older enterprise systems used to manage key business processes within a firm in a variety of functional areas from manufacturing, logistics, finance, and human resources. **Enterprise systems** are corporate-wide systems that relate to all aspects of production, including finance, human resources, and procurement. Many large Fortune 500 global firms have implemented global enterprise-wide systems from major vendors such as IBM, SAP, Oracle, and others. Generally enterprise systems have an inward focus on the firm's internal production processes, and only tangentially are concerned with suppliers. More contemporary cloud-based dedicated B2B software that can be integrated with existing enterprise systems is growing in importance. Companies such as IBM, Oracle, and SAP have developed SaaS (software as a service) or on-demand cloud-based supply chain management systems that can work seamlessly with their legacy offerings. Cloud-based supply chain management revenues are growing at 25% annually, although many firms prefer to maintain their own supply chain management systems on their private clouds rather than use shared public cloud services (Chao, 2015; Accenture, 2014).

12.3 TRENDS IN SUPPLY CHAIN MANAGEMENT AND COLLABORATIVE COMMERCE

It is impossible to comprehend the actual and potential contribution of B2B e-commerce, or the successes and failures of B2B e-commerce vendors and markets, without understanding ongoing efforts to improve the procurement process through a variety of supply chain management programs that long preceded the development of e-commerce.

Supply chain management (SCM) refers to a wide variety of activities that firms and industries use to coordinate the key players in their procurement process. For the most part, today's procurement managers still work with telephones, e-mail, fax machines, face-to-face conversations, and instinct, relying on trusted long-term suppliers for their strategic purchases of goods directly involved in the production process.

There have been a number of major developments in supply chain management over the last two decades that set the ground rules for understanding how B2B e-commerce works (or fails to work). These developments include just-in-time and lean production, supply chain simplification, adaptive supply chains, sustainable supply chains, electronic data interchange (EDI), supply chain management systems, and collaborative commerce (Supply Chain Digest, 2012a).

JUST-IN-TIME AND LEAN PRODUCTION

One of the significant costs in any production process is the cost of in-process inventory: the parts and supplies needed to produce a product or service. **Just-in-time production** is a method of inventory cost management that seeks to reduce excess inventory to a bare minimum. In just-in-time production, the parts needed for, say, an automobile, arrive at the assembly factory a few hours or even minutes before they are attached to a car. Payment for the parts does not occur until the parts are attached to a vehicle on the production line. In the past, producers used to order enough parts for a week or even a month's worth of production, creating huge, costly buffers in the production process. These buffers assured that parts would almost always be available, but at a large cost. **Lean production** is a set of production methods and tools that focuses on the elimination of waste throughout the customer value chain. It is an extension of just-in-time beyond inventory management to the full range of activities that create customer value. Originally, just-in-time and lean methods were implemented with phones, faxes, and paper documents to coordinate the flow of parts in inventory. Supply chain management systems now have largely automated the process of acquiring inventory from suppliers, and made possible significant savings on a

supply chain management (SCM)
refers to a wide variety of activities that firms and industries use to coordinate the key players in their procurement process

just-in-time production
a method of inventory cost management that seeks to reduce excess inventory to a bare minimum

lean production
a set of production methods and tools that focuses on the elimination of waste throughout the customer value chain

global basis. Arguably, contemporary supply chain systems are the foundation of today's global B2B production system.

SUPPLY CHAIN SIMPLIFICATION

Many manufacturing firms have spent the past two decades reducing the size of their supply chains and working more closely with a smaller group of strategic supplier firms to reduce both product costs and administrative costs, while improving quality, a trend known as **supply chain simplification**. Following the lead of Japanese industry, for instance, the automobile industry has systematically reduced the number of its suppliers by over 50%. Instead of open bidding for orders, large manufacturers have chosen to work with strategic partner supply firms under long-term contracts that guarantee the supplier business and also establish quality, cost, and timing goals. These strategic partnership programs are essential for just-in-time production models, and often involve joint product development and design, integration of computer systems, and tight coupling of the production processes of two or more companies. **Tight coupling** is a method for ensuring that suppliers precisely deliver the ordered parts at a specific time and to a particular location, ensuring the production process is not interrupted for lack of parts.

SUPPLY CHAIN BLACK SWANS: ADAPTIVE SUPPLY CHAINS

While firms have greatly simplified their supply chains in the last decade, they have also sought to centralize them by adopting a single, global supply chain system that integrates all the firm's vendor and logistics information into a single enterprise-wide system. Large software firms like Oracle, IBM, and SAP encourage firms to adopt a "one world, one firm, one database" enterprise-wide view of the world in order to achieve scale economies, simplicity, and to optimize global cost and value.

Beginning in earnest in 2000, managers in developed countries used these new technological capabilities to push manufacturing and production to the lowest cost labor regions of the world, specifically China and South East Asia. This movement of production to Asia was also enabled by the entrance of China into the World Trade Organization in September 2001. Suddenly, it was both technologically and politically possible to concentrate production wherever possible in the lowest cost region of the world. These developments were also supported by low-cost fuel, which made both transoceanic shipping and production inexpensive, and relative political stability in the region. By 2005, many economists believed a new world economic order had emerged based on cheap labor in Asia capable of producing inexpensive products for Western consumers, profits for global firms, and the opening of Asian markets to sophisticated Western goods and financial products.

As it turns out, there were many risks and costs to this strategy of concentrating production in China and Asia in a world of economic, financial, political, and even geological instability. Today, managers need to be more careful in balancing gains in efficiency from a highly centralized supply chain, with the risks inherent to such a strategy (Long, 2014). For instance, in the global financial crisis of 2007–2009, relying on suppliers in parts of Europe where currencies and interest rates fluctuated greatly exposed many firms to higher costs than anticipated. Suddenly, key suppliers could

---

supply chain simplification

involves reducing the size of the supply chain and working more closely with a smaller group of strategic supplier firms to reduce both product costs and administrative costs, while improving quality

tight coupling

a method for ensuring that suppliers precisely deliver the ordered parts, at a specific time and particular location, to ensure the production process is not interrupted for lack of parts

not obtain financing for their production or shipments. In March 2011, following the earthquake and tsunami in Japan, key suppliers in Japan were forced to shut down or slow production because of nuclear contamination of the entire Fukushima region where, as its turns out, major Japanese and American firms had automobile parts factories. As a result, General Motors could no longer obtain transmissions for its Volt electric car, and had to shut down a truck factory in Louisiana due to a lack of parts from Japan. Japanese and other global firms could not obtain batteries, switches, and axle assemblies. Production lead times in the automobile industry were very short, and inventories of parts were intentionally very lean, with only a few weeks' supply on hand. Texas Instruments shut down several of its Japanese plants, as did Toshiba, putting a crimp on the world supply of NAND flash memory chips used in smartphones (Jolly, 2011; Bunkley, 2011). Caterpillar, Sony, Boeing, Volvo, and hundreds of other firms that are all part of a tightly coupled world supply chain also experienced supply chain disruptions. And then, in October of 2011, torrential rains in Thailand led to flooding of many of its key industrial regions, and the wiping out of a significant share of the world's electronics components from hard disk drives to automobile subsystems, cameras, and notebook PCs (Supply Chain Digest, 2012b). In recent years, the source of supply chain disruptions shifted to technology, with major disruptions due to failure of cloud-based services and cyberattacks (Rossi, 2015; Rowland, 2014; Gusman, 2013; Zurich Insurance, 2012).

The risks and costs of extended and concentrated supply chains have begun to change corporate strategies (Chopra and Sodhi, 2014). To cope with unpredictable world events, firms are taking steps to create **adaptive supply chains** that allow them to react to disruptions in the supply chain in a particular region by moving production to a different region. Many companies are breaking up single global supply chain systems into regional or product-based supply chains and reducing the level of centralization. Using adaptive supply chains, firms can decide to locate some production of parts in Latin America, for instance, rather than having all their production or suppliers in a single country such as Japan. They will be able to move production around the world to temporary safe harbors. This may result in higher short-term costs, but provide substantial, longer-term risk protection in the event any single region is disrupted. Increasingly, supply chains are being built based on the assumption that global disruptions in supply are inevitable, but not predictable. The focus in 2015 is on optimal-cost, not low-cost, supply chains, and more distributed manufacturing along with more flexible supply chains that can shift reliably from high-risk to low-risk areas. Regional manufacturing means shorter supply chains that can respond rapidly to changing consumer tastes and demand levels (PriceWaterhouseCoopers and the MIT Forum for Supply Chain Innovation, 2015; Cachon and Swinney, 2011).

adaptive supply chain
allows companies to react to disruptions in the supply chain in a particular region by moving production to a different region

ACCOUNTABLE SUPPLY CHAINS: LABOR STANDARDS

Accountable supply chains are those where the labor conditions in low-wage, underdeveloped producer countries are visible and morally acceptable to ultimate consumers in more developed industrial societies. For much of the last century, American and European manufacturers with global supply chains with large offshore production

accountable supply chain
one where the labor conditions in low-wage, underdeveloped producer countries are visible and morally acceptable to ultimate consumers in more developed industrial societies

facilities sought to hide the realities of their offshore factories from Western reporters and ordinary citizens. For global firms with long supply chains, visibility did not mean their consumers could understand how their products were made.

Beginning in 2000, and in part because of the growing power of the Internet to empower citizen reporters around the world, the realities of global supply chains have slowly become more transparent to the public. For instance, for much of the past decade, beginning in 1997, Nike, the world's largest manufacturer of sporting goods, has been under intense criticism for exploiting foreign workers, operating sweat shops, employing children, and allowing dangerous conditions in its subcontractor factories. As a result, Nike has introduced significant changes to its global supply chain.

With the emergence of truly global supply chains, and political changes at the World Trade Organization, which opened up European and American markets to Asian goods and services, many—if not most—of the electronics, toys, cosmetics, industrial supplies, footwear, apparel, and other goods consumed in the developed world are made by workers in factories in the less developed world, primarily in Asia and Latin America. Unfortunately, but quite understandably, the labor conditions in these factories in most cases do not meet the minimal labor standards of Europe or America even though these factories pay higher wages and offer better working conditions than other local jobs in the host country. In many cases, the cost for a worker of not having a job in what—to Western standards—are horrible working conditions is to sink deeper into poverty and even worse conditions. Many point out that labor conditions were brutal in the United States and Europe in the nineteenth and early twentieth century when these countries were building industrial economies, and therefore, whatever conditions exist in offshore factories in 2014 are no worse than developed countries in their early years of rapid industrialization.

The argument results in a painful ethical dilemma, a terrible trade-off: cheap manufactured goods that increase consumer welfare in developed countries seem to require human misery in less developed countries. Indeed, these jobs would never have been moved to less developed parts of world without exceptionally low, even survival level, wages.

Notwithstanding the argument that having a job is better than being unemployed in low-wage countries, or any country, there are some working conditions that are completely unacceptable to consumers and therefore to firms in developed countries. Among these unacceptable working conditions are slave or forced labor, child employment, routine exposure to toxic substances, more than 48 hours of work per week, harassment and abuse, sexual exploitation, and compensation beneath the minimal standard of living leaving no disposable income. These practices were, and are, in some cases typical, and certainly not atypical, in many low-wage countries.

A number of groups in the last decade have contributed to efforts to make global supply chains transparent to reporters and citizens, and to develop minimal standards of accountability. Among these groups are the National Consumers League, Human Rights First, the Maquilla Solidarity Network, the Global Fairness Initiative, the Clean Clothes Campaign, the International Labor Organization (UN), and the Fair Labor Association (FLA). The FLA is a coalition of business firms with offshore production and global supply chains, universities, and private organizations. For member firms, the FLA conducts interviews with workers, makes unannounced visits to factories to track progress, and investigates complaints. They are also one of the major international labor standard-setting organizations (Fair Labor Association, 2012).

In March 2012, the FLA released its investigation of Hon Hai Precision Industry Company (a Taiwan-based company known as Foxconn), which is the assembler of nearly all iPhones and iPads in the world. Foxconn operates what is alleged to be the largest factory in the world in Longhua, Shenzhen, where over 250,000 workers assemble electronics goods. The audit of working conditions at Foxconn was authorized by Apple, a member of the FLA, and was based on 35,000 surveys of workers at the Longhua factory. The report found over 50 legal and code violations (sometimes in violation of Chinese laws) including requiring too many hours of work a week (over 60), failing to pay workers for overtime, and hazardous conditions that injured workers (Fair Labor Association, 2012). Similar violations of labor standards continue to be found in the Middle East and Asia (Fair Labor Association, 2015).

SUSTAINABLE SUPPLY CHAINS: LEAN, MEAN, AND GREEN

Sustainable business is a call for business to take social and ecological interests, and not just corporate profits, into account in all their decision-making throughout the firm. No small request. Since the United Nations World Commission on Environment and Development (WCED) published the first comprehensive report on sustainable business in 1987, firms around the globe have struggled with these concepts and in some cases ignored or resisted them as simply a threat to sustained profitability. The commission's report (*Our Common Future*) argued for a balance of profits, social community development, and minimal impact on the world environment, including of course, the carbon footprint of business. Today, the consensus among major firms in Europe, Asia, and the United States has become that in the long term, and through careful planning, sustainable business and **sustainable supply chains** are just good business because it means using the most efficient environment-regarding means of production, distribution, and logistics. These efficient methods create value for consumers, investors, and communities.

sustainable supply chain
involves using the most efficient environment-regarding means of production, distribution, and logistics

Notions of sustainable business have had a powerful impact on supply chain thinking. In part, these efforts are good risk management: all advanced countries have substantially strengthened their environmental regulations. It makes good business sense for firms to prepare methods and operations suitable to this new environment.

For instance, all the major textiles brands and retailers have announced plans for a more sustainable supply chain in textiles. One of the world's truly ancient industries, textiles supports millions of workers while consuming extraordinary resources: it takes 1,000 gallons of water to make one pound of finished cotton (your jeans, for instance). While growing cotton has its issues (fertilizer), the subsequent dying, finishing, and cleaning of cotton makes it the number one industrial polluter on Earth. It's not a small matter then that Walmart, Gap, Levi's, Nike, and other large players in the industry are taking steps to reduce the environmental impact of their operations by improving the efficiency of the entire supply and distribution chains.

With the help of IBM, SAP, and Oracle, other firms and entire industries are working to develop sustainable supply chains. McKesson, North America's largest distributor of drugs, uses IBM's Supply Chain Sustainability Management Solution (SCSM) to minimize carbon dioxide emissions throughout its supply chain, while lowering its distribution costs. SCSM (a business analytics package that works with IBM's B2B software) can determine low-cost refrigeration alternatives for certain medicines (such as insulin and vaccines), identify the environmentally least harmful way to bring new products into its distribution network, and determine the best way to transport pharmaceuticals to customers.

ELECTRONIC DATA INTERCHANGE (EDI)

As noted in the previous section, B2B e-commerce did not originate with the Internet, but in fact has its roots in technologies such as EDI that were first developed in the mid-1970s and 1980s. EDI is a broadly defined communications protocol for exchanging documents among computers using technical standards developed by the American National Standards Institute (ANSI X12 standards) and international bodies such as the United Nations (EDIFACT standards).

EDI was developed to reduce the cost, delays, and errors inherent in the manual exchanges of documents such as purchase orders, shipping documents, price lists, payments, and customer data. EDI differs from an unstructured message because its messages are organized with distinct fields for each of the important pieces of information in a commercial transaction such as transaction date, product purchased, amount, sender's name, address, and recipient's name.

Each major industry in the United States and throughout much of the industrial world has EDI industry committees that define the structure and information fields of electronic documents for that industry. Estimates indicate that B2B e-commerce EDI transactions will total about $3.1 trillion in 2015, about 49% of all B2B e-commerce (U.S. Census Bureau, 2015; authors' estimates). In this sense, EDI remains very important in the development of B2B e-commerce (Cecere, 2014).

EDI has evolved significantly since the 1980s (see **Figure 12.5**). Initially, EDI focused on document automation (Stage 1). Procurement agents created purchase orders electronically and sent them to trading partners, who in turn shipped order fulfillment and shipping notices electronically back to the purchaser. Invoices, payments, and other documents followed. These early implementations replaced the postal system for document transmission, and resulted in same-day shipping of orders (rather than a week's delay caused by the postal system), reduced errors, and lower costs. The second stage of EDI development began in the early 1990s, driven largely by the automation of internal industrial processes and movement toward just-in-time production and continuous production. New methods of production called for greater flexibility in scheduling, shipping, and financing of supplies. EDI evolved to become a tool for continuous inventory replenishment. EDI was used to eliminate purchase orders and other documents entirely, replacing them with production schedules and inventory balances. Supplier firms were sent monthly statements of production requirements and precise scheduled delivery times, and the orders would be fulfilled continuously, with inventory and payments being adjusted at the end of each month.

In the third stage of EDI, beginning in the mid-1990s, suppliers were given online access to selected parts of the purchasing firm's production and delivery

FIGURE 12.5   THE EVOLUTION OF EDI AS A B2B MEDIUM

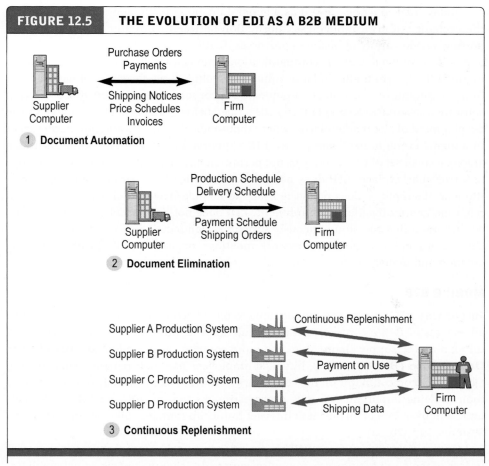

EDI has evolved from a simple point-to-point digital communications medium to a many-to-one enabling tool for continuous inventory replenishment.

schedules, and, under long-term contracts, were required to meet those schedules on their own without intervention by firm purchasing agents. Movement toward this continuous real-time access model of EDI was spurred in the 1990s by large manufacturing and process firms (such as oil and chemical companies) that were implementing enterprise systems. These systems required standardization of business processes and resulted in the automation of production, logistics, and many financial processes. These new processes required much closer relationships with suppliers and logistics partners (shipping and ground transporters), who were required to be more precise in delivery scheduling and more flexible in inventory management. This level of supplier precision could never be achieved economically by human purchasing agents. This third stage of EDI enabled the era of continuous replenishment. For instance, Walmart and Toys"R"Us provide their suppliers with access to their store inventories, and the suppliers are expected to keep the stock of items on the shelf within prespecified targets. Similar developments occurred in the grocery industry.

Today, EDI must be viewed as a general enabling technology that provides for the exchange of critical business information between computer applications supporting a wide variety of business processes. EDI is an important industrial network technology, suited to support communications among a small set of strategic partners in direct, long-term trading relationships. The technical platform of EDI has changed from mainframes to personal computers, from corporate data centers to cloud-based software-as-a-service (SaaS) platforms (described below). EDI is not well suited for the development of Net marketplaces, where thousands of suppliers and purchasers meet in a digital arena to negotiate prices. EDI supports direct bilateral communications among a small set of firms and does not permit the multilateral, dynamic relationships of a true marketplace. EDI does not provide for price transparency among a large number of suppliers, does not scale easily to include new participants, and is not a real-time communications environment. EDI does not have a rich communications environment that can simultaneously support e-mail messaging, video conferencing, sharing of graphic documents, network meetings, or user-friendly flexible database creation and management.

MOBILE B2B

Bring Your Own Device (BYOD) policy
employees use their personal smartphone, tablet, or laptop computer on the company's network

Just as with B2C commerce, mobile devices have become increasingly important in all aspects of B2B e-commerce, through all steps of the procurement process and throughout the supply chain. More and more companies have adopted a **Bring Your Own Device (BYOD) policy**, in which employees use their personal smartphone, tablet, or laptop computer on the company's network, which has helped contribute to their growing importance in B2B. Cisco estimates that by 2016, mobile traffic will represent over 25% of all business Internet traffic, up from less than 5% in 2011 (Cisco Systems, Inc., 2015a).

On the procurement front, B2B buyers are increasingly using mobile devices for all phases of the purchase process, from discovery to decision-making, to actual purchase. One study found that over 50% of B2B decision-makers surveyed used a mobile device to research products, equipment, services, and suppliers. B2B buyers want to be able to place orders using mobile devices just as they do in the B2C arena, and increasingly expect B2B e-commerce sites to be readily accessible from such devices, to be able to start an order from a device and finish it on their desktop and vice versa, and to be able to get online customer service on their mobile devices (eMarketer, Inc., 2014; Forrester Research, 2013).

On the supply chain front, many supply chain network and software providers are enhancing their offerings by providing support for mobile devices and applications. For instance, Elementum provides a variety of mobile apps running on a cloud platform to track various aspects of the supply chain and enable supply chain visibility. For instance, Elementum's Exposure App enables companies to identify and respond to risks in their supply chain, providing real-time alerts on events that may impact the supply, manufacture, or distribution of components of their products. Elementum's Perspective App helps companies monitor the health of their supply chain by providing a dashboard that provides real-time tracking of key performance indicators (KPIs) in the supply chain.

B2B IN THE CLOUD

In the traditional approach to B2B enterprise systems, firms build on their existing on-premise, enterprise production systems that keep track of their manufacturing and distribution processes to include new functionality connecting them to their suppliers' systems. This is a very expensive process that involves connecting suppliers one at a time, establishing the telecommunications channels, and managing the data quality issues, not to mention the cost of building the infrastructure of computers and telecommunications to support coordination of suppliers and B2B transactions. Cloud computing (described in Chapter 3) is increasingly being used to greatly reduce the cost of building and maintaining B2B systems.

In **cloud-based B2B systems**, much of the expense of B2B systems is shifted from the firm to a B2B network provider, sometimes called a data hub or B2B platform (see **Figure 12.6**). The cloud platform owner provides the computing and

cloud-based B2B system
shifts much of the expense of B2B systems from the firm to a B2B network provider, sometimes called a data hub or B2B platform

| FIGURE 12.6 | CLOUD-BASED B2B PLATFORMS |

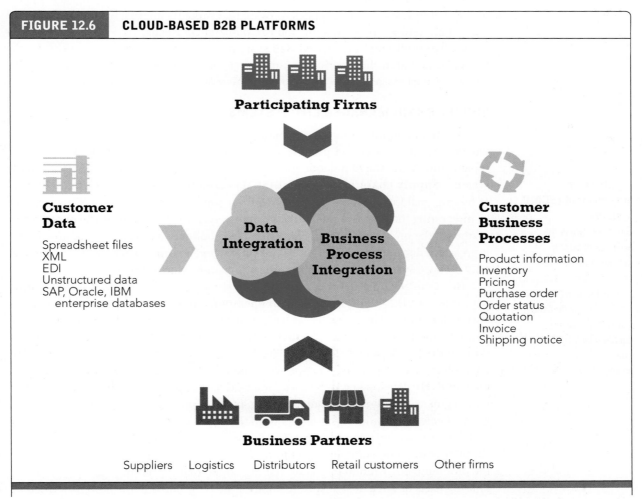

Cloud-based B2B platforms integrate a firm's customer data, business processes, and business partners into a cloud-based software system. Businesses are charged for the hardware and software platform on a utilization basis, reducing their costs significantly.

telecommunications capability; establishes connections with the firm's partners; provides software on-demand (software-as-a-service or SaaS) to connect the firm's systems to its partners' systems; performs data coordination and cleaning; and manages data quality for all members. Network effects apply here: the cost of these tasks and capabilities is spread over all members, reducing costs for all. B2B network providers also provide communication environments and file storage services that allow partners to work together more closely, and to collaborate on improving the flow of goods and transactions. B2B network providers charge customers on a demand basis, rather than on a percentage of their transactions' value, depending on their utilization of the network. Suppliers of traditional on-premise B2B and supply chain management systems have responded by purchasing cloud-based B2B networks in the last few years. For instance, SAP purchased Ariba, one of the first and largest cloud-based B2B transaction networks, in 2012 for $4.6 billion. Ariba's global network automates more than $700 billion in commercial transactions, collaborations, and business intelligence among a wide range of suppliers, shipping, and logistics firms. SAP, the largest supplier of firm enterprise systems, supplies software that supports internal business processes. Other B2B network providers include E2Open and GT Nexus.

Unlike traditional firm-based B2B systems, cloud-based B2B data networks can be implemented in short periods of time to respond to corporate mergers and rapidly changing markets, as *Insight on Technology: Your Shoes Are in the Cloud* illustrates.

SUPPLY CHAIN MANAGEMENT SYSTEMS

Supply chain simplification, just in time and lean production, focusing on strategic partners in the production process, enterprise systems, and continuous inventory replenishment are the foundation for contemporary supply chain management (SCM) systems. **Supply chain management (SCM) systems** continuously link the activities of buying, making, and moving products from suppliers to purchasing firms, as well as integrating the demand side of the business equation by including the order entry system in the process. With an SCM system and continuous replenishment, inventory is greatly reduced and production begins only when an order is received (see **Figure 12.7**). These systems enable just-in-time and lean-production methods.

Hewlett-Packard (HP) is one of the largest technology companies in the world, with sales of $112 billion in 2014. With operations in over 150 countries, sales in 43 currencies, and 15 languages, HP is truly a global firm with global supply chain issues that became even more complicated as HP expanded by making over 200 acquisitions in the last decade. In 2015, HP has the largest supply chain among information technology manufacturers. To cope with one of the most complex supply chains in the world, HP developed a Web-based, order-driven supply chain management system that begins with either a customer placing an order online or the receipt of an order from a dealer. The order is forwarded from the order entry system to HP's production and delivery system. From there, the order is routed to one of several HP contractor supplier firms. The supplier's system then verifies the order with HP and validates the ordered configuration to ensure the PC can be manufactured (e.g., will not have missing parts or fail a design specification set by HP). The order is then forwarded to

supply chain management (SCM) systems

continuously link the activities of buying, making, and moving products from suppliers to purchasing firms, as well as integrating the demand side of the business equation by including the order entry system in the process

INSIGHT ON TECHNOLOGY

YOUR SHOES ARE IN THE CLOUD

Have you ever worn Keds, Hush Puppies, Merrells, Sebagos, Sperry Topsiders, or Sauconys? If so, you've had a product made by Wolverine World Wide Inc. on your feet. Although you may not be familiar with its name, Wolverine is one of the world's largest designers, manufacturers, and marketers of footwear for sports, casual wear, and work. The company's business is divided into three segments: its Lifestyle Group includes Sperry Topsider, Stride Rite, Hush Puppies and Keds. Its Performance Group includes Merrell, Saucony, Chaco, and Patagonia. The Heritage Group comprises brands such as Wolverine, Cat, Bates, Sebago, Harley-Davidson, and HyTest Safety. Wolverine was founded in Grand Rapids, Michigan, in 1883, and originally made the boots that built America's railroads, skyscrapers, and highways. Since then the company has expanded largely by purchasing well-known name brand manufacturers. The company sells its footwear through national retailers, catalog sales, and consumer direct businesses at various e-commerce Web sites.

In 2014, Wolverine generated almost $2.8 billion in revenue. In 2012, it purchased a total of four brands, including Saucony and Keds, that increased its revenue by $1 billion in a single year. The company has 6,600 employees worldwide. Today, Wolverine sources production of more than 100 million pairs of shoes from 110 factories located in 20 countries. The company's major competitors are Nike (the global giant with $28 billion in revenue) and Deckers (with $1.8 billion in revenue). The global footwear market is estimated to be $248 billion, with a 4.4% annual growth rate.

Like many global consumer goods manufacturers, Wolverine has faced a number of challenges

in managing its global supply chain with both the supply and retail fronts. In the early 2000s, Wolverine's supply chain management capability was based on SAP's BusinessSuite enterprise software. The SAP software centralized and consolidated its operations across all its brands and created an integrated system platform for managing the supply chain, customer relationships, orders, and financial reporting. However, the system could not recognize multiple currencies, languages, or global standards. Signing up new suppliers or retail outlets was an expensive and sometimes lengthy process. Out-of-stock situations were growing as the company could not respond to retailer demands for specific styles. Matching inventory to actual demand was becoming more difficult as fashions changed rapidly. Working with global retailers was difficult at times because the existing system could not work with different languages and currencies. Many of the company's largest global retailers were not comfortable transacting in dollars. In response, Wolverine expanded its SAP enterprise system by adopting the software firm's SAP Retail solutions. This new system had global capabilities that enable different languages and currencies to be used for transactions and communications. The new system also allowed Wolverine managers as well as their retail partners to gain increased, real-time visibility into consumer demand, supply chain, and store operations. As a result, stock outs have declined, and revenues at retail stores have increased 15 to 25% in various segments.

On the supplier side of its operations, Wolverine also faced significant challenges. Its 2012 acquisition of Saucony and Keds brought in an additional $1 billion worth of transactions to process, and might have quickly overwhelmed its domestic supply chain's systems. Its SAP enter-

(continued)

prise system was a traditional on-premise, very large system that was designed to enhance Wolverine's supply chain, and not the entire ecosystem of manufacturing, logistics, and financial firms that work with Wolverine to manufacture and distribute shoes. Wolverine in fact had over 200 suppliers in 120 countries that had their own supply chain software, and integrating them into a single platform was unimaginable, costly, and time consuming. There was no easy (or inexpensive) way to scale up its existing supply chain system to include all its partners, and their millions of transactions. It was difficult for its global suppliers to sign up to Wolverine's domestic system, the payment system was outdated, and logistics and finance were not supported in the existing system.

For help Wolverine turned to GT Nexus, a provider of a cloud-based supply chain platform. GT Nexus is a network of supply chain networks that allows firms to tie their own supply chain systems into a global platform and communicate with their partners, who may be manufacturers, shipping companies, finance firms, and retailers. Unlike with traditional enterprise software, Wolverine does not buy the package, or pay monthly rental costs, or host the software on its servers. Instead, GT Nexus provides an on-demand, pay-as-you-go, software-as-a-service (SaaS) model. Some of the services provided include supplier enablement, purchase-to-payment financial tracking, tracking of packing and shipping, financing of transactions, freight contracting, auditing, documentation and customs, and in-transit tracking. GT Nexus bills itself as an on-demand, cloud-based,

global supply chain management platform. Currently, GT Nexus supports supply chain management at 25,000 companies, has over 100,000 users, and manages an estimated $100 billion in trades. It also facilitates more than $20 billion in payments between buyers and their suppliers in 90 countries and in eight currencies. In addition to Wolverine, GT Nexus customers include Adidas, Nike, Caterpillar, Columbia Sportwear, DHL, Home Depot, Levi Strauss, Pfizer, and UPS, among many others.

Using GT Nexus, Wolverine can provide its suppliers, retailers, logistics, and financial partners a single login to the global Wolverine supply chain. Wolverine managers and their supply partners can see the entire supply chain from suppliers of raw materials, to manufacturers, transporters, and ultimately retail store orders.

In August 2015, Infor, one of the world's leading suppliers of enterprise resource planning software, announced that it would acquire GT Nexus for $675 million. Infor's current business focuses on applications within an enterprise, and it currently counts among its customers 18 of the top aerospace companies, all of the top 10 pharmaceutical companies, and 17 of the top 20 industrial distributors. Adding GT Nexus will enable Infor to expand its reach beyond the walls of an organization into its supply chain and allow businesses to better integrate merchandising, marketing, and demand data into supply chain management. Infor currently uses Amazon Web Services to deliver its cloud SaaS ERP software, and plans to add GT Nexus's software to that platform as well.

SOURCES: "Infor Seeks to Strengthen Cloud Footing with $675 Billion GT Nexus Buy," by Katherine Noyes, Cio.com, August 11,2015; "About Us," Wolverineworldwide.com, accessed July 21, 2015; "About GT Nexus," Gtnexus.com, accessed July 21, 2015; Wolverine World Wide, Inc. Form 10k for the fiscal year ended December 31, 2014," March 3, 2015; "Wolverine Worldwide Warns Investments to Hurt Earnings," by Josh Beckerman, *Wall Street Journal*, January 12, 2015; "Cloud Hub is a Good Fit for Footwear Company," by Mary Pratt, CIO.com, May 29, 2014; "Wolverine World Wide Achieving Business Clarity to Grow Retail Globally," SAP Transformation Study, SAP.com, May 6, 2014; "Powering the World's Most Responsive and Adaptive Supply Chain Networks," Gtnexus.com/about, May 2014; "Global Footwear Manufacturing: Market Research Report," IBISworld.com, March 2014; "Wolverine World Wide, Inc. Form 10k for the fiscal year ended December 31, 2013," February 25, 2014; "Shoe Supply Chain Has Sole Version of Truth," by Jane Bird, *Financial Times*, January 29, 2014.

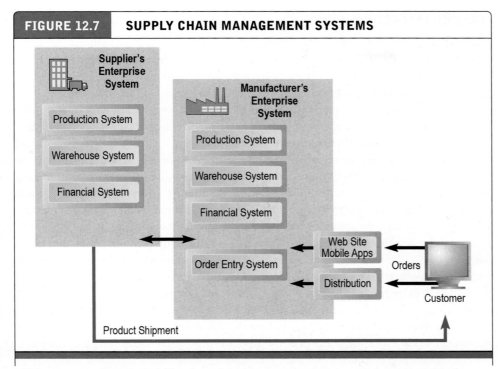

FIGURE 12.7   SUPPLY CHAIN MANAGEMENT SYSTEMS

SCM systems coordinate the activities of suppliers, shippers, and order entry systems to automate order entry through production, payment, and shipping business processes. Increasingly customers, as well as employees working throughout the supply chain, are using smartphones, tablets, and mobile apps to place and coordinate orders.

a computer-based production control system that issues a bar-coded production ticket to factory assemblers. Simultaneously, a parts order is forwarded to the supplier's warehouse and inventory management system. A worker assembles the computer, and then the computer is boxed, tagged, and shipped to the customer. The delivery is monitored and tracked by HP's supply chain management system, which links directly to one of several overnight delivery systems. The elapsed time from order entry to shipping is 48 hours. With this system, HP has eliminated the need to hold PCs in inventory, reduced cycle time from one week to 48 hours, and reduced errors. HP has extended this system to become a global B2B order tracking, reporting, and support system for HP B2B customers (Hewlett-Packard, 2014, 2015).

It isn't just huge technology companies that use supply chain software. There's nothing quite so perishable as fashionable underwear given the rate of fashion change. Under Armour, which is the world's No. 1 performance athletic brand, uses software from SAP to predict sales, plan inventory, and coordinate suppliers (Gilmore, 2014; Booen, 2011). Prior to using these tools, Under Armour often missed sales because it did not produce enough of popular items, or overproduced items that were not selling.

COLLABORATIVE COMMERCE

collaborative commerce

the use of digital technologies to permit organizations to collaboratively design, develop, build, and manage products through their life cycles

Collaborative commerce is a direct extension of supply chain management systems, as well as supply chain simplification. **Collaborative commerce** is defined as the use of digital technologies to permit firms to collaboratively design, develop, build, market, and manage products through their life cycles. This is a much broader mission than EDI or simply managing the flow of information among organizations. Collaborative commerce involves a definitive move from a transaction focus to a relationship focus among the supply chain participants. Rather than having an arm's-length adversarial relationship with suppliers, collaborative commerce fosters sharing of sensitive internal information with suppliers and purchasers. Managing collaborative commerce requires knowing exactly what information to share with whom. Collaborative commerce extends beyond supply chain management activities to include the collaborative development of new products and services by multiple cooperating firms.

A good example of collaborative commerce is the long-term effort of Procter & Gamble (P&G), the world's largest manufacturer of personal and health care products, from Crest toothpaste to Tide soap, to work with suppliers and even customers to develop 50% of its product line over time. In the past, for instance, P&G would design a bottle or product package in-house, and then turn to over 100 suppliers of packaging to find out what it would cost and try to bargain that down. Using Ariba's procurement network, P&G asks its suppliers to come up with innovative ideas for packaging and pricing. Taking it a step further, P&G's Web site, Pgconnectdevelop.com, solicits new product ideas from suppliers and customers. About 50% of P&G's new products originate with substantial input from its suppliers and customers (Vance, 2010). P&G is also collaborating with its biggest online customer, Amazon, by co-locating their operations. P&G sets aside warehouse space for P&G products purchased by Amazon customers. Amazon ships the products to its customers directly from the P&G warehouses rather than shipping them first to Amazon warehouses, and then to the consumer. This collaboration results in Amazon reducing its costs of shipping and storing goods, becoming more competitive on price compared to Walmart and Costco, and reducing the time it takes to arrive at consumers' homes. For P&G collaboration means savings on transportation costs incurred trucking products to Amazon warehouses, and Amazon's help in boosting online sales of P&G products. Other well-known companies using collaboration to develop and deliver products include Lego (DesignByMe), Harley Davidson, Starbucks, and GE's Ecomagination program (Carlozo, 2015; Winston, 2014; James, 2012; Esposito, 2012).

Although collaborative commerce can involve customers as well as suppliers in the development of products, for the most part, it is concerned with the development of a rich communications environment to enable inter-firm sharing of designs, production plans, inventory levels, delivery schedules, and the development of shared products (see **Figure 12.8**).

Collaborative commerce is very different from EDI, which is a technology for structured communications among firms. Collaborative commerce is more like an interactive teleconference among members of the supply chain. EDI and collaborative commerce share one characteristic: they are not open, competitive marketplaces, but

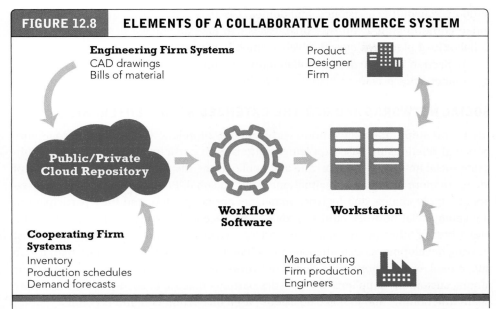

FIGURE 12.8 **ELEMENTS OF A COLLABORATIVE COMMERCE SYSTEM**

A collaborative commerce application includes a cloud repository where employees at several different firms can store engineering drawings and other documents. Workflow software determines who can see this data and what rules will apply for displaying the data on individual workstations.

instead are, technically, private industrial networks that connect strategic partners in a supply chain.

Collaboration 2.0: Cloud, Web, Social, and Mobile

The technology of collaborative commerce has changed greatly since its inception over thirty years ago with tools like Lotus Notes, which was used almost entirely within firms to establish an environment where employees could share ideas, notes, and ideas, and work on projects together. What's new about collaboration tools today is that the software and data are stored on cloud servers where it is less expensive, and easy to update; social networks like Facebook and Twitter are commonly used by employees in many firms, while other firms deploy their own social network platform; the Web enables very inexpensive collaborative environments; and the mobile platform of smartphones and tablets means that collaboration can take place in many more places and times (Computerworld, 2015; Gohring, 2014). Collaboration technologies have expanded collaboration from a within-the-firm platform to a primary tool of inter-firm B2B collaboration.

Broadband video networks like Cisco's TelePresence Studios also play a role in enabling frequent, long-distance, collaboration among supply chain partners. TelePresence is one of several high-bandwidth video systems from different vendors that give users the impression they are sharing physical space with other participants who are in fact located remotely, sometimes on the other side of the globe. Cisco's @CiscoLiveDesk's Twitter feed enhances the TelePresence experience by adding face-to-face support, scheduling assistance, and demos (Cisco Systems, Inc., 2015b). Using Skype video conferencing, even tiny businesses can take advantage of very inexpensive collaborative platforms over the Web, or mobile platforms.

In Section 12.5, we discuss collaborative commerce in greater depth as a technology that enables private industrial networks.

SOCIAL NETWORKS AND B2B: THE EXTENDED SOCIAL ENTERPRISE

It's a short step from collaboration with vendors, suppliers, and customers, to a more personal relationship based on conversations with participants in the supply chain using social networks—both private and public. Here, the conversations and sharing of ideas are more unstructured, situational, and personal. Procurement officers, managers of supply chains, and logistics managers are people too, and they participate in the same social network culture provided by Facebook, Twitter, Tumblr, Instagram, and a host of other public social networks as we all do. Being able to respond to fast moving developments that affect supply chains requires something more than a Web site, e-mail, or telephone calls. Social networks can provide the intimate connections among customers, suppliers, and logistics partners that are needed to keep the supply chain functioning, and to make decisions based on current conditions (Demery, 2015; Red Prairie, 2012).

Participants in the supply chain network are tapping into their tablet computers, smartphones, and social network sites for purchasing, scheduling, exception handling, and deciding with their B2B customers and suppliers. In many cases, supply chain social networks are private—owned by the largest firm in the supply chain network. In other cases, firms develop Facebook pages to organize conversations among supply chain network members.

Some examples of social B2B include TradeSpace, a UK-based business social network where business people can share experiences and ideas, and buy and sell products. Cisco is using its Web site and Facebook pages to run new product campaigns for its business customers using social networks exclusively. Dell, like many businesses, uses its YouTube channel to engage suppliers and customers in conversations about existing products, and ideas for new products. Social networks are beginning to be common tools for managers engaged in B2B commerce. Public social network sites like Facebook and Twitter can be excellent for coordinating the flow of information among business partners through the supply chain.

12.4 NET MARKETPLACES

One of the most compelling visions of B2B e-commerce is that of an online marketplace that would bring thousands of fragmented suppliers into contact with hundreds of major purchasers of industrial goods for the purpose of conducting frictionless commerce. The hope was that these suppliers would compete with one another on price, transactions would be automated and low cost, and as a result, the price of industrial supplies would fall. By extracting fees from buyers and sellers on each transaction, third-party intermediary market makers could earn significant revenues. These Net marketplaces could scale easily as volume increased by simply adding more computers and communications equipment.

In pursuit of this vision, well over 1,500 Net marketplaces sprang up in the early days of e-commerce. Unfortunately, many of them have since disappeared but some still survive, and they are joined by other types of Net marketplaces—some private and some public—based on different assumptions that are quite successful.

CHARACTERISTICS OF NET MARKETPLACES

There is a confusing variety of Net marketplaces today, and several different ways to classify them. For instance, some writers classify Net marketplaces on the basis of their pricing mechanisms—auction, bid/ask, negotiated price, and fixed prices—while others classify markets based on characteristics of the markets they serve (vertical versus horizontal, or sell-side versus buy-side), or ownership (industry-owned consortia versus independent third-party intermediaries). **Table 12.3** describes some of the important characteristics of Net marketplaces.

TYPES OF NET MARKETPLACES

Although each of these distinctions helps describe the phenomenon of Net marketplaces, they do not focus on the central business functionality provided, nor are they capable by themselves of describing the variety of Net marketplaces.

In **Figure 12.9**, we present a classification of Net marketplaces that focuses on their business functionality; that is, what these Net marketplaces provide for businesses seeking solutions. We use two dimensions of Net marketplaces to create a four-cell classification table. We differentiate Net marketplaces as providing either indirect goods (goods used to support production) or direct goods (goods used in production), and we distinguish markets as providing either contractual purchasing (where

TABLE 12.3	CHARACTERISTICS OF NET MARKETPLACES: A B2B VOCABULARY
CHARACTERISTIC	MEANING
Bias	Sell-side vs. buy-side vs. neutral. Whose interests are advantaged: buyers, sellers, or no bias?
Ownership	Industry vs. third party. Who owns the marketplace?
Pricing mechanism	Fixed-price catalogs, auctions, bid/ask, and RFPs/RFQs.
Scope/Focus	Horizontal vs. vertical markets.
Value creation	What benefits do they offer customers or suppliers?
Access to market	In public markets, any firm can enter, but in private markets, entry is by invitation only.

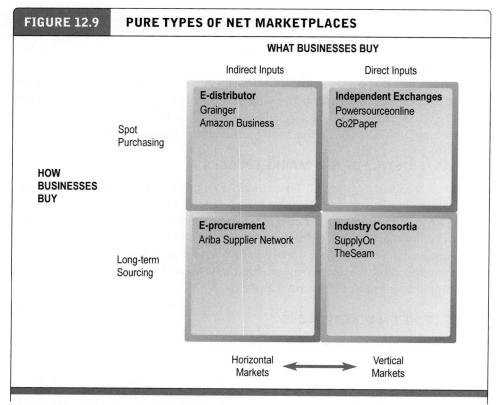

FIGURE 12.9   PURE TYPES OF NET MARKETPLACES

There are four main types of Net marketplaces based on the intersection of two dimensions: how businesses buy and what they buy. A third dimension—horizontal versus vertical markets—also distinguishes the different types of Net marketplaces.

purchases take place over many years according to a contract between the firm and its vendor) or spot purchasing (where purchases are episodic and anonymous—vendors and buyers do not have an ongoing relationship and may not know one another). The intersection of these dimensions produces four main types of Net marketplaces that are relatively straightforward: e-distributors, e-procurement networks, exchanges, and industry consortia. Note, however, that in the real world, some Net marketplaces can be found in multiple parts of this figure as business models change and opportunities appear and disappear. Nevertheless, the discussion of "pure types" of Net marketplaces is a useful starting point.

Each of these Net marketplaces seeks to provide value to customers in different ways. We discuss each type of Net marketplace in more detail in the following sections.

e-distributor

provides an online catalog that represents the products of thousands of direct manufacturers

E-distributors

E-distributors are the most common and most easily understood type of Net market-place. An **e-distributor** provides an online catalog that represents the products of

---

FIGURE 12.10 **E-DISTRIBUTORS**

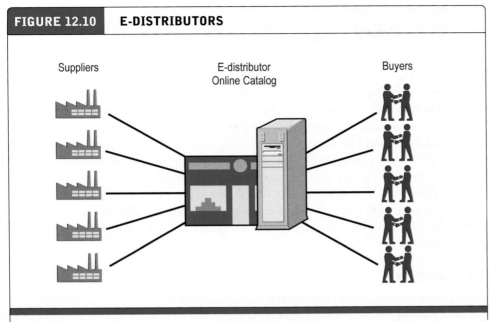

E-distributors are firms that bring the products of thousands of suppliers into a single online catalog for sale to thousands of buyer firms. E-distributors are sometimes referred to as one-to-many markets, one seller serving many firms.

---

thousands of direct manufacturers (see **Figure 12.10**). E-distributors are independently owned intermediaries that offer industrial customers a single source from which to order indirect goods (often referred to as MRO) on a spot, as-needed basis. A significant percentage of corporate purchases cannot be satisfied under a company's existing contracts, and must be purchased on a spot basis. E-distributors make money by charging a markup on products they distribute.

Organizations and firms in all industries require MRO supplies. The MRO function maintains, repairs, and operates commercial buildings and maintains all the machinery of these buildings from heating, ventilating, and air conditioning systems to lighting fixtures.

E-distributors operate in horizontal markets because they serve many different industries with products from many different suppliers. E-distributors usually operate public markets in the sense that any firm can order from the catalog, as opposed to private markets, where membership is restricted to selected firms.

E-distributor prices are usually fixed, but large customers receive discounts and other incentives to purchase, such as credit, reporting on account activity, and limited forms of business purchasing rules (for instance, no purchases greater than $500 for a single item without a purchase order). The primary benefits offered to industrial customers are lower search costs, lower transaction costs, wide selection, rapid delivery, and low prices.

W.W. Grainger is one of the most frequently cited examples of an e-distributor. Grainger is involved in long-term systematic sourcing as well as spot sourcing, but its emphasis is on spot sourcing. Grainger's business model is to become the world's leading source of MRO suppliers, and its revenue model is that of a typical retailer: it owns the products, and takes a markup on the products it sells to customers. Grainger's Web site and mobile apps provide users with a digital version of Grainger's famous seven-pound catalog, plus other parts not available in the catalog (adding up to around 900,000 parts), as well as a complete ordering and payment system. In 2014, Grainger recorded $2.8 billion in e-commerce revenues (28% of its total sales), up 13% from 2013 (W.W. Grainger Inc., 2015). McMaster-Carr, a New Jersey-based industrial parts mecca for machinists and manufacturers around the world, is a similar e-distributor. In 2013, Amazon also entered the B2B distributor market with AmazonSupply, aiming to leverage its global B2C fulfillment infrastructure into the B2B arena, and in 2015, rebranded it as Amazon Business. Other examples of e-distributors include B2Buy and NeweggBusiness.

e-procurement Net marketplace

independently owned intermediary that connects hundreds of online suppliers offering millions of maintenance and repair parts to business firms who pay fees to join the market

E-procurement

An **e-procurement Net marketplace** is an independently owned intermediary that connects hundreds of online suppliers offering millions of maintenance and repair parts to business firms who pay fees to join the market (see **Figure 12.11**). E-procurement Net marketplaces are typically used for long-term contractual

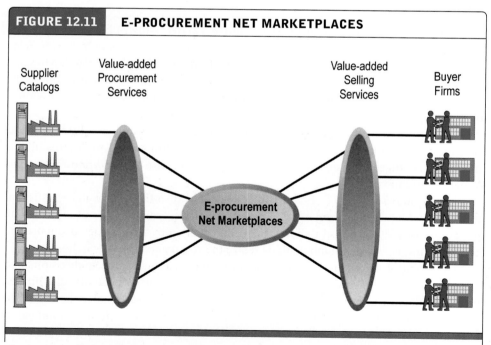

FIGURE 12.11   E-PROCUREMENT NET MARKETPLACES

Supplier Catalogs   Value-added Procurement Services   Value-added Selling Services   Buyer Firms

E-procurement Net Marketplaces

E-procurement Net marketplaces aggregate hundreds of catalogs in a single marketplace and make them available to firms, often on a custom basis that reflects only the suppliers desired by the participating firms.

purchasing of indirect goods (MRO); they create online horizontal markets, but they also provide for members' spot sourcing of MRO supplies. E-procurement companies make money by charging a percentage of each transaction, licensing consulting services and software, and assessing network use fees (Trkman and McCormack, 2010).

E-procurement companies expand on the business model of simpler e-distributors by including the online catalogs of hundreds of suppliers and offering value chain management services to both buyers and sellers. **Value chain management (VCM) services** provided by e-procurement companies include automation of a firm's entire procurement process on the buyer side and automation of the selling business processes on the seller side. For purchasers, e-procurement companies automate purchase orders, requisitions, sourcing, business rules enforcement, invoicing, and payment. For suppliers, e-procurement companies provide catalog creation and content management, order management, fulfillment, invoicing, shipment, and settlement.

E-procurement Net marketplaces are sometimes referred to as many-to-many markets. They are mediated by an independent third party that purports to represent both buyers and sellers, and hence claim to be neutral. On the other hand, because they may include the catalogs of both competing suppliers and competing e-distributors, they likely have a bias in favor of the buyers. Nevertheless, by aggregating huge buyer firms into their networks, they provide distinct marketing benefits for suppliers and reduce customer acquisition costs.

Ariba stands out as one of the poster children of the B2B age, a firm born before its time. Promising to revolutionize inter-firm trade, Ariba started out in 1996 hoping to build a global business network linking buyers and sellers—sort of an eBay for business. With little revenue, the stock shot past $1,000 a share by March 2000. But sellers and buyers did not join the network in large part because they did not understand the opportunity, were too wedded to their traditional procurement processes, and did not trust outsiders to control their purchasing and vendor relationship. In September 2001, Ariba's share price tanked to $2.20. Ariba survived largely by selling software that helped large firms understand their procurement processes and costs. Finally, by 2008, large and small firms had become more sophisticated in their purchasing and supply change management practices, and Ariba's original idea of a global network of suppliers and purchasers of a wide variety of industrial goods came back to life. In 2012, SAP, the largest enterprise software firm, purchased Ariba for $4.3 billion in an effort to strengthen its B2B e-commerce suite. Today, Ariba (now owned by SAP AG) is a leading provider of collaborative business commerce solutions that includes an e-procurement Net marketplace called the Ariba Supplier Network. Other players in this market segment include Perfect Commerce, BravoSolution, A.T. Kearney Procurement & Analytic Solutions, and IBM Emptoris Sourcing.

Exchanges

An **exchange** is an independently owned online marketplace that connects hundreds to potentially thousands of suppliers and buyers in a dynamic, real-time environment

value chain management (VCM) services
include automation of a firm's entire procurement process on the buyer side and automation of the selling business processes on the seller side

exchange
independently owned online marketplace that connects hundreds to potentially thousands of suppliers and buyers in a dynamic, real-time environment

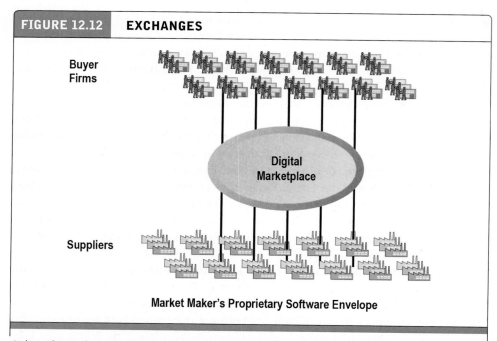

FIGURE 12.12   EXCHANGES

Independent exchanges bring potentially thousands of suppliers to a vertical (industry-specific) marketplace to sell their goods to potentially thousands of buyer firms. Exchanges are sometimes referred to as many-to-many markets because they have many suppliers serving many buyer firms.

(see **Figure 12.12**). Although there are exceptions, exchanges generally create vertical markets that focus on the spot-purchasing requirements of large firms in a single industry, such as computers and telecommunications, electronics, food, and industrial equipment. Exchanges were the prototype Internet-based marketplace in the early days of e-commerce; as noted previously, over 1,500 were created in this period, but most have failed.

Exchanges make money by charging a commission on the transaction. The pricing model can be through an online negotiation, auction, RFQ, or fixed buy-and-sell prices. The benefits offered to customers of exchanges include reduced search cost for parts and spare capacity. Other benefits include lower prices created by a global marketplace driven by competition among suppliers who would, presumably, sell goods at very low profit margins at one world-market price. The benefits offered suppliers are access to a global purchasing environment and the opportunity to unload production overruns (although at very competitive prices and low profit margins). Even though they are private intermediaries, exchanges are public in the sense of permitting any bona fide buyer or seller to participate.

Exchanges tend to be biased toward the buyer even though they are independently owned and presumably neutral. Suppliers are disadvantaged by the fact that exchanges put them in direct price competition with other similar suppliers around the globe, driving profit margins down. Exchanges have failed primarily because suppliers have refused to join them, and hence, the existing markets have very low liquidity, defeating the very purpose and benefits of an exchange. **Liquidity** is typically measured by the number of buyers and sellers in a market, the volume of transactions, and the size of transactions. You know a market is liquid when you can buy or sell just about any size order at just about any time you want. On all of these measures, many exchanges failed, resulting in a very small number of participants, few trades, and small trade value per transaction. The most common reason for not using exchanges is the absence of traditional, trusted suppliers.

liquidity
typically measured by the number of buyers and sellers in a market, the volume of transactions, and the size of transactions

While most exchanges tend to be vertical marketplaces offering direct supplies, some exchanges offer indirect inputs as well, such as electricity and power, transportation services (usually to the transportation industry), and professional services. **Table 12.4** lists a few examples of some current independent exchanges.

The following capsule descriptions of two exchanges provide insight into their origins and current functions.

Global Wine & Spirits (GWS) is unique among independent exchanges, not only as a start-up that has managed to survive, but also as a latecomer to the B2B e-commerce community. GWS opened in 1999, but did not begin to trade products online until May 2001. Based in Montreal, Quebec, GWS is operated by Mediagrif Interactive Technologies Inc., a Canadian company that operates a number of independent exchanges in a variety of industries. GWS offers a spot marketplace for wines, where wine and spirit producers offer wines for sale; a call for tenders market, where members make offers to purchase wines and spirits; a trade database with listings of thousands of industry professionals; and a wine and spirits catalog with over 35,000 products and 6,700 companies (Globalwinespirits.com, 2015).

Inventory Locator Service (ILS) has its roots as an offline intermediary, serving as a listing service for aftermarket parts in the aerospace industry. Upon opening in 1979, ILS initially provided a telephone and fax-based directory of aftermarket parts to airplane owners and mechanics, along with government procurement professionals. As early as 1984, ILS incorporated e-mail capabilities as part of its RFQ services, and by 1998, it had begun to conduct online auctions for hard-to-find parts. In 2015, ILS maintains an Internet-accessible database of over 85 million aerospace and marine industry parts, and has also developed an eRFQ feature that helps users streamline

TABLE 12.4	EXAMPLES OF INDEPENDENT EXCHANGES
EXCHANGE	FOCUS
PowerSource Online	Computer parts exchange
Converge	Electronic components
IronPlanet	Used heavy equipment
EquipNet	Used industrial equipment
IntercontinentalExchange	International online marketplace for over 600 commodities

their sourcing processes. The network's 23,000 subscribers in 93 different countries access the site over 75,000 times a day (Inventory Locator Service, 2015).

Industry Consortia

industry consortium
industry-owned vertical market that enables buyers to purchase direct inputs (both goods and services) from a limited set of invited participants

An **industry consortium** is an industry-owned vertical market that enables buyers in the industry to purchase direct inputs (both goods and services) (see **Figure 12.13**). Industry consortia emphasize long-term contractual purchasing, the development of stable relationships (as opposed to merely an anonymous transaction emphasis), and the creation of industry-wide data standards and synchronization efforts. Industry consortia are more focused on optimizing long-term supply relationships than independent exchanges, which tend to focus more on short-term transactions. The ultimate objective of industry consortia is the unification of supply chains within entire industries, across many tiers, through common data definitions, network standards, and computing platforms.

Industry consortia sprang up in part as a reaction to the development of independently owned exchanges, which were viewed by large industries (such as the

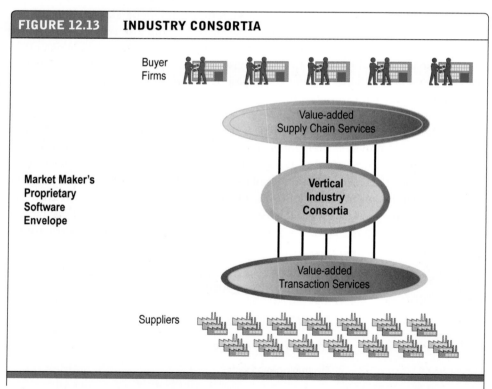

FIGURE 12.13 | **INDUSTRY CONSORTIA**

Industry consortia bring thousands of suppliers into direct contact with a smaller number of very large buyers. The market makers provide value-added software services for procurement, transaction management, shipping, and payment for both buyers and suppliers. Industry consortia are sometimes referred to as many-to-few markets, where many suppliers (albeit selected by the buyers) serve a few very large buyers, mediated by a variety of value-added services.

automotive and chemical industries) as market interlopers that would not directly serve the interests of large buyers, but would instead line their own pockets and those of their venture capital investors. Rather than "pay-to-play," large firms decided to "pay-to-own" their markets. Another concern of large firms was that Net marketplaces would work only if large suppliers and buyers participated, and only if there was liquidity. Independent exchanges were not attracting enough players to achieve liquidity. In addition, exchanges often failed to provide additional value-added services that would transform the value chain for the entire industry, including linking the new marketplaces to firms' ERP systems.

Industry consortia make money in a number of ways. Industry members usually pay for the creation of the consortia's capabilities and contribute initial operating capital. Then industry consortia charge buyer and seller firms transaction and subscription fees. Industry members—both buyers and sellers—are expected to reap benefits far greater than their contributions through the rationalization of the procurement process, competition among vendors, and closer relationships with vendors.

Industry consortia offer many different pricing mechanisms, ranging from auctions to fixed prices to RFQs, depending on the products and the situation. Prices can also be negotiated, and the environment, while competitive, is nevertheless restricted to a smaller number of buyers—selected, reliable, and long-term suppliers who are often viewed as strategic industry partners. The bias of industry consortia is clearly toward the large buyers who control access to this lucrative market channel and can benefit from competitive pricing offered by alternative suppliers. Benefits to suppliers come from access to large buyer firm procurement systems, long-term stable relationships, and large order sizes.

Industry consortia can force suppliers to use the consortia's networks and proprietary software as a condition of selling to the industry's members. Although exchanges failed for a lack of suppliers and liquidity, the market power of consortia members ensures suppliers will participate, so consortia may be able to avoid the fate of voluntary exchanges. Clearly, industry consortia are at an advantage when compared to independent exchanges because, unlike the venture-capital-backed exchanges, they have deep-pocket financial backing from the very start and guaranteed liquidity based on a steady flow of large firm orders. Yet industry consortia are a relatively new phenomenon, and the long-term profitability of these consortia, especially when several consortia exist for a single industry, has yet to be demonstrated. In fact, the number of firms that can be defined as purely industry consortia has declined since the early 2000s, with many firms broadening their mission to encompass more than one industry, or more commonly, being sold by the original industry founders to private investors. For example, GHX, originally founded in 2000 by companies in the pharmaceutical and medical supply industry, is now owned by a private equity firm. E2open, originally founded by IBM, Seagate, and Hitachi as an industry consortium for companies in the high technology industries, has since become a public company and now provides a cloud-based B2B platform and services for a wide variety of industries.

However, a number of industry consortia do remain. One example is The Seam, which was founded in 2000 by leading global agribusiness companies such as Cargill, Louis Dreyfus, and others. The Seam focused initially on creating a cotton trading

TABLE 12.5	INDUSTRY CONSORTIA BY INDUSTRY
INDUSTRY	NAME OF INDUSTRY CONSORTIA
Agribusiness	The Seam (Cotton Consortium)
Automotive	SupplyOn
Chemical	Elemica
Food	Dairy.com
Hospitality	Avendra

exchange, and has since added peanuts, grains, and excess USDA farm commodities. The Seam has handled over $4 billion in transactions since inception and more than 90% of the cotton buyers in the United States are active participants in its Cotton Trading system. **Table 12.5** lists some additional examples.

12.5 PRIVATE INDUSTRIAL NETWORKS

Private industrial networks today form the largest part of B2B e-commerce, both on and off the Internet. Industry analysts estimate that in 2015, over 50% of B2B expenditures by large firms will be for the development of private industrial networks. Private industrial networks can be considered the foundation of the extended enterprise, allowing firms to extend their boundaries and their business processes to include supply chain and logistics partners.

As noted at the beginning of this chapter, private industrial networks are direct descendants of existing EDI networks, and they are closely tied to existing ERP systems used by large firms. A private industrial network (sometimes referred to as a private trading exchange, or PTX) is a Web-enabled network for the coordination of trans-organizational business processes (sometimes also called collaborative commerce). A **trans-organizational business process** requires at least two independent firms to perform (Laudon and Laudon, 2014). For the most part, these networks originate in and closely involve the manufacturing and related support industries, and therefore we refer to them as industrial networks, although in the future they could just as easily apply to some services. Private industrial networks can be viewed as extended enterprises in the sense that they often begin as ERP systems in a single firm, and are then expanded to include (often using an extranet) the firm's major suppliers. **Figure 12.14** illustrates a private industrial network originally built by Procter & Gamble (P&G) in the United States to coordinate supply chains among its suppliers, distributors, truckers, and retailers.

In P&G's private industrial network shown in Figure 12.14, customer sales are captured at the cash register, which then initiates a flow of information back to distributors, P&G, and its suppliers. This tells P&G and its suppliers the exact level of demand for thousands of products. This information is then used to initiate production,

trans-organizational business process
process that requires at least two independent firms to perform

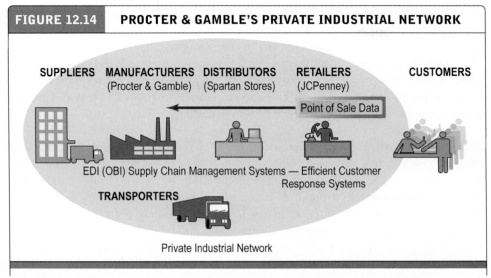

FIGURE 12.14 **PROCTER & GAMBLE'S PRIVATE INDUSTRIAL NETWORK**

Procter & Gamble's private industrial network attempts to coordinate the trans-organizational business processes of the many firms it deals with in the consumer products industry.

supply, and transportation to replenish products at the distributors and retailers. This process is called an efficient customer response system (a demand-pull production model), and it relies on an equally efficient supply chain management system to coordinate the supply side (Gartner, Inc., 2015).

GE, Dell, Cisco, Microsoft, IBM, Nike, Coca-Cola, Walmart, Nokia, and Hewlett-Packard are among the firms operating successful private industrial networks.

OBJECTIVES OF PRIVATE INDUSTRIAL NETWORKS

The specific objectives of a private industrial network include:

- Developing efficient purchasing and selling business processes industry-wide
- Developing industry-wide resource planning to supplement enterprise-wide resource planning
- Increasing supply chain visibility—knowing the inventory levels of buyers and suppliers
- Achieving closer buyer-supplier relationships, including demand forecasting, communications, and conflict resolution
- Operating on a global scale—globalization
- Reducing risk by preventing imbalances of supply and demand, including developing financial derivatives, insurance, and futures markets

Private industrial networks serve different goals from Net marketplaces. Net marketplaces are primarily transaction-oriented, whereas private industrial networks focus on continuous business process coordination between companies. This can include much more than just supply chain management, such as product design, sourcing, demand forecasting, asset management, sales, and marketing. Private industrial networks do support transactions, but that is not their primary focus.

Private industrial networks usually focus on a single sponsoring company that "owns" the network, sets the rules, establishes governance (a structure of authority, rule enforcement, and control), and invites firms to participate at its sole discretion. Therefore, these networks are private. This sets them apart from industry consortia, which are usually owned by major firms collectively through equity participation. Whereas Net marketplaces have a strong focus on indirect goods and services, private industrial networks focus on strategic, direct goods and services.

For instance, True Value is one of the largest retailer-owned hardware cooperatives with operations in 54 countries, 4,500 stores, and 12 regional distribution centers. The logistics are staggering to consider: they routinely process over 60,000 domestic inbound loads, and over 600 million pounds of freight. True Value imports roughly 3,500 containers through 20 international ports and 10 domestic ports. The existing inbound supply chain system was fragmented, did not permit real-time tracking of packages, and when shipments were short or damaged, could not alert stores. The supply chain was "invisible": suppliers could not see store inventory levels, and stores could not see supplier shipments. Using a Web-based solution from Sterling Commerce (an IBM company), True Value created its own private industrial network to which all suppliers, shippers, and stores have access. The network focuses on three processes: domestic prepaid shipping, domestic collect, and international direct shipping. For each process the network tracks in real time the movement of goods from suppliers to shippers, warehouses, and stores. The system has led to a 57% reduction in lead time needed for orders, a 10% increase in the fill rate of orders, and an 85% reduction in back orders. If goods are delayed, damaged, or unavailable, the system alerts all parties automatically (True Value, 2015; IBM, 2011).

Perhaps no single firm better illustrates the benefits of developing private industrial networks than Walmart, described in *Insight on Business: Walmart Develops a Private Industrial Network*.

PRIVATE INDUSTRIAL NETWORKS AND COLLABORATIVE COMMERCE

Private industrial networks can do much more than just serve a supply chain and efficient customer response system. They can also include other activities of a single large manufacturing firm, such as design of products and engineering diagrams, as well as marketing plans and demand forecasting. Collaboration among businesses can take many forms and involve a wide range of activities—from simple supply chain management to coordinating market feedback to designers at supply firms (see **Figure 12.15**).

One form of collaboration—and perhaps the most profound—is industry-wide **collaborative resource planning, forecasting, and replenishment (CPFR)**, which involves working with network members to forecast demand, develop production plans, and coordinate shipping, warehousing, and stocking activities to ensure that retail and wholesale shelf space is replenished with just the right amount of goods. If this goal is achieved, hundreds of millions of dollars of excess inventory and capacity could be wrung out of an industry. This activity alone is likely to produce the largest benefits and justify the cost of developing private industrial networks.

A second area of collaboration is *demand chain visibility*. In the past, it was impossible to know where excess capacity or supplies existed in the supply and distribution chains.

collaborative resource planning, forecasting, and replenishment (CPFR)

involves working with network members to forecast demand, develop production plans, and coordinate shipping, warehousing, and stocking activities to ensure that retail and wholesale shelf space is replenished with just the right amount of goods

INSIGHT ON BUSINESS

WALMART DEVELOPS A PRIVATE INDUSTRIAL NETWORK

Walmart is a leader in the application of information technology to coordinate its supply chain. Walmart's supply chain is the secret sauce behind its claim of offering the lowest everyday prices. Walmart is able to make this promise because it has possibly the most efficient B2B supply chain in the world. It also doesn't hurt to be the largest purchaser of consumer goods in the world. With sales of $482 billion in 2014, Walmart has been able to use information technology to achieve a decisive cost advantage over competitors. As you might imagine, the world's largest retailer also has the world's largest supply chain, with more than 100,000 suppliers worldwide. In the United States, Walmart has more than 5,200 retail stores (including Sam's Clubs). The larger stores stock as many as 200,000 different items. Internationally, Walmart has over 6,200 additional stores in 27 countries, giving it a total of over 11,500.

In the late 1980s, Walmart developed the beginnings of collaborative commerce using an EDI-based SCM system that required its large suppliers to use Walmart's proprietary EDI network to respond to orders from Walmart purchasing managers. In 1991, Walmart expanded the capabilities of its EDI-based network by introducing Retail Link. This system connected Walmart's largest suppliers to Walmart's own inventory management system and required large suppliers to track actual sales by stores and to replenish supplies as dictated by demand and following rules imposed by Walmart.

In 1997, Walmart moved Retail Link to an extranet that allowed suppliers to directly link over the Internet into Walmart's inventory management system. In 2000, Walmart hired an outside firm to upgrade Retail Link from being a supply chain management tool toward a more collaborative forecasting, planning, and replenishment (CFPR) system. Using demand aggregation software, Walmart purchasing agents were now able to aggregate demand from all of Walmart's separate stores in the United States into a single RFQ from suppliers. This gave Walmart tremendous clout with even the largest suppliers. The software helped Walmart purchasing agents select a winning bid and negotiate final contracts. In addition, the software enabled suppliers to immediately access information on inventories, purchase orders, invoice status, and sales forecasts, based on 104 weeks of data, with data available by item, by store, and by hour. The system did not require smaller supplier firms to adopt expensive EDI software solutions. Instead, they could use standard browsers and PCs loaded with free software from Walmart. In 2002, Walmart switched to an entirely Internet-based version of EDI, and the result was a radical reduction in communications costs.

Beginning in 2012, and continuing through 2015, Walmart began a transition to a new supply and inventory management platform called Retail Link 2.0 or Global Replenishment System (GRS). It has currently been deployed to about 80 vendors, with the goal to bring all vendors on board by the end of 2015, and close down the existing Retail Link by 2018. Retail Link 2.0 has all the functionality of the first Retail Link and builds on that foundation with real-time, online data and analytics that is available over the Web to vendors and employees.

Retail Link 2.0 uses Microsoft SharePoint, which is a collaborative Web-based collection of software services that can store and share documents, keep track of changes, and provide corporate search and enterprise social networking tools

(continued)

to connect employees with one another. SharePoint is integrated with Office 365. In Walmart's Retail Link 2.0, the SharePoint platform is used to create an online Web-based facility that enables vendors to respond to orders, track shipments, and sales in a near-real time manner. Vendors and Walmart managers can use business intelligence tools to predict sales rather than simply react to empty shelves or low inventory.

The transition to Retail Link 2.0 requires a massive retraining effort for Walmart's 100,000 suppliers, and tens of thousands of Walmart managers. Problems have developed in the supply chain as the number of new products in stores has mushroomed. Without a history of sales that can be used to predict future sales, some stores have too much inventory, and others not enough.

Despite its success in building a world-class supply chain to support its retail stores, Walmart was not well prepared to deal with online sales or to compete with the online champion, Amazon. From the beginning, Walmart separated out its fledgling e-commerce operation as a separate company with a much lower priority for investment than its physical stores. It was late to invest in an Internet supply chain because the separate companies could never agree on whether it was a good investment. As a result, Walmart's Internet supply chain remains a work in progress, relying on employees at some of the stores to pick online orders and ship from the store, while other orders are handled by a few Internet order warehouses. Last year, Walmart had $12 billion in online sales (compared to Amazon's $79 billion), representing only about 2% of its $482 billion in sales. In 2013, Walmart finally began creating a new inventory and logistics system that will combine the inventory information from its stores and warehouses and then decide the most efficient way to pick and ship online orders.

Like other large global firms, Walmart's global supply chain has been criticized for exploiting labor in underdeveloped countries where it buys products and in home markets where it sells them, bribing officials to look the other way, destroying environments, and wasting energy. In response to critics, Walmart has taken a number of steps. Walmart has set a goal of reducing carbon emissions in its supply chain by 20 million metric tons by 2015, and a goal of 100% renewable energy use in the United States. Walmart has made less progress in its labor policies: In 2012, the ABP pension fund blacklisted Walmart for failing to comply with the United Nations' Global Compact principles that include a set of core values relating to human rights, labor standards, the environment, and anti-corruption efforts. In 2014, the National Labor Relations Board issued a complaint against Walmart claiming that it had illegally retaliated against workers who took part in protests about working conditions and a U.S. Department of Justice investigation into allegations that Walmart bribed Mexican officials to expand its stores and supply chain in Mexico remains ongoing. In 2015, to counter critics of its labor policies, Walmart launched a billion dollar program to raise wages, improve health care policies, and improve scheduling or work.

SOURCES: "Corporate & Financial Facts," Walmart.com, accessed September 1, 2015; "Wal-Mart Builds Supply Chain to Meet E-Commerce Demands," by Kim Nash, *Wall Street Journal*, May 7, 2015; "Walmart U.S. CEO: Fresher Food, Fill Empty Shelves and Lower Prices," by Phil Wahba, *Fortune*, April 2, 2015; "Wal-Mart Acknowledges Inventory Woes in U.S. Stores, Seeks 'Fresh' Fix," by Kim Souza, Thecitywire.com, February 12, 2015; "The Supply Side: Welcome to the Supply Chain Revolution," by Kim Souza, Thecitywire.com, February 2, 2015; "The Scoop on Retail Link 2.0," by Sheldon Cwinn, Linkedin.com/pulse, September 15, 2014; "Wal-Mart Looks to Grow by Embracing Smaller Stores," by Shelly Banjo, *Wall Street Journal*, July 8, 2014; "Biggest Lessons Listed for New Wal-Mart Suppliers," by Kim Souza, Thecitywire.com, November 20, 2013; "Walmart's SPARC initiative in Spotlight Again," Retailingtoday.com, October 10, 2013; "Wal-Mart's E-Stumble With Amazon," by Shelly Banso, *Wall Street Journal*, June 19, 2013; "The Trouble Lurking on Walmart's Empty Shelves," by Bill Saporito, *Time Business*, April 9, 2013; "Walmart's Secret Sauce: How the Largest Survives and Thrives," by Chris Petersen, Retailcustomerexperience.com, March 27, 2013; "Wal-Mart Toughens Supplier Policies, " by Shelly Banjo, *Wall Street Journal*, January 21, 2013; "How Walmart is Changing Supplier Sustainability—Again," by Aran Rice, Renewablechoice.com, May 30, 2012; "Wal-Mart's Dirty Partners," by Josh Eidelson, Salon.com, July 6, 2012; "The Walmart Model and the Human Cost of Our Low Priced Goods," by Juan De Lara, *The Guardian*, July 25, 2012; "Supply Chain News: Walmart, Sustainability, and Troubles in Mexico," by Dan Gilmore, *Supply Chain Digest*, April 26, 2012; "Retail Giant Optimizes Supply Chain Processes With Quintiq Software," *Supply&Demand Chain Executive*, February 15, 2012.

| FIGURE 12.15 | PIECES OF THE COLLABORATIVE COMMERCE PUZZLE |

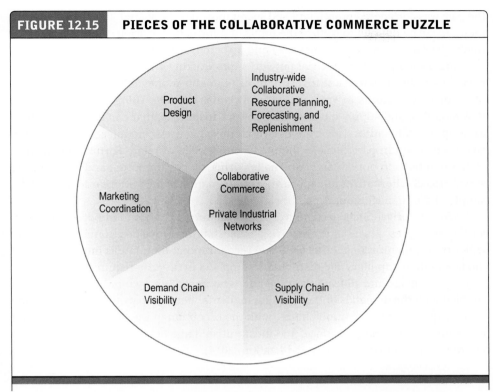

Collaborative commerce involves many cooperative activities among supply and sales firms closely interacting with a single large firm through a private industrial network.

For instance, retailers might have significantly overstocked shelves, but suppliers and manufacturers—not knowing this—might be building excess capacity or supplies for even more production. These excess inventories would raise costs for the entire industry and create extraordinary pressures to discount merchandise, reducing profits for everyone.

A third area of collaboration is *marketing coordination and product design*. Manufacturers that use or produce highly engineered parts use private industrial networks to coordinate both their internal design and marketing activities, as well as related activities of their supply and distribution chain partners. By involving their suppliers in product design and marketing initiatives, manufacturing firms can ensure that the parts produced actually fulfill the claims of marketers. On the reverse flow, feedback from customers can be used by marketers to speak directly to product designers at the firm and its suppliers. For the first time, closed loop marketing (customer feedback directly impacting design and production) can become a reality.

IMPLEMENTATION BARRIERS

Although private industrial networks represent a large part of the future of B2B, there are many barriers to its complete implementation. Participating firms are required to share sensitive data with their business partners, up and down the supply chain. What in the past was considered proprietary and secret must now be shared. In a digital environment, it can be difficult to control the limits of information sharing. Information a firm freely gives to its largest customer may end up being shared with its closest competitor.

Integrating private industrial networks into existing enterprise systems and EDI networks poses a significant investment of time and money. The leading providers of enterprise systems to Fortune 500 companies (Oracle, IBM, and SAP) do offer B2B modules, and supply chain management capabilities, that can be added to their existing software suites. Nevertheless, implementing these modules is a very expensive proposition in part because the procurement side of many Fortune 500 firms is so fragmented and out-of-date. For smaller firms, cloud computing and software as a service (SaaS) alternatives are appearing on the market, which offer far less-expensive supply chain management capabilities.

Adopting private industrial networks also requires a change in mindset and behavior for employees. Essentially, employees must shift their loyalties from the firm to the wider trans-organizational enterprise and recognize that their fate is intertwined with the fate of their suppliers and distributors. Suppliers in turn are required to change the way they manage and allocate their resources because their own production is tightly coupled with the demands of their private industrial network partners. All participants in the supply and distribution chains, with the exception of the large network owner, lose some of their independence, and must initiate large behavioral change programs in order to participate (Laudon and Laudon, 2014).

Elemica:
Cooperation, Collaboration, and Community

I t may seem unusual to refer to an entire industry as a community, a word reserved typically for collections of people who more or less know one another. Trade associations are one example of an industrial community. Trade associations form in an effort to pursue the interests of all members in the community although usually they do not include customers in the community. Elemica is a B2B cloud-based, supply chain platform aiming to revolutionize the entire supply chain of the chemical, tire and rubber, energy, and other process industries worldwide. Elemica's purpose is not just to foster cooperation on a one-to-one inter-firm basis, or just to foster collaboration on multi-firm projects, but instead to lift all boats on an industry tide by providing an inter-firm platform for communicating B2B information, and thereby making all firms more efficient. Elemica calls itself a supply chain operating network ecosystem. Elemica is one of the few survivors of the early B2B e-commerce years. Elemica today processes approximately $350 billion in annual transactions across more than 7,500 process industry trading partners. Clients include BASF, BP, Continental, The Dow Chemical Company, DuPont, The Goodyear Tire & Rubber Company, LANXESS, Michelin, Shell, Solvay, Sumitomo Chemical, and Wacker.

Elemica was founded by 22 leading corporations in the chemical industry (including oil and industrial gases) to provide cloud-based order management and supply chain applications and services. A single platform provides one-stop shopping so that companies can buy and sell products to one another through their own enterprise systems or using a Web alternative. It also helps companies automate all of their business processes, creating efficiencies and economies of scale that lead to an improved bottom line.

How does Elemica achieve community among a diverse, global collection of firms where firms are often both customers and vendors to one another? It unites community members by linking together their enterprise systems. This is the "social glue" that sets Elemica apart. This "super platform" permits companies to communicate with one another and to conduct transactions, handle logistics, and keep the books. The Elemica commerce platform has effectively standardized industry business transactions for all network members regardless of the type of enterprise system they have, and it's leveled the playing field for trade partners who are less technically sophisticated. This neutral platform facilitates millions of transactions for industry suppliers, customers, and third-party providers. In this sense, Elemica is one of the most sophisticated technology platforms in the B2B space.

One of the largest investments for a company is its enterprise system. Despite these investments, intercompany relationships—the backbone of its supply chain—are often left to outdated and unreliable processes. These shortcomings cost billions in lost productivity, revenue, and profit. Elemica's eCommerce platform changes that. It helps its clients leverage their enterprise system investment by incorporating transactions to external trade partners. Elemica's QuickLink ERP connectivity enables companies to link their internal IT systems through a neutral platform so that information is moved into each company's database while maintaining confidentiality and security. The chemical and oil industries were among the first users of enterprise systems (referred to in the early years as manufacturing resource planning systems). These large-scale systems were developed by single firms in order to rationalize and control the manufacturing process. They achieved this objective by identifying the outputs, inputs, and processes involved in manufacturing and automating key elements including inventory control and planning, process control, warehousing and storage, and shipping/logistics. If a company needed to produce 10 tons of polyethylene plastic, its enterprise system could tell it precisely how many tons of petrochemical inputs were required, when they should be delivered to manufacturing, the machinery and labor force required to manufacture the product, how long it would take, where it would be stored, and sometimes how it would be shipped. The systems can estimate the cost at any stage.

Elemica facilitates transactions of all types including order processing and billing, and logistics management. However, unlike some other companies in the field, Elemica does not buy, sell, or own raw material products. Instead it acts as an intermediary, or network, linking companies together to automate confidential transactions. Like eBay or a credit card company, Elemica's revenue comes from charging transaction fees on a per-transaction basis. Its network of clients opens the door for companies to do business with all other connected buyers and sellers.

Elemica offers a variety of services for suppliers, customers, and logistic partners, enabling them to automate both their business processes and internal purchasing. A modular, cloud-based solution simplifies sales, procurement, and financial processes; integrates supply chain partners to diminish communication barriers; and reduces overhead and errors.

Elemica integrates information flow among global trading partners using a cloud-based business process network called the QuickLink network. This is often referred to as platform as a service (PaaS). Each client needs only a single connection to Elemica, and Elemica manages the connections to that company's external trade partners. That means a company needs only maintain one connection to Elemica (important when it's time for enterprise system maintenance or upgrade) rather than maintain a variable number of connections and infrastructure to all its trade partners. Once a company connects to Elemica, it can have access to thousands of other trading partners, including suppliers, customers, and logistics firms. Clients are charged for the service based on volume of usage. This is much more efficient than older EDI solutions to inter-company transactions. Elemica provides the platform for collaborative commerce through a fully automated integrated network of suppliers, customers, and third-party providers.

Elemica offers cloud-based solutions for four areas: Logistics Management, Customer Management, Supplier Management, and Sourcing Management. Using these solutions, companies can automate ordering, invoicing, shipment tracking, and day-to-day business operations. Companies can sign up for one or more solutions depending on their needs. The software applications are software as a service (SaaS) applications residing on Elemica cloud servers, and therefore do not require participating firms to buy any hardware or software. Firms are charged on the basis of how much of the service they use, on a demand basis.

Here's an example of how Elemica works. Let's say you need to order vinyl acetate from one of your suppliers. You put the order into your internal enterprise system, the order is automatically routed to Elemica's QuickLink network, Elemica routes the order to your supplier's internal enterprise system, and you get a confirmed receipt of the order. Elemica's QuickLink Network ensures the accuracy of the item number and purchase order number and sends an alert if there's an issue. Once an order is confirmed, Elemica's platform can be leveraged to plan and coordinate delivery and automatically send an invoice and submit payment. For small or medium firms that may not have an enterprise system, Elemica has a Web portal with online software that allows firms to participate in the community with suppliers and customers. The platform offers a closed-loop process, end to end, from the purchase order, to acknowledgments, load tenders and responses, carrier status updates, and dock scheduling. All of this takes place in a few seconds with little or no human intervention. Elemica has even developed a solution that allows a customer to send a purchase order via e-mail or a print driver (alleviating fax processes) that is then routed to Elemica. The company then routes it to the supplier in its preferred format, integrated with its enterprise system as though it were a true electronic order. This holistic approach to order management allows suppliers to automate the process with both strategic and core customers, without asking its customers to change their processes. It's a win-win situation for suppliers and customers. Elemica's QuickLink Network is sometimes referred to as Come as You Are network because it allows firms to use whatever communication tools they currently use, such as EDI, XML, and even e-mail, or formats associated with their enterprise systems.

Unlike the automobile industry or the airline industry, where a few companies dominate, the $5 trillion global chemical industry is made up of many companies of all sizes. In addition, unlike many other industries, chemical companies often buy the output from other chemical companies to use as raw materials for their products. Thus, chemical companies are often customers of one another as well as competitors.

Senior leaders at some of the larger chemical companies were aware of changes in technology that made the adoption of information technology and the tools of e-commerce more appealing. The questions were how to best use these advances to benefit their businesses and how to establish industry standards for electronic transactions to make them accessible and attainable for all. Leaders from companies such as Dow Chemical and DuPont began discussing this subject and determined that a cooperative alliance would be the most efficient way to move forward. They were met with initial skepticism by marketing and sales staff, worried that online procurement would negatively affect relationships. Further, senior corporate leadership wasn't sure that e-commerce would have any use in the chemical industry at all.

And companies were cautious about the expense of investing in the infrastructure necessary for e-commerce.

However, there were compelling opportunities that were impossible to dismiss, including lowering costs, creating closer connections with customers and suppliers, and differentiating companies on something other than price. At the same time, new start-ups like e-Chemicals and PlasticsNet were making traditional chemical companies nervous. What would happen if their efforts to use information technology to streamline an inefficient supply chain helped them capture market share? In other words, if the more traditional companies didn't move forward, they might end up losing the revenue race.

When Dow began looking at start-ups that were using e-commerce and talking to their customers, they found that customers were concerned about making an investment to establish online connections with multiple firms. Dow and DuPont decided that the best and most economically efficient option was to offer customers the choice of a neutral one-to-one link. This would remove the obstacle of multiple connections. A strong, third-party network addressed the community concern about loss of control. The two companies decided to create and invest in a neutral e-commerce company, partnering with other companies to create the critical mass needed to make it viable.

In 1999, the corporate boards of Dow and DuPont agreed that there were major advantages to online transaction processing and additional online connections among buyers and sellers. Because time and cost considerations made multiple connections unattractive to customers, a hub concept was adopted. It was also decided that a neutral community was the best approach.

All participants shared the common goal of creating a neutral platform to facilitate inter-company transactions and enhance business processes. Dow and DuPont also reviewed the concept with the relevant regulatory agencies and received up-front approval. Ultimately, 22 global chemical companies were involved in the launch of Elemica.

When Elemica opened its doors in 1999, there were around 50 start-up B2B e-commerce companies in the chemical industry. Nearly all of these B2B companies were third-party-owned Net marketplaces suitable at best for short-term sourcing of some direct inputs. In 2016, only a handful of these Net marketplaces for the chemical industry remain. Elemica focuses on building longer-term business relationships by creating committed and contractual supply chains. The company acts only as a facilitator of business transactions and does not directly buy and sell chemical products.

Elemica's business model has been successful primarily because it addresses the needs of chemical, tire and rubber, energy, and selected process companies of all sizes. It does this by offering multiple options for connecting to its hub system, multiple products that can be used alone or in combination, and by ensuring that only one connection integrated with a client's enterprise system is needed for all transactions. Customers can use Elemica, and take advantage of the technology it offers, without purchasing an additional internal system.

With Elemica, companies benefit from improved operational efficiency, reduced costs due to elimination of redundant systems and excess inventory, and a much

SOURCES: "SmartLink Applications," Elemica, accessed July 8, 2015; "Elemica is a Supply Chain Operating Network," Elemica, accessed July 8, 2015; "Clients Meet Sustainability Goals by

higher percentage of safe and reliable deliveries. The flexibility of Elemica's solutions and network combines simplification, standardization, and efficiency. And clients have increased their profitability and improved cash flow through faster payment.

A number of very large companies use Elemica's platform. In Europe, Shell Oil started using Elemica after recognizing that it had ongoing problems with the coordination of paperwork processing and deliveries. Truck drivers would arrive at delivery sites and wait up to two hours while paperwork was filled out. These delays were costing Shell money. Once Shell began using Elemica, things improved. Today, paperwork is processed 24 hours a day, and truck waiting time has been cut from an average of two hours to an average of 15 minutes. Given this success, Shell continues to expand its relationship with Elemica.

Dow Chemical began to transition to full procurement automation with Elemica in 2007. More than 300 of their MRO suppliers are now linked to Elemica's platform. Errors are down 75%, and Dow has achieved economies of scale that have led to meaningful financial savings. Elemica helped Dow unify multiple, disparate business processes, reduced the cost of getting contracted items from suppliers, and increased efficiency in procurement, operations, IT, and accounts payable.

Air Products & Chemicals, Inc. is a global provider of gases and chemicals with 22,000 employees worldwide, and $10 billion in revenue. A major customer asked them for online ordering, but the initial method proposed would have required considerable additional work for both parties. Because both companies were connected to Elemica, there was a better option—the Elemica Supply Chain Hosted Solution.

Elemica has also developed a sustainability program. In 2015, Elemica received the Food Logistics 2015 Top Green Provider Award for its efforts in promoting sustainable supply chains. Elemica automated all inbound and outbound invoices for a global chemical company, eliminating over one million paper invoices. Elemica also eliminated the costs of archiving and storing paper records, saving additional costs.

Elemica has added social tools to its Supply Chain Operating Network (SCON). The idea is to give clients the ability to discover, create, and build social business networks—just as Facebook provides its users the ability to build online social networks. SCON provides its clients with a cloud-based network for establishing business relationships and SaaS (software as a service) applications to carry on trading once the relationship is established. Instead of creating hundreds of one-to-one EDI connections with partners, and then building their own software applications, firms can now more easily just connect to the network and find all the tools they need to trade with many partners. And in May 2014, Elemica introduced its Process Control Tower, a graphical interface that offers a consolidated view of transactional data across all a customer's business partners. Based on the metaphor of an airport control tower, the idea is to give managers a near real-time view of their entire supply and logistics systems. In the past, and still in many firms today, this kind of supply chain information comes in many different forms, from faxes, to e-mails, spreadsheets, and EDI messages. The Control Tower eliminates these difficult-to-interpret messages, and greatly enhances supply chain visibility.

Automating Paper-Driven Processes," Elemica, June 25, 2015; "Elemica Shell Global," Royal Dutch Shell, PLC, June 2015; "Building Effective Business Networks in Process Industries Improving Supply Chain Value Networks," by Lora Cecere, Supply Chain Insights, LLC, January 2015; "Elemica Introduces New Supply Chain Process Control Tower," Elemica, May 7, 2014; "Top Ten Supply Chain Initiatives for 2014 That Are Reimagining How Companies Conduct Commerce," Elemica, January 13, 2014; "Elemica: Shifting From a Shared Services Bazaar to Platform 'PaaS' Standard," by Jason Busch, Spendmatters.com, November 18, 2013; "Elemica Announces Launch of New 'Delivery Schedule' Solution," Elemica, September 24, 2013; "The Social Side of Supply Chain Management," by Adrian Gonzalez, Supply Chain Management Review, August 2013; "Next Generation Supply Chain Networks Enable More Robust Collaborative Workflows Across Trading Partners to Increase Value," Becky Boyd, Market Wired, July 2, 2013; "Elemica Named to Inbound Logistics Top 100 Logistics IT Provider Awards," Wall Street Journal, April 24, 2013; "Elemica Introduces Transportation Management Solution," Elemica, February 16, 2012; "Elemica Procurement Case Study: Dow," Elemica, September 2010; "Elemica Order Management Case Study: BP," Elemica, September 2010; "Elemica Case Study: LanXess," Elemica, September 2010; "Elemica and Rubber-Network Merge," SDCExec.com, August 25, 2009; "Case Study: Elemica," Ebusinesswatch.org, August 25, 2009; "Once Elemica Tackled the Hard Part, the Rest Was Easy," SupplyChainBrain.com, August 5, 2009; "Elemica Merger with Rubber Network," Philly.com, August 3, 2009; "Elemica Automates B2B Transactions Between Trading Partners—Speeding Up Orders by 78%," Softwareag.com, January 2009; "Top Chemical Company Selects Elemica's Business Process Network to Automate Global Procurement," Redorbit.com, December 18, 2008.

Case Study Questions

1. If you were a small chemical company, what concerns would you have about joining Elemica?

2. Elemica provides a community for participants where they can transact, coordinate, and cooperate to produce products for less. Yet these firms also compete with one another when they sell chemicals to end-user firms in the automobile, airline, and manufacturing industries. How is this possible?

3. Review the concept of private industrial networks and describe how Elemica illustrates many of the features of such a network. In what ways is it different from a private industrial network?

12.7 REVIEW

KEY CONCEPTS

■ **Discuss the evolution and growth of B2B e-commerce, as well as its potential benefits and challenges.**

- Before the Internet, business-to-business transactions were referred to simply as *trade* or the *procurement process*. Today, we use the term *B2B commerce* to describe all types of inter-firm trade, and the term *B2B e-commerce* to describe specifically that portion of B2B commerce that is enabled by the Internet and mobile apps.
- In order to understand the evolution of B2B e-commerce, you must understand several key stages:
  - *Automated order entry systems*, developed in the 1970s, involved the use of telephone modems to send digital orders.
  - *EDI* or *electronic data interchange*, developed in the late 1970s, is a communications standard for sharing various procurement documents including invoices, purchase orders, shipping bills, product stocking numbers (SKUs), and settlement information for an industry.
  - *B2B e-commerce Web sites* emerged in the 1990s along with the commercialization of the Internet. They are online catalogs containing the products that are made available to the general public by a single vendor.
  - *Net marketplaces* emerged in the late 1990s as a natural extension and scaling-up of the electronic storefront. The essential characteristic of all Net marketplaces is that they bring hundreds of suppliers, each with its own online catalog, together with potentially thousands of purchasing firms to form a single Internet-based marketplace.
  - *Private industrial networks* also emerged in the late 1990s with the commercialization of the Internet as a natural extension of EDI systems and the existing close relationships that developed between large industrial firms and their suppliers.
- Potential benefits of B2B e-commerce include lower administrative costs; lower search costs for buyers; reduced inventory costs; lower transaction costs; improved quality of products; decreased product cycle time; increased opportunities for collaborating with suppliers and distributors; greater price transparency;

and increased visibility and real-time information sharing among all participants in the supply chain network.

- Potential risks and challenges include lack of real-time data, environmental impacts, natural disasters, labor concerns, and the impacts of economic, financial, and political instability.

■ Understand how procurement and supply chains relate to B2B e-commerce.

- The *procurement process* refers to the way business firms purchase the goods they need in order to produce the goods they will ultimately sell to consumers. Firms purchase goods from a set of suppliers who in turn purchase their inputs from a set of suppliers. These firms are linked in a series of connected transactions. The *supply chain* is the series of transactions that links sets of firms that do business with each other. It includes not only the firms themselves but also the relationships between them and the processes that connect them.
- There are two different types of procurements (purchases of direct goods and purchases of indirect goods) and two different methods of purchasing goods (contract purchases and spot purchases).
- The term *multi-tier supply chain* is used to describe the complex series of transactions that exists between a single firm with multiple primary suppliers, the secondary suppliers who do business with those primary suppliers, and the tertiary suppliers who do business with the secondary suppliers.

■ Identify major trends in supply chain management and collaborative commerce.

- *Supply chain management (SCM)* refers to a wide variety of activities that firms and industries use to coordinate the key players in their procurement process.
- *Just-in-time production* is a method of inventory cost management that seeks to eliminate excess inventory to a bare minimum.
- *Lean production* is a set of production methods and tools that focuses on the elimination of waste throughout the customer value chain.
- *Supply chain simplification* involves reducing the size of the supply chain and working more closely with a smaller group of strategic supplier firms to reduce both product costs and administrative costs, while improving quality
- *Adaptive supply chains* allow companies to react to disruptions in the supply chain in a particular region by moving production to a different region.
- *Accountable supply chains* are those where the labor conditions in low-wage, underdeveloped producer countries are visible and morally acceptable to ultimate consumers in more developed industrial societies.
- *Sustainable supply chains* involve using the most efficient environment-regarding means of production, distribution, and logistics.
- EDI remains very important in the development of B2B e-commerce.
- Mobile B2B has become increasingly important in all aspects of B2B e-commerce, through all steps of the procurement process and throughout the supply chain.
- *Cloud-based B2B systems* shift much of the expense of B2B systems from the firm to a B2B network provider, sometimes called a data hub or B2B platform.
- Contemporary *supply chain management (SCM) systems* are based on supply chain simplification, just in time and lean production, focusing on strategic partners in the production process, enterprise systems, and continuous inventory replenishment.
- *Collaborative commerce* involves the use of digital technologies to permit firms to collaboratively design, develop, build, market, and manage products through their life cycles, and is a direct extension of supply chain management systems, as well as supply chain simplification. Collaborative commerce today involves cloud servers, social business tools, and mobile devices.

- Social networks are providing intimate connections among customers, suppliers, and logistics partners.

■ **Understand the different characteristics and types of Net marketplaces.**

- Characteristics of Net marketplaces include their bias (seller-side vs. buy-side vs. neutral), ownership (industry vs. third party), pricing mechanism (fixed priced catalogs, auctions, and RFPs/RFQs), scope/focus (horizontal vs. vertical), value creation (customers/suppliers), and access to markets (public vs. private).
- There are four main types of "pure" Net marketplaces:
  - *E-distributors* are independently owned intermediaries that offer industrial customers a single source from which to make spot purchases of indirect or MRO goods. E-distributors operate in a horizontal market that serves many different industries with products from many different suppliers.
  - *E-procurement Net marketplaces* are independently owned intermediaries connecting hundreds of online suppliers offering millions of MRO goods to business firms who pay a fee to join the market. E-procurement Net marketplaces operate in a horizontal market in which long-term contractual purchasing agreements are used to buy indirect goods.
  - *Exchanges* are independently owned online marketplaces that connect hundreds to thousands of suppliers and buyers in a dynamic real-time environment. They are typically vertical markets in which spot purchases can be made for direct inputs (both goods and services). Exchanges make money by charging a commission on each transaction.
  - *Industry consortia* are industry-owned vertical markets where long-term contractual purchases of direct inputs can be made from a limited set of invited participants. Consortia serve to reduce supply chain inefficiencies by unifying the supply chain for an industry through a common network and computing platform.

■ **Understand the objectives of private industrial networks, and their role in supporting collaborative commerce, and the barriers to their implementation.**

- Objectives of private industrial networks include developing efficient purchasing and selling business processes industry-wide; developing industry-wide resource planning to supplement enterprise-wide resource planning; increasing supply chain visibility; achieving closer buyer-supplier relationships; operating on a global scale; and reducing industry risk by preventing imbalances of supply and demand.
- Private industrial networks are transforming the supply chain by focusing on continuous business process coordination between companies. This coordination includes much more than just transaction support and supply chain management. Product design, demand forecasting, asset management, and sales and marketing plans can all be coordinated among network members. Some of the forms of collaboration used by private industrial networks include the following:
  - *CPFR* or *industry-wide collaborative resource planning, forecasting, and replenishment* involves working with network members to forecast demand, develop production plans, and coordinate shipping, warehousing, and stocking activities.
  - *Supply chain and distribution chain visibility* refers to the fact that, in the past, it was impossible to know where excess capacity existed in a supply or distribution chain. Eliminating excess inventories by halting the production of overstocked goods can raise the profit margins for all network members because products will no longer need to be discounted in order to move them off the shelves.
  - *Marketing and product design collaboration* can be used to involve a firm's suppliers in product design and marketing activities as well as in the related activities of their supply and distribution chain partners. This can ensure that the parts used to build a product live up to the claims of the marketers. Collaborative commerce applications used in a private industrial network can also make possible closed-loop marketing in which customer feedback will directly impact product design.

QUESTIONS

1. Explain the differences between total B2B commerce and B2B e-commerce.
2. What are the key attributes of a B2B e-commerce Web site? What early technology are they descended from?
3. List at least five potential benefits of B2B e-commerce.
4. Name and define the two distinct types of procurements firms make. Explain the difference between the two.
5. Name and define the two methods of purchasing goods.
6. Define the term supply chain and explain what SCM systems attempt to do. What does supply chain simplification entail?
7. Explain the difference between a horizontal market and a vertical market.
8. How do the value chain management services provided by e-procurement companies benefit buyers? What services do they provide to suppliers?
9. What are the three dimensions that characterize an e-procurement market based on its business functionality? Name two other market characteristics of an e-procurement Net marketplace.
10. Identify and briefly explain the anticompetitive possibilities inherent in Net marketplaces.
11. List three of the objectives of a private industrial network.
12. What is the main reason why many of the independent exchanges developed in the early days of e-commerce failed?
13. Explain the difference between an industry consortium and a private industrial network.
14. What is CPFR, and what benefits could it achieve for the members of a private industrial network?
15. What are the barriers to the complete implementation of private industrial networks?
16. What is EDI and why is it important?
17. Describe six major trends in supply chain management and collaboration.
18. Describe the challenges inherent to B2B e-commerce.
19. What is a multi-tier supply chain and why does it pose a challenge for B2B e-commerce?
20. What is a cloud-based B2B platform and what advantages does it offer?

PROJECTS

1. Choose an industry and a B2B vertical market maker that interests you. Investigate the site and prepare a report that describes the size of the industry served, the type of Net marketplace provided, the benefits promised by the site for both suppliers and purchasers, and the history of the company. You might also investigate the bias (buyer versus seller), ownership (suppliers, buyers, independents), pricing mechanism(s), scope and focus, and access (public versus private) of the Net marketplace.

2. Examine the Web site of one of the e-distributors listed in Figure 12.9, and compare and contrast it to one of the Web sites listed for e-procurement Net marketplaces. If you were a business manager of a medium-sized firm, how would you decide where to purchase your indirect inputs—from an e-distributor or an e-procurement Net marketplace? Write a short report detailing your analysis.

3. Assume you are a procurement officer for an office furniture manufacturer of steel office equipment. You have a single factory located in the Midwest with 2,000 employees. You sell about 40% of your office furniture to retail-oriented catalog outlets such as Quill in response to specific customer orders, and the remainder of your output is sold to resellers under long-term contracts. You have a choice of purchasing raw steel inputs—mostly cold-rolled sheet steel—from an exchange and/or from an industry consortium. Which alternative would you choose and why? Prepare a presentation for management supporting your position.

4. You are involved in logistics management for your company, a national retailer of office furniture. In the last year the company has experienced a number of disruptions in its supply chain as vendors failed to deliver products on time, and the business has lost customers as a result. Your firm only has a limited IT department, and you would like to propose a cloud-based solution. Go to the web site of GT Nexus. Explore the Why GT Nexus tab, and the Solutions By Industry/Retail tab. Read several case studies on the site. Write a report to senior management why you believe that a cloud-based B2B solution is best for your firm.

REFERENCES

Accenture, Inc. "Supply Chain Management in the Cloud." (June 25, 2014).

Antai, Imoh. "A Theory of the Competing Supply Chain: Alternatives for Development." *International Business Research* Vol 4, No. 1 (January 2011).

Ariba Inc., "Ariba-Spot-Buy-Powered-by-Ariba-Discovery." (May 13, 2014).

Barlow, Alexis. "Web Technologies and Supply Chains." Glasgow Calendonian University, Scotland. In *Supply Chain Management: New Perspectives*, edited by S. Renko. (2011).

Beard, Alison and Richard Hornik, "It's Hard to Be Good," *Harvard Business Review Magazine,* November 2011

Bolukbasi, Hande. "Putting the Business in the Palm of Your Hand." SAPInsider.com (January 2011).

Booen, Brett. "The Under Armour Success Story: How SAP Improves the UA Supply Chain." SupplyChain-Digital.com (March 10, 2011).

Bunkley, Nick. "Lacking Parts, GM Will Close Plant." *New York Times* (March 17, 2011).

Cachon, Gerard, and Robert Swinney, "The Value of Fast Fashion: Quick Response, Enhanced Design, and Strategic Consumer Behavior." *Management Science* Vol. 57 778–795 (April 2011).

Carlozo, Lou. "Crowdfunding: A New Frontier for Investors." U.S. News and World Report (May 6, 2015).

Cecere, Lora. "Supply Chain Visibility in Business Networks." Supply Chain Insights, LLC (March 11, 2014).

Cecere, Lora. "EDI Workhorse of the Value Chain." Supply Chain Insights, LLC (November 20, 2013).

Chao, Loretta. "Supply Chain Management in the Cloud." *Wall Street Journal* (May 22, 2015).

Chopra, Sunil and MamMohan Sodhi. "Reducing the risk of Supply Chain Disruptions." *MIT Sloan Management Review* (Spring 2014).

Cisco Systems, Inc. "Cisco Visual Networking Index: Global Mobile Data Traffic Forecast Update 2014–2019" (2015a).

Cisco Systems, Inc. "@CiscoLiveDesk." Twitter.com/CiscoLiveDesk (accessed August 30, 2015b).

Computerworld. "Healthcare IT's Seismic Shift: How Collaboration is Changing Cyber Insurance and More!." Computerworld.com (May 28, 2015).

Demery, Paul. "Salesforce.com Rolls Out a Portal for Selling B2B Mobile Apps." Internetretailer.com (January 5, 2015).

eMarketer, Inc. "B2Bs Face a Mobile-First Future: Smartphones and Tablets Invade the Workplace Thanks to Trends Such as "Bring Your Own Device." (April 2, 2014).

Enright, Allison. "B2b E-commerce is Poised for Growth: More Than a Third of Business Buyers Plan to Spend More Online Next Year." InternetRetailer.com, May 31, 2013.

Esposito, Carl. "What Are the Best Examples of Crowdsourcing." Crowdsourcing.org (2012).

Fair Labor Association, "Independent External Monitoring of the Hestle, Olan, and Balsu Hazelnut Supply Chain In Turkey, 2014–2015. (2015).

Fair Labor Association. "Independent Investigation of Apple Supplier, Foxconn Report Highlights." Fairlabor.org (March 30, 2012).

Fauska, Polina, Natalia Kryvinska, and Christine Strauss. "E-commerce and B2B Services Enterprises." 2013 International Conference on Advanced Information Networking and Application Workshops, IEEE (2013).

Forrester Research, Inc. "Mobile Workforce Adoption Trends." (February 4, 2013).

Gartner, Inc. "Gartner Announces Rankings of Its 2015 Supply Chain Top 25: Amazon Takes the Top Spot in Top 25 Rankings; Apple and P&G Move into New Masters Category." (May 14, 2015).

Gilmore, Dan. "Under Armour's Athletic Supply Chain." *Supply Chain Digest* (April 3, 2014).

Globalwinespirits.com. "About GWS." Globalwinespirits.com (accessed August 30, 2015).

Gohring, Nancy. "Collaboration 2.0: Old Meets New." *Computerworld* (April 10, 2014).

Gusman, Phil. "Most 2012 Supply-Chain Disruptions Were from Tech-Related Events, Not Weather." *Property Casualty Journal* (September 9, 2013).

Hewlett-Packard. "Fact Sheet: Realize Better Outcomes." (2015).

Hewlett-Packard. "Form 10-K for the fiscal year ended October 31, 2014." (December 17, 2014). Hewlett-Packard.

IBM Corporation, "True Value Company: True Value Optimizes Their Inbound Supply Process with IBM Sterling Supply Chain Visibility." (July 2011).

Inventory Locator Service LLC. "About Us." ILSmart.com (accessed August 30, 2015).

James, Henry. "Crowdsourcing Trends in 2012." Crowdsourcing.org (April 9, 2012).

Jolly, David. "Long Pause for Japanese Industry Raises Concerns About Supply Chain." *New York Times* (March 16, 2011).

Kaplan, Steven, and Mohanbir Sawhney. "E-Hubs: The New B2B Marketplaces." *Harvard Business Review* (May–June 2000).

Kumaran, S. "A Framework-Based Approach to Building Private Trading Exchanges." IBM Systems Journal (July 2002).

Laudon, Kenneth C. and Jane P. Laudon. *Management Information Systems: Managing the Digital Firm.* 13th edition. Upper Saddle River, NJ, Prentice Hall (2014).

Long, Gene, Jr. "Supply Chain Resiliency: From Insight to Foresight: Sustaining Shareholder Value by Hardening the Enterprise Against External Risks. *IHS Quarterly* (March 2014).

Melnyk, Steven, et al. "Supply Chain Management 2010 and Beyond." APICS Educational & Research Foundation (2010).

PriceWaterhouseCoopers and the MIT Forum for Supply Chain Innovation. "Making the Right Risk Decisions to Strengthen Operations Performance." (2015).

Red Prairie, Inc. "The B2B SoLoMo Imperative." (September 2012).

Rosenzweig, et al., "Through the Service Operations Strategy Looking Glass: Influence of Industrial Sector, Ownership, and Service Offerings on B2B E-marketplace Failures." *Journal of Operations Management* (29) (2011).

Rossi, Ben. "How to Protect the IT Supply Chain From Cyber Attacks." Information Age (March 24, 2015).

Rowland, Daryk. "Combating Cyber Risk in the Supply Chain." Scmagazine.com (November 11, 2014).

Supply Chain Digest. "Building the Supply Chain from the Shelf Back Research." (April 4, 2012a).

Supply Chain Digest. "Global Supply Chain: Toyota Taking Massive Effort to Reduce Its Supply Chain Risk in Japan." (March 7, 2012b).

Trkman, P.; McCormack, K.; "Estimating the Benefits of Implementing E-Procurement," Engineering Management, IEEE Transaction, Volume 57, Issue 2 (May 2010).

True Value. Annual Report 2014. (March 2015).

U.S. Census Bureau. "eStats." (May 28, 2015).

Vance, Ashlee. "For an Online Marketplace, It's Better Late Than Never." *New York Times* (November 20, 2010).

Winston, Andrew. "GE Is Avoiding Hard Choices About Ecomagination." *Harvard Business Review* (August 1, 2014).

W.W. Grainger. Inc. Form 10-K for the fiscal year ended December 31, 2014, filed with the Securities and Exchange Commission (February 27, 2015).

Yoo, Byungjoon; V. Choudray; and T. Mukhopadhyay. "Marketplaces or Web Service: Alternate Business Models for Electronic B2B Commerce." *Proceedings of the 44th Hawaii International Conference on System Sciences* (HICSS) (2011).

Zarroli, Jim. "In Trendy World Of Fast Fashion, Styles Aren't Made To Last." Npr.org (March 11, 2013).

Zurich Insurance. "Outsourcing Failures Now in Top 3 as Causes of Supply Chain Disruption." *Insurance Journal* (November 8, 2012).

Index

A bolded page number indicates that the term is defined on that page

Credits

Video Cases